Pendleton District and Anderson County, S.C.

Wills, Estates, Inventories, Tax Returns and Census Records

Compiled By:

Virginia Alexander
Colleen Morse Elliott
Betty Willie

Southern Historical Press, Inc.
P.O. Box 1267
Greenville, S.C. 29602

ISBN # 0-89308-143-4
Library of Congress Card Catalog # 79-67499

Printed in the United States of America

PREFACE

It should be called to the reader's attention that the 1820 Pendleton District Census and the Anderson District Tax Returns 1835-1861 have not been included in the full name index for the remainder of this book. The tax returns are already basically in alphabetical order so the reader should not have difficulty with this. The 1820 Census will have to be carefully studied since it appears in the same order as the enumerator took the census.

Two of the interesting features about this book concern the abstracting of the wills which were found in Deed Book A of Pendleton County 1790-1792, and the list of estate records and Revolutionary War soldiers who were found in Pendleton District Deed Books A - P, 1790-1822.

Mrs. Charles Willie, who is one of the compilers of this volume, is presently at work abstracting the deeds of Pendleton District from 1790 to 1826. This book of deeds will be available in the late Fall of 1980.

Related material to supplement this volume are the following titles and all of these may be obtained from Southern Historical Press:

> Marriage & Death Notices From The Pendleton (S.C.)
>   Messenger, 1807-1851, Brent Holcomb
> Early Anderson Co., S.C. Newspapers Marriages &
>   Obituaries, 1841-1882, Tom C. Wilkinson
> Marriage & Death Notices From The Keowee Courier,
>   1849-1871 and 1878-1883, Colleen M. Elliott
> History of Old Pendleton District & Genealogy of
>   Leading Families, R. W. Simpson

It is with deep appreciation that I thank Virginia Alexander, Colleen Elliott and Betty Willie for the vast number of hours they spent at the microfilm reader abstracting this material.

Also, my thanks go to Aurora Shaw of Jacksonville, Florida, former editor and publisher of the Southern Genealogist Exchange Quarterly for her allowing me to use the 1820 Pendleton District Census which had appeared in an earlier edition of her magazine and copyrighted by her.

The Publisher

March 1980

INTRODUCTION

In 1826, Pendleton District was divided into Pickens and Anderson Counties with the name Pendleton disappearing as a contemporary legal entity.

Previous to the year 1768 the only court held in South Carolina was in the City of Charleston. In that year the State was divided into six districts, and Courts of General Sessions and Common Pleas were thereafter established and held in each of the said districts. The judges were authorized to build court houses and other necessary public buildings in some convenient place in each. A court house was established at Ninety-Six, at Cambridge, (See State Statutes, Vol. 7, p. 197.)

At the close of the Revolutionary War all the territory embraced in the present counties of Greenville, Anderson, Oconee and Pickens belonged to the Cherokee Indians, although embraced within the State lines. Many adventurous white people had founded settlements within this territory, and, for their protection from the Indians, the State had built forts in several places, and maintained garrisons therein. All of this territory, except the extreme upper portion of Oconee and Pickens counties was ceded to the State by the Cherokees shortly after the close of the war by a treaty negotiated by Gen. Andrew Pickens near his home on Seneca River. Tradition points out a large oak tree, near the banks of the Seneca River, under which General Pickens met the Cherokee chiefs and made with them the treaty by which the State secured the exclusive possession of this territory.

By Act of 1789, Vol. V., p. 105, the new counties of Pendleton and Greenville were allowed representation in the legislature, each to have one senator and three members in the lower house. At the same session commissioners were appointed to locate a court house for the County of Pendleton. The commissioners were Andrew Pickens, John Miller, John Wilson, Benj. Cleveland, Wm. Halbert, Henry Clark, John Moffett and Robert Anderson. These commissioners purchased from Isaac Lynch a tract of land, about as near the center of the County of Pendleton as practicable, containing eight hundred and eighty-five acres. And the same was conveyed to the said commissioners in trust for the County of Pendleton, as appears by deed dated April 8, 1790, and recorded in book "A", page 1.

Upon this tract of land the Town of Pendleton is located. This tract of land, or a part of it, was laid out into streets and village lots, which were numbered, and the remainder of the tract was divided into what were called "out-lying" lots.

By the Act of 1791, Vol. 7, p. 262, Gen. Andrew Pickens, Col. Robert Anderson, Capt. Robert Maxwell, John Bowen, James Harrison, Maj. John Ford and John Hallum were appointed to purchase land and superintend the building of a court house and jail for the district of Washington. Washington District was composed of the counties of Pendleton and Greenville. The court house was located at Pickensville, near the present Town of Easley.

By the Act of 1798, Vol. VII, p. 283, the name County was changed to District. And at the court house in each of the several districts there shall be held after 1800, Courts of Sessions and Common Pleas , to possess and exercise the same powers and jurisdiction as is held by the district courts. By the same Act, it was enacted that the court for Pendleton District should be held at Pendleton Court House.

TABLE OF CONTENTS

ANDERSON COUNTY, SOUTH CAROLINA
PROBATE JUDGE ESTATE RECORDS, 1793-1799
LETTERS OF GUARDIANSHIP BOOK, 1801-1819
BOOK C

Pendleton records have been inherited by Anderson. In 1828, Pendleton
was divided into Anderson and Pickens Districts. Pendleton County and
District records were transfered to the custody of Anderson District
which explains the presence of Pendleton documents among the records
of Anderson County.

ORDINARY'S BILL OF FEES

For each citation.	$ .50
For qualifying executor, Adm'r or Guar'n issuing letter to either & recording it.	2.50
For taking bond from Adm'r or Guard'n and recording same.	1.00
For issuing warrant of appraisements and oath.	.50
For proving will in common form, certifying and filling same.	1.00
For proving will in solemn form, certifying and filling same.	5.00
Recording will, probate, & certificate per copy sheet of ninety words.	.09
Filing and entering renunciation of Executor.	.50
Dedimus Potestatem to prove will or qualify as Executor.	1.00
Recd'g each inventory & apprais't or acct. of sales, each fig. a word per C.90 word.	.09
Recd'g & exam'g & filing the annual account of each Adm., Exr. or Guardian for 1st year.	3.00
Recd'g & exam'g & filing for each succeeding year.	1.00
Recording said account per copy sheet of 90 words.	.09
Hearing and filing petition for sale of personal estate and order.	1.00
Hearing and filing petition for Guard'ship and appointm't of Guardian.	1.00
Entering a Caveat or withdrawing the same.	.50
Hearing very litigated case.	3.00
Swearing and examining each witness.	.50 (?)
Certifying copy of any paper on file in this office.	.50
Copying such paper per copy sheet of ninety words.	(?)
Every rule issued against defaulting witness or party failing to act.	(?)
Every attachment issued on return of such rule.	(?)
Furnishing and certifying copy of proceedings in case of a (page torn).	(?)
Every order of revocation of letters, or substitutions of other security.	(?)
Every search.	(?)
Every certification not hereinbefore specified.	.25
Service in proceedings for sale or division of real estate.	12.00
Taking bonds in cases of guardianship of minors, or such division of real estate.	3.00
Moneys collected on sale of real estate and paid over by him.	.01
Printers fee for twice publishing citation.	2.00 (?)

(Note: This appears at the first of this book, and where there is a
question mark the figure was illegible on the microfilm, but may have
shown up on the original. The page seems to have been turned up or
torn when copied.)

ESTATE OF JOHN LINDLEY - pp 1-2
List of appraisement of the estate of John Lindley, deceased. Among
other things listed were 280 acres on Saluda River at mouth of Big
Creek, 300 acres on Twenty-three Mile Creek, 100 acres on Big Creek,
90 acres on branch of creek. Taken on 13 Nov. 1790 for deceased, by
John Robinson, James Starrett, John Rose (?).
Recorded 15 April, 1893.

ESTATE OF THOMAS HALLUM - pp 2-3
Inventory and appraisement of goods, chattles, negroes, rights, credits
etc. belonging to the estate of Thomas Hallum late of the county of
Pendleton, deceased, as directed and shown by John Hallum and Elizabeth
Hallum administrator and administratrix to said estate. Negroes named
Nat, Cubit, Bob, Binah, Teenah and her child Vensus, Big Tennah and
her child Hannah, and Sarah was being appraised. Appraisement made
5 Feb. 1791 in Pendleton Co. by Tilley Merrick, Robert Baker, David
Hamilton.

ESTATE OF JOHN JOHNSTON - pp 3-4
Appraisement of John Johnston's estate. Had negro named Ben. Appraisers: James (X) Gilliam, William Jolley, John Turner. No date.

WILL OF JOHN POLLOCK - p 4
Will of John Pollock of Pendleton, dated 1 Nov. 1791. Wife Elizabeth,
daughter Elizabeth, daughter Ann, sons James, Samuel and John. Daughter
Sarah, daughter Mary. Child unborn, if a boy to be named William, if a
girl to named Keziah. Executors: Elizabeth and James Pollock.
                         (Signed) John Pollock
Wit: Anthony Laughlin
      Robert Gray
      Elizabeth Jones   (Pollock had land on Broadway)
Proven in court 15 April, 1792 by Anthony Laughlin.

ESTATE OF JOHN POLLOCK - p 5
Appraisement of Pollock's estate.

WILL OF SAMUEL DALRUMPLE - pp 5-6
Will of Samuel Dalrumple of Abbeville Co. Wife Sarah to have 1/3 of
plantation and land whereon I now live and 1 negro boy to help raise
the children, also 1/3 moveable estate for lifetime then to revert to
son James. Daughter Rachael Laughlin. Daughters Sarah, Mary and
Elizabeth to have land on head of Coldwater a branch of Rocky River.
Nephew Samuel Dalrumple. Four youngest children: Ann, Glenor (?),
Rosannah and Rebeckah land on Bush (?) River. All my children. Exe-
cutors wife and brother John Dalrumple. Dated 21 Nov. 1791.
                         (Signed) Samuel Dalrumple
Wit: James Pollock
      George Dalrumple
      Lewis Sherrill
Proven 15 April, 1792 by Lewis Sherrill.

ESTATE OF SAMUEL DALRUMPLE - p 6
Appraisement of Samuel Dalrumple dec'd appraised 10 July, 1792 by Lewis
Sherill, Robert Gray, Lewis Jones.

ESTATE OF JOHN TWITTY - p 7
Appraisement of estate of John Twitty dec'd 10 June, 1791, by Alexander
Kilpatrick, William Mackey, William Nevill. Notes on Uriah Conner,
James Gillison, a cow and calf from Mr. Miller.

WILL OF MATHEW THOMPSON - pp 7-8
Washington District - Will of Mathew Thompson of said district. Wife
Mary, to have 1/3 of plantation and 1/3 of mill that is to be built,
during her widowhood. Allow her whole of land and mill until youngest
son is 18, also 1 negro named Silvey. Oldest daughter Rachael Thompson,
2nd daughter Hannah Thompson, 3rd daughter Mary Thompson, daughter
Anne Thompson; 3 sons Mathew, Joseph and John. John is youngest and
Mathew oldest. Mentions negro boys Bob and Sam. Executors: Wife Mary
and Col. Robert Anderson. Dated 2 Feb. 1792.

Wit.:   Joseph Swaringen
        James Long
        William Thompson

Before signing I allow the land I have on Shilloody to be sold by Col.
Robert Anderson my executor and by him equally divided between my wife
and children.

ESTATE OF MATHEW THOMPSON - pp 8-9
Pendleton Co. - 15 Sept. 1792 - Appraisement of Mathew Thompson dec'd
delivered by Mary Thompson executrix. Signed James Long, Wm. Thompson,
James Thompson.

WILL OF GILES GANT - p 9
Will of Giles Gant of Pendleton. Wife Elizabeth to raise and school
children. Son William when he comes of age; sons Hugh and John; all
my children. Nephew Abigail if she stays till she is 18. Executors:
Robert Telford and my wife Elizabeth.
Dated 1 July 1792   (Signed) Giles Gant
Wit.:   Wm. Gant
        Wm. (X) Armstrong
        Margaret Armstrong (signed with X)
Proven 24 Jan. 1793

ESTATE OF ASA TOURTELLOT - pp 10-12
Inventory and appraisement of estate of Asa Tourtellot dec'd. Book
debts: Thomas Hamilton, Tilly Merrick, David Clark, Robert Kennan,
George Forbes, Robert Glenn, Thomas Boyd, John Prater, John Evans,
George Paine, Ratcliff Boon, William Griffin, John Wilkinson, William
McMahen, Benjamin Cornelius, William Hamilton, Robert Pickens, Jacob
Visage, William Burney, William Rankin, John Pattison, Junr., John
Mayfield, James Anderson, Thomas Cary, Andrew Tounihill, John Land,
John Johnston, James Rogers, Henry Burch, James McKimmey, John Hellon,
John Perkins, John Hallum, John Hunnicutt, Hugh McVea, David Neal,
John Yager, Archibald Boyd, Thomas Lofton, Nathaniel Clark, John Tennison,
David Stevens, Richard Farrar, James McBride, Charles Sinclair, Charles
Oliver, James Jett, William Henderson, Solomon Roe, James Smith, Thomas
Henderson, Stephen Caldron, James Kemptool, James Farras, Adam Wright,
Messick (?) Stevens, Samuel Lofton, William Smith, Joseph Smith, William
Hodges, David Cruise, John Morrow, John Brady, Henry Norton, Thomas
Finley, George Erskine, Richard Hood, William Pen, John Smith, William
Riggs, James Beatty, John Townihill, William Cruise, Henry Dobson, John
Godfrey, Joel Foster, Mila Brady, Thomas Brady, Charles Lay, Benjamin
Brown, David Hillhourn, James Agnew, John Ubanks, Thomas Robinson,
Thomas Raper, William Haney, Hardy Owens, Benjamin Land, Isaac Lon (?),
William Holderby, John McCeab, John Hood, Reuben Piles, Randell Hunnicutt,
John Scott, John Stewart, Peter Broomberry, James Brady, Robert Baker,
John Row (?), William Jackson, Seth Waddel, John Glenn, John McDowell,
Stephen Mayfield, John Whitney, James Hubbard Connel, William Farras,
Henry Simpson (?), John Miller, Hugh Rogers, John McKensie.

Notes of hand viz...David Smith, William Davis, Gabriel Harding, Jonathan
Clark, Jonathan Hicks, Sr., James Hamilton Senr., Elias Hollingsworth,
John White, Philip Prater, John Huggins, John Pattison Senr., Jonathan
Hicks Junr., Daniel Boon, John Hudson, Levi Pierce, Ambrose Mayfield,
Christopher Graham, Joseph Clark, William Gillam Bennet Combes, Morgan
Osborne, John Ward, William Osborne, Isaac Miller, Thomas Case, Willis
Jones, Samuel Jones, Ransom Thacker, John Movillar, John Robinson, William
McCaleb.

Bonds viz...Henry Mitchell, Alexander Erwin, Francis Miller, William
McCaleb.

Pendleton County, 1 Feb. 1793 - John Willson, Thomas Garvin and Tilley
Merrick made inventory and appraisement of Asa Tourtillot as produced
by Mrs. Avis Tourtillot, administratrix.

RIGHT OF DOWER OF SUSANNAH BRICKELL - p 12

3

Susannah Brickell of St. John's Parish, S. C. appoints Joseph Johnson attorney to ask, demand and receive our right of dower to lands of Major Ephraim Mitchell, late Surveyor General of the State, which Susannah Brickell is entitled to by law, as being the widow of said Ephraim Mitchell and the said James Brickell by his inter-marriage with her.
Dated 11 June 1793   (Signed)   James Brickell
                                                  Susannah Brickell
Wit.:   Sarah Burdell
        Robert Burdell

A true copy examined 4 July 1793. (Signed) Robert Anderson

I appoint my friend Mr. Samuel Dickson my attorney to represent me in obtaining within mentioned dower. (Signed) Joseph Johnson
Present: Robert Anderson
Dated 4 July 1793.

PROPERTY OF JOHN LINDLEY - pp 13-14
Purchasers at the sale of property of John Lindley, 11 Dec. 1790:
William Pyle, Sarah Lindley, Christopher Brunk, Jonathan Crews, Thomas Raper, Robert Gilliland, Andrew Rose (or Row or Ross ?), William Dosse, Benjamin Cornelius, Robert Moore, John Perkins, Benjamin Waldrop, Henry Lenderman, William Reed, William Musteen, John Hughs, Frederick Farmer, Benjamin Farmer, John Wilson, William Farris, Sturdy Garner, Nicholas Pyle, James Starrett, William Harper, Edwin Smith, Henry Cobb, Jesse Gray, Peter Acker, Richard Ship, Ambrose Blackburn, Daniel Ship, James Millnose (?), William Poore, William Halbert, Esq., Joel Charles, Benjamin Bowen (or Brown), Martha Alexander, Robert Maxwell.
Recorded 14 Sept. 1793.

ESTATE OF SAMUEL DALRUMPLE - p 14
Sales of estate of Samuel Dalrumple, dec'd: Purchasers: Lewis Sherrill, Mary Dalrumple, Sarah Dalrumple, Elial Moore, William Laughlin, Reuben Pybas (or Pyles), John Dalrumple, Pheneas Creton, William Jolley, Samuel McCulley, Elizabeth Dalrumple.
Recorded 14 Sept. 1793.

ESTATE OF JOHN TWITTY - p 14
Sale list of estate of John Twitty, dec'd. Purchasers: Ann Twitty, John Twitty, John Parsons, William Twitty, John Rottan, John Adday, R. Powell. (Negro woman named Jude and girl named Esther being sold.)
Recorded 14 Sept. 1793.

ESTATE OF JOHN POLLOCK - p 15
Sale list of estate of John Pollock deceased. 19 June 1792, by Elizabeth Pollock.

WILL OF ROBERT PICKENS - p 15
Will of Robert Pickens of Greenville County, St. Bartholomew's Parish, dated 20 Jan. 1783. Son Robert Pickens, executor. Miriam Pickens my other executor to have mare colt, 2 young cows with calf, and 3 sows when she leaves plantation. Grandson and granddaughter John and Martha Pickens; grandchildren Margaret and Elizabeth Pickens. To Elinor Prater 1 silver dollar. Daughter Jane Norwood. Son Andrew Pickens 1 cow and calf if he ever comes here for them.
                              (Signed)   Robert (X) Pickens
Wit.:   James Seawright
        Samuel Reed
        Margaret (X) Sharp

Abbeville Co., S. C. - On 1 June 1793 before us Adam C. Jones and Hugh Wardlaw two of justices for said county personally appeared Capt. Samuel Reid and Margaret Jones and made oath that they did see Robert Pickens sign will and did also see James Seawright sign.
                              (Signed)   Samuel Reed
                                         Margaret (X) Jones
Recorded 14 Sept. 1793.

INVENTORY OF GEORGE BENNESON - pp 16-17

26 Jan. 1786 - Ninety Six District, Abbeville County - Inventory of
George Benneson, dec'd, by Abel Pearson, James Hamilton, Hugh Baskin.
27 Jan. 1786 - Articles of estate of George Beneson dec'd sold at Public
Vendue by Sarah Beneson Administratrix. Purchasers: Sarah Beneson,
Mary Files, Jeremiah Files, William McCaleb.

Paid on note Robert Muehuny (?)
George Beneson received for Moses Liddle to his part for carrying land
warrants to town.
Proven accounts of: James Alexander, Joseph Jolley, John Strain,
Thomas Finley, James Seawright, Daniel Stringer, William McCaleb,
John Mackey, William McCarter, Daniel Keith.
To a note of Thomas Winn's (?)

Memorandum of service done for estate - Of George Beneson:
5 days to Jeremiah Files
4 days to David McCluskey's (or McClesky's)
4 days to 96 Court House
3 days at Court House
3 days in Georgia at David McClesky's
1 day of James Gillison's
1 day at James Partin's
3 days at Thomas Gordon's
1 day at Moses Liddles
4 days at Col. Thomas' at Fair Forrest
2 days to Benjamin Laurence
2 days at Capt. Baskins
4 days for Hugh Baskin
4 days at Wm. Benesons
3 times at Georgia 12 days
4 days at General Pickens'
2 days at Wm. McCaleb's
1 day at Col. Anderson's
4 days for Abel Pearson

Cash paid to Hugh Baskins.
Cash paid to Abel Pearson.
For service done for estate of George Beneson by Sarah Beneson.

Foregoing is true copy of inventory and appraisement and sale bill and
other accounts respecting administration of Sarah Beneson on estate of
George Beneson and as filed in clerk's office of Common Pleas for
District of Ninety-Six. Dated 22 Jan. 1793.
Recorded 16 Sept. 1793   Julius Nichols, Junr., C. C. P.

ESTATE OF JOHN COBB - p 17

Inventory of estate of John Cobb, dec'd. Henry Cobb administrator.
Notes on Henry Cobb, Jacob Reed, Robert Parker, Pheneas Creton, Aaron
Broyles, Samuel Cobb, Asa Cobb. Dated 5 July 1793. Appraised by Peter
Acker, William Hall, Hugh Brown (?).
Recorded 17 Sept. 1793.

ESTATE OF ROBERT RALSTON - p 18

Inventory of estate of Robert Ralston, deceased, late of Pendleton,
23 Jan. 1794, by Nathaniel Perry, Godfrey Isbell, Henry (X) Barton,
appraisers.

INVENTORY AND APPRAISEMENT OF GILES GANT - p 19

8 Nov. 1793, inventory and appraisement of property of Giles Gant,
dec'd, by Joseph Brown, Jr., Wm. Fowler, Caleb Conaway, appraisers.

ESTATE OF ROBERT PICKENS - p 19

19 Nov. 1793, estate of Robert Pickens, appraised by John Willson,
Robert McCann, Benjamin Smith, as shown to them by Robert Pickens, Jr.

INVENTORY AND APPRAISEMENT OF SOLOMON ROE - p 19

Inventory and appraisement of Solomon Roe, late of Pendleton, dec'd,
by John Hallum, David Hamilton, George Miller. 8 Jan. 1794.

BOOK ACCOUNTS OF SOLOMON ROE - pp 20-22
List of book accounts of Solomon Roe, dec'd: David Clark, Seth Farrar, William Muleon (?), Willis Jones, Hugh McVey, Williby Pugh, John Hunnicutt, Eli Hunnicutt, Jno. Broomberry, Wm. Anderson, Jno. Briant, Richard Morrow, Roland Hunnicutt, David Smith, Wm. Brison, Jas. Hill (?), Jno Sanders, Jno Jackson, Col. Anderson, Jno Evans, Jno Cothem (?), Israel Mayfield, Benj. Cornelius, Jno McMahan, Howel Doddy (?), Adolph (or Asalph ?) Bradley, Philip Sutton, William Hunney, Jas. McDaniel, Robert Warnock, Jeremiah Abel, Jas. Mulur, Robert Obar, David Stinger, Charles Loyd, George Nelson, George Fought (?), Henry Watts, Jas. (?) McKinsey, Jno White, Jos. Dunn (?), Jas. Jolley, Jno Wilson, James Faris, James Mulur, Jno Wilkeson, Jno Lewis, Jacob Capehart, James Gillispie, Peter Thompson, William Crain, Misheck Stevens, William Ross, Thomas Hood, William Twitty, Thomas Watts, Shadrick Noling (?).

Thomas Lofton Dr. to Sol. Roe - warrants against Peter Broomberry, Daniel Stringer, Williby Pugh.

Thomas Bradley Dr. to Sol. Roe, for summoning two witnesses, same for Chapman.

A return of amount of sale of Solomon Roe. 25 Feb. 1794. Purchasers: Rozanah Roe, B. Roe, E. Mayfield, Jno Roe, Ambrose Mayfield, E. Norton, Thos. Boyd, Rd. Richardson, Isaac Miller, Robt. Glenn (?).

WILL OF CHARLES SINKLER - p 22
Will of Charles Sinkler, wife Sarah, 3 sons, Robert, John and Charles. Wife to have estate until children are raised, then to be divided between her and all my children. Youngest son Charles is under 21. Executor: wife Sarah and trusty friend William Murphree. 8 Jan. 1793.
Wit.: David Kiniman   (Signed) Charles (X) Sinkler
       Jesse Murphee
       Wm. Boner (?)
Pd. 24 June 1794
Inventory and appraisement of Charles Sinkler's estate by Bailey Anderson, Wm. Murphee, James Murphee.

WILL OF JAMES THOMPSON - p 23
Will of James Thompson of Pendleton 8 Nov. 1794 (NOTE: He signed his name Thompson, but clerk wrote the name Tomson). Daughter Abigail Alexander, daughter Mary Dilworth, wife Ablis (?), she to have estate her lifetime then to be divided between son Samuel Tomson, Edward Tomson, William Tomson, James Tomson, Ann Tomson, Elizabeth Tomson, and Ablis Tomson. Executor : Wife Ablis.
Wit.: James Nowlin   (Signed) James Thompson
       Richard Oldham
       Jesse Cobb
Rec. 26 Jan. 1795

ESTATE OF JAMES THOMPSON - p 24
James Thompson's estate appraised Apr. 6, 1795, by William Hall, Joseph Brown, George Oldham.

ESTATE OF WILLIAM LESSLEY - pp 24-26
Inventory of estate of William Lessley, late of Pendleton, appraised Feb. 1794, by James Shields, John Henderson, Thomas Lesley. Recorded 20 Apr. 1794 by B. Earle, Clerk.

WILL OF JONATHAN WEST - pp 27-28
Will of Jonathan West of Pendleton, wife Sophiah, oldest son Robert to have half a dollar if required, son Aquila half dollar, son Bennet half dollar, son Jonathan to have plantation. Son Michael, daughter Fanny, son James Grahams (?) to have half dollar, youngest daughter (not named). Executors: Wife Sophiah and Jacob Vishage. 5 Feb. 1794.
Wit.: Andrew Warnock   (Signed) Jonathan West
       James Warnock
Rec. June 24, 1795

INVENTORY OF JONATHAN WEST - p 28
Inventory of Jonathan West, 10 Sept. 1794, by Elias Hollingsworth, John Robinson, Hugh Rogers.

WILL OF RANDLE GIPSON (GIBSON) - pp 28-29
Will of Randle Gipson (Gibson), of Pendleton. Wife to have negroes Jesse and Bob as long as she lives. Son Jacob Gibson, grandson Landy (?) James, son James Gibson, son Willi Gibson, son John Gibson, daughter Elizabeth, daughter Mary, daughter Nella, grandson Joseph Gibson, sons Randle and Jacob Gibson. Dated 27 Jan. 1794.

Wit.: William Brice (?)   (Signed)   his
      Jesse (X) Gibson   Randle (R) Gipson
      George (X) Gibson   mark
Rec. 24 June 1794

ESTATE OF RANDLE GIBSON - pp 29-30
20 Oct. 1794, Henry Clark, James Gibson, W. W. Bruce (?) appraised estate of Randle Gibson.

WILL OF JAMES COMPTON - pp 30-32
Will of James Compton, 11 Feb 1794. Half of lands to friend Benjamin Smith, other half to friend Jane (or Jean) Campble, to Charles Wilson, to Baziel Hallum Sr., to John Wilson, Esq. Executors: Friends John Wilson, Esq., and Benj. Smith.

Wit.: William Owens   (Signed)   James (X) Compton
      Mary Willson
      Charles Willson
      Bazzel Hallum
Rec. 25 June 1794

INVENTORY AND APPRAISEMENT OF JAMES COMPTON - p 33
Inventory and appraisement of James Compton, deceased by John Willson, Benj. Smith, executors, certified by James Agnew, Alexander Oliver, and Job Smith.
22 Aug. 1794

SALE OF JAMES COMPTON - pp 33-34
Aug. 22,1794, sale of James Compton. Purchasers: Benjamin Smith, Robert McCann, Job Smith, Elijah Kidwell, Jno Willson, David Smith, Alexander Boyse, William Downin (?), James Agnew, John Wilkinson, John Huggins, Mary Doven (?), Job Dowen (?), Patrack Silver (?), Josiah Dowen (?), Alexander Hamilton.

INVENTORY OF JOHN MCAMBRIDGE - pp 34-35
14 June 1794. Inventory of property of John McAmbridge, dec'd, by James Brice, James Dobbins, Charles McClure, appraisers.

RETURN OF SALE OF JOHN MCCAINBRIDGE - pp 35-37
8 July 1794. Return of sale of John McCainbridge. Purchasers: Elub (?) Moore, William Hillhouse, James Hughston, Moses Holland, John McClain, Francis Jones (?), Andrew Riddle, John Corrom (?), John Warnock, Henry Houston, John Hanney, Elub Moore, Andrew Pickens, Alexander Moore, James McClure, Samuel Houston, Charles McClure, El Moore, Stephen Whitmire, William Grayham, Joseph Land, John Henry, John McFalls, Samuel Amberson, Thomas Houston, John Houston, Mattan)(?) Anderson, John Gorge, Robert Stevenson.

WILL OF PETER CORBAN - pp 37-39
Will of Peter Corban. Wife Elizabeth. Son Samuel. Son John. Gannoway Johnson owes me two cows. Children: Samuel, John, Judy, William, Sarah, Elizabeth, David, Elijah, Jesse (?), and James. Executors: friends John McClure and Charles Bowen.

Dated 7 June 1794.   (Signed)   Peter (X) Corban
Wit.: Enoch (X) Williams
      Ganoway Johnson

SALE OF ROBERT PICKENS - p 39
Sale of Robert Pickens (not dated). Robert and Polly Pickens were only purchasers of feather bed and pewter dishes.

WILL OF LEWIS SHELTON - pp 39-40
Will of Lewis Shelton. Daughter Nancy to have negro girl named Leah
and her increase. Daughter Sukey to have negro girl Diley and her in-
crease. If either daughter should die without heir, negroes to be
divided amongst the rest of my children. Estate to be kept together
until youngest son comes of age, then divided between my six sons:
Aron, Taliaferro, Spencer, Lewis, David and Vincent. Executors: William
Martin and Taliaferro Shelton.
Dated 18 Jan. 1794.   (Signed) Lewis Shelton
Wit.: Johnston Willborn
       William Smith
Recorded 25 June 1794

RETURN OF PROPERTY OF LEWIS SHELTON - p 41
Return of property of Lewis Shelton dec'd made by Mary Shelton, administratrix, 2 Aug. 1794. William Clark, John Smith, John Barton, appraisers.

ESTATE OF ISHAM FRANKLIN - p 42
15 Sept. 1794 - Inventory of estate of Isham Franklin shoen by Ann
Franklin to appraisers James Hambree, James Long, Samuel Houston.
Purchasers at sale: The widow Agnes Franklin the only one on 28 Feb.
1795.
Rec. Jan 1795.

APPRAISEMENT OF EASEN GEE - p 43
11 Sept. 1794. Appraisement of Easen Gee, by John Sallings, Jordan
Reaves, Jacob Chamberlan, and Lacy Walker. Made in April 1794.

INVENTORY OF JAMES WATSON - pp 43-44
Inventory of James Watson, Nov. 3, 1794, by John Nicholson, John Pepper
and William Parsons.
Rec. 26 Jan. 1795.

INVENTORY OF JAMES GARNER, SR. - pp 44-45
Inventory of James Garner, Sr., by Stephen Willis, Roger Martin and
Robert Harkness, appraisers. 18 Jan. 1795. Among other things had
negro wenches named Hanah and Sandy.

SALE OF GILES GANT - p 46
Nov. 8, 1794 - Book of sale of Giles Gant, dec'd. Purchasers: Richard
Hall, Robert Telford, Henry Gotcher, Joseph Brown, William Gotcher,
Elizabeth Gant, Wm. Halbert, Wm. Fowler, Benj. Bowen, Wm. Armstrong,
Andrew Kenedy.
Rec. 24 Jan. 1795.

WILL OF SAMUEL FINDLEY - pp 46-48
Will of Samuel Findley, son John, daughter Mary Bowen, Daughter Agnes
Moore, son Samuel. Three youngest daughters Elizabeth, Margrat and
Jane Findly. Wife, Anna. Youngest son Alexander Findly. Executors:
Wife Anna and Richard Hall. 1 Sept. 1794.
Wit.: Robt. Sloan   (Signed) Samuel Findly
       Edwin Smith
       Daniel (X) Cook
Proven 24 Jan. 1795 by Robt. Smith.

WILL OF JAMES SIMMS - pp 48-49
Will of James Simms, Yeoman, Itenerant trader. Three sisters Catharine,
Jean and Elizabeth Simms. Two brothers Thomas and Joseph Simms.
Executors: friends James Love and Thomas Hunter. 28 June 1794.
Wit.: Andrew Warnock   (Signed) James Simms
       James Warnock
Rec. Jan. 1795.

ESTATE OF JAMES SIMMS - pp 49-53
Appraisement of estate of James Simms held at the house of Andrew
Warnock. (A most interesting estate, all kinds of cloth, clothing,
books, such as a peddlar would carry, plus two horses and a wagon.)
31 Jan. 1795, by W. Steele, John Willson, J. McGehee.

WILL OF ISAAC PERKINS - pp 53-54
Will of Isaac Perkins. Wife. Son Richard. 10 Feb. 1794.
Wit.: John C. Kilpatrick   (Signed) Isaac Perkins
       Alexander Kilpatrick
       Bartholomew Wollom (?)
Rec. Apr. 1795

ESTATE OF WILLIAM MCVEY - pp 55-56
Inventory and appraisement of estate of William McVey, sworn to by two
of the appraisers, Fenton Hall and James Holmes 20 Nov. 1794. Elijah
Brown made oath that he saw most of the articles and believes them well
appraised.
Rec. Apr. 1795.

WILL OF JAMES GREER - pp 56-58
26 Jan. 1792. James Greer of Pendleton, planter makes his will. Son-
in-law John Hambleton and his wife. Son-in-law Jacob Gilliam and Mary
his wife. Samuel Wiley and wife Jane. Grandchild Jane Greer, daughter
to my son William Greer. Daughter Martha.
Wit.: Thomas Henderson   (Signed) James Greer
       James (X) Compton
       Stephen   (?)
Rec. Apr. 1795.

ESTATE OF SETH FARRAR - pp 58-59
William Young, Samuel Jackson and Bennett Combs appraised estate of
Seth Farrar. Notes on Thomas Finley and Joel Terrell. 20 Feb. 1795.
Sale list: Leonard Farrar and William Murphee purchasers. Actt. against
Nicholas Perkins.

INVENTORY OF JOHN MCCLAIN, JR. - p 60
Inventory of John McClain, Jr., by James Clements, John Jenry and
William Wardlaw.
Rec. June 1795.

ESTATE OF GION GIBSON - pp 60-61
Appraisement of estate of Gion Gibson by Joshua Presbudge, Edward
Grayham, Thomas Dunken.
Rec. June 1794.

PROPERTY OF GUION GIBSON - pp 62-63
Memorandum of property of Guion Gibson sold at public sale. (No purchasers
listed.)
Rec. June 1795.

ESTATE OF HENRY COBB - pp 63-65
Estate of Henry Cobb, appraised 29 July 1794. Negro man Peter, yellow
wench Hannah, black negro Hannah, negro girls Fan, Milla, Sal and Lettie,
and negro boys Toney, London, Dick, Peter. Appraised by Thomas Garner,
Benj. Farmer, William Harper.
Rec. Jan. 1795.

SALE OF HENRY COBB - pp 65-67
Purchasers at sale of Henry Cobb 2 Mar. 1795: Rachel Cobb, Elizabeth
Cobb, Samuel Cobb, Jno Coram, Wm. Halbert, Chas. Clements, Jno Pepper,
Colliver (?) Clements, Hezekiah Rice, Joseph Jolly, Aron Broyles, George
Reed, Joseph Kenedy, Wm. Bell, Asa Cobb, Obediah Estrage, Thos. Thaxton.
Rec. 27 June 1795.

INVENTORY OF JESSE CLEMENTS - pp 68-69
Inventory of Jesse Clements appraised by Nathaniel Reed, John Oldham,
George Reed. (Large estate, must have been merchant.)
Rec. 20 Apr. 1795.

ESTATE OF SAMUEL DALRUMPLE - p 70
Appraisement of estate of Samuel Dalrumple 9 July 1795 by Lewis Sherrill,
Robt. Gray, Lewis Jones.
Rec. July 1795.

SALE LIST OF DAVID LOWRY - p 70
Amount of sale list of David Lowry dec'd.
Rec. 27 June 1795.

PROPERTY OF JESSE CLEMENTS - pp 70-76
5 June 1795. Return of property of Jesse Clements dec'd. Purchasers:
Benj. Clements, James Clements, Charles Clements, Cullver Clements,
Reubin Clements, Peter Turrine (or Sarvin?), benj. Bowen, Mathew
Alexander, Thos. McCann (?), Aron Alexander, John Fillpot, Callion (?)
Clements, Claiborn Harris, Benj. Boyar, James Mankins (?), Mathew
Alexander bought bible and hymn book, John McClain, John Reed Long,
John Todd, Reubin Brock, Thos. Thackston, Jno McFall, Jno Bowen, Cubi (?)
Clements, Thos. McCann, Nathan Nall, John Gotcher, Jno Cowin, Othneal
Rice, John Brown, Joseph Brown, Elijah Graham, Joshua Broils, John M.
Lain, Ruben Clements John Moore, Peter Hall, Moses Holland, Stephen
Bennett, Abram Mafield, Hugh Haskins, Alex. Snell, Walter Bell, Thos.
Thaxson, Saml. Brown, James Park (?) Odin (?), Wm. Woodon (?), David
Barnhill, Isaac Brick (?), Anthony Laughton, Isaiah Brock, Reuben Brock,
Robt. Graham, George Reed, William Thompson, William Hall, Jacob Reed,
James Jack, James Madkins, Wm. Wooten, Stephen Bennett, Wm. Armstrong,
Thos. McHants (?), James Alexander, John Moon (or Moore), Robert Wood,
Petter Griffin. Certified by Benj. Clements, Charles Clements and
Culliver Clements.
25 Jan. 1795.

WILL OF DAVID ALEXANDER - pp 77-78
Will of David Alexander, dated 25 Aug. 1795. To all my children that
are married: Ann Gotcher, Jane Moore, David Alexander, Margaret Davis,
Catharine (Bowen or Brown, could not decipher), Eliner Reed, James
Alexander, Elizabeth Woods, to each of them five shillings. To my son
John Alexander, to son William Morrison Alexander, daughter Ruth
Alexander. Wife Margaret Alexander. Executors: Wife Margaret and
Stephen Willis.
Wit.:   John Reed Long   (Signed) David Alexander
        Alexander Snell
        Martha (X) Snell
Proven 22 Sept. 1795 by John Reed Long before B. Earle, J. P.

SALE OF JAMES GARNER - pp 78-79
Amount of sale of James Garner dec'd. E. Garner bought negro woman
named Sandy and a girl. Thomas Garner, Johannah Garner, James Garner,
William Hillhouse, George West, James Thompson.
Rec. 18 Nov. 1795.

SALE OF JAMES WATSON - p 79
Articles of sale of James Watson, dec'd. Purchasers: William Bennett,
Ann Bennett, Dickson Barnett (?).
Rec. 25 Jan. 1796.

WILL OF JAMES TURNER - pp 79-80
Will of James Turner, dated 12 July 1793. Brother Thomas Turner, niece
Janet George, Niece Agnes Gordon, nephew James Young, brother Alexander
Young. Executor: brother Alexander Young.
Wit.:   Jno Moffat   (Signed) James Turner
        David Watson
        Robt. Sayer
Rec. 26 Jan. 1796.

ESTATE OF JONATHAN THOMSON (?) - p 81
5 Feb. 1796. Appraisement of estate of Jonathan Thomson (?) by Moses
Liddle, Thomas Morrow, Mathew Martin. Mary Liddle and other two
appraisers came before E. Browne (?), J. P. 2 April 1796.

APPRAISEMENT OF MOSES ANDERSON - p 81
15 April 1796. Appraisement of Moses Anderson by Robt. Rankin, Caleb
Edmondson and William Townsend.

WILL OF GRIFFITH JAMES - 82
Will of Griffith James, dated 20 April 1795. Son Joseph James to have

10 lbs. of money due Griffith in the State of Maryland. Daughter
Hannah Seanor (?). Daughter Jenny Dean. Daughter Mary Cummins. Son
John James. Son Samuel James. Wife Mary. Executors: sons John and
Samuel.
Wit.:   Owen McCorkel   (Signed) Griffith James
        Jane (X) Lesley
        James Jones
Proven 12 April 1795.

SALE OF MOSES ANDERSON - p 83
Return of sale of Moses Anderson by Mary Anderson, administratrix.
Rec. June 1796.

INVENTORY AND APPRAISEMENT OF WILLIAM SLOAN - p 84
Inventory and appraisement of William Sloan as shown by David and Polly
Sloan administrator and administratrix. Negro man Zen (?), negro woman
Ponny, Mulatto boy, 3 negro fellows and 1 wench. Appraised by Alexander
Kilpatrick, James Fergason and John Burks.
Dated 18 June 1796.

WILL OF JOHN PICKENS - pp 84-85
Negro girl named Phillis to my wife. Son Joseph. Daughter Hannah
Coldwell. Son John if ever he returns to have $100.00 at the expiration
of two years from the date. Daughters Elenor and Sarah. Executors:
wife and son Joseph. Dated 22 Sept. 1795.
Wit.:   John McElister   (Signed) John Pickens
        James Gordon
        Alexander McElister
Proven June 27, 1796.

WILL OF JESSE WOOD - pp 85-86
Will of Jesse Wood of Pendleton, farmer, dated 18 Jan. 1795. Wife
Margaret to have plantation to raise and school children. After her
death or re-marriage to be divided among all my children. Executors:
Wife Margaret and Robert Rankins.
Wit.:   Jno Willson   (Signed) Jesse Wood
        Elizabeth (X) Tate
Proven June 27, 1796.

pp 87-88
Thomas Sidney Reese, William Steele and John Hallum are bound unto
J.G. Guignard, Treasurer of the State of South Carolina in the sum of
$6428.57. Reese has been commissioned sheriff of Pendleton County.
24 June 1796.

ESTATE OF SOLOMON ROE - p 88
16 Oct. 1795. John Hallum and David Hamilton appraised estate of
Solomon Roe, a horse produced by Berry Roe, administrator.
Rec. 19 Sept. 1796.

ESTATE OF CLEMENT DEALE - pp 89-90
As directed by John Baylis Earle, Esq., Daniel Ship, J. Whitner and
Wm. Steele appraised estate of Clement Deale 24 Aug. 1796. He had negro
woman named Petty and Child Alice. Negro girl Kate, negro boys Romeo
and Tower.

INVENTORY AND APPRAISEMENT OF HARRIS MAULDIN - pp 90-91
Inventory and appraisement of Harris Mauldin 14 July 1796. Had negro
man George. Appraised by Daniel Pitchford, William Brown, John Hall.
Rec. 19 Sept. 1796.

WILL OF BEVELY COX - pp 91-92
Will of Bevely Cox, 13 Sept. 1794. Wife Mary to raise and school child-
ren. After her death or when all are raised estate to be divided among
all children. Executors: Wife Mary and trusty friend James Jones.
Wit.:   Thomas Turner   (Signed) Bevely (X) Cox
        John Cox
        James Shields
Proven Sept. 1796.

11

WILL OF THOMAS REESE - pp 92-95

Will of Thomas Reese, Clergyman, of Pendleton. Among other matters, Reese requested that "no spirituous liquor be used at my funeral but least this should be thought to proceed from a covetous temper, my executors are hereby directed to take as much money out of my estate as they suppose might have been sufficient for purchase of said liquor, and bestow on those whom they deem real objects of charity." Wife Jane to have negro lad named Mosey, wench Rose and girl Hannah. Land on north side of Twenty-three Mile Creek where I now Live. Son Edwin to have negro fellow Derry. Son Thomas Sidney to have negro lad Jack. Son Elihu Harris to have negro fellow Sam. Daughter Leah to have negro fellow Couar, child Caesar, wench Cola and girl Maria. Daughter Lydia to have negro girls Nanny and Mary. Son Henry Dobson to have negro boy Cyrus, boy Toney and girl Daphne. Henry Dobson, after receiving a good English education, to be bound out as an apprentice to such trade or profession as my executors think best. Daughter Susannah to have negro boy Prince, girl Chloe. Negroes Cato and Candis to be sold. Executors: Wife Jane, Ezekial Pickens, George Reese, John Harris of Connoross and Robert McCann. Dated 28 April 1796.

Wit.: W. Steele   (Signed) Thomas Reese
       Wm. Hunter
       Elizabeth Miller
Proven 19 Sept. 1796.

SALE OF CLEMENT DEALE - pp 95-98

Sale of Clement Deale 28 Oct. 1796. Purchasers: Jane Deale, Patty Deale, Alexander Deale, John Deale, Polly Deale, Willaim Griffin, Abner Steele, George Reese, Willaim Crews, Joseph Whitner.
Rec. 4 Nov. 1796.

ESTATE OF DAVID ALEXANDER - pp 98-99

Hugh Brown, William White and George Read met at the plantation of David Alexander, deceased and appraised his estate as shown them by Stephen Willis, executor.
Rec. 11 Nov. 1796.

INVENTORY AND APPRAISEMENT OF JOHN PICKENS - p 100

Inventory an appraisement of John Pickens, dec'd. 26 Sept. 1796. Negro man James, negro girl and child. Appraised by Elial Moore, Robert Lowder and Patrick Norris, James Brice and Peter Greenlee.
Rec. 10 Nov. 1796.

p 100

Cash received of James Simms: paper money, gold, Pennsylvania money, French Crowns, French Guineas. James Love and Thos. Hunter, Executors.
Rec. 11 Nov. 1796.

INVENTORY OF JAMES SIMMS - p 101

Inventory of James Simms, balances of accounts as they stand Jan. 7, 1793. In North Carolina the following: Charles Grant (bad debt), Samuel Anderson, James Anderson, Colo. Gordon, Mr. Carruth, Miss Clemmy Grant, James Morris, Jonathan Carter (?), Wm. Armstrong, Linn Estridge, Capt. Gordon, David Anderson, James Downey, Joseph Sloan, Squire Ladd - Germantown, Widow David, Wm. Mullin, Maj. James Holland, John Irwin, Jimmy Cooper, Colo. Every, Saml. McFadin (bad debt), Alexr Bailey, Alexr. Gilbert, Wm. Grant, James Finley, James Erwin, Thos. Rowland, James Love, James Logan, Esq., Thomas Hunter.

In South Carolina: Zacharaha Thomson, David Crews (note), Thomas M. Hights (?), Wm. Farris (?), Job Smith, Wm. Blair, Mrs. (?) Ritchey, Frederick Little, Mr. (?) Wardlaw, Sam & Robt. Means, Wm. Crews, James Moore, Geo. Harrison, Mr. Thomas (Sawer ?), Peter Broomberry, Mrs. Bowen, Squire Edmondson, Wm. Edmondson, Jas. Bavia (?), Michael Smith, Samuel Norwood, Wm. McMahan, John Alterons (?), James Curry, John Winter, by James Love and Thomas Hunter, Executors.

(Note FROM COMPILER: The North Carolinians were of Rutherford County, at least many of them. James Love made his will in Rutherford in 1802, named his daughter Nancy Sims, and his friend Thomas Hunter, a merchant of Pendleton, S. C., and also Clementina Grant.)

WILL OF MICHAEL WHITMIRE - pp 101-102
Will of Michael Whitmire. Son Henry to have part of land originally
granted Daniel Kelly, including small plantation made by John Wright.
Sons Christopher and William. Charles Whitmire to have land. Wife
Catharine. Sons and daughters and grandson (to wit) Stephen, Michael,
Henry, Samuel, Christopher and William Whitmire, and grandson John
Whitmire, and Catharine Whitmire and Rebekah Wright my daughters.
Executors: Nathaniel Newman, Wm. Young. Dated 8 Oct. 1795.
Wit.: John Bynum   (Signed) Michael (X) Whitmire
       Elizabeth (X) Bynum
Proven 24 Jan. 1797.

WILL OF JOHN NORRIS - pp 102-103
Will of John Norris of Rocky River, Pendleton County. Wife to have
negro man Bob and woman Charlet. Daughter Mary to have negro girl Jenny.
Daughter Nancy to have negro girl Lucy. Daughter Elizabeth to have
negro girl Minder. Son John land on Long Cane. Son James land on
Long Cane. Son Robert Brown. Son Ezekial land on Rocky River. Son
Jesse (?) land on Rocky River. Executors: Brother Patrick Norris,
Charles McCluer and James Thompson. Dated 10 Jan. 1797.
Wit.: Thomas Hays   (Signed) John Norris
       Elizabeth Thompson
       James Hays
Rec. 24 Jan. 1797.

WILL OF WILLIAM BROWN - pp 103-104
Will of William Brown. Wife Hannah the plantation her lifetime or till
she wishes to give it up, then to devolve to William Brown, son of
Alexander Brown. Wife to have negroes. Executors: Wife. Dated 1 Aug.
1792.
Wit.: John River   (Signed) William Brown
       Abraham Cremin (?)
       Benj. Tyree (?)
       Jacob Fannin

WILL OF NATHANIEL HALL - pp 104-105
Will of Nathaniel Hall. All estate deeded me by John Falkner as may
be seen in records of Laurence County if ever it is obtained equally
divided among all my children. Negro woman Ufley (?) and her daughter
Jinny. Wife Elizabeth. Son Nathaniel. If other boys stay with their
Mother until they reach 21 she shall furnish them horse, saddle and
bridle. Property not to be sold out of family. Dated 19 Oct. 1793.
Executors: Brothers Fenton and John Hall.
Wit.: Robt. Noris   (Signed) Nathaniel Hall
       Jos. Erwin
       Benj. Hall
Proven 24 Jan. 1797.

ESTATE OF EVAN THOMAS - p 105
Alexander Ramsey, david Dunlap and John Adair appraised estate of
Evan Thomas 9 Jan. 1797.

INVENTORY OF THOMAS TURNER - pp 106-107
Inventory of Thomas Turner appraised by Thomas Lesley, Isaac Steele,
and James Brown 17 Nov. 1796 at the house of Thomas Turner, deceased
as shown them by Priscilla, James and William Turner administrator and
administratrix.
Rec. 24 Jan. 1797.

SALE OF HARRIS MAULDIN - pp 107-108
Amount of sale of Harris Mauldin 10 Oct. 1797. Purchasers: Robert
Patterson, Hannah Mauldin, Benjamin Hall, Richard George, John Mauldin,
Elizabeth Hall, Daniel Pitchford, Laud (?) Hall, John Lauderdale, Robert
Norris, Fenton Hall, Bartlet Tucker, James Thompson, Wesley Mauldin.
Rec. 24 Jan. 1797.

SALE OF JOHN STEVENSON - p 108
Sale of John Stevenson 16 Feb. 1797. Purchasers: James Morrow, John
Weems, James Stevenson, Moses Liddell, Sarah Morrow, R. Stevenson,

James Henderson, Alex. Stevenson, Jno. Russell, Thos. Blair. Alex.
Stevenson, Admr.
Rec. 23 Feb. 1797.

INVENTORY OF ROBERT KING - pp 108-109
Inventory of Robert King 16 Mar. 1797. Had one negro wench. Appraised
by Oliver Charles, Barnabas (B - his mark) Fair, Joseph Smith.

ESTATE OF WILLIAM SLOAN - pp 109-110
Whereas a difference is now subsisting between David Sloan of the one
part and Polly Sloan, widow of William Sloan, deceased, of the other
part. Subject in dispute submitted to our arbitration 29 June last.
Arbitrators met with said parties 21 Sept. 1796. David Sloan produced
a bill of sale of two negro boys named Sambo and Joe executed by William
Sloan 18 July 1794 and visiting right of said negroes in him. Bill of
sale sufficiently proved to have been executed by William but no consideration was proved to have been given by David nor delivery of property
to have been made by William. Polly Sloan produced several witnesses on
her part whose testimony substantially proved that one Hunter in Georgia
at the first settlement of this country had employed William Sloan as
deputy surveyor, and had put warrants from Georgia land office into his
hands to survey a quantity of land, which was not done by William to the
satisfaction of said Hunter who commenced suit for damages in this state
vs. the said William, who obtained a nonsuit in our court vs. said
Hunter who renewed his suit by writ of attachment in Georgia, that said
William attended court to which said writ was returned. That the attachment was overruled in court as illegal or somehow improper on or about
the 15th of July 1794. Said William informed by his council or his
friends or both, that writ was preparing by said Hunter to take him in
Georgia, and he was advised with all possible speed to cross the river
into South Carolina which he did, but told a witness he would immediately
make over his property, least Hunter should recover unjustly against
him. That the bill of sale bears date 16 July, 1794. That William
afterwards told witness and several others that he had made over his
property to his brother David - or that he had given a bill of sale of
the two negroes on purpose to secure them from Hunter in case he should
recover against him. That William did offer to sell both negroes more
than a year after date of bill of sale and but shortly before his death.
That witness told this to David Sloan after death of William. That
David replied that if his brother had sold them the sale would have
been good, that his brother was always at liberty to take them back again
any time in his lifetime. That he never intended to have taken them
from the widow, nor did he claim them as having paid money for them.
We are of the opinion if William had intended David to have the negroes
he would have bequeathed so in his will. Negroes awarded to the estate
of William Sloan. 3 Oct. 1796. Benj. Cleveland, Andw Pickens, Robert
Anderson.
Rec. 17 Apr. 1797.

INVENTORY OF JOHN COBB - p 110
Inventory of John Cobb. Cash in hands of Rachel Cobb. Notes on Jacob
Reid, administrator. Note on Aaron Broyles. Appraised by William Halbert,
Edwin Smith, Hugh Browne.
Rec. 17 Apr. 1797.

ESTATE OF SAMUEL MYRES - p 110
Samuel Myres estate appraised 24 Mar. 1797 By William Hickman, Saml.
Rowan, (or Bowan ?), and Alexr Kilpatrick.
ec. 17, Apr. 1797.

INVENTORY OF JOHN NORRIS - p 111
Inventory of John Norris by Robert Dowdle, James Nash, Stephen Willis.
21 Mar. 1797.

SALE OF JOHN NORRIS - pp 111-113
Sale of John Norris, 5 Apr. 1797. Purchasers: Thomas Hanks, Thomas
Hays, John Lauderdale, Alex. Erwin, Jane Norris, Dan Williamson, Moses
Bean, John Cambell, Stephen Harris, Benj. Hall, Chas. McClure, Wm.
Jackson, James Thomson, Peter Greenlee, John Callahan, Patrick Norris,

Eliel Moore, Jas. Atkins (?), Roger Martin, John Haney, John Fillpot,
Danl. Williams, Stephen Waynie (?), Stephen Willis, James Hays, Saml.
McGill, John Hainy, James Nash, James Long, James Allen, Moses Holland,
John Hall, Benj. White, Benj. Fuller, Wm. Simpson, Eaker Thacker, David
Parker, Stephen Hains, John Matthews, Edward David, John Bermingham,
Lewis Edward, Saml. Matthews, James Hays, Robert Stevenson, Dan. McCoy,
Geo. Nelson, Eli Litchfield, Thomas Garner, Polly Norris, James Thompson,
Joesph Warnock, John McFalls.
Rec. 17 Apr. 1797.

WILL OF JOHN MIDDLETON, SR. - pp 113-114
Will of John Middleton, Sr., freeholder, of Pendleton County, dated
25 July, 1795. Wife Elizabeth to have two negroes of her choice.
Daughter Elenor Patterson. Sons John and Richard. Three grandsons
Samuel, John and Richard Norwood. Beloved children Susannah Margaret
Buchannon, Frances Patterson, Elizabeth Buchannon, John Middleton,
Richard Middleton, Ann Middleton, Arrabella Canty (?) Middleton.
Executors: Wife Elizabeth, Samuel Porter and Nathaniel Lusk.
Wit.: Nathaniel Lusk   (Signed) John Middleton
      Wm. McCurdy
      Robt. Bond.
Rec. 17 Apr. 1797.

(NOTE FROM COMPILER: Susannah and Margaret may be two daughters. There
was no comma between and it could have been Susannah Margaret Buchannon.
Last names given for other children, so it is likely that Susannah
Margaret was one daughter.)

INVENTORY OF MICHAEL WHITMIRE - p 114
Inventory of Michael Whitmire. By appraisers Michael Whitmire, William
Brown, Archer Harris.
Rec. 17 Apr. 1797.

SALE OF SAMUEL MYRES - p 115
Sale of Samuel Myres 2 May 1797. Purchasers: John Myres, George Shields,
Alexander Barren (or Bowen ?).
Rec. 26 June 1797.

APPRAISEMENT OF WILLIAM BROWN - p 115
Appraisement of William Brown 23 Feb. 1797 by Patrick Norris, Daniel
Pitchford and James Nash. Had negro fellow Simon, negro wench Cresey
and child, boy Simon, girl Mima, girl Susa and boy George. (All of these
negroes.)

WILL OF DAVID BROWN - pp 115-116
Will of David Brown of Pendleton. Wife Jane. Sons John and Joseph to
have land at their mother's death if they have taken care of her. If
they do not, land to go to one of sons that will. Daughter Jane.
Daughter Elizabeth. All my children. Executors: Wife Jane and brother
Joseph Brown. Dated 7 June 1796.
Wit.: John Reid   (Signed) David Brown
      Wm. (X) Reid
      Wm. Bain (?)
Proven 26 June 1797.

p 116
Peter Perkins of Pittsylvania County, Virginia is bound unto Harry
Terrill in sum of $4000 current money of Virginia, dated 23 Nov. 1791.
Perkins to make title to lands in Pendleton to Terrill: tract of 250
acres on Big Eastatoe deeded to Miller, also 640 acres joining the above,
purchased by Perkins from James Martin. Also tract called Col. Earle's
on waters of Twelve Mile supposed to contain 250 acres which Perkins
bought of Earle. Also tract bought of William Young called the Mill
Tract on Little Eastatoe, 157 acres. Also 250 acres joining same.
Also one tract bought from William Young on same waters, 252 acres.
Also 80 acres on South side Big Eastoe. My mill survey joining Dyer on
both sides Big Eastatoe, 800 acres. My little survey up the branch,
137 acres. Also 1 tract purchased of M. Langford on Crow Creek, 300
acres.

Wit.: Bailey Anderson   (Signed) Peter Perkins
      Elisha Dyer
      Joshua Dyer
Rec. 24 Jan. 1798.

SALE OF THOMAS TURNER - pp 117-119
Sale of Thomas Turner 4 Apr. 1797. Purchasers : Priscilla Turner,
William Turner, James Turner, Aaron Turner, Moses Turner, Alexander
Turner, James Kerr, Jacob Skelton, John Moffett, Robert Beard, Joseph
Willson, Aaron James, Alex. Young, Andrew Young, James Brown, William
Stephenson, Matthew Martin, Thomas Lesly, William Manson, John Simpson,
John Roberts, Francis Hamby, William McCune (?), Isaac Steel, Thomas
Buchannon, James Buchannon.
Rec. 26 June 1797.

INVENTORY AND APPRAISEMENT OF JOHN MIDDLETON - p 120
Inventory and appraisement of John Middleton shown by Elizabeth
Middleton, Samuel Porter and Nathaniel Lusk 13 June 1797. Negro man
Jim, negro woman Old Jinny, negro man Big Tom, negro woman Jinny and
child, negro woman Silvey and child, negro boy Little Tom, negro boy
Cyrus, negro boy Prince, negro boy Lewis, negro girl Philis. Appraised
by Alexander Loggan, David Loggan, Jno. Moffett.
Rec. 18 Sept. 1797.

ESTATE OF ROBERT KING - p 121
List of sale of estate of Robert King 27__1798, recorded 18 Sept. 1797.
Negro wench Rose purchased by Elizabeth King, who bought all items sold.

WILL OF ROBERT HALL - pp 121-122
Will of Robert Hall, dated 1 Aug. 1797. Wife Mary to have negro girl
Rachel, wriding chair, household furniture, stock, etc., for support
of herself and children until sons James R. Hall and John Hall are 21,
then to be disposed of at discretion of executors. James Roddy Hall and
John Hall shall have 3 cows and calves when they reach 18. Widow to
have legal share of land during widowhood or until son John is 21.
Son James Roddy Hall to have plantation on Goldings Creek lately purchased of James Brown of Noly Chucky, also negro boy Charles, except
that profits from plantation and labors of Roddy and his boy Charles
be applied for support of family in common until he reaches 25 years
of age. To son John plantation whereon I now live and negro boy Israel.
To my child of which my wife is now pregnant supposing it to live,
Negro girl Rachel. Executors: Robert Bowen, Esq., Capt. David Hamilton,
and W. (?) Mathews, and wife Mary Hall.
Wit.: Francis Dover   (Signed) Rob. Hall
      Wm. Pugh
      Robert Glenn
Proven 18 Sept. 1797.

INVENTORY OF JOHN MOORE - p 122
Inventory of John Moore, 22 July 1797, appraised by Henry King, John
Hillhouse, Lewis Edwards.
Rec. 18 Sept. 1797

INVENTORY OF MR. JOHN WOODSIDE - pp 122-123
Inventory of John Woodside, by Thomas (X) Harrison, Mich. (X) Darnall,
Nathl. (X) Perry. 15 Aug. 1792.
Rec. 18 Sept. 1797.

SALE OF JOHN WOODSIDE - p 123
List of sale of John Woodside. Purchasers: Valentine Martin, Henry
Myres, John L. Davis, John Harrison, Jane Woodside, John Burks, Nathaniel
Perry, William Stephenson, Nicholas Darnall, Martin Hewlett, Wm. Perkins,
Elijah Oliver, Philamon Hawkins, Nathan Durran, Robert Carter, Joshua
Lee.
Rec. 18 Sept. 1797.

16

APPRAISEMENT OF WILLIAM GALLOWAY - p 124
Appraisement of William Galloway's estate by David Hamilton, James
Hamilton, Job Smith and Ezekial Pilgrim 28 July, 1797.
Rec. 24 Jan. 1798.

WILL OF HENRY TERRILL - pp 124-125
(Note: Name written very plainly Henry, but when he signed name it was
definitely Harry Terrill. There was a man by the name of Harry Terrill
in 1790 census of Stokes County, N.C. No man by name of either Henry
or Harry in 1790 census of South Carolina.) Son Joel to have lands where
he now lives - that Peter Perkins make him a deed on his paying $200
to my executors. Lend to wife Sarah Terrill 6 negros: Isham, James,
Milly, Aggee, Pate and Edmond. Henry and Patsy Terrill my two children
by my wife Sarah are underage. Children by first wife. Land on
Eastatoe and Crow Creeks be sold and my 3 sons Samuel, Washington, and
William Terrill be schooled. Six children by first wife: Garlant,
John, Samuel, Washington, William and Elizabeth Terrill. Appoint
trusty friends and relatives to be my executors, now living in the State
of Georgia (to wit) Thomas Terrill, Peter Terrill, David Terrill and
Joel Richardson. Dated ____April 1797.
Wit.: Thomas Barnett   (Signed) Harry Terrill
       John Simmons
       Robert Dowdy
       John (X) Lamb
Proven 20 Jan. 1798.

ESTATE OF SARAH ROBINSON - pp 125-126
Richard Robison appeared before John Willson, J.P., and swore
that Sarah Robinson his mother departed this life 17th day of this instant (February) and that he often heard her say in her lifetime and
shortly before her death that her son Ephriam Robinson should have a
negro girl named Hager and her furniture and part of cattle.
Dated 19 Feb. 1798   (Signed) Richard Robinson

WILL OF THOMAS LIDDELL - pp 126-127
John Liddell, son of Andrew Liddell to have 250 acres out of a 1000
acre tract near Lexington, Ky. known by the name of Manchester Spring.
Jerrett Liddell, son of Andrew Liddell to have 250 acres out of same
tract. Remainder of that land sold and divided among remainder of
Andrew Liddell's children and Moses Liddell's children. Land lying at
the Falls of Ohio, 3 miles square (except a part where a town stands
known by the name of Clarkesville) 300 arising from that sale to William
Liddell, son of John Liddell. Remainder divided among children of
Andrew and Moses Liddell. To William Liddell, son of John Liddell,
320 acres on Duck River in Cumberland. Moses Liddell son of Moses to
have horse, saddle and bridle. Tools divided between Moses and William
Liddell. 20 Feb. 1798.
Wit.: Jno Simpson   (Signed) Thomas Liddell
       Elijah Nicholson
       Alexander Young
Proven by oath of Rev. Jno. Simpson 26 Feb. 1798.
Rec. Apr. 16 1798.

pp 127-128
James Martin of York County, S. C. bound unto Thomas Reese of Pendleton
in sum of 300 sterling 19 Sept. 1793. Martin shall make deed to Reese
for 640 acres in Pendleton on Twenty-three Mile Creek at the mouth of
Garvin's Creek.
Wit.: James Ross   (Signed) James Martin
       Thos. S. Reese
Rec. 28 May 1798.

p 128
Andrew Pickens to Alexander Sherard for 29 ₤1 shilling 4 pence sterling,
a negro man named Sambo, about 45 years of age, near 4 ft. 9 inches
high, formerly the property of Thomas Lesley. Dated 16 Apr. 1798.
Wit.: W. Steele   (Signed) And. Pickens
       Wm. Richards
Rec. 28 May 1798.

16 May 1798. William Rankings of Frederick County, Va., To Robert
Harkness a negro fellow named Bene.
Wit.: Thomas Milsaps   (Signed) William Ranking
       John Hartness
       Jas. Harkness
Rec. 17 Aug. 1798.

WILL OF PHILLIP PHAGINS - p 129

Wife Ann. Bond of Isaac Mitchell be given up if they do not molest or
disturb the estate. Son Phillip Phagens. Daughter Rebecah Phagens to
have some land and negro boy Sam. Daughter Lydia Phagens. Daughter
Margaret Phagens. Estate to be equally divided among all my children.
Moses Phagens and Martha Tilman have already received a part of their
portion. Estate to be valued by Thomas Jones, Isaac Mitchell and James
Crowther. Executors: George Tillman and Jeremiah Starks. Dated 5 Oct.
1796.
Wit.: James Crowther   (Signed) Phillip Phagins
       Phillip Phagens
Proven April 1798.

WILL OF THOMAS SIDNEY REESE - pp 129-130

Brother Edwin. Brother Henry D. Mentions negro boy Jack. Land where
Mother now lives.
Wit.: Lewis D. Martin   (Signed) Thomas S. Reese
       John Taylor
Dated 29 Jan. 1798
Proven 16 April 1798.

SALE OF JOHN MIDDLETON - p 130

Purchasers: Richard Middleton, John Patterson, Thomas Buchannon, Francis
Gillaspie, John McGowen. Elizabeth Middleton bought negro man Jim and
woman Jinny, William Pickens bought negro Jenny, Richard Middleton bought
boy Prince. Thomas Patterson bought negro boy Lewis. Agness Middleton
bought negro girl Fillis. Arabella Canty Middleton bought negro girl
Betty. Andrew Pickens bought negro girl Jenny. Sold 17 Oct. 1797.
Rec. 16 Apr. 1798.

APPRAISEMENT OF THE ESTATE OF MATHIAS CLEVELAND - pp 130-131

By order of court 25 Jan. 1798 appraisement of the estate of Mathias
Cleveland ordered. Notes on Absalom Cleveland, Abner Files, Geter Linch,
Isaac Harnage, William Richards. Appraised by William Richards, James
Blair, Jessey Coffee.
Rec. 16 Apr. 1798.

SALE OF WILLIAM GALLOWAY - p 131

Articles sold at William Galloway's sale. Purchasers: William Wallace,
Edward Saterfield, Edward Norton, James Stevenson, John Morris, Jobe
Smith, Gideon Nortin, Michael Smith, Jeremiah Saterfield, William Galloway,
William Henderson, Jane Galloway. 4 Oct. 1797.
Rec. 16 Apr. 1798.

INVENTORY OF ROBERT LINN - p 131

Inventory of Robert Linn by W. Bowen (?), Samuel Jackson, Benj. Burton
(?), as shown by Bennett Combs and John Jinkins administrators 9 Feb.
1798.
Rec. 15 May 1798.

SALE OF JOHN MOORE - p 132

14 Oct. 1797. Sale of John Moore dec'd by Nancy Moore administrator.
Purchasers: Nancy Moore, Jesse Edwards, William Pickens, Nickles Welch,
Benjamin Dickson, Benj. Bowen, Lewis Edwards.
Rec. 30 May 1798.

INVENTORY OF PHILLIP PHEAGANS - p 133

Had 2 negros. Bond on Isaac Mitchell, notes on John and William Anderson.
28 Apr. 1798 by Isaac Mitchell, Thomas Jones, James Crowther, appraisers.
Rec. 25 June 1798.

A list of notes: (NOTE FROM COMPILER: Not clear as to whether or not this is a continuation of Pheagan's inventory and sale.) Nathan Turner, Camp & Langford, Abraham Duff, James and Wardlaw, Champ Langford, James Jackson, Wm. Owens, Wm. Boran (?), Saml. Jackson, James Jett, Sarah Right, Nathan Nations, Abraham Duff, Bennett Combs, Josiah Marchbanks, James Wardlaw, William Kirbee, Lewis Reeder, Hezekiah Johnston, Elijah Mayfield, Sarah Linn, Thomas Langley, John Terrell.

RETURN OF PROPERTY SALE OF ROBERT LINN - p 134
Return of property sale of Robert Linn, By Bennett Combs 25 June 1798. (Note: Above notes may have been in Robert Linn's estate.)

ESTATE OF LEWIS SHELTON - p 134
9 June 1798 - Negro man Nim belonging to the estate of Lewis Shelton appraised by James (X) Davenport and John Barton. Rec. 25 June 1798.

INVENTORY OF SALE OF WILLIAM SLOAN - p 134
Inventory of sale of William Sloan. Purchasers: John Barton, Polly Sloan bought negro man Joe, man Ben, woman Penney, man Sam, and girl Cloe. Nathaniel Perry bought mulatto bound boy named Isaac Williams. Jesse Coffee, Mathew Hooper, James C. Kilpatrick, James Furgason. Polly Sloan, administratrix certified sale to be correct. Rec. 25 June 1798.

ESTATE OF ABIJAH DAVIS - pp 134-135
11 June 1798. Estate of Abijah Davis appraised by Elial Moore, Robt. Stevenson, Jesse Brown. Rec. 26 June 1799 (?).

WILL OF SAMUEL TAYLOR - pp 136-137
Will of Samuel Taylor, Planter. Wife Elenor to have negro man Dave and wench Vilet. Taylor lives on East side Seneca River. Sons John and Samuel to have land in Abbeville County on Savannah River, some lately purchased of Jos. Sanders. To John B. Earle land on west side Seneca River above mouth of Seneca Creek if Earl makes title to son William Taylor to land adjoining land where I now live. Son Joseph. Son John to have negro boy Henry. Daughter Dilly to have negro wench Milly and Nance. Daughter Elizabeth to have wence Molly and girl Sinah. Mentions children under age. Granddaughter Hannah Earle to have girl Marian. If any of my last sons die underage and without issue their share to be divided equally between the rest of brothers and if either daughter die under age or without issue share to be divided amongst surviving daughters. Executors: Son John and Andrew Pickens, William Steele and George Reese. Dated 20 April 1798.
Wit.: James Wood   (Signed) Samuel Taylor
       Robt. Glenn
       Sarah Pickens
Rec. 27 June 1798.

ESTATE OF SARAH ROBINSON - p 137
Before Michael Dickson, J. P., appeared Elizabeth Ship and being duly sworn as the law directs saith on oath that on the 26 December last the said Elizabeth Ship and her grandmother Sarah Robinson being only present that she said Sarah Robinson told the said Elizabeth that she allowed her Ephriam to have her negro girl and her bed and furniture and further her grandmother said she would have settled her affairs in shurer way if it was not for fear of son John Robinson turning her off. Sworn to this 14 Aug. 1798.   (Signed) Elizabeth (X) Ship

Ann Adin appeared before Michael Dickson, J. P. and swore that she was in company with Sarah Robinson and in course of their discourse she told her she allowed her son Ephriam to get her negro girl Hager at her death and her bed and furniture and that she would have given girl to Ephriam before now if it was not for fear of John Robinson disposing her as she had no other place to go. Sworn to 14 Aug. 1798.
                                 (Signed) Ann (X) Eaden

INVENTORY OF MAJ. SAMUEL TAYLOR - p 138-140
Negroes: fellow Harry, fellows Big Charles, Sampson, Pompey and Frank,
Little Charles. Negro women Moll and Violett, boys Dave, Lewis, Henry.
Girls Mille and Nancy. A wench & family to wit: Patty, Peter, Ester,
Isaac London, Marion. Fellow George. Girl Sinah, Boy John, Old Jack,
Kate his wife and 2 children Ester and Lancaster. Nero, his wife Dinah
and 2 children Ransom and Frank. Notes on John McDow, James Hamilton,
John Clark, William Steele, John Wardin, Wm. McCaleb, Isaac Williams,
Old Sam Isaacs, John Diviney, Ledford Payne, James Yowell. Appraised
by Wm. McGriffin (?), Alex. Ramsey, Wm. McCaleb.
Rec. 17 Sept. 1798.

WILL OF PHILLIP PRATER - pp 140-141
Will of Phillip Prater, dated 5 Feb. 1796. Son John, son Thomas, son
Phillip. Daughters Sally and Polly. Son William. Wife Susannah.
Land to be divided when youngest child reaches maturity. Executors:
Wife and son John and William Hubbard.   His
Wit.: Robert McCann   (Signed) Phillip (PP) Prater
       James C. Griffin   Mark
Proven 17 Sept. 1798.

WILL OF CURTIS MOORE - pp 141-142
Wife Mary. Three daughters Winney Moore, Rachel and Synthea. Executors:
Wife Mary and Son Levi Moore. Dated 6 Apr. 1798.
Wit.: Edward Williams   (Signed) Curtis Moore
       Saml. (X) Thacker
Proven 17 Sept. 1798.

INVENTORY AND APPRAISEMENT OF JOHN MOORE - p 142
Inventory and appraisement of John Moore as shown by Elial Moore, adm.
Had 1 negro woman. 28 Aug. 1798. Appraised by Robt. Dowdle, Hezekiah
Davis, Jo Pickens.
Rec. 17 Sept. 1798.

SALE OF JOHN MOORE - p 143
Sale of John Moore 1 Sept. 1798. Purchasers: Robert Love, Elial Moore,
James Simpson, John Wardlaw, Samuel McCalley (?), Elias Oldham, Robt.
Stevenson, James Holland, Nathaniel Timmons, Richard Majors, James
Allen, John Dowdle, William Drennan, John Ross, Stephen Willis, Robt.
Dowdle, Nancy Wardlaw, Purcy Blagg.
Rec. 17 Sept. 1798.

INVENTORY OF SARAH ROBINSON - p 144
John Robinson ordered by court 29 June 1798 to take inventory of Sarah
Robinson, dec'd. Made by David Watkins, Thos. Black, Andrew Warnock.
Rec. 17 Sept. 1798.   Had one negro wench.

INVENTORY OF ABIJAH DAVIS - pp 144-145
Purchasers at sale: Hezekiah Davis, Elizabeth Davis, Hermon Cummins,
James Hilhouse, William Jackson, Richard Dodd, Wm. Linnard, Benj. Brumer,
John Reeves, David Dickey, Alex. McClusky, Eliphas Davis, Willaim Dickey,
Jesse Brown. Certified by Jesse Brown.
Rec. 17 Apr. 1798.

INVENTORY OF THOMAS REESE - pp 146-148
19 negroes. Fellows: Cesa, Sam, Derry, Cato. Boys: Jack, Mose, Cyrus,
Bosen, Prince, Tony. Wenches: Rose, Ola, Hanna. Girls: Maria, Nanny,
Cloe, Daphne, Candis, Mary. Appraised by Michael Dickson, John Griffin,
Joseph Whitner. 8 Feb. 1797.
Rec. 17 Sept. 1798.

INVENTORY OF HARRY TERRELL - pp 149-150
Negroes: Old Sam, Old Lydia, Sally Lucy, Peter, Anna, Young Sam, Tom,
Milley, Simon, Daniel, Little Tom, John Lyde, Molly, James, Patty,
Isham, Azza, Edmond. Appraised by Elisha Dyer, John Cockran, James
McKinney.
Rec. 8 Oct. 1798.

WILL OF NATHANIEL REED - p 150-151

Will of Nathaniel Reed of Pendleton. Wife Elizabeth to have negro
wench Nan. Three youngest daughters Elizabeth Brown, Winifred Hood,
Sade (?) Shotwell. Two eldest daughters Rachel Adams and Anne Adams.
Eldest son William Reed to have negro fellow Will. Second son Nathaniel
Reed to have negro fellow Peter. Third and last son Stephen Reed to have
negro boy Jess. Executors: Sons William and Nathaniel Reed and Hugh
Brown. Dated ____Sept. 1798.   His
Wit.:   J. Keith   (Signed) Nathaniel (NR) Reed
        George Keith   Mark
        Cornelius (X) Keith
Rec. 24 Jan. 1799.

WILL OF MESHACK GREEN - pp 151-152
Wife Creasy to raise and school children. Sons Thomas, Daniel, Joney
and Henry. Nancy. Son John. Land on Coxes Creek. Son-in-law John
Horton to have land where he now lives joining Charles Goodwin, Christopher Crider and Isaac Horton. To John Caldwell land where he lives
joining George Anderson and Goodin and Horton. To Elizabeth Smith
land where she lives joining George Anderson. To Isaac Horton land where
he now lives. Executors: Wife Creasy and son Thomas my trusty friend.
Dated 19 March 1798.
Wit.:   George Anderson   (Signed) Mesheck Green
        Lemuel (or Sameil ?) Thompson   (made his mark)
        Moley (X) Anderson
Rec. 24 Jan. 1799.

INVENTORY AND APPRAISEMENT OF PHILLIP PRATER - p 153
Inventory and appraisement of Phillip Prater by John Hallum, Robert
Baker, Andrew Pickens 22 Jan. 1799.
Rec. 24 Jan. 1799.

WILL OF JOHN VERNER - p 154
Son George Verner. Wife Mary. Son Charles. Wife to have negro man
her lifetime then to go to Charles. Son Samuel. Sons David and John
to have land on Rocky River. Daughters Jenny Verner, Nancy Verner,
Dianna Wakefield, Sarah Montgomery and Mary Ewing. Executors: Wife
Mary and son David.
Dated 10 Feb. 1798.
Wit.:   Thomas Morrow   (Signed) John Verner
        William Stevenson
Proven 24 Jan. 1799.

p 155
January Term of Court 1799. Personally appeared Ambrose Hudgins in open
court and duly sworn made oath that about thirty years ago to the best
of his recollection he was at the house of William Cannon that the said
William Cannon took in his arms his granddaughter Nancy Hudgins who was
about one year old and who is now Nancy Brooks and then asked this
deponent to walk into his kitchen and when they had got into the kitchen
that the said William Cannon said to him, he had asked him to walk in
to see him deliver a negro male child called Jim to his granddaughter
then Nancy Hudgins, but now Nancy Brooks, that the said William Cannon
did then in the presence of this deponent take and deliver the said male
child to the said Nancy Hudgins now Nancy Brooks to be her right and
property when she should marry or come of age. And he further saith
that he hath since seen Ann Cannon widow of William Cannon deceased
deliver the said negro Jim to the above mentioned Nancy Brooks.
Rec. 24 Jan. 1799.   (Signed) Ambrose Hudgins Senr.

p 155
January Term, 1799, personally appeared Mrs. Elenor Taylor and made
oath that she frequently heard William Cannon in his lifetime say that
a certain negro man Jim now in the possession of John B. Earle did
belong to her daughter Nancy Brooks, then Nancy Hudgins, and that said
negro was always considered and called the property of said Nancy Brooks
and she further saith that she was present and saw Ann Cannon widow of
William Deliver the said negro Jim to the above named Nancy Brooks.
B. Earle, Cl. ____Earle, D. Cl. (Signed) Elenor Taylor
Rec. 24 Jan. 1799.

SALE OF PART OF ESTATE OF PHILLIP PHAGAN - pp 156-157
Purchasers: Lydda Phagan, Ann Phagan, Moses Phagan, Rebeccah Melford,
George Tilman, Margret Phagan, James Crowther, Jno. Milford, Jack (?)
Starks, Harbert Tucker, John Calahan, Isaac Mitchell, Phil. Phagan,
David Parker, Wm. Pitts, Jno Hall (or Kell?), Thomas Jones. Appraised
by Isaac Mitchell, Thomas Jones, James Crowther. Nov. 1798.

SALE OF PHILLIP PHAGAN - pp 157-158
Purchasers: Daniel Putman, Lydia Phagan, Phil Phagan, Augusta Harris,
Moses Phagan, Ann Phagan, Mary Phagan, Jno. Fowler, Jacob Pruet, Robert
Beard, James Neil, Jno. Letherdiel (?), Abraham Benhoton (?), Charles
Baine (?), Auguston Harris, William Stephens, Margret Phagan, Archeble
McKee, George Tillman, William Blackdon, George Rogers, William McKune,
William Hambleton, Isaac Mitchell, Rebecca Phagan, Robt. McLough, Benj.
George, Benj. Hall. Sold 18 July 1798. George Tillman, Administrator.
Rec. 24 Jan. 1799.

INVENTORY AND APPRAISEMENT OF ROBERT SWAN - p 158
Inventory and appraisement of Robert Swan as shown by Rebecca Swan,
executrix, to appraisers William Wilson, Charles Wilson, Jas. Stevenson.
Rec. 24 Jan. 1799.

SALE OF SARAH ROBINSON - p 158
Purchasers: Ephriam Robinson, John Robinson, Mary Ward, Richard Robinson.
Rec. 24 Jan. 1799.

INVENTORY OF LEVI MURPHY - pp 158-159
1 negro fellow, 1 negro girl. Appraised by Nathaniel Newman, James
Wardlow. Notes on William Powell Riggins, and Joel Moody.
Rec. 24 Jan. 1799.

SALE OF LEVI MURPHRE - pp 159-161
Sale of Levi Murphre 22 Oct. 1798. Purchasers: Eliga Murphre, Mary
Murphere, Hennery Wolbanks, Jessee Ellis, Jacob Vance, Isaiah Murphere,
Abner Robinson, John Beynum, Solomon Smith, Seth Marchbanks, John Hawks,
Solomon Murphre, Black Seaser. Mary (X) Murphre certified it to be
correct.
Rec. 24 Jan. 1799.

SALE OF PART OF ESTATE OF MAJ. SAMUEL TAYLOR - pp 161-162
16 Oct. 1798. (Purchasers not named).
Rec. 24 Jan. 1799.

WILL OF MARY THOMPSON - pp 163-164
Will of Mary Thompson of Washington District. Three sons Mathew, Joseph
and John Thompson to have plantation whereon I now live it being granted
to Gilbert Neel and sold to me by Maj. Thomas Farrar. It is to be valued
when son John reaches age of 18. Youngest daughter Ann. Dated 7 Nov.
1798. Executors: beloved friends William and James Thompson.
Wit.: John Tippin   (Signed) Mary Thompson
      George Tippin
Proven 28 Jan. 1799.

WILL OF ROBERT CRAIG - pp 164-165
Wife Sarah to have plantation whereon I now live on south side Saluda
River on Rocky Branch. Daughter Martha not of age. Brother John.
Executors: wife Sarah and John Craig. Dated 1 Oct. 1797.
Wit. John Wilson, Jr.   (Signed) Robert Craig
     Samuel Barkley
Proven 29 Jan. 1799.

WILL OF HENNERY WAKEFIELD - pp 165-167
Will of Hennery Wakefield of Abavel County, planter. Wife Jenny to have
plantation and negro fellow Robert her lifetime. At wife's death Robert
to be freed. Son Allen Wakefield. I will that a plantation be bought
of that 150 ₺ that is coming for my land in North Carolina and that it
be for son William. Daughters Jane and Mary to have equal portion to
daughters Marget and Nancy. After the death of my Jane, place I now
live on to be sold and money remaining if there be any divided between

my six daughters: Nancy, Marget, Betsy, Rachel, Mary and Jane.
Executors: son David Bug (?) and Allen Wakefield. Dated 5 Sept. 1790.
Wit.: Ledford Payne   (Signed) Henry Wakefield
      William Wakefield
      Janes (X) Payne
Proven 30 Jan. 1799.

INVENTORY AND APPRAISEMENT OF JOHN FOX - p 167
Inventory and appraisement of John Fox 5 Mar. 1799 by Andrew Liddell,
Benj. Dickson, Lewis Cobb.
Rec. 15 Apr. 1799.

SALE OF EVAN THOMAS - pp 168-169
Sale of estate of Evan Thomas 4 April 1797. Purchasers: Samuel Taylor,
Robert Miller, Saml. Robertson, William Hamilton, John Thomas, Mary
Dagly, Joseph Reed, John Thomas, Ambrose Foster, David Dunlap, William
Bates, Nicholas Bishop, Samuel Robinson, John Knox. Samuel Robinson and
William Hamilton, administrators.
Rec. 15 Apr. 1799.

INVENTORY OF MARY THOMPSON - p 169
Negro woman and two children. Appraised by Robert Dowdle, Joseph Pickens,
Peter Keys. 1 Feb. 1799.
Rec. 15 Apr. 1799.

INVENTORY OF ARCHABALD BOYD - pp 169-170
Inventory of Archabald Boyd 6 Apr. 1799. Notes of Epperson and Brown.
Accounts on James Wallace (?), John Chanler, Rose Reese, Jeremiah
Thompson, James Thompson, Joseph Harrod, Moses Murphee, Elijah Mayfield,
John Barnard. Appraised by Moses Murphree, Alexander Bivins, Jacob
(X) Light. Certified by James Jett, adm.
15 Apr. 1799.

pp 170-171
James Martin of York County, Planter, bound unto Elieb Moore in sum of
500 ₺ dated 29 Nov. 1794. Martin to make deed for 640 acres on Rocky
River to Moore. Except what may fall into Martin's own tract which lies
joining, and Robert Dowdle's tract that may fall into said tract. Land
granted to John Traverse on Rocky River, joins William Forbes, Robert
Dowdle, Elieb Moore and Saml. Dalrumple's land in Pendleton County.
Wit.: John Linn   (Signed) James Martin
      George Ross
Rec. 18 June 1799.

SALE OF ARCHABALD BOYD - pp 171-172
Sale of Archabald Boyd 30 Apr. 1799. Elizabeth Boyd, widow. Thomas
Edwards, Hester Boyd, James Jett, Daniel Alexander, James Barnett,
William Rose, John Edwards, John Powell were purchasers.
Rec. 24 June 1799.   James Jett, Adm.

SALE OF JOHN COX - pp 172-173
Sale of John Cox, dec'd 1 May 1799 by Elizabeth and Hennery Cox,
administrators. Purchasers: Elizabeth Cox, Hennery Cox, Capt. George
Reeves, Fereby Cox, Beverly Cox, Hollingsworth Candiver (?), Thomas
Davis.   Hennery Cox, Adm.
Rec. 24 June 1799.

WILL OF ELIJA ISAACS - pp 173-174
Youngest son George to have negro boy Isaiah when he reaches age of 21.
If he dies without issue negro goes to Jinny and Winney. Daughters
Rebecka Isaacs, Abbee, Jinny and youngest daughter Winney. Executors:
James Blair and Samuel Isaacs. Dated 4 Apr. 1799.
Wit.: Thomas Gibson   (Signed) Elijah Isaacs
      William Isaacs
      Hayes Blair
Proven 24 June 1799.

WILL OF WILLIAM HEATON - pp 174-176
Wife Esther. Youngest son James. Son Salathal. Son Thomas A.,
daughter Mary, daughter Sary and son Benjamin Heaton to have 1
English shilling a piece to paid two years after my death. Son
William. Son Smith. Son Joseph. Daughter Anna Heaton. Executors:
Wife Esther and James Hembree. Dated 11 Jan. 1799.
Wit.: Thomas Riddel   (Signed) William Heaton
       Mark (X) Pitts
       James Heaton
Proven June term 1799.

WILL OF PATRICK EARLY - pp 176-178
Eldest daughter Mary, money lent her at her marriage. Eldest son James.
Youngest daughter Ruth Early. Wife Pheby. Youngest son Enoch Early.
Daughter Lettece Early. Executors: Wife Pheby and Moses Hayns. Dated
10 June 1798.
Wit.: Hugh Simpson   (Signed) Patrick (X) Early
       Thomas Seales
Proven 19 Sept. 1798.
Rec. Sept. 1799.

To the Honorable Court of Pendleton - Gentlemen, being obliged to attend
(by Supenia) the Court of Elbert County in the State of Georgia I cannot
attend to the will of Patrick Early late deceased. Therefore I shall
not act as executor on that case. I am, Gentleman, yours, etc.
                              (Signed) Moses Hayns
Apr. 2, 1799.

HENRY TERRAL, MINOR AND PATSY TERRAL, MINOR - p 179
In pendleton District Court of Ordinary March 1, 1802 (?). Joshua Dyer
was appointed guardian of Henry Terral a minor and Patsy Terral a minor.

ALLSIMEDON (?) THOMPSON, MINOR - p 180
31 Oct. 1803 - Allsimedon (?) Thompson a minor more than 14 years of
age asks that Tarley Thompson be appointed his guardian. Allsimedon
was 14 the 8th of June last. John Harris, Ordinary.

THEANY DAVIS, MINOR - p 181
1 Aug. 1804 - Nedom Truman appointed guardian of Theany Davis a minor
aged 6 months and 2 weeks old.

SIMEON WEBB, MINOR AND ELIZABETH WEBB, MINOR - p 182
4 May 1810. John Green appointed guardian of Simeon Webb 8 years of
age 3 Dec. 1809, and Elizabeth Webb a minor 7 years of age 31 July next.

p 183
Miller's letters of guardianship for the ??? (Nothing more.)

p 184
William F. Spears (?) letters of guardianship for William B. Todd (?).
(Nothing more)

WASHINGTON KEES - p 185
21 April 1813. Mr. Elijah Kees, Jr. (?), and Poyndexter Payne appointed
guardians of Washington Kees a minor 14 years of age last March. They
being chosen by said minor.

p 186
Capt. Samuel Tate's letters of guardianship. (Nothing more.)

WILLE SANDERS, MINOR - p 187
3 Feb. 1812. John Craige appointed guardian of Wille Sanders a minor,
she is 17 years of age last December.

ROBERT TATE, MINOR - p 188
July 8, 1813. Mr Samuel McClure appointed guardian of Robert Tate a
minor 12 years old last October.

HUMPHRES CHAPPLE, MINOR - p 189
2 Aug. 1813 - Mr. Thomas appointed guardian of Humphres Chapple a minor

18 years old last December. Thomas appointed a Chapple's application.

p 190
Cunningham letters of guardianship. (Nothing more on this page.)

BILLY G. DILWORTH, MINOR, GEORGE DILWORTH, MINOR, AND BENJ. DILWORTH, MINOR - p 191

3 Feb. 1817. On application and choice of two minors above the age of 14 the Rev. James Douthet appointed guardian of them and a younger brother under the age of 14. Billy G. Dilworth, a minor 17 years of age 26 day of last November. George Dilworth 14 years of age 9th of last June and Benjamin Dilworth 11 the 13th of December last. Douthet to be guardian of Billy G. and George until they reach the age of 21. Benjamin may choose his guardian at the age of 14.

NANCY BRUSTER, MINOR - 192

3 March in the Year of Independence the forty-first. On application of Margaret Edmondson appoint James Dickeson guardian of Nancy Bruster 9 years of age 24 June next. He to be guardian until she is 21 or chooses other guardian at age of 14.

THOMAS WATSON, MINOR - p 193

27 Oct. 1818. Anselem Roe appointed guardian of Thomas Watson, age 13 the 4th of January last.

ROBERT W. REEVES, MINOR, FRANCES REEVES, MINOR, JANE REEVES, MINOR, PATIENCE REEVES, MINOR, AND ELIZABETH REEVES - p 194

14 Sept. 1819. On application of Robert W. Reeves, age 15, Mr. John Reeves is appointed guardian. Also guardian of 4 other minors: Frances Reeves, age 13, Jane Reeves, aged 11, Patience Reeves, aged 9, and Elizabeth Reeves, aged 7.

THIS CONCLUDES BOOK C

WILL OF PETER LEBOON - pp 1-2
Wife Hannah. Daughters: Catharine and Elizabeth Leboon. Son Peter.
Daughter Mary Waters. Dated only Oct. No day or year.
Wit: John Terrall   (Signed) Peter Leboon
   William Terrall
Proven 7 June, 1800 by James Head who swore that he saw Peter Leboon
sign the will.

WILL OF WILLIAM GRIFFIN - pp 3-4
Planter, of Pendleton. Wife Elizabeth to have slave Charles aged about
55. Son John Griffin. Son Henry. Son William. Son Serjeant, to have
land on Twelve Mile on middle fork. Son Orswell. Daughter Rebeca
Brazeal. Daughter Rosana Blocker. Daughter Hasky Brazeal. Daughter
Martha. Daughter Elizabeth Griffin. Negroes named Jo, George, Nance,
and Belinda (aged 3). My last wife's children to receive remainder of
estate. Executors: Wife Elizabeth and trusty friend Elnathan Davis.
Dated 5 Oct. 1800.
Wit: J. D. Meroney   (Signed) William (X) Grifin
  Tho. Hunt
  And. Tawnyhill
  Charles Morgan
Proven 14 Oct. 1800.

WILL OF AMBROSE HUDGENS - p 5
Wife Joanah. Son Ambrose. Daughters Phebe Anderson and Margaret Millwee.
One shilling to Sarah Robertson (?). One shilling to son John. One
shilling to son Robert. Executors: John Brown and Abednego Green, Sr.
Dated: 21 Sept. 1799.
Wit.: John Brown
  Nancy Tarrant
  Anna (X) Brown
Proven 13 Nov. 1800.

WILL OF GEORGE HOGE - pp 6-7
Dated 3 Nov. 1798. To John Ross. To daughter Barbara Ross. Son
George Hoge to have big Bible. Daughter Georrecte (?). Two sons John
and George. 4 children. Son-in-law John Ross. Son George. Daughter
Georreotte (?). Executors: Son-in-law John Ross and Son George Hoge.
Wit.: John Woodall, Sr.
  John Woodall, Jr.
  Judeth (X) Woodall
Proven 14 Apr. 1881.

WILL OF WILLIAM GREEN - pp 7-9
Farmer, names wife Ann. Son John to have negro March. Wife and son to
raise younger children. Dated 26 Jan. 1801.
Wit.: Aaron James   (Signed) William Green
  James Turner
  Rhody (X) McCurary
Proven 9 Mar. 1801 (?)

WILL OF JOSEPH MCCLUSKY - pp 9-11
Abbeville County. To Joseph McClusky son of David McClusky, 1 bay mare
which was received in payment for 50 acres of land which I give to said
Joseph. Remainder of land to be sold and half of the money received
divided equally between my grandsons Joseph and Joseph Hall, sons of
Alexander and William McClusky. The other half of price of lands to go
to daughter Agnes. If daughter Agnes died single to go to two grandsons
above named. Remainder to go to 3 granddaughters all named Nancy,
daughters of my sons David, Alexander and William McClusky. Executors:
Wife Agnes, son Alexander and Nathan Lusk.

27

cont;
Dated 25 Oct. 1798.
Wit.: Alexander White   (Signed) Joseph McClusky
       William Kerr
       Nathan Lusk
Amendment- The second article altered to read: Money divided in three
equal shares between two grandsons Joseph and Joseph Hall, sons of
Alexander, and William McClusky. Dated 9 Dec. 1799.
Wit.: Alex (X) White
       Nathan Lusk
       John Ferguson
Proven 13 Oct. 1802.

WILL OF THOMAS HOUSTON - p 12
Wife. Sons Thomas, Josiah and John. Executors: Wife and Samuel Houston.
Dated 26 Apr. 1800.
Wit.: Wm. Woods   (Signed) Thomas (X) Houston
       Wm. Henry
       Jas. Hillhouse
Proven 14 Oct. 1800 by Wm. Hennery and John Hilhous.

WILL OF ROBERT GABEE - p 13
Daughter Elizabeth. Sons Robert and Moses. Executors: Thomas Stribling
and Joseph Gabee. Dated 6 Feb. 1802.
Wit.: Richard Speak   (Signed) Robert Gabee
       Saml. Tate
       Thos. Stribling.
Proven 11 June, 1802.

WILL OF CALEB EDMISTON - pp 13-15
Pendleton, a farmer. Wife Margaret. Daughters Elizabeth, Ann and
Haster to have plantation where Moses Whitly lives, to be rented until
one of the daughters marries, then sold and divided amongst the three.
Let their schooling be paid out of the rent. Son Joseph. Executor:
Wife Margret and Nicholas Welch. Dated 26 Sept. 1799.
Wit.: Robert Rankin   (Signed) Caleb (X) Edmiston
       John Watson
Amendment - 3 Oct. 1799. Wife to have plantation her lifetime or widow-
hood.
Wit.: Robert Franklin
       William Welch
       Jonathan Montgomery
Proven 14 Oct. 1800.

WILL OF MOSES LIDDLE - pp 15-17
Pendleton, Yeoman. Executors: Elizabeth Liddle, John Henderson, Andrew
Liddle and Daniel Keith., Wife Elizabeth. Two sons Moses and James.
Owns plantations where Thomas Blair, James Jones and Wm. McClusky live.
Owns negro wench Sarah and child Carlott, fellow Jacob and wife Sylva
and fellow September. Daughter Elizabeth. Son Moses. Son James.
Daughters: Esther, Isabella and Joan. Niece Mary Lidle to have horse
and saddle and bed if she lives with wife Elizabeth until a mature age.
Dated 1 May, 1802.
Wit.: Wm. B. Ross
       Thomas Morrow
Proven 21 Aug. 1802.

WILL OF PETER GREENLEES - pp 17-19
Daughter Nancy Johnson gets negro girl Hannah. Daughter Elizabeth
Oldham to have negro girl Sharlott. Son Willis to have negro woman
Grace and child. Daughter Margaret Greenlees to have negro girl Suck.
Son William to have negro boy James. Daughter Mary Oldham to have negro
girl Vilet. Wife Deborah to have negroes Jane, Dick, Clay, Sissia
(or Sipia), Stephen and Daniel. Wife to have these negroes for support
of herself and my children: James Greenlees, Shadrack Greenlees, John
Greenlees, Duley Greenlees, Milly Greenlees. She and my 5 youngest child-
ren. Executors: Son William and Reuben Johnson. Dated 28 June, 1798.
Wit.: Stephen Willis
Proven 3 Sept. 1802.

WILL OF DAVID WADE - pp 19-21
Wife Anges. Children: Elizabeth Wade, Thomas Clement Wade, Anna Wade,
Edward Wade, David Wade, Polly Wade, Richard Wade, Agnes Wade, William
Wade and James Wade. Those of my children that has received part of
estate previous to these presents. Executors: Wife Agnes and son
Richard Wade. Dated 8 Mar. 1802.
Wit.: James Cooper
      Thomas Hanks
      Timothy Orr
      Claborne Harris
Proven 3 Sept. 1802.

WILL OF ROBERT HENDERSON - pp 21-22
Pendleton. Wife Isabell. Son Nathaniel. Son David. All my children.
Three hundred acres on waters of Packolet divided betwixt my 4 sons
John, William, James and Robert. Executor: Son David. Dated 7 Oct.
1800.
Wit.: Saml. Berdine   (Signed) Robert Henderson
      Wm. Canselar (?)
      Wm. Henderson
Proven 13 Oct. 1801 (?).

WILL OF JOHN EWING CALHOUN - pp 22-31
St. John Parish, Attorney at Law. To wife Floride negroes Johnsy, Dina,
Suckey and her children, and 1/5 part of all my negroes her lifetime.
Wife is possessed of in her own right considerable real property to wit
house in Charleston, Santee lands in St. Stephens Parish, and one half
western part of Lot #1 of the Ferry Tract where I now live. Son John
Ewing Calhoun to have plantation at the mouth of Twelve Mile River in
Pendleton where I usually reside in the summer season, about 3700 acres.
If he dies under age or without issue goes to my son James Edward Calhoun.
If he dies to my son Wm. Sheridan Calhoun. If he dies to daughter
Floride Calhoun. Son John to have 1/5 of negroes including boys Isaac
and Scipio. Son James Edward to have 550 acres on Little River in
Abbeville Dist. lately bought of Ezekial Calhoun, also 640 acres granted
Frances Bonneau of Charleston on Twenty-three Mile Creek in Pendleton,
also 1/5 of negroes including Tom, Palidores son and little New Venuses
son. To son William Sheridan Calhoun, plantation called Trotters Mill
seat on Savannah River in Abbeville Dist. containing 540 acres, and also
150 acres on the River three miles below bounded on the south by John
and Samuel Taylor, land originally granted Andrew Norris. Also 200
acres three miles from Trotters Mill adjoining Mr. Cain. (or McCain?),
originally granted Charles Skinner. He also gets 1/5 of negroes including Billy the son of Polydare and the boy Squirrel. Daughter Floride
to have 1/5 negroes including mulatto Rose and Bina, Polydares daughter.
My will is that three sons get collegiate education at some college of
note and respectability. My will is to keep my negroes together to work
my lands to support and educate family. Ferry Tract at No. 1 on west
side of Chayrant's Creek. Executors: Gen. Andrew Pickens, Henry Wm.
Disaussure, John Ball, Andrew Norris and Joseph Calhoun. Dated 20 May,
1092.
Wit.: Ezekial Noble
      John C. Calhoun
      Alexander Noble.
Amendment dated 21 Oct. 1802 - In addition I appoint Ezekial Pickens one
of my executors.
Wit.: Robert Anderson   (Signed) John E. Calhoun
      John Simpson, Jr.
      B. Green, Jr.
(List of land, value and fromwhom purchased not copied.)

WILL OF BENJAMIN SILMON - pp 31-32
Wife Isabell plantation where she now lives, joins Drury Hutson, James
Baren (?), Tarrants Branch. Son John Silman. Wife to have negro girl
(name illegible). Son David Silman land known as the Dyer place. Son
Benjamin Silman land known as Owns place. Son William land known as
Nations place. Youngest son John to have land on Little Eastatoe. Two
daughters Rosy and Juda. To brother Thomas Silman my still, saddle and
saddle bags. Executors: Wife Isabell, son David, son Benjamin and

cont;
brother Thomas. Dated 15 Dec. 1802.
Wit.: Benj. Silman
    John Cochram
    David (X) Hutson
Proven 25 Jan. 1803, by John Cochran and Drury Hutson.

WILL OF ABEL HILL - pp 33-34

Pendleton, a farmer. Every one of my living children. Sons and daughters of my loving wife Elizabeth to have 5 shillings. To son James lands and negroes. Son Ruben (?) Hill and wife Elizabeth Hill executors. Dated 18 July, 1799.
Wit.: Thomas Cureton   (Signed) Abel (X) Hill
    Mary (X) Cureton
    Rachel (X) Harkens
Proven 14 Mar. 1803. Elizabeth qualified as executor 26 Mar. 1803.

WILL OF ISAAC STEEL - pp 34-35

Wife Grizzle. Sons Michael, William, John, Isaac, Moses and James. Daughters, Margaret, Ruth and Jenny. Executors: Wife Grizzle and William Turner. Dated 13 Mar. 1802.
Wit.: Nathan Lusk   (Signed) Isaac Steel
    John Hamilton (?)
Proven 15 Mar. 1803 by Nathan Lusk, Esq.

WILL OF JAMES FOSTER - pp 35-37

Wife Mary. Son Gabriel land on Twenty-three Mile Creek. Son James. Daughters: Sally Merritt, Abbigail Merritt, and Rachel Foster. Executors: Son Gabriel and Robert Orr, Senr.
Wit.: Robt. McCann   (Signed) James Foster
    Thomas (X) Brown
    Elizabeth (X) Wigganton
    James Foster
Proven 4 Jan. 1802.
    (Note: This will was extremely difficult to read. If it was
    dated I could not make it out.)

WILL OF JOHN ROE - pp 37-38

Camden Dist., Craven County, dated 20 Apr. 1778. Son John to have negro girl Sue. Son Andrew to have negro girl Philhs (?). Son Solomon to have negro girl Rose. Son Benjamin to have girl Lucy. Son Joseph to have negro man James. Son Hansill to have woman Hannah. Daughter Mary. Daughter Martha. Daughter Nancy, to have negro woman Rachel. Daughter Sarah. Daughter Frances.
Wit.: John Roe   (Signed) John (X) Roe
    Andrew Roe
    Ande Roe
Proven 5 Feb. 1802.

WILL OF BENJAMIN BRIMER - pp 38-39

Wife Rebecah. One third to Jessey Brimer. One third to Nancy Maus (?). One third to Betsey Lenard. $50 to Caty Gober. 5 ₺ sterling to Rebecah the child of Samuel Brimer deceased. Five shillings apiece to William Brimer, Polly Haney, James Brimer. Desire that William Leonard see to the business. Dated Jan. 13, 1803.
Wit.: J. L. Brook   (Signed) Benjamin (X) Brimer
    Jonathan Watson
Proven 30 Sept. 1803.

WILL OF WILLIAM HALLUM - pp 39-41

Wife Mary to have negro woman Jude and boy Job. Daughter Rebeccah to have boy Dick and girl Minie and man Landon. Daughter Rebeccah is under age. Land next to Widow Praytor. Brother James, to have mulatto boy Gib. Brothers James Hallum and John Hallum and sister Martha Bracker. Negro man Peter to go free to be his own master on the day of my wife's marriage or death. On his becoming free he is to have 50 acres of land, a cow and calf and a gun. Executors: Wife Mary, Andrew Pickens and James Hallum. Dated 15 Sept. 1803.
Wit.: James Chapman   (Signed) William Hallum

cont;
          William Hallum
          Basel (X) Smith
Proven 11 Oct. 1803.

WILL OF JACOB EARNEST - pp 41-42

Before John Wilson, one of the Justices for Pendleton District, personally appeared William Allen and being duly sworn sayeth that (he) was
sent for by Jacob Earnest to write his (?) will on 5 day of this instant
November and this deponent went and did begin to write the will but
before he had done the speach of the sick man William Earnest failed
and deponent did not finish the will but remembers well how the said
Earnest wished to dispose at the time he began to write will and believes
that at that time said Earnest was of sound mind and memory and in
disposing of his said Jacob Earnest property he did it in manner following. To daughter Jenny Earnest stock, furniture and negro man. To son
Lodwick Earnest. Asked if he did not intend to give his son-in-law
William Meeds (Muds?) some land Jacob Earnest replied yes he must have
the place we talked about. To son Nathaniel Earnest one note of $100.
To son-in-law Thomas Coddle another note of $100. Dated 9 Nov. 1803.
Proven 16 Dec. 1803 by William Allen.
          (Note: Name written William Earnest once, but must have been
          Jacob, because it was written that way several times.)

WILL OF JOSHUA BURRESS - pp 43-44

To Sarah Burress plantation and lands as long as kept in good repair.
When out of repair John Burress and another good man to be chosen and
lands to be sold if not during her widowhood his daughters Elizabeth
Casselbury and Nancy Burress to have lands at their mothers decease.
Sarah Burress to have stock and furniture. Nancy to have feather bed
and furniture. Mary Shamly to have cow and calf. All property not
mentioned to be sold and divided between children. Dated 3 Jan. 1804.
Executor: Joseph Irving.
Wit.: Elisha Herring   (Signed) Joshua (X) Burress
       Wm. Herring
       John Burress
Proven 4 Feb. 1804.

WILL OF JAMES GASSAWAY - pp 44-47

Wife Elizabeth land I live on - 2 tracts, a 200 acre grant to Samuel
Lofton and 105 acres purchased from William Griffin, her lifetime.
After her death divided among my 3 youngest sons, Benjamin, Samuel and
Daniel. All my children. Daughter Rebeccah Gassaway. Daughter Hannah
Gassaway. Daughter Lucy Gassaway. Son Samuel. Executors: Son Thomas
and Mr. Jonathan Reeder. Dated 14 Feb. 1804.
Wit.: Saml. Dickson   (Signed) James Gassaway
       Simon Reeder
Proven 26 Mar. 1804.

WILL OF JOHN NEWMAN - pp 47-48

Dated 13 Aug. 1791. Wife Frances. Executor: Wife Frances. Friend
Moses Haynes is to be overseer of my will.
Wit.: Charles Bond   (Signed) John Newman
       Daniel Putman
Proven 13 Mar. 1804.

WILL OF JAMES DUFF, SR. - pp 48-50

Son Samuel C. Duff to have negro girls Decy and Viny. Wife Agnes to have
negro woman Nann. Son Walter. Son.Abraham. Son-in-law John McCrossey
(?). Son-in-law William Halam. Daughter Nancy to have negro girl Winny.
Son James to have land joining Thomas Henderson and a negro girl Patty.
Son Robert to have land bought of William Gillaspie whereon Samuel Black
lived. Land on Georges Creek joining Joshua Fowler to be sold. Execu-
tors: Sons Samuel C. and James. Dated 27 Mar. 1804.
Wit.: John Hamilton   (Signed) James Duff, Senr.
       John Armstrong
       Nathaniel Henderson
Proven by oath of Nath. Henderson 18 Apr. 1804.

WILL OF HENRY LEDBETTER - pp 50-51
Pendleton. Dated 1 Apr. 1804. Wife Patience. Executors: Trusty
friends Elijah Brown, Esq. and James Jones.
Wit.: Jonathan Brown   (Signed) Henry Ledbetter
Proven 23 Apr. 1804.

WILL OF CHARLES ELLIOTT - pp 51-52
Son William. Son James to have 90 acres on Buck Island Creek in Stokes
County, N. C. Daughter Sarah. Wife Juriah to raise and support rest
of younger children. Executors: Wife Jurial (?) and Son William.
Dated 17 Sept. 1799.
Wit.: John Nickelson   (Signed) Charles (X) Elliott
      James Elliott
Proven 28 Aug. 1804.

WILL OF JAMES FOSTER - pp 53-54
Land joining ____ Simpson and Pickens Mill, crosses wagon road, given to
me by Father, and that part I got of Humphreys. Executors: Brother
Gabriel Foster. Mother to have land if she does not remarry. Sister
Sarah Merritt's son John. Sister Rachel Foster. Brother Gabriel's
oldest son John. Gabriel's daughters Elizabeth and Aggey. Dated 17
July 1804.
Wit.: John Booth   (Signed) James Foster
      Wm. Pigg
Proven 26 Sept. 1804.

WILL OF WILLIBOUGH BROUGHTON - p 55
Dated 28 Oct. 1804. Land to wife Joanna her lifetime then divided be-
tween Frederick Johnston "his son in law" and Elijah Smith, Frederick
Johnston step son. N. B. it to be equally divided between them. To
eldest daughter Catharine Holkam $1.50. To Jesse Broughton heirs $1.50.
To Job Broughton $1.50. To youngest daughter Winefret Davis $1.50.
Executors: Wife Joanna, Frederick Johnston and James Garvin.
Wit.: Thomas Garvin   (Signed) Willibough (X) Boughton
      James Garvin
Proven 5 Nov. 1804.

WILL OF EDMUND SPEARMAN - p 56
Wife Dinah. 4 daughters Sarah, Jane (or June?), Mary, and Patsy. Son
David. Executors: Wife Dinah and son David and daughter Sarah. Dated
30 May, 1804.
Wit.: George Oldham   (Signed) Edmund (X) Spearman
      William Oldham
Proven 5 Nov. 1804.
      (Note: This page very faded and difficult to decipher.)

WILL OF ASA KEMP - pp 57-58
Planter, of Pendleton. Executors to make title to Thomas Harris for land
sold him on Little Beaver Dan Creek. Make deed for balance of land
purchased of Bodeng (?) originally granted Major Mott, to Dr. Handy Harris.
To wife Mary, negro woman Abb. To oldest daughter Juda negro boy Ned.
To daughter Martha negro girl Winney. To child that wife is now preg-
nant with, negro boy Will. Executors: J. C. James and Alexander Kil-
patrick. Dated 26 Dec. 1802.
Wit.: Charles Rice   (Signed) Asa Kemp
      John Burchfield
Proven 21 Feb. 1805.

WILL OF DANIEL DOUGHTY - pp 58-59
Planter. Wife Rachel. 2 sons Joseph and Laban. Executors: Father
Joseph Doughty, Jeremiah Doughty and Alexander Kilpatrick. Dated 24 Nov.
1804.
Wit.: J. C. Kilpatrick   (Signed) Daniel Doughty
      Thomas McKey
      Joseph Doughty
Proven 25 Feb. 1805.

WILL OF HARRY HASEL - pp 59-60
Wife Sarah to have negro man Ned. Daughter Barbara to have negro boy
Isaac. Executor: Friend Daniel Earp who is to be guardian of daughter
Barbara. If Barbara die without issue, her part goes to Sterling Hasel.
If Sterling dies without issue goes to Darling Hasel. My 4 daughters
Feribee, Roda, Fanny and Lily Hasel shall be content with what they
rec'd and 1 shilling each. Dated 29 Sept. 1804.
Wit.: Jesse Chappell   (Signed) Harry (X) Hasel
       Charles Varner
       John Malcolm

WILL OF SEASOR AGUSTA - pp 60-61
Planter, of Pendleton. Wife Holley to have land her widowhood then
divided between children when they come of age: John, Patsey, Peggey,
and Jenny. Land joining John Cochran. Son John to have shoemakers
tools. Dated 5 Dec. 1804.
Wit.: Joab Lewis   (Signed) Seasor (X) Agusta
       Joseph (X) Woods
       James Hughs

WILL OF PATSY MCDANIEL - p 61
Two youngest sons John and Philip McDowel (later spelled McDaniel) Ex.:
Caleb Balden (?), David Sloan and John McDaniel. Dated 20 May, 1805.
Wit.: Ann Stribling   (Signed) Patsey (X) McDaniel
       Mary Ann Terry
       Thomas Stribling
Proven 18 June 1805
       (Note: Believe the name is McDaniel and not McDowell.)

WILL OF JOHN CHESTAIN - pp 62-63
Wife Mary. 2 youngest children Violet and William. Son Benjamin
Christain. Son John Christain. Son Edmond Chestain. Son Joseph
Chestain. Daughter Cloe and her daughter Polly. Daughter Nancy. Rest
of children to have no part in my estate more than they have received.
Executors: Sons Edward and John. Dated 15 June, 1803.
Wit.: None   (Signed) John (X) Chestain
       (Note: Believe the name is Chestain instead of Christain.)

WILL OF HANDY HARRIS - pp 64-65
Sister Anna McCurdy. Land sold John Montgomery. Wife Ann. Son Nathan-
iel land on Little Beaver Dan Creek. Two daughters land in Abbeville
purchased of William Callaham. Executors to have direction of son
Nathaniel until he reaches age of 21, and to purchase for two daughters
when they are 21 a well bound Bible and Hymn Book of Presbyterian Church.
Executors: Wife Ann, Brother John and Brother Thomas Harris with
Brother Joseph Irvin. Dated 27 May, 1805.
Wit.: William Davis   (Signed) Handy Harris
       Mary Harris
       Martha Harris
Proven 17 July 1805.

WILL OF JOHN ANDERSON - pp 65-66
Daughter Nancy Gibbens. Son James to have negro girl Jen. Son Samuel
to have negro woman Belly and child Ned. Son David to have negro woman
Joan. Daughter Mary Dickson. Daughter Rosannay. Daughter Rebeccah
Cunningham. Daughter Martha Dickson to have negro girl Suck. Grand-
daughter Caroline Cunningham. Granddaughter Catharine Dickson. Negro
girl Hannah. Dated 15 Sept. 1805.
Wit.: Thomas Stribling   (Signed) John Anderson
       John Hamilton
       Frederick Brown
Proven 3 Oct. 1805.

WILL OF DANIEL MCALSTER - p 67
Wife Nancy. All my children. Executors: two eldest sons Daniel and
William. Dated 3 Sept. 1804.
Wit.: Thos. Coldson (or Paldson?) (Signed) Daniel (X) McAlster
       Mary Ann Terry (?)
       Stephen Fuller
Proven 26 Nov. 1805.

WILL OF SAMUEL SMITH - pp 68-69
Wife Martha. Daughter Elenor (?) Elexander. Daughter Margaret Wilson.
Daughter Nancy White. Daughter Elizabeth McIntire. Daughter Martha.
Son Robert. Daughter Polly. Daughter Ann. Executor: Son Robert.
Dated 5 Oct. 1804.
Wit.: John Moore   (Signed) Samuel Smith
       Luke (X) Spruile (?)
       Robert Telford
Proven 6 Jan. 1806.

WILL OF ALEXANDER BOYSE - pp 69-71
Wife Jane to have negro woman Dinah. Daughter Jane McClusky. Son
William Boyse. Son John land on south side Hurricane Creek. Son McClan
land joining Joshua Smith, also land known as Darses old place. Sons
Alexander and George Thompson Boyse. Son Thompson is youngest son.
Sons Alexander and George Thompson Boyse to be schooled. Daughter Agnes
Boyse. Executors: John Cochran, Esq., and son William Boyse. Dated
14 Jan. 1806.
Wit.: William Hunter   (Signed) Alexander Boyse
       John Y. Mozley
       William Brown
Proven 3 Feb. 1806 by Doctor William Hunter and Capt. William Brown.

WILL OF MICHAEL LEATHERS - pp 71-72
Sons Elijah and Nimrod. Daughter Rody. Executor: Son Nimrod. Daughter
Frances Seal (or Teal, or Leathers ?, so faded, difficult to read), to
live on in house as long as she pleases or until she marries. Dated 12
May, 1805.
Wit.: John Cleveland   (Signed) Michael Leathers
       Daniel Cleveland
       Ann (or Aaron ?) Downs.
Proven 21 Feb. 1806.

WILL OF JOHN WOODALL, SENR. - pp 72-73
Daughter Sarah Power. Son William. Son Joseph. Daughter Ann McCucheon.
Son John. Executors: Sons Joseph and John Woodall, Jr. Dated 2 Mar.
1806.
Wit.: Christian Fricks   (Signed) John Woodall
       James Cooper
       Stephen B. Suwinny (?)
Proven 7 Mar. 1806.

WILL OF SAMUEL MCCULLEY - pp 73-74
Farmer. Wife Jennet. Land to be divided among my children after wife's
death. Mary Deviney and Margaret Wardlaw already received their part.
Grandchild Samuel Diviney to have a part equal with my children. Ex-
ecutors: Wife and John McFall. Dated 2 Oct. 1805.
Wit.: John George   (Signed) Samuel McCulley
       James Wardlaw
Proven 2 June, 1806.

WILL OF RICHARD BARRY .- pp 74-76
Executors: John Kilpatrick, James Wood, Sarah Gandy. Sister Sarah
Gandy to have land her lifetime or widowhood, then divided among brothers
and sisters: George Barry, Hugh Barry, John Barry, William Barry,
Ellenor Davis, Joseph ___?___ Barry, Sarah Gandy. David Gandy to have
wearing clothes. Dated 8 Sept. 1806.
Wit.: Wm. Millsaps   (Signed) Richard Barry
       John Shannon
       Joseph Glenn
Proven 28 Oct. 1806.

34

WILL OF BENJAMIN CLEVELAND - pp 76-78

Son Absoaom land on Tugalo River and negroes Jim, Lucy, Venus, Bess and
Tom. Grandson John Cleveland (son of Absalom) to have negro boy.
Betsey Smith (daughter of Absalom Cleveland). Benjamin Cleveland (son
of John Cleveland, dec'd) to have negro boys Tom and Charles. To Chapley
R. (or Chasley R.?) Wilborn a negro woman named Charlotte and a child
named Ben. To grandson Absalom Fauche (?) Cleveland (son of John Cleve-
land, dec'd) negro boys Quam and Joe. To Betsey Cleveland (daughter of
John Cleveland, dec'd) negroes Aquilla and Liza. To Patsey Cleveland
(daughter of John Cleveland, dec'd), negroes Jane and Ned. To Bedlery
(?) Franklin a negro fellow Jack. Blacksmith tools to son Absalom.
Rest of property divided between children of John Cleveland, dec'd, and
children of Absalom Cleveland except one stud horse to Jesse Coffee he
being my friend and relation. Executors to dispose of two old negroes
York and Dinah as they think most advisable for said negroes and that
they be taken good care of. Executors: Absalom Cleveland, Jessee Coffee,
and Bickley (?) Franklin. Dated 10 Sept. 1806.
Wit.: Wm. Hawkins   (Signed) Benjamin Cleveland
       Daniel Cleveland
       Nimrod Leathers
Proven 26 Oct. 1806.

WILL OF ROBERT EASLEY - pp 78-80

Daughter Elizabeth Blassingame the wife of John Blassingame to have
negro Great Ned. Grandaughter Mary Blassingame (daughter of Elizabeth
and John) to have negro girl or woman near her own age. Negroes Ben,
Flora, Lucy, Jo, Abram, Jess, Sam, Rose, Alcy, Morning and James to be
equally divided between two sons Samuel Easley, John Easley and my
daughter Nancy Blassingame (wife of Thomas Blassingame). To son Samuel
negro men Isham and Ralph. To son John negro men Little Ned and Daniel.
To granddaughter Mary Blassingame (Daughter of Nancy), a negro girl Amy.
Wife Catharine to have during the life of her father Enuch Benson negro
woman named Suck and at the death of Enuch Benson negro woman Suck to
go to daughter Nancy Blassingame. At death of Nancy, Suck and her increase to go to granddaughter Polly Blassingame (daughter of Nancy).
If son Samuel dies without issue negroes divided among children of Nancy
Blassingame. If son John dies without issue negroes to go to children
of Nancy Blassingame. Land on Saluda River and Georges Creek. Execu-
tors: Major John Blassingame and William Easley of Greenville Dist.
Not dated.
Wit.: Thos. Lorton   (Signed) Robert Easley
       John Dyres
       Samuel Townes (or Lownes ?)
Proven 9 Dec. (no year given, but must have been 1806.

WILL OF THOMAS EDWARDS - pp 80-81

Wife benefits of plantation for purpose of raising children. Son William.
Dated 3 Sept. 1805.
Wit.: Joseph (X) Watkins   (Signed) Thomas Edwards
       Dan (X) Wall
       Robert Taylor

WILL OF JAMES NASH - pp 81-83

Wife Ann. To son Larkin a negro boy Philip and girl Bina. To son James
a negro man Sam and woman Esther. To son George, a negro boy. To son
Valentine, negro boy Peter and girl Beck. To daughter Nancy Nash, negro
boy Ben and girls Lyddia and Sarah. Negro man Tom to be free to go and
live where he shall choose and enjoy profits of his own labor. Executors:
Wife Ann and sons Larkin and George. Dated 1 July, 1805.
Wit.: John Lauglin   (Signed) James Nash
       Burgess (X) Reeves
       John Reeves, Jr.
Proven 19 Jan. 1817.

WILL OF MARY WAKEFIELD - p 83
Daughter Violet. Enuch Berry of the Tennessee State shall take my
daughter Violet under his immediate care and protection. Executors:
David Pugh and John Varner, Esq. Dated 2 Dec. 1806.
Wit.: Thomas Stockdale (?)   (Signed) Mary Wakefield
       Thomas Shelton   (?)
       Jacob Laudermilk (?)
Proven 23 Jan. 1807
        (Note: Very faded and difficult to read.)

WILL OF JOHN MCCOLLOUGH - p 84
Wife Elizabeth to have plantation until youngest children come of age.
Two stepdaughters Mary Cash and Betsy Cash. Executors: James Crawther
and John Mills (?). Dated 4 May, 1806.
Wit.: David Steel   (Signed) John (X) McCullough
Proven 2 Mar. 1817.

WILL OF MARGARET WEED - pp 84-85
Dated 10 Mar. 1807. Daughter Sarah. Daughter Mary. Son James. Son
John. Daughter Peggy. Executors: Leonard Simpson, Esq., William
McCurdy and Peggy my daughter.
Wit.: William Simpson   (Signed) Margret Weed
       John McCurdy
Proven 15 June, 1807.

WILL OF ABRAHAM CRENSHAW - pp 85-86
Wife Nancy. Some of my children got part of their share at marriage.
Betsey, Aggy, Sukie, Abraham and Nancy to have at their marriage or
coming of age. At death of wife estate divided equally between leg-
atees except 1 negro man named Daniel which my son Robert is to have.
Robert is to live on land with his mother. Executors: My trusty friends
Nancy, my wife and John McClure. Dated 6 Mar. 1807.
Wit.: Francis Freeman   (Signed) Abraham (X) Crenshaw
       Henry (X) Hester
Proven 6 July, 1807.

WILL OF JOSEPH JOLLEY - pp 87-88
Wife Jean to have estate her widowhood for use of herself and her children.
If my beloved and present wife should marry estate to be sold and divided
among her and her children, she to have child's part. Daughter Elizabeth.
Executor: Wife Jean, brother William Jolley and Alexander Moorhead.
Dated 2 Nov. 1807.
Wit.: George Nash   (Signed) Joseph Jolley
       Jonathan Smith

WILL OF WILLIAM MAY - pp 88-90
Carpenter. Wife Lucy to have plantation for life or widowhood. To son
William May a negro girl Fillis and 370 acres on Thompson's Creek. To
son Philip May, negro boy George. To son John May, negro boy Charles.
To son Daniel May negro girl Amey. Sons John and Daniel to have land
on James Creek and the upper side of Stanfills big branch joins McCray
and Adams spring branch. To daughter Judith Byrd, negro boy Harry.
To daughter Mary Pou (?), negro girl Laney. Rest of estate divided
between all my children at Lucy's death or marriage. Daniel to have
negro woman Mary in his part. Executors to sell lands in North Carolina containing two tracts only. Executors: Sons William, Philip, John,
and Daniel May. Dated 12 Nov. 1807.
Wit.: Andw. Harris   (Signed) William May
       H. Kilpatrick.
Proven by John C. Kilpatrick 1 Dec. 1807.

WILL OF JOHN MILLER - pp 90-91
Dated 16 May, 1807. To two sons John Miller and Crosby Wilks Miller,
plantation on 18 Mile Creek. To granddaughter Marian Edwards land on
Conneross or its waters known by the name of the Bare Swamp. All of the
rest of the estate divided between my four children, (to wit) John,
Crosby Wilks Miller and Elizabeth and my granddaughter Mary Ann (?) Hutson.
Executors: Two sons John and Crosby and friend Col. John B. Earle.
Wit.: William Robertson   (Signed) John Miller

cont;
Wit.:   James Wood
        Joseph B. Earle
Proven by Capt. Wm. Robertson, 4 Jan. 1808.

WILL OF JOHN SIMPSON - pp 91-94
Of great age. Wife Mariah to have negro woman June (?). Youngest son
David. Children: James, John, Leonard Jean, George W., Archibald,
and David. Schoolbooks to go to grandson John Simpson of Dr. Simpson.
Executors: Wife Mariah and trusty friend John Moffitt. Dated 6 Jan.
1808.
Wit.:   Obadiah Trimmer   (Signed) John Simpson
        Saml. Tate
        George Brook
Proven 22 Feb. 1808.

WILL OF JOHN SHIRLEY - p 94
Sons William and Joshua to be my executors. My dearly beloved wife to
have a decent support out of my estate during her life or widowhood.
Three daughters who are not yet married. All my children: Niper,
William, Rhody, Joshua, James, John, Betsey, Robert, Sara, Polly,
Leanah. Dated 11 April, 1808.
Wit.:   John (X) Wakefield   (Signed) John Shirley
        Wm. Read
Proven 6 June, 1808.

WILL OF ISHAM GREEN - pp 95-96
Wife Nancy to have estate for life or widowhood for use of her and her
children, then divided among children: Polly Green, Betsey Green,
Nancy Green, Lemuel Green, and Rebecca Green, to raise and educate
them. Executors: Wife Nancy and trusty friends Joseph Thompson and
Ransom Thompson. Dated 28 April, 1808.
Wit.:   Joseph Johnson   (Signed) Isham Green
        Joseph Green
        Benjamin Harris
Proven 6 June, 1808.

WILL OF GEORGE ANDERSON - pp 96-97
Wife Molly to raise and school children, to have negroes Buds, Dan,
Sally and Jacob. My son David L. Anderson. My daughter Margaret
Burnsides. Son James Anderson. Each of these to have a negro apiece.
Judey Weacan (?) to have balance of price of land I give her also all
the other she has had, as for Jean to her lifetime and then to fall to
heirs of her body if any, if none, to her brothers and sisters and not
to have sold out of the family. Son John Anderson to have land down the
creek and a negro boy Harry. To daughter Polly Anderson a negro girl
Cunckey, (?) and half the Meeting House tract of land. To daughter
Sally a negro girl Siley. To son Sexon Anderson a negro boy Gilbert.
Executors: Wife Molly, son David and brother Lewis Sexon (?). Lands
on Herricane waters to be sold. Also there is balance of money from Jo
and Jas. Dickson, also a negro named Nobeg and this money to be put to
interest. Dated 14 July, 1807.
Wit.:   Lewis Sherrill   (Signed) George Anderson
        John Dickson
        James Dickson
Proven 4 July, 1808.

WILL OF JOHN ARMSTRONG - p 98
Son John. Daughter Mary to have negro girl Lucy. Son Charles. Dau-
ghters Isabella and Sarah. Rest of my estate divided among all my chil-
dren, to be paid when they come of age or marry. Executors: Joab
Mauldin, John Broun. Dated 6 Mar. 1808.
Wit.:   Jas. Fuming (or Fanning?) (Signed) John (X) Armstrong
        Joseph (X) Pilkey (?)
        Andrew Hughes
Proven 1 Aug. 1808.

WILL OF WILLIAM DICKEY - pp 99-101

Wife Ann to have estate to raise and instruct family or as long as she
is a widow. Son John to have plantation on Rocky River. Legacies left
to children by their grandmother: Daughter Ann, daughter Martha Turner
having already received her part. Son William. Two sons William and
Alexander to have plantation and mill. All my other cattle, property
and plantation got from James Kerd (?) equally divided between my other
children Sarah Jane and Elizabeth and Jennet. Executors: Wife Ann
and brother Alexander Sherrard. Dated 29 Jan. 1806.
Wit.:   Robert Irvin   (Signed) William Dickey
        John Stewart
        Elizabeth (X) Stewart
Proven 15 Aug. 1808.

WILL OF JOHN HUMPHRIES - pp 100-101

Wife Catharine. Son William. Daughter Betsey Jones. Daughter Rebeccah
Thomas. Son Isaac. Son John. Son Jacob. Daughter Catharine.
Executors: Wife Catharine and John Humphries. Dated 1 Oct. 1808.
Wit.:   David Glenn   (Signed) John Humphries
        Thomas (X) Gratin (?)
Proven 25 Oct. 1808.

WILL OF ALEXANDER SHERRARD - pp 101-103

Dated 7 May, 1806. To oldest son John property bought of Edmiston.
To son Alexander plantation on Big Generstee bought from Andrew Hamilton.
To daughter Ann $600 to be managed by her mother. Son James to have land
bought from John McReady and James Kerr. To son William and his mother
her lifetime or widowhood lands bought from Alexander McReady, William
Simpson, Thomas Buchannan and John Stuart. Executors: Wife Martha and
John Hamilton. Dated 7 May, 1806. Proven 9 Feb. 1809.
Wit.:   Robert Irvin   (Signed) Alexander Sherrard
        Robert Love
        William Watson

WILL OF WILLIAM HALBERT - pp 103-105

Wife Elizabeth. To son Joel land bought from Ralph Owens and Elijah
Owens that he has now in his possession and 2 negroes Sol and Mose.
To son John negroes Gean and Mille and other goods he has in his possession. To son Enos land in his possession bought from Henry Burdine and
a negro Rhoda. To son Arthur's children land where he died to be divided
between them viz Harry Halbert, John Halbert, Linda (or Sinda?) and
Arthur when they come of age. To son James land joining where Arthur
died and young negro Peter. To son William land including mill on Big
Creek and land called Dotoral (?) and 1 young negro. To son Joshua land
joining James and 1 young negro and Mill Shoal on Saluda River purchased
from William Ackar. To daughter Martha Grisham 2 young negroes with
what other property I gave in her possession. To daughter Frankah
Garrison 2 young negroes with what other property I gave her. To daughter
Elizabeth Berry 2 young negroes with what other property I gave her.
To daughter Mary Halbert 2 young negroes. To daughter Lucinda Halbert
2 young negroes. Executors: Joel Halbert, John Halbert, Enos Halbert
and John Grisham. Dated 30 July, 1806. Proven 6 Mar. 1809.
Wit.:   William Harper   (Signed) William Halbert
        James Brown
        David Brown

WILL OF BARTHOLOMEW WHITE - pp 105-106

Wife Liddy. Son Charles. Daughter Liddy Nichols. At wife's death
estate divided between son Solomon, son John, daughter Caty Little,
daughter Margret Little, daughter Liddy Nichols. Executors: Wife Liddy
and trusty friend George Nash. Dated 30 Nov. 1808.
Wit.:   Benjamin White   (Signed) Bartholomew (X) White
        Milley Bruster
        Henry Funderburk
Proven 6 Mar. 1809.

WILL OF THOMAS EDMONDSON - p 107
To wife Ann land where John Powell now lives and 1 negro choice of Punch,
Taney, Tery, Jeffrey and George. To sons William and James and daughter
Elizabeth Boulware $3.00 each. To sons George and Benjamin remainder
of estate. Executors: Col. John Brown and Henry Norton. Dated 16 Mar.
1807.
Wit.: Henry Norton   (Signed) Thos. Edmondson
       John Powell
Proven 29 Mar. 1809.

WILL OF JAMES TATE - p 108
To wife Anne negroes Jack, Venus and Prince, Thomas, Biley, Buck and Ned.
Son Samuel. If ever my son William should come into this country and be
in majority wife and son Samuel to give him comfortable way of living
during his lifetime. Son Samuel to give money to John Burton to purchase land to live on. If any of the heirs of my sister Ann who was
married to William McConnell should appear son Samuel is to give them
2 ₺ sterling. Executors: Wife Ann and son Samuel. I have made over
also their shares to wit of my two daughters Margret and Elizabeth by
deeds of gift. I allow my son-in-law Farler Thompson to pay executors
the sum of $300.00 that is $100.00 to my grandson George Camble, Tate
Burton and $100.00 to Richard Speak to help to relieve my negro Tamer
who is mortgaged in his account and $100.00 to my son Samuel Tate the
same Farley Thompson is indebted to me on account of sale of my negro
Isaac which helped him obtain his land. Dated 4 June, 1807.
Wit.: Thomas Sherrar   (Signed) James Tate
       George Bruton
       William Tate Speak
Proven 13 Apr. 1808.

WILL OF JOHN MOORHEAD - pp 109-110
Wife Elizabeth. Son William. Son John. Son James. Son Joseph.
Daughter Ellinor Robertson. Daughter Jean Jolley. Daughter Elizabeth
Lewis. Son Alexander. Executors: Sons James and Alexander. Dated
18 April, 1809.
Wit.: George Nash   (Signed) John Moorhead
       John Watson
       Mills Glascoe (?)

WILL OF DAVID DRENNAN - pp 110-111
Wife Mary Whems Drennan. Two sons James Wilson Drennan and Billy
Gilliland Drennan under age of 21. All my children to share in estate
if wife dies or remarries. Executors: James Anderson and wife Mary
Wheems Drennan. Dated 29 April, 1809.
Wit.: Nathan Lusk   (Signed) David Drennan.
       Arthur McAdow
       Abner A. Steel
Proven 8 July, 1809.

WILL OF ELIZABETH COX - pp 112.113
Son James Cox. Granddaughter Elizabeth Cox (daughter of John Cox).
Granddaughter Lucinda Riley. Son John Cox. Balance of money equally
divided between all my legatees except James Sims, Charles White and
Hollingsworth Oander (?). They should each have 5 shillings and nothing
else. Thirty dollars I have in hands of Benjamin Dickson shold be got
by legatees or executors and pay to James Sims, Davis McCutchen, Henry
Cox, Gambred Cox and Nimrod Bartlett the sum of $2.69 each and the balance
to go to my son John Cox. Son James Cox to have crops growing. Executors: James C. Griffin and son John Cox. Dated 22 July, 1809.
Wit.: George (X) Riley   (Signed) Elizabeth (X) Cox
       James (X) Cox
Proven 7 Aug. 1809.

WILL OF JOHN MORRIS, SENR. - pp 113-114
Wife Baylis. Daughter Elizabeth Ragan. Son John H. Daughter Nancy
Roe. Daughter Susannah May. Daughter Frances King. Executors Wife
Baylis and son John H. Dated 29 May, 1809.
Wit.: James Jett   (Signed) John Morris
       Bryant (X) Mayfield
       Simon Smith
Proven 15 Aug. 1809.   39

WILL OF SAMUEL BRUSTER - pp 114-115
Wife Margret. Children: Lucinda Bruster, Henry Bruster, Harriet Bruster,
Melinda Bruster, Mary Bruster, Nancy Bruster, John Bruster and the one
that my wife is now quick with at this time. Executors: Wife Margret
and brother William Dunlap. Dated 8 Feb. 1810.
Wit: George Nash   (Signed) Samuel Bruster
     Archd. Collins
     Meridith (X) Hunnicutt
Proven 10 Mar. 1810.

WILL OF DAVID WATKINS - pp 115-116
Son David to have negro boy Dug. Wife to have negro girl Sackah. Wife
to have property until youngest child is of age, then equally divided
among all my children including what I have given them. Son John has
received $100., Son Jospeh. Executors: Wife and Joseph. Dated 1 Feb.
1810.
Wit.: John Atkins   (Signed) David Watkins
      Thomas Smith
Proven 2 April, 1810.

WILL OF JESSE CHAPPEL - pp 116-117
Wife Martha to have estate her lifetime or widowhood. If she marry she
is to have negro boy Washint (?) and furniture. Rest sold. After deducting from Sarah Thomas dividend $20 out of Robert Chappel $7.00 and
out of Ann Morris $23.00 and balance equally divided between my children
to wit: Sarah Thomas, John Chapel. Executors: wife, John Chapel and
Charles Webb. Dated 6 Apr. 1810.
Wit.: T. Stribling   (Signed) Jesse Chappel
      Charles Webb
      Thos. (X) Chappell
Proven 18 Apr. 1810.

WILL OF ROBERT SEGO - pp 117-118
Executors: William Chamley son-in-law who is to be chief executor, and
wife. Wife to have half of plantation of 321 acres and son Benjamin to
have other half. William Chamley to have 100 acres where he now lives.
At wife's death son Robert to heir her land. Robert is youngest son.
Daughter Sally. Rest of the children. Two youngest daughters Faithy
(?), and Polly to have feather beds when they need them. Balance of
household stuff divided equally among daughters at death of wife. Dated
26 May, 1810.
Wit.: Morgan Morgan   (Signed) Robert (X) Sego.
      Mary (X) Morgan
Proven 6 July, 1810.

WILL OF JOSEPH THOMPSON - pp 118-119
Robert Thompson, Randsom Thompson, Nancy Green, Betsy Garner, Z. Thompson
and Joseph Thompson to have 5 shillings each. Rest to go to wife Molly
her lifetime then equally divided between my three youngest children
Rebeccah, John and Polly Thompson. Executors: Robert Thompson and
Molly Thompson. Dated 25 Feb. 1810.
Wit.: Zachariah Thompson   (Signed) Joseph Thompson
      Joseph Thompson
      Randsom Thompson
Proven 9 Oct. 1810.

WILL OF JOHN STEPHENS - pp 119-120
Son Edward. Son John. Daughter Sarah Pendergrass. Son Jeremiah.
Daughter Rebeccah Stephens. Son Joseph. Son Zachariah. Daughter
Frances Stephens. Son William Stephens. Daughter Nancy Stephens.
Daughter Elizabeth Stephens. Daughter Susannah Stephens. To my dearly
beloved Lucy whom I make executrix and Daniel Stephens executor of my
will. Lucy to have lands lifetime or widowhood. Dated 31 May, 1810.
Wit.: William Cannon   (Signed) John (X) Stephens.
      Benjamin Barton
      Joseph (X) Stephens
Proven 22 Oct. 1810.

WILL OF VANN DAVIS - pp 121-122

My 12 children have all left me and received their full portion (viz)
Hezekiah, Abijah, dec'd, Nathan, Jesse, Eliphas and Vann my sons and
Martha, Rachael, Hannah, Melea (?), Jean and Rhoda my daughters. To
each of them $1.50 . I had given my grandson John Davis something con-
siderable in my will of 11 December last but as he has proved disobed-
ient and has left me I will give him nothing more than a mare and saddle
he has in his possession. To wife Lucy plantation and negro woman Beck
and all other property to be at her disposal. Executors: Wife Lucy.
Dated 14 April, 1810.
Wit.: James Hembree, Sr.   (Signed) Vann (X) Davis
       Marks (X) Pitts
       Susannah Pitts
Proven 23 Nov. 1810.

WILL OF MICHAEL HAMMOND - pp 123-126

Of the Village of Pendleton, in contemplation to set out from this place
in a few days and travel through and see some of the southern and
western parts of the United States. House and Lot N. 40 in Pendleton
to be sold. If they cannot get $700.00 for it, it is to go to my bastard
son, Alberto Hammond, otherwise called Alberto Martin, being the bastard
son of Louisa Martin, daughter of Major Lewis D. Martin of Pendleton
District. I do own and acknowledge and believe to have begotten him.
Six negroes to son Alberto: 13 yr. old Cullah, woman Mary and her 4
children Susan, Preanna, Minerva and Evelina. Slaves to be hired out
until Albert is of age. House to be rented out if cannot be sold. Rest
of estate sold and to go to Alberto at age 20. Alberto is to be schooled
and when he has progressed far enough to undertake the languages to
place him in some seminary or under some good teacher where he may be
prepared for college and if sufficient money I wish him to take degrees.
If son Alberto dies without issue I bequeath to three brothers John,
Thomas and David Hammond all my estate. Executors: two friends John
Martin and Jonathan Reeder (?). Dated 4 April, 1810.
Wit.: William Brown   (Signed) M. Hammond
       A. Lawhorn
       D. Cherry
       N.B. My said son Alberto Hammond was born 24 June, 1807.
Proven 28 Dec. 1810.

WILL OF ANDREW WILSON - pp 126-128

Wife Mary, Samuel A. Easley and Joab Mauldin my executors. Negro wench
Letty and her three children to be sold. Son Benjamin. Daughter Lucy.
Daughter Elizabeth. To each of my children of age or as they arrive at
age 21. Wife Mary to have property lifetime or widowhood for use of
infant children. Youngest child named William was born July 14, 1809.
Estate divided amongst all my children if wife marries. She to have
child's part. Infant children to receive reasonable good English educa-
tion. Dated 18 June, 1810.
Wit.: John A. Easley   (Signed) Andrew (X) Wilson
       Thos. Blasingame
Proven 7 Jan. 1811.

WILL OF EDWARD TATUM - pp 128-129

Son Luke. Daughter Martha to have negro woman Jude and America. Wife
Martha. Daughter Elizabeth Hendrick to have negro woman Hannah. I leave
out the names of the rest of my children having already given them their
portion. Executors: Friends William Curl and Solomon Murphree. Dated
5 June, 1804.
Wit.: Hamilton Reid   (Signed) Edward (X) Tatum
       Charles (X) Durham
       Joseph Stephens.
Proven 28 Dec. 1810.

WILL OF WILLIAM LEONARD - pp 129-130
Five youngest children: Elizabeth Leonard, Samuel Leonard, Mary Ann
Leonard, Agness Leonard and Honor Malinda Leonard. Executor: George
Leonard. Dated 12 Feb. 1811.
Wit.: William Hillhouse   (Signed) William (X) Leonard
      Tamison Barron
      James Dobbins, Junr.
Proven 29 Mar. 1811.

WILL OF BURGESS REEVES - pp 130-131
Wife Fanny. Children: John Reeves, Mauldin Reeves, Leathy Reeves and
William Reeves. Executor: Wife Fanny, son John Reeves and John Mauldin.
Dated 6 Mar. 1811.
Wit.: Jas. Thomson   (Signed) Burgess (X) Reeves
      Jonathan Brown
      Elizabeth (X) Hanna
Proven 3 June, 1811.

WILL OF SAMUEL NEEL - pp 131-132
Wife Rebecca to have negro fellow John. Daughter Mary Armstrong wife
of James Armstrong. Son David. Daughter Ann Miller, wife of Crosby
W. Miller. Daughter Fanny Ernest, wife of Nathaniel Ernest. Executors:
friend Dr. Wm. Hunter and Crosby W. Miller. Dated 25 Sept. 1811.
Wit.: C. Miller   (Signed) Saml. Neel
      R. Anderson
      Wm. Hunter
Proven 7 Oct. 1811.

WILL OF LEONARD SAYLOR (OR TAYLOR?) - p 133
Wife Mary to have plantation her life or widowhood. Son George's child-
ren to have $3.00 each. Daughter Margret. Daughter Eve. Son Abraham.
Son Leonard. Executor: Samuel Black, Esq. Dated 14 Oct. 1811.
Wit.: Permenis (X) Davis   (Signed) Leonard Saylor
      John (X) Davis
Proven 29 Oct. 1811.

WILL OF ARCHABALD HAMILTON - pp 133-135
Planter. Wife Jean. Sons William, Andrew, Vincent, and Lemuel Green-
lee and my daughter Ann. Wife Jane. Daughter Nancy Greenlee to have
$1.00. Executors: Trusty friends Samuel G. Barr and Andrew Hamilton.
Dated 8 Sept. 1811.
Wit.: John Willson   (Signed) Archabald Hamilton
      Mary Barr
      Wm. (X) Hamby
Proven 2 Sept. 1812.

WILL OF BENJAMIN RAINEY - pp 135-138
To wife Nancy her life or widowhood negroes: boy Ben, girl Jenny, old
women Rose and Senar, and man Moody. After her death divided between
all my children. I charge Michael Hall $375.00 for land deeded him on
Haw River. I charge Neill B. Rose $300.00 for land deeded him on Haw
River. To daughters Nancy, Sally and Milly and son John land in Tenn.
on Turnbull Creek containing 400 acres, each to be charged $200 in the
division of the estate. To my sons and sons-in-law (to wit) John King,
Isaac Rainey, Benjamin Abel Rainey and William Hall, land in Orange
County adjoining Granville Co. line, Anthony Cobb, Jr. and others 300
acres at the price of $300.00 to be accounted for. I gave my interest
in land held by an entry in company with Gibson and Ray unto John King,
Isaac Rainey, Benjamin Able Rainey and William Hall. To my grandson
Austin, 100 acres in Orange County joins widow Ryke and others. Executors
to being from the State of Tennessee all my negroes that remain there
(to wit) Dinah and Bob and their increase to be removed from Tennessee
to this county of Orange, then with remainder of negroes not lent to my
wife to be sold and divided equally amongst my children. My surveying
instruments to son Isaac. Executors: Son Benjamin Able Rainey and son-
in-law William Hall. Dated 17 April, 1811.
Wit.: John Grant   (Signed) Benjamin Rainey
      Mason Tarpley

cont.
Will of Benjamin Rainey of North Carolina produced to me for the
purpose of the executors obtaining letters testamentary so being
sent (?) in this District.   (Not dated)

WILL OF WILLIAM HARRING (HERRING) - pp 138-139
Grandaughter Matilda Harring. My leasehold dwelling house in Pendleton
District where Elijah Harring occupies. Estate divided among all my
children. Executors: Son Elisha Harring. Dated 15 June, 1812.
Wit.: Elijah Harring   (Signed) William Harring
       James Drennan.

WILL OF ROBERT TROTTER - p 139
Wife Susannah. Executors: Robert Trotter, Jr. and wife Susannah.
Wife to have property for life or widowhood then divided equally among
my lawful heirs. Dated 1 Feg. 1812.
Wit.: L. Solomon (X) Hays   (Signed) Robert (X) Trotter
       Nathl. Davis
Proven 7 Sept. 1812.

WILL OF SAMUEL ROSAMOND - pp 140-143
Executor to sell plantation I now live on consisting of 3 small tracts
with mill thereon and a plantation priced at not more than $1000.00
purchased in Abbeville or Pendleton Districts convenient to some place
of public worship for my wife and family. At her death or second marriage to fall to my male heirs. Negro women Teeney, Janney and Sign to
be sold and 3 young wenches purchased in their place. Negro Peter to
be sold or to remain with family as executors see fit. Money put to
interest until 5 of my children come of age or marry and have issue.
Remainder of money to remain at interest until remaining children shall
arrive at such state as first five, then equally divided amongst minor
children. Negro Will by his late mistress will at my death have priv-
iledge of choosing his master or mistress amongst my children. William
Pyles and wife were given choice of 2 negro girls. This is to be part
of their portion. Make title to Robert Young for 279 acres sold him in
Abbeville where I formerly lived upon his paying up. Executors: Son-
in-law William Pyles of Abbeville and Robert McCan, Esq. of Pendleton.
Dated 2 Sept. 1808.
Wit.: John Westfield   (Signed) Samuel Rosamond
       John Jones
       Ambrose Jones
    Codicil - Negroes Peter, Jim and Dudley with Tench Sinah, Jenny and
    Charlott to be sold. Daughter Polly Rosamond to have equal share
    with other children. Executors to pay wife Sarah 5 ₺ yearly for
    each minor under age. Executors: Robert McCann, Esq. and Capt.
    Barksdale Garrson. Dated 17 June, 1812.
Wit.: William Fraip
       Samuel Tucker
       David Thomas
Proven 5 Oct. 1812.

WILL OF JOHN MORROW - p 143
Executors: Wife Mary and Thomas Walker. 3 sons Samuel, John, and
Archabald to have $4.00 each. After wife's death estate divided among
my 4 children: Betsy, Nancy, Jane and Mary. Dated 14 Sept. 1812.
Wit.: Samuel Maverick   (Signed) John Morrow
       Wm. Walker
Proven 28 Oct. 1812.

WILL OF ROBERT ANDERSON - pp 144-154
Dated 25 Jan. 1810. Eldest daughter Mary Carruth to have $50.00 to buy
her a suit of mourning. To Anna Anderson Maxwell a negro woman Nan and
her children Cato, Mose, Ralph, Fanny and Rozetta, all in the possession
of her mother Mary Carruth. She is also to have June a boy, the younger
son of old Nancy now in my possession. All of these negroes to granddaughter Anne Anderson Maxwell. To grandson John Maxwell a negro boy
Tony, the son of Molly. To granddaughter Elizabeth Maxwell a negro girl
Hannah the daughter of old Nancy. If Elizabeth dies without issue
Hannah goes back to her surviving sister or half sister. Hannah and

43

cont.
increase to be divided between them but not to be sold. To granddaughter
Louisa Carruth a negro girl Fanny now my house servant. If Louisa dies
without issue Fanny and her increase goes to her half sisters Anne and
Elizabeth. In behalf of my daughter Jane, of blessed memory, I bequeath
to William Shaw, Esq., to whom she was married, a yellow wench Cloey
and a girl Rachel. To daughter Anne Hunter a negro woman Sue and a girl
Sylvia. To grandson John Hunter negro girl Rose the daughter of old
Mourning now in the possession of Dr. Hunter, John's father. If John
should die without issue to go to his younger brother Robert Anderson
Hunter. To grandson Robert Anderson Hunter a negro boy June, son of old
Mourning. If he die without issue descends to youngest children of the
family yet unborn. Not to be sold out of the family. To granddaughter
Mary Hunter a negro child Celey, child of Affee my house wench. If
Mary dies without issue goes back to brother Robert A. Hunter. Not
sold out of the family to strangers. To grandson William Hunter a negro
boy Peter a son of Affey my present house wench. If he die to younger
branches of the family. Not sold out of the family. To daughter
Elizabeth Maverick a negro girl Lucy and a boy David. To grandson
Samuel Agustus Maverick a negro girl Jane, daughter of Molly and now
house girl with me. To granddaughter Mary Elizabeth Maverick a negro
girl Queen, a child of Moll's. If Mary Elizabeth dies without issue
goes to the younger members of the family or if none back to Samuel
Agustus. To son Robert Anderson 7 negroes: Tom a fellow and Venus his
wife, Nema, Bug and Adam boys and Jude and Caley girls. To granddaughter
Martha Anderson a negro girl Winney the child of Moll. If she die
without issue to younger branches of the family but not sold out of the
family. To grandaughter Anne Anderson the next child Moll has(and she
is very big.) If she die without issue to elder sister or younger
children but not sold out of the family. There are several old and
decrepit negroes which are of little or no value but which must be supported while they live viz: Monday, Solomon, old Cato and young Cato,
Old Dede and old Nancy. My wish they be supported and made comfortable
on the plantation while they live. My will is that Ben, Sawny, Cyrus,
John, Jim, (viz Nancy's Jim), Salem, Joe, Martin Cato and Jeff(excepting
as may be hereinafter directed) all mine grown, but Joe and he is nearly
so, and Dina (Sawney's wife), Mourning, Martin Cato's wife, Affy, lame
Nancy, Peggy her sister and Tabby, Affy's oldest child, all women and
girls with their children (only those otherwise disposed of in this will)
and the offspring of the families shall all remain on the plantation
under the direction of my son Robert Anderson. None to be sold unless
they turn out to be thieves and unless they cannot be restrained by
good treatment, friendly cautions, admonitions and a merciful use of the
rod of correction. Then it is my will they be sold. Land on Keowee
River granted to George McBeth and Lewis D. Martin. Land sold to Willaim
Chalmers. Land granted to Gen. Pickens and Francis Greenwood. Some
part I plan to sell old Mr. Cunnenham and part to Luke Hubbert. Cunningham has lived on the land several years but has never paid a cent for it.
The old man shall live on the land his lifetime if he chooses. Another
part I agreed to sell Luke Hubbert many years ago, believe he lived
nearly one year upon it and left of his own accord which he has done
several times since when he came back he always asked my liberty to
take possession and promised payment but he never staid much longer time
on the land than was necessary to build a cabbin since the first time
he settled on it and is now gone from it. The eight tracts above specified amount to 2514 acres. Plantation where I live on west side Keowee
to be kept settled with negroes thereon and superintended by son Robert
Anderson until grandson Robert Anderson Maxwell is 21. Grandson to be
educated. $50.00 to Mary Lemmons the wife of Robert Lemmons to buy a
suit of mourning or any way she may choose. She was chiefly raised in
my family and this is only a small acknowledgement on my part a testimony
of my approbation of her conduct then and since. Son Robert to collect
debts. To enable him to do this there is 640 acres on Twenty Mile Creek,
118 acres whereon John Pound now lives with a small stock of cattle of
mine. This land joins the Indian boundary line. Also 200 acres which
takes in a shoal on Conneross above Mrs. Kilpatricks and also 466 acres
joining last mentioned tract mortgaged me by Maj. Parsons. No expecta-
tions money will ever be paid. Also some indents founded in the Branch
Bank in Charleston. These lands amounting to 1420 acres with funds in

cont.
bank to son Robert to enable him to pay my funeral expenses, debts I
owe and cash legacies. My ever honored wife of blessed memory had in
her own right when she married me (by the name of Jane Reese), two
negroes, old woman Rose, Hannah her daughter and four children the offspring of Hannah. And although the negroes are my legal right Mrs.
Reese had children no better provided for than mine are. And as my own
children are well enough off, I give to Lydia Fendly Charlotte. To
Susannah Cherry I give Ester. (Mrs. Finley and Mrs. Cherry are daughters
of my deceased wife by former marriage and Charlotte and Ester are two
eldest children of Hannah.) To Dr. Edward Reese the next child of
Hannah, a negro girl named Anne. If he dies without issue to go to
Henry Dobson Reese, youngest son of my deceased wife. To Henry Dobson
Reese, youngest son of my deceased wife, Hannah and her two youngest
children. If Hannah has other children to go to Anne Reese a daughter
of George Reese. If Anne dies without issue negro goes to next youngest sister, if not to two elder sisters but not sold out of the family.
I do will an bequeath to son Robert as a restitution for raising a
family, for only the service of a mother, who, by breeding and child
bearing, is but of little service. ....If Dr. Edward Reese returns to
this country and takes up house I will Old Rose should live with him,
and then returned to my plantation. I will not have her sold in her
old age, as she was always a faithful servant to her old Mistress, they
were raised together and were of an age. I traded for Jeffe (Jesse?)
the husband of Hannah at considerable disadvantage on account of his
great attachment to his wife and children. And now although they have
differed and are now apart if they should compromise their differences
and desire to be together again it is my will that Mr. Reese buy Jeffe
from Robert or Robert buy Hannah and her two children as they may agree
themselves. Executors: Son Robert with trusty neighbors George Reese,
Joseph Whitner, Ezekial Pickens, Esq.
Wit.:   Jonathan Harris   (Signed)   Robert Anderson
        Richard Harris
        Daniel Mason
        Robert A. Maxwell
Dated 25 Jan. 1810.
Proven 9 Jan. 1813.

WILL OF MATHEW RUSSEL - pp 154-156
Wife Verlinda. 2 sons Ozburn and Josiah. Rest of my children viz:
Thomas, Elizabeth, David, Marth, Mathew, Sarah, James, Jane, and Lenny
(or Tenny?). Executors: Wife Verlinda and son Thomas. Dated 25 July,
1812.
Wit.:   Thomas Russel   (Signed)   Mathew Russel Sr.
        Ozburn Russel
        Nancy (X) Haney
Proven 1 March, 1813.

WILL OF JACOB LAWRENCE - p 156
Negro fellow Abram at my death to be his own free man. To my brother
John Lawrence's son Joab. To Benjamin Ashworth's son Joab. To brother
Benjamin Lawrence. Executor: Brother Benjamin and friend Col. John B.
Earle. Dated 8 April, 1803.
Wit.:   Joseph B. Earle   (Signed)   Joab Lawrence
        Sarah Earle
        Wm. Taylor
Proven 24 March, 1813.

WILL OF AARON SHELTON - p 157-158
All my children by name: Lewis Shelton, Aaron Shelton, Absalom Shelton,
Polly Shelton, Betsy Shelton and David Shelton to have 2 years schooling
each, and Mary Carson be allowed $10.00 per year for life. Executors:
William Clarke and Spencer Shelton. Dated 6 March, 1813.
Wit.:   David Humphreys   (Signed)   Aaron (X) Shelton
        Patsey Dooley
Proven 23 July, 1813.

WILL OF GEORGE DILWORTH - pp 158-159
Planter, deceased, and declared by him by word of mouth on 20 July, 1813.
His daughter Rachel to have as much property as he had given his daughter
Jenny Orr. Wife Frances to have home as long as she is a widow. When
his wife gets old if his children left her he had money enough owing him
to buy a negro to take care of her but would rather if she could make it
without purchase of negro. To son Billy Green Dillard. Sons George and
Benjamin. Son Anthony. Executors: Wife and son Billy. Billy is too
young at present but to act as soon as he is capable. Jacob Boyer and
John Morgan made oath to nuncupative will of George Dilworth dec'd and
spoken to them being by the dec'd personally called. George Dilworth
died 1 day of this inst. Sworn to July 24, 1813.
                              (Signed) John Morgan
                                        James (X) Merret
                                        Jacob (X) Boyer
Proven 11 Aug. 1813.

WILL OF EZEKIAL PICKENS - pp 159-161
Of St. Thomas Parish. Wife Elizabeth to live on plantations in lower or
upper county and have 10 negroes and household furniture except silver
marked with initial letters of my deceased wife which I give to my daughter Elizabeth Bonneau Pickens. Eldest son Ezekial to have my share in
the Library Society in Charleston. All my children: Ezekial Pickens,
Samuel Bonneau Pickens, daughter Elizabeth Bonneau Pickens, children by
my first wife, and my sons Thomas Jones Pickens, Andrew Calhoun Pickens
and my daughter Mary Barksdale Pickens, children of my present wife.
If wife Elizabeth is now pregnant and should have issue within nine
months such issue entitled to equal share. Children of present wife
will be entitled to considerable property under the will of their grandfather George Barksdale. Sons to have regular collegiate education.
Eldest son Ezekial to be at all times watchful of and attentive to the
welfare of his mother-in-law and show her all due respect, that he will
always entertain a proper affection for his brothers and sisters and be
attentive to their interest. Daughters to have a suitable and proper
education. Wife and friend Mrs. Floride Calhoun to be guardians of my
daughters. It is my will that executors purchase landed property in
Abbeville District for my wife and children. Executors: Wife Elizabeth,
brother, Col. Andrew Pickens, Friends John Caldwell Calhoun of Abbeville
and Samuel B. Jones of Charleston. Dated 19 May, 1813.
Wit.: P. Weston   (Signed) E. Pickens
       Geo. P. B. Hasell
       Rosser Pinckney
Proven 13 Sept. 1813.

WILL OF ELIZABETH EVENS - pp 161-162
Brother John Evens Cineau $65.00 it being notes due me by Adam Davis.
Also note of $20.00 on Daniel Earp to said John Evans. To Elizabeth
Evens, daughter of John Evens. To Hannah Barnet. To Jane Evens daughter
of John Evens. Clothing divided between Ames Barnett's two daughters
and John Evens daughters. To beloved sister Hannah. To Ealey Evens
wife of John Evens. Dated 9 Feb. 1814.
Wit.: William Turner   (Signed) Elizabeth (X) Evens
       John Barnet
Proven 18 June, 1814.

WILL OF LODOWICK DOBBS - pp 162-163
Sons Joshua, David, John, Silas, Charles, Peter. Daughters Nancy, Jane,
Lucy. Wife Sarah and six youngest children: Lewis, Dotia, Lodowick,
Stephen, William and James. Wife to school six youngest, who are to be
under the care of David Humphries and Jesse Dobbs my son who shall be
executors. Dated 21 Sept. 1813.
Wit.: McCaja (X) Turner   (Signed) Lodowick (X) Dobb
       Jane England
       Dile Nichols
Proven May, 1814.

WILL OF WILLIAM WOOD - pp 163-164

Planter. Son Oliver $1.00. Son Robert 25 cents. Daughters Jannet,
Ann, and Agnes $1.00 each. To three youngest daughters Martha, Margaret,
and Rachael $1.00 each. To wife Margaret all lands, goods, chattels,
etc. She to be sole executrix. Dated 13 Feb. 1804.
N. B. My will is that Martha, Margaret and Rachael be clothed and
furnished out of my property.
Wit.:   Robert Dowdle, Sr.   (Signed) William Woods
        Robert Love
        Samuel Given Dowdle
Proven 29 Mar. 1814.

WILL OF JAMES DUFF - p 164

Wife Mary land and negro fellow Jess and girls Jane and Charity. Estate
to be kept together until youngest children are of age, then sold and
divided equally between wife and surviving children or their heirs.
If wife marries before youngest child of age then estate sold and divided at that time. Wife to educate youngest children. Executors Wife and
her brother David Brown. Dated 19 June, 1814.
Wit.:   Isaiah Kirksy   (Signed) James Duff
        Philip May
        Mark Kirksey
Proven by oath of Isaiah Kirksey. No date.

WILL OF ARON TERRILL - pp 165-166

Wife Hannah to have estate lifetime or widowhood then sold and equally
divided between sons Aron, Moses and William Steele Terrill having
already given daughter Elizabeth Kaylor (Hayloe?) as much as she is
entitled to. Also having given daughter Sally Mahe (?) her part and
have given daughter Nancy Davis her part. Also done justice to son
Joseph. I have raised granddaughter Polly Davis and feel great fond-
ness for her therefore I give her a negro girl Dolly and should Polly
die Dolly descends to her sisters. Executors: Wife Hannah and trusty
friend John Varner, Esq. Dated 29 July, 1814.
Wit.:   O. B. Trimmer   (Signed) Aaron Terrel
        Robert Hackett
        Ephm. B. Osburn
Proven by oath of Robert Hackett, no date.

WILL OF JAMES YOWEL - pp 166-167

Of great age. Wife to have plantation, negroes, stock, etc., her lifetime. To son Joel negro woman Lucy at the decease of his mother. Balance after the death of wife equally divided between son Joel and the
children of my son Joshua and my daughter Martha Rainey (?). Land originally intended for my son Allen and which he sold to Joshua having never
been conveyed by me I rest in the children of said Joshua reserving
the use of it to his widow during her widowhood. Land son-in-law Lewis
Jones lives on to descend to children of daughter Polly. Land given son
William. Moiety of deer in my park to friend Col. Obadiah Trimmer.
Other moiety to Dr. Osborn. Son Joshua's children. Executors: Son
Joel and son-in-law Lewis Jones. Dated 21 July, 1814.
Wit.:   O. B. Trimmer   (Signed) James Yowel
        Alexander Shaw
        Ephm. B. Osborn
Proven 5 Mar. 1814.

Will of Joseph Brown - 167 -(Will is actually six pages long, but pages between 167 and 168 unnumbered.)

Of Broad Mouth Creek, Pendleton District, planter, aged 78 years or
thereabouts. Wife Mary. Son David. Wife to have among other things,
1/13 share with children. Son David to care for his mother and is to
have tract of 400 acres on Broadmouth whereon I now live. Also land
purchased from William Reed on Broad Mouth. Also land whereon Thomas
Crow formerly lived on south fork of Broad Mouth. Son James to have
140 acres on south fork of Broad Mouth where he now lives, also part of
land where Thomas Crow formerly lived. To daughter Fanny Lester, negro
girls Suck and Kate. I have on the marriages of my children William
Brown, Hugh Brown, Joseph Brown, Deceased, Margaret, wife of Benjamin
Starritt, Violet, wife of William Reed, Elizabeth, wife of James Reese,

47

cont;
Mary wife of James Duff, Jane wife of John Hall, and Fanny wife of
Moses Lester advanced and promoted their interest respectively in
life, as far as my circumstances admit of. I have been of great expense in the education of my son George A. Brown. The above named
children or the children of my deceased son Joseph not entitled to any
other share of my estate than an equal 1/13 of the residue mentioned.
William Brown the eldest son of Joseph, deceased, shall draw lot for
his brothers and sisters except my granddaughter Mary Brown who now
lives with me and for whom I have provided separately. Granddaughter
Mary Brown, (Daughter of son Joseph, dec'd) to have negro girl Violet.
Jemimah the widow of son Joseph Brown. Executors: Sons Hugh and
David and friend and neighbor Robert Telford. Dated 17 Jan. 1810.
No probate date.
Wit.: Aaron Broyles,   (Signed) Joseph Brown.
      Benjamin Bowen
      James Harkin

WILL OF BALLARD DAY, SENR. - pp 168-169
Wife Silvey remaining part of land I have deeded my sons supposed to
be 150 acres including plantation whereon I now live, and two negro
boys Isaac and Jesse. She to have this for life or widowhood, and is
to school my children that are yet living with her. Each child now
living with me whenever they marry that my sons receive equivalent with
my son Johnson that is married and my daughters equal to Mary Brezeal.
At wife's death or division, land I now live on goes to son Meddleton.
Executors: Wife Silvey and Abraham Mayfield.
Dated 13 Jan. 1815. No probate date.
Wit.: Reuben Clements   (Signed) Ballard Day
      T. W. Burford
      Rich. Harrison

WILL OF THOMAS LOVE - pp 169-170
Wife Rebecca. Nephew Robert D. Love the son of Robert Love. Executors:
Wife Rebecca and Thomas Drenan. Dated 2 Sept. 1814. No proven date.
Wit.: John Warnek   (Signed) Thomas Love
      Samuel Dowdle
      Jms Keith (?)

WILL OF JOSEPH DOUGHTY, SENR. - pp 170-171
Wife Nancy. Two sons Jeremiah and Joseph. All my children: Jeremiah
Doughty, Joseph Doughty, Sarah Kilpatrick, Rhody Clayton, Nancy Barnett.
Jeremiah and Joseph to pay to Joseph and Daniel Doughty, the children
of Daniel Doughty, deceased, $50.00 each when the arrive at age of 21.
Executors: James Kilpatrick, Jeremiah Doughty and Joseph Doughty.
Dated 5 Jan. 1810.
Wit.: J. C. Kilpatrick   (Signed) Joseph Doughty
      Thos. B. Singleton
Proven 14 April, 1815.

WILL OF ISAAC WILLBANKS - pp 171-172
Wife Sarah. Two sons Thomas and William. Gun and Smith tools to be
sold. All I have after debts paid to be used for raising and schooling
my children. Daughter Terasa to have household furniture at wife's
death or remarriage. Executors: A. McElroy, Marchell Willbanks and my
wife Sarah. Dated 27 June, 1815.
Wit.: Jno. Mays   (Signed) Isaac (X) Willbanks
      James Bond
Proven 4 Sept. 1815.

WILL OF JOHN HALLUM - pp 172-175
Planter. Wife Ann to have negro Harry and girl Lucy. To son Bazzel
$1.00. To daughter Martha Bowen $1.00. To son Richard $1.00. To
daughter Rachel Hallum the wife of William Hallum, $1.00. To daughter
Mary Overby $1.00. To daughter Nancy Hamilton $1.00. To daughter
Elizabeth Hallum two negro girls Kate and her child and Crease and my
boy Peter. To son John $1.00. To son William a negro man Big Peter
and a boy called Ben. To son Thomas two negro men Allen and Buck and
a mulatto boy Sampson. To daughter Sally Hallum negro woman Rose and

cont;
the little orphan child Elias and a girl Jenny and a boy Sie. Son
Thomas is to live with his mother and provide for her. Executors:
Wife Ann and sons Bazzel and Richard. Dated 27 July, 1815.
Wit.: John Willson   (Signed) John Hallum
       Wm. Hubbard
       Regnal Odell
Proven 7 Nov. 1815.

WILL OF JOHN ADAIR - pp 176-179
Wife Jean to have negro man Friday and woman Old Jenny. Land at Flat
Shoal Little River below Fish Trap called Walters Trap, joins Kye's line.
Son Samuel. Son Walter to have one third of debts due me in the
Cherokee Nation which he is about to collect. Walter to make title
to Thomas B. for plantation where I now live. To daughter Charlotte.
To son John 224 acres on Conneross purchased of James Baird. Son
Edward owes me considerable sum. I also purchased note from James
Head paid $42.00 for relapsing and carrying through some lands. This
I request him to make title to my son Thomas B. I also give to my
daughter (did not name her) a negro woman Pegg. To son James land
where I now live, joining Cane Creek, John Moore and Sloan. To daughter
Jane (?) a negro woman Jenny. To son William Henry land on Rusk's
Still House Branch. To son Charles D. To son Washington, a negro
man Harry. Son Elbert Earle. Daughter Mary Ann to have negro girl
Susan. Son Benjamin Franklin. Son John Alexander to have negro boy
Peter and land in fork between Cane Creek and Little River. I owe
debt to Adam Tunneau. My still and property to be sold for money
sufficient to release negro Harry from Thomas Reid from the present
embarrassment. Furniture and stock kept together and plantation
cultivated for support of children until they marry or come of age.
Dated 4 Nov. 1815.
Wit.: Samuel Boystun   (Signed) Jno. Adair
       Thomas Lanier
    N. B. I appoint Joseph Reid, Esq., and Samuel Boydston and Capt.
    David Sloan my executors.
Proven 4 Dec. 1815.

WILL OF WARREN TALIAFERRO - pp 180-183
Executors to sell land in the State of Georgia and purchase other land
more convenient to the residence of my family. Estate to be kept together for the support and education fo my family until my son Zacharias
is 21. If he dies then until son Charles is of age. That is if my
wife Mary M. continue to be a widow and my daughters Mary Elizabeth
Taliaffero and Lucy Gilmore Taliaferro remain unmarried and then be
divided. Executors: Wife Mary M., Brothers Zacharias and Richard,
and brothers-in-law Teachy R. Gilmore and George R. Gilmore. Dated
6 Oct. 1815.
Wit.: Josiah D. Gailard   (Signed) Warren Taliaferro
       Edmund Martin
       Anna (X) Martin
Proven 4 Dec. 1815.

WILL OF LOUIS D. MARTIN - pp 183-186
Land on 18 Mile Creek. John, son, to have two mulatto boys Bill and
Andrew, a watch, a sword and hangings and uniform clothes. Lot in
village of Pendleton near the gaol whereon Stephen Hopkins now lives
to daughter Caroline Martin. She also to have negro girl Milly. To
daughter Polly Martin, 234 acres on Conneross joining John Harris,
Esq. Also to Polly a negro man Isaac and a girl Nelly. To daughter
Margaret Crow a negro man Old Bill. Daughter Hannah Smith is well
provided for, so to her $40.00 for suit of mourning. To daughter
Louisa Martin 25¢. Executors: Samuel Cherry, Dr. William Hunter and
John Martin. Dated 29 Sept. 1815.
Wit.: John Taylor   (Signed) Louis D. Martin
       Madison E. Lewis
       Jo. B. Earle
Codicil 4 Oct. 1815. Daughter Caroline to have household goods for
attending me in my sickness. Also running gear of cotton machine in
the Village of Pendleton, on a lot occupied by Stephen Hopkins. Son

cont;
John left a horse in my care when he left the district. I omitted to
give him satisfaction in my will.
Wit.: James C. Griffin
       James Dodds
       Jo. B. Earle
Proven 4 Dec. 1815.

WILL OF JOHN PEPPER, SENR. - pp 186-188
Wife to have estate her lifetime then divided equally between my child-
ren: Daughter Ruth, sons Samuel, William, Elijah, John, Jesse, Elisha.
Daughters Polly and Fanny. My six oldest negroes Lucy, Tony, Dave,
Major, Charles and Reuben to be sold. To daughter Betsey a negro girl
Sooky and boy Sam. Betsey to be raised and supported in the family
until she is 18 or marries. Executors: Son Elijah and Thomas Bennett.
Dated 25 Jan. 1816.
Wit.: William Harper   (Signed) John (X) Pepper
       John Wilson, Jr.
       Edward Harper
Proven 4 Mar. 1816.

WILL OF JOHN BRUSTER, SENR. - pp 189-191
To children of my deceased son Samuel Bruster 100 acres, part of
plantation whereon I now live. John Dunlap Bruster, youngest son of
my deceased son Samuel. To granddaughter Hariot Bruster. Peggy
Bruster, widow of Samuel. To children of my son William Bruster $100.00
to be paid to them out of a note of hand which I have drawn on William
Dunlap for $600.00 payable to me. Son Hugh Bruster. Children of my
son John Bruster. Children of my son Sheriff Bruster. To children
of daughter Jinny Gray $50.00 which she had to David Gray to be paid
to them out of the above mentioned. To children of daughter Peggy
Camp. Children of daughter Betsey Flenniken. Children of my son James
Bruster deceased. Children of my son Henry Bruster deceased.
Executors: Son William Bruster and friend William Orr. Dated 1 June,
1813.
Wit.: Alexander Moorhead   (Signed) John (X) Bruster
       James Moorhead
       Jonathan Smith
Proven 4 March, 1816.

WILL OF SAMUEL BARR - pp 191-193
Wife Mary to have estate her life or widowhood, then sold and divided
equally between my children: James Sidney Barr, Andrew, Leroy, John
Milton and Felix Barr, and daughters Ellend and Polly Addaland Barr.
Wife to have negro woman Alse and children and negro fellow Joe until
youngest son Felix is of age, then equally divided between my five sons.
Executors: Wife Mary and Andrew Warnock, Jr. Dated 19 Nov. 1813.
Wit.: Chas. Wilson   (Signed) Samuel Barr
       Jesse (X) O'Brient
Proven 4 March, 1816.

WILL OF NEWMAN MOORE - pp 194-196
Merchant. Body to be interred by the Society of Free and Accepted
Masons in which I have been recently a member. Mother Mary Moore.
Three sisters Martha, Jane, and Leah Moore. Land and property mort-
gaged to Wm. Scott. Executors: Mr. James Crawford and John McFall,
and Peter Keys and John Bryce, Esq. Dated 19 March, 1816.
Wit.: Lent Hall   (Signed) Newman Moore
       Robert Neill
       Elijah Brown
Proven 21 March, 1816.

WILL OF JOHN COX - pp 196-199
Wife Sarah to have negro man about 29 years of age named Jacob and a
woman Marget and a girl about 11 named Mariah, also land on Savannah
River on Jenorostee Creek or at least 300 acres including my Irelands
and mill for life or widowhood. Eldest son William. Daughter Elizabeth
Skelton. Son Ned. Son John. Son James. Daughter Naomi not yet 18.
Daughter Alley when she is 18. Minors to be clothed and fed, and

cont;
schooled for two years. Daughter Casiah under age 18. Daughter
Delilah when she is 18. Daughter Sarah when she is 18. Son Tilman
when he is 21. Son Azariah when he is 21. Son Israel when he is 21.
Son Hiram when he is 21. Dated 18 August, 1815.
Wit.: Jesse Couch   (Signed)   John Cox
      Edward Cox
      Samuel Fitzgerald.
Proven 9 August, 1816.

WILL OF JOHN BEATY, SENIOR - pp 199-202
To son William negro wench Lett. To son John. To daughter Margaret
B. Beaty negro girl Sinthy. To son Samuel W., negro boy Harry. To
daughter Mary McCarly negro girl Kate. Executors: Brothers William
and Thomas Beaty and son Samuel W. Dated 29 Jan. 1816.
Wit.: John Reid   (Signed)   John Beaty
      Thomas Beaty
      William Beaty, Senr.

WILL OF BENJAMIN HOLLAND - pp 202-204
Wife Peggy all estate lifetime or widowhood then divided among all
my children. To eldest daughter Rutha Holland a negro woman Rose.
To daughter Polly Holland negro boy Peter. To son Thomas a negro
boy Dick and land whereon I now live. To third daughter Sally Holland
$400.00 or valuation of a negro of that amount. To sons John Shannon
Holland a negro boy Moses. To son Jacob Holland a negro boy Aaron.
Executors: Wife Peggy and Ambrose Mason. Dated 3 August, 1816.
Wit.: Joshua Inman   (Signed)   Benj. Holland
      John A. Blackburn
      J. H. Perryman
Proven 9 Oct. 1816.

WILL OF ABRAHAM DUKE - pp 205-206
Wife Rosanna land lifetime then to son Abraham Martin Duke and his
heirs and assignes. Wife to have negro woman named Rhoda to wait on
her during lifetime and at Rosanna's death Rhoda to be set free.
Executors: Wife Rosanna, John Tatum and William Cox. Dated 3 July,
1816.
Wit.: Jesse Miller   (Signed)   Abraham Duke
      John H. Roe
      Hugh Tatum
Proven 9 Oct. 1816.

WILL OF ISAAC CLEMENT - pp 206-210
To son Aaron Clement lawfully begotten by the body of Ann Clement my
lawful wife, a negro man Phil, girl Suse, boy Israel and benefits he
has received by Jacob. To son Stephen lawfully begotten by Ann, a
negro wench Silale, a boy Dave, a girl Rose, and a boy Julas. To son
Hugh lawfully begotten of wife Ann, a negro man Harry, girl Fillis and
girl Barbery. To daughter Rachel Butterworth lawfully begotten by
lawful wife, a negro wench Moll, and girls Milly and Dinah. To son
Isaac lawfully begotten by Ann, a negro wench Fan, a boy Bill and
girl Alse. To son Daniel lawfully begotten of Ann, a negro boy Philip,
a young wench Silvia and a girl Anne. To son Benjamin lawfully begotten of Ann, a negro girl Grace. Land not to be sold our of family.
To son Stephen Clement, Stephen Butterworth, Hugh Clement and Isaac
Clement, now Jr., 636½ acres in Pittsylvania Co., Va. If I should
chance to take a companion, and should die before them they are to
have reasonable maintenance during their life. Executors: My son
Stephen Clement, Hugh Clement, and my son Benjamin. Dated 30 Oct. 1805.
Wit.: James R. Webster   (Signed)   Isaac Clement
      H. Webster
      James Hathorn, Jr.
N. B. May 18, 1812. Son Aaron to have negro girl Cloe. Daughter
Rachel Butterworth to have negro boy Ned. Son Stephen to have negro
girl Easter. Son Hugh to have negro boy Jack. Son Isaac to have negro
girl Viannah. Son Daniel to have negro boy Joshua. Son Ben to have
next young negro or like value.
Wit.: William Hay, Jr.
      James R. Webster
Proven 27 Jan. 1817

WILL OF FENTON HALL - pp 210-213
To wife Hannah 3 negroes, furniture, tools, etc., to support her and
her family. After her death sold and equally divided among my children:
Polly Hall, William Hall, Jonathan Hall, Fenton Hall, Rhoda Hall, James
Hall, Johnson Hall, Lemuel Hall, Peggy Hall, Flemming Hall, Hannah Hall.
Young children who has had but little should be made equal with those
who had most. Executors: sons Johnson and Fenton. Mentioned negroes
Annas and Lidd. Dated 20 Nov. 1809.
Wit.: Harbert Tucker   (Signed) Fenton Hall
      Wm. Pickens
      James Hodge
Proven 25 March, 1817.

WILL OF JOSEPH BARTON - pp 213-214
Wife to have plantation her lifetime. At her death moveable property
divided in four parts amongst children Rebecke, James, Cassey and
Pheby. John Head to have that part of land that was laid off for him
by a conditional line between me and him. My son James to have upper
part joining Benjamin Sego. Executors: Wife and Morgan Morgan.
Dated 23 March, 1816.
Wit.: Benj. Sego   (Signed) Joseph (X) Barton
      Henry Cobb
      Jacob Chamlee
Proven 18 April, 1817.

WILL OF JAMES DOBBINS - pp 215-217
Wife Elizabeth land where I live for lifetime or widowhood, then to
go to son James, Jr. Balance of land joining William Henery and
John Dobbins to be sold and divided in seven shares. These shares
to go to son Robert B., son John, daughter Mary Morris, daughter
Elizabeth Hillhouse, daughter Sarah Calaham, daughter Jean Liddle,
son James Jr. Executors: Wife Elizabeth and son James. Dated 11
March, 1813.
Wit.: John Bryce   (Signed) James Dobbins
      Abraham Barron
      Wm. Hillhouse
Proven 26 July, 1817.

WILL OF GEORGE HEAD - pp 217-220
Far advanced in age. Son-in-law Stephen Liddal. To granddaughter
Nancy Liddal. To granddaughter Elizabeth Williams. To granddaughter
Rebeckah Yancy. To granddaughter Mary Yancy. Granddaughter Sally
Liddal. Grandson John Liddal. After paying the small legacies above
bequeathed I will that real and personal estate equally divided among
all my children with following exceptions. First that $150.00 be
deducted out of part that may come to my son-in-law William Pigg for
tract of land he now is living on. Second that part of estate that
may come to daughter Elizabeth Williams be divided into 8 parts. One
eighth of which I give to daughter Elizabeth Williams and her husband
John Williams, the other 7 parts to the 7 children she had by her first
husband Amos Adkinson. Children of Stephen Liddal that he had by my
daughter his first wife the part of estate that would be due their
mother was she living to be equally divided among them all. Executors:
Sons George and John Head. Dated 8 March, 1817.
Wit.: James Douthet   (Signed) George (X) Head
      Susannah Douthit
      Elijah Satterfield
Proven 2 March, 1818.

WILL OF JOHN TIPPEN - pp 220-222
Son William. Son George. Daughter Sarah Ballard. Daughter Mille
Prichard. To grandchildren Nancy, George, Mary, Betsey and Rhoda, the
children of Samson Tippen deceased. To wife Eleanor bed, furniture,
sow and pigs, corn, and the black cattle she took to Georgia. Land I
now live on to be rented out. Negro Dick to be hired out. Son John
not of age. Daughters Betsey and Abigail. To Elijah Weems, son of
Eleanor Tippen. To Leander Tippen, $1.00. Executors: William Tippen
and Silas Macey. Dated 3 Feb. 1818.
Wit: W. McGoger   (Signed) John Tippen

52

George Stevenson
Richd. Speake
William Tippen and Silas Massay qualified as executors.
Proven 9 March, 1818.

WILL OF BENJAMIN BARTON - pp 223-225

Wife Darkus. Two youngest sons Benjamin and James Matison Barton, to
have lands at death or marriage of wife. Oldest son Jona (?) Barton.
Oldest daughter Sela Kannon. Daughter Jeane Brown. Daughter Vashti
Kirksey. Daughter Averillah Griffin negro wence Nance and her youngest
boys Spencer and Green. To son Baley a negro man Adam. To son Thomas
negro man Mager. To daughter Darkey. To daughter Eliza a negro girl
Clarace. To son Benjamin negro boys Kalep and Jeremiah. To youngest
daughter Sarah negro woman Candus and her boys Sampson and John. To
youngest son James Matteson a negro boy martin and girl Suckey. To
wife a negro woman named Hester, a man Minna, a boy Stephen, a man
Arter and a wench Patty. Executors: Wife and Son Baley and Sargin (?)
Griffin. Dated 8 Feb. 1818.
Wit.: Jacob Guyton   (Signed) Benjamin Barton
       Wm. Baker
       Richard Baker
Proven 24 March, 1818.

WILL OF JONATHAN WATSON, SR. - pp 225228

Son David. Youngest son Stephen. David shall raise my two youngest
children Stephen and Nancy and is to have a negro woman named Mary and
the use of the plantation. Then negro to be sold and equally divided
amongst legatees. David to give Stephen two years schooling and Nancy
one year schooling. Land on Mountain Creek. John McCown and Nancy
McCown to have equal share with the rest of my children. Executors:
James Burriss and son David Watson. Dated 23 July, 1818.
Wit.: Joseph Taylor   (signed) Jonathan Watson
       W. McGriger
       Joseph Land
Proven 21 Sept. 1818.

WILL OF HENRY WILLBANKS - pp 228-230

Of Pendleton District, being weak in body and at a distance from home.
Wife Ruth to have one third of estate. Son Solomon has received part
of his share. Daughter Ibbey Gentry, wife of Bartley Gentry, has
received part of her share. Daughter Zilpha Dollar, wife of John
Dollar, has received part of her share. Rest of my children: Tempy
Willbanks, Hiram Willbanks, Elim Willbanks, Abijah Willbanks, Elijah
Willbanks, Gideon Willbanks, Richard Willbanks to have the remainder
of estate. Each to receive part when they arrive at the age of 21 or
marry. Executors: Sons Hiram and Elim. Dated 24 Sept. 1818.
Wit.: Charles Crow   (Signed) Henry (X) Willbanks
       William West
       Henry Langston
Proven by oath of Rev. Charles Crow 7 Oct. 1818, who swore he was
present at the decease of Henry Willbanks which happened on a journey.

WILL OF CHRISTOPHER KIRKSEY, SR. - pp 230-233

Wife Perthany to have negroes Joseph and his wife Jamima and girl Patsey
for life or widowhood. At death or remarriage to be sold and divided
equally among my children William Kirksey, John Kirksey, Elisha Kirksey,
Isaiah and Mark Kirksey, Lucy Pace and the lawful heirs of the body
of Nancy Davis and Sarah Foster (to wit) whole of heirs of said Nancy
Davis to have a share equal to one of the above legatees to be equally
divided among them as they arrive at lawful age. Heirs of Sarah Foster
to have share equally divided among them as they reach 21. To daughter
Nancy Davis one horse bruit. To daughter Sarah Foster one horse bruit.
Negro girl Phebe and her increase equally divided among heirs of Nancy
Davis at her death. Executors: sons William, Isaiah and Mark. Dated
13 Aug. 1814.
Wit.: Philip May   (Signed) Christopher Kirksey
       Andrew Davis
       Jonathan Davis
Proven 27 Oct. 1818

WILL OF JAMES BRUCE, SENIOR - pp 233-234
Wife Mary to have estate her lifetime, then sold and equally divided
between lawful heirs. Executors: Stephen Adams, William Bever. Dated
13 Feb. 1818.
Wit.: John Popham   (Signed) James Burce
       Gabriel Sisk
Proven 10 Feb. 1819.

WILL OF WILLIAM T. BARRY - pp 235-236
Wife Nancy to have Ceasar and wife Genny. Eldest daughter Catharine
Barry to have Scinda and Maria. Only son Bartley Barry to have Jordan
and all land consisting of part granted me by Spillers. Youngest
daughter to have Margaret and Ally. Wife to have estate her lifetime
to support and educate children. Executors: B. C. Barry and John
Barry. Dated 29 Aug. 1818.
Wit.: Jonathan Reader   (Signed) William T. Barry
       William Brown

WILL OF JESSE MILLER - pp 237-238
Wife Patsey to have entire estate her lifetime or widowhood. All lands
south of Wolf Creek then go to son Archibald. Lands north of creek
sold and equally divided between my five other sons: William, George,
Emson, Dowel, and James. Household property if any remaining to my
six daughters: Sarah Bruce, Amy Young, Susannah McColm, Rebeckah Tatum,
Peggy Perts, and Mary Miller. Executors: friends William Colm and
Patsey Miller. Dated 17 April, 1819.
Wit.: William Miller   (Signed) Jesse Miller
       Rebecah (X) Tatum
       Wm. McCollum
       Wm. (X) Tatum
Proven 2 March, 1819.

WILL OF THOMAS STRIBLING - pp 238-240
To wife Ann negroes Rachel, Alse and Cato for lifetime. At her death
Cato to son Thomas Stribling. Alse to son Jesse Stribling. Daughter
Ann Tate. Son-in-law Charles Webb. Rest of property sold and divided
between Frances Buchanan, Clayton Stribling, Elizabeth F. Farr, Thomas
Stribling, Lucy Trimmier and Sigizmond Stribling, allowing son Thomas
double amount of the rest of my children for his service to me.
Executor: son Thomas. Dated 24 Sept. 1818.
Wit.: T. Stribling, Jr.   (Signed) Thomas Stribling
       Frances Stribling
Proven 7 June, 1819.

WILL OF JAMES BAILY - pp 240-242
Wife Mary to have house and household furniture, all stock, one half
plantation tools and one half cleared land if Wiatt stays with her.
If not she shall have land until she marries, one third of furniture,
one third of stock and Grace and her child Daniel to work for her.
At her decease Lizabeth Knop (?) Knap (?) Kross (?) shall have Grace
and her daughter Eliza Knop shall have bed and furniture. Son Wiatt
Bailey shall have land joining Joseph Celly and Widow Anderson. To
granddaughter Mary Baily, the daughter of Wiatt and Peggy Bailey, bed
and furniture at decease of her grandmother. To daughters Frances
Fleming and Martha Garrerson negro Daniel and rest of stock and furniture except one bed and furniture to my woman Grace. Dated 31 July,
1810.
Wit.: Levi Garrason   (Signed) James Baily
       John P. Knop
       Frances B. Fleming
Proven 4 Oct. 1819.

WILL OF THOMAS CARADINE - pp 243-245
To wife Elizabeth negro girl Charlotta forever. Whole estate to wife
her lifetime or widowhood. After decease or marriage to son Joberry
E. Caradine, negro boy Joe. Negro girl Nancy to daughter Evalina
Caradine. Negro girl Arrena to daughter Patsey. To son Thomas, negro
boy Billey. Negro man Peter to choose his own master among my children.
My desire is that none of my black family be sold but to continue and

54

be among my children. Daughters Polley, Elizabeth, Sarah, Patsey and
Avaline. All my children. Extra to before mentioned young children.
Executor: Wife Elizabeth. Dated 26 April, 1820.
Wit.: Thomas Lamar Hirum   (Signed) Thomas Caradine
       Jane (X) Wright
       P. Cardine
       Elizabeth Caradine
Proven 19 May, 1820.

WILL OF JOHN MULLIANAX - pp. 245-247
Wife Alsey. All property during widowhood. Son Matthew. Four younger
children as they come of age: William G., Emanuel G., Jincy G., and
Fanny G. My eight children: Nancy Smith, John Mullinnax, Lawson
Mullennex, Matthew Mullinnax, William G., Emanuel G., Jeny G., and
Fanny G. Mullianax. Executors: James Gaines and Jno. Mullianex, Jr.
Dated 3 Oct. 1819.
Wit.: William Evatt   (Signed) John Mullianax
       Samuel McDow
       Thomas Evatt
Proven 5 June, 1820.

WILL OF NATHANIEL DAVIS - pp. 247-249
Wife Piety. Son Thomas. Grandson Armstead, the son of my daughter
Piety to be schooled. Each of my children: Thomas Davis, Elizabeth
Burriss, Nancy Cox, Piety Hobson, Judy Hix, and Rebecka Davis.
Executors: Son Thomas Davis and Enoch Davis. Dated 14 June, 1817.
Wit.: John Mays   (Signed) Nathaniel (X) Davis
       Archibald McElroy
       Martha McElroy
Proven 5 May, 1820.

WILL OF ROBERT DOWDLE, SR. - pp 249-252
Wife Mary to have negro wench Sally and a fellow Maurice. Wench Betty
to be under the care of wife for life then to be provided for by son
Samuel and his heirs. At wife's death Maurice to be manumitted from
servitude for life. Two daughters Margaret Dowdle and Esther Liddle.
Daughter-in-law Martha Dowdle. Negro boy Nathan after wife's death
goes to son Samuel and after Samuel's death to Samuel's son James.
Negro girl Lucy to son Samuel. Son Robert. Daughter Elenor Warnock.
Grandson Robert Barr, son of my son Samuel, to have negro boy Cato.
Also to Robert Barr, Pegg and James, sons and daughter of my son Samuel,
I give $50.00 each. To grandson William, son of Samuel, $25.00 to
assist in their education to be exclusively for tuition. To son James
a negro fellow Tom. To daughter Margaret Pickens a negro boy Sambo.
To son John, a negro girl Susan. My nine children. Executors: Wife
Mary, son-in-law John Warnock, and William Achor, Esq. Dated 2 Sept.
1819.
Wit.: Joseph Whitner   (Signed) Robert Dowdle, Sr.
       Major Lewis
       Adam Todd
Proven 7 Aug. 1820.

WILL OF WILLIAM NICHOLSON - pp. 252-255
Wife Martha to have negroes Leath, Fabe, Elijah, Jack and Robert along
with plantation, tools, stock, etc., for the purpose of raising the
children during her natural life, then sold and equally divided among
children. Slaves not to go out of the family nor to be slaves longer
than until they are 50 years of age provided that they conduct themselves in a suitable manner to be free. To daughter Sarah Nicholson
a negro girl Loosey until she is 50. To daughter Martha a negro girl
Veney until she is 50. To daughter Harriet a negro girl Sarah until
she is 50. To daughter Belinda a negro girl Ony until she is 50. To
son William part of plantation on the other side of the creek from where
this house stands. To son Lemuel land on this side and house and the
three tracts bought from the state on Cravens Creek. Other two plantations to be sold and divided. To daughter Mary a negro woman Mary to
be given to her against the 25 of December next and to belong to her and
the heirs of her body. The child that negro Mary is now with if it lives

55

not to belong to Mary Norton but to be returned to the rest of the family at the age of two. Executors: Wife and sons Evan and William Nicholson. (Will not dated.)

Wit.: John McWhorter   (Signed) William Nicholson
      Robert (X) Partain
Proven 7 Aug. 1820.

WILL OF WILLIAM COX - pp 255-256
Wife Mary. To William Bolen Cox and John Wesley Cox plantation where I now live. Rest of property divided equally among rest of my children. Garner Broocks I leave him nothing but his son William Tomson Broocks I leave him equal share with the rest of last mentioned children. Executors: Richard Madden and Isaac Steat (?). Dated 16 April, 1821.

Wit.: Thomas Jones   (Signed) William (X) Cox
      Ezekial Madden
      Thomas Wiley
Proven 25 May, 1821.

WILL OF THOMAS COOPER - pp 256-257
Wife Elizabeth to have estate her lifetime then divided among my three children John Cooper, James Cooper and Johannah Perry. To William Rea the son of my wife Elizabeth after her death a feather bed and furniture. Executors: sons John and James. Dated 2 April, 1821.

wit.: John Edmondson   (Signed) Thomas (X) Cooper
      William Singleton
Proven 2 July, 1821.

WILL OF WILLIAM STEELE - pp 258-261
Wife Esther to have negro woman Candice and child Moses for life or widowhood. Son Aaron Steele to have mills on Twenty-three Mile Creek with land granted me by Daniel Shipp and land on Millwee (?) Creek joining William Dodds and David Boyd. He also to have old negro Jim, negro fellow Stephen and boy Jacob. Daughter Polly L. Steele to have negro woman Drilla and son Benjamin. Daughter Elizabeth Steele to have negro girl Fanny and boy Cato. To son Joseph Steele plantation I now live on and negro men John and Sawny. To son James 700 acres near the mouth of Eighteen Mile Creek including the old mill seat, also to have negro man Ben and boy George. To son William Steele who ran away and is as I suppose at sea, $1000.00 to be held in reserve and at interest for him until he may return but if he should not return within ten years after my decease money to be divided and given his surviving brothers and sisters or to the child or children of any who may die. To daughters Polly L. and Betsy Steele the house where Benson lives on both sides of Eighteen Mile Creek and adjoining the Court House lands. Negro woman Rhoda to be sold and divided equally among Polly L., Elizabeth, Joseph L., and James Steele. Executors: friends James C. Griffin, Esq., Benjamin Dickson, Esq., and my son Joseph L. Steele. Dated 26 Jan. 1818.

Wit.: Benj. Dickson   (Signed) W. Steele
      David L. Boyd
      Job Rainwater
Proven 6 Aug. 1821.

WILL OF SARAH BROWN - pp 261-263
Widow. Son Joseph. Daughter Ann Hughs. Daughter-in-law Sarah Brown wife to my son Andrew. Daughter Sarah Hughs' daughter Sarah. A negro girl Rhoda to daughter Sarah Hughs. Negro boy Absalom jointly to son Andrew and daughter Ann Hughs. Granddaughter Ann Brown, daughter of my son Andrew. Executors: John Hughes. Dated 20 Feb. 1821.

Wit.: John McWhorter   (Signed) Sarah (X) Brown
      Benj. Hughes
Proven 6 Aug. 1821.

WILL OF WILLIAM CLEVELAND - pp 263-267
To daughter Patsey Wright $300.00 in cash or in some degree indemnify her for the negro wench Phillice I gave her and she had the misfortune to lose. To daughter Fanny Wright a negro woman Milley now in her possession but with the condition that should she die without issue the negro and all her increase equally divided among her brothers and sisters.

To daughter Catharine Wright a negro woman Dicy. To daughter Nancy
Cleveland, wife of George Cleveland, negro boy Andrew now in her
possession. To son Robert Harrison Cleveland, negro boy Sampson. To
daughter Polly Cleveland negro boy Allen. To daughter Jane Cleveland
negro boy Daniel. To son Oliver F. Cleveland, negro boy John. To
daughter Lucinda Cleveland, negro boy Green. To daughter Elizabeth
Cleveland, negro boy Jim. To son William Earl Cleveland negro boy
Hugh. Negro fellows Williston and Jacob to be hired out. If their
hire amounts to $300.00 before they are sold I want that amount paid
to Thomas Wright, the remainder divided among remainder of children
including my daughter Patty Wright. Remainder of negroes Coop and
Moll and Chester, Jack and Hannah and Peter Tom and Cato, Dick and Luse
I wish to remain on the place and labor and support my wife and children.
Land on Toogooloo. If wife be alive when youngest child is of age
she shall have so many negroes as will be able to support her comfortable and should she find negroes troublesome she may give them up to
be divided among the children. Land on Beaver Dam remain in hands of
my three sons-in-law as they now have it, until younger children of age,
then divided equally among my children. Larkin Wright shall have same
benefit of land on which he lived on at the Beaver Dam that his brothers
has for the execution of my will. Executors: Wife Nancy, son Robert
H. Cleveland, son-in-law Thomas Wright, and Benjamin Harrison. Dated
31 July, 1820.
Wit.:   Samuel Earle   (Signed)   William Cleveland
        Jeremiah Cleveland
        Osburn Cleveland
Proven 22 Oct. 1821.

WILL OF WILLIAM POOR, SENIOR - pp 267-269
Wife Mary to have house and plantation her lifetime or widowhood, then
to go to my five daughters. To son Samuel land where he lives on
Toneys Creek waters of Saluda River, 206 acres. To youngest son Lemuel
Poor, land where I now live except as given to his mother. Oldest
daughter Delilah Poor to have 173 acres where she lives during her life
or celibacy and at her death or marriage to go to her son Harper Poor.
Executors: Mary Poor, Samuel Poor and Lemuel Poor. Dated 31 Dec. 1820.
Wit.:   William Poor, Jr.   (Signed)   Wm. Poor
        Cain Broyles
        John (X) Connway
Proven 3 June, 1822.

WILL OF DAVID LEWIS - pp 270-271
Five shillings each to son Isaiah. Daughter Priscilla which married
Thomas Field. Son Jacob Lewis. Son Joab Lewis. Son Neriah Lewis.
Son Benjamin Lewis. Daughter Elizabeth Lewis which married Micajah
Alexander. Daughter Cozby which married Ezekial Norton. To son Daivd
Lewis and daughter Rosannah Lewis and wife Penelopy Lewis I give all
personal property to be divided between them. Executors: wife
Penelopy. Dated 19 Jan. 1822.
Wit.:   Gabriel Barron   (Signed)   David Lewis
        Samuel Barron
        George W. Liddell
Proven 2 Sept. 1822.

WILL OF ADAM KILBY - pp 271-273
To daughter Sarah Kilby $300.00, beds, furniture, cows and calves. To
Nathaniel Duncan $100.00, mare, cow and calf and all farming tools,
bed and furniture. Rest of furniture equally divided between Sarah
Kilby and Nathaniel Duncan. To my three sons William, Edward, and
James Kilby $1.00 each. To daughters Fanny White and Nancy Harris
$1.00 each. Executors: Daniel Duncan and John Morris, Jr. Dated 5
Sept. 1819.
Wit.:   John Morris, Jr.   (Signed)   Adam (X) Kilby
        Daniel Duncan
Proven 11 April, 1823.

WILL OF ELIAS EARLE - pp 273-276
To daughter Elizabeth R. Earle negroes Nimrod, Elijah, Phillip and
Rose. To daughter Nancy McClanahan negroes Andrew and wife Betty and
all their increase. To son Samuel G. Earle, negroes Jacob, Prince,
Charles, Phillip, Little Charles and Milley with 23 children and future
increase. To daughter Sally Harrison, negroes Kranky, Mary and Feilding
with their future increase. To son Robinson M. Earle, negroes Randol,
Frederick, Abraham, Virgin, Trulove, Jack and several small children
of Virgin. To grandson Elias Henry Tillinghast, negroes Joannah and
her four children. If he dies, negroes go back to estate and equally
divided between my sons Elias Earle and John Baylis Earle. Land on
Twenty-three Mile Creek near Court House Road and Mrs. Rosamond.
Land purchased from Robert Anderson near Carter's fence and
Carter's Branch. To James Harrison and Samuel G. Earle lands purchased
of James Lawson including town of Andersonville. Youngest sons Elias
and John B. Earle. Wife to have third of estate. Executors: son
Elias. Dated 2 Feb. 1823.
Wit.: Josiah McClure   (Signed) Elias Earle
       James Clarke
       Thomas Stribling
Proven 2 June, 1823.

WILL OF MICAJAH SMITHSON - pp 276-277
Son Asa to have all land and negroes. To son Marson Cox Smithson
$100.00 also be it remembered that in the year of 1798 or 1799 I
payed him $60.00 in full of all claims. To Albert Francis Smithson
$57.00 with 13 Ł Virginia money that I lent him long since if anywhere
to be found. To son Basill Coleman Smithson $100.00 if to be found.
Executors: son Asa Smithson and David Pugh. Dated 29 July, 1822.
Wit.: John Verner   (Signed) Micaja Smithson
       Squire Hughes
       David R. Verner
Proven July, 1823.

WILL OF FRANCES MCKINSTRY - pp 277-279
Spinster. Two sons Thomas and Newman M. McKinstry be sent to school,
Thomas 9 months and Newman M. 18 months. I will that out of what I
possess Thomas and Newman shall have in the first place to the amount
of what sum the other heirs was entitled to out of the personal estate
of their father and remainder except bed and furniture equally divided
amongst all my children male and female. Whichever of my daughters
remaining with me and takes care of me longest to have aforementioned
bed and furniture, or if more than one stays equally divided.
Executors: John George, Sr., and Alexander Moorehead. Dated 4 July,
1822.
Wit.: Abraham Massey   (Signed) Frances McKinstry
       John Richardson
       Robert (X) McCallister

WILL OF ROBERT IRWIN - pp 279-283
Minister of the Gospel in Pendleton District. Wife Eleanor plantation,
furniture, etc., for life or until she marries. She may live on plantation after marriage buy not to waste estate. To John Black who was
bound to me by indenture by his mother according to civil law if he
continue to fulfill his time till he comes of age to have $40.00
besides sum specified in his indenture which is $60.00. If he is
obedient to my wife and after his time is fulfilled will live with and
rent land from her I desire her to favor him before any other. If he
marries prudently and stays on plantation I bequeath to him feather bed
and necessary covering and she may either rent him land or shew some
part on plantation where he may clear a field and live there for four
years until he may provide a place but he shall have no power to rent
or sell it but at the will of my wife. If he leaves her to receive
only sum in indenture and sum bequeathed him and a pocket Bible. To my
brother John Irwin's sons in the State of Georgia, viz. Samuel and
Robert, I leave plantation I live on at the death of Eleanor if they
or either of them be then in the land of the living and if they come
and live on it. They have no power to sell it if they will not come
and live on it. If they died before wife it goes to Associate Reformed

Congregation of Little Generostee. To rest of brother John Irwin's children in the State of Georgia, and to my sister Sarah Pendrey's son John Pendrey 400 acres of pine land on Duheart's Creek in Jefferson County, Georgia. What household furniture left at wife's death sold for purpose of purchasing pocket Bible with psalms for each of my wife's brothers and sisters children then alive and unmarried in this state and in Elbert County, Georgia, and for each child of my after mentioned executors and balance given to that one of brother's sons who may not get the plantation. Executors: James Sharard of Pendleton District and John Gordon, Esq., of Elbert County Georgia and my wife Eleanor. Dated 7 June, 1822.

Wit.: William B. Patterson   (Signed) Robert Irwin, G. M.
       Thomas Henderson
       James Henderson
Proven 22 Dec. 1823.

WILL OF WILLIAM CLARKSON, JR. - pp 283-284
Of Charleston. Wife Esther Susannah Clarkson. Children born and unborn. Sons to receive their share at age 21, daughters also at age 21 or at marriage. Executors: friend Lewis Ciples and wife Esther Susannah. Dated 20 March, 1815.

Wit.: Peter Dubois   (Signed) William Clarkson, Junior
       Thomas W. Carne
       Elizabeth Carne
Codicil. Dec. 16, 1823, I appoint my dear cousin, William Clarkson, Sr., executor of my will.
Wit.: John D. Carne
       Cornelias P. Dupre
       Mary Dupre

WILL OF ABSALOM HALL - pp 285-286
Wife Sarah. Children under age. Executors: John Hall and Ezekial Hall. Dated 18 Feb. 1824.

Wit.: David Hall   (Signed) Absalom Hall
       Dg. Tucker
       Hannah (X) Hall
       Sarah Hall
Proven 26 April, 1824.

WILL OF MARY HUNTER Senior - pp 286-288
To three daughters Mary Hunter, Mandanna (Maudonna?) Hunter and Ethelinda Hunter, house and lot #41 in Village of Pendleton, purchased by me from Leonard Capeheart. To each of my children not heretofore mentioned, 25 cents. Executors: friends David Cherry and Elam Sharpe. Dated 15 March, 1822.

Wit.: Mary D. Hunter   (Signed) Mary (X) Hunter
       Martha Whitfield
       J. T. (?) Whitfield
Proven, no date.

WILL OF ELIZABETH JAMES - pp 288-289
Wife of Thomas James, deceased. Son James Brown. Daughter Nancy Brown. Plantation whereon I now live equally divided between them. Executor: James Dobbins. Dated 4 Jan. 1824.

Wit.: James Dobbins   (Signed) Elizabeth (X) James
       Martha Dobbins
No Proven date.

WILL OF JOHN WILSON, SENIOR - pp 289-291
Wife Elizabeth. Son Robert. Daughters Sarah, Mary Ann, Jennet, Agness, Elizabeth and Hannah. To youngest sons John and Hugh, 200 acres on Saluda River. Executors: Sons John and Hugh. Dated 5 April, 1812, (or 1822?).

Wit.: Samuel Houston   (Signed) John Wilson
       Henry Cobb
       William (X) Rogers
No proven date.

WILL OF JOSPEH WHITNER - pp 291-295
To be buried on plantation whereon I now live if I die at home. Wife
Elizabeth to have all her lifetime, then to three daughters Rebecca,
Elizabeth and Sarah. Have already given son Benjamin Franklin Whitner
a collegiate education which I estimate cost $1100.00 and other things
including a negro boy Ben, the son of Silvey, about 15 years of age.
Have given son Joseph Newton Whitner a collegiate education, other
things and negro boy Abraham. Joseph Newton became of age the 11th
day of April last. Daughters to have Jenny and her children, Nelly and
her children, with exception of Abraham already bequeathed. If one of
daughters die before marriage or coming of age, her share goes to her
surviving sisters. Negroes possessing families to be divided without
separating mothers from younger children as far as practicable.
Executors: Son Jospeh Newton Whitner and friend Col. Robert Anderson.
Dated 1 Feb. 1921.
Wit.: William Anderson   (Signed)   Joseph Whitner
     F. W. Symmes.
     Warren R. Davis
No probate date.

WILL OF RUSSELL CANNON - pp 295-297
Wife Jean to have negro Simon for her own and Rose and Cato her life-
time. At her death sold and equally divided among my lawful heirs.
Daughter Harriet Duke to have negro Ann. All other property disposed
of and equally divided amongst my children. Executors: Wife Jean and
son Elijah. Dated 10 July, 1824.
Wit.: James Hunter   (Signed)   Russel Cannon
     James E. Hart
No probate date.

WILL OF LUKE HAMILTON - pp 297-299
Wife Elizabeth. Daughter Margaret McCallester. Daughter Jane Hamilton.
Daughter Leah Hamilton. Daughter Mary Reid. Daughter Nancy Hamilton.
Daughter Letitia Long. Daughter Sarah Cason. Daughter Fanny Hamilton.
Son William Hamilton. Son Luke Hamilton to have 150 acres on north-
west side of the road leading from Montagues to Baskins ford. To daugh-
ter Jane Hamilton a negro girl Flora. Executors: James Thompson and
sons William and Luke Hamilton. Dated 22 Feb. 1822.
Wit.: Jas. Thomson   (Signed)   Luke (X) Hamilton
     Fenton Hall
     Math. Thomson
No probate date.

WILL OF THOMAS HUNTER - pp 300-302
To daughter Mary Anderson a negro woman Esther and her four children
Nero, Frank, Lucy and Milley. To son John Hunter, 400 acres in Ruther-
ford County, North Carolina, on Waters Creek. To wife Sarah, one third
of real and personal property for life. At death to go to son John.
If son John should die without issue, his share to his sister Mary.
Executors: son John and friends Samuel Cherry and James C. Griffin.
Dated 4 April, 1825.
Wit.: George E. W. Foster   (Signed)   Thomas (X) Hunter
     N. R. Webb
     H. W. Davis
No probate date.

WILL OF ALEXANDER CALHOUN - pp 302-306
Wife Susannah (?). Two youngest sons Alexander and George. Susannah
to have negro woman Mille to dispose of as she pleases. Son John
Calhoun. Son-in-law George Cammel. Son-in-law Abner Ledbetter. Son-
in-law William Bell. To daughter Elizabeth, negro girl Nancy Dawson.
Negro girl Melicy to son Alexander. Negro girl Mary Ann to son George,
also to George negro child Henry. Negro man Willis to remain on
plantation and help support widow, after widow's death to go to son
Alexander. Executors: son Alexander Calhoun. Dated 27 May, 1825.
Wit.: Daniel Ledbetter   (Signed)   Alexd. Calhoun
     Asa Castleberry
     Benjamin Dickson
No probate date.

WILL OF DAVID L. BOYD - pp 306-308
Wife and children shall live on my 300 acre tract. If she marries she
may have one third. Negro girl Hagar to wife until youngest child
is 21. Then divided between wife and children. Executor is to collect
$200.00 of Uriah Beatonbough for land sold in Union District, and get
my daughter Amey (?) to make title and pay over to daughter Amey Boyd
said $200.00 with interest. Executors: friend Thomas Townsend and
my wife Elizabeth Boyd. Dated 11 July, 1825.
Wit.: James C. Griffin   (Signed) David L. Boyd
      Major Wilbanks
      Reuben Cason
No proven date.

WILL OF JOHN N. SIDDAL (LIDDAL?) - p 309
Dated 15 Oct. 1812. Father Jesse Siddall, all my slaves his life time,
to wit: Peggy, Toney and Abraham. After his death equally divided
between the heirs of Elizabeth Head and Rebecca Shotwell. Land on
Twelve Mile Creek. Executor: father Jesse Siddall and John A. Easley.
Wit.: Thomas Blasingame   (Signed) Jno. N. Siddall
No proven date.

WILL OF DAVID STEVENSON - pp 310-311
Wife. Youngest son Hamilton Stevenson. Negro man Jack to be sold and
another fellow purchased. Son William. Daughter Mary Ann. Son James.
Son Samuel. Daughter Jeane. Daughter Elizabeth. Executors: William
Simpson, James Stevenson and my wife. Dated 30 Dec. 1821.
Wit.: E. B. Benson   (Signed) David Stevenson
      Joseph Taylor
      James Stevenson

WILL OF MARGARET DICKSON - pp 212-213
Of great age.. Negro man Dick having been a faithful servant I wish to
place him in as pleasant circumstances as laws permit, and direct
that he shall choose a master which master shall pay $400.00 to my
son William Dickson and his legimate sons by equal shares. Daughter
Mary. Daughter Jean. Son Robert. Executor: friend William Simpson.
Dated 15 April, 1823.
Wit.: Rebecca (X) Simpson   (Signed) Margaret (X) Dickson
      O. B. Trimmier
N. B. Negro man Dick at my decease.to obtain his freedom by an act of
the Legislature, petitioned in my name made to legislature by my
executor. Dated 18 Oct. 1824.
Wit.: Simpson Dickson
      William Sanford
No proven date.

WILL OF ELIAB MOORE, SENIOR - pp 314-315
Wife Rebecca. Two sons Samuel and Eliab. Executors: George Manning
and Thomas Hays, Esq. Dated 13 Feb. 1826.
Wit.: E. Browne   (Signed) Eliab Moore, Senior
      Thomas Taylor
      Archibald Keaton
Proven by Elijah Browne, Esq.
No proven date.

WILL OF ALEXANDER RAMSAY - pp 315-318
Wife Mary to have negroes Bristo and wife Silvia, boy Jacob and girl
Mary Ann. To son Andrew, negro boys Thomas and Adam. To daughter Jane
McDow, negro boy Dulinser and girl Lucinda. To daughter Elizabeth Gates,
negro girl Mary Ann at death of her mother. To son Alexander, plan-
tation. He is to look after his mother as long as she lives. To son
Alexander, a negro boy Ivery. If Alexander should die without issue,
equally divided among other children. Executors: Son Alexander and
friend Col. Robert Anderson. Dated 14 Aug. 1824.
Wit.: J. C. Kilpatrick   (Signed) Alexander Ramsey
      Josiah Wright
      Ezl. Harris
No proven date.

WILL OF BENJAMIN LAURENCE - pp 318-325
Farmer. To wife Rachel, negroes Frank, Hannah and Bill. Sons James
and Elisha to take care of mother. To son James negro fellow Cyrus
usually called Cye. To son Elisha, negro fellow Abram. To daughter
Sarah Speed, wife of William Speed, negro boy Bill, unless she would
prefer girl. Daughter Margaret Deal, wife of Alexander Deal. To
granddaughter Rachel Speed who now lives with me. Land on Conaross.
Executors: sons James and Elisha and Robert Anderson, Esq. Dated 17
July, 1819.
Wit.:   John T. Lewis   (Signed) Benjn. Laurence
        John Hunter
        Warren R. Davis
No proven date.
Codicil: Negro Cyrus to go to son Elisha, and Abram to go to son James.
Sarah Speed to receive $300.00 instead of negro. Dated 19 Sept. 1821.
Wit.:   George W. Boggs
        M. T. Anderson
        Ann T. Anderson
Codicil proved by Martha Anderson
No probate date.

WILL OF NICHOLAS HEATON - pp 325-327
Brother David Heaton. Nancy Gordon holds note on me. Brother William
Heaton. Sister Matilda Heaton. Sister Sally Heaton. Brother Timothy
P. Heaton. Wife Linney (?). Executors: Bryan Burriss. Will not dated.
Wit.:   David Gambrell   (Signed) Nicholas (X) Heaton
        Robert Black
        George W. Masters
No proven date.

WILL OF THOMAS K. EDWARDS - pp 327-328
Land on Friend (?) St. in Charleston is mortgaged to Messrs. Matthews
and Bonneau. If sold and amount to more than mortgage, it is to go
to Elizabeth Ashby Shackleford. To Susan Rose, $1500.00 and girl to
be purchased by executors. After bequests if anything left it is to
go to Thomas Asby of St. John's Parish, Planter, with the exception
of my wearing apparel which I give to Francis W. Kane. I hold a negro
boy James and a small gold watch under the gift of my mother. These I
give to Thomas Ashby. Executor: Thomas Ashby. Dated 18 March, 1826.
Wit.:   Leroy Barr   (Signed) Thos. K. Edwards
        Milton Barr
        Frs. W. Kane
No proven date.

WILL OF HENSLEY STIGALL - pp 329-330
Children I have had by Fanny Holeman, the woman with whom I now live:
Spencer, Caroline, Mary, Elizabeth and William Warren. If Fanny Holeman wishes she may live on plantation and raise children there until
youngest is 21. If my father Richard Stegall who is now living should
at his death leave any part of his estate to me, I do will that same
be equally divided among above named children, each to receive his
part as he becomes of age. Dated 10 July, 1826.
Wit.:   James Douthit   (Signed) Hensley Stigall
        Susannah Douthit
        Elias Elrod
Proven by oath of Rev. James Douthit, no date.

WILL OF DAVID SLOAN, SENIOR - pp 330-338
Planter, dated 29 Oct. 1821. To be buried at the burial ground on
plantation whereon I now live. To wife Susannah, one third part of 54
negroes and house we live in or if she prefer the house Jesse Stribling
lately lived in, her lifetime. My ten children. Eldest son David,
negroes in his possession and land whereon he lives on north side of
Cane Creek, being 950 acres, and 50 acres on south side Cane Creek to
include his mill and pond, but he is to grind free of toll all grain
brought by Jesse Stribling to the mill. To Jesse Stribling and his
wife Elizabeth, my eldest daughter, negroes in their possession and 950
acres on south side Cane Creek, whereon he lives. To son David and
Jesse Stribling, land on Cane and Richland Creeks, about 340 acres,

originally granted to self and Talley. To Robert Bruce and my daughter
Susannah Bruce his wife, land on Toogaloo River and Gum Log Creek in
Franklin County, Georgia, about 1250 acres, and the negroes in their
possession. To son Benjamin Franklin Sloan, 13 negroes and five tracts
of land on Toogaloo River and Pains Creek in Franklin County, Georgia,
being about 1643 acres. To son Thomas M. Sloan, 22 negroes, and 2000
acres where he now lives purchased from Joseph Taylor on Keowee or
Seneca River about five miles from Pendleton. To youngest son James,
under age of 21. To son William, 2000 acres where I now live. Wife
and son David to be guardians of James Madison. Two youngest sons
William and James Madison, both under 21. To Joseph Taylor and wife
Nancy all personal property heretofore placed in his possession by me,
and $1000.00. To Joseph B. Earle and wife Rebecca my daughter, negroes
in their possession. A note of his I paid cash for to James Rucker
dated 16 Oct. 1817. To John P. Benson and wife Catharine, my youngest
daughter, negroes in his possession and $2314.00. To grandson David
S. Taylor, a negro boy Bob aged about 14. To granddaughter Susannah
Taylor, a negro girl Elvira aged about eight. To grandson Charles
Burce, a negro boy Edward aged about 16. Executors: Wife Susannah and
son David.
Wit.: Joseph Grisham   (Signed) David Sloan
       James Harrison
       John Matthews
Proven by Col. Joseph Grisham. No date.

WILL OF JOHN MILLER, SENIOR - pp 338-341
Wife Jane to have all of my estate for raising younger children. At
her death to go to unmarried daughters or sons as may be in need.
If she marry her future husband prevented from spending or disposing
of my estate. Four daughters now single. Sons Joseph, George, James
and William to have land west of Seneca River. To children whom I have
given nothing I express an affectionate regard and regret I am unable
to leave them legacies. Executors: Wife and son Charles. Dated 7
Aug. 1826.
Wit.: Martha M. Dart   (Signed) Miller
       Susan Dupre
       Joseph Grisham
No proven date.

WILL OF WILLIAM BENNETT - pp 341-343
Wife A____ (page turned back when microfilmed and wife's name not
legible.) Son Coper Bennett to have negro man Robin. Daughter Daliceh
Johnson. Son Hardemen Bennett. My property including present crop of
tobacco sold. My cropper James M. Posey (?) (page turned back here.)
to have one fifth I grew on the old land and one fourth of that grown
on new land. Executors: friend William McGregor. Dated 19 Nov. 1826.
Wit.: Benj. Dickson   (Signed) William Bennett
       Jeremiah D. Gee
       Samuel Gee
No proven date.

WILL OF DANIEL LEDBETTER - pp 343-349
To wife Nancy 350 acres where I now live and a negro woman Sarah and
negro man Robert her lifetime or widowhood. Son Abner is a cripple.
Daughter Ede Russel to have negro woman Sarah and child Eliga. Daughter
Rhoda Gordon. To Leah Tippen $457.50 as her part of my estate. Son
William. Daughter Nancy Calhoun. Daughter Jenny. Daughter Lavena.
After death of my daughter Rhoda Gordon her part devolves to the chil-
dren she has had by Jacob Gordon. Friends John L. North and Rev.
Sanford Vandiver and Edmon Webb to be commissioners to settle contro-
versy that might arise among legatees. Executor: Son Abner.
Dated 6 August, 1824.
Wit.: Benj. Dickson   (Signed) Daniel Ledbetter
       Thomas G. Dickson
       Charles Alexander
Codicil - Daughter Jenny is now married and land I willed to her re-
voked as she is now provided for. Dated 21 Dec. 1825.
Wit.: Benj. Dickson, Thos. G. Dickson, Ralph E. Dickson. No date.

WILL OF JEHU ORR - pp 349-351
Wife Jane B. to have one third of estate. Other two thirds to legal
heirs. Executors: Wife Jane B., and son Christopher, and son-in-law
Thomas Hays. Dated 15 Feb. 1827.
Wit.: William F. Clinkscales   (Signed) Jehu Orr
      John Martin
      Amaziah Rice
No proven date.

WILL OF EPPS MAJOR - pp 351-352
Wife Susannah all estate during her widowhood for her support and
support of my children until they come of age. Have given daughter
Dorothy McWhorter property. Also given son George Major property.
Rest of children: Rebecca Major, Elijah Major, Marian Major, Tarey
(or Sarey?) Major, Elizabeth Major, Nancy Major. Executors: Wife
Susannah, Barnett H. Algood, and Isaac Miller. Dated 12 April, 1827.
Wit.: David Hendrix   (Signed) Epps (X) Major
      Henry Sarjeant
      Isaac Miller, Jr.
No proven date.

WILL OF WILLIAM PERKINS _ pp 353-355
To daughter Rutha Philips one shilling for her disobedience. To son
Moses Perkins one shilling for his disobedience. To sons Josiah and
Joshua Perkins, land whereon my mother lives. Rest of estate equally
divided between my wife and children as they come of age, Rutha and
Moses excepted. At wife's death or re-marriage to go to children except
Rutha and Moses. Executors: John C. Kilpatrick, Peter Kilpatrick
and Josiah Foster. Dated 29 March, 1816.
Wit.: R. H. Grant   (Signed) William Perkins
      Aaron Terrell
      Aaron Shannon
Codicil - I, William Perkins, have made my will dated 29 Mar. 1816
giving to my daughter Sarah Harrison, wife of Shadrack Harrison, an
equal part of estate with my wife and all my children except my daughter
Ruth Philips wife of Aaron Philips and my son Moses Perkins. I revoke
the said part of estate to Sarah Harrison and in lieu to said Sarah
and heirs of her body (if she should ever have any) a negro girl Hannah
the right of which is to be placed in the hands of John C. Kilpatrick,
Peter Kilpatrick, William Simpson and Asa Smithson, Trustees for her
use and benefit and not subject to debts of her husband. If Sarah die
without issue, negro to go to other children. I give daughter Ruth
Phillips and heirs of her body a negro girl Melinda placed in the hands
of the same trustees. To son Moses Perkins I give 100 acres off of the
lower or east end of a 300 acre tract on both sides of Colonels Fork
of Coneross Creek.
Wit.: John C. Dench   (Signed) William (X) Perkins
      Birdwell Hill
      Richard Carvet
No proven date, no date on codicil.

WILL OF JAMES CUNNINGHAM - pp 355-356
Brother John Cunningham and Elizabeth Wandsly his daughter to have all
money coming to me in the State of Georgia by note. To sister Jane
Moore who I have lived with for many years my plantation bought of
Samuel Taylor on Weems Creek waters of Savannah River. Also to sister
Jane the lands I possess in the State of Georgia granted to Moses Flemm-
ing but which is my right. As John Moore has left my sister who was
his lawful wife for many years and without cause in a distressed
situation taking everything comfortable, that said John Moore not re-
ceive any part of the estate bequeathed to my sister Jane Moore.
Bequests to be for Jane independent of her husband John Moore and at
her disposal at her death. Executors: friends James Thompson, William
Underwood, and Joseph Taylor. Dated 10 Nov. 1826.
Wit.: Joseph Taylor   (Signed) James Cunningham
      Joseph T. Earle
      Samuel J. Taylor
Proven by oath of Col. Joseph Taylor.
No proven date.

WILL OF ABRAHAM MAYFIELD - pp 357-359

Wife Peggy. Second daughter Suffy. Oldest son Austin. To Elijah 47 acres when he pays demands Austin has against him. To Epraigm, land on south side spring branch. At wife's death or marriage property to be sold and equally divided among all my children. Dated 21 Oct. 1826. Executor: William Magee.

Wit.: William Magee   (Signed) Abraham (X) Mayfield
   Samuel McCoy
   Sanferd Vandiver
No proven date.

WILL OF ROBERT COBB, SENIOR - pp 359-362

Son Robert. Daughter Catharine Kirksey and her husband William Kirksey. Daughter Penelope Moore and her husband William Moore. My three granddaughters the children of my son Tobias Cobb deceased that is to say Penelope Cobb, Elizabeth Cobb and Leah Cobb. To grandson Jesse G. Cobb, son of Robert Cobb, negroes Stephen, Cherry and Silvey. To grandson Presley G. Cobb negro woman Pink and girls Emilia and Nancy. To grandson Samuel P. Cobb negro girl Martha, boy James and girl Phebe. If daughter-in-law Jemima Cobb should need support, Jesse G. Cobb, Samuel P. Cobb and Presley G. Cobb are to support her in an equal proportion out of the negroes which I have willed them. Executors: Moody Burt and Jesse G. Cobb. Dated 30 March, 1823.

Wit.: James C. Griffin   (Signed) Robert Cobb
   Jesse G. Cobb
No proven date.

WILL OF JOHN GEROGE - pp 362-366

Wife Margaret to have land and a negro man Jack her lifetime or widowhood. Each of my sons to have equal share to wit.: James, William, Francis, John and Thomas. It is uncertain where my son Thomas is. Executors to keep his share for him if he should apply within four years after my decease either in person or by his attorney. If he does not apply equally divided among rest of sons. To daughter Margaret $100,00 in hands of Andrew McFall, (lent money) but never to receive the same or any part in the life time of John Bryce or until she finely seperates from said Bryce and in case Bryce outlive Margaret then money divided among my sons. To Ezekial George, son of William George, $20.00 for schooling. Negro man Jack is to have his freedom at the death of my wife Margaret. Executors shall aid and assist said Jack in choosing a guardian to act for him in defending his freedom. Executors: son William and friends Benjamin Dickson and Samuel McElroy. Dated 1 November, 1827.

Wit.: Herbert Hammond   (Signed) John Geroge.
   James Todd
   John McElroy
No proven date.

WILL OF WILLIAM STEVENSON - pp 366-368

Wife Jane. Sons John and Thomas. Daughters Peggy and Martha to have land where son James lives. Executors: Wife and sons John and Thomas. Dated 14 Jan. 1828.

Wit.: Andw. Young   (Signed) William (X) Stevenson
   William B. Patterson
   John McPherson
Proven by oath of Capt. Wm. B. Patterson. No date.

WILL OF PETER LABOON, SR. - pp 368-370 (Two pages numbered 368)

Wife Rachel to have all estate her lifetime or widowhood, then lands divided equally with my three sons or their heirs, Peter, Joseph and Moses Canada Laboon. If wife marry property to be divided with my children or at her death two daughters Sarah and Rebecca to have feather bed and furniture whenever they marry or when the property is divided to make them equal with my other daughters Anna Wadkins, Mary Robins, Rachel Elrod, and Frances Daulton. To two sons Joseph and Mason Canada Laboon as much of property as will make them equal with propety I have give to my sons John and Peter when they marry or call for it. Son John's two children Eada and Susannah. Executor: Wife Rachel. Dated 9 Jan. 1828.

Wit.: Benk (?) Williams   (Signed)   Peter Laboon
      Solomon West
      Joseph (X) Cason
No proven date.

WILL OF GEORGE KENNEMORE - pp 370-372
Wife Elizabeth. Son Michael. Daughters Ruth Mullennix, Nancy Gibson,
Temperance Mayfield, Rosannah Kennimore, Judith and Vicey. Youngest
son Lot Kennemore all lands at death of his mother. Executor: Son Lot.
Dated 7 Dec. 1824.
Wit.: William Clanahan   (Signed)   George (X) Kennemore
      Andw. Hamilton
      James Henderson
Proven by oath of Major Andrew Hamilton. No date.

WILL OF JOHN KNOX - pp 272-276
Wife Fanny to have negro girl Phillis to dispose of as she thinks
proper. She is also to have plantation and girls Jenny, Celia, Mattey
and Hannah and negro boy Bob for her life or until she marries. At
death or marriage plantation goes to two sons Washington and Andrew.
To son Isaac, negro girl Jenny. To son Matthew, negro girl Celia.
To son James, negro girl Mattey. To daughter Sarah McClure, negro girl
Lame. To daughter Elizabeth Dandy, negro girl Lucinda. To son William
negro boy Bob. To daughter Mary Ann, negro girl Mariah on the day of
her marriage or at wife's death or marriage. To daughter Susannah,
negro girl Frances at her marriage or at death or marriage of wife.
To son Samuel, negro girl Hannah. First increase of Jenny or Celia
shall be property of son Washington. Second increase from Jenny or
Celia to son Andrew. Plantation in the State of Georgia to be sold.
To son John, $150.00. To son James $50.00. Executors: Wife and
son Samuel. Dated 20 Jan. 1828.
Wit.: Alex. Ramsey   (Signed)   John Knox
      William Knox
      Thomas Lamarr
      Jacob (X) Frederick
No proven date.

WILL OF JESSE SIDDELL (OR TIDDELL? OR LIDDELL?) - pp 376-380
Wife. Grandson Jesse Shotwell to have blew frock coat I have had lately
made and one vest. Servant James to have two coats, a great coat and hat.
Balance of clothing divided between two bound boys now living with me
and my servant James. Property not wished to be retained by wife is to
be sold except servants James and his mother Agga. At her death they
should have the liberty of providing a livelihood for themselves under
the direction of my executors provided James provides for and takes
care of his mother. Also if there is enough property besides them to
pay all debts. If they must be sold and any money left it is to go to
daughter Rebecca Shotwell and her three children and the children of
Richard Head deceased being the whole of my children and grandchildren
now living. I do not include any property originally belonging to my
present wife leaving it at her own disposal. Executors: friend
Benajah Dunham, William Sitton, and my son-in-law Nathaniel Shotwell.
Dated 22 April, 1828.
Wit.: William Holcombe   (Signed)   Jesse Siddall
      Thomas Edmondson
      Jordan Holcombe
No proven date.

WILL OF SERAH HARKINS - pp 380-381
Being old and full of days. Two sons John and Hugh Harkins my one third
of land that fell to me at the death of my husband. Daughter Serah.
Dated 2 Jan. 1819.
Wit.: Robert S. Telford   (Signed)   Serah (X) Harkins
      William Telford
      Robert Telford, Sr.
No proven date.

WILL OF WILLIAM CANTRELL - pp 382-383
Of Pickens County. Executors: Benjamin Haygood and my wife Elizabeth.
Estate to wife until youngest child is of age, then divided equally
among the children. Dated 3 July, 1828.
Wit.: Jacob Lewis   (Signed) William Cantrell
       Abner Lewis
       Annor (?) or Amos (?) Waldrop
No proven date.

WILL OF WILLIAM TIPPINS - pp 383-384
Son Matthew Tippins. Negro boy Bill to be sold. Wife Mary to have
negro boy and negro girl Violet. Daughters Elizabeth Bishop and Mary
Bishop. To Milly Sanders negro girl Rachel. To daughter Matilda negro
girl Jane. If debts satisfied, remainder equally divided between John
Tippens, Matthew Tippens, Milly Sanders, and Matilda Tippens. Dated
4 Oct. 1828.
Wit.: A. Evins   (Signed) William Tippens
       George Tippens
       John Tippins
Proven 20 Oct. 1829 (?).

WILL OF ISRAEL PICKENS - pp 384-387
Oldest child (?). Daughter Elizabeth Steward (?) to have negro girl
Winna her lifetime and then to go to all my children. To daughter
Matilda and my daughter Sally Williams, negro girl Rachel. Son Ezekial
Andrew. To grandchildren the offsprings of Dilly and Rebecca land where
I formerly lived on Rocky River. Son John has received a negro man.
William has received land. Israel has received horses and cows.
Daughters Ellender has received furniture, cow and calf; Mary received
furniture, cow and calf; Matilda received furniture. Wife to have
child's part her widowhood. Executors: James Casper and David Boyd.
Dated 5 Jan. 1829.
Wit.: John Davis   (Signed) Israel Pickens
       Samuel John
       John Bevill (?)
Proven 2 March, 1829.

WILL OF HUGH REID - pp 387-390
To wife Elizabeth plantation and negro man Cesar and girl Lavica her
lifetime or widowhood. At her death or marriage land to go to three
youngest daughters: Jane, Elizabeth and Ann. Land joins Andrew Mc-
Donald and William Colwell. Ann to have part of land whereon she now
lives. Stepdaughter Susanna McDonald. Each of my children: Ellider
McDonald, William Reid, Margaret Colwell, Jane Shelton, Martha Colwell,
Elizabeth Reid, Ann Heaisee (?). Daughter Elizabeth shall keep and
provide for support of my brother Alexander Reid. Executors: friend
Benjamin Dickson and my son William Reid. Dated 1 July, 1828.
Wit.: Charles Dilday   (Signed) Hugh Reid
       Samuel Buchannan
       James (X) Colwell
No proven date.

WILL OF MATHIAS RICHARDSON - pp 390-391
Sons and daughters: Charity Gilliland, Catharine Stanton, John Richard-
son, Mathias Richardson, Jr., Frances Claridy, Elizabeth Ward, Mourning
Tarrant, Anna Dossett. My three grandchildren: Aaron, Mathias and
David, (sons of my daughter Martha Garrison, deceased). Executors:
John and Mathias Richardson, my sons, and William Stanton. Dated 27
June, 1827.
Wit.: John Wilson   (Signed) Mathias (X) Richardson
       Saml. Wilson
       Clark Wilson
Proven 27 Dec. 1828 (or 1829 - looks like 8 written over 9.)

WILL OF ROBERT TELFORD - pp 392-393

To wife Isabell estate her lifetime then divided between Elizabeth, Eliza C. and William. My lawful heirs: James, Robert L. (?), Mary B., William, Elizabeth and Eliza C. To heirs of John (L?) Telford, cow and calf. Land joins Asa Clinkscales, John and Hugh Harkins, R. L. Telford, G. A. Moore, and A. O. Toomer (?). Executors: Three sons James, Robert L. and William. Dated 21 Sept. 1829.

Wit.: John B. Anderson   (Signed) Robert Telford
       John Harkins
       Henry Cobb
Proven 28 Sept. 1829.

WILL OF JONATHAN SMITH - pp 394-395

Of Anderson District. To sons Whitaker Smith, Aaron Smith, Gideon Smith and my daughters Hannah Lewis, Mary Ducksworth, Catharine Harden, Aney McCully, and Lettice Dickson one shilling each and what I have already given them. Wife Elizabeth to have plantation for purpose of raising the younger children. As they come of age she may give them what she thinks proper. Youngest children: David Smith, Jesse R. Smith, William Smith, John Athanot (?) Smith and Artemissa Smith. Executors: sons Whitaker and Aaron and my wife Elizabeth. Dated 12 Sept. 1829.

Wit.: Alexr. Moorehead   (Signed) Jonathan Smith
       John Kay
       Nancy Kay
Proven 28 Sept. 1829.

WILL OF JOHN WHITTEN - pp 396-397

Of Anderson District. Plantation to wife until the children are of age, then sold and one half to wife and one half to children. Executors to collect from my mother the price of the millstones, millwheel and the iron that is on it to help in paying my just debts. Executors: friends David Hendrix, Senr., and James Whitten. Dated 21 May, 1829.

Wit.: William McMurry   (Signed) John Whitten
       James A. Wilson
       Alfred Ekes
No proven date.

WILL OF MOSES HOLLAND - p 397

Of Anderson County, wife Gracy all property her lifetime or widowhood then divided between my lawful heirs of her body. Moses, Ann (?), Aaron, Caleb, Joshua, Tabitha, and Eleb. I also give to my daughter Ellender $1.00, to James $1.00, to heirs of Chesly Holland $1.00, to John $1.00, to Fanny $1.00, and to Thomas $1.00. Executor: William Acker, Esq. Dated 4 Sept. 1829.

Wit.: Henry Cobb   (Signed) Moses (X) Holland
       William Magee
       H. Rice (?)
Proven 9 Nov. 1829.

WILL OF DAVID RYKARD - pp 398-399

Each of my children: Mary Ann, Elizabeth Caroline, Sarah Catharine, and Martha Hannah the youngest one years schooling. All I may be entitled to as a legacy from my father's estate. Wife Rebecca. Executors: Wife and David Ruff (or Russ?). Dated 22 Dec. 1829.

Wit.: Peter Dilleshaw (?)   (Signed) David Rykard
       Susannah Ruff
       Saml. R. Evins (?)
No proven date.

WILL OF JESSE CRENSHAW, SR. - pp 400-401

Son Nathaniel. Son Anderson $5.00. To Giles and Jane Collins heirs $5.00. To Edmon Martin and wife Christian $5.00. To John Martin and wife Elizabeth $5.00. To Lucy Mullins $5.00. Sons Jesse Jr., Stephen, Nathaniel, Matthew and Grif Crenshaw. Executors: Sons Jesse, Stephen, Matthew and Grif. Dated 14 Nov. 1827.

Wit.: David V. ?   (Signed) Jesse Crenshaw
       Caleb V. ?
       Solomon Skelton
No proven date.

WILL OF ABNER LEDBETTER - pp 401-404

Wife Sarah to raise and educate children as far as the English grammer.
Children to have $1200 and negro boy Pinckney and girl Mary divided
between them on the coming of age of the oldest. Executors: Alexander
Calhoun and Joseph N. Whitner. My interest in my mother's estate at
her death to be paid to my wife. Dated 4 May, 1830.
Wit.: George Reese, Jr.   (Signed) Abner Ledbetter
      William Miller
      John Mullenix
Proven 7 August, 1830.

WILL OF ROBERT PICKENS - pp 405-411

Two old negro women Rachel and Mima to go to my wife Dorcas to be dis-
posed of at her death as she thinks proper. Son Robert. Daughters
Margaret and Elizabeth who now live with me. Son Andrew. Robert
and Andrew may each choose a negro. Rest of negroes divided by lot
among the balance of my children: John Pickens, John Smith, Margaret
Pickens, Elizabeth Pickens, Mary Bowman, Dorcas Paris and Ann Balding.
Executors: Wife and sons Adrew and Robert. Dated 3 Jan. 1823.
Wit.: J. Douthet   (Signed) Robert Pickens
      Jas. Oliver
      Jas. Smith
Codicil - 6 April 1828. My wife has died. Child who gets negro man
Cato by lot shall have his mother Rachel. Negro man Abraham and his
mother Mima to go to son Robert.
Proven by James Smith, 6 Sept. 1830.

WILL OF LEWIS F. GIBBES - pp 411-413

My children to share and share alike. Executors: John L. North, Lewis
R. Gibbes and Charles D. Gibbes and the two last named shall be guard-
ians of their younger brothers and sisters. Dated 11 Aug. 1828.
Wit.: James Stuart   (Signed) Lewis F. Gibbes
      Rodolphus Dickinson
      Anthony W. Ross
      George Hall
Codicil - 15 Aug. 1828. To my __?__ Lucinda $10.00 to be paid on
Christmas of each year.
Proven 3 Dec. 1830.

WILL OF HENRY BURROW - pp 414-418

Wife Anny (or Amy?) negroes Isaac, Lila and Wilson. To daughter Nancy
Langston, negro man Steven. To daughter Rebecca Hollidy negro girl
Chainy. To daughter Amy (or Anny?) Gray, negro woman Dolly. To son
Henry Burrough, negro girl Mary. To Lewis Burrow, negroes Sam, Jeffer-
son and Clary. To son Thomas Burrow, negroes Levi, Jack, Tony and
Rhoda. To daughter Tabitha Burrow, five negroes Jimsey, Darky, Emily,
Aster and Anthony. To son William Burrow, property already given him.
To son Green Burrow property already given him. Daughter Susanna Gib-
son has already received her part. Daughter Mary Harris already re-
ceived her part. Have given to son Joel Burrow his part already.
Negro man Isaac to be freed at wife's death. Executor: Amy Burrow.
Dated 12 Oct. 1829.
Wit.: Lewis Sherrill
      Joseph Mahow
      J. C. Anderson
Proven 21 Dec. 1829.

WILL OF ALLEXANDER OLIVER - pp 419-421

Dated 28 Nov. 1821. Wife Mary to have negro woman Lett. Son John
Oliver. Daughter Favre White. Son Samuel Oliver. Daughter Jamima
Casin. To son James Casin negro girls Charlotte and Ann. To daughter
Mary Oliver. Daughter Susannah Oliver. To son Andrew Oliver, Old Sam,
Ben, Candis, Leah, and Lett at the death of my wife. Son Andrew to pay
legacies and debts and execute my will.
Wit.: Rt. McCann   (Signed) Alexander Oliver
      Susannah (X) McMahan
      Dorcas (X) King
Proven 16 Aug. 1830.

WILL OF JOHN LEDBETTER - pp 422-424
Wife Mary. Sons Henry, James and John. All my minor children.
Children now with me: Joel, Chatherine, Hester (?), David, Mary
Caraline, Daniel L., and George Montgomery. Executors: Two oldest
sons Henry and James. Dated 20 Jan. 1831.
Wit.: Benj. Dickson   (Signed) John (X) Ledbetter
      John Binning
      James Gilmore
Proven by James Gilmer (?) 7 March, 1831.

WILL OF BURWELL CARPENTER - pp 424-426
Wife Elizabeth. Children of Laban Massey by my deceased daughter Polly.
Son Willis Carpenter. Daughter Elizabeth Stone. Daughter Delaney
Crawford. Daughter Gean (?). Hath not pleased God to bless my son
Burwell with forsight to enable him to proced for himself. Heirs of
my son Asbery Carpenter deceased. Son Thomas F. Carpenter. Son Alfred
M. Carpenter. Son John Carpenter. Executors: sons Alfred M. and John.
Dated 20 Aug. 1830.
Wit.: William Acker   (Signed) Burwell Carpenter
      Eli Bowes (or Burress ?)
      Henry D. Acker
Proven 24 Jan. 1831.

WILL OF DAVID DURHAM - pp 426-428
Wife Sina. Son Littleberry. Executor: Son Littleberry. Dated 2 June,
1828.
Wit.: Benj. H. Douthet   (Signed) David (X) Durham
      Susannah Douthet
Proven 7 Feb. 1831.

WILL OF SPENCER BROWN - pp 428-430
Wife Catharine. Son Robert M. Negro Diner to live with any of my
children she pleases at wife's death. Rest of negroes drawn by lots
by my children. Dated __ Aug. 1830.
Wit.: Richard F. Harden   (Signed) Spencer (X) Brown
      William (X) Guest
      John C. Aderhold
Proven 4 Apr. 1831.

WILL OF MATHEW DICKSON - pp 430-431
Son Alexander. Four daughters now living with me: Polly, Nelly, Jane
and Peggy. Executors: Son Benjamin Dickson and Hugh Gaston. Dated
20 May, 1827.
Wit.: Hugh Gaston   (Signed) Mathew Dickson
      John C. Eliott
      Wm. B. Dickson
Proven 2 Aug. 1830.

WILL OF ZACHARIAS TALIAFERRO - pp 432-436
Daughter Elizabeth Ann Broyles. Land bought of John Robertson and John
Hamilton and his wife Martha. Negroes Shandy, Terry and Mary Ann go
to daughter Elizabeth Ann. To grandson Edward Broyles negro girl
Amanda. To grandson Zacharias Broyles. To daughter Lucy Hannah Taylor,
land bought of John Turner. Negroes Bartlet, Jane and Susan to daughter
Lucy Hannah Taylor. To daughter Margaret Taliaferro land bought from
John and James Dixon. To Richard Taliaferro, Osa B. Broyles and
David L. Taylor as trustees the following negroes: Banister, David,
Bob, Kipa, Jesse, Randal, Tilda, Daniel, July, Grace, Lucy, Hester,
Tony, William, Isaac, Martha, Sall, Eliza, Augustus, Joe and Nick for
the benefit of my daughter Margaret Taliaferro. If she dies without
issue then negroes to the relations living at the time. To daughter
Caroline Taliaferro land bought from William Hunter and Ed. Kemp.
To Richard Taliaferro, Osa R. Broyles and David Taylor, as trustees
negroes Rose, Brooks, Aleck, Nunly (?), Henry, Frances, Elizabeth,
Charles, Charity, Celia, Beck, Polly, Shadrick, Edmond, and Tray for
the benefit of daughter Caroline. If she dies without issue negroes
go to relation living. Daughter Sarah Ann Broyles. Executors:
Richard Taliaferro, Osa R. Broyles and David S. (or L?) Taylor. Dated
14 Jan. 1831.

WILL OF CHARLES WEBB - pp 436-439
Son Edward to have negro girl Rachel. Son William to have negro boy
Lowry. Son Thomas to have negro boy Moses. Son Micajah to have negro
boys Ben and Sandford. Son Warren Robinson Webb to have negro boy
Elias. Son Clayton to have negro boy Phill and negro girl Nancy.
Son Elijah to have negro boys Sims and Baylis. Son Elisha to have
negro man Edmond and his wife and children. To son Charles Baldwin
negro boy Mark and girl Caroline. Daughter Nancy Terry (?). Daughter
Frances Clark negro girl Hannah and negro boy Lifus. Wife Mary Ann to
have negro fellow Jerry and wife Nan and a negro wench Ally. Sons
Elisha and Charles Baldwin to have land on Sececa River whereon I now
live, including part I purchased from Ed. Young. Negroes Bowes and
Alee to be sold. At wife's death old man Jerry and wife Nann shall be
at liberty to choose which of my children they will go to. Executors:
Warren Robison Webb and Eligah Webb. Dated 14 July, 1828.
Wit.:   Aaron Mills   (Signed)   Charles Webb
        Nancy B. McDaniel
        Martha _____

Pages 440-449 missing when this book was microfilmed.

Pages 450-452 were numbered incorrectly, beginning with page 452.
Numbered 352. This numbering continued for several pages, but will
be numbered here as they should be, in the 400's instead of 300's.

WILL OF GEORGE W. REED - pp 450-452
Land whereon I live on Tugaloo to wife Amy in conjunction and common
use with my sons that now reside with me: Jesse, George B., Moses
and Joseph Benjamin Reed. Youngest son Benjamin is under 21. Daughter
Elizabeth Reed. Daughter Rhoda Reed. Daughter Nancy Reed. These
daughters unmarried. Son Tolivar Reed living in the State of Georgia.
Daughter Rachel Dyer. Daughter Amy Salmon. Son Jesse Reed to be
executor. Dated 19 Nov. 1831.
Wit.:   Abraham Coffin   (Signed)   George W. Reed
        Hartwell Jones
        Wm. King
Proven 4 June, 1832.

WILL OF WILLIAM MCPHERSON - pp 452-455
Wife Elizabeth. Son Elijah. Negroes Basdel, Rose and Sooky remain
with wife and at her death or marriage divided between my several
children. To children of Elizabeth Stevenson deceased, six in number:
Sarah, William, John, Joseph, Elijah and James $24.00 each in lieu
of a negro girl Judith I intended to give my daughter Elizabeth
Stevenson. Daughter Nancy Brown. To Arther McFall 450 acres where he
now lives. To youngest son Elijah land whereon I now live, plat drawn
by John McPherson D. S. dated 20 Oct. 1829. $160.00 deposited in the
hands of my executor for benefit of my daughter Milly Migee and her
children. To Alexander McPherson. All other property sold and equally
divided among my several children. Executors: Wife and sons William
McPherson, Jr. and John McPherson. Dated 9 July, 1830.
Wit.:   James Armstrong   (Signed)   William McPherson
        Adam Stuart
        George Stuart
Proven 20 Aug. 1832.

WILL OF ROBERT MCCANN - pp 455-457
Dated 6 April, 1831. Son Hugh to have negro boy Andy. To son James L.
plantation on which I now live and granted in my own name, also land
bought from Freneu and Breamer, also servants Humphrey, Abraham,
Julanna and her children, Caroline and Merdy (?). To daughter Martha
Orr negro woman Pomelia and a walnut chest I bought of Rev. Mr. Orr.
To son Thomas H. McCann plantation bought of the Olivers and J. P.
Archer, and a small tract granted to me, also servants George,

Caroline, Lucey, Lucinda, Anderson and Louisa. To son Thomas H. land
on Preather Creek where it is suspected there is a gold mine. Servant
woman Byna to live with any of my children she may choose, not as a
slave for if the law would permit her emancipation I would do it for
she has been a trusty, honest, faithful servant to me and I give her
one cow and calf to be her own. If she is displeased after her choice
she may remove to any of my other children. My grandchildren by my
daughter Jane Hamilton is made provision for by will wrote by W.
Whitfield (?), and my son James executor, it which I establish and
confirm as a part of this my will dated 20 May, 1829. Executor to have
stones placed on graves of each of my wives engraven the year they
died and at my grave my age and departure from time to eternity.
$20.00 to Theological Seminary at Columbia. Balance to be divided
equally between son Hugh, daughter Martha, sons James and Thomas
Hampton. Executors: sons James L. McCann and Thomas Hampton McCann.
Wit.:   John R. Smith   (Signed) Robert McCann
        Kezia Donnelly
        Hannah Linn
Proven 4 July, 1831.

WILL OF WILLIAM FELTON - p 457
Wife Mary. Son Cary. Son-in-law John Richland. Dated 18 Nov. 1828.
Wit.:   Sarah (X) Harden   (Signed) William (X) Felton
        David Moor, Jr.
        John Crocker
Proven 10 Oct. 1832.

WILL OF ANDREW MCCOLLISTER - pp 459-460
John, Alexander, Nathan, William and Robert McAlliester each to receive
$1.00. Thomas McAlister to receive $15.00 to school him. Jinny
McAlister to receive $20.00 to school her. Andrew to receive $25.00
to school him. Equal divide to be made betwixt Elizabeth, Fanny, Sarah,
Polly, Rassey, Thomas, Ginny and Andrew McAlister till each receives
$150.00. Remainder divided between all my sons and daughters, Nathan
excepted. Executors: John McAllister and Alexander McAllister. Dated
14 Dec. 1831.
I will my son Thomas to Alexander, Ginne To Sarah and Andrew to John
each to be bound according to law.
Wit.:   Lewis McAllister   (Signed) Andrew McAllister
        Matilda McAllister
Alexander McAllister resigned as executor and John qualified.
Proven 6 March, 1832.

WILL OF JOHN FOUNTAIN - pp 460-462
Wife Nancy to have furniture and stock except that reserved for grand-
daughter Matty. After her death divided between all my children. Son
Littleton. Matty, the daughter of my daughter Hannah. Son Simpson.
Executor: Brother-in-law Daniel Mason until Simpson comes of age.
Dated 28 July, 1831.
Wit.:   Thomas Pinckney   (Signed) John (X) Fountain
        John Armstrong
        Mary Anne (X) Lambert
Codicil - Son Littleton co-executor with brother-in-law Daniel Mason.
Dated 8 Sept. 1832.
Wit.:   Hannah (X) Winn
        John Bruce
        Thomas Pinckney
Proven by Col. Thomas Pinckney 10 Nov. 1832.

WILL OF JOHN MAULDEN - pp 462-464
Wife Mary. Son Godfrey. Male servant Thomas and female servant Patsey
to remain with wife for life and at her death all personal property
sold. To daughter Sarah Hughs $300.00, balance equally divided between
my other three daughters Mary, Elizabeth and Frances. Daughter Mary
to have servant boy Riley. Daughter Elizabeth to have servant Mary,
and daughter Frances to have servant Sam. Three youngest daughters
are now unmarried. Lots of land heretofore given sons Joab, Taliaferro
and Frances to remain as their property. Land given son James to
remain his. Executors: Sons Joab and Taliaferro. Dated 3 Dec. 1831.

Wit.: John Liddall.   (Signed) John Mauldin
       Samuel Mauldin
       R. M. Briggs
Proven 5 March, 1832.

WILL OF WILLIAM WILSON .- pp 464-466
Son James P. Wilson, daughters Jane and Rebecka. Negro girl Eliza
to be sold. If my land in Hall Co., Ga., 8th District, is obtained
it is to be sold and divided between Jane and Rebecka. Executor:
Daughter Jane Wilson. Dated 21 June, 1832.
Wit.: John Herron   (Signed) William (X) Wilson
       Wm. B. Fowler
       John Hall
          If any difficulty arises about the division of my property
          the executor is to sell all property and divide the effects
          with what ready money is now on hand and what is in William
          E. Wilson's care in Hall Co., Ga., equally divided between
          my two daughters.
Jane Wilson relinquished her right as executor and letters of administration with will annexed granted to John Herron.
25 June, 1832.

WILL OF JOHN MILLS - pp 466-468
Wife Elizabeth to have personal property and half of land for life or
widowhood. Remaining one half of land to Berry Beasly commonly called
Berry Mills and Lucinda Williams the wife of Evil (?) Ellias (?)
Williams and their heirs to be equally divided. Also to Berry Beasly
a negro man Arch and the half of land I gave my wife after her decease
or marriage. To Berry Beasly commonly called Berry Mills and Lucinda
Williams the balance of property given to my wife. She is to have
at her own disposal a negro woman Amy. Executors: Wife and friend
Sampson Pope. Dated 31 August, 1825.
Wit.: James Dickson   (Signed) John Mills
       Shadrick Wilbanks
       Sampson Pope
Proven 24 Sept. 1832.

WILL OF JOHN SIMPSON - pp 468-469
Wife Lydia. To son-in-law Herron all his notes payable to me at my
decease. To James English $5.00. To son James Simpson the crop which
I left with him in Alabama. Desire that my wife removed to my grandson
John Herrons and that she be provided with a decent house and the
expenses paid out of notes of my executor that those payable to me and
there to have annual support out of the interest of the balance of said
notes. To James Herron the balance of said monies. Executors: Grandson John Herron and David Herron. Dated 25 March, 1831.
Wit.: Thomas McCurry   (Signed) John (X) Simpson
       Wm. B. Fowler
       Elizabeth C. (?) Johnson
Proven 8 August, 1831.
       (Note: The clerk often left off the s when meaning the word son
       or daughter to be plural, so the above could be grandsons instead
       of grandson.)

WILL OF ALEXANDER STEPHENSON -. pp 470-471
To son John one bed and furniture and no more. To son John's three
sons William, Alexander and John, and his one daughter Hanna, 50
acres. To son Joseph balance of my land. Son John's children,
above named, are not of age. My five sons: James, Samuel, Alexander,
Joseph and Jonithan to have the balance of my money. Executor:
Sanford Vandiver (?). Dated 4 Oct. 1831.
Wit.: V. D. Fant.   (Signed) Alexander (X) Stephenson
       John Killpatrick
       John Moore
Proven 7 Nov. 1832.

WILL OF ROBERT MCLINN - pp 471-473
Wife Sarah to have for life and after her death to go to sons James and
Alfred, a negro Frank and his wife Big (?) Nancy and her child Lewis.
To son James negroes David and Ann, Jeff, Sharlot, Delphy, Harriet. To
son Alfred, negroes Beryman, Fanny, Zack, Caroline, George and Margaret.
Negro girl Polly to be sold. Executors: James T. and Thomas H. McCann
and Garrison Linn. Dated 22 Oct. 1832.
Wit.:   Thos. L. Carpenter   (Signed) R. McLinn
        Thos. McDonald
        James Dannelly
Proven (no date except 1832.)

WILL OF JACK BASKINS - pp 473-475
(A free man of color of Anderson County.) To my former master Robert
McKinley Baskin I give all my land consisting of 180 acres except 50
acres to be laid off which I give to my son Day (or Davy ?). To daughter Giney my best feather bed and one quilt which she made a present
of to me. To my bound boy Hamilton two quilts, two blankets and one
small bed and cord. To son Davy second choice of beds and remaining
bed clothes. Executors: friend J. H. Baskin. Dated 5 March, 1831.
Wit.:   John Milford   (Signed) Jack (X) Baskin
        Thomas McCollough
        James H. Baskin
Proven 13 Feb. 1833.

WILL OF ROBERT HACKET - pp 475-477
Wife Lucinda. Three daughters Harriet, Frances and Sophronia. To
wife a negro woman Sarah. Son Albert Hacket to be trustee for all of
my children, those by my first and present wife included for their
support and education. Executor: son Albert Hacket and Garrison Linn.
Dated 14 Nov. 1832.
Wit.:   J. T. (?) Whitfield   (Signed) Robert Hacket
        Gideon Smith
        Silvanus Minton
Proven 17 Dec. 1832.

WILL OF THOMAS GIBSON - pp 478-480
Late of Culpepper Co., Va., but now of Anderson District, S. C.
Son John $1.00. Son Thomas Gibson $1.00. Son-in-law William Duke
$1.00. Grandchildren the descendants of my daughter Elizabeth Duke
$1.00 each viz Thomas Montgomery her son by her first husband, John,
Feagan, Bathsheba, Hannah and Nancy her children by her second husband,
and Mark (?), James, Gibson and July her children by Mr. William Duke
her third husband. To my daughter Polly Tompkins. Dated 13 Nov. 1830.
Wit.:   James Douthit   (Signed) Thomas Gibson
        B. H. Douthit
        Sarah R. Douthit
Proven 4 May, 1833.

WILL OF ANDREW YOUNG - pp 480-483
Daughter Janey McCully (or McCally ?), $1.00. Daughter Patsy Hinson
(or Hutson ?), $1.00. Land to son John Young. Daughters Nancy Karr
(?) and Jane Karr land for 15 years then to be sold and equally divided
among all my children. Daughter Eleanor Holmes $1.00. Executors:
Francis Beaty and Archibald Simpson.
Wit.:   George Brown   (Signed) Andw. Young
        Thos. O'Briant
        Andrew J. O'Briant
Will not dated, but proved 1 July, 1833.

WILL OF ANDREW LIDDELL, SR. - pp 484-487
Wife Jane Liddell, calls herself Jenney Liddle, to whom I was married
and who lived with me about 4 years and who then voluntarily left my
house, bed and boarding and hath not returned any more to me nor been
in my house for upwards of 10 years and on this account I give her one
cow to her and her heirs and assigns forever. To my oldest son John
Liddle 110 acres joining land of my own and Andrew Liddle, Jr. on
Twenty Six Mile Creek. Son Andrew J. Liddle, Esq., land whereon he
now lives, being 100 acres. To son George Liddle land whereon he now

74

lives, 100 acres. Also to son George a negro girl or female slave named Tabb about 25 or 40 years of age. To son Moses Liddle $1.00 to be paid by son James S. Liddle. To son Francis Liddle $30.00, $2.00 to be paid by my son George and rest by son James S. To my daughters Jean Mauldin, widow of Joab Mauldin; Elizabeth Miller the wife of John Miller; and Mary McGehee wife of Willes McGee each $1.00 in addition to what I have already given them, namely one negro shortly after marriage. To son James S. Liddle the land I now live on and a negro boy Jack aged 4, and negro Jeffry aged 6 months. Executor: son James S. Dated 25 Jan. 1820.
Wit.: John Harris   (Signed) Andrew Liddell
      Joseph Grisham
      Wm. Grisham
   Codicil - I have been long afflicted and my son James S. has been at great trouble with me. I revoke bequest to son Frances, except the $2.00 to be paid him by son George. Dated __Oct. 1832.
Wit.: John B. Earle, Jr.
      Randolph Brown
      C. Gaillard
Proven 6 May, 1833.

WILL OF LUCY HAMMOND - pp 488-489
Aged and infirm. All property to son Herbert Hammond who is to execute this will. Dated 30 August, 1832.
Wit.: Mathew Gambrell   (Signed) Lucy Hammond
      John Willingham
      Wm. B. Willingham
Proven 19 Nov. 1833.

WILL OF ANDREW MCCALLISTER, JR. - pp 489-491
Brother Nathan McCallister $1.00. Neqhew Andrew Todd $200.00. Rest of estate divided dqually between Robert Todd's six children, Robert McCallister's 4 children, William McCallister's 3 children and John McCallister's one child vix: Robert Todd's 6 children: Jane M. Gordon, Mary Ann Todd, Elizabeth Todd, Margaret Todd, James Todd, and John Todd; next to brother's children: Elizabeth McCallister, Andrew McCallister, Syrena Emaline McCallister and Mary McCallister. Next my brother William's children Jane McCallister, Mary McCallister and William McCallister. Next to brother John's child James McCallister. If brother Nathan pays money he owes me he shall have the land back that I sold a sheriff's sale and bought. Executor: Andrew Todd and Robert Todd. Dated 28 March, 1829.
Wit.: Thomas Hanna
      Andrew McCallister, Sr.
      John McPhail
Proven 23 July, 1833.

WILL OF ROBERT MCCANN - pp 491-493
Grandchildren Samuel Morrow Hamilton, Hannah Linn Hamilton and Thomas Morrow and Martha A. Hamilton, a negro woman Sally and her 3 children Winney, Bearnice (?), and Bailus. Negroes to be held by executors until youngest grandchild of age. Executor will hire them out and after paying into my estate $300.00 the amount paid by me to their father K. Hamilton for his trouble in raising of the negro children. When grandchildren come of age an equal division made between my four grandchildren. Executor: Son James L. McCann. Dated 28 May, 1827.
Wit.: Joseph T. Whitfield   (Signed) Rt. McCann
      John Millekin
      Wm. Anderson
      John R. Smith
Proven 15 July, 1831.

WILL OF ELISHA BENNETT, SR. - pp 493-495
Son John to have $250.00 to make him equal with my other children that have left me. To son Archibald a negro boy Nathan and furniture to make him equal. Then an equal distribution of all my property among all my children. The part that should fall to my daughter Jenny shall be for her and her increase alone and that my son Stephen or Adam shall have the disposition thereof for her and her children. My family of

negroes consisting of Sam and wife Lucy with all her children except
Nathan are to be valued by disinterested persons and taken by my
children at valuation only it is my wish that Sam and wife not be
seperated and that Charles select home for himself if such can be,
if not to be sold at public sale. Executors: Wm. Magee and my son
Archibald. Dated 17 Sept. 1833.
Wit.: James Majors   (Signed) Elisha Bennett
       John Vandiver
       Robert Brown
Proven 31 Oct. 1833.

WILL OF JAMES MERRETT - pp 496-497
Daughter Rebeckah Hambrick, horse worth $40.00 to make her equal to
that received by other children that have left me. Daughter Sarah
now living with me. Wife Sarah. Negro man Sam to choose own master
provided person chosen will be willing to take him. Remaining property
equally divided among all my children. Executor: son and trusty
friend Josiah Merritt. Dated 24 Feb. 1832.
Wit.: David (X) Durham   (Signed) James (X) Merrett
       James H. Atkenson
       Wm. Holcombe
Proven 2 Dec. 1833.

WILL OF JOHN SWORDS, SR. - pp 498-499
Land on Cuffy Creek and 5 negroes to be sold amd money put out at interest for use of wife as long as she remains widow. Then divided as
follows: To son Andy Swords $1.00. To son-in-law John Pilgrim $1.00.
To son John Swords $1.00. To daughter Esther Moore $1.00. After these
payments rest equally divided among following: Son William Swords one
share. Son Jonathan Swords one share. Son-in-law William Elrod one
share. Son-in-law Willis Newton one share. Son-in-law John Elrod one
share. Son-in-law Samuel Morris one share. Executors: William Swords
and son-in-law William Elrod. Dated 15 Jan. 1834.
Wit.: E. B. Benson   (Signed) John (X) Swords
       Fair Kirksey
       John S. Sloan
Proven 15 Jan. 1834.

WILL OF JOHN GAMBRELL - pp 500-501
Wife Barbara to have slaves Jane and Frank. After her death to go to
son Frank Gambrell. Executors to have in trust a negro Meshack and
Eliza and her children Rachel, Grace, Mariah and Jenny, and also land
on Broadmouth Creek joining Reuben Cox in trust for benefit of my son
Henry. At his death divided between heirs of his body and Susannah
his wife. All my children: William Gambrell, Henry Gambrell, John
Gambrell, James Gambrell, David Gambrell, Mathea Gambrell, Elizabeth
Cox and Nancy Brazeal. Executors: sons John and Mathew, and J.
Hammond. Dated 10 March, 1830.
Wit.: Saml. J. Hammond   (Signed) John Gambrell
       Elijah Griffin
       Barbara Casey
Proven 29 Sept. 1834.

WILL OF DANIEL R. TOWERS - pp 502-505
Negro girl Betsy to be held in trust by executors for my daughter
Margaret Elvira. Betsy to continue with wife until daughter marries
or comes of age. Wife Margaret to have residue of estate for life or
widowhood then divided between all my children. Wife to educate
children. Negroes and property sold if executors think best.
Executors: brother Silas Towers and friend Joseph N. Whitner. Dated
12 Nov. 1834.
Wit.: Francis Posey   (Signed) D. R. Towers
       Samuel P. Hillhouse
       S. L. Westmoreland
       Codicil - Since execution of will on 12 Nov. 1834 it has pleased
       God to add to my family an infant daughter for whom I desire to
       make a similar provision with that made for older daughter. I
       give negro child Amanda about 6 months old and her future in-
       crease to be held in trust for my infant daughter Rebeckah.

76

Rebeckah to be included in division of estate with all my children.
Dated 27 Dec. 1834.
Wit.:   Samford Vandiver
        Samuel Brown
        Ibyan (?) Rice
Proven 9 Feb. 1835.

WILL OF THOMAS LYNCH DART - pp 506-507

Wife Mary Louisa Dart and her children herein named: Isaac Mott,
Elizabeth Martin, Arabella Ann Reid, Mary Louisa, George Ann,
Henrietta and Cathrine Barnwell Dart all my estate including negro
man Richard, woman Cors and her children Amos, Fanny, Ben, Lucinda
and Franklin. Land on Garven's Creek to be held by executor until
eldest child of age. Son Isaac Mott Dart my gold watch. Executors:
Wife Mary Luisa Dart, C. C. Pinckney, Sr., and C. L. Gaillard. Dated
2 May, 1835.
Wit.:   Thos. S. Reese   (Signed) Thomas L. Dart
        Wm. Sanders
        Wm. T. Porter
Proven 25 June, 1835.
     (Note: No punctuation was used, so it is difficult to make out
     names of children. Were they all double names, as son Isaac Mott
     Dart ?)

WILL OF DAVID PRESLEY, SR. - pp 508-512

To daughters Jane M. and Rachel M. bed and furniture, horse, saddle
and bridle, and cow and calf to make them equal with other daughters.
Sons James Presley and Alexander E. Presley $20.00 each to make them
equal with other children. Daughter-in-law Elizabeth Presley wife of
James Presley to be supported on plantation were she now lives and
at her death equally divided between David A. Presley and William A.
Presley sons of James Presley. Grandsons called for me, namely David
P. Porter, son of Charles B. Porter; David P. Porter, son of Richard E.
Porter; David W. Presley, son of Alexander Presley; David W. Presley,
son of David Presley Jr., and my name sake David, son of Laughlen
Johnson, Esq., to each of them $5.00. On account of my son-in-law
Elijah Willbanks kindness to me when unable to manage own business I
will to his son David Presley 50 acres of land, part of tract where
I now live, joins Widow Crawford and Robert Cowen. Other land to
Elijah Willbanks, joins James Baskens and William Scott. Beloved
children: Lauchlen Johnson, Charles B. Porter, Richard E. Porter,
David Presley, Jr., Elijah Willbanks. My sister Esther is to be
supported on plantation as long as she chooses. To daughter Jane M.,
negro girl Amanda about 12. To daughter Rachel M., negro boy
Cornelius and $250.00. To nephew John S. Presley bed and furniture.
Executors: Wife Ann and trusty friend the Rev. Ebenezer E. Presley and
my Nephew John S. Presley. Dated 12 Jan. 1834.
Wit.:   Mathew Young   (Signed) David Presley, Sr.
        Lewis McAllister
        Elijah Wilbanks
Proven 14 June, 1834.

END OF WILL BOOK 'A'

WILL OF CHARLES STOREY - pp 1-5

Wife Susannah to have negro man Jackson, his wife Lydia and their
children Nancy and Jim, Nero and his wife Alice and her eight children:
Fany, Carolina, Moses, Eliza, Ann, Sarah, Matilda and Phoebe. Also
a negro man James, a man Billy and his wife Mary and her child Isabella.
Also a negro boy Irwin. Plantation on 23 Mile Creek. To niece Mary
Elizabeth Cherry a negro girl Harriet and a boy Ben and a boy Clifton
(known on the plantation by the name of Henry). Also to have a man
Isham and his wife Delilah and her children Alexander and Purcy.
Also negro man Ned. If Mary Elizabeth dies without issue slaves go
to her brothers and sisters whether of the whole or half blood.
To sister Anna Reese a negro man Munday. To Dinah Winter, widow of
Jeremiah Winter dec'd, a negro girl Mary her lifetime and after her
death to Dinah and Sarah Winter, daughters of said Jeremiah Winter.
To sister Esther Witherspoon should she be living at the time of my
death $1750. In case sister is not living at my death said money
to go to the children of Esther Capels. To friend the Rev. Aaron
Foster $200. To Charles Storey Willson, son of Jeremiah Willson
$150. for board and schooling. Plantation except on 23 Mile Creek
sold after death of wife that land sold and divided between Rev.
Aaron Foster, my nephew Nathaniel Harris, Rev. David Humphries and
Dr. Nathaniel Harris of Abbeville District. Nephew Thomas Sidney
Reese one fourth part of the rest of my estate. Nephew James E.
Reese, Esq., ¼. Niece Mary Elizabeth Cherry ¼. Executors: Wife
Susannah, Dr. James A. Cherry and Thomas Sidney Reese. Dated 11 Jan.
1835.
Wit.: Miles M. Norton   (Signed) Charles Story
       Thomas R. Cherry
       Samuel E. Lawhorn.
Proven 19 Mar. 1835.

WILL OF GAVINNEY (or GWINNEY ?) DEAN - pp 6-7

Widow. Grandson James M. Deane to have a negro girl Caroline aged
about 11. Daughter Miriam McGregor, widow, to have negro woman Lue.
Grandson Liles (or Silas ?) McGregor a mulatto boy about 18 months
old named Anderson. To granddaughter Mariah McGregor the future
children of negro Lue. After my decease executor to pay to my children
here below named: Thomas Deane, Joseph Deane, Richard Deane, Aaron
Deane, Samuel Deane, Grifhett Deane, Moses Deane and to the heirs
of John Deane dec'd and to the heirs of Polly Hillhouse 5 shillings
sterling each. Executors: son Thomas Deane and James Burrough, Sr.
Dated 6 Dec. 1834.
Wit.: Benj. Dickson   (Signed) Gavinney (X) Deane
       John W. McGregor
Proven 7 Sept. 1835.

WILL OF JOHN MORRIS, SR. - pp 8-10

Wife Leenah (or Seenah ?). Daughter Margaret Cornilious has already
received a negro girl Selah. Son Adam has received money from me
paid to John Turner and Christopher Hargraves and James Hart. Have
given daughter Janny Holly a negro girl Liza. Have paid money to
Feraline Cox for my son Amos. To son John plantation where he lives
which has been designated to him in the presence of Matthew Clark,
James Rosmond and Thomas Thomas. Have paid money to James Wood,
John Gentry and Henry Cox for my son John. To son James the plantation where he now lives. To son David J. the plantation where I
now live at the death of his mother, also negro boys Harry and Frank.

Executors: sons James Morris and David J. Morris. Dated 27 April, 1830.
Wit.: A. J. Liddell   (Signed) John Morris
       Mary Liddell
       James G. Clarke
Proven 15 Mar. 1835.

WILL OF JAMES BURRISS' - pp 11-14
Wife Susannah to have negro woman Rachel. Son James to have negro man John. Executor to pay debt owed Bryan Burris for his services and also reasonable compensation to my son Jacob for his services. Jacob to be guardian for my son James during his minority. Son-in-law Elliot Eskew. Son Bryan Burress. Son John Burress. Three youngest children of Joseph Heaton by my deceased daughter. My daughters: Nancy Massey, Elizabeth Brown, Mary Hall, Sarah Masters and Catherine Eskew. If note of Saml. McMurtray is not collected daughter Nancy Massy's share $100. less. Dated 28 Mar. 1835.
Wit.: Joseph N. Whitner   (Signed) James Burress
       Thos. Holland
       Danl. Gentry
Codicil - Son Bryan to be co-executor.
Wit.: Thos. Holland
       V. D. Tant (or Fant ?)
       James (X) Chasteen.
Proven 22 Feb. 1836.

WILL OF JOHN BURRESS - pp 15-17
Son Thomas. Son Orrong (?). Son Davis. Son Milford. Son Elbert. Daughter Polly Burress. Son Aaron. Land bought of J. Brown. Daughter Nancy. Daughter Becky. Executor to pay my children legacies as they come of age. Wife Elizabeth. If wife remarries she to get 7 negroes: Esther and Sarah, Ben and Washington, George and Mariah and Jane. Two youngest sons Milford and Albert. Executors: Aaron Burress, Thomas Burress and Peter Keys. Dated 16 July, 1828.
Wit.: Jesse Davis   (Signed) John Burress
       Solomon Ruth
       Wm. Hall
Proven 29 Feb. 1836.

WILL OF JOHN B. EARLE - pp 18-20
Silver Glade, Anderson District, having arrived at my 70th year. I believe I have made a just and equitable distribution amongst my children who have married or arrived at full age of all the property of which I was possessed clear of debt at the time of my marriage to my present wife and that what I now own has been saved by means of the fortune which she brought me. To sons-in-law Thomas Harrison, Benj. F. Sloan and George Seabron in trust for my daughter Georgie Washington Earle and heirs of her body, slaves Aaron and wife Jinsy and their children Caroline, Ransom, Harriett, Washington, Elizabeth and Christie. To wife Nancy Ann. Son Joseph. As a small testimonial of my respect for my brother officers of the Brigade I will and bequeath to Genl. Waddy Thompson my military bridle, breast plate and martingale, to Lt. Col. David L. Taylor a pair of brass barrelled horsemens pistols. To Maj. Thomas H. McCann my dress sword and to Capt. Elias D. Earle a horseman's sabre. Executors: Sons-in-law Thomas Harrison, Benj. F. Sloan and George Seaborn. Each to have a gold headed cane. Dated 1 Feb. 1836.
Wit.: O. R. Broyles   (Signed) J. B. Earle
       R. L. Hannon
       Jesse P. Lewis
Proven 22 Feb. 1836.

WILL OF WILLIAM TURPIN - pp 21-35
Charleston, S. C., a citizen of the United States now residing in the City of New York. Dated 20 April, 1833. All my negroes in South Carolina are free. My executors in South Carolina are to protect their freedom. Those now living in South Carolina: Will, Jenny, all her children and grandchildren, Lund, Juda, Leah, Abram, Ben Boston, Cesar, Hector, Mary, Edward, Tom, March and Feb. To my

freed black woman Jenny land conveyed to me by deed from Christian
Belzer with the two story brick house and all improvements on said
lot on the South side of Federal St., now called Society St., joins
Cox and my lot. One room in the house is reserved for black man Will
his lifetime. Jenny's heirs to inherit as her legal heirs without
any regard to her being legally married to their fathers as negroe's
marriages cannot be easily proved. I give to freed black people
Tom, March, Feb, Mary and Edward during their lives lot of land
conveyed to me by deed from Elizabeth You together with a two story
wooden house and all other improvements on North side Magazine St.
in Charleston, joins Wilson, Wolf and Mackinfee's lots. I give to
Sarah Gray, daughter of Henry Gray, the use of one tenement in this
house during her lifetime on condition only that she reside therein
and act as guardian and protector of these colored people.
   To the two nieces of my wife, Mary Yeadon (?) and Sarah Gelzer
(Belzer ?) equally to each of them a lot of land conveyed to me by
deed from their mother Elizabeth You on the West side of Meeting St.
one mile from Charleston, bounded to the East on Meeting, South on
Spring St., West on heirs of Thomas and Elizabeth You, and North on
Columbus St. Likewise all that lot of land by deed from Elizabeth
You on East side King St., Homesteed (?), one mile from Charleston.
To Mary Yeadon and Sarah Gelzer and their brother John You equally
one third each of house and lot conveyed to me by deed from Elizabeth
You on North side Lynch's Lane, corner of Zigzag Alley in Charleston.
To Edward B. Weyman's three children: Lydia Catharine Weyman,
Elexander Wayman and Mary Rosilla Weyman land from Elizabeth You on
North side of Trot St. called Wentworth St. in Charleston, South on
Wentworth, East on Langstaff, North on my lot left to Jenny and West
on Miller's lot. On this lot there is a wooden two story house and
other improvements. I appoint their grandmother Catherine Weyman in
trust for them until the youngest is twenty-one.
   To Samuel Augustus Maverick and his sister Lydia Ann Maverick a
three story brick house and lot conveyed by deed from Erasmus Rathmaler
on East side of King St., Wraysboro, near Charleston, bounded on West
by King St. and other sides by land lately owned by heirs of John
Wray.
   To Hanna Turpin my brother's widow during her life, interest on a
bond due me from her son William Turpin, Jr. Bond is for safety kept
by Catharine Weyman in Charleston.
   To Willim Turpin, Jr., his bond for $2784.00 if he pays his mother
interest her lifetime. Also to William land conveyed by Charles James
Air's deed on West side of King St. near Boundary St. in Charleston
with the three story brick house and other great improvements thereon,
bounded on East by King St., North by Gennerick's lot, West by Maverick
and South by Cunningham's lot. William Turpin, Jr. or his heirs to
take possession of this lot after the death of his sister Catharine
Weyman as during her life I give her the use, rent and profit of said
house and improvements. To William, Jr. all that farm on Charleston
Neck conveyed to me by deed of Isaac Teasdale, 16 and ¼ acres, two
and a half miles from Charleston, East by King St., North by land
lately held by John M. Errick, West on Delamotta's land, South by
land formerly Osborn's. To take possession after the death of his
sister Catharine Weyman.
   To my two nephews Samuel Maverick and William Turpin, Jr., and
my niece Catharine Weyman, 386 acres on Brook's Mill Creek, Spartanburg
District, including Little David's Mountain, the gold mine and iron
ore bed, said land was granted by Gov. Pinckney to Wadsworth and
Turpin on 3 March, 1788, for full description refer to Samuel H.
Dickson's plat of resurvey 3 March, 1804, also refer to William Benson's
plat to the original grant annexed. To my two nephews Samuel Maverick
and William Turpin the residue of real estate in South Carolina.
Executors: Catharine Weyman, Samuel Maverick and William Turpin, Jr.
to executor that part of my estate that lays in South Carolina and in
no other place.
   All my colored people in the State of New York are free: Joseph,
Thomas, Turpin, Land Turpin, Lucy Bates and her children. These I
recommend to the kind protection of my executor and Juda Jackson to
their particular care but Charles Augustus, Martin Luther and John
Piper are absent.

To my faithful friend my freed black man Joseph Thomas Turpin a
lot conveyed to me by deed of master in Chancery Court in City of
New York, Lot #18 South St., bounded on West by James Leat, East by
Isaac Clayson and Stephen Whitney, in rear by Elbert Rosevelt. Have
given long lease on lot to William and John James. Also to Joseph
Thomas Turpin a dwelling house on East side of the Bowery known as
#271, joins David Marsh and John Farris. Conveyed to me by Effingham
W. Marsh. Also to Joseph Thomas Turpin a lot from David Lydig on
South St. and Front St. with the four story brick house, #253 Front
St. Lot is next to corner of Dover St., joins Delaplaine and Lydig.
Joseph Thomas Turpin to have wearing apparel and one silver teapot,
sugar dish and one quart bowl, one tankard and one plated milk pot.
To Juda Jackson my freed black girl and her brother Edward Butter
(or Butler ?), provided they live to be 21, land conveyed by Elbert
Anderson on West side of Broadway near Franklin St. known as #371
Broadway, East by Broadway, South by Fowler, West by an ally. Lot is
leased to Luke Kep (or Kess ?). Dr. Kissam now owns Kep's lease.
If Juda and Edward both die property is to go to freed black woman
Lucy Bates. I appoint Charles Collins and his son George B. Collins
guardians to Judah Jackson and Edward Butler.
To my sister's son, Samuel Maverick, and to my brother's son
William Turpin, Jr., a four story brick store #173 South St., by deed
from J. M. McDonald, also four story brick at #174 South St. Catharine
Weyman is to have one third of the rent or income for her lifetime.
To Mary Flandrau (?), a two story brick house at #386 Pearl St.
conveyed by John Lenacree's deed, joins Franklin and Mount's land.
Also to Mary Flandrau land now leased to James Flandrau containing
two acres on road leading from New Rochelle landing back to the high
water mark bounded to the East by farm sold to Catharine Weyman,
South on the marsh, West on Constant's land. Also to her a small
sliver tea pot, sugar dish and milk pot.
To my mother's brother's son Barnabas Brown and equally to his sons
Peleg Brown and William Turpin Brown one third to each of them land
conveyed to me by Jacob Stout on Greenwich St., across Washington St.
to the channel of North River, together with a three story brick
house #62 Greenwich St. and a three story brick at #63 Washington St.
To my brother's grandson William Peter Turpin a two story brick
house #466 Broom St. in New York City conveyed by Robert Pearsall,
joins McCrady. Also to him lot adjoining with 2 story brick house,
joins Lorillard, Addison and McCrady.
To William Turpin and his heirs in the male line my large Bible
containing our family record and list of slaves set free under my
protection. Also to him books of accounts and papers relating to
business in South Carolina. $900.00 to be paid to either of my
executors in South Carolina or to Richard Yeadon of Charleston either
of their receipts shall be a complete discharge to my executors in
New York. This at the request of my (late) wife: is to be paid
$150.00 to the heirs of Tucker Harris and $150.00 to the heirs of
Alexander Alexander, $200.00 to the Fellowship Society, $200.00 to
Mount Zion Society in Charleston.
To William Fuller of Graves County, Kentucky, for the sole use of
his wife and children, $2000.00.
To Mary Turpin Champney (?) and her heirs $500.00. To my most
beloved friend Rachel Malin (if living to receive it) and her heirs
$6000.00 to be carried by Barnabas Brown or Peleg Brown as quick as
possible and paid to her at her house in Jerusalem, Yates County,
and if she is not then living, money goes to James Brown for his own
use in the same house.
To my freed black man Lund (or Land ?) Turpin (a Methodist Preacher)
$1000.00. To Henry Drayton a full discharge for debt he owes me.
$8000.00 to the 21 slaves set free by will of my partner Thomas
Wadsworth in 1799, their heirs and assigns as a proper renumeration
for their services when slaves to Wadsworth and Turpin. Executors
are authorized to pay to any persons hereinafter named, executors
to pay to those free people in South Carolina after deducting 12½%
for his expenses in paying at the houses where each family resides.
My executor shall pay it to Samuel Maverick or William Turpin, Jr.
or to Samuel Augustus Maverick or to Charles Collins the person
that undertakes to go and pay those free people must divide the money

82

into 21 equal parts and pay one part to each family, say to seven
families now living in Newberry District: (1st) family James and
Bets, (2nd) family Priss and 3 children, (3rd) family Jenny and 3
children, (4th) family John and 2 children, (5th) family Betty and
4 children, (6th) family Mike, (7th) family Fanny and 2 children.
To two families in Abbeville District: (8th) family Let and 5 children,
(9th) family Rachel and children. To 11 families in Laurens District
(10th) family Sarah Kain Jones and 8 children, (11th) family Liz and
7 children, (12th) family Line, (13) family Chloe and 5 children,
(14) Philes, (15th) family Charlotte and 2 children, (16th) Thomas,
(17th) Edmund, (18th) Miley, (19th) Martha, (20th) Rubin; and one
family in Union District (21st) family Silvey and 2 children.
  I give to Edward B. Weyman full discharge of the debt he owes me.
To Mary Rosella Weyman $500.00. To Joseph T. Weyman and wife Elizabeth
and Robert Howard Weyman one cent to each of them. To Phebe Johnson
$500.00. To Jane Ward $500.00. To Benjamin Lunda (?) editor of a
paper called The Genesis (?) of Universal Emancipation $1500.00.
To William Loyd Garrison editor of The Liberator $500.00. To Charles
Collins 100 shares in Mechanics Bank of New York. To Peleg Brown 100
shares. To Dr. William Beach the medical reformer $500.00. To
Theodore Dwight (?) editor of The Daily Advertiser $1000.00. Executors
to pay $600.00 to Charles Collins or to his son George B. Collins
to have printed in phamplet form 600 copies of this will and send
copy to each person herein named.
  To Jesse Torrey of Philadelphia if living $4000.00 and a bundle of
papers sealed up and directed to him. To Barnabas Brown and his sons
Peleg and William Brown silver bowls and spoons. Books to black man
Joseph Thomas Turpin. Remainder of library to William Turpin, Jr. and
his son William Peter Turpin. Household and kitchen furniture divided,
half to William Peter Turpin, one fourth to Mary Flandrau, one fourth
to Joseph Thomas Turpin.
  To Peter Williams, church minister (black man) $500.00. To Arthur
Tappan and Israel Course 200 shares in Mechanics Bank in trust that
they transfer to such society will best promote education and welfare
of the descendants of Africa.
  To Peter A. Jay, Thomas Hale and Charles Collins, 100 shares bank
stock to be transferred to the New York Society for promoting manu-
mission of slaves for the benefit of the African free school.
  To Peleg Brown $4000.00 I lent him. To William Mower $200.00 to
be divided between his 2 daughters.
  To Willie (or Miller ?) Hickson $1000.00. To Morris Robinson
$2000.00. To Isaac Lawrence $1000.00, this gift to Hicks, Robinson
and Lawrence who I shall name co-executors is on condition they are
living at time of my death. If not, null and void. Residue of my
estate after legacies paid divided into four equal parts. One fourth
to my six cousins: To Thomas William Turpin Bicknall, to his brother
George A. Bicknell, to his sister Almira Wheeler, to the widow Mehitable
Atwell, to Angeline Post, to Anna Dunlap; to my friends George B.
Collins and Rachel Malin. Barnabas and Peleg Brown to take Rachel
Malin's part and pay to her or James Brown at her house in Jerusalem,
Yates County at their discretion to aid poor friends.
  One fourth to my old friend Frances Depau. Remaining one fourth
to my sister's son Samuel Maverick, to my brother's daughter Catharine
Weyman and her brother William Turpin, Jr.
  My executors will note there is no person living of equal degree
of kindred to me as the three last named. Executors: Francis Depau,
Morris Robinson, Willet Hicks, Isaac Lawrence, my cousin Barnabas
Brown of Chenango, his son Peleg Brown and my brother's son William
Turpin, Jr. of South Carolina. Dated 14 May, 1833.
Wit.: Issac Bell   (Signed) Will Turpin
      Miles R. Burke
      C. Botton
      (all of the City of New York).
  I certify the foregoing printed on 21 pages to contain true copy
from last will of William Turpin formerly of Charleston, deceased.
Filed and of record in this office the same having been proven in New
York County 12 Mar. 1835.
Filed Anderson Co., S. C. 3 Oct. 1835.

WILL OF DAVID MOORE - p 36
Wife Margaret to have half of estate. Other half to David Anderson
and Margaret Anderson, the children of Elizabeth Crook. Executor:
Wife Margaret Moore and Elizabeth Crook the wife of Jesse Crook.
Dated 19 Jan. 1836.
Wit.: Henry (X) Cole   (Signed) David Moor
       John Crocker
Proven Mar. 8, 1836.

WILL OF ELIJAH BROWNE - pp 37-40
Wife Sally all land, stock, furniture and negroes Barney, Dover and
Silvy for life or widowhood. Then to be sold and equally divided
between my children by her. To granddaughter Kitty Carpenter a negro
girl Milley now in possession of my daughter Selina in the State of
Tennessee about 5 years old on condition she does not get one of her
mother's estate when her brothers come of age.
     The other negroes in Tennessee to remain as they are subject to the
contract now existing between Selina Browne and myself. Executors:
Much respected friend George Manning, Esq., Elisha McPherson and Col.
Amaziah Rice. Dated 22 Aug. 1828.
Wit.: Whitefield Anthony   (Signed) E. Browne
       Wm. Magee
       Thomas Taylor
     Codicil - One wagon to wife Sally; 1 gold brooch to son Sidi (?)
H. Browne. Silver knee buckles to Elijah the son of Jonathan Browne.
Executors to see that four youngest children receive tolerable good
English education and that son Sidi Hamet be taught mathematics and
art of surveying. Daughter Selina has deceased. Negroes Eliab or
Louisa, whichever he may choose, go to son Darius Q. Browne. The
other 3 negroes in Selina's care (subject to Kitty Carpenter's claim
as named in will) to be kept in trust with Darius Q. and Jonathan
Browne for benefit of such of their brothers as have not received
equal part of property acquired by their mother.
     Having selected spot of ground back of the potato patch for family
burying ground, my will to be buried beside my child already buried
there. If land sold one half acre around graves reserved. My grave
to be covered over so as to prevent rain falling on it and that my
coffin be laid on sticks of durable wood to prevent its touching
the ground and pailings kept up around graves from time to time at
the expense of my estate. Dated 2 May, 1833.
Wit.: James Gwinn (?)   (Signed) E. Browne
       Robert C. Harkness
       Elizabeth (X) Welch
Proven 21 Mar. 1836

WILL OF NATHAN MCALLISTER - pp 41-42
To Nathan McAllister Arnold a child raised by me 293 acres where
David Gordon now lives. To Nathan McAllister, son of Andrew McAllister
700 acres of land where I now live on condition he pay Frances
McAllister my brother $5.00 and to his son Nathan McAllister $95.00
in one year and a day after his taking possession of land, and the
said Nathan, son of Andrew, is immediately after my death to take
possession of aforesaid premises with all my personal estate. He is
to pay $100.00 to be equally divided among the heirs of Andrew
McAllister that may be living at the time of my decease, also $100.00
to Elizabeth Emberson my only living sister, also $100.00 to Thomas
McAllister and William McAllister, my brothers, to each, also that he
pay $100.00 to the heirs of Rosa McAllister to be equally divided
among them. $100.00 to be paid to Allen Arnold. Executors: Nathan
and John. Dated 10 June, 1836.
Wit.: Robert Todd   (Signed) Nathan McAllister
       Andrew Todd
       A. Evins
Proven 13 June, 1836.

WILL OF JAMES HARRIS - pp 43-44
If wife Sarah survives me she is to have furniture, stock and negro
Caesar and wife Lizey. Daughter Mary E. Harris shall have one seventh.
Son William Harris to have negro boys Dick and John. Son James C.

Harris to have negro boys Mose and Daniel and the land called the
Watt tract. Daughter Jane Amanda Harris to have negro girls Suckey
and Louisa. Son Thomas Alonzo Harris to have land where I now live
and negro boys Aaron and Tom. My own grave and the grave of my former
wife shall be neatly fixed with brick or stone and a neat marble headstone be placed to each. Executors: M. Black of Abbeville District.
Dated 13 June, 1836.
Wit.: Jno. W. Connor   (Signed) James S. (?) Harris
       Robertson Smith
       Robert McAllister
Proven 5 Sept. 1836.

WILL OF JESSE MCGEE - pp 45-50

Daughter Polly Herron land on Big Generostee granted Wm. Lesley, Jr.
in 1784. Also to Polly one third of the Mills Shoal and land attached
to said mills. Also to Polly a negro girl Marandy. To son Willis
McGee, plantation where he now lives originally granted Holcomb and
Lesley. Also to Willis one third of mills shoal. To son Elias
McGee land where he has made improvements on Generostee and one third
of mills. To son Samuel McGee land where he now lives. To daughter
Ruthy Smith land where she lives and a negro girl Cary. To daughter
Elenor McFawson (?) land conveyed to me by Matthew Dunlap on Savannah
River, and a negro girl Lucy. I give a bill of sale for girl to
William McFawson.
   To daughter Gilly Riley land on Big Generostee conveyed by James
Long and also to Gilly a negro girl Fanny. To my wife Nancy McGee
the plantation where I now live, furniture, stock and negroes not
already willed. To be held by wife until children of age, then to
give each child $1100.00 or if not that much equal amount in slaves.
My six children: Tabitha McGee, Jesse McGee, Hudockey McGee, Betsy
McGee, Nancy McGee and Emmeline McGee to be educated by wife. If wife
shall marry property sold and she to have child's part and balance
divided between my six children by my wife Nancy provided no more
than $1100.00 each. Children by my first wife: Willis McGee, Polly
Herron, Elias McGee, Samuel McGee, Eleanor McFawson, Ruthey Smith,
Gilly Riley to receive equal share. Have tried to make equal shares
in division of property among all my children. Executors: Wife
Nancy and sons Willis and Jesse. Jesse not being of age I will that
he be fully informed to act as executor when he comes of the age of 20.
Dated 27 Sept. 1828.
Wit.: Miles Hardy   (Signed) Jesse (X) McGee
       James W. Hardy
       Joseph Taylor
Proven 6 Feb. 1837.

WILL OF LEWELING GOODE - pp 51-53

I will negroes Douglass, Ezekial, Shade, Annakey and Clarinda be sold.
Necessary property be sold for maintenance of my wife and children,
divided equally at the coming of age of youngest child. Executors:
Friends John Maxwell and Thomas Paine. Dated 17 Nov. 1836.
Wit.: John Ramsey   (Signed) Leweling Goode
       John B. Earle
       William Steele
   Codicil - Land known as Thomas Benton tract sold. Dated 8 May,
1837.
Wit.: Moody Burt
       Whitaker Smith
       Joseph Hillhouse
Proven 6 June, 1837.

WILL OF JOSEPH STEVENSON - pp 54-55

Wife Mary the plantation and property for life or widowhood. Then
sold and $100.00 to Joseph S. (?) Hearston. To my two nephews Alexander
Stephenson of Abbeville District and William Stephenson of Anderson
$100.00 each. Rest of estate equally divided between my two brothers
John and Samuel Stephenson. Dated 13 Sept. 1836. Executor: F. D. Fant.
Wit.: John Haynie   (Signed) Joseph (X) Stephenson
       George Burrough
       Elizabeth (X) Hearston
Proven 10 Oct. 1836.

WILL OF FRANCIS BURT - pp 56-58

Pickens District. Negro woman Charlotte and her two children Martha
and Stephen sold. To wife Catharine plantation where I live on 18
Mile Creek and negroes Stephen, Milly, Sam, Rose, Israel, Moses, Archer,
Dick and Ede. To her for life. At her death divided in two parts.
To son Francis Burt upper tract and my daughters Eliza and Parmelia
the part where I live. Slaves to be divided between Matthew Burt,
Oswee Burt, Armistead Burt, Francis Burt, Eliza Burt, Catharine
Roberts, Pamelia Burt, and Erasmus Burt. To my daughters Eliza and
Pamelia I give slaves Jacob, Patt, Zeny, Backey, Lorra, Esther, Mariah,
Isom, Margaret, Alleck, Pindee, Lucy, and Spencer. To son Erasmus I
give negroes Roger, Humphries, Warren and Mary Ann. Slaves to remain
with his mother until he is of age. Executors: sons Armistead and
Francis Burt. Dated 13 Mar. 1836.
Wit.: D. S. (?) Taylor   (Signed) Francis Burt
      Lucy H. Taylor
      Caroline V. Talliaferro
   Codicil - notes held on Samuel Reed, John Davis and Francis Burt,
Jr. be applied to payment of balance due for land in which I now reside,
and I bequeath land for equal division among four of my children:
Francis, Erasmus, Eliza and Parmelia. Dated 8 June, 1837.
Wit.: F. W. Symmes
      Moody Burt
      Moody Wright
Proven 3 July, 1837.

WILL OF AMBROSE MASON - pp 59-60

Debts paid, and residue to Jenny Payne. Dated 14 Apr. 1837.
Wit.: James Young, Sr.   (Signed) Ambrose Mason
      Jesse Bradberry
      Abraham (X) Meredith

WILL OF NATHANIEL HARRIS - pp 61-63

Wife Susan to have house and lot where I now live in village of
Pendleton, also negro fellow Adam and woman Hannah and her third child
named Henry for her lifetime. At her death to be sold and equally
divided between my children. If wife and executor think best to sell
or dispose of property they are at liberty to do so. Son Edwin Handy
Harris under age 21. Son George Reese Harris under 21. To daughter
Mary S. (or L. ?) Harris negro girl Lucy and boy Mat and $500.00 to
be given her when she marries or reaches 21. Executors: Wife, friend
David Cherry and Thos. R. Cherry. Dated __ May, 1837.
Wit.: Wm. Hubbard   (Signed) Nathl. Harris
      John B. Sitton
      A. H. Reese
Proven 31 July, 1837.

WILL OF STEPHEN WILLIAMS - pp 63-65

Wife Martha W. Williams to have house and lot in village of Anderson
and land joining the village where I now live, for purpose of educating
the three youngest children: Francis, Amanda and Ann. My four children:
Rachael, Francis, Amanda and Ann. Negro Silva to my wife Martha.
Executor: Wife. Dated 27 Nov. 1835.
Wit.: Elijah Webb   (Signed) Stephen Williams
      Caroline Webb
Proven 2 July, 1837.

WILL OF JOHN RICHEY - pp 65-67

After my death and death of wife Elizabeth land sold and divided into
5 equal parts, 1 to each of my sons: James Richey, Joseph Richie,
John Richie, Charles Richie, and 1 equal share to my grandson Charles
Almond Richie. My 3 daughters Nancy Blagg, Sally Mason and Elizabeth
Hix. Obligation I have this day given Wm. Steele for $112.00 shall be
taken out of share to son Joseph Richie. Dated 2 Jan. 1834. Executors:
Wm. Adams and Wm. Steele
Wit.: Whiteaker Smith   (Signed) John (X) Richie
      E. Clark
      Wm. Adams
      Wm. Steele
Proven 6 Mar. 1837.

WILL OF SARAH DALRYMPLE - pp 67-68
Trusty friend Herbert Hammond trustee for Rosannah Lewis the plantation
on which Elisha Lewis and Rosannah Lewis now reside, 160 acres. At
their decease land goes to their children. Dated 26 Jan. 1837.
Wit.: Lewis Sherrell   (Signed) Sarah (X) Dalrymple
       James M. Lewis
Proven 20 Feb. 1837.

WILL OF JOHN SCOTT - pp 69-70
Wife Sarah land on West side Willson's Creek where I now reside.
Grandson John Stephens 200 acres where Shadrick Stephens now lives.
John Stephens is to maintain my 2 daughters Mary and Elizabeth Scott
their lifetimes. I give to my daughters Mary and Elizabeth land that
falls to me by estate of Thomas Scott deceased. To daughter Margaret
White $50.00. To daughter Jane Stephens $50.00. Whatever else remains
divided between Jane Stephens and David Scott. Executors: Penuel
Price and David Scott. Dated 5 June, 1833.
Wit.: Lewis Bozeman   (Signed) John Scott
       D. Beaty
       Elisha Brown
Proven 22 May, 1837.

WILL OF JOHN MILFORD, SR. - pp 71-72
Wife Rebecca. Son Philip. Son Henry. Balance of personal property
sold and equally divided amongst my children John, Robert, Sally,
Martha, and Mary, the balance of my children being already provided
for. Executors: Charles Stark. (Will not dated).
Wit.: Blackman Burton   (Signed) John Milford, Sr.
       John M. Saxon
       Peyton Burton
Proven 12 Dec. 1837.

WILL OF JESSE OBRIANT - pp 73-74
Dated 14 May, 1837. Wife Joice to have land her lifetime then sold
and equally divided amongst all my children. Executors: Wife Joice
and Jesse H. Obriant and Andrew Obriant.
Wit.: Andrew Reed   (Signed) Jesse (J. B.) Obriant
       Alex. McCallister   (his mark)
       Andrew T. Obriant
Proven 1 Jan. 1838.

WILL OF FRANCIS CLINKSCALES, SR. - pp 75-76
My 9 children: Catharine Campbell, Priscilla Clement, Jane B. Orr,
Wm. F. Clinkscales, Elizabeth Kay and Polly Kay deceased, John Clink-
scales, Levi Clinkscales, Francis B. Clinkscales. The share that is
coming to Katharine Campbell dec'd I give to heirs of her body and
appoint my son Wm. F. their guardian. The share of Polly Kay dec'd to
heirs of her body, with my son Francis guardian. Executors: Sons Wm.
F. and Francis. Dated 18 Nov. 1831.
Wit.: S. (?) D. Kay   (Signed) Francis Clinkscales, Sr.
       Daniel Mattison
       Aaron Davis
Proven 15 Jan. 1838.

WILL OF ELIZABETH MILLS - pp 76-78
To William Steel and E. B. Benson a negro woman Amey (or Anny (?).
To Polly Robins 10 acres on tract where she now lives and purchased by
me from Wm. Steel. Desire my executors to build a cabin on land
purchased from Steel and 3 acres cleared and fenced and Amey allowed
to live there her lifetime. Amey to have use of cow and calf, sow and
pigs and their increase her lifetime and at her death may be permitted
to dispose of them as she may please. At Amey's death balance of land
purchased from Wm. Steel except the 10 acres to Polly Robbins I give
to her son Wm. Jesse Robbins. Should Amey die before the child Wm.
Jesse Robbins is of age, land rented out for his benefit. To Caleb
Edmondson $100.00 if that much is left. To James Green $60.00 after
Edmondson has received his $100.00. Executors: Wm. Steel and E. B.
Benson. Dated 6 July, 1837.
Wit.: Jeremiah (X) Willbanks   (Signed) Elizabeth Mills

W. H. D. Gaillard
Thos. L. Carpenter
Proven 29 Jan. 1838.

WILL OF FRANCIS POSEY - pp 79-80

Addison Francis Posey the son of my brother B. L. Posey. Sister Sarah
Findley. Brother Robert B. Posey. James Willis Posey the son of
Charles Posey is under 21. John Allen Posey, son of Charles, is under
21. Harriet Amanda Posey, daughter of Charles. My friend and pastor
Reed Sandford Vandiver. $20.00 to Deacons of Baptist Church at Anderson.
Sister Nancy Robison. Negro man Pike to be sold at private sale. Wife
Polly Posey. Executors: Valentine D. Fant and Elijah Webb.
Dated 26 Dec. 1837.
Wit.: John Haynie   (Signed) Francis Posey
       A. O. Norris (or Harris ?)
       Wm. Long
Proven 5 Feb. 1838.

WILL OF AUGUSTINE E. SCUDDY - pp 81-82

Gentleman, dated 2 Feb. 1838. Wife Sintha and two small sons Augustine
and Henry, land where I now live and negro girl Jane. Son-in-law
Ledford Beauford. Marta Harris to have her board free with my wife
Sintha. Daughter Lucy by my first wife. Negro Judy Ann to be put up
and sold. Negroes Winston and Miley to stay on place this year for
benefit of wife, then sold. First wife's children: Jane, Clarissa,
John, Nancy. Executors: Wife Sintha, Jesse C. McGee and Ledford
Buford.
Wit.: Henry Holmes   (Signed) Augustine E. (X) Scuddy
       E. Cuchan
       A. Beatrice (X) Sanders
       Thos. T. Gibbs
Proven 12 Oct. 1838.

WILL OF GEORGE REESE - pp 83-85

Wife Anna a lifetime estate in land, part of it where Mrs. Story former-
ly lived. Wife to have negroes Old Sabina, Big Jim, Derry and Wezon.
Son Horation Reese negroes Charlotte, Mary, Emily and Jackson. Son C. M.
Reese to have house and lot in Pendleton where he now lives. Daughter
Mary Cherry. Daughter Susan Harris. Son D. A. Reese to have negro boy
Jeremy (?). Son George Reese. Son Thomas S. Reese to have negroes
Ransom and Bina and all her issue. Son J. E. Reese. Son Edwin Reese
to have negro boy Carter. Son A. H. Reese to have negroes Fanney and
Cyrus. Negro Sylvia and her daughter Leaner to be sold. Laurens M.
Reese and Charles Edwin Reese to be educated, money to Thomas S. Reese
for this purpose. Executors: Sons George and J. Eliju Reese. Dated
14 July, 1830.
Wit.: Rm. M. Cherry   (Signed) George Reese
       W. B. Finley
       John Mullinax
Proven 30 April, 1838.

WILL OF JAMES CARSON - p 86

Two of my children, William and Narcissa are married and have left me,
already received their part. My other children: James Madison, Lemuel,
John, Sarah Ann and Allen. Wife Tolley (?). Hope she can keep younger
children together. Executors: Wife Tolley and friend Wm. Steele.
Dated 15 Apr. 1838.
Wit.: Whiteaker Smith   (Signed) James (X) Carson
       Charles Bell
       Dudley White
Proven 18 June, 1838.

WILL OF WILLIAM MCCURDAY - pp 87-89

Wife Sarah land where I now live and 65 acres joining A. Simpson and
Harris and my old place, and one negro girl Caroline and child Nancey
and Miles. After her death or widowhood land and negroes to be sold
and divided equally amongst my children. I will my daughter Elizabeth
an equal share with rest of my children, she already received $400.00.
Son James. Son H. L. Daughter Margaret Aston. Daughter Sarah McCurday,

a negro girl Mary. Son-in-law Stephen Carsey and Polly Carsey his wife.
Son William McCurday. Grandson William McCurday, Jr. $100.00 to
Generotee Church. Executors: William Sherard. Dated 28 Nov. 1837.
Wit.:   Robertson Smith   (Signed) William McCurday
        Andrew W. Beaty
        David Parker
Proven 2 July, 1838.

WILL OF RACHAEL M. PRESSLY - pp 89-90
Sister Elizabeth Porter of the State of Alabama, a note I hold on
legatees of my father's estate. To my mother Ann Presley the use and
services of a negro boy Cornelius aged about 9. After mother's death
the boy to go to my sister Jane M. Pressley. Brother-in-law Elijah
Willbanks. Executor: Elijah Willbanks. Dated 20 June, 1838.
Wit.:   Hugh Porter   (signed) Rachael M. Presly
        Nancy Crawford
        Jane L. Brownlee
Proven 22 Apr. 1839.

WILL OF JOHN JENNINGS - pp 91-92
Wife Jane. All my children. Executors: Roberson Smith and Joel H.
Berry. Dated 15 Jan. 1839.
Wit.:   A. Simpson   (Signed) John (X) Jennings
        Ezekial George
        John B. (X) Winfield
Proven 4 Mar. 1839.

WILL OF JOHN CARR, SR. - pp 92-94
Wife Polly to have land where I now live and 3 negroes: Baalum, Chance
and Lewis. At wife's death sold and divided between all my children.
Executors: Wife Polly and sons John Carr, Jr. and Laban Carr. Dated
17 July, 1837.
Wit.:   John M. Barns   (Signed) John Carr
        John Moore
        Robt. B. Lewis
Proven 7 Apr. 1839.

WILL OF TURNER RICHARDSON - p 94
All estate to be equally divided among my children and my wife. Three
good men to appraise estate. Executors: Peter Belott and Saxon Anderson.
Dated 13 Mar. 1838.
Wit.:   John T. Humphreys   (signed) T. Richardson
        Martha W. Humphreys
        Mary Humphreys
Proven 21 Jan. 1839.

WILL OF CHARLES BOWIE - pp 94-96
Son Wesley. Wife Catharine. Son Charles 50 acres in trust for use of
Mary C. and John T. McCulough the children of my daughter Catharine.
Their mother may reside on premises if trustee sees fit. Daughters
Nancy, Catherine, Mary and Jane. To grandson John M. White, the son
of my daughter Nancy, my colt, the increase if any to his brothers and
sisters. My sons William and Charles have received their share.
Daughter Sarah has received her share. Executors: Sons William and
Charles. Dated 22 Oct. 1837.
Wit.:   E. B. Gibert   (Signed) Charles Bowie
        Peter Gibert
        A. Hunter
Proven 7 Oct. 1839.

WILL OF WESLEY BOWIE - pp 96-97
Half of estate to wife Lavona and half to brother William Bowie.
William to take care of my mother Catherine Bowie as long as she lives.
Dated 30 Sept. 1839.
Wit.:   Jno. W. Conner   (Signed) Wesley (X) Bowie
        David Martin
        D. Tucker
Proven 7 Oct. 1839.

WILL OF ROBERT POOLE - pp 98-99
Property remain together on plantation for use of wife Elizabeth and my
children. Executors: Wife Elizabeth and Joseph M. Jolley. Dated 26
Mar. 1830.
Wit.: Alex. Moorhead   (Signed) Robert (X) Poole
      Robert Alexander
      Edw. W. Burford
Proven 27 Jan. 1840.

WILL OF ELEANOR LEWIS - pp 99-100
Daughter Julia Hannah to have a female child of Peggy named Maria.
To my children Julia Hannah, Henry Talliaferro, Samuel Wilds, Thomas
Harrison and Benjamin Franklin Lewis, my negroes Prince, Warren and
Peggy. Also to my five children my interest in lands of my deceased
husband. Dated 29 Sept. 1839.
Wit.: William Golden   (Signed) Eleanor Lewis
      James J. Willson
      George G. Elrod
Proven 24 Mar. 1840.

WILL OF GEORGE OLDHAM - pp 100-101
Wife Susannah. Son Thomas. Daughter Nancy. Son William. Sons Thomas
and Garland. Executors: Sons William and Thomas. Dated 24 Nov. 1829.
Wit.: Hugh Wilson   (Signed) George Oldham
      Thomas Bennett
      John Murphey
Proven 24 Mar. 1840.

WILL OF ROBERT JUNKINS - pp 102-103
Wife Milley to have one third. Balance divided among my five children:
Mary Jane, Margaret, Elizabeth, Westley and William. Executors:
Friends Jesse Dobbins and E. S. Norris. Dated 1 Apr. 1840.
Wit.: William Skelton   (Signed) Robert Junkin
      Van Tate
      Jacob (X) Hays
Proven 27 Apr. 1840.

WILL OF HUGH POOR - pp 103-105
Wife Anna. Children: Andrew J. Poor, George W. Poor, John J. Poor,
Hugh Poor, Samuel E. Poor, Sarah V. Poor and Mary E. Poor. Any money
that may hereafter fall to me or my children by kinship in and through
my father John Poor's estate to be settled on wife and children in same
manner. I wish executors to keep interest until children of age.
Executors: My brother John Poor and brother-in-law William Holland.
Dated 24 Jan. 1840.
Wit.: Joseph Cox   (Signed) Hugh Poor
      Elijah Browning
      George W. Poor
Proven 11 May, 1840.

WILL OF CROSBY W. MILLER - pp 105-108
Wife Elizabeth and her children, youngest not of age. Son-in-law John
Cammorand (or Cammonard ?). Son-in-law Josiah N. Boggs. Son Enos
Kelsey Miller. Son Crosby Wilksmilleer. Son John F. Miller. Land
known as Colds Old Fields. Have made personal advances to some of the
other children. Executor: E. B. Benson. Dated 28 Apr. 1840.
Wit.: F. W. Symmes   (Signed) Crosby W. Miller
      John T. Sloan
      Thos. M. Sloan
Proven 8 June, 1840.

WILL OF JOHN GENTRY - pp 108-109
Nuncupative will. Declared by word of mouth 28 Mar. 1840. Estate to
remain in possession of wife Elizabeth her lifetime and that Elizabeth
Ellen Wood have bed and furniture.
Wit.: Mathew Parker
      Hiram Howard
      Zechariah Gentry
Widow, Elizabeth, filed for probate 6 June, 1840.

WILL OF WILLIAM ELLIOT - pp 109-110
Wife Rosannah, to have negro girl Edey and her offspring. Executor:
Wife Rosannah. Dated 5 June, 1840.
Wit.: Henry Cobb   (Signed) William Elliot, Jr.
      Wm. Bennett
      Azariah P. Cobb
Proven 14 Sept. 1840.

WILL OF LARKIN WRIGHT - pp 110-112
To wife Catharine negroes Dice, Gin, George and Daniel, Mariah and
Caroline for lifetime or widowhood, division amongst children made when
youngest of age. Sons Oliver H. and Alexander R. J. Daughter Frances
Hix to have negro woman Kiz and after her death equally divided among
her children. Daughter Julia M. Holland to have negro girl Mary.
Daughter Nancy C. Wright to have negro girl Charity. Son Oliver H.
Wright to have boy Eli. Daughter Lucinda E. J. Wright to have girl
Modesty. Son Alexander R. J. Wright to have boy Coly. Daughter Mary
Ann Wright to have boy Ben. Daughter Catharine Wright to have girl
Eliza. Executors: Wife Catharine, William Holland and Benjamin Magee.
Dated 23 Mar. 1840.
Wit.: Martin S. McCoy   (Signed) Larkin Wright
      J. R. Cox
      Livingston Isbell
Proven 19 Oct. 1840.

WILL OF SAMUEL MAGILL - pp 112-113
Son William. Two daughters Sarah and Mariann Magill. Executors: Son
William and daughter Sarah. Dated 1 June, 1839.
Wit.: L. Bozeman   (Signed) Samuel Megill
      Ezekial McGill
      Samuel H. (X) McGill
Proven 30 Dec. 1839.

WILL OF JAMES R. WEBSTER - pp 114-119
First Will. Wife Jane negro man Harry, women Rinda and Sarah. She is
to raise the families of the children of Rinda and Sarah for Ann and
Margaret Webster which I give to them. At wife's death or marriage
property sold and after deduction of $780.83 from proceeds which amount
to be equally divided between her five own children according to her
mother's will viz: John Robinson, Hugh Robinson, Elizabeth Armstrong,
Ann and Margaret Webster. After deduction balance equally divided
between my heirs: two youngest daughters Ann and Margaret Webster to
have negroes Thompson, Louisa, Minerva and Mahala and increase from
Rinda and Sarah. To daughter Henrietta Webster bed and furniture.
Woman Beck, man Edmund, woman Eve and her children sold and divided as
follows: One share to daughter Ethelender Loveless; one share to heirs
of my son James R. Webster; one share to son Henly Webster; one share
to Arthur and Polly Smith my daughter. One share to Andrew J. and
Elizabeth Reeve my daughter. One share to daughter Henrietta Webster.
One share to heirs of dec'd daughter Nancy Kay. Executors: Friends
Hugh Gantt and Arthur Smith. Gantt is to attend to Ann and Margaret
and Smith to rest of heirs. Dated 19 Apr. 1837.
Wit.: George Mattison   (Signed) James R. Webster
      Wm. Long
      Wm. P. Martin
Second Will. Wife Jane. Mentions grandson Posey Webster, not mentioned
in first will. Daughter Henrietta has married Joel Kay. Executors:
Hugh Robinson and Arthur Smith. Dated 3 Aug. 1840.
Wit.: Geo. Mattison   (Signed) James R. (X) Webster
      Hampton Stone
      John M. Branyon
Proven 14 Dec. 1840.

WILL OF LEWIS SHERRILL - pp 199-122
Wife Mary to have 6 negroes for life: Daniel, Frank, Ben, Franky, Lucy
and Joe. Also to have land which goes to son Lewis at her death.
Have given son John a boy George of whom he has disposed. To son David
a slave Isaac. To son Lewis a negro Ephraim. To daughter Eleanor
Campbell slave Polly. Have given daughter Judah Anderson a slave Nancy.

After Judah's death to go to heirs of her body by her second husband.
To daughter Rachel Moorhead a slave Susan. Have loaned daughter Ruanna
Crow and her husband a slave Betsy. I now give same to Ruanna. To
daughter Polly Matthews a girl Cindy. To daughter Esther Cullins a
boy Amos. Many of my children are scattered to distant parts and may
not apply for provisions of this will. Executors to make reasonable
exertion to locate them for a period of two years after my death.
Executors: Dr. William Anderson and my sons David and Lewis Sherrill.
Dated 24 July, 1838.
Wit.: James Campbell   (Signed) Lewis Sherrill
       G. W. Masters
       Elisha Lewis
Proven 28 Dec. 1840.

WILL OF WILLIAM ELLIOT, SR. - pp 122-123
Wife Peanny to have plantation and negroes Fillis, Elleck, Dick and
Saml. for life. Then negroes go to son Charles Elliot. To granddaughter
Sinthy Ann Owens the daughter of my daughter Nancy Owens, at the death
of my wife, a negro girl Frankey. Also at the death of wife, my sons
James Elliot and Aiky (?) Elliot to have plantation. Executors: Hugh
Willson and my wife Peanny. Dated 9 Jan. 1841.
Wit.: Wm. Bennett   (Signed) Wm. Elliott
       Martin Welborn
       Aaron Welborn
Proven 8 Feb. 1841.

WILL OF BARTLY TUCKER - pp 123-125
Wife Nancy and children (not named). To John Smith $100.00 for his
support placed in the hands of James Thompson. Executors: Wm. and
Reuben Tucker. Dated 10 Mar. 1841.
Wit.: J. Thompson   (Signed) Bartly (X) Tucker
       Wm. B. Newell
       G. F. Stiefel (Steifel)
Proven 5 Apr. 1841.
    Reuben D. Tucker, Alexander D. Gray and wife Elizabeth; Robert D.
Gray and wife Nancy; Abner Clinkscales and wife Rebecca; William Newill
and wife Jincy; Dejarnet Tucker and wife Sarah; James Tucker; Fenton
Hall and wife Polly; heirs of Bartley Tucker late of said District,
dec'd, and Nancy Tucker, widow of Bartley, appoint Reuben D. Tucker and
Wm. Tucker to administer estate of Bartley Tucker. Dated 26 Mar. 1841.
Wit.: M. Thompson
       J. Thompson

WILL OF ROBERT GUYTON - pp 126-127
Wife and children to remain upon place I now occupy and family be kept
together, both black and white, and that my man Isaac be allowed a
reasonable share of direction and management of my farm for raising
of my children so long as he shall conduct as well as he has done heretofore. Wife to have entire control of estate for life or widowhood.
At death divided among my children when youngest of age or married,
provided all other children are of age at the time. Titles be made
by executors to land recently sold to Henry Keasler and Nimrod Smith.
Monies arising from estates of my father-in-law Benjamin Ducksworth
and from estate of my father be put to interest for benefit of my
children. Children should be well raised and educated. Wife Hester.
Executors: John W. Guyton and William Webb. Dated 4 Apr. 1841.
Wit.: Wm. Steele   (Signed) Robert Guyton
       G. W. Masters
       Wm. Anderson
Proven 3 May, 1841.

WILL OF MATTHEW CLARK - p 127
Son Thomas B. Clarke. Son James G. Clarke. Son Benjamin Clarke. Son
Abner Clark. Son James G. to have man Washington on condition he pay
out of value of said negro $300.00 to Thos. B. Clarke. Daughter Martha
Jane to have one half of plantation where I live, also 2/3 of plantation
on 23 Mile Creek (except 1 acre which I give to John Barrett whereon
the Methodist Church stands and ¼ acre for each graveyard for use of
the Methodists, adjoining lands of J. B. Earle, D. J. Morris and others)

92

or half lease or sale of plantation. Man Henry to be sold and money
put to interest. If Martha Jane dies without issue property divided
equally between my sons Thomas, Benjamin, James G. and Ambros Clark's
three orphan children. Wife Jinsey to have ½ of plantation whereon I
now live and 1/3 of plantation on 23 Mile Creek, also negro fellow
Archy and ½ of the services of a girl Ellen. This girl Ellen I got my
wife and I found she was about $500.00 more in debt that she expected
which debts I have since paid out of my funds. Wife is now pregnant
with child. Executors: Joseph N. Whitner, Elijah Webb and Elias
Earle. Dated 15 Dec. 1840.
Wit.:   Warren R. Webb   (Signed) Mathew Clarke
        A. Evins
        John W. Broddy
Proven 9 June, 1841.

WILL OF WILLIAM PRICHARD - pp 130-131
Wife to have all except $1.00 to each child. Executors: David Russell,
Rev. John Vandiver. Dated 25 Aug. 1837.
Wit.:   Robert Brackenridge   (Signed) Wm. (X) Pritchard
        H. R. Brackenridge
        S. H. Browne
Proven 11 June, 1841.

WILL OF SARAH LEWIS - pp 131-133
Of Pickens District. $100.00 in trust for Methodist Episcopal Church
in village of Pendleton. To Joseph Black of Rutherford Co., N. C.,
$500.00. 1/6 to daughter Mary A. McDowell and heirs of her body except-
ing her daughter Nancy. 1/6 to daughter Anne E. Shanklin and heirs of
her body; 1/6 to daughter Sarah Ann Reese and heirs of her body. 1/6
to son James O. Lewis. 1/6 to son John E. Lewis and 1/6 to son Andrew
F. Lewis. Executors: Joseph Van Shanklin of Pendleton and John
McDowell of Rutherford Co., N. C.
Wit.:   Jesse P. Lewis   (Sarah Lewis, by Jesse P. Lewis)
        Wm. J. Knauff
        John Canunade (?)
    Codicil - To son Andrew F. Lewis a woman Milley he received in the
division of his father's estate and since has been transferred by him
to me. Property I have given Sarah Miller Lewis be decucted from part
which James O. Lewis is entitled. Said property is a girl Jeanette,
a cow and furniture. Dated 7 Nov. 1836.
Wit.:   Jesse P. Lewis
        Susan M. Lewis
        W. Werner
Proven 2 Nov. 1841.

WILL OF AARON GUYTON - pp 134-138
To each of my 5 daughters: Polly Sherrill, Hannah Smith, Betsy Webb,
Margaret Steele and Sally Duckworth one negro and other property already
given them. To son Robert Guyton 185 acres on Milwee Creek, also part
of Shirley tract containing 50 acres, joins Robert's own land just below
and near Hopewell Meeting House. Son Joseph Guyton to have land where
he lives in Hall Co., Ga., a negro woman Leah and child. To son Aaron
W. Guyton, a boy Lawson, he having received land he sold to Thos.
Duckworth. To son John W., 500 acres beginning at the ford of branch
between my house and the meeting house, to include all the Ervin and
Shirley tracts except that willed to Robert. Also to John W. a negro
boy Adam. To son Guyton Guyton a boy Orange. Land on Beaverdam Creek
adjoining Thomas Green to be sold. Wife Margaret is to have residue
of estate her lifetime, at her death negro man Bill to son Guyton
Guyton. Rest sold and divided among my children. Executors: 3 sons
Robert, Aaron W. and John W. Dated 14 Feb. 1840.
Wit.:   Jas. Wilson   (Signed) Aaron Guyton
        Charles Irby
        Thomas H. Garrett
    Widow, Margaret, asked that property be sold as there was to much to
maintain her. She reserves negroes Dan, Rose and Jince as hers. Dated
17 Dec. 1841.
Wit.:   G. W. Masters   (Signed) Margaret (X) Guyton
        James J. Barron

Legatees of Aaron Guyton accept relinquishment of their mother
Margaret and empower John W. Guyton to dispose of estate. Dated 17 Dec.
1841.
Wit.: G. W. Masters   (Signed) Wyatt Smith, Hannah Smith
       James J. Barron   Wm. Webb, Elizabeth (X) Webb
                                        Wm. Steele, M. N. Steele
                                        Thomas Duckworth, S. M.
                                                       Duckworth
                                        A. W. Guyton
                                        G. Guyton
                              Wm. Steele atty. for David Sherrill
                                        and wife Polly.
                              Wm. Webb as executor of est. of Robt.
                                        Guyton.

Proven 20 Dec. 1841.

WILL OF MARGARET JUNKIN - pp 139-140
Daughters Elizabeth Ann and Sarah Jane Junkin to have 40 acres described
in deed from Robert Junkin dated 14 Sept. 1839. All my property to be
equally divided between said daughters after deceased of my beloved
father and mother William and Elizabeth Junkin. Executors: Friends
John McFall and Andrew O. Norris. Dated 1 Oct. 1841.
Wit.: Moses Dean   (Signed) Margarette (X) Junkin
       Edward Yeargin
       John Bennett
       A. B. (X) Harbin

WILL OF JAMES WARNOCK - pp 140-141
To wife Mary her lifetime all negroes: Keziah, Alexander, Jake and
Susan. After death of wife go to daughter Mary. Granddaughter Nancy
Elizabeth Borough. Daughter Matilda Borough. Sons LeRoy and Alfred
Warnock. Executors: Friend Dr. Wm. Anderson and my wife Mary. Dated
24 Aug. 1841.
Wit.: James Bell   (Signed) James Warnock
       Battle Mayfield
       S. R. McFall
Proven 4 Jan. 1842.

WILL OF SAMUEL WARREN - pp 142-144
Of the Parish of St. James, Santee. To Lydia Ann Miller my silver and
plated ware and gold watch. To John Miller her husband of Pendleton,
my wearing apparel and gold sleeve buttons. To Samuel Fenner Warren
Miller of Pendleton my mahogany writing desk, 3 seals and what books I
may have at Soldier's Retreat, Pendleton. Friend Rebekah Verree. To
Warren DuPre 2 book cases at Echaw Grove. Books to College at Columbia.
Books to Samuel Warren White. The use of 30 negroes at Soldier's
Retreat, Pendleton to Lydia Ann Miller her lifetime, then to her children
by John Miller. Slaves: October, August, June, Prince, Cruso, Geddis,
Bacchus, Cesar, William, Pollidore, November, Ajax, Teresa, Camilla,
Sylvia, Magdalen, Hagar (or Hugar), Witty, Binky, Sucky, Little William,
Jack, Matilda, Daphne, Mira, Mary, Nero, Cardenio, Hannah and Rachel.
Plantation of 450 acres near Pendleton Village called Soldier's Retreat
to Lydia Ann Miller, also 5 acres bought of Smith Heaton, also my half
of adjoining mill of which John Miller owns half. After death of Lydia
for the use of all of her children until they come of age, then goes
to Samuel Fenner Warren Miller. Plantation called Ehaw Grove with all
negroes to be sold.
Wit.: R. A. Jerman   (Signed) Sam. Warren
       John S. Palmer
       Sam. Cordes (?)
(no date)
    Charles L. Gaillard sworn in as administrator of estate of Samuel
Warren 28 Dec. 1841.
    Codicil - To Col. Saml. Warren's Will - To my friend Alfred Huger of
Charleston my pair of crutches made with some of the live oak which was
taken out of our Friagete Constitution when Pres. Jackson ordered her
thoroughly repaired, which crutches I put great value on, as I know of
no friend which I think will take more care of or value for them. I
have always supported the Constitution to the best of my ability and now

I am old, weak and infirm, the Constitution supports me.
Wit.: John Robinson, M. D.
       Henry Clark
       A. E. Clark
Proven at same time Chas. L. Gaillard sworn as administrator. 28 Dec.
1841.

WILL OF WILLIAM HARPER - pp 144-145
Wife Nancy. Son John to have negroes Andrew and Juda after wife's death,
also to have Mary and her increase. All my children. Executors: Wife
and son John. Dated 19 Aug. 1841.
Wit.: James Telford   (Signed) William Harper
       James H. Telford
       Joseph Cox.
Proven 25 Jan. 1842.

WILL OF DAVID MARTIN - p 146
Wife Phebe to have land her lifetime or widowhood to raise children,
then sold and divided among all my heirs. Each son to have $60.00
as he comes of age. Daughter Sally Gabbs. Executors: Son James O.
Martin and John Spearman. Dated 4 Jan. 1842.
Wit.: David Whitman   (Signed) David Martin
       David Martin
       John A. Martin
Proven 7 Feb. 1842.

WILL OF SAMUEL MCAFEE - p 147
Wife Sarah. Heirs: Elizabeth Trussel, wife of R. Trussel; Henderson
McAfee; Anny, wife of D. Williamson; Nancy, wife of Joseph Baker;
Washington McAfee and my grandchild Abner Mattison the son of my daughter
Susan and William Mattison. Dated 11 Nov. 1841.
Wit.: Chester Kingsley   (Signed) Samuel (X) McAfee
       John Wright
       John W. Wright
Proven 19 Mar. 1842.

WILL OF DINAH WINTER - pp 147-148
Son-in-law Elisha C. B. Christain and wife Polly. Son Charles Winter.
Son-in-law John Adams and wife Sarah. Son-in-law Thomas J. McKee and
wife Dinah. Son Jeremiah Winter. Son James C. Winter. Daughter
Frances Winter. Executors: James Gaines, Esq. and Rev. Wm. G. Mullinax.
Dated 16 June, 1840.
Wit.: W. W. Knight   (Signed) Sarah Winter
       Amanda Knight
       Susan Symmes
Proven 6 June, 1842.

WILL OF JOHN WARNOCK - pp 149-150
Wife Ellenor to have estate her lifetime, then to children. Daughter
Jane is to have girl Lucy. Daughter Margaret to have boy Jim. Daughter
Frances to have girl Tena. Dated 22 Sept. 1835.
Wit.: Jos. N. Whitner   (Signed) John Warnock
       Wm. R. Sanders
       Robt. A. Archer
Proven 4 July, 1842.

WILL OF EBENEZER BUCHANNAN - p 150
Body to be interred by the side of wife. If I die before the end of
the present year daughter Polly and her daughter Abigail shall have
their support out of my estate until the end of the year. Rest of
estate divided between daughter Polly and my son Samuel Buchannan.
Am giving Polly land to make her equal with my children who have married
and left me. Have given lands to Polly and Samuel for waiting on me in
my affliction. Executors: Neighbor Abner Clinkscales. Dated 26 Feb.
1842.
Wit.: Hubbard Partin   (Signed) Ebenezer (X) Buchannan
       John Stewart
       Saml. M. Buchannan
Proven 5 Sept. 1842.

WILL OF JOHN MOORHEAD - pp 151-153
To wife Sarah the plantation her lifetime or as long as she lives on
it, then goes to sons Major and Ira. Have purchased colt from Widow
Jolly. Estate to be used to maintain family until children are of age.
Daughters Clarissa, Syrenia, Violet and Jane with granddaughter Sarah
Ann, R. Griffin to continue to enjoy priviledges of my house and
family while single and at marriage to have equal part of stock ,
household and kitchen furniture to make them equal with my daughter
Elizabeth Whitmire. Executors: Wife Sarah and son Maxey Moorhead.
Dated 12 Mar. 1836.
Wit.: James Jolly   (Signed) John Moorhead
       Alexander Jolly
       Alexander Moorhead
Proven 16 Sept. 1842.

WILL OF THOMAS WATSON - pp 153-155
Land where I live and adjoining and 3 negroes bought of W. N. Gaillard
to be sold and small farm purchased in Pickens or wherever she and
executors think best to make home and raise children. Not to be sold
her lifetime or widowhood or during minority of my children. Children
to be given good English education. Executors: Wife and dear friend
and brother Joseph Grisham. Dated 19 Sept. 1842.
Wit.: Mary L. Grisham   (Signed) Thomas Watson
       Daniel Wiseman
       Robert A. A. Steele
   Codicil - Dated 8 Nov. 1842. If debts can be paid without selling
farm where I now live, I leave to discretion of executors about selling
and buying smaller farm.
Wit.: Thomas Dickson   (Signed) Thomas (X) Watson
       M. T. Miller
       Delphia Herndeon
   Melinda C. Watson declined to qualify as executrix and asked that her
brother Joseph Grisham act for her.
Proven 21 Nov. 1842.

WILL OF DAVID GUTHRY - pp 155-157
Wife Mary to have whole estate lifetime or widowhood. At her death
to son Benjamin Guthry 100 acres. At death of wife to two daughters
Penelope and Agnes and in trust for their sister Mary Williams, land
where I now live. At death of wife, to son Stephen, 100 acres joining
Murphy. Balance of estate sold. To Obediah Duckworth and wife $1.00
each. To William K. (or R.) Williams and wife $1.00 each. To son
Henry Guthry .50 cents. To son William Guthry $30.00. Balance equally
divided among my five daughters: Temperance Elrod, Milly Elrod, Penne-
lope Guthry, Agnes Guthry and Sarah Flemming. One part to Temperance
and husband Phillip Elrod, principal to be kept by them and divided
among children of Temperance as they come of age. One equal part to
Samuel and Milly Elrod. One part to William and Sarah Flemming. Three
equal parts to Penelope and Agnes Guthry, one third in trust for the
use of Mary Williams. Executors: Sons Nelson and Benjamin Guthry.
Wit.: John M. Moore   (Signed) David Guthrie
       Noah T. Richardson
       Elizabeh Moore
Proven 31 Oct. 1842.

WILL OF FRANCE A. RAGSDALE - pp 157-159
Wife Priscilla to have 1/3 of estate for life. Balance to sons Francis
A. and John F. Ragsdale. At wife's death sons to inherit. Daughter
Elizabeth $100.00 and every other daughter $75.00. Sons to have negro
boy Benjamin. Executor: Son Francis. Dated 13 June, 1841.
Wit.: Halbert Acker   (Signed) Frs. A. Ragsdale
       Peter Walker
       Nicholas (X) Balkham
Proven 13 Jan. 1843.

WILL OF JEREMIAH ELROD - pp 159-160
Wife Sarah and daughter Elizabeth. My daughter Elizabeth is illegiti-
mate, but it is my will that she inherit as though legitimate.
Executors: John P. Amach and friend Dr. William Anderson. Dated 7 May,

1843.
Wit.:   Jeptha Wilson   (Signed)   Jeremiah (X) Elrod
        Hardy Briant
        Abram Martin
Proven 29 May, 1843.

WILL OF JESSE FANT - pp 160-162

To wife Mary land where I now live, 110 acres, joins Moses Chamblee,
Peter King, James King and George W. King, to be used for benefit of
herself and family her lifetime, then she is to dispose of as she sees
fit. Executor: James Major, Sr. Dated 23 Sept. 1842.
Wit.:   Wm. Acker   (Signed)   Jesse Fant
        W. Magee
        Geo. W. King
Proven 1 Sept. 1843.

WILL OF DAVID WATSON - pp 162-163

To son J. J. Watson the Cross Roads Tract whereon he now lives. To
son John D. the Junkin and Harbin tracts when he comes of age, his mother
having the use of it until then. To son David M. the Magee and Gaillard
tracts and part of the Brimer tract, joins Daniel Watson, and the Gentry
tracts, his mother having use of it until her death or marriage. To
son William G. the balance of land, his mother to have use of it until
death or marriage. Rest of estate to wife Mary for life or until she
marries. My daughter Malissa is to have $1000.00 to be placed in hands
of my sons Jackson and John and they care for her. At her death the
money goes back to estate. Each of my other daughters is to have at
the death or marriage of their mother property equal to my sons and if
there is overplus equally divided between my sons and daughters. Dated
6 Aug. 1843.
Wit.:   Geo. Tippen   (Signed)   David Watson
        Geo. Stephenson
        Drury Snipes
Proven 21 Aug. 1843.

WILL OF LEVI CLINKSCALES - pp 163-166

Wife Polly to have 2 plantations known as homeplace and the tract purchased from Bullock, granted originally to Johnson, also 2 men Bob and
Zach for her life or widowhood. She shall support and educate minor
children with common English education such as other children received.
At her death or marriage sold and divided among all my heirs, portion
to which my daughter Terissa Manning may be entitled to be invested as
executors see best for interest of her children. To friend Amaziah
Rice girl Sarah about 7 or 8 for the benefit of my daughter Terissa
Manning and after her death to her children. Rest of estate sold. To
wife Polly 1/3. 2/3 equally divided among all my children. Executors
must charge what I have already given John Clinkscales, Terissa Manning,
Sally Geer, Wm. Franklin Clinkscales, Adaline Martin, Jane Burton,
H. R. Clinkscales. My minor children: Amaziah P. Clinkscales, Christo-
pher C., Levi Newton, Thos. Leftwich and Fleetwood. Executors: Son
Ibzan Clinkscales to be guardian of the 5 minor children. Wife Polly
to serve as executor also. Dated 12 Sept. 1842.
Wit.:   Christopher Orr   (Signed)   Levi Clinkscales
        H. Rice
        Frances M. Kay
    Codicil - Amaziah Rice, my friend, to serve as additional executor.
Dated 31 Mar. 1843.
Wit.:   Frances M. Kay
        M. R. Manning
        A. M. Carpenter
Proven 1 Sept. 1843.

WILL OF WILLIAM COX, SR. - pp 166-168

Property divided between wife Elizabeth and each of my children:
Barbary, John, Polly, Thomas, Elizabeth and William. Son William to
be guardian of Barbary Harper. Executor: Son William Cox. Dated 15
June, 1843.
Wit.:   Ira G. Gambrill   (Signed)   William (X) Cox
        James Cox

97

Airis (?) (X) Cox
Proven 25 Sept. 1843.

WILL OF WILLIAM KEOWN - pp 168-172
Nephew William M. Keown the plantation whereon I now live with tract
on this side of Bowman Ferry Road that is the road leading from Fellow-
ship Church to the Mineral Springs and also my negro woman Rachel with
her 6 children and Nathan, Lewis and William. Also to have tanyard
tools and 3 stills, stock and furniture and rifle gun at John Ables,
and cotton gin and the furniture a James Stevens shop. Cotton at James
Speers. To friend James S. Able 225 acres on Bowman Ferry Road not to
cross Abbeville line. To friend William Kelly as trustee for his son
G. W. Kelly 49 acres on South side Abbeville line, joins tract left to
heirs of Mr. White now belongs to John W. Brown. To nephew George W.
Keown 80 acres where Rody Evans lives, also tract where Wm. M. Keown
lives, joins Gwinn tract and Robeson and tract whereon brother Robert
lives. Also to him negroes Betsy Ann, Adrend and Alexander. Also to
George W., 200 acres where Lennard Gwinn lives at Gwinn's decease, but
Gwinn is to enjoy land his lifetime. To brother Robert Keown, land
where he lives, joins Oliver's land. At his decease to his youngest
child Oliver. To nephew James A. Keown of the State of Georgia, 202½
acres in Henry Co., Ga., drawn by Stephen Carp (?) of Elbert Co., also
40 acres in Cherokee Co. drawn by Mary Haly, widow, of Elbert Co., Ga.
To John Able, Jr., 90 acres where he lives. To friend John Back 254
acres on Senora River bought of Newton White including the Miller tract.
(Note: Believe the name is Black instead of Back. Written Black most
of the time in this will.) Two tracts in Pickens Dist. on Connaross to
John Black as trustee for Reuben Haly. This land was bought of John
Pullem. At Reuben Haly's decease to Henry Casper. To John Black as
trustee for Liza Casey (or Carey ?), $400.00 when she is of age. To
friend Frances A. Young a woman Lizar. To friend Col. A. Bowin, formerly
of Abbeville District, attorney at law, $1500.00. To friend and brother-
in-law Henry Casper two children and $100.00 when collected. To friend
John Morgan $200.00 when collected. To John Black, Wm. M. Keown, Geo.
W. Keown and James S. Able and Henry Casper, balance of all my property.
Executors: John Black, Wm. M. Keown and George W. Keown. John Black is
to collect and pay out all monies that is bequeathed; in the case of the
death of said Black or his refusing to act, the management of business
falls to Wm. M. Kewon. Dated 11 Sept. 1843.
Wit.:   Robt. E. McBride   (Signed) Wm. Keown
        John Abell
        Hiram Burdett
Proven 3 Oct. 1843.

WILL OF JAMES C. GRIFFIN - pp 173-177
Executors: Friends Robt. A. Maxwell, Thomas J. Pickins and Richard
Simpson. Sons William and Joseph N. to have real estate conditioned
that wife Sophia shall have possession for life or widowhood or until
son William is 20 years of age. If sons died without heirs, equally
divided between my children by my first wife. To daughter Sarah Ann
Griffin, slaves Orelius and Synthia. To daughter Margaret Griffin,
slaves Jeffrey and Mary. To daughter Narcissa Griffin, Jane and Rose.
To daughter Rebeccah Griffin slaves Sealey and Mariah. To daughter
Georgeanna Griffin slaves Jackson and Sarah. If daughters die before
marrying or coming of age, equally divided between surviving daughters
by my last wife. Wife to have household furniture. Rest of estate
sold and divided: to sons Clark, James, Goodman, Washington, Larkin;
daughters Patsey Whitefield, Elizabeth Tarrant, Lucy Cobb and Malissa
Cobb. Dated 5 July 1842.
Wit.:   Larkin Griffin   (Signed) James C. Griffin
        Wm. Fant
        Thos. K. Hamilton
   Codicil witnessed by J. V. Shanklin, John B. Ferrell, and Robt. O.
Barr 6 Sept. 1842. Another codicil dated 30 Mar. 1843. Daughter
Margaret has died. Daughter Sarah Ann is now a Robertson.
Wit.:   F. W. Symones
        John Maxwell
        Thomas Hamilton
Proven 6 Oct. 1843.

98

WILL OF MOODY BURT - pp 177-180
To William Toney and David G. Rainey a slave Jack aged 22 in trust for
my daughter Sarah Pope for her lifetime, then to heirs of her body,
also in trust for Sarah Pope lands in Florida where I formerly lived
adjoining lands of Col. Wm. Toney and others. Daughter Martha Goode
and son-in-law Lewelling Goode executors. Dated 6 Aug. 1834.
Wit.: Mathew Burt
       Alex. Evans
       Isaac R. Towers
   Codicil - Daughter Martha H. Goode and husband are both deceased.
Their part to their 4 children: Sarah Goode, Martha Goode, Thomas Goode,
and John Goode. Appoint Thomas Payne and John Maxwell executors. Dated
27 Mar. 1841.
Wit.: Jesse McKinny
       Wm. Steele
       Micajah Anderson
Proven 6 Nov. 1843.

WILL OF ISAAC ELROD - pp 180-182
Son George to maintain my wife Nancy. Son Adam. Three daughters:
Leviny, Sarah and Mary. Deceased daughters: Rachel and Elizabeth.
Executors: Son Adam. Dated 23 May, 1843.
Wit.: W. E. Welborn   (Signed) Isaac Elrod
       T. M. Welborn
       Lemuel H. Welborn
Proven 20 Nov. 1843.

WILL OF HUGH MCLINN - pp 182-184
Daughter Manerva Jane. Sons Pickens, John and James Gamble. Manerva
Jane's husband Lewis Christopher. Daughter Mary Eliza. Wife is deceased.
Executors: Sons John and Pickens. Dated 14 Feb. 1843.
Wit.: T. J. Shackelford   (Signed) Hugh Mecklin
       John Barrett
       David Humphreys
Proven 15 Dec. 1843.

WILL OF JOSEPH MAJOR - pp 184-185
Wife Nancy and my only daughter Mary Elizabeth to have negroes Harriet
and Caroline and notes on Nathan C. Rochester and Samuel Millwee. Dated
14 Apr. 1844.
Wit.: P. McPhail   (Signed) Joseph M. (X) Major
       N. T. Smith
       J. W. Major

WILL OF WILLIAM FORSYTHE - pp 185-187
As much of land as cannot be cultivated is to be rented out until the
youngest child is of age, then sold. Wife Cinthia to receive one third
for life or until she marries, then divided among my children. All my
three children: Mary Harrenton Forsythe, Sarah Morgan Forsythe and
Warren Davis Forsythe. Executor: Wife Cynthia. Dated 22 Apr. 1844.
Wit.: Archibald Todd   (Sgined) William (X) Forsythe
       Herbert Hammond
       Jesse George
   Codicil - 22 Apr. 1844. Friend William Magee to be executor in ad-
dition to wife.
Wit.: Gideon W. Land
       John Moore
       Dycy Duckworth
Proven 3 June, 1844.

WILL OF JAMES MCCOY, SR. - pp 188-189
Wife Quffy (Luffy ?). Have given to Peggy, Dorcas, Catharine, James
and Samuel what I intend for them to have. My 3 other children: Ephraim,
Kelsey C., and Sally. Son James to have land where I live joining Todd's
line to Brown's Road, thence to brother Samuel's line, including house
where James now lives. Balance of home tract at wife's death to sons
Ephraim and Kelsey and Samuel may have privilege of settling on the
piece of land that me and my wife inherited from her father Abraham
Mayfield to use and cultivate until death of my wife. Daughter Sally

99

is under age. Three oldest daughters Peggy, Dorcas and Katharine receive amount that may arise out of sale of their grandfather Mayfield's land that now Peggy Mayfield has the use of. Executor: James McCoy, Jr. Dated 20 July, 1843. Proven 6 May, 1844.
Wit.: J. L. Todd   (Signed) James McCoy
      Harrison Latimer
      Wm. Magee
Proven 6 May, 1844.

WILL OF ANDREW ROBERT TODD, SR. - pp 190-192
Land sold except tract where David Gordon lives called the Jarret tract and other tract where James Jarret lives called the Old McDaniel tract that I bought from Wm. M. McKee. The Jarret tract I will to heirs that now is and that will come from the body of my daughter Jane M. Gordon, contains 230 acres. Jane M. is to live on the land her lifetime. McDaniel tract to son-in-law James Martin. To my wife Olive 1/3 of estate. Balance of equal share coming to James Martin beside the land be given to his heirs, all heirs that come from my daughter Mary Ann Martin's body, and that money be put to interest and paid to heirs as they become 21. Andrew Todd's son, my grandson, Robert Todd, is not 21. Grandson Robert C. Presley, the son of David and Elizabeth Presley, is under 21. Grandson Robert Gordon, son of David and Jane M. Gordon, is under 21. Grandson Robert Todd Branyan, son of Henry and Margaret Branyan, is under 21. Brother John Todd that is in Ireland or on his way from there to the United States I give $400.00 when he arrives. Sons Andrew and John Todd and son-in-law Henry Branyan and David A. Presley. Executor: Son Andrew Todd. Dated 13 June, 1844.
Wit.: James Herron   (Signed) Robert Todd
      Geo. W. Long
      John McPhail
      Nathan McAlister
Proven 26 July, 1844.

WILL OF ELISHA KELLY - pp 192-194
Wife Elizabeth all estate for lifetime or widowhood. At her death or marriage executors make distribution among those of my children that has not received their part so as to make them equal with those that has received their part. The remainder equally divided among all my children. If any child leave my wife while she is a widow she should give them their part if it can be done without injuring herself. Executors: Wife Elizabeth and Alford and Allen Kelly. Dated 10 Feb. 1838.
Wit.: Josiah W. Cobb   (Signed) Elisha Kelly
      Williamson Breazeale
      Hugh Poor
Proven 8 Nov. 1844.

WILL OF GEORGE BROWN - pp 194-195
Wife Rachel to have estate her lifetime, then sold. Sons Isham, Jesse, Elijah. Elijah to manage affairs and if anything is left divided among all my heirs. Dated 19 July, 1844.
Wit.: James Hembree, Sr.   (Signed) George (X) Brown
      Daniel Gentry
      James Hembree, Jr.
Proven 13 Jan. 1845.

WILL OF SAMUEL EMERSON - pp 196-197
Wife to have child's part. Children: James Emerson, Mary McLellan, Elizabeth Carpenter, Rosey Ann McLellan, John A. Emerson. Grandson Joseph Yancy Hall. Eldest daughter Margaret Clark. Executor: Son James. Dated 16 July, 1841.
Wit.: Z. Hall   (Signed) Samuel (X) Emerson
      Conrad Wakefield
      Jacob Sligh (or High ?)
Proven 24 Jan. 1845.

WILL OF ROBERT GORDON - pp 197-199
Wife Agnes. Son John. Son James. Son Robert. Daughter Eliza to have negro girl Rose. Daughter Mary Caroline to have negro girl Julia. Son Robert to have boy George at death of his mother. Son John at mother's death to have boy Eli. To Robert Alexander Morehead (?), my infant

grandson, a negro child Elias. Negroes Edmund, Line and Lucy to remain
with widow. To Frances Crawford, a negro girl Martha. To William
Crawford $200.00 at his grandmother's death or marriage. My old servant
negro Cherry (?) shall live with any of my children that she may wish
after my death. Executors: Son James and Alexander Evans. Dated 15
Apr. 1844.
Wit.: John Creswell   (Signed) R. Gordon
       Elijah Webb
       Alfred Holt
Proven 27 Jan. 1845.

WILL OF GEORGE STANTON - pp 199-200
Wife Lurance (?) to have estate for lifetime or widowhood. At her death
equally divided among the whole of my children, my grandchildren, the
children of my daughter Elizabeth Payne, deceased, to have their mother's
part. Executor: Caleb Payne. Dated 4 Aug. 1837.
Wit.: James Douthit   (Signed) George (X) Stanton
       Berry Durham
       Anderson Durham
Proven 21 Apr. 1845.

WILL OF JOHN HARPER - pp 200-202
Wife Martha. Three daughters now with us, namely Mary, Zilpha, and
Martha, to remain with their mother. If they marry they are to receive
their part, as much as has been given those already married. Oldest
daughter Nancy. Estate to be sold after death of wife and unmarried
daughters and equally divided among all my children. Executors: Sons
John and Thomas and daughter Mary. Dated 15 Nov. 1844.
Wit.: Alfred Kelly   (Signed) John Harper
       Jasper Williams
       Lewis Cooly
Proven 2 May, 1845.

WILL OF WILLIAM COX - pp 202-204
Wife Frances to have estate her lifetime or widowhood. Then to son
William David Cox the real estate after Jesse Cox has 100 acres. Two
sons Reuben Berry and Thomas Cox. Daughter to have girl Anny. Daughter
Hulda. After death or marriage of wife estate is to be sold and divided
among all my children both male and female to have an equal share.
Executors: Wife Frances and eldest son Reuben B. Dated 10 Feb. 1845.
Wit.: David R. Reese   (Signed) William Cox
       R. N. Wright
       Wm. F. Clinkscales
Proven 5 May, 1845.

WILL OF JOHN HARRIS, ESQ. - pp 204-205
Son Andrew. Heirs of son John deceased. Son Nathaniel. Son Ezekial.
Son Thomas Handy. Son Joseph Pickens. Son Benjamin to have boy Adam.
Daughter Rebecca Reese is to have girl Clarisse. Daughter Mary H. Noble
is to have girl Jane. Daughter Eliza C. Burrus is to have girl Nan.
Wife Mary is to have girl Phillis and the services of woman Sarah her
lifetime. Remainder of estate divided equally among all my children.
Sons Joseph and Nathaniel to act as trustees for wife. Executors:
Sons Nathaniel, Joseph P. and Benjamin. Dated 17 Feb. 1845.
Wit.: Charles Bruce   (Signed) John Harris
       Wm. S. Woolbright
       Handy H. Bruce
Proven 23 June, 1845.

WILL OF JOHN INGRAM - p 206
Wife Delila to have all estate unless she marries, then divided equally
between wife and heirs of her body that has arrived from her marriage
with me. Executor: Peter Johnson. Dated 21 Aug. 1845.
Wit.: M. B. Williams   (Signed) John (X) Ingram
       Jas. T. Wilson
       George G. Elrod
Proven 8 Sept. 1845.

WILL OF THOMAS ELROD - pp 207-208
Wife Mary to have estate her lifetime or widowhood, then sold and

divided among our children. Ex.: Friend Jesse W. Norris. Dated: 6 Sept.
1845. Pr. 26 Sept. 1845.   (Signed) Thomas Elrod
Wit: M. B. Williams
      Jas. T. Wilson
      George G. Elrod

WILL OF WILLIAM TRIPP - pp 212-213
Wife Ann. Son Harvey. All my children. Executors: Wife and son
Harvey. Dated 2 Oct. 1845.
Wit.: Henry Cobb   (Signed) William Tripp
       John Gambrell
       Robt. Tarrant
Proven 7 Nov. 1845.

WILL OF JOSEPH CLARK - pp 213-215
Wife Nancy. Joseph Clark Carpenter (minor son of Alfred M. Carpenter).
Katharine S. Carpenter, wife of Alfred. Monies due me from Amaziah
Rice. To friend Alfred M. Carpenter land near Cumberland River in
Sumner Co., Tenn. Executor: Friend Alfred M. Carpenter. Dated 27 Oct.
1845.
Wit.: P. D. Major   (Signed) Joseph Clark
       A. T. Carpenter
       Herbert Hammond
Proven 1 Dec. 1845.

WILL OF WESLEY EARP - pp 215-217
To wife Mourning a negro Sarah aged 9. Son-in-law James M. Henderson
(?). Friend Henry Tyler of the State of Georgia. My mother Mrs. Jane
Earp. Two orphan children William Joshua Reed and James Lany Reed.
If Mourning marries all estate sold and divided as follows: 1 moiety
to said Mourning. The other moiety to be divided between my brothers-
in-law and sisters. If Mourning dies my widow, one moiety to my brothers-
in-law and sisters and the other moiety divided between the brothers
and sisters of Mourning. Executors: Friends Francis Gaines and William
Glenn. Dated 2 Aug. 1845.
Wit.: Jas. M. McLees   (Signed) Wesley Earp
       Moses W. Hazlitt
       A. Campbell
Proven 1 Dec. 1845.

WILL OF GEORGE CRYMES - pp 217-220
Greenville District. Wife Nancy to have land in Anderson lately pur-
chased of Cooper Duckworth on Big Creek, also slaves Peter, Eliza and
Washington. To Philip C. Lester and Robert D. Crymes in trust for
Edward (or Edmund ?) Crymes during his lifetime, land in Laurens County
on which Edward (Edmund ?) now lives. After his death land sold and
divided between the children of said Edmond. Children of deceased son
William M. Crymes. Children of deceased daughter Mary Cureton. Children
of my son John Crymes. Son Robert. Land to Robert Crymes and Philip
C. Lester in trust for Benjamin F. Crymes and after Benjamin's death
to his children. To William Smithson in trust for Elizabeth Smithson
and after her death to her children. To daughter Nancy Lester. Children
of Thomas Crymes deceased. Balance of estate equally divided between
Elizabeth Smithson, Nancy Lester, Robt. D. Crymes, the children of
B. F. Crymes and the children of Thomas Crymes deceased. Executors:
Philip C. Lester and Robt. D. Crymes. Dated 6 Dec. 1844.
Wit.: Josiah Kilgore   (Signed) George Crymes
       Daniel Wood
       John Kershaw
Proven 10 Dec. 1845.
     Wilborn Duckworth, Esq., made oath on 17 Dec. 1845, that he was with
George Crymes in one of the months of the summer or fall of 1845, and
heard him say he had erased the name of Robert D. Crymes out of his will
and afterwards had become satisfied for him to be executor and inserted
the name where it was erased. Duckworth had been requested to write a
new will, but George Crymes did not execute the one written by him.

WILL OF RICHARD M.LEWIS - pp 220-222
Of Cherokee Co., Ala. Executors to get 3 or 4 of my neighbors to
appraise my estate. Executors may dispose of property as they see
fit to benefit my wife and educate my ____?____ . If my wife or
daughter should marry or die executors make division according to the
act of the state which provides for the division of estates. I direct
that my dear Miss Sarah B. Lewis and my friend Harrison Clark be executors. My friend Jonathan B. Lewis of Anderson District to control
accounts and notes in my favor. Dated 20 Sept. 1843. On 4 March,
1844 in Cherokee Co., Ala. clerk certified this to be true copy of
will.
Wit.:   Waddy Thompson   (Signed) R. M. Lewis
        James M. Gambrell
        Richard Barry
Filed in Anderson Co. in 1846.

WILL OF JAMES ERSKINE, SR. - pp 222-224
Dated 7 Feb. 1845. Wife Nancy. Executors: Sons William and James
Erskine. Daughter Martha Dobbins. Daughter Nancy Lowe. Daughter
Polly Shirley. James E. Shirley my grandson and the son of my daughter
Margret is under the age of 21. Appoint Aaron Shirley his father to
be his guardian. I reserve one square acre for a graveyard. Plantation
to be divided in three equal parts and either of my sons William, James,
John or Thomas may chose one. Daughters and grandson to receive $300.00
each. My five sons: Thomas, Hugh, William, James and John.
Wit.:   Wm. Carlile   (Signed) James Erskine
        J. L. Todd
        James Major
Proven 6 Apr. 1846.

WILL OF ANDERSON BURNS - pp 224-225
Wife Leah to have estate her lifetime for her benefit and benefit of
our children. At her death estate sold and equal division made except
that sons none of whom had the advantages of an education shall each
have $100.00 more and each daughter now under age of 10 yrs. (3) shall
have $50.00 more. If as I expect another is added to the number, either
boy or girl, to be included in provisions. Executors: Wife and her
brother James A. Doyle. Dated 26 Jan. 1846.
Wit.:   F. W. Symmes   (Signed) A. Burns
        John Maxwell
        Wm. Fant
Proven 6 June, 1846.

WILL OF WILLIAM NEWELL - pp 225-226
Two daughters Susannah and Jincy and my son Izaah each to have $100.00
after which I desire estate equally divided between my wife Jincy and
sons William, John, Thomas, Reuben, Newton, Samuel, Izaah and my daugh-
ters Hannah, Susannah and Jincy. Executors: Wife Jincy and son William.
Dated 2 June, 1843.
Wit.:   John M. Hamilton   (Signed) William (X) Newell
        John M. Thomson
        Luke Hamilton
Proven 5 Oct. 1846.

WILL OF JAMES MCCARLEY - pp 227-228
To daughter Rachel a negro girl and boy Eliza and Jefferson. If she
dies without heirs negroes to my son Hugh W. Sons William, John and
Elias. Daughter Rachel is unmarried. To son Hugh, a negro woman Rachel.
To Elias, a girl Margaret. Daughter Mary Ann Henderson (?). Executors:
Sons Elias and Hugh. Dated 5 Sept. 1845.
Wit.:   John McFall   (Signed) James McCarley
        James Todd
        Jno. C. Griffin
Proven 9 Oct. 1846.

WILL OF SAMUEL CUNNINGHAM - pp 228-230
Daughter Catharine Cunningham. Son Thomas. To daughter Catharine a
woman Rachel and a man Jim. All my children. My grandson Samuel C.
Humphres. Grandson Samuel Lockhart. My other children: Margaret

Williams, Jane Williams, Rebecca Humphres, Lucinda Lockhart, and the
heirs of deceased daughters Polly Wilks and Dorcas Gray. Executors:
Son Thomas and Dr. M. J. Lockhart. Dated 3 Sept. 1843.
Wit.: David Simpson   (Signed) Saml. Cunningham
       Jas. J. McLees
       David Sadler, Jr.
Proven 16 Nov. 1846.

WILL OF THOMAS SPRAY - pp 230-232
Plantation of 262 acres on Little Broadway Creek joining land of S. J.
Hammonds, Wm. Davis, H.H. Wardlaw and John Knox to be for the use of
my nephew John Leavell and wife Peggy Leavell their lifetimes and at
their decease to their children, each to share alike except Richard
Leavell. He is not to receive any part.
   Beloved friend and adopted daughter and daughter of John and Peggy
Leavell, Elizabeth. Nephew and niece John and Peggy Leavell. Executor:
John Leavell. Dated 24 Apr. 1844.
Wit.: Wm. Magee   (Signed) Thomas (X) Spray
       Wm. Holmes
       Ann Amanda Holmes
Proven 2 Jan. 1847.

WILL OF NIMROD SMITH - pp 233-234
All to wife Jane H. Smith and young son John Gaston Smith who is under
21. Executors: Sons William and Wyatt Smith. Dated 30 July, 1846.
Wit.: J. T. Whitefield   (Signed) Nimrod Smith
       Joseph Taylor
       Robert Smith
Proven 4 Jan. 1847.

WILL OF CHARLES BENNETT, SR. - pp 235-236
Nephew Charmes M. Bennett son of my brother Thomas to have a negro boy
Wade, a woman Dolly and land whereon I now live. Executor: Nephew
Charles M. Dated 17 Oct. 1840.
Wit.: John Harper, Jr.   (Signed) Charles Bennett
       Micajah B. Williams
       John Wilson
Proven 1 Feb. 1847.

WILL OF JOHN FRETWELL - pp 236-237
To each child of my daughter Polly Ann Gentry $50.00, also to Polly
Ann Gentry $50.00. To daughter Elizabeth Fretwell a negro girl Eller
and a boy George. If Elizabeth should die the negroes go to two sons
Joseph Y. and Bry. Fretwell. To my two grandchildren by my daughter-
in-law the wife of Bry Fretwell, Martha and Josephine, I give a negro
girl Rachael. To granddaughter Caroline Matilda the daughter of Joseph
Y. Fretwell, a negro boy Isaac. My three children: Joseph Y., Bry and
Elizabeth. Executor: Son Joseph Y. Dated 11 July, 1847.
Wit.: A. P. Carter   (Signed) John (X) Fretwell
       Elijah Webb
       John W. B. Skelton
Proven 2 Aug. 1847.

WILL OF FLEMMING WALTERS - pp 238-239
Wife Rebecca. All my children: Ibzan, Williford and Macklin and son-
in-law Willis Stacks. Macklin is in possession of a tract of land in
Thomas Co., Ga. To be returned to estate and divided with other chil-
dren. Executors: Wife Rebecca and son Ibzan. Dated 27 Sept. 1847.
Wit.: A. Reid   (Signed) Flemming Walters
       Wm. Obriant
       R. H. Reid
Proven 2 Aug. 1847.

WILL OF ASA CLINKSCALES - pp 240-241
Wards John and Katharine Kay. Land bought of my father-in-law's estate.
Wife Nancy, to raise and educate our children. My six children: William
Berry, Robert Marshall, Silers Wesley, Alexander Evins, Benjamin Thaddeus,
Abner Lewis. Dated 23 Oct. 1847.
Wit.: Amariah Felton   (Signed) Asa Clinkscales

Mary Clement
Elizabeth Hall
Proven 5 Nov. 1847.

WILL OF JAMES WATSON - pp 242-244
To wife Mary a negro woman Tilda her lifetime and then to son Andrew.
To son Andrew P. land whereon I now live on 26 Mile Creek, being 400
acres, and negroes Joe and Adam. He is to support his mother. To
children of my deceased daughter Cynthia Bennet a house worth $65.00.
To sons Samuel and Andrew P. in trust for my daughter Polly Oliver a
negro woman Letty for her lifetime unless she becomes again a single
woman, then the negro in fee simple to her. Sons Robert and James.
Rest of estate divided in eight parts. To sons Samuel, Robert A.,
James M. and Andrew P. one share each. To the children of my deceased
daughter Cynthia Bennett one share. To Andrew P. and Samuel in trust
the remaining three shares. One of each for the use and benefit of my
married daughters Eliza Berry, Sarah Ann Couch and Polly Oliver. If
eigher daughter becomes single again the share at once to them absolutely.
Executors: Sons Samuel and Andrew P. Dated 4 Jan. 1844.
Wit.:   John P. Benson   (Signed) James Watson
        Jno. B. Wynne
        J. N. Whitner
Proven 22 Nov. 1847.

WILL OF HENRY PARIS - pp 245-247
Of Greenville Dist., Farmer. To son William a negro girl Caroline.
Negro girl Suffrona and her four children and their increase to remain
with my daughter Lurany Jenkins her lifetime and at her death to be
equally divided between my daughter Elander Cobb and my son William Paris
or their heirs. Negro girl Ann to be left in the hands of Amaziah B.
Cobb as trustee for my daughter Mary Mauldin and that she be hired out
and proceeds apply to the support of my daughter. After her death to
be equally divided between my daughter Elander Cobb and my son William
Paris. Daughter Nancy Paris is to live with my daughter Elander Cobb
and slaves Betsy and her children Jess, Susannah, Mary, Jenny and Matilda
to remain with her. At her death to my daughter Elander Cobb.
    To my granddaughter Elizabeth Cobb a negro girl Salley. To my grand-
daughter Mary Paris, daughter of William Paris, a negro girl Harriet.
    Plantation and a negro boy Hence are to be sold. To son Moses a
negro girl Emily and her two children, negro Frank and infant not named.
To son John Paris $5.00. To daughter Elizabeth Gordon $1.00. Executor:
Grandson Amaziah B. Cobb. Dated 28 Apr. 1843.
Wit.:   W. P. Turpin   (Signed) Henry Paris
        Charles Lark
        Joseph Powell
Proven 26 Nov. 1847.

WILL OF WILLIAM BEATY - pp 247-249
Land whereon I now live divided in two tracts. It lies on Market Road
leading to GoodHope Church and contains 370 acres. Part to son John and
part to son Elias. To son John a negro boy Jacob and girl Jane. To
son Elias a negro boy Andrew and a girl Esther. To daughter Martha
Beaty a negro girl Isabella. To daughter Margaret Spearman a negro girl
Sarah. To sons John and Elias Beaty a negro girl Harriet in trust for
my daughter Elizabeth McCullough and in no way to be controlled by her
husband Daniel McCullough and after her death to be divided between her
children.
    To wife Ann for her lifetime a negro man March, a woman Rebecca and
a child Julia. After her death divided among my children. Executors:
Sons John and Elias. Dated 23 Feb. 1844.
Wit.:   W. Hattan   (Signed) Wm. Beaty
        Dejarnant Tucker
        Charles Bowie
Proven 27 Dec. 1847.

WILL OF JEREMIAH W. RODGERS - pp 250-252
Wife Elizabeth to have negroes Sam, Isabel and Melinda. To daughter
Anna negroes Rhina, Margaret and Hall. To daughter Sarah negroes Emeline,
Warren and Ben. To son Jacob negroes Whit, Butler and Molsie. To

daughter Ruthy negroes Bill, Frances and Patsey. To daughter Hester
Jane negroes Winny, Rose and Noah. If any of negroes should die or
become incapable of service previous to the marriage of any of the above
legatees they are at liberty to choose another negro. Balance of negroes
to remain with my wife. Land whereon I now live on Beaverdam Creek to
go to wife her lifetime or widowhood and then to son Jacob. Younger
children are to be raised and educated. To Mary Owens whom I believe
to be my illegitimate daughter $300.00. (This crossed out.)
   To Robert Owens whom I believe to be my illegitimate son land on
northeast Side Beaverdam Creek. To Robert Owens a negro boy Charles,
(this crossed out). To Piney Owens and to Dicy Rogers one negro each
which I have heretofore delivered to them. Executors: Wife Elizabeth
and friend John P. Rodgers. Dated 1 Apr. 1847.
Wit.: Dr. Wm. Anderson   (Signed) J. W. Rodgers
      R. H. Anderson
      James J. Barron
   Welborn Duckworth made oath that the clauses which appear crossed
out were made by Joseph Cox, Esq. in his presence by the direction of
J. W. Rodgers.
Proven 15 Jan. 1848.

WILL OF MARTHA BEATY - pp 253-254
My estate to Rev. David Humphreys in trust for the education of pious
young men for the ministry in the Presbyterian Church under charge of
the South Carolina Presbytery. Rev. Humphreys is to be sole executor.
Dated 1 Mar. 1847.
Wit.: Thos. O. Hill   (Signed) Martha (X) Beaty
      Jinny (X) McCearly
      Arch. Simpson
Proven 10 Mar. 1848.

WILL OF JOHN LAURENS NORTH - pp 255-256
Of Pendleton, Planter. Wife Eliza Elliott North to have all estate.
She is sole executrix. Dated 20 Jan. 1826.
Wit.: John E. Calhoun   (Signed) John L. North
      Jno. G. North
      Joseph N. Whitner
Proven 24 Mar. 1848.

WILL OF JAMES W. KAY - pp 256-258
Wife Susannah to remain on land until youngest child is 21 or marries.
At her death or marriage estate sold and divided between my children.
Executors: Wife Susannah and oldest son James E. If either should die
the next oldest son is to act as executor. Dated 16 Dec. 1847.
Wit.: Albert W. Kay   (Signed) James W. Kay
      James L. Brock
      R. N. Wright
Proven 3 Apr. 1848.

WILL OF ELIZABETH MCPHERSON - pp 258-259
My several children: William, Phebe, Nancy, John, Selina, Ellener,
Elijah to each 1/12 of my estate. To my grandchildren the heirs of my
daughter Sarah Brown 1/12. To my grandchildren the heirs of my son
Elisha, 1/12. To my granchildren, heirs of my daughter Mary, 1/12.
To daughter Malindah 1/12, not for her husband. To daughter Lucy 1/12
to be kept for her and not her husband. Executors: Daughter Malindah
McGee and Jane Moore. (Will not dated.)
Wit.: Saml. Lovinggood   (Signed) Elizabeth McPherson
      John T. Shehane
      James Gunnin (?)
   Witnesses swore on 9 June, 1848 that they saw Elizabeth sign her name
they believe on 6 June, 1843.

WILL OF BLACKMAN BURTON - pp 260-261
Wife Jane Y. to have plantation and negroes Julias and Ned her lifetime.
To my children: Lucinda Spaulding, Peyton T. Burton, Louisa McCullough,
Henry J. Burton, Adelia Hampton and Blackman L. Burton I have already
given their part. Children at home: Adeline, Jane W., German and James
D. Burton. Executors: Friend A. G. Latimer and my son German Burton.

Dated 25 Feb. 1848.
Wit.: John Milford   (Signed) Blackman Burton
       Thos. Simpson
       James McKee
Proven 15 Aug. 1848.

WILL OF NANCY GRISSUP - pp 261-262
Dated 17 May, 1848. To colored woman Rebecca Stewart all household and
kitchen furniture and stock and all other things which belong to me.
Wit.: Kelly Sullivan   (Signed) Nancy (X) Grissup
       Robt. B. Alexander
       Wm. M. Aston
Proven 27 Sept. 1848.

WILL OF JOHN SMITH - pp 263-264
Son-in-law James D. Simes. Son-in-law Levi B. Bowman who married my
daughter Talith deceased. Son Sidney. Son-in-law Benjamin M. Smith.
Son John C. Smith. Daughter Mary Ann Smith. Son Andrew M. Smith.
Son James D. Smith. Wife Elizabeth shall have all property she was
possessed of when I married her. Executor: Son James D. Smith.
Dated 26 Dec. 1840.
Wit.: Wm. Mullikin   (Signed) John Smith
       Jacob Pickle
       Benj. Mullikin
Proven 24 Oct. 1848.

WILL OF DAVID RICHARDSON - pp 265-266
All to wife Esther her lifetime, then to daughter Esther M. Amick and
son A. W. Richardson. Executor: John D. Amick. Dated 4 Mar. 1848.
Wit.: Elijah Webb   (Signed) D. Richardson
       John Martin
       Jesse Gray
Proven 15 Dec. 1848.

WILL OF SAMUEL MCCOY, SR. - pp 266-268
Wife Polly to have estate for her use and benefit of those of my children
that may live with her. To be sold at her death and divided among each
of my children. Executors: Wm. Magee, Michael Magee and Strother Kay
or either of them. Dated 28 Sept. 1843.
Wit.: Wm. Magee   (Signed) Samuel McCoy
       Thos. L. Rice
       Harrison Latimer
Proven 1 Jan. 1849.

WILL OF WILLIAM SMITH - pp 268-269
Wife Mariah along with Joseph Cox and my son Daniel to be executors.
Wife to live on plantation for lifetime or widowhood. If wife marries
to be sold and wife to have 1/3 and as the children come of age they
receive two slaves. All property divided equally between my children.
Dated 22 Feb. 1849.
Wit.: Wyatt Smith   (Signed) William Smith
       J. L. Wilson
       Harvin Vandiver
Proven 26 Mar. 1849.

WILL OF NANCY BROWN - pp 270-272
Widow. Children of my daughter Artimasa now deceased, not of age.
Children of my deceased daughter Lucretia not of age. Son Ovid P. Brown.
Son George R. has the care of my person and estate in my old age and
last sickness, and is to have negro woman Sally and her oldest child
Elep a boy. Also to George a negro girl Harriet in trust for little
granddaughter Edney Emeline Brown the youngest daughter of George R.
Brown by his first wife Edney. Executor: Son George R. Dated 16 Dec.
1844.
Wit.: Enoch Breazeale   (Signed) Nancy Brown
       Wm. Smith, Jr.
       J. P. Reid (also spelled Reed)
Proven 27 Mar. 1849.

WILL OF NANCY HALL - pp 272-275
Land whereon I now live, 200 acres, the larger part received as my share
out of the estate of my late husband, William Hall, deceased. Negroes
to be sold and divided in six shares. One share to son James Eugine
Hall. Share to son Edward M. Hall. Share to daughter Susannah M. Hall.
Share to Harriet M. Martin. Share to my grandchildren Elvira Geer,
Marthilia Geer and George Alexander Evins Geer, the children of my
deceased daughter Sarah Ann Geer. They are to receive their share as
they arrive at age of 21 or marry. The remaining share to my daughter
Susannah Hall in trust for my son William Burt Hall his lifetime and then
to the heirs of his body. No executors named. Dated 22 Jan. 1846.
Wit.: James L. Orr   (Signed) Nancy Hall
      James King
      Alfred Fant
Proven 15 June, 1849.

WILL OF HUBBARD PARTAIN - pp 275-277
Dated 1 May, 1849. Wife Elizabeth. Note on James Wiley. Three children:
Luisa, John, Elizabeth. Daughter Jincy Evans. John Henley Partain.
Son John Jennings Partain. Daughter Elizabeth's husband, Lemuel Buchanan.
Executors: Kelly Sullivan and son John J. Partain.
Wit.: John C. Tucker   (Signed) Hubbard Partain
      Mark W. Havird (Harird ?)
      John W. Stuart
Proven 9 July, 1849.

WILL OF JAMES MATTISON - pp 278-280
To son William 300 acres whereon he now lives, also the Talton Lee tract
of 140 acres, also $50.00 to pay for his lot at Anderson Village. To
the three children of my son James deceased after his widow's 1/3 taken
of which is 140 acres, the other 300 acres I gave my son James to be
divided among his children. Land is on Rocky River.
     To son Daniel 640 acres and two half acre lots in Anderson Village,
also the French tract joining him, and also half the profits from the
store, also profits from saw and grist mills, also interest in four
negroes which he has bought.
     To son Wyatt Mattison in trust the plantation where I now live with
mills and mill tract, also the Nimrod Smith tract and the William Gambrell
tract, also the Shaw tract for life, then to his children.
     To daughters Malinda Townsen, Elizabeth Carpenter, Lettice Gambrell,
Mariah Smith and Mary Cox the balance of my land consisting of the
Flowers tract, the Williamson tract, the Round Meadow tract and Townsen
tract, to equally divided between them and to each of them one negro girl.
Personal property of 25 negores, tools, furniture and my one half of the
store sold and equally divided between my children. Executors: Sons
William and Daniel. Dated 30 Jan. 1848.
Wit.: Wm. P. Martin   (Signed) James (X) Mattison
      Jas. F. Mattison
      James M. Carpenter
Proven 30 July, 1849.

WILL OF REV. JAMES HEMBREE - pp 281-283
Black woman Peggy and her son Grief Presley have the liberty to choose
their master and that one of executors give them a pass for 5 days to
look out a person of their choice and as Peggy is near 47 years old and
not very sound and Grief will be 12 on the 25th of Aug. next I value
them myself the purchaser to give $600.00 to have same credit and terms
as those who buy at my public sale. Balance of estate sold. I have no
claim to anything in Peggy's house except the cotton wheel and cards
and old table.
     Four of my children has been advanced above the rest: John and James
Hembree and Winney Heaton and Polley Bowen. Son Amariah Hembree. Job
Rainwater who married my daughter Hephzibah and his daughter Betsey
Lavina my granddaughter. Daughter Sally Day lives in Texas. Executors:
Sons John and James Hembree. Son James to be guardian for his mother
as she is not capable of trading and doing business for herself. Dated
5 May, 1847.
Wit.: Jno. C. Griffin   (Signed) James Hembree, Sr.
      C. D. Gaillard
      J. T. Whitefield
Proven 20 Aug. 1849.

108

WILL OF JOHN WILSON - pp 283-285
Wife Elizabeth whole estate her lifetime. She is to reside with any of
my children she may choose and her expenses paid out of estate. Negro
Silvia and her present and future increase to my 4 youngest children.
Namely William D. Wilson, Martha Durham, Betsey Gambrell and Nancy
Sutton. All my children. Minerva Jane Copeland to receive equal share
which would have given to my deceased daughter Mary C. Copeland.
Executors: Sons-in-law Reid Gambrell and John P. Sitton. Dated 2 Feb.
1848.
Wit.:   Jno. Watson, Sr.   (Signed) John Wilson
        R. E. Blassingame
        Allen O. Merritt
Proven 1 Oct. 1849.

WILL OF JAMES MATTISON, SR. - pp 285-288
This will recorded on pages 278-280 also.

WILL OF JOSEPH HIPPS, SR. - pp 288-290
Granddaughter Rebecca Hipps, daughter of Elizabeth and Joseph Hipps.
Son James Hipps. Daughter Anna Simpson, wife of Mathew Simpson. Daugh-
ter Sarah Neighbors, wife of William Neighbors. Son Joseph Hipps.
Daughter Rutha McInteer, wife of Samuel McInteer. To grandson Abner Hipps,
son of Elizabeth and Joseph Hipps. Grandson Joseph Hipps, son of Eliz-
abeth and Joseph Hipps. Grandson James Hipps, son of Elizabeth and
Joseph. Grandson John Hipps, son of Elizabeth and Joseph. My son James
Hipps. Executor: Joseph Hipps. Dated 25 Mar. 1848.
Wit.:   James Cleghorn   (Signed) Joseph (X) Hipps
        Lewis Sherrill
        Robert Scott
    Admitted to probate in Cass Co., Ga. Joseph Hipps obtained letters
testamentary. 9 Jan. 1850.

WILL OF SUSANNAH MCMAHAN - pp 290-292
To Alexander McKinney's son Robert Phelix McKinney 140 a. whereon I now
live after my decease or at his becoming 21. To Samuel Van McKinney a
mare. To James Oliver McKinney a horse. To Robert Phelix McKinney a
mule. To Samuel Van McKinney, James Oliver McKinney and Robert Phelix
McKinney a negro girl Adaline and her increase divided amongst them.
To Peter Franklin McKinney, son of James McKinney, 55 acres on his coming
of age including house and field they now live in. Family not to be
disturbed before he is of full age. To Susannah McKinney furniture and
$10.00. To William McKinney, Jr. $10.00. To Robert McKinney $10.00.
To Jane McKinney, Sr. one heifer and one blue table. To Perry McKinney's
daughter Susannah McKinney furniture and 5 acres where they now live
including the land that is on South East side of big road. To my brother
and sisters Mary Oliver, Jane Oliver, Jemima Bates and John Slater .50
cents each. Negro woman Tilda to be sold. Friend Perry McKinney executor. Dated 6 Feb. 1847.
Wit.:   G. W. Rankin   (Signed) Susannah (X) McMahan
        A. J. Floyd
        Z. B. Floyd
Proven 23 Jan. 1850.

WILL OF W. R. NELSON - pp 292-294
Wife Sarah whole estate her life or widowhood. At her death to son James
O. Nelson negro boy Jim. To son Wm. R. Nelson boy Bob. To son John
H. Nelson negro boy George. At death of wife, or at her marriage, estate
sold. Daughter Harriet Amanda Nelson to have $800.00 and furniture.
Daughter Permelia McAllester to have $5.00. Daughter Sarah McGee have
$5.00. Remainder of estate divided equally amongst my 3 sons above named
and my daughter Harriet Amanda Nelson. If she leaves no heirs her share
goes to 3 sons. Executors: Sons James O. Nelson and William R. Nelson.
Dated 11 May, 1849.
Wit.:   Wm. A. Glenn   (Signed) W. R. Nelson
        Henry H. Scuddy
        James Gilmer
Proven 4 Feb. 1850.

WILL OF JANE WILSON - pp 295-296
Brother William Fagan. To Elizabeth Waters representatives. Brother
James Fagan. Brother George Fagan. Remainder of estate put in hands
of Bryan Boroughs in trust for use and benefit of Nancy Gibson her lifetime and at decease to be equally divided between her three children to
wit: Sarah Ann Sitton, Susannah Bowen and William B. Gibson. Further
if my brothers or sisters or their legal representatives does not apply
for their amounts it is to be applied according to last bequest. I
appoint Bryan Boroughs executor. Dated 1 Sept. 1843.
Wit.:   John H. Rosamond   (Signed) Jane (X) Wilson
        G. W. Wigginton
        Joseph Laboon
Proven 28 June, 1850.

WILL OF WILLIAM ROGERS, SR. - pp 296-297
Sons Joseph T. Rogers and John Rogers in trust for benefit of my daughter
Polly Rogers land on Camp Creek a branch of Big Creek, waters of Saluda
River containing 300 acres, with the house and 10 acres whereon Sally
Rogers now lives which she is to have possession of during her lifetime
then land returns to sons Joseph and John my trustee for the benefit of
said Polly. Land conveyed to me by William Duckworth, bounded by Samuel
Williams, John McColister, Hugh Wilson. Dated 3 Nov. 1847.
Wit.:   Henry Cobb   (Signed) William (X) Rogers
        Ozea B. Rogers
        Amanda E. Rogers
Proven 2 July, 1850.

WILL OF HEZEKIAH RILEY - pp 298-300
Village of Anderson. Wife Ruth to have 2 lots in Anderson Village her
lifetime. To friend Stephen McCulley money in trust for wife Ruth, and
at her death he pay executors entire sum received. At death of wife
property sold. Step-son John Davis. To children of my son Daniel Riley
surviving my wife Ruth. Heirs of body of deceased daughter Nancy Gregg,
late wife of Francis Gregg. Son Ira Ellis Riley. Remainder to my
children or representatives of those not surviving to be equally divided.
Executors: Friends Leverett A. Osborn and Jacob P. Reed. Dated 20 Mar.
1847.
Wit.:   C. L. Gaillard   (Signed) Hezekiah Riley
        Elijah Webb
        Jno. C. Griffin
Proven 15 July, 1850.

WILL OF JULIUS HUFF - pp 301-302
Dated 15 Dec. 1849. Six children: Tamar Huff, maiden name, Julius Huff,
Patsy Huff, maiden name, John Huff, Abigail Huff, maiden name, and
Samuel A. Huff all my property. Executor: Son Samuel A. Huff, and if
he should fall by accident, I will that my son Julius should act.
Wit.:   Micajah B. Williams   (Signed) Julius Huff
        Elizabeth Martin
        Abram Martin
Proven 1 Aug. 1850.

WILL OF BETSEY RICHARDS - pp 302-303
Daughter Eleanor Brecenridge. Son Dr. William Richards. Daughter Polly
Todd. Daughter Jane Erskine. All of these bequest to come from money
coming to me. Funds which I may have on hand be used to support me
while I live and defray the necessary expenses after my decease.
Granddaughter Elizabeth B. Todd. Granddaughter Katharine J. Todd.
Son-in-law James Todd to be executor. Dated 22 Mar. 1844.
Wit.:   Archibald Todd   (Signed) Betsy (X) Richards
        G. W. Land
        W. R. Erskine
Proven 25 Aug. 1850.

WILL OF CHARLES BROWN - pp 304-306
To Ruth Brown the wife of my son Isaac Brown, 1/5 of tract whereon I
now live containing 200 acres. To my daughter Jane Brown, the wife of
Clem Brown, 1/5 of tract where I live. To heirs of my daughter Elizabeth
Dunlap, formerly wife of Matthew Dunlap but now dead another 1/5. To

110

Charity Brown , the wife of my son Cornelius Brown 1/5. To Kizziah
Brown, the wife of my son George Brown 1/5. Executor: Andrew Reid.
Dated 26 Sept. 1846.
Wit.: R. H. Reid   (Signed) Charles (X) Brown
      Isaac M. Adams
      John E. Adams
Proven 30 Aug. 1850.

WILL OF JOHN MAGEE - pp 306-308
Wife Nancy to retain portion coming from her former husband's estate for
division and as we have in our possession a portion of said estate in
property for which I stand indebted it is my will that she retain in her
hands said property and that it not be sold as a part of my estate,
but that the debt be paid out of my property which I now possess exclusive of all debts against me at the time of my death. An equal share
with each of my children hereafter named, except son Michael. Son
Samuel. Heirs of son Jesse. Benjamin Mattison an equal share. Theodotia
Amanda Harkness an equal share. Caroline Richey an equal share. Gabriel
an equal share. James an equal share. Elizabeth Siddle an equal share.
Nancy an equal share. Harriet Martha an equal share. John an equal
share. Lucy Christian an equal share.
     (NOTE: After Gabriel should come William an equal share, and Hillman
an equal share). If present wife Nancy should have a living heir or
heirs it or they are to have equal shares, but if either of my minor
heirs depart life before they arrive at mature age their portions to
revert to other children and their children. Executors: Sons Gabriel
L. Magee and William Magee. Dated 21 June, 1850.
Wit.: Michael McGee   (Signed) John Magee
      E. J. Earle
      Nathan Harris
Proven 7 Oct. 1850.

WILL OF JOHN ADAMS - pp 309-310   329-330
Children of my daughter Charlott Adams and as they live in a distant
country I know not their names. They to receive as they reach 21.
Three sons James Adams, John Adams, Asa Adams. Executor: Dejarnet
Tucker. Dated 29 Oct. 1850.
Wit.: John (X) Seigler   (Signed) John (X) Adams
      Asa Partain
      Martha Partain
Proven 8 Nov. 1850.

WILL OF REV. JAMES DOUTHIT - pp 310-314
Shortly after marriage of daughter Mary H. to Elias Elrod I let her
have negro girl Harriet not as her own but to remain my property. I
now give girl to Mary H. Gave girl Lucy to daughter Elizabeth A.
Kimbrough shortly after marriage to Marmaduke Kimbrough. Same terms.
Did let daughter Susanna E. Gambrell at time of marriage to Larkin
Gambrell have girl Jane, same terms. Jane is dead, but had issue. I
did let daughter Sarah R. at time of marriage to Thomas J. Wilkinson
have girl Talitha Cumi, same terms. I let daughter Maria H. have girl
Carline at time of marriage to Henry L. Gaines, same terms. After my
death balance of my negroes shall be appraised by three dis-interested
men chosen by executors. The two oldest ones with their youngest child
have the privilege of disposing of themselves to any person in or out of
the family that they may choose to live with that will take them at their
valuation and give approved security to secure payment at 12 months
credit. My wife shall keep whichever of the girls she pleases and if
she wishes to do so the oldest boy Elsly to do for and take care of her.
The rest of my children they may choose to live with that will take them
at their valuation. They are human beings and have high claims upon the
humanity of those in whose hands they are and I wish those of them that
have fallen into my hands to have all the priviledges of suiting themselves that their situation and the laws of the country will justify.
Those my wife chooses shall have the same privilege at her death of
choosing their future homes. Wife may keep plantation except part given
to son Samuel to cultivate. Son Benjamin. Son John. Samuel. Grandson
James D. Elrod. Grandson James Garrison Douthit. After sale of property
divided into 9 equal parts. 1 part to son James H. Douthit and his

children, and then 1/9 to each of my other children. If any of my
negroes refuse or fail to dispose of themselves as they have the priv-
ilege to do then they will have to be sold at public sale as my other
personal property will be. Executors: Three sons Benj. H. Douthit,
John W. Douthit, Samuel D. Douthit, and my son-in-law Elias Elrod.
Dated 25 Mar. 1848.
Wit.: Harrison Givens   (Signed) James Douthit
       Orsborn R. Tripp
       William Langa
Proven 24 Jan. 1851.

WILL OF HARMON CUMMINS - pp 314-317
Son Thomas Cummins. Daughter Sarah Trainer. Daughter Mary Simpson (?).
Daughter Hannah Davidson and her husband John L. Davidson. Son Griffith
Cummins. Son Samuel Cummins. Harmond Cummins. Son John Cummins.
Daughter Malinda Junkin. Samuel Cummins the son of Griffith Cummins.
Executors: Neighbors Aaron Hall and Andrew W. Norris. Dated 16 May,
1843.
Wit.: John Moore   (Signed) Harmon (X) Cummins
       James Stevenson
       George Stevenson
Proven 3 Mar. 1851.

WILL OF ARTHY GENTRY - pp 317-319
Daughter Rebecca Gentry all my estate her lifetime. After her death to
be sold and disposed of as follows: To son Daniel Gentry, to daughter
Winnifred Hembree, to Allen Gentry, to Tabitha Vandiver. Grandson
Aaron F. Hembree, to see after myself, Artha Gentry and daughter Rebecca.
My 4 children: Daniel, Winnifred, Allen and Tabitha. Executor: James
Hembree. Dated 8 Sept. 1849.
Wit.: Jacob Burris   (Signed) Arthy (X) Gentry
       George Tippen
       James Buroughs
Proven 5 May, 1851.

WILL OF HANNAH HARRISON - pp 319-320
Son James T. Harrison and Benj. F. Sloan trustees for my daughter Rose
Earle Harrison. Executors: Son James T. Harrison and Benj. F. Sloan.
Dated 3 Nov. 1841.
Wit.: W. H. D. Gaillard   (Signed) Hannah Harrison
       A. C. Campbell
       J. A. Shanklin
Proven 5 May, 1851.

WILL OF JAMES CONWILL - pp 321-323
Wife Rebecca. Children: Daniel, Katharine, Elizabeth, Clarissa Caroline,
Malissa Ann, Malinda, Mahala, to be equally divided between them. I
give portion belonging to daughter Katharine who married Zadok Skelton
to her two daughters Eliza Reid and Thursa Elrod, wifes of Robert Reid
and Elijah Elrod. Portion falling to my daughter Elizabeth who married
Mr. Woods I give to her children. Portion falling to daughter Malissa
Ann who married John Rainey I give to her 2 sons James Thomas Rainey
and William Hulban (?) Rainey. Executors: Daniel E. Conwill and David
McConnell.
Wit.: Wm. S. Shaw   (Signed) James (X) Conwill
       Saml. W. Williford
       Silas P. Shaw
   Codicils - lands not sold during wife's lifetime. Malissa Ann's part
to go to her instead of her sons. Dated 23 Nov. 1849.
   One codicil witnessed by John Herbert, another by James T. McClinton,
in addition to other two witnesses. No date on will proper.
Proven 12 June, 1851.

WILL OF BENJAMIN MULLIKIN - pp 324-325
Three sons, James, William and Benjamin. Daughter Nancy the wife of
James Israel. Executors: Sons James and William. Dated 25 Dec. 1847.
Wit.: Elijah Owen, Jr.   (Signed) Benjamin (X) Mullikin
       Elizabeth Owen
       Alanson Forbes
Proven 4 Aug. 1851.

WILL OF BETSEY WARDLAW - pp 325-327
George Newton Ballantine, son of my sister Polly Ballantine. Daughter
Betsey Francis Wardlaw, daughter of my brother Hugh H. Wardlaw. Betsey
Satira Ballantine, daughter of my sister Polly Ballantine all the bed-
clothes she has made since she has lived with me at my fathers, and all
that she may make as long as she may continue with me. Betsey Wardlaw
Major, daughter of my sister Nancy Major. Remainder of estate equally
divided between John M. Wardlaw, Nancy Major, Hugh H. Wardlaw, Polley
Ballantine, Betsey Wardlaw Major, and Betsey Satira Ballantine. If
my mother should survive me she shall retain such portion of my estate
as she may desire for her use and at her death to be distributed as
before directed. Executor: Nephew William Nevitt Major. Dated 1 July,
1851.
Wit.: Herbert Hammond   (Signed) Betsey Wardlaw
       Peter G. Acker
       Matthew P. Gambrell

WILL OF ELIJAH MOORE, SR. - pp 328-329
All my children except Tabitha Slaten share in estate, and I desire that
Tabitha's eldest daughter Sarah have 1/3 of what is coming to her mother,
and likewise will that Sarah Taby the eldest daughter have the amount
of that note that I hold on Stephen Slaten, Tabitha's husband, given
1838, due 1840. Executors: Adam Elrod, Grant A. Moore, John Morgan.
Dated 16 Mar. 1844.
Wit.: John Slaten   (Signed) Elijah Moore
       John D. King
       John Murphy
Proven 6 Sept. 1852.

WILL OF JAMES MAJOR, ESQ. - pp 330-332
Daughter Lavina Vandiver negro girl given in trust to Pinckney Major.
Son Pinckney Major. Daughter Caroline Smith, have made advances to her
husband. Son Hiram B. Major. Daughter Heskey Clement, wife of
Washington Clement. Son James A. Major. E. Jenkins Major. Salley
Shirley wife of Stephen Shirley. Son Jabo W. Major. Son David R.
Major. To my wife Peggy Major my home plantation and the Burton planta-
tion adjoining my home, and 1/3 or a child's part. Foregoing bequests
shall be paid to children at age 21. Executors: Sons Hiram B. Major
and James A. Major. Dated 26 Dec. 1851.
Wit.: John Erskine   (Signed) James Major
       Thomas Erskine
       William Major
Proven 27 Sept. 1852.

WILL OF WILLIAM WEBB - pp 333-334
Wife Elizabeth to have all estate her life or widowhood with hope that
she may be able to raise and educate our children. At her death or
marriage to be sold and equally divided among my children. My negro
girl Mary which I loaned to my son-in-law John Wilson I still wish my
wife to suffer him to keep as assistance and help for our daughter
Caroline his wife. Executor: Wife Elizabeth. Dated 18 Feb. 1844.
Wit.: Wm. Steele   (Signed) Wm. Webb
       Wm. Anderson
       J. W. Guyton
Proven 18 Nov. 1852.

WILL OF JOSEPH TAYLOR - pp 335-336
Son David S. Taylor all negroes and the plantation whereon he now lives.
To daughter Susan Lewis all negroes and other property of mine now in
her possession. To wife Nancy Taylor my lands and negroes and all other
property that may be at her disposal, knowing and believing she will
do the same justice to my children as if I were living and to dispose
of them myself to my children being satisfied of her prudence in that
respect I freely submit the whole of my property to her management and
disposal, and if my wife should die without a will I will that my daughter Eleanor receive a thousand dollars worth of property. Balance of
property to be equally divided between my 7 children: Samuel, Eleanor,
Baylis, Joseph, William, Benjamin and Robert. Executors: Wife Nancy
and my son David S. Taylor. Dated 29 Mar. 1828.

Wit.: Elias Earle   (Signed)   Joseph Taylor
       Alexr. Evins
       Sion (X) Holley
Proven 6 Dec. 1852.
     The will of Col. Joseph Taylor, with David S. Taylor qualifying as
executor.

WILL OF THOMAS SKELTON - pp 337-339
Wife Elizabeth all plantation whereon I now reside except small piece
whereon Charles K. Williford is now building and has dug a well, the
said reserved lot joins estate of Samuel Maverick dec'd, contains 5
acres. To wife her lifetime negroes Jinny, Sela, Bob, Mariah, Amaline,
Sam, Jim, Stephen, Liz and her 3 children Tilda, Leah and Thomas. After
death of wife public sale of all property, and equally divided amongst
my children viz. James M. Skelton, Thomas T. Skelton, John W. B.
Skelton, Archibald B. Skelton, Mary T. McLees the wife of James J.
McLees, Eleanor M. Nelson the wife of William R. Nelson, Oliver P.
Skelton, Elizabeth Williford the wife of Charles K. Williford, and
David H. Skelton. Executors: Son Thomas T. Skelton and James J.
McLees. Dated 3 Nov. 1852.
Wit.: Mary Seawright   (Signed)   Thomas Skelton
       Andrew McLees
       James Gilmer
Proven 6 Dec. 1852.

WILL OF WILLIAM WILLIAMSON - pp 340-341
Wife Rosanna to have property at my decease for lifetime or widowhood.
Proceeds above what she may need to be kept by son David Williamson
whom I appoint to take charge of and manage for her use and at her
death the remainder sold and my son to serve as executor and make equal
distribution among all my children viz. Mastin, James, William, David,
Polly, Nancy, Sarah, and Jane. Dated 31 July, 1844.
Wit.: William Magee   (Signed)   William Williamson
       Asenath Magee
       David (X) Haynie
Proven 10 Jan. 1853.

WILL OF BENJAMIN GASSAWAY - pp 341-343
Wife Margaret all estate her lifetime or widowhood, except a lot of
land in Cobb Co., Ga. containing 40 acres which I give to my son Lemuel
H. Gassaway on which he now lives. Also I give to each of my daughters
that are unmarried at my decease bed and bedding, and side saddle apiece
to make them equal to those of my daughters that is married and had the
above named articles. After death of wife Margaret I give to my son
Benjamin Franklin Gassaway half of land whereon I now live containing
265 acres on East side of Rocky River adjoining lands of John Hall,
S. C. Fisher and others. Other half divided between other children.
Executors: Sons William and Benj. F. Gassaway. Dated 8 Oct. 1850.
Wit.: S. C. Fisher   (Signed)   Benjamin Gassaway
       John Hall
       H. L. Fisher
Proven 11 Feb. 1853.

WILL OF ARCHIBALD MAULDIN, SR. - pp 343-344
Formerly of Abbeville District but now of Anderson. Wife Elizabeth M.
my whole estate. Executor: Arthur A. Bowie.
Wit.: T. A. Evins   (Signed)   A. Mauldin
       J. C. Garrison
       S. M. Hagood
Witnesses thought they saw him sign will on or about 6 June, 1852.
Proven 21 Feb. 1853.

WILL OF JACOB PRUET - pp 345-346
Property be sold. Only real estate at this time is a declaration by
probate sent to the City of Washington for a patent land warrant which
if said warrant returns I order to be sold at public outcry. To be used
to support wife and raise children. Executor: A. X. Todd, Esq. Dated
3 Mar. 1851.
Wit.: A. D. Gray   (Signed)   Jacob Pruit

Joshua Buchanan
Thos. Simpson
Proven 29 Mar. 1853.

WILL OF MARTHA S. JOHNSON - pp 346-347
To Martha O. Stevens (daughter of John B. and Jane K. Ferrell deceased)
all of my wearing apparel and the drawers and trunks that contain them,
also furniture. To Lizzie, daughter of Martha O. Stevens my satinwood
work box and stand. To Florence daughter of William L. and Jane H.
Jenkins 7 bank stock, gold spectacles, the house wherein I now live and
the residue of articles not mentioned. Nephew Wm. L. Jenkins to be
executor. Dated Oct. 9, 1852.
Wit.: Mary Louisa Dart   (Signed) Martha S. Johnson
      Mary Louisa Barnes
      Henrietta D. Dart
Proven 28 Apr. 1853.

WILL OF FRANCES LORTON - pp 348-349
Of Pendleton Village. Son John S. Lorton house and lot where I now live
and negroes Adam, Dan and Rhoda. Daughter Mary. Remaining property
divided between my two surviving children. Executor: John S. Lorton.
Dated 1 Apr. 1842.
Wit.: E. B. Benson   (Signed) F. Lorton
      F. W. Symmes
      Fair Kirksey
Proven 6 June, 1853.

WILL OF JOHN PERRY MAJOR - pp 350-351
Sons John Westly Major and Samuel B. Major in trust for benefit of my
daughter Martha Eliza Smith and her children 100 acres to be laid off
from tract of 204½ acres which I bought of Joseph Cox and wife and others,
this I desire for a home for daughter Martha Eliza and her husband
Nimrod Smith as long as they live. If she die first goes to her children.
Wife Mary Major. Estate sold after her death and proceeds go to children:
Nancy Black, Rebecca Talbert, Isabella Talbert, Samuel B. Major, John
W. Major, Mary Ann Hendricks, Martha Eliza Smith and Jane Carpenter.
Daughter of my dec'd son Jospeh M. Major. Executors: Sons John Westly
and Samuel B. Major. Dated 19 Jan. 1852.
Wit.: R. M. Morris   (Signed) John P. (X) Major
      Samuel Craig
      James Webb
Proven 24 June, 1853.

WILL OF JOSEPH MCCARLEY - pp 352-353
Sons William and Robert B. Daughter Elizabeth. Son Elijah. Executors:
Daughter Elizabeth and son Elijah. Dated 9 Jan. 1849.
Wit.: James Stuart   (Signed) Joseph McCarley
      George Stuart
      Samuel Yeargin
Proven 19 Aug. 1853.

WILL OF JOHN BROWN, SR. - pp 354-357
Daughter Hannah Smith, wife of Robert Smith land known as Burford tract
and pieces added to it by purchase from Aaron Vandiver and John Warnock,
containing 670 acres on Robert Smith's giving to other heirs $1000.00.
To daughter Hannah negro woman Catharine and child Elias about 4 years
old. My son Joseph Brown and his wife Mary are deceased but they left
five children viz. Susan B. Brown, Eliab Brown, Nancy Brown, John Brown,
and Samuel Brown. I give to them 303 acres on Broadway Creek where the
said Mary Brown resided with exception of 12 acres sold to John Warnock,
it being tract I purchased from William Lesley. To daughter Nancy Moore
her lifetime 2 tracts whereon she now lives containing 150 acres which
was purchased by me from Col. Eliab Moore, Sr., the other tract purchased
at sheriff's sale which was sold at the property of her husband Eliab
Moore, Jr. The two tracts join. Also to Nancy Moore her lifetime
tract of 157 acres adjoining known as the Bowen tract. At Nancy's death
all th her children. To son Robert B. Brown 226 acres purchased of
Peter Acker. To John Brown a son of Catharine Lefoy (Leroy ?) (now
Catharine George), a negro girl named Mary a child of Anna's, but if

115

John Brown should die before coming of age girl reverts back to estate.
To the 4 children of Alamine Atkins viz. William Penn Brown, Jane
Czarena Brown, Martha Ann Brown, and Elvira Brown, all household and
kitchen furniture. To William Penn Brown son of Alamine Atkins, male
slave Jerry about 27 years of age. Remainder of estate sold and divided
amongst my children as follows: Daniel Brown, Hannah Smith, Samuel
Brown, the children of Joseph Brown, children of Nancy Moore, Robert B.
Brown, and Elizabeth Smith. Executors: James Gilmer and James Gunnin.
Dated 18 Nov. 1851.
Wit.: Charles Haynie   (Signed) John Brown
       David D. Earp
       M. R. Manning
Proven 22 Aug. 1853.

WILL OF MARY SNIPES BOONE - pp 358-359
Relict of Thomas Boone, deceased. To my nephew Dr. Henry W. DeSaussure
my servant girl Delia as a small return for his long and kind attendance
upon me as a physician. To my executor hereinafter named $280.00 now
in hands of my sister Mrs. Maria Glover to and for the following purposes:
a broach for my sister Susan DeSaussure, a broach for sister Maria
Glover, one or more pieces of silver for my best friend Henry A. De-
Saussure, Esq. as a token of my sincere gratitude for his kindness to
me a widow and to my orphan children. Executor: Friend Henry A.
DeSaussure, Esq. Dated May 1853.
Wit.: Wm. J. Boone   (Signed) Mary S. Boone
       Phoebe C. Boone
       Eliza P. Boone
Proven 23 Aug. 1853.

WILL OF DANIEL MAY - pp 360-361
Both tracts of land sold, namely the one on Big Creek containing 200
acres and the tract of 234 acres on Hencoop Creek where I now live.
Debts paid and $50.00 reserved for wife Polly, balance divided among
my children viz. Elizabeth Saylors, Sally Bird, Rachel Cunningham,
Asenath Wright, Anna Queen and my son George W. May.
    Son Washington is to have Canadian filly and mule colt for his long
and strict attention to his mother and myself. Several amounts bequethed
to my daughters in hands of executors. If either should die without
children the amount divided among those already named. Executors:
Friend William Magee and Son George W. May. Dated 9 July, 1853.
Wit.: J. Wilson   (Signed) Daniel May
       T. W. Price
       William J. Taylor
Proven 15 Sept. 1853.

WILL OF NANCY M. CALDWELL - pp 362-365
Body to be intered in Baptist churchyard at Columbia by the side of my
deceased husband and my grave covered with a stone similar to his.
    To daughter Fanny Jeanette Caldwell my slaves Winny and Becca and her
child. To Howard H. Caldwell my slaves Harvey and Lizzy, and they have
been faithful servants and I request my son to treat them kindly and
when they are no longer able to work to make their old age comfortable.
    To my executor $1500.00 in trust to pay over to my sister-in-law
Mary A. Caldwell the interest of that sum during her life and at her
death to divide the principal among my four youngest children or such
as may be living at the time of her death. Remainder of property sold
and divided into five equal parts, one part of which I give to a trustee
appointed by the Court for benefit of my son Howard H. Caldwell during
his life and at his death the trust to be executed in such child or
children of his as may then be living.
    One part in trust for my son James Fitz James Caldwell his lifetime,
then to his children, and if he leaves no living children to his next
of kin.
    One part in trust for son Hall Calhoun Caldwell, then to his children.
    The remaining part I give and bequeath to my daughter Fanny Jeannette
Caldwell, not subject to the debts of any husband she may have and at
her death to her next of kin.
    Executor: Friend John A. Moore of Columbia and desire him to procure
the appointment of trustees for my four youngest children. Dated 1 Apr.
1851.

Wit.: W. L. Roach   (Signed) N. H. Caldwell
       J. M. Roach
       Mary C. Hughes
     Codicil - I revoke the bequest to John A. Moore in trust for the
benefit of Mary A. Caldwell and give the said sum of $1500.00 to my
children Howard H. Caldwell, James Fitz Caldwell, Hall C. Caldwell and
Fanny Jeanette Caldwell, and I desire that executors sell my house and
lot in Anderson and divide proceeds among the four children above
named, and I further desire that the sum of $500.00 be taken from the
amount bequeathed in trust for the benefit of Luther M. Caldwell and
divided in the same manner among my other children.
Wit.: Amanda H. Chapman
       Joseph Glenn
       Robert W. Craig
Proven in Richland District 3 Nov. 1853 by oaths of J. M. Roach and
Amanda H. Chapman. Admitted to probate in Richland District.
     (NOTE: Nowhere is Luther M. Caldwell mentioned in the will, but from
reading the codicil he must have been a son because the estate was
divided into 5 shares and only 4 heirs named in the will. He would make
the fifth.)

WILL OF LEONARD S. HAMILTON - pp 366-367
Wife Elizabeth and children. At her death or marriage estate divided
among all children. Executor: Wife Elizabeth. Dated 27 July, 1853.
Wit.: E. Alexander   (Signed) Leonard S. Hamilton
       Joseph Hill
       Henry Keasler
Proven 7 Jan. 1854.

WILL OF MATTHEW PARKER - pp 368-370
Wife Martha during her lifetime my plantation whereon I now reside on
waters of Little Genorostee adjoining lands of Abner Clinkscales, Jacob
Mochat and others containing 207 acres. Remainder of estate sold and
divided between my 3 sons and the bodily heirs of my 3 daughters (to
wit) Matthew G. Parker, Samuel E. Parker and Henry Parker and the bodily
heirs of Mary Obriant, Martha Obriant and Lavina Scott. Shares to heirs
of daughters in trust until they reach 21.
     At wife's death land sold and divided as follows: 1/6 to Matthew G.
Parker, 1/6 to Samuel E. Parker, 1/6 to Henry Parker, 1/6 to heirs of
Martha Obriant, 1/6 to heirs of Mary Obriant, 1/6 to heirs of Lavina
Scott. Executor: Abner Clinkscales. Dated 28 Nov. 1851.
Wit.: Herbert Hammond   (Signed) Matthew Parker
       Sanford V. Gentry
       David White
Proven 4 Feb. 1854.

WILL OF RALPH E. ELLIOTT - pp 371-373
Of Chatham Co., Ga. All my estate in trust for support, maintenance and
education of my wife and children until my youngest son reaches age of
16, then to be distributed to wife and children as law directs.
     As I have 300 or 400 acres of tide swamp lands not under cultivation
I direct that any surplus proceeds of my property after providing for
wife and children as above directed be invested in purchase of negroes
for the purpose of bringing said vacant swamp lands under cultivation.
     To the Bishop and convention of the Protestant Episcopal Church in
the State of Georgia $1000.00 in trust for support and maintenance of
widows and orphans of deceased Protestant Episcopal Clergymen of the
Diocese of Georgia.
     In case of the marriage of any of my daughters I direct that the share
of my estate which she may receive be settled to her separate use and
benefit by ante nuptial contract.
     I appoint Robert Habersham, Robert Mackay, Stephen Elliott Habersham
and my son William Henry Elliott (from and after the time he shall attain
the age of 21 yrs.), executors of this my last will and testament. Dated
29 Aug. 1853.
Wit.: John Rea Habersham   (Signed) Ralph E. Elliott
       Alfred Woodbridge
       Woodbridge Hudson
Proven 3 Mar. 1854.

WILL OF JOHN HARKNESS - pp 374-375
Three sons Robert C., John N. and James J. Harkness.
  Children of my daughter Rosa Ann Clinkscales.
  Children of my daughter Eliza Jane Gaillard.
  Daughter Nancy N. Pratt. Executors: Sons Robert C., John N., James
J. Harkness. Dated 26 Dec. 1853.
Wit.: John Hall   (Signed) John Harkness
      J. W. Norris, Jr.
      R. B. Doyel
Proven 7 Apr. 1854.

WILL OF ELIZABETH G. STARKE - pp 376-379
Of Pendleton Village. To my nephew Wardsdell Avery my negro woman Marea
and her daughter Elizabeth in trust and use of my niece Elizabeth S.
Gaither of North Carolina during her lifetime and after her death to her
daughters.
  To my executors in trust for my niece Elizabeth C. Sharpe of Pendleton,
half of my house and lot in Pendleton, furniture, negro man Cornelius
and girl Elsey and her child.
  To my nephew William Sharpe negro boy John in trust for use of my
brother David Sharpe his lifetime and at his death John sold and proceeds
invested by my nephew in trust for David Sharpe's daughters.
  Negro boy Alfred to be sold and proceeds along with notes due me in-
vested by nephew in trust for David Sharpe's daughters.
  $300.00 to nephew William S. McGuire for use of my niece Louisa Bevens
and her heirs and not to be subject to control of her husband.
  Nephews Wm. O. Sharpe, Wm. R. Sharpe, Marcus L. Sharpe, Edwin A.
Sharpe, Elam Sharpe, Jr. of Pendleton.
  Executors: Nephews Elam Sharpe, Jr. and Marcus L. Sharpe. Dated 9
Oct. 1848.
Wit.: Thos. J. Sloan   (Signed) Elizabeth G. Starke
      John C. Cherry
      S. F. W. Miller
  Codicil - To niece Matilda Sharpe $200.00, and to nephew E. A. Sharpe
in addition to what I have given him, $100.00.
Proven 15 May, 1854.

WILL OF WILLIAM KING - pp 380-383
Wife Nancy plantation on which I live as belongs to the grant of Peter
Horry, 300 acres, also the slaves Phebe, Tom and Matilda, for her life-
time or widowhood.
  To son Robert A. King slaves Mark, Rosa and Sylvia. He is to live
with and take care of my wife for life or widowhood.
  Daughter Martha King is not married. She is to have land on Seneca
River adjoining lands of Thomas White, Thomas Bruce and Wm. Palmer con-
taining 230 acres, also slaves Caroline, Peter, Clarissa and Lewis.
  Slaves Fanny, George, Sam and Moses to be sold and of the proceeds
of sale Hiram King, Solomon King and Eliza Kay be paid $700.00 and Nancy
Webb $600.00. If they have died same be paid their issue then living,
remainder of proceeds equally divided between all my children, including
the said Hiram King, Solomon King, Eliza Kay and Nancy Webb and excluding
Robt. A. King and Martha King who have already been provided for.
  To granddaughter Nancy Mary King, daughter of Robt. A. King, a small
negro girl Cloe. To his son William John King a little girl Jane.
  To granddaughter Nancy Carter, wife of James Carter, at death or
marriage of said wife the slave Phebe in addition to which I will her a
share of the residue of my estate under the fourth clause of this will
equal to the share of each of my children therein provided for.
  My reasons for making this will are as follows - I made a will in
1849. On reflection I think my health was then too feeble to arrange
my affairs properly and I find that two of my slaves Sam and Moses were
left out of that will. I therefore intend this will as a revocation of
that one. Executors: Hiram R. and Robt. A. King, my sons. Dated 28
Sept. 1853.
Wit.: Jonathan Pickrell   (Signed) William King
      Matthew Martin
      D. J. Hix
Proven 12 June, 1854.

WILL OF JAMES WARDLAW - pp 384-386
Dated 24 July, 1848. Wife Peggy to have negro woman Creasey and children
she now has or may have, and boys Daniel and George her lifetime.
Daughter Betsey. Property sold after death of wife and equally divided
among my children. If my son E. A. Wardlaw does not return to get his
share or in the event of his death then it is my will that his share be
equally divided among my other children. My executors to reserve out of
E. H. (?) Wardlaw's share $100.00 to be paid to my great grandchild the
son of Peggy Lewis now deceased when he attains the age of 21. Executors
to put the share of Polly (or Dolly ?) Balentine my daughter out at
interest and to pay it to her bodily heirs as they come of age. Executors:
John M. Wardlaw and Hugh A. Wardlaw.
Wit.: Williamson Breazeale   (Signed) James Wardlaw
       William Smith
       John B. Nevitt
Proven 14 July, 1854.

WILL OF THOMAS DEAN - pp 387-389
Wife Elizabeth to have negro girl and woman of her choosing for her life-
time. At her death sold and divided amongst my five children: Sally
Stevenson, the wife of George Stevenson, Jr., Mary Hall, wife of Jackson
Hall, Elizabeth Jones, wife of William Jones, Samuel Dean and Thomas Dean.
   Negro man Berry to son Samuel Dean for that tract of land I conveyed
to him known as the Elrod tract on Wilson's Creek containing 460 acres.
   To son Thomas Dean one of my negroes of his choosing, and land where
I now reside containing 1184 acres, to be his at death of wife Elizabeth.
   To daughter Sally Stevenson a negro girl Cinda.
   To daughter Mary Hall a girl Eliza.
   To daughter Elizabeth Jones a girl Gwinney.
   Rest of my estate, including negro girl Vina which I loaned to my
daughter Sally Stevenson and girl named Hepsy loaned to daughter Mary
Hall, and girl Hester loaned to daughter Elizabeth Jones to be sold and
equally divided amongst my wife and my five children. Executors: Sons
Samuel Dean and Thomas Dean. Dated 11 Apr. 1848.
Wit.: William Long   (Signed) Thomas Dean
       James Stevenson
       James Gilmer
Proven 31 July 1854.

WILL OF ABSALOM HALL - pp 390-392
Dated 27 May, 1854. Notes due me for my practice as a physician with Dr.
William Wilburn in 1852-1854, I bequeath to my mother Sarah Tucker. All
interest I have in medicines, books, instruments and my one half share of
the shop at Williamston in which I am in co-partnership with Dr. William
Wilburn be disposed of and used for benefit of my mother. Also own a
third part of tract in Anderson District bought from Alford Lewis con-
taining 30 acres. Executor: Maj. Abner Clinkscales.
Wit.: K. Sullivan   (Signed) A. Hall
       Wm. Hatton
       John C. Tucker
Proven 7 Aug. 1854.

WILL OF WILLIAM ELROD - pp 393-394
Personal property equally divided between my wife Dorcas and Mary E.
Brothers.
   To Samuel T. Elrod, Jr. land where he now resides, joins M. B.
Williams, Pickensville and Greenville Road and road leading to Snow Hill
Church. Executors: Wife Dorcas and M. B. Williams. Dated 17 Aug. 1854.
Wit.: John Golden   (Signed) Wm. (X) Elrod
       Abram Martin
       George G. Elrod
Proven 4 Sept. 1854.

WILL OF SUSAN SLOAN - pp 395-398
Daughters Elizabeth Stribling, Susan Bruce, Nancy Taylor and Catharine
Benson.
   Sons James M. Sloan a note in favor of Sion Holly, dec'd. To sons
B. F. Sloan, T. M. Sloan and Thomas J. Linton (?) of Florida the following
negroes: Modesty and her children, 3 negroes purchased by me of Moses

Linton viz. Clarissa, Jordan and Jerry, also negro girl lately purchased
of M. M. Norton and W. D. Steele named Marie (which girl is substituted
for Ely who I had divised to them in my former will) with their issue all
the aforesaid negroes being now in the state of Florida in the possession
of Rebecca Sloan wife of my son James M. deceased in trust for the children of aforesaid James M. dec'd. Their mother may enjoy use of them as
long as she remains a widow or until children shall arrive at full age
or marry.
　　To son B. F. Sloan negro man Hiram on his substituting his man Peter
or some other negro.
　　Balance of estate divided between my 9 children or their representatives.
　　To daughter Elizabeth Stribling 2 negroes Ester and her child Bob
Hampton and boy Peter, substituted by B. F. in lieu of Hiram.
　　To son B. F. land whereon I now live including both sides of the river.
　　To Nancy Sloan, wife of my son David dec'd and her children one equal
share.
　　To my granddaughter Susan Vivian and Mary Earle, children of my
daughter Rebecca each one third of one share to be paid in money and the
other one third of one share in trust for use of my granddaughter Eliza
Gaines during her life and then to her children.
　　Balance of negroes I give to my sons Thos. M. Sloan, William Sloan
and daughters Nancy Taylor and Catharine Benson.
　　Executors: Sons B. F. and Thomas M. Sloan. Dated 9 May, 1849.
Wit.: Robt. W. Poe　　　　　　　(Signed) Susan (X) Sloan
　　　A. Cornog
　　　John J. J. Sheppard
Proven 11 Sept. 1854.

WILL OF WILLIAM G. REECE (REESE) - pp 399-400
All to wife her lifetime or widowhood, then equally divided between
children then living or their representatives. Dated 4 Oct. 1854.
Wit.: F. F. Mauldin　　　　　　(Signed) William G. Reece
　　　J. E. Holaday
　　　G. R. Brown
Proven 16 Oct. 1854.

WILL OF NANCY SLOAN - pp 400-401
Of Pickens District. I have 8 living heirs of my body: William D.
Sloan, Sarah M. Bomar the wife of John Bomar, John T. Sloan, Emily C.
Bomar wife of George W. Bomar, Susan A. Lewis wife of A. F. Lewis, Lucy
C. Maxwell wife of R. D. Maxwell, Thomas J. Sloan and Benj. F. Sloan.
Equally divide my property among them. Executors: John T. Sloan, A.
F. Lewis, and R. D. Maxwell. Dated 2 Sept. 1846.
Wit.: Eliza C. Maxwell　　　　　(Signed) Nancy Sloan
　　　Saml. E. Maxwell
　　　Edmund M. McCreary
Proven 3 Nov. 1854.

WILL OF DAVIS SMITH - pp 402-403
Dated 28 July, 1854. Estate equally divided between my brothers and
sisters Jeremiah Smith, Martin Smith, A. W. Smith, and R. S. Smith,
Elizabeth Branyan, Rebecca Holland, Sarah Ann Russell and Martha Brock
and my father and also Rebecca Ann Poor the eldest daughter of Terresa
Poor to be made equal with my brothers and sisters.
　　I appoint A. W. Smith to take charge of my father's and Rebecca Ann
Poor's parts and manage them. Martha Brock's part is to be taken out of
the amount her husband owes me.
　　To my sister Ellen Brock $4.55 and balance on note paid to M. McGee,
Esq. on a judgement.
　　William Davis Holland and Davis Smith Branyan each to have $25.00.
　　Executor: A. W. Smith.
Wit.: W. T. Holland　　　　　　(Signed) Davis Smith
　　　H. C. Wardlaw
　　　C. B. Stanton
Proven 6 Nov. 1854.

WILL OF LAZARUS TRAYNUM - pp 404-405
Wife Frances H. Traynum, 100 acres including improvements where I now

live and 5 negroes namely Suckey, Matilda, Sam,Alex. and May her lifetime
or widowhood and at her death or marriage to come back to my two children
Lucinda and John P.
  To daughter Lucinda negroes Jack, Diner and Martha. To son John P.
negroes Bary and Julia.
  Executors: Jacob Pickel with my wife Frances H. Dated 22 July, 1852.
Wit.: J. M. Smith   (Signed) Lazarus Traynum
       P. F. McKinney
       H. A. Smith
Proven 1 Dec. 1854.

WILL OF THOMAS WHITE - pp 406-407
Daughter Laura White to have $1200.00 in trust and my son Henry White to
act as trustee. I have given off to my children already about an equal
share. After paying Laura her legacy I direct that property be sold
and divided as follows: among my 7 children: Daniel White, Henry White,
Betsey Whitefield the wife of David Whitefield, Martha King, wife of Hiram
King, Julia Brown wife of Wm. J. Brown, Polly Whitefield wife of Benjamin
Whitefield, and Lucinda Whitefield wife of Thomas Whitefield.
  Executors: Sons Henry and Daniel. Dated 5 Aug. 1854.
Wit.: John Martin   (Signed) Thomas White
       Andrew Todd
       Elijah Webb
Proven 29 Dec. 1854.

WILL OF MARGARET ABBOTT - pp 408-409
Daughter Elizabeth Abbott. Son John Abbott. Executor: Daughter Eliza-
beth. Dated 26 Nov. 1828.
Wit.: James Mullikin   (Signed) Margaret (X) Abbott
       Joseph Pitts
       Malinda Mullikin
Proven 6 Aug. 1855.

WILL OF GEORGE ELROD - pp 410-411
Wife Elizabeth and daughters Sarah M. and Mary E. to have tract of land
where I now live during the time they are single. Should they not wish
to make it their home sold and divided among my heirs: Wm. A. and John
M. and Elijah B. Richardson, and Thomas H. and Adam F. and Sarah M.,
Lavina E. and Mary E. and when the land is sold I will that if there is
so much that last named 5 heirs should have $50.00 a piece and then equal
division among all heirs made.
  My executors shall pay my daughter Mahala Ann one dollar. Executors:
Wife Elizabeth and son John M. Elrod.
Wit.: Wm. E. Welborn   (Signed) George Elrod
       Wm. B. Millwee
       Adam Elrod
Proven 17 Aug. 1855.

WILL OF ELIZABETH ABBOTT - pp 412-413
My 40 acre tract originally belonging to my father Thomas Abbott, dec'd
and bequeathed to my mother Margaret Abbott dec'd and joining land of
James Mullikin, Martin Slone and others, I will to John Buller Abbott,
son of my brother James Abbott, dec'd.
  I wish the remaining part of my estate equally divided between the six
other children of my brother James, viz. Thomas W. Abbott, Elijah Abbott,
James Abbott, Jane E. Abbott (now Jane E. Simmons), Franklin Abbott and
Lucinda Abbott.
  Executor: James Mullikin. Dated 27 June, 1855.
Wit.: James Mullikin   (Signed) Elizabeth Abbott
       Thomas H. Martin
       Stephen (X) Ford
Proven 24 Aug. 1855.

WILL OF DAVID GRIER (GREER), SR. - pp 414-416
Wife Polly to have 1/3 of land where I now live and proceeds that may
remain at my decease of the sale of a family of negroes which myself and
her sold to Armstrong and McGee except so much of the proceeds as I have
and may settle with her children in my lifetime of which I have already
settled the following named children: Thomas S. Greer, John and Martha

121

Dunlap, James S. Greer. At wife's death property sold and equally divided
among my 4 sons: John M. Greer, Benjamin Greer, Nimrod J. Greer and
Robert S. Greer, or their children.
I give to son David 100 acres of land and negro woman Sabra.
To son John M. 146 ½ acres and negro man Billy, boy Penn and girl
Doshey.
To son John M. in trust for my son Benjamin, 150 acres joining James
Armstrong and David Greer, Jr.
To son Thomas S. 200 acres on Hencoop Creek.
To daughter Polly Greer 50 acres which she has received and sold to
Dr. John Wilson.
To daughter Eliza Lee and her children negro girl Ann.
To Daughter Eleanor Cobb, $20.00.
To Son James S. Greer $300.00.
The remaining part of property at my decease to be sold and after debts
paid and above specified amounts which I give to my son Thos. S. Greer,
Eleanor Cobb and the children of Jane Lee dec'd then my wife Polly to
have 1/3 and the balance equally divided between my sons John M. Greer,
Robt. S. Greer, Benj. Greer and my daughters Eliza Lee and Martha Dunlap,
or their children.
Executors: Son John M. Greer and friend Wm. P. Martin. Dated 13 Feb.
1852.
Wit.: Charles Murphy   (Signed) David Greer
      Hampton Stone
      A. J. Brock
Proven 17 Sept. 1855.

WILL OF MARY CASEY - pp 417-418
20 July, 1852. Daughter Melinday Casey the plantation whereon I now
live of 130 acres. To my son-in-law James Masey and daughter Sarah Ann
Masey $5.00. To son-in-law Sugar Bonds and daughter Mariah J. Bonds
$5.00. Balance of property put to sale and divided between Melinday
Casey and Mary E. Prince and Mariah H. Bonds.
      Executor: William Sherard.
Wit.: Thomas A. Watt   (Signed) Mary Casey
      Dr. A. G. Cook
      Allen (Haverd)
Proven 1 Oct. 1855.

WILL OF THEODOSIA STRAWTHER - pp 419-420
Bequests to Dolphus Warren Coal, Sarah Frances Coal, Robert Franklin Pain,
Martha Wilson.
Notes on David Kellar and Robert Wilson to be used for the benefit
of Dolphus Warren Coal and Robert Franklin Pain, also for benefit of
Sarah Frances Coal as long as she sees fit to live on the same. What-
ever else, I give and bequeath to the above named children.
      Executor: Alexander Avery. Dated 28 Sept. 1855.
Wit.: B. D. Kay   (Signed) Theodosia (X) Strawther
      John Burdett
      W. A. Presly
Proven 11 Oct. 1855.

WILL OF JAMES GAMBLE MCLIN - pp 421-422
Wife Harriet Nesbit McLin and our children. Executors: Wife Harriet N.
and friend Lewis C. Clinkscales.
Wit.: Lindsay A. Baker   (Signed) James G. Mecklin
      D. O. Mecklin
      Henry M. Willbanks
      Codicil - Should my wife marry again she is to have child's part.
Proven 7 Jan. 1856.

WILL OF ELIZABETH COX - pp 423-424
Property of every kind to be sold by my son William Cox whom I appoint
my executor, and divide among each of my children, he being one.
Heirs of John Cox, dec'd 1 share. 1 share to Thomas Cox, 1 share to
Polly Ellison, 1 share to Elizabeth Davis. 1 share to William Cox.
1 share to Barbary Harper and at her death to her children.
John Harper and William C. Harper the sons of my daughter Barbary
Harper. Dated 14 Apr. 1848.

Wit.: M. McGee   (Signed) Elizabeth (X) Cox
       J. P. McGee
       W. Magee
Proven 4 Feb. 1856.

WILL OF DR. F. W. SYMMES - pp 425-428
My just debts and those of my deceased son F. W. Symmes, Jr. be paid.
My five surviving children to inherit. One moiety being 500 to 530 acres
known as the mill lands. Land near Village of Pendleton bought of
Martin Palmer containing 384 acres. House and lots joining where I live
in the Village, and share in S. C. Railroad and Bank. My interest in
Shoal Creek Manufacturing Co. in Hart, formerly Franklin Co., Ga.
    Slaves shall be divided into 5 lots. Property be appraised by John
S. Lorton, Richard F. Simpson, G. T. Symmes, Thomas D. Garvin and W. H.
D. Gaillard or any three of them. Mothers not to be separated from
young children if it can be avoided.
    John S. Lorton and G. T. Symmes, one or both, may act as trustees for
my daughters and as guardians of my two older sons till they come of age,
and Wm. R. Jones may act as guardian of my younger daughter and younger
son till each comes of age, and also of my nephew Jones F. Evatt whose
guardian I now am and who has certain property enumerated in the office
of the Commissioner of Equity for Pickens.
    Executors: G. T. Symmes, John S. Lorton, Wm. R. Jones. Dated 8 Oct.
1855.
Wit.: M. S. McCoy   (Signed) F. W. Symmes
       J. L. Shanklin
       S. S. Cherry
    Codicil - F. W. Symmes of Village of Pendleton, declare that I choose
to give my two daughters property as follows: To my daughter Cornelia
the wife of Wm. R. Jones I give negro woman Martha and her 3 youngest
children Tallula, Henry and Alonzo, and to my daughter Mary the woman
Mary Ann, Ellen and her child Baylis, and a girl named Anna, Martha's
oldest daughter. Codicil dated 12 Jan. 1856.
Wit.: W. H. D. Gaillard
       W. L. Jenkins
       J. B. E. Sloan
Proven 15 Feb. 1856.

WILL OF SAMUEL J. HAMMOND - pp 429-432
Wife Ann W. during her lifetime the home tract and 6 or 7 negroes at her
discretion, income from the mills. After death of wife property except
mills sold and proceeds divided into 8 shares. To Benj. F. Hammond,
Clarinda C. Broyles if then living, if not to lineal descendant one share
to the children of my wife's deceased daughter Cornelia Webb (to wit)
Louisa C. Wilkes and Dudley H. Webb. One share to Eliza D. Webb if then
living or to her lineal descendants. One share to Wm. L. Hammond. One
share to my executors in trust for use of my daughter Aleathea L. Gaillard
and her descendants. One share to my son Samuel J. Hammond and one
share to my daughter Amanda P. Earle.
    I have stipulated with sons Wm. and Samuel J. for rebuilding the Mills
where they recently stood on Broadway Creek. Mills join lands of James
Wardlaw, William Smith and others, lands bought from Matthew Gambrell.
Two sons to have mills.
    Executors: Sons Wm. Leroy Hammond and Samuel Jenkins Hammond. Dated
22 Sept. 1852.
Wit.: John Wilson   (Signed) S. J. Hammond
       Elisha Webb
       Herbert Hammond
Proven 8 Aug. 1856.

WILL OF NANCY ROGERS - pp 433-434
Brother-in-law Elias Miller. Nancy Caroline Miller. Martha Green
Shearer. Martha Jane Shearer. My brother Elihu Rogers. Bed clothing
to my sisters. My brother-in-law Gillum Shearer. If Martha Green
Shearer dies before she is 21 her part to go to Gillum Shearer and his
heirs. Sister Malinda Lyndsa. Executor: Gillum Shearer. Dated 30 July,
1856.
Wit.: Jas. McLeskey   (Signed) Nancy (X) Rogers
       Shola Ann Crenshaw
       P. A. Wilhite
Proven 18 Aug. 1856.

WILL OF THOMAS CUNNINGHAM - pp 435-439
Son John Cunningham slaves Moses, Jerry, Alcy and her children Frank,
Wm., Jim and Caroline. Money coming to me from the estate of Thomas
Hood, deceased of Laurence District.
   Wife Elizabeth B. Cunningham land whereon I now reside known as the
Widow McPherson tract containing 233 acres and the slaves Jack, Bob, Lucy,
Laura, David and Dick. To her for life, then divided among her surviving
children.
   To son John a negro woman Hannah and her 2 children Ann and Henrietta
in trust for my daughter Mary Jane Cunningham. To son John 2 girls
Charlotte and Mary in trust for my daughter Martha L. Cunningham. To
son John 2 negro girls, Catharine and Matilda, in trust for my daughter
Annie Maria Cunningham.
   Sons Samuel Cunningham and Thomas H. Cunningham and Joseph G. Cunning-
ham.
   Daughter not of age or married. Sons Samuel, Thos. and Joseph not of
age.
   I give (should my said wife who is enciento) hereafter bear to me a
living female child, to my son two negroes Linda and Harriet in trust for
such child. If child is male to share with other sons.
   Executors: Son John Cunningham and my wife Elizabeth B. Cunningham
and they to be guardians of my children. Dated 21 Apr. 1856.
Wit.: E. S. Norris   (Signed) Thomas Cunningham
      Margaret Williams
      Samuel M. Wilkes
Proven 12 May, 1856.

WILL OF JOSEPH HILLHOUSE, Rev. - pp 440-441
Wife Harriet Hillhouse to have all my estate including my tract of land
on which I am now living on Six and Twenty Mile Creek and also 2 negro
slaves named Charlotte and her daughter Mariah. Dated 13 Nov. 1855.
Wit.: C. L. Gaillard   (Signed) Joseph Hillhouse
      J. D. Gaillard
      Saml. P. Hillhouse
Proven 11 Oct. 1856.

WILL OF POSEY TRUSSELL - pp 441-442
Wife Elizabeth, land where I now live, 374 acres on Broadmouth Creek,
waters of Saluda River, and negroes Margaret and her child in her arms,
William, John, Eady, Dick, Jensie, Harriet, Martha and her child, Ander-
son, Jenny, George, Asbury and Creasy.
   Executors: Hampton Stone and James F. Mattison. Dated 23 June, 1849.
Wit.: Joseph Cox   (Signed) Posey (X) Trussell
      Thomas J. Cox
      Mary Cox
Proven 20 Oct. 1856.

WILL OF NANCY HARPER - pp 443-444
Widow of the late Wm. Harper, Sr., deceased. To Joseph Cox, Esq. I give
my old colored servant woman Juda, also to him $20.00 because Juda is
old and may become a burden and expense to him and is is my will that
she should remain with him and his family during the term of her life.
   Rest of property I give to Jonathan B. Lewis and Elizabeth Wilson,
wife of Hugh Wilson of Big Creek.
   Executor: Jonathan B. Lewis. Dated 12 Dec. 1856.
Wit.: Geo. B. Telford, Belton, S. C.
      G. R. Brown, Belton, S. C.
      J. Wilson, Williamston, S. C.
                                (Signed) Nancy (X) Harper
Proven 2 Jan. 1857.

WILL OF JOS. B. HARBIN - pp 445-446
Wife Agnes Lavinia Harbin my negro girl Lucy, and land in Anderson Dist.
purchased from Alfred Huger.
   My notes I wish placed in hands of J. B. Earle to be kept at interest
and interest paid to wife for benefit of herself and children until the
Court of Equity shall appoint a trustee.
   I wish each of my children on coming of age receive $100.00 out of
my estate and at decease of my wife the residue of my property equally

divided between them.
    Executors: Wife and Henry Clarke, Sr. Dated 3 Sept. 1856.
Wit.: H. E. Ravenel   (Signed) Jos. B. Harbin
       Aaron Boggs
       J. W. Hillhouse
Proven 22 Dec. 1856.

WILL OF ELEANOR DICKSON - pp 447-448
Sisters Jane and Mary Dickson and Margaret C. Smith all my claim and title
to land left me by my father Matthew Dickson. At death of survivor of
them to my nephew Alexander A. Dickson.
    I appoint Dr. C. L. Gaillard my executor. Dated 18 May. 1856.
Wit.: Charles S. Davis   (Signed) Elener (X) Dickson
       David M. Watson
       Jacob Burriss
Proven 13 Jan. 1857.

WILL OF GEORGE B. MATTISON - pp 450-452
Body be interred by side of my oldest sister Matilda in Abbeville Dist.
To my two sons Reuben Mattison and Benjamin Thompson Mattison all tract
of land purchased by me from my brother Archibald, some 50 acres. The
remainder of the tract I expect to sell to James King and Wm. B. Mattison
before my decease.
    To the 3 children of my deceased daughter Frances Risener one half of
the remainder of my personal estate provided that half does not exceed
the value which I have given my sons Reuben and Benjamin Thompson Mattison
in land, if it does then I desire the excess above the value of the land
to be divided into four shares and given each to Reuben, Benj. T., to
Frances' children and one to my son Wm. B. Mattison's children that may
be living at my death.
    To grandson Abner Mattison $5.00 above his brothers and sisters.
    Executor: Friend R. N. Wright. Dated 28 Dec. 1847.
Wit.: A. Mattison   (Signed) George B. Mattison
       James A. Mattison
       James L. Orr
Proven 21 Mar. 1857.

WILL OF REUBEN HALEY - pp 452-454
All estate sold. To Andrew Reid, Esq. my negro boy Charles. To William
Haley my son, Elenor Haley my daughter, the children of Reuben Haley
deceased, and the children of Kitty Buffenton deceased, Willis and
Archibald Haley and the children of Melinda Seigler my daughter dec'd,
John Haley, Orange B. Haley, Rufus Haley, James Haley, Matilda Haley,
Thomas Haley my children $5.00 each. To Polly Yous $5.00.
    Rest of my estate divided equally among my several children, the
children of a deceased child taking their parents share, except Willis
and Archibald Haley herein before named together with Polly Yous who is
to have an equal part with them for her own use.
    Executor: Andrew Reid. Dated 5 Mar. 1857.
Wit.: Henry M. Willbanks   (Signed) Reuben Haley
       Thos. G. Campbell
       J. W. Campbell
Proven 11 May, 1857.

WILL OF JOSEPH T. WHITEFIELD - pp 455-457
Wife Martha. Son John C. He is to be trustee for my daughter Margaret
G. Gaines, whose surviving female children inherit from her. Stock in
Greenville and Columbia Railroad.
    Executor: Friends the Hon. Joseph N. Whitner, Col. Herbert Hammond
and my wife Martha Whitefield. Dated 28 Mar. 1855.
Wit.: James L. Orr   (Signed) J. T. Whitefield
       T. A. Evins
       A. B. Towers.
Proven 25 May, 1857.

WILL OF WILLIAM ERSKINE - pp 458-459
Dated 8 May, 1857. Wife Elizabeth to have plantation and at her death
sold and equally divided among my children.
    Executors: Jas. M. Erskine and W. W. Erskine my two sons. My daughter

Nancy L. Erskine to be made equal with the others is to have a bed, cow
and calf and side saddle.
Wit.: Wm. M. Kay   (Signed) Wm. Erskine
      L. D. Stringer
      B. T. Irby
Proven 1 June, 1857.

WILL OF JAMES E. ALLEN - pp 459-460
Wife Mary C. Allen to have all property for life or widowhood, then sold
and equally divided between her and my children then living or their
heirs.
    Executor: Wife Mary C. Allen. Dated 3 June, 1857.
Wit.: B. F. Mauldin   (Signed) James E. Allen
       Alexander Acker
       G. R. Brown
Proven 15 June, 1857.

WILL OF ANDREW STEVENSON - pp 461-462
Daughter Jane Richey wife of Reuben Richey $1.00, she having received of
my sister Margaret Stevenson's estate over $600.00.
    Estate sold and divided between my wife and children, to wit:
Elizabeth, Mary, William, Anna, John, Nancy, Vilet, Robert Ebenezer, with
the exception of Jane Richey as set forth. The share given to wife
Elizabeth is a child's part.
    Executors: Son-in-law W. B. Bailey and my son Robert Stevenson.
Dated 16 May, 1856.
Wit.: Elijah Webb   (Signed) Andrew Stevenson
       J. C. Whitefield
       C. A. Webb
Proven 28 Aug. 1857.

WILL OF SARAH HUNNICUTT - p 463
Daughter Sinthey Hunnicutt, my two other daughters Elizabeth Hunnicutt
and Mary Ann Jones, and Mary Ann Jones children. Dated 27 Mar. 1857.
Wit.: Martha Milwee   (Signed) Sarah (X) Hunnicutt
       Sophia C. Millwee
       John Hunter, Sr.
Proven 5 Oct. 1857.

WILL OF PETER MC MAHAN - pp. 208-210
Wife Susannah. Bro. William McMahan. Bro. John McMahan. Sis. Catharine
Wright. Sis. Elisabeth Forbes. Sis. Peggy Wilkinson's children.
Dated: 11 Apr. 1838.   Pr. 26 Sept. 1845.
                                   (Signed) Peter (X) McMahan
Wit: Wm. McMurray
      Thomas Orr
      James McKinny

WILL OF AMBROSE H. JONES - p. 210
Wife Happy to have entire estate her lifetime or widowhood, then to heirs
living. Ex.: Wife and son William. No date. Pr. 5 May 1845.
                                   (Signed) Ambrose H. Jones
Wit.: Jno. Watson
       Robt. McKay
       James Goodlett

WILL OF WILLIAM WADDLE - pp. 211-212
Wife Hannah to have estate for life or widowhood, then sold and divided
equally among all of my children. My dau. Delanah Simpson has received
her part. Son William shall have colt. Dated 18 Feb. 1828. Pr. 13 Oct.
1845.   (Signed) William Waddle
Wit.: Robt. Norris
      John Smith
      Sidney Smith
                        End of Book

ANDERSON COUNTY, SOUTH CAROLINA

PROBATE WILL

BOOK 3

1857-1880

Abstracted by Mrs. Charles E. Willie
3610 Fleetwood St.
Amarillo, Texas 79109

INDEX WITH ORIGINAL BOOK PAGE NUMBERS

WILL OF REDMON GRIGSBY WYATT - pp 1-2
Names six children by first wife, who were mentioned under will of
their grandfather, James Richey, deceased, viz: James E. Wyatt,
William Franklin Wyatt, Mary Jane Wyatt, Harriet Elizabeth, John
Newton, Samuel Thompson. Wills home place, 228 acres, to wife, Nelly
Ann; five minor children, Margaret Louisane, Eugenia Ann, Andrew
Seawright, Redmon Caldwell, Rebecca Josephine. Executors: Wife,
Nelly Ann and son, James E. Wyatt. Dated 26 Sept. 1856.
Wit.:   John A. Weir
        B. M. Cheatham
        A. H. McGowan
Probate: 9 Nov. 1857.

WILL OF JOHN S. CARTEE - pp 3-4
Names eight children, to wit: Falby A., Cornely A., Juda C., Milly C.,
Hester E., Oliver S., Warren A., Martha J. Cartee. Executors: Wife
Mary Cartee and uncle, Caleb Cartee. Dated 17 Nov. 1857.
Wit.:   Willis Allen
        J. C. Martin
        S. L. Westmoreland
Probate: 30 Nov. 1857.

WILL OF PEMBROKE S. JOHNSON - pp 4-5
Names wife, Ann Johnson, "to have one sixth share, if marries again",
children who were minors, (unnamed). Executors: Brother, Benj. R.
Johnson and Jas. H. Ware. Dated 8 Sept. 1857.
Wit.:   W. O. Alexander
        W. C. Brown
        L. P. Featherstone (sworn to by William O. Alexander).
   Codicil dated 8 Sept. 1857, "Executors to have power to sell Real
   Estate at public or private sale" (same witnesses).
Probate: 28 Jan. 1858.

WILL OF MARY E. DANIELS - p 6
Nuncupative will, "in presence of witnesses about 2 o'clock in the
morning of 28 Aug. 1857" names mother and sisters (unnamed), Aunt
Phebe Paine, Mrs. Ann Morris (no rel. stated), Aunt Sarah Paine.
Executor: Mr. Daniel Brown.
Wit.:   Elizabeth Johnson
        R. E. Webb
        Mrs. Rice
Probate: 2 Jan 1858.

WILL OF JOHN HIX, SR. - pp 6-8
Daughter Judah C. Hix, "for long continuation with me and her trouble
with her mother in her sickness", all my children: William Hix,
Baylus Hix, Gibson Hix, Rebecca Masters, John Hix, Elias Anderson Hix,
Judah C. Hix. Son, Baylus to be trustee for Rebecca Masters. Executors:
Sons, Baylus Hix, William Hix. Dated 6 June, 1857.
Wit.:   Bryan Buroughs
        A. T. Shirley
        Baldwin Thomas
   Codicil (no date) names son, Granderson Hix, "over-looked and
forgotten".
Wit.:   Bryan Buroughs
        J. C. Tunno (?)
        William N. Tunno (?)
Probate: 5 Feb. 1858.
   (John Hix, Sr. signed his mark).

WILL OF KENON BREAZEALE - pp 9-11
Names wife Lucy Breazeale, tract of land, including homestead, 165
acres, among bequests, a book case made by Hiram Major (no rel. stated).
Children: Enoch Breazeale, dec'd, Aiken Breazeale, Peggy Major, Griffen
Breazeale, Sarah Pepper, Williamson Breazeale, David K. Breazeale,
Laura Cox, Matthew Breazeale. Executors: Sons, Griffen Breazeale,
Matthew Breazeale. Dated 10 Mar. 1854.
Wit.:   Elijah Webb
        A. Evins
        Herbert Hammond
Probate: 5 Feb. 1858.

WILL OF JAMES TELFORD - pp 11-12
Names beloved wife and her three sons (un-named), "now with her",
homestead, 190 acres; my son Robert, my daughter Caroline, "the
children of my first wife", eight in number, four sons and four
daughters", mentioned funds from a court judgement. Executors: Sons
George B., James H. and Robert C. Telford. Dated 19 Dec. 1857.
Wit.: G. W. McGee
       E. M. Gable
       A. P. Taylor
Probate: 16 Feb. 1858.

WILL OF ELIJAH WYATT - pp 12-14
Names wife, Mary; sons James F., William N., Redmon G. Five eldest
daughters, Eliza Mattison, Esther Mitchell, Milly Cox, Susan S. Kay,
Harriet Mauldin, and daughter Matilda. Executors: Son James F.
Wyatt, son-in-law Abner Cox. Dated 13 Oct. 1847.
Wit.: William Magee
       Matthew T. Gambrell
       Michael Lawless
Probate: 10 Mar. 1858.

WILL OF SARAH MILLER - pp 14-15
Names children: Maria Jane Coffe of Cherokee Co., Ga., Mary Ann Wright,
wife of William Wright, Andrew Jackson Lowery, Theresa Pullen, wife of
Leroy Pullen, John Franklin Miller. Executor: Son Andrew Jackson
Lowery. Dated 6 Jan. 1858.
Wit.: H. R. Vandiver
       H. H. Bruce
       Laban Carr
Probate: 10 Mar. 1858.

WILL OF WARREN R. WEBB - pp 16-18
Brother Elijah Webb, in trust for his third son, Elijah R. Webb, when
he is 21...Samuel M. Wilkes, in trust for his son, Willie Webb Wilkes,
when he is 21...Louisa C. Wilkes, wife of Samuel M. Wilkes...nephew,
Warren H. Webb, son of Eliza Webb...my brother and sisters: Elijah
Webb, Elisha Webb, Clayton Webb, Nancy Terry and Frances Clark,
Warren E. Webb, son of Dr. Edmund Webb, Warren Elijah Webb, son of
Micajah Webb, dec'd, James Warren Webb, son of Elisha Webb, Samuel
Warren Webb, son of Clayton Webb, Dudley H. Webb, son of Elijah Webb
"judgement and interest he owes me from 2 Sept. 1855, recorded in
Clerk's Office, Anderson Co.", Samuel M. Wilkes, lot purchased from
A. M. Holland to care for his wife, Louisa C. Wilkes. Executors:
Elijah Webb, Samuel M. Wilkes. Dated 23 Feb. 1858.
Wit.: A. O. Norris
       Thos. S. Crayton
       J. W. Harrison
Probate: 2 April, 1858.

WILL OF JOHN WESLEY FEATHERSTON - pp 19-23
"When any of my sons or daughters come of age or marry"...sons: L. P.
Featherston, John C. C. Featherston...Daughters: Hellen H. Williams,
Emma E. Young. Executors: Sons, L. P. Featherston, John C. C.
Featherston. Dated 11 Feb. 1858.
Wit.: John Wilson
       R. N. Wright
       John M. Mattison
Probate: 31 May, 1858.

WILL OF THOMAS H. GARRETT - pp 23-25
Wife, Clarissa Garrett to have plantation of 240 acres...daughter
Samantha Garrett...Sion Garrett...Lucinda Sego, (no rel. stated)...
son, Wyatt Garrett...daughter, Elizabeth McCarley...son, Seaborn...
son, Bandiver Garrett...son, Calvin...son-in-law Thomas S. Leavell...
orphan children of Ruel Garrett...orphan children of Tillmon Garrett...
Polly Reid, (no rel. stated)..."John Garrett and Bluford Garrett, to
be guardians of two orphan children of Benjamin Johnson, (no rel.
stated), in my stead." Executors: Son, Bluford Garrett and son-in-
law, John Garrett. Dated 3 Jan. 1858.

Wit.: A. P. Cater
        Dudley H. Webb
        Elijah Webb
Probate: 2 April, 1858.

WILL OF LEWIS PRICHARD - pp 25-27
Wife, Harriet...Sons: James Prichard...Berry Prichard...William
Prichard...Cornelius T. Prichard...Lemuel M. Prichard. Daughters:
Nancy Bolt...Martha Ann Prichard...Sarah E. Prichard...Eliza J. Prichard
...Mary C. "Daughters when they marry or reach age 21". Executor:
Bryan Buroughs. Dated 3 Feb. 1858.
Wit.: Asa Avery
        Wm. M. Keown
        James H. Hembree
Probate 13 Aug. 1858.

WILL OF JANE PETTICE - p 27
"Give to Mr. Daniel Osborn (no rel. stated), all property I possess,
after his death and all the funeral expenses and necessary debts paid,
the proceeds shall be given as follows: To Brother Murry Woodson...
his children by his first wife, Katy". Executors: William Telford,
J. Madison Gambrell. Dated 22 Feb. 1858. Testement: Mathias Roberts.
Wit.: G. Horton
        M. G. Cox
        John Ashley
    (Grief Horton and Matthew G. Cox, in oath).
Probate: 27 Aug. 1858.

WILL OF MICHAEL O'NEILL - pp 28-29
Names wife, Catherine, to have house and lot in Anderson, S. C.
Executor: Wife, Catherine O'Neill. Dated 28 Oct. 1857, in Town of
Columbia, S. C.
Wit.: C. Montague
        Charles McKenna
        John Roche
Sworn by Charles McKenna, 24 Sept. 1858, before Jacob Bell, Ordinary
of Richland Co., S. C.
Probate: 27 Sept. 1858, Anderson Co., S. C.

WILL OF JAMES WILSON - pp 30-31
"To beloved wife, land known as Belotte farm, lying at Cross Roads
between Anderson Court House and Williamston or Mineral Springs"
(440 acres)...eldest daughter, Sarah Avary...daughter Elizabeth Avary,
widow of Jesse Avary...Margaret Coker (no rel. stated), wife of Edwin
A. Coker. Executors: Wife (unnamed), son John Wilson, M. D. and Geo.
B. Telford. Dated 13 Aug. 1853.
Wit.: J. B. Lewis, Belton, Anderson District
        P. T. Southern, Belton, Anderson District
        J. H. Telford, Belton, Anderson District
    (J. Harvey Telford in Oath).
Probate: 13 Oct. 1858.

WILL OF ELIZABETH PICKENS - pp 31-32
Names brother Andrew Pickens...sisters, Margaret Pickens, Darcus Paris
(?)...heirs and representatives of Martha Smith, Mary Boman, Anna
Boland, John Pickens. Executor: Brother Robert Pickens. Dated 15
Mar. 1849.
Wit.: W. D. Sitton (William D. in Oath)
        Mary Ann Wilson
        Sarah Ann Sitton
Probate: 15 Oct. 1858.
    Robert Pickens qualified 3 Jan. 1859.

WILL OF MARY LIDDELL - pp 33-34
Names daughters, Amanda Dickson, widow of Alex Dickson...Rachel Emily
Stephenson, wife of James Stephenson, both living in the State of Miss.
...daughter Mary Caroline Liddell, "now living with me, tract of land
I now live on, being third part which husband, A. J. Liddell, Esq.,
deceased, possessed, laid out by Commissioners of the Ordinary of

Anderson District...daughter Eliza Reeves, wife of R. W. Reeves.
Executors: daughter Mary Caroline and son-in-law, R. W. Reeves, Esq.
Dated 17 Nov. 1849.
Wit.: R. D. Gaillard
      S. R. McElroy (Sarah R. McElroy in Oath)
      Wm. Steele
Probate: 17 Dec. 1858.

WILL OF LEWIS WHITFIELD - pp 34-37
Names daughters Martha Whitfield, Rebecca Whitfield...sons, Peter
Whitfield, Lewis Whitfield, Benjamin Whitfield, all to have land lying
west of Burket Creek between Samuel Brown and Jordan Burns, bounded
by William Wright, 490 acres...Son Deny (?) Whitfield, land where he
now lives in Heart (sic) Co., Ga., adjoining Jonathan Weldon, John
Wright and others...William Whitfield, land where he now resides in
Pickens District, surveyed by M. S. McCoy, adjoining Baylus Hix, S.
Isbell and others, also 10 acres whereon Jeptha Whitfield now lives,
lying on left side of road leading from Fairplay to Livingston Whit-
field's, (no rel. stated)...son, Jeptha Whitfield, land adjoining
Joberry Meritt, J. Gibson and others...daughters Mary Gibson and
Rebecca Whitfield, land whereon Jackson Gibson now lives adjoining D.
Stribling, John Hendrix and others...son-in-law John Hendrix. Executor:
H. R. Vandiver. Dated 22 Oct. 1858.
Wit.: William Fant
      Walter C. Dickson
      J. H. Harris
Probate: 3 Jan. 1859.

WILL OF MARY DICKSON - pp 37-38
Names sisters, Elenor and Jane Dickson...Margaret Smith...mentions
late father, Matthew Dickson...nephews, Alexander H. Dickson, Benjamin
W. Dickson. Executor: Dr. C. C. Gaillard. Dated 18 May, 1856.
Wit.: Charles S. Davis
      David W. Watson
      Jacob Burris
Oath dated 26 Jan. 1859, Charles L. Gaillard qualified.
Probate: 12 Mar. 1859.

WILL OF WILLIAM HOLLAND - pp 38-39
Son, William Davis Holland to take control of estate when age 21,
until youngest child becomes 21. Executor: Benjamin F. Mauldin.
Dated 10 Feb. 1859.
Wit.: Hugh Wilson
      W. F. Gaines
      Elizabeth Wilson
Probate: 15 Mar. 1859.

WILL OF WILLIAM MCMURRY - pp 40-41
Names grandson, Joberry McMurry, and grandson, Greenberry Langston to
be educated to age 16. Executors: William M. Willson, Joberry McMurry.
Dated 25 Dec. 1852.
Wit.: Perry McKinney
      P. F. McKinney
      James McKinney
Probate: 22 Apr. 1859.
                              (Signed) William McMurry, Sr.

WILL OF JAMES W. GLEN - pp 41-42
To mother, Pyrena McDaniel, land intersecting road leading from John
Stevenson's to Anderson C. H. adjoining Wilson Hall, Milford Burris,
John Armstrong...wife, Martha...6 children until age 21. Dated 12 Apr.
1859.
Probate: 20 May, 1859.

WILL OF ADAM ELROD - pp 43-44
"Wife, Sarah O. Elrod to have place where I now live, containing 500
acres"...son Richard, land known as Tripp place...son Elijah, land where
he now lives,(180 acres)...daughter, Emily. Executor: son, Richard
T. Elrod. Dated 30 Nov. 1857.

Wit.: Elias Elrod
      A. B. Holland
      W. S. Howell
Probate: 5 Aug. 1859.

WILL OF HENRIETTA WHITLEY - pp 44-46
Spinster, names "my daughters (sic), Jamimah Whitley, Nancy Toler,
Esther Whitley...sons, Adam Whitley, George Whitley". Executors:
Jamimah Whitley, Nancy Toler, Esther Whitley. Dated 8 July, 18<u>32</u>.
Wit.: Alexr. Moorhead
      Walter Poole
      William Poole, Jr.
Probate: 31 Aug. 1859.
   Esther <u>Wilson</u>, qualified.

WILL OF SAMUEL HARRIS BAKER - pp 46-48
Names wife, Margaret...son, James Hamilton Baker...daughter, Elenor N.
Paden, wife of Martin W. Paden...daughter Esther E. Paden, wife of
John M. Paden...children of deceased son, A. W. R. Baker...children of
son, Lindsey A. Baker...daughter Margaret E. Beaty, wife of Thomas N.
Beaty...daughter Penelopy N. Baker...son James Hamilton Baker...son,
Laurence F. Baker...son, James W. Baker, deceased, his wife and
children. Executors: Son, James Hamilton Baker, James Gilmer.
Dated 22 Jan. 1855.
Wit.: Thomas T. Skelton
      P. K. Norris
      Jas. J. McLees
Probate: 12 Dec. 1859.

WILL OF WILLIAM F. CLINKSCALES (WILLIAM FRANKLIN IN OATH) - pp 48-53
Names five children: Asa Clinkscales, Polly, wife of Stephen Clements
...Betsy Hunnicutt, wife of W. P. Hunnicutt, land where they reside in
Gwinnett Co., Ga., Lot No. 270, 6th District, 250 acres...Chloe Towns,
wife of William W. Towns, land where they reside on east side of Hen
Coop Creek, bounded by Noah Cobb, heirs of Mazyk and others, 165 acres
...Berry Mandeville..."illegimate son of Ann Harper, whom she calls
William Franklin Clinkscales, born 7 April, 1848"...Bequests to the
children of Asa Clinkscales, Polly Clements, Betsey Hunnicutt, Chloe
Towns. Executors: James Lawrence Orr, Berry Clinkscales, Franklin
D. Towns. Dated 17 Nov. 1852.
Wit.: William H. Acker
      J. G. Gantt
      Joel Cox
      Abner Cox
   Codicil: William Franklin Clinkscales, Sr., "In will dated 17
Nov. 1852, I named Franklin D. Towns one of my executors. His name
should be written Julius Franklin Towns. I appoint Wm. Clement, my
grandson one of the executors". Dated 27 Feb. 1854.
Wit.: Abner Cox
      J. S. Acker (Joshua S. Acker in oath)
      Christopher Clement.
Admitted to probate 25 Nov. 1859, Berry Clinkscales qualified 19 Dec.
1859.   (This is a long detailed will).

WILL OF ISAAC NEWTON - pp 54-55
"To be decently buried by the side of my departed wife"...bequest to
daughter Martha Newton "for kindness shown in my old age"...children:
Willis Newton...Martha Newton...Catherine, wife of Mitchel Swords...
Frances, wife of Jesse Ingram...Isaac Newton. Executors: Son, Willis
Newton, grandson, Larkin Newton. Dated 28 May, 1859.
Wit.: R. F. Simpson
      Thos. C. Watkins
      B. F. Glenn
Probate: 27 Dec. 1859.

WILL OF THOMAS BLASSINGAME - pp 55-57
Pickens Co., S. C. Names wife, Sarah Blassingame...Children: Mary
Harmon...John Blassingame...Robert Blassingame...Elizabeth Fields...
Obedience Fields "have all been provided for"...daughter, Pertheny
Ariel, daughter, Jane Woodruff, son, Thomas Blassingame, land bought

134

from John Couch, situated on lower end of my land in Anderson District, near Saluda River, (100 acres)...son, David, land adjoining my land, 200 acres...son, William, land adjoing my land, 200 acres...sons, Carr, Franklin and Harrison, each 200 acres when they come of age...Daughter, Eliza. Executors: Wife, Sarah and son-in-law, John Ariel. Dated 29 July, 1833.
Wit.: John Watson
      W. H. Watson
      L. W. Watson
Probate: 31 Dec. 1859.
    John Ariel qualified 31 Jan. 1859.

WILL OF HEZEKIAH RICE - pp 58-59
(Called Hezekiah Rice, Sr. in oath)...wife Polly Rice...children: Polly Clinkscales...Ibzan Rice...Thomas L. Rice...Amaziah Rice... William Magee and Asneth, his wife...children of dec'd son, Hezekiah Rice...Abner H. Magee and his wife, Louisa...Fleetwood Rice...Wiley Latimer and his wife, Irena Smith. Executors: Son, Amaziah and son-in-law, Abner H. Magee. Dated 5 April 1846.
Wit.: John R. Towers
      Harrison Latimer
      George W. Nelson
Probate: 18 Jan. 1860.

WILL OF E. B. BENSON - pp 59-61
(Enoch B. in oath), of Village of Pendleton. Wife, Esther Benson... refers to a reciept book, "I have advanced to John T. Sloan, James W. Earle, James W. Harrison, Andrew P. Cater and John B. Benson, $2000 dollars to each of them, I now direct my executors to collect from each of them $2000 dollars or a total of $10,000 dollars to be added to my estate"...Daughter Esther W. Moore, wife of Hulet Moore, "advanced money to build house in Lawerence District...son, John B. Benson...son, Thomas B. Benson...Rebecca G. Sloan, wife of Frank Sloan...grandson, Samuel Moore. Executors: John B. Benson, James W. Harrison, Thomas B. Benson. Dated 6 May, 1856.
Wit.: J. L. Lorton
      S. F. W. Miller
      John W. Clark
Probate: 17 Mar. 1860.

WILL OF WARREN H. WEBB - pp 62-63
"Give five equal shares to Samuel J. H. Webb, Charles L. Webb, Charlotte A. C. T. Webb, Benjamin F. Webb, (no relation stated)...sister, Ann W. Pepper, wife of John H. Pepper...mentions guardians of minor children to be named. Executor: "to be named by Ordinary". Dated 6 Sept. 1859.
Wit.: Samuel W. Wilkes
      Isabella Reeve
      Louisa M. Reeve
Probate: 9 Mar. 1860.
    Noah R. Reeve qualified 25 Mar. 1860.

WILL OF DAVID HALL - pp 63-67
Farmer...names wife Hannah Hall...three oldest sons, Fenton S. Hall... David L. Hall...Aaron W. Hall. Three youngest sons, Absolom J. Hall... John M. Hall...William C. Hall...daughter Martha Barksdale...daughter Louisa Wildes...daughter Lucinda Hall...daughter Licena Tucker... daughter Mary Bell...mentions land in Anderson District called the Speer tract, lying on fork of Generostee Creek, adjoining lands of James Wiley, Johnson Hall and others (340 acres), Mosely tract adjoining lands of John Speer (250 acres), Worthington tract adjoining lands of Harrison Tucker, W. M. Cook and others (120 acres). Homestead adjoining Howery Hall, Ian Robinson, Levi Gable and others. The Gabel tract on waters of Wilson's Creek, known as Widow Gabel tract, adjoining Manning Belcher, R. Norris, Nathan McAlister. Executors: Sons, David L. Hall, Absolom J. Hall. Dated 26 May, 1859.
Wit.: James Tucker
      P. R. Price (Penuel R. Price in oath)
      Newton J. Newell
Probate: 23 April, 1860.

WILL OF RUTH RILEY - pp 68-69
Names nephew, Sanford V. Gentry...friend Andrew O. Norris, Esq....
niece, Malissa Wilcox, wife of James B. Wilcox. Executor: Andrew O.
Norris. Dated 27 April, 1858.
Wit.: Elijah Webb
      Joberry Sloan
      T. A. Evins
Probate: 18 May, 1860.

WILL OF NATHANIEL PARROTT - pp 69-71
Heirs: Martha G. Watt, wife of Samuel S. Watt...William D. Hewin...
Elvira O. Keown, wife of Robert Keown, Jr...Postell Hewin...Olin T.
Hewin...Pinkney W. Hewin, (no relation stated on any of these).
Executor: Kelly Sullivan. Dated 4 June, 1860.
Wit.: James D. Watt
      Hudson B. Sullivan
      James W. Watt
Probate: 11 July, 1860.

WILL OF ISAAC CLEMENTS - pp 71-74
Wife Pricilla...mentions W. H. Acker, Esq., Dividing land into three
plats, tract no. 1, where Jackson Shaw now lives, situated on Bear
Creek (200 acres), to friend Enoch Drake, in trust for daughter Sally
Shaw, and after her death to be divided between children of her
present and former husband...tract no. 2, where daughter Polly Mattison
resides (116 acres), to friend, Reuben Clinkscales, in trust for Polly
Mattison...tract no. 3, whereon my dwelling house is located (260 acres),
to daughter Rachel Burris...Daughter Anna Keatts, wife of William
Keatts of Pittsylvania Co., received her portion years ago. Executors:
William H. Acker, James L. Orr. No date recorded.
Wit.: L. W. Tribble
      William J. Taylor
      Rolly Banister
Probate: 10 Aug. 1860.

WILL OF OBADIAH MERITT - pp 74-75
Names wife Zilpha Meritt...daughter Lucy, and her two daughters Mary
and Printha...daughter Sarha (sic)...daughter Nancy. Executor:
Ritchard (sic) T. Elrod. Dated 13 June, 1860.
Wit.: John Long
      Elias Elrod
      G. W. Elrod (George in Oath).
Probate: 31 Aug. 1860.

WILL OF A. N. MCFALL - p 76
Of High Shoals, Anderson Co., wills estate to daughters: Elizabeth,
Caroline and Lucretia McFall. Dated 4 May, 1860.
Wit.: S. R. McFall (Samuel in Oath).
      E. E. Thomson (Elizabeth in Oath).
      Jas. Thomson
Probate: 20 Sept. 1860.
   (Andrew N. McFall in index).

WILL OF JAMES DOBBINS - pp 77-79
Wife Mary, to have land known as Felton tract, where I formerly lived...
youngest daughter Jane...4 sons: James J. Dobbins...John B. Dobbins...
William L. Dobbins...Henry E. Dobbins...afflicted daughter Mary E.
Dobbins. Executors: Sons, James J. Dobbins, John B. Dobbins.
(James Dobbins signed by mark). Dated 9 Sept. 1860.
Wit.: Jonathan Pickrell
      James L. Stewart
      John D. M. Dobbins
   Codicil: Names wife, Mary and son-in-law, Joseph McLeskey, dated
   9 Sept. 1860.
Probate: 2 Oct. 1860.

WILL OF JAMES ARMSTRONG, SR. - pp 79-80
Names sons, N. H. Armstrong and John R. Armstrong...wife, Polly...sons,
Wm. B. Armstrong and C. C. Armstrong...four daughters: Margaret, wife

of Benjamin W. Chamblee...Lucinda, wife of Jas. C. Williams...Polly
A. E., wife of H. A. Cobb...Elizabeth Armstrong. Executors: Sons,
N. H. and John R. Armstrong. Dated 4 Dec. 1857.
Wit.: Jas. Armstrong
       Robert H. Branyon
       Joseph J. Copeland
Probate: 31 Oct. 1860.

WILL OF MARY ELLIOTT - pp 81-82
Bequest to Emily Margaret, "a free woman of color in consideration of
the kindness and support in my helpless state"...D. T. Rainwater,
trustee of land (117 acres) granted to William Gaston, 22 Jan. 1822
and deeded to me 3 Feb. 1827, "in trust for said Mary Margaret (later
called Emily Margaret, again), and after her death to her heirs".
(Mary Elliott signed by mark). Executor: Richd. F. Simpson. Dated
3 Feb. 1858.
Wit.: Aaron Smith
       N. T. Smith
       David J. B. Craig
Probate: 10 Nov. 1860.

WILL OF JAMES WILEY - pp 82-83
To Jane A. Wiley and E. M. Wiley, (no relation stated), tract of land
on Beard's Creek, (286½ acres), where I now live on Little Generostee
Creek, (360 acres). Executors: Jane A. Wiley and Elizabeth M. Wiley.
Dated 26 June, 1858.
Wit.: James H. McConnell
       Elias McGee
       Joel A. Partain
Probate: 16 Feb. 1861.

WILL OF JANE DICKSON - pp 83-84
Jane Dickson gives sister, Margaret C. Smith, "tract whereon we now
live which was left to me by my father, Matthew Dickson, dec'd, and
at her death to Alexander A. Dickson and Permelia Dickson (no relation
stated). Executor: Charles L. Gaillard. Dated 5 June, 1859. (Jane
Dickson signed by mark).
Wit.: S. F. McConnell
       Wm. J. Brown
       Jacob Burris
Probate: 27 April, 1861.

WILL OF JAMES WESLEY EDWARDS - pp 84-85
Names wife, Martha Ann Edwards, "if she dies without children"...
children of my brother John M. Edwards. Executor: John Wilson.
Dated 13 May, 1861.
Wit.: Thomas Cox
       Jas. Gambrell
       Harper Gambrell
Probate: 24 May, 1861.

WILL OF DAVID ANDERSON - pp 85-88
Mentions note on Gen'l J. W. Harrison for $700 dollars. Wife, Lucinda
Matilda Anderson...two youngest children, Edward M. Anderson and James
G. Anderson, when full age...child or children of a deceased child to
represent the parent...other children, Robert Anderson...Martha
Anderson...David Anderson...mentions land lying next to town of
Anderson and lot now occupied by Edmund Murrah, across the General's
Road. Executors: Jacob R. Reed and Samuel M. Wilkes. Dated 23 June,
1860.
Wit.: A. T. Broyles
       S. Bleckley
       T. S. Crayton
Probate: 5 July, 1861.

WILL OF THOMAS J. CUMMING - pp 88-89
Mentions land in Anderson District and property in City of Charleston,
on Pritchard Street. Wife Fredrica (?) E. M. Cumming. Bequest to Miss
Rosa Hannah Duglas, "for kindness and regard to my wife and myself"...

137

children of Adeline Alley, (no relation stated)...brother, George A.
Cumming...sister, Agnes Cumming. Executors: Friends, Joseph Poulnot
and John B. P. Alley. Dated 7 Sept. 1861.
Wit.: P. A. Wilhite, M. D.
       Wm. C. Lee
       George Roof
Probate: 20 Sept. 1861.

WILL OF CHESLEY M. MARTIN - pp 90-91
To Addie Ann Martin "child of the wife I once lived with, but now
separated, and which child I don't recognize as my own, $10 dollars.
Some two years ago, my wife who the law recognizes separated for life,
and upon settlement, paid her 1/3 of my whole estate"...balance divided
among my brothers and sisters, the daughter of Richard Mary Frances
(sic), taking share of her mother if she were living. Executors:
J. C. Martin, Richardson Elrod. Dated 26 Dec. 1861.
Wit.: S. Bleckley
       M. H. Brock
       Elijah Webb
Probate 10 Feb. 1862.
   Jacob C. Martin qualified.

WILL OF LARKIN ROGERS - pp 91-92
Names children: W. N. Rogers...Sarah E. Rogers...D. J. S. Rogers...
Eben Z. Rogers...Thomas Rogers...Benjn. H. Rogers...John S. Rogers...
Joseph W. Rogers, when age 21...Daughter July A. Rogers...Matilda M.
Rogers, "she has a lame arm", when she is age 16...David C...Terry F.
Rogers, when they come of age...mentions wife (not named). Executors:
Sons, W. N. and D. S. Rogers. Dated 19 Mar. 1862. (Larkin Rogers
signed by mark).
Wit.: Chesley Rogers
       J. F. Rogers (Jacob in Oath).
       W. W. Rogers (Wm. in Oath, he signed by mark).
Probate: 5 May, 1862.

WILL OF POSTELL L. HEWIN - pp 93-94
Names wife Sarah Emily, to have all estate. Executor: Robert B.
Alexander. Dated 14 Nov. 1861.
Wit.: Kelly Sullivan
       T. M. Fisher
       R. J. Alexander
Probate: 5 May, 1862.

WILL OF ARCHIBALD ARMSTRONG - pp 94-95
Was of Anderson Co., S. C., will written in Hart Co., Ga., wife to
have homestead, (300 acres)...nine children: Elizabeth Shirley...
Daniel B. Armstrong...Isabella L. Ellis...Mary J. Shamble...Arty E.
Armstrong, she being a cripple...Margaret L. Hays...Andrew T. Armstrong
...Rachel R. Armstrong...John A. Armstrong. Executors: Sons, Daniel
B. Armstrong and Andrew T. Armstrong. Dated 4 April, 1862.
Wit.: Wm. R. Pool, Hart Co., Ga.
       Henry Ford, Hart Co., Ga.
       A. H. Floyd, Hart Co., Ga.
       Henry Ford made oath in Anderson Co., S. C.
Probate: 12 May, 1862.

WILL OF AMARIAH FELTON - pp 96-97
Wife and children, when they become 21 years of age. Executor:
Joseph Y. Fretwell. Dated 14 April, 1861.
Wit.: J. H. Whitner (James H. Whitner in Oath).
       Thos. S. Crayton
       W. H. Nardin (Waller H. Nardin in Oath).
Probate: 3 July, 1862.

WILL OF A. R. N. GILMER - pp 97-98
Wife, Ellen F., three children, Sarah Jane...Elizabeth Emma...Tacula
(?) T. Executor: James Gilmer. Dated 4 Jan. 1862.
Wit.: S. W. Williford (Samuel W. Williford in Oath).
       W. M. Buchanan

H. B. Major
Probate: 7 July, 1862.

WILL OF ANDREW H. SUBER - pp 98-99
Wife Ellen C. Suber. Executor: H. R. Vandiver. Dated 28 Dec. 1861.
Wit.: Jonathan Pickerell
R. O. Tribble
W. H. Holland
Probate: 23 June, 1862.

WILL OF LEVI N. GEER - pp 99-100
Wife Margaret. Dated 8 Nov. 1861.
Wit.: W. C. Norris
George M. Bigby
William Williamson
Sworn to by W. C. Norris, 9 July, 1862, in Richmond, Va. T.
Atkinson, N. P.
Probate: Admitted in Anderson District, 28 July, 1862.

WILL OF WILLIAM R. BOROUGHS - pp 100-101
Wife, Mariah F. Buroughs...daughter Julia...appoint John B. Watson,
her guardian until age 21. Executor: Reubin Burriss. Dated 17 July,
1861.
Wit.: W. S. Sharpe
J. T. Snipes
P. K. Norris
E. S. Norris, John B. Watson and J. T. McCown all appeared to swear
that the signatures were those of the witnesses.
Probate: 4 Aug. 1862.

WILL OF J. V. SHANKLIN - p 102
"To be decently interred in Episcopal Church yard in Pendleton"...
wife, Ann E. Shanklin...surviving four children of son, Augustus,
deceased...son E. Henry Shanklin...son Julius L. Shanklin. Executors:
wife, Ann E. Shanklin and son, Julius L. Shanklin. Dated 8 Oct.
1856.
Wit.: J. B. C. Sloan
John L. Lewis
B. Frank Sloan
Probate: 1 Sept. 1862.

FRANCIS M. BREAZEALE - pp 104-105
Names brothers and sisters, also deceased wife's brothers and sisters,
viz: Gambrell Breazeale, Kenon Breazeale, E. W. Breazeale, Barbary
Dean, Nancy Latham, children of Griffen Breazeale, dec'd., G. W. Cox,
Elizabeth Breazeale, Lucy P. Breazeale, Margaret A. Cox. Executor:
brother, Kenon Breazeale. Dated 4 Sept. 1861.
Wit.: J. B. Lewis
M. Breazeale (Matthew in Oath).
W. P. Martin (William in Oath).
Probate: 26 Sept. 1862.

WILL OF THOMAS C. WATKINS - pp 105-106
Wife and children, (unnamed). Executors: B. J. Watkins, Warren J.
Martin and Aaron John Smith. Dated 15 Jan. 1862.
Wit.: J. A. Boggs
D. O. Watkins
Felix Watkins
Probate: 14 Oct. 1862.

WILL OF JOHN B. SLOAN - pp 106-109
John B. Sloan, of Town of Anderson, names friend, Thomas S. Crayton,
trustee for wife and children until age 21, or when daughters marry
(unnamed). Executors: Wife and Jo Berry Sloan. Dated 21 Aug. 1858.
Wit.: J. M. Partlow
J. D. M. Dobbins
J. A. Partlow.
Codicil: Revoke appointment of Jo Berry Sloan as executor and desire
wife to be sole Executrix. Dated 17 July, 1861.
Wit.: J. R. Smith

```
                A. B. Towers
                J. B. Clark
        Probate:  16 Oct. 1862.
          Mrs. Lucille Sloan qualified.
```

WILL OF WILLIAM MULLIKIN - pp 109-111
Mentions wife's aunt, Elizabeth Fielding, dec'd, was a resident of
State of Ga., legacy from her...children: James Monroe Mullikin...
William Haynie Mullikin...Benjamin Washington Mullikin...Martha
Malvina, wife of John W. B. Orr...Laurence Mullikin...Sarah Jane,
wife of Jesse Robins...Hugh Dickson Mullikin...Emily Cornelia Mullikin
...Francis Marion Mullikin...Executors: Son, James Monroe Mullikin
and son-in-law, John W. B. Orr. Dated 22 July, 1862.
Wit.: James Mullikin
       Wm. M. Orr
       Anderson A. Smith
    Codicil: Names unmarried children: Benjamin Washington, Laurence,
    Hugh Dickson and Emily Cornelia. Dated 22 July, 1862, same witnesses.
    Second Codicil: Jesse Robins, husband of daughter Sarah Jane is
    in the Army and John B. Orr, husband of my daughter Martha Malvina
    will immediately be taken by conscript act. Dated 6 Oct. 1862.
    Same witnesses.
Probate: 31 Oct. 1862.

WILL OF JOSEPH T. ROGERS - pp 112-113
Names children: William Avory Rogers...Clary Annis Duckworth...
Sarah Elizabeth Nichols...Mary Caroline Breazeale...Oze B. Rogers...
Dicey Emily Murphy...Matilda Ann Welborn...Amanda Elender Duckworth
and her two children, Mary and Dicey Emily...Joseph Cannon Breazeale,
son of Mary Caroline Breazeale...William Avory Roger's two children,
Thomas Rogers and Elvian Murphy. Executors: Oze B. Rogers and David
K. Breaseale.
Wit.: J. J. Duckworth
       Chesley Rogers
       B. F. Crymes
Probate: 7 Nov. 1862.

WILL OF MRS. NANCY TAYLOR - pp 113-117
Widow of the late Joseph Taylor and principal legatee under his will
dated 29 Mar. 1838. To son-in-law, William Poe, by deed of trust,
tract on School House Branch adjoining John Chamblee, Sloan's Ferry
Road, and Crawford tract, (650 acres)...daughter Ellen C. Poe...
son, Dr. Joseph Taylor, tract known as Towns tract, (297 acres)
conveyed to late husband by Martha Towns, 22 Nov. 1834, Hunt tract
conveyed by Herbert Hammond, Esq., 8 Jan. 1849, Dean Tract of 80
acres conveyed to late husband by J. B. E. Taylor, 6 Oct. 1848...
other children: David S. Taylor...Susan M. Lewis...Samuel J. Taylor...
John B. E. Taylor...William S. Taylor. Executors: sons David S.
Taylor, William S. Taylor, and son-in-law, William Poe...Dated 2 July,
1853.
Wit.: John B. Sloan
       P. S. Vandiver
       Sarah E. Hackett
    Codicil: Mentions notes advanced to sons, J. B. E. Taylor and
    William S. Taylor to be deducted from their shares. Dated 4 Feb.
    1856.
    Wit.: William Sloan
           A. T. Broyles
           A. M. Sloan
    Second codicil: Son-in-law, William Poe has departed this life.
    His wife, Ellen C. Poe to take 460 acres which was described in
    will as 650 acres, now represented by plat of survey made out by
    James Gilmer, 17 Dec. 1856. I have conveyed to Joel A. Roberts
    by deed of trust for benefit of William S. Taylor, four negroes.
    Dated 28 April, 1857.
    Wit.: J. L. Shanklin
           T. J. Pickens
           J. B. E. Sloan
No Probate date.

WILL OF SILAS CROW - pp 118-119
Wife, Mary E. Crow...children when they become 21 years of age. Dated
17 Mar. 1862.
Wit.: R. W. Reeve
       L. M. Tilly
       C. B. Gilmer
Probate: 15 Dec. 1862.

WILL OF DANIEL LEDBETTER - pp 119-120
Wife, E. E. Ledbetter...children, (not named)...H. R. Vandiver,
trustee. Executors: O. H. P. Fant, Joseph N. Brown, John C. Miller,
Samuel Brown, Sr. Dated 18 July, 1861.
Wit.: Jno. Peter Brown
       C. C. M. Bruce
       D. E. Brown
Probate: 26 Jan, 1863.

WILL OF WILLIAM MARVIN KAY - p 121
Wife, Sarah Ann Kay...Children, when 21 years of age. Executor:
Father, Charles Kay. Dated 26 Nov. 1862.
Wit.: W. B. Long
       J. P. Stone
       W. D. Jones (Signed his mark).
Probate: 26 Jan. 1863.

WILL OF SAMUEL BROWN - pp 122-123
Names wife, Helena T. Brown...Joseph N. Brown, trustee for granddaughter,
Emma E. Feaster...six sons: Joseph N. Brown, S. F. Brown, John Peter
Brown, D. E. Brown, J. M. Brown, W. S. Brown. Executors: Sons, Joseph
N. Brown, Samuel F. Brown. Dated 13 July, 1861.
Wit.: H. R. Vandiver
       D. A. Ledbetter
       B. F. Gantt
Probate: 2 Mar. 1863.

WILL OF SUSAN VANDIVER - pp 124-126
Mentions late husband, Sanford Vandiver...children: Hezekiah R.
Vandiver...Helena Brown, wife of Samuel Brown...James M. Vandiver...
Mary C. Bruce, wife of C. C. M. Bruce...Elizabeth N. Ledbetter, wife
of Daniel A. Ledbetter...Jane E. Cox, wife of Jacob E. Cox...Grand-
daughter, Ann E. Simpson. Executor: Son, Hezekiah R. Vandiver.
Dated 24 April, 1857.
Wit.: Thos. Bruce
       S. P. Bruce
       Emma Bruce
Probate: 2 March, 1863.   (Susan Vandiver signed her mark).

WILL OF WILLIAM A. CASON - pp 126-127
Wife, Nancy E. Cason, to raise children: John W. Cason, Syntha Jane
Cason, William James Ostin Cason. Dated 3 Mar. 1863.
Wit.: Wm. D. Sitton
       J. A. M. Cason
       B. J. Spearman (Benjamin J. Spearman in Oath).
Probate: 31 March, 1863.

WILL OF SOPHIE HAYNIE - pp 127-128
Wife of William Haynie, "by virtue of the power given me by a Decree
of the Court of Chancery in Anderson District, S. C., June term 1852,
in settlement of my share of Estate of my late mother, Julia White"...
Nieces: Sophia Jane Watters and Julia Ann Watters. Executor: Friend,
Andrew O. Norris. Dated 25 Aug. 1858.
Wit.: P. A. Wilhite
       T. S. Crayton
       J. W. Harrison
Probate: 8 May, 1863.   (Sophia Haynie signed her mark).

WILL OF L. PRESLY GAINES - pp 128-129
Wife, Elizabeth E. Gaines. Dated 18 April, 1862. No executor named.
Wit.: Nathan Whitmire

F. M. Daniel
T. E. Whitmire
Greenville District, S. C., by Robert McKay, Esq., Ordinary, appeared
Nathan Whitmire, witness, made oath he saw L. Presly Gaines sign his
will.
Probate: 23 May, 1863.

WILL OF ANNA WILLIAMS - pp 129-130
Names children: Austin Williams; Humphrey Williams; John B. Williams;
Ira C. Williams; Lewis A. Williams, son of Lewis A. Williams; Harriet
Horton, wife of John C. Horton; Elizabeth Clement, wife of William
Clement; Mary McDavid, wife of James McDavid; Matilda Acker, wife of
Joshua Acker; children of Mrs. Laura Ann Calhoun; Ira Allen Gilkerson,
son of daughter Louisa A. Gilkerson..."to be interred at the burying
ground where my late husband is laid in Greenville District. Executor:
Son-in-law, James McDavid. Dated 12 April, 1862.
Wit.: Elijah Webb
Abner Cox
John Harkins
Probate: 9 Mar. 1863.

WILL OF WILLIAM F. HARRIS - pp 130-131
Names wife, Margaret...children: Lucinda Rebecca, Livonia Ann,
Katherine Jane (elsewhere mentions two above named children). Executor:
Father, Nathan Harris. Dated 19 July, 1862.
Wit.: Kelly Sullivan
Hudson B. Sullivan
J. P. Sullivan
Probate: 1 June, 1863.

WILL OF ELIZABETH LEWIS - pp 132-133
Names children: Emily R. Goss...Melissa Shackleford...Moses Dean,
wife Narcissa Dean...James C. Keys, wife Louisa...children of Robert
B. Lewis, dec'd.,...viz: Rosalie E. Lewis, J. B. Lewis, Arabella Lewis.
..children of Major J. Lewis, viz: Waddy T. Lewis, Crawford Lewis,
Thomas L. Lewis, Major J. Lewis...children of William A. Lewis, viz:
Major J. Lewis, William W. Lewis, Gilbert E. Lewis. Executors:
James C. Keys and Moses Dean. Dated 22 Dec. 1862.
Wit.: M. C. Munro
S. E. Munro
J. W. Harrison
Probate: 2 July, 1863.   (Elizabeth Lewis signed her mark).

WILL OF JOHN S. PRESLY - pp 134-135
Reverend in oath. Names wife Martha Jane Presly, mentions note held
on James P. Weed. Executors: Wife, Martha Jane and friend, William
A. Presly of Lowndesville, Abbeyville District. Dated 5 May, 1855.
Wit.: Jas. C. Chalmers
Elijah Willbanks
Mary A. Cook
Probate: 10 June, 1863.

WILL OF JOHN O. LONG - pp 135-136
"At the call of my country, have volunteered for it's defence". Wife
Caroline Long to be sole executrix. Dated 29 July, 1862.
Wit.: James N. Campbell
W. O. Campbell
J. A. Hutchinson
Mrs. Martha Campbell made oath that the signatures of James N.
Campbell and W. O. Campbell are genuine. Mrs. Eveline Hutchinson
made oath that the signature of J. A. Hutchinson is genuine.
Probate: 1 July, 1863.

WILL OF JAMES MCMURTRY - pp 137-138
Of Laurens District, S. C. names wife, Dorothy executrix, and father-
in-law, Elijah Teague, executor. Dated 17 Aug. 1835.
Wit.: Joseph Hipps, Jr.
William McMurtry
John Dalrymple
Anderson District, Lewis Dalrymple made oath that signature of John

Dalrymple is genuine. W. H. McMurtry made oath that signature of William McMurtry is genuine. Elijah Teague made oath that the signatures of Joseph Hipps and William McMurtry are genuine.
Probate: 3 Aug. 1863.

WILL OF MASTIN RILEY WILSON - pp 138-139
Names wife, Nancy Elizabeth Wilson, "my own children" (unnamed).
Executor: Wife, Nancy Wilson. Dated 15 Nov. 1862.
Wit.: R. B. Robinson
      Robert Woods
      William N. Fulks
Probate: 24 Aug. 1863.

WILL OF WILLIAM M. CELY - pp 139-140
Names wife, Sarah E. Cely...children when they come of age. Executor:
Wife, Sarah E. Cely. Dated 11 Mar. 1863.
Wit.: Elias Elrod
      Benj. H. Douthit
      Mary A. M. Elrod
Probate: 11 Sept. 1863.

WILL OF WILLIAM GIBBS - pp 140-141
Names wife, Eliza Gibbs, children (unnamed). Executor: Wife, Eliza
Gibbs. Dated 27 July, 1863.
Wit.: B. F. Mauldin
      A. F. Weldon
      Jas. E. Pickle
Probate: 23 Oct. 1863.

WILL OF ALFRED FANT - pp 141-143
Names wife, Sarian (?) Fant...youngest son, Alfred Preston Fant, when
he becomes full age...other children unnamed. Executor: John C.
Horton. Dated 14 Sept. 1858.
wit.: E. J. Major
      Elam Vandiver
      Wm. King
Probate: 23 Oct. 1863.

WILL OF REVEREND ANTHONY W. ROSS - pp 143-145
Names wife, Elizabeth Ross...sons, Anthony W. Ross, Julius N. Ross...
daughter Sally...granddaughters, Elizabeth W. Harrison, Sarah Harrison,
Antoinette Harrison...grandson, James Harrison. Executors: Wife,
Elizabeth Ross and sons, Anthony W. and Julius N. Ross, and nephew
James H. Whitner. Dated 26 March, 1859.
Wit.: Amos P. C. Whitner
      B. F. Whitner
      Toccao Whitner
Probate: 4 Nov. 1863.

WILL OF ADAM STUART - pp 145-146
Names wife, Sophia...wife's daughter Margaret McCartney...my brothers
and sisters, (unnamed). Executor: Hugh Gregg, Sr. Dated 30 Oct.
1863.
Wit.: W. A. Glenn
      V. A. Gregg
      M. C. McCarley (Signed her mark).
Probate: 6 Nov. 1863.   (Adam Stuart signed his mark).

WILL OF JAMES N. CAMPBELL - p 147
Wife, (unnamed)...father, Jesse Campbell...mother, Sarah, "to have my
interest in her estate". Executor: Wm. Sherard. Dated 9 May, 1862.
Wit.: J. W. Sherard
      J. A. Gray
      J. W. Sherard
Probate: 30 Nov. 1863.

WILL OF LEROY W. MATTISON - p 148
Names John Allen Spotts, the grandson of Clarissa Loveless, (no relation
stated) "to have all my estate, if he dies before age 21, bequeath to

to Elizabeth Taylor and her children, viz: Martha Emeline, Margaret Ann, Louisa Salina Taylor. (No relation stated). Executor: Gabriel M. Mattison. Dated 2 Sept. 1861.
Wit.: Thomas W. Traynham
       John W. Rowland
       J. G. Gantt (John G. Gantt in Oath).
Probate: 17 May, 1863.   (Leroy W. Mattison signed his mark).

WILL OF AARON M. HALL - pp 149-150
"Volunteer in the Confederate States:, names brother, F. S. Hall, other brothers and sisters, (unnamed). Executor: Hampton Tucker. Dated 8 Jan. 1862.
Wit.: Willis Craft
       Joshua Boroughs
       Alfred Gailey
Probate: 15 Dec. 1863.
       Fenton S. Hall qualified as executor.

WILL OF HUGH WILSON - p 150
Names wife, Elizabeth Wilson...son, James R. Wilson...J. B. Lewis, Dr. John Wilson and B. F. Mauldin, trustees for Mary Wilson, daughter of dec'd. son, John H. Wilson and her children. Dated 4 Sept. 1862.
Executors: Wife, Elizabeth Wilson and son, James R. Wilson.
Wit.: B. F. Mauldin
       A. L. Abernathy
       J. J. Barron
Probate: 11 Dec. 1863.

WILL OF ALEXANDER MOORHEAD - pp 151-153
Wife Rachel Moorhead to have house and land...son, Robert Moorhead... three grandsons, James L. Gentry, Lewis Gentry, Methusulah B. Gentry... grandson, James L. Campbell...grandson, John Starnes...sons, John and Lewis Moorhead "to have tract of land in Pickens District known as Samuel Adair's Indian Reserve, also 27 acres deeded by Jesse Stepp"... son, William Moorhead...son, James Moorhead " to have 165 acres of land, where he now lives"...daughters, Sarah B. Burriss and Susan G. Knauff... grandson, William Alexander Knauff, his parents being Henry J. and Susan G. Kauff (sic), to be his guardians. Executors: William and Robert Moorhead. Dated 20 Dec. 1862.
Wit.: Jacob Burriss
       James Jolly
       W. G. Smith
Probate: 7 Dec. 1863.

WILL OF NATHANIEL ROCHESTER - pp 153-154
"Not being blessed with children", wife, Louisa Rochester. Executors: Wife, Louisa Rochester, D. T. Rainwater. Dated 22 April, 1862.
Wit.: Jeremiah Smith
       Wm. R. Duckworth
       Elijah Webb
Probate: 4 Jan. 1864.

WILL OF JOHN JOSEPH COOLEY - pp 154-155
Names wife, Sarah V. Cooley, brothers and sisters, (not named). Executor: Hugh Poor. Dated 21 April, 1862.
Wit.: B. F. Mauldin
       Lewis Ellison
       Martha A. Whitt
Probate: 11 Jan. 1864.

WILL OF ASBURY BROOKS - pp 155-156
Names wife, Laura N. Brooks. Executors: Wife, Laura N. Brooks, Kelly Sullivan. Dated 12 Oct. 1863.
Wit.: William Teat
       H. B. Sullivan
       Mary Herring (Signed her mark).
Probate: 12 Feb. 1864.

WILL OF SARAH CRESWELL - pp 156-158
Son, Pickens Creswell, tract containing 550 acres...son, Eliju Creswell,
dec'd., mentions items received from his estate...granddaughter,
Sallie Brownlee...son, Henry Creswell...daughters, Margaret Anderson,
wife of Dr. Michael M. Anderson...Caroline Brownlee, wife of James
Brownlee...Elizabeth Waller, wife of Albert Waller, dec'd...grand-
daughter, Sallie Creswell, daughter of dec'd. son, John H. Creswell.
Executors: Sons, Pickens Creswell and Henry H. Creswell. Dated 6
Sept. 1859.
Wit.:   A. B. Towers   (Alexander B. Towers in Oath).
        Thos. M. White
        W. W. Humphreys
        John V. Moore
Probate: 22 Feb. 1864.

WILL OF JOHN MCPHAIL, JR. - p 159
Names wife, Mary L. McPhail..."Wife's heirs, George Shrimp and said
John McPhail's heirs, (unnamed) share and share alike". Executor:
Col. Charles S. Mattison. Dated 1 Feb. 1864.
Wit.:   James Emerson
        John Herron
        Martha J. Elrod
Probate: 22 Feb. 1864.

WILL OF BENJAMIN F. JOHNSON - pp 160-161
"Names Hasting Johnson, (no relation stated), trustee for wife, Mary
Eliza Johnson and all my children, (unnamed)". Executor: Wife, Mary
Eliza Johnson. Dated: 14 Dec. 1861.
Wit.:   A. P. Martin
        John Milam
        W. H. Martin
Probate: 27 Feb. 1864.

WILL OF HIRAM COOLEY - pp 161-163
Son, Newton W. Cooley, plantation known as James Cooley place, 240
acres...B. F. Mauldin, trustee for daughters Lizzie and Mary Ann Cooley
...daughter Martha Ann Bruce...Nancy Jane Hall, Francis Emeline Jordan.
..son-in-law, A. J. Hall...B. F. Mauldin, trustee for daughter Frances
Emeline Jordan, one quarter section of land in Cherokee Co., Alabama,
being place whereon she now lives...son, John H. Cooley, land surveyed
for him...other children: William L. Cooley, Emory T. Cooley, Jacob
M. Cooley, Jasper Cooley, H. C. Cooley. Executor: B. F. Mauldin.
Dated 11 Feb. 1862.
Wit.:   David Rogers
        W. M. Cooley   (William in Oath)
        Lucind Cooley
Probate: 21 April, 1864.

WILL OF JAMES MATTISON COX - pp 163-164
Wife, Mary H. Cox...two children: John F. Cox and James C. Cox, when
age 21. Executor: Alfred Campbell. Dated 9 Mar. 1864.
Wit.:   Belvarida Pickett
        Martha A. Cox
        Joseph Cox
Probate: 25 April, 1864.

WILL OF JUDGE J. N. WHITNER - pp 164-166
(Later Joseph Newton)...wife, Elizabeth Hampton Whitner...children
unnamed. Executor: Wife. Dated 17 Aug. 1861.
Wit.:   Albert A. Morse
        A. B. Towers
        A. O. Norris
Probate: 23 May, 1864.

WILL OF ANDREW T. STEVENSON - pp 166-167
Wife, Louisa Asenath Stevenson...children unnamed. Executor: Wife.
Dated 24 Nov. 1862.
Wit.:   Thos. A. Sherard
        W. Y. Sherard
        William Sherard
Probate: 6 June, 1864.

WILL OF BENJAMIN ADAMS - pp 167-168
Wife, Elizabeth...daughters: Mary H. Tucker, Permelia E. Wasson,
Martha R. C. Hall, Lucinda M. Presley, Sarah Ann A. Adams, Nancy L.
Adams. Executor: Gabriel M. Mattison. Dated 24 Dec. 1862.
Wit.:   J. C. Gantt
        J. M. Greer
        J. A. Brock
Probate: 10 June, 1864.

WILL OF ROBERT COLEMAN - pp 168-170
"Caroline Davis, for keeping house for me, lot lying West of road
leading from Williamson Grubbs' to Barkers Creek Church, adjoining
John Massey, being part of Lee tract, upon her death to revert back
to estate"...tombstones to be put at graves of my wife, Sarah Coleman,
Robert, William and Thomas Coleman, all now dec'd...Children: John
Coleman, David Coleman, Henrietta Coleman, Isabella Austin, Jane
Campbell. Executor: Gabriel M. Mattison. Dated 2 April, 1863.
Wit.:   Samuel Donnald
        David Moore
        R. R. Seawright
    Codicil: Dated 2 April, 1863, Abbeyville District, revoking all
legacy to Caroline Davis. Dated: 4 Dec, 1863.
Wit.:   J. F. Kellar
        M. J. Mattison
        M. R. Mattison
Probate: 30 June, 1864.

WILL OF LOUISA ROCHESTER - pp 170-171
Wm. Rochester, Sr., of Cobb Co., Ga....John Addison Greggory of Union
Co., S. C....William G. Smith, conductor on G&CR Railroad, (no
relation stated). $1500 dollars for fixing up three graves in Hopewell
Baptist Church in Anderson District, (not named)...Mother, unnamed...
sisters, including Aaron John Smith's wife, my dec'd. sister's children
...brothers and sisters or their heirs. Executor: D. T. Rainwater.
Dated 1 June, 1864.
Wit.:   John M. Carlisle
        Charles Kay
        L. P. Carson (Signed his mark).
Probate: 4 July, 1864.

WILL OF SAMUEL BOWEN - pp 172-173
Wife, unnamed...daughter Sarah Mahala Bowen...mentions land known as
Crenshaw tract...other children unnamed. Executor: David Tillotson
Rainwater. Dated 29 April, 1864.
Wit.:   Samuel F. McConnell
        A. A. Whitaker
        W. E. Eskew
Probate: 4 July, 1864.

WILL OF LUCINDA COOLEY - pp 173-174
Mentions tract of 71 acres adjoining Widow Poor, John Poor and others..
.niece, Elizabeth Mattison and her husband, John Mattison. Executor:
Benjamin F. Mauldin. Dated 12 Sept. 1859.
Wit.:   B. F. Whitner
        J. A. Harrison
        J. W. Norris
Probate: 7 July, 1864.

WILL OF JOHN MCCALISTER - p 175
Wife, Nancy E. McCalister...children when they come of age. Executor:
Wife, Nancy E. McAlister. Dated 10 Feb. 1864.
Wit.:   A. Reid
        Thomas Beaty
        J. H. Reid
Probate: 25 July, 1864.   (John A. McAlister in index).

WILL OF W. W. WELBORN - p 176
Names William and John Welborn, when they come of age...wife, Zilpha...
four children: Mary E. Welborn, J. A. Welborn, M. L. Welborn, Nancy
Jane Welborn. Executor: Zilpha Welborn, F. M. Welborn, Thomas Harper.

Dated 2 July, 1863.
Wit.:   Jas. E. Pickel
        J. B. Rogers
        A. F. Welborn
Probate: 1 Aug. 1864.

WILL OF HOLBERT A. COBB - pp 177-178
Wife, Mary Ann Cobb...children, when they come of age. Executors:
Wife, Mary Ann Cobb and son, Wm. H. Cobb. Dated 9 Sept. 1863.
Wit.:   G. W. Cox (George W. in Oath)
        E. W. Breazeale
        L. H. Richardson
Probate: 5 Aug. 1864.

WILL OF MARY ELIZA NORTH SMITH - pp 178-179
Names sisters, Sarah Edith Ann Smith, Emily Hayne Smith, Alice Talmadge,
...half sister, E. S. V. Wilson...niece, Mary Edith Talmadge, daughter
of John A. Talmadge...niece, Laura Benjamin Wilson, daughter of S. M.
Wilson, "she bears name of her two uncles who have fallen in defence
of their country"...half sister, Elizabeth Wilson (may be same as E.
S. V. Wilson). Executors: Brother, William C. Smith and sister,
Sarah E. A. Wilson. Dated 16 July, 1864.
Wit.:   E. Emily Thurston
        John B. Adger
        Wm. C. Ravenal
Probate: 18 Aug. 1864.

WILL OF AARON JOHN SMITH - pp 180-182
Wife, Ann Elizabeth Smith..."either or both children until marriage
or reach majority"...mother Mary Smith, widow, "property I may devise
from her". Executors: Wife, Ann Elizabeth Smith, William Newton
Smith, David T. Rainwater. Dated 28 April, 1862.
Wit.:   John Wilson
        J. B. McGee
        A. O. Norris
    Codicil: Dated 29 April, 1862, "Either or both" children should
read, one or more of my children, it being my purpose to provide for
the birth of future child or children of my present marriage, having
now but two children.
Wit.:   B. F. Whitner
        J. B. McGee
        A. O. Norris
Probate: 29 Aug. 1864.

WILL OF JOHN HUNTER, JR. - pp 182-183
Names wife, Eleanor Hunter and children, (unnamed). Executor: Wife,
Eleanor Hunter. Dated 29 Aug. 1863.
Wit.:   W. B. Long
        W. Duckworth
        W. L. Bolt (William L. Bolt in Oath)
Probate: 30 Aug. 1864.

WILL OF DANIEL E. BROWN - pp 183-184
Names mother, Helena F. Brown...mentions sale of father's property,
in 1863...brothers, Joseph N. Brown...S. F. Brown...John P. Brown...
J. M. Brown...William S. Brown...niece, Emma E. Feaster. Executor:
Joseph N. Brown. Dated 23 Mar. 1864.
Wit.:   H. R. Vandiver
        William Pitts
        Jordan Burns
Probate: 12 Sept. 1864.

WILL OF SAMUEL F. BROWN - pp 185-186
Names wife, Mollie Brown...brothers and Emma Feaster, "all the property
that I received from my father and his estate, which will appear in
Ordinary books in Anderson Court House"...Brothers, John Peter Brown,
Joseph N. Brown, Seph N. Brown. Executor: Joseph N. Brown. Dated
27 Jan. 1863.
Wit.:   David Simmons

147

Bird Pullen
Thos. B. Palmer
Probate: 12 Sept. 1864.

WILL OF JOHN H. NEWELL - p 187
Names brother, Samuel Newell, "tract of land where we now live, that
we purchased at my mother's sale, also land I purchased from Thos. J.
Newell...other brothers and sisters, (unnamed)...N. J. Newell, trustee
for nephew, John James Tucker. Executors: N. J. Newell, Samuel Newell.
Dated 26 Aug. 1863.
Wit.: J. D. M. Dobbins
       Elijah Webb
       S. V. Gentry
Probate: 19 Sept. 1864.

WILL OF SAMUEL J. HAMMOND, JR. - pp 188-189
"To be buried at Baptist Church in town of Anderson, suitable tombstone
to be erected:...mentions Deed of Trust executed to James L. Orr, 17
Nov. 1863...wife, Louisa O. Hammond...brother, W. L. Hammond...sisters,
Aleathea Gillard, Amanda Earle, Eliza Reeves...friend, Elias Earle,
trustee for Eliza Reeves. Executor: John D. M. Dobbins. Dated 6
Sept. 1864.
Wit.: John Dalrymple
       Milford Burress
       M. Kelly
       James L. Orr
Probate: 19 Sept. 1864.

WILL OF JAMES EMERSON, ESQ. - pp 189-191
Names son, Samuel "to have Garner tract where he now lives", (250 acres)
John Allen Emerson, "to have tract where I now live, bounding Rocky
River, William P. Hawkins, (250 acres)...son, Samuel to be guardian of
James Harvey Emerson, who is mentally deranged...daughters, Jane Drake,
Sarah Ann Elizabeth Rice, Lucinda E. Magee. Executors: Son-in-law,
James A. Drake and son, Samuel. Dated 23 Aug. 1864.
Wit.: John Martin
       F. M. Kay
       A. Rice
Probate: 23 Sept. 1864.

WILL OF WILLIAM O. CAMPBELL - pp 191-192
(Called Obediah Campbell in body of will)...mother, Sarah Campbell
"to have share of my father's estate. Executor: Sarah Campbell.
Dated 17 Sept. 1864.
Wit.: Jacob Mouchet
       George Stevenson
       John A. McMahan
Probate: 27 Sept. 1864.

WILL OF JAMES F. MATTISON - pp 192-193
"To be buried at Shady Grove Burying Ground"...wife, Elizabeth Caroline
Mattison, land where she now lives known as Calhoun Place, (260 acres),
a tract known as Hawkins tract, (270 acres)...mentions co-partnership
with Daniel Mattison in firm of D. & J. F. Mattison...four children,
John Robert Mattison, Isabella, Letitia, Emeline Mattison. Executors:
wife, Elizabeth Caroline Mattison and Daniel Mattison. (Signed at
Sullivan's Island). Dated 5 Nov. 1862.
Wit.: Jas. C. Keys
       Thos. Parks
       William H. Haynie
Probate: 6 Oct. 1864.

WILL OF EDWARD C. PRINCE - p 194
Names wife, Mary E. Prince. Executor: William Sherard. Dated 10 Jan.
1862.
Wit.: S. A. Hutchinson
       G. F. Burditt
       R. N. Boyd
Probate: 7 Oct. 1864.

WILL OF ISAAC BARNETT - p 194
Names wife, Nancy S. Barnett and children (not named). Executors:
J. D. M. Dobbins and wife, Nancy S. Barnett. Dated 31 Aug. 1863.
Wit.: William S. Hall
      Henry Clark
      Elisha Webb
Probate: 8 Oct. 1864.

WILL OF JOHN P. ROGERS - pp 196-197
Names wife, Ann Rogers, "to have land lying N. W. of Williamston Road
and E. of Five Notch Road, (300 acres)...eldest son, J. F. Rogers,
when he comes of age or marries..son, H. C. Rogers. Executor:
Friend, Austin Williams. Dated 29 Feb. 1864.
Wit.: R. R. Hudgins
      J. B. Rogers
      A. F. Welborn
Probate: 12 Oct. 1864.

WILL OF DAVID M. CAMPBELL - pp 197-198
Names "two of my sisters", viz; Nancy R. Campbell and Fanny B. Campbell.
Executor: James Gilmer. Dated 16 Jan. 1862.
Wit.: A. S. McClinton   (David M. Campbell signed his mark).
      Jas. J. McLees
      Jas. L. Simpson
Probate: 2 Dec. 1864, Nancy R. Campbell, qualified.

WILL OF SAMUEL R. MCELROY - pp 198-199
Names wife, Mary Montgomery McElroy, and children when they come of
age...Executors: Wife, Mary M. McElroy and her father, Thomas Dickson.
Dated 12 Mar. 1863.
Wit.: J. E. Bellotte
      Robert A. Steele
      William M. Belotte
  All witnesses were residents of Pendleton, S. C.
Probate: 18 Nov. 1864.

WILL OF HUGH HARKINS - pp 199-200
Names wife, Martha Harkins. (No executor listed). Dated 12 Jan. 1852.
Wit.: William Carlisle
      James McDavid
      Alexander Stevenson
Probate: 25 Nov. 1864.

WILL OF BAYLIS H. MATTISON - pp 200-201
Wife Elizabeth Mattison to be executorix. Dated 17 Nov. 1864.
Wit.: W. M. Gaines
      W. S. Davis
      D. W. Hawthorn
Probate: 29 Nov. 1864.

WILL OF P. R. PRICE - pp 201-202
Names wife, Margaret E. Price...nine children: Josiah D. Price, John
J. Price, James A. Price, Martha J. Price, William O. Price, Claudius
G. Price, Rufus E. Price, Joseph L. Price, Salina R. Price. Executor:
Josiah D. Price. Dated 11 Sept. 1864.
Wit.: H. P. Price   (P. R. Price signed his mark).
      R. R. Beaty
      Wm. J. Millford (Dr. Millford in Oath).
Probate: 14 Nov. 1864.

WILL OF DR. EDMUND WEBB - pp 202-205
Names Martha Ann Webb, "support for herself and such of my children
as may continue to live with her"...son, Thomas J. Webb...Trustee,
James L. Orr...mentions daughters share. Executor: Wife. Dated
26 Mar. 1860.
Wit.: Samuel M. Wilkes
      J. D. M. Dobbins
      S. Bleckley
Probate: 5 Dec. 1864, Martha Ann Webb qualified.
   Codicil: "If wife, Martha Ann should remarry, I direct my trustee,

James L. Orr to take all property into his hands, as trustee".
Dated 21 June, 1860.
Wit.:   J. M. Dobbins
        S. Bleckley
        Elijah Webb.

WILL OF NANCY FINLEY - pp 205-206
"Debt to John C. Carpenter to be paid, also additional $200.00, if
he returns from the Army", the rest equally divided between brothers
and sisters, (not named)...Samuel Herring, $20.00, (no relation
stated). Executor: Kelly Sullivan. Dated 18 Nov. 1864.
Wit.:   William Teat   (Nancy Finley signed her mark).
        Laura N. Brooks
        Margaret E. Sullivan
Probate: 29 Nov. 1864.

WILL OF J. AUGUSTUS LEWIS - pp 206-207
Names wife, Catherine J. Lewis...mentions interest in mercantile firm
in town of Honea Path. Firm called Shirley and Lewis. Executors:
Brother J. B. Lewis and friend, J. J. Shirley. Dated 18 July, 1861.
Wit.:   W. W. Roland
        Alfred Holt
        W. P. Martin
Probate: 12 Dec. 1864.

WILL OF JOHN E. NORRIS - pp 207-208
Names wife, Catherine D. Norris...granddaughters: Cindarella Keys,
Martha Keys...Daughter, Clementine, wife of Aaron Hall...children of
A. O. Norris...children of J. H. Norris...children of Sarah Crumley.
..children of Clementine Hall...children of dec'd. daughter, Harriet.
Executor: Brother Jesse W. Norris. Dated 15 Feb. 1861.
Wit.:   B. F. Crayton
        Alfred M. Ayers
        John B. Wilson
Probate: 3 Jan. 1865.

WILL OF JOHN B. POOR - pp 209-210
Names wife, Elizabeth E. Poor and children when oldest comes of age.
Executor: Wife. Dated 23 Feb. 1863.
Wit.:   J. N. Whitner
        M. T. Whitner
        E. H. Whitner
    "J. W. Harrison and F. E. Harrison swear that J. N. Whitner is
dead and that M. T. Whitner and E. H. Whitner are absent from limits
of this state. They are acquainted with signatures of said men and
they are genuine". Dated 9 Jan. 1865.
Probate: 9 Jan. 1865.

WILL OF JOHN SHERIFF - pp 210-211
Names wife, Sarah E. Sheriff...mentions land on Three and Twenty Mile
Creek, adjoining lands of James D. Smith, James B. Pegg and others,
(150 acres)...children to share and share alike. Executor: James
Gambrell, Jr. Dated 27 May, 1863.
Wit.:   Wm. D. Sitton (Esq. in Oath)
        Alexander Moore (signed his mark)
        William Waddle
Probate: 16 Feb. 1865.

WILL OF JAMES HARDY - pp 212-213
"Having heretofore made advances to my children and intending in the
future as I may think proper, to advance further any child or grand-
child, hence this will. Estate to be divided amongst my children and
lineal descendants of any deceased child or children". Executors:
Sons, Richard B. Hardy, John Hardy and son-in-law, John F. Sadler.
Dated 13 July, 1849.
Wit.:   Elias McGee
        Dickson L. Baker
        Lyndsay A. Baker
Probate: 17 Mar. 1865.

WILL OF JOHN MCCOWN - pp 213-214
Names wife, Mary McCown...daughters: Amanda and Cindarella...son,
William. No executor named. Dated 17 May, 1865.
Wit.: Bryan Boroughs
       J. T. Dean
       J. F. C. Jones
Probate: 2 June, 1865.

WILL OF MARY HERRING - pp 214-216
Mentions real estate of late husband...daughters: Mrs. Laura N.
Brooks, Mrs. Sarah Ann Tilly...sons: James Herring, Francis Herring,
Jefferson Herring, Jesse Herring, Elijah Herring...James M. Herring
to be trustee for Sarah Ann Tilly...grandchildren: Francis A. Beaty,
David Milton Beaty, children of my dec'd. daughter, Rutha Ann Beaty,
when reaching full age. Executors: Son, James M. Herring and John
M. Burriss. Dated 11 April, 1856.
Wit.: T. A. Evins   (Mary Herring signed her mark).
       Ansel Strickland
       J. W. Harrison
    Codicil: Dated 17 Nov. 1857, release James M. Herring as trustee
for daughter Sarah Ann Tilly, she to take her full share free from a
trustee.
Wit.: B. F. Crayton
       T. S. Crayton
       J. W. Harrison
Probate: 5 June, 1865.

WILL OF MARY TODD - pp 217-218
Names children of dec'd. son, Archibald Todd...children of dec'd.
daughter, Mary Amanda George...children of dec'd. daughter Jane Rice.
..children of dec'd. daughter Ellen Jones...sons: R. Willis Todd,
John L. Todd, William P. Todd, James Auson (sic) Todd, Joseph Addison
Todd...daughter Mrs. Elizabeth McFall...daughter Sarah Ann Roof, wife
of George Roof. Executors: Sons, R. Willis Todd, W. P. Todd. Dated
7 Feb. 1861.
Wit.: J. W. Harrison
       J. D. M. Dobbins
       A. O. Norris
    Codicil: Dated 7 Sept. 1862, "John L. Todd and Joseph Addison
Todd have died since execution of will. The legacies bequeath to them
should fall into my estate".
Wit.: A. O. Norris
       M. H. Brock
       Herbert Hammond
Probate: 17 June, 1865.

WILL OF JAMES T. LATTA - p 219
Mentions "that portion of my father's estate which by the 5th section
of his will I am entitled, upon the death of my mother, to my three
sons": Edward D. Latta, William P. Latta, Walter W. Latta. Executor:
Wife, Angela W. Latta. Dated 27 May, 1865.
Wit.: Wm. Henry Treascott
       W. A. Haynie
       Carver Randall
Probate: 11 July, 1865.

WILL OF JONN C. MASSEY - p 220
"If I die in battle, to be brought back and decently interred and
expenses paid by my executors"...wife, Mary Ann Massey...children
(not named). Dated 14 Jan. 1864.
Wit.: Samuel F. Fisher
       A. B. Holland
       Elijah Webb
Probate: 14 July, 1865.

WILL OF WASHINGTON S. BLAKE - pp 221-222
Names wife, Harriet Ann Blake...sons: William Austin Blake, Andrew
Lee Blake. Executors: Wife, Harriet Ann and friend, Austin Williams.
Dated 4 Mar. 1865.

Wit.: W. K. Clement
       Aaron Welborn
       Richardson Garrett
Probate: 7 Aug. 1865.

WILL OF ELBERT J. STEVENSON - pp 222-223
Names first wife's son, Luther E. Stevenson, (also called "my oldest
son")...wife Elmira C. Stevenson...five children by present wife:
Margare J. Stevenson, Cindarella L. Stevenson, Francis A. Stevenson,
Elmira A. Stevenson, and a son not named yet, until all come of age..
.No date, oath said sometime in Feb. 1863. No executor named.
Wit.: B. D. Kay
       G. F. Burdett
       John Morgan
Probate: 23 Sept. 1865.

WILL OF THEODORE M. FISHER - pp 223-234
Names wife, Sarah Ann Fisher...three children now living: Mary,
William and James S. Executors: William L. Wharton, James H. Wideman,
Hezekiah Burnett. Dated 25 Feb. 1863.
Wit.: Kelly Sullivan
       James H. Sullivan
       William Teate
   Codicil: Dated 1 Sept. 1863, "If my wife should have another
child, it should have equal share with the three children named".
Wit.: Kelly Sullivan
       James H. Sullivan
       William Teate
Probate: 16 Oct. 1865.

WILL OF ALEXANDER H. GLENN - pp 225-226
Sister, Eleanor Jane Smith, wife of S. F. Smith...sister, Margaret
E. Glenn...Cynthia, wife of dec'd. brother, B. F. Glenn, and his two
minor children, James Lawrence and William Henry Glenn, guardian to
be named for them...Uncle, F. M. Glenn, trustee for sister, Mary C.
Snipes, wife of Mathew A. Snipes. Executor: Brother-in-law, S. F.
Smith. Date: , 1864.
Wit.: John C. Whitfield
       B. F. Crayton
       Herbert Hammond
Probate: 18 Oct. 1865.

WILL OF ROBERT GILMER - pp 226-229
Names wife, Jane Gilmer...sons, Abner R. N. Gilmer, Crawford W. L.
Gilmer...Daughter, Mary M. S. S. C. Todd, wife of James A. Todd.
Executor: Brother James Gilmer. Dated 28 Oct. 1856.
Wit.: B. F. Crayron
       H. N. Reid
       J. H. Maret
   Codicil: Dated 15 April, 1857. "A deed of trust bearing date, 15
April, 1857, I have given my son, Abner R. N. Gilmer, a negro girl,
Senthor, for sole use of my daughter, Mary S. S. C. Todd, and appoint
Abner R. N. Gilmer, Trustee.
Wit.: James L. Orr
       Thomas S. Crayton
       John M. Partlow
   Second Codicil: Dated 31 July, 1862, "my two sons, Abner R. N.
Gilmer and Crawford W. L. Gilmer have both departed life, since
execution of will, I hereby revoke bequests made to them, but in no
way to effect the share intended for my daughter, Mary M. S. S. C.
Todd in trust, except as modified by this codicil: After death of my
wife, one half of entire estate to the two children of son, Abner R.
N. Gilmer, one half to daughter Mary.
Wit.: Rebekah Herbet
       Sarah Gunnin
       J. W. Harrison
Probate: 15 Nov. 1865.

WILL OF ANDERSON A. SMITH - pp 229-230
Names father and mother, John A. Smith and Rhoda C. Smith, tract of
land adjoining C. McSmith, (118 acres)...two sisters: Amanda A.
Smith and Cimela H. Smith, (also spelled Chimela)...other sisters
and brothers...H. G. Smith, dec'd. brother, John L. Smith. Executors:
Sisters, Amanda A. Smith and Chimela Smith. Dated 23 Feb. 1863.
Wit.:   William D. Sitton
        Fannie J. Sitton
        Mary K. Kay
Probate: 24 Nov. 1865.

WILL OF BEVERLY L. THOMPSON - p 231
"Interest in my father's estate to my wife, Mary L. J. Thompson,
until youngest child becomes 21 years of age". Executor: Wife, Mary
L. J. Thompson. Dated 15 June, 1863.
Wit.:   B. F. Mauldin
        Joshua Smith
        Wm. Thompson
Probate: 5 Feb. 1866.

WILL OF JOHN SITTON - p 232
Names wife, Eliza A. Sitton...daughter, Mary C. Sitton. "I have
provided for my other children before making this will". Executor:
Eliza A. Sitton. Dated 4 Dec. 1865.
Wit.:   B. F. Mauldin
        John Wilson
        R. W. Todd
Probate: 25 May, 1866.

JOHN W. DANIELS, CLERK OF COURT, NOW ACTING ORDINARY.   HERBERT HAMMOND,
FORMER ORDINARY.

WILL OF HERBERT HAMMOND - pp 233-234
Names wife, Elizabeth Hammond, "all her children to share and share
alike"..."In transaction of the business of the Ordinary Office of
Anderson District, there are numerous claims which have not been
regularly charged to the parties and to the intent that all such
be made available, I authorize that recourse be had by my executor
to the journal or minute book and the estate papers of parties filed
and where any such administers, executors, guardians and so forth
may be in default in paying their regular fees, such measures may
be adopted as to bring them to legal settlement with my Estate".
Executor: Son, John P. Hammond. Dated 25 Apr. 1866.
Wit.:   John Wilson
        Elijah Webb
        J. D. M. Dobbins
        Geo. F. Round
Probate: 13 July, 1866.

WILL OF FLORIDE CALHOUN - pp 235-245
Pendleton...Daughter Anna Mariah, wife of Thomas G. Clemson, of
Maryland, "to have land in Pendleton, purchased by me from Mr.
William Adger"...mentions prayer book presented to me by the Church
at Newport, Rhode Island...granddaughter Floride Elizabeth Clemson.
..sons, John and William and their children...cousin, Edward Boisseau
...grandson, John Calhoun Clemson, "a book of the funeral ceremonies
of his Grandfather, presented to me by Mr. R. Pinkney, of Charleston"
...daughter-in-law, Kate P. Calhoun and her children...grandson, John
C. Calhoun, child of dec'd. son, John...grandson, Benjamin A. P.
Calhoun, child of dec'd. son, John, "his Grandfather's work on
Government"...grandson, Lownd Calhoun, child of dec'd. son, William
Lownd...son, Andrew P. Calhoun, his father's portrait painted in
Europe, now hanging at Ft. Hill...granddaughter, Margarite Calhoun,
daughter of son, Andrew...dec'd. daughter Cornelia...grandson, Duff
Green Calhoun...grandson, John C. Calhoun, son Andrew's child...
grandson, Andrew P. Calhoun, to have "The Carolina Tributes to
Calhouns", presented to me by the author...grandson, James Edward
Calhoun, grandson, Patrick Calhoun...granddaughter Mary Lucretia
Calhoun...Floride Rion, "my namesake", daughter of James C. Rion of

Winsboro...Emma Floride Cunningham, "my namesake", daughter of Floride
C. Cunningham, of Charleston...mentions debt due me by son, Andrew,
for purchase of Ft. Hill, amounting to about $40,200.00, and unreserved
interest in gold mine at Dalonega, Ga. belonging to the Estate of my
late husband, also interest in estates of dec'd. son, Patrick and dec'd.
daughter.Cornelia...Legacy to Calhoun Clemson...Trustee, Edward Noble,
of Abbeyville. Executors: Edward Noble of Abbeyville and Thomas J.
Pickens of Pendleton. Dated 27 Jan. 1863.
Wit.: Rev. A. H. Cornish
       William Henry Trescott
       Eugene Parker
    Codicil: Dated 22 Jan. 1866, "Termination of the late war having
deranged all property matters and in great measure destroyed the
wealth of the country, and as such has been it's effects upon the
extent and value of my estate, it is necessary that my will hereto
attached be altered to conform to the condition of the country".
(Continues with five pages of changes).
Wit.: Rev. A. H. Cornish
       James Hunter
       S. B. Pickens
Probate: 7 Aug. 1866.

WILL OF DANIEL OWENS - pp 246-247
"Note I hold on Thomas McCartha, for $800.00 given 4 Dec. 1863, due
23 Dec. 1865 and note on Julius R. Earle for $100.00 to be divided
between said Thomas McCartha and Julius R. Earle, or their lawful
heirs share and share alike". Executor: Charles Haynie, of Anderson
District. Dated 12 July, 1866.
Wit.: P. R. Haynie
       Charles Haynie
       John Pickens (Pickens signed by mark)
Probate: 21 July, 1866. Charles Haynie renounced appointment as
executor.

ROBERT JUNKINS IS NOW ORDINARY

WILL OF ROBERT MCLEES - pp 247-248
Names wife, Susan Elizabeth McLees...her full brother and sister:
Jonathan Burr Werts and Sarah Olivia Werts...my brothers: James
McLees, George M. McLees...my sisters: Jane McLees, Elizabeth McLees
and Mrs. Sarah Ann Mills...niece, Jurushia Amanda McLees...nephew,
George Robert McLees..."should wife leave a child or children, I
desire children to have one half of entire estate". Executors:
Wife, Susan Elizabeth and brother, James McLees. Dated 20 Nov. 1865.
Wit.: Tapley Anderson
       Aaron C. Dobbins
       James Gilmer
Probate: 17 Aug. 1866.

WILL OF ROBERT B. NORRIS - pp 249-252
Robert B. Norris, names wife, Frances B. Norris...daughter, Eliza
A. W. Clinkscales, wife of John Clinkscales...son, William P. Norris
...son, James P. Norris...daughter, Mary A. M. Clinkscales, wife of
Hezekiah R. Clinkscales...son, Ezekiel B. Norris...daughter, Frances
L. Peoples, wife of John O. Peoples...daughter, Louisa J. Zimmerman,
wife of John Zimmerman...John H. Zimmerman, trustee for daughter,
Nancy H. Gaines, wife of William O. Gaines...and daughter, Caroline
Rutledge, wife of Ritchmond T. Rutledge...and son, Jesse W. Norris
and his wife, Jane Norris...and son, Andrew M. Norris...and son,
Robert Evins Norris. Executors: Son, James T. Norris and son-in-
law, John O. Peoples. Dated 14 April, 1856.
Wit.: B. F. Crayton
       John Wakefield
       B. F. Whitner
    Codicil: Dated 25 Jan. 1868, "Mrs. Louisa Jane Zimmerman is dead,
leaving surviving children, whereby I bequeath one equal share. I
do by this codicil will that my son, James T. Norris and son-in-law,
John O. Peoples shall not be executors, preferring other person or
persons to administer my estate. (Did not name another executor).

Wit.: B. F. Whitner
      P. A. Masters
      J. W. Harrison
Probate: 25 Jan. 1868.

WILL OF STEPHEN LIVERETT - pp 254-255

Farmer, names nephew, John B. Liverett, son of John and Ursley Liverett,
tract of 307 acres situated on Wilson's Creek, waters of Rocky River,
bounded by Nathan McAlister, Andrew Todd, Esq., A. D. Gray, Jackson
Hall and G. L. Magee. Executor: John B. Liverett. Dated 1 Oct. 1866.
Wit.: Andrew Todd
      Lewis McConnell
      Dudley C. Howard
      Waller Small Norris
Probate: 8 Oct. 1866.

WILL OF ELIZA ELLIOTT NORTH - pp 255-258

Of Rusticella...names grandnieces of my dec'd. husband: Sarah Ann
Edith Smith and Emely Haynie Smith, sisters, "to have plantation at
Rusticello, share and share alike"...husband's nephews and nieces:
Dr. Richard Lawrence North, James Hayward North, Eliza Emily Thurston,
Ann Jane Bee, and Valaria M. North, widow of Dr. Edward North...Edward
North, son of Dr. Edward North and James Thurston, "all my realestate
in Village of Washington, near Charleston"...husband's grand niece,
Alice Elliott Dreyton Smith...Alice D. Talmadge, and at her death to
her daughters Alice Hylah and Mary Edith Talmadge, (no relation stated).
Mrs. Edith Ravenel, (no relation stated). Executors and Trustees:
Dr. Richard L. North, James H. North, and Josiah Edward Smith. Dated
13 July, 1865.
Wit.: W. Alston Hayne
      J. E. Adger
      Margaretta L. Heyne
Probate: 26 Oct. 1866.

WILL OF DAVID TILLOTSON RAINWATER - pp 258-259

Wife, (unnamed) "to have legacies from wife's father's estate and my
father's estate"...wife's brothers and sisters...my brothers and
sisters, to share and share alike. Executors: Wife and wife's brother,
Aaron John Smith and my brother, John Milton Rainwater. Dated 14 Feb.
1862.
Wit.: Herbert Hammond
      A. O. Norris
      C. C. Langston
Probate: 13 Nov. 1866. Violet Rainwater qualified. John M. Rainwater,
    stated he was unwilling to qualify.

WILL OF JANE HAMILTON - pp 260-261

Gives to Sarah E. Taylor, land where I now reside and Sarah must take
care of her mother. (no relation stated). Executor: Dr. Wm. Millford.
Dated 5 May, 1866
Wit.: Levi Gabel   (Jane Hamilton signed her mark).
      William Hamilton
      P. L. Millford
Probate: 5 Dec. 1866.

WILL OF MARTIN H. HALL - pp 261-262

Names wife, Margaret Caroline Louisa Hall...children when they come of
age to marry. Executor: Amaziah Rice (called Col. A. Rice in probate)
Wit.: Z. Hall
      L. M. Hall
      Levi Gable
Probate: 23 Jan. 1867.

WILL OF GEORGE POOR - pp 262-264

Names wife, Sally Poor, "to have land on both sides of Long's Creek,
where I now live, (113 acres)"...daughters, Malissa C. Poor, wife of
John H. Poor...Frances E. Glines...children of John Milton Poor, dec'd.
.."bequeath to trusty friend, Joshua S. Acker, land and tools in trust
for daughter Malissa C. Poor". Executor: Matthew Breazeale. Dated

19 Oct. 1866.
Wit.: Joseph Cox
       C. P. Dean
       Samuel Poor
Probate: 31 Jan. 1867.

WILL OF NANCY BREAZEALE - pp 264-266
Widow, names son, Kenon Breazeale...daughter Sarah Keys, wife of Robert
A. Keys...son, Gambrell Breazeale...Barbara Dean, wife of B. P. Dean,..
.son, Enoch Breazeale...daughter Lucy P. Breazeale...daughter Nancy L.
Breaseale...son, F. Marion Breazeale...dec'd. son, Griffen Breazeale,
his children. Executor: Son, Kenon Breazeale. Dated 2 Dec. 1857.
Wit.: H. N. Reid   (Nancy Breazeale signed her mark).
       Jo Berry Sloan
       J. W. Harrison
Probate: 13 May, 1867.

WILL OF WILLIAM VAN WYCH - pp 266-268
Anderson District. Will written in Abbeyville District..."will to be
admitted to probate in proper offices in State of New York."...son,
Samuel Van Wyck...son, William Van Wyck...granddaughters, Zoe Banks
and Lydia Ann Banks, children of dec'd. daughter Zernah (?) E. Banks...
son, Augustus Van Wyck...son, Robert A. Van Wyck...daughter Lydia Ann
Van Wyck...son, Benjamin S. Van Wyck, "a piece of land in town of Hunt-
ington, County of Suffolk, on Long Island, adjoining land of late James
Harrison---, said parcel of land surveyed by my parents to my brother,
Samuel A. Van Wyck and myself, said brother conveyed his moiety to me,
deeds recorded in Clerk's Office in Suffolk Co."...Executors: Wife,
Lydia Ann Van Wyck and friend, Robert P. Lee, Esq., "Counsellor at Law
and nephew of my old friend, John H. Lee, of New York, guardians of my
minor children. Signed at Abbeyville Court House, 1 May, 1867.
Wit.: S. McGowan
       Thos. Thomson
       R. A. Farr
Probate: 11 July, 1867.

WILL OF EZEKIEL MURPHY - pp 269-273
Names wife, Charity Murphy, "to have tract of land on Hurricane Creek,
(580 acres)...daughter, Hester Richardson, wife of Noah T. Richardson..
.daughter Nancy, wife of Albert S. Welborn...son, Thomas M. Murphy...
son, Charles Murphy...daughter Polly Pickle, wife of Chesley W. Pickle.
..Elizabeth Pickle, wife of Crawford W. Pickle...son, Chesley Murphy...
daughter Ruth Gambrell, wife of Matthew Gambrell...Katy Elrod, wife of
Benjamin Elrod...daughter Lucinda E. Gore, wife of R. S. Gore. Executor
Noah T. Richardson and Crawford Pickle. Dated 4 April, 1860.
Wit.: Wm. Bennett
       J. J. Acker
       Chesley Rogers
       Wm. H. Mauldin
    Codicil: Dated 1 Aug. 1867, "having purchased tract of land contain-
ing 234 acres, which is part of my home tract"...makes changes in be-
quests.
Wit.: B. F. Mauldin
       Wm. Bennett
       J. J. Acker
Probate: 1 Aug. 1867.

WILL OF POLLY CLINKSCALES - pp 273-275
Names children of dec'd. daughter Sally Geer, wife of Thos. Geer...son,
T. L. Clinkscales...son-in-law, Josiah Burton, husband of Sally Jane
Burton, dec'd....granddaughter Mary Jane Burton. Executors: Thomas L.
and Fleetwood Clinkscales, sons. Dated 2 Mar. 1866.
Wit.: F. M. Kay   (Polly Clinkscales signed her mark).
       A. Rice
       Two witnesses only.
Probate 5 Aug. 1867.

WILL OF WILLIAM HARRISON - pp 275-276
Names wife, Abi Harrison, and son, William T. W. Harrison. Executors:

Son, William Thomas, Whitner Harrison, when he is age 21, and Alexander
B. Tamers (?). Dated 23 Jan. 1867.
Wit.:   John Wilson
        Sylvester Bleckley
        Elijah Webb
Probate: 18 Aug. 1867.

WILL OF HENRY F. SUBER - pp 276-277
Names wife, Jane L. Suber. Executor: H. R. Vandiver. Dated 1 June,
1861.
Wit.:   Samuel Brown
        D. A. Ledbetter
        Joel M. Brown
Probate: 7 Aug. 1866.

WILL OF JESSE LEWIS - pp 278-280
"Home tract of land, (160 acres), resurvey made by W. G. Smith, 2 Jan.
1860 on Milwee Creek, bounded by J. B. Sitton, Thos. Dickson, R. A.
Steel, James Couthit and Blackmon D. Elrod"...also, "tract known as Pope
tract purchased from Sampson Pope bounded by Dr. Gillard, J. B. Sitton,
and Peter McPhail"...daughters Amanda Jane and Eliza Hannah, until mar-
ried...other children: Elizabeth Mariah Smith, wife of W. G. Smith...
J. Berry Lewis...Katy G. Moorhead...Jesse Augustus Lewis...Aaron B.
Lewis...Polly M. Lewis...Anna McPhail...children of dec'd. daughter
Rachel Gibson. Executors: Sons, J. Berry Lewis and Jesse A. Lewis.
Dated 21 Sept. 1860.
Wit.:   J. M. Smith
        J. H. Marshall
        James L. Orr
Probate: 2 Sept. 1867.

WILL OF CHARLES KAY - pp 280-284
"Wife to retain in her own right, property she held at time of our mar-
riage"...wife, Charlotte...children:J. Harrison Kay...W. Marvin Kay...
Teresa E. Smith, wife of Jery (sic) Smith...E. Henry Kay...C. Wesley
Kay...Silas Kay...Eldred J. Kay...Mark M. Kay...Mary C. (?) Welborn,
wife of Edwin Welborn...two grandchildren: Mary E. Moorhead and Lewis
Moorhead, children of daughter Caroline Moorhead, dec'd. (minors)...
four grandchildren: Harriet Stone, Lewis E. Campbell, Mary J. Campbell,
L. C. Campbell, children of dec'd. daughter Louisa C. Campbell. Exec-
utor: Son, W. Marvin Kay. Dated 23 May, 1862.
Wit.:   Wm. M. Archer
        J. B. McGee
        Herbert Hammond
   Codicil: Dated 12 Sept. 1866, "son W. Marvin Kay, being dead, now
appoint friend, John W. Daniel, executor".
wit.:   A. Evins
        James B. Moore
        Jno. L. McLinn
Probate: 6 Sept. 1867.

WILL OF AUSTIN WILLIAMS - pp 284-285
Names wife, Mary Williams...son, John L. Williams, "land lying in Green-
ville District, S. C. known as my old homestead, a part of Kelly place
described in deed made by Harriet A. Blake, Excutrix of Estate of W.
L. Blake, dec'd. to myself"...daughter, Nancy Jane Anderson "to have
one half of the Chickey Moga and Elrod place"...son, Samuel, "the other
half"...daughter Harriet A. Blake, house and lot in Williamston.
Executors: Wife, Mary Williams and sons, James L. and Samuel Newton
Williams. Dated 4 April, 1867.
Wit.:   James E. Pickel
        D. L. Donnald
        W. K. Clement
Probate: 27 Sept. 1867.

WILL OF DAVID K. BREAZEALE - pp 286-287
Names wife, Mary C. Breazeale...three minor children: Dicy Ann Elizabeth, Joseph Kenon, Misouri Elendor Breazeale, (there was no punction
between these names)...two married daughters, Minerva L. Majors and

Mariah Vandiver. Executors: Wife, Mary C. Breazeale and brother Matthew Breazeale. Dated 18 Aug. 1866.
Wit.: J. C. Nichols
       E. S. Pepper
       J. J. Copeland
Probate: 8 July, 1868.

WILL OF WILLIAM C. BENLEY - pp 287-290
Town of Anderson...wife, Catherine D. and children "begotten by me".
Executor: Wife, Catherine D. Benley. Dated 6 May, 1868.
Wit.: Thomas A. Evins
       John Wilson
       Eliza E. Evins
Probate: 18 May, 1868.

WILL OF JOSEPH B. WEYMAN - pp 288-290
Wife, Emmely Maxwell Weyman...wife's sisters: Mary L. Maxwell, Anne M. Maxwell, Miriam M. Maxwell...to John H. Maxwell for use of Ammala Weyman Lewis, daughter of Thomas L. Lewis, until she attains age of 21 or marries...her mother, Eliza Lewis, and brothers and sisters of said Emmala Weyman Lewis. (no relation stated on these)...sister, E. A. M. Houston, wife of G. J. Houston. Executor: G. J. Houston, (but Emmala M. Weyman qualified). Dated 21 Oct. 1860.
Wit.: J. D. Smith
       L. R. Smith
       G. W. Fullerton
Probate: 27 July, 1868.

WILL OF THOMAS WELBORN - pp 290-291
Wife, Mary "who is aged"...daughters Hester...Francis, "sorely afflicted" ...other children: Elizabeth, William, Thomas, Aaron, Rebecca Savilla and James. Executor: Son, James and Aaron. Dated 11 April, 1868.
Wit.: Allen W. Clement
       D. L. Dolland
       J. B. Rogers
       All residents of Williamston, S. C.
       D. L. Donnald made Oath.
Probate: 28 Aug. 1868.

WILL OF GEORGE POOR - pp 292-293
THIS IS SAME WILL RECORDED ON PAGE 262.

WILL OF CHARLES HAYNIE - pp 294-295
Nuncupative will...names sister-in-law, Miss Betsie Reed, "she is to remain in his family as a member of the same and to receive like protection as she has done for years."...Wife, Mrs. Ann Haynie. Executor: Dr. S. R. Haynie. Dated 17 Nov. 1867.
Wit.: J. P. Caldwell
       Bird Phillips
       J. H. Little
Probate: 5 Dec. 1867.

WILL OF ANDERSON BRADBERRY - pp 295-296
Names wife, Amarintha Bradberry, and children, as they arrive at age 21, or daughters when they marry. Executor: Amarintha Bradberry. Dated 12 Oct. 1866.
Wit.: J. W. Brannon
       Elijah F. Tribble
       Jeptha Hutchins
Probate: 22 Jan. 1868.

WILL OF MATTHIAS STANTON - pp 297-298
Names wife, Mary Stanton and four children, (not named). Executors: Wife, Mary Ann and brother O. B. Stanton. Dated 5 July, 1862.
Wit.: William H. Stone
       Peter Johnson
       Wm. P. Martin
Probate: 27 April, 1868.

WILL OF JAMES F. WYATT - pp 298-300
Wife, Nancy "to have homeplace, tract of land adjoining Martin Phillips,
John Burdine and others...son, Wm. R. Wyatt...son, Ludy (?) A. Wyatt...
Virginia C. Burdine, wife of James H. Burdine, tract (100 acres) known
as Saw Mill tract, adjoining John Burdine..."five oldest and four young-
est children" of dec'd. son, Redmon F. Wyatt...four children of dec'd.
daughter, Epe E. Martin, formerly wife of Thomas W. Martin. Executors:
Wife, Nancy Wyatt, James H. Burdine. Dated 24 Feb. 1868.
Wit.:   W. R. Reeves
        H. A. Richey
        Wm. D. Sitton
Probate: 20 Mar. 1868.

WILL OF MARY OLIVER - pp 301-302
Names nieces: Amanda Caroline Couch, and Mary Elizabeth Ann Mullikin.
Executor: Andrew P. Watson. Dated 18 Aug. 1859.
Wit.:   James Mullikin   (Mary Oliver signed her mark).
        J. R. Spillers
        Malinda Mullikin
Probate: 10 Mar. 1868.

WILL OF REDMON FOSTER WYATT - pp 302-304
Names wife, Nancy Ophelia and children age 21, or when daughters marry.
Executors: Wife, Nancy Ophelia, James F. Wyatt, and John W. Rosmond.
Dated 6 April, 1863.
Wit.:   J. J. Acker
        E. H. Acker
        Jas. D. Smith
Probate: 25 May, 1868.

W. W. HUMPHREYS IS NOW PROBATE JUDGE

WILL OF OLIVER TODD - pp 304-306
Names son, Andrew Todd...Jane M. Gordon...James Martin and wife, Mary
Ann Martin...Henry Branyon and wife, Margaret Branyon...John Todd...
Elizabeth Presly's four children viz: E. E. Presly, James C. Presly,
R. C. Presly, M. E. Presly, "now married to a man by name of Spruel".
Executor: Son, Andrew Todd. Dated 7 Aug. 1866.
Wit.:   J. J. Branyon   (Oliver Todd signed his mark).
        J. J. Findley
        James W. McPhail
Probate: 9 Oct. 1868.

WILL OF JANE ELIZABETH STRANGE - pp 306-308
Mentions late husband, William P. Strange, dec'd...Mrs. Lucinda Strange,
(no relation stated)...father, Thomas F. Skelton...sister, Susannah
Skelton...sister, Florence Skelton...sister, Mrs. Juliett Burriss.
Executor: Friend, Charles W. Williford. Dated 10 Aug. 1868.
Wit.:   M. T. Humphreys
        P. D. McClinton
        James Gilmer
Probate: 6 Nov. 1868.

WILL OF CATHERINE BENSON - pp 308-311
Names son, Thomas Prue (?) Benson...daughter Mary Prince Sloan, widow,
and her three children: Edward Postel Sloan, John David Prue Sloan,
Esther Rebecca Sloan...son-in-law, Thomas M. White and wife, Nannie
Taylor White. Executor: Son, Thomas Prue Benson. Dated 17 Aug. 1867.
Wit.:   A. P. Cater
        Wm. M. Archer
        J. B. Clack
Probate: 9 Nov. 1868.

WILL OF ISAIAH J. NEWELL - pp 311-313
"Tombstones to be put to the graves of my sister, Susan M. Tucker and
Thomas A. Newell"...mentions tract of land known as"Thomas A. Newell
tract, (149 acres) to sister, Jincy L. Newell"...brother Reubin (?) D.
Newell...mentions brothers and sisters. Executor: Brother Newton J.
Newell. Dated 2 Feb. 1869.

Wit.: Ezekiel Hall, Jr.
       E. Hall, Jr.
       W. Morrison
Probate: 6 Mar. 1869.

WILL OF JAMES C. ADAMS - pp 313-315
Mentions "I sold John E. Adams 50 acres laid off by my executor on N. E.
corner of my land adjoining J. N. Burriss"...son, E. N. Adams, a portion
of home tract adjoing J. L. Bryan...Wm. Jones, trustee...son, J. Frank
Adams, land where he now lives, his three children: Susanna Josephine
Adams, James Edward Calhoun Adams and Thomas Joel Williamson Welborn
Adams...daughter, Mrs. Elvira McAllister...daughter, Bethia McMahan....
grandson Columbus Bryan..daughter Emily W. Jones..."I have been appointed Executor of the late Will and Testament of Rafil (?) L. Hardin, of
Abbeyville District and have transacted business of the Estate__I would
suggest my worthy son-in-law, Wm. Jones as executor, in my place". Ex-
ecutors: Wm. Jones and John A. McMahon. Dated 13 Nov. 1868.
Wit.: A. G. Cook
       James T. Stuckey
       Jas. S. Beaty
Probate: 24 Nov. 1868.

WILL OF ELIJAH TEAGUE - p 315
Names daughter Dorothy McMurtry...other four daughters: Sarah Barksdale,
Nancy Teague, Mary Teague, Elizabeth Teague...mentions tract of land
known as Chevis (?). Executors: Daughters, Sarah Barksdale, Nancy
Teague, Mary Teague, Elizabeth Teague. Dated 20 Nov. 1867.
Wit.: James McClesky
       W. B. Harbin
       James F. McClesky
Probate: 4 Aug. 1869.

WILL OF JOHN WIGINTON - pp 317-319
Names wife, Agnes Wiginton..."my children when they marry or leave home"
Executor: Wife, Agnes Wiginton. Dated 10 Nov. 1840.
Wit.: J. B. Gambrell
       Ezekiel Murphy
       George V. Gambrell
     "I, Elihu Wiginton swear that Agnes Wiginton, so named in above will,
has departed this life, prior to the death of her husband, John Wiginton.
I will truly execute the above will." Dated 27 April, 1869...David D.
Spearman swears he has examined the signatures, and is well acquainted
with the handwriting of J. B. Gambrell and Exekiel Murphry and John
Wiginton...he believes the signatures to be genuine. Exekiel Murphy departed this life, J. B. Gambrell and George V. Gambrell removed from the
limits of this state, before the death of John Wiginton. Dated 27 Apr.
1869.

WILL OF WM. P. KAY - pp 319-322
Names wife, Elizabeth Kay...son, Robert P. Kay...son, Samuel R. Kay,
when he is 21 years old...son, W. H. Kay...son, M. V. S. Kay...other
children: Mary E. Land, Sarah A. Kay, Cynthia M. Kay, Nancy A. Kay,
Lewis F. Kay...Carrie E. Kay...Milton A. Kay...when youngest child
arrives at age 21. Executors: W. Asbury and M. Veninal (?) S. Kay.
Dated 22 Sept. 1868.
Wit.: Michael Burts
       S. J. Burts
       G. M. Mattison
Probate: 13 Sept. 1869.

WILL OF DANIEL MATTISON - pp 322-324
Wife, Ann Mattison, to have all estate and to be executor. Dated 10
Feb. 1869.
Wit.: Robert Dugan
       W. T. Traynham
       A. M. Mattison
Probate: 6 Oct. 1869.

WILL OF HIRAM HOWARD - pp 324-327

...To be buried at family burying groung near my dwelling...wife, Sarah
Howard...grandsons, Daniel H. Howard and Taylor Howard, "to live with my
wife and be her dutiful children as they have been to me."...children:
John Howard...children of Hiram Howard, dec'd...Patsey Teet, wife of
William Teet...daughter-in-law, Sarah Howard, wife of Enos Howard, equal
shares with George Howard, John Howard, Dudley Howard, Barbara Howard.
Executor: Son, Dudley C. Howard, and to be trustee for Patsey Teet and
children of Hiram Howard, dec'd. Dated 2 Sept. 1859.
Wit.:   J. D. M. Dobbins
        Dudley H. Webb
        Elijah Webb
Probate: 20 Oct. 1869.

WILL OF JAMES J. HARKNESS - pp 327-330
Wife Letitia C. Harkness...children as they come of age: Ida Corrie...
Frances Perry...James Calvin...William Benton...Jesse Paullie...Pauline,
"and any other child or children born of my present marriage:..."In case
the law determined me to be the lawful owner of any part of the estate
of John T. Wallace, my wife's former husband then the same is bequeathed
to my wife and children". Executors: Wife, Letitia C. Harkness, and
friend and kindred, John N. Harkness and Andrew C. Hawthorne. Dated 20
May, 1868.
Wit.:   Wm. F. Pearson
        E. D. Pruitt (?)
        Conrad Wakefield
Probate: 22 Oct. 1869.

WILL OF GEORGE CAMPBELL - pp 331-333
Wife, Mary Campbell...two daughters, Nancy A. Campbell and Fannie B.
Campbell...Executor: Friend, John D. M. Dobbins. Dated 12 June, 1868.
Wit.:   John Wilson   (George Campbell signed his mark).
        W. H. Nardin
        J. W. Harrison
Probate: 20 Nov. 1869.

WILL OF ELIAS EARLE - pp 333-338
Names daughter, Fannie H. Earle, "to have plantation on both sides of 23
Mile Creek, known as Saw Mill Tract, (140 acres), also, house and lot in
Town of Anderson, on Main Street whereon Mrs. Gibbs now lives, also
tract near Town of Anderson purchased at Estate of John R. Benson, dec'd.
opposite home of N. C. Cely (?), and land owned by Mrs. Creswell...daugh-
ter, Mary R. Sloan, house and lot in Town of Anderson, whereon I now
live, also tract adjoining property devised to daughter Fannie H. Earle,
thense along Greenville Road, (120 acres)...son-in-law, Thomas B. Lee
and daughter Marion B. Lee, tract opposite Pinkney Burris on the Pendleton Road, along line to McConnell Road, thence to Centerville Road, including the Russell Scott and Dickson places, (600 acres)...son, Preston
E. Earle tract situated in Pickens Co., S. C. known as Beverdam Place
including the Maret and Myers tracts, (1000 acres)...daughter Florence
L. Earle, plantation including Hembree place, (600 acres), all the remainder of the Anderson Tract, (150 acres), also three houses and lots
in Town of Anderson on Main Street opposite residence of Dr. A. P. Cater.
..grandson, Joseph Lee, tract of land in Pickens Co., called Hardins
tract, (250 acres)...grandson, Walton Lee, tract of land near the Picken
line called the Stone Place, (174 acres)...granddaughter, Harriet Lee,
lot in Town of Anderson on Manning Street, whereon Buchanan, (or Birch-
man), now lives...granddaughters, Hattie Sloan and Mary Sloan, two tracts
near Centerville known as Bryson Place, and Ferry Place adjoining each
other, (1000 acres). Executors: Son-in-law, Thomas B. Lee and son,
Preston E. Earle. Dated 7 May, 1866.
Wit.:   John T. Sloan
        Jno. B. Earle
        J. W. Harrison
Probate: 26 Jan. 1870.

WILL OF WM. K. HARRIS - pp 338-340
Names wife, Eliza J. Harris, formerly Eliza J. (smeared), probably
Browne...youngest daughter Willie, "fruit of our intermarriage"...my
children, daughter Eliza Jane...daughter Mary Ann Harris...son, Jonathan

161

W. Harris...son, Larkin F. Harris. (No executor named in will). Dated
10 Mar. 1870.
Wit.: John W. Daniels
      P. A. Wilhite
      F. M. Murphy
   E. M. Taylor, swears to take true inventory, John W. Daniels quali-
fied as executor.
Probate: 1 April, 1870.

WILL OF JONATHAN T. HARRISON - p 340
Names wife, Eliza and son, Wm. O. Executor: Wife, Eliza. Dated 8 Mar.
1870.
Wit.: Jacob Burris
      David M. Watson
      Joseph Felton
   Inventory by E. M. Harrison, W. O. Harrison on 2 May, 1870.
Probate: 8 Mar. 1870.

WILL OF ELIZA D. REVE - pp 342-344
Eliza D. Reve...sons: Charles S. Webb, Benjamin Webb...daughter Ann W.
Pepper...mentions "land whereon I now live...granddaughter Sally Pepper.
..daughter Charlotte Maddox...grandson, Charles Simpson...grandson,
Hammond Webb. Executor: Son, Charles S. Webb. Dated 22 Mar. 1871.
Wit.: Nancy Bolt
      Prudence C. Bolt
      John C. Whitfield
Probate: 29 April, 1870.

WILL OF A. C. JACKSON - pp 344-348
Names wife, Elvira T. Jackson...six children: John Arthur...Mary Marr-
illa Reid...Thomas Carruth (?)...Samuel Orr...Alice Florrie...James
Seland...mentions 50 or 60 acres on both sides of Rocky River...children
as they come of age or marry...James A. Reid, trustee for son, John
Jackson. Executors: Wife, Elvira T. Jackson, son-in-law James A. Reid,
son, Thomas C. Jackson. Dated 16 Feb. 1870.
Wit.: Jas. Thompson
      W. D. Gray
      Wm. F. Pearson
Probate: 21 July, 1870.

WILL OF WM. OLDHAM - pp 348-350
"Mary Oldham to have all my personal property and Real Estate, 100 acres
lying on Hurricane Creek, waters of Saluda River, and to her bodily
heirs that she may have by Thomas Oldham, Jr., her husband, that my
brother, Thomas Oldham, shall have his lifetime maintence. At death of
Mary Elizabeth Oldham, will above named property to July Ann Adaline
Oldham." Executors: Mary Elizabeth Oldham, John Garrett, and Thomas
Oldham, Sr. Dated 11 Mar. 1859.
Wit.: J. D. King   (Wm. Oldham signed his mark).
      R. O. Elrod
      A. F. Elrod
Probate: 22 July, 1870.

WILL OF JOHN HOPKINS - pp 350-353
Names three sons: Washington S. Hopkins...James N. Hopkins...John H.
Hopkins...Samuel Bar Alexander (no relation stated), and his wife, "a
note of hand on William O. and Hugh Alexander."...daughter Diana Alexan-
der...Jane Hopkins, Elizabeth Kay....Polly Ann Avory or her daughter
Marietta Avory, when she is 21 years of age...daughter Ellen Caroline
Hopkins...daughter Nancy Wadkins, "or her bodily heirs provided they can
be found". Executor: Rev. Willson Ashley. Dated 4 Feb. 1864.
Wit.: G. W. L. Mitchell
      R. G. Kay
      William J. Taylor
Probate: 16 Nov. 1870.

WILL OF BRYANT BURROUGHS - pp 353-355   (Signed Bryan Burriss)
Brother Jacob Burriss...mentions credit on books of Watson and Brother..
.wife, Mary...daughter Savilla (later spelled Cavilla) A. Potts, her
husband, Jas. A. Potts...wife and daughter, to have interest in estate

162

of John Wiginton, Sr., dec'd. Executors: Polly (sic) and brother,
Jacob Burris. Dated 13 Oct. 1870.
Wit.: Joseph Y. Fretwell
       David M. Watson
       John Brown
Probate: 19 Oct. 1870.

WILL OF WILLIAM HIX - pp 356-357
"I desire all my goods and estate to be disposed of as the law directs".
(no heirs named). Executor: Friend, B. F. Crayton. Dated 16 April,
1870.
Wit.: Bryan Burroughs
       Reuben Burris
       W. T. McCown
       John W. McGregor
Probate: 28 Nov. 1870.

A. O. NORRIS, JUDGE OF PROBATE

WILL OF AMANDA DALRYMPLE - pp 357-358
Names granddaughter, Louisa Jane Slaton,...daughter, Nancy Elizabeth
Dalrymple...daughter Matilda Norris (or Harris) Dalrymple...son, John
Wesley Dalrymple...son, William L. Dalrymple...son, Hugh A. Dalrymple..
.daughter Martha Jane Slaton...mentions late husband, Lewis Dalrymple.
Executor: C. L. Gaillard. Dated 30 Dec. 1870.
Wit.: L. L. Gaillard
       M. A. Robbins
       John C. Whitfield
Probate: 9 Jan. 1871.

WILL OF ROBERT HOLLAND - pp 359-361
"To be buried by the side of my wife and our graves to be enclosed by a
house of stone or some lasting material. All Real Estate to be sold,
except ¼ acres of land including my grave which I reserve for a grave
yard"...surviving children: Jincy Harrison...Benjamin...Thomas......
Jefferson...Peggy...Stanley...William W....Robert...Jacob T....Elizabeth
Lattimer...Jas. W....Sarah Merritt...N. H. Holland. No executor named.
Dated 6 Feb. 1856.
Wit.: William C. Norris
       William H. Waid
       John Hix
   Benjamin Holland states witnesses William C. Norris and John Hix are
   dead and William Waid left this country and has not been heard from
   for more than seven years...Benjamin Holland qualified as executor.
Probate: 10 Mar. 1871.

WILL OF BARTHOLOMEW WHITE - pp 361-363
Names wife, Polly...trustee for wife to be friend, John B. Watson.....
heirs: Johnathan (sic) White, my son...Sally Williams...son, Matthew
G. White...four grandchildren, viz: Matthew...Charles...Martha Jane...
James..."together with three great (sic) grandchildren of John White,
dec'd., representatives of my son, James, their father, dec'd.".....
granddaughter Kizzah Jane Grubbs, daughter of my son John, dec'd....
four grandchildren: Alverda...Franklin...Alice...and Frances (sic),
children of my dec'd. daughter Martha Smithen (?), when they come of age
...mentions tract known as Hip's tract, (100 acres), North East of my
homestead, bounded by lands of William Milwee, Henry Jolly and others.
Executors: Sons, Johnathan and John B. Watson. Dated 3 May, 1870.
Wit.: Jacob Burris
       Corrie Watson
       Reede Watson
Probate: 24 Mar. 1871.

WILL OF REUBEN J. NEWELL - pp 364-365
Mentions land known as Stephen Liverett's tract, (211 acres)...William
B. Newell, (no relation stated)...sister, Jincy L. Newell, while single,
...brother Newton J. Newell...brother Samuel L. Newell...sister, Hannah
E. Price...nephew, John J. Tucker. Executor: Brother, Newton J. Newell.
Dated 10 Jan. 1871.
Wit.: James Tucker

```
                    J. J. Tucker
                    V. A. L. Moore
          Probate:  25 April, 1871.
```

WILL OF MAXEY MOORHEAD - pp 366-368

Names sisters: Serena Griffen and Clara Moorhead...nephew, Maxey John,
son of Major L. Moorhead, dec'd....Major Lewis Moorhead's heirs at law.
..Iry Griffen Moorhead's heir at law...sister, Violet, wife of Alexander
Harris...Jane, wife of Elijah F. Martin...Polly Martin, granddaughter
of my sister, Serena Griffen. Executor: Robert Moorhead. Dated 20
Oct. 1870.
```
Wit.:  Jacob Burriss              (Maxey Moorhead signed his mark).
       Solomon L. Jones
       John B. Watson
Probate:  12 May, 1871.
```

WILL OF THOMAS MORGAN - pp 368-370

Mentions land, (200 acres) on Big Road leading from Union Church to
Newton Burriss...wife, Sarah Lucretia...children: Sarah Giles..Malissa
Jane...John Thomas...Louisa...James Robert...William Marbry. Executors:
Brother, John Morgan and son, John T. Morgan, also to be guardians of
minor children, Cynthia Louisa, James Robert and William Marbry. Dated
14 Jan. 1871.
```
Wit.:  B. D. Kay
       R. A. Every
       M. D. Galbreath
Probate:  26 May, 1871.
```

WILL OF MATHIAS RICHARDSON - pp 370-372

Heirs now living: children of Abraham Nettles, Joseph Nettles, to have
his dec'd. mother's share, and Richardson Nettles...wife and my children
...son, Sion Richardson. No executor named. Dated 25 Oct. 1861.
```
Wit.:  Elijah Webb
       J. B. Lewis
       A. O. Norris
Probate:  12 July, 1871.
```

WILL OF CHILES MCGEE - pp 372-373

Of Madison Co., Ga.,will written in Camp Lamar, Warwick Co., Va.......
names wife, Rebecca McGee, and children to share and share alike. Ex-
ecutor: Brother, Joseph McGee. Dated 20 Feb. 1862.
```
Wit.:  Wm. R. Collins
       Isaac B. Simmons
       John C. Collins
       J. M. Matthews
```
Court of Ordinary, Madison Co., Ga., Aug. term, 1862. "Last will of
Chiles McGee, dec'd. has been duly proven at Court on oath of John
M. Matthews.
Recorded 7 Aug. 1862. R. H. Bulloch, Ordinary, W. H. Griffith, Deputy
Ordinary.
    (There is no explanation as to why this is included in Anderson Co.
records).

WILL OF JAMES MCNINCH - pp 374-376

"To Caroline Crawford, my house and lot for 12 years or during her life-
time or widowhood for nursing me in my last illness. Property on 23
Mile Creek."...my legal representatives, viz: Mary Bryson...James Mc-
Ninch,Jr....Heirs of Samuel McNinch and Martha McNinch...mentions land
bought in Missippi (sic) to be brought to sale. Executors: William
Bryson, and John Martin. Dated 10 May, 1871.
```
Wit.:  James McLesky
       James Bryson   (his mark)
       David Reece    (his mark)
Probate:  4 Aug. 1871.
```

WILL OF HARRIET HILLHOUSE - pp 376-378

Names daughter Eliza S. Hillhouse, "to have Real Estate and personal
property as long as she remains unmarried. After her death or marriage
to be equally divided between my children or their representatives,

share and share alike"...daughter Elizabeth G. Bowden, wife of A. B.
Bowden, her share in trust to son, William G. Hillhouse. Executors:
Sons, John Peter Hillhouse, William C. Hillhouse. Dated 15 June, 1867.
Wit.: Wm. W. Smith
      J. L. Elgin
      D. L. Richey
Probate: 30 Mar. 1869.

WILL OF J. WILLIAM MILLS - pp 378-380
Daughter Mary Juliett Humphrey, wife of Samuel C. Humphrey...grandson,
John McClintock Humphrey, son of daughter Mary Juliett Humphrey.....
"dearly beloved, but deformed and helpless daughter Elizabeth Jane Mills."
Executor: Son-in-law, Samuel C. Humphrey. Dated 7 Mar. 1862.
Wit.: B. F. Crayton
      S. Bleckley
      Elijah Webb
Probate: 23 Oct. 1871.

WILL OF JANE MILLER - pp 381-382   (Jane F. in Oath)
Of Pendleton...niece, Amanda Boggs...sister, Martha Wilson...nephew,
Freddie E. Wilson...niece, Mattie Bowden...nephew, Dr. M. L. Sharpe.
"Executor to make good and sufficient title to my portion of a tract
of land in Oconee Co., S. C., sold by my sister, Mrs. Charlotte Kay and
myself to Richard Fletcher and Shedrick Taylor when they comply with
their contract". Executor: Dr. M. L. Sharpe. Dated 29 Aug. 1871.
Wit.: W. M. Belotte
      C. W. Young
      Charlotte Kay
   All residents of Pendleton, S. C.
Probate: 6 Nov. 1871.

WILL OF ASA HARPER - pp 383-387
"Previous to the Matrimonial Alliance between my present wife, Martha
E. Harper and myself, each of us by deed of marriage settlement, did
reserve unto ourselves all rights and titles...it became necessary for
her to leave her own home and her friends in the State of Georgia...as
she has been a good and faithful wife, I, therefore give and bequeath
all that tract of land lying in Anderson Co., S. C. on waters of Millwee
Creek bounded by lands of William Harper, J. Williams and others, (123
acres), same tract purchased by me from John G. Smith, Deed of Conveyence
15 Feb. 1861. At death of my wife, to revert back to estate." Executors:
"My two sons", William Harper and L. L. Welborne Harper, the name Harper
being stricken before signing." Dated 15 Nov. 1864.
Wit.: B. F. Whitner   (Asa Harper signed his mark).
      John Wilson
      L. D. Harris
   Codicil: Makes changes in cash bequests "due to great changes in my
   circumstances on account of the issues of the late war."
   Dated 23 May, 1867.
Wit.: John Wilson
      James E. Harper
      S. M. McCully
Probate: 9 Nov. 1871.

WILL OF WILLIAM HUNT - pp 387-390
Names wife, Jany (?) Hunt, and "lawful heirs both male and female"....
later mentions seven daughters. Executor: Son, John Hunt. Dated 1
June, 1845.
Wit.: James E. Robinson
      Thomas Cox
      R. N. Wright
Probate: 13 Nov. 1871.

WILL OF WILLIAM SPENCER MOORE - pp 390-392
Names wife, Emily Moore and children: Preston E. Moore, "should he be
living"...Harlston Perin Moore, Commodore Worth Moore, William Brewster
Moore and Anna Jurussa Moore. No executor named. Dated 25 July, 1865.
Wit.: W. B. Long
      J. N. Shirley
      L. D. Harris
Probate: 9 Jan. 1872.

WILL OF REBECCA LOVE - pp 392-394
Son, John M. Baily, "in trust for my daughter Anna Bailey, wife of
William C. Bailey...all my grandchildren: Eliza Ann Bailey...Robert S.
Bailey...William B. Bailey...Thomas L. Bailey...Jane M. Bailey, wife of
James L. Brown. Dated: 27 Sept. 1860.
Wit.: Joshua Holland   (Rebecca Love signed her mark).
      Elizabeth Hammond
      Herbert Hammond
Probate: 24 Jan. 1872.

WILL OF MARY C. MCMAHAN - pp 395-397
Grandson, Alexander Capers McMahan, homestead (254 acres) adjoining
John M. Craft to Craft Ferry Road...rest of land to be sold to J. M.
Craft...daughter Sarah Boseman. Executors: William O'Briant and
Claudius Beaty to be guardians of grandson until 21 years of age. Dated
31 Jan. 1872.
Wit.: B. D. Kay   (Mary McMahan signed her mark).
      William A. Craft
      George A. Craft
Probate: 19 Mar. 1872.

WILL OF DILLY CASEY - pp 397-399
"To Thomas A. Sherard, my land (160 acres), he is to put up tombstones
on my grave and Eliza A. Casey, dec'd." (no relation stated). Executor:
Thomas A. Sherard. Dated 26 Nov. 1866.
Wit.: C. S. Beaty   (Dilly Casey signed her mark).
      R. H. Reed
      T. A. Stevenson
Probate: 8 April, 1872.

WILL OF PETER JOHNSON - pp 399-402
Wife, Nancy A. Johnson...children: N. Caroline Mattison...W. Willis
Johnson...Mary A. E. Ellison...B. Lewis Johnson...Sara T. Johnson.
Executor: Lewis Johnson. Dated 1 Mar. 1872.
Wit.: Allen W. Clement   (Peter Johnson signed his mark).
      C. B. Stanton
      C. C. Poor
Probate: 18 May, 1872.
    Joseph N. Brown, Esq. commissioned by A. O. Norris, Esq. Judge of
    Probate, examined witnesses and qualified B. Lewis Johnson executor.

WILL OF M. H. DALRYMPLE - pp 403-404
Called Matilda H. Dalrymple in oath. Names brother W. L. Dalrymple...
"aunt, Mrs. Martha Harkins has given brother John D. W. Dalrymple and
sister Martha J. Seaton (or Sluter) a tract more than the rest of my
living brothers"...sister, Nancy E. Dalrymple. Executors: Sister,
Nancy E. Dalrymple and cousin, Lorenza D. Harris and Dr. C. C. Gaillard.
Dated 15 May, 1872.
Wit.: Wm. C. Martin
      O. W. Casey
      John Harper
Probate: 7 Aug. 1872.

WILL OF JAMES STEVENSON - pp 405-406
Wife, Jane Stevenson, tract where I now live, bounded by J. J. Stevenson,
W. E. Padget, John B. Armstrong and others...our son, D. L. Stevenson..
..children of dec'd. daughter Eliza E. Brown...children of dec'd. son,
Andrew T. Stevenson...children of dec'd. son, Samuel J. Stevenson...
mentions "land I own in Pontotoc, Miss., containing 160 acres now in the
hands of John Stevenson to sell by Power of Attorney." Executors: Wife,
Jane Stevenson and son, D. L. Stevenson. Dated 10 Oct. 1871.
Wit.: Wm. H. Haynie   (James Stevenson signed by mark).
      R. B. Junkins (his mark)
      John C. Haynie
Probate: 21 Nov. 1872.

WILL OF RICHARDSON O. ELROD - pp 407-408
"I am now going to the Army of the Confederate States"...Thomas Martin,
in trust for daughter Mary Frances Elrod, "all my estate, tract of land

166

lying near White Plains, (140 acres)". No executor named. Dated 15
Aug. 1863.
Wit.:   J. D. M. Dobbins
        B. F. Crayten
        Elijah Webb
Probate: 23 Nov. 1872.

WILL OF WILLIAM TUCKER - pp 408-410
Names wife, Sallie Tucker...children: Hannah Barnes...Ella Hall.....
Reuben D. Tucker...Elias Tucker...William B. Tucker...Nieces: Emily
Hall...Martha Ann Hall...Margaret Ann Hall. Executors: Nephew, Newton
J. Newell, and son-in-law, Samuel Hall. Dated 17 Jan. 1870.
Wit.:   James Tucker
        J. J. Tucker
        Wm. B. Newell
Probate: 22 Nov. 1872.

WILL OF E. A. BOWEN - pp 410-412
Names three children: Whitner, Mary and Milford. Executor: Wm. Burriss.
Dated 2 Dec. 1872.
Wit.:   R. M. Burris   (E. A. Bowen signed her mark).
        J. J. Thacker
        John Eskew
Probate: 5 Dec. 1872.

WILL OF THOMAS A. EVINS - pp 413-417
(Called Dr.Evins in oath). Names wife, Eliza E. Evins...three children:
Thomas Earle Evins...Martha Elizabeth Evins...Samuel Holcombe Evins...
mentions guardian to be named for children. Executors: Brother John
H. Evins, of Spartanburg Co., S. C. and William Sharpe, of Anderson Co.
Dated 5 Oct. 1872.
Wit.:   W. J. Ligon
        W. H. Nardin (called Dr. in oath)
        A. Evins
     Codicil: Mentions interest in father's estate, Samuel N. Evins, late
     of Spartanburg, S. C., now dec'd. to be divided by heirs...mentions
     agreement signed with brothers and sisters to sell Real Estate of
     dec'd. father to Thos. Fielder and one third interest in brick store
     house and lot in Town of Reidville, Spartanburg Co. Dated 21 Oct.
     1872.
Wit.:   W. J. Ligon
        W. H. Nardin (called Dr. in oath)
        A. Evins
Probate: 20 Dec. 1872.

WILL OF NANCY E. SLOAN - pp 417-421
Names son Robert E. Sloan...son, Benjamin Sloan, to be trustee for three
daughters: Mary E. Sloan...Septima Sloan...Julia Octavia Sloan. Exec-
utor: Benjamin Sloan. Dated 5 Dec. 1871.
Wit.:   Thomas S. Crayton
        Nancy S. Crayton
        W. K. Easley (called W. K. Earle in oath)
Probate: 6 Dec. 1873.
     Maj. Benjamine Sloan qualified.

WILL OF AUGUSTUS SIMPSON - pp 421-423
Names wife, Roda Simpson and children, (unnamed). Executor: Friend,
Jeptha F. Wilson. Dated 2 Dec. 1872.
Wit.:   Mrs. E. J. Wilson
        E. E. Jones
        Harry Jenkins (his mark)
Probate: 11 Jan. 1873.

WILL OF WILLIAM MATTISON - pp 423-427
Mentions homestead on Brod Mouth Creek, reserving ¼ acre as family
burying ground, rest to be sold and divided among children of J. F.
Mattison and P. E. Mattison...other heirs: Francis Sherley...Martha
Cox...Mary J. Garrison...John J. Mattison...Wm. H. Mattison...daughters
shares to be held in trust. Executors: Sons, John J. Mattison,

William H. Mattison. Dated 20 July, 1870.
Wit.: J. B. Cox
      E. S. Gantt
      R. N. Wright
Codicil: Mary Jane Garrison to have full control of her share.
Dated 26 July, 1870.
Wit.: J. B. Cox
      E. S. Gantt
      R. N. Wright
Probate: 14 Jan. 1873.

WILL OF NANCY O. WYATT - pp 427-428
"Last will and testament of Redmon Foster Wyatt admitted to probate 15
Jan. 1873. Nancy O. Wyatt qualified as Executor. Will recorded on
page 302.

WILL OF JOHN B. CHASTAIN - pp 429-431
Son, F. Garvin Chastain, tract where he now lives...son, Jas. L. Chastain
tract where he now lives...youngest son, Joshua B. Chastain, other tract,
adjoining first named tracts, (3 tracts each containing 45 acres)....
mentions lean (sic) on F. G. Chastain and James L. Chastain to be paid
when Joshua becomes 21 years of age...wife, Elizabeth Chastain, to have
home plantation...other children: Frances E. Chastain...Stephen
Chastain...Martha E. J. Chastain. Executor: Wife, Elizabeth Chastain.
Dated 8 Feb. 1872.
Wit.: James McLeskey
      James F. McLeskey
      R. D. Williams
      Amos C. Chastain (his mark)
Probate: 11 Feb. 1873.

WILL OF ANNIE ROBINSON - pp 432-434
Headed Abbeyville District, (she is called Miss Anna in oath)..."to be
buried in graveyard near father and mother"...Brother, James Robinson,
"tract where I now live, (319 acres) conveyed to me by A. O. Norris, Esq.
Commissioner in Equity in Anderson Co., District on 19 July, 1859, recorded in Book E. E., page 26, and upon his decease to his living children. It is my earnest wish for them not to sell same, but that one or
more may live on the place, which was the home of their grandparents"...
friend, John R. Wilson, trustee, for five grand nephews and nieces:
Sally A. Pearman...Wilson C. Pearman (later called Weldon Pearman)...
John B. R. Pearman...Isaac Henry Pearman...Leta Larinda Pearman, when
she becomes 21...Rachel Carr, formerly Pearman. Executor: Brother,
James Robinson. Dated 8 Oct. 1859.
Wit.: James Adams   (Annie Robinson signed by mark).
      Wm. Duncan
      James L. Orr
Probate: 7 May, 1873.
R. B. H. Robinson made inventory.

WILL OF JESSE REED - p 435
Sister, Elizabeth Reed to have all my estate. Executor: Elizabeth Reed.
Dated 16 Aug. 1858.
Wit.: Joab L. Mauldin
      J. W. Harrison
      B. F. Whitner
Probate: 24 Mar. 1873.

WILL OF MARY RANKIN - pp 437-440
Mentions one fifth interest in tract of land, whereon I now live as by
Deed of Conveyence from Thomas F. Rankin, James C. Rankin, Geo. W. Rankin,
F. N. Garvin and wife, Letitia K. Garvin, made to me and my four daughters,
viz: Eliza B. Rankin, Margaret P. Rankin, Mary J. Rankin, and Martha A.
Rankin on 9 Jan. 1855, (410 acres)...my daughter Mary J. Rankin died in-
testate and by if bylaws of inheritance, I am entitled to her interest,
bequeath to surviving three daughters...All other children (mentioned in
Deed) have received full share of husband's estate. Executors: Sons,
Geo. W. Rankin, daughter Martha A. Rankin. Dated 9 Jan. 1873.
Wit.: J. A. Boggs   (Mary Rankin signed by mark).

Joseph N. Hembree
J. Perry Glenn
W. T. Bryant
Probate: 17 Apr. 1873.

Page 441 blank

WILL OF DAVID K. HAMILTON - pp 442-452
Names grandchildren: Jacob Hamilton...Elizabeth Jane and Charles Thomas
Martin, children of dec'd. daughter Mary E. Martin, (who are minors).
Their father, William N. Martin...children of daughter, Martha Jane
Russell, wife of Thomas H. Russell, to wit: David Hamilton, Thomas
Wallace, William Walker, Edward Alexander, George Washington, Benjamin
Franklin, and Emma, as they come of age...mentions "balance of Calhoun
tract (266 acres), the rest of the tract (187 acres) having been conveyed
by me to trustees for daughters Martha Jane and Mary E....wife, Jane
Hamilton, home tract known as Whitten place, (340 acres). Executors:
Thomas H. Russell and T. Hamilton Boggs, Esq. Dated 7 Nov. 1854.
Wit.: Thos. Rogers
       Thos. H. McCann
       James L. Orr
    Codicil: "In addition to home tract, give wife, Jane Hamilton adjoin-
ing tract of land called Orr tract, (100 acres). Additional grandchil-
dren: Benjamin Carlos Martin, son of Mary E. Martin...children of Martha
Jane Russell, viz: Marion Augustus...Mary Jane...John Andrew...Matilda
Adelaide...Louisa Ann, when full age or girls marry. Dated 2 Mar. 1864.
Wit.: Jas. W. Earle
       Wm. H. Ford
       Jas. Mulliken
    Second Codicil: I originally bequeathed home tract known as Whitten
tract together with Orr tract containing 400 acres to my wife, J. E.
Hamilton. I now revoke this bequest and give to my three grandchildren,
to wit: John Andrew Russell, Matilda Adalaide Russell, Louisa Ann Russ-
ell, the aforesaid tract...Trustees for children to provide for wife,
J. E. Hamilton. Trustees: T. M. Russell and William Ford. Dated 11
Aug. 1870.
Wit.: Jas. E. Earle
       E. A. Russell
       Benj. F. Barnett
    First Codicil: Have surveyed land to be divided during my life. I
give to my daughter Martha Jane Russell 160 acres in plat by J. J. Garvin,
21 Dec. 1854...to children of dec'd. daughter, Mary E. Martin, who may
be surviving, 108 acres in plat by J. J. Garvin, 21 Dec. 1854. Date of
codicil, 8 May, 1855.
Wit.: M. McGill
       A. Evins
       James L. Orr
    (This codicil was recorded out of sequence, BW).
    On 29 Mar, 1873, Dr. Alex Evins made oath in Spartanburg District to
Benj. Wofford, Probate Judge, of Spartanburg.
Probate: 18 April, 1873.

WILL OF RICHARD DAVIS - pp 453-456
Names wife, Jane Davis...sons: F. M. Davis...Jas. P. Davis...Matthew J.
Davis...John N. Davis...Wm. F. Davis. Executor: Son, Wm. F. Davis.
Dated 4 Oct. 1872.
Wit.: C. W. Smith   (Richard Davis signed by mark).
       E. M. Mauldin
       R. N. Mauldin
Probate: 26 April, 1873.

WILL OF RUTH ODELL - pp 457-459
Of Town of Williamston...daughter Emily Teresa McCorkle, wife of W. A.
McCorkle, place where I now live with family of W. A. McCorkle, consist-
ing of a town lot in Williamston with buildings, bounded West by Pickens-
ville Road, South by Julius (?) L. Williams, East by Wilson Bridge Road,
North by T. J. Zenlu (?)...heirs: Sarah E. Fuller, wife of Dr. F. G.
Fuller...heirs of Frances M. Mitchell, wife of Peter Mitchell. Executors:
Daughter, Emily Teresa McCorkle, and son-in-law, Dr. W. A. McCorkle.

Dated 1 June, 1871. No witnesses signed.
John L. Williams made oath that James W. Carlile and John M. Gambrell
witnessed the will with him.
Probate: 21 June, 1873.

WILL OF JAMES ELLISON - pp 460-463
Names wife, Mary...sons, Hugh A. Ellison...Joel....daughters, Barbara..
.Nancy...heirs of son, William...heirs of son, Matthew...heirs of son,
James W...daughter Mary Prater, "note I had against her husband for the
purchase of land to be forgotten". Executors: Son, Hugh A. Ellison,
and grandson, James M. Ellison. Dated 7 Jan. 1873.
Wit.: W. S. Perkins   (James Ellison signed by mark).
       L. B. Jones (or Janes)
       B. C. Johnson
Probate: 10 July, 1873.

WILL OF JOHN L. HOLLAND - pp 463-465
Written at Sullivan's Island, Charleston, S. C....names wife, Martha
Ellen Holland..,mentions notes against John Holland and G. W. White.
Executor: Wife, Martha Ellen Holland. Dated 6 July, 1863.
Wit.: J. F. Shirley
       J. H. Long (or Lang)
       J. R. Bridgefirth (?)
Probate: 11 Aug. 1873.

WILL OF MARTIN HALL - pp 465-468
Names wife, Elizabeth Nancy Hall...nephew, John Smith Lipscomb Nance.
Executor: Wife, Elizabeth Nance Hall. Dated 5 Feb. 1867.
Wit.: B. F. Crayton
       E. P. Earle
       J. S. Murray
Probate: 11 Aug. 1873.

WILL OF JOHN J. STEVENSON - pp 468-470
Names Levi Burriss, trustee for wife, Margaret Stevenson..."tract of land,
where I now live on waters of Generotee Creek, waters of Savannah River,
bounded by Wm. G. Watson, Baxter Hays, Estate of James Stevenson, dec'd.
and others, to be property of daughter. "Harriett Emeline McFarland,
her husband and family take charge of plantation and all other property
on 15 May, 1873 and support, feed, cloth, care for myself, my wife,
Margaret Stevenson, and daughter, Margaret Florella Stevenson". Executors:
Levi Burriss and David McFarland. Dated 15 May, 1873.
Wit.: Wm. H. Haynnie   (John J. Stevenson signed mark).
       D. L. Stevenson
       C. C. Armstrong
Probate: 20 Oct. 1873.

WILL OF A. BENSON LEWIS - pp 471-473
"Two sisters, Amanda Jane and Eliza Hanah Lewis, (282½ acres) on Mullin's
(?) Creek, one acre is never to be sold, to be used as a graveyard"...
nephew, Gilky Augustus Moorhead, "to have home with them until 21, and
treated as one of the family"..."to place headstone on my grave, and
brother Robert B. Lewis grave, and my sisters, Catherine G. Moorhead,
and Mary M. Lewis' graves. Executors: Brother, J. Berry Lewis and
sisters, Amanda Jane and Eliza Hanah Lewis. Dated 10 June, 1873.
Wit.: James G. Douthit
       R. B. Brock
       W. P. Martin
Probate: 16 Oct. 1873.

WILL OF LARKIN (?) GASAWAY - pp 474-476
Names wife, Louisa Gasaway, and children, unnamed. Executor: Friend,
N. P. Martin. Dated 3 Jan. 1874.
Wit.: Joseph D. Pinson   (Larkin Gasaway signed by mark).
       A. R. Cox
       J. N. Cox
Probate: 15 Jan. 1874.

WILL OF JOHN GAMBRELL - pp 476-478
Names wife, Mary Gambrell...son, Harper Gambrell...son, James Gambrell.
..daughters: Ann Duckworth...Elizabeth Wilson...Nancy Williams...Mary
Lewis...son, William Gambrell...children of dec'd. son, John Gambrell...
mentions Copeland Tract of land. Executor: John Wilson. Dated 4 Jan.
1866.
Wit.: John M. Gambrell
       Jeremiah Spearman
       J. B. Wilson (John R. Wilson in oath)
Oath 13 Mar. 1866.
No Probate date.

WILL OF ESTER VANDIVER - pp 478-479
Estate to Harriet W. Horton and her daughter, Lucy J. Horton, wife and
daughter of John C. Horton. Executor, John C. Horton. Dated 20 Feb.
1873.
Wit.: Moses Chamblee   (Ester Vandiver signed her mark).
       Elisha Chamblee
       James C. Horton
Probate: 20 Feb. 1874.

WILL OF JAMES L. WARDLAW - pp 480-487
"Being feeble at this time from soar (sic) in face and neck."..Brothers:
Andrew C. Wardlaw and Carrol B. Wardlaw, "my interest in tract of land
where I now reside, being same tract lately owned by my father, H. H.
Wardlaw, dec'd., my interest 1/7 part, containing 260 acres, bounded by
Peter Acker, Louisa Gambrell, B. B. Breazeale and others...Carrel B.
Brown, (no relation stated)...Fannie E. Wardlaw...Josephine Erskin, wife
of James W. Erskin...America Drake, wife of James F. Drake...Cassie E.
Gambrell...Martha L. Erskin, wife of John N. Erskin...Andrew C. Wardlaw,
trustee for Martha...Lucy C. Major, wife of D. N. Major...Sarah Simpson,
wife of A. H. Simpson...Amanda A. Smith, wife of E. L. Smith...Mary M.
Burford, wife of D. P. Burford. (No relation stated on any of these)..
.wife and children of dec'd. brother, H. C. Wardlaw. Executor: Brother
Andrew C. Wardlaw. Dated 11 July, 1873.
Wit.: John B. Moore
       E. M. Brown
       Peter G. Acker
   Codicil: "My last expenses to be paid out of bequests to five
sisters: Fannie E. Erskin, Americus Drake, Ailesse (?) E. Gambrell,
Josephine Erskin and Martha L. Erskin...the name Carral B. Brown was in-
tended to be Carral B. Wardlaw. Dated 14 Feb. 1874.
Wit.: John B. Moore
       J. S. Kay
       Peter G. Acker
Probate: 23 Feb. 1874.

WILL OF JOHN POOR - pp 487-491
"Tract of land on Big Creek, waters of Saluda River, (287½ acres), plat
executed by Joseph Cox, surveyor in Nov. 1871, being tract I now reside
on, to friend B. F. Whitner, in trust for wife, Annie Poor...daughter
Anna Dean, wife of J. T. Dean...children of Andrew Jackson Poor...chil-
dren of Samuel E. Poor...children of Hugh Poor, "all sons of my wife,
by former marriage"...mentions tract adjoining the above tract, (180½
acres). Executor: B. F. Whitner of Town of Anderson. Dated 14 Jan.
1873.
Wit.: D. Sloan Maxwell
       B. F. Crayton
       M. B. Green
Probate: 19 Mar. 1874.

WILL OF GEORGE S. CAMPBELL - pp 492-493
Of Pendleton, names wife, Carrie P. Campbell, to have all estate. Ex-
ecutor: Carrie P. Campbell. Dated 26 May, 1873.
Wit.: W. H. D. Gaillard
       J. T. Shubrick
       Jno. H. Maxwell
Probate: 4 April, 1874.

171

WILL OF JOSEPH W. CARPENTER - pp 493-495
Names mother, Catherine Carpenter, "to have my interest in tract of land
in Oconee Co., S. C. known as the Real Estate of my two brothers: Thomas
J. and John T. Carpenter, also 1/3 interest in store known as the firm
of Carpenter and Anderson, and note on Fredrick Owen for $30.00"....
two sisters: Elizabeth P. Albertt (?) and Nancy A. Gadd (?). Executor:
Samuel Brown. Dated: 28 June, 1873.
Wit.: R. H. Anderson
       John F. Mitchell
       Joshua Jamerson
Probate: 13 April, 1874.

WILL OF MINERVA C. BRANYON - pp 495-498
"To children of my first husband", A. B. Armstrong, viz: Mary B. Carwile,
wife of Z. H. Carwile...Delila P. Armstrong and Minerva A. Armstrong,
tract of land whereon I now live, (180 acres), conveyed to me by A. O.
Norris, Court of Equity, from Estate of my first husband, and one small
tract purchased from John McAdams, conveyed to me by name of Minerva C.
Armstrong during my widowhood...children by my last husband, A. W. Bran-
yon, to wit: William W. Branyon, Louisa Ellen J. Branyon, Jefferson
Davis G. Branyon. Executor: Son, Andrew M. Armstrong. Dated 23 Apr.
1871.
Wit.: R. W. Wright
       John McAdams
       M. T. Hughes
Probate: 1 May, 1874.

WILL OF SIMON S. BRYANT - pp 498-501
(Briant in some places), wife, Susann, 1/3 share...sister Mary Mayfield,
remaining 2/3 share. Executors: Brother, John M. Bryant and John W.
Nally. Dated 13 Feb. 1874.
Wit.: W. S. Pickens
       Catherine E. Spearman (her mark)
       B. J. Spearman
Probate: 10 May, 1874.

WILL OF WM. GLENN - pp 501-507
Being now about 76 years of age...to be buried beside my wife at Rhuh-
umah (sic) Church and plain but decent tombstones to be erected at our
head and feet...Real Estate to be laid off in four tracts, one tract,
(100 acres) bounded by land belonging to my son, John F. Glenn, James
C. Winters, on South side of road leaving from A. M. Holland's store to
Brown's Ferry, (now J. B. Earle's Ferry), land I leave to son, John F.
Glenn...balance of land in three other tracts of 200 acres each, each
to bind on Savannah River...one tract to son, Jas. W. Glenn...one tract
to William A. Glenn...one tract to son, Matthew F. Glenn...other bequest
to: heirs of my son, Joseph B. Glenn, dec'd...Mary E. Taylor, daughter
of my daughter, Serephtha A. Winter...Mary Herman...heirs of daughter
Elvira Martin...Lucy E. Parks...Mourning E. Scales, wife of John Scales
...grandson, Hugh W. Gregg, in lieu of mother's share. Executors: Two
sons, John F. Glenn, William A. Glenn. Dated 3 Sept. 1870.
Wit.: Wm. E. Watters
       Benj. F. Wilson
       John Wilson
    Codicil: My son, James W. Glenn is now in Mississippi in humble
circumstances, as he may sell his bequeathed land, John F. Glenn and
William A. Glenn to have first choice of the lands. Dated 3 Sept. 1870.
Wit.: Wm. E. Watters
       Benj. F. Wilson
       John Wilson
Probate: 23 July, 1874.

WILL OF JOHN W. MCGREGOR - pp 507-510
Names wife, Mary E. McGregor, and four children: Miriam F., William
T., Eliza J., and Emma D. when they come of age or marry. Executors:
Friend, John A. Reeves and wife, Mary E. McGregor. Dated 17 May, 1874.
Wit.: James McFall
       Reuben Burriss
       William Burriss
Probate: 23 July, 1874.

WILL OF ANN HAYNIE - pp 510-513

Widow...executors to erect tombstone similar to that of my late husband, Chas. Haynie...sister, Elizabeth Reid, homestead tract, (212 acres), adjoining lands of John Holland, Julia Burriss and others, and Caldwell tract, (100 acres), adjoining my place, Brooks tract, Wm. Buchanan and others...after death of Elizabeth Reid to nephew, J. Harvey Little...tract known as Brooks place, (256 acres), adjoining Caldwell tract, lands of J. E. Earle and others to Charles Haynie Little and Francis Pinckney Little, sons of J. Harvey Little...to former servant, Manuel Haynie (freeman), after death of Elizabeth Reid, tract, part of Hugh Reid place conveyed to me by Sheriff McGukin, 9 April, 1869...nephew, Joseph P. Caldwell...my young friend, Caroline Heller. Executor: J. Harvey Little. Dated 12 Feb. 1872.

Wit.: Thos. H. Anderson   (Ann Haynie signed by mark).
      J. R. Earle
      E. E. Whitner
Probate: 29 Dec. 1874.

WILL OF POLLY SMITH - pp 513-516

"Tombstone to be placed on my grave. I have sold greater part of my property and divided it between my children and grandchildren"...mentions William G. Smith, grandchild who received a share of my husband's Estate ...Executor: James Webb.

Wit.: Wm. M. Rampley
      M. G. Scott
      Alex. A. Dickson
Probate: 1 Feb. 1875.

WILL OF JOHN POOR - p 516

Regarding Will of John Poor, dec'd.: B. F. Whitner declines to be executor of will. Dated 26 Jan. 1875.

WILL OF OZEY R. BROYLES - pp 517-523

(Doctor, called Sr. in oath)...named wife, Sarah Ann Broyles, "my full estate, whether in State of S. C. or State of Tenn., or else where"...have advanced to son, Augustus T. Broyles...son, Charles E. Broyles...daughter, Margaret C. VanWyke...son, William Henry Broyles...son, Ozie Robert Broyles, Jr...daughter Sarah A. Williams...son, Thomas T. Broyles ...son, John P. Broyles. Executors: Three eldest sons, Augustus T. Broyles, Charles E. Broyles, William H. Broyles. Dated 21 Sept. 1868.

Wit.: W. J. Ligon
      Jos. D. Taylor
      Z. T. Taylor
   Codicil: Changes amounts of money advanced to children to be taken into account by wife, when dividing estate. Dated 20 Apr. 1871.

Wit.: W. J. Ligon
      G. T. Hammond
      E. T. Murrah
   Second Codicil: Appoint wife, Sarah Ann Broyles to be executrix, in addition to executors named. Dated 8 Jan. 1874.

Wit.: P. F. Stevens
      W. J. Stevens
      R. F. Simpson
Probate: 15 April, 1875.

WILL OF JOHN CARPENTER - pp 524-526

Son, Albert Carpenter, tract where I now live, (250 acres) on Neal's Creek of Broadway Creek of Rocky River, waters of Savannah River, bounded by J. W. Norris, James Callaham, Aron Vandiver and others...wife, Elizabeth Carpenter...daughter, Miss Martha Jane Carpenter...son, Albert A. Carpenter...daughter, Sarah Ann Elizabeth Todd...son, Sam'l Newton Carpenter...daughter, Mary Emaline Hall...daughter, Rosa Elvira Hopkins ...son, John James Carpenter...son, Benjamin F. Carpenter. Executors: Son, Albert A. Carpenter and relative, James B. Carpenter. Dated 4 June, 1874.

Wit.: Wm. H. Haynie
      J. B. Carpenter
      Wm. L. Haynie
Probate: 2 May. 1876.

WILL OF SAMUEL MORRIS - pp 526-528
Children: Richard M. Morris...Salina M. Wright...Tinsey A. Estus...
Leanor E. Elrod...Rebecca C. White...Dorcas C. Stribling, Rutha L. El-
rod...Mary E. Clark, last two named being dec'd., their children to re-
ceive their share. Executors: Sons, Richard M. Morris, and son-in-law
D. A. Elrod. (No date).
Wit.: J. W. Major
      W. A. Y. McHorten (McWhorton in oath)
      W. A. Major
Probate: 3 May, 1875.

WILL OF SIMION SMITH - pp 528-531
Wife, Any (sic) Smith...daughter, Lucinda McElreath...daughter, Elizabeth
C. Wyatt...son, Miles H. Smith...son, Joshua Smith...son, Edward Smith
...daughter, Margaret E. Martin. Executors: Son, Joshua Smith and son-
in-law, John N. Wyatt. Dated 6 Mar. 1871.
Wit.: W. S. Pickens
      P. E. Pickens
      James B. Newberry
Probate: 3 April, 1875.

WILL OF ELLEN C. POE - pp 531-532
Of Pendleton Village, children unnamed. Executors: D. B. Sloan, and
J. T. Poe. Dated 20 June, 1874.
Wit.: W. C. D. Gaillard
      Jas. F. Green
      B. S. Gaillard
Probate: 15 July, 1875.

WILL OF THOMAS OLDHAM, SR. - pp 533-534
Mary Elizabeth Oldham, all Real Estate and personal property, 147 acres
on Hurricame Creek, waters of Saluda River...her husband Thomas Oldham,
Jr...Brother, William Oldham to have lifetime maintenance...Jewly Ann
Adeline Oldham...Executors: Mary Elizabeth Oldham, and John Garrett.
Dated 11 Mar. 1859.   (Thomas Oldham signed mark).
Wit.: J. D. Kay (J. D. King in oath)
      R. O. Elrod
      A. T. Elrod
Probate: 27 July, 1875.

WILL OF MARY ANN KAY - pp 535-537
Names three children: Lucinda E. Ragsdale...John B. Massey...Franklin
G. Massey. Executor: Franklin G. Massey. Dated 17 April, 1875.
Wit.: Wm. McGukin   (Mary Ann Kay signed her mark).
      R. S. Bailey
      Cindarella McGukin
Probate: 6 Aug. 1875.

WILL OF JOHN RICHARDSON, SR. - pp 537-539
John Kelly 190 acres bounded by J. B. King, S. T. Richardson and others.
...mentions note on J. F. Wiginton, date 15 June, 1875, $200.00...note
on Elihew Wiginton...note on Laurens Mulliken...note on Harry P. Wilson
...on Harry E. Neill, (or Null)...note on Wm. S. Gentry...D. P. Robinson and J. W. Robison...on Greer Ellis...on J. B. King...on S. Burgess
and Jo A. Bats...Executors: Jobert Biant (sic) and S. J. Richardson.
Dated 13 July, 1875.
Wit.: W. W. Seawright
      W. R. Richardson
      J. M. Richardson
Probate: 12 Aug. 1875.
      W. J. Bryant and S. J. Richardson, qualified.

WILL OF JOHN DALRYMPLE - pp 539-541
Names four sisters: Margaret Dalrymple...Nancy Dalrymple...Lucinda
Dalrymple...Elizabeth Ann Dalrymple...Walter Quincy Hammond, his mother,
Caroline Hammond, (no relation stated)...four children of Jesse George,
dec'd.: Sam'l George, Mary Elizabeth Webb, James Dalrymple George,
and Willie Baxtur George. Executor: Sister, Lucinda Dalrymple. Dated
14 July, 1875.

Wit.:   W. Bar Bailey
        G. W. Hammond
        W. H. Drennan
Probate: 2 Oct. 1875.

WILL OF JOHN HARKINS, SR. - pp 542-544
Names nephew, John Harkins, now living in State of Texas...Matilda
Branyon...Sarah Jane Branyon...Essa Cornelia Branyon...John Robert Lee
Branyon, (no relation stated).   Executor: Andrew Jackson Stringer.
Dated 20 June, 1875.
Wit.:   W. C. Brown   (Dr. in oath)
        A. R. Cox
        J. P. Davenport
Probate: 18 Oct. 1875.

WILL OF PRIMUS (?) JACKSON - pp 544-547
Names wife, Hester and children, who are underage, (unnamed).   "Guard-
ians of my property, James Babb, Sr. and Robert Conners, posited by
Robert Jackson" to pay W. S. Pickens out of present crop...son, David.
Signed by Primus Jackson, his mark and Hester Jackson, her mark.   No
date.
Wit.:   Elias Pickens
        Kerksey Blassengame   (his mark)
        Buris Halloms   (his mark)
Probate: 8 Nov. 1875.
        J. W. Babb and Robert Conners qualified.

WILL OF JAMES M. LANDRESS - pp 547-549
Names wife, Jane Landress...children: Thomas L. Landress...A. J. Lan-
dress...Henry Landress...Pinkney Landress...W. F. Landress.   Executors:
Dr. John Wilson and son, A. J. Landress.   Dated 19 Oct. 1875.
Wit.:   J. G. Knight
        Silas Kay
        J. D. Rogers
Probate: 20 Nov. 1875.

WILL OF GRIFFEN BREAZEALE - p 549
The undersigned named as Executor of last Will of Griffen Breazeale,
late of Anderson Co., dec'd., declines to accept.   Dated 14 Oct. 1875.
Signed: J. J. Copeland.

WILL OF CATHERINE D. NORRIS - pp 550-551
Bequeath all my estate, including rent and interest on J. F. Wilson
bond to my granddaughter, Cindarella Keys, for sole use and benefit of
my daughter, Catherine Norris.   Executor: Cindarella Keys.   Dated 1
Mar. 1875.
Wit.:   W. L. Maroney
        Oliver Y. (?) Watson
        D. E. Maroney
Probate: 11 Dec. 1875.

WILL OF DAVID JORDAN MORRIS - pp 563-565
Names wife, Elizabeth Morris...daughter, Mary A. Hillhouse, who received
all her mother's estate...four daughters by my last wife, viz: Jane D.
Brown...Susan M. Mays...Fannie Mays...Elizabeth P. Morris.   Executor:
Wife, Elizabeth Morris.   Dated 4 April, 1873.
Wit.:   James McLesky
        Abram Bolt
        Mary Bolt
Probate: 19 Feb. 1876.

WILL OF JAMES BAGWELL - pp 566-568
Names wife, Sarah Bagwell...other heirs: Malinda Morrison...Caroline
S. Smith...Mary J. Gunnels...Margaret A. Bagwell...Francis C. Bagwell..
. William F. Bagwell...Louisa J. Lollis...children of Pleasant Bagwell,
dec'd....James Gunnels, son of Martha Gunnells, dec'd....mentions notes
given by Robert Gunnels, W. P. Bagwell, Wm. F. Bagwell and Calloway
Lollis.   Executor: Friend, Gabriel M. Mattison.   Dated 22 Nov. 1875.
Wit.:   Wm. Gambrell
        J. H. Austin

M. J. Austin

(James Bagwell signed his mark)

Probate: 4 Mar. 1876.

WILL OF MANNING BELCHER - pp 568-569
Names heirs: Sarah Maxwell Gray "to have her mother's wearing apparrel
left at her decease"...George W. Belcher...Wallace D. Gray...Sarah Jane
Belcher, relict of Charles D. Belcher, in trust for her children. Ex-
ecutors: George W. Belcher and Wallace D. Gray. Dated 12 Jan. 1861.
Wit.: Benjamin Aug McAllister (Augustus in oath)
       James F. Morris
       F. E. Vandiver
Probate: 23 Oct. 1868.

WILL OF ASA COX - pp 570-571
Two daughters, Mary Ann Cox and Manerva White to have all estate and to
be executrix. Dated 29 Mar. 1873.
Wit.: R. Lewis Moorhead
       W. L. Bolt
       John W. Daniels
Probate: 30 May, 1876.

WILL OF ALLEN MATTISON - pp 572-573
Names son, Robert Mattison, for his care of me...balance of children,
I consider I have given their full share. Executor: Son, Robert Matt-
ison. Dated 28 April, 1876.   (Allen Mattison signed his mark)
Wit.: J. Wilson (Dr. John in oath)
       Virginia E. Keith
       S. A. Wilson
Probate: 4 July, 1876.

WILL OF SAMUEL D. MCCOLLOUGH - pp 574-575
(SAMUEL DAVID in oath)...Brother, John McCollough...sisters, Margaret
McCollough and Nancy McCullough. Executor: Nephew, Alexander W. McCu-
llough. Dated 10 June, 1876.
Wit.: Jas. B. Burris   (Samuel D. McCullough signed his mark)
       F. F. Burton
       A. C. Beaty
Probate: 14 July, 1876.

WILL OF JOHN ROGERS - pp 576-578
Wife, unnamed...five oldest children: Duck, Dicy, Lizie, Washington,
and Jack...Howard Duck Rogers, tract, (140 acres) known as Canada Place
...Jefferson Washington Rogers, piece of land formerly belonging to
Joseph T. Rogers, North of the Wilson Ferry Road, down said road to
Drawburrows (?)...son, Jack Harrison Rogers, piece of land South of
Wilson's Ferry Road, adjoining Wm. W. Rogers, Chesley Rogers, J. C.
Rogers...daughter, Gussie Ann Rogers...son, Munrow (?) Patterson
Rogers. Executors: H. D. Rogers, and Wm. S. Murphy. Dated 7 Aug.
1874.
Wit.: H. B. Rogers   (John Rogers signed mark)
       J. C. Rogers
       J. M. Duckworth, Jr.
Probate: 22 Aug. 1876.

WILL OF MRS. CHARLOTTE C. PEGG - pp 578-580
Having seperate estate from my husband, Capt. S. M. Pegg...should I die
leaving no child or children, estate to go to my brothers and sisters,
and to my husband, Capt. S. M. Pegg. No executor named. Dated 31 Dec.
1875.
Wit.: Wm. Waties
       M. E. Williams
       Zenobia Waties
    Oath says Miss Lizzie M. Williams as witness. Sallie C. Bowie and
Cornelia Langston swore this was Mrs. C. C. Pegg's will. John W. Daniels
qualified as executor.
Probate: 13 Sept. 1876.

WILL OF J. F. RAGSDALE - pp 581-583
(Signed John F. Ragsdale), names wife, Elizabeth S. Ragsdale...children,
when youngest comes of age...four sons, Charley M. Ragsdale, John W.
Ragsdale, William Gustavus Ragsdale, James Clifford Ragsdale. Executor:
Wife, Elizabeth Ragsdale and M. F. Elgin. Dated 24 Mar. 1873.
Wit.:   J. M. Shirley
        C. C. Smith
        Nancy A. Shirley
Probate: 28 Sept. 1876.

WILL OF DORCAS BISHOP - pp 583-584
Sister, Jane Bishop, Real Estate, consisting of ½ tract of land we live
on, lying on Garvin's Creek, waters of 23 Mile River (450½ acres),
bounded by J. Owen Trescott and Simpson. Executor: Friend, W. W.
Knight. Dated 7 Sept. 1868.
Wit.:   W. W. Knight   (Dorcas Bishop signed her mark)
        R. S. Smith
        M. J. Martin
Probate: 12 Oct. 1876.

WILL OF F. C. V. BORSTEL - pp 585-588
Of Town of Anderson, names daughter, Alice Maxwell, lot on Brick Range,
with store rooms and offices and buildings connected...her husband,
trustee, D. S. Maxwell...daughter, Christine Borstel. Executors: Friend,
Joseph W. Brown, and guardian for daughter, Christine until age 21.
"Give old colored nurse, Caroline Spann, who attended me in my illness,
house and lot where she resides". Dated 30 Nov. 1876.
Wit.:   Julius Poppe
        J. L. Tribble
        J. A. Brock
Probate: 9 Dec. 1876.

WILL OF WEST A. WILLIAM - pp 589-591
Of Anderson County,...wife, Georgie C. Williams...daughter, Maggie C...
.son, West A. Williams...mentions house and lot in Abbiville Co., in
Village of Greenwood, containing 2 acres bounded by James G. Gaillard
and others, 1/6 interest in Presbyterian Chappel in said town and county.
Executors: Aaron M. Guyton, to take charge of estate in Anderson Co.,
and W. B. Millwee and A. McMeil to take charge of my estate in Abbiville
County. Dated 3 Jan. 1877.
Wit.:   A. W. Pickens
        Mattie Jameson
        Joshua Jameson
Probate: 8 Jan. 1877.

WILL OF SUSANNAH ACKER - pp 591-592
Children: son, Alexander Acker...son, P. N. Acker...son, Halbert Acker
...son, Alexander Acker...son, Joel M. Acker...Teressa McDaniel...Lucinda
McGee...heirs of Francis Hammond...heirs of Elizabeth Mattison...heirs
of Mary Townsend. Executor: P. N. Acker. Dated 13 Apr. ____.
Wit.:   Joseph Cox
        Samuel Poor
        F. M. Poor
No Probate date.

WILL OF WILLIAM CYMS MARTIN - pp 593-594
Names wife, Sarah Elizabeth Martin...two daughters, Mary Florence Martin
and Lucy Floronia Martin. Executor: Sarah Elizabeth Martin. Dated 11
Sept. 1876.
Wit.:   James McLeskey
        Levi W. Garrison
        Nancy Martin
Probate: 24 Feb. 1877.

WILL OF WM. L. BROYLES - pp 595-597
Of Fork Township, Anderson Co. "Expenses of children who are off at
college to be paid"...wife and each child to share and share alike.
Executors: Wife, Mary, brother, A. R. Broyles, and N. O. Farmer. Dated
1 July, 1876.

Wit.: John C. Gantt
      Harvey Routh
      D. S. White
    (Dr. WM. L. BROYLES in oath)
Probate: 3 July, 1877.

WILL OF ELIZABETH ROBERTSON - pp 597-599
"Feme sole"...daughter, Sarah C. Speer, wife of E. H. Speer of Abbey-
ville County...daughter, F. Jane Beaty, wife of C. S. Beaty, of Anderson
county...mentions tract of land, (486 acres), situated on East side of
Savannah River, lying in both Anderson Co. and Abbeyville Co., being
my old homestead bounded by J. W. Wiles, Anderson and Abbeyville lines,
Col. J. W. Lomax and others. Executor: C. S. Beaty, of Anderson Co.
Dated 10 Feb. 1876.
Wit.: S. W. Sherard
      R. N. White
      M. M. White
Probate: 15 Aug. 1877.

WILL OF WILLIAM H. FORD - pp 599-601
Wife, Mary Ford...children as they come of age. Executors: Wife, Mary
and friend, V. F. Glenn. Dated 31 Aug. 1863.
Wit.: Sam'l N. Williams
      A. F. Welbourne
      Austin Williams
Probate: 30 Aug. 1877.

WILL OF NANCY HOLMES - pp 601-603
Only daughter Kason Caroline Griffen, her present husband, Kenon Griffen
...house and lot in town of Belton, where she now lives, (4 acres),
bounded by B. D. Dean, J. W. Poor and lot of Baptist Church...2 grandsons, William P. Holland and Holmes Holland, house and lot in Belton
where Sam Hall now lives, (4 acres), bounded by B. D. Dean, Academy lot
and lands of Hiram Williams...granddaughter, Martha Jane Gentry...step
daughters, Mary M. Geer and Martha Emeline Vandiver. Executors: Daughter, Kason Caroline Griffen and grandson-in-law, D. D. Gentry. Dated
29 March, 1877.
Wit.: Wm. H. Haynie
      J. J. Poore
      G. W. Hyde
Probate: 22 Dec. 1877.

WILL OF JOHN BLAIR PREVOST - pp 604-605
Names wife, Mary Orr Prevost..."should I have child or children living
at time of my death, wife to be guardian". Executor: Wife, Mary Orr
Prevost. Dated 2 June, 1876.
Wit.: Jas. L. Orr
      J. G. Cunningham
      F. E. Harrison, Jr.
Probate: 15 Aug. 1877.

BLANK _ p 606

WILL OF JOHN HOLLAND - pp 607-609
Names wife, Martha A. Holland...daughters, Martha C. S. Lauless (?)...
Emma C. Lauless...Nancy L. Hall...Elizabeth M. Walker...Samanther J.
Grant...Mary M. Lawless...Elizer A. Dove...three sons, E. M. Holland...
L. F. Holland...G. W. Holland...heirs of son, John L. Holland, dec'd.
Executor: John C. Horton. Dated 14 May, 1877
Wit.: Allison Langston
      J. A. Langston
      John C. Horton
    Dated 14 May, 1877..."Advancements I have made to my children, E. M.
Holland, and son-in-law, W. D. Grant, John E. Dove."
Probate: 12 Sept. 1877.

WILL OF JAMES R. DRENNAN - pp 610-612
Mother, Mary Drennan, to have Real Estate consisting of one tract of land
about 3 miles Northwest of Anderson, on Blue Ridge Railroad, (153 acres),

bounded by John O'Neal, Mrs. David Watson, Mrs. Elizabeth Felton, William Burriss, and others...at her death to brothers and sisters then living. Executor: James H. McConnell. Dated 5 Sept. 1877.
Wit.: D. White
       W. J. Drennan
       Jno. E. Breazeale
Probate: 4 Oct. 1877.

WILL OF JAMES ADAMS - pp 613-617
Names wife, Mary Imma Adams...son-in-law, A. S. Armstrong, and wife, Mary Ann Armstrong to have 60 acres taken from tract purchased from John B. Armstrong...daughter, Lenorah A. Adams, 50 acres lying along Broadside of Janes Robinson's land on Northeast side of hometract, along road to Shirley's Mill, adjoining Sally Robinson...daughter, Margaret Parker, 51 acres on West side of branch, adjoining Joshua Ashley and others...daughter, Larinda H. Benton, 60 acres from tract purchased from John B. Armstrong, adjoining land set off for Mary Ann Armstrong, as plat will show...son, William C. Adams, (150 acres), adjoining lands of Larinda H. Benton...son, James W. Adams...daughter, Rhoda Elizabeth Lindsey...daughter, Lety A. Driver, her eight children: Lety, Mary Ann, Lenorah, Margaret, Elizabeth, Hosettin (?), William and Weldon. Executors: Sons, William C. Adams and James M. Adams, son-in-law, B. F. Driver. Dated 14 Mar. 1876.
Wit.: R. N. Wright
       R. G. Kay
       E. R. Kay
Probate: 25 Oct. 1877.

WILL OF MRS. NANCY HOLMES - p 617
Last will and testament of Mrs. Nancy Holmes, dec'd. was admitted to probate, 4 Aug. 1877 on oath of Wm. H. Haynie and D. D. Gentry. Mrs. K. C. Griffen qualified. 22 Dec. 1877.

WILL OF J. L. KENNEDY - pp 618-620
Wife, Mrs. E. D. Kennedy to have house and lot where I reside in Williamston, at her decease equally divided among children: M. D. Kennedy...
J. L. Boggs, son of D. C. and H. R. Boggs...J. C. Kennedy...E. P. Long..
...S. J. Wycough...A. R. Kennedy...J. L. Kennedy...L. F. Clayton...D. H. Kennedy...J. W. Kennedy...Stepdaughter, Mary F. Simpson. Executor: John M. Glenn. Dated 25 Oct. 1875.
Wit.: W. F. McCorkle
       F. P. McCorkle
       T. F. Anderson
Probate: 18 Jan. 1878.

WILL OF MOSES DEAN - pp 620-622
Wife, Narcissa Dean...daughter, Evalina N. Morrow; her daughters, Magie N. and Emily Josephine...W. H. Dean; his living daughters, Ella L. C. Elizabeth Alice Palmyra West, (no punctuation)...Samuel and Lucinda Dean, their daughters, Rosemond E. and Lucinda N...John H. and Mariah L. Jones; their daughters, Sallie and Louisa D. Jones...Rufus R. and Annie E. Beaty, their daughter, Ida V. Beaty...R. D. and Amanda Dean; their daughters, Leanora P., Amy, and Anna...Fleetwood and Elizabeth Rice, dec'd.; their daughters, Frances E. and Cornelia McFarland Rice. Executor: Son, Robert B. Dean. Dated 16 Dec. 1877.
Wit.: Reuben Burris
       M. J. West
       E. E. West
Probate: 20 Mar. 1878.

WILL OF JESSE C. MORRIS - p 623
Wife, Margaret Morris, to have all estate. Dated 24 Dec. 1877.
Wit.: Tapley Anderson
       John T. Cook
       Jesse W. Morris
No executor named, and no probate date.

WILL OF JOHN J. MARTIN - pp 624-625
Wife, Lucy Francis Martin and son, Charley Luther Martin. No executor named. Dated 22 Feb. 1878.

Wit.: W. L. Dalrymple
       O. W. Casey
       M. H. Casey
    Codicil: Dated 23 Feb. 1878, appoint father, Wm. C. Martin, Thomas
H. Martin, Sanford M. Martin, executors.
Wit.: M. E. Deal
       O. W. Casey
       M. A. Casey
Probate: 21 Mar. 1878.

WILL OF WILLIAM LEVERETT - pp 626-627
"I have deeded son, John Wesley, 95 acres, dated 26 Dec. 1877"...wife,
Bethena Leverett...daughters: Martha Jane, Nancy Ann L., Sarah Eliza-
beth M. Executor: Son, John Wesley Leverett. Dated 20 Apr. 1878.
Wit.: J. R. O. McKee   (William Leverett signed his mark)
       John B. Leverett
       John McCullough
Probate: 3 May, 1878.

WILL OF JOHN LEVERETT - pp 628-630
Formerly of Anderson Co. (there is no explanation for Formerly, BW)...
grandson, John Bradley Leverett, son of J. B. and L. C. Leverett, tract
of land, 35 acres, on waters of Wilson's Creek, bounded by John B.
Leverett, Carrie Norris, G. L. McGee, to be held in trust until he arr-
ives at age 21...five children: Mary E. Dobbs...J. Baylis Leverett...
N. E. Olliver...E. M. Leverett...Heirs of S. F. Dobbs. Executor: John
Baylis Leverett. Dated 6 Feb. 1878.
Wit.: G. L. McGee
       Stephen Taylor
       B. A. McAllister
Probate: 10 May, 1878.

WILL OF RICHARD S. HILL - pp 630-632
Names wife, Marion Gourdine, interest deeded to her in house and lot on
which I now live and farm known as Fairyard (?) shown in books of Clerk
of Court...daughter, Mary Jane...son, Thomas F...son, Rufus S...little
daughter, Richardine Gourdine. Executors: Wife, Marion Gourdine, son,
Rufus S. Hill. Dated 24 July, 1877.
Wit.: Joseph B. Simpson
       John B. Watson
       T. J. Leak
Probate: 31 May, 1878.

WILL OF JAMES ARMSTONG - pp 633-637
Names wife, Elizabeth Armstrong...Nariza C. Branyon, wife of Davis S.
Branyon...Elizabeth J. Johnson, wife of Wm. G. W...mentions tract sit-
uated on Barker's Creek, bounded by lands of A. Cowan, George Grubbs,
and others, (290 acres)...Palestine Brock, wife of William Brock and
James L. Lindsey, children of Mary Lindsey...Executors: Richard B.
Robertson and James L. Lindsey. Dated 27 Mar. 1869.
Wit.: J. G. Gantt
       R. B. A. Robinson
       G. M. Mattison
    Codicil: Revoke appointment of R. B. A. Robinson as executor and
appoint in his stead, (with James L. Lindsey), D. L. Branyon, William
G. W. Johnson and Palestine Brock. Dated 5 Sept. 1874.
Wit.: J. C. Williams
       R. H. Branyon
       J. C. C. Featherston
...Personally appeared J. C. Williams and upon oath says that the name
Jas. L. Lindsey, one of the named executors to the best of his knowledge
is a misnomer. It should be James A. Lindsey as he is not aware that
there is any person by the name of James L. Lindsey...James A. Lindsey
being one of the children of Mary Lindsey. 29 May, 1878.

WILL OF LEMUEL HALL - pp 638-641
Son, L. M. Hall...daughter, Roseanna Hamilton...mentions tract of 39
acres on Governer's Creek...dec'd. son, Robert's children. Executor:
Rev'd. A. Rice. Dated 14 Dec. 1865.

Wit.: Z. Hall
         John Wakefield
         A. E. Rice
   Codicil: Makes changes in some bequests. Dated 20 Dec. 1871.
Wit.: Z. Hall
         W. E. Walters
         Josiah Hereford
Probate: 1 July, 1878.

WILL EXECUTED - JAMES ADAMS - p 642
"I, J. W. Adams, now being of age, do solomnly swear to execute the will
of James Adams, dec'd. Dated 5 Aug. 1878.

ESTATE OF JOHN POOR - p 643
B. F. Whitner, In Regards: Estate of John Poor, dec'd. - partition for
Letters Testamentary. Dated 18 July, 1878.

WILL OF AMAZIAH RICE - pp 644-648
Two youngest daughters, Ann C. and Rachael A., tract, (300 acres), bound-
ed on North by lands belonging to me, on Belton Road, Mrs. Keaton to
Welch Spring Branch, down Rocky River, J. M. Brown, Dr. Jasper Brown and
L. N. Clinkscales...son, Addison E. Rice...daughter, Mrs. Elizabeth
Gassaway...daughter, Sarah C. Cheatham...daughter, Polly E. Ranson, her
five children: John J. Ranson, Eliza Ann Ranson, Marion P. Ranson,
Eunice Ranson, Willie Ranson. Wm. Ranson, trustee for Eunice and Willie.
..Dec'd. son, James F. Rice's two children: Lucy Ann Rice and James T.
Rice...dec'd. daughter, M. C. L. Hall's three children: Lucinda J. Mont-
gomery, Juliet Ann Hall, and Sallie T. Hall. Dr. Lucius Montgomery, of
Micanopy, Fla., guardian...Henry Wakefield, a Freedman, now in my service,
tract of land, (50 acres), bounded by Col. John Martin, Belton Road,
Samuel J. Emerson and Mrs. Cowan, if he stays in my service...mentions
friends, J. Scott, Murray, and Dr. Jasper Brown. Executors: Son, Addi-
son E. Rice and Friend, F. L. Clinkscales. Dated 19 Feb. 1873.
Wit.: Samuel J. Emerson
         James W. Brothers
         Christopher C. Reed.
Probate: 5 Aug. 1878.

WILL OF ALFRED ELKIN REED - pp 649-652
Names wife, Elizabeth Holbert Reed...mentions Smith tract of land on
West side of Rocky Creek on Fair's Bridge Road...six sons: Columbus C.
Reed...J. Pink Reed...Erasmus F. Reed...Joel H. Reed...Henry G. Reed...
Dudley A. Reed. Executors: Sons, Columbus C. Reed, and J. Pink Reed.
Dated 9 Mar. 1878.
Wit.: H. O. Henick
         M. L. Sharpe
         James B. Pruitt
Probate: 10 Aug. 1878.

J. BLAIR PREVOST - p 653
Mary O. Prevost swears to will of J. Blair Prevost and will execute same.
Dated 4 Sept. 1878.

WILL OF ANDREW MCLEESE - pp 654-658   (McLees)
Two daughters, Eliza E. McLees, Susan W. McLees, tract (207 acres) adjoining T. H. Anderson, J. J. McLees and my other lands, as shown on plat
made by James Gilmer, DS, 19 Feb. 1867...mentions tract, (149 acres) adjoining Mrs. Fowler and my other lands, as shown on plat made by J. R.
Earle, Surveyor, 29 Apr. 1876...granddaughter, Mary J. Stovall of Ala-
bama...my three children: John McLees, Mrs. Jane Sadler, wife of David
Sadler and Mrs. S. C. Seawright...mentions homestead, (353 acres) to
son Hugh McLees, and two daughters, Eliza E. McLees and Susan W. McLees.
...dec'd. daughter, Mrs. Mary L. Black's four children...son, J. J.
McLees. Executor: Hugh McLees. Dated 29 April, 1876.
Wit.: Thos. A. Anderson
         J. B. Anderson
         W. W. Humphreys
   Codicil: Dated 29 April, 1876, to J. J. McLees another tract of land.
Wit.: Sue W. McLees
         John B. Anderson

Thos. H. Anderson
Probate: 20 Sept. 1878.

WILL OF DAVID D. SPEARMAN - pp 659-661
Wife, Nancy Spearman...children: Susan Corbin...Levi Spearman...Sarah
Adcock...James Spearman...Mary Moore...heirs of Edmund Spearman, Dec'd.
...Jeremiah Spearman, heir of David D. Spearman, Jr., dec'd...Nancy
Durham...Frances A. Spearman...John C. Spearman...Calvin O. Spearman.
Executors: Wife, Nancy Spearman and son, John C. Spearman. Dated 3
Nov. 1877.
Wit.: D. E. King
      S. F. Richardson
      S. J. Brown
No Probate date.

WILL OF JACOB MOUCHET - pp 662-664
Wife, Mary Mouchet to have Real Estate in Anderson Co., and Clay Co.,
Alabama. (40 acres)...daughter, Matilda, formerly widow of Thomas D.
Cook, but now widow of John C. Tucker...daughter, Louisa, wife of James
W. Spearman...son, Tyler Mouchet...three children of dec'd. daughter,
Malinda, formerly wife of John McMahan, viz: Elizabeth and William
McMahan, and Mary C., wife of John Adams. Executors: Son, Tyler Mouchet
and wife, Mary Mouchet. Dated 14 Mar. 1878.
                              (Jacob Mouchet signed his mark)
Wit.: Wm. Jones
      G. Stevenson
      Col. Jess McGee
Probate: 31 Oct. 1878.

WILL OF MIKE C. RENIX - pp 665-666
Of Pendleton Village...wife, Polly Renix, Real Estate consisting of lot
of land, (12 acres), lying in Village of Pendleton, purchased by me from
D. B. Sloan, adjoining J. D. Smith, L. L. Green, Estate of Mrs. Poe, D.
B. Sloan, Carver Randall and Mrs. Worley. Executor: Wife, Polly Renix.
Dated 4 Feb. 1878.
Wit.: W. H. D. Gaillard
      W. L. Jenkins
      J. M. Duke
Probate: 29 Nov. 1878.

WILL OF AARON VANDIVER - pp 667-670
Wife, Martha E. Vandiver, tract laid off by J. C. Horton, (282 acres),
already deeded to her, 12 dec. 1873...mentions note of S. M. Geer to
Aunt Lucy Breazeale, to be forgiven, as compensation for waiting on her
for several years...step-daughter, Martha Jane Geer...to children, (un-
named), share and share alike, the share of A. W. Vandiver, dec'd. to
go to his children. Executor: Kinsman, Joseph N. Brown. Dated 22
Sept. 1875.
Wit.: J. A. Brock
      J. L. Tribble
      B. Frank Mauldin
Probate: 17 Dec. 1878.

WILL OF WILLIS ALLEN - pp 671-672
Wife, Fannie S. Allen...grandson, Willis Allen, son of Johnathan D. All-
en...children to share and share alike. Executor: Son, Johnathan D.
Allen. Dated ___ __, 1878.
Wit.: A. F. Elrod
      P. L. Gunley
      T. F. Pace
Probate: 17 Dec. 1878.

WILL OF WILLIAM SMITH - pp 673-675
Wife, Matilda, homestead tract, (230 acres) on Broadway Creek adjoining
lands of B. B. Breazeale, Samuel Smith, Gambrell Smith, Lewis Smith,
Robert Campbell...daughter, Louisa...daughter, Lula...daughter, Sarah..
.son, Samuel...grandson, Harrison, son of my daughter, Martha Geer, widow of Thomas Geer, when age 21...Gambrell Smith, (no relation stated)...
"after these bequests, eleven children to share and share alike". No

executor named. M. G. Smith qualified. Dated 11 Sept. 1871.
Wit.:   John W. Daniels
        Wm. McGukin
        Sam'l Crawford
    All of Anderson Courthouse.
Probate: 3 Jan. 1879.

WILL OF JOSIAH KING - pp 676-678
Wife, Nancy A. King...oldest son, H. O. King...son, John Michey King,
when 21 years of age..."heirs of my wife, when 21 years old". Executors:
Wife, Nancy A. King and Wm. C. Brown. Dated 25 Mar. 1872.
Wit.:   G. W. Cox   (Josiah King signed his mark)
        A. J. Stringer
        G. W. McGee
Probate: 27 Jan, 1879.

WILL OF JOHN M. DUNLAP - pp 679-680
Wife, Martha A. Dunlap...children, (unnamed) to share and share alike.
Executor: Wife, Martha A. Dunlap. Dated 9 Dec. 1873.
Wit.:   N. M. Greer (or Green)
        John N. Kay (his mark)
        G. M. Mattison
Probate: 5 Mar. 1879.

WILL OF ROBERT KING - pp 681-683
"To be decently interred in Baptist Cemetery at Neal's Creek, by the side
of my late wife, Francis...my Rev'd. Brothers, A. Rice and J. S. Murray
preach my funeral...as a Soldier of War of 1812, my burial to be conduct-
ed with military honors - and that Mayor John B. Moore to deliver an
address upon the occasion."...granddaughter, Alice Hosletine Taylor...
grandson, Robert H. Gaines...daughter, Nancy L. Gaines, Robert's mother,
to have tract of land adjoining Josiah King, James P. Haynie, Nancy L.
Gaines, E. K. Pepper, and John Williangham...daughter, Susan J. A. Taylor,
tract whereon I now live, adjoining Lucy P. Stringer, John Willingham and
others..."sons and daughters not mentioned, have been provided for prev-
iously."...Executor: Son, W. H. King. Dated 25 Jan, 1878.
Wit.:   John B. Moore   (Robert King signed his mark)
        L. B. Hall
        Wm. C. B. Hall
Probate: 17 Jan. 1879.

WILL OF LIZZIE WARDLAW - pp 684-686
Nephew, Albert Latimer, son of Wesley Latimer..."balance of estate equ-
ally divided between my legal representatives." Executor: Albert Latimer. Dated 6 Sept. 1871.
Wit.:   Jas. Wilson   (Lizzie Wardlaw signed her mark)
        W. F. Sutherland
        G. M. Mattison (called Gabriel M. Mattison in oath)
    "To R. N. Wright, Esq., by W. W. Humphreys, Judge of Probate - give
you full power and authority to examine the witnesses to last will of
Lizzie Wardlaw." Dated 21 Jan. 1879....Present: R. N. Wright, Trial
Justice for County of Anderson - George Strother Adams swears to the
writing in above will and took oath as executor, 30 Jan. 1879.

WILL OF JACOB BURRISS - pp 687-691
Grandson, Luther J. Burriss, to have choice of one half of tract, (279
3/4 acres) on both sides of road leading from Anderson to Pendleton, plat
made by W. S. Hall, 24 Dec. 1874...son-in-law, John Eskew, as trustee for
granddaughter, Ophilla Burriss...John Eskew and his wife, my daughter,
Amanda...mentions 984 acres and residue of estate consisting of stores on
Granite Row and the Cater house and lot in Anderson, also Steele tract..
.other living children: Wm. Burriss...Martha E. Watson...Eliza Watson,
wife of John B. Watson...Martha E. Watson's son, Belton...Executors:
Son, Wm. Burriss, and "friend and attorney for me in my lifetime," Joseph
N. Brown. Dated 19 Sept. 1879.
Wit.:   William B. Watson
        Wm. Henry Strickland
        Vasti B. Keys
    Codicil: "J. Belton Watson, has agreed with his mother, Martha E.

Watson to decuct sum advanced, etc." Dated 28 Dec. 1878.
Wit.: W. B. Watson
       J. R. Earle
       W. B. Hembree
Probate: 11 Feb. 1879.

WILL OF JAMES HARRISON - pp 692-696
Mentions acquisition of land recently in Florida...daughter, Elizabeth
H. Whitner...son, James W. Harrison, land where he resides adjoining
Town of Anderson, which was purchased by my dec'd. son, Elias...son,
Francis D. Harrison, has possession of land at Andersonville, adjoining
each side of Seneca and Tugaloo River, deed to him...son-in-law, Joseph
N. Whitner...mentions investments made in Mississippi by dec'd. son,
William H. Harrison..."demand by B. J. Earle, though I have never re-
garded the claim addressed to myself."...granddaughters: Sallie F.
Rucker, eldest...Elizabeth Tocoa Whitner...Mary Talulah Whitner...Bettie
Harrison...Mary Lucie Harrison...Ida Harrison...Nina Harrison...Eliza-
beth W. Harrison...Sallie E. Harrison...Antonette Harrison. Executors:
Son-in-law, Joseph Whitner and sons, James W. Harrison and Francis E.
Harrison. Dated 30 June, 1858.
Wit.: R. Munro
       L. A. Osborn
       Abi Herndon
   Personally appeared Mrs. Abi Harrison, (nee Herndon), witness to
above will to make oath.
Probate: 2 May, 1879.

WILL OF WILLIAM ALLEN - pp 697-698
Wife, Sarah M. Allen. Executors: Wife, and friend, A. F. Elrod. Dated
2 April, 1879.
Wit.: P. L. Ginley
       W. R. Ginley
       A. F. Elrod
Probate: 12 May, 1879.

WILL OF AMOS ACKER - pp 699-701
Wife, (unnamed)..."Martha Jane Smith, of Indiana and her husband, Jas.
D. Smith having collected money of the Halbert Estate in Indiana, by
virtue of Power of Attorney and due myself and wife amounting to near
$300.00 which money has never been paid to either of us. To said Martha
Jane Smith, the Fiftieth (sic) part of my estate to be equally divided
among my other eight children, viz:"...Mary Williams...Elizabeth Reed.
..Albert S. Acker, of Alabama...Herbert F. Acker, of Alabama...Teresa M.
Reece, of Texas...J. J. Acker...Rob Acker...S. W. Suratt(?). Executors:
Sons, J. J. Acker, R. V. Acker. Dated 7 June, 1876.
Wit.: George A. Green   (Amos Acker signed his mark)
       A. J. Bradley
       W. T. Green
       All residents of Williamston, S. C.
Probate: 25 Nov. 1880.

WILL OF DANIEL BROWN - pp 702-706
Of Town of Anderson...wife, Eleanor St. Clair Brown, tract where I now
reside lying between the General's Road and the road running South out
to the end of McDuffie's Street, of the town, in the rear of my resid-
ence in the direction of Mrs. M. Archer...mentions late, William Waller,
father of my wife...John S. Bird, trustee...step-son, Dr. Waller H.
Nardin, trustee for daughter, Ida St. Clair Brown, to complete her ed-
ucation...son, Samuel Brown, trustee for daughter, Theresa Clementine
Brown...grandsons, children of John J. Brown, dec'd. Executors: Wife,
Eleanor St. Clair Brown. Dated 28 Jan. 1864.
Wit.: J. P. Reed
       Elijah Webb
       Herbert Hammond
Probate: 2 July, 1879.

WILL OF B. F. LOW - pp 706-708
Called BENNETT F. LOW in oath...wife, unnamed, tract of land bought from
John D. Alewine...sister, Emaline Alewine...Carry Taylor, who is now

184

living with and bound to me, when age 21...children: Susan C. Banister.
..John B. Low...Elizabeth Brock...Nancy Strickland...Ivy C. Low...Margaret Pruitt. Executors: Friend, R. B. A. Robinson, and son, Ivy C. Low.
Dated 9 June, 1879.
Wit.: James B. Pruitt
      D. B. Dunlap
      H. Robinson
Probate: 11 July, 1879.

WILL OF ELIZABETH REID - pp 709-711
"To be interred in cemetery at Robert's Church near where my sister, Ann
Haynie is buried, and to erect a tombstone similar to that on the graves
of Charles Haynie and his wife, my sister, Ann Haynie"...friend, Mrs.
Martha Lucretia Little...Carrie Elloise Little, eldest daughter of J.
Harvey Little...Annie Elizabeth Little, second daughter of J. Harvey
Little...afflicted nephew, Joseph P. Caldwell..."my especial friend, J.
Harvey Little", tract of land (65 acres), bounded by Wm. Buchanan, Miss
Julia Burriss, Estate of Ann Haynie and others. Executor: J. Harvey
Little. Dated 1 Nov. 1876.
Wit.: Wm. H. Haynie   (Elizabeth Reid signed her mark)
      Bascom B. Sharpe
      L. W. Fleming
Probate: 24 July, 1879.

WILL OF JOHN COX - pp 711-714
Names wife, Sarah Cox, "150 acres to be cut off from my Fork place to
embrace the homestead and lower portion of tract joining lands of Estate
of Col. F. E. Harrison"...Mary Ann Cox, widow and formerly wife of my
brother, W. G. Cox...Trustees of Methodist Episcopal Church, Anderson
Station, S. C...Cynthia C. Busby, wife of J. T. Busby, (no relation
stated)...mentions land sold to me by Oliver Bolt, Thomas McGukin and
others. Executors: Joseph W. Prevost and John W. Daniels. Dated 23
Jan. 1879.
Wit.: C. A. Reid
      Wm. L. Bolt
      J. R. Vandiver
Probate: 21 July, 1879.

WILL OF ELEANOR ST. CLAIR BROWN - pp 714-718
Wife of Daniel Brown of Town of Anderson...son, Dr. Waller H. Nardin,
house and lot of land where myself and husband and family now reside,
situated South of the Town of Anderson, (24 acres), bounded by North by
S. H. Langston, East by street running in front of residences of R. E.
Belcher and T. O. Heinck (?), South by lands of D. J. Bohannan, West by
the General's Road or Main Street of Town of Anderson. Dr. Nardin to be
trustee for daughter, Ida St. Clair Brown...John Feaster Brown, grandson
of my husband...stepson, Dr. Benjamin F. Brown...stepdaughter, Nancy C.
Belcher...step daughter, Teresa C. Brown...Georgia Brown, widow of dec'd.
stepson, John H. Brown...stepson, Samuel Brown...stepson, Elijah W.
Brown. "Bequests with approval of my husband, Daniel Brown." Executor:
Son, Dr. Waller H. Nardin. Dated 24 July, 1876.
Wit.: James A. Hoyt
      Chas. W. Webb
      R. C. Webb
   Codicil: "I, Eleanor St. Clair Brown, now widow of late Daniel Brown,
dec'd. make this addition: Sister, Caroline Waller, bond in possession
of Col. Joseph N. Brown...sister, Mary Waller...granddaughter, Eva Nardin,
daughter of son, Dr. W. H. Nardin, when she is age 21...daughter-in-law,
Lucy Nardin, wife of my son, Dr. W. H. Nardin. Dated 18 Aug. 1877.
Wit.: J. P. Reid
      Chas. W. Webb
      Robt. C. Webb
Probate: 22 July, 1879.

THOMAS ERSKIN - pp 719-722
"To be interred in family burying grounds according to the rites of the
Presbyterian Church."...wife, Elizabeth...children: Margaret Jane
Erskine...Letty E. Shearley...Sarah Kay...Martha Kay...Ugenia Lafoy...
Hugh C. Erskine..."homestead on South side of Greenville and Columbia

Railroad, (125 acres). Executors: Sons, Hugh C. Erskin and James W.
Erskin. Dated 24 Dec. 1878.
Wit.: John B. Moore
       J. N. Erskin
       J. M. Elgin
Probate: 4 Aug. 1879.

WILL OF WILSON HALL - pp 723-725
Names wife, Elizabeth...nine children: Mary A. E. Speers...Lety C.
Wright...Nancy A. Whitaker...Maranda J. Brown...William D. Hall...James
A. Hall...Dargin W. Hall...Gracy C. McKinney...son, James A. Hall,
trustee for daughter Cornelia G. McKinney. Executors: Sons, William
D. Hall and John W. Hall. Dated 19 Feb. 1879.
Wit.: J. T. Stuckey
       Jas. S. Bouchillon
       T. M. Nelson
Probate: 4 Aug. 1879.

WILL OF STEPHEN MARTIN - pp 725-726
Bodily heirs: William Whitner Martin...Lucinda Hester Martin...Emma
Cornelia Martin...Louisa Jane Martin...mentions Duckett Plantation.
Executors: Friends, T. M. Glenn and son, William Whitner Martin. Dated
1 April, 1879.
Wit.: John B. Rowland   (Stephen Martin signed his mark)
       James K. Robinson
       W. F. Broughton
Probate: 2 Sept. 1879.

WILL OF SARAH SEABORN - pp 727-728
Daughter, Mrs. Mattie Richards, wife of G. G. Richards...daughter,
Eliza Seaborn...daughter, Hannah Seaborn...daughter, Sue Seaborn.
Executors: Col. J. B. E. Sloan, and Dr. Paul H. E. Sloan. Dated 20
Mar. 1879.
Wit.: Amanda Redmond (signed her mark)
       P. H. E. Sloan
       Thos. G. Cuthbert
Probate: 16 Sept. 1879.

WILL OF ABRAHAM MEREDITH - pp 729-731
Wife, Clarissa Meredith, tract of land, (200 acres) on Martin's Branch,
waters of Tugaloo River adjoining J. H. Price, Mary Dobbins, John B.
Meredith, Abraham Meredith, Jr., Lewis Cromer and J. R. Meredith.
Eleven children: Katherine Osborne...Elizabeth Bradberry...William
Meredith...Rebecca Holbrooks...Emily Meredith...J. Robert Meredith...
Abraham Meredith, Jr...Susan Meredith...John Meredith...Amanda Stoulaker
(?), (only ten named, BW)...mentions children by first wife. Executor:
G. W. Hammond. Dated 25 June, 1879.
Wit.: John Himbree   (Abraham Meredith signed his mark)
       Marion Dannell (signed his mark)
       D. W. Patterson (signed her mark)
       G. W. Hammond
Probate: 25 Sept. 1879.

WILL OF JOHN J. COOLEY - pp 732-733
Names wife, Sarah V. Cooley...brothers and sisters, "or their children
in the event of their death before division"..."In the event of my wife
leaving child or children by second marriage, at her death, I direct
the entire proceeds of my estate to be paid to such child or children
at age of 21." Executor: Hugh Poor. Dated 21 April, 1862.
Wit.: B. F. Mauldin
       Lewis Ellerson
       Martha A. Whitt
Probate: 28 Oct. 1879.

WILL OF ALONZO THOMPSON - pp 734-735
Wife, Clara Thompson, lot of land and houses in Garvin Township, (two
acres) and carpenter tools. Executor: Clara Thompson. Dated 18 Mar.
1879.
Wit.: Carver Randall   (Alonzo Thompson signed his mark)

186

C. J. Hascall
S. S. Cherry
Probate: 7 Nov. 1879.

WILL OF EMILY C. WATERS - pp 736-737
Husband, Armsted J. Waters to have all property. Executor: Armsted
J. Waters. Dated 14 Dec. 1878.
Wit.: Solomon S. Jones
       John Simpson (signed his mark)
       Samuel Simpson (signed his mark)
Probate: 20 Nov. 1880.

WILL OF BENJAMIN J. SPEARMAN - pp 738-739
Names wife, Catherine E. Spearman, at her death, property to two daugh-
ters: Mary A. Spearman and Nancy E. Spearman...two sons, Jacob Spear-
man and David J. Spearman...to take care of daughter, Nelly Ann Spear-
man as long as she lives. Executors: Sons, Jacob J. Spearman, and
David J. Spearman. Dated 12 Sept. 1879.
Wit.: N. S. Reeve
       W. T. Dickerson
       W. B. Smith
Probate: 1 Jan. 1880.

WILL OF MATTHEW DUNLAP - pp 740-741
Ann Dunlap, "my present wife"...daughters, Nancy E., Malinda, Cynthia
Jane, Amanda N...rest equally divided between all my children. Exec-
utor: Wife, Ann Dunlap. Dated 12 June, 1873.
Wit.: A. Reed   (Matthew Dunlap signed his mark)
       Thomas Beaty
       P. H. Reid
     Oath says Dr. J. H. Reed was subscribing witness.
Probate: 5 Jan. 1880.
       A. E. Dunlap qualified and signed her mark.

WILL OF JOHN B. ADGER, JR. - pp 742-743
Nuncuperative Will..."We the subscribing witnesses certify that on 24
Jan. 1880, at Rivoli, in Anderson Co., S. C. at the residence of John
Adger, Jr. did declare that his will was to leave all his property to
his sister, Susan D. Adger.
Wit.: W. Walker Russell
       Theron Earle
       J. Lawrence Reynolds.
Probate: 28 Feb. 1880.
     Jno. B. Adger swore to the will and to make a perfect inventory.

WILL OF LUCINDA CAROLINA DEAN - pp 744-747
Widow of the late Charles Pinkney Dean, of Anderson Co., S. C..."funds
to fix up my own grave and the grave of my late husband, C. P. Dean,
and my departed son, Thomas L. Dean"...son, Julius Franklin Dean, all
my one half interest in the Mill and Mill tract of land, also ½ interest
in tract known as a part of Elijah Pepper land, situated near town of
Williamston on waters of Big Creek, adjoining Wm. Cooley, Allen Clement
and others - trust agent to manage Real Estate. If he dies without
marrying to be divided between his brothers: George R. Dean...J. L.
Dean...and sister, Anna L. Brown...mentions interest on cotton which
is to be paid by Mr. James Gambrell and his son. Executor: Son, George
R. Dean. Dated 3 Mar. 1880.
Wit.: E. H. Acker
       A. R. Cox
       W. C. Brown
     To G. W. Nicholls, Esq. of Spartanburg Co., S. C. , "I empower you to
administer usual oath to George R. Dean, named Executor of this will
of Lucinda C. Dean, dec'd. Dated 12 Mar. 1880, signed by W. W. Humphreys,
Judge of Probate of Anderson Co., S. C.
Probate: 16 Mar. 1880.

WILL OF JAMES B. CHAMBLEE - pp 747-749
Names wife, Nancy Agnes Chamblee, to have tract of land known as Keowee
place, (517 acres) on Generostee Creek, waters of Savannah River, bounded by Dr. James T. McFall, D. K. Watson, Reuben Burriss, Col. Wm. S.

Shaw and others...son, Robert T. Chamblee...son, James M. Chamblee...
son, David S. Chamblee...daughter, Eleanor Frances Carter...Jesse P.
McGee and wife...Wm. T. Chamblee...three sisters: Ann Elizabeth Cham-
blee, Mary Frances Chamblee, Nancy Jane Chamblee, minor children of
dec'd. son, John Alexander Chamblee to have jointly the tract of land
where they and their mother now live, (202 acres), in Anderson Co. on
Richland Creek, waters of Savannah River, bounded by Estate of James
Gilmer, dec'd., Dr. J. T. Cook, Mrs. Lucinda Reamor, Estate of George
Campbell and others..."two children not herein named". Executors: Wife,
Nancy Agnes Chamblee and son, James M. Chamblee. Dated 30 May, 1872.
Wit.: Wm. H. Haynie   (James B. Chamblee signed his mark)
      H. G. Scudday
      R. L. Moorhead
Probate: 20 Mar. 1880.

WILL OF MARTHA B. SIMPSON - pp 750-751
(Will was not included. BW)
   Codicil: To will made Dec. 1874, bequeath to certain heirs of dec'd.
son, Jas. L. Simpson. Now do bequeath to my daughter, Louisa C. Simpson.
Dated 6 Dec. 1874.
Wit.: Jas. J. McLees   (Martha B. Simpson signed her mark)
      D. M. Simpson
      Hugh McLees
Probate: 28 Apr. 1880.

WILL OF JAMES J. CLEMENT - pp 752-753
Names wife, Elizabeth Clement and two daughters, Sarah E. and Mary L.
Executor: Wife, Elizabeth Clement. Dated 9 Mar. 1880.
Wit.: C. C. Grubbs
      M. B. Wright
      J. Marshall Dunlap
Probate: 30 Apr. 1880.

WILL OF SUSANNA M. BARNES - pp 754-756
Member of Methodist Episcopal Church in Pendleton Village...sister,
Eliza F. Dupre...niece, Dena Kennedy...sister, Esther M. Dupre...niece,
Susanna C. Bellotte...step-daughter, Rosanah Morrow, formerly Rosanah
P. Cromer...Mattie Cromer and her twin sister, Mollie Cromer...Mrs.
Thursa Hammond, (no relation stated)...brother, John David Carnes'
five children, viz: Margaret, John David, James Bland, Eliza Martha,
and Mary Jane...Sallie Bellotte, (no relation stated). Executors:
Julius F. C. Dupre, and John E. Bellotte. Dated 25 Oct. 1872.
Wit.: J. B. Traywick
      W. L. Jenkins
      S. S. Cherry
Probate: 7 May, 1880.

WILL OF SHADERICK D. DEAL - pp 759-761
Planter, names wife, Licenor Catherine..."In event of the adoption of
an orphan, as is now contemplated, said orphan shall receive education
and be provided for." Executor: Wife, Licenor Catherine. Dated 21
Mar. 1870.
Wit.: C. E. Horton
      D. L. Donald
      James H. Nash
Probate: 9 July, 1880.

WILL OF AARON HOLLAND - pp 761-763
Wife, Malinda Holland, at her death or remarriage, to children equally.
Executor: Son-in-law, N. G. Ellison, and wife, Malinda Holland. Dated
25 Nov. 1878.
Wit.: R. T. Elrod
      L. G. Elrod
      A. B. Elrod
Probate: 20 July, 1880.
   Greenlee Ellison and Malinda Holland qualified.

WILL OF DAMARIS GRAY - pp 763-765
Son, Hezekiah H. Gray...mentions other children (unnamed). Executor:
Hezekiah H. Gray. Dated 18 Sept. 1869.

Wit.: W. S. Moore   (Damaris Gray signed his mark)
      John W. Kay
      H. P. Moore
Probate: 14 Aug. 1880.

WILL OF BOB JAMESON - pp 766-767
(Freedman)...sister, Milley Arnold, (freedwoman)...sister, Haret West-
feild, (freedwoman). Executor: Joshua Jameson. Dated 25 Aug. 1867.
Wit.: W. Y. Croft   (Bob Jameson signed his mark)
      J. P. Traynum
      L. V. Jones
Probate: 17 Aug. 1880.

WILL OF JACOB P. REED - pp 767-772
Town of Anderson...wife, Teresa Caroline Reed...son, Clifton A. Reed...
son-in-law, B. Frank Mauldin...daughter, Lucy E. Reed...son, J. P.
Reed, Jr., when 21 years of age...infant children: Teressa Hammond
Reed, and Clifton A. Reed...mentions salary due me by State of S. C...
mentions law library and office furniture, residence and three truck
patches, and farm, three miles from town, which John Williams resides
on, (152 acres), and place known as Julia White tract, also 20 acres
in town of Williamston, S. C...tract purchased by me from C. B. Gilmer,
on which daughter Emala T. Miller and family reside...Town property
known as Waverly House, a hotel. Executors: Wife, Teressa Catherine
Reed, and son-in-law, B. Frank Mauldin. Dated 18 June, 1880.
Wit.: J. L. Tribble
      W. H. Nardin
      J. A. Brock
Probate: 7 Sept. 1880.

WILL OF MARION G. HILL - pp 772-773
(Called Mrs. M. G. Hill in oath)..."being greatly afflicted"...daughter,
Mrs. Pet A. Orr and her husband to have care and custody of minor daugh-
ter, Richardine G. Hill...son, John E. Allen..."to be buried after
rites of Methodist Episcopal Church". Executor: Samuel M. Orr. Dated
12 Aug. 1880.
Wit.: L. C. Gaillard
      M. A. Allen
      John E. Allen
Probate: 8 Sept. 1880.

WILL OF RICHARD B. ROBINSON - pp 774-777
Mentions my interest in homestead where I now live, being Old Homestead
of my father, John Bar Robinson, dec'd. and bought by my brother, James
A. Robinson, now dec'd., (324 acres) to sister, Hannah Kay and her
children and Benjamin F. Robinson, my nephew, who lives with me, and
his own children...Ezekiel Harris, and his heirs, tract known as Evans
tract, (50 acres), (no relation stated)...my interest in Nelson tract
(72 acres) to dec'd. sister, Adeline Ashley's five children...my interest in L. O. Williams tract, where my brother, Henry Robinson lives,
to him and his children...niece, Elizabeth A. Kay...dec'd. sister, Polly,
...sisters: Rachel Kerr, Eliza McClain...dec'd. sister, Jane Hog.
Executor: Ezekiel Harris. Dated 19 July, 1880.
Wit.: Geo. M. McDavid
      J. W. Green
      R. N. Wright
Probate: 1 Nov. 1880.

WILL OF ALBERT MCCRARY - pp 777-779
Mentions three tracts of land, the Home Place, the Maxwell Place, the
Rolletten Place...wife, Mary C. McCrary...three single daughters, Mary
A. McCrary, Sallie H. McCrary, Celestine McCrary...three sons: Samuel
McCrary, Langdon McCrary, William H. McCrary. Executors: Sons, Samuel
McCreary, and William H. McCreary. Dated 28 Sept. 1880.
Wit.: B. F. Gantt
      John R. Zachary
      C. G. Davis
Probate: 1 Nov. 1880.

                         END OF RECORD

PENDLETON COUNTY, SOUTH CAROLINA

CONVEYENCE BOOKS

WILLS
BOOK A

1790-1792

Abstracted by Mrs. Charles E. Willie
3610 Fleetwood St.
Amarillo, Texas   79109

WILL OF MRS. KITTY BURRIS - p 175
Mrs. Kitty Burris made oath that her duaghter, Jean Burris, now Jean
Glenn was first married to John Evans who died and left one daughter,
Letitia, and something considerable in property, as he was a careful,
well managing man...daughter then married William Brummett who was not
so attentive of his worldly concerns and spent the full half of what
first husband had left, without adding to the stock, but left issue of
two sons...when said William Brummett was on his death bed, she asked
him how he wished to have his worldly affairs settled...he replied that
he wished Letitia to be made whole, if there was property enough left,
signifying that what was left should be applied to the use of the first
husband's child...John Burt was also present. Dated 21 July, 1790.
Robert Anderson, J. P.

WILL OF RALPH WILSON - p 178
Abbeyville Co., S. C...wife, Jane Wilson...children: Elizabeth Wilson,
George G. Wilson, James W. Wilson, Sarah D. Wilson..."care and educa-
tion of children under executor until son, James Wharey Wilson is 21.
Executor: Thomas Wharey, John Wharey, and Stephen Wilson, Jr. Dated
9 Oct. 1788.
Wit.: Jesse Wood
       Aaron Derney
Probate oath on page 180, not signed or witnessed.

WILL OF R. RALSTON - pp 178-181
Pendleton Co.,...wife, Frances...sons, Lewis and John Raulston, tract
of land lying on Tugaloo River adjoining tract called Village Tract.
(150 acres). Dated 17 May, 1879.
Wit.: Jesse Walton
       Benj. Harrison
   (no executor named)

WILL OF JOHN JOHNSON - p 181
Yeoman of Pendleton Co.,...wife, unnamed...son, Joseph, 200 acres lying
on Greatsaltketchers in Winton Co., in Orangeburg Dist., S. C...daughter,
Elizabeth, 100 acres on Three Mile Creek, waters of Big Saltketchers.
Executor: Andrew Jones. Dated 15 Aug. 1790.
Wit.: Stephen Sullivant
       Elizabeth Jones (her mark)
       Joseph Dunklin
Oath, 8 Nov. 1790.

WILL OF JOHN LINLEY - p 182
Yeoman of Pendleton Co...wife, Sarah Linley...unmarried children. Ex-
ecutor: William Pyle, Jr., and wife, Sarah. Dated 9 Sept. 1790.
Wit.: John Robinson
       Joel Halbert
       Jacob Visage
Oath, 11 Nov. 1790.

Will of Sarah Lindley - p 305
Sarah Lindley made oath that her husband, John Lindley was lying on
his death bed, he said there was one thing he forgot...son, John should

191

have a colt. Dated 31 Dec. 1790.
Wm. Halbert, J. P.
Recorded 9 June, 1791.

WILL OF ROBERT GOODWIN - p 305
Farmer...son, Mecager Goodwin, all goods, chattels and dwelling house.
Dated 1 Mar. 1791.
Wit.: Nathaniel Bullard
      John Langley
Recorded 9 June, 1791, by John Wison, J. P.

WILL OF ALICE LOWE - p 351
Children: William Roberts, Richard Roberts, James Roberts, John Roberts,
Thomas Roberts and Alice Roberts. Dated 9 Sept. 1791.
Wit.: Elizabeth Miller   (Alice Lowe signed her mark)
      Jno. Miller
Recorded 26 Oct. 1791, by John Wilson, J. P.

DEED OF GIFT, ISREAL PICKENS - pp 371-372
Pendleton Co., 96 District...daughters: Ellender Pickens, Mary Pickens,
Elizabeth Sherd, (could be Stord) Pickens, Metildy Pickens...sons:
John, William and Isreal Pickens, Jr. Dated _____, 1791.
Wit.: Sam'l Brown
      John Burchfield
Recorded 8 Oct. 1791, by Elijah Browne, J. P.

WILL OF WILLIAM BROOKS - pp 417-418
"taking into consideration that I have a growing family and that I am
subject to excess use of spiritous liquors whereby I am liable to be
departed of my property by designing men, by which I may be unable to
find support for my wife and children..therefore this indenture, between William Brooks, farmer and Sarah and Margaret Brooks, both daughters of William Brooks...tract of land which I now live, on Tugaloo
River, (200 acres). Dated 6 Feb. 1792.
Wit.: Wm. McCaleb
      Henry Barton
Recorded 13 Feb. 1792.

BOOK B

1791-1795

WILL OF ARCHIBALD GILLISON - pp 63-64
Abbeyville Co., S. C...wife, Jean Gillison...children: Elizabeth Price,
Mary Harris, James Gillison, Karenhappuch Harris...daughter, Ann Gilli-
son, tract where I live at wife's decease or remarriage, (125 acres)...
John Gillison, son of daughter, Ann Gillison. Executors: Three friends,
James Nash, Stephen Harris, Larkin Nash. Dated 3 Jan. 1792.
Wit.: George Nash
      James Thornhill
      Valentine Nash
Recorded 20 Sept. 1792.

WILL OF JAMES WILSON - pp 126-127
Brother, John and his oldest son, Robert...wife, Keziah, to be sole
executrix. Dated 16 April, 1790.
Wit.: Frances Nunn   (James Wilson signed his mark)
      William Lowe
      Robert Maxwell
Recorded 24 Jan. 1793.

DEED OF GIFT, JOHN LAUDERDALE - p 365
For sum of 50 lbs. stg. of my son, James Lauderdale left him by his
grandfather, which I have wasted and run through, give to son, James,
½ of tract of 300 acres that I now live on and other goods and chattels.

Dated 2 Jan. 1795
Wit.: Harris Mauldin
       Robert Norris
       John Mauldin
Recorded 26 Jan. 1795.
       Deed of Gift to daughter, Sarah Lauderdale, (same wording), one
half tract of 300 acres, etc. Same date and witnesses.

BOOK C-D

1795-1799

DEED OF GIFT, JOHN SMITH - p 24
Planter...wife, Anna Smith, whole estate, including 300 acres of land.
Dated 27 Mar. 1795.
Wit.: Nath'l Perry
       Susanna Perry
Recorded 24 June, 1795.

DEED OF GIFT, FRANCIS ROSE - p 305
Wife, Pricilla Rose, all my property both real and personal, including
tract lying on Savannah River bounded by Samuel Rose, Col. John Moffett,
75 acres...$1.00 to my brother, John Rose or his oldest son, if living.
Dated 25 June, 1796.
Wit.: Thos. McCune
       Wm. McCune
Recorded 24 Jan. 1797.

WILL OF MATTHEW HARE - p 472
"In consideration of long journey...all of my brothers and sisters...
to orphant chile that is bound to me...wife, Elizabeth to be sole
executrix." Dated 26 Sept. 1776.
Wit.: David Looney
       John Adair
     State of North Carolina, Sullivan County, November session, 1780,
Elizabeth Hare cohibitted in court, last will of David Hare, dec'd.
Proven by teste, Matthew Rhea, Sullivan County, Tenn., 18 Feb. 1799.
Recorded, Pendleton County, 11 Mar. 1799.
     Betty Haire of Sullivan Co., Tenn., have land in State of South
Carolina coming to me by virtue of my husband, Matthew Haire, dec'd.
in late American War, and property he took into ____State. Appoint
John Tally of Sullivan Co., Tenn. my attorney to recover and dispose
of these lands. Dated 18 Feb. 1799. Signed Betty Hare.
Recorded 11 Mar. 1799.

END OF BOOK

SOUTH CAROLINA, PENDLETON DISTRICT

CONVEYENCE, ESTATES AND REVOLUTIONARY SOLDIERS

BOOK A

1790-1792

Extracts abstracted by Mrs. Charles Willie,
3610 Fleetwood St., Amarillo, Texas 79109

p. 115
Soldier...PATRICK FORBIS, planter of Abbeyville Co. to JAMES MOORE, of
Abbeyville Co., 200 acres in 96 District above ancient boundary line,
in waters of Hencoop, waters of Rocky Creek, granted sd. Patrick Forbis
for being a soldier in Continental Line. 5 Mar. 1787.
Wit.: Patrick Buchanan
      Philmon Waters
      Robt. Stevenson

pp. 190-192
Soldiers...JOHN SWORDS, late Soldier of Continental Line of this State
to LEWIS DANIEL MARTIN, late Captain of sd. Line, 200 acres in 96 Dis-
trict on Martin's Creek, waters of Keowee River. 21 Jan. 1785.
Wit.: Richard Taliferro
      John Bowie
      John L. Swords
Sworn 5 Jan. 1791, to Alexander Hamilton, Abbeyville District.

pp. 292-294
JOHN DICKESON and ELENOR DICKESON, his mother to ROBERT DICKESON, all of
Pendleton 100 acres on 26 Mile Creek, waters of Savannah River, 100
acres granted to Michael Dickeson, husband of Elenor Dickeson. 17 Jul.
1790, adj. Edward Camp.
Wit.: Thomas Case
      Moses Jones
Lyddia Dickeson signed with John and Elenor Dickeson.
Rec.: 6 June, 1791.

p. 352
Soldier...FRANCIS WELCHEL, of Union Co., S. C. to JOHN DAVIS, "In deed
31 Sept. 1785, Francis Hollan and his son, John Hollon sold Francis
Welchel 200 acres in 96 District." Welchel now sells land to Davis on
both sides of Shoal Creek, branch of Saluda River, originally granted to
Dominic Hollon (Soldier), recorded in Union Co. Book A., No. 1, page
500, on 24 Sept. 1787. Dated 4 Aug. 1791.
Wit.: Davis Welchel
      J. Whitner
Rec.: 3 Nov. 1791.

BOOK B

1791-1795

p. 34
Soldier...ELEANOR WEITZEL, Executor to JOHN WEITZEL, Surgeon, dec'd. to
SABRA PERKINS, 300 acres on North Fork Choestoe Creek, waters of Tuguloo.
Tract granted to John Weitzel, surgeon in Continental troops of this
State, 16 July, 1784. Dated 27 Oct. 1791.
Wit.: Wm. Sloan
      John Shannon
      Jno. Sitton
Rec.: 25 June, 1792.

p. 60
Soldier...FIELD FARRAR, of Fairfield Co., S. C. to ROBERT BOX of Pendle-
ton Co., 200 acres on Noyewee (?) Creek, Tugaloo River, near Tugaloo
Old Town, bd. by S. Edwards, Robert Miscampbell and vacant lands,
originally granted to Jesse Grouter (Soldier), 21 Jan. 1785. Dated 9
Sept. 1790.
Wit.: John Clark Kilpatrick
      Jno. Barton
Rec.: 25 Jan. 1792.

p. 81
Soldier...CHARLES COTSWORTH PINKNEY, of Charleston, late Brigadier
General of the Armies of United States, and MARY, his wife, to GENERAL
ANDREW PICKENS, COL. ROBERT ANDERSON, CAPTAIN ROBERT MAXWELL, MR. JOHN
BOWEN, MAJOR JOHN FORD and MR. JOHN HALLUM of Washington District for
5 shillings, all that square tract of 60 acres on waters of Brushy
Creek, branch of Saluda River. Dated 7 Sept. 1792.
Wit.: Anne Louisa Smith
      Willm. Johnson
      p. 82 - General Assembly of this State, by their act on 19 Feb. 1791,
appoint the commissioners to superintend building of Goal and Courthouse
in the District of Washington...and to form a town by the name of Rock-
ville...same date and witnesses.
      p. 83 - plat of town certified by Saml. H. Dickson, deputy surveyor.
Rec.: 14 Nov. 1792.

p. 189
Soldier...JAMES ROBERTSON of Washington Co., Ga. to JAMES TERRELL of
Pendleton Co., tract in Pendleton on Chauga Creek, waters of Tugaloo
River, originally granted to James Robertson, a soldier bearing date
21 Jan. 1785, Book BBBB. Dated 1 Dec. 1792.
Wit.: Saml. Taylor
      Blake Mauldin
Rec.: 1 Dec. 1792.

p. 203
Soldier...BENJAMIN DENTON of Greenville Co., N. C. (sic) to JOSEPH
MARTIN of Henry Co., Va. tract in Pendleton District on Tugaloo River
about 2 miles above Col. Benjamin Cleveland, adjoining Robert Looney and
others, being tract which Robert Denton of S. C., dec'd. devolved to
Benjamin Denton as heir at law to Reuben Denton, his brother, grant
to Rueben as a soldier's right, 200 acres. Dated 6 April, 1790.
Wit.: Henry Potter
      John Craft
      Wm. Martin
Rec.: 13 Nov. 1793.

p. 326
Soldiers...JERVIS HENRY STEPHENS of Charleston, Gentleman, to BENJAMIN
CLEVELAND, of Pendleton District, Planter, 200 acres on Toxaway Creek,
branch of Chagua, waters of Tugaloo, tract granted to Henry Hyrne, Esq.
for his faithful services during the war as a Lieutenant in State Cavalry
commanded by Col. Hezekiah Maham. Dated 22 Mar. 1793.
Wit.: John Davidson
      James Blair
Rec.: 15 Sept. 1794.

p. 339
Soldier...ROBERT ANDERSON, ESQ. to ROLAND and RICHARD BURKS, 200 acres
on both sides of Conoros Creek, waters of Keowee River, bounded by Capt.
Uriah Goodwine, land granted to George Bough on the bounty of his service
in the late war, on 10 July, 1784, recorded in Book BBBB, page 27.
Dated 30 May, 1794.
Wit.: David Sloan
      Job Hunter
Rec.: 26 Nov. 1794.

pp. 352-353
Soldier...JOSEPH WILLIAMS, of Rutherford Co., N. C. to JOHN EARLE 200
acres on Middle Fork of Connross Creek, branch of Keowee River, orig-
inally granted to John Williams on bounty, now dec'd, died intestate
and having no issue, Joseph Williams is his brother and lawful heir.
Dated 7 Sept. 1794.
Wit.: William Hannon
       Robert Young
       George W. Earle
Rec.: 26 Jan. 1795.

p. 365
Deed of Gift...JOHN LAUDERDALE for 50 lbs. stg. of my son, JAMES
LAUDERDALE, left him by his grandfather, which I have wasted and run
through, give to JAMES LAUDERDALE ½ tract of 300 acres where I now live
and other goods and chattels. Dated 2 Jan. 1795.
Wit.: Harris Mauldin
       Robert Norris
       John Mauldin
Rec.: 26 Jan. 1795.
       Same page, same wording...JOHN LAUDERDALE to SARAH LAUDERDALE, his
daughter, ½ tract of 300 acres and other goods and chattels. Same date
and witnesses.

p. 379
Soldier...ROBERT ANDERSON and LYDIA, his wife, to JOHN SHANNON, farmer,
200 acres on both sides of Conneross Creek, waters of Keowee River,
originally granted to John Davey (on bounty for service of Daniel Davey,
dec'd in late war), on 16 July, 1784. Recorded Book BBBB, page 24.
Dated 9 June, 1794.
Wit.: William Sloan
       Joseph Jenkins
Rec.: 28 Jan. 1795.

p. 388
Soldier...JOHN MOSS to WILLIAM LEWIS, 200 acres granted to John Moss on
his bounty, 4 July, 1791, bounded by William Lewis, and unknown on
Milwee Creek, waters of 23 Mile River. Dated 2 Feb. 1795.
Wit.: Saml. Neil
       William Hobbs
Rec.: 10 Feb. 1795.

                              BOOK C-D

                             1795-1799

p. 39
Heirs of Estate of HENRY WAKEFIELD, dec'd, free a slave named Bob former-
ly slave of Henry Wakefield. Signed by William Mathis, Allen Wakefield,
William Wakefield, Enoch Barry, Henry M. Whorton, Willoughby Pugh, David
Pugh, Mary Wakefield. Dated 20 Feb. 1795.
Rec.: 13 July, 1795.

p. 51
Soldiers...FIELD PREWETT, SR. and FIELD PREWETT, JR. name Benjamin
Ingram, Atty. to recieve all money due us for public service mentioned
in our discharges from Lt. David Mosley. Dated 17 Apr. 1795.
Wit.: Benj. Whorton
       James Hendricks
       Francis King
       John King
Rec.: 6 Aug. 1795.

                                197

p. 75
Soldier...STEPHEN DRAYTON, of Charleston to JOSIAH LEE, tract on
Choestoe Creek, branch of Tugaloo River, granted Drayton as bounty from
State for his Army service, 500 acres. Dated 18 Feb. 1793.
Wit.: John McKee
       Stephen Ravenal
Sworn to in Charleston.
Rec.: 3 Oct. 1795.

pp. 147-148
Soldier...JOHN NORWOOD, of Abbeyville Co., planter, to COLLIN CAMPBELL,
planter, 200 acres being tract granted to John Norwood, heir-at-law of
Daniel Norwood, Soldier late of the Army, on waters of South fork of
Saluda River. Grant 15 Oct. 1784. Dated 27 Oct. 1791.
Wit.: William Leonard
       Honour Leonard
Rec.: 27 Jan. 1796.

p. 156
Soldier...THOMAS STONE to JAMES BOURLAND, grant dated 2 Oct. 1786 to
John Logan, heir-at-law of Thomas Logan, dec'd. for his services on
bounty, tract of 200 acres on Little George's Creek, waters of Saluda,
recorded Book BBBB, page 241, conveyed by Logan to Stone. Dated 9 Nov.
1794.
Wit.: John Bourland
       Enoch Smith
       William Bourland
Rec.: 9 Feb. 1796.

p. 166
Heirs...MARY HARRIS and HANDY HARRIS, both of Abbeyville Co. and JOHN
HARRIS, of Pendleton Co. to JOSEPH WHITE, of Pendleton. John Harris,
dec'd. of Abbeyville, minister of the gospel in his lifetime was possess-
ed of tracts of land, one of which, by his last will directed to be sold
by his executors, 250 acres on East side of Keowee River, bounded by
River, all other sides vacant, granted John Harris, 15 Oct. 1784, Grant
Book AAAA, page 178. Dated 10 July, 1794.
Wit.: Saml. H. Dickson
       Rebekah Dickson
       Jno. Dickson, Sr.
Rec.: 10 Mar. 1796.

p. 247
Deed of Gift...THOMAS EDMONDSON to MARY POWELL, trustee for NANCY
EDMONDSON, wife of Thomas Edmondson, tract 200 acres including plantation
where John Powell now lives, part of tract purchased by Edmondson from
Thos. C. Russell, to be held in trust after my decease, my heirs and
executors to maintain said Nancy Edmondson. Dated 2 May, 1796.
Wit.: W. Thompson
       Wm. Norton
Rec.: 25 June, 1796.

p. 344
Heirs...PETER BAYLEY, late of Charleston, Atty. at Law, by his last will,
dated 13 June, 1785, among other bequests gave to Thomas Drayton, second
son of William Drayton, Esq. Barrister at Law, his tract of 640 acres
in 96 District. Thomas Drayton has since departed life, intestate,
said lands became right of Jacob Drayton, Hannah Drayton, Mary Charlotte
Wilson, widow, Sarah Motte Drayton and William Drayton, his surviving
brothers and sisters, who agree to sell this land to Peter Keys, of
Pendleton Co. 640 acres on branch of Big Generostee Creek, branch of
Savannah River, originally granted to Peter Bayley 15 Oct. 1784. Dated
6 July, 1797.
Wit.: James Long
       W. Young
Rec.: 22 Aug. 1797.

p. 348
Soldier...COLIN CAMPBELL to CORNELIUS KEITH of North Carolina, 100 acres
where Joseph Dunn lives, part of tract granted to John Norwood, heir-
at-law of Daniel Norwood, (a soldier), dec'd., containing 200 acres
bearing date, 15 Oct. 1784, lying on both sides of Oolinoy (?) Creek of
Saluda River. Dated 23 Apr. 1795.
Wit.: William Keith
       John Keith
Rec.: 25 Apr. 1795.

p. 357
Heirs...ISABELLA MCCHESNEY, WILLIAM ASHER (sic) and wife, WILLIAM YOUNG
and wife to WALTER MCCHESNEY, 100 acres in State of Virginia, Rockbridge
Co., waters of Walker Creek, being plantation of Walter McChesney, dec'd.
adjoining Henry Camponels (?), William Wardlaw. Dated 10 Nov. 1791.
Signed Isabel McChesney, William Asherst, Mary Asherst, William Young,
Jean Young.
Wit.: Robt. Akin
       Thomas Hood
Rec.: 20 Nov. 1797.

p. 473
Soldier...DANIEL DO'YLEY of Charleston to FREDRICK LANIER, 200 acres in
96 District on Beaverdam Creek, waters of Tugaloo River, granted as
bounty land to said Do'yley as Lt. in First Continental Regiment of the
State of S. C. Dated 7 Mar. 1799.
Wit.: Geo. Caborne
       Francis Bremar
Rec.: 23 Mar. 1799.

p. 485
Soldier...ROBERT SMYTH of Abbeyville Co., to JAMES LAFOY of Pendleton
Co., 200 acres granted to Nathaniel Bradwell of Charleston District as
his soldier's bounty, 3 Sept. 1784, in 96 District on North fork of
Choestoe Creek, waters of Tugaloo. Dated 24 Dec. 1798.
Wit.: Turner Harris
       John Lively
Rec.: 22 June, 1798.

BOOK E

1799-1800

Much of this book is very dim, most unreadable.

pp. 51-52
Soldier...Abbeyville Co., JOHN WILLIAMS, of Abbeyville to JOHN MCMILLIN
of Pendleton, 200 acres granted to Williams as bounty land, 7 July, 1788,
on West branch of Generostee Creek, waters of Savannah River, bounded
by David Jordin and vacant lands. Dated 24 Aug. 1799.
Wit.: Samuel Weems (?)
       William Yorbrough
Rec.: __ Sept. 1799, by Samuel Foster, J. P., Abbeyville Co.

p. 96-97
Soldier...WILLIAM MCCALEB to WILLIAM HUGHES LACY, 400 acres, originally
granted to James McIlwee as bounty, tract on Choestoe Creek, waters of
Tugaloo River. Dated 20 June, 1795.
Wit.: David Sims
       Brooks Davis
Rec.: 22 Nov. 1799.

p. 139-140
Soldier...JOHN HOLLAN to JOHN DAVIS, 200 acres granted to Dominic Hollan
(soldier) by Patent, 21 Jan. 1785, on Shoal Creek of Saluda River.

Dated 9 Mar. 1793.
Wit.: Bennet Combs
       William Whelchel
Rec.: 5 Jan. 1800.

p. 207
Soldier...JOHN BAYLIS EARLE to ASA MEEKS, 200 acres originally granted
to John Williams as bounty 24 Jan. 1785, on fork of Cain Creek. Dated
17 Mar. 1800.
Wit.: James Wood Gilbert
       ____ Hancock
Rec.: __ Mar. 1800.

BOOK F

1800-1802

Much of this book is unreadable.

pp. 269-271
Heirs...JOHN ROBERTS, ELSA GROWGAN, THOMAS ROBERTS, WM. LAWRENCE, lega-
tees of Widow ELSA LOVE to JACOB CAPEHART, 222 acres granted to Samuel
Love, 6 Nov. 1786, conveyed from Samuel Love to Thomas Love, at death
of Thomas Love to his wife, Elsa Love and from her to said legatees.
Dated 29 Oct. 1800.
Wit.: Moses Liddell
       Sam'l Tate
       Joseph Roberts.

BOOK G

1801-1804

p. 120
Soldier...CAPT. BENJAMIN BROWN to JOHN MCMAHAN, 300 acres, being land
granted to Capt. Brown for his services during the last war, land on
branch of Conoross Creek, a branch of Keowee River. Dated 18 Jan. 1802.
Wit.: William Brown
       Hezekiah Morris

pp. 145-146
Soldier...GODFREY ISBELL, of Franklin Co., Ga., planter, to JAMES
ALEXANDER of Pendleton, 100 acres granted to John Atterson, soldier,
21 Jan. 1784, conveyed by Atterson to Minor Winn, Esq., and by Winn to
Isbell, on branch of Cain Creek, branch of Tugaloo. Dated 13 Feb. 1794.
Wit.: James Clark
       John Alexander
Rec.: 22 July, 1802.

pp. 190-191
Soldier...HENRY BURDINE to WILLIAM HALBERT, 120 acres, part of tract
granted to William Davis, soldier, 21 Jan. 1785, conveyed from Davis to
Aaron Boggs and by Boggs to Burdine, land on head branches of South fork
of Big Creek, waters of Saluda River. Dated 7 Nov. 1801.
Wit.: Jocob Buzbey
       Thomas Hall.
Nancy Burdine rel. dower.
Rec.: 11 Oct. 1802.

p. 209
Heirs...SAMUEL CHERRY of Chester District, ELIZABETH WEIR, of Chester

District, SAMUEL TARBERT, of York District, JAMES LOGGINS, of Pendleton District, and WM. HALL of Union District, having only right to tract of land surveyed for our father, Sam'l Tarbert, Sr. on 2 June, 1784, sell to GEORGE DILLWORTH of Pendleton District, 200 acres on North fork of Brushy Creek, waters of South side of Saluda River. Dated 24 Jan. 1803.
Wit.: Thomas Cherry
      Richard Addis
Rec.: 22 Feb. 1803.

pp. 280-281
Soldier...CAPT. FIELD FARRAR, dec'd., who died intestate, he being entitled for services to Military bounty land from the goverment of U. S., THOMAS FARRAR, heir-at-law, appoint Thomas Tucker, Treasurer of U. S. my lawful attorney to take out and recover these warrants. Dated 14 May, 1803.
Wit.: Joseph Taylor
      Samuel Cherry
Rec.: 14 May, 1803.

p. 305
Deed of Gift...JESSE HALL to my (son ?) ZACHARIAH HALL, all my real estate and personal property including 150 acres. Dated 7 Jan. 1803.
Wit.: Thomas Lofton
      John Adair
Rec.: 10 June, 1803.

pp. 424-426
Soldier...DAVID MCCALEB, ESQ. Sheriff of Pendleton District to HENRY BIRCH, ESQ...whereas, Richard Brooks Roberts, now dec'd., in his life-time was possessed of tract of 300 acres granted to him as Military bounty, land on West side of Keowee River...judgement against property by Morton Brailford and Sebastian Huly, merchants, dated 31 July, 1790. Adm. on Estate of Roberts, James Kennedy sold at public auction, 7 Nov. 1803 to said Henry Birch.
Wit.: Thos. Stribling
      Wm. Hamilton
Rec.: 28 Jan. 1804.

p. 489
Soldier...JOHN MCMAHAN, of Abbeyville District to WILLIAM STEELE and JAMES WOOD, both of Pendleton, tract of 300 acres on both sides of Richland Creek, branch of Conneross, waters of Keowee, being land granted to Capt. Benjamin Brown for his services in the late Revolutionary War, conveyed to McMahan 11 Jan. 1802. Dated 15 Mar. 1804.
Wit.: Wm. Hunter
      J. C. Kilpatrick
Rec.: 21 Mar. 1804.

p. 525
Heirs...THOMAS GARNER, JAMES GARNER, JOHN GARNER and WILLIAM GARNER to THOMAS WILLIAMS, 133 2/3 acres on Rocky River originally granted to James Barr, being part of real estate of James Garner, dec'd. being same, where Thomas Garner now lives, which became inheritance at death of their father, James Garner. Dated 9 Jan. 1804.
Wit.: Jonathan Ruth
      George Taylor
Jane Garner and Elizabeth Garner, wives of James and Thomas Garner rel. dower.
Rec.: 12 Mar. 1804.

BOOK H

1804-1807

pp. 6-7
Soldier...PETER GRAY, of Spartan District to BENJAMIN STARRETT of

Pendleton District, 300 acres which was County Right from State of
S. C. to Peter Gray for services during the War, land on waters of
Coneross, in 96 District. Dated 10 Oct. 1803.
Wit.: Benjamin Hawkins
       William Montgomery
Hannah Gray rel. dower.

p. 18
Heirs...WILLIAM DAVIDSON, JOHN DAVIDSON and ANDREW THOMAS DAVIDSON,
heirs of James Davidson, dec'd., late of Meclenburg Co., N. C. to JAMES
TUFFENELL, of Pendleton District, 20 acres being part of 835 acres
granted to said heirs, children of James Garner, dec'd., 4 Sept. 1786.
Dated 28 June, 1804.
Wit.: Samuel Cherry
       Moses Liddell
Rec.: 2 July, 1804.

p. 20
Heirs...Heirs of JACOB WEST, dec'd. to JONATHAN WEST of Pendleton
District, 33 acres part of 150 acre tract purchased by Jacob West from
John Robinson on 23 Mile Creek of Keowee River. Heirs were: HANNAH WEST
and CHARLES WEST of Pendleton District, ZACHARIAH MORGAN and POLLY WEST
(she signed Mary West), both citizens of N. C. Dated 28 Jan. 1804.
Wit.: Wm. Sims
       Wm. Passmore
       James Grimes
Rec.: 11 July, 1804.

p. 38
Heirs...CHESTER ATKINS for himself and legatees of John Atkins, dec'd.,
sell to JACOB, formerly called HENRY for balance of his servitude...
Dated 29 July, 1803. Signed by: CHRISTIAN ATKINS, ROBERT ATKINS, WILLIAM
ARNOLD, BARTIES (?) ATKINS, SARAH THOMASON, ANN HOOKER, JOSEPH ATKINS,
LUCY ATKINS, MARTHA ATKINS.
Rec.: 13 Mar. 1804.

p. 62
Soldier...Affidavit, personally appeared ADAM THOMPSON, who made oath
that Robert Lin, now dec'd. was the lawful heir of John Lin, who fell in
the late American War and that SARAH LIN, now wife of William Murphree
and JOHN LIN, JR. is lawful heirs of above Robert Lin. Dated 6 Mar. 1804.
Rec.: 14 Mar. 1804.

pp. 115-116
Heirs...ANN MATHEWS, JOSEPH MATHEWS, POLLY MATHEWS, NANCY MATHEWS, and
JNO. MATHEWS, heirs of Isaac Mathews, dec'd. of Abbeyville District to
THOMAS HANAY of Pendleton District, 154 acres bounded by Savannah River,
lands laid out for Joseph Calhoun and lands laid out for Wm. Love. Dated
19 Dec. 1804.
Wit.: Hugh Simpson
       Isaac Evans
       Jos. Hutton
Rec.: 10 Oct. 1804.

p. 116
Heirs...ANDREW PICKENS, ROBERT ANDERSON, and JOHN WILSON, Commissioners
for laying off land adjoining Pendleton Court House, sell lot of land to
JANE MARCHBANKS, MARGARET WILLIAMS, JOHN YOUNG, SARAH YOUNG, ANNE YOUNG,
JAMES YOUNG, NANCY YOUNG, DICEY YOUNG, heirs of William Young, dec'd.
of the State of Tenn. Dated 9 Oct. 1803.
Wit.: James Jett
       Sam'L Cherry
Rec.: 10 Oct. 1804.

p. 129
Deed of Gift...ABIEL COBB to son, LEWIS COBB, all my lands, goods, and
chattels. Dated 15 Dec. 1804.
Wit.: A. Patterson
       Mary Patterson
       Inventory: Tract of land on East side of 23 Mile Creek, waters of

Keowee River, 191 acres bought from Samuel Robinson. (Oath said
Archibald Patterson, one of witnesses).
Rec.: 15 Jan. 1805.

p. 197
Heirs...SAMUEL ORR of Carlagan in County of Monaghan, farmer; ROBERT
ORR of Muhuailghuly, carpenter; ALEXANDER ORR of Bellaheugh in Co. of
Armagh, weaver; ALEXANDER WHITERAFT (?) of Co. of Monaghan, farmer
and ANN WHITERAFT (?), his wife, otherwise ORR, all of the Kingdom of
Ireland, appoint Thomas Orr of Bellaheagh in Co. of Armagh, now age 21,
our lawful attorney to demand and receive from administrator of William
Orr, formerly of Glenehiem (?) in Co. of Monaghan and lately of South
Carolina in America, where he died, and which property, we the brothers
and sister are entitled. Given at Mariaghen in County of Monaghan in
that part of United Kingdom called Ireland. Dated 17 Apr. 1804.
(Agnes Orr signed with above heirs).
Wit.: David Hamilton
Rec.: 15 June, 1805.

p. 238
Soldiers...LEWIS DELLARIN (?) to WILLIAM MAY of Anson Co., N. C., tract
of 400 acres original grant to James Mitchell containing 300 acres
grant for his bounty. Dated 1 Oct. 1805.
Wit.: P. H. May (called Phillip May in oath).
      Wm. Hamilton
Rec.: 1 Oct. 1805.

pp. 326-327
Heirs...HENRY RUKELSEMAN (?), planter, to heirs of Thomas Boyd, dec'd.
JOHN BOYD, WILLIAM BOYD, EPHRAIM BOYD, MARY BOYD, JEREMIAH BOYD, 105
acres at head of Spring Branch of George's Creek, waters of Saluda River.
Dated 22 Feb. 1806.
Wit.: Stephen Merritt
      Abraham Ruklesmer
Rec.: 26 Mar. 1806.

pp. 328-330
Soldier...JAMES CROFFORD to JOHN ELSTON, 100 acres on Tugaloo River,
part of tract originally granted to Aron Smith, Lieutenant in Army of
U. S. in Revolutionary War, 15 Oct. 1784. Bounded on Tugaloo River
above Walton's Ford at mouth of Spring Branch. Dated 10 Sept. 1803.
Wit.: Deveriue (?) Jarrett
      James Gibson
Rec.: 27 Mar. 1806.
      Elizabeth Crawford rel. dower. (2 deeds).

p. 395
Soldier...DANIEL BROWN of Kershaw Co., S. C. to MATHEW HOOPER, 200
acres on Choestoe Creek, waters of Tugaloo River, originally granted
to John Skelton, a soldier, 21 Jan. 1785. Dated 8 Mar. 1799.
Wit.: John Fisher
      John Brown
Rec.: 9 June, 1806.
      Mary Brown rel. dower.

p. 410
Soldier...DANIEL MAZYCK, eldest Captain in the late Second Regiment of
Foot (Soldier?) of the State of S. C., a Continental Establishment
commanded by Lt. Col. Commandant Francis Marion to JACOB HOLLAND, farmer,
remaining part of 300 acres on Beaverdam Branch, waters of Tugaloo,
granted to Mazyck on the bounty of the State. Dated 24 Nov. 1801.
Wit.: James Gillison
      Thomas W. Mazyck
Rec.: 28 Oct. 1806.

p. 432
DANIEL MAZYCK to BURRELL GREEN (same wording) 200 acres in 96 District
on South Branch of Coneross Creek, waters of Keowee River, bounded by
George Slator, which was granted to Lt. Stephen Mazyck, 2 May, 1785,

on bounty of the State, conveyed to Daniel Mazyck 2 May, 1785, duly
registered in Charleston Dist., Book P, no. 6, page 100-102. Dated
3 Nov. 1795.
Wit.:   James Gillison
        Thomas W. Mazyck
Rec.:   28 Nov. 1806.

p. 434
Heirs...ARMSTEAD BERRY, KESIA BERRY, WILLIAM BERRY, POLLY BERRY,
FREDRICK MOSS, all of Pendleton District are firmly bound for debt
to Robert Walton and Swift Mullins, both of Franklin Co., Ga. Armstead
Berry and Kesia Berry, appointed administrators of Estate of Andrew
Berry, dec'd. in 1802. Dated 13 Jan. 1807.
Wit.:   Samuel Earle
Rec.:   2 Feb. 1807.

p. 462
Soldier...Essey Meeks to James Starrett, 200 acres on Middle Fork of
Cain Creek, originally granted John Williams as a bounty grant, 21 Jan.
1785. Dated __, 1802.
Wit.:   Littleton Meeks
        Issac Grabtree
Signed: Nassey (?) Meeks, Fannie Meeks, his wife.
Rec.:   28 Oct. 1806.

BOOK I-J

1807-1809

p. 193
Heirs...JOHN D. TERRELL, JOEL TERRELL, DAVID MOZLEY, GEO. W. TERRELL
and WILLIAM H. TERRELL, all of Franklin Co., Ga. being heirs of Sam'l
D. Terrell, late of Franklin Co., Ga. nominate George W. Terrell our
attorney to sell tract on Big Estotoe in Pendleton District. Dated
30 Dec. 1805.
Rec.:   4 Apr. 1808.

p. 335
Will...HARRELL FELTON bequeath to son, HEZEKIAH FELTON, all my estate,
land, stock, and house hold furniture, at time of his becoming age 21,
to divide my estate between two daughters, MARY and ELIZABETH, and wife,
EMELIA to have her living from estate. ELIJAH GENTRY to be guardian.
Dated 26 Jan. 1809.
Wit.:   Wm. Wooddall
        John Woodall
        Elijah Gentry
        William Busclark (?)
Rec.:   6 Feb. 1809.

p. 401
Heirs...REBECCA FOSTER, adm. of Estate of BENJAMIN ALDRIDGE, dec'd to
LEONARD SAILOR, 109 acres originally granted Benjamin Aldridge, 5 Feb.
1798. Dated 3 Dec. 1808. At request of REBECCA ALDRIDGE, AGNES ALD-
RIDGE, JOSEPH ALDRIDGE, BENOM ALDRIDGE, MARY ALDRIDGE, JOHN ALDRIDGE,
and SARAH (LINDER?), plat laid out on Barker's Creek, waters of Savanna
River, bounded by Mr. Vanderhorst, Nathaniel Aldridge, Leonard Winters.
Rec.:   27 Mar. 1809.
Plat included.

p. 433
Heirs...JOHN YOUNG, HENRY YOUNG, ELIZABETH YOUNG, of Greenville Co.,
S. C., also HUME (?) R. FIELD, and WILLIAM ____, wife, JANE TAYLOR
and JAMES YOUNG of Mecklinburg Co., Va., heirs of JOHN YOUNG, dec'd. to
FREDRICK OWEN of Mecklinburg Co., Va. tract in Pendleton District,
formerly Abbeyville Co., in 96 District on 26 Mile Creek, 400 acres,

John Young, dec'd. of Granville Co., N. C. purchased. Dated 3 Dec.
1808.
Wit.: Lazarus Treynum
       Wiley Owens
       John Y. Young
Rec.: 1 May, 1809.

p. 466
Heirs...Power of Attorney...WILLIAM COCKERHAM, DRURY COCKERHAM, JOHN
COCKERHAM, being part of heirs of EDEY COCKERHAM, late of Virginia,
dec'd. appoint PETER COCKERHAM of Franklin Co., Ga. our attorney to
collect from administrator of Estate of RICHARD STONE, late of Va.,
dec'd. a sum of money bequeathed in his last will to said EDY COCHERHAM.
Dated 21 Aug. 1809.
Wit.: Francis Junkins
       Wm. Vernon
Rec.: 25 Aug. 1809.

                              BOOK K

                            1809-1810

pp. 51-52
Heirs...Abbeyville District, NIPPER SHIRLEY, WILLIAM SHIRLEY, WILLIAM
GRUBBS, JOSHUA SHIRLEY, JAMES SHIRLEY, JOHN SHIRLEY, HEZEKIAH WAKEFIELD,
ROBERT SHIRLEY, JOHN WAKEFIELD to SAMUEL MCKINNEY, of Abbeyville
District, mill and appurtences on Little River of Pendleton District,
formerly belonging to John Shirley, Sr., dec'd., tract 100 acres lying
part in Pendleton District, part in Abbeyville District, beginning on
Barker's Creek, bounded Goudy's line, Hackleman's line, Nathaniel
Aldridge, Sr., part of tract granted to said Aldridge, and recorded
in Secretary's Office. Dated 6 Aug. 1808.
Wit.: Abel Wakefield
       David Greer
Rec.: 24 Jan. 1810.

pp. 146-147
Heirs...ABRAHAM DUKE, HUGH TATUM, JOHN H. ROE, NANCY ROE, heirs of
SOLOMON ROE, dec'd. to ANDREW HAMILTON, 180 acres granted to SOLOMON
ROE, 4 Feb. 1788, on both sides of Rockhouse fork of 18 Mile Creek,
waters of Seneca River, bounded by Leonard, Henderson, 200 acres granted
to John Henderson, by Henderson to Roe, 2 Jan. 1792. Dated 17 Nov.
1809.
Wit.: Moses Hendrix
       Robert Wilson
       George Cannemor
   Rosannah Duke, wife of Abraham Duke, Nancy Tatum, wife of Hugh
Tatum, Cynthia Roe, wife of John H. Roe, rel. dower.
Rec.: 12 May, 1810.

p. 167
Power of Attorney...THOMAS STRIBLING, of Pendleton District, appoint
CLAYTON STRIBLING, of Union District, S. C. my lawful Attorney to
collect legacy from Estate of JOHN KINCHLOE, dec'd. late of Prince
William Co., Va. who bequeathed to my wife, ANN STRIBLING, formerly
ANN KINCHLOE, daughter of JOHN, legacy to be kept by my wife's mother,
ELIZABETH KINCHLOE, relict of John, until her death, which did not
take place until after the second marriage to EDWARD EMMS. At death of
ELIZABETH EMMS, legacy was left in hands of CORNELIUS KINCHLOE, trustee
for my wife, Ann. Dated 27 Aug. 1810.
Wit.: Thos. Stribbling, Jr.
       Cornelius K. Stribling
Rec.: 3 Sept. 1810.

p. 248
Soldier...Power of Attorney, BENJAMIN HARRIS, late of N. C., more

recently of Pendleton District appoint RICHARD MAJOR and WALTER BELL,
of Jackson Co., Ga. attorney to receive lands in State of Tennessee,
claimed by CLAIBORN HARRIS, dec'd. for services done by him as a regular
soldier in Revolution then a citizen of Greenville (sic) Co., N. C.
under command of Col. William Taylor. Dated 5 Sept. 1810.
Wit.:   Josiah Prewit
        Polly Harris
Rec.:   6 Nov. 1810.

BOOK L

1810-1812

pp. 126-127
Indenture...JAMES BEARD, SR. having arrived at very old age and having
a son born to me in my old age...it is my duty to provide for raising
and education of infant son, ISAAC BEARD...household goods and cattle.
Dated 4 Oct. 1810.
Wit.:   James Beard, Jr.
        Francis Beard
Rec.:   2 Apr. 1811.

p. 172
Heirs...WILLIAM NORTON, planter to heirs of THOMAS BOYD, dec'd.,
JOHN BOYD, WILM. BOYD, EPHRAIM BOYD, MARY BOYD, JAMIMAH BOYD, 304
acres on Little River, of Keowee River, bounded by McCann, granted
to William Norton, 8 Mar. 1799.
Wit.:   Stephen Merritt
        William Brevart
Rec.:   5 Aug. 1811.
        (Date of deed, 16 July, 1808).

p. 225
Heirs...JOHN TAYLOR sold to WILLIAM DUNLAP, in trust for WILLIAM MILWEE
and his wife, MARTHA, during their lifetime and at their death to
their sons, JOHN MILWEE, WILLIAM MILWEE, JAMES MILWEE, SAMUEL MILWEE,
reserving to ELIZABETH MILWEE and PATSY MILWEE, daughters of William
and Martha Milwee, a maintenance until they marry, on branch of 26 Mile
Creek, including place where Milwee now lives. Dated 3 July, 1811.
Wit.:   Tho. Harrison
        John Miller
Rec.:   2 Dec. 1811.

pp. 234-235
Soldier...WILLIAM STEEL and JAMES WOOD merchants, to ISRAEL GILLISON,
50 acres part of tract originally granted to Capt. Benjamin Browne
on Bounty, for 300 acres on North Fork of Coneross Creek, branch of
Keowee River. Dated 30 Dec. 1811.
Wit.:   Jo B. Earle (Joseph in oath)
        Jno. McEntire
Rec.:   14 Dec. 1811.

pp. 327-328
Soldier and Heirs...JOHN C. KILPATRICK, JAMES KILPATRICK, ALEXANDER
KILPATRICK, Executors of Estate of ASA KEMP, dec'd., 19 acres on East
side of Little Beaverdam Creek of Tugaloo River, part of 330 acres,
taken from prior grant to Maj. Saml. Wise for his bounty, also 55½
acres being part of tract granted to Maj. Charles Mott. Dated 29 May,
1805.
Wit.:   John Clayton
        Nancy Clayton
        Mary Hunt rel. dower to tract sold by executors of Asa Harris, dec'd.
to Anna Harris, widow of Dr. Handy Harris, dec'd. in prior deed, on
2 Feb. 1807.

pp. 369-370
Deed of Gift...JAMES BARNETT to children: REBECCA PITTS, TILMON
BARNETT, LANDY BARNETT, ASA BARNETT, WYLY BARNETT and JANE BARNETT,
stock, furniture, farm utinsels, etc. Dated 2 May, 1812.
Wit.: William Richards
      Adam Richards, Jr.
Rec.: 16 June, 1812.
   Next Deed of Gift...JAMES BARNETT to SILAS PITTS, son-in-law and
REBECCA, his wife, TILMON, LANDY, ASA, WILEY (sic), and JANE BARNETT,
tract on Tugaloo River, 200 acres, condition that I live on land, after
my death to be sold to highest bidder and money divided equally.
Dated 2 May, 1812.
Wit.: William Richards
      Adam Richards, Jr.
Rec.: 16 June, 1812.

pp. 371-372
Deed of Gift...THOMAS HARRISON, SR. "Having one unfortunate son,
WILLIAM, who I respect as much as any child...follows path of dissapa-
tion and thoughtless dealing that to me appears folly for me to give
him the property for which I have labored hard...which would be squand-
ered to the certain reduction of his helpless family...mentions
William's infant children...give to son, BENJAMIN HARRISON, in trust,
plantation tools, other goods and chattels, on condition...if son,
William reforms within ten years, Benjamin, at his satisfaction, make
right to property...otherwise to heirs of William, by his present wife,
ELIZABETH, as they come of age or marry, and she to have maintenance...
notes due me by John Varner, Duncan McKenzie, John Patrick (?), give to
son, BENJAMIN"...Dated 4 April, 1809.
Wit.: John Cleveland
      Clary Cleveland
      Peggy Perkins
Rec.: 18 June, 1812.

p. 412
Heirs...Heirs of WILLIAM MCCARLEY, SR., dec'd: MOSES MCCARLEY, SAMUEL
MCCARLEY, JOHN MCCARLEY, JAMES MCCARLEY, WILLIAM MCCARLEY, JOSEPH
MCCARLEY, JANNETT MCCARLEY, FRANCES BEATY and WILLIAM BEATY, all of
Pendleton District, except John McCarley of Logan Co., Ky. to DAVID
MCCARLEY, tract where he lives, on branch of Big Generostee Creek,
waters of Savannah River, 200 acres surveyed for Moses McCarter (sic)
6 June, 1784, 138 acres surveyed for William McCarley, Sr. 4 Dec. 1797.
Dated 20 Oct. 1809.
Wit.: David Beaty
      Samuel McGill
Rec.: 8 Sept. 1812.

p. 444
Deed of Gift...ELIZABETH FOSTER, of Prince William Co., Va. to CORNELIUS
GAINES, of Prince William Co., ELIJAH WYATT of Pendleton Co., S. C. and
JAMES MUNDAY of Roberson Co., Tn., 640 acres in Pendleton District,
according to last will of JAMES FOSTER, dec'd. bequests to wives of
above named. Dated 9 Feb. 1812.
Wit.: Daniel Foster
      John Prince
      Wm. Gaines
   All of Prince William Co., Va.
Rec.: Pendleton District, 13 Oct. 1812.

pp. 514-515
Heirs...JOHN HAYNIE to heirs of STEPHEN and MARTHA HAYNIE: POLLY HAYNIE,
LUKE HAYNIE, JOHN HAYNIE, JR., LUCINDA HAYNIE, STEPHEN HAYNIE, JR.,
and MALINDA HAYNIE, tract whereon Stephen Haynie now lives, 200 acres
on both sides of Robinson Creek, bounded by Nancy South, Lucy Harris,
Othenal Rice, granted John Haynie, 1799. Dated 20 May, 1809.
Wit.: George Taylor
      Thomas Taylor
      Anthony Haynie
   Elizabeth Haynie, signed Betsey, wife of John rel. dower.
Rec.: 2 Oct. 1809.

p. 30
Deed of Gift...RACHEL CUNNINGHAM, Excx. of Estate of FRANCIS CUNNINGHAM, dec'd. to my children, heirs of Estate: ELIZABETH, SARAH, PAUL, AGNES, RACHEL, ALEXANDER...negroes. Dated 18 Mar. 1807.
Wit.: William McKee
Aaron Holston
Rec.: 2 Dec. 1812.

p. 60
Heirs...Sheriff's sale, JOHN MCMILLION, Esq. Sheriff to SAMUEL CHERRY, whereas CLEMENT DEAL possessed tract of land which descended to JANE DEAL, widow and other heirs of Clement Deal, dec'd: ALEXANDER DEAL, HENRY COX and MARY his wife, THOMAS DEAL, MESHACK DEAL, ABNER STEEL, ELIZABETH his wife, EPHRAIM ROBINSON, survivor of his wife, PATSY, late PATSY DEAL, dec'd., JAMES DRENNAN and MILLEY, his wife, dec'd, HUGH GASTON and CHARLOTTE his wife, JOHN SCHISM (?) and SUSAN, his wife,...sell tract to divide with heirs. Dated 21 Nov. 1812.
Wit.: Elam Sharpe
David Cherry

p. 68
Heirs...WILLIAM MARCHBANKS, wife, JENNY, now dec'd; SAMPSON WILLIAMS, wife PEGGY; NATHANIEL RIDLEY, wife, SALLY; GEORGE WHITE, wife, ANN; WILLIAM THOMAS, wife, NANCY; NATHANIEL HAGGARD, wife, BODDECEA; and JAMES YOUNG in his own right, all of Jackson Co., Tn. heirs of WILLIAM YOUNG, dec'd. to WILLIAM GRIFFEN, land on 12 Mile River, 525 acres being part of four seperate tracts, granted to William Young in his lifetime and sold to William Griffen. Dated 25 Aug. 1812.
Wit.: W. T. Wherry
Bailey Barton
Rec.: 23 Feb. 1813.

pp. 100-101
Deed of Gift...STEPHEN HOPKINS to children: DAVID HUDSON HOPKINS, BENJAMIN HOPKINS, JOHN HUBBARD HOPKINS, RHODA PEOPLES HOPKINS, NANCY A. HOPKINS, PATSEY TAYLOR, land on Little River of 100 acres, furniture and cattle. Dated 4 Feb. 1813.
Wit.: Thos. Lamar
Mary Lamar
Rec.: 24 Mar. 1813.

p. 105
Heirs...BENJAMIN SHIRLEY, MOSES HUGHES, STARRETT DOBBINS, GEORGE BROWN, EDWARD HUGHES, WILLIAM HUGHES, JOHN HUGHES, heirs of Widow REBECCA NEAL, dec'd. to SAMUEL CHERRY of Pendleton Village, Merchant...sell negro. Dated 16 Mar. 1813.
Wit.: Jos. Grisham
George W. Reece
Rec.: 14 Apr. 1813.

p. 136
Soldier...EZEKIEL BUFFINGTON to ISAIAH BECK, 200 acres on Little Creek, branch of Tugaloo River, bounded by Eliaser Turner, granted to Matthew Hare, Soldier, 21 Jan. 1785, now dec'd. Dated 9 Jan. 1813.
Wit.: Patrick Calla (called Patrick Kelly in oath)
Jeoffry Beck
Rec.: 6 Sept. 1813.

p. 146
Soldier and Heirs...JOHN HAMMOND, of Concord Co., La.; DAVID HAMMOND,

of Williamson Co., Tn; LARKIN CLEVELAND of Morgan Co., Ga.; THOMAS
HAMMOND, legal heirs of MICHAEL HAMMOND, Esq., dec'd., to DR. JOSEPH
B. EARLE, lot known in General plan of Village of Pendleton by lot No.
40, on which Michael Hammond lately resided. LARKIN CLEVELAND, acting
attorney for Thomas Hammond, now of the U. S. Army. Dated 20 Sept.
1813.
Wit.: Jos. Grisham
       Jonathan Reeder
Rec.: 24 Sept. 1813.

p. 148
Heirs...CHARITY JONES, JOHN JONES, JAMES MOREHEAD, LEWIS JONES, WILLIAM
JOLLY, JR., WILLIS DICKESON, JOAB JONES to ABRAHAM TIMS, tract on West
side of Little 26 Mile Creek, adjoining Richard Meders, Peter Keys,
Benjamin Duck, Venson Tims, Lewis Jones, granted to Luis Jones, dec'd.,
100 acres. Dated 8 Mar. 1812.
Wit.: Anthony Dickinson
       Randolph Hunnicutt
Rec.: 4 Oct. 1813.

p. 149
Heirs...JOHN DODD, MICHAEL SPEED, JAMES DICKSON and WALTER C. DICKSON
all of Pendleton District, except Michael Speed of Abbeyville District
to THOMAS GASSAWAY, 271 acres except tract belonging to heirs of WILLIAM
SWIFT, dec'd., 271 acres belonging to the Estate of HUGH DODD, dec'd.,
at time of decease of his widow, ISABELLA DODD, bounded by unknown,
5 Mile Branch and branches of 18 Mile Creek and waters of Keowee River,
ROLIN HUNNICUTT, heirs of Isabella Dodd, dec'd. Dated 4 Oct. 1818.
Wit.: Matthew Dickson
       Jos. Grisham
Plat included
Rec.: 5 Oct. 1813.

p. 169
Deed of Gift...ELIZABETH GARNER, widow of JAMES GANRER, dec'd., to son,
JAMES GARNER, with whom I live, title to tract, where we live, laid off
to me as my third by consent of the family, 60 acres on Rocky River.
Dated 16 June, 1813.
Wit.: George Taylor
       Micajah Taylor
Rec.: 19 Dec. 1813
    Followed by deed to son James Garner...mentions children of her
late husband, James Garner, then of age, and two youngest sons, JAMES
GARNER and WILLIAM GARNER, both then minors. Dated 16 June, 1813.
Wit.: George Taylor
       Micajah Taylor

p. 175
Deed of Gift...JOHN WALL to PARRUM WALL, goods and cattle, all tract
of land in Edgefield District on Log Creek, waters of Savannah River,
adjoining John Linkling, Reuben Landrum, 175 acres for my wife, AMY
WALL for support and maintenance, and any child she may bear me.
Dated 24 June, 1813.
Wit.: Stephen Anderson
       William Wall
       Reuben Brock
Rec.: 23 Dec. 1813.

pp. 210-211
Heirs...AGNES ALDRIDGE, BENONEY SNIDER and SARAH SNIDER, his wife, to
EDWARD SHIPMAN, 160 acres on Barker's Creek, waters of Savannah River
granted to Benjamin Shipman, 5 Feb. 1798, adjoining Leonard and Phillip
Taylor, Wm. Aldridge, being land left to AGNES and SARAH ALDRIDGE
heirs of said EDWARD SHIPMAN (sic).
Wit.: Thos. Brown
       George Henderson
       Rebecca Foster
Rec.: 5 Feb. 1814.

pp. 246-247
Heirs...Heirs of RICHARD MINTON, dec'd. to JOSEPH MINTON, tract in
Union District, S. C. on waters of Padgett's Creek, 100 acres part
of tract originally granted to Abel Pearson, and conveyed to Richard
Minton, 1786, bounded by Rogers, James Doogen, Hannah Minton, James
Hunter. Dated 22 Nov. 1811. Signed by ESTHER MINTON, ZOPHER TANNER,
THOMAS RIDDELS, SAMUEL MORRIS, RICHARD MINTON, AMARIAH HEMBREE, all of
Pendleton District.
Wit.:   Wm. Heaton
        Amariah Hembree
Rec.:   21 Apr. 1814.

p. 311
Deed of Gift...LEWIS STANLEY, SR. to sons, DAVID AND JOHN STANLEY,
250 acres where I now live, adjoining James Morris, Matthew Clark,
Lewis Stanley, Jr., Rich. Askins. Dated 29 Aug. 1814.
Wit.:   Danl. McCoy
        Wm. Ledbetter
Rec.:   19 Dec. 1814.

p. 312
LEWIS STANLEY, SR. to wife, ADAH STANLEY, household furnishings, cattle.
Dated 29 Aug. 1814.
Wit.:   Danl. McCoy
        Wm. Ledbetter
Rec.:   19 Dec. 1814.

pp. 377-378
Marriage...I certify that on 15th inst. at the dwelling house at Oconey
Mountain, where WM. RICHARDS, lately dec'd. formerly lived I, subscrib-
ing Justice of said District of Pendleton did then and there marry
JAMES MACDANNIAL and ELLENDER RICHARDS and do from said marriage
publicly affirm them to be man and wife, this 17 June, 1809. Signed,
James Starrett.
Rec.:   9 May, 1815.

pp. 380-381
Heirs...Sheriff's Sale, by John McMillion, Esq. Sheriff, petition to
sell Estate of JAMES BRUISTER, dec'd., died intestate, possessed tract
that descended to MILLY BRUISTER, widow and heirs: JAMES BRUISTER;
JAMES DICKSON and his wife, SARAH; WILLIAM GRAY and his wife, ELIZABETH;
RHODAM DOYLE and his wife, JANE; DOWNS BRUISTER; POLLY BRUISTER, JR.;
WILLIAM BRUISTER; CHARLOTTE BRUISTER; HUGH BRUISTER; and MARGRET and
NANCY BRUISTER, widow and daughter of HENRY BRUISTER, dec'd., tract
originally contained 640 acres granted to John Hall, 16 July, 1784,
to be sold at public auction. Dated 17 April, 1815.
Wit.:   James Dobbs
        Colbert Baker
Plat included.
Rec.:   13 May, 1815.

p. 386
Soldier...JOSEPH DORSETT to JOHN DORSETT and ELIJAH DORSETT, 200 acres
on North fork of Coneross, waters of Keowee River, originally granted
Dennis Obrian, a soldier on his bounty. Dated 8 Dec. 1812.
Wit.:   Joseph Dorsett
        Hardy Owens
Rec.:   5 June, 1815.

pp. 393-394
Deed of Gift...HARDY OWENS to children, CYNTHIA ADAMS, wife of JOHN
ADAMS; WILLIAM OWENS; NANCY or ANN (sic) OWENS; SARAH OWENS; ALFRED
OWENS; JOHN OWENS; MARY OWENS and FRANCES OWENS to divide all my person-
al estate between them, whether named or not, (list of cattle, furniture,
etc.). Dated 10 Sept. 1814.
Wit.:   Joseph Grisham
        John Bowie
Rec.:   8 July, 1815

p. 394
Soldier...CHARLES GATES to HARDY OWINS, 200 acres originally granted
to George Slater, on a bounty, recorded Grant Book B, No. 4, page 96,
on fork of Keowee and Tugaloo Rivers, on both sides of middle fork
of Conneross, waters of Keowee, it being plantation Hardy Owens now
lives on. Dated 23 Feb. 1810.
Wit.: Josiah Foster
       Joseph Dorsett
Rec.: 8 July, 1815

pp. 451-452
Soldier...By death of JACOB HOLLAND, late of Pendleton District,
HUGH HOLLAND, entitled as one of the heirs to receive certain monies
and property, appoint my brother, ROBERT HOLLAND to receive from
administrators my portion of estate and to keep same until my expira-
tion of my time of service in United States Army. Dated 17 Jan. 1815.
Wit.: Wm. A. Slaughter
       John Bowie
Rec.: 15 Dec. 1815.

pp. 457-458
Soldier...WILLIAM STEELE and JAMES WOODS, merchants, to JOHN GREEN,
tract of 250 acres part of tract granted to CAPT. BENJAMIN BROWN as
bounty, on Richland Creek, branch of Conneross, of Keowee River. Dated
13 Dec. 1811.
Wit.: Jo B. Earle
       Jno. McIntyre
Rec.: 4 Jan. 1816.

p. 476
Soldier...HENRY GEDDES of Charleston to WILLIAM AUSTIN of Greenville,
tract in 96 District on North branch of Big Creek, waters of Saluda
River, purchased by Geddes from Anthony Duffield as his bounty land
for his services in former War, granted 4 July, 1785. Dated 15 Dec.
1815.
Wit.: Caleb Hughes, of Greenville
       George W. Geedes
Rec.: 8 Feb. 1816.

pp. 484-485
Heirs...JOHN SMITH to lawful heirs of ABRAHAM ANDERSON, dec'd.:
ARONAMIAS (?), ISAAC, ABEL, ZADOCK, JOHN and ABRAHAM ANDERSON and
ROSANNAH KINNEMORE, ELIZABETH ANDERSON, ABA RILLA ANDERSON, 150 acres
on Oolennoy Creek, waters of 12 Mile River. Dated 2 Nov. 1815.
Wit.: James Barrett
       Jesse Barrett
Rec.: 4 Mar. 1816.

p. 495
Heirs...DANIEL VANOY and JOHN RAGSDALE of Cherokee Nation and MICHAEL
RAGSDALE of Ga. and SUSANNAH HAMBLETON and THOMAS RAGSDALE of Pendleton
District, legatees of Estate of BENJAMIN RAGSDALE, dec'd. to JAMES
BARRETT, 175 acres on 23 Mile Creek, waters of Savannah River, adjoining
Estate of Archibald Hamilton. Dated 4 Dec. 1815.
Wit.: Jas. Hogan
       John Smith
       Thomas Odell
   SUSANNAH RAGSDALE, widow of BENJAMIN RAGSDALE, dec'd. rel. dower.
Rec.: 25 Mar. 1816.

pp. 514-515
Heirs...WILLIAM HASSELL GIBBS, Esq., Master of Court of Equity for
Eastern Circuit, at Charleston to SILAS MASSEY, of Pendleton District
...SUSANNAH MCILHENNY, administrator of Estate of REV. JAMES MCILHENNY,
dec'd. made complaint 1 Feb. 1814, against JANE MORE MURPHY, JAMES
MCILHENNY, MORTON W. MCILHENNY and EMILY MCILHENNY, the last three by
guardian...said JAMES MCILHENNY, late of St. Paul's Parish, departed
life 4 Oct. 1812., intestate, leaving widow, the complainant, and
four children...several debts are unsatisfied, tracts to be sold for

payment, at public auction...one in Pendleton District on Big Generostee Creek, waters of Savannah River, 100 acres conveyed by Archibald Gilmer to McIlhenny, 1 Nov. 1811, bounded by Stringer, Big Generostee Creek, James Bruce, Thomas McGregor, Abigale Gee, Robert Gilmer and John Carrick...another tract on Big Generostee, 34½ acres. Dated 1 Aug. 1814.
Wit.:   Allston Gibbs
        Washington Gibbs
        Wm. Hassell Gibbes, Jr.
Rec.:   26 Mar. 1816.
    Same to JOHN BURRIS, 500 acres originally granted James Martin, then to Jonathan Hemphill then to James McIlhenny, on both sides of Generostee Creek, bounded by _____ Armstrong, Sr., Gregory Chamberlain, Saxon. Same dates and witnesses.

p. 550
Soldier...JAMES DAVENPORT, of Franklin Co., Ga. to JAMES YOWELL, 95 acres on Tugaloo River, being part of tract of 200 acres granted Gilbert Grooms (Soldier) adjoining John Smith and Davenport. Dated 13 Dec. 1801.
Wit.:   James Blair
        Joel Yowell
        J. W. Barton
Rec.:   1 July, 1816.

p. 600
Heirs...JONATHAN and WILLIAM SWIFT, ARCHY MAYSON and ELIJAH CRESWELL, trustees for ELIZABETH SWIFT, now ELIZABETH BALL, heirs of WILLIAM SWIFT, DEC"D. to HENLY EVATT, tract originally granted to William Swift, 3 Nov. 1788, 491 acres. Dated 23 Mar. 1816.
Wit.:   James H. Swift
        James L. Mayson
    MARY SWIFT, wife of Jonathan Swift, rel. dower...in Abbeyville District MARY ANN SWIFT, wife of William Swift, rel. dower. Plat included.
Rec.:   7 Oct. 1816.

p. 606
Heirs...JAMES STEPHENSON to heirs of MATHEW MARTIN, dec'd: AGNES MARTIN, wife and widow of Mathew Martin, MARY MORROW, JOHN MARTIN, SAMUEL MARTIN, MARGET MARTIN, JANE MARTIN, AGNES MARTIN, KATHERINE MARTIN and REBECCA DUNON MARTIN, children, 320 acres on Devil's Fork, branch of Big Generostee Creek, conveyed to James Martin, Esq. 8 Apr. 1789. Dated 5 Jan. 1804.
Wit.:   John Henderson
        Saml. Tate
    ELINOR, wife of James Stephenson rel. dower.
Rec.:   15 Oct. 1816.

BOOK N

1816-1818

p. 12
Soldier...JOHN HARRIS, SR. to HENRY D. REESE, tract on Keowee River, North side of Conoross Creek, part of two tracts, one granted to James Hamilton (Soldier), the other granted to Ephraim Mitchel, Major in Continental Army, 200 acres adjoining John Harris, Thom. B. Singleton. Dated 11 Oct. 1816.
Wit.:   James L. Sloss
        Nathaniel Harris
Plat included
Rec.:   23 Nov. 1816.

212

pp. 24-25
Heirs...Power of Attorney SAMUEL GIBSON, THOMAS GIBSON of Bedford Co.,
Tenn. appoint WILLIAM G. GIBSON , our attorney to recover land in
Pendleton District by right of inheritance from our father, JOHN GIBSON,
late of S. C. dec'd. Dated 18 Sept. 1816. Acknowledged in Bedford
Co., Tenn., by JAS MCKISACK.
Rec.: 10 Dec. 1816.
   ELIZABETH GIBSON, relict of JOHN GIBSON, dec'd.; JAMES JENKINS, in
right of his wife, SALLY, formerly GIBSON; WILLIAM REED, in right of
his wife, NANCY, formerly GIBSON; ROBERT GIBSON all of Madison Co.,
Mississippi Territory, appoint WILLIAM C. GIBSON, atty. Dated 11 Oct.
1816, sworn to in Miss. by GEORGE HALLMARK.
   pp. 27-28...JOHN GIBSON, appoint my brother, WILLIAM C. GIBSON,
attorney in same matter. Dated 27 Sept. 1816.
Rec.: 10 Dec. 1816.

pp. 72-73
Heirs...WILLIAM OLIVER, PETER M. OLIVER, JANE OLIVER to ROBERT MCCANN,
200 acres granted to JAMES OLIVER, dec'd., by his last will, bequeathed
to his wife and two sons, on 23 Mile Creek, bounded by Peter McMahen,
Aaron Clemon. Dated 25 Sept. 1816.
Wit.: Alexander Oliver
      Peter McMahen
   LYDIA C. OLIVER, wife of PETER OLIVER, rel. dower.
Rec.: 27 Jan. 1817.

p. 89
Heirs...Deed of Gift., LYDIA FINLEY to her children, a negro...was
property of BARKELY W. FINLEY, dec'd., gave to his mother, JANE GILKEY
of N. C. during her lifetime, Finley made deed to LYDIA FINLEY, widow
and JANE ELVIRA FINLEY, MIRA ELIZA FINLEY, and BARKLEY W. FINLEY,
children of BARKLEY FINLEY, dec'd. entitled to said negro on determi-
nation of Estate of JANE GILKEY...I, LYDIA FINLEY now give to mentioned
children. Dated 23 Sept. 1816.
Wit.: Sarah Hunter
   In oath, Mrs. LYDIA FINLEY now Mrs. LYDIA MARTIN.
Rec.: 8 Feb. 1817.

pp 156-158
Heirs...THOMAS HENDERSON, SR. to heirs of JOHN HENDERSON, dec'd:
MARTHA HENDERSON, widow of JOHN HENDERSON, MARY HENDERSON, ANN
HENDERSON, ROBERT HENDERSON, HANNAH HENDERSON, children of JOHN
HENDERSON, 100 acre part of tract of 500 acres granted Thomas White,
7 Sept. 1795, recorded Book R., No. 5, page 31-32, on branch of Little
Generostee, fork of a branch of Savannah River. Dated 11 June, 1816.
Wit.: J. McMahan
      Mary Henderson
      Rebecca Henderson
   REBECCA HENDERSON, wife of THOMAS HENDERSON rel. dower.
Rec.: 8 Apr. 1817.

pp. 183-184
Heirs...JOHN POWELL, POLLY POWELL, his wife, DAVID POWELL, THOMAS POWELL,
EDMOND POWELL to JAMES OSBORN, tract bounded by Jas. Osborn, Wm. Wilson,
Purcell, and Sproute, 58 acres part of tract willed to us by A___
(in fold of book) EDMONDSON, 2 Dec. 1810, on Middle Fork of Brushy
Creek, waters of Saluda River. Dated 4 Feb. 1816.
Wit.: Christopher Smith
      Sally Powell
Rec.: 24 Apr. 1817.

pp. 211-216
Deed of Trust...WILLIAM SCOTT to JOHN ROBERTSON, who is nominated
trustee...WILLIAM SCOTT, now of Pendleton District, but shortly ex-
pecting to leave this state...is endebted to S. C. Bank of Charleston,
Estate of SAMUEL ROBERTSON and ELIZABETH BIGGELOW...make provisions
for wife, REBECCA E. SCOTT, and to pay debts...mentions plantations
on Savannah River, near Andersonville, containing 1000 acres which he
recently sold...tract on Conoross Creek, waters of Keowee River,

649 acres to be sold...mentions wife's mother, ELIZABETH BIGGELOW.
Dated 28 Apr. 1817. "The name JOHN ROBERTSON should be JOHN ROBINSON"
...followed by inventory of property belonging to WILLIAM SCOTT.
Rec.: 15 May, 1817.

p 222
Heirs...JAMES DALRYMPLE, ROBERT THOMPSON, RANSON THOMPSON, JOHN MILWEE,
ELISHA LEWIS, SARAH DALRYMPLE, REBECCA DALRYMPLE to JAMESON BARROW,
200 acres on Rocky River, part of tract granted SAMUEL DALRYMPLE,
dec'd., bounded by Dobbins, Jesse Davis, John Dowdle and John Dobbins,
bequeathed to heirs. Dated 25 Dec. 1816.
Wit.: Joseph F. Comer
      William Barron
Rec.: 7 May, 1817.

pp. 271-273
Heirs...ARCHY MAYSON and ELIHU CRESWELL, trustees for ELIZABETH SWIFT,
late ELIZABETH BALL, dec'd. and JONATHAN SWIFT and WILLIAM SWIFT, to
SAMUEL MAVERICK, tract on 18 Mile Creek, 625 acres. Dated 22 Nov. 1816.
Wit.: Austin Pollard
      James L. Mayson.
Plat included.
    MARY SWIFT, wife of JONATHAN, MARYANN SWIFT, wife of WILLIAM, rel.
dower.
Rec.: 31 July, 1817.
    p. 274...JONATHAN SWIFT sells land to SAMUEL MAVERICK, granted to
my father, WILLIAM SWIFT, 6 Nov. 1786, tract conveyed to me by my
brother, WILLIAM SWIFT, ARCHY MAYSON, ELIJU CRESWELL, trustees of my
mother, ELIZABETH SWIFT, since ELIZABETH BALL. Dated 5 July, 1817.
Wit.: John T. Lewis
      Enoch B. Benson
Rec.: 31 July, 1817.

p. 279
Heirs...HANNAH WEST, REBECCA WEST and MARY WEST, heirs of JACOB WEST,
dec'd. to AMOS GARRETT ROBINSON, 100 acres part of 640 acres on 23
Mile Creek, bounded by Amos Robinson, lands lately owned by Rhodam
Doyle, Mrs. Elizabeth Morgan, part of tract sold by John Robinson to
Jacob West, other part being sold to Jonathan West by Jacob West in
his lifetime. Dated __, 1817.
Wit.: Edward Williams
      Wm. Doyle
Rec.: 5 Aug. 1817.

pp. 317-318
Heirs...WILLIAM TUBS and JEREMIAH SMITH, of Hickman Co., Tenn. to
ANDREW WILSON of Pendleton District, tract formerly belonging to
William Sanders (?), dec'd, being legatees of Estate, WILLIAM TUBS
having full power from: SION SANDERS, WILLIAM SANDERS, MILLY (?)
SANDERS, JOHN SANDERS, NICHOLAS FISHER, DANIEL TUBS, ___DDY SANDERS
and JOHN SIMPSON, of Hickman Co., Tenn. has sold three shares of land
of Estate of WILLIAM SANDERS, dec'd.,that is VINSON SANDERS, KINCHEN
PERRY and NATHAN NUNNAY, tract on Little River, 177 acres originally
granted to Thomas ___per (?), 4 Feb. 1799. Dated 20 Nov. 1816.
Wit.: Andrew McCallister
      John Sanders.
Rec.: 26 Sept. 1817.
    (This deed is disjointed, in wording, and part of the names are in
the margin of the book, and can't be made out. BW)

BOOK O

1817-1820

p. 40
Heirs...Sheriff's Sale. JAMES GARNER, dec'd. owned tract 180 acres,

bounded by lands of Patrick Norris, Thomas Taylor, George Manning,
William Pritchard, originally granted to Blake Mauldin, land sold to
JOHN GARNER for distribution to heirs: THOMAS GARNER; POLLEY, wife of
JOHN STOGNER; BRADLEY GARNER; ELIZABETH, wife of DANIEL WILLIAMS;
LUCRETIA, wife 'of WILLIAM HILLHOUSE; SUSANNAH, wife of JAMES MYERS;
WILLIAM GARNER; JAMES GARNER; children of JAMES GARNER to give each
distributive shares. Dated 7 Nov. 1817.
Wit.:   E. B. Benson
        Jesse P. Lewis
Rec.:   24 Jan. 1818.

p. 56
Soldier...HUGH ROBINSON to DAVID HAMILTON, 200 acres granted to Reuben
Bolden, 3 Mar. 1788 (?), recorded in Sec. Office in Bounty Grant Book
BBBB, page 486, on branches of 23 Mile Creek, waters of Savannah River.
Dated 5 Mar. 1816.
Wit.:   Thos. Hamilton
        Lettice Hamilton
Rec.:   10 Feb. 1818.

pp. 72-73
Heirs...Legatees of JACOB HOLLAND to Legatees of RICHARD CHILDRESS,
dec'd. tract on Tugaloo River, bounded by James Perryman to mouth of
Hurricane Branch, John Holland's land on branch of River a little below
Big Beaverdam Creek, 200 acres. Dated 3 Nov. 1817.
Wit.:   Sarah Thomson
        William Crow
Signed by legatees of JACOB HOLLAND: MARY HOLLAND, ROBERT HOLLAND,
ARCHIBALD HOLLAND, JOHN HOLLAND, ALLEN GUEST.
Rec.:   25 Apr. 1818.

pp. 75-76
Deed of Gift...WILLIAM MONTCASTLE, of Pendleton Village, boot and shoe
maker...3 negroes to GEORGE EGGLESTON MONTCASTLE, JOHN RICHARD MILTON
MONTCASTLE, JEANNETTE ARIETTA MONTCASTLE, ANDREW MONTCASTLE and SUSANNAH
MONTCASTLE, my wife, said children to support thier mother after my
death, and divide with any future issue by me. Dated 20 May, 1818.
Wit.:   Lemuel Whyte
        Mathew Burt
Rec.:   21 May, 1818.

p. 86
Heirs...JOHN NICHOLS, THOMAS NICHOLS, and ARCHIBALD NICHOLS, heirs of
AMBROSE NICHOLS, dec'd. for fee paid by George Nelson, have sold to
JEHORDA HUNNICUTT, son of ROLIN HUNNICUTT, tract on Reedy Branch, 150
acres. Dated __, 1816.
Wit.:   Jas. Anderson
        Rolin Hunnicutt
Rec.:   19 Mar. 1818.

p. 117
Heirs...SUSANNAH BOYD, administrator of THOMAS BOYD, dec'd. together
with my father, WILLIAM NORTON, administrator of same...as I am endebted
to Estate, relinquish my claim, unto said WILLIAM NORTON, and give up
property, household furniture, cattle, in full payment, and overplus
to be put into hands of JEPTHA NORTON as guardian of my daughter,
LOUISA BOYD. Dated 10 Dec. 1811.
Wit.:   Jacob Capehart
        William Nicholson
Rec.:   25 Mar. 1818.

pp. 122-123
Heirs...SAML. ELROD, MARY MCCOY, JAMES MCCOY, SARAH SMITH, ELIZABETH
SMITH, WILLIAM ELROD, PEGGY MCCOY, HENRY LINDUM (?) to ISAAC TIMMS,
208 acres on 26 Mile Creek of Savannah River, originally granted to
John Hunnicutt, 7 Apr. 1788, Hunnicutt conveyed to Patrick McCoy, 10
June, 1792, bounded by Jacob Duckworth, Jr., Daniel Pittman, Wm. Carter,
Daniel Green, Joseph Timms. Dated 1 July 1817.
Wit.:   Mark K. Hollems
        James Orr
Rec.:   31 Mar. 1818   215

pp. 183-186
Heirs...Sheriff's Sale for distribution of Estate of BARKLEY W. FINLEY,
dec'd, died intestate...heirs: LYDIA FINLEY, widow, now wife of
JOHN MARTIN, JANE ELVIRA FINLEY, MARIA ELIZA FINLEY, and BARKLEY W.
FINLEY, lot No. 39, 1 acre in Village of Pendleton, 21 acres adjoining
John Taylor, Samuel Cherry, and others, purchased from William Shackle-
ford. Land sold at public sale to Samuel Maverick and divided among
heirs. Dated 4 Sept. 1818.
Wit.:   Jos. Shanklin
        Joseph Grisham
        Jesse P. Lewis
Rec.:   3 Sept. 1818.

p. 195
Power of Attorney...NANCY BOX, widow of EDWARD BOX, dec'd; REBECCA BOX,
wife of JOHN WEATHERFORD; PEGGY BOX, wife of PHILMER RULE; ELIZABETH BOX,
wife of JOHN MORRIS, all of Bedford Co., Tenn., appoint WILLIAM BOX,
of Bedford Co., Tenn. our attorney to sell tract in Pendleton District
which formerly belonged to EDWARD BOX, dec'd. 260 acres on Nove (?)
Creek, waters of Tugaloo River, now in possession of Samuel Rowan and
Drury Jeffres. Dated 22 July, 1818.
Wit.:   Rice Hughes
        Robert Hughes of Bedford Co., Tenn.
Rec.:   10 Sept. 1818.

p. 220
Heirs...FLORENCE POWER, THOMAS POWER, JAMES POWER, ALEXANDER POWER,
MARGARET CHANDLER heirs of Estate of ALEXANDER POWER, dec'd. to BENJAMIN
MATTISON, 105 acres on 23 Mile Creek and 26 Mile Creek, waters of
Savannah River, bounded by David Moris. Dated 1 Oct. 1818.
Wit.:   Archibald Patterson
        John Nash
Rec.:   2 Oct. 1818.

pp. 255-256
Heirs...Widow MARY MORROW, THOMAS WALKER, ELIZA WALKER, ISAAC MELSON,
AGNES MELSON, JANE MORROW and MARY MORROW, 5 acres, part of survey of
330 acres on tract originally surveyed for Thos. Hallums, now occupied
by Thomas Walker, sell to SAMUEL MAVRICK, tract owned by Estate of JOHN
MORROW, dec'd. on 18 Mile Creek, adjoining original survey bought lately
by S. Maverick from Starrett Dobbins. Dated 9 Nov. 1814.
Wit.:   Jeremiah Pope
        John L. Weaver (?)
Rec.:   27 Nov. 1818.
Plat included.

p. 302
Soldiers...HENRY DOBSON REECE to JOHN MAXWELL, 200 acres being part of
2 tracts, one granted to James Hamilton (a soldier), and the other
granted to Ephraim Mitchell, a Major in the Continental Army, bounded
by Keowee River and Conoross Creek, Thomas B. Singleton and John Harris.
Dated 26 Dec. 1818.
Wit.:   Joseph Grisham
        Joseph Whitner
    BECKY REECE, wife of HENRY D. REECE rel. dower.
Plat included
Rec.:   22 Jan, 1819.

p. 349
Heirs...MARGARET ECHOLS, widow of JOSHUA ECHOLS, dec'd., JOHN ECHOLS,
DARIOUS ECHOLS, JAMES ECHOLS, JOSHUA ECHOLS, ABRAHAM ECHOLS, E. V.
ECHOLS and RICHARD BROWN, heirs of JOSHUA ECHOLS, dec'd. to GEORGE
CLEVELAND, 350 acres originally granted JOSHUA ECHOLS, adjoining
Tugaloo River and lands of Lewis Botston (?), except 20 acres conveyed
to JOSHUA ECHOLS, JR. by MARGARET ECHOLS, 23 Oct. 1818. Dated 31 Oct.
1818.
Wit.:   J. G. Cleveland
        R. H. Cleveland
Rec.:   19 Apr. 1819.

p. 429
Heirs...JAMES LINN, ROBERT M. LINN, SARAH LINN, wife of JAMES LINN,
dec'd. to MOODY BURT of Abbeyville District, 80 acres, part of tract
of 102 acres conveyed by MARTHA VANN to JAMES LINN, dec'd., 12 Dec.
1803, balance being taken away by an older grant to Lawyer Yancy,
land on 26 Mile Creek, waters of Keowee River. Dated 27 April, 1819.
Wit.:   Sary Shirley
        James Shirley
Rec.:   22 Sept. 1819.

p. 466
Heirs...JOHN MULLINAUX, 366 acres originally granted to me on Keowee
River, bounded by Anderson Thomas, all other sides vacant...was
equitable the right and property of RATLIFF BOON, dec'd., have granted
and released unto NANCY BOON, widow of Ratliff Boon, POLLY CANDLER (?),
JOSEPH BOON, TRYAN (?) BOON, KISIER HARBIN, KADER (?) BOON, NANCY
PALMOUR, RATLIFF BOON, DANIEL BOON, LUCINDA BOON, BETSY BOON, CELIA
BOON (also spelled BOONE). Dated 11 Jan. 1819.
Wit.:   Thomas Alexander
        Robt. Stewart
Rec.:   30 Oct. 1819. (very dim)

p. 534
Heirs...JOHN, JOSIAH, JOSEPH, AARON, JEREMIAH PRATOR, sons of PHILLIP
PRATOR, dec'd. to JOHN CHAPMAN, 57 acres, part of 710 acre granted
to ROBERT M. MCCANN and conveyed to PHILLIP PRATOR, on 18 Mile Creek.
Dated 25 Dec. 1819.
Wit.:   Benjamin Smith
        Benjamin Chapman
Rec.:   19 Jan. 1820.
Plat included.

                        BOOK P
                      1820-1822

pp. 23-24
Power of Attorney...SAMUEL BARRON, his wife POLLY, formerly POLLY
LEONARD, and MICAJAH BEAL, his wife, MALINDA, formerly MALINDA LEONARD,
both daughters of WILLIAM LEONARD, dec'd., late of Pendleton District,
appoint ANDREW KEITH of Giles County, Tennessee, our attorney to
dispose of the land we are entitled to by will of WILLIAM LEONARD,
dec'd. Dated 15 Sept. 1819.
Wit.:   Barnard M. Patterson
        Geo. McConnell of Giles Co., Tenn.
Rec.:   25 Feb. 1820.

pp. 28-29
Soldier..."In pursuance of an Act of the General Assembly passed 26 Mar.
1784, for purpose of securing and granting land within this State to
Officers and Soldiers, we have granted to the REV. HENRY PURCELL a
plantation or tract of land containing 450 acres in 96 District on
North Fork of Conoross Creek", Witness, his Excellency Benjamin
Guerard, Governor and Commander in Chief of the State, at Charleston,
21 Jan. 1785. (Plat included).
Certified: 9 Oct. 1784.
Recorded in Pendleton District 13 Mar. 1820.

pp. 29-30
Heirs...13 Dec. 1819, conveyence between THOMAS HUNT, ESQ. Commissioner
of Court of Equity for Southern Circuit at Charleston and AMOS ROBINSON
...MRS. SARAH B. PURCELL, EDWARD HENRY and JAMES S. PURCELL, minors,
by their mother, SARAH B. PURCELL, JOHN WHITE' and other heirs of
HENRY B. PURCELL, dec'd, bill of complaint against MRS. ANN GILLON,
HENRY PURCELL and MRS. SARAH SERISIER (?), co-heirs of several tracts
of land...would be productive for lands to be sold at auction, or
private sale...Indenture, all tract in 96 District, 450 acres on

North Fork of Conoross Creek, conveyed to AMOS ROBINSON.
Rec.: 3 Mar. 1820.

p. 49
Heirs...JESSE CORBIN and ELIZABETH GORMAN, his mother, heirs to
Estate of PETER CORBIN, dec'd. to SIMION WADE, 35 acres part of tract
owned by PETER CORBIN, dec'd. originally granted to JAMES FLEMMING,
5 Aug. 1787, on branch of North Fork of George's Creek, waters of
Saluda River, bounded where John McCroskey now lives. Dated 24 Mar.
1820.
Wit.: James Crawford
       Richard Burdine
Rec.: 27 Mar. 1820.

pp. 60-61
Heirs...DANIEL SYMMES, AVES SYMMES, his wife; ADAM HILL, NANCY HILL,
his wife; ELIZABETH TOURTELLOTT, joint heirs of ASA TOURTELLOTT to
JOHN DICKSON, 300 acres bounded by Richard Hallums, Daniel Symmes,
Adam Hill, Andrew Pickens, originally granted ASA TOURTELLOTT, 4 Oct.
1790, on 18 Mile Creek. Dated 10 Dec. 1819.
Wit.: William Walker
      John Dickson, Jr.
Rec.: 29 Mar. 1820.
      Deed on p. 66 names JOHN DICKSON and his wife, LYDIA, as heirs.

p. 74
Heirs...WILLIAM COX, his wife ANN and ELIZABETH HARBIN, heirs of
SAMUEL HARBIN, dec'd. to NATHANIEL HARBIN, 300 acres on Keowee River,
at Burches Ford, part of 3 tracts, one on river, originally granted
JESSE HARBIN, the other granted to HENRY BURCH, one granted JAMES
GILLISON, bounded by Burch, James McDaniel, William Cox. Dated 22
April, 1820.
Wit.: John Grisham
       William Lusk
Rec.: 6 May, 1820
...pp. 74-75...NATHANIEL HARBIN (called Capt. in oath), his wife,
BARBARY; WILLIAM COX, his wife ANN, heirs of SAMUEL HARBIN, dec'd. to
ELIZABETH HARBIN, land on Keowee River at mouth of Fall Creek, 279
acres bounded by Cox and River. Same dates and witnesses. pp. 65-66.
..NATHANIEL, and BARBARY HARBIN, ELIZABETH HARBIN to WILLIAM COX, 322
acres on both sides of Keowee River, bounded by Nathaniel Harbin,
Elizabeth Harbin, John Price and River. Same dates and witnesses.

pp. 80-81
Sheriff's Sale...Heirs of WILLIAM T. SPEAKE, dec'd. land descended to
JESSE JOLLY, his wife, MARGARET SPEAKE; ANNE C. SPEAKE; SARAH SPEAKE;
RICHARD SPEAKE, SR.; GEORGE T. SPEAKE; RICHARD SPEAKE, JR.; WILLIAM T.
SPEAKE ask for land to be sold at public auction to be divided...
land on Devil's Fork of Generostee, where RICHARD SPEAKE, SR. now lives,
166 acres originally granted to JOHN SMITH 16 July, 1784, bounded by
Mrs. Gilmer, Mrs. Shamblee, Major Lewis, Maverick and Lewis. Dated 1
May, 1820.
Wit.: William Grisham
       John Adams
Rec.: 11 May, 1820.
      (Next deed sells land to William Houston of Rock Mills, Pendleton
      District.)

p. 85
Heirs...JAMES HOBSON; CHRISTOPHER RAIMEY, and BETSEY, his wife;
HANNAH WOODALL, by her attorney, JAMES HOBSON; SAMPSON BARNETT and
ESTHER his wife; MARY HOBSON; RACHEL HOBSON; ISAAC HOBSON; THOMAS
HOBSON, all heirs of JAMES HOBSON, SR., dec'd. to JAMES C. GRIFFEN, Esq.
tract whereon James Hobson now lives on 23 Mile Creek, 153 acres bounded
by David Boyd, Nathaniel Davis, also 8 acres on 23 Mile Creek where
Grist Mill, saw mills and cotton gins are erected bounded by Col.
Samuel Warren and others. Dated 8 May, 1820.
Wit.: J. Miller
       William Grisham
...PIETY HOBSON, wife of ISAAC HOBSON, BETSY RAIMEY and ESTHER BARNETT
rel. dower.
Rec.: 16 May, 1820.

p. 91
Heirs...ELIZABETH LIDDLE, widow, ELIZABETH BARRAN, MOSES LIDDLE, JAMES
LIDDLE, ESTER DAVIS, ESBEL LIDDLE, JENNY LIDDLE, all legatees of
Estate of MOSES LIDDLE, dec'd. all of Pendleton District, except
Elizabeth Barran of Murry Co., Tenn. to MARTHA RUSSELL, widow and sole
legatee of JOHN RUSSELL, dec'd., 200 acres on Devil's Creek, branch of
Big Generostee, waters of Savannah River, part of 640 acres originally
granted to JAMES BLYTHE, 16 July, 1784. Dated 18 Sept. 1809.
Wit.: James Morrow, Sr.
    Abel Skelton
    Jacob Clearman
    James Russell
    Also signed by Jane Lesly, Daniel Liddle with other heirs.
Rec.: 25 May, 1820.

p. 112
Marriage Contract and Deed of Trust...Dated 6 June, 1820, between
WILLIS HUNNICUTT and CATHERINE MCGUFFIN to WILLIAM CARSON, Esq...
marriage intended to shortly be solomnized between WILLIS HUNNICUTT
and CATHERINE MCGUFFIN...CATHERINE being possessed with considerable
Real Estate in her own right consisting of farm where she resides,
100 acres on West side of 18 Mile Creek, bounded by Joseph Grisham,
William Steele, Thomas Richards. It being agreed to sell WILLIAM
CARSON all tract in trust for CATHERINE MCGUFFIN, and MRS. SARAH
MCGUFFIN and her daughter, MARY MCGUFFIN, sister of CATHERINE shall
remain on property and receive all profits for remainder of her
natural life.
Wit.: Joseph Grisham
    William Miller
Rec.: 12 July, 1820.

p. 135
Deed of Gift...JOANAH LANXTON, widow of JAMES LANXTON, dec'd. now in
good health and reasonable senses convey all my property to my two
children, JOANNAH LANXTON and WILLIAM D. T. LANXTON...Dated 8 June, 1820.
Wit.: George W. Liddle
    Thos. B. Reid
Rec.: 4 Sept. 1820.

pp. 136-137
Heirs...JOHN YEATMAN and MARY his wife; GEORGE RIGGS and MARGARET his
wife; JAMES KENNEDY; JOHN KENNEDY; SAMUEL KENNEDY; SARAH KENNEDY, all
of Pendleton District; and JOSEPH KENNEDY of Bedford County, Tenn.;
and SAMUEL REED, NANCY his wife, of the Creek Nation to GEORGE KENNEDY
all our distributive shares, tract on Beaverdam Creek of Savannah
River, 214 acres, descended to us from JOSEPH KENNEDY, dec'd. originally
granted to JEAN (JOHN ?) MILLER. Dated 29 Aug. 1816.
Wit.: Isaac Matthews
    John Sherrill
    John Milwee
    John Matthews
    (Plat included, all above signed, as did Hery Drummond and Sarah
    Drummond).
Rec.: 4 Sept. 1820.

pp. 179-180
Soldier...Power of Attorney GOLDMAN HARRIS, of N. C., now "residenter"
of Pendleton District appoint RICHARD MAJOR and WALTER BELL, of
Jackson County, Ga. my attorneys to recover from any person in possession
of lands in State of Tennessee, claimed by GOLDMAN HARRIS for services
done as a regular soldier in Revolutionary War, then a citizen of
Granville Co., N. C., under command of Col. William Taylor. Dated 7
Sept. 1810.
Wit.: Elisha Bennett
    George Hall
Rec.: 4 Sept. 1820.

p. 196
Deed of Gift...17 Jan. 1821, JAMES BEARD, SR. having arrived at a
very old age and having three children by name of ANNA, EDWARD GARDNER,
and WILLIS BEARD and it being my duty for raising and educating same,
grant to two sons, tract where I now live, 262 acres on 18 Mile Creek,
also cattle and household goods...two sons to make and raise their
sister, ANNA an equal part.
Wit.: Reuben Mitchell
       Thos. Gassaway
Rec.: 22 Jan. 1821.

p. 205
Heirs...Quit Claim, EZEKIEL LONG to WILLIAM TIPPEN, guardian for JOHN
TIPPEN, ELIZABETH TIPPEN, ABBIGALE TIPPEN, heirs of JOHN TIPPEN, dec'd.
all part of tract conveyed to LONG by ELENOR TIPPEN, on Generostee
Creek on North side of road leading from Sloan's Ferry to Lee Shoals
on Rocky River. Dated 21 Aug. 1820.
Wit.: Joseph Taylor
       Ansel Prewett
Rec.: 5 Feb. 1821.

p. 227
Marriage Contract and Deed of Trust...16 Feb. 1821, THOMAS WILLIAMS
to JANE MOORE and MARY MOORE, the mother of JANE, all of Rocky River...
marriage is intended and will be shortly solomnized between THOMAS
WILLIAMS and JANE MOORE, said JANE is in possession of considerable
real and personal property, as one of the heirs of her late brother,
NEWMAN MOORE, which estate has not been divided between her mother and
her sisters, and is still in hands of Exc., plantation where late NEWMAN
MOORE lived on Rocky River, near Lee Shoals, adjoining Lewt Hall, Mrs.
Cavin (?) and others, 150 acres to MARY MOORE, in trust for bodily
heirs of JANE MOORE and the child she now has, ARABELLA FRANCES...
Wit.: Reuben Grisham
       Joseph Grisham
       (Signed Jeane Moore).
Rec.: 16 Feb. 1821.

END OF BOOK

ANDERSON COUNTY DISTRICT, S. C.
INVENTORIES, APPRAISEMENTS AND SALES

BOOK 1

1839-1845

MFM C 1053

Abstracted by Colleen Morse Elliott

4/28/1979

"This book contains a record of all the Inventories, Appraisements
and Sales which have been returned to this office since the 27th day
of January 1840, the time at which P. S. Vandiver commenced writing
in the Ordinary's office. Witness my hand and Seal."

P. S. Vandiver   (Seal)

INDEX WITH ORIGINAL BOOK PAGE NUMBERS

RAGSDALE, FRANCIS A. 233
RANEY, JOHN 272
RYKARD, DAVID 424
ROBERSON, JOHN 433
SHERRILL, LEWIS, SR. 108
SOUTH, LUKE H.? 134
SWORDS, JOHN 245
SMITH, JAMES 410
STUART, JAMES 429
TAYLOR, MICAJAH 98
TUCKER, BARTLEY 100?
TODD, JAMES, JR. 202
TODD, ROBERT 391
WILES, FREEMAN 7
WILLSON, CHARLES 40
WEBSTER, JAMES R. 66
WEST, DEMPSEY 118
WARNOCK, JAMES 137?
WARREN, SAMUEL 170
WINTER, DINAH 196
WARNOCK, JOHN, SR. 199
WATSON, THOMAS 211
WEBB, MARY ANN 234
WILLSON, CHARLES, SR. 273
WARLEY, J. M. 349
WATSON, DAVID 361
WALLER, WILLIAM 435
WARREN, SAM'L 462?
YOUNG, FRANCIS 161

INVENTORY: Goods & Chattels & Personal Estate of ROBERT POOL, late
of Anderson Dist., yeoman, dec'd. Made 30 Jan. 1840. Negro woman
and 2 boy children, Henry and Sampson. Appr's: J. L.? Whitefield,
James Chamblee, Andrew Stevenson, Alex. Moorehead, David Hendrix, Jr.

APPRAISEMENT: Estate of JAMES A. HASLETT, dec'd. John Barrett,
Admr. 15 Feb. 1840. Book acct's on Hug Rush, J. L. W. Vernon, Wm.
M. Haslett, Mrs. Hannah A. Haslett, David C. Haslett, Moses W. Haslett,
Simeon Goodwin, G.? W. Haslett, Milton M'Lees, A. Gilliland, Benjamin
Carroll, Maberry Snipes; Notes on hand: William Mitchell, Hugh
and Wm. Rush, Hannah Caroline Vernon, J. L. W. Vernon, Hannah H.
Haslett; female slave Cloay?, about 32 years old, female slave
Frances, about 3 years old. John Barrett, Admr. Appraised: 18
Feb. 1840. Appr's: Thomas Skelton, Charles Haynie and Simpson Hagood.

SALE BILL: Estate of JAMES A. HASLETT, dec'd. Anderson Dist. John
Barrett, Admr. (could be Barnett). Purchasers: Thomas A. Paterick,
Alexander Gilliland, Revd. Levi Garnson?, Thomas L. Skelton, William
Bullman (rented house and plantation), B. G. Dilworth, Mrs. E. R.
Haslett, James V. Ledbetter, L. W. B. Skelton, Charles Haynie, Silas
Massey, C. B. Webb, Osborn? Garnson, Moses W. Haslett, Rev. J. B.
Chappell, A. S. McClinton, J. L. W. Vernon (transferred to Jno.
Barrett), Lewis Pritchett, Thomas Reynolds, Elisha Burris, (bought
slaves Cloay and Frances), Samuel McCollum, John Young, John Simpson,
David Sadler, Sion? Holly, William Bullman. James Gilmer, Clerk.

INVENTORY: Goods & Chattels of FREEMAN WILES, dec'd. 2 Dec. 1839.
(Numerous books of unusual titles) Negroes: Mimery?, Nelly, Martha,
Simon. Notes on: James A. Hall, John Caldwell, Wm. Hutchison, Wm.
O'Briant, W. R. Sanders. Appr's: Jas. Wiley, A. Reid, Blackman
Burton, Hiram Cowen.

BILL OF SALE: Estate of FREEMAN WILES, dec'd. 5 Dec. 1839. Pur-
chasers: E. Wiles, J. Burriss, R. Haley, Wm. O'Briant, Jas. E.
Anderson, Jas. Wiles, John G. Caldwell, B. Burton, St.? Jones, R.
Giles, Jas. R. Winfield, J. Burrows, R. Boid?, Jas. Wiley, J. Winfield,

J. M. Simpson, H. Cowen, William Young, J. Whitman, M. Howard, William
Latham, J. C. Anderson, J. H. Wiles, John Fowler, J. E. Anderson, P.
Burton, J. H. Drennan, B. Burton, C. Bowie, R. Haley, M. Prince,
Jas. H. Wiles, M. Kennedy, J. Whitman, S. Mitchel, Wm. Cook, John
Winfield, Jane Sherard, D. O'Briant, Wm. Soat?, J. McCalister, G.
Young, G. W. McCullough, William Scott, J. Rowsey, S. Lindsey, Wm.
Saunders, Wm. H. Simpson, D. O. Macklin, A. Molden?, Wm. R. Saunders,
Jas. E. Anderson, M. W. Lackey, M. Kennedy, M. W. Lackley, John Watt
(bought Nelly, Martha and Simon, negroes), E. Wiles (bought negro
woman Memory), Wm. Jackson, Wm. Bond, Wm. M. Paschal, Wm. Hatton,
H. Cowen, C. Bowie, A. Buchanan, A. Gray, J.? Hall, Wm. Milford, Wm.
Arnett, J. Speer. (E. Wiles bought Bible and Sp.? Wiles bought
Testament). Notes on: Jas. A. Hall, John G. Caldwell, Wm. Hutcheson,
Wm. O'Braint, Wm. R. Sanders. Dated: 6 Dec. 1839. Jas. Wiley, Clerk.

INVENTORY: Estate of SAMUEL CHERRY, dec'd. Notes, Judgements &
Accounts: D___Stevens, Israel Gillison, John Bruce, V. A. Lawhon,
James Dickson, William Frasier, Wm. H. Frasier, Jno. Elrod, Jeptha
Robinson, Billy Stevens, Manning Belcher, Abner Howell, L. R. Vick-
ory, Ezekiel George, Wm. Golden, Sr., Wm. Hubbard, Geo. Reese, Willis
Dickinson?, Willis Burket, L. K. Cherry, L. R. Cherry (negro woman
Jenny), Jesse Lewis, A. P. Cater, W. B. Cherry, J. A. Cherry, William
Roach, Col. Jas. Taylor (signed by Samuel Taylor), Cleveland Estes,
Th. Wayland, Robt. M. Cherry, James Dickson, Matthew Dickson, Joel
Kelly, James Cherry (of North Carolina), Mary Mullinax, Edward Martin,
Mary Robbins, Jno. C____, R. T. Wilson, Thos. G.? Carradine?, James
Hopkins, Andrew Elrod, Robt. R. Dickeson, Dr. Wm. Anderson, Thomas
Hunnicutt, Moody Wight, James & Jesse Palmore, Sr., Henry Howard,
B. S. Britain (of North Carolina), James Brownlow, Sally Farris, Wm.
Abbott, Thomas Bryce, John Miller, James McGuffin, Leroy B. Gaston,
Wm. Frasier, L. R. Cherry, Sidney H. Reese, F.? Reese, James Caradine.
Accounts: G. R. Harris, Susan Harris, Wm. C. Elrod, R. L. Wilson,
William Hubbard, Jno. B. Sitton (Litton?), Elisha Christian, Mrs.
Hamnett, Mrs. Forbes, Mr. Wayne, Mrs. Starks, Wm. J. Knauff, Wm. Waller,
Miss Mary Hunter, F. Burt, Caroline Hall, B. Batcheller, (above notes
due the firm of L. R. Cherry & Co., half of which belongs to S.
Cherry). Firm of L. R. & W. B. Cherry. 1 Jan. 1839. Appr's: J.
S. Lorton, David Cherry, Andrew F. Lewis. 9 Apr. 1840.

APPRAISEMENT: Property of SAMUEL CHERRY, dec'd. Negroes: John,
Rebecca, Giles, Sarah, Eliza, Andy, Joe, Esther, Frank, George,
Dick, Scipio, Jenny, Bob (blacksmith), Emily, Israel, Harriet,
Frances, Creasy, Andrew, Laurence, Bob (yellow boy), Elijah, Christy
and child, Eliza Ann, Martha, Rachael. (All sold with exception of
Esther, Frank and George.) L. R. Cherry, Admr. 9 Mar. 1840. Appr's:
David Cherry, Benj. D. Dupre, A. F. Lewis, J. S. Lorton.

BILL OF SALE: Estate of SAMUEL CHERRY, dec'd. Purchasers: Susan
Cherry, L. R. Cherry, William Sloan, Archibald McElroy, Jesse Lewis,
Sr., A. Hill, B. D. Dupree, Jas. Wilson, Sam. S. Cherry, _____Smith.
(Estate had many books, the classics, etc.) Sarah A. Cherry, Mary E.
Cherry, James Richard, Jacob Bellotte, Wm. B. Cherry, Eliju D. Cherry,
_____ Crenshaw, Eben Smith, Thomas R. Cherry, Jno. Elrod, John Hop-
kins, Wm. Sloan, Abner Russell, Henry Clarke, Jno. Rofflander, James
Lockery?, J. Hickman, Col. Samuel Warren, J. J. Duke, M. Rusten,
Thomas Dodel, Samuel Marench?, J. C. Griffin, L. Lockery, R. Max-
well, Wm. McMurry, Thos. Watson, A. Russell, Archibald McElroy, Wil-
liam Swords, A. Philips, F. Howell, Jno. Williams, Aaron Boggs, Jno.
Hopkins. These purchased the negroes: David Cherry (Christy and
child; Eliza Ann and Martha), Thos. Gasaway (Andy), Baylis Earle
(Sarah), Thomas M. Sloan (Eliza), L. R. Cherry (Creasy, Lige and Bob),
Daniel Brown (Emily and Frances), J. D.? Lewis (Bob, blacksmith),
L. R. Cherry (Scipio), Mrs. Nardin? (Jenny and Harriet), L. R. Cherry
(Israel, Andrew, Laurence and Dick), Wm. Sloan (Joe), W. B. Cherry
(John, Becky and Giles), Mention of "Old Rachel".

INVENTORY: Estate of STEPHEN CASEY, dec'd., late of Anderson Dist.,
S. C. 27 Jan. 1840. Appr's: Fra. S. Young, Thos. O. Hill, J. H.
Berry, W. Connor. Notes due estate: (includes cash due): Joel H.

223

Berry, Israel P. David, Wm. H. Bowie, Matthew Young, John W. Connor, Flornoy W. Davis, Marion J. Davis, William Hutcherson, Uriah Baron, William Cook, Alexander McKinney, dec'd - due estate, Stephen Cash, A. Molden, Robert Boid, Pickens Davis.

RETURN OF GOODS SOLD: Estate of STEPHEN CASEY, dec'd. 28 Jan. 1840 by Wm. Sherrard. Purchasers: Mrs. Aston, J. W. Connor, F. A. Young, Mary Casey, widow, David Simpson, F. Young, Sr., Robertson Smith, Joel Gilbreath, J. B. Shackleford, John B. Winfield, Mrs. McCurday, Francis Beaty, F. W. Davis, Wiley Shackleford, A. Simpson, Francis Young, Sr., Arthur Bowie, John Moffett Simpson, John Young, William Athias?, John Stuart, Henry Adams, John M. Bonds, Elisha Beard.

APPRAISAL: Estate of the late CHARLES WILLSON, Anderson Dist., S. C. 28 Nov. 1839. (Receipt on James Willson, son of Charles Willson), James W. Drennan, Solomon Taylor, James Bell, Lucretia Ambrose, William Willson (his son), Admr. Appr's: David Geer, Wm. M. Nevitt, James Todd.

BILL OF SALE: Estate of CHARLES WILLSON, dec'd. Purchasers: William Willson, his son, Adm'r. 29 Nov. 1830. George Willson, Ibzan Rice, Duff Willson, David Geer, John Smith, Samuel Bell, Jane Willson, Solomon Geer, Saml. R. McFall, Lewis Willson, Andrew Shearer, Thomas McConnel, Martha Wright, Jesse R. Smith, Wm. M. Archer, John Erskine, Ambrose Milwee, William Nevitt, William Erskine, John H. Hammond, Jesse R. Smith, Ezekiel George, Christian Orr, Thomas Spray, Thomas George, James George, Jesse Gray, Enoch Magers, R. B. Brown, Col. H. Hammond, Osborn Jarrett, James W. Drennan, Solomon Taylor, James Bell, Lucretia Amborse. (Note: carried to p. 271...this refers to page in original book).

APPRAISEMENT: Estate of WILLIAM OWEN, dec'd. (Preceded by a statement of R. A. Maxwell, made 27 Feb. 1840) (William Owen was once overseer to Maxwell, Jan. 1836). Thos. R. Cherry, James McCann, J. Caradine, L. R. Cherry. Appr's: J. S. Lorton, B. D. DuPree, John Hastie. Pendleton. 27 Feb. 1840. John Martin, O.A.D.

APPRAISEMENT: Estate of GEORGE OLDHAM, dec'd. Appr's: Jno. Murphy, Geo. Elrod, John Harper. (No date).

INVENTORY: Land & Chattels of ROBERT JUNKIN, dec'd. 2 May, 1840. Notes on: Jesse Dobbins, Jackson Howel, William Holland, Margaret Junkin, Van Tate, John A. Tate, John Herbert, Jacob Hays. William Long, David (his x mark) Tate, Appr's.

APPRAISEMENT: Estate of HUGH POOR, dec'd. 26 May, 1840. Lewis Cooley, Samuel Poor, William Stone, Appr's.

INVENTORY: Estate of ELEANOR LEWIS, late of Anderson Dist., S. C. dec'd. 5 May, 1840. Negroes: Puggy, Prince, Warren. Francis Burt, David S. Taylor, Geo. Seaborn, Wm. Hubbard, Appr's. B. F. Slaon, Wm. Sloan, ____Bowen, ____Rolleter.

INVENTORY: Estate of SARAH BROWN, dec'd., wife of E. Brown, dec'd. Negroes: Barny, Aaron, Silvy, Jeffry, Peter (evidently the young children of Aaron), Elizabeth, John. A. Rice, Ex'r. Last Will & Testament of E. Brown, dec'd. Appr's: Wm. Sanders, James Emerson, John Harkness.

BILL OF SALE: Property of E. BROWN, dec'd, as sold 5 May, 1840. Samuel Browne, J. M. Browne, A. Rice, A. M. Carpenter, John N. Harkness, Elijah Majors, James Emerson, James Baskins, James Thompson, Sr., Danton Brown, Thos. Geer, (Sam'l Brown bought the family Bible), John Martin, John M. Thompson, Alfred S. Tucker, Robert Todd, James M. Hamilton, Lidi H. Browne, J. M. Browne, James Thompson, Sr., Solomon Geer, Mat. Thompson, Josiah D. Gaillard, Zach. Hall, Jonathan Shirley, Wm. Sanders, Levi Clinkscales, Phebe McFall, Joseph Clark, William Geer, R. C. Harkness, Leonard Sailors,

William Rampey, Luke Hamilton, Robt. Hall, Craven Frasier, Jas.
H. Baskins, Arch. Gaillard, Ephraim Alewine. Sam'l Browne (the
negro man Barney); J. M. Thompson (negro man Aaron); A. Rice
(negro girl Elizabeth); Phebe McFall (negro girl June); 1 negro
woman & 2 children. Signed: Jerry Browne, John Martin.

BILL OF SALE: of ROBERT JUNKIN, dec'd. 16 May, 1840. Purchasers:
William Junkin, James Stevenson, Levi Burris, Jesse Dobbins, the
Widow Junkin, John Stevenson, Wm. C. Richards, William Long, David
Watson, Jonathan Shirley, Van Tate, Capt. Haynie, Thomas Heaton,
Harmon Hays, Milford Burris, Thomas Elrod, Harmon Kennedy, Thomas
Dean, Mathew Galloway, James Fowler, Levi Burris. 6 July, 1840.
E. S. Norris, Clerk.

INVENTORY: Estate of C. W. MILLER, late of Anderson Dist., S. C.
24 July, 1840. Appr's: Thos. M. Sloan, John T. Sloan, G. T.
Anderson, J. Overton Lewis.

SALE OF PROPERTY: Estate of C. W. MILLER, dec'd. John C. Miller,
Auctioneer. E. B. Benson, Exr. 24 July, 1840. Purchasers: D. K.
Hamilton, Bird Lanear, John Cammanade, D. S. Taylor, William Owens,
Eli Moore, Mrs. E. Pickens, John L.? Sloan, John Rolida (Holida?),
Daniel Pike, William Walker, L. S. Hamilton, Mrs. Prioleau, Wallace
Miller, Thos. H. Miller, J. O. Lewis, E. B. Benson, J. P. Lewis.

APPRAISEMENT: Personal Property of BAILY FRICKS, dec'd. Christopher Fricks, Admr. 12 Sept. 1840. Appr's: Williamson Dollar, R.
B. Lewis, Hugh Gregg.

NOTES: Estate of BAILY FRICKS (FRICK), dec'd. Abner Liddle, William Dooley, Joshira Harris.

MEMORANDUM: Personal Property of BAILEY FRICK, dec'd, sold on 12
Sept. 1840. Christopher Frick, George Stevenson, Jane T. Harris,
Jesse O'Brian, Henry Parker, George Stephenson, Garner Brook, Thos.
George, William Glenn, Asbury Brooks, W. R. Nelson, John McLees,
Thomas Burriss, James Burriss, D. D. Earp, Hugh Gregg, D. W.? Beaty,
Moses Pruit, D. P. Martin, Samuel Mitchel, R. B. Lewis, W. F. Phil-
ips, Thompson Brooks, Cornelius Latham, James T. Harris, James Pat-
terson, George Varner. Elijah Elrod, salesman of Estate. David
D. Earp, Clerk.

SCHEDULE OF ESTATE of LARKIN WRIGHT, dec'd. Negroes: George, Ellick, Cole, Daniel, Caroline, Ben, Dicy, Jenny, Mariah, Charity,
Modesty. Benjamin Magee, W. W. Holland, Catharine (Wright?), Exr.
& Exr'trx. 28 Nov. 1840. Appr's: Robert Holland, Levinston Isbell, Samuel Isbell, Pendleton Isbell.

APPRAISEMENT: Real & Personal Estate of JAMES R. WEBSTER, dec'd.
28 & 29 Dec. 1840. Negroes willed to Widow: Rinda, Sarah & Harry.
Portion willed to Ann & Margaret Webster: Negroes - Thompson, Louisa,
Minerva, Mahala, Harriet, Dala, Emaline, Michael. Property (negroes)
appraised for benefit of other legatees: Rebecca, Edmund, William,
Westley, Samuel, Eve and her 2 small children, Mary, Maria, Caroline
and Mark. Notes on hand: William P. Martin, W. B. Trayham, J. E.
Williamson, R. Williamson, G. French. Appr's: Wm. Kay, Jr., Wm.
Mattison, H. Acker, J. F. Wyatt. Hugh Gantt, Clerk.

BILL OF SALE: Estate of JAMES R. WEBSTER, dec'd. Sold 30 Dec.
1840. Purchasers: John L. Davis, Joel Kay, A. Bigbee, Hampton
Stone, A. Hathhorn, William Mosely, William Roberson, A. W.
Smith, William Clement, T. Stephens, R. Searight, Benj. Shirly,
John J. Robinson, Vincent Shaw, John Gilkemon, William Robertson,
R.? Shirley, A. Armstrong, George Bigbee, William P. Kay, Johnston
Clement, William Long, Sr., A. G. Latimer, A. N. Ware, Jas. L.
Killingsworth, Andrew Brock, Samuel Kinnon, E. D. Mitchel, Reuben
Case, William Arnold, M. Brock, John Gilkeyson, N. Shirley, Rich-
ard Smith, A. W. Smith, R. C. Sharp. Richard Smith bought woman

Becky; William Longs, Sr. bought boy Edmund; A. W. Smith bought
boy William; R. C. Sharp bought boy Westley; Jane Webster bought
woman Eve and 2 children, and boys Mark and Samuel; Joel Kay
bought girl Caroline, and Mary; A. W. Smith bought Maria; William
P. Martin, Ethellender Loveless. Hugh Gantt, Clerk.

SALE of Portion of Personal Estate of L. GOODE
Jacob Belot, Lewis Belot (bought boy Alston); John C. Black (girl
Leathy); Sam'l Brown (girl Winny). Maj. M. Burt, A.? Burriss, W.
P. Cannon, Dr. A. P. Cater, Carter Clayton, William Clayton, (bought
Easter and child, and girl Louisa); Eliju Creswell (negro boy
Luee? (Luse?); John Dalrymple (negro girl Polly); A. Harper, Jesse
Lewis, Joseph Majors (woman Harriet and child); Peter McPhail, L.
Milwee (boy Jerry); W. N. Moore (man Ben, wife Kizia? and 2 children;
also Kiziriah, Stephen, Margaret, Frank, Gene? and child, and boy
Scott); Alfred Wright.

PROPERTY RENTED & HIRED - L. GOODEE dec'd Estate - Maj. M. Burt:
Plantation, Mill & Miller; Negroes: Dolly and 2 children; Charlotte; Patty; Jim; Cyrus; Betty and 2 children. Wm. Steele.

APPRAISEMENT: JOHN HALL, JR., dec'd. 29 Jan. 1841. (Personal
goods). A. D. Gray, Appr.

BILL OF SALE: Estate of JOHN HALL, JR., dec'd. 29 Jan. 1841.
Purchasers: James M. Bell, Robert McCown, John Hall, Sr., John
Dunlap, Wesley Dunlap, Dr. Steifle?, Robert McKeown, Wm. Magee,
Fenton Hall.

SALE PERSONAL PROPERTY: L. RICHARDSON, dec'd. 20 Nov. 1840.
Purchasers: J. L. Belotte, Peter McPhail, M. L. Richardson, D. H.
Cochran, Whiteaker Smith, Jacob Burriss, A. O. Norris, A. E. Thomp-
son, A. P. Cater, David Richardson, W. R. Webb, Thomas Duckworth,
Wyatt Smith, John B. Earle, Milford Burriss, Elisha Burriss, Hiram
Waters, Elias Earle, William Fant, Reuben Gentry, W. G. Johnston,
J. P. Benson, Elias Tillinghast, Richard Felton, Nancy Moorhead,
Joseph Major, Lewis Prichard, Jesse Gray, Samuel Milwee, John Barks-
del, Stephen McCulley, Samuel McFall, Wm. Richardson, John Davis.

APPRAISEMENT: Property of SAMUEL POOR, dec'd. Samuel Poor, Exr.
of the Will of William Poor, dec'd. 19 Jan. 1841. Includes a
large family Bible.

BILL OF APPRAISEMENT: SAMUEL POOR, dec'd. (same date) shown by
Willis Johnson. Appr's: J. L. Acker, Lewis Cooley, John Poor.

SALE OF PROPERTY: SAMUEL POOR, dec'd. 5 Feb. 1841. Purchasers:
John Poor, Widow Poor, Sarah Poor, P. N. Acker, James Harkins,
Austin Williams, Hampton Hand, J. W. Lewis, Wm. H. Braswell,
Mathias Roberts, Joseph Hughs, James Kay, Grant Moor, Lewis Cooley,
Grief Horton, Wm. Poor, Humphrey Williams, Reuben Poor, J. L.
Acker, J. E. Allen, M. Roberts, Banister Stone, Lawson Harris,
Saml. Poor, Sr. (bought Bible), Reuben Philips, Robt. Halladay.

APPRAISEMENT: Estate of WILLIAM ELLIOT, dec'd. (No date) Includes 5 negroes not named. Household & farm goods. Appr's:
Josiah W. Cobb, John Harper, Wm. Bennett.

ESTATE OF WM. & ELIZ. GEORGE. James George, Admr. Saseon? And-
erson, John Dalrymple, M. J. Berry, Benson H.? Bomar, Elijah Webb,
John P. Holt, Dr. Anderson, T.? L. Scott, John Brown, F. W. Symmes,
Nathan Jeffers, Wm. M. Archer, A. Todd, Wm. Wilson, S. McCulley,
C. Orr, R. Prince, C. P. McKinney, Daniel Campbell, John Pilgrim,
John Harris, R. B. Norris, James George, John Haynie, John Brown,
J. N. Whitner, B. F. Hammond, L. J. Hammond, Francis George.

DEBTS PAID FOR ELIZ. GEORGE: Thomas Davis, Daniel Brown, John
Harris, William Campbell, W. R. Webb, John P. Benson, L. J. Hammond,
Dr. Wm. Anderson, J. B. Clark, A. Evins, Wm. George, Eliz. George.
_____ Vandiver.

INVENTORY APPRAISEMENT: Goods of CATHARINE BOWIE, dec'd. 20 Jan.
1841. Appr's: Jas. Wiley, Hugh Porter, Uriah Baron.

BILL OF SALE: CATHARINE BOWIE, dec'd. 20 Jan. 1841. Wm. H. White,
John W. Beaty, A. R. White, Wm. H. Bowie, U. Baron, A. McCullough,
R. Pettigrew, D. McCullough, Wm. Bondy?, H. Burton.

APPRAISEMENT: Estate of JOHN POOR, dec'd. 28 Jna. 1841. Appr's:
Mathias Stanton, Samuel Poor, William H. Stone. Reuben Poor. Notes
on John Poor, R. Roor, Wm. Reece, M. Poor.

BILL OF SALE: Estate of John Poor, dec'd. From Thursday 11 Feb.
1841 to following Saturday. Purchasers: Samuel Poor, Jr., Reuben
Poor, H.? Avory, Joseph Case, G. W. Poor, Amos Acker, Ed. Glaspy?,
J. W. Lewis, Samuel Poor, Sr., D. R. Whitt, Jos. Bagwell, John Ashley,
Mason Kay, John Hunt, Wm. Avory, Ez'l. Vincent, John Cooley, Lewis
Cooley, Hampton Hand, J. H. Kay, Presley Pernell, Capt. W. Case?,
Joseph Cox?, David R. Whitt, James Bagwell, P. N. Acker, Lawson
Harris, J. L. Rogers, Jas. C. Duck, Sam'l Heaton, Wm. Smith, C. P.
Dean, E. Pepper, Thos. Bennett, L. P. Massey, Asariah Cobb, Henry
Cobb, W. H. Stone, John Harper, Sr., J. P. Reed, W. Shearman, George
Gambrell, H. M. Gaines, W. Welborn, Lawson Harris, Dan'l Ragsdale,
Ann Poor, W. Smith, John Harper, W. H. Stone, Jos. Cox, P. N. Acker,
E. Eskew, W. Holland, Samuel Clark, W. B. Mattison, S. Roberts, Polly
Davis, Joshua L. Acker, Wm. Tripp, Wm. Garrett. __Mar. 1841.
Joseph Cox, Clerk.

APPRAISEMENT: of Estate of P. B. RIMMER, dec'd. ____ Adams, Wm.
H. Harrison, James Harrison, John Cox, Lucinda Rimmer, John K. Lilley
(Tilley?). Appr's: John B. Chappell, A. B. Skelton, William Dobbs.

BILL OF SALE: Estate of P. B. RIMMER, dec'd. John K. Lilly (Tilly?)
and Lucinda Rimmer.

BILL OF SALE: Estate of JESSEE MC GEE, dec'd. 23 Mar. 1841. Pur-
chasers: Martin Smith, Hiram Frost, Henry Homes, Elias McGee, Abner
Liddel (Siddel?), Willis McGee, Mark Havard, Jesse C. McGee, John
McGee, E. Aldridge, William Pashel, Wm. McGee, A. W. Aldrige, Thomas
Burriss, Nathan Harris, William Sherard, Thomas Stowers, Mrs. McGee,
Garner Brook, (Mrs. McGee took negro woman. Ester; William Sherard
took boy Lewis; Martin Smith took boy Bob; A. J. Wakefield took
girl Amanda.)

APPRAISEMENT: Personal Property of WILLIAM MC GILL, dec'd. 12 April,
1841. James Emerson, Admr. Appr's: R. Breckenridge, Tho. Taylor,
E. Ashley, A. Keeton.

BILL OF SALE: Property of WILLIAM MC GILL, dec'd. Mary McGill, widow
took entire lot of goods.

INVENTORY: Goods & Chattels, of MICAJAH TAYLOR, dec'd. 17 Apr.
1841. James Emerson, Admr. Appr's: R. Breckenridge, Tho. Taylor,
E. Ashley, A. Keeton.

BILL OF SALE: Estate of MICAJAH TAYLOR, dec'd. Purchasers: John
Martin, Robt. Shirley, James Emerson, Nancy Taylor, David Roof?.
Samuel McCoy, Clerk.

APPRAISEMENT: Estate of BARTLEY TUCKER, dec'd. Held at his late
residence. 26 Apr. 1841. (Very large estate). Testament & Bible
included; also tracts on Prickley Pear Shoals, McCright place and
Abbeville. Includes mills. Appr's: M. Thompson, Z. Hall, J. Taylor.
Negroes: Jack, Dina, Milly and 3 boy children; Simon, Olive, Old
Frank, Darkey, Ned, Emaline, John, Emily, Caroline, Young Frank, Jacob.

SALE OF ESTATE of BARTLEY TUCKER, dec'd. 28 Apr. 1841. A. D. Gray (bought Bible), James Tucker (took Milly and 3 children), John M. Hamilton, John Bowen, Gabriel McGee, R. D. Gray (took Jack & Dinah), Ezekiel Hall, J. J. Lepford, Wm. Long, John C. Tucker, Major Porter, R. D. Tucker, (took Simon, Olly, Ned), S. D. McCullough, Mark Prince, Caleb Burton, Z. Hall, Jas. Burriss, Robert McKeown, David Hall, Drury R. Hall, John Harkness, Jonathan Shirley, Wm. Newell (took girl Emily), Matthew Thompson, Dejernett Tucker (took Old Frank), Jas. D. Houston, Jacob Hill, Wm. C. Richards, Daniel Cochran, Woody Bowen, Sterling Bowen, Thomas Law, Jas. Dixson, John Surling?, Andrew Todd, Nancy Tucker (took Caroline), S. C. Fisher, Elizabeth Allen, Thomas Taylor, F. P. Robertson, A. Russell, Fenton Hall, Sr. (took Darky), G. W. Beasley, Wm. Ware, Robert Duncan, George Milford, Wm. Carr, Jas. Thomson, Jas. R. Rampey, Wm. Tucker (took the Testament), Thomas M. Curry, Alford Tucker, Jno. W. Elrod, Wm. Hall, Peter Glenn, Abner Clinkscales, Lemuel Hall, R. H. Hall (took Emaline), Jno. Crowther, John Davis, Thos. McCadams, E. Man (Maw?), E. P. Hollyman, Wm. Hall, Jr., A. McMahon, Jas. McKee, Houston McNair, David Russell.

APPRAISEMENT: Estate of LEWIS SHERRILL, SR., dec'd. Anderson Dist., S. C. 25 Jan. 1841. (Includes family Bible and a lot of Baptist books.) Negroes: Frank, Ben, Daniel, Franky and child, Josep?. Exr's. Dr. Wm. Anderson and Lewis Sherril. Appr's: Herbert Hammond, G. W. Masters, Robert Guyton.

BILL OF SALE: Estate of LEWIS SHERRILL, SR. dec'd. Sold 26 & 27 Jan. 1841. Purchasers: Joseph Jolly, Thomas McConnel, Jr., William Erskine, Dr. Wm. Anderson, Whiteaker Smith, Lewis Sherrill (took family Bible; negro Frank), John Williams, Alexander Ray, Daniel Campbell, Thomas Garrett, Calvin Garrett, G. W. Masters, Jonathan White, Benj. L. (T.?) Rodgers, Robert Guyton, Charles Irby, William N. Fant, Martha Dobbins, Nancy Lolar, Samuel Milwee, David Jones, Valentine D. Fant (took Frankey and child), Samuel Bell, James Willson, John Erskine, Jeremiah Rodgers, John Smith, Thomas Maddox, Stephen McCulley (took negro man Ben), James Wardlaw (took Daniel), Andr'w Stephenson, H. H. Wardlaw, Polly McDowell, Samuel Dawson, Lewis Moorhead, John Davis, B. L. Mitchell, J. H. Hammond, James Burgess, John Dalrymple, Hiram White, William Wellborn, Gilleson Harris, __. T. Whitefield, William Harrison, __. A. Harrison, Charles Kay, T. Rodgers, James Chamblee, Elisha Lewis, ___llson, Vermillion, __eon Anderson. Herbert Hammond, Clerk.

APPRAISEMENT: Estate of ROBERT GUYTON, dec'd, late of Anderson Dist., S. C. Negroes: Isaac, Betsey, Caroline, Eliza, John, Ben, Warren. 315 acres land. John Martin, Esq., Ordinary of Anderson Dist. John W. Guyton and William Webb, Exr's. 15 May, 1841. Appr's: Wyatt Smith, James C. Duckworth, G. W. Masters.

NOTES & OPEN ACCOUNTS: Estate of ROBERT GUYTON, dec'd, of Anderson Dist., S. C. E. D. Duckworth, Samuel Martin, Thomas Duckworth, D. M. Stott, Abdiel Stott, J. R. Hunnicutt, William Elrod, Samuel Martin, William Masters, David Jones, William Vermillion, Col. John W. Guyton, Esq. Signed: Wyatt Smith, James C. Duckworth, Herbert Hammond.

MEMORANDUM: Goods & Chattels appraised of Estate of WILLIAM PRICHARD by Robert Brackenridge, Gabriel Kay and Ebenezer Ashley. David Russell, Exr. 15 Oct. 1841.

INVENTORY - BILL OF SALE: Estate of WILLIAM PRICHARD, dec'd. 15 Oct. 1841. Eliz. McCoy, Gabriel Kay, Valentine Davis, William Haynie, John Martin, E. Prichard (widow), Mercer B. Hembree. James Emerson, Clerk.

INVENTORY: Estate of DEMPSEY WEST, dec'd. 27 Aug. 1841. Appr's: Robert Reid, Joseph Caldwell, Hugh Reid, Elias (his x mark) Findley.

RESALE: of Property of B. TUCKER, dec'd. (no date) Jas. Tucker, Abner Clinkscales, G. W. Hall, Ezekiel Hall, Wm. Tucker (mostly land resold.)

INVENTORY: Estate of HEZEKIAH RICE, JR., dec'd. 10 Nov. 1840.
Negro boys: Philip, Peter. Notes: John E. Norris, Thos. Geer,
Rice & Cater, Archibald Todd, Jas. Chastain, Jas. B. Clark, Cornelius
Keys, William Mitchell, J. W. Drennan, Thomas Holland, E. Martin,
John Archer, J. Flowers. (Notes listed as "good", "doubtful" and
"desperate".) A. Rice, Admr. M. Vandiver, Ibzan Rice, Wm. M. Nevitt,
C. Orr, Appr's.

BILL OF SALE: Property of H. RICE, JR., dec'd. 10 Nov. 1840.
Purchasers: Jane Rice, Elijah Webb, J. T. Whitefield, A. Rice.
Jane Rice bought man Philip; Abner Fant bought boy Peter. Mention
also made of "real estate of Todd."

INVENTORY: Goods & Chattels of Doc't JOHN ROBINSON, dec'd. Late of
Pendleton Village, So. Carolina. 15 Oct. 1841. Notes: Robert
Anderson, A. B. Campbell, Wm. D. C. Daniels, Sam'l Crookshank, William
Hunter, A. Hester, Nath'l Sheriff, Rich d Underwood, C. P. DuPree,
Goven G. Smith, Jesse Richards, William Fraser, Anthony Horton, F. R.
Donald, (Dowald?), Wm. Vandiver, Wm. Crenshaw, Enoch Payne, Wm. J.
Parson, Arthur Barrett, John Brissy, James Brownlow, Aaron Cantrell,
Elisha Christian, John Cansetter, Michael Dickson, Philip Campbell,
R. E. Dickson, Bradwell Day, John Dunn, James Dickson, Jeremiah Elliot,
Thos. Gibson, Jacob Genim?, Elijah Mayfield, Jeptha Norton, Thomas
Nichols, James Lesley, David Pinson, Daniel Pike, David Reid, Thomas
Turner, Thos. Rockley, Wm. Peoples, Jesse Stansil, Travis Smith, Larkin
Satterfield, Elizabeth Turner, Daniel Towes?, John Strawhorn, Peter
Edwards, W. H. Simonds, Hampton Smith, Joshua Smith, George Smith,
David Serjeant, Wm. Vowell, James W. Edmondson, Pryor Alexander,
Morgan Dowald, Wm. S. Burge, Wm, Barrett (Stiller), Hall. Vandiver,
Enoch Payne, Charles Roper, John Henderson, John Perry, Enoch Chapman,
Cannon Simon, James Gibson, George Shearman, Hamilton Hamby, John A.
Smith, Fair Smith, Andrew Smith, James Smith, John W. Wilson, Govin G.
Smith, Pinckney Hall, Kennedy Hughes, Field Mullinax, Thos. Barnett,
Ambrose Bradley, Isaiah Trotter, Benj. Barton, Thos. M. Clyde, Moses
Hollis, Edward Norton, Rial Kennemore, Laban Maulden, Thos. Gibson,
John Gunter, Michael Kennemore, Lewis Barrett, Madison Barton, Joshua
Smith (Hamp's son), Jno. Forgerson, Mrs. Abe Duke, Claiborn Wilkinson,
Wm. O. Dell, Elijah Watson, Reuben McClanahan, Stephen Akin, Leverett
Osborn, Josiah Kilgore, John Couch, Jr., Maj. A. Hamilton, Jacob
Gensin, Rich'd Underwood, James Wood, James Mariam?, Leroy Barr, Philip
Huff, Pleasant Ladd, Alva Griffin, John Gossett, William Kirsey.

APPRAISEMENT: Estate of Dr. JOHN ROBINSON, dec'd. Negroes: Peter,
Valentine, Mary, Mahala, George Violet, Sattira, Louisa & Ned, Harriet,
Milo, Judge, Martha (Jude and Martha given to Holcombe). Medical
books. Instruments. Medical Acc'ts due: Mrs. Sloan of (Cain Creek),
Wm. Hubbard, James Laurence, Robert Patterson, Rev. B. DuPree, Asa
Philips, Francis Burt, John T. Sloan, William Knauff, Sarah Doyle,
Patrick Miller, Thos. Christian, Sam'l Maverick, Mrs. Susan Harris,
Lyney R. Cherry, Old Mr. Lee (near Cain Creek), Mrs. Ann Hunter, Francis
Howe, Thomas Dodd, Col. D. S. Taylor, Col. J. E. Calhoun, Col. Sam'l
Warren, William Daniels, Jesse P. Lewis, William Waller, Edmund Martin,
Elijah Alexander, Edmond Singleton, James Steele, Thomas Hamilton,
John F. Maw, Doc't R. Maxwell, Miss Frances Conyers, Benson Stephens,
David Cherry, Crosby Miller, Elisha Christian, Bird Lanear, Abel Mauldin,
William Doyle, Elijah Watson, Henry Clarke, William Gibson, William
Stribling, Jacob Gearin, John Masters, Mr. Thompson, Sam'l Hall,
Andrew Lewis, Elisha Laurence, Col. Harleston, James Harrison, Thos. M.
Clyde, John Caviward?, Walter M. Gipson, Mr. Carson, John Hopkins,
Elias Mullinax, Rich'd Wilson, William Murphree, Madison Barton, Mr.
Col. Lewis, Horatio Bruice, Amos Wootton, John Hays, James C. Griffin,
Benj. Dilworth, Jacob Warley, Shelby Bates, Thomas Hallum, John Young,
John Sitton, (Litton?), Mrs. McClure, Robert Gains, Porter Y. Dupree,
Mrs. Dennis, John C. Miller, Old Mr. Bruce, Mr. Moore, Mr. Van Wyke,
William Smith, Samuel Reid, Thos. M. Sloan, Elijah Webb, Calvin Hall,
Milton Reese, Robert Anderson, E. B. Benson, Jackson Lewis, Mrs. Harris,
Thornton Rodgers, Mr. Rutledge, Miss Mary Hunter, Joseph Harris,
Mr. Hood, Arch'd Campbell, John B. Ferrell, Joel Patterson, Mrs.
Hammett, Paschal Williams, Mrs. Reese, William Singleton, William

Holcombe, Bird Abbott, William Sloan, Hundley E. Campbell, Thos. McCoy, James Swords, Michael Keesler, Mrs. Susan Cherry, Miss Martha Carne, Addison Holcombe, .Anderson Vandike, Franklin Laurence, Major Elam Sharpe, Joseph Prator, James O. Lewis, Geo. W. Liddell, Andrew Spence, Farro Kirksey, Mrs. Duff, Thos. R. Cherry, Miss Masters, Andrew Bennett, Mrs. Gaillard, Elizabeth Starke, Field Mullinax. Signed: E. B. Benson, Wm. Hubbard, Thos. R. Cherry, Appr's.

BILL OF SALE: Personal Estate of DR. JOHN ROBINSON, dec'd. By Willis Robinson, Admr. Purchasers: Mrs. Robinson (Mary and 3 children), Willis Robinson (negro Bob), Earle Holcombe, E. B. Benson, G. T. Anderson, L. M. Sloan, Geo. Seaborn, R. A. Maxwell, John Miller, Thos. D. Garvin, Leonard Hamilton, Doc't Elliot, Andrew Lewis, John Owens, Jos. V. Shanklin, B. F. Sloan, Col. B. Hagood (boy Milo, 12 years old and man Valentine), Dr. R. D. Maxwell, J. O. Lewis, Thos. Christian, John Couch (man Peter), Col. F. A. Garvin (Satyra and 2 children), Wm. Mulligan (girl Harriet, 12 years old), Dr. Jenkins, Dr. Symmes, John. Litton (Sitton?), ____Campbell,Earle Holcombe (2 negroes given him by Dr. Robinson - Judy and Martha).

APPRAISEMENT: Property of ABRAHAM HILL, dec'd. 20 Feb. 1841. Appr's: J. J. Robinson, John W. Gantt, James Adams.

BILL OF SALE: Property of ABRAHAM HILL, dec'd. 20 Feb. 1841. Negro boy: Andrew. Appr.: John Watt.

APPRAISEMENT: Estate of MARGARET ASTON, dec'd. 18 Nov. 1841. Purchasers: James E. Massey, Willis McGee, John Watt, James Abel, H. D. McCready? (negro boy Andrew), A. Simpson, Berry Burdit, John Young, Wm. L. Young, J. W. M. Hays, John Howie, Dan'l McCullough, Minors (children of Margaret Aston), James S. Stewart, Amaziah Frost, Jared Howard, Wm. M. Paschal, Wm. Stewart, Joel Galbreath, Wm. Cook, Wm. Fant, H. B. Shackelford, Mrs. Tucker, Daniel Brown. Note on Jacob Whiten.

INVENTORY: Personal Estate of MARGARETTE JUNKIN, dec'd. Appr'd 12 Jan. 1842. Appr's: Van Tate, Aaron Hall, David (his x mark) Tate.

INVENTORY: Personal Property of AMBROSE BROWN, dec'd. William Berry, A. Simpson, W. R. Nelson, J. M. Simpson. Property bought by William Berry. Certified by M. A. Gregg.

APPRAISEMENT: Estate of LUKE H. SOUTH, dec'd. 17 Dec. 1841. Notes: Thomas Duncan, Wm. Reed, L. H. Elrod, W. T. Hopkins, John Taylor, L. Vandiver, (interest in a bridge on Little River). Appr's: W. R. Webb, John P. Benson, A. Evins. David Brown, Admr.

APPRAISEMENT: Bill of the fruit belonging to the Estate of JOHN POOR, SR. (Orchards) 17 July, 1841. Orchards owned by deceased, and locations. John Martin, Esq., Ordinary of Anderson District. Signed: Samuel Poor, M. Stanton, Lewis Cooley, Mag't (Seal).

SALE OF FRUIT: Orchards....belonging to the Estate of JOHN POOR, SR. 17 July, 1841 (on a credit of 12 mo's). Reuben Poor (fruit orchard above the thresher), John Poor (orchard by the "Crib") George W. Poor (orchard East of New cotton gin), John Poor (orchard known as "Cosey Bottom"), George W. Poor (young orchard), Reuben Poor (Sanders Turner orchard and House lot orchard).

RENT OF THE LANDS: of JOHN POOR, dec'd for one year at the highest bidder. 27 Nov. 1841. Reuben Poor (the Holbert tract), David R. Whitt (the Garrett tract), William E. Sledge (the House tract), William Shearman (the River tract). Lewis Cooley, Mag't.

PRAISE BILL: Estate of MOSES J. GORDON, dec'd. Appr's: R. Smith, John Stewart.

BILL OF SALE: Estate of MOSES J. GORDON, dec'd. Purchasers: Widow, Henry Atkins, Henry Holmes, Wm. Sherard, George N. White, John Stewart, Ezekiel White, Williford Waters, Wm. Atkins. Robertson Smith. 17 Dec. 1841.

APPRIASEMENT: Estate of SARAH LEWIS, dec'd. (good inventory of household articles room by room). Includes family Bible and the Hymn book. (Negroes excepted). J. V. Shanklin, Exr. 16 Nov. 1841. Appr's: E. B. Benson, David S. Taylor, Thos. R. Cherry.

NOTES DUE, CREDITS, ETC: Estate of MRS. SARAH LEWIS, dec'd. J. O. Lewis, A. F. Lewis, Wm. Abbott, S. M. Lewis estate, Jno. E. Lewis, dec'd, Col. Rich'd Lewis, dec'd. J. V. Shanklin, Exr. 10 Nov. 1841.

VALUATION & ALLOTMENT OF NEGROES: J. V. Shanklin, Exr. Last Will & Testament of SARAH LEWIS, dec'd. Classification of Negroes belonging to estate: Lot 1 - Betsy, Rhody, Elisha (Elisa), Clinker. Lot 2 - Virginia, Lewis, Kelly, Billy. Lot 3 - Louisa and child, Miller, Nancy, Geo. Ann. Lot 4 - Davy, Emily, Francis, Henry. Lot 5 - Fodge, Judy, Lida and child, Haly, Bob. On casting the five lots (John E. Lewis, one of the children of the testatrix having died after the making of said will and before the death of the Testatrix without any lineal descendant). It appeared that Lot 1 was cast to and for Edwin Reese and Sarah Ann his wife; Lot 2 to John McDowell and Mary M. his wife; Lot 3 to J. V. Shanklin and Nancy his wife; Lot 4 to A. F. Lewis and Lot 5 to J. O. Lewis. Negro woman Milley bequeathed to A. F. Lewis... ...negro girl Janette mentioned in codicil of said will, given to Sarah M. Lewis estate (estate valued at $10,030.00) 11 Nov. 1841. E. B. Benson, David L. Taylor, Thos. R. Cherry, appr's.

SALE OF ESTATE: of MRS. SARAH LEWIS, dec'd. 12 Nov. 1841. Purchasers: Jno. & Mary McDowell, Edwin & Sarah Ann Reese, Andrew F. Lewis, Charles Miller, Mrs. E. Pickens, John T.? Sloan, Mrs. Sarah Blasingame, G. T. Anderson, John Miller, Printer, C. C. Pinckney, David S. Taylor, E. C. B. Christian, W. C. Smith, Mrs. Cook, David Cherry, Thos. H. Russell, Jno. L. North, Robt. Anderson, J. Rohledder, Sr., J. Rohledder, Jr., Jas. C. Griffin, John Cammanade, Dan'l Pike, T. R. Cherry, Thompson Miller, Jno. Hall, Andrew Pickens, John C. Miller, John C. Sitton (Litton?), Francis Howell, J. O. Lewis (family Bible), J. V. Shanklin.

INVENTORY: Goods & Chattels of JOHN JAMES, dec'd. Notes: Jacob Burriss. 1 Feb. 1842. John Haynie, W. M. Archer, Jno. E. Norris.

BILL OF SALE: Estate of JOHN JAMES, dec'd. Sold at the residence of John E. Norris on 18 Feb. 1842. John J. Stevenson, Wm. Stevenson, David Tate, Elias Cannon, James Thacker, John Davinson, Van Tate, Wm. M. Archer, John E. Norris, Joseph Crawford, Mary Cummings, and signed: W. M. Archer.

APPRAISEMENT: Estate of AARON GUYTON, dec'd. Appr'd 12 Jan. 1842. Negroes: Davis (David?), Jince, Rose, Bill, Will, Berry, Nice, Patsey, Sarah, Jo, Mary, Lear?, David, Cinda and 2 children, Candy, Chloa and 2 children. Very large estate. Appr's: Welborn Duckworth, Benj. Rodgers, Lewis Sherrill.

BILL OF SALE: Estate of AARON GUYTON, dec'd. 13 Jan. 1842. Purchasers: Jas. Chamblee, Charles Irby, Whiteaker Smith, Thos. Duckworth, J. W. Rodgers, Benj. Rodgers, Lewis Sherrill, S. F. McConel, J. W. Guyton, Welborn Duckworth, A. W. Guyton, Andrew Shearer, John McFall, John Creswell, __. J.? Whitefield, Wyatt Smith, Jas. Campbell, G. Guyton, Larkin Rodgers, Robert Jolly, Jas. B. Pegg, Wm. Steele, Jas. Wilson, William Campbell, Joseph Guyton, Marion Kay, Wm. W. Seawright, Harrison Kay, G. W. Masters, B. F. Hammond, J. M. Erskine, Wm. Archer, Thos. Hunnicutt, Wm. Richey, Wm. Webb, J. T. Rodgers, John Moorhead.

INVENTORY: Goods & Chattels of EPHRAIGM CANNON, dec'd. Rent of plantation whereon James Cannon now lives. Notes: George Stevenson, T. S. Scott, John Chambers, Luke H. South, Aaron Dean, James Fowler. 24 Jan. 1842. Appr's: John J. Stevenson, A. H. Waddell, Aaron Hall.

BILL OF SALE: Estate of EPHRAIGM CANNON, dec'd. 25 Jan. 1842 to
25 Dec. next. Mary Cannon, Elias Cannon, Willis Hembree, John Haney,
Robert Keys, Wilson Hall, John Herring, Aaron Hall, John Burriss,
Kindred Massey, Matilda Junkin, Levi Burriss, John Dunkin, John J.
Stevenson, Van A. Tate, George Stinson, Thomas Burriss, Milford Burriss,
Sam'l Williford, Robert Dunkin, Henry Crawford, J. E. Norris, Benj.
Watson, J. M. Brown, Robert Gray, T. L. Scott, John A. Thompson. Sale
of EPHRAIM CANNON's property, dec'd, made by me on the 25th of Jan.
1842. Reuben Burriss, Clerk.

INVENTORY: Personal Estate of MATTHEW CLARKE, dec'd. 8 Feb. 1842.
Note on Benjamin Clarke; (Benjamin Clark of Alabama), James G. Clarke
of Mississippi. Some property willed to Mrs. Clarke by Matthew Clarke.
Negroes: Ellen, Archy. Some property willed to Martha Jane Clarke.
8 Feb. 1842. Wyatt A. McMillion, Clayton Webb, Daniel Gentry, John
W. B. Skelton, A. B. Gentry.

INVENTORY & SALE: Personal Estate of MATTHEW CLARKE, dec'd. By E.
Webb, Exr. 9 Feb. 1842. John Moorhead, Stephen McCulley, James C.
Keys, Col. Joseph Taylor, Mrs. Jincy Clarke, Lewis Prichard, Clayton
Webb, William Brady, Moses Gamison, Christopher Orr, Daniel Brown,
William Tucker, James Dickson, John Skelton, (negro boy Henry), Elijah
Webb, Jos. C. Keys, Alexander Evins, John P. Benson, Dan'l Gentry.
Elijah Webb, Exr.

INVENTORY & APPRAISEMENT: Estate of JAMES WARNOCK, late of Anderson
Dist., S. C., dec'd. 26 Feb. 1842. Thomas Borough?, James A. Harrison.
Negroes: boy Ellick, boy Jacob, woman Hezekah and child. John Martin,
Esq., O. A. D....James Warnock, dec'd...S. R. McFall, S. J. Hammond,
William Harrison, Herbert Hammon.

INVENTORY: Estate of A. MASON, dec'd. (No date). Negro boy Barnett.

BILL OF SALE: Estate of A. MASON, dec'd. Abraham Meredith, J. Brad-
berry, Esther Mason, S. E. Maxwell, Perry Bradberry, William Hudson,
Pendleton Barton, Seaborn Moore, R. D. Maxwell, John Hughs, Ezekiel
Stanley, Edward McCann, C. H. Whitworth, Jackson Lowery, Jesse Brad-
berry, John Brooks, William Lanear, A. P. Reeder, Allen Guest, Robert
Holland, H. F. Chandler, J. R. Fant, Wm. Wright, Hiram Whitworth, M. S.
McCoy, Levi Herring, James Simmons, Frederick Moss (negro boy Barnett).

INVENTORY & APPRAISEMENT: Estate of FRANCIS YOUNG, dec'd made 16 Oct.
1841. Negroes: ____, Jerry, Joe, George, Rose, _____, Sarah and
child. 10 Feb. 1842. William Sherrard.

NOTES & ACCOUNTS: due FRANCIS YOUNG, dec'd. Francis Thornton, G. B.
Burdet, L. W. McAllister, James Turner, William Hutcheson, M. Young,
John Robinson, J. W. Shackleford, F. A. Young, J. E. Calhoun, N. A.
Lawhon, Spring Company, James Turner, William Sherard, R. Pettigrew,
William McAllister, A. Mauldin, Sr., John Stevenson, Robertson Smith,
William Cook, William Galloway, Jno. N. Young, E. Turnbull, V.? A.
Lawhon, F. A. Young, Wm. H. Simpson, A. Frost, Flornoy Davis, Robert
Simpson, William Ransom, Robert Willson, Mineral Spring Company,
Robert Berry, B. R. Taylor, William Keown, H. B. Shackleford, John
Stewart, B. R. Taylor, Samuel Stuart, F. Y. Baskins, Jno. Stewart,
James Stewart, Uriah Barron, John Stephenson, Robertson Smith, William
C. Simpson, Robert Keown, Jno. W. Brown, William Buchanan, Alex. Mc-
Allister, William Galloway, William B. Patterson, Stephen Cash, John
Young, Hezekiah Butler, Robert Keown, Jno. Bonds, A. McKinney, David
Calhoun, John Speer, Flournoy Davis, Jno. W. Shackleford, Samuel W.
Beaty, John Watt.....found in the possession of Francis Young at the
time of his death. This 10th Feb. 1842. Matthew Young, F. A. Young,
James Turner.

SALE BILL: Personal Estate of FRANCIS YOUNG, dec'd. Sold on 16 & 17
Nov. 1841. P. L. Byrum, J. N. Young (bought majority of estate),
H. B. Shackleford, F. A. Young, T.? O. Hill, James Turner, O. Clarke,
S. P. Beaty, M. Young, M. Kennedy, Wm. H. Simpson, F. Y. Baskins,
Jno. H. Chafin?, T. W. Gantt, A. McCullough, Rev. M. Chalmers, W. Barron,

Mr. Buckland, Spring Company, James Speer, Wm. Fant, E. Stephens,
J. Moff (Moss?) Simpson, Jno. Baskins, J. S. Baskins, Anderson Dist.,
S. C. Van A. Lawhon, Clerk. 10 Feb. 1842.

INVENTORY: of SAM'L WARREN, dec'd. A list of the Negroes appraised
at Soldiers Retreat, the plantation of the late Col. Sam'l Warren:
Pollidore, Camilla, October, Sylvia, Jack, Rachel, November, Magdalen,
Geddes, Binkey, Hannah, Isaac, Frankey, Matilda, Thomas, Lydia, Sesur,
Suckey, Adam, Mana, Bill, Andrew, Lucy, Caty, Bacchus, Mina, Elizabeth,
Leah, Hagar, Mary, Cardeno?, Sarah, Edward, Teresa, William, Daphne,
Nero, August, June, Prince, Tabor, Flora, William, Sam, Smith, John,
Grace, Felix, Tira, Twin?, Pollidore, Mary, Sabina, Marth, Rebecca,
Henry, April, Paris, Clansa?, Trice?, Cyrus (the last two in the low
country). Other property. Soldiers Retreat, 30 Dec. 1841. C. L.
Gaillard, Admr. Appr's: Edward Harleston, B. F. Sloan, William C.
Smith, Wm. Steele.

BILL OF SALE: Personal Estate of SAMUEL WARREN, dec'd. Leonard
Hamilton, John Rothlander, Jr., Henry Clarke, John Miller, Sarah Miller,
John Rothlander, Sr., William Sanders, Jno. T. Sloan, E. E. Tillinghast,
J. C. Griffin, Zach. Power, Ebenezer Smith, W. S. Burrage, E. Earle,
John Dickson, John Hix, C. P. DuPre, Aaron Smith, A. D. Gaillard, J.
C. Miller, Geo. Seaborn, Jesse Martin, Lewis Belotte, John Caminade,
Thomas Crenshaw, S. S. Cherry, D. S. Taylor, John Maxwell, Sam Maverick,
G. T. Anderson, J. V. Shanklin, R. D. Maxwell, James Emerson, Jacob
Belotte, Hugh Tatum, T. M. Sloan, Dr. O. R. Broyles, Mrs. Burns,
John Capehart, J. J. Duke, Thomas Pickens, S. W. Miller, Will. Hubbard,
A. McElroy, S. E. Maxwell, Dan. H. Cawhon, James Steele, Nat Roberts,
P. J. Miller, Thomas Garner, Ed. Harleston, James Harrison, John Hastie,
Dr. J. McElory, Charlotte Miller, Dr. F. W. Symmes, D. A. Thompson,
W. H. D. Gillard, Michael Keazer?, Benj.? Smith, J. N. Whitner, S. G.
Earle, J. B. Earle, Robert Norris, M. T. Trimmer, Willis Robinson,
J. B. Sitton, John Qualls, John Garner.

APPRAISEMENT BILL: of DAVID MARTIN, dec'd. Notes on: Henry Gable,
Joshua Goodwin, Andrew Buchannon, Charles Bowie, Levi Gable. 22 Feb.
1842. R. Smith, William Cook, Wm. H. Bowie, D. Tucker, Appr's.

BILL OF SALE: Personal Estate of DAVID MARTIN, dec'd. Sold 24 Feb.
1842. Levi Gable, Phebe Martin, James O. Martin, William Sherard, D.
Tucker, P. Byram, S. Whitman, J. McClenon, A. R. White, Wm. Cook.
Jas. Wiley, Clerk.

INVENTORY: of JOHN COOLEY, dec'd. 7 Negroes (not named). Appr's:
J. C. Duckworth, Elijah Pepper, James Cooley.

BILL OF SALE: Estate of JOHN COOLEY, dec'd. Ann Cooley (took the 7
Negroes), John Gambrell, Martha Cooley, James Gambrell, Wm. M. Cooley,
Alfred Kelly, Lewis Cooley, J. C. Duckworth, Wm. W. Rodgers, Presley
Pimrell, Wm. Elingbury, Wm. Scott, Wm. Glasby, Wm. Bennett, Thomas
Barnett?, Spencer Carter, Wm. Glasby, J. B. Gambrell, J. L. Lewis,
....Notes: M. B. Williams, Edward Whitt, John Ashley, Boothe Dalton.
James Gambrell, Clerk. Alex'r Moorhead, John Dalrymple, David Hendrix.

INVENTORY: Estate of MANNING POOL, late of South Carolina, Anderson
Dist...yeoman, dec'd. Made 9 Mar. 1842. 5 Negroes. (not named.)

BILL OF SALE: Estate of MANNING POOL, dec'd. Anderson Dist. Sold
10 Mar. 1842. Wm. H. Pool, John Dalrymple, Mary Pool (girl Sarah, boy
Abram.*), Edmund Martin, L. Milwee, W. A. Milwee, Bartley White,
Jesse Gray, James Jolly, D. H. Cochran, Benjamin Mitchell, N. Ro-
chester, Wm. Entrican, Wm. Erskine, E. George, Wm. Baley, George Martin,
Berry Lewis, T. R. Smith, Adam Pool (boy Julius, girl Fanny and child*),
Alex. Moorhead, Alfred Henry. A. Moorhead, Clerk.

APPRAISEMENT: Property of WILLIAM (WM.) HARPER, dec'd. as shown to
appraisers by Exr.'x. Negroes: Andrew, Juda his wife, and Mary their
daughter. Note: J. (Joseph) Cox. 4 Feb. 1842. Joseph Cox, Matthew

Gambrell, Hugh Wilson, James Telford, Charles P. Dean, Appr's.

INVENTORY & APPRAISEMENT: Estate of S.? (L?) W. CATLIN, dec'd. 17 May, 1842. C. Orr, Gleetwood Rice, Elijah Webb, Appr's. Includes Bible. Notes on: Joesph Pritts, Daniel Lucius, Anderson Dist., S. C.

BILL OF SALE: Sold at Public outcry on Personal .Effects of S. W. CATLIN, dec'd. 23 May, 1842. C. Orr, A. A. McFall, P. S. Vandiver, Fleetwood Rice (took Bible), J. L. (T?) Whitefield, J. P. Reed, Jesse W. Norris, Hiram B. Major, D. H. Cochran, James P. Cochran, Wm. Jackson, W. R. Webb, Jesse R. Smith, A. P. Cater, E. George, Wm. McCoy, Elijah Webb, D. Humphreys, John Langston, Larkin Moore, Jno. H. Creswell, Jno. B. Wynne, Jno. Towers, Stephen McCulley. James L. Orr, Clerk.

APPRAISEMENT: Estate of SAMUEL MC FEE, dec'd. 16 & 19 April, 1842. Appr's: Wm. Acker, A. Mattison, William Williamson. Notes on: Archibald Mattison, Toliver Flowers, Benjamin Morgan, William Sadler. Signed: Wm. Acker, Mastin Williamson, Wm. Williamson.

BILL OF SALE: Estate of SAMUEL MC FEE, dec'd. Sold 19 Apr. 1842. Strother Kay, Wm. O. Alexander, Wm. P. Todd, Washington McFee, Wm. A. Trussell, Rhodam Trussell, John Wright, Wm. B. Hall, Chester Kingsley, John Hanks, David Williamson, Michael Magee, John Hunt, Meredith H. Brock, George Grubbs, Harrison Latimer, Wm. Williamson, John Mattison, Abner Magee. Rhodam Trussell, Clerk.

APPRAISE BILL: Personal Estate of JACOB DUCKWORTH, dec'd. 5 Mar. 1842. (Includes Bible). Negroes: Mariah, Rhoda, Fanny and child Elizabeth, Margaret, Jane, Eliza, Berry, Catharine, Sam, Chany, Andy, Joe. Signed: Charles Irby, Wm. (his x mark) Elrod, Wm. (his x mark) Webb, J. M. Guyton.

BILL OF SALE: Estate of JACOB DUCKWORTH, dec'd. Anna Duckworth, (took Fanny and child, Sam, Joe & Chany; also Bible), Wm. Duckworth (girl Margaret), Benj. Duckworth (took Jane & Katherine), Benj. T. Rodgers (took girl Lize & boy Berry), Thomas Duckworth, Welborn Duckworth, Joseph Rogers, Abraham Martin, Wm. W. Rogers, Jas. Chambers, Perry Rogers, J. W. Rogers (took man Andy), Terrel Bryant, Jacob Duckworth, Wm. Martin, Simon Bryant.

MEMORANDUM: Goods & Chattels, Estate of DINAH WINTER, dec'd, late of Anderson Dist., S. C. 12 July, 1842. Signed: D. K. Hamilton, W. W. Knight, H. B. Fielding.

APPRAISEMENT: Goods & Chattels of JAMES B. FANT, dec'd. 14 Sept. 1842. 1 black woman, 1 child. Notes on : Archibald Davis, Wm. __. Z. Davis. Signed: Elijah Major, David Duncan, Moses Chamblee.

SALE BILL: Estate of JAMES B. FANT, dec'd. 15 Sept. 1842. Elizabeth Fant (negro woman Sal), James Major, Esq., Daniel Major, Robert M. Davis, P. D. Major, Elijah Major, Sr., Elijah Eubanks, Archibald Davis, Wiley C. Smith, David Duncan, Geo. W. King, Alfred Fant (negro child Phillip), Moses Chamblee, Enoch Major.

APPRAISEMENT: Goods & Chattels of JOHN WARNOCK, SR., dec'd 23 Aug. 1842. Negroes: Dick, Scipio, Henry, Betty and infant child, Zechaniah, Manda, Jane, Lucy (willed to daughter Jane), Jim (willed to daughter Margaret), Tena (willed to daughter Frances). Acc'ts on: Carter Scott, James George. Note on: John Warnock, Mary Langston, Elijah Major, Jr., G. V. & F. Gambrell, Benson & Wynne, John Vandiver. S. R. McFall, Archibald Todd, Mary Todd, Jas. Dickson. Appr's: A. O.? Norris, L. L. Hammond, John Vandiver, William M. Nevitt.

INVENTORY & APPRAISEMENT: Estate of JOHN MOORHEAD, dec'd. 3 Nov. 1842. Maxcey Moorhead, Exr. Signed: Alex'r Moorhead, Andrew Stevenson, David Hendrix, James Jolly.

APPRAISEMENT: Estate of JAMES TODD, JR., dec'd. Notes on: Wm. A.
Presley, David Gordon. Signed: Robert Todd, John McPhail, Nathan
McAllister.

SALE BILL: Estate of JAMES TODD, JR., dec'd. A. Todd, Admr. Purchasers: John Todd, A. Todd, Robert Todd, John Herron, John A. Tate,
James Martin, David Gordon. John Todd, Clerk.

SALE BILL: Goods & Chattels of JOHN MOORHEAD (MOREHEAD), SR., dec'd.
Late of Anderson Dist. William Archer, James Dalrymple, James Chamblee,
William Erskine, Hezekiah Gray, W. M. Goode, William Gibson, Syrena
Griffin (took the old Testament), Herbert Hammond, Charles Kay, Ira
G. Morehead, Major Morehead, Maxsey Morehead, Sarah Morehead, Widow;
Clarisa Morehead, John Morehead, Janes? Morehead, Pinckney Masters,
Wyatt Smith, William Smith. Signed: Alex. Moorehead.

APPRAISEMENT: Goods & Chattels of Estate of EBENEZER BUCHANON, dec'd.
Notes on: John Evans, Asa Evans, William Berry. Signed: R. Smith,
Henry Atkins, Matthew Parker. 10 Nov. 1842.

SALE BILL: Estate of EBENEZER BUCHANON, dec'd. 11 Nov. 1842.
Samuel Buchanon, Abner Brown, Lemuel Buchanon, William Sherrard,
Willis McGee, Lamal? Parker, Jacob Mushat, Hubbard Parton, Forester
Roach, John McMahon, Berry Roach, Henry Roach, A. Elliot, Nathan Harris,
Hen. Atkins, James Bostick, William Roach. K. Sullivan, Clerk.

APPRAISEMENT: Estate of DAVID GUTHREY, dec'd. 11 Nov. 1842. Notes:
Samuel Elrod, Norman Clardy, Richard Fleming, W. A. Williams. (Includes family Bible). Signed: Ezekiel Murphy, John M. Moore, Philip
(his x mark) Smith.

APPRAISEMENT: AGNES CASEY dec'd as shown by Kindred Massey, Admr.
17 Nov. 1842. (25 bushels corn only). Signed: A. Simpson, Jno.
W. Connor, Wm. N. Fant.

INVENTORY: Estate of THOMAS WATSON, Esq., late of Anderson Dist.,
dec'd. Joseph Grisham, Exr. 30 Nov. 1842. Negroes: Moses and Rachel,
his wife; Jacob and Dinah, his wife; Eliza and her female child;
Milly, about 13 years old; Leah, about 10 years old. Signed: Wm.
Steele, Thomas M. Sloan, M. T. Miller.

APPRAISE BILL: Estate of SAMUEL POOR, dec'd., late of Anderson Dist.
23 Nov. 1842. Notes on: John Ashley, John W. Spearman, Robert Ashley,
David Cochran, George Poor, John Rogers, Jos. L. Archer. Appr's:
J. L. Archer, John Poor, Lewis Cooly. Joseph Cox, Clerk.

SALE BILL: Property of SAMUEL POOR, dec'd. Sold 24 & 25 Nov. 1842.
Nancy Poor, Andrew Brock, John Poor, Joseph Cox, Albert Acker, George
R. Brown, Henry Barney, Samuel Poor, Perry Rodgers, Harbert Acker,
Austin Williams, Reuben Poor, William Harper, William Reese, John Poor,
Willis Johnson, Lewis Cooly, John Gambrell, Holland Poor, Hampton Poor,
H. M. Gaines, William Slaton, Daniel Ragdale, P. N. Archer, Lewis
Bennett, Hyram Cooly, William Holland, Jacob Duck, William H. Stone,
John Ashley, Allen McDavid, Jasper Williams, Humphrey Rodgers, Larkin
Rodgers, Thomas Harper?, Miles Ellison, William Poor, Wm. Tripp, V.
Shaw, R. B. Cox, James Bagwell, William Avery, Joshua J. Acker, N.
Acker, William Telford, E. Brazeale, Reuben Philips, Milly Poor, James
Stone, John H. Harper, Charles Kay, E. Pepper, James M. Griffin;
Anderson Dist., S. C. 26 Nov. 1842. Joseph Cox, Clerk.

INVENTORY: Estate of BENJAMIN GRIFFIN, dec'd. (Bible and Testament
included). John C. Griffin, Adm'r. Appr's: Samuel Swelling, Allen
Baily, John T. King, John M. Grubbs.

SALE BILL: Estate of BENJAMIN GRIFFIN, dec'd. 22 Dec. 1842. John
C. Griffin, Adm'r. H. Branyan, Jno. C. Griffin (Bible & Testament),
L. M. Kay, J. M. Grubbs, A. J. Wakefield, Z. Masters, J. Pearman,
Jas. Bradberry, Elisha Rogers, Elias D. Prints, Robt. Swilling, L.
Bradberry, Eben. Smith, John C. Griffin, Clerk.

ACC'T. OF THE PROPERTY: of MARY ANN WEBB, dec'd. Negro woman, Ally.
Boy, Tim, negro girl Caroline 16 or 17 years old. Benjamin Dickson,
Esq., Maj. Jas. Gilmore, Maj. William Dickson, Appr's. 18 Jan. 1843.

SALE BILL: of THOMAS WATSON, dec'd. 22 Dec. 1842. Archibald Mc-
Elroy (small Bible), M. C. Watson, (Family Bible) (Testament), M. R.
Hunnicutt, Thomas Christian, William Steele, John B. Sitton, Jackson
Stephens, B. F. Sloan, Mrs. Richardson, John T. Sloan, N. H. Steele,
Alex. Burns, John O. Grisham, Joseph Eaton, Joseph Barnett, E. G.
Mullinax, Peter McPhail, M. M. Norton, ___ Tillotson, Wm. Smith, B.
Watson, Joseph Williams, Phillip Goode, B. Mulliken, Thomas Anderson,
Sam'l Milwee, M. T. Miller, Col. T. Barnett, Chs. Thompson, A. Harper,
Lewis Belotte, Maj. Geo. Seabourn, Barnet? Gaines, Miles M. Norton,
Edw'd Martin, Carter Clayton, Patt. Miller, E. G. Mullinax, Thomas
Dickson, Lach'n Powers, Mrs. S. Oliver, Joseph Williams, Elias Tilling-
hast, A. Barns, John B. Letton?, Sidney Cherry, Lewis Belotte, William
M. Gibson, Wm. D. Steele, Charles Thompson, Col. J. Barnett, Wyatt
Smith, Maj. Simpson, Toliver Scott, Henry Recoles?, John Owens, Jesse
Lewis, John Scott, Alfred Moore, James Hunter, Alfred Fuller, A. Moore,
Henry Keisler, Rev. Allen Fuller, Jas. Hunter, Thos. Hunter, E. C. B.
Christian, Greene Stephens, E. G. Robinson, Andrew McFall, Joseph
Grisham, Exr. of Thomas Watson, dec'd. made at Public Vendue...by Ed-
mund Martin at the late residence of dec'd. on 22 Dec. 1842. John O.
Grisham, Clerk.

SALE BILL: Estate of JOHN SWORDS, SR., dec'd. John Pilgrim, William
Owen, William Swords, William Earskine, Wm. McMurry, Willis Newton,
Wm. Elrod, Elizabeth Elrod, Richard Morris, Isaac Newton, Neely Elrod,
Jackson Floyd, Felix Mathews, Samuel Morris, W. C. Elrod, Lefore In-
graham, Franklin Owen, Eli Moore, Mrs. Elrod, Jesse Holbrooks, W.
Elrod, L. N. Garvin (took 1 negro woman and child), Thomas Cherry
(2 negro girls), Willis Newton (1 negro girl). Wm. C. McMurry, Clerk.

SALE OF PROPERTY: HUGH POOR, dec'd. 15 Feb. 1842. John Poor, John
Ashley, Willis Johnson, Jos. Cox, William Holland, George Poor, James
E. Allen, John Gant, E. H. Davenport, Elijah Wyatt, William Telford,
Abner Cox, C. P. Deen? ((Dun?), H. B. Williams, H. Acker, David
Vincent, Sam'l Poor, Thomas Cox, George Stone, William Reese, David
Reese, Murry Woodson, Elias Chapman, William Stone, Joseph Burriss,
B. F. Mauldin, Peter Walker, Mitchell Scott, R. B. Cox, John Acker,
Enoch Brazeale, James Bagwell, James Harkins, Reuben Poor, Grant
Moore, I. W. Poor, Jeremiah Davis, Griffin Smith, Hyram Cooly, William
Poor, Ira? Rea, Allen McDavid, Washington Holliday, Howard Duckworth,
Geor. R. Brown, Geo. Hatton?. John Poor & Wm. Holland, Exr's. Jos.
Cox, Clerk. 1 Dec. 1842.

APPRAISEMENT: Property of FRANCIS A. RAGSDALE, dec'd. Anderson Dist.,
S. C. 7 Feb. 1843. Peter Walker, Joshua T.? Acker, Halbert Acker,
Appr's.

SALE BILL: Property of FRANCIS A. RAGSDALE, dec'd. 9 Feb. 1843.
Francis A. Ragsdale, Jr.?, Peter Walker, Henry M. Gaines, David Reese,
Grayton Nighbours, John L. Davis, Halbert Acker, William Clements,
William Mattison, Elijah Wyatt, Wm. Rees, Vincent Shaw, Wm. C. Harper,
John Gary, John Ashley, William H. Braswell, James Harkins, Michael
Magee, Daniel Ragsdale, Lewis Pyles, John Leach.

APPRAISEMENT - INVENTORY: Estate of NIPPER ADAMS, dec'd. 2 Dec.
1842. Note on: _____ Weldon (could be Hearman?). Appr's: Robt.
Parker, Thomas L. Read, Samuel Brown.

SLAE BILL: Estate of NIPPER ADAMS, dec'd. Sold 23 Dec. 1842.
Reuben Adams, James Adams, Wm. H.? Clinkscales, John Harkness, Sr.,
J. A. Gant, Polly Adams, Jr., Polly Adams, Sr., L. H. Browne, Elizy
Taylor, Rolly Banister, Jonathan Weldon (may be the above Weldon in
Inventory.) T. L. Reid, Robert Parker, John Shirley, William Adams,
J. B. Armstrong, Paris Hawkins, L.? C. Fisher, Wm. Banister, J. D.
Murdock, John Wright, Sam'l Browne, Jasper Browne, J. M. Browne.

APPRAISEMENT: Estate of CALEB EARP, dec'd. David D. Earp, Adm'r. Anderson Dist., S. C. (2 Bibles & 2 Testaments). 8 Dec. 1842. Charles Haynie, Joseph Caldwell, William G_____, Appr's.

SALE OF PERSONAL ESTATE: CALEB EARP, dec'd. 8 Dec. 1842. Martin Smith, James Gilmer, Alexander.McClinton, Joseph Caldwell, Jr., Joseph Caldwell, Sr., Samual Buchanon, Garner Brooks, Wm. H. Bowie, David M. Baity? (Baily?), Cornelius Latham, Thomas Smith, Caleb A. Earp, Elias McKerly, David Sadler, Matilda T. Earp, Lewis Wilson, Levi Burriss, Henry Tyler, John Burriss, Harrison Bulman, James M. Davis, Wm. Hale, John Hale, James Vernon, Archibald Skelton, William Caldwell, Sr., John Rainy, Margaret Earp, David D. Earp, William Caldwell, Jr., (no mention of sale of Bibles). Urban A. Gregg, Clerk.

INVENTORY - APPRAISEMENT: Estate of NATHAN JEFFERS, dec'd. 28 Feb. 1843. (Large Bible). C. Orr, E. Webb, Appr's.

SALE BILL: Property of NATHAN JEFFERS, dec'd. Sold by Fleetwood Rice, Adm'r. 1 Mar. 1843. Mrs. Roda Jeffers (Bible), L. H. J.? Alley, Joseph Crawford, D..H. Cochran, Dr. A. P. Cater, Henry Parker, Elijah Webb, Warren R. Webb, Samuel Bell, James Stephenson, C. Orr, L. V.? Gentry, Jesse R. Smith, Reuben Gentry, William Jackson, Enoch Major, Stephen McCully.

SALE OF PROPERTY: JAMES BURRISS, dec'd. (Second Sale) 16 Mar. 1843. James Burriss, W. E. Eskew,.G. W. Masters, B. Burriss, D. H. Cochran, Jacob Burris; Byran Boroughs, Clerk.

APPRAISEMENT: Estate of CHARLES WILSON, dec'd. Appr's: Sam'l R. McFall, Ibzan Rice, John Haynie.

SALE BILL: Estate of CHARLES WILSON, dec'd. 23 Nov. 1843. H. Whiteker, D. Wilson, B. Grimes, D. Greer?.

APPRAISEMENT: Estate of JOHN RANEY, dec'd. Late of Anderson Dist. Mrs. Malissa Raney, Adm'rx. Slaves: Lela (60 years old), Milly (19 years old), Harriet (3 years old); 1 Aug. 1843. Samuel Cunningham, Lindsey A. Baker, Samuel H. Baker, Appr's.

APPRAISEMENT: Property of CHARLES WILSON, dec'd. 30 Aug. 1843. Negroes: Jack, Elizabeth, Tom, July, Aggey, Martha, Materson, Rily, Andrew, Elizabeth, Caroline, Malinda, Spencer, Blufort, Alfred. Nelly considered worth nothing because of old age; boy Jarrett considered worth nothing due to insanity. Appr's: J. H. Rosamond, John A. Smith, Stephen Watson, Martin (his x mark) Phillips.

SALE OF PROPERTY: Estate of CHARLES WILLSON, dec'd. 31 Aug. 1843. J. A. Smith, Jas. Wilson, H. McGoven, G. G. Smith, Thos. Hollingsworth, Sarah Wilson, William Wilson, Jane Wilson, Boswell Day, Bryan Boroughs, Alex. Mauldin, John Williams, F. P. Smith, E. Holcombe, W. Sherriff, Osbers? Nally, Em. Smith, Joseph Smith, W. B. Gibson, R. D. Wilson (man Jack), Joshua Hughes, A. W. Holcombe (boy Tom and boy July), R. D. Wilson (woman & child, and Jarrett), Wm. Wilson (child Bluifort), W. B. Gibson (Aggy and 2 children)(also boy Materson), H. C. Briggs (girl Martha), Em. Smith (boy. Riley)(girl Caroline), Sarah Willson (boy Andy, Nelly, girl Elizabeth), Stephen Watson, Clerk. Note on: A. M. Hamilton.

APPRAISEMENT - INVENTORY: Estate of WILLIAM KEOWN, dec'd. (Lands excepted). 5 Oct. 1843. Negroes: Lewis, Nathan, William Mary, Mely Ann, Mary Ann, Rachel, Eliza, Lucinda, Charles, Caroline, Sarah Jane, Thomas. (William M. Keown's negroes.) George W. Keown's Lot of Negroes: Betsy Ann, Adriana, Thomas Alexander. One negro woman Elizar F. Young....Wm. Kelly. Notes: Beverly Allen, Henry Adams, James Ables, Jesse Adams, Joseph Ables, A. Shaw, Andrew Obriant, Bery Burditt, John Black, F. G. Baskins, John Baskins, Henry Cosper?, F. Davis, Wm. N. Fant, L. Gwinn?, George Burditt, Jas. E. Evans, John Stewart, R. Davis, K. Sullivan, Clark Fields, Wm. Jennings, Thomas C. Hill, Reuben Haley, George W. Keown, Wm. Keown, W. Tira Mauldin,

Robert Lesley, Robt. H. Petigrew, D. Smith, John Able, John Watt, E.
Willbanks, James Furner (Turner?), Martin Marshall, A. Maulding,
William Hutcheson, L.? Lindsey, Wattson Bond, John W. Brown, George
Burditt, Stephen Burditt, Daniel Brown, David Obriant, Wm. Buchanon,
Wm. Crawford, T. Crawford, Levi Gwin (free man of color), Amaziah
Frost?, Thomas Guest, Joel Galbreath, B. F. Dickson, Wm. Haslett, Wm.
Kelly, Jonathan Rarmard?, John Mecklin, Wm. Simpson, James B. Martin,
James E. Massey, McKenny & Hays, John S. McCollam, Samuel Sherrall,
Hudson Scoggings?, A. Scott, Nimrod Saylor, Daniel Smith, James
Stewart, Wm. B. Scott, John Terrell, Robert Wilson (free man of color),
R. Walker, J. C. Waller?, George Young, Hick Roun (man of color). Bad
Notes: Wm. McKee, James Thomas, James White (out of date and him in
Georgia), James S. Stacht? and S. Cash (both in Mississippi), Silvanus
Scoggins, Michel Kelly, Sela Lowry, J. P. Davis, Jane defur?, John
Goodwin, James C. Griffin, Stephen Cash, John M. Bond, Wm. L. Crawford,
John Brown, Prisy Lay and Joseph, James A. Keown, Esq., H. Armstrong.
Book Acc'ts Good: John Able, James Able, F. Y. Baskin, Berry Burditt,
Mary Casey (widow), Dejernet Tucker, James Turner, John Watt, Cyrus
Bond, Wm. Keown, Jes Adams, D. Connel, Wm. Fant. Notes - doubtful:
Wm. Able, Joshua Brown, James Bostick, Wm. Crawford, Rhoda Evans, Wm.
Fant, James Edwards, Horatio Fields, John W. Brown, Leonard Gwinn
(man of color), Joseph Able, George Able, Samuel Able, John Able, Sr.,
Wm. Simpson, James G. Stewart, Hugh Saxon, Riley Willson (free man of
color), Margaret Hay (free woman of color), Fielding Acock, Rosey
Leppard, Mrs. Lesley, James B. Martin, James E. Massey, James Crawford,
Wm. Kelly, J. P. Davis, Edward May, Tucker May, Ann Everett. John
Black, W. M. Keown & George W. Keown, Exr's of estate of William Keown,
dec'd. R. Smith (M. A. D.), Hiram Burditt and F. Y. Baskin, Appr's.

INVENTORY: Goods, Chattels, Lands, Tenements of the Estate of LEVI
CLINKSCALES, dec'd as taken 6. Nov. 1843. Negroes: James & Miley,
Levina & child, boy Michael, boy Jackson, boy Morris, boy Simon, boy
Phillip, boy Henry. 6 Nov. 1843. John Martin, Wm. Cowen, William
Keeton, S. H. Browne, Appr's.

SALE BILL: Estate of L. CLINKSCALES, dec'd. Sold 8 Nov. 1843.
Polly Clinkscales (negro boy Phillip, woman Mily), William Keaton,
Ibzan Clinkscales (negro boy Jackson), H. R. Clinkscales, Thomas Geer
(negro man Jim), Martin Williamson, Jno. Harkness, Sr., James Thomson,
Jno. Clinkscales, F. A. Manning, Nancy Clarke, Jno. Haynie, David
Williamson, A. Rice, Elias Cannon, Andrew Shearer, Henry J. Sanders,
Wm. Cowen, Jonathan Weldon, Jas. J. Harkness, A. Keaton, Jno. Pratt,
J. D. Gaillard, Robert Gray, Asa Clinkscales, M. R. Manning, Wm. C.
Williams, Jesse Kutage,)Rutlige?), Luke Hamilton, F. M. Kay, Thos.
Branian, J. A. Gantt, J. M. Hamilton, L. Hall, J. N. Harkness, Jno.
Clinkscales, Jr. (negro boy Simon), Josiah Burton (negro woman Levina
& child), Wm. Magee (negro boy Michael), Robt. B. Norris (negro boy
Morris).

APPRAISEMENT: Estate of JOHN M. MOORE, dec'd. Appr's: Lewis Owen,
John Slaton, John Murphy. Negroes: Dick, John, Malinda. Notes on:
Blasingame & Bowen, Phillip Smith, Wm. Smith. 15 Nov. 1844.

SALE BILL: Estate of John M. Moore, dec'd. 17 Nov. 1843. Elizabeth
Moore, Perry Rodgers, Mitchel B. Scott, Lewis Owen, A. G. Welborn,
John Slaton, John M. Elrod, John Murphy, Spencer Carter, John Tripp,
Wm. W. Rodgers, A. Ryly, Stephen Slaton, Benjamin Spearman, E. Murphy,
Esq., Lovin Slaton, Robert Parmer, L. B. Gutry, Wm. C. Pickel, Simeon
Smith, David Durham, Nathan Briant, Wm. Martin, Chesley Martin, George
Slaton, Elijah Moore (took girl Malinda), Ira C. Williams, Capt. L.?
S.? Carter, Abraham Martin (boy John), Benjamin Reagan, Benjamin Rod-
gers, Elizabeth Moore (took boy Dick), Terril Briant, H. J. Roberts,
Thomas B. Moore, Wm. E. Welborn, John M. Elrod.

APPRAISEMENT: Estate of JESSE FANT, dec'd. 30 Dec. 1843. Appr's:
Wiley C. Smith, James King, Robert King, Moses Chamblee, George W.
King.

APPRAISE BILL: Goods & Chattels of GILLISON HARRIS, dec'd. Note:
Isaac Cannon. 20 Dec. 1843. Appr's: Samuel Craig, Wm. Smith,
Robert Smith.

SALE BILL: Estate of GILLISON HARRIS, dec'd. Sold on 21 Dec. 1843.
Widow Harris, Jno. Smith, Jno. Fretwell, H. Harkins, Jas. Chamblee,
Robert Smith, Wm. Smith, Jackson Jones, G. Brazeale, Chesly Martin,
Thos. Erskine, Mr. Deen, Wm. Hunter, D. Dalrymple, Thos. Wilson,
Jno. Kay, H. Parker, Jno. Erskine, Wm. Hunter, S. Milwee. Wm. A.
Archer, Clerk.

APPRAISEMENT: Estate of JANE HOLLY, dec'd. 4 Jan. 1844. Negro:
girl Lizy.

SALE BILL: Estate of JANE HOLLY, dec'd. 11 Jan. 1844. Purchasers:
Caleb Robertson, Margaret Holly, Robert Thomas, John Morris, Wil-
liam Hinton, John B. Earle, Charles B. Webb, Armstead Waters, D. T.
Morris, Henry Pearson, Rachel Johns, Zechanah Masters, Archibald B.
Skelton (took girl Lizy).

INVENTORY: Goods, Chattels, Estate Real & Personal of WILLIAM COX,
dec'd. 21 Nov. 1843. Negroes: Ron, Jubates?, Sarah, Jane, Harriet,
Irena, Grace, Henry, Abram, Anderson, Samuel. Notes: Bill Agee?,
J. W. Leatherston (Featherston?), Robert Stucky, Tilman Hanks, Robert
N. Wright, Stephen Shirley, Ira G. Gambrell, Avis? Cox, Matthew Gamb-
rell, John Gambrell, John E. Brock (Brooks?), Thomas Cox, James
Ellison?, W. Harper, J. H. Harper, John Cox, William Cox, Halbert Acker;
William Cox, Ex'r. Appr's: Ains? Cox (his x mark), M. McGee, Halbert
Acker.

SALE BILL: Goods, Chattels, ETC. of WILLIAM COX, dec'd. 22 Nov.
1843. William Cox, J. L. Davis, William Reese, V. Shaw, Wm. P. Kay,
R. B. Cox, L. (S.?) Robinson, Joel Smith, W. Maw?, B. Davis, T.? Cox,
M. McGee, V. Shaw, J. I.? Robinson, H. L. Harper, Jas. Bagwell, Wm.
Coxsen, M. N. Gambrell, Thomas Cox, Jr., R. Morrison, Jas. McCullough,
L. V. Gambrell, Wm. Harper, A. Hughes, R. B. Cox, Wm. P. Kay, William
Main, Asa Braswell, Urah Nixon, Barbary Harper, Abner Nixon, Abner Cox,
Arch.? Johnson, A. J. Reeve, D. F. Lucious, L. Bagwell, Wm. Telford,
A. Johnson, L. Robinson, Robert Wood, Jas. Thomas, Wm. H. Braswell,
George Stone, Eli Ellis, T. W. Davis, T. & B. Lewis, J. M. Grubbs,
William Stone, B. Davis, Wm. French, Jas. Kay, R. B. Cox, B. McGee,
Mason Kay, W. B. Hall. Purchasers of Negroes: Wm. Cox, (Ron), Jno.
Widow (Jubiter?, Sally), B. Davis (Jane & Harriet & Irena), A. H.
Magee (Grace), Thomas Cox (Henry), Wm. Cox (Abram), Jno. Cox (Anderson,
Samuel), Barbary Harper (Jacob). Sold 22 & 23 Nov. 1843.

INVENTORY: Goods & Chattels of MOODY BURT, dec'd. Appr'd 13 Nov.
1843 by William Steele, W. M. Archer, Ch. L. Gaillard, and Whitiker
Smith. Slaves: Austin, Letha, Jim, Rina, David.

ACCOUNT OF SALES: Portion of Estate of MOODY BURT, dec'd. M. M.
and P. O. Goode (David & Rina), J. L. Orr, J. H. Creswell, E. H.
Tillenhast, J. W. Harrison, J. B. Wynn, J. R. Smith, James Gordon,
D. H. Cochran, Wm. Purcer (Jim), Lewis Morehead (old Austin and Letha.)
S. Millwee.

INVENTORY: Goods & Chattels of KINDRED MASSEY, dec'd. Appr'd: 2
Dec. 1843. Negroes: Kitty and child, Caroline, Dennis, Mary, Harris,
Ben. Notes: J. B. Clark, William Martin. 2 Dec. 1843. Appr's:
Asa Clinkscales, W. B. Latimer, Silas Lewis.

SALE BILL: Estate of KINDRED MASSEY, dec'd. Sold by M. H. Brock on
5 Dec. 1843. Matthew Snipes, James Cochran, E. G. Robinson, James R.
Massey, Widow Massey (took Mary, Dennis and Ben), Milford Burns, Enoch
Major, James Gray, Elbert Burriss, John Haynie, A. H. Waddle, L. A.
Osborn, James Stephenson, Joel A. Hall, Bryan Burriss, W. B. Gibson,
A. T. Hembree, John J. Stephenson, Willis Hembree, J. H. Creswell,
Abner Fant, John H. Tate, Wilson Hall, A. M. Carpenter (took Kitty and
boy child), Peter McPhail (took Caroline), Asa Clinkscales. B. D.

Kay (took Harris).

INVENTORY & APPRAISEMENT: Estate of JEREMIAH ELROD, dec'd. Dr.
Wm. Anderson & John D. Amack, Exr's. Negro boy John, negro woman
Letty (Betty?) and child Charity. 17 Oct. 1844. D. Richardson,
Thomas H. Garret, Chesley Martin, Herbert Hammond, Appr's.

SALE BILL: Estate of JEREMIAH ELROD, dec'd. Sold 8 Nov. 1844.
Dr. William Anderson (took plantation), Tillman Garret, John Ingraham,
Micajah Williams, John Erskine, John D. Amach, Battle Mayfield,
Thomas Duckworth (took boy John), Wm. Erskine, Wm. Elrod, John Wilson,
Samuel Millwee, Chesley Martin, Jackson Wilson, Simon Bryant, John
Bryant, John Mayfield, Wm. Hunter, Sarah Elrod (took woman Letty -
or Hetty? and child Charity), John Young, James M. Erskine, Benjamin
Duckworth, Wid. Resirrer?, Elizabeth Elrod, Daniel H. Cochran, James
Wilson, James Welborn, Wm. Smith, Spencer, Gregory, Terrel Kay, Wm.
Richey, Thomas Garret, Harrison Pilgrim, John Mayfield. 9 Nov. 1843.
Herbert Hammond, Clerk..

APPRAISEMENT: Property of HENRY GAMBRELL, dec'd. John Gambrell,
Adm'r/Ex'r. Negroes: Meshack, Gracy, Rachel, Mariah, Eady, Jane,
Eliza, Abram. James Wilson, B. F. Hammond, Lewis Cooley, Appr's.

SALE BILL: Property of HENRY GAMBRELL, dec'd. John Gambrell, Adm'r
16 Nov. 1843. Purchasers: Asa Cox, Charles Irby, Daniel Major,
B. F. Hammond, P. Majors, J. J. Gambrell, Elijah Majors, Jr., Wm. S.?
Kay, Wm. Majors, John Stinson, John White, M. Lawless, J. Elliot,
Thomas Mattox, John Sullivan, Sam'l Dawson, Lewis Sherril, Wm. Smith,
John Moorehead, Wm. W. Rodgers, Allen Johnson, James Bell, Mrs.
Susan Gambrell,; signed: Harper Gambrell.

SALE BILL: Property (Negroes) of HENRY GAMBRELL, dec'd. (Entry says
John Gambrell property. Probably mistake, as John was the Adminis-
trator....cme) Daniel Major (man Meshack), Mrs. Susan Gambrell (girl
Gracy), Wm. Smith (girl Rachel), Wm. C. Harper (girl Mariah), John
Gambrell (girl Eady), Daniel Brown (boy Abram), A. Kay (girl Eliza),
J. B. Lewis (girl Jane). Wm. C. Harper - land.

APPRAISEMENT: Estate of ISAAC ELROD, dec'd. 14 Dec. 1843. Includes
Bible. Appr's: Thomas Welborn, Caleb Carter, W. E. Welborn.

CASH & NOTES Res'd of the Estate of ISAAC ELROD, dec'd. 14 Dec. 1843.
Notes on: Adam Elrod, George Elrod, Jacob Elrod, Obadiah Merrit,
Wm. Welborn, Thomas Oldham, D. & Frances A. Spearman, J. L. Rodgers,
James Fleming, Lucy Merrit, Phillip Elrod, Wm. Bennett, John Fleming,
Elijah Moore, Wm. L. Moore, Wm. __. Carter, Wm. King, Wm. Barnett,
J. W. Cobb, Richard Fleming, Francis M. Lee*. Signed: Francis M.
Lee. (19 Jan. 1835*states he is greatly indebted - sum given is
$10.00 .

SALE BILL: Estate of ISSAAC ELROD, dec'd. 15 Dec. 1843. Elijah
Moore, Richard Fleming, George Elrod, Abraham Rily, Jeptha Harper,
Spencer Carter, Norman Clardy, Nicholas Tripp, Mrs. Merrit, Elias
Elrod, John Fleming, Lucy Merritt, John D. King, William A. Elrod,
Thomas Carter, Thomas B. Moore, Matthias Richeson, Barsdell Smith,
Harrison Wilbanks, William Clardy, Andrew Barkley, Caleb Payne,
Wm. Oldham, Thomas Welborn, Elias Elrod, Henry Orr, Thomas Harper,
John Murphy, Doc't Kenimore (Kenmon?, Keniman?), James Wilson, Jasper
Wilson, Wm. M. Rodgers, Harva? Welborn, Jacob Martin, Larkin Rains,
William Tripp, Larkin Rodgers, John Bryant, J. W. Cobb, John H. Tripp,
Noah Richardson, Mitchel Scot, William Martin, William King, Lewis
Scot, John M. Elrod, John Harper, Norman Clardy, John Fleming, Small-
wood Dalton, John H. Tripp, John King, Nathan Bryant, Matthias Richard-
son, Andrew Barkley, Alexander Orr, Wm. Masters, James Wilbanks,
Lovin Slaton, Jos. Smith, Jeptha Harper, Thomas B. Moore, Burrel
Dalton, Thomas Bennett, Jasper Wilson, Harrison A. Wilbanks, Benjamin
Harris, Larkin Estes, Wadsworth Fleming, James Thompson, J. W. Cobb,
Reuben Carter, J. H. Garrison, J. M. Merrit, Griffin Hopkins, Howard

Duckworth, Terrel Briant, Jeremiah Rodgers, Samuel Garrison. Signed:
Adam Elrod 15 Dec. 1843.

APPRAISEMENT: Estate of NICHOLAS BISHOP, dec'd. Negroes: Billy and
Nelly; Kate, Cato, Jackson, Jim, Eliza and 2 children, Mariah, Mary
and Ben. James Henderson, Adm'r. 6 Jan. 1844. Appr's: A. C.
Campbell, Wm. C. McMurry, Joseph Watkins.

SALE BILL: Property of NICHOLAS BISHOP, dec'd. 10 Jan. 1844.
H. N. Bishop (man Cato, woman Eliza and child Leah, boy Banister),
Robert Henderson (girl Mariah, boy Jackson), Darcus Bishop (man
Bill and woman Nelly, Jane Bishop (woman Kate), Alexander Waddel.
Fuldix Watkins, Henry Fielding, William Douglas, James Henderson (
boy Jim and girl Mary and boy Ben), William Sloan, G. B. Garvin,
W. L. Jenkins, Wm. Boggs, Edmund Martin, William Brewer, C. M. Lay,
L. M. Sloan, J. Evett, A. Voyles, Joel Newton, Warren Night, John
Lorton, Leonard Hamilton, Wm. McMurry. Note on: B. D. Dupree.
Signed: Stephen Watson, C. B.

INVENTORY & APPRAISEMENT: NANCY JOHNSON, dec'd. Appr'd 5 Feb.
(Monday), 1844. Negro girl: Liza, about 10 years old; Alsey or
Affy - old; Ginny, a woman about 26 years old. Anderson Dist., S.
C. Joseph Cox, James Cooly, John Gambrell, Appr's.

SALE BILL: NANCY JOHNSON, dec'd. Sold 6 Feb. 1844. Personal Pro-
perty. Puchasers: Charles Irby, Joel Johnson, A. Kay, Jos. Cox,
W. Erskine, B. Stone, ___ Ellenberg, W. Bennett, W. Johnson, Allen
Johnson, Clary Johnson, Willis Johnson, John Kelly, Allen Kelly, C.
Johnson, G. Horton, John Ingram, James Stone, Johnson Allen, Ann
Cooly, Elijah Pepper, M. Roberts, T. W. Kinman, Jeptha Harper, A.
Williams, Esq., G. Smith, L. Rogers, Peter Johnson, Jas. Stone (Bible),
A. McDavid, H. Gambrell, Nancy Johnson, Nathaniel Rodgers, Griffin
Smith, M. Stanton, W. Erskin, H. White, Lewis Cooly, A. Kelly, W. W.
Rogers, J. B. Lewis, Edwin Cob?, Reuben Poor, A. Williams, A. Johnson,
E. Pepper, Sanford Heaton, Clarisa Johnson, Larkin Rogers, Jacob
Duck, Miles Ellison, John Gambrell, S. Poor, Banister Stone, Perry
Rogers, Ludy Wyatt, John Ingram, Charles Irby, Sanford Heaton, N.
Rogers, (Nancy Johnson took Lizar, negro girl); J. B. Lewis took
Affy & Ginny). John Ingraham, Anderson Dist. Allen Johnson, Adm'r.

APPRAISEMENT: Estate of ELIZABETH R. HOPKINS, dec'd. Shown by David
Gambrell of Anderson Dist., appr'd 7 Apr. 1844 by Bird Lanier, James
B. Fant, S. Bradberry.

SALE BILL: Mrs. ELIZABETH R. HOPKINS, dec'd. 16 Apr. 1844. Allen
Lenior, Charles Hunt, Benjamin B. Harris, David Gambrell, Abraham
Meredith, John Hopkins, A. Bradbury.

APPRAISEMENT: Estate of JAMES C. GRIFFIN, dec'd. 4 Nov. 1843.
Negroes: (to be sold) Old Jack, Susan and child, Hampton (age 20),
Henry (age 17). Others, willed to: Aurelius (age 15), and Lucinda,
(age 11) to Mrs. Robinson; Jenny, (age 14) and Rosey (age 10),
willed to Nacissa; (Cely and Maria), willed to Rebecca; (Jackson and
Sarah), willed to Georgiana; (Jeffry and Mary), willed to Margaret,
dec'd. Charlotte and child Jacob.

SALE BILL: Estate of J. C. GRIFFIN, dec'd. 7 Nov. 1843. Mrs.
Griffin, Nat. Roberts, Elam Sharpe, Mrs. Mays, Rich'd B. Dupree, Thos.
Christian, Thos. Hamilton, Wm. McMurry, Geo. Seaborn, Nimrod Smith,
D. Gaillard, Alex. Ramsey, Willis Robinson, J. V. Shanklin, Rev. A.
W. Ross, Wm. Fant, Thos. Dickson, D. S. Taylor, Willis Newton, Capt.
A. Smith, Jesse Lewis, Geo. Federick, Fair Kirksey. J. V. Shanklin
bought negro Jack, wife & child; Geo. Federick bought boy Hampton;
Kirksey bought Henry. (N. B. - The negro man Jack and wife Susan and
child sold to J. V. Shanklin for $530 was contested as unsound. The
case was referred to Arbitrators under an agreement if the unsoundness
was established they should take back. The award was against the Estate and negroes returned. - R. A. M.)

241

SALE BILL: of Property of DAVID GUTHREY, dec'd. Sold 24 Jan. 1844.
Benjamin Gentry, William Carter, Ezekiel Murphy, N. Richardson, A.
Riley, Andrew Barkley, J. Burges, A. G. Welbourn, B. Guthrey, J.
Hunt, A. Roberts, A. Guthrey, L. Guthrey, N. Guthrey, H. Roberts, C.
Carter. Certified by Andrew Barkley, Clerk.

SALE of Estate of Gen. EARLE, dec'd that is stock and other articles
surrendered to estate Exr. for sale by Mrs. Ann Earle. 8 Oct. 1842.
at Silver Glades. Sold to : J. P. Benson, S. Smith, J. Wilson, A.
Riley, J. Golden, G. Seaborn, B. F. Sloan, J. Martin, Wm. Ritchie?,
L. Duckworth, M. Williams, J. Bryant, W. Duckworth, A. McFall, Col.
Guyton, W. Webb, D. Winfrey. Sold at A. C. H. (Anderson Court House)
Oct. Court 1842: (Horses, cows, other stock) J. Taylor, E. B. Benson,
Miles Ellison, L. Smith, D. Humphreys, Dr. Jenkins, J. L.? Lorton,
J. V. Shanklin, J. Roleter?, Major Seaborn, E. Smith.

INVENTORY/APPRAISEMENT - Estate of JAMES MC COY, dec'd, late of
Anderson Dist. 24 Aug. 1844. Signed: Strother Kay, P. O. Major and
J. R. Towers?

APPRAISEMENT: Estate of J. (Jacob) W. Worley, dec'd. Anderson Dist.
14 June? (Jan.?) 1844. E. B. Benson, B. F. Sloan, J. S. Lorton,
Appr's.

SALE BILL: Estate of J. W. WORLEY, dec'd. John L.? F.? Sloan, Clerk.
Elam Sharpe, Wm. L. Keith, S. J. Pickens, Geo. Seaborn, R. D. Maxwell,
S. E. Maxwell. (this page very dim...cme).

INVENTORY: Estate of JOSEPH M. MAJOR, dec'd. Late of Anderson Dist.
Negro woman Harriet and child Caroline. Notes on: Nathaniel Roches-
ter, Samuel Millwee, N. T. Smith, Thomas Hunnicut. John Dalrymple,
Adm'r. 20 Nov. 1844. Herbert Hammond, Robert Smith and Samuel Craig.

SALE BILL: Estate of JOSEPH M. MAJOR, dec'd. Sold 21 Nov. 1844.
J. R. Major, B. H. Lee, R. Morris, Wm. Richardson, D. Hendrix, Tho.
Miller, J. W. Major, Nancy Major, Wm. Owen, A. Smith, Walli Richard-
son, D. Reid?, John Hunter, Wm. Simpson, S. Craig, J. Dalrymple, S.
Millwee, H. Hammond, Wm. Erskine. Signed: John W. Major.

APPRAISEMENT: Goods and Chattels of JESSE O'BRAINT, dec'd. Signed:
A. Reid, E. White, R. Smith and M. Parkes.

INVENTORY: Estate of WILLIAM FORSYTHE, dec'd. 4 Sept. 1844. Signed:
William C. Baily, James Todd and L. R. McFall. Notes: Samuel Askew,
James McKinny, C. Orr, Levy N.? Hanby?. Signed: Herbert Hammond.

SALE BILL: Personal Property of WILLIAM FORSYTHE, dec'd. 5 Sept.
1844. Enoch Major, John Erskin, William Baily, Deinchy? Hill, John
Wornock, Alexander Stephenson, Herbert Hammond, C. M. Wilson, James
Todd, Abraham Massy, B. F. Hammond, S. R. McFall, Elizabeth Padgett,
Leytha? Forsythe.

INVENTORY: Estate of BENJAMIN CLEMENT, dec'd made 17 Jan. 1844.
Negroes: James, Tilmon, John, Lauson?, Matilda, negro woman and 2
children, Zachariah and Hagar, Mary, Eliza, L_____, _____ McGee,
_____Wright and John A. Gant.

SALE BILL: Goods and Chattels of BENJ. CLEMENT, dec'd. Sold 18 Jan.
1844. A. L. Clement, A. J. Brock, John Gant, William Clement, John
Gilkey, Jos. Lee, P. Lee, Jincy Clement, Benj. Clement, Stephen
Clement, David Cummings, James King, C. Clement, J. West, V. Shaw,
W. Magee, C. Kingsley, L. Clement, P. B. Mays?, A. Mitchell, John
Hunt, B. Armstrong, W. H. Mattison, Jas. Armstrong, Jhn. McAdams, A.
Braswell, Aaron Davis, Wm. Harper, Jenny Clement, James Bagwell,
Phillip Lee, Wyatt Mattison, L. Wyatt, D. Reese, Doct. Brown, R. A.
Wright, A. Smith, Mason Kay, Lewis Piles, Widow O. Shirley; negroes
bought by: James by Jincy Clement; Tillman by Stephen Clement; Amy
and 2 children by Jancy Clement; Lauson by A. Clement; John by Lucy
Clement; Matilda by B. Clement; Mary by William Clement; Charlotte

By Benj. Clement; Laurence by Wm. Clement. Sold 18 Jan. 1844. Hugh Gant, Clerk.

APPRAISEMENT: Estate of DAVID WATSON, dec'd. Negroes; Bob, Kitty, Isaac, Henry, L____and child,____. Notes: Washington Glenn, J. J. Watson, Samuel Martin, W. G. Johnson, V. D. Gary, Mitchel Dooly, B. J. Dolby, Wm. Crawford, W. Dooly, Elijah Webb, Fenton Hall, W. G. Johns, Willis Stocks?, Wm. Dooly, Drewry Snipes, Cooper Benot?, Margery Gortney?, W. B. Gibson, John Little, J. T. Whitfield, Newton Riddle, George Haynie, William Fite?, James Fowler, Samuel Chastain, Hiram Harbin, Maberry Snipes, Jackson Howe?, Elias Davis?, Daniel McConnel, Stephen Hays, Miles Glasgow, Van Davis, Edward Fillips, Reuben _____, David Gentry, Philip Johnson, James Long, William McDavid, J. M. Murry, B_____ F_____, Samuel Michaels.

SALE BILL: DAVID WATSON, dec'd. Property. 31 Jan. 1844. Moses Deen, James Burriss, Jonathan J. Watson, A. B. Barton, Mary Watson, Alfred M. Neel, John M. Burriss, John Haynie, Milford Burriss, John McGregor, Maberry Snipes, B. C. Haynie, Daniel K. Watson, A. N. McFall, Robert Dunkin, Elbert Burris, John B. Watson, Mathhu? Snipes, J. W. Glenn, R. A. King, Van. D. Gary, Wilson Hall, John G. Watson, Martin Smith, Malinda Junkin, Mary Watson (widow). Signed: Reuben Burriss, Clerk.

INVENTORY & APPRAISEMENT BILL: Estate of James Harkins, dec'd. Negroes: Ben, 6 years old; Lucinda, 9 years old; Frank, 13 years old; Sam, 17 years old; Richard, 19 years old; Daniel, 22 years old; Lucy, 40 years old; Jordan, 24 years old; Peter, 32 years old; Henry, 34 years old. Notes: J. W. Lewis, J. B. Lewis, N. Acker, M. Cooly, M. Roberts, G. Stone, J. Hanks. Judgement against John Ashley. Note on N. Loveless. Certified by Joseph Cox, William Telford, J. F. Wyatt and Abner Cox.

SALE BILL: Estate of James Harkins, dec'd. 5 Dec. 1844. Jane Harkins (took Lucinda and Dick); Sarah Harkins, James W. Lewis (took Ben and Sam), Ephraim Mitchel, James Gambrell, James Lee, W. L. David, John Cox, O. Shirley, Sam'l Poor, B. F. Mauldin, W. Holmes, Wm. C. Harper, James Hollida, Joseph Cox, Benj. Shirley, John Hunt, Austin Williams, William Bennet, R. D. Crymes, James F. Wyatt, J. W. Featherston (took Frank); J. P. Reed, David Rooss?, John Hammond, Charles Kay, John L. Davis, Wm. Smith (took Dan); B. Nabors, J. J. Robinson, R. S. Smith, P. D. Majors, A. Armstrong, John Hunt, William Erskin, John A. Mattison, George Grubs, Francis Ragsdale, John Wardlow, Vincent Shaw, Lewis Cooly, Henry Lawless, R. N. Wright, Abner Cox (took Henry); Michael Magee, R. R. Seareglit (took Jordan); John Sullivan, David Cox, David Cumming (took Peter); Andrew Brock, R. G. Wyatt, A. Acker, David Greer, William Davis, Jesse N. Balentine, R. Trussel, John Harper (took Lucy); William Telford, M. Magee, J. B. Lewis, J. W. Lewis, Isaac Davis, William Holmes. 6 Dec. 1844.

INVENTORY: Goods and Chattels of MATHEW GAMBRELL, dec'd. Appr'd 27 Nov. 1843. Appr's appointed by Court of Ordinary. Negroes: Grantison (37), Martin (39), Thomas (46), Bob (27), Pompey (55), Rebecca (30), Irena Snith? (10), Mary Ann (12), Betty (24), Amanda (5), Sarah and child (35), Caroline (15), Clarinda (11), Malinda (8), Harriet (6), Sally (4). Notes: Howard Duckworth, Gid Land, J. Todd, Hugh H. Wardlaw, Elisha D. Hall, Wm. B. Holland, John Levell, John Stevenson, Albrose? Millwee, J. Bell, Harrison Wilbanks, Michael Lawless, Brooks Lewis, Wm.M. Sears, Jas. Telford, Wm. Erskin, Jas. M. Erskin, Alfred Lewis, Dan'l Major, Jordan Gambrell, Wm. Smith, James M. Griffin, John C. Griffin, David H. Gambrell, Thomas D. Garvin. 28 Nov. 1843. Certified by: S. J. Hammond, B. F. Hammond and James Telford.

SALE BILL: Estate of MATHEW GAMBRELL, dec'd. Sold 28 and 29 Nov. 1843. Lettuce Gambrell, Sam'l Bell, David Gambrell, Jos. T. Rogers, E. Wyatt, H. Latimer, W. Smith, David Duncan, Jas. Bell, Jr., B. F. Hammond, Benj. Mitchel, James Wyatt, H. Major, W. J. Mattison,

M. Magee, John Gambrell, W. Jackson, Joseph Cox, R. Trussell, D. Major,
D. H. Gambrell, Jas. Taylor, John Morehead, John Ashley, C. P. Dean,
G. W. King, W. L. Kay, P. D. Majors, Joseph Cox, D. Mattison, John
Cox, James King, Samuel Smith, C. B. Holland, G. W. King, W. Jackson,
W. Johnson, P. Strop? (Stros?), G. Brazeal, W. B. Hall, L. T. Gambrell,
J. M. McCoy, A. Fant, W. Pagit, Allen Johnson, James Nichols, Charles
Irby, L. McCulley, L. Dalrymple, S. F. Risner, Carter Scott, Jas. E.
Allen, D. Cowhorn, W. Featherston, John Stevenson, James Wyatt, Jas.
Telford, J. W. Featherston, James Chambers, W. Harper, John Towers,
John Haynie, J. M. Wardlaw, L. A. Risner, Wyatt Smith, Joel Kay, Jas.
M. Carpenter, P. Pepper, Robt. Parker, James Gambrell (Bible), N.
Latimer, Jerry Gambrell, J. B. Lewis, L. Gambrell (negro man Pompey
and Bob), David Geer (man Thomas), N. Wilson (grandison), S. J. Hammond
(Martin), E. Mitchel (Becky), S. McCracken (Bets and Amanda), W.
Magee (Irrena), H. Latimer (Mary), L. Gambrell (Harriet, Sally, Sarah
and child, and Caroline), M. L. Gambrell (Clarinda), D. N. Gambrell
(Malinda), Geo. Brown, John A. Dacus. Adm'r: Joseph Cox, L. Gambrell.

INVENTORY: Goods and Chattels of JAMES COOLY, dec'd. H. Cooly,
Adm'r. 26 July, 1844. Dessy Pack. Negroes: Mary, Betsy, Jane
(claimed by Dessy Pack), Henry, Cindy (claimed by Mary Cooly).
Signed by: Joseph Cox (Seal), John Poor (Seal), James W. Lewis (Seal),
J. (Joshua) S. Acker (Seal). Notes: L. Cooly, M. Stanton.

SALE BILL: Estate of JAS. COOLY, dec'd. Sold 29 Aug. 1844. George
W. Devenport, M. Roberts, J. L. (S.?) Acker, William Poor, W. P. Kay,
Joel Kay, James Holida, John Cooly, Geo. Grubbs, Joseph Ellenburg,
H. Cooly, John Harper, W. M. Cooly, Mrs. Ann Cooly, Wm. Holmes, Allen
Kelly, James Bagwell, Jos. Cox, Geo. Poor, C. P. Dean, J. B. Lewis,
James B. Molley, Lewis Cooly, James Gambrell, A. Cobb, Dessy Pack,
Jacob Cooly, A. M. Gaines, Miles Ellison, A. Williams, Jasper Williams,
James Ellenburg, W. Gambrell (large Bible), D. Vincent, Wm. Turner,
John B. Croft, Jos. Burn, M. Brazeal, Carter Chapman, James King,
Wm. Bennett, Wm. Poor, H. Majors, John Poor, Reuben Poor, Banister
Stone, W. P. Kay, Eliz. Pennell, A. W. Smith, W. Welborn, Sam Roberts,
Jos. T. Rogers, A. Lawless, A. M. Gaines (All goods sold first day
of sale). Joseph Cox, Clerk.

INVENTORY: of Goods and Chattles as sold on last day of sale - (JAS.
COOLY, dec'd) - 5 Nov. 1844. Dessy Pack, H. Cooly, Jos. Burns, John
Croft, Mrs. Ellenburg, Eliz. Pennell, E. Cooly, Jacob Cooly, John
Cooly, L. Cooly, M. Roberts, A. Cooly, J. B. Lewis, A. Williams,
Thos. Bennett, W. A. Stone, John Sullivan, A. Brock, A. J. Nichols,
W. B. Turner, J. W. Cobb, J. B. Lewis, E. T. Cooly, A. M. Gains, Jos.
T. Rogers, J. Hughs, James C. Dickworth, Wm. Fleming, J. B. Croft, A.
Cochran, Jacob Duckworth, Samuel Roberts, James E. Allen, Jackson
Nichols, James Rutledge, Thos. Wilbanks, George Poor, Sr. (negro woman
Polly and Mary), E. Pennell (Jane and Betty), A. B. Cobb (boy Henry),
John Wynne, W. Reece. Joseph Cox, Clerk.

APPRAISEMENT: Estate of Robert Todd, Dec'd. 7 Aug. 1844. (Includes
balance of the Arthur McFall tract of land.) Also these tracts:
Cross Road, Chalmers, Bluford McDaniel, Tagaloo, Old Home (disputed),
old Burford, old McDaniel, Little Slip (vacant). Negroes: Tom, Ned,
Caleb (spelled Calep), Katy, Mary Elsy, Mandy, Silbert. (Family Bible
and small Bible.) Notes, etc.: John McDowell, David Gordon, Robt.
Duncan, Thos. Duncan, A. Todd, John Davis, Wm. T. Elrod, Thos. F. Todd,
Elijah Wilbank, J. C. Chalmers, D. A.? Presly, Steph. Haynie, A. N.
McFall, Jse. Elrod, John Duncan, M. R. Manning. Certified by: James
Herren, Nathan McAlister and John McPhail. 2 Jan. 1845.

SALE: of Estate of ROBT. TODD, dec'd. 6 Nov. 1844. Sam'l Brown,
Andrew Todd, James A. Rampy, Henry Branyan, David Gordon, Sam'l M.
Webb, Robt. Duncan, Andrew Latham, Robert Duncan, Jr., John Herren,
John Cantnel, James Stevenson, Joseph Jarrett, Leut.? Hall, David Hall,
Fenton Hall, Olive Todd, John Todd, Fenton J. Hall, John Duncan,
Thos. Duncan, D. A. Presly, John Scott, M. R. Manning, Wm. B. Elrod,
Drewry Hall, Jacob Sligh, James Cochran, Dan'l H. Cochran, Mat. M.

Manning, Nathan McAlister, Lewis Sherrell, James Martin, Benj. F.
Duncan, David Hall, Andrew Todd (table Bible), Olive Todd (Bible and
Psalm book), William Ranson, John B. Wynne (family library), James
Martin, Robt. D. Gray, Stephen Haynie, William Lesly, Jackson Carter,
David S. McKiney, David Scott, James Burten, John McPhail, Elijah
Webb. (Sale con'td 7 Nov.).....John M. Hamilton, John Haynie, Hiram
Howard,.Luke Hamilton, Andrew W. Hawkins, John McFall. Negroes bought
by: David Gordon (Ned), James Emberson (Tom), David Gordon (Ted and
Gilbert, unsound), John Todd (negroes Caleb and Elcy), Henry Branyan
(Mary), Olive Todd (Caty), Lewis Clinkscales (Amanda). Tracts of land
pruchased by: John A. Tate, John Todd, Olive Todd, Andrew Todd. (Sale
cont'd 8 Nov.) D. S. McKinny, James Stevenson, John Cantrell. John
Herron, Clerk. 6 Jan. 1845.

APPRAISEMENT: Estate of ISAAC LONG, dec'd. Shown 4 Dec. 1844.
Appr's: Charles Bowie, John Beaty, Asa Adams, R. Smith.

SALE BILL: Personal Estate of ISAAC LONG, dec'd. 5 Dec. 1844.
Letty Long (widow), Andrew Reid, Joseph Long, Dudly Howard, Miss
Melvina McAlister, William Long, Andrew Todd, Lewis Clinkscales,
James Burroughs, John Black, Henry Gable, John McMahon, Wm. Long, Sr.,
Charles Bowie, Samuel Beaty, Clem Brown, D. S. McKinny, Jacob Whitman,
Wm. Obriant, James Burris. Signed: John Black. 7 Dec. 1844.

INVENTORY: Goods and Chattels of SAMUEL EMERSON, dec'd. Anderson
Dist. 5 Feb. 1845. Negroes: Spencer and Sarah. Tract of land.
Appr's: Z. Hall, Ezekiel Hall, Wm. Tucker and Conrad Wakefield.

BILL OF SALE: Estate of SAMUEL EMERSON, dec'd. 18 Feb. 1845.
Conrad Wakefield, Wm. Hamilton, Z. Hall, S. C. Fisher, J. Alewine,
Wm. russel, Wm. Carwile, Maj. Jas. Thompson, Wm. Hall, Jr., A. D.
Gray, A. Todd, S.? C. Jones, Michael Alewine, Francis Fleming, Martin
Hall, James A. Drake, Luke Hamilton, Owen Burton, R. H. Hall, S.? M.
Davis, L.? H. Gasoway, Dr.?.M. Thompson, R. W. Hall, John Davis, Rbt.
D. Gray, Stephen Haynie, Rev. A. Rice, John N. Harkness, D. S. Mc-
Kinny, Robt. McCown, L. McClellin, Green Fleming, J. C. Black, John
Osborn, Jesse Rutledge, John H. Emerson, R. D. Tucker, Ezekiel Hall,
Ramsy White, John Brownlee, John Hall, Jr., Jos. Y. Hall, James Emers-
on (girl Sarah), Widow E. Emerson (man Spencer), Capt. T. Taylor,
Sam'l Taylor, L. E. Sligh, James A. Rampy, Widow Murry, Janus H. Wiles,
David Williamson, John Newell, C. Wakefield. 19 Feb. 1845. John H.
Emerson.

INVENTORY: Estate of JAMES SMITH, dec'd. Appr'd by Col. John Rankin,
Robt. Pickens and John Pegg on 11 Mar. 1845. Negroes: Will, Gim,
Milly, Harrison, Abe. Acc'ts: Considered good: Andrew Oliver, Thomas
T. Rankin, Wm. Robison, Wm. Hubbar (Hubbard?), Peter McMahon, Benj.
Muliken, Jr., Amos Voiles. Acct's doubtful: James McKinny, Alex.
McKinny, Miss Fanny Martin, Silas Floyd, Thomas Farmer, Pinckerton
Slater. Notes: D.? K. Hamilton, Col. Geo. Rankin, J. W. Earle,
Benjamin Smith, Wm. McMurry, Wm. J. Smith. Campbell & Bird, Nathan
Briant, Nathan R. Briant, John S.? Owen, J. L.? McCann.

INVENTORY SOLD: Estate of JAMES SMITH, dec'd. Sold to highest
bidder on 12 and 13 Mar. 1845. J. H. Smith, J. M. Smith, B. Mullikin,
Jr., Wm. Steel, Warren Smith, William Sanger, Rev. J. Wilson, Benj.
Stafford, James Davis, J. H. McCann, Wm. Martin, Thos. H. McCann,
John Williams, William Stafford, Wm. Orr, Jr., W. W. Rogers, Thos.
Prater, James D. Smith, Benj. Mulliken, Jr. (man Jim), J. M. Smith
(men Will and Harrison), John C. Smith (boy Abram), Terrel Briant,
Jeremiah Hunt, Larkin Mitchum, Rich'd Golden, Simon Briant, J. B.
Pegg, A. M. Smith, Jacob Pickle.

APPRAISE BILL: Estate of ELISHA KELLY, dec'd. 21 Nov. 1844. (400
acres of land); Negroes: James (12), Linda (10), Mary (7), Jacob (5),
and Levi (3). Tract of land on broad Moor? Creek of 104 acres recently
purchased and sold to his son Balis Kelly. Notes: Wm. Eskew, Asberry
Pinnel, Boothe Daulton, Alfred Kelly, Howard Duckworth. 21 Nov. 1844.

John Harper, Clerk. John Harper, Sr. and Henry Cobb.

INVENTORY: Estate of ROBERT GORDON, dec'd. James Gordon, Ex'r.
11 Feb. 1845. Negroes: Edmond (42), Sim (32), Rose (18) and child
Charlet (1), Elias (1), George (14), Julian (10), Lucy (8), Ely/Eliz.?
(6), Martha (4). Acc'ts: A. Moore, C. Prince, Dr. A. P. Cater, Jr.,
James Thomason, L. Osborn, Dr. A. Evins, _____Donal. Land where
Robert Gordon lives. Lot for John Gordon. William Dickson (debt).
Appr's: James C. Keys, Andrew Stevenson, S. McCully, Ruben Richey.

APPRAISEMENT: Goods and Chattels of RUBEN JOHNSON, dec'd. made 18
Feb. 1845. Appr's: Martin (his x mark) Phillips, John Williams and
John P. Litton.

SALE BILL: Estate of RUBEN JOHNSON, dec'd. Jas. W. Lewis, Mrs. B.
Johnson, James Ellison, Martin Phillips.

APPRAISEMENT: Property of WM. ELLENBURG, dec'd. 5 Apr. 1845. Shown
by Mrs. Nancy Ellenburg. Appr's: J. B. Lewis, Willis Johnson and
William Holland.

SALE BILL: Estate of WILLIAM ELLENBURG, dec'd. 8 Apr. 1845. Nancy
Ellenburg, bought entire bill, $36.72.

APPRAISEMENT: Estate of DAVID RYKARD, dec'd. 17 Mar. 1845. Sally
and Charles. Appr's: Andrew Riley, James M. Edwards, and George W.
Blackburn.

BILL OF SALE: Estate of DAVID RYKARD, dec'd. Sold 18 Mar. 1845.
Andrew Riley, E. Davis, Thos. Rykard, Thos. Rily, Jacob Rykard,
G. W. Blackburn, H. Rily, Peter Rykard, E. Cater, J. H. Rykard, Birt
Rily, James Edwards, John Anderson, A. Logan, H. Booger, G. Marshall,
B. White, L. Hinton, David Edwards, Rachel Heughy?, Thos. Edwards,
Dr. Leland, F. Logan, Wm. Anderson, Levi H. Rykard, F. A. Buchannon,
E. Cater (boy Charles), H. Booger (girl Sally), Mary Rykard, A. Rykard,
E. Rykard, John Hinton, James Tolbert, N. Jenkins, D. Edwards. Signed:
Levi H. Rykard.

MEMORANDUM: Property appraised Estate of RUBEN ARNOLD, dec'd. 18
Dec. 1844 by David Gambrell, C. H. Simmons and Asa Grant.

SALE: Anderson Dist. 18 Dec. 1844. Sold by E. B. Benson, Adm'r.
Estate of REUBEN ARNOLD, dec'd. Franklin Reeder, Mrs. Arnold, Thomas
Harris, L. Vandiver, Jno. Coats, Geo. Grant, Thos. Simmons, T. C.
McGee, White Yancy, David Gambrell, Anderson Burns, T. H. Simmons,
Robt. Kenly.

INVENTORY: Estate of JAMES STUART, dec'd. 21 Nov. 1844. Negroes:
Bridget (50), Alfred (7), Robert (17). Family Bible. Appr's: Sam'l
G. Earle, S. H. Baker and Hugh Gregg.

SALE BILL: Estate of JAMES STUART, dec'd. Sold 22 Nov. 1844. Mary
Stuart, James Stuart (family Bible), Adam Stuart, George Stuart, Sam'l
Stuart, John Stuart, David Gortney, Wm. McConel, Joel C. Dyer, Thos.
Dean, A. J. Watson, Hugh Gregg, David Obriant, Mathew Dunlap. (James
Stuart, dec'd. - intestate) Adam Stuart took negro woman; Mary Stuart
took negro boy; George Stuart took small boy.

INVENTORY AND APPRAISEMENT: Estate of E. B. MOORE, dec'd. 11 May,
1844. Appr's: Robert Smith, J.? Carpenter, and James E.? Cochran.

SALE BILL: Estate of E. B. MOORE, dec'd. 11 May, 1844. Nancy Moore.
W. Magee, Clerk.

INVENTORY AND APPRAISEMENT: Estate of WILLIAM WALLER, dec'd. 23
Sept. 1844. Negroes: Scipio, Brister and George. Mariah T. Waller,
Admt'rx. P. Vandiver, James L. Orr, J. P. Reed and Fleet Rice, Appr's.

SALE BILL: Estate of WILLIAM WALLER, dec'd. Sold 23 Sept. 1844.
Terms cash. Mariah T. Waller, James Land, R. H.? Waller, negroes
Scipio and man Brister, R. Patriot. Caroline Waller interest in
boy George, 11 years old. P. S. Vandiver.

APPRAISEMENT: Estate of JOHN GENTRY, dec'd. 10 May, 1844. Widow
Gentry kept certain property at appraisement. Appr's: L. Bozeman,
Sam'l McMaken and Hiram Howard.

SALE BILL: Estate (Property) of JOHN GENTRY, decd. Moody Gentry,
Adm'r. Daniel Watson, A. Todd, A. Latham, L. Bozeman, Moody Gentry,
John Herron, S. M. Webb, John Moore, Geo. Stevenson, James Stevenson,
J. J. Watson, H. Howard, Milton Dunlap, Wm. McConnell, Jr., George
Howard, Jno. A. Tate, Chas. Brown, Chs. McConnell, John Garrett, Dan'l
McConnell, Robt. McCearly, Banks Wright. James Stuart, Wm. Latham, Jr.
and A. Todd, Clerk.

ACCOUNT SALE: Of 15 negroes sold by C. L. Gillard, Adm'r of the estate
of Col. SAM'L. WARREN on the 3rd day of Feb. 1845. Anderson C. H.
Terese to Warren Miller; Nero to Charles M. Lay; Ceaser to P. J. Miller,
as also Mariah, Bacchus, Mira, Darcus, Leah and Elizabeth to Allen
McDavid; Polydore to Elisha Borrough; Camilla to Isariah Hembree.

APPRAISEMENT: Personal Estate of JOHN ROBERSON (ROBINSON), dec'd
13 Mar. 1845. Negroes: George, Mark and Rinda. Note on Estin Brock.
Certified by: R. N. Wright, Archibald Armstrong and Jhn Hunt.

SALE BILL: Personal Estate of JOHN ROBINSON, dec'd. 14 Mar. 1845.
Joel Cox, Sam'l Robinson, Berry Armstrong, James Armstrong, W. P. Kay,
John R. Shirly, Thos. Cox, Jas. E. Robinson, L. Robinson, Jas. N.
Richey, Jas. Searight, M. H. Brock, Hugh Robinson, William Cowen,
Caleb Collins, J. E. Davis, R. N. Wright, James Armstrong, Jr., Jno.
B. Armstrong, Geo. Bigby, William Rees, S. M. Trible, Wm. Armstrong,
J. J. Robinson, Thos. Branyan, Henry Cobb, M. H. Brock, Jas. E. Robinson,
Sr., Jno. B. Robinson, James Adams, William Keer?, A. B. Armstrong,
Jno. B. Armstrong, Jas. W. Richey, Col. J. Martin, Jos. W. Kay, Robt.
Wood, R. W. Grubbs, Jas. McMinn, Rich'd Shirly, David Greer, Sr.,
James Wilson, Thompson Hogg, Archibald Armstrong (negro George); Jno.
B. Armstrong (negro Mark); (also girl Rinda); David Williamson. R.
N. Wright, Clerk.

APPRAISEMENT: Estate of J. L. MAULDIN, dec'd. 4 Mar. 1845. Negroes:
Ambrose, Lewis, Milly and child, Harriet. Notes due: B. F. Crayton,
B. F. Mauldin, V. D. Fant, A. J. Liddle, Josias D. Gillard, Samuel
Mauldin, V. D. Fant, A. J. Liddle, Josias D. Gillard, Samuel Mauldin,
Mrs. S. Creswell. Appr's: James L. Orr, John P. Benson and F. Rice.

SALE BILL: Estate of J. L. MAULDIN, dec'd. Sold at public auction
5 Mar. 1845. John Haynie, B. F. Crayton, B. F. Mauldin, A. Cambrell,
J. R. Smith, William Jackson, D. H. Cochran, J. M. Gambrell, James
Harrison, A. J. Donald, S. R. McFall, E. Smith, W. Magee, A. N. McFall,
James Gray, J. C. Keys, M. Murphy, M. Barroughs, Elijah Webb, M. Burris,
F. Rice, J. T. Whitfield, T. L. McBride, A. Holt, P. L. Byrum, J. R.
Smith, J. R. Towers, H. Rily, Mrs. E. Mauldin, E. George, J. H. Creswell,
J. P. Reed, J. B. Wynn, L. A. Osborn, C. Langston, J. P. Benson, J.
Hillhouse, Jesse Smith, B. F. Crayton (man Lewis), J. Mauldin (took
Ambrose, Milly and child), A. Fant (Harriet). John B. Wynn, Clerk.

APPRAISEMENT: Property of MICHAEL ALEYWINE (ALYWINE), dec'd. Late
of Anderson Dist. 19 May, 1845. Notes: J. J. Fisher, L. S. Barns,
John Jones, Levin Bunton (Burton?), Geo. Ricket, T. B. Foster; William
Duncan, Admr. Appr's: R. D. Tucker, John W. Shirly and Hugh Robinson.

SALE BILL: Property of MICHAEL ALEYWINE, dec'd. Sold 20 May, 1845.
Widow Aleywine, Sion Snipes, Jacob Aleywine, J. B. Armstrong, S. M.
Fisher, E. Aleywine, Jr., James Burton, Isaac Robinson, H. Robinson,
P. S. Burton, Thos. Branyan, Caleb Burton, John Elgan, Wm. Duncan, Geo.
Milford, Charles Jones, L. Branson, James Crowther, James Thompson,
E. Aleywine, Sr., L. V. Jones, E. Barn, J. L. Barnes, Jno. Briant,

Moses Ashley, Jacob Sly, H. Prince, J. N. Harkness, J. L. Sly, A. Aleywine, John Wright, Robt. Hall, J. W. Shirly.

INVENTORY: Goods and Chattels of WM. COX, dec'd. 30 May, 1945. (Bible), Negroes: Esther, Peggy, Hannah and Abner. Notes: W. French, L. Johnson, W. Reece, D. F. Lucus, Thos. Cox. F. and R. B. Cox, Ex'rs. Appr's: Joseph Cox and Halbert Acker. Anderson Dist., S. C.

APPRAISEMENT: Estate of ANDREW MC ALISTER, dec'd. Anderson Dist., S. C. 23 Sept. 1845. Note: Margaret P. McAlister. Appr's: J. D. Gaillard, William C. Baily and Andrew Todd.

SALE: Property of Estate of ANDREW MC ALISTER, dec'd. Margaret P. McAlister, John McAlister, Andrew Todd.

APPRAISEMENT: Estate of ANN DUCKWORTH, dec'd. 17 Dec. 1844. Negroes: Sam, Joseph, Fanny, Charry (Channy?). Appr's: Wyatt Smith, Charles Irby and Wm. Smith.

SALE BILL: Estate of ANN DUCKWORTH, dec'd. 25 Dec. 1845. William Duckworth (man Sam), Benjamin Rodgers, Middleton Stott, Wade Ricardson, J. W. Guyton, Jacob Duckworth, William King, Abram Martin, J. W. Rogers (woman Fanny), Chesley Martin, Thos. Duckworth (woman Channy), Welborn Duckworth, Bery Duckworth (man Joe), Bird Mayfield. Pd. to Jacob Duckworth for old negro Hannah.

SALE BILL: Estate of JOHN POOR, dec'd. (Fruit orchards) 12 July, 1842. William S. Thurman, R. Poor, W. Gambrell, R. Holliday, W. Sheraman?, W. A_____.

INVENTORY: Estate of GEORGE BROWN, dec'd. 5 Feb. 1845. (One black woman supposed to be dying.)

APPRAISEMENT: Estate of JNO. HARPER (no date) One negro boy. Notes on hand. Thomas Welborn, Alfred Kelly and W. A. Williams, M. A. D., Appr's.

APPRAISEMENT: Estate of JOHN INGRAHAM, dec'd. Appr'd 30 Sept. 1845. (Very difficult to read...cme) PP 466 and 467 on mfm. Appr's: James Wilson, M. B. Williams, Wm. Webb and Jacob Martin. Notes and Acct's: Jas. Wilson, Willis and Peter Johnson, B. J. Shearman, Benj. Johnson, Tom Masters, John Golden, Jas. Young, Benj. F. Grymes, Benson Bryant, James Chambers, Phillip Ingram, L_____ Bryant, James Masters, Rich'd Golden, Peter King, Nathan R. Bryant, David Owens, David Watkins, Jr., Ben O. Mayfield, Henry McKennen, William Bracken, Saml. Young, Fertnell Mulligan, Wm. Martin, Wm. Elrod, Wilson Vermillion, J. J. Wilson, Wm. Adkins, G. S. Elrod, Saml. Smith, John Duckworth, Mathew Dickson, Henry Brooks, Saml. Golden, Oswell Golden, Jas. Burgess, Chesley Martin, Terril Bryant and Andr'w Oliver.

SALE BILL: Estate of JOHN INGRAHAM (or INGRAM), dec'd. 30 Sept. 1845. Delila Ingram, Wm. Ingram, J. J. Wilson, Jesse Ingram, James Wilson, Chesley Martin, J. _. Guyton, M. B. Williams, J. W. Brothers, T. Harper, James Ingram. M. B. Williams, Clerk. (p. 468 on mfm.)

END OF BOOK

ANDERSON COUNTY DISTRICT, SOUTH CAROLINA

INVENTORIES, APPRAISEMENTS AND SALES

BOOK 2

1845-1851

ABSTRACTED
BY

COLLEEN MORSE ELLIOTT

28 APRIL, 1979

INDEX WITH ORIGINAL BOOK PAGE NUMBERS

MC CURDY, WILLIAM 483
MITCHELL, EPHRAIM 491
MC ELROY, ARCHIBALD 496
NEWELL, WILLIAM 121 and 122 and
  376
NORTH, J. L. 331
NELSON, WILLIAM R. 392
PARRIS, HENRY 264 and 265
PRESLEY, DAVID 326 and 376
PARTAIN, HUBBARD 340
RODGERS, BENJAMIN 46 and 340
ROBERTSON, JOHN 73
REID, HUGH 95
REEVES, JOHN 114
RAINY, JOHN 128
ROBINSON, JOHN JASPER 177
RICE, wid. JANE 234
RODGERS, J. W. 260
RICHIE, JOHN 320
RICHARDSON, DAVID 321 and 352
RILEY, HEZEKIAH 431
REECE, DAVID 513
RICE, IBZAN 508
STANTON, GEORGE 50
SPRAY, THOMAS 132
SMITH, WILLIAM 141
SMITH, NIMROD, SR. 158
SMITH, ELIZABETH 226
SHIRLEY, NIPPER 285
SMITH, JOHN 314
STANTON, CATHARINE 347
SMITH, WILLIAM 371
SLOAN, THOMAS N.? 433
SAWYER, ELIZABETH 442
SEAWRIGHT, MARY 444
SKELTON, GEORGE S. 446
SMITH, JONATHAN H. 466
SPEARMAN, REV. JOHN 473
SHAW, PEYTON R. 475
TRIPP, JOHN 49
TRIPP, WILLIAM 50
VANDIVER, JOHN 137
VANDIVER, SANFORD 160
WATSON, J. J. 61
WADDLE, WILLIAM 78
WARNOCK, JOHN, SR. 124 to 126
WATTERS (WALTERS?), FLEMING 224
WATSON, JAMES 236
WEBB, C. B. 249
WILSON, JOHN 298
WATKINS, JOSEPH 328
WILLIAMS, THOMAS 348
WILSON, JOHN, SR. 359
WALLACE, NELSON 385
WRIGHT, WILLIAM F. 394

INVENTORY - ESTATE OF FAIR KIRKSEY
Dec'd. (no date). Several pages - appears to be inventory of a mer-
cantile store. Mentions Mrs. Pickens and Mrs. Maxwell. Silas Kirksey,
Administrator. Appr's: E. B. Benson, John S. Larton, John Hastie, Elam
Sharpe, Jr. and Thos. R. Cherry. 1 Aug. 1845. (Takes in pages 11-16
in original book).

INVENTORY OF NOTES AND ACCOUNTS - ESTATE OF FAIR KIRKSEY
Dec'd. 1 Aug. 1845. Notes belonging to estate: J. N. Arnold, G. L.
Anderson, J. S. Lorton, F. Burt, O. L. Carmes? (Canns?), Colin Campbell,
James Chapman, E. B. Christian, Renny? Chastain, Sidney Davis, Abner

Dean, Wm. Enix?, Simpson Fountain, Eli Fitzgerald, Thos. D. Garvin,
Sophia Griffin, H. S. Gains, O. P. Hix? (Hin?), J.H. Hopkins, Milton
Hix?, Elias Hollingsworth, J. J. Duke, Philip Ingraham, Jesse Ingraham,
W. L. Jenkins, A. F. Lewis, Richard H. Lee, Jesse Lewis, John Maxwell,
R. A. Maxwell, Isaac McKee, Martin McCay, John Miller, Robt. McKinney,
J. H. Messer ?, Eli Moore, William Nimmons, Wm. M. Orr, B. F. Reeder,
J. H. Reeder, H. D. Reese, John Simmons?, B. Smith, Wm. Steele, Sr.,
Wm. H. Stribling, Stephen M. Wilson, James C. Winter, Isham Williams,
B. F. Wilson, Wm. Bird, Wm. Cooper, Benjamin Chastain, J. B. C. Lewis,
Nancy Laboon, Wiley Owens, John Slaton, Peter Sharp, _____
Book Acct's: Wm. H. Anderson, Elijah Alexander, Edmund Anderson, George
L. Anderson, Mrs. P. Adams, J. N. Arnold, Mrs. Mary B. Anderson, William
Anderson, O. R. Broyles, Frances Burt, Garner Boggs, Lewis Burroughs,
J. W. Bridwell, Ransom Banks, Sr., Lewis Belotte, Thomas Brice, James
Bawden, Joseph Boggs, ___Barnet (mail rider), J. A. Boggs, Neely Boggs,
A. Burns, Baylis Brown, J. E. Calhoun, Sterling Campbell, John C. Cal-
houn, Miss Mary Cherry, Eli Cherry, Miss Sarah Cherry, James W. Crawford,
William Clayton, Sidney Cherry, O. L. Cann, John Caminade, Miss Rebecca
Chapman, Daniel P. Chapman, Samuel Craig, J. J. Duke, Miss Sarah Doyle,
B. Dupree, Sr., Mrs. Mary Dart, W. D. C. Daniels, John B. Davis, Mrs.
Mary A. Duffries, Thomas Davis, J. H. Dendy, Wm. H. Dorsey, Thomas
Dickson, Dr. R. E. Elliot, M. P. Earle, J. W. Earle, Ezekiel Edgar,
Anderson Elis, Judith Edgar, Samuel M. Earle, Hundley Evatt, Sr., Eli
Fitzgerald, Mrs. Faissen?, George Frederick, Miss Helen Faissen, James
Ferguson, Alfred Fuller, O. H. P. Fant, Thomas Fitzgerald, W. Fain, Mrs.
Sophia Griffin, Mrs. R. W. Gaillard, F. N. Garvin, John M. Grubbs, Ran-
som Grist?, Sarah Goode, Martha Goode, A. Gains, Eliha H. Griffin, C.
L. Gaillard, Thos. H. Gains, Thos. D. Garvin, _____ Gould, William P.
Ganier, J. J. Gilman, Jacob Gea____, James Grant, B. F. Holland, William
Hunter (stone Mason), Edward Harleston, James Hunter, Wm. Hix, J. C.
Hall, John Hix, Sr., Robert Hackett, Joseph P. Harris, D. K. Hamilton,
Mrs. Hodges, Jane Harris?, Richard Hallum, Clark Hallum, Henry Hester,
Sam P. Harris, J. B. Harbin, Wm. Hubbard, Abraham Hester, Anderson Hix,
J. F. Heard, John Hix, Jr., J__y Hollingsworth, M. R. Hunnicutt, Wiley
Hollingsworth, Elias Hollingsworth, Susan Harris, Jno. O. Hendricks, Wm.
Hubbard, Sr., Leon S.? Hamilton, W. L. Jenkins, Eliz. Johnson, Eliz.
Johnston (Irish), Robert Johnston, Robert Isbell, Jesse Ingraham, Wm. J.
Knauff, Wm. Kirksey, Jr., G. W. Kilborn, Wm. Kirksey, Sr., R. A. King,
Robert Kirksey, E. W. Kirksey, Henry Keester, Hiram H. King, A. F. Lewis,
James O. Lewis, Martha Lawrence, Jesse P. Lewis, Bird Lenoir, A. J. Lid-
dell, R. A. Maxwell, Samuel E. Maxwell, Robt. A. Mayson, Elijah Mayson,
Henry Miller, John Maxwell, Robt. D. Maxwell, Mrs. J. Miriam Mays, G. W.
McDow, C. B. Moses, John Mason, J. C. Miller, Benj. Mulliken, Jno. F.
Maw?, Nathan Madden, E. G. Mullinex, Wm. McDow, Benjamin Mulliken, Sr.,
Jno. L. North, James Nal, N. Overby, Wm. Odell, Wm. M. Orr, James Powers,
A. C. Pickens, W. J. Patton, Dan. Pike, T.? J. Pickens, Mrs. E. Pickens,
Jno. Phillips, Sr., Arch. Phillips, C. C. Pinckney, Jery? Prator, Sam.
Parsons, Alex Ramsey, D. Russel, Wm. Robinson, John Boledor?, A. W. Ross,
Willis Robinson, Joseph Ritchey, Elizabeth Ritchie, Wm. Russel, Henry
Russel, Lavina Russel, Wm. Robinson, Geo. Seaborn, Benj. F. Sloan, F. W.
Symmes, Nancy Sloan, Thomas M. Sloan, Wm. Sloan, Abram Sarjeant, J. V.
Shanklin, J. B. E. Sloan, Jno. S. Swords, Wm. C. Smith, Elam Sharpe, Jr.,
Benj. Smith, Jno B. Sitton, Nancy Steele, Jno. T. Sloan, John O. Smith,
James Y. Sitton, Jonathan G. Smith, Green Stephens, Benj. Smith (Slab-
town), Elam Sharpe, Joseph Sheeler, Wm. Steele, Nancy Serjeant, David
Stribling, William Sanders, Harvey J. Smith, Joseph Taylor, David S.
Taylor, Jacob Tanas?, Baldwin Thomas, J. C. Thomas, R. T.? Thomas,
Stephen M. Wilson, Sophia Worley, Mrs. Walker, Jno. Watkins, R. L. Wilson,
Mrs. Worley, Eliz. Worley, Thomas White, Sarah White, James H. Worley,
Frederick F. Worley, Thomas C. Watkins, Henry N. White, Felix Worley,...
Trust Estate of Mrs. Catharine Hallum in account with Fair Kirksey, Esq.
Trustee:........; More Book Acct's: Dupre, Lorton & Kirksey, Wilson F.
Burt, F. M. Adams, Samuel Adams, Anderson Burns, Nathan Bryant, Mrs.
James Brock, Jesse C. Crenshaw, John Wright, Mrs. Mays, Samuel E. Mays,
James B. Mays, Nancy Bains, J. W. Earle, Josiah Dean, Estate of Mrs.
Mayrant?......Andrew Oliver, Thos. Humpreys, Mrs. Harris, Jesse Lewis
(23 Mile), J. C. Miller, Mrs. Maroney, Mary McCrery?, James Mulliken,
Bates Blassingame, R. D. Maxwell, R. A. Maxwell, Jhn. Maxwell, John
S. Lorton, Mrs. Pinckney, Wm. Wright, Zachariah Whitten, Harvey Tripp,

251

Dinah Winter, W. G. Singleton, William Maulden, Mrs. Eliza Robinson,
Wm. Robinson, Joseph Reed (gone), Robert Goins, Joel Newton, Wm. Fard?,
Sr., Lucinda Wright.

SALE BILL - ESTATE OF FAIR KIRKSEY
Dec'd. Filed 1 Aug. 1845: Nancy Sloan, J. W. Bridwell, John Maxwell,
D. S. Taylor, Yancy White, Wyatt Smith, L. J. Hallum, Samuel McFall,
George Fredericks, J. B. Earle, Mrs. Mays, J. H. Smith, Benjamin Mull-
igan, Jr., Samuel Morris, Carter Clayton, Eli Fitzgerald, William Mere-
dith, Thomas M. Stribling, D. C. Daniels, R. D. Maxwell, Wm. Sloan, John
Maxwell, Wm. D. Steele, Rev. A. W. Ross?, C. B. Moses, J. L. Orr, J. B.
Earle, Jesse W. Norris, George Seaborn, J. D. Gassoway, Samuel P. Harris,
J. J. Garvin, J. H. Smith, G. L. Anderson, Jno. Maxwell, Jno. F. Miller,
Samuel E. Maxwell, Robt. D. Maxwell, Joseph Taylor, Elam Sharpe, J. B.
Wynne, Wm. Gaillard, J. L. Kenedy, Dr. Miller, L. J. Hallum, W. D.
Steele, A. M. Holland, W. P. Dennis, M. L. Davis, Thomas Yaw, Yancy
White, J. B. Wynne, Andrew Hamilton, Thomas M. Stribling, Elam Sharpe,
Rev. Pierce, G. Brazille, Robert Hubbard, Eli Fitzgerald, Silas Kirksey,
B. Mulligan, J. F. Maw, W. G. Mullinix, E. H. Cox, Col. Orr, Samuel
Morris, Goerge Sherman, James Davis, Joseph Boggs, L. R. Brackenridge,
W. H. D. Gaillard, L. A. Gow (Yow?), W. H. Stribling, J. F. Maw, J. H.
Smith, Carter Clayton, A. C. Pickens, James Thomason, Calvin Hall, W.
P. Dennis, B. F. Crayton, T. J. Hallum, G. L.? Anderson, Thomas Hamilton,
C. S. Gaillard, B. J. Earle, B. B. Harris, _____ Bryce, ____ Cart
(Cash?), W. C. Lee, Andrew Pickens, H. Hammond, ___Simpson, Franklin
Holland, J. V. Shanklin, Samuel Morris, Willis Newton, Ebin Smith,
Ezekiel George, Felix Watkins, J. E. Calhoun, B. F. Rice, John F. Miller,
Robert Craig, J. J. Duke, J. B. McMurry, John Qualls, Wm. Kirksey, Peter
Stephens, V. H. Oppert?, B. F. Holland, G. W. Howard, John Rolletto, Sr.,
Dempsey Yow,.....(this ends on page 45 of original book; mostly bad
film; difficult to read; most names a repeat...cme).

INVENTORY AND APPRAISEMENT - ESTATE OF BENJAMIN RODGERS
Late of Anderson District, dec'd. Appr'd. 2 Dec. 1845. Negroes: Bidy
and two children; Levi?, Edmund, John Demsey, George and wife Sally
and three children, Wade, Nancy and Anderson, Frank and wife Daphne and
four children: John, Lucy, Judy and Frank, Ann and two children: Peter
and Phebe, Eliza, Parry, Jack, Ester, Maria and Ann. Note on W. Duckworth, Brooks Lewis, John A. Dacus, David Lewis, William Simpson, Wm.
Steele, O. R. Broyles, Benjamin Duckworth, Larkins Rodgers, Jerry?
Rodgers, Julias Huff, Albert Bowlin, James Wilson, Richard Rodgers, W.
W. Rodgers. Hester Rodgers, Adm's. Appr's: Charles Irby, Charles Kay,
and Herbert Hammond.

SALE BILL - ESTATE OF BENJAMIN RODGERS
Dec'd. 3 Dec. 1845. 12 months credit. Hester Rodgers, James Beel,
William Murphy, John Rodgers, Wilburn Duckworth, Terral? Bryant, Josiah
Rodgers, S. R. McFall, J. W. Rodgers, John A. Dacus, Joseph Rodgers,
Andrew Brock, W. W. Rodgers, (1 negro woman and 2 children), (Levi);
John Rodgers, (boy Bob, 18 years old and John); Joseph Rodgers, (boy
Edmund, 16 years old); John A. Dacus, (boy Demsey); Larkin A. Rodgers,
(boy Aaron); Hester Rodgers, (man Geroge and wife Sally and 3 children;
Frank and Daphne and 4 children Elich?, Lucy, Judy and Frank; woman An
and 2 children; girl Eliza and boy Berry.) John A. Davis, Herbert
Hammond.

APPRAISEMENT - ESTATE OF JOHN TRIPP
Dec'd. Negro woman and child, Fanny and Mahaly; Margaret; George. 16
Aug. 1845. Thos. Blastegame, Elihu Rea, William Orr, William Sanger,
Appr's.

SALE BILL - ESTATE OF JOHN TRIPP
Dec'd. 21 Aug. 1845. Pur.: John Tripp, Harrison Givin?, Smith Bradley,
Joseph Laboon, Phillip Huff, G. W. Ruhs?, Hugh McGown, Nicholas Childers,
Rufus Oats, James T. Wilson, Norman Clardy, John W. Douthet, William
Orr, Darcus Tripp, John Smith, Mattison Fangrim?, (could be Ingram?),
Nicholas Tripp.

INVENTORY - PERSONAL ESTATE OF PETER MC MAHON
Dec'd. App'd. 4 Oct. 1845 by George Rankin, James Davis, Thomas Orr
and J. M. Smith. Shown by Susan McMahon.

INVENTORY - ESTATE OF WILLIAM TRIPP
Dec'd. Real and Personal. Appr's: John Gambrell, James Thompson and
W. A. Williams.

INVENTORY - GOODS AND CHATTELS OF GEORGE STANTON
Dec'd. Signed by: Elias Elrod, B. H. Douthit and William S___ga?.
30 April, 1845.

INVENTORY - APPRAISEMENT - PERSONAL ESTATE OF JOHN H. CRESWELL, ESQ.
Dec'd. 16 Oct. 1845. (Library and Portraits; interesting inventory).
Negroes: Harriet and child, George; Kitty; Sandy; Lee. Notes: Peter
Byram, J. P. Benson, M. J. Berry, J. W. Brothers, Wm. Brady, Dan'l
Browman?, J. T. Broyles, Charles Langston, John F. Clinkscales, James
Chamblee, Sarah Creswell, Robert Duncan, Wm. Dickson, J. A. Gantt,
David Gurdin, James Gordon, John Golden, J. D. Gaillord, A. L.? Hembree,
Wm. S. Heaton, Wm. Hudson, Wm. Holmes, H. Hammond, John Black, G. W.
Land, A. Mattison, Abraham Massy, Dorcas McPherson, J. L. Orr, C. J.
Prince, J. B. Poor, John Poor, J. L. Padgett, Reuben Richey, Elihu Rea,
John Reid, Ebon Smith, C. __. Stott, D. W. Stott, Thos. Smith, Mary
Tilly, Elijah Webb, H.H. Whiteker, Miss Rebecca McPherson, J. M. Simp-
son, Edward Vandiver, Ephraim Smith, J. N. Whitner, John Smith, B. F.
Sloan, Sarah Creswell, J. Long; L. J. Hammond, Admr. Appr's: J. P.
Benson, Elias Earle, J. W. Hansin?, and P. S. Vandiver. (This followed
by an appraisement of the Law Books belonging to dec'd.) Signed by:
J. N. Whitner, Jos. W. Hemsin? and P. S. Vandiver.

SALE BILL - PROPERTY OF J. H. CRESWELL ESTATE
Dec'd. 23 Oct. 1845. Samuel J. Hammond, Alitha L. Creswell, (took
negro woman and boy Georg (e); boy Sandy; boy Lee), William Magee, Mil-
ford Burroughs, J. W. Hamson?, V. D. Fant, Elijah Webb, B. F. Hammond,
C. C. Hammond, W. B. Gibson, S.? T. Broyles, Elias Earle, D. H. Cahran,
A. P. Cater, A. D. Donnader?, J. P. Benson, A. O. Norris, J. P. Rice?,
J. L. Orr, A. N. McFall, L. L. McBride, P. S. Vandiver, E. G. Smith,
Sarah Creswell, W. L. Hammond, Fleetwood Rice, J. P. Cockran, John
Haynie, Wm. Hamson, P. D. Major, J. C. Keys, James Gray, Joshua Bour-
oughs, Jas. Brownlee, John H. Burton, (negro girl Kitty).

SALE BILL - ESTATE OF WESTLEY EARP
Dec'd., late of Anderson District, S. C. Sold 23,24, and 25 Dec. 1845.
Thomas Burriss, Cornelius Latham, Richard S. Gains, Reuben L. Tyler,
James Brooks, James Gilmer, James B. Alexander, Reuben Tyler, Jr.,
Joshua Hutcheson, Elias McGee, Alexander Campbell, Charles Barrett, Dr.
A. Thompson, Rily Burriss, William Caldwell, Martin H. Smith, John
Brown, Joseph Caldwell, James Chamblee, (negro man Larkin), David Mc-
Connell, G. V. White, Capt. Joseph Caldwell, Henry Gamson, David L.
Leadbetter, John Hardy, Wm. Ransom, James Taylor, C. Smith, Charles
Haynie, (negro man Charles), James Dobbins, Aaron Dobbins, Reuben Burris,
(negro man Elias), Charles K. Williford, (negro girl Sarah), Marcus
Carter, Frances Harrison, Willis Croft, A. Simpson, Hugh Caldwell,
George Shelton, Francis Wood, Mrs. Reid, Milton McRees, Thomas O. Hill,
James L. Simpson, Capt. W. F. Phillips, Franklin Brice, Moses J. Carden?,
C. B. Webb, Robert West, Isaac West, Mrs. Lucinda Rimmer, Mrs. Mary
Masters, Samuel Fendley, Peyton R. Shaw, A. S. McClinton, John Caldwell,
David Saddler, Capt. Sam'l G. Earle, Joseph B. Glenn, Samuel Buchanan,
James B. Gains, Mrs. Mourning Earle, William Sherrard, Micajah Carter,
Ezekiel White, John Hall, Frances Henning?, Andrew McLees, D. M. Beaty,
William Glenn, Exr. 25 Dec. 1845. James Gilmer, Clerk.

APPRAISEMENT - ESTATE OF WESTLEY EARP
Dec'd., late of Anderson District, S. C. William Glenn, one of the
Exr's. of estate. 20 Dec. 1845. (Methodist magazines and a Bible).
Negroes: Charles, Larkin, Elias, Jenney and child, Tilda, Cenda and boy
Aaron, Betsey, Sarah. Notes due: John Brooks, Reuben Tyler, Rebecca
McDaniels, C. Latham, J. M. Gains, Sam'l G. Earle, W. W. Dooly, Abner
Siddle, Wm. Glenn. 20 Dec. 1846? Signed: Charles Haynie, A. S. Mc-
Clinton.

APPRAISE BILL - ESTATE OF J. J. WATSON
Dec'd. 4 Nov. 1845. (Family Bible). Appr's: Moody Gentry, L. Bozeman, Hiram Howard, Moses Deen.

SALE BILL - ESTATE OF J. J. WATSON
Dec'd. 5 Nov. 1845. J. G. Watson, Hiram Howard, Mary Watson, D.? P.
Neal, M. L. Watson, Thomas Neal, Robt. McCorley, Moses Dean, Wm. Long,
J. P. Neal, J. M. Caldwell, Christopher Neal, D. S. McKinny, L. Boze-
man, John Stewart, S.? E. Parker, Tilman Tate, Thomas Dean, V. D. Gary,
John Haney, Wm. McConnel, A. M. Neal, Lewis Clinkscales, M. Gortney,
E. Norris, Esq., Lent? Hall, H. Canada. 7 Nov. 1845. J. B. Watson,
Clerk.

APPRAISE BILL - GOODS AND CHATTELS OF AMBROSE H. JONES
Dec'd. 18 Nov. 1845. Appr's.: Adam Elrod, William A. Elrod, Burrel
A. Dalton.

INVENTORY AND APPRAISEMENT - ESTATE OF ROBERT GUYTON
Dec'd. 11 Nov. 1845. Negroes: Isaac, (age 42), Betsy and child Margaret Ann, Caroline, (age 14), Eliza, 12 years, John, (age 11), Ben,
(age 8), Warren, (age 6), Henry, (age 3). Signed: Wyatt Smith, Thos.
H. Garret, and W. Duckworth.

SALE BILL - ESTATE OF ROBERT GUYTON
Dec'd. 12 Nov. 1845. Hester Guyton, John Guyton, L. J. Hammond, J. D.
Amack, Charles Irby, Hosea Simpson, S.? V. Simpson, Jesse Crow?, D. H.
Cochran, Samuel Millwee, Wyatt Smith, (boy Isaac),.Hester Guyton, (wo-
man and children, Caroline, Eliza, John, Ben, Warner, Harry), W. W.
Rogers, Benj. Duckworth, Clerk.

APPRAISE BILL - ESTATE OF JOHN HARRIS, ESQ.
Dec'd. Negroes: Priscilla and child; Clarissa; Tom; Jincy?; Willis;
Harry (Henry); Hannah; Lazarus; 218 acres of land. Signed: John Max-
well, H. Ackin, James Steele, J. C. Miller.

SALE BILL - ESTATE OF JOHN HARRIS
Dec'd. J. P. Harris, B. B. Harris, Jno. Maxwell, Jas. Harris, Wm. F.
Woolbright, Jas. J. Coates, H. J. Sanders, Tillman McGee, R. A. Maxwell,
Jordan Burris, Thos. Simmons, Arch Phillips, C. Buttons?, Chas. Whitworth,
Yancy White, C. P. Bruce, Jno. Coates, A. McCray, C. B. Moses, S. W. Kay,
M. R. Hunnicut, Berry Philips, J. C. Miller, Dobsen Reese, (Bible), Al-
bert McCrary, Meredith Speers, E. McCrary, Ira Brooks, Jacob Belot, R. D.
Maxwell, Wm. Kimbell, N. Harris, Samuel C. Maxwell, Daniel Hix, Andrew
Harris, L. J. Pickens, J. C. Reeder, Wm. Hancock, Robert Hays, Thos. N.
Harris, R. E. Elliott, N. Harris, (negroes Lot and Phillis), J. P. Harr-
is, (negroes Jincy and child, Clarrisa), C. B. Moses, (Willis and Laza-
rus), Jas. J. Coats, (Henry), George Seaborn, (Hannah), Levi Herring,
(Mary), B. B. Harris, (Tom), Samuel Brown, Ira Gambrell, Jno. Grubbs,
Mary Harris, Wm. Meredith. Signed: H. H. Bruce.

INVENTORY - ESTATE OF JOSEPH CLARK
Dec'd. 12 Dec. 1845. Large Bible. Note: Wm. Geer. S. M. Carpenter,
Exr. Signed: Olly Mattison, John Carpenter, and William Keaton.

INVENTORY AND APPRAISEMENT - ESTATE OF ANDERSON BURNS
Late of Anderson Dist., dec'd. 7 July, 1845. Extr's, (not named).
Signed: J. A. Moore, J. G. Bowden, and W. Magee.

APPRAISE BILL - PERSONAL ESTATE OF JOHN ROBERTSON
Dec'd. 18 Nov. 1845. Notes: Mark L. Anthony, Wm. Hutchison, Charles
Brown, George B. Burditt, Stephen Cash?; Negroes: Aaron, Lucy, Chat?
and her child Benjamin, Bill, Nelly, Moses, Manda and her child Caroline,
Dinah, Charlet and her child Pinkney, Dick, Samuel, Matilda, Edward,
James, Hannah, Susannah, Aaron, Jr., Simon, Andrew. Signed: Andrew
Reed, Martin Hall, William Sherard, P. Price?, and David Hall.

SALE BILL - PERSONAL ESTATE OF JOHN ROBERTSON
Dec'd. Sold 25 and 26 Nov. 1845. John Adams, Charles Bowie, John Black,
William O. Briant, Rev. J. C. Chalmers?, Lewis Clinkscales, William Cook,

R. D. Brigg?, Martin Hall, John Hall, David Hall, Haggis, (or Hagger?),
(girl Nelly), John Latham, William Lestly, William McKee, David McKinney,
Nathan McAlister, John A. Martin, George P. Pettigrew, (Matilda and
James), Mark Prince, James Robertson, Jane Robertson, (widow), (Aaron,
Sr., Lucy and Andrew, her child, Chat and Benjamin, her child, Bill,
Moses, Manda and her child Caroline, Dinah, Charlot and her child,
Pinkney, Dick, Samuel, Edmund, (or Edward), Hannah, Susannah, Aaron, Jr.,
Simeon), William Sherrard, Andrew Todd, Dr. Matthew Thomson, Maj. James
Thomson, George Young. John H. Reid, Clerk. 5 Dec. 1845.

APPRIASE BILL - ESTATE OF WILLIAM WADDLE
Dec'd. 13 Nov. 1845. Negro: man George considered a chargable. Note:
Yancy Hall. Appr's: James Smith, Robert Pickens, and John Pegg.

BILL OF SAEL - ESTATE OF WILLIAM WADDLE
Dec'd. 14 Nov. 1845. Pur.: Wm. Waddle, James W. Smith, James D. Smith,
John David, John Pegg, Richard Davis, James Henderson, (Wm. Waddle got
George at $100 dollars to take care of him during said negro's life at
the lowest bidder.)

INVENTORY AND APPRAISEMENT OF ESTATE OF WILLIAM MITCHELL
Doods, Chattels, Rights and Credits of Estate of William Mitchell, dec'd.
19 Oct. 1846. Signed: R. N. Wright, William Davis, and Posey Trussell.

SALE BILL - PERSONAL PROPERTY OF WILLIAM MITCHELL
Dec'd. 20 Oct. 1846. Pur.: William P. Kay, Hampton Stone, John L.
Davis, William Davis, Strother Kay, Moses Davis, Samuel V. Gambrell,
Thomas Davis, John Wilson, Matthew A. Davis, Daniel Mattison, Vinson
Shaw, Benjamin Mattison, Joe Kay, J. G. Gantt, William Kay, Sr., William
Davis, Thomas Cox, Jr., Huldah Mitchell, Jesse Gent, Hanson Davis. J.
G. Gantt, Clerk.

APPRAISE BILL - ESTATE OF JAMES ERSKINE, SR.
Dec'd. 30 Apr. 1846. Note: William and James Bell.

SALE BILL - ESTATE OF JAMES ERSKINE, SR.
Dec'd. 1 May, 1846. Morris Erskin, John Erskin, Widow Erskin, William
Erskin, James Major, Sr., William Erskine, Jr., Thomas Erskin, James
Erskin, Rhoda Trussel, John Smith, John Guyton, Washington Erskin, James
Bell, Samuel Dawson, Leroy Hammond, William Holmes, Pinkney Major,
Gideon Land, Widow Dobbins, Hugh Erskin, Enoch Major, S. F. McConnel,
Mary McDowel, (McDavid?), Wm. R. Erskin, Asa Vandiver, Samuel Dawson,
Widow Dobson, Widow McCracken. (Second sale - 2 Nov. 1846) Thomas
McConnel, Sr., Clerk. (Note - the name Erskine is spelled through the
text - Erskin...cme).

INVENTORY AND APPRAISE BILL OF ESTATE OF GEORGE CRYMES
Dec'd. Eight negroes: Hudson, Hannah and child Winny, Peter, Eliza,
Washington, John, Jensy?. P. C. Oates or Lestor?, Exr. 25 Dec. 1845.
Appr's.: W. A. Williams, Hugh Wilson, Elijah Pepper, Miles Ellison.

SALE BILL - ESTATE OF GEORGE CRYMES
Dec'd. Sold 26 Dec. 1845. William Adcock, B. F. Crymes, (family Bible),
Robert D. Crymes, (girl Jinny), Ann Cooly, Nancy Crymes, (girl Eliza),
Pascel Cureton?, (boy Peter), W. M. Cooly, Jacob Duckworth, Miles Ell-
ison, William Galospy, Jeptha Harper, S. Holland, Thomas Harper, Charles
Irby, Allen Kelly, William Kelly, P. C. Lestor, Wm. H. Lester, (negroes
Hannah, Winny, Washington, John), Grant A. Moore, Elijah Pepper, G. W.
Poor, Larkin Rodgers, John Rodgers, R. Rodgers, Mitchel Scot, E. Tripp,
Hugh Wilson, James Woolbanks, W. A. Williams, Thos. Welborn, Rev. Frank
J. Crymes. 3 Jan. 1846. Phil C. Lester, Acting Exr..

APPRAISE BILL - PERSONAL ESTATE OF A. BROYLES
Dec'd. 12 Dec.?, 1845. Negroes: Alse George and Ann?, Baylis, Violet,
Ezekiel, Polly and two children, Mary Ruston Milton Rachel and Will, Sam,
Nancy and Nancy, Matilda Jefferson Lazarus?, Cinda Milford and Jack,
Catherine and Israel, Elias, Monah and Harvey, Manuel and Eliza, Big Jim,
Tennessee Jim, Jesch?, Abram Winny and __?. (Theses names run together).
Appr's.: B. F. Mauldin, Joseph Cox, and Halbert Acker. Appraisement
cont'd.: (Note: This writing very faint and difficult to read). J. D.

255

Lewis, B. Magee, M. J. Brown, C. P. Dean, ...G. Stone, John Ashley,
Milly Jordan, ...D. Cochran, A. Cornelius, J. B. Moloy, Jerry Smith,
A. Brock, Jno. Cochran, Richard Smith. 14 Feb. 1846.

SALE BILL - ESTATE OF A. BROYLES
Dec'd. Sold Dec. 17, 18, and 19, 1845. John B. Póor, G. Horton, (
Manuel and Eliza), Dr. G. R. Brown, Pinkney Todd, Jesse Wardlaw, M.
Lawlis, Capt. J. P. Reid, (one negro girl), Col. A. Welborn, Sally Cox,
W. Southern, David Ruff, Stephen Clement, A. M. Gaines, J. H. Fite?,
Griffin Smith, (Note: p. 88 mostly illegible; very faint), John L.
Davis, Dr. O. R. Broyles, Mathias Roberts, Caleb Holland, B. F. Maulden,
......William Telford, William Holmes, William Phillips, D. H. Gambrell,
A. E. Mitchel, John H. Harper, William Holland, Dan'l. Mattison, Harper
Gambrell, F. A. Ragsdale, H. Tripp,....Capt. John Lewis, Dr. C. C.
Hammond, John Walker, Dr. James Broyles, (Ezekiel, Polly, Emeline, Martha,
Milton, William, Mary, Rachel), William Gibson, (Dick), C. P. Dean, D.
Majors, A. Fant, Josiah King, A. R. Broyles, Geo. Stone, ____ McGown,
Isaac Davis, David Duncan, Vincent Shaw, Michael Magee, Austin Williams,
Jesse French, Joseph Hughs, Samuel Bell, H. Acker, Maj. J. T.? Broyles,
(George and Ann, Violet and Baylis, Big Jim), William Cooley, Joseph
Cox, Miles Ellison, James E. Allen, Nace Morrison, Geo. Kay, Geo. Ruff,
Grant Moore, P. D. Major, J. M. Gambrell, William Smith, Cain Broyles,
David Cummings, Henry Tripp, Jacob Roberts, (Sam, wife and children).

INVENTORY AND APPRAISEMENT - ESTATE OF JOHN MC COY
Dec'd. 9 Dec. 1845. Appr's.: Strother Kay, P. D. Major, and Asa P.
Vandiver.

SALE BILL - ESTATE OF JOHN MC COY
Dec'd. 9 Dec. 1845. Pur.: Widow, H. Lattimer, P. D. Major, A. Mayfield,
Terry Gambrell, W. Holmes, M. Magee, S. Kay, W. P. Todd, W. Trussel, S.
McFall, J. L. Todd. M. McGee.

SALE BILL - ESTATE OF LAVENDER BENTON
Dec'd. 25 Nov. 1845. R. Branyan, William Wilson?, L.? M. Branyan,
James Robinson, A. Branyan, Thos. Sims, C. L. Nelson, Isaac Robinson,
J. Briant, W. Pearman, Bartholomew Notz, Thomas Branyan, James Hopkins,
Eli Barnes?.

INVENTORY AND APPRAISEMENT - PERSONAL ESTATE OF THOMAS ELROD
Dec'd. Taken 14 Oct. 1845. Negro woman Rose and boy Jerry. Anderson
District, S. C. Samuel Smith, John Herron, and A. O. Norris, Appr's.

SALE BILL - PERSONAL ESTATE OF THOMAS ELROD
Dec'd. 15 Oct. 1845. Mary Elrod, John McPhail, Caroline Elrod, Alfred
Elrod, Albert Elrod, David Elrod, Lurna? Elrod, J. W. Norris, James
Fowler, Thomas Dean, John Duncan, Maberry Snipes, John Harkness, John
Haynie, D. S. McKinny, James P. Gray, Ezekiel Elrod, D. H. Cochran,
Sam'l. Smith, J. J. Branyan, J. A. Tate, Wm. M. Archer, Wm. Holmes,
Enoch Major, B. F. Duncan, Henry Branyan, A. D. Gray, James Harrison,
Lucinda Black, John Herron, B. C. Haynie, Wm. Caldwell, John McFall,
Thomas Geer, G. W. Johnson, Alfred Elrod, (woman Rose), Mary Elrod,
(Boy Jerry), John Herron, Clerk.

SALE BILL - ESTATE OF WILLIAM COX
Dec'd. 30 Dec. 1845. R. B. Cox, Joel Kay, John L. Davis, Mason Kay,
Jesse French, Frances Cox, (Peggy and Bible), James Bagwell, Jesse Cox,
Martin Stone, William Kay, Thomas Davis, James Kay, Joseph Cox, David
Reese, Martin Williamson, M. Magee, James Armstrong, Helday Cox, W. S.
Greer, H. Mattox, Thos. Cox, M. E. Mitchel, Washington Clement, W. S.
Phillips, H. Acker, Robert Drake, Ephraim Mitchel, Halbert Cobb, Thos.
Carter, D. W. Lewis, (Esther and Abner), Daniel Brown, (Ann), James
Holeda. 31 Dec. 1845. Joseph Cox, and Abner Cox, Clerks.

INVNETORY AND APPRAISEMENT - ESTATE OF HUGH REID
Dec'd. 9 Jan. 1846. Negro children: Molly, Malissa and Elias. Appr's.:
Joseph Caldwell, Samuel Buchanan, and James Caldwell.

SALE BILL - ESTATE OF HUGH REID
Dec'd. Sold 9 Jan. 1846. Hugh Caldwell, James Caldwell, Charles Haynie,

256

Robert Gilmer, James A. Taylor, George Herndon, John Caldwell, William
F. Philips, Robert Gilmer, Alex. Campbell, George Campbell, Isaac West,
Thomas Burriss, Robert Reid, John Harris, Samuel Buchanan Cornelius
Latham, Wm. H. Bullman, (also spelled Bulware), Daniel Watson, James
Busby, David McConnel, A. S. McClinton, John Brown, Elizabeth Reid, M.
R. Manning, Levi Boroughs, Wm. Caldwell, Wm. Reid, T.? A. Skelton,
Martin Smith, Hugh Caldwell, Wm. F. Phillips, Hiram Gentry, Robert Reid,
Daniel Watson, (man Caeser?), Thomas Skelton, (Lavina?, Mary, Malissa
and Elias), A. S.? Y. Siddle, (Liddle?), A. L. McClinton, Samuel McGee,
John K. Lilly, L. D. Williford. 24 Jan. 1846. Robert Reid, Clerk.

INVENTORY - GOODS, CHATTELS, RIGHTS AND CREDITS OF DANIEL BROOKS
Dec'd. M. McGee, Admr. 1 July, 1846.

SALE BILL - ESTATE OF DANIEL BROOKS
Dec'd. Sold 1 July, 1846. B. McGee, M. McGee, Noel F. Strickland,
Mary A. Brooks, P. N. Wright, G. R. Brown.

INVENTORY AND APPRAISE BILL - CHESTER KINGSLEY
Dec'd. 6 Apr. 1846. Negroes: Sam, (48 years), ____, (48), Martha, (3),
Elizabeth, (20), Jane, (11), Mary, (9), Luanda? (?), Jesse, (22), George
(17), Lemuel, (15), Peter, (14), John, (13), Ned, (18), Grace, (27),
Liza, (10, Elvira?, (8), Emely, (5), Barbary, (15), ____ and child,
____, (2), Cato, (37), ____, (1), Meshack, (25), Polly, (12); large
family Bible. Sale cont'd. on Monday, 4 May, 1846. Acct's: George R.
Brown, Jeremiah Smith, David Mayson, A. Mattison, Thos. Smith, Abram
Hill, Rodam Trussel, Pinkney Mitchel, Milly Stricklin, Jacob and Eliza
(Elza?) Ketsinger?, widow Sintha White, (small pocket Bible),; Notes:
Obadiah Shirley, John Wilson, George Bigbee, Archiabald Bigbee, David
Wright, M. McGee, J. Brown, Mason Kay, T. J. Broyles, Peter King?, Hal-
bert Acker, J. L. Davis, H. Roberson?, W. R. Farley, Henry Cobb, George
Mattison, Nancy Howe?, Dillon? Grimes, Andrew and William Dun, John
Brownlee, R. N. and John Wright, Elijah Webb, Harrison Elgin, R. L. Smith,
Johnson E. Brock, R. G. McClinton?, Asa P. Vandiver, Joshua Hollan, Cain
Broyles, Hampton Stone, W. Long, H. Long, John Moore, J. G. Gant, J. J.
Robinson, C. T. Latimer, D. and A. W. Smith, Wm. Allen, B. Bagwell,
Micajah Gambrell, Wm. Gambrell, John Hughes, James Williamson, Wm. Fant,
Newton Hill, H. Norris, D. Brooks, C. Cook, E. W. Banester, David Duning,
Mary King, Nathan Jeffers, C. Broyles, George Grubb, G. D. King, R.
Trussel, B. Nixon, W. M. Bell, Redman Bagwell, Reuben Flowers, James
Nixon, Ed.... Gains, James Mitchel, Josiah Rutlege, John Leach?, Jesse
Morris, E. Hand, John Morrison?, P. T. Anderson, Thos. Dow?, Wm. Nor-
wood, James Thomas, J.... Johnson, Robt. Maddox, Larkin Maddox, George
Furman?.

SALE BILL - GOODS, CHATTELS OF CHESTER KINGSLEY
Dec'd. as kept and sold 5 May, 1846: Phillip Lee, John Cox, P. D. Major,
Nathan Shirley, A. N. McFall, Z. Hall, Esq., J. E. Robinson, Rody Truss-
el, Obadiah Shirley, M. McGee, Dr. Brown, Henry Steel, L. R. McFall,
Abner Cox, Strother Kay, W. P. Kay, J. W. Featherston, Wm. Cox, George
Ruff, Alfred Carpenter, Thos. Cox, F. Rice, Robert Brownlee, Arch Arm-
strong, E... Wright, Phillip Lee, Isaac Robins, James Wilson, Charles
Evins, George Brown, Henson Posey, Sam'l. Robinson, George Roof, A. M.
Carpenter, Esten Brock, Wm. McGee, Jackson Richey, John Gains, James
Brownlee, Vinson Shaw, Isaac Robinson, J. B. Armstrong, L. M. Williams,
J. Martin, Bery Johnson, A. W. Smith, W. P. Kay, R. O. Treble, A. C.
Hathern, John Donnald, A. N. McFall, David Roof, Ibzan Rice, Ben Johnson,
D. H. Cochran, Elijah Webb, J. W. Agnew, J. P. McGee, Jacob Alewine,
R. W. Todd, R. F. Wyatt, Isaac Robinson, (Bible), H. Latimer, M. McGee,
(Family Bible), John Horton, W. B. Gibson, J. Branyan, Dr. Milford,
Jesse Ghent?, C. P. Dun, S. Adams. Sale Bill cont'd.: 3 Nov. 1846.
J. J. Robinson, Ephraim Mayfield, Stephen Shirley, James Brown, Wm.
Erskine, Arch Armstrong, Alfred Carpenter, Labon Massey, W. Reese, Nimrod
Greer, A. Holt, Rev. J. Wilson, James King, James Armstrong, John Bran-
yan, W. Stone, John Ashley, J. Reid, R. S. Smith, Caleb Collins, Robt.
Parker, G. W. Nelson, Wm. Pruett, James Telford, Jackson Richey, Osten?
Mayfield, Lidd Williams, A. Harper, B. F. Gambrell, Thomas McConnel,
Andrew Webb, J. R. Martin, R. B. McAdams, John Gant, James Gordon, F.
A. Ragsdale, Jeremiah Smith, Wm. Jackson. Negroes Purchased: Albert

Dollar, (Sam, wife and child, Martha; Mary and Lucinda), H. L. Richey, (Lewis?), E. P. Mosely, (Elizabeth), J. R. Wilson, (Ned), B. F. Maulden, (Jess), C. L. Latimer, (George), J. W. Agnew, (Peter), Albert Dollar, (Jane, Tom, John), Geo. Mattison, (Polly, Gracey and child), A.......
Clinkscales, (Lettice and three children), A. McDavid, (Meshack), John McFall, (Eliza), John Wakefield, (Barbary), W. P. Todd, A. M. Elgin, Archy Mattison, Danl. Major, Alfrod Fant, Enoch Major, Abner Clinkscales, John Hanks.

INVENTORY AND APPRAISE BILL - ESTATE OF ELIJAH BROWN
Dec'd. Note on: John Hayne, Elijah Webb, Clayton Webb, Luke Hayne, Thomas Burriss, Sam'l. and Robt. Martin, J. C. Miller, John Dickison, Isham Brown, W. A. McMillan, John E. Norris, Robert Keys, John Butler, James McLeskey, John Morris, James Morris, James G. Brown, Stephen Mc-Cully, J. C. Kays, John Todd, William Haynie, ...Montgomery, Wilson Vermillion, John Archer, E. and D. Stribling, John Butler, Andrew Elrod, John Coker, Stephen Chastain, Hiram Harbin, Elias R. Totter?, Samuel Smith, James Moore, John Carsen. Negroes: Middleton, Nancy and child Lucy Farris?, _____, a girl 16 years old. Appr's.: W. Magee, J. G. Gretwell, and J. B. Skelton.

SALE BILL - PROPERTY OF ELIJAH BROWN
Dec'd. Sold 3 Nov. 1846. B. Buroughs, C. Brown, Reuben Gentry, John Fretwell, John Brown, W. R. Burriss, E. Smith, A. B. Gentry, Joseph D. Scott, L. Orsborn, L. Scott. Negroes sold to: C. Brown, (Nancy and child; Lucy, Mid. and Ann).

APPRAISE BILL - PROPERTY OF JAMES MC CARLEY
Dec'd. 23 Oct. 1846. Negroes: Rachel, Lysa, Margaret, Dick, Ellen. Signed: Samuel Martin, David L. Leadbetter, James Dobbins. Test.: James McLeskey.

INVENTORY AND APPRAISE BILL - GOODS, CHATTELS OF ELIZABETH E. GRAY
Dec'd. 17 Nov. 1846. Negroes: Caleb; woman and child; Allen; Randolph; Elic; Emily. Note on: David Simpson, A. Simpson. Signed: Willis McGee, Thos. O. Hill, and J. Melton Simpson.

INVENTORY AND APPRAISE BILL - ESTATE OF WILLIAM JONES
Dec'd. 4 Nov. 1846. Negroes: Jess, (abt. 28), Tempy and child, Ed-ward; Dick, (abt. 13); Matilda, (abt. 14), and Clorinda, (abt. 10). Signed: J. C. Eaton, Michael Melton, and Berry Mills. Test.: C. L. Gaillord.

SALE BILL - ESTATE OF WILLIAM JONES
Dec'd. 5 Nov. 1846. Wilson Jones, Adm'r. Jackson Jones, C. L. Gail-lard, Joseph Eaton, J. D. Scott, William Owens, William Jones, Berry Mills, Wyatt Smith, J. B. Hunnicut, John Key, Thomas Harper, Michael Melton, Nimrod Smith, Elijah Owens, _. W. Richardson, Bailis Walkins, (Watkins?), Jesse Cox, John Hunter, William Lewis, William Smith, Elijah Teas, Thos. Duckworth, (boy Dick), Ann _____, (Jess, Joshua Wilson, (Matilda), Sam'l. Milwee, (Clarinda), Whitaker Smith, (woman and child).

APPRAISE BILL - ESTATE OF JOHN REEVES
Dec'd. 6 Nov. 1846. Negro: George. A. J. Liddele, Clerk and one of the Appr's.

SALE BILL - PROPERTY OF JOHN REEVES
Dec'd. 17 Nov. 1846. J. A. Reeves, (George), William Hembree, Jacob King, D. W. Smith, R. W. Reeves, James Ingram, C. Barrit, M. Anderson, G. P. Gentry, Charles Bryson, Joseph Moore, A. J. Liddle, H. Lyles, B. Mason, Reuben Gentry, Sam'l. Brown, H. Tyler, J. B. Hays, Elias Brown, John Kay, James Hembree, Charles Todd, J. P. Watson, R. Gentry, Jesse Gray, A. D. Hembree, Andrew Moore, Charles Bryson. E. Smith, Cryer; Isaac B. Hays, Clerk.

APPRAISE BILL - ESTATE OF ANDREW M. BUCHANAN
Dec'd. 10 Oct. 1846. Z. Hall, J. Thomson, and B. Gassaway, Appr's.

SALE BILL - ESTATE OF ANDREW M. BUCHANAN
Dec'd. 16 Oct. 1846. Conrad Wakefield, R. W. Hall, Ezekiel Hall, Wm.
A. Hall, Sam'l Buchanan, Wm. J. Milford, L. M. Hall, B. Calahan.

2nd APPRAISE BILL & SALE - ESTATE OF SPENCER BROWN
Dec'd. Negroes: Moris, Edee and Sonney. Note: Larkin Brown. Sale
Bill: Peter E. Burton, Abraham Burton, B..... Hix, D. J. Hix, R. M.
Brown, Nicholas Brown, A. C. Dobbins, John Dyer, Alex. Connell, William
Dyer, James Carter, H. F. Chandler, John Crocker, Welborn Wilding,
Larkin Brown, Obediah Brown, Lewis Aderholt, William P. King, Mathew
Martin, Lewis Right, Jesse Dyer, Isaac Wilding, William Meredith,
Samuel Bobbo, Wm. Williams, C. Dobbins, John Wakefield, Wm. Dyer, Saml.
Richardson, Dempsey Bobbo, Benjamin Brown, Archibald Cole, Abram
Meredith, Jediah Ayers, Abraham Coffin, Wm. Dyer, B. J. Price

APPRAISE BILL & INVENTORY - ESTATE OF WILLIAM NEWELL
Dec'd. Negroes: Ferriba? and 2 children Harriet and Hiram: Lucy, Ben
and Crawford. Jincy Newell, Ext'rx. 19 Nov. 1846. App'r. by John
Liverett, James Tucker and A. D. Gray.

SALE BILL - ESTATE OF WILLIAM NEWELL
Dec'd. Purs.: Jincy Newell (Pheriba and 2 children), John Newell
(Lucy), William Newell, L. M. Hall, Col. J. Thompson, D. L. McKinney,
Mark Prince, John Liverett, Thomas A. Beaty, Lent Hall, E. Ervin,
Thomas Newell (Ben), Hannah Newell, R. W. Hall, James Tucker, W. J.?
Millford, James Lockhart, John Hall, R. D. Gray, Ezekiel Hall (Crawford).
J. M. Hamilton, Clerk.

SALE BILL- GOODS & CHATTELS - ESTATE OF JOHN WARNOCK, SR.
Dec'd. 18 Nov. 1842. Pur.: Samuel R. McFall, Mary Todd, John Warnock,
David Gear, Eleanor Warnock (girl Tena), S. R. McFall, Admr. 1843 -
Rec'd cash to estate. 21 Dec. 1846. S. R. McFall, Admr.

SALE BILL - ESTATE OF JOHN WARNOCK, SR.
Dec'd. 16 Jan. 1846. John Warnock (woman Betty and 3 children; Mandy,
Lucy and infant; man Dick), Mary Todd (boy Henry), Alexander Stephenson,
A. N. McFall, Strother Kay, J. W. Harrison, S. R. McFall, John
Carpenter, William P. Todd, Nimrod Kay, S. H. Baker (girl Tena), Solomon
Gear (man Scipio), James Todd, Rebekah Love, Wm. P. Hawkins, Thomas
Gear, Mrs. S. McCracken, John M. Hamilton, William Holmes, Samuel
Dawson, P. D. Major, J. L. Pagett, D. Major, Aaron Vandiver, William
Harrison, Meredith Brock, Robert Smith, William Nevitt, B. F. Hopkins,
Rev. W. Carlisle, Dempsey Hill, R. W. Todd, Samuel Bell, Jeptha
Vandiver, A. Todd. S. R. McFall, Adm'r.

APPRAISE BILL & INVENTORY - ESTATE OF SAMUEL CUNNINGHAM
Dec'd. Thomas Cunningham, Ex'r. 19 Dec. 1846. Appr's: Samuel G.
Earle, E. S. Norris, S. H. Baker. Salves: Peter, Allen, Joe, Tom,
James. 300 acres of land.

APPRAISE BILL & INVENTORY - ESTATE OF JOHN RAINY
Dec'd. 29 Dec. 1846. Appr's: Samuel Baker, Lindsey Baker, Williamson
Dollar. Henry Cosper, Clerk.

SALE BILL - ESTATE OF JOHN RAINY
Dec'd. Sold 1 Jan. 1847. Henry Cosper, Daniel E. Connel (Conwell?),
David McConnel, James Taylor, James Phillips, Joseph Caldwell, Robert
Gilmer, M. R. Manning, James Conwell, Allen McConnel, Hiram Frost,
Samuel Williford, Levi Garrison, Jesse C. Magee, A. Harris, Joseph
Caldwell, John Tate, Moses Haslett, William Glenn, Francis A. Woods,
William McConnel, William Long, James Winter, Newton Brown, William M.
Keown, John Hail, Milton Beaty, Francis Gregg, A. Sanders, W. R.
Nelson, Lewis M. Tilley, William R. Nelson, John Tilley, S. G. Earle,
Samuel Baker, Lindsey Baker, James Herron, William L. Jones, Thomas
Duncan, Franklin Brice, Thomas Boroughs, Reuben Estes, Ann Harris,
William Watson, H. Scuddy, F. A. Woods, Martin Smith, A. S. McClinton,
Rebekah McDaniel. Henry Cosper, Clerk.

APPRAISE BILL - GOODS AND CHATTELS OF THOMAS SPRAY
Dec'd. John Leavell, Ex'r. 7 Jan. 1847. Bible and Hymn book. Notes
on: C. P. Deen, Alfred J. Willingham, W. M. Sears. Appr's: James M.
Gambrell, H. H. Wardlaw, John Willingham.

INVENTORY - PERSONAL ESTATE OF E. W. KIRKSEY
Dec'd. Large library of medical books; Bible, medical instruments.
(Note--in latter part of inventory, shows his middle name to be
WINCHESTER...cme) Silas Kirksey, Adm'r. Pendleton, 31 Dec. 1846.
Appr's: E. B. Benson, T. W. Symmes, Thomas R. Cherry, Elam Sharpe, Jr.

MEDICAL ACCOUNTS OF E. W. KIRKSEY
Dec'd. Jenkins Adams, J. W. Bridwell, Mrs. Robert Anderson, Chesley
Brock, Randall Brown, J. C. Calhoun, James Crawford, Miss Louisa L.
Caruth, Mrs. Dart, J. J. Duke, James Dodd, Jarratt Evatt, Jaratt
Augustine Evatt, Alanson Forbes, D. K. Hamilton, Henry Gains, Richard
Hallum, B. F. Holland, J. C. Hall, T. J. Hallum, J. P. Harris,
Christopher Kirksey, William Kirksey, Jr., Wm. Kirksey, Sr., Silas
Kirksey, John M. Lawrence, Mrs. Elisha Lawrence, John S. Lorton, Doct.
J. M. McElroy, Elijah Mason, P. A. Maxwell, Seaborn Moore, Eli Moore,
John A. Moore, J. L. North, Joshua Owen, John Owen, Estate of Col.
Pinkney, T. J. Pickens, Phillip Johnson, Thomas Steward, Mrs. Starke,
Maj. E. Sharpe, ____ Suttles, Mrs. Swafford, W. D. Steel, Dr. F. W.
Symmes, Mrs. Willard Watson. 28 Jan. 1847. List by: F. W. Symmes,
Tho. R. Cherry, E. B. Benson.

SALE OF PERSONAL PROPERTY OF E. W. KIRKSEY
Dec'd. 5 Jan. 1847. Dr. F. W. Symmes, Samuel Maverick, Dr. Eli Cherry,
Elam Sharpe, Jr., J. V. Shanklin, J. T. Sloan, Baylis Watkins (Bible and
Dictionary), Silas Kirksey (Bible and "Paradise Lost"), B. F. Holland,
M. R. Hunnicutt, T. J. Pickens, J. McElroy, Thomas Miller, J. J. Duke,
R. A. Maxwell, P. J. Miller, J. S. Lorton, S. P. Harris, William Hubbard,
Archibald McElroy, J. P. Harris, T. J. Hallum, Elijah Agnew, A. W. Ross,
Zechariah Masters, J. C. Miller. 29 Jan. 1847. Silas Kirksey, Adm'r.

INVENTORY & APPRAISE BILL - PERSONAL PROPERTY OF JOHN VANDIVER
Dec'd. Appr'd: 5 Jan. 1847.........place adjoining John Carpenter.
Anderson Dist., S. C. P. S. Vandiver, Adm'r. Appr's: Robert Smith,
Elijah Major, Wm. Acker.

SALE BILL - PERSONAL ESTATE OF JOHN VANDIVER
Dec'd. Sold 25 Dec. 1847. to 15 Jan. 1847(8?). Asa P. Vandiver,
Wellborn Keaton, Elam Vandiver, Elijah Major, James E. Vandiver, A. M.
McFall, James King, John Haynie, Peggy Vandiver, A. J. Reeve, R.
Trussell, Jepthae Vandiver, Harvin Vandiver, Thomas Gear, Newton
Vandiver (family Bible), (free negro, Morris), J. C. McConnel, S. R.
McFall, Willis D. Jones, W. P. Hawkins, E. Mitchell, William Major,
Wiley C. Smith, James A. Major, Clerk of Sale, 15 Jan. 1847.

INVENTORY & APPRAISEMENT - PROPERTY OF WILLIAM SMITH
Dec'd. Note on Samuel Smith.

SALE BILL - PERSONAL PROPERTY OF WM. SMITH
Dec'd. Sold 11 Dec. 1846. Samuel Smith, Martha Smith, John Smith,
Nancy Smith, William Smith, James Wardlaw, G. W. McDowell, A. Kay, W. M.
Kay, John Erskine, William Erskine, Elisha Hall, A. M. Neal, Samuel Bell.

SALE BILL - ESTATE OF SAMUEL CUNNINGHAM
Dec'd. Thomas Cunningham, Thomas C. Wilks, Asbury Brooks, Edmund
Thacker, Catharine Cunningham, John Caldwell, Cornelius Latham, Wm. R.
Nelson, Jr., Lydall (or Lyall) Williams, Samuel Dean, David Humphreys
(Negro man, Peter), E. S. Norris, Esq. (boys, Joe and Tom), Henry
Brownlee (Boy, Allen).

APPRAISE BILL - PROPERTY OF BENJAMIN CHAMBLEE
Dec'd. 27 Jan. 1847. Negro man, Ben, age 50 or 60 yrs., woman, Kitty,
abt. 70 yrs., woman, Elizabeth, abt. 17 yrs. James Chamblee and Bryan
Boroughs, Admr's. Appr's: James Gunnin, Thos. Burris, Jr., Matthew
Snipes.

SALE BILL - PERSONAL PROPERTY OF BENJAMIN CHAMBLEE
Dec'd. Sold 12 Feb. 1847. William Chamblee, James Chamblee, Esther
Watson, James Driver, John McKown (also McCown), D. K. Watson, Rob.
Chamblee, George Stevenson, C. Webb, M. Snipes, Samuel Williford, James

Burriss, James Stephenson, James Taylor, J. C. Keys, William Teat, B.
Boroughs, J. Broyles, James Taylor, James Brison, John Butler, R. W.
Chamblee, E. Smith, W. D. Smith, Thomas Skelton, John Watson, A. D.
Hembree, Henry Crawford, Jos. Taylor, C. B. Webb, Fenton Hall, B.
Taylor, A. J. Darnold, John Haynie, Charless Barrett, Levi Wilson, A. H.
Townsend, William Williams, Lewis Prichard, L. A. Osborne, James Winter,
Jos. Leather, William Chamblee (old negro woman), Rob. Chamblee (man Ben),
A. J. Dornald (girl Eliza).

APPRAISE BILL - ESTATE OF CHARLES BENNETT
Dec'd. Negro man: negro woman; tract of land. Appr's: John Harper,
Elijah Pepper, W. A. Williams. (M.A.D.) Charles M. Bennett, Ex'r.
26 Feb. 1847.

INVENTORY & APPRAISE BILL - ESTATE OF HIRAM HARBIN
Dec'd. Filed 18 Aug. 1846. Appr's: Wm. E. Eskew, John J. B. Skelton,
Reuben Gentry.

SALE BILL - PERSONAL PROPERTY OF HIRAM HARBIN
Dec'd. Sold 6 Mar. 1847. Mary Ann Harbin, W. B. Harbin, A. B. Gentry,
William Boroughs. Herbert Hammond, (O.A.D.)

INVENTORY - GOODS & CHATTELS OF IBZAN CLINKSCALES
Dec'd. Taken 2 Mar. 1847. Negro boy: Jackson; boy: Michael. Note
on G. Kay. Appr's: James A. Gantt, William Keeton, Gabriel Kay.

SALE BILL - ESTATE OF IBZAN CLINKSCALES
Dec'd. Made 3 Mar. 1847. Polley Clinkscales, Thomas Geer, W. F.
Clinkscales, John Clinkscales, A. H. Magee, William P. Norris, Harrison
Lattimer, Z. Hall (boy Jackson), Josiah Burton (boy Michael), Wilbern
Keeton (note).

INVENTORY & APPRAISE BILL - PERSONAL ESTATE OF DANIEL F. LUCIUS
Dec'd. Late of Anderson Dist., S. C. Shown by Daniel L. Cox and Ackray
Lucius, Admr's of Est. Negroes: Lettuce (70), Harry (65), Ciller (50),
Kesiah and Ciller (32), Hembree (28), Nancy (26), Emanuel (21), Lydia
(11), Jane (9), Minerva (5), George (6). Note on S. D. Philips and
Reuben Philips: Appr's: Aris Cox, Halbert Acker, M. McGee.

SALE BILL - PERSONAL GOODS, CHATTELS OF DAVID F. LUCIUS
Dec'd late of Anderson Dist. Sold 8 Apr. 1847. William Kay, Widow
(took Emanuel and Lydia), D. Mattison, W. Reese, J. C. Horton, John
Bagwell, M. McGee, J. S. Acker, J. W. Bagwell, O. Shirley, J. M. Grubb,
J. Cox, V. Shaw, G. W. Davenport, W. Acker, Wash. Holliday, J. E.
Holliday, R. D. Crymes, D. L. Cox, J. H. Harper, J. W. Featherston,
Joseph Sullivan, A. W. Smith, J. F. Wyatt, H. Johnson, J. Ghent, Aris
Cox, J. H. Davis, Henry Maddox, W. P. Kay, J. R. Jameson, Wm. Reese,
S. Kay, Jesse French, James McCollough, D. F. Lucius, D. Neighbors, H.
Johnson, Thomas Davis, N. Gaines, J. G. Gantt, Wm. Holland (Keziah and
child), J. Cox (Nancy and Harry), L. B. Philips (Lettuce), Wm. Reese
(Hembree), J. R. Smith (Ciller and George), D. L. Cox (Jane and Minerva).
M. McGee, Clerk.

APPRAISE BILL - ESTATE OF NIMROD SMITH, SR.
Dec'd. 28 Apr. 1847. Negroes: Ellen and Aaron. Notes: Armstead
Waters, Alfred P. Hembree, Aaron Smith, L. O. Shirley, Willis Dickinson,
Nimrod Smith, Jr., R. M. Morris, N. S. Smith, William Erskine. Jane
Smith, Adm'trx. Appr's: Barth. White, James Jolley, Aaron Smith,
Robt. Smith.

SALE BILL - PROPERTY OF NIMROD SMITH, SR.
Dec'd. Sold 30 Apr. 1847. Bartley White, Thomas Duckworth, James
Dickson, James Shirley, Capt. Aaron Smith, Robert Smith.

INVENTORY - PERSONAL PROPERTY OF SANFORD VANDIVER
Dec'd. 28 May 1847. P. S. Vandiver, Adm'r. Appr's: James R. Fant,
Lewis Whitefield, Joseph Burns.

261

SALE BILL - PERSONAL PROPERTY OF SANFORD VANDIVER
Dec'd. Sold 29 May 1847. H. R. Vandiver (family Bible), William
Meredith, S. P. Harris, A. Meredith, J. J. Coates, M. L. Davis, P. S.
Vandiver.

INVENTORY & APPRAISE BILL - PERSONAL PROPERTY OF SUSANNAH CHERRY
Dec'd. Appr's: Geo. Seaborn, V. H. Oppert, Elam Sharpe, Jr. 16 Mar.
1847. E. D. Cherry, Adm'r.

SALE BILL - PERSONAL PROPERTY OF MRS. SUSANNAH CHERRY
Dec'd. Sold 20 Mar. 1847. E. D. Cherry, R. A. Maxwell, M. E. Cherry,
J. Smith, J. C. Cherry, M. Harper, J. Belott, S. S. Cherry, M. Fant,
J. Howell, J. Steele, W. Douglass, J. O. Lewis, T. Miller, T. R. Cherry,
George Seaborn, L. Hamilton, D. Cherry, John C. Miller; E. D. Cherry,
Clerk of Sale.

INVENTORY & APPRAISE BILL - ESTATE OF GEORGE HERNDON
Dec'd. Appr's: Andrew McLees, Charles Haynie, Samuel G. Earle.

SALE BILL - PERSONAL PROPERTY OF GEORGE HERNDON
Dec'd. Sold 11 May 1847. Samuel G. Earle, William Glenn, William Hale,
Charles Haynie, Edmund Herndon, John Stephenson, Charles Williford, John
Tilly, William R. Nelson, Harrison Bullman, Robert Gilmer, P. R. Shaw,
J. J. McLees, Lewis Clinkscales, John McDonald, John Caldwell, James
Dobbins, Thomas Brooks, Keys Norris, Charles Haynie, Francis Harrison,
Alexander McClinton, Henry Scuddy, James Leadbetter, Matthew Parker,
Reuben T. Herndon, Cornelius Latham, Peyton R. Shaw, Zephaniah Herndon.
David D. Earp, Clerk.

APPRAISE BILL - PERSONAL ESTATE OF FRANCIS BEATY, SR.
Dec'd. Negroes: Bob, Lyddy and Jefferson, Cyrus, Symes. Note: A. W.
Beaty, David Humphreys, Adm'r. 23 Dec. 1846. William N. Fant, Appr.

SALE BILL - ESTATE OF FRANCIS BEATY, SR.
Dec'd. Widow (took Symes and Cyrus), William G. Speed, John Cown,
David Humphreys, James H. Wiles, William Hatton, D. C. Howard, William
O'Briant, D. Presley, Thomas O. Hill, David Sadler, Fal Davis, Samuel
Beaty, Thomas Fields, William Huchison, F. A. Young, Hany Adams, Charles
Bowie, Wm. N. Fant, Matthew Galloway, James Connel, David Connel, George
Connel, John Burriss, Fenton Hall, Richard Hill, James G. Speer, Mark
Prince, William Sympson (also Simpson) (boy Bob), Dr. Wm. R. Sanders
(girl Liddy), James Donnelly, James Allen, Dr. Walker, Tyre Mauldin,
Mr. Dupree, Ibzan Waters, Elbert Burriss (Jefferson). Wm. N. Fant,
clerk.

INVENTORY & APPRAISEMENT - GOODS, CHATTELS, RIGHTS & CREDITS OF ASA
CLINKSCALES Dec'd. Notes: T. H. Hensley, Wm. Mitchell, J. T.
Whitefield; Anderson Dist., S. C. James L. Orr, Exr. 13 Nov. 1847.
Appr's: A. N. McFall, A. Felton, W. Carlile, V. D. Fant, A. O. Norris.

INVENTORY & APPRAISE BILL - PERSONAL ESTATE OF MARY BROWN
Dec'd. Appr'd 17 Nov. 1846. V. D. Fant, Adm'r. Appr's: Daniel Brown,
David Geer, Robert Smith.

SALE BILL - ESTATE OF MARY BROWN
Dec'd. Sold 17 Nov. 1846. A. A. Mitchell, David Russell, S. Bell,
D. Brown, Nancy Moore, Elizabeth Pagett, James Cochran, W. Keaton,
Harvin Vandiver, V. D. Fant, William Nevitt, Enoch Major, W. Erskine,
W. Trussel, William Geer, O. Martin, Thomas Erskine, W. Smith, James
Dickson, John H. Hammond, William Jackson, Francis Major, A. Stephenson,
David Geer. James Carpenter, Clerk. Herbert Hammond, O.A.D.

INVENTORY & APPRAISE BILL - GOODS OF THE ESTATE OF WILLIAM S. HUNT
Dec'd. Herbert Hammond, O.A.D. and Adm'r. Notes: Chas. Todd, Wilson
Vermillion, James McCleskey, Samuel Martin, Anderson Braswell, James
Chastain, J. McLees, Henry Pearson, Stephen Chastain, Joseph Taylor.
Appr's: Elijah Webb, John Martin, A. O. Norris.

INVENTORY & APPRAISE BILL - GOODS, CHATTELS OF J. J. ROBINSON
Dec'd. Thurs. 9 Sept. 1847. Acct's: William Armstrong, J. W.
Featherston, John Shirley, Miss Caroline Fisher, L. P. Wright, James L.
Owens, Archibald Armstrong, Halbert Armstrong, Colbert Armstrong, J. W.
Wright, P. N. Wright, A. B. Armstrong, James C. Wright, Leonard Saylors,
James Adams, George Mattison, Abraham Saylors, John Saylors, Sr., James
S. Hughes, John Ashley, Sr., William Cowen, B. McGee, Isaac Robinson,
James M. Hopkins, James A. Hall, Nathaniel Pearman, Cyntha Ann Wakefield,
John Bryant, John Cox, Thomas W. Martin, A. H. Magee, Silas Massey,
Thornton Owens, Harvey Brownlee, Stephen Shirley, James A. Gant, R. W.
Grubbs, John A. Branyan, William Green, William Kent, Benjamin Bearman,
James E. Robinson, George Wilson, James L. Fisher, Tucker May, John R.
Martin, Elam Vandiver, Turner T. Wright, Jonathan Pearman, James Nelson,
Jesse Rutledge, Samuel Robinson, George Grubbs, Jane Webster, James
Shirley, Richard Robinson, Jesse Robinson, M. H. Brock, George W.
Brownlee, Robert Drake, Josiah D. Gailard, David Ruff, Curtis W.
Clement, Jeremiah Moore, Reuben N. Shirley, William Callaham, Harrison
Latimer, Francis M. Kay, Richard G. Kay, John R. Kay, Anderson Braswell,
Hezekiah Wakefield, Luke Hanks, Gabriel Kay, Rolly Banister, Thomas
Penold, Hayden Brock, Geo. Nelson, William Martin, O. Shirley, G. W.
Magee, John H. Hopkins, Isaac Clement, William Towns, John Hunt, Wm.
Hunt, Anna Wright, John Hinton, James Wilson, Thompson Hog, John M.
Grubbs, Weldon Pearman, Wm. F. Clinkscales, James Brock, J. C. Black,
Jacob Alewine, Chester Kingsley, John R. Armmstrong, Jane Fisher,
Mastin Cobb, Philip Lee, Elihu Smith, Aaron Davis, Hugh Clement, John
F. Clinkscales, L. Bigbee, Daniel Brown, Halbert A. Cobb, James E.
Brock, John Massey, Robinson Cobb, James Armstrong, Sr., James D. Madoc,
James Richey, Jr., Daniel Wright, Henry Reed, M. Magee, William Pruitt,
S. M. Trible, A. Clement, John W. Shirley, Jeremiah Shirley, Jesse
Martin, Jesse Magee, Saml. K. Jones, Nimrod Greer, James King, John R.
Shirley, James Emerson, James Lindsey, Richard Shirley, James Collins,
Elgin Kay, William Hanks, James Hanks, Toliver Pruitt, L. W. Trible,
S. C. Fisher, Reuben King, Nathaniel Shirley, William Clement, Elias
Kay, John Wakefield, Edney Fisher, William Wilson, Robert Parker, R. O.
Trible, A. G. Latimer, Joshua Pruitt, Willis Pruitt, Abner Branyan,
Benjamin Shirley, Laban Massey, Willia S. Greer, Benjamin Johnson,
A. J. Brock, Henry Robinson, Alex. Elgin, William Owens, John Mattison,
Marion Shirley, Joshua Ashley, Franklin Mattison, Asa Avery, James
Brock, Thomas Branyan, James P. Cochran, Robert Burton, Benjamin Wilson,
William J. Jones, Mary Ann Fisher, Katharine Kay, James Armstrong, John
Lewis, Rhodam Trussel, Asa Vandiver, George W. Weldon, James Banister,
Andrew J. Shaw, Rolen Banister, William P. Saylor, John M. Bolton,
James Taylor, Nipper Shirley, John Wilson, Matthias Smith, Elizabeth
Banister, Mariah Brownlee, Thomas A. Wakefield, John Saylor, Martin F.
Freeman, W. S. Hopkins, Clement Nelson, Alexander Mattison, David Hill,
James E. Brown, Dempsey Hill, Wm. P. Emory, James Vandiver, James
Taylor, Samuel S. Martin, John Robinson, Stephen M. Fisher, P. M.
Gambrell, J. F. M. Massey, Daniel May, Wm. Pruitt, Jr., John Ashley,
Nancy Callaham, John Fields, Rachel McAlister, Henderson Dove, Joshua
Ashley, John A. Saylors, Abner M. Elgin, John Wright, John N. Saylor,
Wm. R. McAlister, William Dove, Pinckney Dove, Edward Ashley, Robt.
Hinton, Allen M. Clark, Samuel Fisher, Polley Hill, Thomas Fields,
James Morgan, William Banister, Thomas Banister, Nancy Taylor, George
Taylor, John Hanks, Wm. D. Weldon, Sally May, Elisha Callaham, Wm.
Fields, Benj. Morgan, John B. Strickland, Peter Rickets, W. J. Taylor,
Nancy Martin, Hiram B. Uldrick, William Tucker, Nancy Nelson, Harrison
Wright, Asenith Stone, Mary Robinson, James Grimes, Simon Massey,
Ebenezer Ashley, Sarah Brownlee, Hugh Brackenridge, Stephen Kitsinger,
Susan Martin, Nimrod Saylors, John Cobb, G. W. May, Lewis McConnell,
David Dove, Eliza Taylor, Caroline Callaham, Isaac Hill, Thos. McClellan,
John N. Saylors, Rachel Callaham, Benjamin Pearman, James Adams, James
D. Murdoc, R. N. Wright, J. G. Gant, J. M. Hopkins, Jno. Ashley, Sr.,
James Drake, G. B. Mattison, Jane and Sam Robinson, Cynthia Ann
Wakefield, James Cullins, J. A. Hall, Abram Saylor, R. W. Grubbs, Thomas
Penald, G. B. Mattison, B. McGee, Jonathan Pearman, Wm. F. Wright, Geo.
Wilson, J. E. Brock, C. W. Clement, T. T. Wright, John Trible, G. W.
May, John Saylor, A. B. Robinson, S. M. Fisher, S. Fields, John
Robinson, A. J. Shaw, Daniel Wheaton, Daniel McCollum, Wm. Russel,
James Patterson, A. Clark, T. Bannister.

ESTATE OF JOHN JASPER ROBINSON
Dec'd. Hugh Robinson and Letty M. Robinson, Adm'r. 15 Sept. 1847.
Appr's: Wm. Cox, Jno. F. Clinkscales, S. M. Trible, and R. N. Wright.
(Note: several more pages of this accounting, including most of the
same names as above.)

2nd INVENTORY OF THE PERSONAL ESTATE OF J. J. ROBINSON
Dec'd. 8 Nov. 1847. Negro: Sam. (Note: same admr's. and same appr's.)

SALE BILL - GOODS AND CHATTELS OF J. J. ROBINSON
Dec'd. 13 Sept. 1847. H. Robinson, W. Cox, G. Grubbs, W. Ashley, R. N.
Wright, J. Buris, J. J. Shirley, J. C. Wright, S. Massey, W. Shirley,
W. K. Clement, S. Robinson, James Armstrong, J. L. Brock, E. Shirley, J.
Alewine, H. Robinson, J. W. Featherston, W. P. Kay, J. Pearman, R. O.
Trible, V. Shaw, Widow, T. F. Branion, L. W. Trible, B. F. Shirley, M.
Bird, J. Drake, J. Bagwell. (Note: this list is almost a duplication
of the preceeding list of names. Mr. Robinson was evidently in the
mercantile business...) 2nd Sale of Property commenced on 9 Nov.
1847 and ended on 10 Nov. 1847. Sold by R. N. Wright. (Takes in pages
177 to 216 on original ledger.)

INVENTORY & APPRAISE BILL - ESTATE OF JOHN FRETWELL
Dec'd, late of Anderson Dist., S. C. 23 Aug. 1847. Slaves: Poll,
Mariah, Bob, Dublin, Cezar, Gabe, Prince, Sam, Toney, Orange.
Real Estate: Home tract (721 acres), old tract (175 acres), Woodall
tract (146 acres), W. C. Dickson tract (260 acres). Joseph Y. Fretwell,
Ex'r. Notes: ....Whitner, L. A. Osborn, E. Webb, C. Webb, J. D.?
Morris, Reuben Richey, James Gordon, D. Russell, R. A. Keys, A. D.
Hembree, Jos. Taylor, B. Boroughs, F. M. Johnston, J. Y. Fretwell, D.
Brown, A. Montgomery, Wm. Pearce, James L. Orr (blacksmith), J. B.
Skelton (blacksmith), Wm. E. Eskew (blacksmith), J. C. Keys. Appr's:
Bryan Boroughs, James C. Keys, Robert A. Keys.

APPRAISEMENT - RESIDUE OF ESTATE OF JOHN FRETWELL
Dec'd. 22 Nov. 1847. Same Appraisers. Also appraisal of 395 acres of
land whereon Bry. Fretwell lives, as property of John Fretwell, dec'd.
Appr'd. 13 Dec. 1847 by Abel Robins, Daniel Innman, Lewis Moorehead.
Samuel Mosely, Clerk.

SALE BILL - PROPERTY OF JOHN FRETWELL
Dec'd. 23 Nov. 1847. Bry. Fretwell, K. Breazeale, J. B. Taylor, J. Y.
Fretwell, G. W. Meritt, A. J. Busby, A. E. Porter, James Burriss, W. J.
Brown, D. H. Cochran, John Haynie, M. M. Anderson, Elbert Burriss,
Haden Elrod, Joseph Taylor, A. D. Hembree, Sanford Sympson, Charles Kay,
W. J. Brown, John McFall, W. E. Escew, W. R. Burriss, A. Felton, T. B.
Garrett, A. Campbell, John Moorhead, W. H. Bulman, Reuben Burriss, A.
Mitchell, Joseph Moore, J. T. Whitfield, G. W. Merritt, G. B. King,
Oliver Bluman, H. M. Barton, W. B. Gipson, J. C. Keys, T. L. Scott,
J. M. Dean, J. P. Benson, Jonthan White, Berry Holland, R. Chastain,
Reuben Gentry, Wm. Erskine, A. P. Cater, John Haynie, E. Webb, Joseph
Taylor, A. J. Donald, John Skelton,: Sale of slaves: K. Brazeale (Polly
and Dublin), G. Brazeale (Mariah), Bry. Fretwell (Bob), J. L. Burriss
(Caesar), J. Y. Fretwell (Sam), Wm. Sherard (Frank), J. Y. Fretwell
(Gabe), Bry. Fretwell (Toney and Prince), John McFall (Orange).
6 Dec. 1847. Bryan Boroughs, Clerk.

INVENTORY & APPRAISEMENT - ESTATE OF FLEMING WATTERS
Dec'd. Notes: Willis Stacks, C. P. Dupree, John Mauldin, Wm. Keown,
Richard B. Cater, Sam'l Beaty, Djt. Tucker, Elijah Willbanks, F. W.
Davis, Wm. N. Fant, Ibzan Watters. Appr's: R. Smith, Wm. Obriant,
James H. Wiles, Wm. Hutcheson, A. Reid. 11 Nov. 1847.

SALE BILL - ESTATE OF JOSEPH CLARKE
Dec'd. Ann Clark, A. M. Carpenter. 6 Dec. 1847. F. G. Carpenter, Clk.

SALE BILL - ESTATE OF FLEMING WATTERS
Dec'd. Sold 30 Nov. 1847. James Speer, J. Watters, R. Smith, Wm. B.
Scott, Mrs. Harris, James Able, R. Pettigrew, Drew Paine, James H.
Wiles, Clerk.

INVENTORY & APPRAISEMENT - ESTATE OF ELIZABETH SMITH
Dec'd. Anderson Dist., S. C. James D. Smith, Adm'r. 25 Feb. 1848.
Note on: J. C. and J. M. Smith, Andrew M. C. Smith, Ann Earl, Robert
Pickens, James B. Pegg, Wm. Turpin. Appr's: John Pegg, James B. Pegg,
Wm. Waddell.

APPRAISAL OF LANDS - ESTATE OF JAMES ERSKINE
Dec'd. William and James Erskine, Exr's. Appr's: Joseph Cox, James
Major, S. J. Hammond. 25 Nov. 1847. Joseph Cox, Dty. Sur'vr.

INVENTORY & APPRAISEMENT - ESTATE OF ROBERT DRAKE
Dec'd. 17 Nov. 1847. 110 acres land. James A. Drake, Adm'r. Appr's:
Wm. Cowan, Thomas Pennal, F. M. Kay, David Ruff.

SALE BILL - ESTATE OF ROBERT DRAKE
Dec'd. Pur.: A. W. Hawkins, Wm. Keaton, A. N. McFall, widow L. Drake
(Bible), James Drake, Jesse Rutledge, John Martin, George Ruff, Hugh
Robinson, Thomas Pennel, John B. Armstrong, James A. Drake, W. F.
Clinkscales, James Emerson, Leonard Saylor, Wm. Cowan, Wm. Martin, J. W.
Featherston, A. Keaton, John A. Saylor, E. Drake, J. M. Brown, N. Brown,
A. J. Hawkins, James Drake (Bible), F. M. Kay, W. R. McAlister, George
Wilson, R. H. Dove, James A. Gant, Olly Mattison, Wm. Keaton, Robt.
Hughins, John Martin, W. G. Johnson. 18 Nov. 1847. James Emerson,
Clerk.

APPRAISE BILL - ESTATE OF EPHRAIM MAYFIELD
Dec'd. Notes: Abram Mayfield, Jepthae Vandiver; Appr's: James Major,
W. C. Smith, John Holland, Grant A. Moore, Wm. Telford. James Telford
and Abraham Mayfield, Adm'rs. 3 Jan. 1848.

SALE BILL - ESTATE OF EPHRAIM MAYFIELD
Dec'd. 6 May 1847. Widow Mayfield, Betsy Mayfield, Jeptha Vandiver,
James Telford, G. B. Telford, James Major, Hiram Major, G. A. Moore,
Marion Mitchell, John Harkins, W. C. Smith, Peter King, Abraham Mayfield,
Wm. Mayfield, Wm. Holmes, J. H. Telford, Thany Mayfield, Enoch Brazeale,
Thomas Kates, H. M. Gaines. Wm. Telford and S. B. Telford, Clerks.

APPRAISE BILL - ESTATE OF A. D. CALDWELL
Dec'd. Shown by William Steele. 24 Dec. 1847. Appr's: J. E. Belotte,
A. Hackett, James Webb.

SALE BILL - ESTATE OF A. D. CALDWELL
Dec'd. Pur.: Joseph Williams, S. Gregory, W. Steele, J. Webb, W.
Rochester, ... Moorehead, A. D. Gaillard, J. E. Belotte. 24 Dec. 1847.
John E. Bellotte, Clerk.

INVENTORY & APPRAISEMENT - ESTATE OF JANE RICE
Dec'd. Amaziah Rice, Adm'r. Appr's: Elijah Webb, S. McCulley, Daniel
Brown.

SALE BILL - ESTATE OF JANE RICE
Dec'd. Sold 4 Nov. 1847. L. A. Baker, Peter L. Byram, E. Webb, W. P.
Todd, J. Gray, J. Thompson, Andrew Shearer, F. Rice, D. Brown, C. J.
Thayer, W. Gibson, E. Major, Ibzan Rice, A. Holt, E. George, D. Cochran,
T. H. Anderson, T. L. Scott, L. A. Osborn, C. C. Langston, A. P. Cater,
R. Brackenridge, Samuel Bell, R. W. Todd, M. Magee, W. Magee (negro man
Philip.)

APPRAISE BILL - PROPERTY OF JAMES WATSON
Dec'd, included in his Will. Negroes: Matilda and her child Juliana,
Letty and Martha Elizabeth, Joe, and Adam. Andrew P. Watson, Ex'r.
12 Jan. 1848. Appr's: James Mulliken, Wm. Richey, Benj. Mulliken, Jr.,
Thos. H. McCann.

BILL OF APPRAISEMENT - PROPERTY OF JAMES WATSON
Dec'd. Not included in his Will. Negroes: Ned, Berry, Mary, Sye, Pris.
Andrew P. Watson, Ex'r. Notes: Moses Meek, Westley H. Potillo,
Jonathan Lindley, Samuel Watson, B. H. Overby, Nicholas Oberby, Jesse
Cox, G. Reed, Elijah T. Wilson, Thomas Wilson, Elijah Timms, Jesse

Timms, Vincent Timms, Ebenezer Reynolds, James Mulliken, Eli Moore,
Amor Voyles.

SALE BILL - PROPERTY OF JAMES WATSON
Dec'd. 14 Jan. 1848. Charles Irby, James Mulliken, Cyrus Hamilton,
Benj. Mulliken, John C. Miller, Andrew P. Watson, James Orr, William
Ford, Harvey Smith, Simeon Smith, James Martin, Mary Oliver, Henry
McKinney, Wm. Birge, Andrew P. Watson (negroes: Ned, Berry, Sye and
old woman Pris); (negro Mary) in trust for Sarah Ann Couch and Mary
Oliver. Anderson Dist., S. C. 6 Mar. 1848. James Mullikin, Clerk.

APPRAISEMENT - GOODS, CHATTELS OF WILLIAM BEATY
Dec'd. Negroes Lucy and 2 children--Amanda and Jerry; boy Ned. Willed
Property Negroes: Rebecca and 2 children--Julia and Francis; Isabella;
Andrew; Sarah; Jain; Jacob; Easter; Harriet. 370 acres land. Appr's:
Andrew Reid, W. Hatton, D. J. Tucker, Charles Bowie.

SALE BILL - GOODS, CHATTELS OF WILLIAM BEATY
Dec'd of Anderson Dist., S. C. 20 Jan. 1848. James Chalmers, Newton
Beaty, James South, David Obriant, Elias Beaty, Ezekiel White, James
Stephenson, Wm. A. McKee, Wm. Webb, James Connel, John M. White, Wm.
Wilson, David Simpson, Stephen Heyney, Margaret Beaty, John Black, Mark
Prince, Elias South, Wm. Obriant, Rufus Yeargin, James Tucker, James
H. Wiles, Lewis Clinkscales, Ibzan Watters, A. G. Lattimer, Wm. Hatten,
Dejernet Tucker, J. W. Beaty, Robt. Hodges, Thos. Simpson, Jesse Camble,
John McMahan, James A. Rampy, Wm. Fant, D. S. McKinney, George Young,
David Whitman, James Wiley, Dr. Wm. Milford, John Spearman, Robt.
Peticrew, Charles Bowie, John T. McKee, Benjamin Burdit, Jasper
Patterson, James Parnel, James Burriss, James McBride, John Stuart,
Martha Beaty, Lewis Bozeman (boy Ned), William Sherard (Lucy and
children--Amandy, Jesse and one not named). H. P. Hays, Clk. 15 Feb.
1848.

INVENTORY & APPRAISEMENT - ESTATE OF WILLIAM BUCHANAN
Dec'd. Appr's: Thomas Watt, James G. Watt, Joseph W. Watt, A. Simpson.

SALE BILL - ESTATE OF WILLIAM BUCHANAN
Dec'd. Sold 6 Aug. 1847. A. Simpson, Wm. Simpson, Elias Magee,
Forrester Roach, Willis Magee, Wiley Powel, L. Buchanan, John J.
Partain, John Sigler, Charlotte Buchana, John Ables. L. Buchanan, Clk.

INVENTORY & APPRAISEMENT - ESTATE OF JAMES BAGWELL
Dec'd. 28 Feb. 1848. Note on Henry Cobb, Redmond Bagwell. Acc't. on
David Cox, Wm. C. Harper, Daniel F. Lucius, William H. Acker, John
Bagwell. Anderson Dist., S. C. Appr's: John H. Harper, David R.
Reece, Wm. G. Reece, W. H. Acker.

SALE BILL - PERSONAL PROPERTY OF JAMES BAGWELL
Dec'd. 29 Feb. 1848. Wm. C. Harper, Adm'r. Mrs. Nancy Bagwell, Hyram
Cooley, James Shumate, Vincent Shaw, M. Trobridge, James S. Lucius,
Wm. G. Reece, Thos. Carter, David Cox, Nace Morrison, Thomas Davis,
Francis Ragsdale, Lewis Cooley, P. N. Acker, Dr. George R. Brown,
George Neighbors, Robert Holida, Daniel Mattison, Drayton Neighbors,
Posey Trussel, John H. Harper, Wm. C. Harper, Wm. F. Dunlap, Holbert
Acker, W. H. Acker, Thomas Harper, Austin Williams, James Holida,
Alexander Austin, John Bagwell. Wm. H. Acker, Clerk.

INVENTORY & APPRAISE BILL - ESTATE OF CHARLES B. WEBB
Dec'd. Anderson Dist., S. C. 25 Jan. 1848. B. F. Hammond and W. L.
Hammond, Adm'rs. Slaves: Keziah and 2 of her children--Martha and
Hannah; Mary; Cloe; Caroline and her child--Maria; Elsa; Hester;
Sanford; Mark; Hamp. Notes: Samuel Martin, A. Campbell, Wm. E.
Caldwell, John A. Simpson, Mrs. Gordon, S. R. Williams, Wm. B. Gibson,
Sejazemond Stribling, Clayton Webb, Henry D. Crenshaw, James C. Winter,
Henry McCrary, James Chastain, John B. Earle, J. T. Broyles, Henry
Terry, Amos Morris, Wm. Dickson, Dr. C. C. Hammond, Elijah Webb, A.
Jackson Martin, Samuel Black, Capt. M. W. Haslett, John Todd, James
Bryson, John Butler, James Morris, Thomas Skelton, Thomas T. Skelton,
A. B. Skelton, David J. Morris, James Chamblee, Samuel Martin, William

Mills, W. B. Gibson. Appr's: James C. Keys, William Mills, Joseph
Taylor, Sr., John B. E. Taylor.

SALE BILL - ESTATE OF C. B. WEBB
Dec'd. Sold 27 & 28 Jan. 1848. Samuel J. Hammond bidding off for
Mrs. Eliza Webb, relict of C. B. Webb, dec'd. Negroes: to Eliza Webb
(Keziah and children Martha and Hannah; Mary; Hester; Sant; Mark) and
majority of estate. Pur.: James Dobbins, A. D. Hembree, James
McCleskey, David Barrett, John Mattison, Maj. J. Harrison, Rev. D.
Humphreys, Thomas Burriss, L. A. Osborn, Samuel O. Boulman, Reuben
Gentry, Levi Wilson, James Bradberry, J. B. E. Taylor, James Burriss,
Clayton Webb, W. H. Boulman, Elisha Webb, Drury Waters, A. Felton,
B. F. Hammond, Samuel J. Hammond (negroes Cloe and Elsa), Samuel W.
Williford (negroes Caroline and Mariah), David Sadler, Jr. (negro Hamp),
Rev. J. McLees, Sam'l. Brown. James Gilmer, Clerk.

APPRAISE BILL - ESTATE OF THOMAS BENNETT
Dec'd. Negro Man: Toney. Charles M. Bennett, Adm'r. Appr'd by:
John Harper, Hugh Wilson, Elijah Pepper. 11 Mar. 1848.

SALE BILL - ESTATE OF THOMAS BENNETT
Dec'd. Ruth Bennett, Charles Irby, Wm. Wellborn, Chas. M. Bennett,
Wm. Avery, Jepthae Harper, Harper Gambrell (man Toney), Samuel Roberts,
Robert Owen, Wm. Bennett, Middleton Stott, Allen Keely, Isaac Wood,
Harvey Tripp, William Ellison. John Harper. Clk.

APPRAISE BILL - ESTATE OF ANNA JONES
Dec'd. Negro boy: Jes. Wm. F. Jones, Adm'r. 21 Jan. 1848. Apr'd.
by: G. Breazeale, Berry Mills, Isaac Cannon.

SALE BILL - ESTATE OF ANNA JONES
Dec'd. Joshua Wilson, M. Stone, George G. Elrod, John Hunter, William
Owen, M. H. Stone, J. E. Dobbins, R. Jones (negro man), M. Robins, Wm.
Jones, T. Garrett, John Smith, B. Mills, R. Shatteen, S. Millwee, J.
Welborn, W. C. Stone, J. S. Wilson, A. Hembree, W. Campbell, G.
Breazeale, J. Hunnicut, W. C. McMurry, Clerk of Sale, W. Poole, Isaac
Cannon.

INVENTORY & APPRAISEMENT - PERSONAL ESTATE OF J. W. RODGERS
Dec'd. (also spelled ROGERS), Negroes willed to Elizabeth Rodgers
(Sam, Izabel, Cinda), willed to Ann Rodgers (Riny), also to Ann
(Margaret and Houl), willed to Sarah Rogers (Emaline, Warren and Ben),
willed to Jacob F. Rogers (Molce, Butler and Whit), willed to Ruth M.
Rodgers (Bill, Patsey and Frances), willed to Hester Jane Rodgers
(Windy, Rose and Noah); negroes left for paying debts and remain in
the care of Elizabeth Rodgers: (Charles, Jim, Cloey, Harett, Lizer
and child Toney, George, Lizie). Notes on: J. P. Rodgers, Herbert
Hammond, Larkin Rodgers, Wm. Duck, Wm. Rodgers, David Spearmin, Alex.
Clements, E. Pickiel, Jerry Rodgers, Terrel Briant, Wm. Anderson,
Nathan Briant, Robt. Parmer, Ira Williams, Edmond Cobb, W. A. Williams,
William Duckworth, Spencer Carter and the Estate of Benjamin Rogers.
J. Paine, Ex'r. and E. Rogers, Extr'x. Appr's: Wm. Martin, Abram
Martin, Wm. Smith.

SALE BILL - ESTATE OF J. W. RODGERS
Dec'd. 18 Feb. 1848. J. P. Rodgers (boy Charles), Larkin Rodgers (Jim),
Howard Duckworth (Cloey), Edwin Smith, Jacob Duckworth, James Ingram,
Thos. Duckworth, Thos. McCarty, John Golding, Wm. W. Rogers, Micajah
Williams, Edward Watson, Benjamin Irby.

INVENTORY - PERSONAL ESTATE OF NANCY HALL
Dec'd. 26 Apr. 1848. Negro woman: Crecy and child Mary; Sampson;
Norris; Flora and child Albert said to belong to E. M. Hall. Acc't.
on A. R. Broyles, Dr. G. R. Brown, W. E. Geer, Josiah King. Notes on:
J. W. Featherston, J. F. Wyatt, J. C. Horton, Wm. Holmes, Elijah
Major. P. S. Vandiver, Adm'r.

SALE BILL - ESTATE PERSONAL OF NANCY HALL
Dec'd. Sold 26 Apr. 1848. A. M. Hall, Josiah King, Peter King,

Wm. Holmes, M. Chamblee (Crecy and child Mary; Sampson; Norris), J. W.
Featherston, J. E. Hall, W. E. Geer, J. L. Todd, A. R. Broyles,
Alfred Fant, E. Brazeale, Basil Davis, J. S. Acker, Jas. King, Sr.,
G. W. King, B. McGee, E. F. Major.

APPRAISEMENT - PROPERTY OF HENRY PARIS
Dec'd. Negroes: Harriet, Ann, Caroline. Appr'd. by: W. A. Williams,
James Thompson, Charles M. Bennett. A. B. Cobb, Ex'r. 5 Feb. 1848.

SALE BILL - ESTATE OF HENRY PARIS
Dec'd. Thomas Welborn, Henry Cobb, Amaziah Cobb, Wallis Ivor?, W. A.
Williams (Clerk of Sale), Jasper Wilson, A. B. Cobb, Andrew Barkley,
John Harper, J. W. Cobb, James Thompson, Thos. Wellborn. 10 Mar. 1848.

INVENTORY & APPRAISEMENT - PERSONAL PROPERTY OF SAMUEL G. EARLE
Dec'd. Appr'd. by Elias Earle, Baylis Earle, John H. Harrison and
James Harrison. Negroes: Lydia (field hand), Austin, Armstead,
Milley, Salley and child, Frances, Thomas, Fielding, Bob (field hand),
Nancy (house servant) and her child, Lucretia (House servant), Julia
(house servant), Louisa (house servant), Rebecca (house servant),
Nancy and Sarah (house servants), Dennis (taylor), Thomas, Sr.
(carpenter), Allen (Blacksmith), Henry (blacksmith), Peter (apprentice),
Dick, (field hand), Ransom, Tom, Jr., Henry, Jr., Jerry, Sam, John,
Smith, Edward (field hands), Taber (coachman and shoemaker), Sophia
(seamstress) and her child. Field hands: Phoeba, Minerva, Charity,
Clarissa, Flora, Hager. Violet and Tabby (cooks), Grace, Rosetta,
Louisa, Daphne, Indy, Jacob (miller), Charles (runaway), Charles, Sr.
(blind). Long list of live-stock, house hold and plantation furnish-
ings. Notes on: Wm. H. Bullman, John M. Barnes, John B. Chappell,
W. W. Dooly, Thomas Duncan, Samuel Dean, Margaret Gilmer, Hiram Gentry,
Wm. and James Hunt, H. G. Harris, George Herndon, John B. Hail,
Richard Bailey, C. C. Langston, W. A. Lewis, R. B. Lewis, Rebecca
McPherson, Oliver Martin, Matthew Martin, Samuel Martin, Francis
Powel, S. Richardson, J. N. Richardson, David Scott, John Saunders,
J. C. Tucker, Jas. T. W. Verner, Ezekiel White, George W. White,
Jos. T. Whitfield, Sam Yeargin, Jr., John Yeargin, Isaac Brown,
Cornelius Brown, John Brooks, Jos. P. Caldwell, Ethelder Costlow,
Tilman Cox, John A. Cox, L. K. Crawford, Rachel Davis, John Dunlap, S.
Earle, C. A. Earp, D. D. Earp, Lewis Evans, Baly Fricks, John Gentry,
Zechariah Gentry, Marjory Gortney, E. George, Levi Garrison, Thos.
Hays, Josiah Herndon, Clement Horner, Wm. Hail, Sampson Haney, N. H.
Ertzberger, Polly Mitchel, C. G. McGregor, Sam Mitchel, Mary Masters,
L. H. McGill, Mary Ann McGill, Hugh McDonald, Jos. O'Briant, Francis
Powel, Sam. Patterson, Moses Pruit, Wm. Rush, Forrister Roach, Wm.
Roach, W. Stacks, S. J. Shackelford, Shad. Stevens, John Stevenson,
Ricket Shiplet, F. A. Skelton, Henry Terry, Benj. Valentine, John R.
West, Jane Williams, Williford Waters. Good notes due estate: H.
Acker, B. F. Mauldin, J. P. Benson, Daniel T. Bozeman, T. C. Harrison,
L. A. Baker, Charles Barrett, Abner Brown, Samuel Buchanan, David R.
Beaty, Thos. Beaty, Garner Brooks, Archibald Bowman, John M. Brown,
Andrew Carter, Micajah Carter, Moses J. Carden, Jesse Campbell,
Barney J. Dooly, Wm. Dooly, Obadiah Dean, W. W. Dooley, W. Dollar,
John F. Early, Christian Fricks, Nancy Fickey, Hugh Gregg, M. W.
Havard, Jas. Harrison, Fenton Hall, Sr., Z. & E. Herndon, Edmund Herndon,
George Herndon, David Humphreys, Robert Howie, Francis Herring, Jacob
Burriss, Edward H. Earle, W. L. Jones, W. G. Johnson, Thomas Jones,
F. G. Stowers, Elizabeth Lewis, Cornelius Latham, John McGee, S. R.
McFall, A. S. McClinton, A. H. McGill, Andrew McLees, Robert McLees,
John Moore, Jas. G. McLin, Nancy McGee, Rebecca McDaniel, A. O. Norris,
J. H. O'Briant, W. R. Nelson, Hubbard Partain, J. P. Reed, Andrew Reid,
Kelly Sullivan, A. S. G. Siddell, Jabez Skelton, A. H. Scuddy, John
Stuart, David Simpson, Robert Simpson, M. H. Smith, Thomas Y. Skelton,
George Stevenson, Mary Tilley, John K. Tilley, E. J. Williams, Elijah
Webb, Robert West, Asa Clinkscales, J. D. Gaillard, B. F. Hammond, W. M.
Nevitt, J. P. Reed, Jesse G. Waters. (Many more pages of accounts,
most a duplication of the above.) Interest in Mercantile firms: M. F.
Berry & Co., in Elbert county, Georgia; Earle & Griffin of Anderson C.
H., Earle & Towers at Evergreen, Anderson Dist.

INVENTORY & APPRAISEMENT - PERSONAL ESTATE OF THOMAS DUNCAN
Dec'd. Appr'd by: John A. Tate, John Herron, John McPhail. 12 May
1848. Notes: Cab. Burton, R. McAlister.

SALE BILL - ESTATE OF THOMAS DUNCAN
Dec'd. 13 May 1848. Martha Duncan, M. M. Duncan, John McPhail, John
Herron, David McConnel, Robert Duncan, D. H. Cochran, John Tate, B. C.
Haynie, Drew Hall, David Tate, B. F. Duncan, John Duncan, Manning
Belcher, Henry Branyan, Ewell Herron, W. H. Haynie, Andrew Todd, John
Findley, Charles McConnel.

INVENTORY & APPRAISEMENT - PERSONAL ESTATE OF JAMES W. KAY
Dec'd. 18 Apr. 1848. Susannah Kay and James E. Kay, Exr's. Appr's:
R. W. Wright, J. B. Robinson, Obadiah Shirley.

SALE OF THE PERSONAL PROPERTY OF JAMES W. KAY
Dec'd. Not disposed of by Will. 20 Apr. 1848. Purs.: Widow, James
E. Kay, O. Shirley, James Armstrong, Benj. Shirley, John Kay, Sr.,
Jonathan Pearman, J. R. Shirley, James Seawright, Marshall Bigby.
R. W. Wright, Clerk.

INVENTORY & APPRAISEMENT - PERSONAL ESTATE OF WILLIAM KERR
Dec'd. 10 May 1848. Notes: Abraham Alewine and George Alewine,
Mattison Bannister. John B. Armstrong, Adm'r.

SALE BILL - ESTATE OF WILLIAM KERR
Dec'd. 10 May 1848. Widow, John B. Armstrong, James Nelson, John R.
Shirley, James M. Hopkins.

APPRAISE BILL - ESTATE OF NIPPER SHIRLEY
Dec'd. 25 May 1848. Notes on: Conrad Wakefield, James Fant, Michael
Davis. Appr'd. by: R. N. Wright, J. D. Gaillard, J. N. Harkness.

SALE BILL - ESTATE OF NIPPER SHIRLEY
Dec'd. 25 May 1848. Margaret P. A. Shirley, James Dixon, S. C. Fisher,
S. K. Jones, Jonathan Pearman. R. N. Wright, Clerk.

INVENTORY & APPRAISEMENT - ESTATE OF JOHN COX
Dec'd. 3 Feb. 1848. Negroes: Solomon, Anderson, Manuel, Hugh, Nervey,
Ede, Sam, Dinah, Jane. Appr'd: R. N. Wright, J. S. Acker, J. F. Wyatt,
Wm. Cox.

SALE BILL - ESTATE OF JOHN COX
Dec'd. 8 Feb. 1848. Widow took (Solomon, Ede and Manuel), J. F. Wyatt,
William Cox, John Geer, J. M. Grubbs, G. Moore Colter, Wm. Kay, Sr.,
W. P. Kay, A. Brock, B. McGee, William Nevitt, P. N. Acker, D. L. Cox,
James Bruce, J. L. Todd, Matilda S. Cox, Benjamin Shirley (took Dinah
and Hugh), Robert McAdams (took Sam), J. M. Grubbs (took Anderson),
J. J. McAdams (took Jane), Allen McDavid (took Nervey).

INVENTORY - ESTATE OF SAMUEL MC COY
Dec'd. 30 Jan. 1849. Appr's: Thomas L. Rice, William P. Todd,
Strother Kay.

INVENTORY & APPRAISEMENT - ESTATE OF ROBERT HOWIE
Dec'd. 22 July 1848. Appr'd. by: Jacob Mouchet, Matthew Parker, A.
Simpson, Ezekiel White.

SALE BILL - ESTATE OF ROBERT HOWIE
Dec'd. Sold by E. J. Earle Adm'r. Pur.: Mrs. E. Howie, Deveraux
Yeargin, E. J. Earle, Hosea Hays, Matthew Parker, Lewis C. Clinkscales,
G. W. South, Samuel Parker. 1 Sept.____

INVENTORY - ESTATE OF DORCAS MC PHERSON
Dec'd. 5 Sept. 1848. Appr's: E. S. Norris, James Jones, George
Stuart.

SALE BILL - ESTATE OF DORCAS MC PHERSON
Dec'd. 5 Sept. 1848. Pur.: Rebecca McPherson, E. S. Norris, Martha

Watson, James Jones, Obadiah Dean, William Ransom, James McPherson,
Charles McConnel, John McPherson, John Stephenson, Jesse Obriant, Thomas
Burriss, Sarah McPherson.

INVENTORY - PERSONAL ESTATE OF MARTHA BEATY
Dec'd. 23 Mar. 1848. (Large Bible). Rev. David Humphreys, Ex'r.
Appr's: Wm. Fant, A. Simpson, Thos. O. Hill, Wm. G. Speed.

SALE BILL - ESTATE OF MARTHA BEATY
Dec'd. Pur.: Thos. O. Hill, David Humphreys, F. Hall, Wm. O'Briant, A.
Simpson, Robert Howie, Wm. Cook, Thomas Fields, Kelly Sullivan, Mrs.
Malinda Cowan, Z. Herndon, James South, Wm. G. Speed, F. A. Young, Moses
Lackey, David Connel, David McKinney, Ginny McKerley, Joel Galbreath,
Dr. J. H. Reid (family Bible), Wm. Sherard, Rev. J. C. Chalmers, Henry
Parker, James H. Wiles, Capt. _____ Elliott, Elias Magee, David Sadler,
Wm. M. Keown, Thomas Morgan, John Morgan, Wm. Grant, Dr. J. T. Baskins,
Jno. R. Worthington. Wm. N. Fant, Clerk.

INVENTORY - ESTATE OF JOHN WILSON
Dec'd. 26 Apr. 1848. Appr's: James Thompson, John Harper, W. A.
Williams. John and Jasper Wilson were in full co-partnership of
contents of this inventory.

SALE BILL - ESTATE OF JOHN WILSON
Dec'd. 27 Apr. 1848. Jasper Wilson, W. S. Stansel, John Harper, Hugh
Wilson, G. Hopson, D. V. Garrison, Wm. Bennett, Sarah Wilson. John
Harper, Clerk. Half claimed by Jasper Wilson.

INVENTORY - ESTATE OF WILLIAM MC PHERSON
Dec'd. James Gunnin, Adm'r. (Will annexed) 25 Aug. 1848. Anderson
Dist. Slaves: Bass (about 45), Sela (about 16). Appr's: S. H.
Baker, John Moore, George Stewart.

SALE BILL - ESTATE OF WILLIAM MC PHERSON
Dec'd. 1 and 2 Nov. 1848. Rev. David Humphreys, Jesse McGee, John A.
Stevenson, George Stevenson, William Jones, Thomas Burriss, Hugh Rush,
David O'Briant, Obadiah Dean, James Burris, Samuel McGee, Elijah
McPherson (Bible and slave, Bass), William McPherson (slave, Sela),
Samuel H. Baker, M. H. Smith, James & George Stewart, Hugh Gregg. James
Gilmer, Clerk.

APPRAISEMENT - ESTATE OF ELIZABETH MC PHERSON
Dec'd. James Gunnin, Esq., Adm'r. (Will annexed) 28 July 1848.
Anderson Dist., S. C. Slaves: Julia & her child Becky; Lots of goods
numbered 1 to 12 and set apart for 12 of the Legatees, viz: Lot #1 -
Lucy Fields; Lot #2 - Pheby McFall; Lot #3 - Sarah Brown's children;
Lot #4 - Lina Earp; Lot #5 - William McPherson; Lot #6 - Milly McGee;
Lot #7 - Elijah McPherson; Lot #8 - Nancy Brown; Lot #9 - John McPherson;
Lot #10 - Eleanor Steel; Lot #11 - Polly Gunnins children; Lot #12 -
Elisha McPherson's children.

SALE BILL - ESTATE OF MRS. ELIZABETH MC PHERSON
Dec'd. James Gunnin, Esq., Adm'r. 1 & 2 Nov. 1848. Pur.: Wm.
Stephenson, Wm. Jones, Sam'l McGee, Thos. Burris, Sr., James Burris,
Geo. Stuart, Sr., Cornelius Latham, James Gunnin, Esq., David O'Briant,
M. H. Smith, Dr. Thos. Lee, Abner Brown, Rev. David Humphreys, John A.
Stevenson, John Dunkin, James Caldwell, Jepthah Brown, Samuel Brown,
Samuel H. Baker, John Jones, James Herring, James Taylor, J. H. Reed,
A. H. Townsend, Jeremiah Brown, Ebenezer Smith, George Howard, E. J.
Earle, Jesse C. McGee, Hugh Gregg, James Gilmer, Wm. Long, Samuel
Buchanan, James Stuart, Newton Brown, John Harris, John Davis, Miss Jane
Gunnin for James Gunnin, Esq. (Julia and Beck), T. D. Cook, Rev. John
Moore. James Gilmer, Clerk. 3 Nov. 1848.

INVENTORY & APPRAISEMENT - ESTATE OF JOHN MORRIS
Dec'd. 21 Nov. 1848. Appr's: Samuel H. McCollum, James Dobbins,
James McCleskey, Joel Ledbetter.

SALE BILL - PERSONAL PROPERTY OF JOHN MORRIS
Dec'd. 23 Nov. 1848. Elizabeth Morris, A. C. Dobbins, Amos Morris,
Joseph Colwell, James McLeskey, Charles Barrett, A. D. Hembree, James
Smith, Levi Garrison, Harrison Bullman, D. J. Morris, Foster Garrison,
W. H. Bullman, Charles Williford, Robert Gilmer, S. P. Hillhouse, H. W.
McCarley, Oliver Bullman, Wm. Hale, F. A. Chastain, Jarrett Busby,
James Winter, James Morris. James Morris, Adm'r.

INVENTORY - PERSONAL ESTATE OF THOMAS CRAWFORD
Dec'd. Notes on: George D. King and V. D. Fant, Henry Crawford,
Stephen McCully, James Gordon, P. S. Vandiver, David Crawford, Samuel
Crawford, Daniel Bagwell.

SALE BILL - ESTATE OF THOMAS CRAWFORD
Dec'd. Pur.: Mrs. Crawford, H. Crawford, James Crawford, Samuel
Crawford, Daniel Bagwell. James Crawford, Adm'r.

INVENTORY - PERSONAL ESTATE OF JOHN SMITH
Dec'd. James D. Smith, Ex'r. 9 Dec. 1848. (Large Bible) Negroes:
Tom, David, Burton, Barbary. Notes: Wm. D. Wilson, Wm. Mullikin,
John C. Smith, A. M. Smith, Wm. Robinson, James Lollir.

SALE BILL - PERSONAL ESTATE OF JOHN SMITH
Dec'd. J. D. Smith (Bible) also (Negro man Tom and woman Barbary),
A. M. Smith, D. W. Wilson, M. H. Barkley, Frank Mitchel, Benjamin
Mullikin, C. W. Pickle, John Berdine, Brad Day, E. W. Pickle, R. F.
Wyatt, D. M. Durham, J. A. M. Cason, F. N. Glenn, Leroy Barr, J. C.
Smith (Burton), John Williams, Wm. S. Birge, J. M. Welborn, Wm. Galasby,
Wm. Orr, Jr., Isaac Davis, Jas. Gambrell, Wm. Tompkins, Wm. D. Wilson
(man Dave). 12 Dec. 1848. Wm. S. Pickens, Clerk.

INVENTORY & APPRAISEMENT - ESTATE OF REUBEN GENTRY
Dec'd. 25 Aug. 1848. Inventory continues to 19 Sept. 1848 by James
McLeskey, A. (Amariah) Felton, Geo. Tippen. 20 Dec. 1848.

SALE BILL - PERSONAL ESTATE OF REUBEN GENTRY
Dec'd. Sold on 19 Sept. 1848. Cassa Gentry, A. D. Hembree, Amariah
Felton, Robert Cochran, William Burris, Sejd. Stribling, James Hembree,
Thomas W. Terry, Early Watters. James McCleskey, Clerk. 21 Dec. 1848.

APPRAISEMENT & INVENTORY - ESTATE OF JOHN RICHIE
Dec'd. Wm. Adams, Att'y Ex'r. Appr's: John Hix, Henry Clark, Peter
E. Belote.

SALE BILL - PERSONAL ESTATE OF JOHN RICHIE
Dec'd. Pur.: Wm. A. Russel, J. B. Earle, W. A. Palmore, G. Hix, Wm.
Steele, C. B. Moses, A. D. Atkins, Elias Brown, J. C. Miller, A. A.
Hobson, S. R. McElroy, Clerk. 30 Aug. 1848.

INVENTORY - PERSONAL PROPERTY OF DAVID RICHARDSON
Dec'd. 25 Jan. 1849. Negro: Tom. Note on B. H. Irby, A. W. Rochester,
Alfred Lewis, Wm. Brewer, John Mathis, Creswell Stott, Peter Elrod, Wm.
Tims, John Duckworth, D. Wimpey; J. D. Amick, Ex'r. Appr'd by: Charles
Irby, Wyatt Smith, N. Rochester, Jesse Gray.

INVENTORY - PERSONAL ESTATE OF ELIJAH HERRING
Dec'd. Anderson Dist., S. C. Levi Herring, Adm'r. Appr's: David
Simmons, H. M. Barton, Abraham Meredith. 3 Jan. 1849.

SALE BILL - ESTATE OF ELIJAH HERRING
Dec'd. Sale on 3 Jan. 1849. A. Meredith, Jesse Herring, Clara Herring,
Elisha Webb, David Simmons, Robert Brown, T. H. Simmons, J. H. Maret,
Wm. Palmer, John Hendrix, Demce Bobo, W. J. Herring, Wm. P. King, R. M.
Brown, John Simmons, Matthew Martin, Samuel P. Harris, Levi Herring,
Salathiel Bradberry, A. J. Lowrey, Robert Maxwell, James Bradberry,
Archibald Cole, Robert King, Berry Hix.

SALE BILL - PERSONAL ESTATE OF DAVID PRESLEY
Dec'd. Pur.: Wm. Obriant, K. Sullivan, Wm. Hatton, E. Wilbanks

271

(Lucinda and child), L. Johnson (Lavinia, Jacob, Emily, John). Note: Johnson and Wilbanks are Legatees. J. H. Reid. 23 Jan. 1849. K. Sullivan, Clerk.

APPRAISEMENT - ESTATE OF HARMAN CUMMINS
Dec'd. 16 Apr. 1851. Appr's: Samuel Dean, Moses Dean, James Stevenson.

2nd SALE BILL - PERSONAL ESTATE OF EPHRAIM MAYFIELD
Dec'd. 21 Dec. 1849. Wm. Mayfield, Austin Mayfield, Wm. Telford, Abraham Mayfield, Thos. R. Cates, James Telford, H. M. Gaines. John C. Horton, Clerk.

SALE BILL - ESTATE OF SAMUEL MC COY
Dec'd. 17 Feb. 1849. Elijah Major, J. L. Todd, K. C. McCoy, N. Kay, J. A. Major, H. Latimer, S. Kay, M. McGee, W. A. Trussel.

APPRAISEMENT - PERSONAL PROPERTY OF JOSEPH WATKINS
Dec'd. Negroes: Moses, Berry and Sarah, Tack, Larkin, Julia. Appr's: F. M. Glenn, H. B. Fielding, Fielding Watkins, John Owen.

SALE BILL - ESTATE OF JOSEPH WATKINS
Dec'd. 8 Mar. 1849. Mrs. Jane Watkins (boy Berry, Moses and Sarah), Rebecca Watkins, Zephaniah Smith, Elizabeth Watkins, Jane C. Watkins, R. Spiller, William Watkins (Tack and Julia), J. Cox, David Watkins (Larkin), T. A. Watkins, Thos. Martin, C. M. Lay, Jesse Martin, Henry Fielding, Elam Sharpe, Jas. Wilburn, Silas Floyd, Warren Martin, Jos. Eaton, Willis Newton, Wm. Sloan, George Seaborn, J. J. Hunt, Benjamin Mullikin, Wm. Smith, G. W. Rankin, Abner Fant, Thomas Crenshaw, A. D. Gaillard, Jno. M. Laurens, F. M. Glenn, Jno. T. Sloan, A. W. Ross. J. T. Sloan, Clerk.

APPRAISEMENT - ESTATE OF J. L. NORTH
Late of Anderson Dist., S. C., dec'd., as shown by Mrs. Eliza Elliott North, as follows: 32 slaves to wit: William, Lucy, Hetty, Maurice, Hannah, Hester, Tombo, Priscilla, Binah, Tom, Nancy, Molley, Mary, Tom, Mary, Robert, Smart, Harrison, Diana, Phillis, Margaret, Symmes, Margaret, Arthur, Elizabeth, George, Linda, Frederick, Henry, Paris, Elias and Mary Ann. 11 Dec. 1848. Signed: E. B. Benson, Robt. A. Maxwell, John T. Sloan.

INVENTORY - ESTATE OF TILMAN B. GARRETT
Dec'd. Appr'd. 31 Mar. 1849. Sarah Garret, Adm'x. Appr's: G. D. King, John B. Quailes, Robt. Smith, James White.

INVENTORY - PERSONAL ESTATE OF A. J. DONALD
Dec'd., late of Anderson Dist., S. C. 20 Nov. 1848. Merchandise, goods, chattels, etc. Notes: J. P. Reed, E. Webb, Gibson F. Fant, Col. John McFalls, Dr. A. Evins, C. C. Langston, W. P. Norris, Robert Keys, Reuben Ritchie, James Cannon, James Dalrymple, A. Holt, Alfred Moore, Dennis Tippen, Eben Smith, Wm. Jackson, J. T. Whitefield, C. D. Gaillard, D. H. Drennan, Wm. Pelfrey, John Reid, M. M. Goode, R. R. Dickison, A. V. Brooks, Mayberry Snipes, Ezekiel George, Wm. Drennan, James Cannon, David Drennan, S. H. Langston, W. B. Bailey. Col. John McFall, Adm'r.

SALE BILL - ESTATE OF A. J. DONALD
Dec'd. Mrs. Donald, Jno. Martin, E. George, John McFall, Thos. Gear, Geo. Tippen, Alex. Kay, A. J. Reeves, Thomas Martin, John Thompson, John Stevenson, James P. Cochran, D. H. Cochran, R. R. Dickerson, A. M. Norris, C. J. Thayer, Alfred Holt, A. B. Gentry, N. Ertzberger, J. W. Guyton, A. O. Norris. 3 Spet. 1849. Samuel Crawford, clerk.

INVENTORY OF PERSONAL PROPERTY OF WILLIAM C. HAYNIE
Dec'd. (Law books and large library) Appr'd. by Thos. R. Cherry, E. B. Benson and J. V. Shanklin. Elam Sharpe, Jr., Adm'r. Pendleton 12 April 1849.

INVENTORY OF ESTATE OF B. T. (?) RODGERS
Dec'd. (BENJAMIN T. RODGERS) 14 March 1849. Negroes: Jack, Esther,

Mariah. Appr'd. by A. M. Neal, J. T. Rodgers and Charles Kay. Mrs.
Hester Rodgers, Admt'rx.

SALE BILL OF PERSONAL ESTATE OF BENJ. F.(?) T.(?) RODGERS
Dec'd. 29 March 1849. Benjamin Irby (boy Jack) (girl Esther and girl
Mariah) Benjamin Duckworth, Clerk.

APPRAISAL & INVENTORY OF ESTATE OF HUBBARD PARTAIN
Dec'd. _____ 1849. Kelly Sullivan, Ex'r. Appr's: W. Hewins(?),
John Stewart and M. P. Havird(?).

SALE BILL - ESTATE OF HUBBARD PARTAIN
Dec'd. 25 July 1849. John Moon (Moore?), L. Buchanan, Jes. Brown,
J. H. Reid, Geo. Stevenson, Wm. G. Speed, K. Sullivan, F. Roache, M.
Dunlap, J. H. Partain, R. B. Alexander, Jennings Partain, F. W. Davis,
H. E. Parker, J. J. Partain, Jincy Evans, D. F. Partain, D. Obriant, J.
Neal, Wm. Hewins, John Seagler, J. L. Burriss, James Stevenson, Joel
Partain, Elias Roach, J. D. Watt, H. Roach, Wm. Simpson, Abner Brown,
John Stewart, William E. Webb. K. Sullivan, Clerk.

INVENTORY & APPRAISAL ESTATE OF DANIEL KELLY
Dec'd. Appr's: J. S. Carter, Elihu Wigginton and Lewis Owen. Joseph
Kelly, Adm'r. 17 Oct. 1849.

SALE BILL - ESTATE PF DANIEL KELLY
Dec'd. 18 Oct. 1849. Francis Kelly, N. Tripp, Joseph Kelly, Elisha
Kelly, Lucinda Kelly, Norman Clardy, Margaret Kelly, W. S. Smith, O.
Caison, Wm. M. Orr, D. C. Kelly, Larkin Rodgers, William McAlister,
Griffin Smith, Abraham Riley, William S. Smith, A. G. Welborn, Franklin
Cobb, Wm. Glasby, A. J. Caison, J. H. Tripp, Aaron B. Holland, Ezekiel
Long, J. J. Hunt, Allen Elrod, Harrison Jones, N. T. Richardson, Edward
Gillespie, John Garrett, Wm. Mullikin, George Elrod, Andrew Smith,
Greenlee Glaspay, Edw. Glaspay, H. J. Roberts, Jesse Garrett, Jefferson
B. Moore, Michael Lowlens, Richard Davis, S. L. Westmoreland, Mary
Gibbs, Nathan Briant, Leroy Barr, Wm. Durham, Wm. W. Wilson, Simion
Smith, Robert Rogers, P. P. Smith.

APPRAISE BILL - ESTATE OF CATHARINE STANTON
Dec'd. Notes due: Joseph Cox, Jasper Williams, John Gambrell, A. B.
Cobb, Wm. M. Cooley, Reuben Poor, C. P. Dean, J. C. Horton, William
Holland, N. H. Welborn, Sion T. Richardson, Gabriel Cox, Joseph Cox,
R. M. Poor, Saml. Wilson, R. M. Stott, Abner Cox, J. M. Cox, John Poor,
C. B. Stanton, Howard Duckworth, Joel E. Ellison, Miles Ellison, Wm.
Holland, A. R. Broyles, G. R. Brown, James C. Nicholas, J. W. Guyton,
Thos. Duckworth, James Gambrell, Harper Gambrell, Thomas Stanton,
Reuben B. Cox, S. R. Williams, William Holland and W. A. Williams.
Herbert Hammond, O.A.D. C. B. Stanton, Adm'r. 24 Nov. 1849.

SALE BILL - ESTATE OF CATHARINE STANTON
Dec'd. 29 Nov. 1849. J. B. Lewis, J. W. Lewis, Reuben Poor, Henry
Lawless. William Tilford, Clerk.

INVENTORY & APPRAISEMENT - ESTATE OF THOMAS WILLIAMS
Dec'd. Negro: woman Liza (also spelled Eliza). Notes: J. P. Benson,
Thos. Hanks, John Cunningham. 28 July 1849. Robert Brackenridge, L.
Haney and James Emmerson, Appr's.

SALE BILL - ESTATE OF THOMAS WILLIAMS
Dec'd. James Brackenridge, Thos. Hanks, "Widow" Williams, George A.
Ruff (woman Eliza), Andrew Hawkins, P. B. Haynie, A. Keaton, Elizy
Ritsinger. 17 Aug. 1849. Anthony Hanks, Clerk.

INVENTORY & APPRAISAL - ESTATE OF ALFRED KELLY
Dec'd. Negroes: Easter, Jim, Fanny, Ben, George. Appr's: John
Harper, Josiah W. Cobb, Elijah Pepper and Dr. W. B. Millwee. Anderson
Dist. Mary Kelly, Adm'rx. W. A. Williams, Adm'r. 29 May 1849.

SALE BILL - ESTATE OF ALFRED KELLY
Dec'd. F. Harbort, S. R. Williams, Jno. Harper, W. A. Williams, Wm.

Cooly, B. F. Crymes, W. J. Kelly, J. W. Poor, W. B. Millwee, J. Wardlaw,
W. L. Harper, Mary Kelly (George and Esther), John Croft, Hiram Cooley
(Fanny), Wm. Gilkyson (Jim), Saml. Wilson, William Poor, Allen Kelly,
William Croft, John Kelly, William Cooley, Frederick Croft. Jeffreis
G. Johnson, Clerk.

SALE BILL - PERSONAL ESTATE OF DAVID RICHARDSON
Dec'd. 3 May 1849. Elijah Teague, Nathaniel Rochester, Jesse Gray,
John D. Amick, J. D. Gaillard, William Webb, Joseph Williams, A. W.
Richardson, W. R. Boroughs, Charles Irby, Thomas Duckworth, William
Campbell, Thomas Harper, Wyatt Smith, A. D. Gaillard, Jesse Gray, J. J.
Barron, James Ingram, Sanford Simpson, Minyard Ball, Samuel Bell.
Herbert Hammond, Clerk.

INVENTORY - PERSONAL ESTATE OF ROBERT DUNCAN
Dec'd. Anderson Dist., S. C. 14 Aug. 1849. (Includes shares in
Columbus & Greenville R.R.) James Emmerson, John McPhail, John Herron
and J. M. Brown, Appr's.

SALE BILL - ESTATE OF ROBERT DUNCAN
Dec'd. 23 Aug. 1849. W. D. Gray, John Duncan, B. F. Duncan, George
Haynie, John Tate, Robert Finley, J. H. Cannon, Jas. Emmerson, Jasper
Brown, John McPhail, A. M. McFall, Stephen Haynie, Martha Duncan,
John Haynie, Charles McConnell, Samuel Webb, Robert Todd, S. J.
Emmerson (shares in R.R.). Jasper Brown, Clerk.

SALE BILL - ESTATE OF ASA CLINKSCALES
Dec'd. James L. Orr, Ex'r. 21 Jan. 1848. Asa Vandiver, J. L. Orr,
D. H. Cochran, John McFall, Robert Duncan, Wm. M. Archer, George Tippen,
John Kay, V. D. Fant, Wm. F. Clinkscales, J. Y. Fretwell, M. M. Anderson,
John Haynie, A. Felton, Andrew Shearer, James P. Gray. P. C. Haynie,
Clerk.

APPRAISAL - PERSONAL ESTATE OF ASA CLINKSCALES
Dec'd. 8 Nov. 1849. Enoch Majors, J. S. Allen and A. H. Waddill,
Appr's.

SALE BILL - ESTATE OF ASA CLINKSCALES
Dec'd. James L. Orr, Ex'r. 1 Nov. 1849. John Haynie, N. M. Ertzburger,
John McGee, Wilson Hall, P. C. Haynie, S. W. Kay, Thos. Gear, B. D. Kay,
William B. Long, Nimrod Kay, E. L. Smith, James S. Magee, F. S. Allen,
Jesse Rutledge, Wm. B. Gibson, J. P. Cochran, J. D. Pritchard, Aaron
Vandiver, W. B. Long, E. P. Smith, J. Pearman, G. Stevenson, W. Carlile,
F. Rice, G. Waddle, W. P. Flowers, J. T. Whitefield.

APPRAISAL - ESTATE OF JOHN WILSON
Dec'd. Anderson Dist., S. C. Notes: John P. Sitton, Reid Gambrell,
David Durham, James Gambrell, John Pegg, Matthew Gambrell, Carr
Blasingame, S. G. Rosemond, John B. Smith, Andrew Smith, Robert Bowen,
A. W. Holcomb, Loven Staten, H. Givens, C. W. Smith, R. E. Blasingame,
B. H. Douthitt, William Mulliken, Simeon Smith, James Ellison, Elijah
Satterfield, Samuel Jones, William Jones, M. F. Mitchell. Reid Gambrell,
Ex'r. 9 Nov. 1849. Wm. D. Sitton, O. P. Carson and J. Satterfield,
Appr's.

SALE BILL - ESTATE OF JOHN WILSON
Dec'd. 8 Nov. 1849. Reig Gambrell, J. P. Sitton, Thomas Davis, W. D.
Wilson, A. Bico, J. Satterfield, Wm. D. Sitton, Clerk.

INVENTORY - ESTATE OF DAVID ALEXANDER
Dec'd. 30 Oct. 1849. M. McGee, Adm'r. Wm. Cox, App'r.

SALE BILL - ESTATE OF DAVID ALEXANDER
Dec'd. 30 Oct. 1849. M. McGee, Stephen Hanks, J. W. McDavid, A. R.
Broyles, Elizabeth Alexander, Wm. Callahan, Matthew Williams, M. E.
Mitchell, A. Mattison, J. L. Todd.

INVENTORY - ESTATE OF WILEY CHASTAIN
Dec'd. 15 Oct. 1849. R. D. Crymes, Adm'r. Posey Trussell, J. G.

Gantt and Joel Cox, Appr's. Wm. Mattison.

SALE BILL - ESTATE OF WILEY CHASTAIN
Dec'd. 19 Oct. 1849. Hampton Stone, Benj. Crymes, Vincent Shaw, Robert
D. Crymes, John G. Gantt, Wm. C. Harper, Thomas W. Davis.

INVENTORY - ESTATE OF BLACKMAN BURTON
Dec'd. German(?) Burton, Ex'r. 18 Dec. 1849. Negroes: Julius and
Ned.

INVENTORY - ESTATE OF JAMES MATTISON, SR.
Dec'd. (DANIEL MATTISON, survivor) 23 Nov. 1849. Negroes: Curry,
Clary, Charity, Sarah, Wesley, Mat, Nelly, Hala, Mary, Betty, Fiely(?),
John, Charles, Nelson, Emery, Arter, Isaac, Milton, Sanford, Berry,
Jim, Martin, Bill, Henry, George and Riah. William and Daniel Mattison,
Ex'rs. Mason Kay, William Kay, Sr., James Gambrell and Posey Trussel.

NOTES AND ACCOUNTS BELONGING TO THE ESTATE OF JAMES MATTISON, DEC'D.,
AND THE FIRM OF SD. DEC'D. AND DANIEL MATTISON, SURVIVOR.
Holbert Acker, Alexander Austin, Joel Arnold, William Adams, Hardyman
Baramore, Dr. M. G. Burry, John Browns lee, Mrs. Nancy Bagwell, John W.
Bohannan, Robert Brownlee, John W. Bigby, David Cummins, Thomas Cox, Sr.,
Reuben B. Cox, Anis Cox, David Cox, Joseph Cox, Thomas J. Cox, Abraham
Cornelius, Robert D. Crymes, John Cullins, Haywood Davis, Aaron Davis,
Thomas W. Davis, William Davis, Jr., Henson Davis, George W. Dove,
James Dick, William B. Davenport, John Freeman, Strouther Flowers,
Toliver S. Flowers, Reuben Freeman, Jesse Gent, Matthew Gambrell, John
Gambrell, Jesse George, James S. Gambrell, Micajah Gambrell, Reid
Gambrell, Mrs. Elizabeth Gaines, John Gray, James L. Greer, John Gaines,
Wm. Gaines, John Henton, John Hughs, Uriah Hughs, George F. Hughs, Wm.
Harper, Gabriel Hand, Jos. Johnston, Albert W. Kay, Larkin Kay, Wm.
Kay, Sr., Mason Kay, William Kinnan, Joseph M. Kinnan, Samuel Kinnan,
Thomas Morgan, Wyatt Mattison, John Moon, Jackson Mattison, Absolum
Morrison, William Morrison, George Mattison, Sr., Allen Mahorn, Colbert
Mattison, Joel Morrison, John Morrison, James Morgan, Wm. P. Mattison,
Albert E. Mattison, Jas. F. Mattison, Elizabeth Mattison, Elizabeth
Monroe, Peter E. Mattison, Wyatt Norwood, James F. Nabors, Drayton D.
Nabors, Martin Nabors, William Nabors, Austin D. Nabors, Edwin Nabors,
Blufort Lawson, William Long, Sr., John Leach, William Long, Jr.,
Harrison S. Long, Clarissa Loveless, Daniel Lovin, James S. Lucius,
Philip Lee, Reuben Leach, Vincent Gambrell, Alexander Paget, Wm. S.
Philips, Lorenzo D. Phillips, Lewis Pyles, William Poor, E. Penn, E.
Penn, Nancy Robinson, John Richey, Francis A. Ragsdale, John B.
Robinson, David B. Stone, David Smith (in Greenville), James Mattison,
Daniel Mattison, Richard Smith, John W. B. Scott, John B. Sutherland,
Vincent Shaw, Hampton Stone, John W. Smith, Elizabeth Stone, Rhodain
Trussel, Wesley Trussel, Robt. O. Tribble, John Wright, John Wilson,
Norris Wright, Franklin Wright, Henry Loveless, Mrs. Margaret Long,
Henson Posey, Elizabeth Long, Burkley Bagwell, Reuben Long, Benjamin
Jordan, Lucinda Bagwell.

INVENTORY OF ESTATE OF W. SMITH
Dec'd. Joseph Cox and M. Smith, Ex'rs. 11 Apr. 1849. Negroes: Bob
and John, Washington, Gloucester, Ben, Nero, Margaret, Adaline, Jane,
Lucy, Becky, Alexander, Alfred, Mary Ann and 2 children, Isabella and
2 children, Mary, Dorcas and 2 children, Dick. Wyatt Smith, James
Wilson, Wm. Webb and Abram Martin, Appr's.

SALE BILL - ESTATE OF WILLIAM SMITH
Dec'd. 12 Apr. 1849. James Burgess, Jno. W. Guyton, Joseph Cox,
Berry Mills, Ed. Smith, Wm. Erskine, Lettice Gambrell, Battle Mayfield,
Thomas Duckworth, James Ingram, Thomas Harper, Reuben Richey, John
Smith, Anderson Cason, Jesse Lewis, Charles Irby.

INVENTORY - ESTATE OF NANCY GILMER
Dec'd. 25 Dec. 1849. James Gilmer, Adm'r. James McLees and Thomas L.
Skelton, Appr's.

275

SALE & INDENTURE - ESTATE OF NANCY GILMER
Dec'd. 19 Jan. 1850. Margaret Gilmer, John F. Early, William Campbell,
Robert Gilmer, Sr., Silas Massey, William McLees.

INVENTORY ESTATE OF DAVID PRESSLEY
Dec'd. 22 Jan. 1849. Negroes: Lucinda and child, Luvina, Jacob, Emily,
John. Rev. E. E. Pressley.

INVENTORY - ESTATE OF WILLIAM NEWELL
Dec'd. Jincy Newell, Extr'x. 9 Oct. 1849. Negroes: June, Dock and
Dicey. James Tucker, John Leveritt and A. D. Gray, Appr's.

INVENTORY - ESTATE OF JAMES P. GRAY
Dec'd. 26 Feb. 1849. Negroes: Washington, Polly and Betsy, her 2
children: Langston and Martha. John McFall, Adm'r.

SALE BILL - ESTATE OF JAMES P. GRAY
Dec'd. 27 Feb. 1849. Mary A. Gray (took negroes), John McFall, W.
Zachary, John McGregor. Wm. M. Archer, Clerk.

APPRAISAL & INVENTORY - ESTATE OF A. J. LIDDELL, ESQ.
Dec'd. Negroes: Mariah, Harriet, Sampson, Ned, Elbert and Elizabeth.
25 Aug. 1849. Wm. Steele, J. D. Gaillard and C. L. Gaillard, Appr's.

INVENTORY - ESTATE OF REV. JAMES HEMBREE
Dec'd. Negro: Peggy (about 49 yrs. old). Grief Pressley (about 14
yrs.). 6 Sept. 1849. Bryan Boroughs, C. L. Gaillard, Amariah Felton
and Jos. D. Scott, Appr's.

SALE BILL - ESTATE OF REV. JAMES HEMBREE
Dec'd. 15 Jan. 1850. James Hembree, A. D. Hembree, John Hembree, James
McLeskey, Jesse Waters, Samuel Bowen, Sally Wallace, Robert W. Reeves,
Micajah Anderson, Wm. Anderson, A. F. Hembree, A. B. Gentry, John Hix,
Miss Wallace, James McLeskey, Clerk.

INVENTORY - ESTATE OF THE 'WIDOW" SARAH KERR
Dec'd. 20 Jan. 1849. John B. Armstrong, Adm'r. R. N. Wright, James
M. Hopkins and Benjamin Shirley, Appr's.

SALE BILL - ESTATE OF SARAH KERR
Dec'd. 20 Jan. 1849. Welden Pearman, Jacob Aleywine, John Ashley,
J. B. Armstrong, R. N. Wright, Reuben Kay, George Wilson, Jr., Thomas
Bannister, John B. Robinson, J. R. Wilson, Polly Robinson, Peter
Rickets, Stephen Fields, George Grubbs, Polly Banister, W. S. Hopkins,
David Dove, Jas. A. Hall, John B. Saylors, J. R. Shirley, James Martin,
Jonathan Pearman, Joshua Ashley, Berry Sherman, Michel Taylor, Jacob
Rickets, William Fields.

APPRAISAL - ESTATE OF BIRD LANIER
Dec'd. 16 Nov. 1849. John F. Sloan, Adm'r. Thos. R. Cherry, Andrew
F. Lewis and Green Stephens, Appr's.

SALE BILL - ESTATE OF BIRD LANIER
Dec'd. 16 Nov. 1849. E. M. Cobb, J. T. Sloan, Mat. Lanier, Rev. A. W.
Ross, Mrs. Lanier, G. B. Whitten, T. B. Rodgers, John Maxwell, J. C.
Cherry, A. M. McElroy, Geo. Seaborn, Robt. Lanier, Jos. Rolander, C. B.
Moses, J. O. Lewis, E. Sharpe, Archibald Phillips. Anderson Dist., S. C.

INVENTORY - ESTATE OF WILSON WALLACE
Dec'd. 30 Oct. 1849. Mrs. Sally W. Wallace, Admt'rx. John Dalrymple,
Robert Bolt and Henry Steele, Appr's.

SALE BILL - ESTATE OF W. WALLACE
Dec'd. 1 Nov. 1849. Sally W. Wallace, Jesse George, Saml. Millwee,
G. W. Masters, Dr. A. P. Cater, Henry Steele, A. P. Hembree, J. H.
Hembree, William C. Bailey, John Warnock.

INVENTORY - ESTATE OF JAMES BROCK
Dec'd. 12 Feb. 1850. M. H. Brock, Adm'r. R. N. Wright, J. L.
Armstrong and George Grubbs, Appr's.

SALE BILL - ESTATE OF JAMES BROCK
Dec'd. 13 Feb. 1850. Geo. Grubbs, Robt. Cummins, A. J. Brock, B. F.
Shirley, Jonathan Pearman, M. H. Brock, R. N. Wright, B. T. Shirley,
James Martin, James Brock, James Massey, Newton Brock, J. R. Shirley,
Caleb Cullins, A. Webb, J. A. Branyan, James Elgin, Elgin Kay, E. D.
Pruitt, Joseph Howthorn.

INVENTORY - ESTATE OF JAMES O. MARTIN
Dec'd. Late of Anderson Dist., S. C. John A. Martin, Adm'r. 23 Jan.
1850.

SALE BILL - ESTATE OF JAMES O. MARTIN
Dec'd. 24 Jan. 1850. Melissa Martin, John A. Martin, Charles Bowie,
Jos. O'Brian, Joshua Buchanan, C. D. Giles, William Cook, R. Boyd,
A. J. Smith, Alexander Gray, J. Abels, Joel Galbreath, H. J. Stevenson,
John Spearman, R. Simpson, Wm. Sherard. E. S. Martin, Clerk.

INVENTORY - ESTATE OF W. R. NELSON
Dec'd. S. H. Baker, Wm. Dollar and H. Gregg, Appr's. 14 Mar. 1850.

SALE BILL - ESTATE OF W. R. NELSON
Dec'd. W. R. Nelson, M. H. Smith, E. J. Earle, A. W. Harper, D.
McConnell, L. Shiflett, E. P. Sanders. 14 Mar. 1850.

INVENTORY - ESTATE OF WM. F. WRIGHT
Dec'd. R. N. Wright, Adm'r. 9 Jan. 1850.

SALE BILL - ESTATE OF WILLIAM F. WRIGHT
Dec'd. 9 Jan. 1850. R. N. Wright, Jos. Elgin, M. H. Brock, Samuel
Robinson, "Widow" Wright, James Armstrong, Jonathan Pearman.

INVENTORY - ESTATE OF JOHN M. KEYS
Dec'd. Late of Anderson Dist., S. C. 16 Mar. 1850. Negro: George.
Henry Crawford, Samuel M. Wilkes, John W. McGregor and J. Y. Fretwell,
Appr's.

SALE BILL - ESTATE OF JOHN M. KEYS
Dec'd. "Widow" Keys, E. S. Norris, Joshua Burris, A. Felton, Reuben
Burris, Wm. P. Strange, E. J. Smith, William Holmes, J. Fretwell, A. E.
Thompson, W. D. Smith, Henry Crawford, Peter McPhail, K. Breazeale,
Moses Dean (boy, George). 26 Mar. 1850.

INVENTORY & APPRAISEMENT - ESTATE OF ALBERT T. CARPENTER
Dec'd. 21 Nov. 1849. Negro: Caroline. James M. Carpenter, Adm'r.

SALE BILL - ESTATE OF ALBERT T. CARPENTER
Dec'd. 21 Nov. 1849. Mrs. C. Carpenter (girl, Caroline), Alfred
Carpenter, William Holmes, James A. Major, George Roof, David Geer,
A. M. Carpenter.

SALE BILL - PERSONAL PROPERTY OF JOHN GENTRY
Dec'd. R. B. McCarley, James Burris, Moody Gentry, Henry Moore,
Dempsey Lewis, John Henson, John Moore, J. R. Moore. 27 Apr. 1850.

INVENTORY - ESTATE OF DANIEL BAGWELL
Dec'd. 14 May 1850. Appr's.: Matthew Snipes, Henry H. Crawford,
James Crawford.

SALE BILL - ESTATE OF DANIEL BAGWELL
Dec'd. 24 Dec. 1850. "Widow" Bagwell, Samuel Crawford, James Crawford.

SALE BILL - ESTATE (PERSONAL PROPERTY) OF JAMES MATTISON, SR.
Dec'd. 1 Jan. ___ William K. Clement, B. T. Shirley, Vincent Shaw,
Thomas Cox, L. W. Branyan, William Gambrell, John M. Cox, Henry F.
Harper, John L. Davis, Chester Bagwell, Strouther Kay, Alexander Austin,
John Hunt, John M. Cox, James M. Gambrell, Robert O. Tribble, William
C. Harper, William Robinson, William Reece, Mason Kay, Burry Coker,
Ephraim Cobb, Peter G. Acker, Nimrod Kay, Reuben B. Cox, J. C. Gambrell,
William Mosely, William Nabors, D. L. Cox, Noah R. Reeves, S. N. Tribble,

William Clinkscales, G. C. Gambrell, John Wilson, Henry Maddox, P. A.
Acker, Henry Loveless, James Adams, R. N. Shirley, James N. Richey,
Jackson Mattison, Joel Smith, William Kay, Sr., William Mattison, John
W. Featherston, J. E. Hollida, Rev. Alexander Acker, William Smith,
Edwin Nabors, Leroy W. Mattison, Benjamin Clement, B. Davenport, Hyram
Cooley, Daniel Gent, William Holmes, Benjamin F. Moseley, Thomas
Mattison, Francis A. Ragsdale, Aris Cox, William Holland, John M. Cox,
David L. Donald, Charles Mattison, James McCullough, Marion Mitchell
(woman Clary), Elizabeth Carpenter (Charity and Mahala), E. B. Gambrell
(Sarah, Wesley and Mat), Lettice Gambrell (Feely and Henry), Daniel
Mattison (Isaac and wife), William P. Kay (Mary), Joseph Cox (Betty,
Sanford, Bursy (Burry?)), Wyatt Mattison (Charles and Nelson), Mariah
Smith (John), Thomas Hathorn (Emery), William P. Martin (Arter), Robert
Scott (Milton), Malinda Townsend (Bill and Jim), James M. Carpenter
(George), Daniel Mattison (Marion, unsound), William Kay, Sr., Abner
Cox, Albert E. Mattison, Absolom Morrison, John Greer, James F. Mattison,
James Brock, Jonathan Pearman, Mary Mattison, Charles Mattison, James
W. Youngblood, Albert W. Kay, Andrew Monroe, Isaac Clement, Holbert A.
Cobb, Robinson Cobb, Edwin Mattison, John Hinton. 21 Mar. 1850.

SALE BILL - PROPERTY BELONGING TO THE FIRM OF JAMES MATTISON, SR.,
DEC'D. AND DANIEL MATTISON, SURVIVOR.
1 Jan. 1850. Elizabeth Carpenter, Asa Avery, Daniel Gent, Redmund
Hughes, James W. Richey, John Richey, Thomas Robinson, Albert E.
Mattison, J. W. Youngblood, William Gambrell, Daniel Mattison, William
Mosely, Allen McDavid, Vincent Shaw, William Kay, Sr., James Nabors,
James M. Gambrell, John Wilson, Wyatt Mattison, Isaac Clement, Noah R.
Reeves, Joseph Cox, William P. Martin, Meredith Brock, John B. Armstrong,
Alexander Austin, Lewis F. Weights, Wm. Holmes, James McCullough,
Hampton Stone, Archibald Armstrong, Joel Kay, Hyrum Cooley, Christopher
Clement. 21 Mar. 1850. James F. Mattison, Clerk.

SALE BILL - GOODS IN STORE BELONGING TO THE FIRM OF JAMES MATTISON, SR.,
DEC'D. AND DANIEL MATTISON, SURVIVOR
3 Jan. 1850. M. H. Brock, Jane Webster, Newton Mitchell, G. G. Majors,
Micajah Gambrell, M. Trowbridge, R. S. Greer, David Duncan, Nace
Morrison, John Brownlee, R. N. Wright, Matthew Bagwell, W. D. Gilkerson,
Sanford Gambrell, Franklin Greer, Henry Pope, Tilman Maddox, William
Brownin, Joel Arnold, Elihu Acker, L. D. Phillips, Jno. Seawright,
Redmund Wyatt, Rec. C. P. Dean, T. B. Barnwell, Wm. Welborn, Wyatt
Norwood, J. W. Medlock, etc. (Note...numerous pages of this sale,
which include almost all the before named persons from the sales of
estate and firm...cme) 23 Feb. 1850. W. P. Martin, Clerk.

INVENTORY - PERSONAL EFFECTS OF HEZEKIAH RILEY
Dec'd. Negro: Ephraim (17) Notes: S. V. Gentry, S. McCulley, F. L.
Scott, Thos. S. Wilkes, Thos. F. Swan, Robert Wilson, Levi Garrison,
V. A. Lawhon. J. P. Reed, Ex'r. 22 July 1850. Appr's.: John R.
Harsey, A. O. Norris, J. W. Guyton, Joseph Cox and Elijah Webb.

INVENTORY - PERSONAL ESTATE OF THOMAS M. SLOAN
Dec'd. Appr's: John T. Sloan, William Sloan, Saml. E. Maxwell and
W. H. D. Gaillard. 1 Dec. 1849. Negroes: Young Matt (27), Charles
(23), Rhubin (26), Harry (48), Sam and Sue, old Frank-Blacksmith (25),
Jim (36), Wallace (18), Hyram (12), Silvy (35) and 1 child (1), 1
child (3) and 1 child (5), Rose (8), Henry (14), Jake (4), Chany (44)
and 1 child (4 mos.) and 1 child (2 years), and old woman, mother to
Chany, Sue (5), Peggy (6), Isaac (10), Hannah (13), Flora (15), Joe (9),
Mary (21) and 1 child (1) and 1 child (2), Emily (24) and 1 child (4)
and 1 child (6), Nancy (60), Elijah (28), Andy-carpenter (35), Silvy
(22) and 1 child (1), Sarah (14), John (7), Letty (60), Cely (14),
Charlotte (10),... Notes: E. B. Benson, Jas. M. Crawford, J. F.
Gould, Bird Lanier, C. B. Moses, R. A. Maxwell, Mrs. Stephens, J. T.
Sloan, T. J. Sloan,... Acc'ts. due estate: A. C. Campbell, Thos.
Davis, Miss Mary Hunter, William Sloan, William Hubbard, Jno. B. Sloan,
Miss Alice E. D. Smith, Benj. S. Smith, Emily H. Smith, Mrs. Elisha
Lawrence, W. J. Knauff, David M. Sloan, Earle Holcombe, Jack Haze,
Mrs. Hodges, Mrs. Burriss, Benson and Son, Jno. L. N. Smith, Sara E. A.
Smith, William C. Smith, John M. Lawrence, C. B. Moses. Anderson Dist.,

S. C. Benj. F. Sloan, Adm'r. 1 Dec. 1849.

SALE BILL - PERSONAL ESTATE OF THOMAS M. SLOAN
Dec'd. 9 and 11 Jan. 1850. M. R. Hunnicutt, W. A. Cox, Nancy Sloan,
B. F. Sloan, Jno. T. Sloan, Edward Cobb, E. G. Mullinix, Jno. B.
Benson, William Sloan, W. G. Mullinix, C. B. Moses, A. F. Lewis, Geo.
Seaborn, R. A. Maxwell, J. V. Shanklin, Samuel Early, Benjamin Leathers,
Jno. S. Lorton, Bratton Dickson, R. O. Jarrett. Negroes purchased by:
Jas. W. Crawford (Charlotte and Andy), Jas. Daniels (Frank), Nancy
Sloan (Cely, Alfred, Letty, Sarah, Jim, Silvy and 3 children), N. L.
Harper (Rose), Thos. J. Sloan (Henry), John B. Sloan (Sue, Harry,
wife and 3 children), Burt. McGee (Peggy), D. M. Sloan (Flora), Samuel
Easly (Hannah), J. F. Moseley (Isaac), G. W. Liddle (Mary and 2 children)
E. B. Benson (young Matt), J. H. Blassingame (Old Matt and Hiram),
W. M.? Lewis (Rhubin), John T. Sloan (Sam and Sue), Ed. Cobb (Eliza),
J. W. Harrison (old Isaac), J. B. Benson (Charles, Emily and 3 children),
John Bourge (Jo), Saml. E. Maxwell (Nancy), Sarah Stephens (Silvy and
child), J. O. Lewis (Wallace), J. W. Crawford (John).

APPRAISAL - ESTATE OF CORNELIUS LATHAM
Late of Anderson Dist., S. C. 21 Aug. 1850. Matthew Dunlap, Adm'r.
Appr's.: K. Sullivan, Hugh Gregg and M. H. Smith.

SALE - PERSONAL PROPERTY OF CORNELIUS LATHAM
Dec'd. 22 Aug. 1850. John Burriss, Riley Harper, Mr. Manning, Matthew
Dunlap, Elihu Sanders, "Widow" Latham, Elias Findley, E. Herring, N.
Gilmer, M. H. Smith, James Gaines, John Abels, Wm. Latham, Lewis
Shiflett, Joel Partain, Kelly Sullivan, Clerk.

INVENTORY - GOODS & CHATTELS - ESTATE OF ELIZABETH SAWYER
Dec'd. Elam Sharpe, Jr., James Hunter and J. B. Sitton, Appr's. Wm.
L. Knauff, Adm'r. 4 Sept. 1850. (family Bible).

SALE BILL - ESTATE OF MRS. ELIZABETH SAWYER
Dec'd. 20 Sept. 1850. Dr. Symmes, James Hunter, W. L. Knauff, J. C.
Miller, J. M. Arnold, T. Werner, H. Campbell, A. Hawkins, R. L. Terry,
T. Christian, L. Gibbs, J. Johnston, R. Johnston, (Mr. Knauff bought
various articles for "the family"). Thomas Christian, Clerk. Sold at
public sale at Pendleton. 20 Oct. 1850. John B. Sitton, N. P.

INVENTORY - ESTATE OF MRS. MARY SEAWRIGHT
Dec'd. James McLees, Adm'r. 21 Nov. 1850. Anderson Dist., S. C.
Appr's.: William Mills, Thomas T. Skelton, A. S. McClinton and W. S.
Shaw.

SALE BILL - ESTATE OF MARY SEAWRIGHT
Dec'd. 22 Nov. 1850. Miss Polly Seawright, W. S. Shaw, A. S. McClinton,
James Busby, James McLees, William McLees, Thos. T. Skelton, Alexander
Campbell, Robert Chamblee, Jms. Harbin. James Gilmer, Clerk.

APPRAISAL - ESTATE OF GEORGE S. SKELTON
Dec'd. Late of Anderson Dist., S. C. John W. B. Skelton, Adm'r.
31 Aug. 1850. Acc'ts. H. Stevenson, J. J. Ray, J. H. Nelson, J. N.?
Tilly, L. Tilly, J. E. Todd, Mary McLees, Mary Pagett, Marion McMullin,
Berry Long, Tom Buffington, Warren Webb, Henry McGentry. P. R. Norris
and James McLees, Appr's.

SALE BILL - ESTATE OF GEORGE S. SKELTON
Dec'd. 31 Aug. 1850. Thomas Skelton, William Campbell, A. S. McClinton,
D. M. Simpson, James Gilmer, Clerk.

APPRAISAL - REAL & PERSONAL ESTATE OF JOHN MAGEE
Dec'd. 25 Nov. 1850. Negroes: Ben, Peter, George, Mary, Jenny and
child, Hannah, Linda, Elvira, Henry. 2 tracts of land. G. L. and
W. P. Magee, Es'rs. Appr's.: K. Sullivan, M. H. Smith, E. J. Earle
and J. M. Burriss.

SALE BILL - ESTATE OF JOHN MAGEE
Dec'd. 26 Nov. and 27 Nov. 1850. J. Neal, Geo. Stevenson, G. L. Magee,

W. Dyer, L. Butler, J. L. Carter, E. J. Earle, Thos. O. Hill,
Buchanan, N. Harris, E. Sanders, M. H. Smith, J. G. Watson, S. Abels,
Thos. Davis, James Gaines, S. Scales, D. Chaoman, J. W. Puckett, R.
Baker, N. Ertzberger, J. H. Partain, J. O'Briant, A. H. McGill, J. H.
Strange, Julian Neal (309 acres), John Stewart (270 acres), Rufus
Sadler, K. Barron, W. P. Magee, N. Richey, Chiles Magee, D. C. Howard,
James Magee, D. M. Beaty, B. M. Magee (negro man George), Saml. A.
Magee (Mary), Wm. Stevenson (Peter), B. M. Magee (Ben), A. Simpson
(Henry, Jinney and child), A. Y. S. Siddle (Hannah), Burrel Magee
(Malinda), G. L. Magee (Elvira), J. Harkness, James Gaines, C. D. Giles,
Wm. Sherard, J. Clinkscales, H. Herndon, A. Wakefield.

APPRAISAL - ESTATE OF JAMES BURRISS
Dec'd. 18 Nov. 1850. Negroes: Bouze?, Abbe, Clara, Joseph, Caesar,
Milley, Nancy, Charles, Crockett, Calvin, Conny, Sylva, Julia, Jim
(June?), Frances, Mary and child George, Appr's.: Wm. S. Shaw, James
Jones, Bryon Burroughs, and Wm. Jones.

LIST OF NOTES - ESTATE OF JAMES BURRISS
Dec'd. 18 Nov. 1850. Samuel Eargain?, Manning Belcher, Henson
Scoggins, Andrew H. McGee, Obadiah Dean, Geo. W. Singlefort, Clem
Brown, Samuel Martin, J. H. and Loice O'Brian, Croft B. Hannier?,
Robert Marshall, John W. Young, Harriet McAlister, David McTolen,
David Gordon, Edward Yeargan, Thos. L. Elrod, Anderson Braswell, T. H.
O'Brian, James Ataway, Nathan Yeargin, N. McAlister, William Beaty,
Samuel Martin, T. McClennon, Robert L. Robertson, John Scoggins,
Andrew Latham, David O'Brian, John Stewart, James Thompson, John
Hammond.

SALE BILL - ESTATE OF JAMES BURRISS
Dec'd. 19 Nov. 1850. "Widow" Burriss, Thomas Davis, Geo. Stevenson,
T. N. Burriss, James Junkin, Samuel Dean, Joshua Burriss, M. A.
Galaway, E. E. Henson, Reuben Burriss, Wm. A. Glenn, J. M. Simpson,
J. B. McLees, B. F. Burriss, J. R. Kay, B. Boroughs, Levi Burriss, N.
McAlister, David McConnel, J. A. Massey, James Taylor, Moses Dean,
J. B. South, Moody Gentry, E. Shaw, Zechariah Hall, J. J. Beaty, Robert
Chamblee, H. H. Ertzberger, James Jones, Jesse O'Brian, D. H. Cochran,
Andrew Stevenson, Wilson McCoy, Benj. Sloan, S. N. Webb, Dr. Milford,
D. R. Watson, Wilborn Burriss, Newton Burriss, Alfred Neale, E. Ervin,
Jackson Hall, Wm. Tate, John Milford, J. J. Partain, Robt. Findley,
E. P. Holyman, Samuel Parker, James Wiley, B. F. Sloan, Samuel Dean,
J. N. Burriss, H. McGill, Hiram Howard, E. W. South, David Gordon,
W. B. Gibson, John Allen, F. A. Young, William Sherard, Wm. Dyer,
Martin Hall, C. D. Giles, Thomas Hill, "Widow" took (Clary, Caesar,
Calvin, Julia & June), S. W. Cunningham, Matthew Snipes (Bowser and
Abby), Thomas Burriss (Joseph), J. N. Burriss (Milly), Elias McGee
(Nancy), B. F. Burriss (Charles), J. A. Stevenson (Crockett), Julian
Neal (Canny), A. M. Neal (Sylva & Franky), Burrel McGee (Mary & child).
6 Jan. 1851. Levi Burris, Clerk.

APPRAISAL - PERSONAL PROPERTY OF ESTATE OF JAMES MC ALISTER
Dec'd. Anderson Dist., S. C. 18 Sept. 1850. Note on J. A. Tate.
Jasper Elrod, open acc't. A. Todd, Adm'r. John Henson, Nathan
McAlister and T. P. Elrod, Appr's.

SALE BILL - ESTATE OF JAMES MC ALISTER
Dec'd. 18 Sept. 1850. A. Todd, Harriet McAlister, Croft B. Hanna,
N. McAlister, Sr., James McPhail, S. E. Leopard. John Herron, Clerk.

APPRAISAL - PERSONAL PROPERTY - ESTATE OF JOANA BROWN
Dec'd. late of Anderson Dist., S. C. Peter, old negro man, and Patsy.
Isham R. Bond, Adm'r. 1 Oct. 1850. Wm. G. Speed, D. Tucker, Thomas
Morgan and John Morgan, Appr's.

SALE BILL - ESTATE OF MRS. JOANA BROWN
Dec'd. Isham R. Bond (Peter and Patsy), William O'Briant, Thomas
Morgan, B. D. Kay, John W. Prince, A. Simpson, N. P. and John Speer,
Clk.

APPRAISAL - PROPERTY OF JULIUS HUFF
Dec'd. Griffin Elrod, Adm'r. Note on Tabitha Huff, William Duckworth,
John Guyton, James Dickson, M. B. Williams. Appr's.: James Mulliken,
James J. Wilson and Abram Martin.

SALE BILL - ESTATE OF JULIUS HUFF
Dec'd. G. G. Elrod, Adm'r. Lafayette Eaton, John Golden, Thomas P.
Winn, James Wilson, Thomas Harper, James Brothers, James J. Wilson,
Ebenezer Smith, James Martin, John Smith, David Ingraham, William Webb,
William Richie, Harbin Vandiver, James H. Mulliken, Garrison Elrod,
William Elrod, Jeptha Watkins, Wilborn Duckworth, Baylis Voyles, Jacob
Martin, Samuel Elrod, Patrick Riley. James Milliken, Clerk.

INVENTORY - ESTATE OF JOHN ADAMS, SR.
Dec'd. Anderson Dist., S. C. 29 Nov. 1850. Notes: Charles Bowie,
Asa Adams. A. Simpson, R. D. Gray and F. A. Young, Appr's.

SALE BILL - ESTATE OF JOHN ADAMS, SR.
Dec'd. R. D. Gray, Asa Adams, James McKee, Dr. Sloan, J. P. Tucker,
James Gable, W. Beaty, James Stinson, A. Elgin. D. L. Bozeman, Clerk.

INVENTORY - ESTATE OF JONATHAN H. SMITH
Dec'd. Appr's.: George Rankin, Robert Pickens, A. P. Watson, Benj.
Mulliken and James Mulliken. 20 Nov. 1850. Negroes: Emily, and
Albert.

SALE BILL - ESTATE OF JONATHAN H. SMITH
Dec'd. 21 Nov. 1850. J. B. Pegg, P. E. Smith, R. Pickens,.F. M.
Glenn, W. Smith, T. F. Runils, B. R. Briant, B. Mulliken, P. McKinney,
M. F. Mitchell, S. Simpson, J. M. Smith, B. J. Watkins, R. Parmer, J. B.
McCurry, J. M. Glenn, W. Orr, E. Wigginton, J. Pilgrim. J. J. Owens,
Andrew Harris, B. H. Arnold, H. B. Fielding, L. Barr, ...sold one negro
boy named Albert, and girl named Emily. 3 Dec. 1850. James D. Smith,
Clerk.

INVENTORY - ESTATE OF CHARLES BROWN
Dec'd. 8 Nov. 1850. 200 acres land. Andrew Reid, Esq., Ex'r. K.
Sullivan, J. H. Reid and George Stevenson, Appr's. (Mentions Will of
deceased and legatees).

SALE BILL - ESTATE OF CHARLES BROWN
Dec'd. 12 Nov. 1850. Abner Brown, Charles Brown, Edward Brown, Isaac
Brown, Matthew Dunlap, John Dunlap, Thomas Cook, John Evins, Andrew
McGill, Jacob Moshet, John McMahan, David O'Briant, Henry Parker,
Samuel E. Parker, Milton Dunlap, George Stevenson, John Stewart, J. H.
Reid, S. D. M. Young, Robert Todd. J. H. Reid, Clerk.

INVENTORY - PERSONAL.ESTATE OF REV. JOHN SPEARMAN
Dec'd. 29 Nov. 1850. Negroes: Sarah and two children: Amanda and
Andy. Margaret Spearman, Ext'rx. Kelly Sullivan, J. W. Beaty and W.
Hatton, Appr's.

SALE BILL - ESTATE OF JOHN SPEARMAN
Late of Anderson Dist., S. C. Dec'd. Margaret Spearman, (negro woman
and children), Levi Gable, S. D. McCullough, J. H. Wiles. J. W. Beaty,
Clerk.

APPRAISAL - ESTATE OF PEYTON R. SHAW
Dec'd. Wm. S. Shaw, Adm'r. Appr's.: Charles Haney, John Stevenson
and M. W. Haslet. 14 Nov. 1850. Negro: boy Henry.

SALE BILL - ESTATE OF PEYTON R. SHAW
Dec'd. 15 Nov. 1850. Silas M. Massey, James C. Winter, William Glenn,
Sr., Thomas A. Skelton, Robert Gilmer, J. J. McLees, Jane Shaw, M. R.
Manning, Mrs. Rebecca McDaniel, Jno. Harbin, Jno. Tilley, Milley Evins,
Elijah Herron, Nancy Shaw, Levina Shaw, William Hale, Ransom Snipes,
Joel Cunningham, (negro boy), Silas P. Shaw, Clerk.

281

INVENTORY - ESTATE OF HENRY COBB
Dec'd. Negroes: Dick, Reed, John, Jackson, Jo, Berry, Harry, Jinny
(old), Betty and Rial, Susan, Mary, Jerry, Jesse. Notes: Mary Ann
Dalrymple and Hezekiah Gray. W. A. Williams, J. S. Carter, Thomas
Welborn and W. E. Welborn, Appr's. 29 Nov. 1850.

SALE BILL- ESTATE OF HENRY COBB
Dec'd. 3(10) Dec. 1850. Mrs. Cobb, John A. Davus, A. B. Cobb, J. W.
Cobb, Aaron Welborn, J. H. Wright, E. P. Cobb, John M. Sailors,
Benjamin Tarrant, Harrison Jones, Joseph Richards, Larkin Rogers, A. M.
Neale, Franklin Cobb, Dr. William E. Cobb, Mrs. Cobb (took Dick and
Reed), E. M. Cobb (John and Jackson, and Joe), T. L. Scott (Harry and
Jane), E. M. Cobb (Susan, Mary, Berry and Jerry), Mrs. Cobb (Betty and
Rial), E. M. Cobb (Jesse). John Harper and Wallace B. Ivor, Clerks.
A. B. Cobb, Adm'r.

APPRAISAL - BALANCE OF ESTATE OF WILLIAM MC CURDY
Dec'd. 5 Nov. 1850. Negroes: Miles, Nancy, Celia, Tilda, Liza, John,
Caroline and boy child, Wm. William Sherard, Ex'r. Appr's.: Kelly
Sullivan, Wm. Hatton and Willis McGee.

SALE BILL - ESTATE OF WM. MC CURDY
Dec'd. H. L. McCurdy, James D. Watt, Geo. Burditt, Mary Casey, David
Sadler, Sarah Rice, Berry Partain, Joel Galbreath, William McCurdy, Jr.,
(Celia and Tilda), Maj. Stowers (Miles), Fenton Hall (Eliza), H. L.
McCurdy (John), Ibzan Watters (Caroline and child), Sarah Rice (Nancy).

INVENTORY - ESTATE OF JORDAN HOOD
Dec'd. Negro girl: Adaline. T. W. May, Adm'r. 8 Nov. 1850. S. C.
Fisher, J. N. Harkness and John Hall, Appr's.

SALE BILL - ESTATE OF JORDAN HOOD
Dec'd. 29 Nov. 1850. A. Hood, Robert A. Tucker, J. S. Barnes, J. W.
Stokes, Jos. Fowler, W. G. Johnson, T. W. May (Adaline), Michael Taylor,
William Bell, James Brackenridge, James Thompson. James Emmerson,
Clerk.

INVENTORY - ESTATE OF GABRIEL KAY
Dec'd. F. M. Kay, Adm'r. James Emmerson, Clerk. John Martin, Wm.
Cowan, James A. Drake and William Keaton, Appr's.

SALE BILL - ESTATE OF GABRIEL KAY
Dec'd. 28 Nov. 1850. Jesse Rutledge, "Widow" Kay, Samuel J. Emmerson,
F. M. Kay, Stephen D. Kay, Jane Kay, C. Kay.

INVENTORY - ESTATE OF EPHRIAM MITCHELL
Dec'd. 21 Dec. 1850. Negro: Rebecca (42 years old). Saw mill acc'ts.
William N. W. Mitchell, Adm'r.

SALE BILL - ESTATE OF EPHRAIM MITCHELL
Dec'd. 23 Dec. 1850. Thomas Gear, Wm. N. W. Mitchell, Widow Mitchell,
(took Rebecca), M. E. Mitchell. B. S. Mitchell.

INVENTORY - ESTATE SALE - JAMES HEMBREE, SR.
Dec'd. 9 Jan. 1851. John Hix, Newton Bryson, Charles Bryson, Daniel
Gentry, A. B. Gentry, William Myers, Polly Bowen, Samuel Bowen, John
Hembree, John Martin, Asneath Hembree, Aaron F. Hembree, David H.
Hembree, M. L. Hembree, M. B. Hembree, Hardy Williams, A. Felton,
Jesse Waters, David L. Rainwater, W. McMillion, James Hembree, A. D.
Hembree.

INVENTORY - PERSONAL PROPERTY OF A. MC ELROY
Dec'd. (Family Bible) Negroes: Philip, Phebe, Hannah and Rice,
Joshua, Miles, Ann, Sarah, Mariah, June, Henry, Ben, Elijah, William,
Orange, Warren, Frankey, Amanda, Dinah. Notes: W. D. Steele, M. M.
Norton, A. L. McElroy, J. M. McElroy, C. Webb, T. C. Wilkes, B. F. and
T. S. Crayton, J. L. Carpenter, W. Davis, M. Barnett, Mrs. Liddell, J.
Hillhouse, Dr. Boone, W. Dennis, W. Rochester, B. Smith, O. P. Hix,
J. W. Reid, C. B. Moses, W. P. Dennis, H. Morgan, N. Elrod, S. Gregory,

J. D. Gaillard.

ARTICLES SOLD OF PERSONAL PROPERTY OF ARCHIBALD MC ELROY
Dec'd. J. M. McElroy, A. L. McElroy, S. R. McElroy, J. E. Belotte, C.
Webb, G. V. White, W. D. Steele, A. McCrary, Henry Clarke, F. Morgan,
S. Millwee, _____ Champness, W. Hix, A. D. Gaillard, B. S. Bee, N.
Elrod, Mr. Latta, B. Morgan, J. O. Lewis, N. Bryson, J. R. Clarke, J.
Roleter, E. Holcomb, G. V. White, B. E. W. Bee, B. Thomas, J. Reames,
W. D. Steele, John Hix, H. L. McGill, W. S. Stribling, O. J. Pickens,
S. R. McElroy (family Bible) (Phil, Phebe and 2 children, Hannah and
Rice, Dinah.) L. Gaillard, Thos. Dickson, A. L. McElroy (June, Miles,
Ann, 2 children - Sarah and Maria), W. D. Steele (Joshua and Warren),
R. Felton (William), T. C. Wilkes (Elijah and Henry), S. Millwee
(Orange and Frankey), J. N. Reeder (Ben), J. M. McElroy (Amanda), P.
McPhail, A. D. Gaillard, B. F. Sloan. 31 Dec. 1850 and 1 Jan. 1851.
J. E. Bellotte, Clerk.

INVENTORY - ESTATE OF ENOCH BREAZEALE
Dec'd. 30 Dec. 1850. (Blacksmith equipment and shop acc'ts.) 30
Negroes (not named) (Note - see Sale Bill for names of negroes...cme).
Appr's.: B. McGee, J. F. Wyatt, M. McGee and Wm. Cox.

SALE BILL - ESTATE OF ENOCH BREAZEALE
Dec'd. Personal Property. 1 & 2 Jan. 1851. "Widow" Breazeale, A. J.
Brock, E. King, William Ellison, M. Roberts, Silas Anderson, Kenon
Breazeale, Griffin Breazeale, A. Fant, Henry Kay, E. W. Breazeale,
P. S. Johnson, S. Dawson, T. Erskine, Miles Ellison, J. W. Treble,
Allen Kelly, Samuel Robinson, G. W. Magee, M. H. Brock, R. A. Keys,
Saml. Emmerson, Wm. Acker, George Roof, F. P. Robertson, E. D. Pruitt,
Gambrell Breazeale, Henry Maddox, W. G. Reese, G. Horton, "Widow"
took (Frank, Esther, Charles, Young Frank, Tempy and 2 children,
Elias, Perry and Emma), Kenon Breazeale (King), Griffin Breazeale
(Winney and Berry), Gambrell Breazeale (Mashie?), E. W. Breazeale
(Clarisa), James A. Drake (Spencer, Edith and Minerva), G. R. Brown
(Colbert), Milford Burriss (Anderson and Henson), F. A. Conner (Abram),
R. A. Keys (Milton), F. A. Conner (Charity), Nancy Breazeale (Mahala
and child; Huldah), William Holmes (Grace and 2 children), H. Queen,
R. C. Harkness, Albert Johnson, J. N. Harkness, B. Shirley, W. A.
Archer, W. P. Hawkins, Robert Archer, W. T. Holland, Jno. Callahan,
Daniel Major, B. Irby, W. N. W. Mitchell, James Gambrell, Williamson
Breazeale. M. McGee, Clerk.

INVENTORY - ESTATE OF IBZAN RICE
Dec'd., late of Anderson Dist., S. C. 7 Feb. 1851. Negroes: Bob (56)
and Sylva, his wife (49), Buck (25), Elijah (19), Stewart (20), Simon
(15), Mattison (15), Philip (15), Joe (37), Eliza (30) and child Polly
(3), Amanda (7), Phebe (5), Clarisa (20) and Joan and Perry, her
children, Margaret (21) and 2 children--Isaac (3) and Sally (18 mos.),
Hiram (9), Martha (5), Sim (14), Anne (35), Elias (4) and Elihu (7 mos.),
Brooks (11), Fain? (8), Winnie (42) and Emily (3), Lecia (5), Jane (8),
Linda (10), Mary (12).

INVENTORY - NOTES AND ACCOUNTS DUE ESTATE OF IBZAN RICE
Dec'd. V. D. Fant, J. P. Benson, J. C. Keys, J. P. Reid, C. C. Langston,
S. H. Langston, Elijah Webb, Saml. Smith, Frank Harlow, Saml. M. Wilkes,
David White, Alexander Johnson, Wesley Leverett. 7 Feb. 1851. Appr's.
John P. Benson, J. Y. Fretwell, J. W. Harrison, Jas. C. Keys and Saml.
M. Wilkes.

SALE BILL - ESTATE OF IBZAN RICE
Dec'd. 12 Feb. 1851. Mrs. Barbara Rice, widow (Buck, Elijah, Steward
(a mulatto), Joe-carpenter (a mulatto), Eliza and child, Amanda, Phebe,
Anne and 2 children and Tommy), Clayton Webb, William B. Gibson, James
P. Cochran, M. B. Scott, Charles C. Langston, William N. Fant, William
Holmes, Fleetwood Rice, Samuel M. Webb, Welborn Keaton, Samuel Bell,
Gambrell Breazeale (Malinda), Daniel H. Cochran, J. B. Sloan, Zechariah
Hall, J. P. Benson, A. M. Neal, John McFall (Clarisa and 2 children,
Matilda and 2 children, Margaret and 2 children, and Martha), William
Magee (Hiram and Brooks), V. D. Fant, A. Garvin, Lewis Moorhead,

Samuel J. Emmerson (Licy?), J. W. Harrison, Rev. William Carlisle, Dr. J. D. Gaillard, Rev. Amaziah Rice, J. H. Cannon, Dr. A. P. Cater (old negro man Bob and wife), Griffin Breazeale (Simon), Ibzan J. Rice (mulatto boy, Mattison), James Carter (Philip), John Pratt, (Simon), E. P. Holliman (Winney and child), Kenon Breazeale (Jane), Ezekiel Hall (Mary). 31 Mar. 1851. F. Rice, Clerk.

APPRAISAL - ESTATE OF JAMES DOUTHIT, SR.
Dec'd. 11 Mar. 1851. Negroes: George and his wife, Lavina and her youngest child, Guy, Martha, Mary, Sarah Adaline, Susannah, Elzy, George, Jerry and Lavina. Appr's.: Ezekiel Murphy, James Gambrell and J. H. Rosemond.

SALE BILL - ESTATE OF JAMES DOUTHIT, SR.
Dec'd. 11 Mar. 1851. B. H. Douthit (Mary and Susan), John Cooper, R. T. Elrod, R. F. Wyatt, Ezekiel Long, Col. Ervin, G. F. Townes, James Long, John W. Douthit, Samuel D. Douthit (George, Lavina, Guy, girl Lavina and boy George), H. L. Gaines (Jerry). Wm. D. Sitton and H. L. Gaines, Clerks.

APPRAISAL - ESTATE OF DAVID REECE
Dec'd. Notes on Silvanus Adams and John Williams. Appr's.: W. H. Acker, William G. Reece, H. A. Cobb and R. B. Cox.

SALE BILL - ESTATE OF DAVID REECE
Dec'd. 22 Feb. 1851. Elizabeth Reece, widow; William F. Clinkscales, Alexander Austin, William G. Reece, William S. Philips, Abner Cox, Martin Cobb, James W. Medlock, James F. Massey, Holbert A. Cobb, S. V. Gambrell, William Coker, John H. Harper, V. Shaw, L. H. Davis, William Davis, Mason Kay, Gabriel Cox, James Nabors, William Cummins, Sam Robinson, W. H. Acker, Matthew Cox, Joel Kay, Matthew Bagwell, James Greer, Rhodam Trussel, Francis A. Ragsdale, Nicholas Balkum, Roberson Cobb, Henry J. Harper, Thomas W. Davis. Elizabeth Reece and M. Cobb, Admr's.

SOUTH CAROLINA

PENDLETON DISTRICT

U. S. CENSUS

1820

Transcribed by Darleen Jolly and Anne Thiem, May, 1968.

Submitted by Mrs. W. D. Thiem, 231 Mockingbird Lane, San Angelo, Texas.

Due to the length of this Census with the names and age brackets included, it is not possible to print all of this county in one issue, as is our usual policy, but feel that the age brackets as included by the compilers are too worthwhile to omit.

EXPLANATIONS: Transcription of this census from microfilm does not contain the occupation nor slaves of the enumerated "Heads of Households." The numbers below following the "Head of Households" indicated the age categories in which the household members belong:

MALES
Column 1 - Under 10 years of age
Column 2 - 10 to under 16 years
Column 3 - 16 to under 18 years
Column 4 - 18 to under 26 years
Column 5 - 26 to under 45 years
Column 6 - 45 years and over

FEMALES
Column 1 - Under 10 years of age
Column 2 - 10 to under 16 years
Column 3 - 16 to under 26 years
Column 4 - 26 to under 45 years
Column 5 - 45 years and over

NAME	MALES	FEMALES	NAME	MALES	FEMALES
Anderson, Robert	400010	12110	Vandever, Landford	300010	20010
Allen, Robert	000200	01101	Wormack, John	011101	01311
Brayele, Joel	100701	01001	Burten, Robert	110001	20101
Broyler, Cain	211110	20010	Browne, Elijah	400201	11210
Bennett, Charles	000001	01001	Davis, John	311301	11101
Cobb, Henry	221010	31010	Garner, John	400010	10010
Duckworth, Howard	200010	00001	Hall, Lent	211321	21001
Johnson, Reuben	120101	33201	Harkness, Robert	000101	00100
Poor, John	211301	32110	Hayes, Thomas	000021	41011
Pepper, Elijah	000010	00100	McGee, Burrel	000200	00100
Smith, James	400010	10010	McGee, John	220010	10100
Wilson, John	230002	20011	Noris, Robert B.	100010	51010
Cox, John	110010	30101	Norris, Ezekiel	100010	10100
Clement, Benjamine	320010	10010	Pickens, Israel	010001	11010
Christian, Thomas	010010	01101	Rice, Hezikiah	120111	11001
Grant, Widow	010020	01001	Todd, Adam	201110	13010
Horten, Grief	100010	22010	Boasman, Louis	200200	00101
Key, Wilm, Jr.	111110	11010	Beaty, Thomas	000201	00211
Nicholas, Willis	200010	00100	Baskins, Jack	(none listed)	
Strickland, Burrel	120001	10010	Casper, James	100100	00101
Telford, James	200010	20010	Armstrong, Benj.	101110	12110
Trussel, Posey	000010	00010	Bailey, Wiate	200010	10101
Beal, James	111201	21010	Brayele, Cannon	101301	01002
Brice, James	000110	10110	Bennett, Thomas	201401	11110
Bennett, Elisha	221101	01001	Copeland, Wilm.	300010	20010
Browne, Jameson	300010	11010	Duckworth, Joseph	001101	00001
Day, Silvery	120100	11010	Ganbriel, John	310010	11010
Grier, Solomon	230101	11110	McAllister, Wilm.	110100	00100
Gambriel, Mathew	301010	00100	Pepper, Elisabeth	000000	00101
George, William	320010	20010	Pepper, John	100010	00100
Gambriel, David	410010	10010	Williams, Richard	300010	20100
Hammond, Samuel	200010	21010	Anderson, John B.	100010	10010
Moore, Eliab	000201	00001	Clement, Hugh	411101	11001
Majors, Elisabeth	111200	21110	Clinkseales, Wilm.	701110	12010

285

NAME	MALES	FEMALES
Paget, James	100010	10110
Richerson, Robert	201201	12101
Taylor, William	400010	01010
Matteson, Wilm.	000010	00000
Poor, George	000010	11210
Telford, Robert	000101	11001
Trussel, Henry	000001	00010
White, William	000100	20100
Carpenter, Asberry	200010	10100
Browne, John	021201	01001
Bailey, William	100100	10101
Boudle, Robert	000001	00101
Doudle, Samuel	310010	11010
Gambriel, Henry	101110	32110
George, John	000001	00001
Gambriel, John Sr.	000001	00001
Hall, Anthony	221110	10010
Hammond, John	000010	20010
Majors, James	200010	20010
McFall, John	002401	01011
Rice, Amesiah	000100	00100
Stephenson, Thomas	000210	10010
Vandever, Aaron	200010	10100
Wardow, James	000201	00111
Wilson, Charles	301201	21010
Browne, Davis	100100	10100
Brayele, Enoch	300010	10100
Granelee, Widow	000010	00011
Hall, Lemuel	200010	01010
Hall, John	110110	41010
Harkness, John	201101	30110
Hall, James R.	000010	20010
McGee, William	000200	00100
Martin, John	300010	00100
Norris, Widow	000100	00001
Norris, Patrick	000201	00101
Rutledge, Jessee	100001	03101
Thompson, James	110001	01102
Adair, Elisabeth	000000	00001
Brison, John	000001	00101
Browne, Hamilton	310001	10010
Copper, Jacob	101101	30001
Cavin, Margarette	000000	00001
Davis, John	300010	11010
Hardin, Ralph	200001	20110
Hall, Fleming	100100	10100
Hamilton, Luke	000101	10501
Hall, Ursley	000200	01101
Long, Isaac	200010	00100
Milford, Robert A.	300200	00010
Montague, John	000110	00000
Moore, Milly	000100	00201
Prince, Hudson	211201	21101
Tucker, Bartley	110102	11111
Armstrong, Wilm.	110010	21010
Brice, John	000001	00000
Chamberlain, Lewis	210110	20110
Cain, John	410010	00110
Doudle, John	110101	01101
Dean, Thomas	000001	00000
Crawford, William	310011	11010
Davis, Jessee	320001	11001
Dean, Samuel	000201	00001
Gunnin, James	000010	10100
Hillhouse, Wilm.,Jr.	000010	10010
Ewin, Thomas	000100	00101
McPherson, Elisha	100010	30010
Brock, Andrew	110010	10010
Harkins, James	311201	10110
Harper, William	000101	00001
Hilhouse, Wilm.	000101	00212
Keas, Peter	200101	22110
Massey, K.	201200	00100
Long, Matthew	010010	31110
Tilly, Widow	000100	00101
Tilly, Lazerus	000001	00000
Law, Wilm. Bennett	000001	00001
Burress, Elisha	220001	04010
Clark, Matthew	010101	01001
Calhoune, John	300010	10010
Gordin, Robert	100010	21010
Holly, Leon	110101	31101
Morris, James	200000	40010
McCluska, Joseph	110010	00010
Towns, Reuben	000500	00011
Lawe, Jesse, Chas. Sr.	000201	00000
Chapel, John	000010	00110
Dobbins, Jesse	110010	41010
Glen, William	000010	20100
Lewis, Major	312722	12110
Seelton, Thomas	320011	20010
Simpson, David	200010	30010
Shelt, Daniel	200010	00110
Turner, John	210010	41010
Wilson, Hugh	000111	50011
Allgodd, Barnett	111110	23011
Boggs, David H.	000000	00100
Boggs, Aaron	100010	00100
Boggs, Thomas G.	100010	00100
Duff, Mary	011100	21202
Hendrix, David	120210	20200
Humphrey, John	100010	20100
Norton, Edward	000011	11001
Odel, Regnal	200010	30010
Raines, Brinkly	000010	30100
Bruce, Jonathan	200010	10010
Davis, Elnathan	000101	00001
Fegason, James	020201	00201
McCollum, Samuel	100010	21010
Tatum, Hugh	210010	02010
Berry, David	100010	42010
McGee, Jessee	100101	41110
Briant, Thomas	200010	00100
McPherson, William	000010	10100
Emmerson, Samuel	401201	01301
Hall, David	200010	00100
Heuston, James	100101	00001
Hall, Hannah	001110	01101
Leverett, Stephen	101411	02111
Allen, Elisabeth	010102	00102
McAllister, Andrew	000201	00001
Mirchel, Anna	100000	11111
Mewel, William	100010	00100
McFall, Arthur	200001	20010
Thompson, Mathew	100100	20100
Buress, John	310210	11110
Burress, Thomas	211110	11010
Robertson, James	010201	00101
Cockerham, Wilm.	210010	31010
Pickens, William	110101	11101
Tam, Doctor	Left Blank	
Pew, David	000001	10011
Barnes, James	000101	00001
Farrow, James	Left Blank	

1820 SOUTH CAROLINA PENDLETON DISTRICT CENSUS

NAME	MALES	FEMALES	NAME	MALES	FEMALES
Tilly, Stephen	200010	30020	McClurr, Charles	000010	10100
Tippon, William	020001	41010	Redmond, Thomas	000006	10011
Watson, David	110010	31110	Calhoune, David	110010	00110
Darah, John	000001	00000	Earle, Samuel	200101	13010
Bates, Alexander	320010	01010	Harrison, Thomas	120001	41101
Chamberlain, Zadock	211110	21010	Hide, Austen	300010	10011
Fretwell, John	100110	10010	McKinney, Kineth	12001	31010
Hammilton, Barton	110001	60010	Frederick, Moss	100010	10010
Hammilton, James	000011	00011	Pickens, Andrew	010010	01000
Morris, John Sr.	000011	00001	Reader, Jonathan	311101	12010
Taylor, Joseph	310010	11010	Whitehead, Burrell	011210	01101
Webb, Charles	031121	00002	Castleberry, Asa	010001	20200
Calhoune, Alexander	020001	00201	Grant, Wilm. (Rev.S)	211101	11010
Copper, Henry	410010	12010	Hunt, Charles Sr.	301207	10010
Gentry, John	210101	21001	Hawkens, Pleasant	100010	20110
Ledbetter, Daniel	000011	00201	Johnson, Mrs.	010000	01201
McDaniel, Phillip	020010	30010	Harden, Reuben	000100	00100
Seright, Andrew	000010	50010	Lanear, Robert	200010	21110
Sadler, David	100001	02201	McKinley, James B.	200110	22010
Shockley, Prudence	100010	00001	Mason, Nathan	100001	30000
Wells, James	110001	10001	May, William	010001	00001
Webb, Micajah	0000100	00100	Nauls, Elisabeth	070100	00111
Barnett, Elijah	300011	11010	Stribling, Thomas	100010	10010
Boggs, John R.	100010	21010	Bailey, Thomas	110001	30010
Conimore, Michael	200010	23010	Bowman, Archibald	110002	11110
Claton, William	010201	00201	Bruce, John	000010	20100
Humphrey, Caty	000000	01001	Felton, William	020002	10101
Humphry, William	410010	11101	Farrow, Thomas	000001	01001
Kirksey, William	220201	11010	Holland, Mary	100100	00000
Odel, John P.	010001	00101	Harris, Mrs.	000000	00001
Parsons, James	030010	50010	Harrison, James	310010	01010
Boyd, Robert	200001	11000	Holland, Robert	411011	11010
Cannon, Richard	001201	11201	Isbel, Robert	111210	42011
Duke, Rosanah	000100	00101	Isbel, Livingston	210010	21010
Hill, George	100010	21919	King, William	210010	3201
Tatum, John	010001	01212	Robertson, Jacob	000010	00011
Dollar, Reuben	000201	01201	Stribling, Jesse	410001	21010
Stewart, James	011202	01002	Swilling, George	200010	10101
Hardy, James	311101	11001	Vandever, George	000101	00001
Brooks, Thomas	200010	20010	White, Thomas	110015	50010
McDill, James	131220	12010	White, James	310010	21010
Latner, John V.	100100	00011	Abbett, Sarah	132400	01201
Berry, William	210110	21010	Craig, Arthur	000100	00100
Roades, Mosses R.	100010	10010	Lesley, Elisabeth	020000	00010
Beaty, David	012301	51010	Stone, David, Jr.	210210	21011
Varner, John	311201	11001	Cannon, William	310010	12301
Dench, John C.	010310	00110	Hany, Thomas	000002	00001
Clark, William	000101	00001	Finley, Samuel	101110	02000
Step, Jesse	010101	01201	Smith, Samuel	110110	41010
Shell, Henry	000001	00001	McCray, Henry	200001	21001
Harris, Richard	000010	10110	Craig, John	000101	12201
Barton, William	000001	00010	Guthrey, James	000010	00100
Gorden, William	200010	10100	Liddle, George W.	000200	00000
Robertson, David	100010	10010	Beaty, Samuel	200110	00101
Standage, James	200101	10301	Beaty, Samuel	200110	00101
Leatherer, Benjamine	210001	22010	Bowe, John	200010	10010
Terrill, Aaron	100010	30100	Bond, Sugar	310011	00111
Baty, Widow	010000	20010	Moffett, John Sr.	000001	00000
Dean, Richard	000000	00000	McCurdy, James	110010	00010
Edmondson, George	220101	02110	Morgan, William	010010	00101
Leathers, John	010010	00100	Simpson, George W.	200110	32110
Massey, James	300010	21010	Sherrard, James	000100	10100
Cleveland, Geo.C.	100010	10100	Carter, Edward	0000010	01020
Claton, John	010110	00011	Dart, Thomas L.	0000010	01000
Guest, Allen	200010	20100	Daniel, Chesley	000010	01101
Harbin, Widow	010100	01101	Evett, Humley	200001	20010
Lonney, Robert	000201	00101	Gaines, James	000010	43110

NAME	MALES	FEMALES	NAME	MALES	FEMALES
Mercer, Samuel	200010	10010	Gaines, Henry	000001	00001
McGee, Benjamine	110001	41310	Hunter, William	34001	11010
Richards, Adam	100100	00100	Hammond, John B.	010020	00100
Tilley, Burges	100010	00010	Larton, Thomas	043660	11111
Bruce, Charles	000001	01000	Maverick, Samuel	010001	11000
Grindol, John	100010	03311	McDow, William	312501	22010
Harris, John Sr.	021101	01001	McGreggor, Laurence	110001	23110
Harden, Griffen	200007	23010	Palmore, Martin	110020	30010
Harris, Nathaniel	200010	20110	Hunter, Thomas	001101	00110
Jones, John	111207	11002	Simmons, Daniel	000001	01011
Kilpatrick, John	010010	00002	Mauldin, John	000200	00100
May, Moody H.	000010	10100	Winters, Jeremiah	210110	22010
McClure, James	000101	00011	Walker, William	100201	01201
Marlen, Samuel	000101	00101	Cobb, John	101110	21101
Manwell, John	200110	00100	Fields, John	100001	00011
Portwood, Robert	310101	12010	Fields, Samuel	320101	10010
Tiler, Even	000011	20200	Custer, Mary	None Listed	
Browne, Spencer	011101	01101	Ladd, John	020010	22010
Bruce, Charles	100010	20100	Lay, James	500010	00010
Dabbs, Samuel	010010	10010	McKinny, John	000010	00001
Fields, Caleb	300030	10100	Whitmire, William	000002	00011
Guest, John	200020	31020	Pitts, Joseph	000100	10100
Holland, Margaret	200000	00001	Hunt, Else	000010	00000
Harris, John (Rev.S)	210010	20100	Hester, John	110100	10100
Holland, Archibald	300010	20010	Hagwood, John	000010	11010
Holland, Jacob	000100	11000	Hagwood, James, Sr.	110001	00121
Isbel, Daniel	300010	00100	Lathem, John	001201	00201
Jones, William	000101	10010	McAdams, James	000000100001	
Mason, Ambrose	001210	01011	McAdams, James, Jr.	200010	30010
Perriman, James H.	010001	01010	Robertson, James	400010	10100
Lewis, David Slone	020101	00101	Scott, Samuel	200010	11010
Talbert, L. C.	010010	20101	Bowen, William	400010	12010
White, William	000001	10000	Flemming, George	200010	20100
White, Isaac	110201	12210	Harrison, Jesse T.	110111	10001
Adair, James	000010	00010	McCollum, Daniel	020101	10100
Carson, John	101110	00002	Turner, Stephen	000010	00110
Oliver, Peter M.	100001	20100	Beal, George	120201	11101
Oliver, Alexander	000111	00101	Hallum, Wilm. A.	101110	32110
Lemmon, Robert	001201	03101	Roberts, Littleberry	200010	11010
Owens, Banister	000010	20010	Arches, John	310410	01010
Leach, Joseph	100010	20020	Evans, George	120201	11101
Trimmiar, Obediah	110001	02101	Hamilton, David	100101	00002
May, Cobb	000001	01010	Taliaferro, Richard	010001	00000
Barton, Lewis	000010	00010	Watson, James	110001	20201
Beaty, William	21001	11201	Wormack, Andrew	210011	31010
Beaty, Francis	000001	00020	Rankin, Lettier	001110	00001
Davidson, James H.	100210	10010	Murphy, Ezekiel	200010	20010
Moffett, John, Jr.	100010	10100	Martin, Thomas	111110	01101
McCurdy, William	010101	01101	Stribling, Robert	000010	30100
Simpson, Archibald	200010	20010	Hardkin, Thomas	200010	20010
Simpson, Leonard	210301	01101	Danda, James H.	000010	20100
Cherry, David	100010	00010	Torree, Alphin	(none listed)	
Dickson, Samuel H.	000101	01101	Williams, Martin	110201	00101
Dickson, John	110011	30010	Martin, Jacob	000010	20010
Eaton, John	001201	21210	Owens, Frederick	000211	02201
Gasaway, Benj.	210010	30010	Jones, Jacob	210001	21010
Gaines, Robert	101101	13010	Humphry, John T.	200010	10100
Goruen, James	100001	40010	Goreten, Thomas,Sr.	000101	00001
Hall, John	000020	00100	Allen, Betsey	(None listed)	
Hunter, Widow	000000	00301	Reaves, John	110010	23011
Lewis, John L.	300010	10010	Steele, Aaron	110010	00100
Miller, Crosby W.	311101	02300	Earle, Elias	101201	00001
Mosley, David	100100	00100	Morgan, John	520010	01110
Pilgrim, John	700010	22010	Whitfield, James T.	010010	01100
Prater, John	301210	12000	Eavers, Lewis	000101	20010
Johnson, Robert	122301	20010	McKleroy, Archibald	111110	21010
Sharp, Elam	100010	00010	Stribling, Mark M.	000010	10100

1820 SOUTH CAROLINA PENDLETON DISTRICT CENSUS

NAME	MALES	FEMALES	NAME	MALES	FEMALES
Towers, John	300301	32010	Setten, John	000210	30100
McGreggor, Jane	000000	00010	Stribling, Thomas	000101	00301
Clark, Micajah	000001	00001	North, John L.	000010	01010
Cobb, Robert, Jr.	200001	00010	Miller, John, Jr.	100010	00100
Fields, John, Jr.	011110	00000	Lawhon, Archibald	320010	00010
Guster, John	000000	01010	Grisham, Joseph	121310	21010
Jones, Elis	022300	03310	Smith, Benjamine	000010	00000
Linch, Ann	000100	00001	Howell, Enoch	100010	22110
Moore, Burt	010101	10101	Rufe, George	101301	01001
Palmore, John	100110	20010	Pickens, Elijah	020100	10010
Bruce, William	010201	00002	Story, Charles	000001	10001
Freeman, Jepthah	001101	10010	Bruster, William	120101	21101
Hunt, William	000001	10010	Guiton, Willm. W.	000100	00001
Hunt, Helm	200010	00010	Anderson, James	320010	00010
Hunt, John	210110	10010	Bruster, Margarett	010000	22201
Hagwood, Zachirias	200110	10010	Daremple, James	020010	31110
Lathem, James	0000010	00010	Orr, James	200001	10011
Mincy, Aaron	210101	32101	Wallace, Patsy	000100	00011
Pew, Henry	120010	12010	Moorhead, Alemander	300010	10101
Robertson, Allen	101201	02001	Sherrill, Louis	010001	01101
Blasingame, John	211301	33010	Harrison, John	020101	01201
Easley, Samuel A.	000110	02110	Lamethan, Micajah	000011	00001
Jemeson, William	400010	10010	Perry, Benjamine	110101	01010
McCrossky, John D.	110101	22000	Smith, John	120101	11110
Taliaferro, Zacharias	010001	12101	Dickinson, James	201210	21010
Clarkson, William	200210	22010	Linn, Robert	210001	00110
Gregory, David	220110	42010	Griffin, James C.	210001	00110
Roberts, Wily	411210	00012	Carpenter, Thomas	100100	00100
Miler, John	000201	00101	Turner, John	000001	00001
Webb, William	000010	00100	Peerly, Nicholas	200010	10010
Smith, Nimrod	220101	02301	Townsend, Thomas	400010	10010
Davis, Lucy	000000	00001	Morris, John	000200	00100
Boyd, William	100010	10010	Robertson, Ephriam	101101	33110
Thompson, Mary	000000	01101	Gray, William	001210	00110
Gaines, John	420010	00110	Goodman, Charles	100101	23101
Barton, Bailey	100200	20100	Miller, Hugh	210001	10102
Barton, Benjamine	101100	00100	Gailord, Theodore	000010	00100
Kirksey, Isiah	000010	00001	Carson, Jiles	110101	10101
Hagwood, Benjamine	000010	00000	Burt, Moody	000001	00000
Claton, John	000010	10010	Hilhouse, James	000010	10010
Smith, Avat	100010	10010	Wadkins, Temporince	010210	00101
Barton, John	100010	00010	Hunter, James	401120	20010
Holden, Isaac	000010	00001	Griffin, Sargint	420010	00110
Chamberlain, Daniel	220010	22010	Hester, Gudeon	000101	01001
Whisenhunt, Chrstp.	100200	00111	Murphey, Mosses	000011	11211
Laden, Thomas	100200	00111	Kirksey, Mark	000010	00001
Humphry, David	000201	12101	Geron, Jacob	100120	10100
Poore, Francis	100000	31110	Cannon, Certer	000010	21010
Carson, James Sr.	000001	00001	Cannon, Russel	010011	00111
Steele, William	001201	00021	Cox, William	220001	00101
Gailord, Charles	110010	11010	Barton, Widow	010000	01101
Michen, Frances	300110	10010	Fresuir, Richerson	000100	10100
Brady, Luten	210010	11010	Chapman, Joseph	000101	00001
Liddle, Andrew, Jr.	100010	21110	Patterson, Nancy	011001	00001
Whitner, James	000001	00301	Murphy, Isaac	200010	10010
Rosamond, Sarah	020100	10001	Laurence, Benjamine	000001	00101
Gailord, Josias D.	200010	10011	Giles, Robert	100010	20010
Cobb, Robert	001101	00000	Boone, Nathan	000110	03101
	000010	00011	Kirksey, Elisha	000020	40100
	001101	00000	Nicholdson, Martha	010100	01301
Gailord, John	000010	00000	Leydy, John	210001	21010
Warren, Samuel	000000	00000	Heady, Elis	220010	21010
Hunter, John	100010	21010	Waddle, John	100001	11010
Cherry, Samuel	420001	10011	Palmore, Solomon	010111	00201
Cooper, James	310101	01101	Rankin, George	120010	40010
Pinkney, Thomas	000010	10020	Wilson, John	300001	00101
Story, Mary	000000	00001	Terrell, Henry	000010	00000

NAME	MALES	FEMALES	NAME	MALES	FEMALES
Barnes, John	230201	11010	Smith, James	300010	10010
Jones, John	200010	10001	Hallem, Ann	000100	00101
Milew, William	001301	00111	Wilson, Robert	200010	20010
Guiton, Aaron	221101	11001	Johnson, Fredrick	001101	00001
Speed, William	300010	01010	Stanton, William	220001	22101
Duckworth, Benj.	210101	22001	Wilson, William	000101	10001
Anderson, Mary	000100	00101	Gambriel, James	220010	10010
Heuston, Samuel	100101	00210	Gibson, Thomas	100010	20011
Orr, William	310101	01110	Nally, Aaron	420010	01211
Stephenson, Andrew	110010	22100	Richenson, Mathias	000100	10001
Sherrill, David	300010	10010	Cortis, Namon	111101	41010
Kirksey, Jared	000100	00100	Laurence, Elisha	10010	20010
Terrell, Moses	000010	20001	Baker, Gray	100010	12010
Jolly, William	000001	00001	Sotherland, Wilm.	210010	10101
Roper, Benjamine	201301	22101	Ried, Nathaniel	100100	10010
Sotherland, James	001111	01321	Ried, Joseph B.	000100	00100
Hardin, Joseph	100001	20002	Ried, Stephen	000100	00101
Blithe, Absolam	000001	00010	Sutherland, Amos	10010	20010
Kieth, Allen	100010	10100	McClure, John	211201	11110
Norton, Stephen	100010	22010	Kieth, Wilm. L.	000100	0 101
Beck, Jesse	000011	00001	Ladd, Amos	100001	40011
Nicholdson, Ira	100010	30010	Holdman, Henry	000001	00000
Noe, Ansil	120201	23010	Glen, Duke W.	110010	10100
Burch, Henry	000001	000001	Capheart, Jacob	101211	01302
Weems, John	130001	10002	McDaniel, James	000301	00110
Nicholdson, Evan	300020	20100	Holdin, John	200010	20010
Merrett, Obediah	010001	00100	Rogers, James	120201	01201
Russ, Henry D.	3200010	21010	Alexander, Elijah	020101	10101
Martin, Jacob	000010	20010	Holden, Joshua	010101	01002
Gaston, Hugh	120210	40010	Grogan, Thomas	100001	00011
Tatum, William	100010	20010	Couch, John	110110	22010
Redmon, Thomas	0000001	00011	Terrell, William	201201	22110
Brackenrige, Robert	230020	11010	Gasten, William	020010	10010
Kirsey, Stephen	000000	00001	Carnes, William	001101	02001
Tidmore, Henry	100010	20100	McCrosky, David	100310	00100
Hendrix, David	120021	11100	Jackson, James	(left blank)	
Pickins, Robert	000001	00021	Harris, Alex	010010	00100
Johnson, Joel	000010	00000	Hall, John	000020	00100
Pickens, Andrew	000001	00001	Hembrue, James	000001	00101
Evett, James	011211	21001	Hendrix, William	100011	01301
Barton, Joshua	200010	10100	Easley, John	000010	00001
Griffin, Elisabeth	000100	00101	Hammilton, Jane	010000	01010
Baker, William	011401	21010	Hammilton, Wilm. A.	200010	01010
Chapman, John	511101	51101	Whitten, John	100200	00100
Judor, Isaac	210101	10001	Wilson, Charles	021101	00001
Oliver, William	110010	20010	Hamby, Micijah	000200	00000
Knox, John	220101	31010	Bolding, John	110010	50010
Nicholdson, Stephn.	000100	10100	Pickens, Andrew	100010	01000
Norton, Barack	410010	21010	Clement, Aaron	210001	21110
Hughes, John	410010	21011	Williams, Jeremiah	010101	01021
Reed, John	100010	10100	Rosamond, John H.	000010	00010
Lay, Charles	010101	00101	Abbett, John	000010	00011
Coane, Philemon	130010	31110	Cason, Mary	000000	00001
Orr, Thomas	100010	20100	McKinney, James	300010	20110
McMurry, William	000010	02301	Liddle, Stephen	100001	21120
Henderson, James	100100	10100	Briggs, Robert H.	100110	21200
Wilson, John, Jr.	220010	21010	McAems, James	000001	00001
Hulbard, William	000001	00001	Cannon, William	000001	00000
Merritt, Nathaniel	000110	10000	Keas, Joshua	222120110001	
Williams, Jeremiah	300010	20100	Gittem, Phillip	100110	20100
Smith, Benjamine	410010	10010	Browne, John	211101	22201
Jones, Samuel	020110	12101	Chandler, John	000010	10010
Douthel, James	21010	12110	Benson, Thornton	000100	10100
Head, John	310010	11010	Stansil, Jessee	400110	00100
Moore, Elijah	020201	02001	Earle, John B.	101101	02110
Liddle, John N.	000111	000010	Browne, Samuel	000001	00001

1820 SOUTH CAROLINA PENDLETON DISTRICT CENSUS

NAME	MALES	FEMALES	NAME	MALES	FEMALES
Ganes, Richard	100201	10011	Calhoune, John E.	000010	00000
Hall, Elisha	210010	10110	Lewis, Richard	110011	01201
Hendrix, Mosses	300010	30100	Ramsey, Alexander	000101	00001
Kieth, James	000010	20100	Johnson, John	000010	10010
Kersey, Thomas	(left blank)		White, Joseph	310001	12010
Hughes, Andrew	020001	00001	Burdine, Polly	(left blank)	
Head, Richard	100001	31210	Smith, James	(left blank)	
Meritt, James	000101	00011	Hughes, John	001100	02010
Key, William	201110	02010	Orsbourne, James	110110	04110
Laterfield, Elijah	120010	20010	Hughes, Elisha	000100	00100
Morgan, Elisabeth	000000	00001	Burdine, Thomas	(left blank)	
McMoun, James	(left blank)		Burdine, John	(left blank)	
Simpson, Thomas	510010	01010	Copland, William	220111	01100
Richenson, Mathais	110100	30110	Wilson, John	011201	12000
Caredine, Elisabeth	110100	11101	Elrod, Isaac	001201	22011
Edwards, Elisabeth	000100	01010	Chesteen, Abner	000100	10100
Pickens, Aaron	000201	00021	McAlister, Edward	000100	10010
Whitmire, Henry	110101	12001	Barkley, James D.	400010	02011
Thomas, Isaac	412201	23110	Crosley, William	000001	00002
Woodall, Abelle	010000	00001	Sanford, John	100010	30100
Beck, Isarel	001110	01010	Cobb, Roland	000100	10100
Langston, Jesse	420201	00110	McKinny, James	010321	01103
Harrison, Thomas	100010	01010	Boone, Ratlife	101100	01101
Murphy, Roger	000201	12001	Boone, Joseph	100100	20101
Duckworth, Jacob	120001	31010	Vickry, Christopher	010101	00101
Pickens, John	230101	11110	Lewis, Tarlton	11010	21010
Ackor, Peter	302201	13011	Smith, Elisabeth	000200	00101
Cox, Isaac	110201	42001	Slaton, George	000001	00111
Matteson, James	020101	00201	Calhoune, John	020001	00001
Key, William Sr.	200101	22110	Browne, James	000101	00001
Massey, Noel	000011	11000	Broyles, Aaron	000101	00210
Clinkscater, Francis	000101	00001	Lucius, Daniel F.	020001	00001
Wiat, Elijah	011201	31001	Cox, William	010101	00001
Hughes, Redmond	000100	20010	Key, Catherine	121300	31011
Howard, Ezekiel	110010	00010	Key, James Jr.	210100	21010
Howard, William	000010	10100	Wilister, James R.	000101	30101
McCan, Robert	010201	00101	Gambriel, William	320201	02110
Waddle, William	100001	23401	Grier, David	31101	32010
Mathews, John	000100	00110	Robertson, John Sr.	000120	01210
Pickle, William	310010	30210	Wiganton, John	200010	21110
McMahon, Peter	000001	00001	Brock, Reuben	000101	00101
Framun, Lazarus	000001	00001	Norris, Burrel	200010	21010
Keas, William	100100	00100	Winters, Leonard	000001	10111
Timms, William	000001	02201	Saddler, William	001111	00110
Chambers, Andrew	311101	00110	Davis, Edward	210101	21101
Stigall, Richard	100001	10100	Tucker, Dyrant	000100	00100
Maulden, Jane	410010	00100	Keaton, Archibald	100200	10001
Burdine, Abram	210011	21010	Greenlee, William	000010	00011
Thirston, Burly	100010	00100	Taylor, Thomas	000001	00001
Burdine, Lewis	000001	00001	Davis, Thomas	010101	11110
Cooper, Thomas	000001	00001	Hill, Adam	000100	00100
Jones, Plisent	300010	11010	Taylor, Abram	000101	01101
Conger, Benjamine	001101	00001	Orr, John	0000101	00001
Mauldin, John	111201	12001	Clinkscales, Levi	210110	31010
Liddle, Andrew	000001	00000	Hall, William	011201	20101
Hale, George	010001	11010	Dupree, Benjamine	0200001	01211
Ried, Joseph	001301	00001	Calhoune, Mary F.	000000	00001
Shirley, James	101201	02002	Menwilt, Robert	000100	00000
Henderson, Thomas	000011	00001	Crawford, Thomas	210010	10010
Burdine, Daniel	(left blank)		Graham, John	300110	00100
Barr, Richard	(left blank)		Bunnel, Russel	0000010	30100
Adams, James Sr.	0000001	20101	Herndon, James	101110	00100
Smith, John	310010	12100	Mays, Levi	010010	30010
Erskin, William	001210	10100	Welch, Joseph	000010	40100
Jones, John	1100001	01101	Matthews, John	311301	21201
Turner, Jonathan	010001	00000	Strickland, Wilm.	100100	00100

NAME	MALES	FEMALES	NAME	MALES	FEMALES
Jolly, Wilson	000001	010000	Welch, William	011311	31011
Nicholas, John W.	0000001	00001	Turner, Elijah	100200	00200
Black, Samuel	000010	00010	Witicher, Hugh	320001	10010
Hardin, William	000010	00100	Gray, John	000001	22101
Busclark, John	000101	00001	Miluse, Ambros	000010	10100
Morgan, Edmund	001201	00111	Brasden, James	100001	00000
Bickry, Russel	100100	00100	Moore, Orin	021110	00301
Gilstrap, Lewis	010201	20101	Johnson, Richard	200010	22010
Davis, Gabriel	000210	20100	Forbus, William	010110	10200
Morrison, James	100110	30010	Elliott, Polly	000100	00101
Miller, William	300001	21110	Morten, Jacob	110001	11010
Donaldson, Wilm.	120001	12101	Langston, James	000010	20100
Rich, John	000001	10001	Moore, Thomas	000010	01010
Ellard, Thomas	000010	00010	Young, Joseph	010010	50010
Kinsey, William	230001	21110	Powel, Allen	210010	21010
Copland, John	010010	32010	Howard, Ezekiel	300110	12201
Rutlege, Joseph	010200	01001	Terry, Abner	000010	00001
Hamby, William	111401	21210	Hollingsworth, Jacob	100010	11100
Lamkin, Lewis	320110	22010	Dillard, James	120010	11000
Pilgrim, William	310010	10100	Davidson, John	001300	00001
Bowman, George	411110	11110	Hammond, William	210010	21010
Elliott, John	120001	51010	Smith, Job	000011	10101
Smith, John	100100	00100	Wilkinson, William	200100	00100
Winner, James	000010	01010	Hollingsworth, David	100010	01010
Parks, James	100010	21110	Timms, Thomas	000100	10100
Simpson, Alexander	201311	00201	Orr, William	000011	00201
Wade, William	400010	10100	Barkley, Andrew	000120	01101
Duncan, William	000301	02201	Rogers, Joseph T.	100020	10010
Cunningham, Andrew	000110	00100	Arnold, David	000010	00100
Fowler, Benona	111101	02001	Wimper, Daniel	000010	32110
Montague, Philip	000020	10100	Howard, Leth	200010	31110
McKieth, William	000101	00201	Price, Richard	000110	00100
Orr, Christopher	000101	00101	Browne, William	000301	00011
Clemett, Isaac	121110	12101	McDowel, John	000100	00100
Pickens, John	101201	02301	Duglass, Joseph	010210	02110
Davis, John	200010	21010	Hall, Drury	000010	01000
Keaton, Abner	210001	20010	McEarley, Joseph	101101	00101
Hanks, Robert	000010	21010	Stephens, Shedireck	210110	21010
Marsh, Larkin	121101	00201	Taylor, William	121301	01101
Williams, Thomas	000001	00110	Lisley, Edward	200010	10010
South, Luke	1000010	30010	King, Robert	300101	14010
Cain, Robert	100010	30010	Prewite, Drury	001111	00001
Smith, William	120010	00301	Seelton, William	201101	10001
Crofly, Joshua	1000010	30011	Aires, Gadwell	001101	01010
Hobson, James	210010	12110	Johnson, Evin	000100	00100
McAllister, John	110010	00010	Armstrong, James	300010	02000
Hunt, William	200010	00010	Blankenship, Thomas	411110	01010
Garven, Thomas	111111	31010	Crumpton, Robert	200001	10010
Liddle, John	321101	20110	Earpe, David	000200	00100
Dickson, James	020010	30010	Welsh, Samuel	100010	20200
Fountaine, John	100001	02101	Duncan, Susanna	011300	01201
Fowler, William	100110	20110	Justice, John	000010	00000
Winpeo, Adem	130010	41010	Marlow, John	010010	10100
McIntire, Felix	200100	10100	Rice, John	100100	10100
Gregory, Griffin	000200	10100	Murk, George	211101	11101
Norris, John E.	010010	20100	Burts, Joshua	100100	00100
Colbreth, Joel	000010	21010	Davis, Nathaniel	200010	00100
Brooks, George	010011	01001	Prater, Josiah	300010	00110
Frost, Edward	221110	10010	Largent, John	120210	00100
Carson, William	100010	30020	Atwood, James	010010	00001
Nicholds, John	101201	11201	Cantrell, Aaron	100100	00100
Shed, William	200001	11021	Hill, Henton	200110	10110
Mason, James	021210	30110	Jullen, Joseph	310010	10010
Mason, Thomas	210010	30010	Simmons, George	100100	00100
McGatha, Ferrel	200001	00211	Crawford, Thomas A.	120010	50010
Strother, James	000001	00001	Sanders, Abrem	430110	20010

1820 SOUTH CAROLINA PENDLETON DISTRICT CENSUS

NAME	MALES	FEMALES	NAME	MALES	FEMALES
Adair, John	100110	10100	Crooks, William	110001	11010
Barton, Henry	000001	01001	Visage, Thomas	200010	12011
Holbrooks, Alen	000010	30010	Pitt, Charles	020201	01001
Owens, Hardy	110101	01101	England, Abner	100201	32010
Ramy, James	100100	00100	Green, John O.	210010	20010
Claton, Warren	400001	01110	Kelly, Soloman O.	200110	10010
Logens, John	210001	10101	Henson, John	110010	41100
Denington, W.	120101	01001	Watkins, Henry	110110	31010
Fuller, Stephen	101201	01301	Adair, Wilm. Jr.	000100	00100
Wright, Josiah	301101	11110	Garner, Thomas	000200	20100
Carter, David	100010	00100	Jenkins, Thomas	210101	11010
Lowery, James	100010	30010	Prestley, Wilj.	000010	10100
Rusk, David	211101	21001	Bibb, Thomas	210201	11210
Vann, David	110010	00100	Hunter, John	000110	00010
Dagen, William	210001	01210	Mirees, Sarah	000010	00101
Evans, John	300110	10010	Browne, William	300010	00100
Donaldson, Wilm.	120001	11210	Miars, Henry	001201	01301
Morgan, Edward	110001	20101	Browne, Larkin	000010	20010
Lisk, John	220001	00101	Cross, Thomas	110001	10201
Wilson, Andrew	2000010	10200	Mason, Andrew	200010	42010
Anderson, Stephen	000001	00000	Strange, Coleman	000010	00100
Howel, William	000001	10011	Durham, James	000001	00000
McCollum, Allen	100010	10010	Evans, James	200010	20100
Simpson, John	221111	01111	Caldwell, David	001401	00111
Shires, Joseph	200010	21010	Garret, John	210010	10100
Cary, John	110010	31010	Rusk, John	101101	22010
Gassaway, Samuel	000210	00011	Waters, Thomas	000010	00010
Gasaway, Thomas	410010	12010	White, Aleander	210110	11401
Miller, William	010010	10100	Anderson, Peter	000001	00001
Richards, Thomas	0000001	00110	McAllister, Andrew	220201	21210
Defrece, John	100010	10100	Peoples, George L.	110001	01010
Hendrix, John	000201	01010	Langley, John	100100	00100
McGinoris, Daniel	200101	20010	Browne, William	100010	10100
Simpson, Thomas	220010	20010	Erskin, Hugh	000010	00100
Tucker, Thomas	100100	00100	Gaines, Reubin	000010	10100
Chapman, James	000001	10010	Hopkins, Stephen	110110	32010
Keas, Nealy	000001	00001	McKey, William	000100	10101
Blankenship, Wilm.	000100	00100	Browne, Samuel	010001	00001
Bilda, Charles	310001	30210	Alexander, Daniel	200010	00110
Glen, Joseph	300010	00000	Dier, Elisha	210010	21210
Pea, James	100200	01000	Parks, William	310201	00101
Cary, James	000100	10010	Langston, Levi	131202	20010
Eades, John	211101	20201	Barrot, Thomas	000201	00311
McCollum, Wilm.	400110	30000	James, Joel	400110	00100
			Nicholds, Chris.	100100	00200
			Chapman, James	200101	21201
			Borbus, Samuel	100300	00100
			Smith, Thomas	200010	10010
Junkin, Samuel	100010	00110	Chambers, John	200110	10011
Medlin, Francis	211101	00000	Sanders, Joshua	000001	00101
Harris, Sarah	100000	00011	Hughs, William	000010	30010
Harris, Mark	000100	10100	Robertson, Joshua	100010	31010
Culpeper, Joel	110011	10010	Tyner, John	300100	10100
Blackstone, Mary	310000	11001	Smith, Thomas	000100	10101
Rankin, Nathaniel	500010	30020	Fowler, Moses	100100	10100
OBriant, John	000010	00010	Browne, Aaron	000110	00010
Perry, Thomas	010101	10010	Etris, Peter	100010	00100
Harirn, Fredrick	200010	00010	Collett, Greene	200010	20100
Crawford, Margret	221200	00001	Eaton, Meshack	411101	11101
Browne, Thomas	501110	00110	Pinson, Joseph	000101	00201
Copland, James	000100	00100	Rigdon, Francis	110001	30301
Rollins, Nicholas	000100	10100	Huff, Stephen	001211	00001
Knop, Fredrick	100001	20011	Nicholds, James	200010	10010
Owens, Thomas	100100	10100	Connelly, L.A.L.	000010	30010
Rogers, William	200100	00100	Chumley, Thomas	000201	01210
Hopkins, James	000010	01100	Moore, David	121401	10011
Davis, Richard	000011	00011	Grover, Joseph	100001	10100

NAME	MALES	FEMALES	NAME	MALES	FEMALES
White, Robert	200001	00301	Lego, Benjamine	100010	20010
Adkins, William	300010	11010	Sullivan, Pleasant	000301	22001
Austen, James	020011	10101	Tedwell, Anderson	200010	10100
Adams, Nancy	101200	00101	Tredway, William	400010	10010
Beaty, John	110010	11010	Waters, Thomas	000010	00010
Buckhamon, Ebenezr.	001201	02001	Watkins, Joseph	000001	00101
Buckhamon, George	100010	00010	Watkins, Thomas	221101	21010
Buckhamon, Joseph	000010	10100	Adams, Robert	011201	20101
Bowe, Charles	001201	12001	Averett, Andrew	000100	00100
Cowan, Hiram	110010	30010	Bostick, James	000100	00100
Cook, William	000110	10101	Browne, Joshua	320101	30010
Duncap, Jonathan	000001	01101	Buckhamon, Wilm.	200001	31101
Duncan, William	100001	12010	Buckhamon, John	000001	00001
Evans, Leroy	000100	10100	Boyd, David	110010	10010
Greene, John	220010	02010	Browne, Cronelius	100100	00100
Hamby, Samuel	300010	21010	Cowan, Charles	101111	10101
Henderson, James	200010	20010	Duncap, Mathew	100100	00010
Hood, Andrew	000001	00201	Dickey, William	000110	00100
Kirsey, William	000100	00100	Landers, William	000110	00100
Carr, John L.	200010	01010	Gulley, Richard	010001	01001
Lusk, Robert	100100	00010	Henderson, Widow	000000	00001
McKinney, Alin	301110	10100	Harris, Moses H.	100100	10100
McKee, William	210010	30010	Howel, Mrs.	211200	11110
McKee, Ezekiel	010010	01010	Erwin, Robert	010001	00010
Milford, Nancy	000200	00101	Lusk, James	100010	40010
McCurdy, Elisabeth	000010	21010	Lusk, Widow	000100	00301
Obriant, Jesse	511101	22110	Moore, John	000100	00100
Pickens, Isarel	300010	10010	McClennon, Mollida	100010	30010
Durham, Berry	200010	30010	Glover, William	000010	20010
Durham, William	110101	10101	Haney, William	200100	00100
McAllister, James	100010	10010	Vandever, Jonathan	000001	00011
West, John	100010	00100	Wakefield, Wilm.	000010	50010
Elrod, John	000010	00100	Fields, Elisabeth	00000?	00101
West, Solomon	110010	31110	Trible, Elijah	100100	00100
Dodson, Richard	001100	00100	Shirley, Wilm.	200001	12211
Dileworth, Wilm.	010010	00100	Weldon, Wilm. D.	410010	30010
Biram, Caty	200000	02001	Sprowel, Gabriel	200010	20100
Cobb, Robert	200010	20010	Townely, Morris	200010	20100
Nally, Worleton	200010	00100	Hall, Caleb	220010	21001
Wimpee, Levi	220101	32101	Keaton, Wilm.	000011	01001
Edmonson, Thomas	410010	11010	May, Tucker, W.	200010	11010
Tripp, Nicholas	000010	00100	May, Coleman	000010	10010
Carter, Caleb	000010	30100	Hughes, Charles	100100	02010
Dalton, Randolph	012301	00102	Jones, Lemuel	200001	03101
Adams, Jamce C.	100010	20010	Smith, Thomas Jr.	220101	21210
Mastingale, Ephraim	210010	41010	Hunt, William	220110	41010
Couch, John	111110	22011	Malloy, James	100100	10100
Siddle, John	100100	00100	Miller, Hugh	130201	12012
Ford, James	410010	11010	Cambell, Holmes	100010	10100
Wilbourne, Wilm.	100100	00100	Glover, Hezekiah	210001	12000
Boyer, Jacob	000001	10101	Vandever, Ambros F.	200100	20010
Nally, Aaron	420010	01211	Taylor, Jeremiah	100010	40010
Wilboourne, Samuel	010010	21110	McGuffe, John	310001	01010
Nally, Barksdale	300010	30010	Foster, Rebecca	000100	00001
Dickinson, Michiel	220010	30010	Shirley, James	021200	20000
Parris, John	300010	00100	Adams, Nepor	321101	11101
Welsh, Susana	000000	22210	Hays, Gilbert	100010	30010
Head, Henry	110010	30010	Vernum, Isaac	000001	00001
Robins, Albert	200001	11101	Townley, Thomas	110010	21100
McCalley, Samuel	000001	00110	McKinney, Franklin	000010	20100
Douglass, John	101201	22101	Ried, Richard	310001	01401
Morten, Elenor	101100	02010	May, Edmund	000010	00100
Merett, Stephen	100011	00011	May, Elisbeth	000000	00111
Gorden, William	200001	01001	Pritchard, Wilm.J.	000001	00101
Harris, Clabourne	110010	32010	West, Peter	120001	21001
Posey, Wheeler	220001	00001	Kelly, Joshua	211110	21001

NAME	MALES	FEMALES	NAME	MALES	FEMALES
Holden, James	000100	00100	Varnum, James	230010	12110
Dramond, James	121101	01101	Barnett, Sampson	221101	20210
Richards,William	200100	10100	Gibson, Thomas	100010	00100
Hall, Hugh	000010	20010	Carson, James	400010	10010
Louden, Jesse	100010	10200	Dodds, William	020001	01201
Hede, Widow	00000	30101	Vann, Martha	000100	01101
McGriffon, Mary	000000	00010	Dickson, Walter	220010	31010
Gorden, Thomas F.	000010	30100	Brownlow, John	0000001	00011
Williams, Joseph	220010	31010	Wilson, George	200010	30110
Etris, Samuel	110010	20010	Pool, Robert	000010	00020
Nelson, John S.	100010	00110	Gorden, Jane	000000	00111
Louden, William	000100	00100	Dobbs, Sarah	031100	00201
Rider, John	200-01?	33110	Dabbs, Lewis	100100	10100
Newston, John	000200	00100	Farrow, John	211301	00101
Chambers, Phillip	100101	00021	Smith, Jessee	010201	02101
Enlow, John	000001	30010	Bates, William	000001	00311
Carson, William	100010	00010	Honey, Abel	310001	02001
Hays, Isaac B.	200010	30010	Shed, Thompson	011201	01001
Browne, Randolph	410001	41010	Lile, David	100001	10010
Adams, Parker	100100	10100	Beard, James	210010	22010
Barnett, William	000001	00001	Landford, Asa	000201	00001
Richey, Polly	200000	10100	Dickson, Benjamine	131101	01001
Waldrope, Shederack	010011	22001	Lambert, James	010101	00101
Palmore, Jesse	020101	10101	Palmore, Jesse	000100	00100
Putman, Joseph	010001	22210	Barnett, Ezekiel	110010	31011
Ramy, Christopher	121101	11001	Boyd, David	400010	02010
Robertson, Isham	312201	10010	Heaton, Smith	001201	22210
Kimbell, Elisabeth	330000	10010	Hopson, Rachel	200000	11010
Vandever, Hollsngwth.	321210	01110	Griswould, John	000010	10010
Butler, Hosia	200010	10010	Starnes, Sliter	210001	23110
Dickson, Matthew, Jr.	112201	30110	Liddle, James	000001	10100
Mullian, John	100010	10100	Hays, Thomas	111202	20010
Liddle, George	120010	30100	Hix, John	320010	10010
Butler, Abasolm	000100	20010	Whitley, Henrietta	011100	01201
Rainwater, Abasolm	000100	20010	McElroy, Samuel	220010	20010
Howell, Ames	011101	20001	Glasgo, William	000001	00001
Cunningham, Wilm.	000001	00000	Edmundson, Widow	000000	10011
Dodd, James	500010	00010	Jolly, Joseph	000001	00001
Hopson, Isaac	210010	20010	Riggs, Widow	001200	00001
Davis, Enoch	010010	20010	Campbell, William	000111	00011
Dickson, Mathew Sr.	010011	00031	Moorhead, John	200101	31110
Putman, Isabel	000100	01000	Grist, Willis	000100	30020
Richey, James	020010	00010	Thompson, William	201110	02110
Carter, David	300111	00201	Mullinan, Manuel	000001	00001
Pullen, William	320101	10201	Jenkins, Thomas	210101	11010
Voyles, John	111101	01101	Mason, William	100010	02010
Toomer, Isaac	110101	20011	Tombolin, Wilm.	000100	01000
Deal, Thomas	200010	20100	Landford, Mary	011100	02001
Dealton, Elijah	300010	00010	Lutter, John	000001	12010
Dickson, William	220101	10110	Morris, Benjamine	111201	01002
Hull, Joseph	000011	01001	Quailes, John	111101	32001
Massey, James	000001	02000	Early, Enoch	120110	21110
Nevel, Jesse	000011	00001	Fulton, Jessee	100010	20100
Robertson, Amos	310010	11102	Gilmore, Widow	010100	11001
Simpson, William	010001	01002	Cowan, Andrew	300010	00010
Watson, Jacob	000011	00001	Hughs, John	300010	00100
Barton, Caleb	201201	32010	Hatcher, Daniel	000010	41010
Barry, John	200010	21010	Henderson, Widow	001200	00301
Cleveland, Jerimiah	211210	21010	Jones, Isaac	100010	20100
Cleveland, Benj.	120010	31010	Johnson, William	000001	00201
Fuller, Telitha	100000	20010	Laroo, John	111110	22010
Wallace, Jacob	111101	11101	Morton, Samuel	500110	10110
Richey, John Jr.	100010	20010	McLusse, Andrew	310010	20011
Barnes, Samuel	000100	00100	Mayberry, Eaton	100010	00100
Dodds, Milly	000000	21010	McCollum, Daniel	210010	30010

NAME	MALES	FEMALES	NAME	MALES	FEMALES
Shelton, Kegiah	000000	01001	Mullenan, William	000010	20100
Hays, John	200100	00100	Mills, Aaron	100001	00101
Jolly, John	100010	30010	Care, Polly	200000	00100
Moorehead, James	311201	12110	Leright, William	011111	21201
Johnson, Cloe	021100	11110	Jewell, Abel	200020	02110
Canady, George	300010	10010	Honeycutt, John	010001	00001
Milwuce, John	100010	20010	Mastin, John	020010	20010
Barron, William	220010	10010	Melton, David	210010	20110
Jolly, Henry	210010	41010	Cason, Jedethon	100010	00100
McKinney, Jane	220010	11010	Honeycutt, John	200010	20010
Cox, Larkin	100010	20010	Elrod, William	000010	10010
Smith, Fiedling	201101	01101	Jolly, William	201200	00101
Gilbert, Josiah	020101	20001	Massey, Anna	001100	00002
Greene, Thomas	211210	22110	Elrod, Levi	100010	30010
Massey, Abram	100010	40010	Cox, Asa	000010	20111
McKinstry, Widow	110100	00031	Floyd, Lee	000001	23111
Lewis, Elisha	310010	10030	Boldin, Samuel	000110	10101
Horten, Abram	000100	10100	Greene, Mary	310000	00100
Heusten, Samuel	100101	00210	Greene, Henry	220010	21010
Collins, M. R.	210010	10010	Campbell, Daniel	220110	30010
Drammond, Daniel	210001	10010	Drammond, Henry	100100	00101
Canady, Samuel	300110	10100	Sherman, Charles	111401	12101
Pool, Walter	21001?	10010	Kelly, Amos	000010	10200
Steele, Aaron	310001	00011	Morris, Samuel	000001	10201
Wallace, Patsy	000100	00011	Hopkins, Kidia	000010	10111
Canady, John	100010	10100	Forsithe, William	000010	00000
Tippin, George	110110	12010	Rolen, Landale	100010	30010
McCulla, Baranabus	111101	00101	McCoy, Mary	100000	30110
Black, Robert	211100	30110	Wilbanks, Shaderick	310010	41010
Anderson, John	010010	02101	Jones, John	0000100	00100
Glasgo, Miles	200010	20010	Shelton, Joseph	000001	30000
Murry, William	300010	20100	Lewis, Sarah	000100	22110
Land, James	100010	00100	Sims, Mary	000001	00110
Prescott, Isaac	000100	01010	Wilbanks, Hosia	221201	11001
Kelly, James	010001	22001	Wilbanks, Ave	000000	00101
Beard, James	210001	10010	Finderburck, M.	200001	00002
Voce, Robuck	120010	20000	Lewis, Jesse	200010	40010
Williams, Mary	310000	20010	Stephens, Samuel	111501	12101
Clark, Thomas	400010	10100	Porter, James	100010	20100
Hooper, Obediah	310010	21010	Thompson, Joshua	110010	31110
Boman, John	110001	22010	Evett, John	100010	30010
Burgess, James	200001	10001	Preist, John	300010	11011
Burchfield, James W.	020011	30111	Murphey, Levi	220010	32110
Morris, Jorden	420001	11101	Stephens, William	000100	10200
Jackson, Carter	210010	32010	Howard, Abram	000101	10002
Tate, James	300010	10011	Davis, Andrew	120001	21101
Dollar, Ambrose	200010	00100	Durham, Charles	211101	20301
Fulton, Widow	101200	01301	Wilbanks, Joseph	110010	52001
Goodwin, Thadius	120001	31010	Riber, James	110010	22010
Hughs, William	100010	30010	Smith, Caleb	300110	20010
Hale, John	200111	21210	Montgomery, John	200010	00100
Hancock, David	100010	31010	Finderburck, Isaac	500010	00110
Jolly, Jessee	000010	10100	Jones, Jesse	020010	20010
Ledbetter, John	230010	20010	Swords, William	110010	01010
McWilliam, Wiat	000100	00100	West, John	000010	30010
Morton, Matthew	100010	20010	Swords, John Jr.	000100	10100
Mayberry, Dudly	300010	00010	Smith, Barnett	100010	40010
McCollum, James	120101	20201	Smith, Jonathan	311101	01210
McCollum, Ellison	100010	10100	Timms, Isaac	400010	10010
Horton, Widow	000000	00301	Honeycutt, Mirdy	210110	11110
Phillips, John	330101	01110	Honeycutt, Randolph	100201	00107
Ried, William	200010	20010	Hembree, James	300010	30010
Shockley, Widow	210010	00110	Dickenson, Robert	011201	10111
Dickenson, Willis	210010	10011	Lewis, Brooks	000010	00010
Camp, Daniel	400010	10010	Jolly, Joseph	100010	20100

NAME	MALES	FEMALES	NAME	MALES	FEMALES
Dilda, Noah	000010	10100	Lively, Thomas	200001	00011
Matthews, James	101101	21101	Claton, Stephen	100010	40010
White, Charles	100201	11101	Murphey, Daniel	301110	22011
Mongomery, James	100010	10100	Crawther, Harper	100100	10100
Tomson, Zacharias	000010	00101	Miller, Isaac	010201	11202
Voyles, Amos	000010	20010	Morton, Joel Jr.	110010	20010
Dickinson, Levi	100010	00100	Durham, Daniel	410001	21111
Moore, James	200010	30010	Con, Asa	000100	00100
Barton, Charles	000010	00100	Matthews, Thomas	000010	10100
Mongery, Jonathan	100110	00100	McDaniel, Mary	030100	00001
Turner, Benjamine	000001	00001	Greene, Daniel	231110	11021
Minton, Sylvanus	200010	10011	Mongomery, William	000001	00110
Tuffnele, James	000001	00001	Ellenbrug, John	100100	000010
Heaton, William	100101	10001	Stephens, Joseph	200100	00100
Canada, Samuel	120001	10001	Suggs, Jesse	010201	01101
Smith, Aaron	410010	10010	Crane, William	400010	00010
Morris, Saml. Jr.	1000010	10010	Cooper, Ansel	0000010	20100
Starnes, Greene	000100	00100	Hopkins, William	200010	00100
Dupree, Benjamine	000100	00100	Porter, Hugh	400010	21010
White, Bartholmew	400010	10110	Smith, Joshua	000001	00001
Elrod, Jeremiah	000101	00010	Rees, Ross	000001	00001
Timms, Joseph	011110	11010	Ried, John	100010	10010
Duckworth, Zabird	100010	00100	Thacker, Mary	010200	01001
Mathews, Thomas D.	100100	00100	Howel, Abram	100010	10100
Risner, Amy	120000	11011	Patterson, Joseph	300010	10100
Butler, William	021201	10111	Smith, Hiram	100100	10100
Elrod, William Jr.	100100	30010	Phillips, Lemuel	010001	31001
Pitman, Daniel	111101	42010	Johnson, William	110001	11001
Patterson, Archibld.	220010	01010	Youngblood, Samuel	000010	20010
McKee, Elisabeth	300000	01001	Smith, John	200010	31010
Porter, Philip	020101	10011	Cooper, Leon	000101	01201
Latmer, Nicholas	000001	01101	Goodwin, Lazerus	240201	21111
Robertson, Aaron	300001	12000	Kilgore, John	211301	13101
Browne, Amos	400010	20100	Lewis, William	100001	00010
Stephens, James	200110	20010	Mitchell, Joseph	010101	02110
Murphey, William	200100	00100	Epps, Edward	000001	10201
Patterson, Jeremiah	000100	10100	Mays, William	110011	01301
Fowler, Jeremiah	000100	40100	Calhoune, Elijah	200010	20010
Fielding, James	200010	20010	Arnold, Reubin	100010	20100
Hembroc, Edward	121110	40010	Prince, Solomon	100010	00100
Minton, Thomas	320001	10110	Ellison, Joseph	200010	01010
Smith, Whitaker	100010	41010	Roe, Andrew	001101	30010
Moore, Edward	100010	20100	Howard, Ezekiel	300010	00100
Harden, Aaron	421201	21001	Adams, James	000010	10100
Gibson, Elijah	000110	00100	Howard, Abram	000001	10002
Shirley, Smith	100200	00200	Ladder, William	520010	11010
Cason, Abner	300010	20010	Chistorn, John	000100	00100
Wadkins, Joseph	300010	11010	Allen, James	200010	20010
Orr, Ladewick	010010	32210	Edams, Samuel	010010	01101
Swords, John Sr.	001101	01012	Edens, William	000200	00100
King, James	210010	31010	Simmons, Isaac	410001	01101
Elrod, Samuel	01101	10011	Crane, George	111101	21101
Smith, Aaron Sr.	220001	21010	Chistern, Asir	100010	00100
Montgomery, Jonathan	000001	20001	Chistern, Obediah	200010	20010
Boyd, Molly	000000	00001	Stafford, Elenor	001100	00001
Forbus, Wilm. Sr.	120001	11111	Masters, Richard	000110	00000
Timms, Vincent	100010	40010	Powel, Sarah	200000	30010
Hembree, Polly	010100	00101	McClure, Robert B.	100100	00100
Ellis, Gedion	510110	03010	Robertson, Peter	200010	41010
Lively, John	200010	21010	Kieth, Cornelius	520010	20010
Davis, Henry	000010	10100	Chistern, John	011101	02001
Morgan, George	200010	10100	Ried, Ambros	000010	30010
Roach, Elenor	001110	01001	Powel, Abram	200010	30010
Majors, Eps	020001	41120	Kieth, William	010201	01101
Thompson, James	100100	00100	Chistern, Hannah	001200	01010
Durham, Joel	000010	00100	Latner, Nicholas	300001	01101

NAME	MALES	FEMALES	NAME	MALES	FEMALES
Odel, William	100100	00100	Roberts, John	110010	21010
Jeffrey, Mary	300100	00002	Salter, William	420010	10010
Roper, Charles	000201	00011	Howard, Isaac	300010	00010
Fortune, Timothy	510010	00010	Adams, Stephen	220201	10011
Roper, Aaron	220010	30010	Adams, Henry	101301	12001
Turner, John	200010	30100	Howard, James	100010	10200
Alen, Samuel	210010	20010	Hawks, John	100001	21001
Stephens, William	000010	10100	Castle, Ephraim	000021	00001
Tate, James	100100	00010	Ried, Sarah	110100	12111
Suggs, Allen	100100	10100	Adams, Mathew	300010	11010
Moses, James	011101	11101	Jeffery, John	000001	00201
Cooper, Alexander	000100	20100	Wade, Nancy	001200	00101
Frasure, Richenson	000100	10100	Terry, Lewis	220010	10101
Frasure, Lewis	100001	21301	Bearden, Elisabeth	010000	11110
McIntire, Philip	100010	10100	Collins, Nathaniel	200001	23010
Fowler, Jeremiah	000101	40101	Dawson, Jonas	010101	01101
Banks, Jacob	021110	11011	Dawson, William	000010	00100
Howard, John	000100	00100	Capeheart, Leonard	120101	00210
Priest, John Jr.	000100	10100	Boone, Daniel	100100	00100
Patterson, George	200010	20100	Richey, John	100001	10111
Hendrix, Moses	110110	20010	McCollum, Jacob	100010	31210
Prince, John	001111	00110	Howard, Nathan	200010	10100
Durham, Isaac	000010	10100	Nix, Jacob	000100	00100
Chapman, Isaac	100100	00200	Price, John	100010	10010
Smith, Basel	211301	31010	Baker, John	100100	20100
Hood, Nathan	421201	12201	Barron, Samuel	400010	11010
Sinclare, James	111210	31010	Dawson, Enoch	100010	30100
Epps, Richard	100100	00100	Moody, William	320010	01010
Cobb, Stephen	011101	00010	Quals, David	000100	10100
Hellen, Lewis	000100	00100	Barnes, Gabriel	000100	10100
Thomas, Briant	110010	20010	Harbin, Jesse	200001	32010
Kelly, Andrew	200010	00100	York, Lemore	201110	00010
Mitchell, Reuben	000010	20100	Doomes, Andrew	300010	10100
Miller, Joseph	100010	20010	Powel, Josias	100010	20010
Roland, Amond	210010	21010	Gibson, Joseph	011101	00201
Hughs, William	200001	20010	Alexander, Garland	000010	10100
Roland, Amond	210010	21010	Lee, Grsey	001100	01001
Hughs, William	20001	00001	Suirry, George W.	000010	11100
Allen, John	000100	00100	Grogan, Austin	100100	10100
Clopton, Richard	000010	00001	Strahan, James	420001	10010
Ladd, Wilm. C.	200010	10100	Stewart, Robert	310010	30010
Hill, Abel	100010	20100	Kitchens, James	200100	10100
Adams, William	100100	00100	Harris, John	000101	13201
Castle, John	300010	30010	Doegen, Elisabeth	000000	00011
Turner, Ransom	200010	20010	Keith, John	011201	20101
Sotherland, Pascal	000100	00100	Harris, John	000101	13201
Sotherland, Wilm.	000001	00010	Deadman, William	110010	22010
Yates, James	100101	00101	Canady, William	300010	20010
Gazette, William	400010	20110	Giller, Francis	010201	00101
Chistern, Abram	300001	03110	Bevert, William	311110	01110
Stafford, Wilm.	120010	21010	McGriffin, James	300010	52020
Turner, Sarah	030100	01201	Pingston, John	001101	00010
Barlow, Elisabeth	200000	00010	Moore, Elisabeth	310010	11010
Kieth, McKee A.	100100	10100	Parton, Robert	210010	20011
Allen, William	000101	01101	Visage, Jane	000000	20010
			Owens, Polly	110000	11010
Kinsey, William	100010	20011	Redman, Nancy	000000	30010
Visage, William	100010	00011	Ellis, Stephen	310010	23110
McWherter, John	211201	21010	Richey, John	100001	10012
Prince, James	100010	20010	Harpen, James	020010	01001
Greene, Shederack	000101	01001	Lusk, Elenor	010200	01001
Harris, John	000020	00001	Visage, Jacob	000001	00000
Witt, John	100100	00100	Nicholdson, Hannah	200000	01310
Davis, Isaac	000001	00020	Corben, John	310010	12300
Hammond, Moses	420010	01010	Harris, Samuel	100010	10010
Moss, Jeffery	120211	01101	Croft, James	100010	10100

1820 SOUTH CAROLINA PENDLETON DISTRICT CENSUS

NAME	MALES	FEMALES	NAME	MALES	FEMALES
Oliver, Michiel	200001	10010	Ray, David	000010	40010
Framium, Pricilla	000000	00001	Harris, John	200010	20011
Abbett, Mathew	002511	02011	Gilla, Oner	000000	31010
West, John	000100	10100	Norton, William	210001	10011
Smith, Buckner	310101	01001	McAllister, Andrew	000001	20010
Kele, James	110010	32010	Kele, Robert	000101	00201
Herrin, Joshua	320020	01210	West, Solomon	000001	00001
Rolen, David	000101	02001	Lanener, Benjamine	400010	10010
Hubbord, John	100100	001-0	Smith, Henry	410010	11010
Robertson, David	000110	00201	Simms, Beentt	100010	10010
Mauldin, Rucker	201200	00100	Wernack, Mathew	210010	31010
McFarlin, William	200201	12001	Wilson, James	000010	00100
Grisham, John	000001	10201	Lastley, John	011201	20101
Hughes, William	100100	00100	Hubbord, David	500010	00011
Hammond, William	210001	20001	Welsh, Benjamine	100010	02010
Boone, Daniel Sr.	000011	01001	Smith, James	200010	10100
Hughes, James	200010	70010	Edmundson, John	211101	21101
Hunsom, William	300010	20010	Poole, Clabourne	110101	41110
Baker, Isaac	200100	20100	Feggans, William	000100	10100
Alexander, Daniel	100100	10100	Varette, James	010201	11101
Alexander, William	100100	20100	Fennel, Clement	210110	21010
Grogan, Henry	000100	00100	Hughes, James W.	100100	00100
Holden, Elijah	000100	10100	Pickens, Robert	100100	20100
Holden, Richard	000100	00100	Smith, Charles	000001	00201
Rogers, Hugh	000100	10100	Rollins, Samuel	210101	22101
Griffis, John	200001	20010	Wilson, John	210001	32100
Woodall, John	121110	60010	Smith, Hamton	211301	11001
Mauldin, Susanna	011100	01010	Pegg, William	300010	01102
Rich, Jeremiah	000001	01001	Boyd, Joseph	101110	00100
Baker, Thomas	310010	21010	Hughes, John	000010	20100
Baker, James	000101	00001	Clardy, Langsworth	300010	00110
Gursley, John	100100	00100	Williams, John	101201	32101
York, John	220010	31010	Morgan, John	000001	00011
Grogan, Henry	000010	30010	Oldhem, George	000011	00021
Doves, Morgan	010010	20010	Simpson, John	100010	10100
Boone, Tyre	100010	40100	Adcock, John	100100	11010
Russ, Levi	200010	10010	Barkley, William	000010	00100
Crow, Francis	100010	20010	Barkley, John	000010	20100
Hugens, William	210010	31010	Brownan, John	000101	23202
Prince, James	100010	31010	Brownan, William	100010	01100
Roberts, Abram	200100	00100	Conaway, Elisabeth	101100	11001
Williamson, James	100010	10100	Duckworth, Patrick	100100	10100
Ellerd, James	310102	10001	Elliott, William	111101	00101
Brico, John	100001	12010	Garretson, Levi	200010	32010
Watkins, Joseph	000100	10100	Gray, William	100200	10010
Pickens, Andrew	300101	02010	Galespe, Cootney	100100	12110
Knox, James	321301	01110	Hopkins, Sarah	100000	10010
Haney, Thomas	310110	21211	Carder, Sarah	011100	01001
Hopkins, John	100001	00111	Conaway, John	000100	10100
Hamby, Polly	000000	20010	Davis, Polly	00000	20100
Thompson, William	100010	10100	Elrod, Adam	200010	10010
Kelly, John	200010	11000	Gorden, Vincent	300010	01010
Kelly, Elisha	200010	11000	Greene, Henry	110010	40010
Lawless, Asa	210010	30010	Gaskin, James	000010	00101
Owens, Littier	100000	10100	Hamby, Francis	010001	00001
Pack, Simon	000001	10001	Harper, William	210010	21010
Roberts, Elisabeth	010010	00002	Harper, John	120110	22110
Rains, Drury	211101	22110	Allen, Joshua	100010	10100
Smith, Tobias	100010	11010	Johnson, Francis	001100	00110
Slatton, Wade	020010	10010	Knop, Peter	010101	40010
Slaton, William	130010	20110	Lawless, Henry	410010	31111
Slaton, Uriah	310001	30110	Nichols, Archibald	210010	40310
Turner, Landers	310101	10010	Pack, Patsy	200000	10010
Wilbourne, Thomas	200001	20010	Person, George	01001?	01001
Wilbourne, Moses	210010	30010	Rogers, Joseph T.	100020	10010
Whitlock, Thomas	011101	00001	Rollins, Thomas W.	310001	40110

NAME	MALES	FEMALES	NAME	MALES	FEMALE
Armstrong, James	300010	20010	Stone, Jeremiah	100010	40010
			Sears, Kinchen	000010	00001
			Slaton, George Jr.	000200	10100
			Smith, William Jr.	000100	00100
Broyles, Joshua	010011	10001	Smith, John	200002	30010
Bagwell, Jessee	100011	30011	Williams, William	000100	10100
Cox, John	110010	30101	Wilson, Hugh	000110	00000
Childirs, William	000100	10100	Ashley, Thomas	000100	00100
Camp, William	200010	22111	Ackos, Amos	000010	30101
Crowther, John	110010	20010	Brock, Enos	100100	01100
Davis, Robert	401110	21010	Bagwell, George	410010	51010
Duncan, David	100010	30101	Cobb, Niah	110010	20010
Ellison, Miles	000100	00100	Cornelius, Abram	200010	33011
Yancy, Miles	000100	10200	Holdman, Lewis	000010	10100
Wright, John	000001	20010	Cox, William	200110	31010
Jackson, John	100010	20100	Davis, Moses	000100	10100
Hughes, Gilson	100100	00100	Duncan, Dabney	100100	10100
Russel, Robert	100701	00101	Dawson, Samuel	000101	00111
Hughes, Micah	300010	01010	Fowler, Andrew	110010	30010
Gilliand, Thomas	110010	21010	Harkins, Widow	000020	00011
Smith, Elijah	210010	02110	Horten, Daniel	100100	20020
Smith, Wade	000010	01100	Chandler, Jesse	220010	10010
Morris, Andrew	000010	10010	Land, Plyah	000100	20100
Wilbourne, Wilm.	000100	00100	Lee, Tarlton	012210	21010
Cason, Joseph	100010	20110	Morris, Burrel	200010	21010
Littleton, Mark	301110	10110	Massey, Simon	300010	10100
Arial, John	210001	10001	Mayfield, Elijah	200100	11100
Guthery, Nelson	000010	00010	Poor, Samuel	500010	10010
Balden, John	2000010	50010	Robertson, John	000100	00100
Adams, Nathaniel	212210	22102	Smith, Mosses	010010	20010
Tucker, Samuel	100301	12201	Strickland, Malacl	100010	10100
Durham, David	300010	10010	Telford, Robert Jr.	000100	00100
White, Jesse	100010	10100	Walker, Peter	100010	10100
Barkley, Samuel	000101	00101	Davis, James	000100	10100
Pack, James	011110	11001	Carpenter, Urrel	010201	00101
Brazete, Elijah	110201	21301	Valentine, George	201110	11010
Browman, James	000010	20100	Burress, John	100100	00100
Burton, Archibald	100010	20100	Crow, Jonathan	110010	31010
Bailey, Robert	300110	14001	Ried, Henry	100010	21010
Day, Johnson	100010	20100	Ackos, Alexander	000010	00000
Erskin, James	020101	10301	Clemment, Isaac	000010	10100
Gier, David	000100	00100	Barford, Thomas W.	100010	10010
Griffen, John	111301	00110	Burton, Charles	001101	00001
Holland, Nancy	000010	10100	Bowen, Benjamine	001201	00101
Leonard, Samuel	200110	10100	Dobbins, James	110010	20001
McFarlin, George	100010	31010	Davis, William	110010	32010
Majors, Elijah	000010	00100	Eastridge, Nathaniel	121121	03001
McAllister, Wilm.	001200	10010	Fante, Thomas	100010	40010
Mayfield, Samuel	000001	00101	Hilhouse, Samuel	210010	21010
Parker, Reuben	100010	11010	Huff, Joshua	400010	00010
Stephenson, David	000100	11110	George, Francis	000010	00010
Strickland, Henry	200010	10200	Dowel, John	100201	01111
Shiay, Thomas	000101	01001	McRight, Robert	200110	10110
Todd, James	100201	00101	Moore, Samuel	310110	21010
			Norrell, James	100010	10010
Vandever, William	100010	20100	Parker, John	001101	00200
Vandever, John	220010	10010	Stephenson, Robert	110201	00301
Kitsinger, Jacob	100100	10010	Smith, William	220001	30110
Wardlowe, John	000100	00100	Smith, Thomas	201301	21210
Wilson, James	000001	00011	Taylor, Solomon	100100	10100
Bannister, Mattison	310010	30100	Vandever, Edward	020201	00101
Davis, Bennett	200100	00100	Wade, Agnes	100000	20020
Davis, William	300010	00201	Winingham, Sarah	210100	01010
Davis, Jesse	200011	10110	Wade, James - (not to be found)		
Frost, Gorum	100100	30100	Ackor, William	110201	00201
Howard, Hannah	00000	20101	Christain, John	000100	10100
Hayney, John	0012000	00100	Davis, John	310010	40020

NAME	MALES	FEMALES	NAME	MALES	FEMALES
Harris, Archibald	100110	10100	Davis, Charles	100010	20100
Harris, John	010001	10001	Elrod, William	111201	31001
Haney, Stephen	000101	00101	Gunlee, Widow	000010	00011
Hanks, George	210010	40010	Hale, Absolm	000800	00100
Holland, Thomas	000010	10100	Raney, Anthony	020010	01000
Jackson, William	400010	00010	Harris, Joshua	100100	21010
Keaton, John	201110	40010	Haney, Charles	b32201	20210
King, John	200100	10100	Haney, Luke	100010	00100
Manning, George	221201	22010	Holland, Moses	400001	00010
Mayfield, Abram	000001	00002	Jackson, Robert	200010	10010
Leright, James	100011	00011	King, Peter	200010	30010
Taylor, John	000010	20100	King, Robert, Jr.	200010	20010
Cox, Thomas	100100	00100	Middleton, John	100100	10100
Hill, Demsy	200010	20010	Manning, Richard	010001	01000
Key, Morten	100100	00100	McCoy, Daniel	010001	00001
Land, William	300010	10010	Priest, Solomon	211101	32010
Lee, Lewis	100010	01011	Ried, John	200100	10010
McAllister, Nathan	210010	01001	Sigman, John	000101	00101
Massey, Laben	101110	52010	Taylor, John Sr.	000101	00001
Massey, Ansel	000100	00100	Simms, William	111101	41310
Murphey, Rober	000001	00011	Payne, Moses	001201	21001
Robertson, James E.	100010	20100	Davis, Joseph	101101	30010
Strickland, Mathew	100010	00011	Stedham, Zacharias	200010	00010
Smith, George W.	100100	00100	Clanhan, William	300100	20010
Lemon, James	000110	10100	Capin, Silas	231201	01201
Broom, Mark	141101	11010	Stephenson, Henry	100100	10100
Billingsly, James	200100	00100	Townsend, John	231210	20100
Browne, Levi	010001	21101	James, Phillip	100001	10011
Browne, Levi	010001	21101	Payne, Sarah	10000	01010
Browne, Hezekiah	000010	10100	Dickson, William	100010	10010
Butt, Jacob	000010	00000	Martin, James	120101	21001
Cole, John	200100	00100	Jenkins, Francis	331101	10110
Camp, Thomas	100010	11100	Anderson, Noble	230201	10010
Weldon, William	310010	12010	Butt, John	010101	00011
White, Hiram	200100	20010	Browes, John	100010	10100
Wade, Edward	311101	01010	Barnes, Isaac	200100	20100
Bird, Henry	400010	11010	Browne, John	000010	00100
Calhoune, John	000001	00200	Browne, William	200010	10100
Cuningham, Caty	000000	03120	Bryan, Jesse	220001	30301
Cunningham, James	000001	00001	Cole, James	510010	30010
Davis, Orange	200101	10010	Williams, William	300011	30010
Duncan, Robert	320011	11111	White, John	320001	21210
Blair, William	010001	23010	White, William	210010	32010
Gable, John	110010	31010	Browne, Daniel	100010	20101
Hull, Jonathan	300010	00010	Browne, James	110101	10101
Cole, John	110010	31010	Cuminbs, Samuel	100100	00101
Hull, Jonathan	300010	00010	Cunningham, Colly	000100	00101
Cole, John	221101	42111	Cunlap, Robert	200010	01100
Sanford, William	010010	10010	Duncan, John	110001	31201
Chambers, Henry	000010	40100	Elrod, Thomas	321201	11010
Chandler, Abigale	310000	10010	Hanna, William	010010	00001
Yam, Samuel	000100	00100	Herren, James	101302	20102
Fairley, Stewart	00001	00101	Howard, Hiram	320010	11010
Mason, Joseph	000100	10010	Shed, Thompson	100100	10010
Davis, Eli	000001	00101	King, Elijah	300010	30010
Hughes, John	000101	01301	Herden, Francis	011200	01001
Laterfield, Bedwell	000110	00010	Step, Colby	000100	00100
Beaty, James	100100	00100	Wooten, Daniel	120001	10201
Fitzgerald, Ambrose	000101	00011	Fairley, Jesse	200010	20011
Fullerton, John	010010	00101	Clenhan, David	000100	00100
Hays, Willis	300100	10010	Harrison, Shedreck	000010	00100
Hamilton, Wilm.	100010	10100	Minton, Richard	101110	20301
Hall, James	120010	30010	Jolly, John	100010	30010
Jared, Joseph	000010	20100	Fairley, Robert	110010	20010
Lo, Louden	320010	10010	Jones, Jacob	001101	00201

NAME	MALES	FEMALES	NAME	MALES	FEMALES
McKee, Archibald	210101	21100	Guest, Tilmon	000100	20010
McDowell, Wilm.	400010	10010	Hannah, John	000100	00100
Milford, Thomas	200010	10010	Hall, Wilm. A.	210010	41010
McKey, Hugh	000010	10100	Jared, James	010001	01101
McEarly, David	310010	12010	Canada, Pricilla	210001	12001
McCullah, Robert	121301	21101	McCulla, John	000100	10100
McKee, Jane	010000	11201	McKee, William	000001	00001
Wright, William	000010	00100	Milford, John Jr.	000010	20200
Furr, James	300101	11110	McCurry, Thomas	000010	10100
Shirley, Nathaniel	000001	00101	McAllister, Nathan	000010	01002
Rogers, Adam	001101	31501	Milford, John Sr.	010001	01111
Crosby, Anes	000010	00100	Mitchell, Polly	020000	10110
Hughes, George	100100	10100	McCulleh, James	100100	10100
Cain, William	000010	00110	Leathers, Elisha	210001	00010
Camron, Archibald	300010	20010	Capheart, William	600010	10101
Duncan, Geo. A.	221101	20010	Collins, George	000100	10100
Roach, Francis	000000	10010	Harris, Samuel	000010	20010
Queen, Amy	000000	00111	Rankin, Nathaniel	210010	31010
Neese, Peter	000001	00101	Morris, Jorden	320101	10210
Bagwell, John	121201	00101	Browne, Benjamine	210010	21101
Bagwell, Robert	200011	00100	Morgan, Malen	100100	00100
Chunshaw, Anderson	020001	31010	Briscoe, John	200010	10010
Swords, Andrew	100100	10100	Binam, Jane	010000	01001
Elrod, Phillip	110010	01010	Lamar, Thomas	211101	32131
Golden, William	220001	31010	Wilbourne, Aaron	010001	00001
Newton, Isaac	100001	21010	Howard, Delilah	100000	00010
Newton, William	021201	11001	Sizemore, John	110101	00101
Murphy, John	100100	00100	Misner, Joshua	210010	12110
Parris, William	110010	60010	Scott, Francis	210000	10010
McKinney, Hugh	300110	20010	Nise, John	000100	10100
Martin, William	000010	20100	Anderson, William	000001	00000
Nation, Abram	121101	21001	Carder, Thomas	010011	21000
Leathen, Nimrod	200010	30010	Adams, Jacob	121201	01010
Robertson, William	000100	10100	Cambell, Abram	230101	11201
Step, Joseph	211101	20110	Gray, Hulda	010000	01401
Holden, Richard	311210	31010	Gambriel, John	100100	10100
Woody, James M.	100100	20100	Davis, Thomas	000100	10101
Littleton, Mark	100100	30010	Adams, William	000010	00100
Bagwell, William	100011	21011	Vandike, Anderson	000010	00001
Brock, Elisabeth	200000	00010	Raiser, David	100010	10010
Mulligan, Benjamine	021201	11201	Vandevier, Thomas	400010	10010
Briant, John	120010	30010	Richey, John Sr.	000001	01001
Dilling, Thomas	100001	4110	McCrary, Henry	000010	10100
Newton, Willis	000100	00100	Nix, James	000001	00001
Cambell, Robert	210001	20001	Brownlow, James	400010	10100
Wigginton, George	500010	20010	Voyles, Jessee	200100	00010
Farmer, Joshua	000100	02201	Tarrant, Richard	000010	21010
Wisener, Joshua	210010	21110	Brownlo, James C.	000100	00100
Pilgrim, Thomas	100010	00100	Dunlap, Gilbert	220001	30010
Smith, Job	100010	20100	Johnson, Phillip	121201	12101
Birum, Jesse	210001	31201	McDow, Arthur	100101	11101
Craig, William	210010	10010	Nevel, William	200010	00000
Hinkle, John	110401	42110	Steel, Abner	110001	20320
Lofton, Thomas	000101	00101	Terrell, James A.	100010	00010
Chambers, Barrock	200010	20100	Watson, William	41001?	11001
Nations, Daniel	000100	30100	Barry, Widow	100000	01010
Shelton, Aaron	100200	01101	Browne, William	140010	20010
Powel, Almond	200010	00010	Cleveland, William	000001	00000
Parker, David Sr.	211201	11001	McAllister, Elisab.	230000	00010
Moore, Lazarus	000010	00001	Morten, Elenor	300000	01210
Stenson, Moses	000100	10010	Morris, Garret	200010	20110
Stenson, James	100100	00100	Patterson, Wilm.	110001	54010
Hancock, James	310010	12100	Parker, David	000100	00100
Caldwell, William	000010	20020	Parker, James	200010	00100
Collins, Thomas	311201	12010	Rice, Andrew	200010	00100
Collins, George	000100	10100	Stenson, William	011101	00211

1820 SOUTH CAROLINA PENDLETON DISTRICT CENSUS

NAME	MALES	FEMALES	NAME	MALES	FEMALES
Massey, James	300010	20100	Chamberlain, Benj.	000101	12010
Fullerton, Thomas	100010	21010	Davis, Joel	000100	00100
Mason, John	200001	01001	Davis, Van	00010?	41010
Smithson, Marsen C.	100101	00121	Dean, Griffith	100010	10100
Logsand, John	100010	00201	Fricks, Christain	100010	30010
Beaty, Robert	110001	31110	Gentry, Matthew	410001	20010
Cole, Elenor	001200	00010	Gorden, Jacob	110010	21010
McDaniel, Thomas	121201	11111	Gentry, Cain	100011	00220
McDaniel, Thomas Jr.	300010	10010	Gentry, Bart	100010	00010
Step, William	400001	03010	Gentry, Archibald	000100	10100
Browne, William	101200	00101	Nicholds, Patsy	310000	21010
Robertson, John	200010	10100	Long, James	020010	40010
McGee, Samuel	000100	20100	MdGee, Willis	100100	20100
McCulla, Elisabeth	010100	00001	Herrin, Francis	000010	30010
Prewit, Jacob	100010	01000	Jergan, Thomas	100010	20100
Scott, John	000001	00012	Cox, James	000100	20100
Scott, Thomas	010001	00010	McCollum, Samuel	100010	20010
Todd, Robert	101110	31010	Cox, Westley	100100	00200
Waters, Flemming	111110	00010	Evans, John	210101	00101
Fowler, Willm. B.	300100	10100	Herrin, Isiah	100010	20100
Clark, Ephaim	121101	01010	Wason, Joseph	110110	12010
Askin, Samuel	400010	20010	Cox, George	300010	21010
Bennett, Patunee	101100	11201	Hall, Joseph	101201	02010
Burress, Briant	200100	10100	Hays, Gilbert	100001	20110
Bowen, Samuel	200100	00100	Hays, William	110010	11010
Caldwell, Robert	320010	31010	Hays, Jacob	100010	10100
Cox, Edward	111101	20010	McDaniel, Archibald	010010	20100
Williams, Reubin	000001	00001	McDaniel, Henry	100110	10010
Crooks, William	110001	11010	Williams, Grief	110010	32010
Howard, Rome	120000	30011	Browne, William	101200	00101
Wilbanks, Ruth	030200	10110	Nations, Thomas	000100	00100
Crompton, Thomas	100010	40010	Shed, James	100010	00100
Herrin, Elbert	100100	00100	Prier, Pennel	110010	01010
Willey, Thomas	300010	11010	Ried, Mary	010200	01101
Cox, Edward Jr.	100010	30100	Steele, David	001201	32300
Steele, Moses	100010	30100	Scott, David	000010	20010
Wright, Joseph	010001	00101	Still, William	100100	20100
Clanshan, Robert	000001	01000	White, Newton	100100	10100
Bremar, Joseph	010201	01001	Dodd, Joel	020110	51110
Chamberlain, Wilm.	110100	20010	Cordell, Jesse	110101	12201
Cenwall, James	000101	12010	Armstrong, William	010010	00201
Bennett, Holly	000000	20010	Stigall, Spencer	300100	00100
Burress, James	110101	12201	Trotter, Robert	320010	41011
Ballard, William	000100	00100	Yondling, John	220101	12110
Caldwell, George	100010	30010	Madden, Richard	010201	12201
Evans, John	210010	10100	Barnett, Amos	000001	01001
Brooks, Berry	310010	10010	Cox, Levi	310010	20010
Corirs, Iverson	120001	10010	Harris, Edward	100001	43110
Lathern, William	101101	32001	Wells, John	000010	20110
McGregory, Thomas	010001	01011	McConald, William	430010	10010
Turner, William	010001	21201	Browne, George	000100	10100
Crompton, James	000001	00001	Kieth, Thomas	100100	00100
Berry, William	000100	00100	McGill, Ezekiel	100010	00010
Stewart, Samuel	000010	10100	Landers, Edward	100001	21111
Steele, Isaac	200010	10010	Pickins, Samuel	200010	40010
Roach, Henry	221110	20010	Parks, Mathew	200001	21010
Spriggs, Reason	000001	10101	Roberts, John	010101	12101
Bremar, Benjamine	220100	21010	Roberts, Sterling	300010	20010
Bishop, Wily	111201	11002	Laster, John	221101	20110
Cannon, Ephraim	100100	00100	Stephenson, James	200010	00100
Commings, Harmon	101201	00111	Still, Robert	100010	10011
Davis, Widow	011100	00201	Stephenson, Alen	000011	00001
Driver, Christiana	00000?	01001	Seelton, Sadock	000010	20100
Davis, John	400010	10010	Tippen, John	100010	00100

303

NAME	MALES	FEMALES	NAME	MALES	FEMALES
Fountain, Jonathan	120010	20010	Tippen, Widow	110000	10110
McGee, Jeremiah	300010	11010	Wood, Wiat	100001	21011
Gentry, John	020001	01101	Jackson, William	410001	31010
Gentry, Moody	000100	10100	Jenkins, Richard	000001	01001
Payne, Margaret	010200	00100	League, Elisha	101201	01102
Hays, William	001101	01111	McKlerath, Mitchel	400001	01301
Bennett, Rebecca	210000	32001	Norell, Francis	100000	10201
Brooks, Mary	100000	10010	Price, William	300100	00010
McDonald, George	100010	40010	Popham, John	001111	00011
Simpson, John	500010	10100	Prince, William	100010	40010
Yergan, Samuel	200010	10100	Pearson, John	010010	01110
Roach, William	000100	00100	Phillips, Peter	110010	21010
Cox, Wilm. B.	100100	00100	Rackley, William	200010	01010
Wilson, David	000010	10100	Rackley, Jesse	310010	10010
Latham, David	000100	00010	Laterfield, Thomas	022401	21201
Herrin, Zachius	100100	00010	Stephenson, John	200010	10010
Carter, Thomas	000010	10010	Wilson, Robert	000201	10001
Carter, Absolm	220210	30310	Wilson, William	00101	00202
Landers, Thomas	400010	20010	Williford, John	300010	10010
Hall, Johnson	510010	10110	West, Robert	000001	00001
Hays, James	120010	10011	Wood, Marvel	200010	00100
Hays, Thomas	100010	00101	Gray, James	000001	21010
Hays, Stephen	400010	20010	Jones, Elisabeth	000000	00002
Keaton, William	400010	10010	Burrel, Hardy	000100	00100
Johnson, Levi	010010	01110	Browne, Jesse	100100	20100
Long, William	000100	00100	Browne, Isham	100100	00100
Land, Joseph	121101	01001	Burnett, Elijah	200010	20100
Manor, Hosea	000100	00100	Duncan, Nathaniel	100002	20020
Minor, John	300010	10100	Keaton, Thomas	100010	12010
McCown, John	100100	20100	Jolly, William	000010	10010
Payne, John	000100	00100	Long, James, Jr.	000101	10201
Prewite, Ansel	000010	10100	Massey, Phillip	000100	00100
Manor, Elijah	100100	00200	Crane, John	201301	02101
McGregor, William	131201	31110	Duncan, John	110001	31010
Keaton, Lalethiel	010011	00011	Freeman, Mark	000100	30100
Payne, Lindsey	200010	10020	Freeman, Needham	000101	01101
Standley, John	210001	21010	Fowler, Joshua	000101	01001
Trotter, Isham	300010	21010	Griffen, Henry	311201	01001
Trotter, James	310010	01010	Guest, Sopheah	001200	20001
Washborne, David	101110	10010	Guest, James	1000010	30010
McDaniel, Andrew	211201	20010	Glaze, David	100010	20010
Barnett, John	100102	02111	Howard, William	300010	21010
Steel, Widow	010001	00011	Hendrix, Moses	000101	00101
Davis, Mark	100010	41010	Hood, Robert	330010	12010
Jones, Thomas	100010	10010	Hays, Solomon	010001	00201
Yergin, Edward	210001	01010	Burrele, Jesse	010001	00001
Browne, John	000100	00100	Chistern, John	400010	10010
McGill, Samuel	010011	00311	Chistern, David	000010	20010
McGill, William	100010	10010	Dunningham, Mary	100000	21021
Prewet, David	000001	10001	Duncan, Daniel	000001	00001
Perry, William	000101	01201	Fuller, Isaac	300010	11010
Bishop, Wilm. N.	100100	00100	Fulton, Ameriah	100001	10001
Roberts, John Jr.	100110	20100	Gentry, Arthur	300101	10121
Driver, James	31001	21010	Heston, James	000001	00001
Smith, George	100100	00100	Hembru, John	320010	10110
Stephenson, George	101101	02101	Heaton, Joseph	302201	03010
Seelton, Solomon	100010	30100	Heaton, Joseph	000010	01010
Stephenson, Jonathan	100010	10100	Sayent, Ephraim	120201	37101
Still, Dennis	010101	01102	Smith, Enoch	101101	10010
Tuggle, George	000100	10100	Thomas, Rebecca	231001	21110
Tate, David	320010	11110	Tatum, Edward	100010	30011
Waters, Robert	300010	32010	Mark, Baloes	200100	00100
Julan, William	000101	00120	Watson, Robert	110001	00110
Langston, Solomon	211110	10010	Browne, Lewis	200010	11010
Little, Mathias	320010	20110	Black, Mitchel	300010	00100

1820 SOUTH CAROLINA PENDLETON DISTRICT CENSUS

NAME	MALES	FEMALES	NAME	MALES	FEMALES
Miller, Patsy	000100	00201	Bruce, Daniel	201110	23110
Poe, Richard	020101	11101	Chistern, James	310010	01100
Price, Daniel	210010	30010	Corban, Elijah	200010	30010
Prince, Joshua	221301	21110	Chapman, John	200010	10010
Prince, John	210110	40010	Cantrell, Moses	100001	22110
Phillips, Jacob	000001	00010	James, John	000001	00000
Roper, Joshua	420110	21110	Kilpatrick, Hugh	100010	01010
Rackley, Thomas	200010	00010	Morris, John	110010	21010
Singleton, James	000010	40010	McClure, Joseph	110001	01201
Lisk, Gabriel	121210	10010	McHugh, Charles	200010	20010
Watson, Jonathan	100100	20100	Masters, Polly	212301	30110
Watson, Daniel	000100	10100	Pool, Manon	110010	30110
Wood, Charles	100010	20100	Prewit, Thomas	111101	11001
Williford, Wright	000001	10001	Rainwater, Solomon	110100	00301
Wood, Edward	010001	00101	Renalds, Aaron	200010	21020
Seelton, Hosea	200100	00100	Smith, Joseph	110010	42010
Cumings, Griffin	100010	20100	Winters, John	001110	51110
Driver, Jacob	000001	00100	Murk, Daniel	000100	00010
Bello, James H.	010010	01001	Mansil, James	321101	21110
Browne, George	010101	01101	Miller, Isaac	000010	10110
Busclark, Abram	110010	20010	Martin, Absolm	000110	30100
Burdet, Humphrey	410011	30010	Mullenan, Mathew	120011	20101
Case, Jesse	220101	30101	Mayfield, Briant	200010	13010
Morten, Marshal	010102	21012	Randolph, Widow	000000	00011
Barrett, Mary	211200	20010	Wilbanks, Sarah	110000	01001
Odel, James	200010	32110	Waters, Armsted	200010	31010
Payne, Charles	220010	21010	McKinney, Daniel	220101	02101
Prater, Aaron	100010	30010	McCollum, David	240110	31101
Crane, John Jr.	420101	11010	McWhirter, Robert	020101	11010
Edwards, Lemuel	100010	10010	Martin, Margaret	000000	00011
Freeman, Barny L.	100100	10100	Mullenan, Mathew Jr.	300010	10100
Freeman, Reding	000100	10100	McCollum, James	000010	00100
Hollis, Jacob	021101	00201	Mark, John	000010	10100
Gilliand, James	401110	42010	Odel, John	200010	10100
Jenkins, Sheperd	230010	20010	Jorden, Mary	010000	21010
Guest, William	200010	10010	Prater, Jospeh	201200	10100
Gilstrap, Wily	200020	00121	Stewart, Mary	010000	21010
Hendrix, David	310110	10010	Wilson, Winneford	000000	41010
Hollis, Marshal	100100	00100	Roe, John	210010	10010
Hood, Enoch	310010	20011	Wilson, John	000001	30010
Bell, Thomas	120010	01101	Young, James	000001	00001
Clark, Benjamine	000100	00100	Bennett, Cooper	010101	00101
Chistern, Stephen	010101	00001	Binman, John	110001	01100
Cooper, Joseph	000010	10100	Bennett, William	100010	30100
Collins, Thomas	100010	00100	Bell, William	0000010	00100
Ditlda, Amos	100010	00100	Beddleton, Eleanor	000000	00001
Chappel, Robert	400010	20010	Caldwell, Joseph	100010	10100
Gentry, Daniel	200010	10010	Campbell, George	200001	40010
Heaton, William	000100	20101	Cox, Beverly	300010	00100
Hembru, James	300110	10010	Chanley, Widow	001100	00201
Harbin, Catherine	011100	0002	Chistern, Samuel	100010	20100
Heaton, David	100100	00010	Canimore, Moses	(left blank)	
Johns, Arthur	000201	00100	Canimore, Lott	000100	20100
Smith, Suana	211200	01010	Cason, John	100010	50010
Taylor, Chap	020301	00121	Day, Benjamine	311201	10110
Youngblood, Henry	000010	00000	Gilstrap, Zilpah	100000	00100
Vandignf, Jared	00001?	00100	Edwards, William	300101	01100
Watson, Thomas	100100	20010	Gibson, James	000010	30010
Watson, Ansel	000100	00100	Gilstrap, Hardy	100101	11001
Black, Thomas	020001	30211	Goss, Sanders	000100	00100
Black, John	000100	00100	Hendrix, Henry	021101	10301
Bruce, Mary	200000	10021	Hamilton, Andrew	000010	00100
Carder, Richard	000100	20100	Kilbourne, Zibly	100000	00111
Corban, Samuel	110101	12001	Lindsey, George	400100	10010
Cannon, Russel	100100	00100	Earpe, Caleb	201301	40101
Cantrell, Jesse	000100	10100	Varner, David	000201	01101

305

NAME	MALES	FEMALES	NAME	MALES	FEMALES
Johns, John	101110	20010	Vann, Jarirs	000101	11110
McMillion, John	000001	01110	West, Isaac	210001	02001
Morris, William	2000010	00010	Anderson, Shodock	100100	00100
McClure, William	031201	00001	Black, Isaac	100010	00110
Moore, Alen	100100	10100	Blithe, Charles	100010	10010
Phillips,Richard	300010	10010	Black, Grovey	000100	10100
Pool, William	031201	00001	Boggs, Aaron Sr.	100101	01101
Moore, Alen	100100	10100	Boggs, Thomas	000100	00100
Phillips, Richard	300010	10010	Banks, George	200010	10010
Pool, William	000010	00000	Banks, Joseph	310010	11010
Prewit, John	000010	00100	Camp, Wlliam	200010	50010
Rainwater, Joshua	000110	00100	Devina, John	010001	32301
Davis, Henry	101201	13010			
Fitzgerald, Thomas	000010	30010	Boggs, William	110010	01010
Franklin, Thomas	100010	00100	Briant, Sterling	300010	10011
Heuston, Henry	010010	00010	Banks, Ransom	320010	10110
Hays, Council	000010	00010	Conncellor, Wilm.	10011	00100
Aabbett, James	211210	31101	Shed, John	200010	21010
Erwin, John	310010	23010	Evans, William	310001	10010
Kirby, Joel	100010	10010	Morhead, Elisabeth	200000	20010
Kelly, John	300010	30010	Fontain, Stephen	100010	00100
Land, William	100100	10100	Gasaway, Henry	200101	31010
Leathers, Samuel	100010	20100	Hinson, William	220201	10001
Land, Widow	000100	00111	Jackson, John	100010	10100
Moon, William	000101	00001	Davis, John	120201	41201
McClure, William	200010	10010	Fountain, John	121101	33101
Moore, Eli	100010	20010	King, Stephen	100010	30010
Sigmore, William	000110	4110	Lovelace, Amy	000000	11110
Orr, Samuel	000100	30100	Land, Isaac	000110	00010
Orr, David	210010	40010	Leathers, Abram	200010	20110
Pinyon, St okes	310010	22010	Lee, Mary	000000	30010
Phillips, Reubin	200010	10010	McClure, Charles	000101	00101
Roland, Peter	020001	10101	McClure, John	100010	40010
Woodall, Miley	000000	10110	Ladin, William	000010	00100
Young, Edmund	110010	21010	Johnson, Benjamine	120110	32110
Adkins, Patsy	000100	02001	Orr, David, Sr.	100101	20211
Ballard, Stephen	400001	22010	Pound, John	000001	00101
Bennett, Leon	000010	10010	Palmore, Simon	200010	20100
Brooks, John	100001	20011	Phillips, James	310010	00001
Beddleton, Polly	000000	00001	Quailes, Robert	100010	20010
Beddleton, Joshua	000111	01100	Quales, David Jr.	000010	10100
Care, David	111101	10110	Rotherford, Larkin	000100	10100
Cittle, Jacob	000001	10201	Roach, Jeremiah	100100	10100
Chrinshaw, Jesse	300010	20010	Raney, Thomas	100001	10001
Cittle, Samuel	000100	10100	Strickland, Alen	000010	00100
Caldwell, John	210010	30010	Standford, James	101201	01100
Canimore, Goerge	000001	00121	Swafford, Moses	000100	00100
Chapman, Joshua	400010	30010	Shed, William	100100	00100
Claton, Phillip	100010	20010	Tally, Prior	001101	00101
Dean, Elisha	422201	22001	Tally, Henry	000010	10100
Hamilton, Margaret	410000	21121	Roberts, Abram	200100	00100
Edwards, Peter	200010	20010	Woodall, Joseph	321110	10210
Gibson, Thomas	100100	00100	Waller, Drid	210001	22201
Gilstrap, John	000100	10100	Garner, John	000100	10100
Hamilton, David W.	000010	10110	Sullivan, James Sr.	001101	01100
Hamilton, David	000010	10110	Abbett, William	201201	33010
Mullenan, Absolm	200001	31210	Adair, William	00001	00101
Hamilton, James	000100	00010	Beck, William	110010	41110
Earpe, Wesley	000010	10010	Beck, John Jr.	100100	10100
Tippen, Leah	010000	12110	Black, William	111101	01001
Varner, David Jr.	200010	20100	Coffer, Ann	000200	00121
Varner, Charles	110001	30010	Dunn, Thomas	1011000	11101
White, Wilm. H.	000100	00100	Evans, David	000100	10100
Black, Caty	001200	00001	Forgeson	222201	10101
Blithe, Robert	001301	01101	Garner, Thomas	010001	10101
Black, David	100010	00100	Haynes, Thomas	100100	00100

NAME	MALES	FEMALES	NAME	MALES	FEMALES
Lampkins, John	400101	32321	Thompson, James	100100	00100
Bailey, Mrs.	100000	10110	Whitsworth, Chas.	100010	10010
Allen, Wilm. L.	000110	00110	White, George	100100	00100
Browne, Vincient	220001	41010	Winningham, John	100100	20010
Blackbumel, John A.	100010	30100	Young, Phinias	(removed)	
Browne, John	100100	21100	Barton, Lewis	100001	21010
Browne, Thomas	300010	00100	Bradberry, James	210010	12010
Hardy, John	200101	31010	Bradberry, Jesse	310010	20010
Clement, Adam	100010	30010	Bailey, James	410010	00014
Casper, J.	500100	10100	Bates, Stephen	211101	21010
Crow, William	010010	10100	Buba, Dency	010100	10100
Durham, James	000010	00111	Browne, Levi	120010	30010
Dearham, George	400001	00010	Clement, Aarom	210001	21110
Felton, Wilm. Jr.	000100	20100	Clement, John	100100	20010
Guest, William	010101	20100	Cord, Benson	100100	10100
Goode, William	110001	00110	Henrdon, John	221201	11201
Harden, Morten	000100	00100	Devins, Dicey	100000	02201
Hays, William	200111	00302	Coggans, Westley	000100	00100
Hix, Daniel	301210	20010	Goowin, John	100100	00100
Holland, John	210010	40010	Gilbert, Benjamine	020001	00201
Herrin, Gideon	100100	00100	Guest, Squire	211110	10110
Herrin, Elijah	021201	31001	Hutchins, Micheil	110101	21101
Harris, Sarah	020000	21010	Herrin, William	000100	20100
Isbel, Pendleton Jr	000100	10100	Hagood, Mary	020000	21010
Butler, Aaron	000101	00200	Hutchins, Thomas	000100	20100
Butler, Moses	000010	10100	Hughes, John	110020	21010
Barton, David	311101	21110	Pucket, Harris	030010	31110
Denny, Joshua	110010	22201	Isbel, James	210010	31020
Eaton, Joshua	000101	00000	Johnson, Josiah	001101	11110
Carpenter, Willia	030010	10101	Browne, Isaac	000001	00000
Colling, John	000010	00011	Bradley, Francis	100001	10100
Brice, Allen	011101	01101	Barton, Rebecca	101100	01002
Beard, William	000001	00001	Denny, Ehul	100100	00100
Chambers, Wilm.	000001	00001	Evens, David	000100	10100
Dunn, William	200010	10010	Coby, Jesse	200010	00100
Brice, John	000100	00100	Cannon, James	110010	22110
Fredrick, Jacob	110001	11001	Chamberlain, Jacob	200010	20010
Farr, Robert	000001	00001	Bailey, John	000100	20100
Graham, Unity	211010	10010	Cox, Phillip	01001	00101
Gilbert, Amos	111101	10010	Collins, Watson	100010	40010
Hunt, Charles	000001	00001	Fountain, Littleton	200100	00100
Harden, Greene B.	000100	00100	Frix, John	100100	10100
Kent, Mark	200010	10100	Frix, Jacob	111110	21001
Lanier, Bird	300010	12010	Gray, Thomas	200100	00100
Lowery, John	100001	21201	Gorby, Isham	000100	10100
Miars, John	000100	00100	Herrin, Elisha	301200	01101
Hays, Henry	000001	00110	Fretwell, Jane	2000000	10010
Hall, Jesse	000311	01201	Frix, Mathias	300010	20100
Hix, Robert	100111	01211	Gray, John	000111	10011
Jenkins, Francis	401301	32010	Gorby, John	000010	00111
Jolly, James	000001	00001	Gorby, Isham Sr.	000001	00101
Kitchens, David	300010	00010	Hubbard, Jeremiah	020001	10100
Manning, Polly	001010	01110	Hall, Zacharius	300010	01010
Morgan, Morgan	200001	00101	Hall, David	000100	00100
McWhister, John	221101	10111	Howel, William	110101	31001
Peterson, John	020001	10100	Jackson, Robert	410010	32010
Rufus, David	200010	10100	Kelly, James	500010	12010
Renalou, Archibus	010001	11100	Morgan, William	410010	11011
Stancil, James	000100	00100	McEarly, Samuel	010101	12001
Lisk, Joseph	000100	00100	Morgan, David	100010	10100
Stephens, Joshua	000100	10100	Priestly, Richard	000100	00100
Lego, Ellenos	010000	00101	Peterson, Tobias	000010	10010
Sharpen, John	000010	10100	Rainwater, John	100010	00100
Tredway, Ezekiel	200010	10100	Rufus, George	000200	00100
Voyles, James	221101	32001	Stephens, Isiah	210101	12010
White, Samuel	100100	00100	Suttles, Phoeby	020000	10010

1820 SOUTH CAROLINA PENDLETON DISTRICT CENSUS

NAME	MALES	FEMALES	NAME	MALES	FEMALES
Boggs, Joseph G.	300010	20010	Hull, Daniel	120110	12010
Boggs, William	110010	01010	Heuston, Joseph	200001	41201
Hinsome, Henry	000101	00001	Gillison, Eliijah	000120	00101
King, Isaac	000100	30100	Garner, Ed	100100	10010
King, William	000001	00101	Holland, James	200010	20010
Lee, Randolph	200110	13110	Head, Benjamine	100010	01010
McCollum, James	200010	10011	Hammond, Wilm.	100010	30010
McCollum, Ephriam	211310	30201	Hisone, James	100010	31010
Newle, James	000100	10100	King, Samuel	120210	00001
Phillips, Levi	100001	02401	Linch, John	210010	21010
Phillips, Levi Jr.	000100	00100	Lovelady, Margaret	011200	11001
Pratt, James	000101	20201	McDugle, Mosses	310010	20010
Robertson, William	431301	00001	Morgan, Widow	000200	00101
Randolph, Jacob	000200	20200	Nations, Amos	100201	30011
Richards, Adam	100001	13101	Perkins, Mosses	100200	10100
Sweney, Nathaniel	321101	11010	Perry, Sarah	000000	12010
Watkins, William	110101	11001	Patterson, Elisabeth	000000	00001
Bond, Leonard P.	000010	00010	Rothel, Charles	120101	20111
Barnett, James	100010	43110	Ramey, Isaac	000110	00101
Cockerheim, Drury	400010	11010	Ramey, James	100010	00100
Calliway, Susana	000000	10010	Watson, Willis	000100	30200
Hamilton, John	000201	00012	Abel, Widow	211400	32110
Honey, Abner	000201	01001	Browne, Addis	000001	20101
Hutchinson, Drury	001100	00100	Crinshaw, Fortenatus	220010	10020
Honey, Robert	000010	00100	Cobb, Ellison	000100	30100
Lowry, John	000100	00200	Daniel, Mary	110000	20201
Morrett, Benj.	000001	00011	Honeycutt, Dlijah	220010	21010
Mills, Wilm.	000001	00010	Hatcher, Russel	300010	01010
Morrette, John	200010	20010	Harden, Robert C.	000101	20100
McEarly, William	000010	10010	Janis, Burrel	102301	23010
Smith, William	100010	30110	McKinney, Duncan	000001	00011
Arington, Charles	000100	00000	Morrett, Benjamine	100010	20100
Allen, James	210001	32010	Morgan, Armond	000001	00111
Russell, Osbourne	300010	30010	Morette, Stephen	320010	10010
Quales, David	000102	01002	Ray, William	100010	00010
Robertson, Zach.	100100	10100	Smith, Phillip	300001	00010
Ruth, Adam	100010	20010	Adair, William	121110	30010
Ruth, Marion	100000	10011	Butler, William	110010	20011
Raney, Thomas Jr.	200010	20100	Bates, Daniel	000101	00001
Strickland, Moses	030001	30011	Browne, John	000011	00001
Strouther, James	000001	00001	Blackstock, Richd.	010001	01101
Sullivan, John	000010	00100	Blackstock, John	000100	10100
Taylor, Robert	010001	00301	Davis, Thomas	120010	50110
Tally, Mathias	100010	10100	Burket, Sarah	310000	01001
Tally, Eran	200100	11010	Frasier, James	200101	02201
Ramy, Isaac	400010	10020	Farr, Thomas	100010	10100
Woodall, William	000010	10100	Fortnir, Jabel	000010	00100
Rider, Sarah	001100	01010	Honeycutt, Wilm.	120010	11010
Williams, Francis	000000	00001	Honey, William	201101	22010
Wallis, John	000010	20100	Johns, Henry	011110	51211
Abbett, John	120001	10212	Ledbetter, Wilm	210010	21010
Butler, Aarom	001101	01102	Lanier, Bird Jr.	000100	00010
Beck, John	111101	11201	Miller, Elijah	110001	03201
Bison, Daniel	311201	11310	McGee, Telman	000100	00100
Copland, William	000100	10100	Matson, N.	100001	30000
Crittenden, Jonath.	000001	00001	Morgan, Manes	101110	20100
Evans, Samuel	001101	32010	Medlock, William	000100	10100
Greenwood, James	000010	40010	Powel, John	000201	00211
Doyle, William	311110	20110	Miars, Henry	001101	00101
Nimons, David	000001	31201	Miller, Robert	101101	10001
Sanders, James	410010	01010	Mason, Daniel	340001	11110
Sanders, John	010201	01201	Price, Thomas	300301	11110
Thompson, Samuel	220010	10020	Powel, Edmund	000010	10100
Vandeford, Nathan	000100	01101	Roberts, Willis	300010	10010
White, William	000100	00010	Stone, David	200201	12110
Whitten, Charles	230101	20110	Sanders, William	200010	20010
Yow, Demsy	000010	10010	Thompson, William	000100	10010

1820 SOUTH CAROLINA PENDLETON DISTRICT CENSUS

NAME	MALES	FEMALES	NAME	MALES	FEMALES
King, James	100110	01100	Gorden, Elisabeth	010000	00211
Pilgrim, Amos	200010	20101	Childers, Abram	200010	31010
Johnson, Andrew	000100	01100	Tripp, John	010001	01301
Jackson, William	010010	31010	Ballenger, John	010101	00121
Wallace, James	110010	00001	Fielding, James	011101	10010
Prater, Jeremiah	200010	10100	Durham, William	110101	10101
Dowess, William	100100	20110	Couch, Nancy	00000?	00001
Garner, Henry	010011	11100	Copland, James	000100	00100
Barron, John	000010	20001	Elrod, George	200020	10100
Baldwin, John	110010	50010	Sitten, Ailliam	200010	00010
Wiggington, George	410010	20100	Morett, James	000100	01000
Merret, John	200010	30010	Parks, Mary	110100	10110
Pilgrim, Ezekiel,Jr.	100010	00100	Lindesey, Jesse	100100	00100
Elrod, John	300010	20010	McAllister, John	100010	10010
Duncan, Mathew	300001	11011	Wiggington, Eliza	001100	01101
McAllister, James	100010	01010	Smith, Simon	310100	00100
Owens, Wily	210010	10101	Smith, William	000100	00000
Fielding, Thomas	000010	00000			
Briant, Needham	211210	01101	Walker, Allen	100001	22010
Crinshaw, Stephen	000100	00000	Briant, Nathan	220010	21110
Martin, Ann	020000	01301	Palmore, Messer	200001	20010
Slater, John	020101	23101	Williams, David	110001	32010
McKinney, Patsy	200010	20010	Steele, Hiram	000010	00010
King, James	100101	00110	Mulligan, James	100010	01000
Duckworth, Mary	100000	10010	Morten, Edmund	320010	10010
Newton, Henry	241110	10010	Davis, James	000100	10100
Mathews, John	000001	21001	Clardy, John	210111	01111
Oliver, Elisabeth	100000	00010	Moore, Charles	200001	01010
Owens, George	111201	02001	Satterfield, Wilm.	310101	10011
King, Edward	301201	01310	Couch, George	000001	01101
Briant, John Jr.	030010	30010	Wilson, Benjamine	100010	30010
Owens, George	101110	11100	Mire, Obediah	330100	21110
Timms, Absolm	000010	20100	Thompson, James	012201	20101
Fleming, John	300010	11010	Thomas, Lettice	100000	31010
Corban, James	200010	00100	Coley, John	011101	00001
Alred, Elias	100001	00311	Frasuer, John	100010	20010
Smith, Harmon	100101	01102	Collins, John	100001	00001
Pilgrim, Thomas	000001	00010	Hammond, Mary	000000	00001
Wilson, Leah	120000	10110	Beck, Josiah	001110	11010
Cornelius, Wilm.	100010	10100	Parten, Philomon	010101	00101
Logan, John	000010	42010	Parten, Hiram	100100	10010
Wilson, Benjamine	100010	30010	McCoy, James	300001	03010
Vowel, Obediah	201201	01011	McCoy, Samuel	100001	43010
Stegal, Bird	100010	03010	Mayfield, Aschibald	200010	20100
Stubs, Elisabeth	00000?	20020	Townley, Viney	010000	11210
Conger, Jonas	200010	00100	Hudson, John	010101	10211
Peg, John	100001	22010	Obriant, James	000101	00011
Morgan, Benjamine	101201	02001	Mcelen, Francis	201201	32210
Moore, John	000011	00201	Lewis, David	100001	10001
Wilson, James R.	000100	00100	Arnold, William	000010	00100
Fields, Eli	110010	10010	Patterson, Thomas	010201	01201
Martin, Sarah	00000?	21010	Graham, William	300010	00100
Simpson, James	000010	00100	Matteson, Thomas	300010	21010
Gibbs, Jeremiah	100100	10100	Davis, William	000110	00000
Young, James	110010	30010	Matteson, Nevil	000001	01031
Simpson, Robert	001101	01101	Grier, David	100100	10100
McAllister, John	1100001	00301	Cullens, John	021210	00030
Spearman, David	221101	01101	Donaldson, Wilm.	000001	00001
Taylor, David	300010	10100	Smith, Richard	131110	11110
Love, Wade	200100	00100	Taylor, Wilm.	210010	00200
Durham, David	100101	20011	Smith, Thomas	000001	00021
Corgal, Cornelius	110001	00101	Smith, Blanchy	200000	00010
Hambrick, John	000100	00010	Robinson, Jane	200010	00010
Tripp, John Jr.	200100	00100	Miller, William	100011	00011
Tripp, William	300010	20010	Hill, Abram	000010	30100

NAME	MALES	FEMALES	NAME	MALES	FEMALES
Simpson, William	000001	00000	Linch, Nathaniel	300010	10100
Starson, James	000100	00100	Lay, John	210010	31010
Stewart, John	010201	01101	Moore, David	100100	00100
Sherrard, Jane	100000	10011	McKinney, Charles	100010	10010
Turner, James	120101	31010	Nix, Loderick	210010	20010
Watt, Robert	000010	10100	Nix, Daniel	010010	30010
Watt, Thomas	100100	00100	Nix, James	110110	30010
Watt, James	000001	00000	Nix, Joseph	000001	00010
Watt, William	200010	31010	Stenson, Samuel	200010	10100
Wadsworth, Richard	100010	11010	Sealton, Jeremiah	000100	10100
Wiley, Jane	010000	00101	Simpson, Joana	210000	10010
Young, John	000011	00010	Tucker, Barbert	110001	21010
Young, John Jr.	300010	20010	Willis, Freeman	100101	02101
Bennett, Cooper	410020	20010	Watt, Thomas	300010	00010
Campbell, Ennis	100010	10200	Watt, James Jr.	100010	11010
Chinner, William	100010	30010	Wiley, William	100010	10100
Bailey, Verdery	100100	00010	Watt, Mary	110000	00110
Garner, William	200010	20010	Young, John	310010	12010
Evett, Thompson	000100	00100	Young, Andrew	000101	00201
Evett, Thomas	010211	01211	Spillers, Judith	000000	01001
Garrett, Mrs.	000000	20011	Browne, John	100100	20100
Hillin, Jesse	101201	33101	Cary, Thomas	000001	00000
Honeycutt, Roland	120001	21101	Hollingsworth, Elis	000001	00101
Heraldson, Henry	100010	10010	Dickenson, Anthony	011110	41110
Honeycutt, Willis	000100	00100	Evett, William	000101	00101
Mullinan, John	120200	20010	Evett, John	100100	00100
Mullinan, Lawson	000100	20020	Evett, Mrs.	210000	02001
Pierce, William	000010	10010	Grant, James	110110	22110
Russel, John	210101	21210	Hillin, Samuel	100100	00100
Siratt, James	220101	11110	Hammett, Widow	010000	20011
Smith, Samuel	000010	40010	Yates, William	000010	40010
Tredaway, Richard	100010	40010	Miller, John	010201	30101
White, Asa	300100	00100	Mullinan, Alse	020100	10001
Weaver, John L.	000010	40010	Phillips, John	410010	20010
Hollingsworth, John	410010	11100	Pierce, William	010010	10111
Anderson, John	000100	10100	Crinshaw, Abram	000010	40011
Akins, Archibald	200010	30010	Smith, Samuel Jr.	100100	00000
Anderson, Isaac	300110	01010	Simms, Michael	300010	21010
Ashley, Robert	211201	10201	Stafford, Jacob	100100	00010
Beach, Annis	100000	10010	Wimpee, Archibald	000010	40010
Bruce, James	000010	10100	Willism Mrs.	100000	10011
Barrett, Carwell	100010	00100	Hollingswroth, Wilm.	200100	10100
Butler, George	000100	10100	Anderson, Hrminus	220010	10010
Cantrell, John	300010	00010	Alexander, Micah	211110	22010
Cox, William	111301	12100	Anderson, Moses	310010	20010
Crane, John	021401	00001	Alexander, Thomas	110010	32010
Dier, Elisha	210010	21210	Blithe, John	100100	30100
Eaton, Lewis	011101	12001	Bollen, Joseph	110110	40010
Franklin Abram	100010	00010	Briant, James	011201	01201
Fields, Abner	d10010	21010	Barnes, Polly	100000	20020
Fields, John D.	000010	00100	Cantrell, William	220011	21010
Franklin, John	000001	00201	Crane, John Jr.	200010	20010
Gravelly, John Jr.	100010	10100	Collett, Greene	200010	20100
Head, Abner	200010	10100	Alexander, Daniel	000101	00011
Kieth, Asa	110010	10010	Eadens, Alexander	000101	12001
Franklin, William	200010	20100	Masters, John	210010	20010
*Fowler, James (seeP.46)	000100	00100	Man, John	400010	20001
Gravelly, John	001201	01001	Jones, Thomas	110101	11101
Guiton, Jacob	010101	10101	Medlin, Abram	200100	10100
Jones, Edward	000010	00100	Mulleman, Elisab.	010000	00011
Kelly, William	110101	11201	Norris, Edmund	200010	10010
Lewis, Jacob	110201	11201	Pinson, David	110001	00101
McGuttion, Thomas	011110	42011	Shaw, William	120001	30300
Moore, Joseph	310010	20010	Stokes, Hillery	100010	00100

NAME	MALES	FEMALES	NAME	MALES	FEMALES
Nix, Valentine	001101	00001	Tedmore, Adam	100110	00100
Nix, William	100110	10100	Williams, Joseph	310110	20210
Nix, Ambros	200100	00200	Whitmire, Christophr.	000200	00011
Nix, Robert	110001	12010	Whitmire, Jeremiah	100100	00100
Porter, Joseph	100100	00100	Bryam, Peter	000010	11010
Prince, John	400010	10020	Bradley, Alsose	000101	01001
Rich, William	100010	20010	Couch, Samuel	000200	00200
Rice, Isaac	200101	13101	Corban, David	420010	00010
Russe, Jacob	020001	11001	Corban, Jesse	000010	01001
Stancil, David	000100	00100	Hogan, James	100100	00100
Smith, John	200010	20010	Medlin, Andrew	000010	20010
Tate, William	000001	01201	Hughes, Nancy	310100	02001
Tate, Benjamine	020101	00001	Reggens, Leon	000010	00100
Tate, Asa	100100	10100	Stancil, William	231101	10101
Wood, Joseph	401201	13010	Reggens, Powel	201101	23010
Winchester, Wiloby	020201	11001	Stewart, Abram	300010	20100
Whitmore, Christ.	200100	00100	Stephens, James	110001	32010
Young, Levi	000101	01001	Stewart, Robert	000011	10021
Bird, Shederick	100100	00100	Tate, Simon	000010	10100
Ballard, Shederick	100010	11300	Tate, Asa	000100	20010
Brayele, Elisabeth	100000	02010	Thompson, Adam H.	410001	20010
Canselles, Henderson	110010	21010	Wood, William	100010	30010
Vann, Elisabeth	110000	20011	Winters,John	111101	00101
Clark, George	420010	11010	Wallis, Benjamine	110110	32011
Clark, Alen	100010	30010	Young, Stephen	310010	20010
Elliott, John	000100	00100	Barret, Arthur	300010	00010
Adams, James	200010	10100	Ballard, Jonathan	000201	12011
Finley, James	211101	11111	Barnett, Samuel	100100	00100
Freeman, John	020001	02110	Canamore, Noah	311101	20110
Freeman, Alse	200010	43010	Carrier, James	100010	00100
Gibson, Luke	020001	21201	Cox, Jeremiah	200010	20100
Goltney, Wiatt	200010	11101	Crawford, Thomas	300010	20010
Grant, John	000100	00100	Elliott, William	321110	10010
Hester, Henry	000010	01010	Edemy, Mariah	00000?	10010
Hunt, Jesse	100100	00100	Finley, John T.	000100	00100
Hunt, Nicholas	100100	20100	Freeman, Wily	300010	10011
Hagood, Osbourne	000100	10100	Henderson, Richard	000001	00010
Hood, Francis	210010	21010	Gray, Henry	210010	30010
Hagood, Sarah	101200	11110	Gibson, John	100100	00100
Hagood, Elliet	100100	00100	Gaines, Sherwood	000010	11100
Jones, Francis	000001	10010	Hunt, Thomas	410010	10010
Lessie, Abel	100100	00100	Hester, William	300010	30010
Cobb, William	100010	32110	Howard, Thomas	110010	21110
Looper, Samuel	220101	11001	Hill, James	210010	41010
Looper, Soloman	000010	40010	Hagood, James Jr.	310110	11010
Lathern, Anthony	100010	00100	Hagood, Nancy	00000?	10100
Hester, Thomas	000110	20100	Gibson, Absolm	110001	11101
Looper, Jeremiah	210001	22010	Hood, Lazarus	110101	00101
Lessle, William	300010	00010	Wooten, Dudley	010010	01001
Lassle, Mosses	221101	01101	Wooten, Solomon	000100	10100
Loooer, Daniel	200010	10100	Moody, Allen	100010	31010
Lathern, John Jr.	000100	00100	Quals, Elizabeth	010000	00101
Potts, James	000010	00000	Durham, Isaac	000100	10100
Looper, Joseph	000001	00001	Rankin, Sarah	000200	01101
Fowler, Josiah	210101	11002	Cox, William	300100	10100
Freeman, Westly	100100	00100	Burch, Reuben	220010	20210
Medlin, Stephen	000001	00001	Burch, John	320010	31010
Mences, Nathan	200010	200010	Baker, Jeremiah	110100	00120
Owens, Nancy	200000	11010	Kelly, Patrick	020001	10010
Prince, Edward	200010	10002	Keaton, William	000101	01101
Sitton, Joseph	300010	10010	Pritchard, Phillip	200011	10010
Sealton, William	000100	10100	South, Joseph	011200	00200
Turner, Martha	310100	12210	Haney, John	000100	00100
Whitmire, Michael	000100	00100	Lee, Widow	100000	00101
Whitmire, Samuel	100101	41110	Andirson, Widow	000100	00110
Allred, Levi	100010	00010	Moore, John	100100	00100

NAME	MALES	FEMALES	NAME	MALES	FEMALES
Bowen, William	000100	10100	McCulla, Widow	000000	00001
Bledsoe, Benjamine	100010	30020	Stephenson, Robert	001301	00211
Cargill, Clemment	100010	20100	Williamson, Wilm.	110001	21010
Cobb, Masten	300010	10100	Williamson, Chasten	100100	00100
Elrod, Jeremiah	011101	12001	Maxwell, John	210001	03010
Henderson, Nathaniel	100010	00100	Hill, Dewey	100020	20100
Henderson, John	310010	10010	King, Robert	000101	02200
Harrison, Jesse T.	110111	10001	Keaton, Ephriam	200010	00010
Henderson, David	100001	21010	Johnson, John	000100	10100
Logans, Dixon	000100	00100	Chapman, Mary	00000	00011
Mize, Obediah	331110	30110	Edwards, Stephen	000100	10100
McCollum, James	300010	10100	Prater, Susana	00000?	00101
Pilgrim, Elijah	200100	10100	Logans, Samuel	301201	21210
Rollins, Peter	000010	10100	Mauldin, Francis	300010	20100
Satterfield, James D	200210	40210	Maulden, Jacob	300010	10100
Singleton, Edmund	010111	01001	Nicholds, John	000101	10100
Wade, Telitha	300000	00010	Posey, James	021110	21011
Wade, Simon	100010	00110	Singleton, Wilm.	000010	00100
Yancy, Lewis	100100	10100	Smith, James	32001	01201
Barrot, Jesse	200100	20010	Wade, Sarah	000200	10112
Bailey, Nathaniel	011101	00301	Wade, Henry	200010	30010
Day, William	011101	00000	Watson, Solomon	000100	00100
Floyd, Sales	100100	10010	Yancy, Dabney	100100	10110
Hamilton, Thomas	110101	21221	Barts, Levi	100010	31010
Smith, Anderson	200010	10010	Canamore, Moses	120010	20010
Smith, John	100100	10100	Deckery, Henry	300010	10100
Smith, Archibald	010010	00100	Melson, Isaac	400010	00010
Maulden, Laban	210010	31010	Whitten, Joel	111101	01001
Hollingsworth, Elias	200010	10100	Roberts, Elias	000010	10100
Maulden, Rucker	110101	01101	Maulden, James	400010	10010
Pilgrim, Rebecca	001100	10101	Smith, Tyre	100010	00100
Hendrix, Ann	301100	02010	Smith, Nicholas	000101	00011
Harris, Elisabeth	120000	30110	Smith, Travis	210010	10010
Maulden, Laban	001101	00100	Maulden, Lewis	100010	00100
Howard, Jonathan	110001	01101	Smith, John O.	100010	01100
Holden, Mathew	000100	00100	Smith, Christopher	211101	40120
Hughes, Charles	(left blank)		Farmer, Mary	000200	01310
Pilgrim, Ezekiel	110001	00101	Burdine, Richard	110201	10010
Bates, Widow	100000	01210	Hughes, Andrew	200010	21010
Holden, James	200010	31000	Robins, William	000100	10100
McDougle, Sarah	220000	10101	Browne, William	010010	10100
Baker, John	100100	10100	Roland, Peter	010100	10120
Wooten, William	200100	00100	McMahon, Archib.	130001	00221
Moody, Daniel	130001	40110	Jones, Benjamine	210001	32010
McCoy, Jerusha	010000	01010	Bradley, Ambros	300010	30100
Dowess, George	100010	10010	Wilson, Mary	021100	11101
Johnson, William	110010	11100	Wilson, Manuel	000100	00100
Harbin, Nathaniel	100100	00200	Stegal, Mary	210000	00010
Vandergriff, Peter	210010	20110	Stegal, Blackwell	200100	30100
Burch, Jared	210100	41010	Stegal, Hensley	110010	20101
Jackson, Polly	020000	00101	Pilfrey, Joseph	110101	31121
Sheafford, John	000010	02010	Hays, Thomas	101201	11001
Pritchard, Henry	200100	20100	Morgan, Manus	100010	20010
Taylor, Miciajah	100010	40010	Guthrey, David	111201	12301
Stephenson, John	000100	10100	Laboon, Peter	111201	11301
Harris, Goldman	000001	00001	Dalton, Urael	200010	20010
Haney, Elisabeth	010101	00010	Simpson, Jesse	300010	20010
Hanks, Luke	421101	10010	Greene, Jeremiah	000100	00110
Wakefield, Samuel	100101	01001	Coly, Jacob	400010	10010
Taylor, Abram	100100	00100	Stephens, John	000010	00000
Harris, John	010001	10001	Simpson, John	100010	10100
Davis, Thomas	010001	12001	Owens, Lewis	200111	00010
Williamson, James	000200	10100	Rollins, Nicholas	110201	01101
McClinton, Robert	220001	10010	Rineheart, Daniel	331101	10010
Alexander, David	310201	01100	Adams, George	200010	21010
Ellison, James	200010	30010	Merrett, Joseph	000100	00100

312

NAME	MALES	FEMALES	NAME	MALES	FEMALES
Petty, Alen	000001	33010	Cambell, James	100101	01001
Gaseway, Nicholas	211101	10101	Simikins, John	120001	53201
May, Daniel	100001	33010	Wilson, David	100101	02100
Robertson, Thomas	000101	00201	Vandever, Holnsgwth.	300010	00010
Williams, Elias	111101	11001	Pritchard, Lewis	200010	20010
Wilson, John	010101	00001	Perkens, Abram	000201	00011
McDaniel, John R.	220010	20210	Holden, Richard	000101	00011
Kelly, Sarah	120000	10101	Browne, William	000211	00011
Greene, Benjamine	320001	21010	Morris, Jacob	311201	32101
McCurry, William	010010	30010	Dotson, Amos	121201	22101
Morris, Delilah	010100	01101	Telford, John	110101	00110
Donaldson, Eli	000010	00100			
Tevitty, John	200001	02101	OMITTED: (page 10)		
Davis, John	410010	00010			
Bloodworth, Wilm.	110010	00110	Floyd, Alse	00000?	10201
Flowers, Sarah	200000	10010			
Smith, William	100100	00100			
Donaldson, Elisb.	110000	11010			

ANDERSON DISTRICT TAX RETURNS
1835 - 1861

The tax records contained herein were recorded by the state
comptroller general from the returns which he received from the
district and parish tax collectors. The comptroller general for-
warded the records to the clerks of court in the various parishes
and districts in order that taxpayers might be able to compare
the receipts issued to them by the tax collectors with the amount
recorded on these lists.*

    The records are presented here primarily for their research
value since they pre-date the formation of the county auditor's,
treasurer's, and delinquent tax collector's offices. Having been
filmed as they were found, these records may or may not be complete for the years indicated.**

(* Thomas Cooper and David J. McCord, eds., Statutes at Large
of South Carolina, 10 Vols. (Columbia, S. C.: A. S. Johnson,1836-
1841), No. 2079, 6:10.
 ** Tax returns were not found for the years 1838-1839, 1849-
1852, 1855, and 1857-1860. One set of returns was found which
had no recorded date and it has been determined, with as much
accuracy as possible, that the date of these returns is either
1838 or 1839.)

    As these tax returns are recorded in a loose alphabetized or-
der, they are not included in the master index of this book.
.....Ed.

GENERAL TAX RETURNS FROM ANDERSON DISTRICT OF PENDLETON FOR THE
YEAR 1835 COLLECTED BY EZEKIEL HARRIS, T.C.

Armstrong, James
Adams, Henry
Adams, Asa
...... John
...nold, Allen
Acker, William
Adams, John
Adams, Jacob
Ashley, Joseph
Armstrong, William
Armstrong, James
Armstrong, John B.
Armstrong, Archibald
Armstrong, James Sen.
Ashley, Edward
Acker, Harker(?) C.
Anderson, John B.
......, Susanna
Ashley, John
Acker, Amos
Anderson, William D^r
Anderson, William
Adkinson, James
Adkinson, Aaron A.
Abbott, John
Alexander, Robert
Archer, John P.
Anderson, Layavina(?)
Anderson, John
Anderson, David
Algander(?) David
Addis, Mary
Archer, John, Senr.
Anderson, Larken
Bailey, Allen

Bailey, Henry M.
Brown, Robert
Brown, Catharine
Bradberry, Jesse
Bradberry, Salathiel
Brown, Vinson
Bowman, Archabald
Buroughs, Thomas
Brooks, Thomas
Buchananon,Samuel
Brooks, John
Barret, John
Barret, Charles
Betterten, Julius
Brooks, George
Beaty, John
Bailey, William
Bennett, Cooper
Burroughs, Reuben
Brooks, Garner
Buchanon, William
Burroughs, Orange
Brown, George
Buchanon, Ebenezer
Brown, Charles
Beaty, William
Beaty, John
Beaty, Francis
Barron, Uriah
Barry, Joel H.?
Bryd, David
Beaty, Samuel N.?
Bowie, Charles Senr.
Bowie, Charles Junr.
Beaty, David

315

Bond, Sugar
Bond, Isham A.?
Blackburn, Burton?
Boyd, Robert
Bird, Edward
Bozman, ...(Lewis?)
Brown, George
Burroughs, Bryan
Brown, Isham
Brewster, William
Brown, Daniel
Brown, Thos. T.?
Brown, Jastley?
Brackenridge, Robert
Brown, Joseph
Bell, Charles
Bagnell, Robert
Brown, Elijah
Burdin, Sarah
Brown, Joseph
Burris?, Absalom
Barron, William
Bailey, William
Brock, Meradith H.
Benson, Thornton?
Balentine, George
Balentine, Richard
Bagwell, John
Bagwell, Warren
Bohanon, John N.
Brownlee, Mariah
Broyles, John __
Brock?, Enos
Brown, George R.
Brock, Hayden
Brock, James
Bagwell, James
Balentine, Jesse? H.?
B...mett, Charles
Bennett, Thomas
Barkley, Nancy
Braswell, Harrison
Braswell, George
Braswell, James
Brazeal, Canon?
Brazeal, David K.
Brazeal, Mathew
Brazeal, Griffin
Barkley, Josiah
Barkley, Sarah
Brazeal, William
Brazeal, Enoch
Breeler?, ...
Bill, Samuel
Briant, Terrell
Bryant, Nathan?
Bryant, Simon
Burgess, James
Bowen, Robert
Blasingame, John E.
Barr, Mary M.?
Brewer, John
Brewer, William
Belcher, Manning
Bishop, Nicholas
Brown, Randolph
Belott, Peter E.
Burt, Francis, Senr.
Bowmer, George W.?
Bruce, Charles Senr.
Bruce, Thomas
Brown, Elijah Est.
Buroughs, Elisha
Benson, John P.
Brown, Nancy
Bowen, Samuel
Brown, Robert
Burford, Edward
Barry, William
Burroughs, Jacob
Burroughs, James Est.
Burroughs, John Est.
Buroughs, James

Bruce, Charles junr.
Benson, Enoch B.
Benson & Sloan
...rnes, John
Brown, Samuel
Brown, John
Broyles, Ozias? R.
Bruce, John
Colwell, Geran?
Colwell, James
Colwell, Joseph
Connel, James
Colwell, William
Cox, John Senr
Cox, John Junr
Cox, Laban
Crymshaw, Jesse?
Colwell, John Junr
Calhoun, Alex.
Chappell, John B.
Campbell, George
Campbell, Alexander
Cox, John
Cox, Bevely
Cox, Nancy
Cox, Edward
Christopher, David
Christopher, John
Cowan, Robert
Carsey?, Drucila
Casey, Stephen
Conner, John R.?
Carter. Robert L.?
Carter & Cunningham
Cowan, Hiram
Cosper, Lewis
Casey, William Est.
Clinkscales, Abner
Clark, James G.
Cook, William (may be Cash)
Cash, Stephen
Cosper, Jacob
Cosper, Henry
Cunningham, Robert L.
Clark, Joseph
Christian?, John W.
Crawford, William
Clinkscales, Asa
Carpenter, John
Campbell, Daniel
Campbell, William
Clark, Matthew
Carpenter, Alfred
Creswell, Henry H.
Clinkscales, William F.
Clinkscales, Francis Senr.
Coll, Noah (may be Cobb)
Clement, Isaac
Chambers, John
Cobb?, Martin
Clement, William
Cowan, William
Cumming, David
Clement, Hugh
Clemant, Stephen
Collins, Caleb
Cox, William
Cornelius, Abraham
Clinkscales, Levi?
Cox, John
Clemant, Benjamin
Cox, Thomas
Cox, William
Cox, Sarah
Cobb, Henry
Chamblee, Moses
Cox, Aris
Carter, Caleb
Carter, Spencer
Cooley, John
Cooley, James
Cox, Gabriel
Cox, William

Cesar - Freeman
Cooley, Lewis
Cox, David
Campbell, James
Carder, Thomas
Crenshaw, Stephen
Cowen?, Joseph
Cargill, Clemant
Clardy, John
Clardy, Normon
Cooper, James
Cooper, Washington
Copeland, William Est.
Chambers, Nancy
Casen, William
Cason, Mary
Cason, James
Cason, Sarah
Carpenter, Thomas
Cason, Reuben
Cherry, Thomas R. H.
Cherry, James
Campbell, Archibald C.
Carson, James
Carpenter, Elizabeth
Cummings, Harmon
Cater, Edward
Cochran, Daniel H.
Colwill, Isyah?
Cox, Joseph
Cox, Reuben Est.
Cherry, Samuel
Clark, John B.
Chamblee, Benjamin
Chamblee, James
Chastain, Stephen
Cox, Asa
Carlile, Wm. Rev^d?
Chastain, John
Chastain, Stephen F.
Chamblee, James
Cunningham, Samuel
Cunningham, Thomas
Coats, John
Campbell, Abell? heirs
Cherry, David H.
Clanahan, James
Dobbin, James
Dean, Thomas
Dickson, William
Dobbins, Jesse
Davis, Flunoy? W.
Dean, Aaron
Dean, Samuel D___?
Dobbins, James Est.
Drenon, Thomas Est.
Davis, Jesse
Davis, Valentine
Dalrimple, Samuel
Dickenson, Willis
Dowdle, Robert Est.
Dalrimple, James
Dalrimple, John
Davis, John L.
Dobe?, John
Davis, Moses
Dickinson, James
Davis, Levi
Davis, John
Dawson, William
Day, Silvy
Davis, William
Dawson, Elizabeth
Dawkin?, David
Davis, Archabald
Davis, Levi
Davis, Aaron
Duckworth, Jacob
Duckworth, Howard
Duckworth, Robert C.
Duckworth, James C.
Duckworth, Welborn
Duckworth, Thomas

Hopkins, John
Hunter, John
Hunt, John
Harper, William
Harkins, Hugh
Honea, William
Harper, John
Harkins, James
Horton, Grief
Hunter, Sarah Mrs.
Holcomb, William
Hughs, John
Hamilton, Thomas
Hamilton, David R.
Hicks, John
Hubbard, William
Hilhouse, Joseph
Hix?, Bailey/Bailis
Hembree, James Sr.
Hembree, James Jr.
Hall, John
Harris, John
Harper, Asa
Holt, John P.
Hall, Nancy
Hall, Lent Sr.
Hall, Jesse A.
Hillhouse, Mary
Hann/Hall, Fenton
Houston, William
Hall, Wilson?
Hail?, John
Hardin, James
Hammond, Francis
Harris, John Esqr.
Harris, Benjamin
Harris, William
Humphries, David
Huger?, Francis K.?
Harris, Nathaniel
Harris, Joseph
Harris, Ezekiel
Harris, John Col.
Harlston, Edward
Hewen, Elizabeth
Hunter, Mary Miss
Isbell, Pendleton
Isbell, Robert
Irving, Elenor
Ingram, William
Jones, Elizabeth
Jones, Hartnell?
Jones, Thomas
Jennings, John
Junkin, Robert
Jolley, Jane
Jolley, James
Johnston, Cloe
Johnston, Reuben
Johnston, Peter
Johnston, Nancy
Jolley, Henry
Johnston, Benjamin
Jones, John
Johns, Richard
James, Samuel
Johnston, Allen
Jones, Willis D.
Jolley, Joseph
King, William
King?, William Sr.?
Kay, John A.(H.?)
Keown, William
Kennedy, Lorenzo? G.
Kay, Gabriel
Kay, Robert Est.
King, Peter
Kennedy, George
Kay, John
Kees, James C.
Kees, Robert
Kennedy, Joseph B.
Kay, Jesse

Kay, Strother
Kay, William Senr.
Kerr, William
Kay, James P.?
Keaton, William
King Iziah
King, Mary
Kay, Maston
King, Robert
Kay, Catharine
King, James
K___, Charles
Kelly, Elisha
K___, John
Kay, Alexander
King, John
Kelly, Benjamin
Kelly, Daniel
K___, John
Kay, William Junr.
Keaton, Archibald
Kennedy, L.? Rev
Lowrey, Henry
Lowrey, Jackson
Ledbetter, Mary
Ledbetter, James
Lewis, Major
Long, Harrison
Luck?, Lewis
Love?, Isaac
Latham, Cornelius?
Leverett, Stephen
Leverett, John
Leverett, Thomas
Long, William
Little, Rachel
Lewis, Elisha
Liddell, John
Loveless, Hembree
Lalimer?, Wiley
Leg, Tarlton Est.
Lucas, Daniel Jr.
Lucas, Daniel Sr.
Lewis, Eleanor
Labren?, Joseph
Linn, Garrison
Linn, Robert
Linn, Robert
Long?, Ezekiel
Langston, Solomon
Langston, William
Lewis, Jesse P.
Lewis, James O.
Liddell, Andrew J.
Liddell, James L.
L...., Lowden?
Logen?, John
Lewis, Jesse
Laighen?, Van A.
Lewis, James W. & H.?
Lewis, James/(Mary?)
Ledbetter, John
Lor..., Nathan
Lofton, Frances W.
Lorton, John A.
Jay, James
Merrett, Benjamin H.?
Meredy, Abraham
Moore, David
Mason, Ambrose
McCarley, Joseph
McCorley, James
McGreem?, Samuel D.
McCorley, Robert B.
Minton, Hezekiah
McCollum, Jesse
Martin, Samuel
Maverick, ___ Lewis
Moore, Samuel
Mills, Rebeca
Masa?, Silad?
McLees, James
McPherson, Elijah

McPherson, William
Moore, John
McCaswell, William
McGill, Samuel
McGill, Ezekiel
McGill, John
Macklin, Hugh
McGee, Willis
Mitchel, Samuel
McCullough, Samuel D.
McGee, Elias
McGee, Jesse
McGee, Jesse C.
McKee, Kiziah
McBride, James L.?
McMahan, Samuel
McCurdy, William
Morris, Garrett
Mouchet, Jacob
McMichel, Lewis? W.
McCurdy, Hugh L.
Martin, David
Mitchell, Margarett
Micklin, John A.
Morgan, John
McAlister, Mastan Mc.
McFall, Ait...?
Millard, John Senr.
Milford, Phillip
Milford, Thomas
Milford, Robert
McKee, Archibald
McKee, William
McAlister, Isaac
McPhail, John
Morehead, Alexander
Mattison, James Jr.
Miller?, William
Morris, Jane
McFall, Andrew A.
Mellon, Wyatt
McClinton, Andrew S.?
McAlister, Margarett
Milley, Ezekiel
McAlister, Andrew?
Major, Elijah
Mattock, Thomas
McConnell, Thomas
McFall, Samuel
Massey?, Kindred
Massey?, Abraham
Morehead, Nancy?
Morehead, John
Hollison, Archibald
McCoy, Samuel
Magee, John
Magee?, Benjamin H.?
Mattison, Nevel
Manning, George
Massa?, Laban
McCoy, James
Moore?, Jeremiah
May, Daniel
Mitchell, Ephraim
Mitchell, John
McCollum, Daniel
Martin, John
McFee, Washington
Mattison, Polly?
Mattison, George B.
Magee, Michael
Magee, A. Com.?
McAlister, John
McAlister, Allen
Moore?, Grant A.
Major, James
Major, Elijah
Major, William
Mattison, Wyatt
Moore, John M.
Mattison, James Jr.(Sr.?)
Mattison, J. & Wm.?
Mills, Elizabeth

Martin, Chesley
Murphey, Ezekiel
Martin, Jacob
Martin, William
Martin, Hester
Mills, Thomas?R.
Martin, Elizabeth
Martin, James
Martin, Abraham
Merrett, Obediah
Moore, W.?
Moore, Elijah
Moore, Tilman? B.
Moore, Elijah R.?
Moore, Jeremiah
Murphey, John
Merrett, Josiah
McAlister, James
McAlister, Patsey
Mortin,?, Abell
McMahan, Peter
McKinney, Alexander
Mullikin, Benjamin
McKinney, Patsey
McMurry, William C.
Mullikin, Benjamin
Millon?, Michael
Millon?, David
Mullikin, James
Moore, Robert
McClary?, John
McCann, Thomas R.
Mullikin, William
Mason, Jim
McMurry, William
McMurry, Jane Miss
McMin, Jesse
McClary, Mary
McElroy, Archibald
McClure, Edward J.?
Morris, John
Miller, Matthew T.
Miller, Jane
McGregor, Ann R.
Miles, Susan M..
Miller, John
Morris, Davis J.?
Morris, James
Miller, John
McAlister, Nathan
McDonal, William
McPherson, Nelley
Massa?, Simon
May, Edmond
Miller, John
Murry, William
Mafield, Ephraim
Magee, William
Mafield, Margarett
McDowell, William , Minors
McDowell, Elihu
McKeown, John
Magee, Jesse L.?
McCulley, Stephen
McAlister, John
Masten, George W.
Menfrmary?, Alfred
Mills, Berry
McLuskey, James
McCulley, George R.
McLuske?, Andrew
Miller, Elias
McKay, Hugh
McKay, Jane Est.
Moore, Mary?
McFall, Jas.?
McGregor, Mary
Moore, Joseph?
Magee, Burrell
Major, Enoch
McPherson, Deren?
Miller, Crosby W.
McFall, John Jr.

McDaniel, Phillip
Marrick?, Sam & fam.?
McCann, James L.
Masters, Zachariah
Mackem, Francis B.
Milwee, William
Milwee, Samuel
Newel, George
Newel, Alfred
Norris, Ezekiel
N..lon, William
Norris, Jesse W.
Norris, Andrew O.
Nerrill, James
Nevett, William
Norris, John E.
Nichols, Zachariah
Nichols, Archibald
Newton, Hezekiah
Newton, Isaac
Newton, Samuel
Newton, Willis?
North, John
Norris, Robert B.
Newel, William
Nelson, James O.
O'briant, Jesse
Obar?, William
Owens, Thornton
Orr, Christopher
Orr, Jane B. ...
Oliver, Juneous?Americus?
Overly, Nicholas
Owen, Ashley
Owen, Lewis
Oldham, George
Oldham, John dec'd
Orr, William
Ower, Elijah? Senr
Oliver, James
Owen, Martha
Owen, John
Owen, Banister
Owen, Elijah? Junr.
Orr, Thomas
Ozier?, ...
Owen, Daniel
Obar, Robert
Owen, Hiram
Pullen, William
Pullen, Patten?
Parker, Matthew
Patrick, Thomas A.
Patterson, Samuel
Powell, William
Parrott, Nathaniel
Partin, Hubbard
Prestley, Ann?
Patterson, Thomas H.
Parker, James
Petagrew, Robert C.?
Parker, David
Posey?, Hubbard
Pickens, Sarah Mrs.
Price, Samuel? Tennel?
Pitts, William
Pickens, Elenor
Priest?, Dudley heirs
Pool, Robert
Pool, Manning?
Pool, Walter
Prince, Richard
Parker, Robert
Posey, Harrison
Pritchard, William
Poor, William
Pinson, Elijhie?
Poor, George
Poor, Samuel
Poor, John Senr
Poor, John Junr
Poor, Martin
Phillips, Martin

Potter?, Jane
Poor, Hugh
Pruett, Elizabeth
Parmer, M.....
Pickel, William
Page, John
Pickens, Robert
Pickens, Elizabeth
Pickel, Jacob
Pasmore, William
Padgett, Elizabeth
Prewett, William
Pritchett, Lewis
Posey Francis
Palmer, Martin
Palmer, William
Pinckney, Thomas
Pinckney, Charles C.
Pilgrim, John
Pickens, Thomas J.?
Reed, Jesse
Rusk?, David
Raney, John
Reid, William
Reid, Elizabeth
Rush, William
Riley, Daniel E.
Roach, Henry
Rice, Amaziah
Rainwater?, Joab
Rice, Hezekiah jr
Ramsey, John
Riley, Hezekiah
Rice, Ibzan
Rutledge, Richmond T.?
Rice, Fleetwood
Robertson, James
Robertson, John
Rice, Hezekiah Sr
Reed, Jacob P.
Reid, J. P. &.Co.
Reid, Henry
Richey, James
Reid, Thomas
Ruff, David
Robinson, John J.
Robinson, John B.
Rogers, William A.
Ragsdale, Daniel F.
Ragsdale, Frances F.(A.?)
Richey, Reuben
Rogers, Jerry W.
Rogers, Joseph L.
Rogers, John
Rogers, William Sr
Rogers, Humphrey
Roach, Benjamin
Rogers, William Jr
Rosman?, Jhn. H.
Richardson, Mathias
Richardson, Noah L.
Rogers, Simeon
Rankin, George
Richey, William
Robertson, Hugh
Robertson, David
Robertson, William
Robinson, Ephraim
Reese, Alexander H.?
Richey, John
Riceux?, John
Ross, Anthony W.
Reese, George Sr.
Reese, George Jr.
Roberts, George
Russell, David
Reid, Andrew
Rimmer, Philip
Rampy, Anderson
Reese, Charles M.
Reese, Henry? D.
Rogers, Elizabeth
Swilling, James

Swilling?, William
Swilling, Samuel
Swilling, George
Stanley, Ezekiel
Smith, Faron/Laron? S.
Stewart, James Sr.
Skelton, H.....
Skelton, adlock
Simpson, David
Skelton, William
Sewright, William
Slacks?, Willis
Sanders, Abraham
Siddell, Stephen
Siddell, Abner
Smith, Samuel
Sanders, Thomas
Skelton, Thomas L.
Simpson, Archibald
Sullivan, Kelly
Sherrard, . Sullivan
Sullivan, Nimrod
Stephenson, Jane
Sherrard, William
Simpson, William H.
Sherrard, Jane
Shackelford, John
Stephenson, John
Stephenson, Thomas
Stone, Hampton
Spearman, John
Simpson, William
Smith, Robertson
Simpson, Thomas
Stewart, John Sr.
Stewart, John Jr.
Stewart, Samuel
Sherrard, John
Stewart, James
Stepehn, John
Skifle?, Mary
Scott, David
Scott, John
Smith, Samuel
Shaw, William
Smith, Robert
Stephenson, Andrew
Smith, Sanford L.?
Smith, Ebanezer
Stephenson, Joseph
Sailor, Isaac
Sailor, Abraham
Sherly, John
Stricklin, Rilley?
Sailors, Abraham
Sherly, Obediah
Smith, Richard
Sailor, John
Sailor, Leonard
Sitton, William D.
Shearer, Andrew
Strickland, Matthew
Shirley, John
Sherley, Nipper
Seawright, James
Spray, Thomas
Slatten, William
Slaven, John
Stone, James
Smith, Bazel
Stone, William W.?
Smith, George S.?
Stone, George
Smith, Aaron
Shirley, James ....?
Shirley, Aaron
Shirley, James Ju.
Sherrell, Lewis
Spearman, Benjamin
Spearman, David
Stanton, George
Smith, John
Slatton, Stephen

Spearman, Francis
Sitton, William
Slaten, Loven
Simpson, James T.
Sizemore, Henry
Smith, Mark
Simpson, Jesse
Smith, John
Siddell, John
Stegall, Spencer
Spearman, George
Saterfield, Jeremiah
Smith, James
Smith, O. Benjamin
Smith, Simeon?
Sheriff, Abell
Sharpe, Jane
Smith, Aaron
Smith, Nimrod, Jr.
Shanklin, Joseph
Story, Charles Est.?
S....., Elizabeth G.?
Sloan, Jesse
Sherrod, John L.
Sharpe, Elam
Stuards?, William
Stuards?, John Est.
Stuards?, John N.
Shaw, Paten? R.
Stephenson, James
Stephenson, John
Stephenson, George
Skelton, Thomas
Skelton, John W. B.
Sl..., Luvan?
Smith, Benjamin
Smith, William C.
Steel, William
Snipes?, Mathew
Steel, Nancy
Steel, Charles
Sanders, William
Smith, Wyatt
Smith, William Jr.
Smith, William Sr.
Sadler, David
Simpson, John M.
Simpson, George W. Est.
Scott, Elizabeth
Steel, James
Sloan Benson & Sloan?
Sloan?, John T.?
Smith, Zephaniah
Symmes, Frederick W.
Simmons, James
Simmons, David
Smith, Archibald
Simmons, John
Stanton, Mathias
Stanton, Catharine
Smith, John
Shaw, William
Tiller, Mair?
Turner, James
Tu ks, Dearmett
Taylor, William
Tucker?, Bartlett
Tucker, James
Taylor, Thomas
Tucker?, Reuben D.
Todd, Robert
Todd, Archibald
Todd, Mary Mrs.
Todd, ldam Est.
Thompson, John
Thompson, Elizabeth
Thompson, Matthew
Thompson, Matthew & co.?
Thompson, James
Taylor, James
Todd, James
Todd, John
Townes?, Daniel Est.

Townes?, William W.
Townley, ...
Taylor, Thomas
Trussell, Rhodam
Trussell, Henry
Trussell, Posey?
Turner, John B.
Telford, William?
Telford. Juldah
Timmons?, Isaac
Tripp, John
Tripp, Nicholas
Tompkins?, John
Trainum?, Lazarus
Thompson, James
Tucker, Willis
Taylor, David L.?
Taliaferro, Margaret M.
Taliaferro, Caroline V.?
Tate?, David
Tate, John
Thompson, John
Telford, James
Taylor, John
Terry, Henry?
Taylor, Joseph Sr.
Thayer & Prince?
Tippin, William
Valentine, Benjamin
Vandiver, Edward?
Vandiver, John
Vandiver, William
Vandiver, Larkin
Vandiver, Manning
Vandiver, Edward Jr.
Vandiver, Asa P.?
Vandiver, ...
Vandiver, Holley?
Vandiver, Aaron?
Vandiver, John
Vandiver, Harrin
Vandiver, Sanford
Wright, Larkin
White, William
Wright, Jefferson
Watson, Daniel
Willi nd, John
Watson, Stephen
Watts, Thomas
Winfield, John B.
Watts, Mary
Watts, John
Wilbanks, Elijah
Watt, James
Wiles?, Freeman
Whitman, Jacob
Winfield, James
Wright, Elizabeth
Woords, Joel
Williams, Thomas
White, Bartholamew
White, Charles
Warnach, John Sr.
Wornach, John Jr.
Wallis, Willis
Whitmire, Andrew P.?
Wilson, William
Williams, Stephen
Webb, Elijah
Webb, Warren
Webb, Elijah & Co.
Whitfield, Joseph L.
Whiticar?, Hugh H.
Wyatt, Elijah
Williamson, William
Wyatt, Redman G.
Wyatt, James F.
Wright, John
Webster, James R.
Wright, Robert N.?
Williamson, Mastin?
Wardlaw, James
Wardlaw, John

Walker?, Peter
Willingham, John
Willingham, James
Wilson, James P.
Wilson, James B.
Willson, Hugh
Wilburn, Thomas
Wilson, Sarah
Wardlaw, Hugh H.
Williams, Micajah
Williams, Jasper K.....
Williams, Mary
Wilbrun?, Joel E.
Wilburn?, Sarah
Wilar..., Shadrach
Warnoch, James
Webb, William
Wimpe?, Levi
Williams, V. Cureten?
Wilson, John
Waters?, Mary
Westbrook, Samuel
Waddill, Hannah
Wilson, Charles
William, Thomas R.
William, Hannah & Lucy
Wheten, Rebecca
Walker, Feld?
Winby?, Charles
Wilbanks, Hosea
Waters?, James
Watkins, Balin?
Watkins, Temperance
Win.., Dinah
Willson, John
Willson, Isabela
Willson, Harvey?
Williams, John
Wiginten?, John
Wigenton?, Thomas
Wigeinton, George
Willson, Robert
Worley, Jacob
Watson, Willard
Wright, Martha
Wilson, Richard T.?
Whitner, Joseph N.
Wilson, Charles
Webb. Elisha
White, Julia
Webb, Baldwin
Webb, Clartin? Clayton?
Webb, Maryann
Watson, Jonathan Est.
Webb, Edmund
Watson, David
Waters, Flemming
Waters, Macklin
Willson, Robert
Whitfield, Benjamin
Whitfield, Isaac?
Watkins, Joseph
White, Thomas
White, Newton
Whitfield, Hugh
Werner, William
White, William
Whitner, Elizabeth
White, Daniel
Wardlaw, James
Young, James
Young, John
Yeargin, Samuel
Young, Francis
Yoes?, Mary
Young, John J.
Young, Samuel

Property returned in other
Districts and Parishes:

Abbeville:

Young, Francis
McCurdy, William
M....liett, Jacob
Melford, Thomas
Stiefle?, Phillip Est.
Stiefle, Haris?
Tucker, Bartlett
Young, Samuel
.....ler, Charles
Smith, Benjamin
Smith, William C.
Maverick, Samuel
Harleston, Edward
White, Alexander

Beinville:

Calhoun, John C.

Maverick, Samuel in Man-
chester & Statesburg.....

Edgefield:

Pitts, William

Fairfield:

Maverick, Samuel

Greenville:

Moore, David
Maverick, Samuel
Roper?, Aaron
Masters, Thomas Est.
Blythe, Absalom
Hardin, Joseph
..lan, Irby
Masters?, John

Laurens:

Ferguson, James
Towers?, Larkin
Maverick, Samuel

Lexington:

Maverick, Samuel

Newberry:

Maverick, Samuel

Orangeburg:

Maverick, Samuel

Spartonburg:

Moore, David
Tippen?, William
Maverick, Samuel

Union:

Maverick, Samuel

H. P. & H. Michael:

Maverick, Samuel
Packard?, Chelion?

H. Jas. Santee:

Gaillard, Theodore
Warren, Samuel Col.

Gaillard, Josiah D.

P. G. Wynyan?:

Warren, Samuel Col.

H. Stephens:

Gaillard, C. & J.

321

Adams, William
Adams, Asa
Atkinson, Henry
Adams, John
Adams, Henry
Arnold, Allen
Armstrong, John B.
Ashley, Wilson
Ashley, John
Adams, Sylvanus
Armstrong, James
Anderson, Saxon?
Alexander, David
Alexander, Robert
Acker, William
Anderson, David
Anderson, John
Anderson, George T.
Anderson, Martha
Ashley, Edward
Archer, John
Archer, John P.
Anderson, William
Alewine, Michael
Armstrong, Archibald
Armstrong, James
....., Susanna
Acker, P. N.
Adams, Jacob
Acker, Halbert
Acker, Amon?
Anderson, John B.
Ashley, John
Atkins, Aaron
Atkinson, James
Abbott, John
Adams, John
Bruce, Charles
Bailey, Allen
Bradbury, James
Bradbury, Jesse
Barton, Henry M.?
Bruce, Charles, Senr.
Bruce, Thomas
Bradbury, Salathiel
Burns, John
Brown, Robert H.?
Burns, Bufort W.
Bowman, Archibald
Brown, Obee?
Brown, Catharine
Brown, Larkin
Brown, Vincent
Burt, Francis,Jr.
Burt, Francis, Sr.
Bishop, Nicholas
Bowden, J. G.
Belcher, Manning
Boggs, Nely
Bowman, G. W.
Bomar Hacket & Co.
Brown, Samuel
Betterton, Joshua
Buchanan, Samuel
Barrett, John
Baker, Lindsey A.?
Borroughs, Eliza
Brooks, George
Burroughs, Orange dec'd.
Buchanan, Ebenezer
Brooks, Garner
Brown, Charles
Brown, George
Beatty, William
Buchanan, William
Beaty, John
Bowie, William
Bowie, Charles
Beatty, Francis
Berry, Joel H.

Beatty & Young
Bone, Sugar
Bone, Isham R.
Beatty, David
Burroughs, James
Barron, Uriah
Beatty, Samuel
Boyd, Robert
Bowie, Charles Jr.
Burton, Blackman
Beatty, Thomas H.
Bayley, William (Bagley?)
Bozeman, Lewis
Brown, Elijah, dec'd.
Bannister, William
Brock, Meredith H.
Brock, James
Barclay, Nancy
Bryant, Simon
Bryant, Terrell
Bryant, Nathan
Brown, George
Brown, Leslie
Brownlee, Mariah?
Bagwell, Robert
Burdett, Hiram
Brazil, Enoch
Berry, William
Barrett, Charles
Brown, Samuel
Brown, Joseph
Burford, Edward
Broyles, John T.
Bohanan, J. W.
Breckenridge, Robert
Baggwell, John
Brown, Daniel
Benson, John P.
Brown, John
Brown, Elijah
Brown, Isham
Brown, Thomas J.
Burgess, James
Bowen, Samuel
Barron, William
Burroughs, Jacob
Burroughs, John dec'd.
Burroughs, James dec'd.
Ballentine, George
Ballentine, Richard E.
Brown, Jeremiah
Baily, William
Brown, Robert
Baker, Samuel H.
Bell, Samuel
Burroughs, Elisha
Brasswell, James
Brasswell, George Jr.
Brasswell, George Sr.
Baggwell, James
Brasswell, Harrison?
Brock, Hayden
Brasswell, Asa
Brown, George R.
Broyles, Aaron
Brock, Andrew
Brock, Enos
Ballentine, Jesse H.
Brown, Nancy
Brazil, Williamson
Brazil, Griffin
Bennett, Thomas
Burnett, Charles
Bennett, William
Brazil, Cannon
Brazil, David K.
Barclay, Josiah
Barclay, Sarah
Brazil, Matthew
Blassingame, Thomas

Bowen, Robert
Blankenship, John
......, Wm.
Barr, Mary
Barr, Mary A.
Brewer, John
Brooks, Thomas
Burroughs, Thomas
Benson, Enoch B.
Benson & Sloan
Brown, Randolph
Bennett, Cooper
Bruce, Charles Sr.
Bellotte, Peter E.
Bell, Charles
Bruce, John
Baulding, Stephen
Broyles, O. R.
Coates, John
Clinkscales, Asa
Cater, Edward
Chamblee, John
Coates, Anthony
Cason, Reuben
Cherry, James A.
Campbell, A. C.
Caminade, John
Carpenter, Thomas
Craig, Samuel
Cherry, Thomas R.
Chappell, John B.
Conwell, James
Carpenter, Elizabeth
Caldwell, William
Campbell, George
Caldwell, John
Caldwell, James
Cox, Beverly
Cox, John
Caldwell, Joseph
Caldwell, George
Cleary, Daniel
Cunningham, Samuel
Cunningham, Thomas
Campbell, Alexander
Chastain, Stephen
Chastain, Stephen F.
Christopher, John D.
Corr?, John Sr.
Corr?, John Jr.
Corr?, Laban
Cox, Nancy
Clinkscales, Abner
Comer, John W.
Cash, Stephen
Carter, Robert D.
Cook, William
Casey, Stephen
Cowan, Hiram
Casper, Jacob
Casper, Lewis M.
Cunningham, Catharine
Clarke, Joseph
Clinkscales, Levy
Chambors, John
Carr, William
Cobb, Noah
Clements, Isaac
Cowan, William
Campbell, James
Campbell, Daniel
Campbell, William
Cox, Asa
Casden?, Thomas
Cherry, Samuel
Caston, James
Cummings, Harman
Chamblee, Benjamin
Clarke, John B.
Clarke, Matthew

322

Cobb, Masten
Crawford, William
Crawford, James
Carpenter, John
Chamblee, James
Chastain, Stephen
Creswell, John
Cox, William
Cox, John
Carpenter, Alfred
Chamblee, Moses
Carlisle, William
Cannon, Isaac
Cochran, D. H.
Clinkscales, William
Clinkscales, Francis Sr?
Cullins, Caleb
Clements, William
Clements, Stephen
Cox, Harris
Cox, William
Clements, Benjamin
Clements, Isaac Jr.?
Cox, Thomas
Cox, William Sr.
Cox, Gabriel
Clements, Hugh
Cummings, David
Cox, Abner
Cox, David
Cornelius, Abram
Cooly, John
Carter, Caleb
Cooly, Lewis
Cox, Sarah
Caesar & Jenny Davis
Carter, Spencer
Cobb, Josiah W.
Cox, Joseph
Cox, R. R. & S.
Cooly, James
Carter, Reuben
Chambers, Nancy
Chavely?, John
Cobb, Henry
Cooper, James
Clardy, Norman
Cooper, Washington
Crenshaw, Stephen
Cason, James A. M.
Cason, Sarah
Cason, Mary
Cason, Esther
Cason, William dec'd.
Campbell, Jesse
Broyles, O. R.
Dunham, Benajah
Dunham & Holcombe
DuPree, Benjamin Sr.
DuPree, Benjamin
Dart, Thomas L. dec'd.
Daniels, W. L. ___?
Driver, James
Dollar, Williamson
Dobbin, Jesse?
Dobbin, James
Deane, Aaron
Deane, Samuel dec'd.
Deane, Thomas
Dickson, William
Davis, F. W.
Duncan, Robert
Duncan, Thomas
Davis, Valentine
Davis, John L.
Duckworth, Howard
Duckworth, Jacob
Dalrymple, James
Duckworth, Thomas
Dalrymple, Samuel
Duckworth, James O.?
Davis, Jesse
Dowdle, Robert dec'd.

Doley, William
Dalton, Burrell
Davis, Levy
Dawson, L. D.
Drennan, Thomas, dec'd.
Deane, Moses
Dickinson, Robert
Duckworth, Welbourne
Dobbins, Martha
Dalrymple
Davis, Aarnon B.
Davis, Moses
Davis, William
Davis, Charles
Davis, Zachariah
Duncan, David
Davis, Levy
Deane, Charles P.
Durham, Berry
Durham, William
Douthet, Benjamin H.
Dilworth, Benjamin
Douthet, James
Durham, David
Durham, William
Davis, James
Dickson, Matthew, dec'd.
Donnelly, James
Dickinson, Willis
Dickson, Walter C.
Davis, John
Eaton, Joseph
Eaton, William
Elliott, Mary
Earpe, Wesley
Earpe, David J.
Earpe, Caswell
Earpe, Margaret
Emberson, Samuel
Elrod, William
Elrod, Thomas P.
Elrod, Thomas
Emberson, James
Elrod, George G.
Elrod, William
Elrod, Jeremiah
Elliott, William
Elrod, Philip
Erskine, William
Earle, Samuel G.
Earle.& Lewis
Elliott, William
Elrod, Adam
Erskine, John
Erskine, James, Sr.
Erskine, James, Jr.
Erskine, Thomas
Estis, Larkin
Ellison, Miles
Elrod, Samuel
Elrod, George
Ellison, James
Elrod, Elias
Elrod, Isaac
Elliott, John
Estis, Micajah
Earle, John B.
Earle, Anne
Earle, George W.
Evans, Alexander
Earle, James W.
Fant, James
Forsythe, William
Felton, Mary
Forbes, Henson?
Fowler, Ruth
Finley, Elias
Fowler, William B.
Fisher, Samuel C.
Featherston, J. W.
Felton, Richard
Fricks, Christopher
Fant, M. D.

Forsythe, William
Fant, Alfred
Flowers, Tollaferro
Fant, James B.
French, William
Fleming, Richard
Fleming, James
Ford, William
Ford, Stephen
Floyd, Silas
Fielding, Henry
Fretwell, John
Fretwell, Joseph
Felton, Hamell?
Fraser, W. A. & Co.
Ferrell, J. B.
Frank, William (Grant?)
Gordon, John
Gordon, William
Grubbs, John M.?
Gilbert?, Amos
Gambrell, David
Griffin, James
Griffin, Clarke
Gaston, William
Gibbs, A. L.?
Green, Lemuel
Glenn, William
Gentry, Zachariah
Gilmer, Robert
Gee?, Jeremiah
Gregg, Hugh
Gilmer, James
Gilmer, Nancy
Gentry, John
Gentry, Moody
Green, John
Green, John R.
Gwin, Leonard
Gaillard, Theodore
Gable, Levy
Gable, Henry
Gable, Henry Jr.?
Gable, Harman
Gray, Alexander D.
Gentry, John
Gassaway, Benjamin
Gaillard, Josiah D.?
Gauntt, James M.
Grubbs, George
Gauntt, John W.
Guyton, Aaron
Garnett, Thomas H.
Green, John
Garrett, John
Gambrell, Joel B.
Goulding, John
Gaillard, Charles L.
Gaillard, Jane
Goodrum, William
Giles?, Robert
Greenlee, James
Guyton, Robert
Geer, Solomon
Geer, David
Gordon, Robert
Gable, John, dec'd.
Gentry, Amos B.
Gentry, Allen
Gentry, Daniel
Gumming, James
Gentry, Reuben
George, James
George, Elizabeth
Geer, Thomas
Gray, Hezekiah
Gantt, William
Gantt, John G.(Y.?)
Gantt, Hugh
Gambrell, James
Green, David
Green, John

Gambrell, William
Gantt, John
Gray, William
Gambrell, John
Gambrell, Henry
Gambrell, William
Gambrell, Barbary
Gray, Hulda
Guthry, Nelson
Guthry, Benjamin
Griffin, John
Gibbs, Mary
Gambrell, Henry
Griffin, Elijah
Gambrell, Mathew
Gaines, Henry
Gibson, Thomas
Gambrell, James
Gambrell, Ezekiel
Gambrell, Reid
Gambrell, Larkin
Guthry?, David
Gaillard, William
Gaillard, Rebecca
Goode, Levelling
Gaillard, Cornelius
Hix, Daniel
Harris, John
Hughes, John
Harris, Allen B.
Herrin, Elijah
Herrin, Jesse
Holland, Robert
Herrin, Levy
Hix, Baylis
Hix, Posey
Harris, Joseph
Holland, Jacob
Hubbard, William
Hix, John
Harris, Nathaniel
Hughs, Francis R.
Haney, Charles
Humphreys, David
Herndon, George
Herndon, James
Haslet, James
Henderson, Robert
Haslet, Moses
Holmes, Henry
Herring, Francis
Havind?, Mark W.
Haney, Sampson
Houston, William
Harchy?, James
Howie, Robert
Harris, Sarah
Hatton, William
Heaton, Thomas
Hayes, Winney
Harris, John
Hall, Nancy
Hanks, Luke
Hanks, Polly
Hinton, William
Hammond, Francis
Hannah, Thomas
Hammond, L. J.
Hembree, Azariah
Herring, John
Howard, Hiram
Harper, William
Harper, Asa
Hall, Joseph
Herndon, Zephaniah
Herndon, Edmund
Hall, Aaron
Herring, James
Hale, Wilson
Hamilton, John M.
Hunter, Sarah
Holland, Grace
Haney, Britton C.

Harris, William H.?
Hale, John
Hammond, Herbert
Hunter, John
Holland, William B.
Hank, Tillman
Harris, Benjamin
Hillhouse, Mary
Haney, John
Harris, John
Harkins?, Hugh
Harris, James S.?, dec'd
Hill, Thomas O.
Hall, Martin
Hamilton, Luke H.
Hall, Zachariah
Hall, Lent?
Hall, Henton
Harkness, Robert C.?
Hall, John
Hall, Lent Jr.
Howard, Gerard
Hall, John
Haney, Stephen
Hall, Ezekiel
Hall, Sarah
Hall, William
Hall, Drury
Harkness, John
Hall, Lemuel
Hall, James E.
Hughes, Robert
Hughes, E.
Haney, Luke
Hill, Abram
Hunt, William
Hinton, John
Hunt, John
Hall, Joseph
Haney, William
Hawkins, William P.
Houston, Sarah
Hall, John W.
Hall, William
Hembree, James, Sr.
Hembree, James, Jr.
Holcombe, A. W.
Harrison, James
Harper, John H.?
Harper, William
Hopkins, John
Hunt, William H.
Henderson, James
Harper, John
Holland, Aaron B.
Harkins, James
Holland, John
Hubbard, William
Hallum, J. J.
Hamilton, David K.?
Hamilton, Thomas
Harris, Ezekiel
Hallum, Richard
Hallum, William, dec'd.
Hillhouse, Joseph
Hacket, Albert
Hacket, Robert, dec'd.
Hacket, Lucinda
Harris, Gillison
Holt, John P.
Harleston, Edward
Humphreys, John
Jones, Elizabeth
Jones, Hartwell
Isbell, Samuel
Johnston, Richard
Jones, Thomas
Jones, Joseph B.
Irvin, Elenor
Jennings, John
Jones, Samuel K.
Ingram, William
Jolly, Henry

James, Samuel
Jones, John
Jolley, Joseph
Jolley, Jane
Johnston, Mille
Jenkins, Robert
Johnston, Nancy
Johnston, Allen
Johnston, Peter
James, John
Jones, Ambrose W.?
Johnston, Benjamin
Kay, Robert, dec'd.
King, William, Sr.
Knauff, William G.?
Keys, John M.?
Keown, Wililiam
Kervey?, Greesilla?
Kennedy, Loving G.
Keating, William
Kay, James W.
Kay, Strother
Kinsley, Chester
Kay, Gabriel
Kay, Jesse
Kay, William, Sr.
Keys, James C.
Keys, Robert
King, Peter
King, James
King, Mary
Kay, Alexander
Kay, John
Knox, John
Knox, Charles
Keating, Archibald
Kay, Catharine
Kay, Mason
Kay, Fielding
Kay, William, Jr.
King, Isiah
Kinsley & Mattison
Kelly, Elisha
King, Robert
Kitsinger, Jacob
Kelly, John
Kelly, Daniel
Kirksey, Fain
Lanier, Bird
Looney, John
Lowrey, Jackson
Lewis, James C.
Lewis, Jess P.
Leddell, John S.
Latan, Frances
Latan, John J.
Ledbetter, James
Ledbetter, John
Ledbetter, Mary
Long, Harrison
Lewis?, Major
Lewis? & Maverick?
Long, Isaac
Latham, Cornelius
Leverett, John
Leverett, Thomas
Liddell, Rachel
Linleys?, Nathan
Lewis, Eleanor
Long, William
Lattimer, Wiley
Lewis, Elisha
L....., Hembree
L....., Stephen
Leverett, Wesley
Love?, Linden?
Leary, Henry
Lucius, Daniel F. Sr.
Lucius, Daniel F., Jr.
Lee, James
Lawless, Henry
Leboon, Joseph
Langston, Solomon

324

Long, Ezekiel
Langston, William
Liddell, Andrew J.
Liddell, James S.?W.?
Lewis, Jesse?
Linn, R. M. dec'd.
Linn, Garrison
Moore, Margaret
Merritt, Benjamin W.
Miller, John
Mason, Ambrose
McCay, Martin
McCrary, Mary
Miller, Jane
Martin, Jesse
Miller, John
Miller, Crosby
Mills, Berry
Mason, Daniel
McClure?, Edward J.
McElroy, Archibald
McCarley, James
McCarley, Joseph
McCarley, Robert B.
McConnell, William
McLease, Andrew
McCollum, Jesse
Mills, Rebecca
Massey, Silas
McLease, James
McLease, Margaret
McFall, Arthur
McCroskey, David
Mecklin, Hugh
McGee, Willis
McGee, Jesse C.
McGill, Samuel
McGill, John
Mitchel, Samuel
McPherson, Elijah
McPherson, Elizabeth
McPherson, Elijah
McGee, Jesse, dec'd.
McGee, Elias
McBride, James L.
McAllister, Nathan
Martin, David
McKey, Archibald
McKey, William
McMahan, Samuel
Mecklin, John A.
McCullough, Samuel G.?
McAllister, Lewis
Mitchel, Margaret
Morgan, John
McC..hy, William
McC..hy, Hugh L.
McAllister, Isaac
Millford, John Sr.
Millford, Philip P.
Millford, Robert
Millford, John Jr.
McKee, William M.
McKey, Hugh
McKey, Jane, dec'd.
Moore, Jeremiah
May, Daniel
McCoy, Samuel
McCoy, James
McGee, Michael
McGee, John
McGee, Benjamin M.
McFee, Washington
McAdams, John
Mitchel, Ephraim
McFee, Samuel
Massey, Laban
Melison?, Olley
Martin, Chessley
Martin, Hester
Martin, Elizabeth
Martin, William
McAllister, John

McAllister, Allen
McConnel, Thomas
Murphy, Ezekiel
Major, Joseph M.?
Martin, James
Mattison, James Jr.
McCrum?, John
McGregor, Abriam
Mitchel, Benjamin S.?
McDonald, James
McDonald, William
Major, James
Maddox, Thomas
McFall, Samuel R.
Martin, Samuel
Mattison, Nevil
May, Edmund
Martin, John
Massey, Kindred
Morris, James
Morris, James
Morris, David
McCluskey, James
McGee, William
Mayfield, Margar..t?
McCullough, Stephen
Moorehead, Alexander
McFall, John
Masters, G. W.
McWilliam, Wyatt A.?
McGill, Ezekiel
Massey, Lenior?
McGregor, Samuel L.
McPhail, John
Martin, Abram
Martin, Jacob
Manning, George
Morris, Samuel
Muchet, Jacob
McAllister, Andrew
McAllister, Peggy
McDonald?, Philip
Morris, John
Minton, Hezekiah
McDowel, Polly
Miller, Elias
McPherson, Dorcas
McDonald, Bluford
McDonald, William
Major, Elias?
McFall, John dec'd?
McDowel, William
Major, Elijah
Miller, Edmund
Moorehead, Maxey
Moorehead, John
Major, Enoch
Montgomery, Alfred
McFall, Andrew N.
Mattison, Wyatt
Mattison, James Sr.
Mattison, William
Mattison, Archibald
McConnel, Daniel
Massey, Abraham
McDowel, Esther
Moore, Grant
Murphy, John
Major, William
McGee, Burrell
Mitchel, John
Mayfield, Ephraim
Moore, Elijah
Moore, John M.
Moore, Thomas B.
Merritt, Josiah
McAllister, John
McAllister, Martha
Moon, Jeremiah
Merritt, Obediah
McMahand, Peter
McKinny, Alexander
McKinny, William

McMurry, Jane
Melton, David
Melton, Michael
Martin, Abram
McAllister, James
McCann, T. H.
Mulligan, Benjamin Sr.
Mulligan, Benjamin Jr.
McKinney, Martha
Mulligan, James
Mulligan, William
McMurry, William C.
McElroy, John
Miller, John C.
Miller, Tell? F.
McDowe, Pink
Mylum, Alfred
Mills, Elizabeth
Moore, John
McCoy, Thomas
Maverick, Samuel
McGregor, Ann R.
Millwee, William
Nevil, Alfred
Nevil, George
Nally, Crawford
North, Jhohn L.
Norris, E. S.
Newel, William
Norris, Jesse WS?
Norris, A. C.
Norris, John C.
Nevett?, William
Norrell, James
Norris, Robert B.
Nelson, James C.
Nichols, Zachariah
Nichols, Archibald
Newton, Hezekiah
Newton, Samuel
Newton, Willis
Newton, Isaac
Owens, Hiram
Owens, John
Obar, Robert
Obriant, Jesse
Obar, William
Owens, Thornton
Owens, Ashley
Orr, Christopher
Orr, Jane B.
Ozier?, Jacob
Oldham, George
Oldham, John dec'd.
Oldham, Thomas
Orr, William
Owens, Lewis
Oliver, Andrew
Oliver, James
Owens, Elijah Sr.
Owens, Daniel
Owens, Martha
Owens, Elijah Jr.
Oraby?, Nicholas
Owens, Bannister
Orr, Thomas
Pullem, Peyton
Pullam, William
Pullam, William Jr.
Palmore, William
Pritchett, Catharine
Philips, John
Passmore, William
Parker, Matthew
Presley, Jane
Pettigrue, Robert H.
Parker, David
Partin, Hubbard
Patterson, Samuel
Porter, Hugh
Pitt, William
Posey, Hubbard
Pruitt, William

Parker, Robert
Price, Pennel?
Parker, James
Parmer, Messen?
Pilgrim, John
Parmer, Joshua
Pruitt, Dudley, dec'd.
Poole, Walter
Poole, Manning
Poole, Robert
Pritchet, Lewis
Pickerel?, Jonathan
Pritchard, William
Prince, Richard
Poor, John
Philips, Martin
Posey, Harrison
Paget, Elizabeth
Posey, Francis
Pettis, Jane
Poor, John
Pepper, Elijah
Poor, William
Poor, Samuel
Poor, Martin
Poor, Hugh
Poor, Holland
Poor, George
Pickle, William
Perry, John
Pegg, John
Pickens, Robert
Pickens, Elizabeth
Pickle, Jacob
Pickens, Thomas J.?
Pattison, Hawkins?
Prince, C. J
Pinckney, Thomas
Rodgers, John
Reed, Jesse
Rimmer, Philip B.
Reese, A. H.
Ross?, Anthony W.
Robinson, Ephraim
Reese, Charles M.
Reese, Thomas S.
Ritchie, Elizabeth
Reed, William
Reed, Elizabeth
Rush, Hugh
Reed, Robert
Raney, John
Ri..., Daniel
Roach, Henry
Reed, Andrew
Rease, Hickison
Rampey, James J.
Rutledge, Jas.?
Reed, Thomas
Rice, Amaziah
Rice, Hezekiah
Robinston, John
Robinson, James E.
Robinson, John L.
Rodgers, Joseph
Rodgers, J. W.
Rodgers, Humphreys
Rodgers, William
Rodgers, John
Rodgers, William
Rodgers, William A.
Rice, Ibzan
Rodgers, Benjamin
Ruff, David
Russell?, David
Rosamond, John H.
Rice, Fleetwood
Rainwater, Job
Ritchie, William
Rodgers, William W.
Rice, Jane
Ritchie, Reuben
Rusk, David

Ritchie, James
Robinson, John B.
Reid and Acker
Reed, J. B.
Ragsdale, Francis A.
Reed, Henry
Rodgers, Eliza B.
Richardson, Noah
Rice, Washington
Richardson, Matthias
Rankins, George
Rodgers, ...
Robinson, William
Robinson, David
Reese, Henry J.?
Ramsey, John
Reeves, John
Roberts, George
Reese, George, Sr.
Reese, George, Jr.
Steele, James
Simmons, John
Smith, Aaron L.
Swilling, Samuel
Swilling, James
Swilling, George
Stanley, Ezekiel
Simmons, David
Simmons, Charles
Stone, David
Smith, John E.
Sherriff, Washington
Sherriff, Abel
Smith, Benjamin
Smith, William C.
Swords, John
Story, Charles dec'd.
Story, Susanna
Swords, William
Swords, John dec'd.
Swords, John
Sharpe, Elam
Stokes?, Elizabeth
Smith, Zephaniah
Swain, Jesse
Shanklin, Joseph M.
Symmes, F. W.
Symms, Avis
Symmes, G. T.
Sadler, David
Stephenson, James
Stewart, James
Simpson, David
Skelton, Moses
Seawright, William
Skelton, William
Shaw, H. G.
Shaw, Peyton
Skelton, Thomas
Skelton, Zadack
Skelton, Thomas
Starks?, Willis
Smith, Robert
Sherrard, William
Sullivan, Kelly
Stephenson, Jane
Siddell, Stephen
Siddell, Abner
Scott, David
Scott?, John
Stewart, John
Stewart, John Sr.
Simpson, William H.
Stephens, John
Simpson, Robert
Simpson, James
Scott, Elizabeth
Simpson, Archibald
Stephenson, John
Stephenson, Thomas
Spearman, John
Simpson, John N.?
Shackelford, John W.

Stewart, James
Simpson, William
Stiffle?, Mary
Simpson, Thomas
Smith, Samuel
Sailors, Abraham
Sailors, Abraham
Sailors, Leonard
Sailors, Isaac
Sailors, John
Strickland, Matthew
Seawright, James
Shirley, James Sr.
Shirley, James Jr.
Shirley, Dancy?
Spearman, David G.
Smith, Aaron, Sr.
Steele, Nancy H.
Stevenson, Andrew
Snipes, Matthew
Stephenson, John J.
Stephenson, George
Shirley, John
Smith, Samuel
Shambler, James
Sheander?, Andrew
Skelton, John W. B.
Strickland, Mille
Smith, Isaac
Smith, Ebenezer
Satterfield, Jeremiah
Stephenson, Mary
Smith, William
Smith, Robert
South, Luke H.?
Smith, William
Sherrill, Lewis
Saunders, Abram
Saunders, Thomas
Smith, John
Smith, John
Smith, Wyatt
Scuddy, A. E.
Smith, Wiley C.
Stem?, Haryston
Shirley, Robert J.
Shirley, Nipper
Shirley, John
Smith, Richard
Smith, David
Stone, George
Stone, William H.
Smith, William
Slaton, William
Slaton, John
Smith, Basil
Stringer, William K.
Smith, G... L.?
Spearman, Asbury
Smith, Thomas G.?
Stone, James
Stanton, Catharine
Stanton, Matthias
Slattin, Lovin
Sullivan, Thomas J.
Spearman, David
Stegall, Spencer
Sitton, William D.
Smith, Joseph
Stanton, George
Sitten, William
Spearman, George
Siddel, John
Simpson, Jesse
Slatton?, Stephen
Smith, Benjamin
Swords, Andrew?
Smith, Aaron
Smith, James
Smith, John
Sharpe, Jane
Smith, Simeon
Saunders, William

Sloan, J. T.
Smith, Whitaker
Simmons, James
Sloan, Benjamin
Sloan, Susan
Shirley, Aaron
Sitton, John B.
Simpson, Richard
Tillinghast, Elias H.
Tilley, Mary
Thacker, Edmund
Tucker, Dejarnet
Turner, James
Thompson, Matthew
Taylor, James M.
Thompson, John M.
Tate, John
Tucker, Bartley
Thompson, Elizabeth
Tucker, James
Tucker, Reuben
Taylor, William Sr.
Taylor, Thomas
Tate, David
Towne, William W.
Timms?, Joseph
Timms?, Isaac
Todd, Mary
Todd, Adam, dec'd.
Todd, Archibald
Taylor, Thomas
Todd, Sinai
Taylor, John
Tippen, George
Todd, James
Todd, John
Towers, Margaret
Towers, Larkin
Thompson, James
Terry, Thomas W.
Todd, Robert
Todd, Andrew
Trussell, Henley
Trussell, Posey
Trussell, Rhodam
Telford, James
Tripp, Nicholas
Tripp, John
Turner, John B
Telford, William
Telford, Isabella
Turner, John
Tompkins, John
Tripp, John
Trainem?, Lazarus
Thompson, James
Taylor, Joseph
Taylor, John B. C.
Talliaferro, Caroline
Taylor, George L.
Thompson, John
Vandiver, Sandford
Valentine, Benjamin
Vandiver, Paul
Vandiver, Hollingsworth
Vandiver, John
Vandiver, William
Vandiver, Asa P.
Vandiver, Edward
Vandiver, Ibzan
Vandiver, Larkin
Vandiver, Harvin
Vandiver, Aaron
Vandiver, Edward
Vandiver, Manning
Vandiver, John
Whitfield, Lewis
White, William
White, Thomas
White, Newton
Wright, Larkin
Wilson, Richard
Watkins, Boyles

Watkins, Temperance
Warley, Jacob
Watkin, Joseph
Warren, Samuel
Whitner, Elizabeth
Williford, John
Wilson, Lewis
Watt, Mary
Wright, Elizabeth
Watt, Thomas
Watt, Mary
Whitmore, Jacob
Willbanks, Elijah
Watt, John
Watt, James
Wilcle?, - Freeman
Wiley, William
Wilson, Robert
Wilfield?, J. B.
Winfield, James
Williams, Thomas
Williamson, Masten
Wright, K.? W.
Wright, John
Wright, Anne
Williamson, William
Willbanks, Shadrach
Wilson, James S.
Wilson, James B.
Wamock, James
Welborn, Joel E.
Welbourn, Sarah
Wimpey, Levy
Webb, William
Webb, Elisha
Watson, Daniel K.?
Watson, Stephen
Watson, Jonathan
Watson, David
Wilson, Charles
Warnock, Jesse? Sr.(John)
Warnock, John Jr.
Wilson, Robert
Webb, Edmund
Webb, Clayton
Webb, Elijah
Webb, Warren R.
Webb, E. & Co.
Williams, John
Wilkins, Martha
Wallace, Wilson?
White, Bartholomew
Whitmire, A. P.
Willingham, James
Willingham, John
Wilson, James
Wilson, William
Wuddell?, Alexander
Warwick, William
Webb, Charles B.
Williams, Stephen
White, July Anne
Whitner, Joseph A.
Whitfield, J. T.
Wyatts, E.
Webster, James R.
Wyatts, Redman G.
Walker, Peter
Wardlaw, James
Williams, Mary
Wardlaw, John M.
Wilson, Hugh
Wyatt, James M.
Welbourn, Thomas
Welbourn, William E.

PROPERTY RETURNED IN OTHER
DISTRICTS AND PARISHES:

Abbeville Dist.:

Miller, Charles

Maverick, Samuel & family
Smith, Wm. C.
Smith, Benjamin
McAllister, Nathan
Young, Francis
M'Curchy?, William
Tucker, Bartley
Webster, James R.
Harleston, Edwards

Greenville:

Williams, W. A.
Hagood, Benjamin
Harding, Joseph
Keith, Cornelius
Blythe, Absalom
Roper, Aaron
Wade, Solomon
Maverick, Sam'l. & family
Maxwell, Robt. A.
Greenville Dist.

Laurens:

Maverick, Sam'l & family
Simpson, Richard
Furgerson, James

Spartanburg:

Floyd, Silas
Maverick, Saml & family

Union:

Maverick, Saml. & family
Rusk, John

Newberry Dist.:

Maverick, Saml. & family

Lexington:

Maverick, Saml. & family

Orangeburg:

Maverick, Saml. & family

Fairfield:

Maverick, Saml & family

Edgefield:

Stiffles, Mary
Pitt, William

St. James Santee:

Gaillard, Theodore
Gaillard, Josiah L.?
Warren, Samuel

Prince George ....

Warren, Samuel

St. Philip & St. Michael:

Gibbs?, A. L.(S?)
Maverick, Sam. & family

St. Stephens:

Gaillard, C. L. & Jane
Maverick, Sa'l & family

AVERAGES COLLECTED BY E.
HARRIS IN Pendleton Dist.
Barry, Bartlett

Mullinax, Manuel G.
Moore, Eliab B.
Mason, Jim, Free?

1828-1829-1830-1831-1832-
1833 - Six Years

REMAINDER OF TAX RETURNS
WHICH WERE OUT OF SE-
QUENCE:

Wilson, Samuel
Wilson, Sarah
Williams, M. B.
Williams, Jasper & Newton
Wilson, James
Williams, W. A.
Welbourn, Albert J.
Wilson, Charles
Wilson, John
Wiggington, John
Wiggington, George
Wilson, William
Wigginton, Henry
Waddell, Hannah
Wilson, Robert G.?
Winters, Dinah
Watson, James
Watkins, Felex
Wilson, Isabella
White, Charles
Watson, Thomas
Wight, Alfred
Watson, Willard
Werner, William
White, Dudley
Young, James
Yeargon, Samuel
Young, Francis
Young, John

RETURNS OMITTED:

Moore, Leah
Steele, William

END OF 1836 TAX RETURNS
#

GENERAL TAXES OF 1837 OF THAT PART OF OLD PENDLETON DISTRICT LYING WITHIN THE LIMITS
OF ANDERSON DISTRICT, COLLECTED BY WM. STEELE, T.C.

(Note - This particular section of the tax book was torn or water-marked. Both left
and right margins are missing in some instances and other pages are difficult to read.
.....Ed.)

Adams, Asa
Adams, John
Adams, John (2)
....., Henry
....., Michael
....strong, James
....strong, Archey
...hley, John
...hley, Wilson
...mstrong, Jno. B.
...ms, Sylvanus
Armstrong, James
Acker?, Holbert
Acker, P. N.
Acker, Amos
..ams, Jacob
...ker, Susan
...hley, John
...inson, Jas. H.
...inson, Aaron
....., John
Amack, Jno. D.
Anderson, Saxon
Anderson, Y. Gamble
Anderson, Dr. Wm.
..ddis, Mary
..nderson, Thomas
..cker, William
Armstrong, James
Anderson, Jno. B.
Arnold, Allen
Anderson, David
Adams, Henry
Anderson, Martha
Alexander, David
Acker, Wm. M.
Anderson, Micajah
Acker, John
Brooks, Thomas
Buzby, George
Burris, Thomas
Buchanan, Sam'l.
Barrell, Charles
Butterton, Joshua
Bennett, Cooper
Brooks, George
Burris, Orange (Estate)
Burris, Eliza
Bayley, William
Buchanan, Eben.
Beaty, Francis
Beaty, David
Beaty, William
Buchanan, Wm.
Beaty, Sam. W.
Bowie, Chas. S.?
Brown, Charles
Barton, Blackburn
Barron, Uriah
Berry, Joel H.
Beaty, Young
Beaty, John
Bond, Sugar
Bowie, Chas. Jr.
Bowie, Wm. H.
Bonds, Isham R.
Beaty, Thomas
Bozeman, Lewis
Burdett, Hiram
Bell, James
Brown, Jeremiah
Brown, Samuel
Brock, James
Brock, Miria?
Brownlee, Maris
Bannister, Wm.

Braswell, Asa
Braswell, James
Braswell, George
Braswell, Harrison
Braswell, George
Bagwell, James
Burris-Eliza-(scratched)
Bagnal, Jno.
Ballentine, R. E.
Brock, Heyden
Ballentine, George
Bagwell, James
Boyle, Aaron
Brown, Dr. G. R.
Ballentine, Jesse
Brazel, Matthew
Barclay, Nancy
Bennett, Charl..
Bartley, Josiah
Bartley, Salley
Bennett, Wm.
Brazil, D. K.
Brazil, Henon
Bennett, Thomas
Brazil, Griffin
Brazil, Williamson
Blassingham, Thos.
Blankenship, Jno.
Bemore, Thomas
Bowen, Robert
Bloodsworth, Wm.
Burris, Bryant
Barr, Mary
Brewer, John
Brewer, William
Briant, Simon
Brazil, Enoch
Bellotte, Jacob
Brown, Randolph
Bell, Charles
Belotte, P. E.
Bradbury, Jesse
Bayley, Allen
Burns, John
Bruce, Chas. Jr.
Barton, Henry M.
Bradbury, Lat.?
Bruce, Charles Sr.
....., Thomas
....bury, James
....ens, B. W.
...own, Saml.
...own, Obediah
...own, Catharine
Brown, Robt.
..own, Larkin
Bowen?, Saml.
Briant, Nathan
Briant, Terrill
Burt, Francis
Burt, F. (Estate)
Bishop, Nicho's.
..owden, James
..cher, Manning
..nson, Sloan
..son, E. B.
Bee?, W (Mrs.?)
Brooks, Garner
Brown, Elijah
Bayley, Wm.
Brown, George
Broyles, Jno. F.
Burgess, James
Burriss, Thos. Jr.
Burriss, Melford
Boyd, Robert

Breckenridge, Robt.
Bohanan, J. W.
Brown, Daniel
Brown, Leslie
Bell, Samuel
Benson, Jno. P.
Brown, Isham
Brown, Robt.
Bagwell, Robt.
Brown, Joseph
Berry, William
Baker, Saml. H.
Baker, L. A.
Brown, Eliza
Barron, William
Burriss, Jacob
Burris, Eliz'h.
Burriss, Mary
Brown, Sarah
Brock, Andrew
Beaty, Lydia
Brown, John
Brown, Archey'd.
Broyles, O. R.
Barrett, John
Bruce, Chas. Jr.
Barnett, Ceasar
Campbell, George
Cunningham, Thos.
Cunningham, Sam
Caldwell, John
Cox, John
Caldwell, Wm.
Caldwell, Hugh
Caldwell, George
Cox, Beverly
Caldwell, James
Chappell, Jno. B.
Caldwell, Joseph
Conwell, James
Campbell, Alex'd.
Corr, John
Christopher, John
Clinkscales, Abner
Casey, Stephen
Cowan, Hiram
Cox, Edward
Campbell, Jesse
Conner, Dr. Jno. W.?
Cook, William
Casper, Jacob
Cunningham, Cath'e.
Clark, Joseph
Cobb, Noah
Cox, Nancy
Carson, James
Cox, John
Cobb, Martin
Cobb, James
Clement, Isaac
Clement, Stephen
Clement, Ben.
Clement, Isaac
Cullens, Caleb
Cowan, William
Cox, William
Clinkscales, W. F.
Clinkscales, F. E.
Cummins, David
Cummins, Robt.
Clement, Wm.
Cox, Arris
Cox, William
Cox, Thomas
Clements, Hugh
Clark, Wm.

Cox, Gabriel
Cornelias, Abram
Cox, David
Cox, Abner
Cobb, Henry
Cobb, Josiah W.
Carter, Caleb
Cooley, Lewis
Cooly, John
Carter, Spencer
Chamblee, Moses
Clardy, John
Clardy, Norman
Cooley, James
Childers, Abram
Cooper, James
Cooper, Wash'g.
Chambers, Nancy
Caron, Rev.?
Caron, Sarah
....nter, T. L.
....non, Isaac
...., Asa
....mpbell, James
....mpbell, Daniel
..arden, Thomas
Cox, Sarah
Craig?, Saml.
Cherry, F. R.
....adine, Eliz'h.
Cherry, F. R.
Cherry, David
Campbell, A. C.
Cherry, Saml.
..orr, Laban
..arpenter, Alfred
..rpenter, Eliz'h.
..mmings, Harman
Cannon, Ephraim
Cash, Stephen
Clinkscales, Asa
Cox, Joseph
Cox, R. & Sisters?
Chamberlain, Jno.
Clarke, Matthew
Carter, Dr. A. P.
Clarke, Jno. B.
Cochran, D. H.
Carpenter, John
Cox, William
Chastain, Stephen
Crawford, James
Crawford, Wm. Estate
Crawford, Sarah
Chastain, John
Chastian, Stephen
Chamblee, Ben
Chamble, James
Carter, Edward
Chamblee, James
Clinkscales, Levi
Carter, John
Cason, James
Carson, Wm. Estate
Cason, Hester
Carlisle, Wm.
Calhoun, Alex'd.
Creswell, Sarah
Caminade, John
Driver, James
Davis, Levi
Deane, Thomas
Dickson, William
Dollar, William
Davis, John
Dunlap, Matthew
Dunlap, Robt.
Davis, Jno. L.
Davis, Aaron
Davis, Zac.
Davis, William
Davis, Richard
Dawson, Saml.

Duncan, David
Duckworth, J. C.
Davidson, Jenny
Davis, Levi
Durham, Berry
Douthet, James
Durham, William
Durham, David
Dalton, Burrell
Dalton, Boothe
Dalton, Smallwood
Douthet, Ben.
Davis, Charles
Durham, Wm.
Dickinson, Willis
Dickerson, Thomas
Dalrymple, Jno.
Dickenson, Robt.
Duckworth, Jacob
Duckworth, Wilburn
Duckworth, Howard
Dalrymple, Sam.
Dalrymple, James
Dickson, John
Dickson, Matthew Estate
Dart, Mary L.
Davis, James
Dupree, Ben Sr.
Dove, John
Davis, Jesse
Davis, Elias
Deane, Aaron
Deane, Saml. Estate
Deane, Moses
Dobbins, Martha
Davis, Valentine
Duckworth, Thomas
Dowale, Rt. Estate
Duncan, Thomas
Dalrymple, John
Davis, Moses
Dobbins, Jesse
Duncan, Ivey
Dobbins, James
Dunham, Benajah
Dooley, William
Dupre, B. D.
Daniel, Wm. D. C.
Dickson, James
Emberson, Saml.
Elrod, William
Emberson, James
Earpe, Caswell
Elliott, Wm. Jr.
Elliott, Wm. Sr.
Ellison, Miles
Ellis, Larkin
Elrod, George
Elrod, Isaac
Ellison, James
Elrod, Elias
....., Samuel
....., Adam
...le, Jas. W.
....., Micajah
...rod, Phillip
...skine, Phillip
...rod, William
...on, William
...n, Joseph
Elliott, Mary
Earle, Sam. G.
Earle, J. Lewis
Elrod, Jeremiah
Earpe, Wesley
..rod, George
...od, Thos. P.
...skine, James
...rns, Dr. Alex'd.
Elrod, Thomas
Erskine, Thomas
Erskine, John
Elliott, Dr. R. E.

Erskine, James
Earpe, David D.
Earle, Jno. B.
Eaton & Miller
Earle, Ann
Earle, Geo. W.
Findley, Elias
Fowler, William
Fisher, Saml/ C/
Fisher, Samuel
Flowers, Toliver
Featherston, Jno. W.
French, William
Fant, Alfred
Fant, James
Fleming, Richard
Fleming, James
Ford, Stephen
Forbes, Alanson
Floyd, Silas
Fant, James
Felton, Mary
Ford, William
Fielding, Henry
Fuller, Alfred
Fowler, Ruth
Fant, V. D.
Fant, A. E.
Ferrill, Jno. B.
Felton, Richard
Fricks, Christian
Fretwell, John
Fretwell, Jos. Y.
Forsythe, Wm.
Gilmer, Nancy
Gilmer, Robert
Gilmore, James
Gentry, John
Gentry, Zac.
Gregg, Hugh
Gee, Jeremiah
Gentry, Moody
George, Thomas
Glenn, William
Green, Jno. R.
Green, John
Gwin, Leonard
Gentrey, John
Gaillard, Theo.
Gable, Jno. (Estate)
Gassaway, Ben.
Gable, Harman
Gray, A. D.
Gantt, Jno. W.
Gantt, Jas. A.
Green, W. W.
Gamble, James
Gamble, William
Green, John
Gamble, Sarah
Gambrel, E. B.
Gray, Huldah
Gantt, Hugh
Gantt, John
Grubbs, George
Greer, David
Gantt, William
Gantt, Jno. G.
Gamble, Matthew
Griffin, Elijah
Gutry, David
Griffin, John
Gutry, Benjamin
Gutry, Nelson
Gambrel, John
Gambrel, Wm.
Gambrel, Barbara
Gambrel, Henry
Gibbs, Polly
Gambrel, Ezekiel
Gambrell, R.
Gambrel, Larkin
Gambrell, James

Gibson, Thomas
Green, Lemuel
Golding, John
Garrett, John
Gambrell, Joel B.
Garrett, Thos. H.
Gayton, Aaron
Gaillard, C. L.
Gaillard, Jane H.
Gaillard, Cor.? D.
Gilbert, Amos
Grantt, William
Grubbs, Jno. M.
Gordon, Jno. C.
Gordon, William
Gambrel, David
Gibbs, Dr. A. S.
Gaillard, W. H. D.
Gaston, William
Gaillard, Rebecca
......., James
....., Henry Jr.?
...ble, Henry
.....ble, Levi
......., Solomon
.....ay, Hezekiah
....don, James
....., R.
.....y, Allen
....er, William
...eer, Thomas
Gordon, Robert
Grimes, Mary
Gentry, A. B.
Geer, David
Gentry, Daniel
Godwin, Joshua
Gilliland, Alex'd.
Gentry, John
Gramble, Henry
Gaillard, Jos. D.
Goode, Lewelling Estate
George, James
Griffin, Jas. C.
Greer, David, Sr.
Harvey, Charles
Henderson, Martha
Heeton, Thomas
Houston, William
Holmes, Henry
Honey, Samson
Harvey, Mark
Harvey, James
Herndon, George
Hale, John
Herring, Francis
Herndon, Zepha
Howie, Robert
Hill, Thomas O.
Haley, Reubin
Hall, Thos. A.
Harris, Sarah
Hattin, William
Harris, Jas. S. Estate
Howell, Jackson
Hall, Martin
Hall, Lent Jr.
Hall, Jno. Sr.
Hall, John B.
Hall, Wm. A.
Hall, Zac.
Harkness, John
Hall, Lemuel
Hall, Lent, Sr.
Hamilton, Luke
Haney, Stephen
Harkness, R't. C.
Hall, Ezekel
Harkness, Jno. N.
Herring, James
Hunt, William
Hopkins, John
Hunt, John

Hewens, Robt.
Haney, Luke
Hinton, John
Harper, William
Harper, Jno. A.
Harkins, Hugh
Hanks, Tilman
Holland, Gracie
Harkins, James
Holland, Aaron
Horton, Grief
Harper, John
Henderson, James
Holland, John
Harper, William
Hubbard, William
Hamby, Samuel
Hamilton, D. R.
Hamilton, Thomas
Harris, Gillison
Hunter, Sarah
Hix, Jhohn
Hillhouse, Joseph
Herring, Elijah
Herring, Jesse
Herring, Levi
Hix, Daniel
Hughs, John
Hix, Milton
Harrison, James
Holland, Robt.
Holland, Jacob
Hacket, Albert
Humphries, David
Hembree, Jas. Sr.
Hembree, Jas. Jr.
Hartie, John
Hubbard, William
Harris, Nat.
Harris & Anderson
Hunter, Mary
Hays, Geo. B.
Harris, Ezekel
Harleston, Edward
Haney, John
Hall, Aaron
Hall, Joseph
Hammond, Sam. J.
Holt, Jno. B.
Hill, Abram
Hamilton, Jno. D.
Harris, Lucy
Hall, Nancy
Hanks, Geo. Estate
Hammond, Hubert
Hutchins, Michael
Harris, John
Harris, Ben.
Hipps, Joseph
Hembree, Azariah
Howard, Hiram
...ing, John
....all, Henton
Houston, Sarah
Hembree, Willis
Holland, William
Holland, John
Hannah, Thomas
Herndon, Edmond
Harris, John
Hendricks, David
Hall, James E.
Harper, Asa
Hall, John
Hall, William
Harris, Joshua
Hartlet, James
Hartlet, Moses W.
Humphries, Jno. T.
Hammon, B. H.
Hillhouse, Mary
Hanks, Luke
Henny, John

Hawkins, W. P.
Harris, Wm. A.?
Harris, Jos. P.
Harris, Jno. Estate
Hinton, Wm.
Harrison, Thos. Estate
Huger, T. K.
Hackett, Lucinda
Holbrook, Jesse
Holly, Jane
Hall, Wilson
Jones, Thomas
Jones, Jos. B.
Irvine, Eleanor
Jennings, John
Jones, Saml. K.
Johnston, Nancy
Johnston, Allen
Johnston, Peter
Jones, John
Jones, Ambros H.
Johnston, Benj.
Jolley, Henry
Jones, Elizabeth
Jones, Hartwell
Jones, Anna
Isbel, Samuel
Johnston, Richard
Ingram, Wm.
Jolly, Jane
James, Samuel
Johnston, W. G.
Junken, Robt.
Johnston, Milley
Ingram, Jno. H.
Jeffers, Nathan
Jolly, Joseph
Keown, William
Kennedy, Lorenzo
Keating, Wm.
Keys, John
Kay, James W.
Kerr, William
Key, Mason
Kay, Fielding
Kay, Wm. Sr.
Kay, Strother
Kay, Catharine
Kay, Wm. Jr.
King, Josiah
King, James
King, Mary
Kingsley, Chestine
King, Robert
Kelly, Elisha
King, John
Kelly, Alfred
King, Peter
Kelly, John
Knox, John
Kelly, Daniel
Knight, Warren
Kay, Alexander
King, Wm. P.
King, William
Kirksey, F. & C.
Kirksey, F.
Kirksey, Wm. Sr.
Keys, James C.
Keys, Robt. A.
Kitsinger, Jacob
King, Hiram
Kay, Robt. Estate
Keys, John
Kay, Jesse
Kay, John
Keaton, Archey'd
Lockhart, Dr. J. M.
Long, Harrison
Lewis, Major (Estate)
Ledbetter. James
Ledbetter, Mary
Ledbetter, C..

Long, Isaac
Long, William
Liverett, John
Liverett, Thomas
Little, Rachael
Loveless, Nathan
Lucias, Dan'l F.
Lucias, D. F. Jr.
Lee, Phillip
Lee, James
Lewis, J. W. & M.
Lewis, J. W.
Leboon, Joseph
Lawless, James
Linn, Garrison
Linn, Robert
Long, Ezekel
Lewis, Eleanor
Linn, Robt. (Estate)
...ddle, Jas. S.
Lewis, Jesse
Looney, Isaac
....ry, Jackson
Liddle, Jno. S.
Liddle, A. J.
Lewis, Jesse P.
Langston, Wm.
Lewis, James O.
Lewis, Elisha
Lovelace, Hembree
Latimer, Wiley
Leverell, Stephen
Leverett, Wesley
Low, Lowden
Lorton, Francis
Lorton, Jno. S.
Morris, John
McCroskey, David
McCroskey, Jos.
McCartey, Robt.
Martin, Samuel
McCullam, Jesse
Massey, Silas
McCarley, James
McLease, Andrew
McLease, James J.
McGill, Samuel
McGill, Ezekel
McGill, John
McGee, Jesse C.
McGee, Nancy
McGee, Willis
Meeklin, Hugh
McGee, Elias
Martin, David
M'Culley, Saml.
McBride, Jas. L.
McPherson, Elijah
Mouchett, Jacob
Machum, Saml.
McKee, Wm. M.
McKee, Archibald
McKee, Welt?
Michell, Saml.
McCurdy, William
Meekley, Jno. A.
Meeklyn, A. P.
Morgan, John
McFall, P.
Millford, John
Milford, Robt. A.
Melford, P. P.
Millford, Rebecca
McAlister, Isaac
May, Edmond
Martin, John
Massey, Laban
Moore, Jeremiah
Matteson, Archey
McFee, Washington
McAdams, John
Matteson, Olley
Matteson, James Sr.

Matteson, Wyatt
Mitchell, John
Matteson, William
Matteson, Nevel
Matheson, Eliz.
McCoy, Sam...
McCoy, James
Mitchell, Ephraim
Moore, Grant
McAlister, John
Moore, Jno. M.
Majors, Elijah
Majors, William
Murphy, John
Mayfield, Ephraim
Moore, Jeremiah
Merritt, Obediah
Moore, Elijah
McAlister, John
Merrell, Josiah
McAlister, Patsey
Murphy, Ezekel
McCann, F. H.
McKinney, Martha
McMahan, Peter
McKinney, Alex'd.
Martin, James
Martin, Jacob
Milliken, James
McMurry, COm/ company?
Mellekin Com.
Millikin, Benjamin
McAlister, James
Millekin, Ben. Jr.
Martin, Abram
McElroy, John
Martin Co.m
Martin, Hester
Martin, Eliz'h.
Miller, F. R.
Meredith, Abram
Merritt, Ben. W.
Myers, John
Moore, Margaret
McCay, Martha S.
Miller, John
McMurray W.
Martin, Jesse
Miller, Jane
McCrary, Mary
Miller, Jno. C.
McFall, John
McGee, Wm.
Mayfield, Margt.
Moore, John
Moore & Murphy
McCoy, Alex.
Mattox, David
Moorehead, Alex'd.
McKeown
Martin, Abram
McGee, John
Majors, Elijah
...y, F. W.
McConnell, Wm.
Moore, Mary (Estate)
McLeskey, James
McFall, Saml.
Morris, David
Melwee, Samuel
Melwee, Com.
Mitchell, Ben
McDaniel, James
McDaniel com.
Massey, Kindred
Martin, Chesley
Masters, Geo. W.
McCulley, Stephen
MgGregor, Mary
Moore, John
Martin, Samuel
McMillan, W. A.
Massey, Abram

Martin, Hez'h.
Miller, Elias
Moore, Larkin
Majors, James
Majors, Jos. M.
Manning, George
Majors, Enoch
Moorhead, Maxey
Moorhead, John
McGregor, Saml. D.
Morris, Jesse B.
Mills, Rebecca
Morris, James
McDowell, Ester
McDaniel, Phillip
McLease, James
McLease, Margaret
McDaniel, Buford
McAllister, And'w.
McAllister, Margt.
McGee, Burrell
McGee, M.
McConnell, Thomas
McCullam, Danl
McFall, A. N.
Morris, Samuel
Murray, Margt.
McAllister, Nathan
McElroy, Archy'd
Moore, Eli
McPherson, Dorcas
Montgomery, Alfred
McPhail, John
Maddison, Jas. Estate
Miller, M. L.
Miller, Crosby W.
Miller, Jno. Jr.
Meverick, Sam.
Meverick Roch Mill
Mills, Eliz'h. Estate
McMurtry, Wm.
Maw, Jno. F.
Milwee & Gugson
Maxwell, Robt.
McDowell, James
Mason, Jim
Nelson, W. R.
Newell, William
Norris, Jesse W.
Norris, Ezekel
Norris, & Houston
Nichols, Zac.
Nichols, Archey'd.
Newton, Isaac
Newel, Alfred
Newton, Hez'h.
Newell, George
North, Jno. L.
Newton, Sam.
Newton, Wm.
Newton, Willis
Norris, Jno. E.
Norris, And. O.
Nevit, Wm. M.
Norris, Robt. B.
Obriant, A. J.
OBarr, Wm.
Owens, Thornton
Owens, Lewis
Oldham, George
Oldham, Jno. Estate
Oldham, Thomas
Orr, William
Oliver, James
Owens, Elijah
Oliver, Dr. James Est.
Oliver, Andrew
Owens, Martha
Owens, Elijah Jr.
Owens, John
Ownes, Daneil
Owens, Banester
Orr, Thomas

Overly, Nicholas
Owens, Ashley
Owens, Hiram
Osburn, James
Orr, Christ'r.
Orr. Jane B.
Patrick, Thomas
Parker, Matthew
Presley, Ann
Partin, Hubbard
Porter, Hugh
Price, Pennel
Posey, Hubbard
Parker, James
Presley, David
Pritchett, Wm.
Pruett, Wm.
....., Harrison
....., Reuben
....., Jane
....., Holland
....., John
....., William
Poor, Martin
Poor, Hugh
Poor, Samuel
Poor, George
Poor, John Jr.
Payne, Isaac Co.
Pegg, John
Pegg, James
Pickens, Robert
Pickens, Elizabeth
Pickle, Jacob
Pickle, William
Pitts, Charles
Palmer, Mercer
Pilgrim, John
Payne, Jane
Pullum, Leroy
Palmore, William
Pellum, Peyton
Pullum, Wm. Sr.
Pullum, Wm. Jr.
Pickerel, Jonathan
Pettigrew, Robt. H.
Pitts, William
Pasmore, Wm. Estate
Phillips, John
Pike, Daniel
Poole, Robert
Pruett, Dudley Estate
Poole, Manning
Patterson, Samuel
Prince, Charles J.
Phillips, Martin
Prince, Richard
Pagett, Eliza
Pepper, Elijah
Parker, Robt.
Pickens, Thomas J.
Pinkney, C. C.
Pritchett, Lewis
Pinkney, Thomas
Reid, William
Reid, Eliza
Rainey, John
Reid, Hugh
Reid, Robert
Rush, Hugh
Riley, Daniel
Roach, Henry
Roach, Berry
Reid, Andrew
Ramsey, James A.
Rice,Aama.
Russell, David
Robinson, Jn. B.
Robinson, Jno. J.
Rutledge, R. T.
Reid, Thos. L.
Robinson, John
Robinson, James E.

Reese, Jacob
Reed, Henry
Reid & Acker
Reid, J. P.
Ritchie, James
Ragsdale, Francis
Richardson, Mathias
Ritchie, William
Rankin, George
Rosamond, John
Rodgers, Simeon
Robinson, David
Richardson, David
Richardson, N. A.
Richardson, A. W.
Rodgers, William
Rogers, W. A.
Rodgers, Humphrey
Ragsdale, John
Rodgers, Benjamin
Rodgers, William
Rodgers, Eliz. B.
Richardson, Noah
Reid, Jesse
Rogers, Elihiu
Rimmer, Jas. W.
Rimmer, P. B.
Rice, Ibzan
Riley, Hez'h.
Rice, Hez'h.
Rice, Jane
Roberts, George
Ritchie, Reubin
Robinson, E. J.
Rice & Carter
Rice, F.
Reese, Dr. A. H.
Reese, George
Reese, Geo. Estate
Rainwater, Job
Reid, Hugh
Rogers, Jeremiah
Rogers, Joseph
Ruff, David
Ross, A. W.
Richardson, Turner
Ritchie, Eliz'b
Reeves, John
Ramsay, John
Reese, H. D.
Shaw, William
Stewart, James
Sadler, David
Skelton, Zadoc
Skelton, Hosea
Shaw, Peyton
Skelton, Thomas
Skelton, Thos. F.
......, A. E. Estate
....., Stephen
....., Abner
....., Archey
....., William
....,anson, Jane
...man, John
....er, David
...cks, Willis
Sanders, Abraham
Sanders, Thomas
Smith, Robert
Stephens, Shadrick
Simpson, Robert
Simpson, James
Stewart, Jno. Jr.
Stewart, Jno. Sr.
Simpson, Thomas
Sullivan, Kelly
Simpson, William
Stephenson, John
Stephenson, F. W.
Scott, David
Stewart, James
Stiffle, Mary

Smith, Luke H.
Sanders, William
Smith, Samuel
Skelton, William
Strickland, Matthew
Sailors, Isaac
Saylors, Leonard
Sailors, John
Smith, Jeremiah
Smith, Richard
Sailors, Abram
Sailors, Abram
Stone, Hampton
Shirley, Obediah
Shirley, Benjamin
Shirley, Jno. (Estate)
Strickland, Milley
Stone, George
Smith, George S.
Spray, Thomas
Slater, William
Spearman, F. A.
Slater, John
Stone, James
Stone, William
Smith, William
Smith, Basil
Slater, L.
Stringer, Eliza
Smith, Thos. G.
Stanton, Catharine
Stanton, Mathis
Saxon, William
Saterfield, Jeremiah
Sitton, William
Seddle, John
Simpson, Jesse
Shearman, George
Stanton, George
Setgall, Spencer
Smith, Joseph
Stone, Bannister
Sullivan, Thos. J.
Spearman, Benj.
Smith, James
Smith, John
Sheriff, Abel
Sherif, Washington
Smith, Benj.
Sitton, W. B.
Sharpe, John
Spearman, D. D.
Smith, Simeon
Smith, William
Smith, Wyatt
Sherrill, Lewis
Sterling, James Jr.
Shirley, James Sr.
Swilling, Samuel
Swilling, James
Swilling, George
Smith, Aaron S.
Simmons, Charles
Simmons, James
Simmons, David
Simmons, John
Stanley, Ezekel
Smith, John E.
Swords, Andrew
Sharpe, Elam
Starke, Mrs. E. G.
Smith, Wm. C.
Smith, Benjamin
Smith, Aaron
Swords, John
Smith, Zepha
Swords, William
Swords, Jno. Estate
Shanklin, Joseph
Sitton, John
Symms, G. T.
Symms, Susan
Symms, Dr. F. W.

333

Sloan, Jno. T.
Stephenson, Jno. J.
Smith, William
Simpson, David
Smith, Aaron Sr.
Stephenson, James
Stephenson, Andrew
Shackleford, Jno. W.
Stephens, John
Smith, Samuel
Scott, Elizabeth
Snipes, Matthew
Stephenson, George
Shirley, Aaron
Skelton, J. W. B.
Seawright, James
....., John
....., William
....., Robert
....., ... C.
...y, D.
....y, Gillam
...y, Jno. N.
....., Andrew
....., Jesse R.
Smith, Ebenezer
Smith, Whitaker
Simpson, Richard
Steele, Nancy H.
Steele, James
Steele, William
Smith, Nimrod
Sloan, Susan
Sloan, Benjamin
Sloan Benson & Sloan
Thacker, Edmond
Tilley, Mary
Turner, James
Tucker, James
Tucker, James H.
Taylor, James H.
Thomson, Elizabeth
Thomson, Matthew
Taylor, William
Todd, Robert
Todd, Andrew
Tate, John A.
Taylor, Thomas
Tate, David
Tucker, Barkley
Tucker, Reuben
Tucker, John C.
Taylor, Thomas
Todd, Mary
Townes, W. W.
Tupple, Posey
Tupple, Henby
Telford, James
Telford, William
Telford, Isabella
Turner, John B.
Turner, Jonathan
Tomkins, John
Tripp, John Sr.
Tripp, Nicholas
Tripp, John Jr.
Thomson, James
Trainem, Lazarus
Timms, Joseph
Timms, Isaac
Teppens, Elizabeth
Tellinghast, Elias H.
Tippens, Dennis
Taylor, David S.
Thomson, Jno. M.
Thomson, John
Thomson, Jas. & Co.
Thomas, James
Terry, Henry
Tucker, D.
Todd, James
Todd, John
Todd, Simon

Towers, D. R. (Estate)
Taylor, Jno. B.
Taylor, Joseph Sr.
Talioferro, C. V.
Taylor, John
Voluntine, Benjamin
Vandiver, Paul
Vandiver, Thomas
Vandiver, Ibzan
Vandiver, Sanford
Vandiver, Manning
Vandiver, William
Vandiver, Asa P.
Vandiver, Enoch
Vandiver, Larkin
Vandiver, John
Vernon, J. T. W.
Vandiver, Edward
Vandiver, Aaron
Vandiver, John
Watson, Daniel R.
Williford, Jno. Estate
Wyld- Freeman
Winfield, Jas. R.
Wiles, Jesse
Wall, Thomas
Whitman, J....
Wiley, James
White, Ezekel
Wilbanks, Eli....
Waters, Fleming
Wright, Lizzy
Watt, James
Watt, Mary
Winfield,......
Watt, Mary ....
Watt, John
Wiley, William
Williamson, William
Wright, John
Wright, Robt. N.
Williamson, Martin
Wright, Daniel
Wright, Ann
Webster, James R.
Walker, Peter
Wyatt, Elijah
Wyatt, Jas. F.
Wyatt, Red. G.
Wardlaw, John
Wardlaw, James
Wardlaw, Hugh
Willingham, James
Willingham, John
Wilson, Jas. P.
Wilson, James B.?
Wilson, Samuel
........ah
.........,.....ah
....., Thomas
.... E.
....., M. B.
......, Jasper & N.
....., Mary
....., Charles
....son, John
......., Albert
....mphey, Levi
...addle, Hannah
..Wigginton, John
Wiggington, Henry
..tson, James
.ilson, William
Williams, John
Watson, Willard
Wigginton, George
Wilson, Isabella
Wilbanks, Shadrick
Webb, William
Warnock, James
Wilbanks, Thomas
White, Bartholomew
White, Thomas

White, William
Wright, Larkin
White, Newton
Whitworth, Charles
Watkins, Felix
Winters, Dinah
Waller, William
Watkins, Joseph
Warley, Jacob
Wilson, Rich'd. F.
Whitner, Eliza Estate
Werner, William
Watson, Thomas
Warren, Samuel
Whitmore, A. P.
Wallace, Wilson
Watson, David
Wilson, Lewis
Webb, Elisha
Webb, C. B.
Wilson, Thomas
Watkins, Baylis
Watkins, Temperance
Warnock, John Sr.
Warnock, Jno. Jr.
Wilson, James
Wilson, Robert
Webb, Elijah
Wilson, James
White, Jonathan
Welburn, Sarah
Wilson, William
Wilson, Charles
Waddle, Alexander
Warnock, William
Wells, C & C
Webb, W. R.
White, Julia
Webb, Clayton
White, Dudley
White, W. A.
Whitner, Jos. N.
Webb, Edmond
Wright, Alfred
Whitfield, J. T.
Williams, Martha

Abbeville:
Muchett, Jacob
Young, Francis
McCurdy, Wm.
Stiple, Mary
Smith, Wm. C.
Smith, Ben.
Harleston, Edward
Miller, Charles
St. James Santee:
Gaillard, Teho.
Warren, Samuel
St. Stephens:
Gaillard, C. L. & J. H.
Edgefield:
Pitts, William
Robinson, Randal
Gibbs, A. S.
Warren, Saml.
Richardson, Turner
Simp..., Richard
Meverick, Sam
Greenville:
Williams, W. A.
Maveri ck, Sam.
Hagood, Ben
Keith,...
Roper, Aaron
Blythe, Ab.
Hard...Jos.
York:(?)
Rush, John

#

TAX RETURN FOR EITHER 1838 or 1839......(Heading torn away)

Armstrong, James
Adams,.......
Atkins, Henry ?
Adams, John
Adams, Henry
Alewine, Michael
Armstrong, James
Ashley, John
Ashley, William
Armstrong, James
Adams, William
Armstrong, John B.
Alexander, David
Adams, Sylvanus
Armstrong, A. A.
Ashley, Edward
Armstrong, Willm B.
Acken, P. N.
Acken, Amos
Adams, Jacob
Acken, Susanah
Acken, Joshua L.
Acken, Halbert
Avery, Thomas
Atkinson, A. N.
Atkinson, Jos. H.
Adams, John
Amick, John D.
Anderson, Dr. Wm.
Archer, John P.
Ackin, William
Arnold, Allen
Anderson, John
Anderson, David
Acken, William
Abbott, John
Alexander, Wm. P.?
Anderson, Micajah
Anderson, G. G.
Alexander, Saxon
Archer, John
Burgess, James
Beaty, David
Blassingame, Thos.
Blankenship, Jno.
Bennett, Cooper
Brooks, Thos.
Busbey, George
Burris, Thomas
Buchanan, Sam.
Burris, Reubin
Betterson, Joshua
Berry, William
Boyd, Robt.
Buchanan, William
Beaty, Francis
Barron, Uriah
Beaty, William
Beatty, John
Beatty, Saml.
Buchanan, Ebenez.
Burris, Orange D.
Beatty, Lydia
Beatty, Thomas
Bowie, Charles
Bowie, Wm. H.?
Bryant, Joice O.
Brown, Isaac
Bowie, Charles
Burdet, Hiram
Burton, Blackburn
Bozeman, Lewis
Bee?, James M.
Brown, Sam.
Brown, Eliza-Estate
Brock, Meridith H.
Banister, William
Brownlee, S. L.
Brock, James
Brock, Heyden
Braswell, Asa

Bagwell, James
Bagwell, John
Braswell, James
Braswell, Nancy
Brasswell, George
Ballentine, George
Broyles, Aaron
Brazeal, Enoch
Ballentine, Richd. E.
Bagwell, James
Brown, Dr. Geo. R.
Brazeal, Matthew
Ballentine, Jesse H.
Bennett, Thomas
Brazeal, David H.
Bennett, Charles
Brazeale, Kenon
Brazeale, Griffin
Barclay, Nancy
Barclay, Josiah
Barclay, Sarah
Brazeale, Williamson
Bennett, William
Bryant, Terrill
Bryant, Nathan
Bowen, Robert
Barr, Mary
Brewer, William
Brewers, Milley
Burns, John
Barten, Henry M.
Bradberry, Jesse
Bruce, Charles
Bailey, Allen
Brown, Catharine
Brown, Obed.
Brown, Robert
Bowman, Arch.d.
Bradberry, Sal'o.?
Brown, Saml.
Brackenridge, Robert
Bishop, Nicholas
Bownden, James
Bruce, John
Bruce, Charles, Sen.
Benson, Enoch B.
Benson & Sloan
Brown, Daniel
Brown, Elijah
Brown, Larkin
Brown, Isham
Berry, Joel H.
Bonds, Sugar
Bonds, Isham R.
Brown, Robert
Brown, Leslie
Brown, Eliz'h.
Brock, Andrew
Burris, Milford
Bowen, Samuel
Brooks, Garner
Benson, Jno. P.
Burt, Francis
Baker, Lindsey A.
Barrett, John
Barrett, Charles
Bryant, Simon
Baker, Sam. H.
Brown, George
Burris, Thomas
Burris, Jacob
Burris, Elizabeth
Burris, Mary
Burris, Elbert
Broyles, John T.?
Bell, Saml.
Bruce, Thomas
Broyles, O.? R.
Bailey, William
Brown, John
Bellotte, Peter E.

Brown, Randolph
Bell, Charles
Belotte, Jacob
Burris, Elisha
Burris, James
Cater, Dr. A. P.
Craig, Samuel
Colhoun, Alex'd.
Caldwell, William
Caldwell, Hugh
Caldwell, Joseph
Campbell, Alexander
Campbell, George
Carpenter, Eliza'h.
Cunningham, Sam.
Cunningham, Thos.
Caldwell, John
Caldwell, James
Cox, Bevely?
Chappell, John
Conwell?, James
Cowen, Hiram
Cunningham, Catharine
Cox, Edward
Christopher, John
Conner, Doctor Jno. W.
Casey, Stephen
Campbell, Jesse
Clinkscales, Wm. F.?
Cosper, Jacob
Corr, John
Clark, Joseph
Clement, Isaac
Clement, Isaac, Sr.
Clement, Hugh
Cobb, Noah
Cowan, William
Collins, Caleb
Cobb, Martin
Cliankscales, Wm. F.
Cox, William
Cox, Arris
Cox, William
Cox, Thomas
Cumming, Robert
Cox, John
Clement, Stephen
Clement, Berry
Clement, Wm.? R.
Cox, Sarah
Cox, William
Cox, Reubin B.
Cummings, David
Coley, Lewis
Cox, Abner
Cox, Gabriel
Cox, David
Cooley, John
Cobb, Henry
Cobb, Josiah W.
Cobb, A. P.
Carelen?, Thomas
Ceasar (free negroe)
Cox, Joseph
Cox, Rachael & sisters
Cooley, James
Carlin?, Caleb
Carter, Spencer
Chamblee, John
Clardy, Norman
Clardy, Jno. B.
Childress, Abram (Childers)
Clardy, Joel
Coates, Anthony (free neg.)
Cason, Reubin
Cason, Sarah
Cason, James A.
Cason, Esther
Cason, Wm.-Estate
Cox, Asa
Campbell, James

335

Cater, Edward
Coor?, Laban
Coates, John
Campfield, T.?-Estate
Campbell, A. C.
Cherry, Saml.
Cherry, T. R. & W. B.
Carpenter, Alfred M.
Cherry, Thos. R.
Cooper, Washington
Cox, John
Christian, John
Clinkscales, Levy
Cannon, Ephraim
Clinkscales, Abner
Carpenter, John
Chamblee, Benjamin
Clinkscales, Asa
Cobb, James
Campbell, Daniel
Chastian, Stephen
Chastian, Stephen
Crawford, James
Crawford, Wm.-Estate
Crawford, Sarah
Chamblee, James
Carpenter, Thos. W.
Cresswell, Sarah
Cook, William
Cummings, Harman
Cochran, Daniel N.
Clarke, Jno. B.
Clarke, Matthew
Carlisle, William
Cannon, Isaac
Deane, Aaron
Deane, Sam.-Estate
Dollar, William
Dobbins, James
Deane, Thomas
Dooley, Wm.
Dunlap, Matthew
Duncan, Robert
Davis, Aaron
Davis, Jno. L.
Daniel Mary (see page 11
of original return)
Davis, Moses
Duncan, David
Duckworth, James C.
Davis, William
Davis, L....?
Deane, Charles P.
Davis, Rachael
Durham, William
Durham, David
Dalton?, Burrell
Dalton, Smallwood
Dawson?, Solomon (Feb?)
Dowthet, James
Douthat, B. H.
Durham, Berry
Burham, William
Dalton, Boothe
Davis, Charles
Davis, James
Dickerson, Thomas
Dickerson, Willis
Dickerson, Robert
Duckworth, Joab?
Dalrymple, John
Duckworth, Thomas
Duckworth, Wm.
Daniels, W. C. D.
Driven?, James
Davis, Levy
Duckworth, Howard
Davis, Jesse
Davis, Elias
Dobbins, Martha
Duncan, Thomas
Dalrymple, John
Dove, John
Dawson, Samuel

Deane, Moses
Davis, Levy
Driven, James
Davis, E'h.?-Estate
Dickson, William
Dobbins, Jesse
Davis, Valentine
Dickson, John
Dickson, M.-Estate
Dupre, Ben.
Dupre, Ben. D.
Dart, Mary
Dalrymple?, James
Davis?, John
Gilman, James
Gentry, John
Gilland, Alex'd.
Gilmer, Robt.
Glenn, Wm.
Gentry, Lae.?
Gregg, Hugh
Gunning?, James
Gentry, Moody
George, Thomas
Green, Jno. R.
Green, John
Given, Lem. & 2 ch.
Gaillard, Theo.
Gable, Henry, Sr.
Gable, Levy
Greer, David
Gassaway, Ben.?
Gantt, James A.
Greer, Davis, Sr.?
Greer, Martha
Greer, John M.
Grubbs, George
G.....?, W. W.
Gantt, John W.
Gantt, Hugh
Gambrell, James
Gambrell, Sarah
Gantt, John
Gambrell, E. D.
Gantt, William
Gantt, John Y.?
Gambrell, Wm.
Gambrell, John
Gambrell, Will'm.
Gambrell, Barbara
Gambrell, Henry
Gambrell, Martin?
Griffin, Elijah
Griffen, John
Gambrell, James M.
Gentry, David
Gutty?, Nelson
Gibbs, Mary
Gambrell, George V.?
Gutrey, Ben.
Golding, John
Gambrell, Larkin
Gambrell, James
Gambrell, Rich.
Gambrell, Ezekel
Gram.....?, James J.?
Gibson, Thomas
Gurton?, Aaron
Gibson, William
G.....?, Thos. H.
Gibbs, Dr. A.J.?
Gantt, William
Grubbs, John M.
Gilbert, James
Gambrell, David
Grisham, Joseph
Gaillard, Rebecca
Gentry, John
Giles, Robt.
Gray, Hiz.?
Gray, Alex'd.
Greer, David
Greer, William
Gentry, A. B.

Gambrell, J. B.
Gambrell & Anderson
Guyton, Robert
Green, Solomon
Green, Thomas
Gentry, Daniel
Gentry, Reubin
Gentry, John
Gentry?, Allen
Green, Lemual
Gilmer, Nancy
Earle, John B.
Earpe, Wesley
Earle, Sam. G.
Earle & Lewis
Earpe, David D.
Edwards, Robert
Elrod, William
Elrod, Thomas
Emberson, Sam.
Earpe, Caswell?
Elrod, Thos. P.
Ellison, James
Ellison, Miles
Elrod, George
Estes, Larkin
Elliott, William
Elliott, William Jr.
Elrod, Sam.
Elrod, Geo. G.?
Elrod, Phillip
Elrod, Adam
Elrod, Isaac
Eskew, Elijah
Elrod, Elias
Earle, Dr. James W.
Elrod, William
Erskine, William
Elliott, Mary
Elrod, Jeremiah
Elliott, R. E.
Erskine, James
Erskine, John
Erskine, James
Erskine, Thomas
Emberson, James
Estes, Micajah
Eaton, Joseph
Eaton & Miller
Earle, Anne
Earle, G. W.?
Evans, Dr. Allen
Finley, Elias
Fisher, Sam. S.
Featherston, J. W.
Fant, Alfred
French, William
Fant, James B.
Fleming, James
Fleming, Richard
Ford, Alanson
Ford, Stephen
Ford, William
Felton, Mary
Fant, James
Floyd, Silas
Farrell, John B.
Fielding, Henry B.
Felton, Richard
Fisher, Sam. C.
Fowler, Ruth
Forsythe, William
Fant, A.
Fant, Abner
Fuller, Alfred
Fretwell, John
Fretwell, J. Y.
Franklin, E.
Fant, V. D.
George, James
Gordon, James
Gordon, Robert
Griffin, James C.
Gray, Huldah

336

Gaillard, W. H. D.
Gaillard, Charles I..
Gaillard, Jane H.
Gaillard, C. D.
Gibson, Thomas
Goode, L...?-Estate
Gaillard, Josiah D.
Hunter?, John
Humphries, John T.
Haslet, Jas. A.
Herndon, George
Herndon, Edmond
Herndon, Zeph'l.?
Hembree, A. B
Humphrey, David
Hall, Martin
Henderson, Martha
Hale, John
Howie, Robt.
Herrin, Francis
Harris, Sarah
Holmes, Henry
Hill, Thomas O.?
Honey, J. S.?
Harvin, Mark W.
Hardy, James
Hatton, William
Howell, Jackson
Harris, James
Hall, James A.
Haley, Reubin
Hall, John
Hanna, Thomas
Hill, Lemuel
Haney, Stephen
Hamilton, Luke
Harkness, R. C.
Harkness, John
Haney, John
Harkness, John N.
Hall, Wm. A.
Herrin, James
Hall, Fenton
Houston, Sarah
Hall, Lent
Hall, David
Hall, Joshua
Hall, Lent Junr.
Haney, Luke
Hill, Abram
Hopkins, John
Hunt, William
Hughens?, Robert
Hanks, Luke
Hanks, Thomas
Hinton, John
Hunt, John
Harper, John H.
Harper, Wm. C.
Hanks, Tilman
Hall, James
Harkins, Hugh
Henderson, James
Horton, Grief
Harper, Wm. Sr.
Harper, John
Holland, John
Hearkins, James
Holland, Aaron?
Hunt, Jeremiah J.
Hubbard, Wm.
Hamblen?, Dr. R.
Hunter, Sarah
Harrison, James
Hughs, John
Herrin, Levy
Herrin, Elijah
Herrin, Jesse
Hix, Meton?
Hix, Daniel
Hastie, John
Hubbard, Wm.
Hix, John

Harris, Joseph P.
Harris, Lucy
Hawkins, H.
Howard, Hiram
Hembree, James
Hall, Nancy
Harris, John
Hammond, Sam. J.
Harbin, Berry
Hall, Lae.?
Hamilton, John
Hipps, Joseph
Harrison, William
Harrison, James A.
Herrin, John
Hall, Wilson
Holland, Gracie
Hall, Joseph
Harris, Joshua
Harris, John
Hall, Ezekel
Harper, Asa
Hall, Aaron
Hendricks, David
Holland, William
Hembree, Willis
Hunt, Wm. S.?
Holly, Jane
Harris, Gillison
Hamm ond, B. T.
Hammond, Herbert
Harris, Benjamin
Harris, Jno.-Estate
Hall, John
Hall, Will'm.?
Hillhouse, Mary
Haslet, Moses
Holt, Jno. P.
Hinton, Wm.
Hembree, James Sr.?/Jr.?
Harris, Ezekel
Holland, Robert
Harrison, Thos.-Estate
Huger, Francis K.?
Harleston, Edward
Harris, Nath'l.-Estate
Houston, William
Humphries, David
Jones, Thomas
Jones, Jos. B.
Jennings, John
Johnston, Nancy
Johnston, Willis
Johnston, Allen
Johnston, Peter
Ingraham, Wm.
Jones, Ambrose
James, Pleasant
Jones, John
Irby, Charles
Jolly, Henry
Jones, Heartwell
Jones, Elizabeth
Isbal, Sam.? R.
Jones, Wilson
Ingram, Jno. H.
Johnston, Ben
James, Sam.
Jolly, Jane
Jolly, Joseph
Junkin, Robert
Johnston, Milley
Ingraham, James
Johnston, W. G.
Keys, Jno. M.
Kerr, Mary
Keown, William
Kennedy, Jas. H.
Keating, Wm.
Kay, Gabriel
King, James
King, Robt.
Kay, James W.

Kerr, William
Kay, Mason
Kay, James
Kay, Will'm. Senr.
Kay, Will'm, Junr.
Kay, Catharine
Kay, Jerusha
Kay, Fielding
King, Peter
King, Mary
Kelly, John
King, Josiah
Kelly, Elisha
Knox, John
King, Jno. D.
Kelly, Daniel
Knight, W. W.
Kay, Charles
Kay?, Alex'd.
King, Wm.
King, Hiram
King, Wm. P.
Kay, Silas
Kay, Strother
Kingsley, Christian
Keys?, Jesse
Keys, James C.
King, William
Keaton, Arch'd.
Kanauff, Wm. J.?
Kay, F. M.
Kitsinger, Jacob
Kay, John
Long, Harrison?
Ledbetter, Jas. S.
Ledbetter, Mary
Ledbetter, Jas. V.?
Lewis, R. B.
Lockheart, Dr. M. J.?
Lewis, Wm. A.
Latham, Cornelius
Long, Isaac
Lesley?, Robert
Leveret, John
Long, William
Leverett, William
Leverett, Thomas
Lattimer & Featherston
Lucius, Daniel Sr.?
Lucius, Dan'l.
Lee, James
Lee, Phillip
Lewis, James W.
Lewis, Major
Lewis, M. & Co.
Leboon, Joseph
Lawless, James
Long, Exekel
Looney, Jane
Lowrey, Jackson
Lewis, James O.
Lorton, Frances
Lorton, Jno. S.?
Lewis, Elisha
Linn, R.
Liveret, Stephen
Liverett, Wesley
Loveless, H...?
Latimore, W. B.
Loveless, Nathan
Linn, Garrison
Lewis, Elizabeth
Liggen & Motes
Lewis, Jesse P.
Liddell, A. J.
Linn, Alfred
Little, Rachael
Lewis, Eulener? Ealener?
Lewis, Jesse
Lewis, Sarah
McElroy, Arch'd.
McCroskey, David
McLease, James A.

337

McClarney?, Joseph
Mcpherson, Elijah
McPherson, Elizabeth
McCarley, Robt.
McLees, James
McConnell, Wm.
McLees, Andrew
McCollum, Jesse
Massey, Silas
McCarley, James
Metts?, Rebecca
McGee, Elias
McGill, Saml.
McGill, Ezekel-Est.
McGee, John
Mitchell, John
McCullough, Daniel
Martin, David
McAlister, Nathan
Mochett, Jacob
McGee, Willis
McGee, Jesse C.
McGee, Nancy
Mecklen, Hugh
McKee, William
McMahan, Saml.
McPhersson, Dorcas
Mecklin, A. P.
McAllister, Isaac
McKee, Archibald
McKee, Wm. A.
Morgan, John
McCurley, Wm.-Estate
McDonald, William
Melford, Mary
Milford, Phillip P.
McDowell, Wm. Senr.
McFall, Ibby
McCoy, Sam.
Mary Daniel (included in
the "D" section)
McAdam, John
Matteson, Olley
Moore, Jeremiah
McGee, Michael
Mattison, Nevil
Massay, Laban
Mattison, James
Mattison, William
Mattison, Wyatt
Mitchell, Ephraim
Mattison, Elizabeth
Mattison, Bayles H.
McCollum, Daniel
Murphy, John
Mayfield, Eph'm.
Major, Elizabeth-(name
scratched through)
McAllister, John
Moore, Grant A.
Major, William
McAllister, James
Martin, James
Murphy, Thomas M.
McAllister, Patsey
McAllister, John
Moore, James M.
Martin, William
Martin, Hester
Martin, Eliz'h.
Moore, Thomas B.
Murphy, Ezekel
Murphy & Martin
Moore, Elijah
Merritt, Josiah
Merritt, Obediah
McCann, T. H.
McCann & Walker
McKinney, Alex'd.
McMahan, Peter
Martin, Abram
McMurray, William
McMurray, Jane

Mulliken, James
McKinney, Martha
Mulliken, Benjamin
Mulliken, Ben. Sr.?/Jr.?
Mulliken, Will'm.
McElroy, John
Martin, Jacob
Meredith, Abram
Merritt, Benj.
McKay, Martin S.
McKey, Thomas
McCrary, Mary
Martin, Jesse
Miller, Crosby W.
Miller, John
McMurray, Wm. C.
Miller, Jane
Martin, Chesley
Matlock, Thomas
McConnell, Sam. F.
Mattison, Arch.
Major, James
Miller, Thomas R.
Martin, Geo. W.
May, T. W.
McCoy, James, Sr.
McPhail, John
Mattison, Mary H.?
Millwee, Sam'l.
Millwee, Will'm.
Massey, Kindred
Major, Daniel
McConnell, Thomas
McGregor, Miriam
Morehead, Alex'd.
Moore, Jane
McAllister, Andrew
McAllister, Marg't.
Massey, Abram
McMillan, Wyatt A.
Mitchell, Ben. H.
Martin, Sam.
McMurtrey, Wm.
McMutry, Rebecca
McCann, John
Major, James M.
Martin, Abram
Morris, James
Morris, John
Morris, Jesse C.
Martin, Sam.
Millar, Elias
McDonald, Henry F.?
Moore, Mary-Estate
McLeskey, James
May, Edmund
Moorhead, Maxey
Moorhead, John
Morris, David
McFee, Washington
Mills, Berry
Major, Elijah
McDowell, Mary
McGee, Wm.
Mayfield, Marg't.
McCoy, James
McFall, Sam.
McAllister, Nathan
Martin, John
McDonald, Wm.
McFall, John
Moore, John
Manning, George
McFall, A. N.
McGee, Burrell
Montgomery, Alfred
McDaniel, James
McCully, Stephen
Mason, J...?
McBride, James L.
Miller, M. T.?
Miller, Jno. C.
Miller, Patrick J.

Morris, Sam'l.
Mauldin, B. F. & Z.? C.
Maverick, Sam. & family
Maverick for R. M. Con...?
Major, John P.
McClure, Edward J.
Maw, John F.
Moore, Larkin
Maxwell, R. A.
Norris, E. S.
Nelson, W. R. N.
Newell, William
Norris, Jesse W.
Nichols, A. J.
Nichols, Arch'd.
Newell, George
Newell, Sam'l.
North, John S.
Newton, Isaac
Newton, Sam.
Newton, Will'm.
Newton, Willis
Norris, John E.
Nevett?, William
Norris, Robt. B.
Norris, Andrew P.
Obrient, William
Obarr, William
Owens, Thorton
Oldham, George
Oldham, John-Estate
Oldham, Thomas
Owens, Ashley
Owens, Lewis
Orr, William
Oliver, Andrew
Oliver, Martha
Oliver, James-Estate
Owens, Elijah, Jrn.
Owens, Elijah, Senr.
Owens, Martha
Owens, John
Owens, Will'm.
Owens, Daniel
Owen, Bannister
Oliver, James
Orr, Thomas
Overly, Nicholas
Owen, Hiram
Oliver, Wm.
Orr, Chris.
Orr, Jane B.
Pritchard, Lewis
Parker, Matthew
Partain, Hub.
Pettigrew, R. H.
Porter, Hugh
Presley, D. A.
Price, Penner?
Parker, Robt.
Parker, James
Pitts, Will'm.
Pruett, Wm.
Phillips, Reubin
Pettis, Jane
Poor, Sam'l.
Poor, Hugh
Poor, Mary
Poor, George
Poor, Will'm.
Poor, John
Poor, Jno. Senr.
Poor, Holland
Palmer, M.
Pickle, Wm.
Paine, Isaac W.
Phillips, Martin
Pickle, Jacob
Pegg, John?
Pegg, James
Pickens, Robert
Pickens, Eliz'h.
Pickle, James E.

Pilgrim, John
Paine, Jane
Pickerell, Jon'n.?
Pullem, Leroy?
Palmer, Will'm.
Pritchard, Cath.
Pullem, Will'm.
Pritchard, Wm.
Pike, Daniel
Pinkney, C. C.
Poole, Robt.
Posey, Harrison
Paggett, Eliz.
Peppen?, Elijah
Poole, Manning
Posey, Hub.
Prince, Richard
Prince, C. J.?
Passmore, Wm.- Estate
Pinkney, Thomas
Pickens, Thomas J.
Quails, J. B.
Richardson, Jas. W.
Rush, Hugh
Riley, Dan'l. E.
Reid, Will'm.
Reid, Eliza.
Reid, Hugh
Raimey, John
Reid, Robt.
Richards, W. C.
Roach, Henry
Roach, Benj.
Rampey, Jas. A.
Reed, Thos. L.
Reid, Henry
Rice, Amaz.
Robinson, J. J.
Ritchie, James
Rice, Hez.
Rutledge, Jesse
Robinson, Jno. B.
Reid & Acker
Reid, J. P.
Reese, Will'm.
Ragsdale? Ragsdal?, F.A.
Rodgers, Humphrey
Riley, Abram
Richardson, N. T.
Rodgers, Wm.
Rodgers, J..?
Richardson, Mathias
Rea, Elisha
Reeks, Wash'n.
Rosamond, J. H.
Rodgers, Simeon P.
Rankin, George
Robinson, David
Richardson, David
Richardson, Wade
Richardson, Nathan'
Rush, David
Rodgers, Ben.
Reid, Jesse
Rimmer, J. W.
Rodgers, Sarah
Russell, David
Ross, A. W.
Reese, Anne
Reese, Geo.-Estate
Reese, Thos. S.
Riley, Hez.
Rogers, W. W.
Rice, Ibzan
Rodgers, Jos.
Rodgers, Jno.
Reid, Andrew
Rogers, Eliz. B.?
Robinson, James E.
Robinson, Jno.
Rainwater, Job
Ritchie, Will'm.
Remmer, P. B.

Ritchie, Reubin
Rice, Jane
Rodgers, Wm.
Rice & Cater
Rice, Fleetwood
Rutledge, R. T.
Robinson, E. G.
Robinson, S. A.
Reeves, John
Robinson, Jeptha
Reese, H. L.?
Ramsay, John
Ritchie, Eliz.
Richards, Turner-Estate
Seawright, Andrew
Skelton, Zadoc
Seawright, Wm.
Stewart, James
Simpson, David
Sadler, David
Shaw, William
Skelton, Thomas
Skelton, Thos. T.
Shaw, Peyton
Skelton, Wm.
Shackelford, Jno. W.
Smith, Robin?
Simpson, F...?
Saunders, Jno.
Siddell, Stephen
Stevenson, John
Stevenson, Lem?
Stewart, Jno. Jr.
Stewart, Jno. Sr.
Simpson, Wm.
Sadler, David
Saunders, Abram
Siddle, Abner
Spearman, Jno.
Simpson, David
Simpson, Robt.
Simpson, James
Stacks, Willis
Smith, Sherod
Stifles, Mary
Shearand?, Wm.
South, L. N.
Scott, David
Sailors, Isaac
Sailors, John
Sailors, Abram
Sailors, Eliz.
Sailors, Leonard
Seawright, James
Strickland, M.
Smith, Rich'd.
Smith, David
Shirley, Obed.
Shirley, Jno. N.
Shirley, Eliz.
Shirley, Jno.-Estate
Shirley, Ben. E.
Shambley, Moses
Stone, George
Smith, A. W.
Strickland, Milley
Spray, Tom./Fom.?
Stringer, Eliz.
Smith, William
Smith, Wm. C.
Stanton, Cath.
Stanton, Mathias
Stone, James
Stone, Wm. H.
Smith, Basil
Spearman, D. D.
Spearman, Ben.
Spearman, Francis A.
Spearman, David
Smith, Joseph
Smith, Jno.
Smith, Geo. S.
Slaten, John

Slaten, Wm.-Estate
Stanton, George
Saterfield, Jer.?
Slaten, Loven
Sitton, W. D.
Siddall, John
Stone, Bannister
Shearman, Geo.
Sitton, Wm.
Sullivan, Thos. J.?
Smith, Thos. G.
Smith, James
Sprewell, Simeon
Smith, Simeon
Sherriff, Wash.
Smith, Ben.
Sharpe, John
Smith, Wm.
Smith, Wyatt
Sterling, James
Shirley, James
Smith?, Aaron
Sterling, Richard
Smith, Nimrod
Simmons, Chas.
Swilling, Sam.
Swilling, Geo.
Swilling, James
Simmons, Jno.
Stone, David
Simmons, David
Simmons, James
Smith, Stewart
Stanley, Ezek.
Shanklin, Jos. V.
Smith, Ben.
Smith, Wm. C.
Sharpe, Elam
Swords, Wm.
Swords, John
Swords, Jno.-Estate
Sitton, Jno. B.
Symmes, Dr. F. W.
Symmes, G. T.
Symmes, Susan
Starke?, Eliz.
Sloan, Jno. T.
Stevenson, John
Stevenson, Andrew
Stevenson, James
Snipes, Matthew
Smith, Jno.
Smith, A. S.
Stevenson, Geo.
Stegall, Spencer
Smith, Ebnez.
Scott, Eliz.
Simpson, Arch.
Stone, Hampton
Sherrill, Lewis
Smith, Robt.
Smith, Wm.
Shearer, Gillam
Skelton, John
Smith, Sam.
Shambly, Jas.
Saunders, William
Shearer, Andrew
Simpson, Richard
Sullivan, Kelly
Smith, Martin
Smith, Jesse R.
Smith, Hep.?/Lep.?
Steele, Nancy H.
Steele, James
Steele, Wm.
Steele & Gaillard
Smith, Whit.
Sloan, Ben.
Sloan, Benson & Sloan
Sloan, Susan
Shirley, Aaron
Smith, Aaron

339

Stevenson, Mary
Sherrill, Lewis, Jur.
Taylor, J. B. E.
Taylor, Joseph
Tilley, Mary
Taylor, James
Turner, James
Tucker, Bailley/Bartley?
Tucker, Reubin
Tate, Jno. A.
Tate, David
Taylor, Jas. H.
Tucker, James
Tucker, De..?
Tucker, John
Todd, Andrew
Thomson, Matthew
Thomson, Jno. M.
Trussell?, Hensley
Trussell, Posey
Towers, W. W.
Telford, Wm.
Telford, Isabella
Turner, Jno. B.
Telford, James
Tripp, Wm.
Tripp?, Nicholas
Tripp, Jno. Sr.
Tripp, John
Traynum?, Laz.
Thomson, James
Timms, Isaac
Timms, Elijah
Timms, Joseph
Tillinghast, Elias
Tomkins, Carter
Taylor, David S.
Thompson, Eliz.
Taylor, Thomas
Taylor, Wm.
Thacker, Edmond
Todd, Mary
Thompson, John
Thompson, James
Todd, J. L.
Tippens, David P.
Todd, James
Todd, John
Towers, Isaac R.
Tippens, Eliza.
Terry, Henry
Todd, Robert
Trussell, Rod.?
Tippens, Geo.
Taylor, Thomas
Towers, Dan-Estate
Tippens, Dennis
Vernon, J. T. W.
Valentine, Ben.
Vandiver, Paul
Vandiver, Thomas
Vandiver, Ibzan
Vandiver, Sanford
Vandiver, Aaron
Vandiver, Larkin
Vandiver, Manning
Vandiver, John
Vandiver, Asa P.
Vandiver, Harbin
Vandiver, William
Vandiver, John
Vandiver, Edward
Vandiver, Enoch?
White, M...?
Williford, S. W.
Williford, Sarah
Williford, Charles R.
Wilson, Lewis
Waters, Fleming
Winfield, Jno. B.
Wiley, James
Willis?, Freeman
Watts, Thomas
W...?, Mary

Whitman, Jacob
Winfield, Jas. R.
Wright, Lizzy
Willbanks, Elijah
Walls?, John
Walls?, James
Wright, R. N.
Williamson, Martin
Wright, Daniel
Wilson, George
Wyatt, Elijah
Williamson?, Wm.?
Webster, Jas. R.
Walker, Peter
Wardlaw, James
Wardlaw, Jno. M.
Willburn, Thomas
Williams, Mary
Wardlaw, Hugh H.
Wilson, James P.
Wilson, James B.
Wilson, Hugh
Wilson, Sarah
Willbourn, Wm.
Wilson, Barclay
Wilson, James
Willingham?, James
Wellbourn, Wm. E.
Welborn, Albert J.
Williams, Wm. J.
Wilson, Charles
Wilson, John
Wimpey, Levy
Wigginton, John
Wigginton, Henry
Wigginton, Geo. W.
Watkins, Bayles
Watkins, Temp.
Watson, James
Winters, Dinah
Wilson, Isabella
Wilbanks, Shadrack
White, Bartho.
Webb, Wm.
Welborn, Sarah
White, Thomas
Whitfield, Lewis
White, Newton
Wright, Larkin
Watkins, Felix
Walker, Wm.
Warley, Jacob
Warren, Samuel
Wilson, Rich'd. T.?F?
Waddell, Alex'r.
Warnock, James
White, Jona.
Whitmore, A. P.
Webb, Elisha
Watson, Willard
Wallace, Wilson
Warnock, Jno. Sr.
Warnock, Jno. Jr.
Webb, Clayton
Webb, C. B.
Watson, Ester
Williams, Jno.
Wilson, Wm.
Watson, Dan'l.
Wyatts, Jas. F.
Wright, John
Wilson, James
Wilson, James J.
Wellborn, Sarah
Wilson, Robert
Willingham, John
Wilson, Wm.
Wilson, Chas.
Watson, David
Wilson, Thomas
Watt, Mary
Webb, Warren R.
Wyatt, R. G.?

Webb, Dr. Edmond
Watkins, Joseph
Waddle, Hannah
Watson, Thos.
Werner, Wm.
Webb, Elijah
Whitner?, Jos. N.
Whitfield, Thos. T.
Williams, M. B.
Williams?, Jasper & New.?
Young, Jno.
Young, George
Young, Wm.
Young, Francis
Young, Francis A.
Yeargan, Sam'l.
Young, James

#

GENERAL TAX FOR 1840 COLLECTED BY DAVID SIMMONS TAX COLLECTOR FOR ANDERSON DISTRICT.

(Note: This section of the Tax book is very faded and difficult to read. Also has a few torn edges on left side of the pages...Ed.)

Arnold, Allen
Acton?, Margt.
Adams, John
Adams, Asa
Atkins, Henry?
Adams, Henry
Ashley?, ...sson
Ashley, John
Armstrong, ...
Armstrong, Ja..., Sr.
Alewine, Michael
Armstrong, Wm. B.
Adams, William
Alexander?, David
Armstrong, Jacj..?
Armstrong, Jno. B.?
Acker?, .. N.?
Acker, Halbert, Esq.
Acker, Amos
Adams, Jacob
Acker, J. S.
Acker, Susann? Benjamin?
Allen, Jas. E.
Avery, Wm.
Atkinson, Jas. H.
Atkinston, Aaron A.?
Abbott, John
Anderson?, Dr. Wm.
Amick?, Jno. D.?
Adams, Wm.
Anderson, B.? S.?
Acker, Wm.
Anderson, David
Acker?.....Wm. G.?
Acker?, A. P.?
Alexander, Wm. C.
Anderson, John
Anderson, L....
Anderson, Robert
A......, Saml.
Burns, ... Jr.
Bennett, C....?
Busby, George
Burris?, Thos.? Sr.
Burks, Thomas
Brown, John
Beaty, ...
Brooks, ...
Brooks, Wm.? T.?
Beaty, Lydia
Bozeman, ...
Brown, Charles?
Beaty, Wm.?
Bonds, Sugar (of Georgia)
Buchanan, Ebenezer?
Beaty, John, Sr.
Beaty, Francis
Buchanan, Wm.
Bull, James (Bell?)
Burton, Blackman
Burton, Peyton _? _?
Beaty, Thomas
Bowie, Charles
Bowie, Wm. H.?
Baron, Uriah?
Berry, Joel H.
Boyd, Robert
Burdit, Hiram
Brackenridge, R.....
Brown, S. H.?
Brown, Samuel
Brown, J... M.
Brock, Easton?
Bannister, Wm.
Brock, James, Esq.
Ballentine, George
Ballentine, R. E.?
Burch?, M. H.

Burch?, Hayden
Brownlee, L. L.?
Bagwell, John
Bridwell?, George?
Bagwell, Jas.?
Bridwell?, Jas.
Bagwell, James
Bradwell, Nancy
Broyles, Aron?
Brown, W. G.R.?
Brock, Enos?
Berry, Wm.
Brazeale, Kennon
Bennett, Thos.
Bennett, Wm.
Brazeale, H.? R.
Ballentine, Jesse F.?
Brazeale, Griffin
Bennett, Chas. M.
Brazeale, Enoch
Barkley, Jos.? M.
Brazeale, Williams
Brazeale, Martha
Brooks, Andrew
Briant, Simon L.?
Briant, Nathan
Briant?, Le...?
Barkley, Sarah
Barkley, Nancy
Bowen, Robert
Blassinghame, Robt. E.?
Blassinghame, Thomas
Brewer, Wiliam
Burgess, James
Bowden, J. G.?
Burns, Anderson?
Benson & Sloan
Bowden?, C. B.
Bowden?, C. B. & Co.
Blassinghame, S.? M.
Bishop, Nicholas
Bellotte, Jacob?
Burt, Francis
Broyles, ...
Burris?, John
Bruce, Chas.
Bowman, Achs.?
Banton, H. M.
Bradberry, Salathiel Jr.
Bradberry, Jesse
Bradberry, Wm.
Bradberry, James
Bailey, Allen
Brown, Robert
Brown, Larkin
Bruce?, Thos.
Bell?, Sam'l.
Baker, Saml. H.
Baker, Lindsey? A.
Brown, Randal? Rachel?
Brown, George
Bowen, Saml.
Brown, Elijah
Burris, Jacob?
Burris, Tilford?
Burris, Elizabeth
Burris, Elbert?
Burris, James
B...., Robt. B.
......, David
......, Danton?
Bohanan, J. W.?
B...., Jas. S.?
B...., Charles
Bettington?, Joshua?
B..... Elisha
B....., J. P.
B....., Reubin

Beaty, David
Bailey?, Wm.
Belotte, J....
Bell, Charles
Brown, Saml. Jr.
Brown, S......
B....., John
Brown, Catharine
Bruce?, Charles Jr.
Bruce?, John
Bass?, Leroy?
Bivan?, James
B..., Bar.....
B....., Saml.?
Bellotte, Peter E.
Barrett?, John
Brown?, Lesley
Bagwell, James
Chastian, John
Cater, A. P.
Carpenter, John
Carson?, Wm.?
Chastain, Stephen
Campbell, Daniel
Cochran., L.... H.
Clark, Joseph
Campbell, A....
Caldwell, John
Cannon, Epharmiah
Campbell, George
Caldwell, Wm.
Caldwell, Hugh
Connell, J.....
Cuningham, James
Cuningham, ...
Caldwell, ...
Corr?, Mary
Caldwell, James?
Christopher, J....?
Chalmers, Jos. C.?
Cummins, H......?
Cowen?, Hiram
Cook, Wm.
Criley?, Mary
Clinkscales, Abram?
Campbell, Jesse
Conner?, Dr.? J. M.
Carsey?, Nancy
Clinkscales, Wm. F.?
Carpenter, A. M.
Cunningham, Catharine
Clement, Hugh
Clement, C. M.?
Cobb, Martin?
Clement, Wm. H.?
Cox, Wm.
Cummin, ...
Cummin, Robert
Cornelius?, Abram?
Cullins, Caleb
Clement, Isaac?
Cowen, Wm.
Clinkscales, Wm. T.?
Cox, ...
Cobb, N....?
Cobb, Ephraim
Cox, Thomas
Cox, Wm. Sr.?
Clement, Stephen
Clement, Benj. Jr.__?
Clement, Benj. Sr.__?
Cox, Arris
Clement, Abram?
Cox, R. B.
Cox, John
Cox, Abner
Cox, Sarah
Cox, David

Chamblee, Moses
Cobb, J...H.?
Card..., Thos.
Cobb, Hampton
Cox, Gabriel
Caesar (of color...)
Cooley, James
Carter, Caleb
Cobb, Henry
Cobb, A. P.
Carter, Spencer
Clardy, J.... M.
Clardy, Norman.
Clardy, John Sr.
Clardy, Jno. B.
Childers, Moaham?
Chamblee, Nancy
Chastain, R....
Cason, Sarah?
Campbell/Crawford?,Russel
Cason, Jas. A.
Cason, Esk...
Campbell, James
Cox, Asa
Cherry, Saml-Estate
Cherry, T.? R.?
Cherry, Susan
Campbell, Arch.
Craig?, S....
Crenshaw?, Henry?
Cherry, David
Ca.... Eliz'h.
Ca...., Susannah
Cater, Edward
Cox, Jacob _? of Pickens
Coffin, A...
C....., Labon
Coates, John
Crawford?, James
Crawford?, Sarah
Chapel, John B.
Carpenter, Albert? _?
Carpenter Eliz'th.
Clinkscales, Berry/Benj.?
Cox, John
Cox, Beverly
Cannon, Isaac
Corley?, Lewis
Carlisle, Wm/
Corley, John
Chastain, Stephen
Chamblee, Ben...
Clark, Mathew
Chamblee, Jas.
Calhoun, Lewis? of ___
Clinks....., Levi
Co...g, Joseph
....
Clinkscales, Asa
Cobb, Jas.
Clark?, Jno. B.
....
......, James
Davis, Jesse
D....., Williamson
Dean, Obadiah
D...., Wm. of ....
Davis?, J....
D..., Moses?
Dunlap?, Mathew
Duncan?, Robert
Do..., John
Davis, Jno. L.?
Davis, Moses
Davis, Thos. M.?
Davis, Valentin?
Davis, Aaron
Duncan?, David
Duckworth, J. C.
Davis, Wm.
D..son, Sam?
Davis, Zach...?

Dean?, Chas. P.?
Durham, Wm.
Dalton, Booth
Dalton, Smallwood
Duckworth, Howard?
Duckworth, Jacob
Duckworth, Thos.
Dalton, Burrel
Douthit, J....
Dickson, Benj.?
Davis, Chas.
Davis, Arch.?
Durham, Wm.
Douthit, B....
Durham, Banajah
Dilworth?, B....
Dilworth?, Billy G.?
Durham, ...
Duckworth, J.....
Davis, James
D..., John
Dicki.., ...?
Dicki.., James
Dupre?, ...
Dupre?, C....
"   .....
Dart?, Mary ? ...
Daniel, ...
D....., Mo..is
Dalrymple, John
Dobbins, ...
Dalrymple, J....
Davis, Levi
Duncan, Thomas
Davis, F. H.?
Dalrymple, John
D..., James
Di..n, Maj. Wm.
Di..n, Elizabeth?
Der?, Geo. W.
Dobbins, Jesse
Dalrymple, ...
Dickson, W. C.?
Davis, Capt. Jno.
Dalrymple, Mary?
Dobbins, J...
Earpe, ... B.
Elrod, Elijah
Earp, Wesley
Earle, Saml.
Earp, Margt.?
Earp, David? D.?
Elrod, ..., Junr.?
Elrod, Wm.
Elrod, Thos. P.
Emberson, Samuel?
Emerson, James, Esq.
Ellison, Wm.?
Elliott, William dec'd.
Elrod, Isaac
Elrod, George
Elrod, Wm. H.
Elliott, Wm. dec'd.
Elrod, L....
Elrod, Philip
Elrod, Aaron?
Elrod, Elias?
Ellison, James
Estes, Micajah
Earle, Dr. Jno. H.?
Elrod, Geo. G.
Elrod, J...
Elrod, William
Erskine, Wm.
Erskine, James
Eaton, Jno.?
Eaton & Miller
Elliote, Mary
Ellison, Miles
Erskine, Thos.
Erskine, John

Eskew, Wm.
Earle, Elias
Estes,? Larkin?
E..., ...?
Erskine?, James
Findley?, Chas.?/Elias?
Featherston?, J. H.?
Fant, Alfred
Flo..., ...?
French?, Wm.?
Fant?, J...?
Flinn?, Richard
Fant, Jas. B.?
Fleming, John C.?
Fleming, James
Floyd, Silas
F..., Wm.
F.... Adamson
Ford, Stephen?
Franklin, Eliza Ann?
F....., ...?
Fuller?, Alfred
Fielding, Henry?
Fe...., Mary
Fant, Jas. N.
Forsyth, William
Fisher, S.... T.?
Fisher, Thos. dec'd.
Fisher, Saml. C.
Fant, Wm. N.
Fant, Abner
Fant, W. D.
Fowler, Ruth?
Fant, ...
Fretwell, John
Fretwell, J. Y.
Gilmer, Robt.
Garrison?, Levi
Gilliland, Alex'r.?
Gilmer, Saml. Esq.
Gilmer, Nancy
Glenn, Wm.
Grigg?, H....
Gentry, Mosby?
Gentry, Eli'th
Gentry, Zach'h
Gallaway, Mathew
George, Thos.?
Gentry, John
Giles, Robt.?
G..., John P.
G..., Jno.
Gable, L...
Gray, A. D.
Gassaway, Benj.?
Gassaway, Jas. _?
Gable, Henry Sr.
Gable, Henry Jr.
Gilbert, Amos
Gailard, J. _?
Gailard, Anne
Gailard, M...
Gantt, Jno. ...
Grubbs, Geo.?
Gree_, John
Green, J... W.?
Green, D... Jr.
Gantt, R...
Gantt, Wm.
Gambrell, James
Gray?, Huldah
G......, David
Gambrell, Wm.
Gambrell, Sarah?
Gambrell, C. B.
Gantt, Jno.
Gantt, Jno. G.
Gambrell, Matthew
Griffin, Elijah
Gambrell, D. H.
Gambrell, Henry
Gambrell, John
Gambrell, ...

342

Gambrell, Wm.
Gambrell, Barbary?
Griffin, J...
G...., H....
Gambrell, G...
Guttrey?, Posey?
Guttrey?, Nelson
Gambrell, Jas.?
Gambrell, Gabriel/Ezekiel?
Gambrell, James Jr.
Gibson, J....
Gibbs, Mary
Ga....., Reid
Guyton, Robert
Guyton, Aaron?
Gambrell, J. B.
Gailard, Chas. L.?
Gailard, C. L.?
Gailard, C. L. & C. D.
Gailard, W. H. D.
Gailard, Rebecca
Grant, Wm.
Griffin, J. C.?
Gaillard, Sherard Sr.
Gibbs, ...
Grubbs, ...
Geer?, J......
Guttry, David
Gentry, A. B.
Gantt, Jas. ...
Gentry, ...
Geer, Thos.?
Geer, David
Gantt, Thos. H.
Gunnin, ...
Gentry, Daniel
Gentry?, Arthur?
Garrett, Osborn?
George, James
Gordon, Robert
Gray, Hezekiah
Gorden, Saml/James?
Golden, John
Gentry?, Rerden?
Gambrell?, David?
Goode, Lewellen, dec'd.
Hailet?, James, dec'd.
Hix, John
Hillhouse, Jos.
Hembree, Azariah _?
Haygood?, Simpson
H...y, Charles
Hurt?, Wm. L.?
Hale, John
Henderson, Martha
Ha..., Joshua
Herndon?, George?
Haslet, Moses W.
Herring, ////
Herndon, Edmund
Humphries, David
H..l..s, Henry
Hall, Lent, Jr.
Hall, Fenton, Jr.
Hodge?, ... H.
Howard, Moses
H..., D...d
Howard, Hiram
H..., Martin
H..., John
H..., Jno. L.
Harris, Nathan
Hattan, Wm.?
H....ch.s.., _?
Harris, Alonzo
H..., M...
H..ndy, James
H..ndy, _ B.
Howie?, Robert
Hill?, Thos. C.?
H..., John
Hamilton?, J...
Hamilton?, Jane

Hamilton?, Nancy
Hall, Ezekiel
Harris, Thomas
Hall.., Wm. __?
Harkness, ...
Hall, Jno. B.
Hall, J.....
Harkness, John
Hall, Samuel?/ Lemuel?
Haynie, Stephen
Heron, John
Hall, Lent Sr.?
Hunt, ...
Hall, Nacy
Harris, John
Hanks, Luke
Hanks, Thos.
Hopkins?, John
H..., Robert
Hopkins, Jas. M.
Hopkins, W. S.?
Haynie, Luke
H..., John
Hinton?, ...
Hanks, Tilman
Harper, Wm. C.
Harper, Jno. H.
Harkins?, James
Harkins?, Hugh
Ha....., Wm.
Holland?, John
Holland?, Wm. B.
Harten?, Grief
Holland, J..., Jr.?
Harris, ...
Holland, Aron?
Hunt, Jos. J.?
Harper, John Sr.?
Harper, John, Jr.
Hains?, Robt. G.
Ham....s.n, Cyrus? E.?
"   , D. K.?
Hunter?, Sarah
Haselton/Hareleston?,Edward
Ha......, Thos. dec'd.
H....., Susan
"   , John
". Andrew
Harper, Asa
Hall, J. E.?
Holland?, Wm.
Harrison, Jas.
Herring, Elijah
Herring, Jesse
Herring, Levi
Holland, Wm.?
Harris, J. P.
Holly, Fredrick
Hix, Daniel
Hix, Milton
Holland, Robert Jr.?
Hughes, Benj. P.
Harris?, Lieut.? G. J.?
Harbin, A. B.
Holley?, ...
Herring?, David?
Harris, T. ?
Hall, Wm. B.
Harris?, Eli... E.?
Hall, Joseph
Hamilton, John M.?
Harrison, Wm.
Harris, Dill...?
Harrison, Jos....
Hall, ...
Hipps?, J...
Hammond, Herbert
Hembree, Willis
Hanks, Polley?
Harkins?, Wm. P.
Hasey?, R. & P. G...?
Hillhouse, Macy

Hammond, B. F.
Hall, Wilson
Hunter, John
Haslet?, Albert
Hix, Bailey?
Heron?, Jos.?
Houston, Sarah
Hammond, T.? J.
Harkness, Robt. C.
Holland?, B. F.
Haynie, John
Hinton, Wm.
Hembree, James Jr.
Hembree, Jas. Sr.
Hunter?, ...
Hamilton, Leonard?
Hug.., ?, ?.
Jones, Jos. B.
Jones, Thomas
Jennings?, Jane
J...., Cler....
Johnson, Willis?
Johnston, P...
Johnson, Nancy
Ingram, William
Jones, Ambrose
Jones, John
Johnson, Allen
Irby, Charles
Jones, Wm.
Jones, Wilson
Jenkins, Wm. L.
Isbell, Sarah
Jones, Eliz'th
Jones, Harbert?
Isbell, Saml.?
Jolley, Jos. M.
Jolley, Henry
Jolly, James
Jeffres, Nathan
James, Saml.
Johnson, Willis?
Johnson, Milly
Johnson, W. G.
Ingram, James
Keown, William
Karr/Kerr?, Mary
Kay, Gabriel
Kay, ... M.
K.., James
Kay, Miss? S. N.?
Kingsley, Chester?
King, Peter Jr.?
King, Mary K.
K...., Wm.
Ka.., J.....
Keys, Jno. M.
King, Josiah
King, Wm. Jr.?
King, Wm. P.?
King, Jas. H.?
King, Catherine?
King, Mason ?
King, James?
King, Fielding?
King, Rev. Wm.?
(all the above King names
may be KEY..Ed.)
King, Geo. W.?
Knox, John
King, Robert
Kelly, Elisha
King, Wm. T.?
Kelly, Jno.?
Key, Jos. H.?
Kelly, Al...
King, John _?
Kelly, Daniel
Knight, ...
Kay.., Alexander?
Kay.., Charles
Knauff, W. J.
Kirksey, ...?

King, Wm. Sr.?/Jr.?
King, Wm. P.
King, Solomon
King, Hiram
His..., A...
Kay, Jesse
Kay, John
King?, Robt R.? (Keyes?)
Keyes?, Jas. C.
Kin...?, Henry
Ledbetter, Mary
Ledbetter, James
Long, Harrison
Larkin?, Cornelius
Lockhart, M. J.
Lockhart, Thomas
Liverett, Stephen Jr.?
Liverett, John
Liverett, Thos.
Liverett, Stephen, Sr.?
Long?, Wm.
Long?, Isaac
Latham?, Wm.
Little, Ra.....
Li...., Wm.
Lee, Philip
Loveless, ...
L....., Danl. N.? Jr.?
"   "   Sr.?
"   , Jas. S.
Lee?, James
Lewis, Jas. W.?
La...., Jos. (Laboon?)
La''''. Eady
Long, Ezekiel
Lewis, Sarah
Lewis, J. O.
Lewis, Jesse
Lorton, J... S.?
Lorton, Francis?
Lorton & Pink/Kirksey?
Looney, James
Long?, Jackson
Lewis, Elisha
L..., B...
Lewis, Robert
Lewis, Elizabeth
Li_ett, Wesley
Latimer, W. B.
Liddle, Andrew J.
McCardy, James
McLees?, ...
McLees, Andrew
....
McCol....., ...
Mosley?, ...
McCann,.....
McLees, ...
McLees?, Margt.
Moore,....
McGee, Elisha?
McC...., J....
"   , Rbt.
McGee, John
McAllister?, Nathan?
McConnel, ...
McMahan, ...
Mitchell, J.. C.?
McGee, Will..
McC..., Robert
Martin?, David
McGill, Wm.?
McGill, Sarah
McGill, Ezekiel
McKee?, James
Milford, Mary
Milford, John
Milford, J.. L.
Mouchet, Jacob
McKee, A....
McKee, Wm. A.
McCol..., J. D.?
Morgan?, John

McCurdy?, Sarah
McAlister, Nathan?
McAlister, Andrew
McPhail, John
Madison, Mary H.
Murray?, Margt.
McFall, Phebe?
McGee, Wm.
Mayfield, Margt.
McCoy, Saml.?
McCoy, John H.?
Massey, Lab...?
Moore, Je....ah
Mattison, Olley?
McCoy, Jas.
McAdams, John
May, Daniel
Mitchell, Ephraim
McF.., M.....
Matison, A....
Matison, Nevel?
McCol..., Daniel
Mattison, Wyatt
Mattison, James
Mattison, Daniel
Mattison, Wm.
Mattison, Baylis H.?
Mattison, Eliz'th
Major?, Elijah Jr.
Major?, Daniel
Major?, Wm.
Mayfield, Ephraim
McCollister, James
Martin?, James
Martin?, Wm.
Martin?, Hester?
Murphy, Ezekiel E'sq.
Murphy, Ezekiel & Co.
McCollister, ...
M..., J... M.
Martin?, Jacob
Murphy, Thos. H.
McKinney, M...
Murphy, John
M..., Thos. B.
M..., _. Y.?
M..itt, Obadiah
M...., Elijah
McColister, John
McCann, Thos. H.?
....
McCollister?, M.....
McMahan?, Peter
Mulliken?, ...
McMurry, William
McMurry, Jane W.
Martin?, Abram
Mulliken?, Wm.?
Mulliken?, Benjamin
McElroy, John
Mulliken, Benj. Sr.
McMann?, Wm.? C.
McKinney, Alex'r.?
Masters, G. H.
Martin, Chesley?
Martin, Abram
Martin, Jesse?
Martin, Edw'd.? Jr.
Major, Jno. P.
Morris?, Samuel
Miller, M.? T.
Major, Jos. M.
Melton?, Mich'l.
Maverick?, Sam. & sons?
""""   ? ....
McElroy, Arch.
Maxwell?, Robt. A.
McCrary, M... M.?
Miller, John C.
Miller, Charles?
Moore, Eli
Miller, Jane
Maw?, Jno. _?

Martin, Mathew
McGee, Jesse L.
Merritt, B. W.?
Meredith, Abrah'm?
Miller, John
M...y, Kindred
McMillian?, Wyatt
Martin, Saml.?
McCl..., E. J.?
McLesky, Jas.
Moore, Leah
McGrigger, John
McGrigger, Mary
McPherson, Eliz.
McKee, Wm.
Moore, John
Moore, Frank...?
Moorehead, Ma..y
Martin, M..Can.. Esq.
Moorehead, John
Massey, Abram
McMurphy?, Wm.
McMurphy?, Rebecca
Massey, Jos. E.?
Mitchell, J...
Maddox, J...
McFall, John?
Martin, ...
Martin, Wm.?
Martin, Samuel
May, Edw'd.?
May, L... W. ?
McLees,Washington?
Major, James
Major, Elijah?
M....., P....?
....
McDaniel, Geo.?
........, Benj.?
McConnel, Thos.?
M..l..se, Wm. dec'd.
Moore, Larkin?
Maulding, B. F.....
Mauldin, D. T.?
Maulding, J. L.?
McFall, Saml. R.
McCollister, Margt.
Moorhead, Alenr...?
McPhail, Peter
Major, Enoch
Moorehead, S....
Mar...., Hugh?
M..., Benj.?
McCully, Stephen
McPherson, Dorcas
Maxwell, John
McFall, ...
McGee, Burrell
McGee, J...., dec'd.?
M...., James
....
Miller, Elias
N...., E. L.?
Newell, Wm.
Norris, J. W.
Nichols?, Arch.? J.
Nichols, Wm. A.
Nichols, Arch.
Nichols, Js. C.?
Newton, ...
Newton, Willis?
N....., J... L.
Newton, Leml.?
N....11, Geo.
"   , Saml.?
Norris, Jno. E.
Nivett?, Wm.
Norris, Robt. D.
Norris, A. O.
Nelson, Jas. O.
Obriant, William
Obriant, Jos.
Owen, ...

Owen, Elijah
Owen, Daniel
Owen, Lewis
Oldham, Geo. dec'd.?
Oldham, John
Orr, Wm.
Owen, Ashley
Oliver, Martha
Owen, Jno.
Owen, Martha
O...., Elijah
O...., B....
O...., James
O...., Thos.?
Overby?, Nicholas?
Oliver, Andrew?
Orr, C...
Orr, J.... B.
Oliver, James, dec'd.?
Parker, William
Pressley, ...
Partain, Hubbard
Pressley, A...
Pettigrew?, Robt. H.?
Porter, ...
Posey, ...
Parker, J.....
Pitts, ...
P..tt., Wm.
Pearman, Benj.
Pearman, ...
Phillips, Reiben
P....., Geo.
Pitts, J...
Poore, Holl...
Poore, John
Poore, Anna
Poore, Saml.
Poore, John-deceased
Poore, Wm.
Pepper, Elijah
Pickel, William
Palmer, Massey
Pickel, Jas. E.
Pegg, Jas. B.
Pickel, Jacob
Philip, Martha
Pickens, Robert
Pickens, Eliz.
Pegg, John
Passmore, Wm.-dec'd?
Pinkney, Thos.
Pickens?, T. _?
Pal..., Wm. _
Payne?, Jane
Pritchard?, Jon.
Pullam, Leroy
Poole, M.....
P....., Pen...l
Padget, Eli'th
Poole, Eliz.
Parker, Robert
Prichard, Wm.
Pullem, Wm.
Posey, Washington C.
P..., C. J.
" , Richard
Prichard, Lewis
Philips, John
Posey, Ha......
Patrick, Thos. D.?
R....., John
Robison, Jeptha?
Rodgers, Nancy & daughter?
Ryley?, Daniel? E.
Rice, ...
Rice & Cater
Rodgers, Wm.
Richardson?, M... L.
Richardson?, Wade H.?
Richardson?, Wm.
Richardson?, Mary L.
Richardson?, James?-dec'd.

Rice, Wm. (Reid?)
Reid, Eliz'th
Rush, Hugh
Reid, Rcbert
Rainy?, John
Reid, Hugh
Roach, Henry
Roach, Berry
Robison, John
Randon?, Wm.
Ried, Andrew
Richards, W. C. & James?
Richardson?, Green?
Rutledge, Jesse
Rolinder?, J. J.?
Rampy, J....
Rice?, Hezekiah?
Rice?, John L.?
Ruff, ...
Rolinder?, John
Rolinder?, Jas. E.
Rolinder?, ...
R..., Lewis R.
Ritchie, Newton
R..., Wm.
Reid, Henry
.....
Reid, Alfred E.
Reid & Acker
Reid, J. N.?
Ragsdale, Francis
Roberts, Matthias?
Ragsdale, D... J.?
Rodgers, Eliza B.?
Ryley?, Abraham
Rodgers, John
Rodgers, Benj.?
Rodgers, Wm.
Richardson, Noah
Rodgers, Wm. W.
Rodgers, J...
Rea, Elihu?
R..., Wellington?
Richmond?, John
R........, Mathew
Rodgers, J... P.
Ritchie, Wm.
Rankin?,...
(Note - The rest of page
16 of original tax book
is unreadable...Ed.)
Page 17 of original book:
Shirley, Eliz'th
Smith, Richard
Strickland, Matthew
Shirley, Obadiah
Saylors, Leonard
Saylors, Ab....
Saylors, Elizabeth
Shirley, Jno. N.
Seawright, Jas.
Shirley, Benj.
Saylors?, John
Shaw, Vincent
Stone, Hampton
Smith, Wiley C.
Smith, Arthur W.
Smith, J....
Stone, Geo.
Stone, Wm. H.?
Sp...., Thos.
Stone, James
Strickland, Milly
Slaten, Jno.
Spearman, D... T.?
Smith, B....
Spearman, David
Spearman, F.? A.?
Spearman, Benj. F.?
Smith, Philip P.
Smith, Geo. S.?
Satterfield, Jacob?
Slaten, Loven

Sitton, Wm. D.
Sitton, Wm.
Smith, Jos.
Smith, Thos. G.?
Siddall, John
S...man, George
Smith, James
Smith, John
Smith, J. C. & Jesse?
Sp...ll, Simeon?
Smith, Jos. _?
Smith, J.. E.
Smith, Andrew
Sheriff, Washington
Smith, Benj'm.
Smith, Simeon
Sharp, John
Stanton, George
Sherrill, L..., Jr.
Sherrill, Levi - dec'd.
Smith, Wm. N.?
Smith, Wyatt
Shirley, James
Shirley, Richard?
Simpson, Richard?
Shanklin, J. _?
Sloan, B. F.?
Pendleton Manufacturing
    Co.
Sloan,.....
Smith, Bej.
Smith, Wm. C.
Sloan?, Jno. T.
Sloan, ...
Sloan?, Nancy
Swords, Jno. S.?
Steele, Nancy H.
Sharp, Elam, Sr.?
Steele, Eli'th G.
Steele, James?
Sitton, ...
Symmes, Dr. .....
(Note - Most of page 18
of original book faded.)
Taliferro, Caroline N.
Taylor, David ..
Tippen, Eliz.?
Todd, Andrew
Taylor, Jos. Jr.
Thompson, John
Taylor, Jos. Sr.?
Tippen, D....
Todd, James
Todd, John
Tate, Nan?
Taylor, Thos.
Tippen, George
Taylor, Jno. B.
Todd, Jno. L.
Towns?, D. R.-dec'd.
Taylor, Thos.
Tippen, Mathew L.?
Tillinghast, Elias H.
Vernon?, Jas. H.?
Valentine, Benj.
Vandiver, Paul
Vandiver, Thos. E.
Vandiver, Ibzan
Vandiver, Larkin
Voyles, Amos
Vandiver, Sanford
Vandiver, Aaron
Vandiver, Mourning?
Vandiver, John
Vandiver, Asa P.
Vandiver, Edward
Vandiver, Enoch
Vandiver, Wm.
Vandiver, John Jr.
Webb, Clayton
Williford, Saml. R.
West, Isaac
Wilson, Lewis

345

Winfield, Jno. B.
Winfield, Jas. R.
Willbanks, Elijah
Watters?, Ibzan
Watters?, Fleming
Whitman, Jacob
Watt, Thos.
Watt, John
Wiley, James
Watt, Mary
Wright, Eliz'th
Watt, Mary Sr.
Watt, James
Wiles, Sim.....-dec'd.
Wiles, Eliz'th
Wiles, Jas. H.
Wiles, Jesse
White, Ezekiel
Wakefield, Conrad?.
Wyatt, Jas. F.
Wright, Wm. F.
Williamson, Wm.
Wright, Robt.
Williamson, David
Weldon?, Wm.
Weldon?, Crennan?
Wright, James
Williams, Jas. C.
Williamson, Hester?
Wade, Edward Sr.?
Wilson, Geo.
Wright, James
Wyatt, Elijah
Welcher?, Jas. R. dec'd.
Wyatt, R. G.
Williamson, Jno. C.
Walker, Peter
Wardlaw, James
Welborn, Thos.
Willingham, James
Willingham, John
Wardlaw, J...M.
Williams, Jasper
Wardlaw, Hugh H.
Wilson, Hugh
Wigington, John
Wiginton, George
Wilson, Jas. J.
White, Robert
Welborn, Wm.
Welborn, Albert G.
Wilson, Jas. B.
Willbanks, Jas.
Woodson, Wm.
Williams, Micajah B.
Wilson, Sarah?
Wil..., Wm. E.
Williams, J.... C.
Wigington, Henry
Wilson, Jos. P.
Wilson, Barkley?
Williams, W. A.
Wimpey, Levi
Wilson, John
Wilson, Charles
Wilson, Wm.
Williams, John
Watson, James
Wilson, Wm.? M.
Westfield, David
Watkins, David
Wilson, James
Webb, Wm.
Willbanks, Shadrack
Willbanks, Thomas
Wellbourne, Sarah
Willbanks, Hezekiah
Warnock, James
Wilson, Rev. James
Watson, Willard?
Watkins, Bayles
Watson, Thos.
Warley, Sophia

Wa....., Samuel?
Waller, Wm.
Watkins, Peter?
Wilson, R. T.?
Walker, J. P.?
Watkins, Jos.
Warley & Sharp
Winter, Dinah
Whitfield, Lewis
Webb, Elisha
White, Newton
Wright, Catharine
Webb, James
Watson, J. M. B.
White, Bartholomew
White, Jon'n.
Wallace, Wilson
Warnock, John Jr.
Warnock, John Sr.
Watson, David
Waddill, A. H.
Webb, W. R.
Wilson, Robert
Webb, C. B.
Whitmore, Andrew
Webb, Edward?
Webb, Elijah
Wilson, Chas.=dec'd.
Wilson, Thos.
Woodward, Wm.
Whitefield, J. T.
Whitner?, Gen'l. J. N.
Williford, Sarah
Williford, Chas. R.
Watson, Danl. R.
White, Julia
White, Thomas
White, Henry N.
Wright, John
Waddill, Hannah?
Whitworth, Chas. H.
Yeargan, Sarah?
Young, Wm.
Young, Thos.
Young, Francis?
Young, _? A.
Young, James

CAPATATION TAX?

Reid?, Jane
Rouse?, Lucinda
Willams?, C.....
Calhoun, A....
Mason, James
P..ter?, Frances & _ ch
Quinn, Jefferson
Quinn, C..... A.?
Quinn, Polly C.
Washington, John J...
Wilson, Robert & wife

IN OTHER DISTRICTS:

Maverick, Samuel A. & son
"   , Saml. A. & two daus.

ST. PHILIPS ....:

Gibbs, A. L.?

PICKENS:

Washington, ... J.
Johns, Ann?
Whi....., Wm.
Russel, David
Fretwell, John
Wilson, Robert
Dupree, C. P.
Carnes, Eliz'th
Green, John
......, Adam-dec'd.

Washington, Jno. .....
Shanklin, T.? N.
Grant, Wm.
Fielding, Henry
Miller, Jno. C.
Miller, Charles
Berry?, Wm.
Greenlee, Jos.
McCann, Thos. H.
Hubbard, Wm.
Boatner?, ...
Anderson, Wm.
Miller, C..... J.
Gantt?, T. J.

ABBEVILLE:

Harleston, Edward
Smith, Benj.
Smith, Wm. C.
Dickson, Thos.
Pitts, Wm.
Ruff, David
Walston?, Jas. R.-dec'd.
Miller, Chas.
Stiefle, Mary
Mouchet, Jacob

GREENVILLE

Maxwell, Robt. A.
Seaborn, Geo.

ST. JAMES SANTEE:

W...on, Saml.?
Gaillard, Theodore?

GEORGTOWN:

Warren, Saml.

ST. STEPHENS:

Gaillard & Larkin?

#

346

TAXES COLLECTED BY DAVID SIMMONS 1841 IN ANDERSON:

Anderson, M.?
Acker, William
Archer, Wm. M.
Anderson, David
Anderson, John
Amick, John D.
Anderson, Dr. Wm.
Avery, William
Acker, Amos
Acker, P. N.
Acker, P. N. & J. S.?
Ashley, John
Acker, Joshua S.
Acker, Susannah
Allen, James E.
Acker, Halbert
Armstrong, Wm. B.
Armstrong, James
Ashley, Wilson
Ashley, John
Armstrong, Arch'd.
Alexander, David
Alexander, H. C.
Armstrong, John
Armstrong, James
Adams, William
Armstrong, Jno. B.
Adams, John
Adams, Henry
Adams, Asa
Atkins, Henry
Atkinson, James H.
Abbot, John
Anderson, Martha H.
Anderson, G. T.
Anderson, Robert
Alewine, Michael
Arnold, Allen
Barton, H. M.
Bradbury, Salathial
Bradbury, James
Bradbury, Jesse
Bradbury, William
Bailey, Allen
Betterton, Joshua
Burress, Thos. Sr.
Barrett, Charles
Buchanan, Samuel
Bowman, Archibald
Broyles, John L.?
Belle, Samuel
Brown, Robert B.
Burgess, James
Brazeale, Griffin
Bennett, Thomas
Ballentine, J. H.
Bennett, Charles
Brock, Enos.
Bennett, William
Brazeale, Kennon
Brazeale, Matthew
Barkley, Nancy
Barkley, Josiah M.
Barkley, Sarah
Brazeale, D. K.
Brazeale, W.
Brock, Andrew
Brazeale, Enoch
Brown, Dr. G. R.
Broyles, Aaron
Bagwell, James W.
Bagwell, James
Braswell, Nancy
Braswell, George
Bagwell, John
Ballentine, George
Braswell, James
Brackenridge, Robt.
Brock, James
Brown, Lesley
Banister, William

Brownlee, Maria
Brock, Hayden
Braswell, Asa
Brock, M. H.
Brown, Saml. F.
Brown, Lidy H.
Browne, J. M.
Bowie, Charles
Beaty, William
Beaty, Samuel
Beaty, Francis
Boyd, Robert
Blankenship, Wm.
Buckanan, William
Bucanan, E.
Beaty, John
Beaty, Thomas
Baron, Uriah
Bowie, Wm. H.
Burdett, Hiram
Burton, Blackman
Burton, Peyton T.
Browne, Abner
Beaty, David
Brown, Charity
Bozeman, Lewis
Brown, Charles
Branyan, J. J.
Branyan, Henry
Brooks, Thomas
Burress, Thos. Jr.
Brooks, Wm. T.?
Brooks, Garner
Baker, Samuel H.
Beaty, Lidia
Bennett, Cooper
Burns, John
Brayant, Nathan
Bryant, Simon T.?
Bryant, Teril
Blasinghame, Thos.
Bowen, Robert
Blasingame, Robt.
Brewer, William
Blasingame, Mrs.? S. H.?
Bishop, Nicholas
Benson, E. B. & Co.
Benson & Sloan
Benson, E. B.
Bellotte, Jacob
Brown, Randolph
Burns, Anderson
Burt, Frances
Bowden, J. G.
Brown, Elijah
Burris, Jacob
Burris, Elizabeth
Baron?, John
Belle, James H.
Burris, James
Burris, Joshua
Barrett, John
Burris, Elbert
Brown, Daniel
Benson, John P.
Benson, J. P. & Wynn?
Bowen, Samuel
Bellotte, Peter E.
Bellotte, J. L.
Bruce, Thomas
Browne, Catharine
Brown, Robert
Browne, Larkin
Bruce, Charles Jr.
Brown, Samuel
Bee, Mrs. Ann
Bee, Miss Maria
Bailey, Isaac S.
Burt, Moody
Berry, Joel H.
Bruce, John

Broyles, O. R.
Baker, Lindsey A.?
Browne, Danton?
Barksdale, John
Burris, Elisha
Burris, Milford
Berry, William
Browne, George
Burris, Reuben
Bailey, William
Bruce, Charles Sr.
Cord?, Laban
Coffee, Hley?
Coffin, Abraham
Campbell, George
Conwell, Isaac/James?
Caldwell, John
Campbell, Alexander
Caldwell, Joseph
Caldwell, Hugh
Cater, Edward
Cummings, Harmon
Carpenter, Albert L.?
Carpenter, Elizabeth
Cannon, Ephraim
Campbell, David
Campbell, William
Creswell, Sarah
Cooley, Lewis
Campbell, James
Cox, Asa
Cox, Sarah
Cox, Joseph
Cox, Rachel & Sisters
Cox, Joseph & Lewis
Ceasar (Colored)
Cooley, James
Carder, Thomas
Chamblee, Moses
Cummings, David
Cobb, Hampton
Clinkscales, Wm. F.?
Cox, William
Corr, Mary
Chapel, John B.
Caldwell, James
Christopher, John
Caldwell, William
Cunningham, Thos.
Cunningham, Saml.
Cox, Beverly
Coates, John
Cason, J. A.
Cason, Sarah
Cason, Esther
Cason, Wm.
Carter, Caleb
Cobb, Henry
Cobb, A. P.
Cobb, J. W.
Clardy, John
Clardy, Joab
Clardy, Norman
Cates?, Spencer (Cater?)
Chambers, Nancy
Clardy, John B.
Cooper, Washington
Crawford, Russell
Cannon, Isaac
Craig, Samuel
Cherry, T. R.
Cherry, Saml.
Campbell, Arch'd. & Co.
Christian, E. C. B.
Carne, Miss S. M.
Carpenter, Alfred M.
Crawford, James
Clarke, John B.
Cox, Abner
Clements, Wm. K.
Cox, Aris

347

Cox, Wm. Sr.
Cox, Wm. Jr.
Cox, John
Cox, Thomas
Clements, Benj. Sr.
Clements, Stephen
Clements, Alex.
Cobb, Noah
Cobb, Mastin
Cox, Thomas
Cox, Reuben B.
Cobb, Ephraim
Cumming, Robt.
Clements, C. W.
Cobb, James
Clements, Isaac
Clements, Hugh
Cullins, Caleb
Clinkscales, Levi
Chalmers, Jas. C.
Clinkscales, Wm. F.
Clark, Joseph
Cook, William
Cowan, Hiram
Conner, J. W. (Dr.)
Cunningham, Cath.
Clinkscales, Abner
Cunningham, F.
Campbell, Jesse
Crawford, Wm.
Crawford, Sarah
Chambler, James
Clinkscales, Asa
Crenshaw, Henry
Crenshaw, Thomas
Carpenter, John
Clarke, Jane
Clarke, Matthew
Cater, Dr. A. P.
Chamblee, James
Cochran, Daniel H.
Creswell, John H.
Carlisle, William
Clinkscales, Berry
Cherry, Susan
Caruth, Miss Louisa
Chastain, Stephen
Chastain, John
Casey, Mary
Cochran, Robert
Chamblee, Benj.
Cox, Jacob R.
Cox, John
Cox, Grabrael
Cox, David
Chastain, S. F.?
Cowen, William
Crayton, B. F.
Driver, James
Dowdle, Morris
Davis, Jesse
Ducksworth, Thos.
Ducksworth, Jacob
Ducksworth, W.
Davis, William
Dalton, Burrel
Duncan, David
Dean, C. P.
Davis, Zachariah
Davis, Moses
Davis, John S.
Davis, Thomas
Davis, Aaron
Drake, James
Duncan, Robert
Davis, F. W.
Dunlap, Mathew
Duncan, Thomas
Dean, Thomas
Dollar, Williamson
Dooley, William
Dean, Obadiah
Dorr, George W.

Durham, David
Ducksworth, Howard
Dalton, Smallwood
Ducksworth, J. C.
Dilworth, B. J.
Douthit, James
Douthit, Benj.
Douthit, John
Davis, Charles
Drake, James
Davis, Archibald
Davis, Richard
Durham, Clarissa
Durham, B.
Durham, William
Davis, James
Durham, William
Dickinson, Willis
Dalrymple, Lewis
Daniels, Wm. D. C.
Dart, Mrs. Mary
Dupre, B. D.
Dickson, Thomas
Dickson, John
Dupre, Benjamin
Dupre, Susanna H.
Dupree, C. P. & C. D.Gail-
  lard
Dupree, C. P.
Dobbins, Martha
Dalrymple, John
Davis, Valentine
Dawson, Samuel
Davis, Levi
Driver, James
Dalrymple, John
Dalrymple, James
Dalrymple, Mary
Dobbins, Jesse
Dobbins, John
Dickson, William
Dean, Moses
Dickson, Matthew
Dickson, Watty
Duckworth, Jacob
Erskine, Thomas
Erskine, James
Erskine, William
Elrod, G. G.
Elrod, William
Ellison, Miles
Eubanks, Elijah
Emerson, James
Emerson, Samuel
Elrod, William
Elrod, Thos. P.
Elrod, Thomas
Earp, Wesley
Earp, Margaret
Earp, David D.
Elrod, Elijah
Earle, Samuel G.
Elrod, Isaac
Elrod, George
Elliott, William
Elrod, Philip
Estes, Micajah H.?
Elrod, Samuel
Erskine, James Jr.
Elrod, Adam
Elrod, Elias
Elrod, William A.
Ellison, James
Earle, Jas. W.-Dr.
Estes, Larkin
Eaton, Joseph C.
Elliott, Dr. Ralph
Elliotte, Mary
Erskine, John
Eskew, William
Evins, Alexander (Dr.)
Earle, Elias
Earle, J. B.

Elrod, Jeremiah
Earle, Mrs. Ann
Fant, James R.
Fretwell, Joseph
Fant, Alfred
Fant, James B.
Fant, Jesse
French, William
Fisher, Samuel S.
Featherston, J. W.
Fisher, Samuel C.
Findley, Elias
Frick, Christian
Flemming, James
Fleming, J. O.
Flemming, Richard
Ford, Stephen
Floyd, Silas
Fuller, Alfred
Forbes, Alanson
Fielding, H. B.
Ferrell, John B.
Fant, Abner
Fant, Samuel
Forsythe, William
Fant, William N.
Fant, V. D.
Franklin, Miss E. A.
Forssin, Mrs.
Felton, Mary
Felton, Richard
Fretwell, John
Garrison, Levi
Gilmer, Nancy
Gilmer, Robert
Gilliland, Alex.
Gilmer, James
Garrett, Thomas H.
Glenn, William
Gordon, Robert
Gordon, James
Gambrell, Matthew
Guiton, Aaron
Guiton, Robert
Guiton, J. W.
Glasby, William
Gambrell, Harper
Gambrell, John
Gambrell, William
Gambrell, Barbary
Gambrell, David H.
Griffin, Elijah
Griffin, John
Gaines, Henry M.
Gambrell, Sarah
Gantt, William
Gantt, Hugh
Gantt, John
Gambrell, William
Gambrell, James
Gambrell, Enock B.
Greer, John
Gray, Huldah
Greer, David, Jr.
Grubbs, George
Gantt, John G.
Greer, David
Gaillard, Josiah D.
Gaillard, Anne
Gaillard, M. D.
Grubbs, Richard W.
Green, William W.
Gantt, John W.
Gable, Henry
Gable, Levi
Gable, Henry, Jr.
Gasaway, Benj.
Gasaway, James S.?
Gray, Robert D.
Galloway, Matthew
Giles, R.
Gray, Elizabeth
Green, John R.

Gentry, John
Gentry, Moody
Gentry, Elizabeth
Gentry, Zechariah
Gordon, Elizabeth
Gregg, Hugh
Gunnin, James
Gambrell, David
Guttry, Benjamin
Gibbs, Mary
Guttry, Nelson
Golden, John
Guttry, David
Guttry, Stephen B.
Gambrell, George _?
Gambrell, James L.?
Gambrell, Ezekiel
Gambrell, James Jr.
Gambrell, Reid
Givens, Harrison
Gibson, Thomas
Gambrell, J. B.
Gaillard, T. Jr.?
Gaillard, Mrs. R. M.
Gaillard, W. H. D.
Griffin, James C.
Gaillard, C. L.
Gaillard, Mrs. E. R. S.
Gaillard, C. D.
Gentry, John
Geer, Solomon
Geer, Thomas
Gaillard, A. D.
Gray, Alexander D.
Gray, Hezekiah
Geer, David
George, James
Gentry, A. B.
Gentry, Artha
Gibson, William B.
Gentry, Daniel
Gray, James
Gentry, Reuben
Gilbert, Amos
Grant, William
Garrett, Osborn
Green, John
Gantt, James A.
Griffin, J. C. & Co.
Goode, Lewellen, Est.
Grubbs, John M.
Harris, Mrs. S. G. J.
Herring, Levi
Hix, Milton
Holland, Robert
Holland, William
Holland, Robert Jr.?
Haygood, Simpson
Humphrey, David
Henderson, Martha
Harrison, James
Hembree, James, Sr.
Harrison, William
Harris, Thomas C.
Hunter, Sarah
Harkins, James
Holland, Wm. B.
Holland, Caleb
Harper, William
Harkins, Hugh
Holland, John Jr.
Horton, Grief
Holland, John, Sr.
Hanks, Tilman
Harper, Wm. C.
Hinton, John
Hanks, Luke
Hopkins, James M.
Hanks, Thomas
Harris, John, Jr.
Haynie, Luke
Hopkins, John
Hunt, William

Hughens, Robert
Hunt, John
Hall, Lemuel
Hanner?, Thomas
Hamilton, Luke
Hamilton, Jane
Hamilton, Nancy
Hall, David
Harkness, John N.
Hamilton, John M.
Haynie, Stephen
Hall, Lent, Jr.
Harkness, John
Harkness, Robert C.
Hall, Samuel
Hall, William A.
Hall, Lent, Sr.
Hall, Fenton Jr.
Hill, Abraham
Hall, Zachariah
Hatton, William
Hutchison, William
Harris, Alonzo
Howie, Robert
Hodges, R. H.W.?
Holmes, Henry
Harris, Nathan
Hall, John
Hardy, James
Hill, Thomas O.
Havird, Mark W.
Hays, John
Heron, James
Heron, John
Howard, Hiram
Howard, George
Houston, Sarah
Hall, Martin
Herndon, George
Haynie, Charles
Hodges, S. H.
Hale, John
Haslet, Moses W.
Herndon, Edmund
Hardy, R. B.
Hembree, Willis
Harper, John Jr.
Holland, A. B.
Harris, Benjamin
Harper, John
Hunt, J. J.
Haines, Robert G.
Hamilton, Cyrus E.
Hamilton, D. K.
Harris, Gillison
Harper, Asa
Hallum, S. J.
Hypps, Joseph
Hubbard, William
Hamilton, Leonard S.
Hammond, Saml. J.
Hall, Joseph
Hillhouse, Joseph
Hammond, B. F.
Hacket, Albert
Hix, Daniel
Haynie, John
Hendrix, David
Hunt, Wm. S.
Hammond, Herbert
Hembree, James, Jr.
Hall, Aaron
Hall, Nancy
Hall, Wilson
Hall, Ezekiel
Hembree, A. D.
Hughes, B. P.
Harris, John
Harris, Mrs. Susan
Harris, Andrew
Hillhouse, Saml. P.
Harris, Joseph P.
Harris, Eliza,(Miss)

Hix, John
Hastie, John & Co.
Hastie, John
Hunter, John
Hall, John
Herring, Jesse
Herring, Elijah
Herring, Francis
Hanks, Mary
Harper, John H.
Holley, Jane
Hix, Baylis
Haynie, Stephen
Huger, ...? K.
Harleston, Edward
Harris, Benjamin
Hinton, Mary
Isbell, Robert
Isbell, Samuel
Ingraham, James
Junkins, Margaret
James, John
Jolly, Henry
Johnson, Allen?
Jones, Elizabeth (on page
  21 of original book..Ed.)
Jolly, Joseph M.
Irby, Charles
Ingram, William
Johnson, Nancy
Johnston, Willis
Johnson, Allen
Johnson, Peter
Irwin, Eleanor
Jones, Joseph B.
Jones, Thomas
Jones, Ambrose H.
Jones, John T.
Jones, Wilson
Jones, William
Jenkins, Dr. W. L.
Jolly, James
Johnson, W. G.
Jeffers, Nathan
Jones, Elizabeth
King, William P.
King, William
King, Solomon
King, Robert
Kay, Charles
King, Josiah
Kelly, Elisha
Kelly, Alfred
Kelly, Allen
King, George W.
Kay, James H.
Kelly, John
King, James
King, Peter
Kay, Jesse
Knox, John
Kay, Strother
Kay, William, Sr.
Kay, William P.
Kay, Fielding
Kay, William, Jr.
Kay, James
Kay, Catharine
Kay, Joel
Kay, James W.
Kay, Mason
Keatts, Jerusha
Kay, Gabriel
Kerr, William
Keaton, William
Kingley, Chester
Kingsley & Mattison
Kay, Francis M.
Kerr, Mary
Keown, William
Keys, J. M.
Kay, Alexander
Kelly, Daniel

Knauff, W. S.
Keasley, Henry
Knight, Warren
Kay, John
Keys, James C.
Keys, Robert A.
King, William L.?
Keaton, Archibald
King, Hiram
King, John D.
Lowry, Jackson
Ledbetter, Joel
Ledbetter, Mary
Ledbetter, James
Lewis, Elisha
Lewis, J. W.
Lewis, J. W. & Simpson
Lucius, James
Lucius, Danl. F. Sr.
Lucius, Daniel F. Jr.
Lee, James
Lee, Philip
Loveless, Nathan
Latimore, M. B.
Little, Rachel
Latham, William
Long, Isaac
Liverett, William
Liverett, Thomas
Liverett, Stephen Jr.
Long, William
Lockhart, M. J.
Lockhart, Thomas
Long, Harrison
Latham, Cornelius
Lewis, Elizabeth
Langa?, William
Laboon, Joseph
Laboon, James
Long, Ezekiel
Lorton, John S.
Lorton, Mrs. Frances
Lorton & Kirksey
Lewis, Mrs. Sarah
Lanier, Bird
Liverett, Stephen, Sr.
Liverett, John
Latimore, W. B.
Lewis, Jesse
Liddle, Andrew J.
Lewis, Jesse P.
Liverett, Wesley
Looney, Jane
McGee, Jesse S.
Meret, Benjamin
Meret, John
Morris, D. J.
Massey, Silas
McCarley, James
McLees, Andrew
McLees, James J.
McLees, James
Major, Elijah
McConnell, S. F.
Massey, Abraham
Martin, Samuel
Mitchell, John
Maddox, Thomas
McCown, John
McAllister, Margt.
Montgomery, A.
Massey, Kindred
Master, G. W.
Moorhead, Maxey
Moorehead, John
Moore, Grant A.
Murphey, John
Mayfield, Ephraim
Major, William
Major, Elijah
McDowell, Mary
McDowell, Esther
Major, Daniel

Major, James
Maulding, B. F.
Mattison, Nevel
Mattison, James
Mattison, Daniel
Mitchell, Ephraim
Mattison, William
Mattison, Wyatt
McGee, William
Mayfield, Marg't.
McCoy, James
Moore, Jeremiah
McAdams, John
Massey, Laban
McCoy, John
McCoy, Samuel
McGee, Michael
Mattison, Olley
McCollum, Daniel
Mattison, B. H.
Mattison, Elizabeth
McPhail, John
McKee, William
May, Edmund
May, Daniel
McAllister, Nathan
McAllister, Andrew
Mattison, Mary R.
McCurdy, Sarah
McBride, James
McKee, James
McCulley, Saml. D.
McCown, Robert
Martin, Phebe
McGee, Willis
Morgan, John
Milford, John
McKee, Archibald
McKee, William A.
Milford, Mary
Mouchet, Jacob
McCarley, Joseph
McGee, John
McGill, Mary & Sarah
McGill, Henry L.
McMahan, Samuel
McConnell, William
McPherson, Elizabeth
McGee, Jesse C.
McGee, Nancy
McGee, Jesse
McCarley, Robert B.
Mecklin, Hugh
McGee, Elias
McPherson, Dorcas
Martin, Jacob
Murphey, Ezekiel
McCollister, (scratched)
Martin, William
Martin, Hester
Martin, Chesley
McKinney, Martha
McCann, Thomas H.
McCann & Walker
Martin, James
Moore, John M.
Murphy, Thomas M.
Moore, William S.
Moore, Elijah
McAllister, Martha
Merril, Obadiah
McAllister, John
Mullikin, James
Mullikin, Benjamin
McMurry, William
McMurry, Jane W.
Mullikin, Benj. J.
Martin, Abraham
McMahan, Peter
Moore, Eli
Mullikin, William
McElroy, John
Moore, Thomas B.

McCollister, James
Melton, Michael
Martin, Jesse
Martin, Edmund
Miller, M. T.
McMurry, Wm. C.
Maverick, Saml. A. & son;
   Saml. & two daughters
   " Rockwill Property
McKay, Martin S.
McElroy, Archibald
Miller, Mrs. Jane
Martin, Abram
Miller, John
Miller, John C.
Miller, Charles
Miller, Patrick J.
McCrary, Mary
McFall, Samuel C.
McClure, Edward J.
Moorhead, Alexander
Moore, Leah
Major, Joseph
Major, John P.
McLesly, James
Moore, John
McMillan, Wyatt A.
Mitchell, Benjamin S.
McPhail, Peter
McGregor, Mary
McGregor, John
McConnell, Thomas
Millwel, Samuel
McFee, Washington
Millwee, William
Moorhead, Lewis
Maulding, B. F. & Co.
Maulding, J. L.
Major, Enoch
McFall, John
McFall, Andrew N.
Miller, Elias
Morris, James
Martin, Matthew
Meredith, Abraham
Maxwell, Robert A.
Maw, John F.
McElmoyle?, Miss E.
Martin, Samuel
Martin, John (Col.?)
Martin, William
McGee, Burrell
Mattison, Archibald
McCulley, Stephen
Mills, Berry
McCann, James L.
McAllister, Nathan
May, Tucker
McMurtry, William
McMurtry, Rebecca
McFee, Sarah
Maxwell, John
Moore, Larkin
McFall, Phoebe
Newell, George
Norris, A. O.
Norris, John E.
Nichols, Wm. A.
Nichols, James C.
Nichols, Archibald
Norris, J. W.
Norris, E. S.
Nichols, A. J.
Newton, Samuel
Newton, Isaac M.
Newton, Isaac
Newton, Willis
Norris, Robert B.
Nevitt, William
Newell, William
North, John L.
Nelson, James O.
Owen, Towton? (Lourton?)

Obriant, William
Obriant, Joseph
Obriant, Andrew
Owen, Elijah
Owen, Lewis
Owen, Ashley
Owen, Daniel
Oldham, Thomas
Oldham, William
Oldham, John
Owen, Bannister
Orr, William
Oliver, Andrew
Oliver, James
Owen, Joshua
Owen, John
Oliver, Martha
Orr, Thomas
Orr, James
Overby, Nicholas
Owen, Elijah Jr.
Orr, C.
Orr, Jane B.
Osborn, L. A.
Pullen, Leroy
Pullen, William
Payne, Jane
Pickerll, Jonathan
Poole, Elizabeth
Prince, Charles J.
Poore, George
Poore, Samuel
Poore, Holland
Poore, Reuben
Poore, William
Poore, John
Poore, Mary
Poore, John
Poore, Hugh
Pettis, Jane
Phillips, Reuben
Parker, Robert
Pearman, Benjamin
Pennall, Thomas
Pressly, David A.
Posey, Herbert
Parker, James
Pitts, William
Price, Pennel
Pruitt, William
Parker, Matthew
Porter, Hugh
Partain, Hubbard
Pressly, Ann
Pettigrew, Robert H.
Palmer, Messer
Pegg, James B.
Pickens, Robert
Pegg, John
Pickell, William
Pickell, James E.
Pendleton Manuf'er Co.
Passmore, William
Padget, Elizabeth
Poole, Manning
Pierce, William
Prince, Richard
Prichett, Lewis
Palmer, William
Philips, John
Philips, Martin
Posey, Harrison
Pickens, T. J.
Pepper, Elijah
Pearman, Jonathan
Patterson, Matilda
Pinckney, Thomas
Quails, Baylis
Rimare, James H.
Reid, William
Reid, Elizabeth
Rusk, David
Richey, Reuben

Rice & Cater
Rice, Fleetwood
Richardson, David
Rodgers, Benjamin
Rodgers, J. W.
Ragsdale, Daniel F.
Ragsdale, F. A.
Reid & Acker
Roberts, Matthias
Reid, Henry
Reece, David
Reece, William
Richey, James H.
Richey, James N.
Reid, Thomas
Reid, Alfred E.
Rice, Hezekiah
Rice, Thomas L.
Rutledge, Jesse
Robinson, John
Robinson, James E.
Ruff, David
Robinson, John J.
Robinson, John B.
Ruff, John
Richards, J. & Jones
Rampey, James A.
Rice, Amaziah
Rice, Hezekiah Jr.
Robison, John
Roach, Henry
Roach, Berry
Reid, Andrew
Richardson, Green C.
Rainey, John
Ranson, William
Reid, Hugh
Reid, Robert
Ryley, Abraham
Rodgers, Eliza. B.
Richey, William
Rodgers, J. L.
Rodgers, William
Richardson, Noah L.
Rodgers, John
Richardson, M.
Rowley, Milton?
Rea, Elihu
Reeks, Washington
Rankin, George
Robinson, William
Rosamond, John
Rodgers, Simeon P.
Robinson, David
Russel, Thomas H.
Robinson, Ephraim G.
Ross, Anthony W.
Russel, David
Rofflander, John Sr.
Robertson, Jeptha
Richardson, A. W.
Richardson, N. A.
Rainwater, D. L.
Richardson, Unroy? L.
Richardson, Wade A.
Richardson, M. L.
Richardson, Wm.
Rice, Ibzan
Reese, H. D.
Ryley, Hezekiah
Reid, J. P.
Reeves, John
Reid, Jesse
Roberts, Benson
Rodgers, Elihu
Richey, Elizabeth
Robins, Mary
Rodgers, William Jr.
Robison, Caleb
Swilling, George
Smith, Thomas G.
Slaten, Loven
Stanton, George

Swilling, James
Swilling, Samuel
Skelton, Thomas
Skelton, Thomas L.
Shaw, Peyton R.
Skelton, A. B.
Sadler, David (2)
Stevenson, James
Stevenson, John
Snips, Matthew
Smith, Jesse R.
Scott, T. L.
Sherrill, Lewis
Stevenson, Andrew
Smith, William
Spearman, D. D.
Stone, William
Stanton, Catharine
Stanton, Matthias
Spray, Thomas (Sprag?)
Smith, Wiley C.
Smith, William
Stone, George
Shaw, Vincent
Stone, Hampton
Shirley, Elizabeth
Shirley, Benjamin
Shirley, Obadiah
Saylor, Leonard
Shirley, Benjamin
Seawright, James
Saylor, Abraham
Saylor, Elizabeth
Shirley, John N.?
Strickland, Matthew
Smith, Arthur W.
Smith, Richard
Smith, Jeremiah R.
Shirley, Jonathan
Smith, Samuel
Sanders, William
Stiefle, Mary
Spearman, John
Sherard, William
Sullivan, Kelly
Smith, Robertson
Scott, David
Shackelford, H. B.
Stacks, Willis
Speer, J. G.
Speer, J.
Shackelford, John W.
Snipes, Sion
Sanders, Abraham
Simpson, William
Stevenson, John
Simpson, David
Simpson, Thomas
Simpson, Archibald
Stevenson, Thomas
Stuart, James G.
Stuart, John
Stevenson, George Jr.
Stuart, James
Skelton, William
Siddall, A. L. Y.
Stuart, James Sr.
Stuart, George
Stuart, Adam
Siddall, Stephen
Smith, Martin
Shaw, William
Searight, Andrew
Skelton, Thomas A.
Smith, Wyatt
Spearman, Daniel
Slaten, John
Spearman, Benj. F.?
Spearman, Thos.? A.
Smith, Basil
Slaten, Philip P.
Smith, George S.
Scott, M. B.

351

Sitton, William D.
Sitton, John L.?
Sitton, William
Siddall, John Sr.?
Spearman, George
Smith, Joseph
Smith, Edward
Satterfield, Jeremiah
Smith, Simeon
Smith, Benjamin
Smith, Andrew M. C.
Smith, John
Smith, J. C. & J. M.
Smith, John E.
Smith, Joseph W.
Smith, J. H.
Sheriff, Washington
Spruill, Simeon
Smith, Zephaniah
Smith, James
Smith, J. C.
Sloan, Thomas M.
Sloan, John L.?
Sloan, Nancy
Sitton, John B.
Stele?, William
Steele, Nancy H.
Sloan, Susan
Sloan, B. F.
Sharp, Elam, Sr.
Starke, Mrs. E. G.
Swords, John S.
Sharpe, John
Smith, Aaron Jr.
Steele, James
Shanklin, Joseph V.
Swords, William
Swords, John
Shirley, Aaron
Smith, Aaron Sr.
Shirley, Richard
Shirley, James
Stevenson, George
Smith, Robert
Smith, John
Skelton, John W. B.
Smith, Nimrod
Smith, Whitaker
Smith, Elizabeth
Shererd, Andrew
Shirley, James
Strickland, Milly
Shearer, Gillam
Sullivan, John S.
Stanley, Ezekiel
Simmons, Charles
Simmons, Charles H.
Simmons, James
Smith, Benjamin
Smith, William C.
Seaborn, George
Symmes, Dr. F. W.
Saylor, John
Shearer, William A.
Stevens, Green
Simpson, R. L.?
Smith, Ebenezer
Sadler, John
Simmons, Thomas H.
Simmons, David
Smith, A. S.
Tippen, Elizabeth
Thompson, John Sr.
Timms, Isaac
Timms, Elijah
Turner, John B.
Telford, William
Telford, Isabella
Telford, James
Trussell, Henry
Trussell, Posey
Townes, William W.
Todd, Mary

Todd, William P.
Taylor, Elijah
Tucker, James
Taylor, Thomas
Thomson, M.
Thomson, J. M.
Thomson, James
Tate, J. A.
Taylor, Samuel H.
Thomas, Elizabeth
Turner, James
Tucker, D.
Tucker, Nancy
Tate, David
Tate, Tilman
Todd, Andrew
Tate, Van.?
Tilley, Mary
Taylor, James
Thompson, James
Tripp, William
Tripp, Nicholas
Tripp, John
Tompkins, John
Traynum, Lazarus
Taylor, David L.?
Taylor, Joseph Jr.
Taylor, Joseph Sr.
Taylor, J. B. E.
Todd, Robert
Tippen, George
Todd, J. L.
Tucker, John C.
Tippen, Matthew
Todd, James
Todd, John
Towers, D. R.-Estate
Towers, Isaac R.
Tillinghast, Elias H.
Tucker, William
Tucker, R. D.
Taylor, William J.
Taylor, Thomas
Talliaferro, Caroline V.
Vernon, James L. W.
Vandiver, Peter S.
Vandiver, William
Valentine, Benjamin
Voyles, Amos
Vandiver, Manning
Vandiver, Edward
Vandiver, Enoch
Vandiver, John A.?
Vandiver, Adam
Vandiver, John
Vandiver, Sanford
(above spelled VANDIVERE)
Whitfield, Lewis
Webb, Elisha
Williford, Charles K.
Williford, Sarah
Webb, Elijah
Webb, William
Wilson, Rev. James
Wallace, Wilson
Willbanks, James
Willbanks, Shadrach
Wilson, James, Sr.
Wardlaw, John M.
Wardlaw, James
Wardlaw, Hugh
Wilson, Sarah
Wilborn, Thomas
Wilson, Hugh
Welborn, William E.
Williams, Jasper
Wilson, James P.
Woodson, William
Welborn, William
Wilson, Barkley
Willingham, John
Warnock, John
Warnock, John Jr.

Wyatt, Redman G.
Willingham, James
Walker, Peter
Wyatt, Elijah
Williamson, John C.
Webster, Jane
Williams, James C.
Williamson, Mastin
Wright, William F.
Welden, Wm. D.
Wright, James
Wakefield, Conrad
Williamson, William
Wright, R. N.
Wade, Edward
Watt, Mary
Walters, Flemming
Watt, Thomas
Willbanks, Elijah
Winfield, James H.
Whitman, Jacob
Wiles, Elizabeth
Wiles, James H.
Watt, Mary Jr.
Wiley, James
Wiles, Jesse
Watt, John
White, George N.
Watt, James D.
White, Ezekiel
Wright, Elizabeth
Watson, David
West, Isaac
Wilson, Lewis
Williford, Samuel
Watson, D. K.
Wilson, James J.
Welborn, A. G.
Welborn, Sarah
Wilson, James B.
Williams, M. B.
Wiginton, John
Wiginton, George W.
Willbanks, Hezekiah
Williams, Ira C.
Williams, Newton
Wilson, John
Wimpey, Levi
Waddle, Abner
Wynn, Franklin
Wiginton, Henry
Watson, James
Wilson, Elijah?
Wilson, William
Wilson, John N.
White, Bartholomew
Watkins, Baylis
Wilson, Thomas
Warley, Mrs. Sophia
Warley & Sharpe
Watkins, Felix
Winter, Dinah
Wilson, R. L.?
Watson, Willard
Watkins, Joseph
Watkins, William
Warren, Samuel
Wilson, Martha E.
Webb, C. B.
Webb, James
White, Jonathan
Webb, Clayton
Wilson, William M.
Williford, Thomas D.
Wyatt, James L.
Waddle, Alexander
Watson, J. M. B.
William, Woodward *
(*should this be reversed)
Waller, William
Whitner, Joseph N.
Whitfield, J. L.
Webb, Edmund

White, Julia
White, Henry N.
White, Thomas
White, Newton
West, Thomas
Watson, Thomas
Wright?, Catharine
Williams, O. A.
Walker, John S.
Winfield, John B.
William, John
Webb, Warren R.
Whiteworth, C. H.
Williams, Stephen
Young, James
Young, Francis
Young, Francis A.
Yeas?, Polly
Yeargin, Samuel
Young, William
Young, Thomas D. M.
Young, John

(see Maverick other col.:)
do Newbury
do Union district
do Orangeburg

\#

ANDERSON

Property in PICKENS:
Johns, Ann
Pyne, Jane
Harrison, James
Anderson, William
Major, James
Sullivan, Kelly
H....., Henry?
Norris, E. L. & Houston
Davis, Jesse
Hubbard, William
 ames?, Adam
Knight, Warren W.
Miller, John C.
Miller, Charles
Fielding, H. B.
Earle, John B.
G......, William?
Maverick, Saml. A.; son &
  two Daughters
Washington, J. J.
Armstrong, James

Property in GREENVILLE:
Maverick, Saml. A. & son
  two Daughters
Seaborn, George
Howell, Robt. A.

Property in ABBEVILLE:
Webster, Jane
Fisher, Elizabeth
Ruff, David
Stiafle, Mary
Armstrong, John B.
Fisher, Thomas
Mouchet, Jacob
Dickson, Thomas
Miller, Charles
Tucker, William
Tucker, R. D.
Smith, Benjamin
Smith, William C.
Kea....?, Michael
Harleston, Edward

LAURENS:
Clarke, Joseph
Maverick, Saml. A., son
  & two Daughters

CHARLESTON DIS.:
Gaillard, C. L. & .....
....

Maverick, Saml. A.
Son & two Daughters
Do Pine Barren
Do Spartanburg

Anderson, John
Acker, Wm.
Avery, Wm.
Acker, P.? N.
Acker, Susanah
Acker, J. L.
Acker, Amos
Allen, Jas. E.
Armstrong, Wm. B.
Alexander, David
Armstrong, Jas. Jr.?
Ashley, Wilson
Ashley, John
Armstrong, ?
Armstrong, Arch'd.
Armstrong, Jno. B.
Adams, Henry
Adams, John
Adams, Asa
Atkins, Henry
Amick, John D.
Anderson, Wm. P.
Arkinson, Jos. H.
Abbot, John
Archer, Wm. N.
Anderson, Micajah
Acker, Holbert
Alewine, Michael
Arnold, Allen
Anderson, David
Anderson, Robert
Brown, Samuel
Brown, Elijah
Benson & Wynn
Benson, J. P.
Bowlind, Albert
Barkley, Jos. M.
Barkley, Sarah
Brazeal, Kennon
Brown, Dr.? Geo. R.
Brazeale, D. H.?
Ballentine, Jos. J.
Ballentine, Jesse H.
Brazeale, Griffin
Brazeale, Griffin, Jr.
Brazeale, Williamson
Barkley, Nancy
Ballentine, George
Broyles, Aaron
Brock, Enos
Braswell, George
Braswell, James
Brock, Hayden
Braswell, Asa
Bragwell, John (Bagwell?)
Bagwell, James
Braswell, James
Braswell, Nancy
Brown, Lesley
Bannister, Wm.
Brackenridge, Robt.
Brock, James
Brock, M. H.
Browne, L. H.
Branyan, Joseph
Browne, Samuel
Browne, J. M.
Cunningham, F.? L.?
Cunningham, Cath.
Cook, William
Casey, Mary
Clinkscales, Abner
Carr, Mary
Campbell, Jesse
Caldwell, John
Corr, Mary
Conwill, James
Christopher, John
Caldwell, Joseph
Cunningham, Saml?
Cunningham, Thos.
Caldwell, Wm.

Caldwell, James
Campbell, George
Campbell, Alex'r.
Chapel, John
Clinkscales, Berry
Corr, Laban
Cater, Edward
Campbell, James
Cox, Asa
Cooley, John dec'd?
Cobb, Henry, Esq.?
Cobb, Josiah W.
Cobb, Azariah
Carter, Caleb
Ceasar (of color)
Carter, Spencer
Clardy, Joab
Clardy, John
Chambers, Nancy
Clardy, John
Childers, John B.
Clardy, Norman
Cason, James A.
Cason, Sarah
Cason, Esther
Cason, Wm. dec'd.
Craig, Samuel
Cheves, Langdon
Crenshaw, Thomas
Carpenter, John
Chamblee, James
Chamblee, Benj.
Cannon, Isaac
Campbell, Daniel
Cooley, James
Cox, William
Cummins, Harmon
Cox, Gabriel
Cox, John
Caldwell, Hugh
Chamblee, Moses
Chastain, Stephen
Clark, John B.
Cason?Carter?, Delila
Coffee, Iley
Cochran, Danl. H.
Creswell, Sarah
Creswell, John H.
Crawford, James
Crawford, Sarah
Crawford, Wm. dec'd.
Chastain, John
Clark, Mrs. Jane
Cowen, Wm.
Cherry, Thos. R.
Cherry, Susan
Caruth, Louisa L.
Browne, Danton
Branyan, Henry
Bell, James
Beaty, Wm.
Browne, Cornelius
Bowie, Charles
Buchanan, Wm.
Beaty, John
Beaty, Thomas
Bowie, Wm. H.
Baron, Uriah
Beaty, Thos.?
Beaty, Samuel W.?
Burton, Blackman
Burton, Peyton L.?T?
Burdett, Hiram
Bonds, Sugar (of Ga.)
Buchanan, E. dec'd.
Brown, Charles
Brooks, Thomas
Brown, Abner
Bozeman, Lewis?
Bozeman, D. T.
Brooks, Garner?
Baker, Samuel H.

Burress, Thos. Jr.
Buchanan, Saml.
Barret, John
Betterton, Joshua
Bayley, Allen
Barton, Henry M.
Bradberry, Salathiel
Bradberry, Sal'l. Jr.
Bradberry, James
Burns, John
Burgess, James
Borough, Thos.
Bennett, Wm.
Bennett, Thos.
Bryant, Nathan
Bryant, Terrill
Blassingame, Thos.
Bowen, Robert
Blankenship, John
Brewer, William
Bayley, J. S.?
Bryant, Simon
Bishop, Nicholas
Burt, ...?
Bellotte, Jacob
Bellotte, Peter E.
Brown, Randolph
Burns, Anderson
Brazeale, Matthew
Bowen, Samuel
Berry, Joel H.
Burns, Jordan
Barrett, Charles
Burress, Thos. Jr.
Bell, Samuel
Brown, George
Bowen, Jas. G.
Bruce, Charles J_?
Bradberry, Jesse
Bradberry, Wm.
Burriss, Joshua
Burriss, Elisha
Bayley, Wm.
Beaty, David
Broyles, John L.?
Burress, Reuben
Bellotte, J. L.
Brazeale, Enock
Brownlee, Mariah
Baker, Lindsey A.
Bennett, Charles M.
Burress, James
Barksdale, John
Blassingame, R. E.
Burress, Milford
Bowman, Archibald
Bowen, Catharine
Brown, Robt M.
Benson, E. B.
Benson, E. B. & Co.
Broyles, O. R.
Boner?, Thos.
Brown, John
Brown, Wm. P.
Burriss, Jacob
Burriss, Elizabeth
Burriss, Elbert
Brown, Daniel
Bowdoin?, Jas. G.
Brown, Larkin
Burt, Moody
Bruce, Charles Jr.?
Bruce, John
Bennett, Cooper
Berry, Wm.
Bee?, B. E.
Brown, Robert B.
Carlisle, William
Chamblee, James
Cannon, Ephraim B.
Clinkscales, Asa
Crayton, B. F.

Carpenter, Albert L.?
Carpenter, Eliz.
Cater, A. P.
Carpenter, A. M.
Cooley, Lewis
Cox, Sarah
Carder, Thomas
Cox, Abner
Cummins, David
Cox, Thomas
Cox, Reuben
Cox, William
Clinkscales, Wm. F.?
Cummins, Robert
Cobb, Mastin
Clements, Wm.
Cox, Aris
Cox, Wm.
Cox, Thomas
Clements, Benj.
Clements, Isaac
Cobb, Noah
Clements, Benj. Jr.
Clements, Alex'r.?
Cobb, Ephraim
Cullens, Caleb
Clements, Hugh
Clements, C. W.
Cobb, James
Clark, Joseph
Clinkscales, Levi
Chalmers, J. C.
Clinkscales, Wm. F.
Cunningham, Danl.
Cowen, Hiram
Carne, Miss Martha
Cox, Joseph
Cox, David
Cox, Rachael & Sister
Coates, John
Campbell, A. C.
Christian, E. C. B.
Davis, Jesse dec'd.
Dean, Moses
Dawson, Samuel
Doudle, ... free.....?
Davis, Levi
Davis, Wm.
Dean, C. P.
Durham, Anderson
Davis, John L.
Davis, Thos. W.
Davis, Moses
Davis, Aaron
Davis, Valentine
Drake, Jas. A.
Duncan, Robt. M.
Drake, James
Davis, ? W.
Duncan, Thos.
Dunlap, Matthew
Dean, Thomas
Dollar, Williamson
Dooley, Wm. (of Ga.)
Driver, James
Dobbins, James
Ducksworth, Jacob
Ducksworth, Thos.
Ducksworth, Welborn
Dorr, G. W.
Ducksworth, Jas. C.
Durham, David
Davis, Richard
Davis, Archibald
Dilworth, Billy G.
Douthit, James
Douthit, John
Durham, Clarissa
Dalton, Burrel
Douthit, Benj. H.
Davis, Charles
Durham, Wm.
Davis, James

Dickerson, Willis
Dalrymple, Lewis
Dart, Mrs. Mary L.
Duke, J. J.
Dickson, Thomas
Daniels, Wm. D.? C.
Dupree, B.
Burpee, B. D.
Dupree, Mrs. Susan'h.
Dalrymple, James
Dobbins, John
Driver, James
Dalrymple, John
Dickson, Walter C. dec'd.
Duncan, David
Dickson, Matthew dec'd.
Dickson, Wm.
Dobbins, Martha
Ducksworth, Howard
Dunham, B.
Dalrymple, John
Ducksworth, Ama.
Davis, Enock ?
Dupree, C. P.?
Dupree, C. P. & Gaillard
Dobbins, Jesse
Ducksworth, Benj.
Evans, A. (Dr.)
Erskine, Thos.
Erskine, James
Erskine, John
Eubanks, Elijah
Ellison, Miles?
Ellison, Joel
Ellitte, Penney
East, Margaret (Easton?)
Emerson, James
Emerson, Saml.
Elrod, Wm.
Earle, Samuel G.
Earp, Wesley
Earpe, David D.
Elrod, Jeremiah
Elrod, George G.
Elrod, Wm.
Erskine, Wm.
Earle, Mrs. Ann
Elrod, George
Elrod, Samuel
Elrod, John
Elrod, Isaac
Elrod, Wm. A.
Elrod, Philip
Elrod, Elias
Ellison, James
Earle, James (Dr.)
Estes, Larkin
Elliotte, Mary
Eaton, Joseph C.
Eskew, Wm. E.
Elrod, Thomas P.
Earle, Elias
Earle, Jno. B.
Elrod, Adam
Elrod, Thos. Jr.
Erskine, James
Elliotte, R. E.
Estes, Macajah
Fretwell, J. Y.
Felton, Richard
Fant, Jesse
Fant, Alfred
French, William
Fisher, Stephen (of Ab.)
Featherstone, J. W.?
Fant, W. N.
Fricks, Christian
Findley, Elias
Findley, Nancy
Fant, Jas. K.(R.?)
Felton, Mary
Farmer?, Jane
Flemming, James

Flemming, R. M.
Flemming, Jno. O.?
Ford, Stephen
Fant, Elijah
Floyd, Silas
Fuller, Alfred
Forbes, Alanson
Fant, Samuel
Fretwell, John
Fant, Elizabeth
Forsyth, Wm.
Fisher, Samuel C.
Fowler, Ruth
Fielding, Henry
Ford, James
Fant, V. D.
Fant, Abner
Fenell, Mrs. Jane
Gentry, Arthur
Graham, J. B.
Gordon, Robert
Galaspey, Wm.
Gambrell, David H.
Griffin, Elijah
Gaines, Henry M.?
Gambrell, John
Gambrell, Wm.
Gambrell, Barbary
Gray, Huldah
Gantt, William
Gambrell, James
Gambrell, E. B.
Gambrell, Sarah
Gambrell, Wm.
Gantt, Hugh
Gantt, John A.
Gantt, J. G.
Greer, David Jr.
Greer, David
Green, John M. (Greer?)
Green, Wm. W.
Grubbs, George
Gantt, John W.
Gaillard, A. D.
Gassaway, Benj.
Gable, Henry
Gable, Levi
Gable, Henry, Jr.
Gantt, Jas. A.
Galloway, Matthew
Gray, A. D.
Green, John
Green, John R.?
Green, James
Gentry, Moody
Gentry, Zachariah
Gentry, Elias?
Gregg, Hugh
Gunnin, James
Glenn, William
Gilmer, Robert
Garrison, Levi
Garrison, Henry
Gilliland, Alex'd.
Gilmer, James Est.?
Gilmer, Nancy
Grayham, A. J.
Grubbs, John M.
Garrett, Thos. H.
Guiton, John
Guiton, Robt. dec'd.
Guiton, G.
Guiton, Aaron dec'd.
Gambrell, Geo. V.?
Guttry, Nelson
Guttry, David dec'd.
Golden, John
Guthrie, Benjamin
Guthrie, Steph.? B.
Gibbs, Mary
Gambrell, J. B.
Gambrell, Jas. Jr.
Gambrell, Ezekiel

355

Gibson, Thomas
Gambrell, Jas. Jr.
Gambrell, Reid
Givens, Harrison
Gaillard, W. H. D.
Gaillard, Mrs. R.? (A.)
Grant, Wm.
Gentry, John
Gray, James
Gordon, James
George, James
Geer, David
Gentry, Reuben
Gilbert, Amos
Geer, Solomon
Griffin, J. C. & Co.
Gray, Eli__?
Gray, Robert D.?
Gambrell, Matthew
Gray, Hezekiah
Gentry, Daniel
Gambrell, Henry?, dec'd.
Gentry, A. B.
Griffin, Jas. C. dec'd.
Gaillard, C. L.
Gaillard, C. D.
Gambrell, David
Goode, Lewellen dec'd.
Gaillard, J. D.
Gaillard, Mary D.
Gaillard, Anna
Hammond, Herbert
Holland, John Jr.
Holland, Wm. B.
Horton, Grief
Harper, Nancy
Holland, Aaron
Harkins, Hugh
Holland, Caleb
Harkins, James
Holland, John
Harper, Wm. C.
Hunt, John
Harper, John H.
Hughens, Robert
Haynie, Luke
Harris, John
Hinton, John
Hunt, William
Hanks, Luke
Hanks, Thomas
Hopkins, John
Hopkins, James M.
Hamilton, J. M.
Hamilton, Luke
Hamilton, Jane
Hamilton, Nancy
Harkness, John
Harkness, Robt. C.
Hall, Wm.
Hall, Saml. C.
Haynie, Stephen
Harkness, John M.
Hall, Lent, Jr.
Hall, Lent
Heron, James
Hall, John
Howie, Robert
Hatton, Wm.
Hodges, R. H. W.
Hall, David
Harris, Nathan
Havird, Martin? W.
Hill, Thos. O.
Hays, John
Howard, Hiram
Howard, George
Hall, Fenton Jr.
Herndon, George
Herring?, Francis
Hale, John
Haynie, Charles
Hardy, James

Hardy, R. B.
Henderson, Martha
Humphries, David
Hix, Milton
Herring, Levi
Harris, Sarah G. J.
Herring, Jesse
Holland, Robert
Holland, Robert Jr.
Hunter, Sarah
Harris, Benj.
Harper, John
Harper, John Jr.
Harper, Phomas?
Hunt, Jeremiah J.
Hamilton, Cyrus E.
Hamilton, D. K.?
Holland, P. N.
Harper, Asa
Harleston, Edward
Hix, John
Harris, John
Hamilton, Leonard L.
Hall, Joseph
Hammond, Saml. J.
Hammond, W. L.
Hall, Zachariah
Heron, John
Hembree, A. D.
Hanner, Thos.
Hendrix, David
Hunt, Wm. L.?
Hall, Aaron
Hembree, James
Hembree, James Jr.
Hillhouse, Joseph
Harris, Joseph P.
Hughes, Benj. P.
Haynie, John
Harrison, Wm.
Hix, Daniel
Hawkins, Wm. P.
Hall, Martin?
Harris, Gillison
Hipps, Joseph
Hembree, Willis
Hall, John Jr.
Hunter, John
Hall, Lemuel
Hackett, Albert
Hall, Fenton H.
Hall, Ezekiel
Hammond, B. F.
Hillhouse, Saml. P.?
Hall, Willson
Hanks, Geo. dec'd.?
Haynie, Stephen
Harrison, James
Harrison, E. E.
Hanks, Tilman
Hall, Nancy
Harris, Susan
Hastie, John & Co.
Hastie, John
Hager, Frs.? K.
Hubbard, Wm.
Holland, Wm.
Harris, Benjamin
Hunter, Mary
Hix, Baylis
Isbell, Samuel
Jolly, Wm.
Jolly, James
Jolly, A.
Junkin, Margaret
Johnson, Milly
Johnson, Allen
Johnson, Willis
Johnson, Nancy
Johnson, Peter
Jennings, Jane?
J...r?, Eleanor
Jones, James

Jones, Joseph B.
Jones, Thomas
Irby, Charles
Ingram, William
Jones, Ambrose H.
Jones, Samuel
Johns?, John
Jones, Wm.
Jones, Wilson
Jolley, nny?
Johnson, W. D.
Ingram, James
Jolly, Joseph M.
Isbell, Robert
Jeffers, Nathan dec'd.?
Jenkins, W. D.
King, Jacob
Kay, Alexander
Keasler, Henry
Knauff, W. _?
King, Wm.
King, John D.
Kay, John
Kay, F. M.
Keaton, Archibald
Knight, Warren W.
King, Hiram
Kay, D.
Kay, Jas. W.
Knox, John
King, Peter
Kay, Jesse
King, Geo. W.
King, James
King, Robert
Kelly, Elisha
Kelly, Alden? Allen?
Kelly, John
Kay, Jas. H.
Kelly, Alfred
King, Josiah
Kay, Wm. Jr.
Kay, Joel
Kay, Catharine
Kay, William
Kay, James
Kay, Mason
Kay, Fielding
Kay, Wm. P.
Kingsley, Chester
Kay, Strother
Kerr, William
Kay, Gabriel
Keaton, Wm.
Keown, Wm.
Keys, J. M.
Kay, L. W.
King, Wm. P.
Kay, Charles
Kelly, Daniel
Keys, James C.
Keys, Robert A.
Lewis, Elisha
Lewis, J. W.
Lewis & Cox
Lewis & Simpson
Lee, James
Lucius, Danl. F. Jr.
Lucius, Danl. F.
Lee, Philip
Loveless, Nathan
Latimer, M. B.
Liverett, Stephen Jr.
Liverett, Stephen
Long, Isaac
Liverett, John
Liverett, Wm.
Lessley, Wm.
Liverett, Thomas
Lord?, Wm.
Lockhart, M. D.?
Latham, Cornelius
Ledbetter, James

Long, Harrison
Lewis, Elizabeth
Ledbetter, Joel
Ledbetter, Mary
Lowry?, Jackson
Long, Ezekiel
Lanza?, Wm.
Laboon, Eady
Laboon, Joseph
Lorton & Kirksey
Lorton, John L.
Lorton, Mrs. Frs.
Lewis, Mrs. L.? dec'd.
Ledbetter, David T.?
Liddle, Andrew J.
Lewis, Jesse
Little, Rachael
Lucius, Jas. L.
Lewis, J. P.
Latimer, W. B.
Liverett, Wesley
Langston, Mary W.
Martin, Samuel
Moorhead, Alex'd.
Maddox, Thomas
Maulding & Crayton?
Mauldin, B. F. & Co.
Mauldin, J. L.
Mitchell, Caleb
McCulley, Stephen
Massey, Abraham
Major, Elijah Esq.
Major, James Jr.
McDowell, Mary
Major, Enock
Major, Wm.
McFall, John
Mayfield, Ephraim
Major, James
Murphy, John
Moore, Grant A.
Mauldin, B. F.
Massey, Laban
Mattison, Wm.
Mattison, Daniel
Mattison, James
Mattison, Wyatt
Mattison, Elizabeth
Mattison, Baylis
Maddox, Henry
Mattison, Ollay?
Mattison & Kingsley
McCoy, James
Moore, Jeremiah
Mitchell, Ephraim
Mattison, Archibald
McGee, Michael
McAdams, John
McCollum, Daniel
McCoy, Samuel
McCoy, John R.?
May, Tucker W.
May, Edmund
McPhail, Ja...?
McFall, Phebe
McBride, John
Martin, Phebe
McBride, Jas. L.
Milford, John
Mosely, L. P.(T.? P.)
Morgan, John
Massey, Jas. E.
McGee, Willis
Mouchett, Jacob
McKee, Wm. H.?
McKee, James
McKeown, Robert
McCullough, L. D.
Milford, Mary
McCurdy, Sarah
McKee, Wm. A.
McKee, Archibald
McCarley, Joseph

McAlister, Nathan
McCarley, Robt. B.
McMahan, Samuel
McGill, Mary (Mrs.?/Ann?)
McGill, Mary
McConnel, Wm.
McPherson, Eliz.?
Macklin, Hugh
McGee, Elias
McGee, Gabriel
Moore, John
McGee, Jesse C.
McGee, Jesse dec'd.
McLees, Andrew
McLees, James
McCarley, James
McClinton, Alex.? L.
Massey, Silas
McLees, James
McLees, Hanford?
Maret, Benj. W.?
McCoy, Martin L.
Martin, Chesley
Milwee, Samuel
Masters, G. W.
Martin, Abram
McCollister, James
McCollister, John
Murphey, Thos. N.?
McKinney, Martha
Martin, Jacob
Martin, William
Martin, Hester
Moore, Thos. B.
Moore, John N.
Moore, Wm. L.
Murphey, Ezekiel
Murphey, E. & Co.
Moore, Elijah
Merett, Obadiah
McMurray, Wm.
McMurray, Jane W.
McCann, Thos. H.
McCann & Walker
Martin, Abram Jr.
Mullikin, Jas. Esq.
Mullikin, Benj. Jr.
McMahan, Peter
McCollister, John
McElmoyle, Miss E.
Mullikin, Benj.
Martin, James
Moore Eli
Mullikin, Wm.
McCann, J. L. dec'd.
McMurray, Wm. C.
McElroy, John
Morris, Samuel
Major, John dec'd?
Major, Joseph
Melton, Michael
Martin, Jesse
McMurtry, Rebecca
McMurtry, Wm.
McCrary, Mary
Miller, John
Martin, Samuel
McPhail, Peter
Moorhead, Maxwell
Moorhead, John dec'd.
Martin, Edmund
Miller, Elias
McCown, John
Major, Elijah
Moore, Larkin
Moorehead, M. L.
Morris, J. C.
Massey, Kindred
Martin, Matthew
Mitchell, Benj. L.
Moorhead, Lewis
Morris, David J.
Morris, James

Mavrick, Saml. A. & son
  Saml. A. & two dau's.
McGee, Jesse? L.
McGee, John
Miller, John C.
McCollister, Andrew
McCollister, Margt.
Milwee, Wm. A.
Milwee, Eliz. & sister
McFee, Washington
McFee, Sarah
McCurdy, Sarah
Montgomery, Alfred?
McFall, Samuel R.?
McConnel, Thos.
McClure, Ed. J.
McMillion, W. A.?
Mitchell, John
McElroy, Arch'd.
McLesky, James
McConnel, L. H.?
McMurtry, James
McCollister, Nathan
McGee, Burrel
Mattison, Mary
McGriggor, Miriam?
McGreggor, John
Martin, John
Martin, Wm. M.
Moore, Leah
McGee, Wm.
Mayfield, Margaret
Murray, Margaret
McFall, Andrew N.
Mills, Berry
McPherson, Lucas/(Dorcas?)
Maxwell, Rob. A.?
Mason, Elijah
Maw, John F.?
Miller, Mrs. Jane
Miller, M. T.?
Maxwell, John
Mays, Mrs. Miram? D.
Meredith, Mrs. Jane?
Norris, A. O.
Norris, John E.
Nevitt, Wm. M.
Nichols, Wm. A.
Nichols, Archibald
Nichols, James C.
Norris, Robert B.?
Norris, E. L.?
Nelson, W. R.?
Nichols, Alex'r. J.(Arch?)
North, John L.
Newton, Samuel
Newton, Willis
Newton, Isaac
Newell, George
Newell, Wm.
Newton, Isaac
Norris, J. W.
Owen, Thornton
Obriant, Wm.
Obriant, A. J.
Obriant, Josephine
Owen, Elijah
Oliver, Andrew
Oliver, Jas. dec'd.
Owen, Daniel
Oldham, Thomas
Oldham, Wm.
Oldham, John decd.
Orr, Wm.
Orr, Alexxander
Owen, Wm.
Owen, Lewis
Orr, James
Oliver, Martha
Owen, John
Owen, Joshua
Orr, Thomas
Overby, Nicholas

357

Owen, Elijah Jr.
Owen, Bannister
Osbourn, L. A.
Orr, C.
Orr, Jane B.
Poore, Holland
Poore, Geo.
Poore, Wm.
Poore, John dec'd.
Poore, Reuben
Poore, John
Poore, Hugh, dec'd.
Poore, Zachariah
Pettis, Jane?
Phillips, Reuben
Pearman, Benj.
Pruitt, Wm.
Parker, Robert
Pennel, Thomas
Price, Pennel
Parker, James
Pressley, David A.
Pitts, Wm.
Pressley, Mrs. Ann
Parker, Matthew
Porter, Hugh
Pettigrew, Rbt. H.
Pickerell, Jonathan
Palmer, Wm.
Pullen, Leroy
Palmer, Nancy
Pickle, Wm. C.
Pickle, James E.
Pickle, Wm.
Paulman, Ludivick
Pickens, Robert
Phillips, Martin
Pegg, John
Pegg, James B.
Phillips, John
Phillips, Arch'd.
Passmore, Wm. dec'd.
Padgett, Eliz.?
Prince. C. J.
Pearce, Wm.
Pruitt, E. D.
Posey, Herbert
Poole, Manning dec'd.
Poole, Mary
Poole, Adam
Pepper, Elijah
Pickens, Thos. J.
Prickett, Lewis
Pearman, Jonathan
Poole, Elizabeth
Quails, John B.?
Robinson, John J.
Rice, Ibzan
Rice, Fleetwood
Rice & Cater
Ragsdale, Danl. F.
Ragsdale, F. A.
Reese, Wm.
Reese, David
Robinson, John B.
Reid, Henry
Reid, A. E.
Richey, Jas. N.?
Rutledge, Jesse
Risner, Silas F. A.
Rice, Hezekiah
Rice, Thomas L.
Robinson, John
Robinson, Jas. E.
Rice, Hez'h. Jr. dec'd.
Rice, A.
Ranson, Wm.
Rampy?,Jas. A.
Robinson, John
Roach, Berry
Roach, Henry
Reid, Hugh
Rainey, John dec'd.

Reid, Robert
Reid, Wm.
Reid, Eliz.
Reid, Jesse
Rodgers, Elisha
Rochester, Nath'l.
Rodgers, J. 1.
Richardson, David
Rodgers, Benj. L.
Rodgers, Wm.
Rodgers, John
Riley, Abraham
Richardson, Noah
Rodgers, Joseph L.
Richardson, Matthias
Rosamond, John H.
Ray, Elihu
Reaks?, G. W.
Richey, Wm.
Rodgers, Simeon
Rankin, Geo.
Robertson, David
Robinson, Wm. H.?
Russel, Thos. H.
Richardson, Mrs. M. L.
Richardson, Wm.
Rainwater, D. L.
Robinson, E. G.
Reid, Andrew
Russel, David
Richardson, Wade
Richardson, Nathan
Robison, Jeptha
Richey, Reuben
Rodgers, Wm. Jr.
Riley, Hez.
Reeves, John
Ruff, David
Roberts, Matthias
Rodgers, Eliza. B.
Rice, Jane
Rowley, Milton
Rusk, David dec'd.
Reid, J. P.
Richey, Mrs. Eliz.
Reese, Thomas L.
Reese, Geo. dec'd.
Roberts, Benson (of Ga.)
Riman?, Jas. W.
Ross, A. W.
Reese, H.? D.
Scott, T.? L.
Smith, Ebenezer
Sherill, Lewis
Smith, J. R.
Spray, Thos.
Smith, Wiley C.?
Smith, Robert
Smith, Wm.
Stone, Wm.
Stone, Geo.
Smith, A. W.
Smith, R.? L.
Smith, Davis
Smith, Jeremiah
Smith, Richard
Shaw, Vincent
Stone, Hampton
Shirley, Obadiah
Shirley, Benj. E.
Strickland, Matthew
Saylors, Leonard
Saylors, Isaac
Shirley, Benj.?
Saylors, Abraham
Shirley, John
Seawright, James
Sanders, Wm.
Stiefle, Mary
Snipes, Sion
Spear?, James
Spearman, John
Simpson, Robert

Sherard, Wm.
Stevenson, Thomas
Sanders, A.
Simpson, Wm.
Simpson, David
Scott, David
Stevenson, John
Stewart, John
Simpson, Thomas
Stewart, Jas. G.
Simpson, Arch'd.
Stacks?, Willis
Stewart, James
Stuart, Adam
Stuart, George
Stevenson, Geo.
Skelton, Wm.
Stuart, James Jr.
Stevenson, James
Shaw, W. L.
Seawright, Andrew
Siddall, Stephen
Smith, Martin H.?
Sadler, John
Skelton, A. B.
Simpson, David
Shaw, Peyton R.
Skelton, Thos. T.
Skelton, Thos. A.
Skelton, Thos.
Swilling, Saml.?
Swilling, James
Swilling, Robert
Symmes, James (Simmons?)
Simmons, Charles
Smith, Wyatt
Smith, Aaron
Shirley, James Jr.
Shirley, Aaron
Steele, Wm.
Stott?, Drayton
Spearman, David D.?
Stott, John W.
Slaten, John
Smith, Basil
Spearman, Benj. J.
Spearman, David
Smith, Thos. G.
Smith, Phillip P.?
Smith, G. L.
Scott, M. B.
Spearman, Frs.? A.
Smith, J. C.
Smith, J. C. & J. M.
Sitton, Wm. D.
Sitton, Wm.
Sitton, John P.
Satterfield, ...?
Stanton, Geo.
Smith, Joseph
Slaten, Loven
Sheriff, Washington
Smith, Ellis
Smith, Joseph
Siddall, John
Smith, Simeon
Smith, Edward
Sloan, Susan
Stanton, ...?
Stanton, Matthias
Snipes, Matthew
Shirley, Diadama
Smith, Saml. Jr.
.......?, Andrew
Smith, Samuel
Smith, Whitaker
Smith, J. ?
Sloan, Thomas M.
Saylors, John
Saylors, Dorothy
Siddall, A. L. W.?
Steele, James
Sitton, J. B.

Symmes, F. W.
Smith, A...?
Starke, Mrs. E. G.
Sharpe, Elam Jr.?
Sloan, John L.?
Stanley, Ezekiel
Simmons, David
Shearer, Mrs. Wm.?
Sullivan, Kelly
Seaborn, George
Simmons, Thos. H.
Telford, James
Turner?, John B.
Telford, William
Telford, Isabella?
Trussel, Henley?
Towns?, Wm. W.
Trussel, Posey
Todd, Mary
Todd, Wm. P.
Taylor, Richard
Thomson, James
Thomson, J. M.?
Taylor, Elijah
Taylor, Samuel
Thomson, Elizabeth
Thomson, Mathew Dr.?
Tucker, Nancy
Tucker, Wm.
Taylor, Thos. Capt.
Tucker, James
Tucker, Dejarnet?
Tate, David
Tate, Van
Tate, Tilman
Thomson, A. E. H.?(D.?)
Taylor, James
Tilley, Mary
T....., Elizabeth
Timms, Isaac
Thomson, James
Tripp, William
Tripp, J. H.
Tripp, Nicholas
Tompkins, John
Tripp, John
Trayma_, Lazarus
Taliaferro, Miss Caroline
Taylor, David L.
Taylor, Joseph Jr.
Tate, John A.
Todd, James?
Todd, A.
Todd, J. L.
Tucker, ? D.
Teaque, Elijah
Tucker, John C.
Thomson, John
Tippen?, Geo.
Turner, James
Todd, Robert
Todd/Towns?, D. N.? dec'd.
Taylor, Thomas
Taylor, Wm. J.
Taylor, Joseph Jr.
Todd, Thomas
Tippen, Matthew?
Todd, Charles
Tillinghast, Elias Jr.
Taylor, ? Cherry
Taylor, J B. E.
Vandiver, Wm.
Vandiver, Aaron
Valentine, Benj.
Voyles, Amos
Vandiver, John
Vandiver, Edward
Vandiver, Enoch
Vandiver, Sanford
Vernon, Jas. ? ?
Vandiver, Peter C.
Wright, James
Williamson?, David

White, Lydia
White, Jonathan
Webb, Edmund
Webb, Elijah
Webb, Warren
Willingham, John
Willingham, Jas.
Wilson, James
Wardlaw, James
Wardlaw, John M.
Wilson, Hugh
Wilson, James P.
Wilson, Barkley
Wilbanks, Shadrach?
Wyatt, Elijah
Williams, James C.
Williams, Jasper
Webster, Jane
Williamson, Wm.
Wright, H.? N.
Wade, Edward
Welden, Wm.
Wright, Wm. F.?
Williamson, Mastin
Wilson, George
Webb, Samuel
Whitman, Jacob
Watt, James G.
Wiles, Jesse
Wallers, Ibzan (Watters?)
Worthington, J. _?
Wiles, Elizabeth‾
Wiles, James H.
Wiley, James
Wright, Eliz.?
Watt, Thomas
Watt, James D.?
Watt, Joseph W.
Watt, Mary
Willbanks, Elijah
West, Isaac
Wilson, Lewis
Williford, Samuel
Williford, Thos. _?
Wright, Catharine‾
White, Thomas
White, Henry M.
Wallace, Wilson
Webb, William
Wilson, John
Welborn, Sarah
Welborn, Phonas?
Welborn, Thomas M.
Wilson, Sarah
Welborn, Wm. E.
Wilson, James B.
Willbanks, James
Welborn, William
Willbanks, Hez'a.
Williams, W. A.
Williams, Ira.? C.
Wilson, John
Wilson, Wm. M.
Welborn, Albert G.
Watson, James
Wilson, Charles
Wilson, William
Wiliams, John
Watkins, Fein?
Waddle, Amaziah?(Hannah?)
Walker, J. L.
Wiginton, Henry
Wilson, James
Wilson, James J.
White, Bartholomew
Watson, Willard
Wilson, Thomas
Watkins, Baylis
Wilson, R. L.
Watkins, Wm.
Watkins, Joseph
Wilson, Mrs. Martha
West, Thomas

Webb, Clayton
Williams, M. B.
Warnock, John Jr.
Warnock, John dec'd.
Webb, James
Whitfield, Lewis
Webb, Elisha
Winters, Miss Frs.?
Wiginton, John
Wiginton, Geo. W.
Watt, John
Wyatt, Redman G.
Webb, C. B.
Walker, Peter
Williams, Newton
Wakefield, Conrad
Williford, Sarah
Williford, Chs. H.?
Waddle, Alexander
Wyatt, J. F.
Watson, David
Whitfield, J. L.
Whitner, J. N.
Wakefield, Andrew J.
Watson, Daniel K.
Whitaker, H. H. & Co.
Wardlaw, Hugh H.
Waller, William
Waller, Caroline C.
Watson, Thos. dec'd.
Warren, Saml. dec'd.
Warley & Sharpe
Warley, Mrs. Sophia
Whitworth, Chas. R.
Watt, Mary Jr.
White, Newton
Young, Thomas
Young, William
Yeargan, Samuel
Young, James
Young, Frs. dec'd.
Young, Frs. A.
Young, Nancy

ANDERSON 1842

PICKENS DISTRICT:
Major, James
Brackenridge
Keown, Wm.
Green, John
Norris, E. S. & Huston
Armstrong, James
Gunnin, James
Anderson, Wm.
Hubbard, Wm.
Grantt, Wm.
Fretwell, John
Earle, John B.
Whitfield, Lewis
Harrison, James
Fielding, Henry
Vandiver, Sandford
Knight, Warren W.
Johns, Anna
Mays, Mrs. Miriam D.
Sullivan, Kelly
Meredith, A.J.

ABBEVILLE:
Gambrell, James
Webster, Jane
Armstrong, John B.
Stiefle, Mary
Tucker, Wm.
Mosely, T. P.
Hall, David
Mouchet, Jacob
Smith, Wm. C.
Smith, Benjamin
Harleston, Edward
Dickson, Thomas
Todd, James

ARBEVILLE cont'd.:
Fisher, Thomas dec'd.
Ruff, David
Alewine, Michael

GREENVILLE:
Mavrick, S. A. & Co.
Seaborn, George

LAWRENS:
Mavrick, S. A.

ST. PH. & ST. MICH'L.:
Mavrick & Son

ST. STEPHENS:
Gaillard, C. L. & Jenkins

S. A. Mavrick in:
ORANGEBURG
UNION
NEWBERRY
SPARTANBURG

GENERAL TAXES COLLECTED IN THE DISTRICT OF ANDERSON FOR THE YEAR 1843 BY DAVID SIMMONS,
Tax Collector.

Acker, Peter N.	Bagwell, Jas.? W.	Burress, Jno.
Acker, Susannah?	Brown, Lidi H.	Bailey, Wm.
Acker, J. J.	Brock, M. H.	Branyan, Hemp?
Acker, A...?	Brock, Hayden	Branyan, Joseph
Avery, Wm.	Bannister, Rolley?	Barkley, Nancy
Allen, Jas. E.	Braswell, Anderson	Brown, Elijah
Armstrong, Jas. Sr.?	Brock, Jas. Esqr.	Brown, Geo.
Armstrong, Wm. B.	Braswell, Asa	B....?, Jas.
Ashley, Wilson	Branyan, Dr.? A.	Bryant, Simon S.?
Ashley, John	Browne, D.? & J.	Borough, Thos.
Ashley, Edward	Browne, Saml.	Bennett, Wm.
Alewine, Michael	Browne, Jeremiah M.	Bryant, Nathan
Armstrong, Jas.	Brownlee, Maria	Bryant, Nathan R.
Adams, Henry	Burton, Blackman	Bryant, Ford?
Adams, John	Beatty, Wm.	Blasingame, Thos.
Ables, Jas.?	Burdett, Hiram	Blasingame, Robt. E.
Arnold, Allen	Buchanan, Wm.	Brown?, Wm. & Milly?
Acker, Wm.	Brown, Charilty	Blankenship, Jno.?
Anderson, David	Beatty, Frances	Bailey, Isaac L.?
Arnold, Lawson	Beatty, J. _?	Barr, Leroy
Anderson, Dr. Wm.	Beatty, Thos.	Benson, E. B.
Abbott, John	Beatty, Saml. W.	Benson, E. B. & Son
Amick, Wm. D.	Bonds, Sugar	Bishop, Jane
Acker, Holbert	Bowie, Chas.?	Bellote, Jacob
Able, Jno.	Benton, Peyton F.?	Bellotte, Jno. E.
Adams, Asa?	Black, _?	Bolling, Sally
Armstrong, Arch'd.?	Brown, Chas.	Burns, Anderson
Anderson, Micajah	Beatty, David	Bowden, Jas.
Armstrong, Jno.? R.	Bozeman, Lewis	Brooks, Garner
Archer, Wm. M.	Bozeman, Danl. L.	Bell, Samuel
Alexander, David	Baker, Saml. H.	Brackenrige, Robt.
Bowon, Sam	Brooks, Thos.	Burriss, Elisha
Brown, Randolph	Barrett?, Jno.	Burriss, Jacob
Bellotte, Peter E.	Brown, Abner	Betterton, Jno.?
Bellotte, ? L.	Burroughs, Bryant	Brown, Eliz'th
Bollery?, Albert	Burress, Reuben	Burns, Jno.
Barkley, J. M.?	Bennett, Cosper	Brock, Enos
Barkley, Sarah	Burress, Thos. Jr.	Broyles, J. T.?
Ballentine, J. D.	Buchanan, Saml.?	Bowen, Robt.
Bennett, Thos.	Bradbery, Jesse	Brownlee, W...?
Bennett, Chas. M.	Bradbery, Jas.	Brazeale, Gambrell
Brazeale, Enoch	Bradbery, Wm.	Boyd, Robt.
Brazeale, D. K.	Bruce, Chas. P.	Barksdale, Jno.
Brazeale, Griffin Jr.?	Bruce, ...?	Bishop, Nicholas
Brazeale, Williamson	Bailey, Allen	Burriss, Milford
Ballentine, Jesse H.	Bowman, Rich.?	Bruce, Jno.
Brazeale, Griffin	Bradbery, Salathiel	Baker & Lindsey
Ballentine, George	Bradbery, Salathiel, Junr.	Brown, Larkin
Broyles, Aaron	B....?, Jordan	Broyles, O. R.
Brazeale, Math'w.	Barton, Holl?	Burress, Joshua
Brown, Dr. G. R.	Bowen, Jas. G.	Bruce, H...?
Braswell, Geo.	Brazeale, Kinnon	Brown, Saml.
Braswell, Jas.	Burris, Thos. Sr.	Burress, Elbert
Braswell, Nancy	Barrett, Chas.	Burress, Eliz'th
Bagwell, Jas.?	Pickens, Wm. (see also	Brown, Jno.
Bagwell, Jno.	under "P")	Brown, Wm. P.

Bowen, Eliz'th.?
Brown, David
Bell, Jas.
Benson, J. P.
Benson, J. P. & W.
Brown, Robt. B.
Bee, B. C.?
Brown, Auth'?/Cath'e.?
Brown, Robt. M.
Barth, Moody
Cobb, Jno.
Chamblee, Moses
Cooley, Jas.
Cox, Sarah
Cox, Abner
Cox, Wm. Jr.
Cox, Wm. dec'd.
Cummins, David
Clinkscales, Wm. P.
Clements, Wm. K.
Cox, J...?
Cox, Wm.
Cox, Geo.?
Cummins, Caleb
Clements, Alex'r.
Clements, Benj'n.
Cox, Thos. Jr.
Clements, Benj'n dec'd.
Cobb, Martin
Campmire?, George
Cox, Thos.
Clements, Isaac
Clements, Hugh
Clements, C. W.
Cobb, Joab/Noah?
Cobb, Ephraim
Clark, Joseph
Clinkscales, Levi dec'd.
Carpenter, Alfred M.
Clinkscales, Wm. Jr.?
Carr, Mary
Chalmers, J. C.
Cowen, Hiram
Cunningham, Frs.? S.
Casey, Sarah
Conner, Jno. W.
Casey, Delilah
Cook, Wm.
Cunningham, Catharine
Casey, Mary
Cummins, Harmon
Clinkscales, Abner
Caldwell, Joseph
Cox, Mary
Caldwell, John/Joth?
Carpenter, Dr.? W.
Caldwell, Wm.
Conwill, Jas.
Christopher, Jno.
Cunningham, David
Cunningham, Thos.
Caldwell, Jas.
Chamblee, Benj'n.?
Clardy, Norman
Coats, Jno.?
Coffee, Olley?
Corr?, Laban
Clinkscales, Bary?
Carpenter, Alex'r.
Carpenter, Albert L.?
Campbell, George
Clark, Jno. B.?
Conner?, Isaac
Carpenter, Jas. M.
Carlile, Wm.
Chamblee, Jas.
Chastain, Hopper?
Chastain, Jno.
Chamblee, Jas.
Chambers?, Nancy
Campbell, Jas.
Cox, Asa
Cobb, Henry

Cobb, Josiah W.
Cobb, Azaria? P.
Carter, Caleb
Clardy, Joab?
Clardy, John
Ceasar
Carter, Spencer
Childers?, Jno.
Craig, Saml.
Crenshaw, Thos.
Campbell, A. C.(J.? C.)
Carney, Miss J.? M.
Christian, E. C. B.
Cherry, Thos. R.
Campbell, Jesse
Carpenter, Jno.?
Chappell, Jno.? B.
Clinkscales, Asa
Cannon, E. dec'd.
Cooley, Lewis
Campbell, Alex'r.?
Cason, Jno.? J. M.
Cason, Sarah
Cason, Esther
Cason, Wm. dec'd.
Cater, __? J. P.
Cox, Joseph
Cox, Rachel & sister
Crayton, B. F.
Coats, Jas.
Campbell, Danl.
Cooley, Anna
Cooley, Jno.?
Cowen, Wm.
Chamblee, Robt.
Cummins, Robt.
Cox, Reuben B.
Clardy, Jno.? B.
Cox, David
Craswell, J. H.
Cox, Jno.?
Cox, Gabriel
Crawford, Jas.
Crawford, Sarah
Crawford, Wm. dec'd.
Cochran, Danl. H.
Caruth, Miss L.
Craswell, Sarah
Cherry, Susan
Cater, Edward
Cheves, Langdon
Coffin, Abraham
Dawson, Saml.
Davis, Valentine
Duncan, David
Davis, Levi?
Davis, Wm.
Duckworth, J. C.
Dean, C. P.?
Davis, Jno. L.
Davis, Thos. W.?
Davis, Moses
Drake, Jno.?/Jas.?
Drake, Enock
Duncan, Robt. M.
Dunlap, Math'w.
Dean, Thos.?
Dollar, Williamson
Dooley, Wm.
Driver, Jas.
Driver, Jas. Jr.
Dowdle, Morris
Duckworth, Jacob
Dickson, Matthew
Dalrymple, John
Drennan, Wm.
Dickson, Wm.
Dorr?, George
Duckworth, Thos.
Davis, Jno. J.?
Duckworth, Howard
Durham, Wm. Jr.
Durham, Wm. Sr.

Duckworth, Anna?
Durham, David
Dalton, Burrel?
Douthit, Jas.
Douthit, Benj.
Douthit, Jno.
Durham, Anderson
Durham, Clarissa
Davis, Richard
Davis, Chas. R.
Davis, Archd.
Dilworth, Billy G.
Dicksinson, Wilson?
Dart, Mrs. Mary L.
Dupree, Benj.
Dupree, Susanna H.?
Davis, Jno. __?
Davis, Enock dec'd.
Dickson, Thos. dec'd.
Daniels, W. J. C.
Davis, __? W.
Dunham, R.?A.?
Davis, Jno.?
Drake, Jas.
Duckworth, Wilborn
Dalrymple, Jas.
Dalrymple, John
Dalrymple, Mary
Dean, Moses
Duckworth, Benj.?
Davis, Aaron
Dobbins, Aaron C.?
Dobbins, Jas.
Dobbins, Jno.
Dobbins, Martha
Dalrymple, Lewis
Duncan, Thos.
Dupree, B. J.
Dupree, Esther M.
Earle, Baylis
Erskine, __?
Erskine, Jas.
Erskine, Thos.
East, Margt.
Eibanks, Elijah
Elliott, Mrs. Peney
Emerson, Saml.
Elrod, Wm.
Eljan?, Stani___?
Elrod, Thos. P.
Earp, Wesley
Earp, Caleb dec'd.
Emerson, Jas.
Eskew, Wm.
Elliott, Mary
Erskine, Wm.
Erskine, Jas. Jr.
Ellener/Ellenson, Miles
Ellison, Joel
Elrod, Wm.
Elrod, George G.
Elrod, Sarah
Elrod, Samuel
Elrod, Philip
Elrod, George
Elrod, Wm. __?
Ellison, Jas.
Elrod, Elias
Elrod, Jno. M.
Earle, Jas. W.
Elrod, Adam
Elrod, Isaac dec'd.
Eaton, Jas.? C.
Earle, Saml. G.
Estes, Larkin
Evans, Dr. J.
Earle, Elias
Elrod, Thos. JR.?SR.?
Elliott, R. E.
Estes, Micajah
Earle, Ann
Fant, Mary
Fant, Alfred

French, Wm.
Featherston, J. W.
Fisher, Saml. S.
Fant, Wm. N.
Frick, Christian
Felton, Mary
Fant, A. F.? P.
Fant, V. D.
Fleming, Richd.
Ford, Jos.?
Fleming, Jno. O.
Ford, Stephen
Ford, Wm.
Floyd, Silas
Forbes, Alanson
Fenell, Jane
Fant, Jas.? R.
Fisher, Jno. J.
Fant, Abner
Fielding, H. B.
Ford, J. W.?
Fretwell, John
Forsyth, Wm.
Fisher, Sml. C.
Findley, Elias
Felton, Richd.
Fant, Saml.
Fretwell, Joseph
Fowler, Ruth
Fuller, Alfred
Griffin, Elijah
Glaspy, Wm.
Gambrell, Jno.
Gambrell, Wm.
Gambrell, Henry dec'd.
Gambrell, David H.
Gaines, Henry M.
Gambrell, Jas.?
Gantt, Wm.
Gambrell, Jas.
Gambrell, Sarah
Gambrell, E. B.
Gambrell, Wm.
Gantt, Jno.
Garnett?, Hugh
Greer, David Jr.
Gantt, Jno. G.
Greer, David Sr.
Greer, Jno. M.
Green, Wm. W.
Grubbs, Geo.
Gable, Henry Jr.
Gable, Leo'nd
Cassaway?, Benj.
Gable, Henry Sr.
Gray, Eliz'th
Green, Jas.
Gentry, Moody
Gentry, Eliz'th
Galloway, Matthew
Gentry, Zach.
Gregg, Hugh
Glenn, Wm.
Gilmer, Robt.
Gilmer, Nancy
Gilliland, Alex'r.
Gilbert, Amos
Grubbs, Jno.? M.
Graham, Andrew J.
Geir, David
Gentry, Reuben
Gentry, Daniel
Gray, Jas.? P.
Gray, Alex'r. D.
Gunison?, Levi
Geer, Solomon
Gilmer, Jas.
Gaillard, Josiah D.
Gaillard, Mary D.
Garrett, Thos. H.
Golden, John
Guyton, Jno. W.
Guyton, Robt. dec'd.

Guyton, G.
Guthrie, Nelson?
Guthrie, David dec'd
Guthrie, Benjn.
Guthrie, Stephen
Gibbs, Mary
Gambrell, Reid
Gambrell, ____?
Gambrell, Jas. Jr.?
Gambrell, Ezekiel
Givens, Harrison
Gaillard, A. D.
Gaillard, Chas. L.
Gaillard, C. D.
Gaillard, C. L. & C. D.
Garrison, Henry
Griffin, Jas. C. dec'd.
Gantt, Wm.
Gorden, Robert
Geer?, Thos.
Gambrell, Mathew dec'd.
Gambrell, Barbara
Gentry, John
Gentry, Arthur
Gantt, Jas. A.
Gunnin, Jas.
George, Jas.
Gray, Hezekiah
Gentry, J. B.
Gray, Robt. D.
Graham, J. B.
Gordon, Jas.
Griffin, J. C.? & Co.
Gibson, Wm. R.?
Gaillard, Mrs.? R. W.
Gaillard, Wm. H.?
Gambrell, David
Goode, Llewellen dec'd.
Gantt, Jno. W.
Hilhouse, Joseph
Hembree, Jas. Jr.?/Sr.?
Hunt, Wm. S.
Hembree, Wm.
Hillhouse, Saml. P.
Holmes, Wm.
Haynie, Luke
Haynie, Wm. H.
Holland, John Jr.?
Harkins, Hugh
Harkins, Jas.
Holland, Caleb B.
Harper, Jno. Jr.
Harper, Jno.
Holland, John
Horton, Grief
Harper, Jno. H.
Harper, Wm. C.
Hanks, Luke
Hanks, Thos.
Hanks, Tilman
Hunt, Wm.
Hunt, Jno.
Hinton, Jno.
Hopkins, Jno.
Hopkins, Jas. M.
Hamilton, Jane
Hamilton, Nancy
Harkness, John
Harkness, Jno. N.
Harkness, Robt. C.?
Hall, Lent
Hamilton, Wm.
Hall, Saml. C.
Hall, Wm. A.?
Haynie, Stephen
Hall, Jno. Jr.?
Hall, Lemual
Hamilton, Luke
Hanna, Thomas
Hall, Zach?
Hodges, R. H. W.
Howie, Robt.
Havird, Mark W.

Harris, Nathan
Hall, David
Hatton, Wm.
Hill, Thos. O.
Hays, Jno.
Howard, Jared?
Hardy, Jas.
Howard, Hiram
Howard, George
Hewans?, Mrs./Wm.?
Hall, Lent
Fleming, Wm.
Hardy, Richd. B.
Haslett, Moses W.
Haynie, Chas.
Herndon, George
Hale, John
Henderson, Martha
Humphrey, David
Holland, Robert Jr.?/P.?
Holland, Wm.
Holland, Robert Sr.
Herring, Levi
Hanson, James (Harrison?)
Harris, Benj.
Hammond, Saml. S.?
Harrison, Wm.
Herron, Jas.
Hamilton, Jno. M.
Hembree, Jas. Jr.?
Hembree, Willis
Hendrix?, David
Hembree, Azarias D.
Hall, Wilson
Harris, Benjn.
Hunter, Sarah
Hammond, Wm. L.
Hammond, Herbert
Holland, Aaron B.
Hunt, Jeremiah J.
Hamilton, Cyrus E.
Harper, Asa
Harper, Thos.
Hamilton, Leonard J.?
Hix, John
Hix, Milton
Huntor, Mary
Harleston, Edward
Harris, Mrs.? S.
Hughes, B. P.
Hackett, Albert
Hall, Joseph
Hall, Aaron
Hall, Joab
Hanks, Mary
Hall, Nancy
Hall, Ezekiel
Harris, John
Hamilton, Martha J.
Harper, Nancy
Hughens, Robt.
He_on?, John
Hall, Martha
Hall, Fenton?
Hall, A. J.?
Hipps, Joseph
Hunter, John
Hammond, B. F.
Holland, Wm.
Harris, Gillison dec'd.
Harrison, Jas. M.
Harris, Jno.
Haynie, Jno.
Hall, Jno. B.
Hopkins, Jno. H.?
Hugor, Frs.? H.?
Hubbard, Wm.
Hamilton, D. K.
Harris, Joseph P.
Hastie, Jno. & Co.
Hastie, Jno.
Harris, Sarah G.? J.
Ha__, Danl.

Hening, Jesse
Ha__, Baley
Hīx, Wm.
Ingram, James
Johnson, Willis
Johnson, Peter
Jennings, Jane?
Irwin, Eleanor
Jones, Thos.?
Jones, Joseph B.
Isbell, Robt.
Jolly, Joseph M.
Jolly, Jas.
Jolly, Alexander dec'd.
Ingram, Wm.
Jolly, Henry
Irby, Chas.
Jones, Ambrose H.?
Jones, Jno. W.
Jones, Saml.
Jones, Wilson
Jones, Wm.
Jenkins, W. L.
Junkin, Marg't dec'd.
Isbell, Saml.
Johnson, Allen
Johnson, Nancy dec'd.
Johnson, Joel E.
Jones, James
Jolly, Wm.
Jones, John
Jeffrey, Mrs. Rhoda
Johnson, W. G.
King, Robt.
King, Peter
King, Geo. W.
King, Jas.
Kay, Jesse
Knox, ...?
Kelly, Elisha
Kelly, Allen
Kelly, John
King, Josiah
Kelly, Alfred
Kay, Wm.
Kay, Wm. Jr.
Kay, Wm. P.
Kay, Fielding
Kay, Joel
Kay, Cath'e.
Kay, Jno.? W.
Kay, Mason
Kay, James
Korr, Wm. (Kerr?)
Kingsley, Chester
Kay, Strother
Keown, Geo. W.
Keown, Wm. M.
Keys, John
Kay, Silas W.
King, John J.
King, Wm.
King, Wm. P.
King, Hiram
Kay, Alex'r.
King, John D.
Kelly, Danl.
Keys, Jas. C.?
Knight, Warner K.?(Warren)
Keaster?, Henry
Knauff, __?. H.?
Kay, Jas― D.
Kenton, Wm.
Kay, Gabriel
Keaton, Arch'd.
Kay, John
Kay, Chas.
Kay, Fell?
Kay?, Robt. A.
Kirksey & Mattison
Kirksey, Fair
Lawless, Mich'l.
Lewis, Jas. K.

Lewis, Mrs.? J. D.?
Lewis & Simpson
Lewis, & Cox
Lucius, Danl. F. Sr.
Lucius, Danl. D. Jr.
Lee, Jas.?
Lee, Philip
Loveless, Nathan
Liverett, Stephen Jr.?
Liverett, John
Little, Rachel
Latham, Wm.
Leverett, Wm.
Lesley?, Wm.
Long, Isaac
Liverett, Thos.
Liverett, Stephen Sr.
Long, Wm.
Lockhart, M. J.?
Latham, Cornelius
Ledbetter, Jas.
Ledbetter, Mary
Ledbetter, Joel
Ledbetter, David
Long, Harrison
Lewis, Eli'th
Lidole, Andrew J.
Lewis, Elisha
Langa?, Wm.
Langston, Solo'm.
Laboon, Joseph
Laboon, Eady
Long, Ezekiel
Lewis, Sarah
Lewis, Jesse P.
Lanier, Bird
Latimer, W.? B.
Lewis, Jesse
Lewis, Miss H.? E.
Lorton, Jno. L.?
Lorton & Kirksey
Lorton, Mrs.? Fr's.?
Lowry, Jackson
Liverett, Wesley
Morris, David J.
McLeskey, Jno.
Massey, Ab'm.?
Major, Elijah
McDaniel, Mary
Major, Jno.
Major, Wm.
McCollister, Jno.
Mayfield, Eph'm.
Moore, Grant A.
Mauldin, B. F.
Maddox, Henry
Mattison, Wm.
Mattison, Danl.?
Mattison, Jas.
McGee, Mich'l.
Mattison, Eliz'th.
Mitchell, Eph'm.
McCoy, Jas. Jr.
McCoy, Jas. M.
McGee, Burrell
Massey, Laban
May, Geo. W.
Mattison, Richd.
Mattison, Olley
McCollum, Danl.
McAdams, Jno.
Moore, Jeremiah
McCoy, Jno. M.?
McCoy, Saml.
McFall, Benj.?
McPhail, Jno.
May, Tucker
May, ___ Gabriel L.
Milford, Mary
Martin, Phebe
Milford, John
McBride, Jno.
McBride, Andrew J.

McGee, Jas.
Morgan, John
McKee, Archd.
McKee, Wm. D.?
McGee, Willis
McCullough, G. H. dec'd.
McCurdy, Sarah
McCullough, Saml. dec;d?
McCarley, Joseph?
McGee, Jesse C.
McGee, __? J. C.
McCarley, Robt.
McConnell, Wm.
McFill?, Mary J.(McGill?)
McPherson, Dorcas
Mouchet, Jacob
McMahan, Saml.
McPherson, Eliz'th
McGee, Jno.
McDaniel, Rebecca
Mecklin, Jas. G.
Moore, Jno.?
McGill, Mary
McGee, Elias
McLee, Jas.
McLees, Andrew
McCown, Jno.
Massey, Silas
McAlister?, J. S.
McCarley, Jas.
McLees?, Jas.
McLees?, Margt.
Maret, Benj. W.
Masters, G. W.
Moorhead, Maxey
Moorhead, Ira?
Moorhead, M. L.
Moorhead, Sarah
Moorhead, Har....?
Miller, Jno.
Martin, Saml.
Mitchell, Caleb
McFee, Sarah
Mitchell, Benjn. S.
Martin, Mathew
Maddox, Thos.
McConnell, Thos.
Martin, Jacob
Martin, Abram
Martin, Jas.
Moore, David
Milwee, Saml.
Millwee, Wm. J.
Millwee, Eliz'th sisters
McKinney, Martha
Murphy, Thos. M.
Mattison, Eliz'th
Martin, Chesley
Martin, Wm.
Martin, Hester
McCollister, Jas.?
Murphy, Ezekiel
Murphy, E. & Co.
Murphy, John
Moore, Wm.
Moore, Thos. B.?
Moore, Elijah
Mulliken, Benjn. Sr.?
Mulliken, Jas.
McMurray, ___?
Mulliken, Em.
McMahan, Peter
Mulliken, Benj. Jr.
Martin, Abram?
Moore, Jno. M. dec'd.
McElroy, Jno.
Miller, M. __?
McMurtry, Wm.
McMurtry, Rebecca
Major, Jno.? P.
Major, Joseph
Morris, Saml.
Molton?, Michael

McMurray, Wm. C.
McCrary, Mary
McCrary, Albert
McElroy, Arch'd.
Martin, Jesse
Miller, Jno. C.
Maverick, Saml. & children
McCay, Jno.
Meredith, Abraham
McGriggor, Mary
McAllister, Jno.
Major, Elijah
Massey, Jas. E.
Moore, Leah
Mattison, Mary
Massey, Kindred dec'd.
May, Edmund
McAlister, Andrew
McAlester, Margt.
Martin, Jno. Col.
McCann, Thos. H.
McCann & Walker
McCay, Martin L.
Mauldin & Guyton
Mauldin, B. F. & Co.
Mauldin, J. L.
McFall, Saml. R.
McPhail, Peter
McGriggor, Jno.
Mitchell, Jno.
McCown, Robt.
McMillion, Wyatt A.
Morris, Jas.
McCollister, Nathan
McCollister, Andrew
Morris, Jesse C.
McConnell, L.? P.?
Mattison, Wyatt
Motes?, Eliz'th L.
Marett, Obadiah
Miller Elias
Moorhead, Jno.
McCullys, Stephen
McFee, Wm.
Mayfield, Margt.?
Moorhead, Alex'r.
McFall, Andrew
McKee, Washington (McFee?)
McFall, Jno.
McAlister, Nathan
Moorhead, Lewis
Mills?, Berry
Miller, Mrs. Jane
McMurtry, Jas.
Maxwell, Robt. A.
Maxwell, John
Mays, Saml.
Moore, Larkin
Mays?, Miriam D.
Martin, John
McClure, Edwd. J.
Nichols, Wm.
Nichols, Jas.
Nichols, Arch'd.
Newell, Wm.
Newell, Wm. & others?
Norris, Jesse W.
Norris, E. S.
Nelson, Wm. R.
Norris, Robt. B.
Nevitt, Wm. M.
Norris, Jno. E.
Nichols, Archd. J.
North, Jno. L.
Newton, Isaac
Newton, Isaac M.
Newton, Willis
Newton, Saml.
Norris, R.? O.
Norris, M. A.
Newell, George
Oldham, Thos.
Oldham, Wm.

Oldham, Jno. dec'd.
Owen, Thornton
OBryant, Wm.
OBryant, Andrew
OBryant, Joseph
Orr, Wm.
Owen, Elijah
Orr, Thos.
Orr, Andrew
Oliver, Jas.
Owen, Lavis?
Orr, Alex'r.?
Owen, Danl.
Owen, Banister
Orr, Jas.
Oliver, Martha
Overby, Nicho's
Oberby, Benj'n
Owen, John
Owen, Martha
Owen, Elijah Jr.
Orr, C.
Orr, Jane D.?
Osborn, J. A.
Pickens, L. J.
Quails, Reuben
Pritchard, Lewis
Poore, Jno.
Poore, Geo.
Pettis, Jane
Poore, Saml.
Poore, Nancy
Poore, Jno. B.
Poore, Reuben
Poore, Lucind
Poore, Holland
Philips, Reuben
Pruitt, Wm.
Pruitt, Elias
Penall, Thos.
Pearman, Benj'n
Pearman, Jonathan
Presley, David L.?
Price, Samuel (Lemuel?)
Pitts, Wm.
Pressley, Ann
Porter, Hugh?
Parker, Mathew
Palmer, Wm.
Padgett, Eliz'th?
Parker, Jas. ?
Quails, Jno. B.
Parker, Robt.
Poole, Eliz'th?
Poole, Wm. & Mary
Poole, Adam
Palmer, Nancy
Pickle, Wm.
Pickle, Jas. E.?
Pickle, Wm. C.
Paulman, Ludovick
Pickle, Jacob
Pickens, Robert
Pickens, Wm. S.?
Pegg, John
Pegg, Jas. B.
Philips, Martin
Philips, Jno.
Philips, Arch'd.
Passmore, Wm. dec'd.
Pullen, Leroy
Pettigrew, Robt.? H.
Pullen, Wm.
Poore, Wm.
Prince, C.? J.
Pepper, Elijah
Pickerell, Jonathan
Partan, Hubbard
Pearce, Wm.
Price, Harrison
Robertson, Caleb
Reeves, ___ ?
Rogers, J.? L.?

Roberts, Mathias
Reese, Wm. G.
Ragsdale, Frs. A.
Reid, Henry
Robinson, Jno. B.?
Reese, David
Rice, Hezekiah
Rice, Thos. L.
Rutledge, Jesse
Robinson, Jas. E.
Robinson, Jno.
Robinson, Jno. J.
Risner, Silas P.? A.
Rice, Hezekiah dec'd.
Rice, Amazia
Reid, Thos. L.
Reid?, Alfred E.
Ruff, David
Ranson, Wm.
Robinson, Jno.
Roach, Berry?
Roach, Henry
Rice, Sarah?
Riley, Danl.
Rampey, Jas.
Rainey, Jno. dec'd.
Reid, Robt.
Reid, Wm.
Reid, Eliz'th
Reid, Hugh
Reid, Moses
Reid, Jesse
Rogers, ___ ?
Russell, David dec'd.
Rimon, Jas. W.
Russell, David
Reid, Andrew
Rainwater, David
Rochester, Nath'l.
Rogers, John
Rogers, Benj'n. L.?
Richey, Wm.
Rogers, Jeremiah
Rogers, Wm.
Richardson, Noah L.?
Richardson, Mathias
Riley, Abraham
Red, Elihu
Rosamond, Jno. H.
Ricks, Washington
Rogers, Simeon
Robinson, Dr.? Wm.
Rankin, Geo.?
Russell, Ths. H.
Robinson, David
Robinson, Jane
Ross, Anthony ?
Richey, Eliz'th.
Rofllander, Jno.
Reese, Mrs. Ann
Reese, Thos. L.?
Rice, Fleetwood
Reese, Geo. dec'd.
Robinson, E. G.
Robins, Mary
Richey, Jas. N.
Rogers, Wm. Jr.
Richardson, Mary L.
Richardson, Wade A.?
Richardson, Maria C.. S.
Ruff, John
Richardson, A. W.
Richardson, N.? J.
Richardson, David
Richardson, Guen?
Rice, Ibzan
Rice, Jane
Rimar , Lucinda
Rogers, Eliz'th
Riley, Hezekiah
Richardson, Wm.
Roberts, Benson
Reese, H. D.

Reid, L.? P.
Richey, Reuben
Steele, Wm.
Steele, J. L.
Spray, Thos.
Smith, Willeys C.
Stevenson, Mary
Smith, Wm.
Spearman, David
Spearman, D. D.
Stone, George
Stone, Wm.
Shirley, Eliz'th
Smith, Davis
Smith, Wm.
Smith, A. W.
Smith, Jeremiah
Smith, Richd. H.?
Smith, Richd.
Stone, Hampton
Shirley, Obadiah
Shirley, Benh'n
Strickland, Mathew
Saylor, Isaac
Seawright, Jas.
Saylor, Leonard
Shirley, Benjn. Jr.
Steifle, Mary
Smith, Saml.
Spearman, Jno.
Speed, Wm. G.
S__ott, David
Simpson, Wm.
Sanders, Ab'm.?
Simpson, Arch'd.?
Sullivan, Kelly
Stevenson, Jno.
Scott, Jno.
Smith, Robertson
Stuart, Jno.
Stevenson, Thos.
Sherard, Wm.
Simpson, Thos.
Snipes, Sion
Stuart, Jas.
Stevenson, Jas.
Stevenson, Geo. Jr.?
Shaw, Peyton R.
Stuart, Jas.
Stuart, Adam
Stuart, Geo.
Siddall, Stephen
Stacks, Willis
Shaw, Wm. L.?
Skelton, Thos.
Siddall, A. S.? Y.
Smith, Martin H.
Skelton, Thos. A.
Skelton, Thos. S.
Seawright, Andrew
Sadler, David
Sadler, David Jr.
Skelton, Arch'd. B.
Swilling, Robt.
Swilling, Jas.
Swilling, Saml.
Simons, Jas.
Shearer, Gillam
Stevenson, Andrew
Stevenson, Geo.
Snipes, Mathew
Simpson, David
Sullivan, Jno.
Smith, Nimrod
Steele, Nancy
Smith, Thos.
Scott, T.? L.
Sherell, Lewis
Shirley, J. W.? Jr.
Shirley, Aaron
Shirley, J. P.? Jr.
Smith, Aaron, Jr.?
Smith, Jno. M.

Spearman, Benjn.
Spearman, Frs. A.
Smith, Geo. S.?
Slaten, Jno.
Smith, Basil
Slaten, Loven
Smith, Philip L.?
Scott, Mitchell B.
Stanton, Geo.
Sitton, Wm.
Sitton, Jno. P.
Smith, Thos. G.
Smith, Joseph
Smith, Griffin
Siddall, John
Sitton, Wm. D.
Smith, Jno. E.
Satterfield, Jeremiah
Smith, Harvey J.
Smith, Andrew M.
Smith, Jas. D.
Smith, Ephraim
Smith, Benjn.
Smith, Jno. C.
Smith, Jas.
Sharp, Jno.
Spruil, Simpson
Stott, Drayton
Shanklin, J. N.?V.?
Sloan, Thos. N.
Simpson, Richd. F.
Smith, Aaron
Sloan, Benj. F.
Pendleton Mfg. Co.
Smith, Zephaniah
Seaborn, Geo.
Sitton, Jno. B.
Smith, Mrs.? S.? N/
Smith, E. S.? V.
Smith, M. E. D.?
Smith, A. E. D.
Smith, Jno. L. N.
Smith, W. C.
Smith, Benjn.
Smith, S. E.
Smith, B. S.
Smith, Wm.
Smith, Waytt
Sanders, Wm.
Sanders, H. J.
Stevenson, Jno.
Smith, Simeon
Smith, Edward
Smith, Ebenezer
Smith, Jesse R.?
Spear, J. G.
Smith, Whitaker
Shearor, Andrew
Smith, Jno.
Smith, Robert
Strickland, Willys
Saylor, Abraham?
Saylor, John
Sheriff, Washington
Skelton, Jno. W. B.
Sadler, Jno.
Simmons, Chas.
Simmons, Chas. H.?
Smith,Samuel
Stanton, Catharine
Stanton, Mathews?
Sloan, Jno. L.?
Swords, Jno. S.
Sloan, Susan?
Sharp, Elam
Starke, Mrs. E. G.
Symes, Dr. F. W.
Stanley, Ezekiel
Simmons, Thos. H.
Simmons, David
Tillinghast, Elias
Todd, Chas.
Telford, Wm.

Telford, Isabella
Turner, Jno. B.
Trussell, Henton?
Towns, Wm. W.
Trussell, Posey
Todd, Wm. P.
Taylor, Richard
Taylor, Elijah
Thompson, Eliz'th?
Thompson, Mathew?
Thompson, Jno. M.
Taylor, Thos. Jr.
Tucker, Nancy
Tate, Jno. A.
Tucker, Jas.
Taylor, Jno. M.
Tucker, Wm.
Tucker, Dejarnet
Turner, Jas.
Tate, David
Tate, Tilman
Todd, Andrew
Todd, Robert
Taylor, Jas.
Tippen, Eliz'th.
Towers?, Rev. Danl. dec'd.
Towers, Jno. R.
Tate, Van
Thompson, Jas.
To__y?, Henry
Timms?, Isaac
Thompson, Jas.
Todd, Jno. L.
Tripp, Nicholas
Tripp, Jno. Jr.
Tripp, Jno. H.
Tompkins, Jno.
Tea man, Lasarus
Taylor, David S.
Talliaferro, Caroline _?
Taylor, Joseph Jr.
Tippen, George
Todd, Mary
Todd, James
Thompson, Jno.
Taylor, Thos. Junr.?
Tilley, Mary
Tucker, Jno. C.
Tilford, Jas.
Thompson, A. E.
Taylor, W. J.
Taylor, Joseph Sr.?Jr.?
Taylor, Jno. B. E.
Todd, Thos. F.
Teague, Elijah
Taylor, Wm. S.
Tippen, Dennis
Taylor, Saml. H.
Tripp, Wm.
Vandiver, John
Vandiver, Edward
Vandiver, Enock
Vandiver, Wm.
Valentine, Benjn.
Voyles, Amos
Vandiver, Aaron
Vernon, Jas. T. W.
Vandiver, Sanford
Vandiver, Peter S.
Willingham, Jno.
Wilson, Jas.
Wardlaw, Jas.
Wilson, Hugh
Wyatt, Elijah
Wardlaw, Jno. M.
Welborn, Thos.
Welborn, Thos. M.
Williams, Jasper
Wyatt, Redman G.
Wyatt, Jas. T.?
Webster, Jane
Walker Peter
Williamson, Martin

Williamson, Wm.
Wright, Wm. F.
Wilson, George
Wright, Anna
Wright, Jno. L.
Webb, Saml. M.?
Wakefield, Conrad
Wiles, Eliz'th
Wiles, Jas. H.
Wiles, Jesse
Watt, Mary Jr.
Watters, __an?
Watt, Thos.
Watt, Joseph W.?
Whitman, Jacob
Watt, Jas. G.
Watt, Jas. D.
Worthington, Jno. _?
Wiley, Jas.
Watt, Jno.
Wilbanks, Elijah
Wright, Eliz'th
Watt, Mary Sr.
White, Ezekiel
Watson, David dec'd.
Watson, J. J.
Williford, Saml. W.
Williford, Dean
West, Isaac
Williford, Chas. H.?
Williford, Sarah
Whitfield, Lewis
White, Thos.
White, Bartho.
White, Jonathan
Webb, Clayton
White, Fleming N.
Wilson, Barkley
Watson, Danl. H.?
Wilbank, Shadrack
Wilson, Jackson
Wallace, Wilson
Wallace, Martha
Wilson, Jno. N.
Warnock, Jno.
Wilson, Rev'd Jas.
Webb, Wm.
Wilson, Sarah
Wilson, Jas. B.
Wilbanks, Hezekiah
Welborn, Albert G.
Wilbanks, Jas.
Welborn, Wm. E.
Wright, Robt. N.
Wiggington, Henry
Wilson, John
Wiggington, Elihu
Wiggington, Jno.
Wilson, Jane
Wilson, Wm. M.
Wilson, Sarah
Wilson, Robt. D.
Waddle, Hannah
Watson, J. L.
Walker, Jno. S.
Wilson, Wm.
Watkins, Baylis
Watkins, Felix
Warren?, Saml. dec'd.
White, Sarah
Watkins, Joseph
Watkins, Wm.
Wilson, Rich'd F.?
Wright, Cath'e.
Welborn, Wm.
Williamson, David
Williams, Jno.
Warnocj, Jno. dec'd.
Webb, Edmund
Welden, Wm.
Williams, W. A.
Welborn, Sarah
Welborn, Jas.

Williams, Micajah
Webb, Elijah
Webb, C. B.
Williams, Newton
Wardlaw, Hugh H.
Wilson, Chas. dec'd.
Williams, J. C.?E.?
Waddle, Alex'r.
Wilson, Jas. T.?
Wilson, Thos.
Wynn, Franklin
Waitsfelder & Oppert
Whitner, J. N.
Webb, Jas.
West, Thos.
Whitworth, Chas. K.
Whitaker, Harmon H.
White, Lydia
Webb, Elijah
Wallor, Wm.
Wallor, Miss Caroline
Waller, Miss R. H.
Warley & Sharpe
Warley, Mrs. Sophia
Wilson, Martha E. M.
Watson, Thos. dec'd.
Whitfield, J. D.?(L?)
Watson, Willard
Williams, Ira? N.?
Young, Nancy
Young, Frs.? A.
Young, Wm.
Yeargin, Saml.
Young, Jas.
Yeas, Polly
McClure, Edward J.

DOUBLE TAXES:
Rofflander, Jno.
Lanier, Bird
Robbins, Mary
Ruff, John
Yeas, Polly
Boyd, Robt.
Garrett?, Osborn
Lewis, Hannah E.(2)
Coffin, Abraham

PROPERTY IN PICKENS DIST.
Major, Jas.
Sullivan, Kelly
Green, John
Black, John
Huston, Norris (&?)
Burroughs, Bryant
Hall, Wm.
Elrod, Geo. G.
Anderson, Wm.
Hubbard, Wm.
Knight, Warren W.
Grant, Wm.
Brackenridge, Robt.
Todd, Jas.
Armstrong, Jas.
Fielding, H. B.
Fretwell, Jno.
Gunnin, Jas.
Brown, Saml.
Vandiver, Sanford
Johns, Anna
Taylor, Wm. S.
Mays, Miriam D.
Meredith, Abraham
Maverick, Saml.

GREENVILLE DISTRICT
Arnold, Lawson
Seaborn, George
Maverick, Saml.

ABBEVILLE DISTRICT
Gambrell, Jas.
Webster, Jane

Latimer, Macajah B.
Gassaway, Jas.? S.
Stiefle, Mary
Ruff, David
Tucker, Wm.
Hall, David
Keown, Geo. _?
Kelly, Rebecca
Sherard, Wm.
Mouchet, Jacob
Simpson, David
Dickson, Thos.
Miller, Jno. C.
Harleston, Edward
Smith, Wm. C.
Smith, Mrs. S.? N.?
Smith, Benjn.
Armstrong, Jno. B.
Fisher, Thos. dec'd.

LAURENS DISTRICT
Stone, Hampton
Maverick, Saml.

CHARLESTON DISTRICT
Jenkins and Gaillard
Maverick, Saml.

UNION DISTRICT
Maverick, Saml.

ORANGEBURGH DISTRICT
Maverick, Saml.

NEWBERRY DISTRICT
Maverick, Saml.

SPARTANBURGH DISTRICT
Maverick, Saml.

#

Adams, William
Anderson, Micajah
Abell, James _?
Adams, John ‾
Adams, Asa
Adams, Henry
Adams, John
Abells, John
Arnold, Allen
Ashley, Wilson
Ashley, John
Adams, James
Armstrong, James
Alewine, Michael
Armstrong, Archibald
Armstrong, James, sen'r
Armstrong, W. B.
Acker, Amos
Acker, Halbert
Acker, F. N.
Allen, Janes/James? E.
Alexander, David
Acker, Susanna
Acker, Jos.?
Acker, William
Anderson, Dr. William
Archer, Wm. M.
Abbott, John
Amick, John D.
Avery, Thomas
Anderson, David
Atkinson, James
Arnold, Lawson T.
Armstrong, J. B.
Bower/Bowes?, Samuel
Bradbury, Salathiel
Bailey, Allen
Bradbury, James
Bruce, C. P.?
Bradbury, Jesse
Bradbury, William
Bruce, Charles
Bradbury, Salathiel Jr.
Barton, W. M.
Bowman, Archibald
Barrett, Charles
Betterton, John
Buchanan, Samuel
Burris, Thomas
Brown, John
Brown, Wm. P.
Brown, Jane C.
Brown, Martha A.
Brown, Elvira
Brooks, Thomas
Brown, Abner
Breckenbridge, Robert
Brown, Charles
Bozeman, Lewis
Bozeman, Tillman
Brown, John
Beatty, William
Buchanan, William
Beatty, Samuel W.
Beatty, John
Beatty, Thomas
Benton, Blackman
Burdett, Hiram
Bo eis, Sugar
Brown, Johanna
Beatty, Francis
Bowie, Charles
Brown, Samuel
Burton, Peyton T.
Beatty, David
Brannon, Henry
Browne, Lidi H.
Browne, Jeremiah M.
Brock, James
Brock, M. H.
Brannon, Alexander

Braswell, Anderson
Brock, Haiden
Bagwell, James
Ballentine, George
Ballentine, Josiah
Brasswell, Nancy
Bagwell, John
Bagwell, James W.
Brock, Johnson E.
Brasswell, James
Broyles, Aaron
Brock, Andrew
Bennett, Charles M.
Brazeale, Kennon
Bartley, Josiah
Bartley, Sarah
Brazeale, Matthew
Bennett, William
Bartley, Nancy
Brazeale, D. K.
Brazeale, Williamson
Brazeale, Enoch
Brazeale, Griffin
Brazeale. Griffin, Jun'r.
Bennett, Thomas
Ballentine, Jesse H.
Brown, Dr. G. R.
Burris, Reuben
Burris, Thomas Junr.
Brannon, Joseph J.?
Bruce, Thomas
Brownlee, Wm. A.
Brown, Elijah
Brown, Rachel
Broyles, John T.
Burriss?, Milford
Burgess, James
Bryant, Nathan
Bryant, Terrell
Barr, Leroy
Bets, Anth‾
Blassingame, Thomas
Brewer, William
Brewer, Milly
Bailey, Isaac S./L.? Est.
Burriss, Bryant
Belcher, Manning
Bruce, John
Bishop, Jane &? Dorcas
Barnes?, Jovelan?
Bridwell, J. W.
Bellotte, John E.
Bellotte, Jacob
Bowden, Jos. G.?
Benson, Enock B.
Browne, Randolph
Burt, Moody Est.?
Bolling, Albert
Blankenship, John
Brownlee, Maria?
Brown, Larkin
Brown, Samuel
Barnett?, John
Burris?, Elbert
B___is, Elisha
B‾‾is, Joshua
Broyles, Dr. O. R.
Brown, Jasper
Bell, Samuel
Burris?, James
Bellotte, Lewis
Briant, Simon
Brazeale, Gambrell
Brown, Samuel
Baker, Samuel H.
Boyd, Robert
Bennett, Cooper
Brooks, Garner?
Bannister, Rolly
Brown, Robert
Brown, Catharine

Bailey, William
Benson, John P.?
Blassingame, Robert
Bowen, Robert
Bellotte, Peter E.
Bee, B. E.
Berry?, Wm.
Burris?, Jacob
Burris?, Elizabeth
Brown, Elizabeth
Baker, L. A.
Barksdale, John
Brown, David?
Brown, Robert
Bell, John
Burns, Anderson?
Corr, Laban
Coffin, Abraham
Chappell, John B.
Chamblee, James
Campbell, George
Caldwell, Joseph
Caldwell, John
Carpenter, J. W .
Corr, Mary
Christopher, John
Cunningham, Saml. Sr.
Caldwell, William
Caldwell, James
Cunningham, Thos. Jr.
Conwell, James
Campbell, Jesse
Carey?, Mary
Campbell, Thos. C.
Cowan, Hiram
Cunningham, _? S.
Casey, Sarah‾
Cunningham, Catharine
Corr?, Molly
Clinkscales, Lewis
Casey, Delilah
Clinkscales, Polly
Clinkscales, Ibzen
Clarke, Joseph
Cowan, William
Clinkscales, W.? H.?
Cummings, Robert
Cox, William
Cox, Elizabeth
Carr?, William
Clement, W. K.?
Clement, Hugh
Clement, G. W.
Cobb, Noah
Cobb, Ephraim
Clement, Isaac
Clement, Benjamin
Clement, Alexander
Clement, A. J. &? C(Co.?)
Cox, Arris
Cobb, Martin
Clinkscales, Wm. F. Sr.
Cox, David
Cullins, Caleb
Cox, R. B.
Cox, Francis
Cumming, David
Cox, Thomas Sr.
Cox, Thomas Jr.
Cox, Joel
Cox, Gabriel
Cox, Sarah
Clardy, Joab M.
Clardy, John
Cooley, John Est.
Cooley, Anna
Corden, Thomas
Chamblee, Moses
Clinkscales, Asa
Cook, William
Coates, John

Campbell, Daniel
Carpenter, John
Chamblee, Benjamin
Carpenter, A. T.?
Carpenter, James M.
Carpenter, Elizabeth
Campbell, James
Cobb, Henry
Cox, Asa
Cobb, Josiah
Carter, Caleb
Clardy, Norman
Cason, James A. M.
Cason, Sarah
Cason, Esther
Cason, Wm. Cator?/Estat.?
Childress?, John B.
Cobb, Franklin
Cannon, Isaac
Carne, Martha
Craig, Samuel
Caesor (free negro over
    50)
Cherry, Thomas R.
Cherry, Susan
Campbell, Archibald C.?
Cherry, Dr. Eli D.?
Cater, Dr. A. P.
Cobb, James
Cox, John
Cox, Abner
Coffee, Wiley
Clarke, John B.
Cox, Joseph
Cox, Rachael & Rebecca
Cannon, Ephraim
Cummings, Harmon
Carpenter, A. M.
Cresswell, John H.
Chalmers, James
Clinkscales, Abner
Cox, John
Campbell, Alfred
Chamblee, James
Carter, Spencer
Coates, J. J.?
Chastain, Stephen
Carlisle, Wm.
Campbell, Alexander
Crawford, James
Crawford, Sarah
Crawford, Wm. Est.
Cochrane, D. K.?
Cooley, Lewis
Cresswell, Sarah
Cooley, James Est.
Cheves, Langdon
Caruth, Louisa
Crayton, B. F.
Clinkscales, John
Chasti__, James
Chamblee, Robert
Driver, James
Dollar, Williamson
Driver, James Jr.
Deane, Thomas
Dunlap, Matthew
Davis, Flournoy
Duncan, Robert
Duncan, Thomas
Drake, James
Drake, Enock
Davis, John L.
Davis, Moses
Davis, Aaron
Davis, Thomas
Deane, Charles P.
Duckworth, J. C.
Duckworth, Jacob
Dawson, Samuel
Davis, William
Dalrymple, John
Dickson, William

Davis, Valentine
Duckworth, Thomas
Duckworth, Benjamin
Duckworth, Welborne
Duckworth, William
Dalrymple, John
Dorn?, George
Durham, William
Durham, Clarissa
Douthet, James
Davis, Archibald
Douthet, Benjamin
Douthet, John
Dillworth, Wm. E. Est.
Davis, Richard
Durham, David
Dalton, Burrell
Durham, William
Davis, James
Dart, Mary L.
Dupre, B. D.?
Dupre, A. H. M.
Durpe, Benjamin
Daniels, W. S. C.?
Dickson, Thomas
Davis, Charles
Dickson, Matthew Est.
Dowelle, Morris Est.
Dunson/Duncan?, David
Dunham, Benjamin/Benajah?
Dalrymple, Jonas?
Drake, James A.?
Deane, Moses
Dobbins, James
Dacus?, John A.
Dobbins, John
Dobbins, James
Dalrymple, Mary
Dooley, Wm.
Dalrymple, Lewis
Dickinson, Willis
D__t, Jonathan
Dobbins, __? C.
Duckworth, Howard?
Davis, John B.
Davis, Enoch Est.
Drennan, Wm.
Earpe, Wesley
Earle, Samuel G.
Elrod, William
Elrod, Thomas P.
Ellison, Miles
Elgen, Harrison
Ellison, Joel
Estis, Larkin
Eubanks, Elijah
Erskine, James
Erskine, Thomas
Erskine, John
Erskine, William
Emberson, James
Emberson, Samuel Est.
Eskew, William
Elrod, William
Elrod, G. G.
Elrod, Samuel
Elrod, John
Elrod, Allen
Elrod, George
Elrod, Elias
Elrod, Adam
Ellison, James
Earle, Dr. James M.
Elrod, Philip
Eaton, Joseph C.
Elliott, Mary
Earle, Elias
Elrod, Thomas
Erskine, James
East?, Margaret
Erskine, W. R.
Elliotte, R. E.
E____?, Alexander

E____ & Cater
Earle, Ann
Earle, John B.
F__t, James R
Felton, Mary
Finley, Elias
Fisher, Samuel S.?
Featherston, J. W.?
French, William
Fant, Alfred
Fleming, James
Fant, Mary
Fant, Elizabeth
Fant, W. M./N? M.?
Fant, W. D.
Fleming, Richard
Fleming, John O.
Forbes, Alanson
Ford, Stephen
Floyd?, A. L.?
Ford, N.? H.
Feiling?, Henry
Ford, James
Fretwell, John
Fant, Abner
Fant, O. H. P.
Felton, Richard
Fisher, Samuel C.
Fowler, Ruth
Fuller, Alfred
Fretwell, Joseph G./Y.?
Forsyth, Cynthia
Fennell, Jane R.
Gentry, Arthur
Gentry, Daniel
Guyton, John W.?
Guyton, Robert Est.
Griffin, F. L.
Gantt, John W.
Gilmore, Robert
Gilmor?, Nancy
Gilmor?, James
Glenn, William
Gregg, Hugh
Galloway, Matthew
Gentry, Moody
Gentry, Elizabeth
Gentry?, Zachariah
Gray, Robert L./D.?
Gray, Elizabeth
Gable, Henry
Gable, Henry Jr.
Gray, Alexander D.
Gantt, James H.?
Gable, Levy
Greene, John
Green?, David Sen'r.
Gassaway, Benjamin
Grubbs, George
Green, William
Gantt, William
Gambrell, James
Gambrell, Enoch B.
Gambrell, Sarah
Gambrell, Wm.
Gray, Huldah
Green, David Jr.
Gantt, Hugh
Gantt, John
Gantt, John G./Y.?
Glasley?, William
Gambrell, James
Griffin, Elijah
Gambrell, David H.
Gentry, John
Gambrell, James M.
Gaillard, Josias D.?
Gaillard, Mary D.?
Gambrell, Lettie?
Gambrell, Matthew T.
Green, David
Gibson, Wm. B.
Ga____, Thomas

Guyton?, G.
Gentry?, Stephen
Gibbs, Mary
Gutry, Nelson
Gutry, Josia Est. (David?)
Gutry, Benjamin
Givens, Harrison
Gambrell, James Sr.
Gambrell, James Jr.
Gambrell, Ezekiel
Gambrell, Reid
Goletin?, John (Golden?)
Golden, Samuel
Gaillard, C. L. (Dr.)
Grant, William
Goode, L. Est.
Gentry, Reuben
Gordon, Robert Est.
Gordon, James
Grubbs, John M.
Graham, A.? T.?
Gaillard, Theodore heirs
Gray, James
Gaillard, Wm. & L.
Gaillard, Mrs.? R. P.
Gambrell, David
Gambrell, Ira?
George, James
Gambrell, Matthew Est.
Geer, Solomon
Gray, Jesse
Gray, Hezekiah
Gordon, Andrew
Garrison, Henry
Garrison, Foster?
Glenn, ? N.?
Gambrell, John
Gambrell, Wm.
Gambrell, Barbary
Gaines?, H. M.
____, A.? B.
Gentry, Sandford _?
____, Thomas
Griffin, J. C. & Co.
____, F.? W.
____, C. D.
____, Sophia
____, James
____llard, A. D.?
____, J. R.?
Gambrell, Susanna
Hembree, James Sr.
Hembree, James Jr.
Hillhouse, Samuel P.
____, Levy
Holland, Robert
Herring, Jesse
Hughes, B. P.
Harris?, Sarah E./G.?
Herbert, John
Henry, Charles
Herring, Francis
Hale, John Sr.
H____, George
H____, Richard B.
Henderson?, Martin?
Humphreys, David
Howard, Hiram
Houston, William
Hall, Martin
Hall, Fenton Jr.
Howard?, George
Hall, Lent Jr.?
Hodges, Robert
Hatton, Wm?
H___, Nathan
Hardy?, John?
Hardy?, James
Howie, Robert
Havird, Mark P.
Hays?, John
Hill?, Thos. C.
Hall, Lemuel

Hall, David
Hamilton?, John
Hamilton, Wm.?
Hall, Lent Sr.
Harkness, John
Harkness, Robert C.
Hall, Wm. A.?
Hall, Samuel C.
Hall, John
Herron, James
Harkness, John N.
Hamilton, Luke
Hamilton, Jane?
Hamilton, Nancy
Ha_s, Stephen
____, James A.?
____, William
Hopkins, John
Hopkins, James M.
Harper, ? ?
Harper, John _?
Harkins, Hugh
Horton, Grief
Hearkins, James
Hearkins, Sarah?
Harper, Nancy?
Holland, Caleb B.
Harper?, John
Hall, Wm. B.
Haney, Luke
Holland, William
Holland?, John
Holmes?, William
Haney, Wm. H.?
Holland, John
Herron, John
Harrison?, Wm.
Hall, Ezekiel
Hammond, L.? J.
Hanna, Thomas
Holland, Wm.
Harrison, James
Hall, Nancy (Hale?)
Hunter, Wm.
Hendricks, David
Hunter, Sarah
Harper, Thomas
Harris?, Benjamin
Holland?, Aaron R.?
Hunt?, Jane? J.
Hamilton, Martha A.
Hamilton, C___? E.
Hamilton, David R.
Harper?, Asa
Hunter, John
____, John
Harris, Susan
Hamilton, Leonard
Hastie, John & Co.
Hastie, John
Hix, John
Hubbard, William
Hillhouse, Joseph
Hembree, William
Hanks, Mary
H_wis, Robert
Hall, Joab
Hall, Aaron
Hammond, Wm. L.
Hunt, James L.
Hall, Zachariah
Haney?, John
Hammond, Herbert
Hanks?, Tilman?
Harris?, R. B.
Hawkins, Wm. P.
Hall,
Hembree, ? ?
Hanks, Thomas
Hanks, Luke
H___, John Sr.
H___, Matilda
Hagood, Simpson

Hall, Joseph
Hembree, Willis
Hix, Daniel
Hix, William?
Hall, Jackson
Hinton, John
Haslet, Moses W.
Hammond, B. F.
Hammond, Dr. C. C.
H__, Baylis
Harleston, Edward
Harrison, J. W.
Hammond, John H.?
H___, Joseph
Haslet, Hannah
Hewins, Wm.
Hopkins, John
Hackett, Albert
Hinton, Mary
Isbell, Samuel
Jones, J. B.
Jones, Thomas
Irwin, Ealenor
Johnston, Willis
Johnston, Joel
Johnston, Allen
Johnston, Peter?
Johnston, W. G.
Jolly, Wm.
Jones, John W.?
Jones, Ambrose H.?
Ing__?, (Ingraham?) Wm.?
Jones, ?
Jones, William
Jenkins, P. L. _?
Isaacks, Abram
Jolly, Henry
Isbell, Robert
Jenkins, Margaret? Est.
Jones, John
Jones, Samuel
Jennings, Jane?
Johnston, ___?
Irby, Charles
Jones, Wm.
Jolley, Joseph
Jolly, James
King, Wm. P.?
Kay, James D.?
Keown, Wm.? M.
Keown, George W.
Keeton, Wm.
Kay, Gabriel
Kay, Fe__? (F. M.?)
Kay, James W.?
Kay, Wm. Sr.
Kay, Wm. P.
Kay, Mason
Kay, Cathereine
Kay, Joel
Kay, Wm.
Kay, James
____, aldeen?
King, James
King, Robert
Kelly, John
Kelly, Elisha
Kelly, B. J.
Kay, Jesse
Kelly, Allen
Kelly, Alfred
Kelly, E. E.
Knox, John
King, Peter
Kay, Strother
Kingsley, Chester
King, G.? W.
King, Josiah
Kay, Alexander
Kay, Charles
Kelly, Daniel?
Kirksey, Fair
Keister, Henry

Knauff, P.? J.?
Knight?, James C.
Keys, Robert A.?
King, John
Kay, L. P.?
King, Wm. Sr.
King, R. A.
King, Hiram R.
Kay, John
Kay, James H.
Keeton, Welborn
Keaton, Archibald
Kingsley, Mrs.? Delilah?
Knight, Warren W.
Keys, John
Ledbetter, Joel
Ledbetter, James
Ledbetter, Mary
Lewis, Elizabeth?
Lockhart, M
Latham, Cornelius
Latham, Wm.
Long, Wm.
Love___, Stephen(Liverett)
Liverett, William
Liverett, Thomas
Liverett, Stephen
Liverett, John
Little, Rachael
Latimer, Harrison?
Lucius, anl F.? Sr.?
Lee, Philip
Lee, James
Lee, Elizabeth
Lucius, James
Lucius, Danl. F.?
Lewis, James W.?
Lewis & Cox
Lewis & Simpson
Lewis, J. W. & J. B.
Lewis, J. B.(2)
Long, Harrison
Lewis, Jesse
L___, William
Laboon, Joseph
Long, Ezekiel
Lewis, Hannah E.
Lorton, John _?
Lorton, Frances
Lewis, Sarah Est.
Liddell, A. J.
Lewis, Elisha
Lowry, Jackson
Ledbetter, David
Lattimore, Wiley
Lewis, Jesse P.
Lasley?, Wm.

_____, Wesley
_____, John
Morris, James?
Morris, David
Merrett, R. P.?
Meredeth, Abraham
M_tin, Matthew
McCollum, Samuel
Massey, Silas
McCooley?, Elias
McCarley, James
McLease?, J. J.
McLease?, James
McLease, Margaret
McLease, William
McLea_, Anderson
McGee, John
Moore, John
McDaniel, Rebecca
McPherson, Elizabeth
?
McGee, Elias
McCa__y, Joseph
McCartey?, Robert B.
McG___, ___?
McC_____, William

(Note - rest of this page
too blurred to read..Ed.)

Pages containing "M"'s are
all blurred.

Nelson, Wm.? E.
Norris, Ezekiel
Newel, Wm.
Norris, Robert B.
Nichols, Arch.? J.?
Nichols, James C.
Nichols, Archibald
Nichols, Wm. A.
Norris, Jesse
Newton, Willis
Newton, Isaac
Newton, Isaac Jr.
Newton, Samuel
Newton, Larkin
Norris, John E.
Nevell?, Wm.
Newell, George
Norris, A. D.?
Norris, M. A. (Mrs.)
North, John L.
Obriant, Wm.
Obriant, Andrew
Obriant, Josephine
Owens, Thornton
Owens, Daniel
Owens, Bannister
Oldham, Thomas
Oldham, Wm.
Owens, Lewis
Orr?, Wm.?
Orr, Thomas
O___, Elijah Sr.
O___, James
Oliver, Martha
Owen, Elijah Jr.
Owen, Martha
Overby, Nicholas
Overby, B. M.
Oppert, Vincent
Oliver, Martha
Orr, Lawrence. J.
Orr, Christopher
Osborn?, L. A.
Palmore, Wm.
Pullen, Benj.
Peckerel, Jonathan
Parker, Matthew
Presley?, Anne
P___, Hugh
P___, Wm.
P___, Hubbard
P___, Thos.? H/
Pettigrew, Robt. H.
Price, Pennel
P___, David A.
Parker, Robert
Pearman, Benj.
Pun_?, Wm.
Pruitt?, Elias D.
P___, Thomas
Pettis, Jane
Poor, Samuel
Poor, Nancy
P___, J. B.
Poor, George
Poor, William
Price, D. P.?
P___, Henry
Parmer?, Nancy
Pickle, Wm.
Pickle, E/C.? W.
P_man, Lodovick
Pegg, James B.
P___, John
P___, Robert
P_ter, Joseph?
Pickens?, Wm.

Pickle, Jacob
Pickle, Chesley?
Pickle, Elbert?
Pinkney, Thos.? Est.
Passmore, Wm. Est.
Philips, Reuben
Padgett,?, Elizabeth
Pendleton Factory
P_man, Jonathan
Poor, Wm.
Padgett, John L.?
Pepper, Elijah
Poole, Wm. H.
Poole, Mary
Poole, Adam
Pritchet, Lewis
Pearce, Wm.
Poor, Reuben
Philips, John
Philips, Archy?
Pearce, Thos. _?
Prince, C. J. _
Poole, Elizabeth
Parker?, Benj.
Pickens, Thos.? J.?
Reagers?, Elihu (Rodgers)
Reid, Jesse
Reid, Moses
Raney, Milissa
Robinson, John
Rutledge, Jesse
Rice, Amaziah
Rice, H. Estate
R___, Wm.
Robinson, John J.?
Rice, Hezekiah
Rice, Thomas L.
Ritchie, James N.?
Robinson, John Est.?
Robinson, James E.
Robinson, John B.
Reid, Henry
Reid, A. E.
Roberts, Mathias?
Rochester, Nathaniel
Rupele?, David
Richardson, Matthias
Richardson, Sion
Rider?, Abraham
Rodgers, Wm.
Rodgers, Wm. W.?
Rodgers, John
Rodgers, Benjamin
Richardson, Noah
Rodgers, Joseph L.
Rea, Elihu
R___, George W.?
Rosamond, John
Robinson, Wm.? Jr.
Rusk, David Est.
Reid, Wm.
Reid, Elizabeth
Roach,
Roach, Forrester?
Ritchie, Thomas H.
Rodgers, Simeon
Rankin, George
Rainwater, F___son
Richardson, David
Robinson, Jane
Ritchie, Elizabeth
Richardson, Mary? L.
Richardson, Wade
Richardson, Maria L.
Richardson, Wm.
Roach, Henry
Rice, Sarah
Rice, Hazan
Reid, Dr. L.? H.
Reid, Andrew
Reid, J. P.
Riley, Hezekiah
Richardson, A. W.?

Rimmer, Lucinda
Ruff, David
Ragsdale, T.? A.
Rolleter?, John
Ritchie, Reuben
Rodgers, Wm.
Rice, L.?
Reeves, John
Reeves, R. W.?
Reese, Thos. _?
Reese, George_ ?
Robinson, Willis
Reese, Wm.
Reese, David
Ramsey?/Rampey, Anderson?
Rice, Jane?
Ross, A. W.
Reese, H. D.
Smith, Wm. C.
Smith, ___ ? ___?
Smith, Benjamin
Smith, Miss? E. D.
Smith, Sarah E. A.
Smith, Benjamin J.?
Shearer, Gillam
Simmons, David
Swilling, Samuel
Simmons, Charles
Shaw, Wm.
Skelton, Thomas
Skelton, Thos. L.
Skelton, Archibald
Shaw, Reuben/Fenton?
Simpson, David
S____, Milton
Stewart, George
Stewart, James Est.
Stewart, Adam
Siddell, Stephen
Smitn,
Siddell, A. ? Y.?
Simpson, Robert
Stewart, James
Stephenson, George Jr.
S____, Willis
Sh____ard, Wm.
____, John
Stifle, Mary
Sneed?, Wm. G.
Speer?, James G.
Snipes, Sion
Saunders, Abraham
Stewart, John
Simpson, Archibald
Stephenson, John
Simpson, Thomas
Sadler, David
Stephenson, Thomas
Sadler, John
Sauners, William
Saunders, H. J.
Scott, David
Strickland, Matthew
Sailers, Isaac
Sailors, Abraham
Shirley, Benjamin
Sailors, Leonard
Seawright, James
Stone, Hampton
Shirley, Benjamin
Smith, R. L.
Smith, Jermiah
Smith, L.?
Smith, Wm.
Stone, George
Strickland, Milly?
Stone, Wm. H.
Spray?, Thomas
Smith, William?
Smith, Robert
Smith, William
Stephenson, George?
Stephenson, John

Smith, Aaron
Snipes, Matthew
Smith, Samuel
Smith, Nimrod
Smith, Wiley C.
Smith, Zion
Smith, Wm.
Shirley, James
Shirley, James Jr.
Shirley, Richard
Shirley, Sarah
Smith, Wyatt
Smith, John
Sherrell, Lewis
Spearman, Francis? A.
Smith, Basil?
Smith, George S.?
Spearman, David
Smith, Philip L.
Spearman, Benjamin
Spearman, David L./D.?
Scott, M. R.
Slaten, John
Smith, Edward
Slaten, Loven
Stone, James
Siton, J. L.
Smith, Griffin
Siddell, John
Satterfield, Jeremiah
Siton, Wm.?
Siton, Wm. D.?
Smith, Thomas G.
Stanton, George
Smith, Joseph
Smith, C. & J. M.?
Smith, James Est.
Smith, John
Smith, James D.
Smith, John C.
Smith, John A.
Smith, Ephraim
Smith, Andrew M. E.
Sp____, Simeon
Sharpe, John
Smith, J. H.
Smith, Aaron
Seaborn, George
Sitton, John B.
Sharpe, Elam
Starke?, Mrs. E. G.
Smith, Zepheriah
Shanklin, Joseph U.?
Sloan, J____ L.
Swords, John ?
Steele, Nancy H.
Sullivan, Jelly
Smith, Robinson
Simpson, Wm.
S____mond, James
Smith, Joseph
Smith, Robert L.
Smith, J. R.
Sloan, ? L.
Sloan, Mrs.? Susan?
Sailors, John
Stephenson, Andrew
Shirley, Elizabeth
Simpson, R. ?
Sherrif, Washington
Skelton, John W. B.
Stephenson, James
Swilling, James
Smith, Simeon
Stanley, Ezekiel
Simpson?, Thos. H.?
S____, J. W.
S____, Drayton
Smith, ___
Simpson, ___
Simpson, Charles H.
Shirley, Obediah
Sta__, Augustus?(Staul?)

Scott?, Toliver L.
Smith, Ebenezer
Stanton, Mathias
Sharpe, Elam Jr.
____, Thomas? M.?
____, Dr. L. _
S____, James
Steele, Wm.
Shearer, Andrew
Seawright, Andrew
Shirley, Aaron
Smith, Whitaker
Sullivan, John
Todd, Charles
Tippen, Elizabeth
Taylor, James
____, David
____, Van
____, Tilman
Todd, Andrew
Todd?, Robert Est.
Tucker, Djarnet
Taylor, Elijah
Tucker, Wm.
Tucker, James
Tucker, Nancy
Tompson, James
Tate, John A.
Thompson, Elizabeth
Thompson, Mathew
Taylor, Richard
Towns, Wm. W.
Trussell, Possey
Trussell, Haney?
Telford, Wm.
Telford, Isabella
Tripp, Nicholas
Turner, John B.
Telford, James
Telford, George B.
Telford, James H.
Todd?, Wm. P.
Tippen, George
Taylor, J. B. E.
Thompson, John
Timms, Isaac
Thompson, James
Tripp, Nicholas
Tripp, John H.
Tripp, John Sr.?
Tompkins, John
Tra____, L
Taylor, D? L.?
Tucker, R. D.
Taylor, Thomas
Todd, John L.
Tu____, James
Todd, Thomas F.
Taylor, Samuel H.
Todd, Mary
Tilly, May?
Tilly, John
Todd, James
Towers, Danl. R. Est.
Taylor, Joseph
Taylor, Wm. J.?
Taylor, Joseph Dr.
Teague, Elijah
Thompson, Dr. A. E.
Towers?, John R.
Valentin, Benj.
Vandiver, Wm.
Vandiver, Edward?
Vandiver, Enoch
Voyles, Amos
Vandiver, Aaron
Vandiver, Peter L.?
Vandiver, John
Webb, Clayton
Whitfield, Lewis?
White, Thomas
White, Henry
Webb, Elisha

Williford, Samuel P.?
Wright, Elizabeth
Watson, Jackson J.
Watt?, Mary
Watt?, Thomas
Watt?, James
Watt, Joseph
Watt?, James G.
Wiley, James
Wiles, Elizabeth
Wiles, James H.
Wilbanks, Elijah
Whitman, Jacob
Waters?, Ibzan
Wiles, Jesse
Worthington, John
Watt?, John
Wright, R. N.
Williamson, David
Williamson, Wm.
Wakefield?, Conrad
Williams, James C.
Wright, Wm. F.
Wilson, George
Williamson, Mastin?
Webb, Andrew
Wyatt, J. L.
Webster, Jane
Wyatt, Redman
Walker, Peter
Wardlaw, James
Wardlaw, J. M.
Wilson, Bartley
Wilson, Hugh
Wilson, Sarah
Wyatt, Elijah
Wardlaw, H. K.
Willingham, John
Webb, Samuel
White, Bartholomew
White, Jonathan
W llis, Wilson
Wallis, Martha (scratched)
Wright, Catharine
Williams, M. B.
Whitaker, H. H.
Wilson, James
Welborn, Wm. E.
Wilson, J. J.
Wilbanks, Shadrack
Wilson, James
Wilson, John
Webb, Wm.
Wilson, James
Willbanks, Hezekiah
Wilbanks, James
Welbourn, A. G.?
Wilson, John Senr.?
Wildon?, Wm.? M.
Wilbourne, James M.
Williams, John
Wilson, Robert
Wigginton, John
Wigginton, Elihu
Wilson, Wm.? M.
Wilson, James F.?
Walker, John S.?
Watson, James
Wa tey?, Sophia
Watkins, Joseph
Watkins, Wm.
Watkins, Felix
Wilson, Richard
Watt?, Mary
Waddle, D___h?
Wellbourne, Wm.
Warnock, John
Warnock, John Est.
Watson, Mary
Williams, Wm. A.
Williams, Ira G.
Welden, Wm. D.?
Wynne, Franklin

Watson, David
Wright, John L.
Williford, C.? R.
Williford, Sarah
Watkins, Baylis
Williams, Jasper
Williams, Newton
Wakefield, John
Wakefield, H. Est.
West, Thomas
Wakefield, Andrew
Whitner, Joseph N.?
Wakefield, Cynthia
Webb, Elijah
Whitfield, J. L.   .
Watson, Willard
Wilson, Jane
White Isiah?/Sarah?
Webb, C. C.?
Waller?, R. H.
Waller?, C. M.
Webb, Edmund
Wilson, Thomas
Webb, James
Wo son?, Samuel Dec.?
Wilson, Stephen M.
Young, James
Yeargon, Samuel
Young, Francis A.
Young, Nancy
Young, William
Year_?, Polly

St. Helen Parish
(above difficult to read)
Calhoun, E. & L. (free
negroes?)
Warren, Samuel Dec.
Ross, A. W.?
Reese, H. D.
Burnes?, Anderson?
Lewis, Moses P.
Wilson, Stephen M.

FREE NEGROES
Robert & Patsey Wilson
Rosanna Valentine
Leonard Goins? 5 children
Wade Denny/Dennis?
John Buster? & 2 sons
Richmond Pachen?
Henry & Martha Wilson
Eveline & Louisa Calhoun
James Shumake
Caesars Polly
Margaret Merinick
Riley Wilson & wife
Edmund Rome Son & Daughter
Clarke? Oglsby
Jim Mason
Jobesey? & wife Cinda
Mitchael Given
Clarke?, Joseph
Merimick, Samuel

UNION DISTRICT.
Merimick (probably Mav-
erick) Samuel
(also in Newbery Dist.;
Orangeburg Dist.Napa____;
Goon Creek; Charleston
City and N___H?

GREENVILLE DIST.
Merenich, Samuel
Johnston, Willis
Seaborn, George
Est. of Gen'l? Earle
Arnold, L. T.

ABBEVILLE DIST.
Smith, Wm. G.
Smith, Mrs. L.? _?

Smith, Mary E. P.?
Smith, John L. N.
She____, Wm.
Stifle, Mary
Speer?, Wm. G.
Keown, George W.
Kelly, Rebecca
Tucker, Wm.
Gambrell, James
Davis, John L.
Stone, Hampton
Wesbster,___
Miller, John C.
Dickson, Thomas
Smith, Robert S.
Tucker, R. D.
Norris, John E.
Ruff, David
Fisher, Thos. Dec.
Wakefield, John
Harleston, Edward
Armstrong, J. B.

PICKENS DIST.
Meredith, Abraham
Breckenridge, Robert?
Norris & Houston
Major, James
Anderson, D. W.
Elrod, G. G.
Hubbard, Wm.
Bishop, Jane & Dorcas
Fielding, Henry
Shanklin, Jos. V.
Green, John
Hall, Wilson
Mochat, Jacob
Oliver, Martin
Todd, James
Wright, Warren W. (Knight)
Gunnin, James
Earle, John B.
Fretwell, John

St. STEPHENS
Gaillard & Jenkins

#

372

GENERAL TAXES OF 1845 COLLECTED IN ANDERSON DISTRICT BY WILLIAM STEELE T.C.

Armstrong, John B
Anderson, Micajah
Abels, John
Adams, Asa
Adams, John
Adams, Henry
Abels, James
Alexander, David
Ashley, Wilson
Ashley, John
Aiken, Herbert
Armstrong, James
Armstrong, John R.?
Acker, Amos
Allen, James E.
Avery, William
Aiken, Joshua
Acker, Susanna
Anderson, Dr. Wm.
Anderson, David
Acker, William
Abbott, John
Amick, John D.
Alewine, Jacob
Armstrong, A. B.
Atkinson, James
Anderson, John
Archer, William
Armstrong, James
Armstrong, Archibald
Arnold, Lawson T.?
Bowen, Samuel
Burns, Jordon
Burns, Joseph
Bradbury, James
Bradbury, Jesse
Bradbury, William
Barton, H. M.
Bailey, Allen
Bradbury, Salathiel
Bradbury, Salathiel Jr.
Bowman, Archibald
Betterton, John
Bennett, Cooper
Burris, Thomas
Burris, J. M.
Brooks, Thomas
Brown, Charles
Bozeman, Lewis
Bozeman, Daniel T.
Beatty, Samuel
Brown, Cornelius
Beatty, William
Black, John
Buchanan, William
Burdett, Hiram
Brooks, Garner
Beatty, Francis
Bowie, Charles
Beatty, John
Beatty, Thomas
Beatty, David
Burris, Milford?
Browne, Samuel
Browne, Jane M.
Branyan, Henry
Branyan, Joseph
Breckenridge, Robt.
Brock, M. H.
Brock, James
Brownlee, Maria
Bagwell, James
Brock, Hazelen?
Bagwell, John
Brasswell, Nancy
Bagwell, James
Brock, Andrew
Brasswell, James
Bennett, Thomas
Bennett, Charles M.
Bennett, Wm.

Ballentine, George
Ballentine, Josiah
Brazeale, D. K.
Brazeale, Matthew
Brazeale, Williamson
Browne, Dr. George
Ballentine, Jesse H.
Brantley, Josiah (Bantley?)
Bantley, Sarah
Brazeale, Kennon
Burgess, James
Burris, Thomas Jr.
Brown, Elijah
Brown, Rachael
Burris, Reuben
Barrett, Charles
Brown, Si_l? R.?
Brazeale, G.
Bantley, Nancy
Brock, J.? E.
Bailey, Wm.
Brient, Ferel?
Briant, Nathan
Brient, Simon
Bee, Ann
Blassingame, Thomas
Belcher, Manning
Blassingame, Robert
Bowen, Robert
Barr?, Leroy
Boggs, J. L.
Brewer?, Wm.
Brewer, Milly
Boman, John
Bailey, Isaac L. dec.
Bishop, Jane & Dorcas
Bridewell, J. W.
Benson, E. B. A. John
Benson, E. B.
Bellotte, John E.
Boweden, James
Bellotte, Jacob
Bellotte, J. L.
Bowlan, Albert
Burris, Jacob
Burris, Elizabeth
Burris, James
Brown, Abner
Boyd, Robert
Brownlee, Wm. A.
Bakers, S.? H.
Bruce, Charles
Bell, Samuel
Burris, Brient
Brazeale, Griffin
Bruce, John
Branyan, John A.
Brown, Newton
Buchanan, Saml
Browne, Johanna
Brown, Samuel
Bonds, Sugar
Bannister, Rolla
Baker, L. A.
Burton, Blackman
Burton, Peyton T.
Brazeale, Enoch
Broyles, John T.
Benson, John P.
Bruce, C. P.
Brown, Daniel
Browne, Robert
Burris, Joshua
Brown, John
Brown, Wm. P.
Brown, Miss J. C.
Brown, Miss M. A.
Brown, Miss Elvira
Bowen, Elizabeth
Brown, Robert
Brown, Catharine

Brown, Larkin
Bellotte, Peter E.
Broyles, C. R.
Broyles, Aaron dec'd.
Bee, Barnard E.
Brown, Randolph
Burris, Elisha
Cannon, Isaac
Chastain, Stephen
Corr, Laban
Coffin, Abraham
Coffee, Iley?
Campbell, George
Caldwell, James
Chappell, John
Conwille, James
Caldwell, John
Corr, Mary
Caldwell, Joseph
Cunningham, Saml.
Cunningham, Thos.
Cosper, Henry
Casey, Salley
Casey, Dilly
Campbell, Thos.
Campbell, Jesse
Cook, Wm.
Clinkscales, Lewis C.
Cowan, Hiram
Cunningham, Catharine
Chalmers, J. C.
Casey, Mary
Clinkscales, John
Clinkscales, Mary
Clinkscales, Ibzan
Clarke, Ann
Clement, W. K.
Clement, J. C.
Clement, Isaac
Cobb, Noah
Cobb, Marton
Cobb, Ephraim
Clinkscales, Wm. F.?
Cox, Thomas
Cullins, Cullins
Clement, E. W.
Cox, Gabriel
Cummin, David
Clement, Christopher
Clement, Jane
Clement, Benjamin
Cox, Arris
Cox, Joel
Cox, John
Cox, R. B.
Cox, Wm. dec'd.
Cox, Abner
Cobb, Henry
Cox, David
Cox, Thomas
Cooley, Anna
Cooley, John dec'd.
Carden, Thomas
Carpenter, John
Campbell, James
Carpenter, A. T.
Carpenter, Elizabeth
Cox, Anna
Campbell, Daniel
Chamblee, Robert
Cox, Wm. H.
Carpenter, A. M.
Cobb, Franklin
Chamblee, James
Campbell, Alexander
Carter, Caleb
Clardy, Joab
Carter, Spencer
Clardy, Norman
Childress, Nicholas
Clardy, John

Coates, John
Cherry, Dr. E. D.
Caine, Miss J. M.
Cheves, Honlb. Langdon
Clement, Hugh
Cresswell, Mrs. Sarah
Cox, Wm.
Cox, Elizabeth
Cummins, Harmon
Caesar Pugh (free negro)
Chamblee, Moses
Cobb, Henry
Cobb, Josiah W.
Cater, Edward
Cobb, James
Chamblee, Benj.
Crawford, Henry
Crawford, Sarah
Chamblee, James
Campbell, Alfred
Crawford, James
Crawford, Mary F.
Carpenter, J. W.
Cannon, Ephraim
Coates, James
Cowen, Hiram
Cresswell, John dec'd.
Clinkscales, Abner
Cooley, Lewis
Cason, Esther
Conant, Allen
Carlisle, Wm.
Crayton, B. F.
Cowan, Wm.
Clinkscales, Wm. F. Jr.
Carpenter, James M.
Cater, Dr. A. P.
Clinkscales, Asa
Cockram/Cockrane?, Danl.H.
Craig, Samuel
Clarke, J. B.
Clarke, J. B. Jr.
Cox, Joseph
Cox, Rachel & Sister
Cooley, Lucinda
Clement, Alex
Clement, Isaac
Clarke, Jane
Crenshaw, Thomas
Caruth, Miss L. L.
Cherry, Mrs. Susan
Clarke, Henry
Cresswell, J. H. dec'd.
Cooley, Jas./Jos.? dec'd.
Dent, Mrs. M.
Dickson, Thos.
Daniels, W. D. C.
Duncan, David
Dooley, Wm.-Georgia
Dobbins, John
Driver, James
Dobbins, James
Dollar, Williamson
Dunlap, Matthew
Deane, Thomas
Drake, James
Davis, Richard
Drake, James
Drake, Enock
Davis, Aaron
Davis, Moses
Davis, Thomas
Davis, John L.
Duckworth, Wilburn
Duckworth, Thomas
Dobbins, A. E
Duncan, Robert
Dawson, Samuel
Davis, Zachariah
Davis, William
Duckworth, Benj.
Duckworth, Wm.
Duckworth, Jacob

Davis, Charles R.
Douthit, James
Douthit, Benjamin
Dunham, David
Douthit, J. W.
Dunham, Wm. Jr.
Dunham, Wm.
Dickinson, Willis
DuPre, Benjamin
DuPre, Miss L.? H. M.
Dalrymple, James
Duncan, Thomas
Dalrymple, John
Driven, James Sr.?
Dunham, B.
Dobbins, Martha
Davis, John B.
Davis, Enoch dec'd.
Deane, C. P.
Duckworth, Howard
Deane, Moses
Dalrymple, Mary
Dacus, John A.
Davis, James
Dorr?, G. W.
Davis, T.? W.
Dalrymple, Lewis
Dalrymple, John
Duke, J. J.
Dent, Mary
Dent, Henriette
Dickson, Matthew dec'd.
Earle& Towers
Earle, Samuel G.
Elrod, Wm.
Emberson, James
Emberson, Saml. dec'd.
Ellison, Miles
Ellison, Joel
Elrod, George G.
Elrod, Wm.
Estis, Larkin
Eskew, Wm.
Elrod, Samuel
Elrod, John M.
Elrod, George
Elrod, Philip
Elrod, W. A.
Elrod, Adam
Elrod, Elias
Ellison, James
Earle, James W.
Eaton, Joseph
Eubanks, Elijah
Erskine, John
Erskine, Thomas
Erskine, Jas. dec'd.
Elgin, Harrison
Erskine, James
Erskine, Wm.
Elrod, Thos. P.
Erskine, Wm.
Elrod, Thos. dec'd.
Evins, Alex dec'd.
Elliott, Mary
Earpe, Wesley dec'd.
Earle, Elias
Earle, & Griffin
Elliotte, R. E.
Earle, J. B.
Featherston, J. W.
Fant, James
Felton, Mary
Fricks, Christopher
Fant, Alfred
Farmer, John W.
Fleming, James
Fleming, Richard
Forbes, Alanson
Ford, Stephen
Floyd, A. J.
Ford, W. H.
Fenell, Jane K.

Fitzgerald, Martha
Fuller, A.
Fretwell, John
Fowler, Ruth
Fisher, Saml. S.
Fisher, S.? C.
Tinley, Elias
Fant, Abner
Felton, Amariah
Fretwell, Joseph Y.
Fant, Wm. N.
Fant, V. D.
Fant, Mary
Fant, Richard
Fielding, Henry
Gantt, John W.
Grant, Wm.
Gilbert, Amos
Grambell, David
Gilmer, James
Garrison, Henry
Gilmer, Robert
Gilmer, Nancy
Calloway, Mathew
Gentry, Moody
Gentry, Elizabeth
Glenn, Joseph
Gassaway, Benjamin
Gordon, David
Gable, Henry
Gable, Henry Jr.
Gable, Levy
Grubbs, George
Gambrell, James
Gambrell, Sarah
Gambrell, E. B.
Gantt, Wm.
Gambrell, Wm.
Green, John
Gantt, Hugh
Gantt, John
Gray, Huldah
Green, David
Green, James L.
Green, David Jr.
Green, Wm. S.?
Gantt, John G.
Gaines, Henry M.
Gillespy, Wm.
Gambrell, James
Gambrell, D. H.
Griffin, Elijah
Garrett, Thomas
Gambrell, Lettice
Gambrell, M. T.
Gentry, Daniel
George, James
Gantt, James A.
Grubbs, John M.
Graham, A. J.
Green, David
Gentry, Sandford
George, Ezekiel
Guyton, Guyton
Gutherie, Benjamin
Gutherie, Nelson
Gutherie, S.? B.
Gibbs, Mary
Gambrell, James
Givens, Harrison
Gambrell, E.
Gambrell, James Jr.
Gambrell, Reid
Gambrell, Jas. M.
Gray, Elizabeth
Grigg, Hugh
Gentry, John
Gentry, Arthur
Garrison, Foster?
Gutherie, David dec'd.
Griffin, Sophia
Gray, Jesse
Gray, Hezekiah

Green, Wm.
Glenn, J. W.
Gentry, A. B.
Gray, Alex. D.
Gibson, Wm. B.
Gentry, Reuben
Gray, Robert D.
Golden, John
Gambrell, Susanna
Gentry, Zacheriah
Gann ?, James
Gaillard, W.H. D.
Gaillard, Mrs. R. W.
Goode, Philip P.
Gaillard, Josias D.
Gaillard, Mary D,
Gray, James
Green, Solomon
Green, Thos.
Gordon, James
Gordon, James dec'd.
Gambrell, Mat dec'd.
Glenn, Wm.
Gray, John
Gambrell, John
Gambrell, Wm.
Gambrell, Barbary
Griffin, J. C.
Guyton, John Wm.
Gaillard, C. L.
Gaillard, A. D.
Goode, Sarah
Goode, Martha
Hunter, John
Hembree, James
Hembree, James Jr.
Hillhouse, Joseph
Herring, Levy?
Hix, Daniel
Harris, Sarah G.
Harris, B. B.
Holland, Robert
Herring, Jesse
Harrison, James
Herring, Francis
Herndon, George
Howard, Hiram
Hall, Martin
Hall, Lent
Houston, Wm.
Hatton, Wm.
Hall, A. J.?
Humphrey, David
Howee, Robert
Harris, Nathan
Handy/Hardy, R. B.
Hall, David
Havird, Mark W.
Handy, James
Handy, John
Hays, John
Hill, Thos. O.
Hall, Zachariah
Hall, John
Hall, Polly
Hall, Lemuel
Harkness, John
Harkness, Robt. C.
Hamilton, J. M.
Hall, Wm. D./A.?
Hall, Wm. A. Jr.
Harkness, John N.
Hamilton, Luke
Hamilton, Jane
Hamilton, Nancy
Hog, Thompson
Hopkins, John
Hopkins, James M.
Hammond, Herbert
Hall, James A.
Hunt, Wm.
Harper, Wm. C.
Harper, John H.?

Hankins, John
Horton, Grief
Hankins, James dec'd.
Hankins, Jane
Hankins, Sarah
Harper, Nancy
Holland, Caleb B.
Holl, Saml. C.
Hennings, James
Holland, Wm.
Hunter, Sarah
Harper, Thomas
Hall, Aaron
Herrings, John
Haney, Charles
Hall, Nancy
Hall, Joab
Holland, Wm. W.
Hall, Joseph
Hall, Wm. J.?/S.?
Hanks, Stephen
Haney, Luke
Haney, Wm. H.?
Holland, John
Harrison, Wm.
Hembree, A. D.
Hunt, John
Holmes, Wm.
Hammond, J. H.
Hankins, Hugh
Harris, Benjamin
Hunt, Jane J.?
Holland, Aaron B.
Hamilton, Martha A.
Hamilton, C. E.
Hamilton, D. H.
Hamilton, L. L.?
Hunter, Mary
Hastie, John A. C.
Hastie, John
Hopkins, John
Hugens, F. R.
Hewins, Wm.
Hendricks, David
Harper, Barbara
Hembree, Wm.
Henderson, Martha
Harper, Asa
Hanna, Thos.
Haslet, Moses W.
Howard, George
Haygood, Simpson
Hinton, John
Hall, Wilson
Hanks, Luke
Hanks, Thomas
Hammond, S. J.?
Hall, Fenton Jr.
Hall, John
Haney, Stephen
Hall, Drury R.
Harris, Matilda
Harris, Joseph P.
Harris, John dec'd.
Hunter, Wm.
Haney, John
Hammond, B. F.
Hammond, W. L.
Harrison, James Jr.
Hughens, Robert
Hughes, B. P.
Hall, Ezekiel
Harper, Martha
Harper, John
Hammond, Dr. C. C.
Hodge, R. H. W.
Hix, John
Harris, Susan
Harleston, Edward
Hillhouse, Saml. P.
Jones, J. B.
Jones, Thomas
Irvine, Ealenor

Jones, Wm.
Johnston, Willis
Johnston, Peter
Jolly, Henry
Johnston, Walter G.
Johnston, Allen
Jolly, James
Johnston, Joel
Ingraham, Wm.
Jones, Happy
Jones, John W.
Jones, Wilson
Jones, Wm.
Jenkins, Wm. L.
Isaac, A.
Jennings, Jane
Isbell, Samuel
Jonkins, Margaret
Jones, John
John, Samuel
Johnston, Milly
Johnston, A. B.
Jolley, Joseph M.
Johnston, F. M.
Irby, Charles
Kay, Strother
King, John D.
King, Wm. P.
Keys, John
Keown, G. W.
Kerr, Wm.
Kingsley, Cheston
Kay, Gabriel
Kay, Wm. Sr.
Kay, Joel
Kay, Catherine
Kelly, Allen
Kelly, Elizabeth
Kay, James H.
Kay, James Jr.
Kay, Wm. P.
Kay, Mason
King, Robert
Kelly, Alfred
Kelly, Elisha
Kelly, B. J.
King, James
King, Josiah
Kay, Charles
King, Peter
King, G. W.
Kay, Jesse
Knox, John
Kelly, Daniel
Knight, W.
Keasler?, Henry
Kay, S. W.
Kay, John
Kay, J. D.
Keys, James C.
Kay, Alexander
Keaton, Wm.
Keaton, Archibald
Keown, M. M.
Keys, Robert A.
King, J. J.
Kay, Fielding
Keaton, Welborn
King, Robert A.
King, Wm.
Kay, F. M.
Knaupf, Wm. P.
Kinksey, Fair dec'd.
Lowry, Jackson
Leadbetter, Joel
Leadbetter, James
Leadbetter, Mary
Lewis, Elizabeth
Lockhart, M. J.
Latham?, Wm.
Liverett, Thos.
Liverett, Wm.
Liverett, Stephen

Liverett, John
Liverett, Stephen Jr.
Lindsey, James L.?S.?
Lee, Philip
Lucius, Danl Jr.
Lucius, Danl
Lewis, James W.
Lewis, J. W. & J. B.
Lewis, J. B.
Long, Wm.
Longer?, Wm.
Leboon, Joseph
Long, Ezekiel
Leboon, E by?
Lorten, John S.
Lorton, Mrs. Frances
Lewis, Mrs. S.?
Lewis, Jesse
Long, Harrison
Lewis, Elisha
Latham, Cornelius
Lattimer, Wiley B.
Leadbetter, David T.
Latimer, Harrison
Liverett, Wesley
Lewis, Jess P. dec'd.
Lewis, Hannah E.
Liddell, A. J.
Morris, Samuel
McClure, E. J.
Moss, Samuel
Merritt, Benjamin
Merritt, John
Meredith, Abraham
McKay, Martin
Martin, Mathew
Massey, Silas
McCollum, Samuel
McLees, James
McLees, Wm.
McLees, Margaret
McCarley, James
McCarley, Elias
McCarley, Joseph
McCarley, Robert
McGill, Mary
McConnell, Wm.
McGee, John
McKee, James
McBride, James L.
Morgan, John
Milford, John
Milford, Mary
Martin, Phoebe
Morgan, Rebecca
McKee, Wm.
McKee, Archibald
McGee, Willis
Mochat, Jacob
McCullough, S.?/L.? D.
McCarely?, Sarah
McPhail, John
McGee, Gabriel L.
May, Daniel
Mattison, Olley
Massey, Laban
Mattison, George B.
McGee, Michael
Mattison, Archibald
McGee, Burrell
Mattison, Wyatt
Mattison, Daniel
Mattison, James
Mattison, Wm.
Mattox, Henry
Mattison, Elizabeth
Mattison, Sandford S.
Maulden, B. F.
Moore, Grant E.
Mayfield, Ephraim
Martin, Chesley
Martin, Abram
Moore, David

Major, Enoch
McGregor, Miriam?
McGregor, John W .
Mitchell, Mary
Major, Elijah
Major, Wm.
McMillian, Wyatt
NcConnell, Thos. Jr.
Mitchel, Caleb
Masters?, G. W.
McFall, Saml. R.
Mitchell, Benj. S.
Mattox, Thos.
McLeskey, James
Major, William
Major, James
McCoy, James
Murphy, Ezekiel
McAlister, John
Martin, Wm.
Martin, James
McMurtry, Wm.
McAlister, John
Murphy & Martin
Murphy, John
Murphy, W. S.
McAlister, James
Murphy, Thos. M.
Moore, Elizabeth
McGee, Wm.
Mayfield, Margaret
Moore, Thos.
Moore, Elijah
Merritt, Obediah
Merritt, Leroy
McCann, F. H.
McCann & Walker
McKinney, Wm.
Martin, Jacob
McMurry, Wm.
McMurrey, Jane
Mullikens, Benj. Jr.?
Mulliken, Wm.
Mulliken, James
McMaham, Peter dec'd.
Mulliken, Benjamin
Martin, Abram
McElroy, John
Milton, Michael
Miller, M. L.
Miller, John C.
Miller, Jane
Martin, Jesse
Miller, John
McMurray, Wm. C.
Miller, S. F. W.
McCrary, Mary
McCrary, Albert
McLees, James J.
McLees, Andrew
McKeown, Robert
McPherson, Elizabeth
McFall, Phoebe & children
McFall, John
Moorehead, Maxey
Moorehead, Clarissa
Mattison, John M.
McClinton, A. S.
McGill, Mary Ann & Sarah
Massey, Abram
Murphy, Moses
Millwee, Samuel
Millwee, Wm. A.
Millwee, Elizabeth & sister
McAdams, John
Moore, Jeremiah
McGee, Elias
Mitchell, Ephraim
Major, Joseph M. dec'd.
McGee, Jesse C.
McKeown, John
McMurtry, James
McMurtry, Rebecca

Martin, John
Murry, Margaret
Martin, Hester
McCraken, Susan
May, Tucker
Martin, Samuel
Martin, John
Mattison, Mary
McAlister, Nathan
Morris, Jesse C.
Morris, David
Morris, James
Mattison, Elizabeth
Moorehead, M. L.
Miller, Henry C.
Milford, Wm. J. - Dr.
Moorehead, Alex
Moore, John
Mauldin, B. F. & Co.
McAllister, Nathan
Moore, Mary dec'd.
Maverick, Samuel
Mills, Berry
McAllister, Margaret
McMahan, Samuel
McConnell, T. F.
Moorehead, John
McFall, A. N.
Mitchell, John
Major, J. W.
McPhail, Peter
Moorehead, Lewis
McCauley, Stephen
Massey?, Elizabeth
Major, John P.
Maxwell, R. A.
Moses, C. B.
McElroy, Archibald
Maxwell, Jno.
Nelson, Wm. R.
Norris, Ezekiel
Norris, Robert B.
Norris, Jesse W.
Nichols, Archibald
Nichols, James C.
Nichols, Wm. A.
North, John L.
Newton, Isaac
Newton, Larkin
Newton, Samuel
Newton, J. M.
Nevitt?, Wm.
Newton, Willis
Nelson, W. R.
Norris, A. O.?
Norris, Mary Ann
Norris, John E.
Newel?, Wm.
Newel?, George
Obrient, Wm.
Obrient, Andrew?
Obrient, Aaron
Owen, Thornton
Owen, Daniel
Oldham, Wm.
Oldham, Thomas
Orr, Alexander
Owen, Lewis
Orr, Wm.
Orr, Thomas
Owen, Elijah
Orr, James
Owen, Martha
Owen, Elijah
Overby, Nicholas
Owen, John
Oliver, Martha
Osborne, L. A.
Orr, James L.
Orr, Christopher
Overby, B. M.
Pritchet?, Lewis
Palmer, Wm.

376

Pickerel, Jonathan
Pullem, Wm.
Parker, Matthew
Presley, Ann
Parton, Hubbard
Porter, Hugh
Pettigrew, Robt. H.
Patterson, Thos. H.
Price, H. P.
Price, Pennel
Pruitt, William
Parker, Robt.
Penel, Thomas
Philips, Reuben
Poor, Samuel
Pettis, Jane
Poor, Lucinda
Poor, John B.
Poor, Nancy
Poor, George
Poor, Holland
Poor, Reuben
Poole, Elizabeth
Pruett, E. D.
Pickle, C. W.
Pickle, W. C.
Pickens, Wm. S.
Poulman, Ludovick
Pegg, John
Pegg, James B.
Philips, Martin
Prater?, Joseph
Pickle, Wm.
Pickle, Jacob
Pickens, Robert
Philips, John
Poor, John
Pressley, David A.
P____, Henry
Passmore, Wm. dec'd.
Pearman, Jonathan
Padget, Elizabeth
Poole, Wm. H.
Poole, Mary
Poole, Adam
Prince, C. J.?
Pearman, Benj.
Pearce, T. A.
Pendleton Manufacturing Co.
Pickle, J. E.
Poor, Wm.
Pickens, Thos. J.
Pepper, Eliza?
Padget, Jno. L.
Pearce, Wm.
Reid, Moses
Reid, Jesse
Rusk, David dec'd.
Reid, Wm.
Reid, Hugh dec'd.
Raney, Mil__a?
Rice, Sarah
Roach, Henry
Roach, Forester
Reid, Dr. J.? H.
Rutledge, Jesse
Ranson, Wm.
Rice, Amaziah
Rice, Hezekiah dec'd.
Robinson, John B.
Rice, Hezekiah
Rice, Thos. L.
Robinson, Jhn. J.
Robinson, James E.
Robinson, John dec'd.
Robinson, Samuel
Reese, David
Reese, Wm. G.
Ritchie, James N.
Roberts, Mathias
Rodgers, Wm. & Larkin
Russell, David
Rodgers, Elihu

Reid, A. E.
Rainwater, D. L.?
Reeves, Elizabeth
Rodgers, Jane W.
Rodgers, Joseph T.
Rodgers, Jack
Richardson, Mathias
Richardson, Sion
Riley, Abram
Richardson, Noah
Rosamond, John H.
Rea, Elihu
Rix, G. W.
Robinson, Dr. Wm.
Robinson, Jane
Robinson, David
Ritchie, Wm.
Rodgers, Simeon
Rankin, George
Ritchie, John dec'd.
Rooleter?, John
Rice, Ibzan
Rice, Jane
Ragsdale, F. A.
Russell, Thos. H.
Richardson, A. W.
Rochester, Nathaniel
Robinson, Jane
Rodgers, Hester
Reid, Andrew
Rodgers, Wm. W.
Ross, A. W.
Rimmer, Lucinda
Robbins, Polly
Reid, Henry
Reid, J. P.
Rice, Fleetwood
Rice & Earle
Rodgers, Wm.
Richardson, Mary L.
Richardson, Maria
Richardson, Wade
Ritche, Reuben
Ruff, David
Rampey, James A.
Robinson, Willis
Reeves, John
Reeves, R. W.
Richardson, David
Riley, Hezekiah
Smith, Wm.
Steele, Robert A.
Shearer, Gillam
Simmons, Charles
Simmons, Thomas
Swelling, Samuel
Swelling, James
Simmons, David
Simmons, James
Shaw, Wm. S.
Skelton, Thos. T.?
Skelton, Thomas
Skelton, A. B.
Siddell, A. S. Y.
Simpson, David
Smith, Martin H.
Stewart, James
Stewart, George
Stewart, Adam
Stewart, Mary
Sullivan, Kelly
Spearman, John
Smith, Robinson
Speed, Wm.
Scott, David
Simpson, Thomas
Simpson, Wm.
Stephenson, John
Stephenson, Thomas
Stevens/Stewart?, John
Sadler, J. F.
Speer, James G.
Saunders, Abram

Sherrard, Wm.
Sherrard, Jane
Smith, Saml.
Sailors, Leonard
Sailors, Isaac
Stickland, Matthew
Shirley, Benjamin
Seawright, Margaret
Shirley, Obediah
Smith, Joel
Stone, Hampton
Smith, David
Smith, A. W.
Smith, Jeremiah
Smith, R. L.?
Shumate, James J.
Stone, George
Stanton, Catharine
Stone, Wm. H.
Strickland, Milly
Stott, Williamson
Stott, Drayton
Smith, William
Smith, Wyatt
Smith, Jesse R.
Smith, J. R. & Co.
Snipes, Matthew
Stephenson, Andrew
Stephenson, John
Smith, Ebenezer
Smith, Wiley O.
Sp_ory?, Thomas
Smith, Wm.
Smith, Saml.
Smith, Wm.
Spearman, Benj.
Spearman, David
Spearman, David Jr.
Smith, S.? C.
Smith, Basil
Slaten, John
Smith, G. S.
Spearman, F. A.
Smith, Philip P.
Smith, Simeon
Slaten, Lovell
Slaten, George dec'd.
Stone, James
Sitton, William
Smith, Ephraim
Smith, John P.
Smith, Joseph W.
Smith, Griffin
Smith, Joseph
Satterfield, Jeremiah
Smith, J. M.
Smith, Sarah
Smith, J. C. & J. M.
Smith, James dec'd.
Smith, J. H.
Smith, John
Smith, J. D.
Smith, Andrew
Sitton, Wm. L.
Spruel, Simeon
Smith, Edward
Sharpe, Elam Jr.
Starke, Mrs. E. G.
Sharpe, Elam
Sloan, John T.
Seaborn, George
Smith, Benj. dec'd.
Smith, Mary E. N.
Smith, Alice E. D.
Smith, J. L. N.
Smith, Wm. C.
Smith, Sarah E. D.
Smith, B. J.?/S.?
Smith, Mrs. S. N. dec'd.
Swords, John
Sitton, John D.
Shanklin, Joseph V.
Smith, Whitaker

Sadler, David
Simpson, James
Simpson, Archibald
Smith, Aaron
Symmes, Dr. F. W.
Smith, Nimrod
Steele, Wm.
Shirley, Aaron
Sailors, Abram
Smith, John A.
Smith, Samuel
Scott, M. B.
Shirley, Richard
Shirley, Elizabeth
Stephenson, James
Stephenson, George Jr.
Simpson, W. S.?
Shirley, James Jr.
Shirley, James
Smith, John M.
Simpson, R. F.
Stephenson, George
Smith, Zepheniah
Shaw, Peyton R.
Stephenson, John Jr.
Smith, Robt. B.
Siddell, John
Sherriff, Washington
Sloan, Thos. M.
Saunders, Wm.
Stanton, Mathias
Skelton, John
Shearer, Andrew
Seawright, Andrew
Scott, T. L.
Sailors, John
Smith, Thos. G.
Sloan, B. F.
Sloan, Susan
Smith, Aaron
Stanley, Ezekiel
Steele, James
Todd, Charles
Tippens, Elizabeth
Tippens, Dennis
Taylor, James
Tucker, Dejarnet
Todd, Andrew
Todd, Olive
Tucker, Nancy
Taylor, Elijah
Tate, J. A.
Tucker, Wm.
Towns, Wm. W.
Trussell, Wesley
Trussell, Posey
Turner, John B.
Talford, George
Telford, James
Telford, James H.
Telford, Wm.
Telford, Gabella
Tippens, George
Todd, James
Tate, David
Tate, Van
Todd, Wm. P.
Todd, Mary
Trussell, Wm.
Thompson, John
Thompson, James
Todd, John L.
Thompson, James
Tripp, Nicholas
Tripp, John H.
Tompkins, John
Trainem, Lazarus
Timms, Isaac
Tilly, Mary
Taylor, Richard
Tucker, James
Taylor, Joseph
Taylor, J. B. E.

Taylor, Samuel H.
Thompson, Elizabeth
Thompson, A. E. (Dr.?)
Tate, Tillman
Towers, Daniel R. dec'd.
Taylor, David S.
Taylor, Wm. J.
Taylor, Dr. Joseph
Tollinghast, Elias H.
Towers, John R.
Tucker, R. D.
Terry, Henry
Teague, Elijah
Wardlaw, James
Whitfield, Lewis
Wright, Oliver
Webb, Elisha
Watson, Daniel
Williford, Sarah
Williford, C. R.
Wright, Elizabeth
Willbanks, Elijah
Watt, Mary Jrn.
Watt, Joseph T.
Watt, Mary
Watt, James G.
Watt, Thomas
Watt, Joseph
Waters, Ibzan
Willy, James R.
Watt, James
Whitman, Jacob
Watt, John
Wiles, James H.
Wilder?/Wilden?, Wm.
Williamson, Martin
Williamson, Wm.
Wright, R. N.
Webb, Andrew
Wright, Turner
Williams, James
Webster, Jane
Wyatt, Redman
Wardlaw, John M.
Williams, Jasper
Wilson, Sarah
Wyatt, James F.
Wyatt, Elijah
Webb, Wm.
Wilson, James
Williams, W. B.(M.? B.)
Wilson, J. J.
Wilson, John N.
Wardlaw, H. H.
Webb, Samuel
Webb, Clayton
Wright, Catherine
Wilson, Bartley
Willbanks, Hezekiah
Willingham, John
Wilson, James
Wellbourn, A. G.
Wellbourn, W. E.
Wilson, James
Welbourn, Thos.
Wilson, Hugh
Willbanks, James
Welborn, Wm.
Willson,Wm.? M.
Waddell, Wm.
Watson, James
Watkins, Felix
Wiggington, John
Wiggington, Elihu
Wilson, John
Wilson, W. D.
Welborn, James
Walker, John S.?
Wilson, Stephen M.
Wilson, James
Wiles, Elizabeth dec'd.
Warnock, John dec'd.
White, Thomas

White, Henry
Watson, Mary
Waddle, Alex H.
Watkins, Joseph
Watkins, Wm.
Wakefield, John
Wynne, Franklin
Wakefield, Cynthia
Wright, Wm. F.
Warnock, John
Williams, Wm. A.
Watkins, Baylis
Wakefield, Conrad
White, Bart
Williford, Saml W.
Williams, John
Williford, Deane
White, Jonathan
Wallace, Wilson
Wallace, Martha dec'd.
Webb, C. B.
Wakefield, A. F.
Webb, Edmund
Waller, Mrs. R. H.
Whitfield, J. T.
Waller, Mary
Wilson, George
Wilson, Wm. M.
Wilson, Robert D.
Whitner, J. N.
Webb, Elijah
White, Julia
Warley & Sharpe
Warley, Mrs. S.
Whitaker, H.
Willbanks, Shadrack
Welborn, Sarah
Watson, Martha L.?
Williams, Jasper
Webb, James
White, Sarah
Warren, Saml. dec'd.
Webb, Warren R.
Young, James
Yeargon, Saml.
Young, Wm. L.
Young, Francis A.

(Following out of order)
Trippe, Anna
Vandiver, Enoch
Vandiver, Edward
Burris, Elisha

FOR PICKENS DIST.
Earle, J. B.
McClure, J. E.
Meredith, Abram
Harrison, James
Colhoun, John
Norris, Ezekiel
Black, John
Adams, John
Breckenridge, Robt.
Gambrell, James
Anderson, Wm.
Elrod, G. G.
Todd, James
Major, James
Hubbard, Wm.
Watson, A. L.
Sharpe, Elam Junr.
Knight, W.
Bishop, Jane & Dorcas
Shanklin, Jos. V.
Fretwell, John
Morten, Oliver
Zachery, James
Hall, Wilson & Brothers
Vandiver, P. L.?
Reys, R. A.
Gunnin, James
Symmes, F. W.

378

Clement, Alex
Mochat, Jacob
Sherrard, Wm.
Tucker, Wm.
Clement, W. K.?
_____, J. L.
Thompson, James
Smith, Mrs. L. V.? dec'd.
Smith, Wm. C.
Dickson, Thomas
Simpson, David
Fisher, Thos. dec'd.
Wakefield, John
Smith, Robert
Miller, J. C.
Ruff, David
Tucker, R. D.
Armstrong, J. B.
Harleston, Edward

Free Negroes 50

GREENVILLE:
Seaborn, George
Cooley, Lewis
Maverick, Saml.
Lewis, J. W. & J. B.

ST. STEPHENS:
Gaillard & Jenkins

CHARLESTON
Maverick, Saml.

LAURENS
Maverick, Saml.

UNION
Maverick, Saml.

NEWBERRY
Maverick, Saml.

ORANGEBURGH
Maverick, Saml.

WAPAANAPAA
Maverick, Saml.

GOOSE CREEK
Maverick, Saml.

GENERAL TAXES COLLECTED IN ANDERSON FOR THE YEAR 1846 BY WILLIAM STEELE:

Avery, William	Armstrong, Arch'd.	Brown, Jane? M.
Acker, P. N.	Armstrong, John B.	Brown, Saml.
Acker, Susannah	Arnold, Lawson T.	Branyan, Henry
Allen, Jas. E.	Barnes, Rev'd. Z. for	Belcher, Manning
Acker, Amos	Miss D.	Beatty, Wm.
Armstrong, James	Brazeale, Kennon	Bowie, Chas.
Armstrong, John	Brazeale, D. K.	Buchanan, Wm.
Acker, Halbert	Bennett, Thos.	Burdett, Hiram
Ashley, Wilson	Bennett, Wm.	Brown, Johana
Ashley, John	Brazeale, Enoch	Bonds, Sugar
Alexander, David	Brown, Dr. G. R.	Burton, Blackman
Armstrong, Jas.	Bennett, Chas. M.	Beatty, John
Adams, Jas.	Brazeale, Williamson	Beatty, Thomas
Armstrong, And'n.	Ballentine, Jesse _?	Beatty, Margt.
Adams, Asa	Bantley, Nancy	Burton, Peyton
Adams, John (2)	Bantley, Sally	Brown, Samuel
Able, James S.	Bantley, Josiah	Black, John
Able, John	Bagwell, Jas.	Bozeman, Lewis
Anderson, Micajah	Brock, Hayden	Brown, Chas.
Anderson, David	Bagwell, John	Brookes, Thomas
Acker, Wm.	Bagwell, James	Baker, Saml. H.
Archer, Wm. M.	Brock, James	Brown, Abner
Anderson, Dr. Wm.	Brock, Meredith	Baker, Lindsey A.
Abbott, John	Brasswell, Nancy	Buchanan, Saml.
Amick, John D.	Brasswell, Anderson	Brown, John
Acker, J. S.	Brownlee, Maria	Brown, Wm. P.
Alewine, Jacob	Breckenridge, Robt.	Brown, _arina?
Adams, Henry	Brown, Newton	Brown, Nat. A.(Mat.?)

379

Brown, Alvina
Burris, Thos.
Bettenton, John
Burris, Reuben
Bowen, Samuel
Bowman, Arch'd.
Bailey, Allen
Barton, H. M.
Burns, Jas.
Bradberry, Salathiel
Bradberry, James
Bradberry, Jesse
Bradberry, Wm.
Burris, Thos. Jr.
Burris, John M.
Bruce, Thos.
Branyan, Jas. J.(Jos.?)
B_ylos, John T.
Brazeale, Griffin
Burgess, James
Borroughs, Matilda
Briant, Terrell
Blassingame, Thos.
Beco?, Antonio
Brewen, Wm.
Brewen, Milley
Bailey, J. S. dec'd.
Belotte, Jacob
Bishop, Jane & Dorcas
Bridwell, J. W.
Bee, B. E.
Benson, E. B.
Benson & Son
Brothers, J. W.
Brown, Randolph
Bowdon, Jas. G.
Bruce, C. P.
Byrum, Peter
Burris, Milford
Brown, Samuel
Benson, John P.?
Brooks, Garner
Broyles, O. R.
Broyles, Aaron dec'd.
Brownlee, Wm.
Bolling, Albert
Burns, Jordan
Brazeale, Mathew
Bruce, Charles
Beatty, David
Ballentine, Geo.
Barrett, Chas.
Beatty, Saml.
Borroughs, Briant
Brown, G.? dec'd.
Brown, Elijah dec'd.
Bell, Samuel
Briant, Simon
Briant, Nathan
Bailey, Wm.
Boyd, Robert
Brown, Larkin
Brown, Cath'e. dec'd.
Brown, Robert
Bozeman, D. T.?
Barr, Leroy
Borroughs, James
Burris, Joshua
Brannon, John
Brazeale, Gamb'l.
Brown, Danl.
Brown, Robt.
Burris, Jacob
Burris, Mrs. E.
Bellotte, Peter E.
Burns?, Leah
Bellotte, John E.
Bowen, Robert
Bowman, John
Cannon, Isaac
Crymes, Benj. F.
Cox, John
Cox, Thomas

Cox, Wm. H.
Clardy, Joab
Carden, Thos.
Cox, Arris
Crymes, Robt. D.?
Cullen, Caleb
Cobb, Noah
Cobb, Ephraim
Cumming, David
Clement, Christ'r.
Clinkscales, Wm. F
Cox, R. B.
Cox, Mrs. Frances
Cobb, Henry
Clement, Isaac
Cox, Wm.
Cox, Eliz.
Clement, C. W.
Cobb, Maston
Cox, Gabriel
Clement, Wm. K.?
Clement, Jane
Clement, J. C. A.
Clement, Isaac
Carpenter, J. W.
Clarke, Ann
Clinkscales, Ibzan
Clinkscales, Mary
Chalmers, J. C.
Clinkscales, Abner
Clinkscales, Lewis
Campbell, Thos.
Casey, Sarah
Chastain, Stephen
Chastain, James
Coates, J. J.
Chamblee, Moses
Campbell, Alex'r.
Clinkscales, Asa
Campbell, Alfred
Casey, Dilly
Cunningham, Cath'e.
Cowan, Hiram
Casey, Mary
Cumming, Harmon
Cunningham, Thos.
Cunningham, Saml. decd.
Cunningham, Cath'e.
Carr, Mary
Caldwell, John
Caldwell, James
Caldwell, Joseph
_____, James
Campbell?, Wm.
Coates, John
Coffee, Iley?
Coffin, Abram
Cox, Jas.? Jos.?
Cox, Rach'l & Rebecca
Cresswell, Sarah
Carpenter, A. T.
Carpenter, Eliz.
Clarke, Jane
Carpenter, A. M.
Carpenter, John
Clinkscales, John
Cresswell, John dec'd.
Cox, Asa
Crawford, Henry
Crawford, Sarah
Campbell, James
Carter, Caleb
Cobb, Henry
Cobb. J. W.
Clardy, Norman
Carter, J. S.
Cobb, Franklin
Cobb, James
Carlisle, Rev. Wm.
Crayton, B. F.
Cator, Dr. A. P.
Chamblee, Benj. dec'd.
Cherry, S.

Carruth, L. L.
Clardy, John
Childress, Nich's.
Cason, Esther
Cason, John
Craig, Samuel
Cherry, Thos. W.?
Crenshaw, Thos.
Carne, Miss S. M.
Cherry, David
Cherry, Mrs. Susan dec'd
Cherry, Dr. E. D.
Cheves, Langdon
Crawford, James
Cochrane, Danl. H.?
Chamblee, Jas.
Cox, Thomas
Cowan, Wm.
Chamblee, Robt.
Cox, Abner
Cook, Wm.
Cox, Wm.
Clarke, J. B. Jr.
Chamblee, Jas.
Cooley, Hiram
Cooley, Lucinda
Clement, Alexr.
Cannon, Eph'm.
Carr, Laban
Cosper, Henry
Campbell, Jesse
Conant, Allen
Carpenter, Jas.
Cooley, John dec'd.
Cooley, Hannah
Clinkscales, Wm. F.?
Campbell, Danl.
Cox, David
Clarke, J. B.
Chamblee, Zadoc dec'd.
Crumley, Dr. J. L.
Dawson, Saml.
Davis, Zach.
Davis, Wm.
Deane, Chaes. P.
Davis, John L.?P.?
Davis, Moses?
Davis, Thomas
Drake, James A.
Drake, James
Drake, Robert
Drake, Enoch H.
Davis, F. W.
Dunlap, Matthew
Deane, Thomas
Deane, Samuel
Dooley, Wm.
Driven, Jas. Jr.
Driven, James
Dollar, Williamson
Dalrymple, John
Dowell, Morris
Dobbins, James
Dobbins, John
Deane, Moses
Duncan, David
Duckworth, Wm.
Duckworth, Benj.
Duckworth, Thomas
Duckworth, Welborn
Dorr, G. W.
Durham, Wm.
Douthet, Jas.
Douthet, Benj.
Davis, Rich'd.
Davis, C. R.
Durham, David
DuPre, Miss Susan
DuPre, Benj.
Dart, Mrs. Mary
Daniels, W. D. C.
Duke, J. J.
Davis, John B.

Davis, Enoch dec'd.
Dobbins, A. C.?
Duncan, Robt.
Dalrymple, Jas.
Dalrymple, Mary
Duckworth, Joab
Dacus, John A.
Duckworth, Howard
Dalrymple, John
Dalrymple, Lewis
Dobbins, Martha
Davis, Aaron
Duncan, Thos.
Dickson, Thos.
Dickson, Matthew dec'd.
Erskine, John
Eubanks, Elijah
Ellison, Miles
Ellison, Joel
Elrod, Wm.
Elrod, Mary
Elrod, Alfred
Earle & Towers
Earle, Saml. G.
Earle, J. B.
Elrod, Geo. G.
Elrod, Samuel
Elrod, Wm.
Elrod, Sarah
Elrod, John M.
Elrod, George
Elrod, Philip
Elrod, Adam
Elrod, Elias
Ellison, James
Ellison, Joel
Earle, Dr. J. W.
Eaton, Jos.
Erskine, James
Elliott, Dr. R. E.
Estis, Larkin
Elliott, Mary
Erskine, Wm.
Erskine, James dec'd.
Emberson, James
Erskine, Thomas
Erskine, Wm.
Elrod, Thos. P.
Eskew, Wm.
Earle, Elias
Evins, Dr. A.
Earle & Griffin
Entzburgan, W. C.
Emberson, Saml. dec'd.
Fant, Alfred
Fant, Mary
Flowers, G.? S.
Featherston, J. W.
Finley, Elias
Finley, Nancy
Fant, Wm. N.
Fleming, Rich'd.
F 1, Wm. H.
Forbes, Alanson
Ford, Stephen
Floyd, A. J.?
Fitzgerald, Mrs. E. M.
Fretwell, Jas. Y.(Jos.?)
Fant, A.
Fant, James
Fant, O. H. P.
Fisher, Saml. C.
Fant, V. D.
Fowler, Ruth
Felton, Amariah
Felton, Mary
Felton, Richard
Fielding, H. B.
Fretwell, John
Fuller, A.
Gambrell, Lettice
Griffin, Elijah
Gambrell, D. H.

Gambrell, J. M.
Gillespy, Wm.
Gambrell, John
Gaines, Henry M.
Gambrell, Wm.
Gambrell, Barbary
Gantt, Wm.
Gambrell, Jas.
Gambrell, Sarah
Gambrell, E. B.
Gambrell, Wm.
Gray, Huldah
Gantt, John
Green, Wm. S.
Green, David Jr.
Green, David Sr.
Gantt, Hugh
Green, Jas. L.
Gantt & Cox
Gantt, John G.
Grubbs, R. W.
Green, W. W.
Gantt, James A.
Gassaway, Benj.
Gable, Henry Jr.
Gable, Henry Sr.
Gable, Levy
Gaillard, Jos. D.
Gaillard, Miss M. D.
Giles, Robt.
Gentry, Zach.
Gray, Eliz. dec'd.
Galloway, Matthew
Gregg, Hugh
Gentry, Moody
Gentry, Eliz.
Gaines, James M.
Glenn, Wm.
Gunnin, James
Gilmer, Robt.
Gilmer, Nancy
Gantt, John W.
Gilbert, Amos
Grubbs, John M.
Graham, A. J.
Gambrell, David
Grantt, Wm.
Gentry, Arthur
Goode, Philip P.
Gambrell, Mat. dec'd.
Gentry, Daniel
Gray, Robt. D.
Guthrie, Nelson
Guthrie, David dec'd.
Garret, Jesse
Garrett, J. & R.
Guthrie, Steph. B.
Guthrie, Benj.
Givens, Harrison
Gambrell, Jas.
Gambrell, Jas. Jr.
Gambrell, Reid
Gambrell, Ezekiel
Grubbs, Geo.
Glenn, F. M.
Gaillard, C. L.
Gaillard, Mrs. R. W.
Gaillard, W. H. D.
Gentry, Reuben
Geer, Solomon
Golding, John
Green, John M.
Garrett, Thos. H.
Gray, Hezekiah
Gentry, S. M.
Gambrell, M. T.
Gordon, J s.
Gordon, Robt. dec'd.
Gibson, Wm. B.
Gentry, A. B.
Gilman, Jas.
Gray, A. D.
Gray, Andrew

Gambrell. H.
Gambrell, James
Garrison, Henry
Garrison, Foster
Glenn, Jos. B.
Gambrell, Sus'h.
Gambrell, Jackson
Glenn, J. W.
Guyton, J. W.
Gray, John
Guyton, Jesse
Geer, David
Gordon, David
Geer, Thomas
Guyton, Guyton
Gray, Jas. P.
Griffin, J. C.
Griffin, Mrs. Sophia
Goode, Sarah
Goode, Martha
Gaillard, C. D.
Gaillard, A. D.
Hunter, John
Hamilton, Luke
Hamilton, Jane
Holland, John
Holmes, Wm.
Horton, Grief
Hawkins, JAS.? dec'd.
Hawkins, Jane
Hawkins, Sarah
Hawkins, John
Hawkins, John H.
Harper?, Wm.
Hog, Thompson
Hinton, John
Hinton, Alfred? Allen?
Hopkins, John
Hopkins, Jas. M.
Hunt, John
Hall, Jas. A.
Hamilton, John
Hall, Lemuel
Harkness, John
Harkness, C-mmingh.?
Haney, Stephen
Howie, Robt.
Harris, Nathan
Hatten, Wm.
Hodges, R.H. W.
Hall, John
Hall, David
Howard, D. C.?
Hill, Thos. O.
Hall, Ezekiel
Hall, Martin
Howard, Hiram
Hall, Lent
Holland, Geo.
Hughens, Wm.
Hughens, Robt.
Hanks, Stephen
Harris, Jos. P.?
Hall, Wilson
Hammond, Herbert
Hinton, James
Hardy, James
Hardy, John
Herring, Francis
Haney, Chas.
Houston, Wm.
Hardy, R. B.
Henderson, Martha
Harrison, James
Harrison & Wynne
Harris, Sarah G.
Herring, Jesse
Hix, D. J.
Hix, Wm.
Harris, Benj.
Hughes, B. P.
Herring, Levy
Holland, Robt.

Holland, Wm.
Hagood, Simpson
Hembree, James
Hembree, Jas. Jr.
Hillhouse, J. P.
Hillhouse, Rev. J.
Harrison, Wm.
Hammond, S. J.?
Hall, Aaron
Hall, Noah
Hall, Wm. S.
Hembree, A. D.
Haney, Luke
Haney, Wm. H.
Herring, John
Haney, J. C.
Harper, Thomas
Hunter, Mrs. S.
Hamilton, Martha A.
Holland, A. B.
Hunt, J. J.
Hunter, Miss Mary
Harrison, Jas. W.
Hall, Nancy
Hix, Derrill
Hamilton, D. K.
Harper, Asa
Harris, Mrs. Susan
Harris, Nath. dec'd.
Hix, John
Hamilton, L.? S.
Hastie, John & Co.
Hastie, John
Hamilton, C. E.
Hackett, Albert
Harleston, E'd.
Hayes, John
Hall, Zachariah
Hammond, B. F.
Hammond, J. H.
Hall, Jos./Jas.?
Hall, John
Hall, Mary
Harkness, John W.?
Haslet, M. W.
Harvey, John
Hall, Wm. A.
Hall, Wm. A. Jr.
Hall, Saml. C.
Hall, Fenton
Hanks, Thomas
Humphreys, Rev. D.
Hammond, Wm. L.
Hanks, Luke
Hunter, Wm.
Hendricks, David
Harris, Mrs. M. M.
Him n, Nancy
Hawkins?, Hugh
Hall, J.
Hanna, Thos.
Herring, James
Hembree, Wm.
Hammond, Dr. C. C.
Johnston, Willis
Johnston, Peter
Ingraham, Delilah
Johnston, Allen
Jones, Happy
Jentry, John
Irvine, Eleanor
Jones, James
Jones, Thomas
Jones, J. B.
Isbell, Robert
Isbell, Samuel
Jordan, Benson
Jolly, Henry
Irby, Chas.
Jones, John W.
Ingraham, B. H.
Jones, Wilson
Jones, WM. dec'd.

Ingraham, J. H.
Isaacks, A.
Jolly, Jas. M.
Jenkin, Margt. dec'd.
Johnston, W. G.
Jolly, James
Jolly, Wm.
Johnston, Francis
Johnston, Milley
Johnston, A. B.
Jones, Wm.
Jones, Samuel
Jones, John
Johnston, Joel
Jenkins, Dr. Wm. L.
Jeffers, Mrs. Rhoda
Ingraham, Wm.
Johnston, Joel
King, Peter
King, James
King, Robt.
King, G. W.
King, Josiah
Kay, Jesse
Kelley, John
Kelley, Eliz.
Kelley, Allen
Kay, Wm. Sr.
Kay, Joel
Kay, Cath'e
Kay, Wm. B.
Kay, Wm. Jr.
Kay, Mason
Kay, Jas. W.
Kerr, Wm.
Keaton, Wm.
Keown, G. W.
Keown, Wm.
Keese, John
King, John J.
King, Wm.
King, Robt. A.
King, Jas. D.
King, Wm. T.
Kay, S. W.
Kay, Al _?
Knox, John
Kingsley, Chst'n. dec'd.
Kay, Chas.
King, John D.
Kelly, Daniel
Kelly, Elisha
Kelly, B. J.
Kay, Strother
Keese, Robt. A.
Keaton, Arch'd
Keaton, B. F.
Kelly, Alfred
Kay, F. M.
Kay, Gabriel
Kay, John
King, Hiram
Keasler, Henry
Keaton, Welborn
Keese, J. C.
Kirksey, Fair
Knight, W. W.
Knauff, Wm. P.?
Levels, John
Lewis, J. W.
Lewis, J. W. & J. B.
Lewis, J. B.
Lewis & Simpson
Lewis & Cox
Lee, Philip
Lucius, D. F. Sr.
Lucius, James
Lucius, D. F. Jr.
Lindsey, James
Liverett, Wm.
Liverett, Stephen
Lattimer, Wm.
Long, Wm.

Latham, Cor's.
Lewis, Eliz.
Lowry, Jackson
Long, Harrison
Lattimer, Harrison
Langer?, Wm.
Leboon, Jas./Jos.?
Long, Ezekiel
Lorton, John S.
Lorton, Mrs. F.
Lanier, Bird
Ledbetter, Jas.
Ledbetter, Joel
Ledbetter, D. T.
Ledbetter, Mary
Lewis, Jesse
Leboon, Edith
Lewis, Elisha
Liverett, John
Liverett, Thomas
Little, Rachel
Liverett, Stephen
Liverett, Wesley
Liddle, A. J.
Lewis, Jesse P. dec'd.
Lewis, Hannah E.
Major, Wm.
Major, James
Major, Elijah
Mitchell, M. C.
McCoy, Ephraim
Mitchell, Benj. S.
Mayfield, Eph'm
Murphy, Thos.
Moore, G. A.
Maulden, B. F.
Massey, Laban
McCoy, Ann
Matthison, Wm.
Mattox, Henry
Mattison, Danl?
Mattison, James
Mattison, Eliz.
Mattison, S. J.
Moore, Jer'h
McAdams, John
Mattison, G. B.
May, Danl
McPhail, John
McGee, G. L.
McBride, Jas. L.
Morgan, John
McGee, W. H.
Martin, Phoebe
McCullough, S. C.
Milford, Mary
Milford, J. W. Co.?
Mochat, Jacob
McGee, Willis
McCardy?, Sarah
McCardy?, Jos.
McGill, Mary
McGill, Sarah & sisters
McCollum, Saml.
Morris, John
Morris, James
Millwee?, W. A. & sister
Moss, Samuel
Mitchel, Larkin
Mitchel, Caleb
Moore, John
McConnell, Wm.
McAllister, Nath.?
McCarley, P.?(R.?) B.
McCarley, Elias
McGee, John
McGee, Elias
McGee, Nancy
McGee, Jesse C.
McClinton, A. S.
McPherson, Eliz.
Massey, Silas
McLees, J. J.

McLees, Andrew
McLees, James
McLees, Wm.
McLees, Robt.
McLees, Margt.
McKeown, John
Merritt, Benj.
Merritt, John
Martin, Matthew
Meredith, A.
Merritt, J. H.
McKay, Martin S.
McMilliam, Wyatt
McCarley, H. W.
McGee, Michl.
Massey, Abr'm
Martin, Abram
McAllister, John
McConnel, Thos. M.
McConnel, S. F.
Morris, J. C.
McGregor, John
Mattox, Thomas
Major, Wm. M.
Morris, David
McLeskey, Jas.
Murphy, Moses
Morehead, M. L.
Massey, Eliz.
McGee, Burrell
McFall, A. N.
McFall, John
Moorehead, John
Martin, Chesley
Martin, Jacob
Moore, David
Martin, Jas.
McCarty, Thos.
McAllister, John
Murphy, Ezek'l.
McAllister, Jas.
Martin, Wm.
Martin & Murphy
Martin, Hester
Murphy, Thos.
McMurtry, Wm.
McCann, J. H.?
McCann & Walker
Murphy, Wm. S.
Moore, Eliz.
McAlister, John
Moore, Elijah
Moore, Thos. B.
Moore, Elijah
Merritt, Obed'h.
Maulden, Sus'h
McKinney, Sarah
McKinney, Martha
Mulliken, Benj. Sr.
Martin, Fanny & sister
McElroy, John
Mulliken, Benj. Jr.
Mulliken, Wm.
McMahan, Sus'a.
McMurry, Wm.
Mulliken, Jas.
Martin, Jesse
McWharter, Robt.
Melton, Mich'l.
McMurtry, Jas.
Morehead, Alex'r.
McAllister, M.? E.
Millwee, Saml.(2)
McFee, Sarah
Martin, John
Major, John
McMurtry, Reb'a
Miller, Warren
Miller, Mrs. Jane
Miller, Jane
McCrary, Mary
McCrary, Albert
McMurry, Wm. C.

Miller, Dr. Henry C .
Master, G. W.
Major, J. A.
McPhail, Peter
McElroy, Arch'd
Maverick, S. & family
McKee, Arch'd
McKee, Wm. A.
McKracken, Susan A.
Milford, John
Mary?, T. W.
Mitchell, Eph'm
McGee, Wm.
Major, Wesley
Miller, J. C.
Mattison, J. M.
Mattison, Wyatt
Mattison, Olley
McNeely, David
McCullough, Hep
Morehead, Maxey
Morehead, Clarissa
Major, D. dec'd.
Mattison, Mary K.
McClure, E. J.
Martin, Saml
Murry, Margt
McFall, Saml R
Martin, John
McAllister, Nath.
Major, Elijah
Moses, C. B.
Miller, T. S.
Morris, Saml
McMahan, Saml
Mills, Berry
Maxwell, John
Maxwell, Robt. A.
Norris, Robt.
Nichols, Arch'd.
Nichols, James C.
Nichols, W. A.
Norris, Ezekiel
Nelson, Wm. R.
Nelson, Wm.
Newell, Geo.
North, John L.
Newton, Willis
Newton, Larkin
Newton, Samuel
Newton, Isaac
Newton, Isaac Jr.
Norris, John E.
Norris, Mary Ann
Nevitt, Wm.
Norris, A. O.
Nevill/Newell?, Wm. dec;d,
Norris, Jesse W.
Mays, Mrs. M. D.
Owen, Thornton
Obriant, Wm.
Obriant, Josephine
Owen, Lewis
Oldham, Wm.
Oldham, Thomas
Owen, Martha
Orr, Wm. M.
Orr, Alexander
Orr, Wm.
Orr, John
Owen, Daniel
Oliver, Andrew
Orr, Thomas
Oliver, Martha
Owen, Elijah
Orr, James
Owen, John
Owen, Elijah
Overby, B. M.
Overby, Nicholas
Orr, Jas. L.
Orr, Christopher
Osborn, L. A.

Pendleton Factory
Philips, Arch'd
Philips, Wm.
Pinckney, Thos. dec;d.
Paget, J. L.
Pepper, Elijah
Pettigru, Robt. H.
Pinnell, Eliz.
Poole, Eliz.
Pickle, C. W.
Pickle, Chesley
Pearman, Benj.
Prichard, Lewis
Pickens, Thos. J.
Poor, Geo.
Poor, Samuel
Poor, Nancy
Poor, Hampton
Poor, J. B.
Poor, J. W.
Poor, John
Pettis, Jane
Poor, Holland
Phillips, Reuben
Pruett, Wm.
Parker, Robert
Penel, Thomas
Pressley, D.? A.
Parker, Matthew
Prince, Mark
Price, Pennel
Price, H. P.
Parten, Hubbard
Pressley, Anne
Patterson, Thos. H.
Pruett, Eli S. D.
Palmer, Wm.
Pickerel, Jon.
Paget, Eliz.
Paris, Henry
Pugh, Casar (free)
Pickle, Wm.
Pegg, Jas. B.
Paulman, Lud'k
Phillips, Martin
Paulman, A.
Pegg, John
Pickens, Robert
Pickens, Wm. S.
Prater, Jos.
Pickle, Jacob
Poole, Wm. H.
Poole, Mary
Pullen, Wm.
Posey, Benjamin
Poor, Wm.
Prince, C. J.
Pearman, Jon'n
Poor, Reuben
Ragsdale, D. F.
Roberts, Matthias
Robinson, John B.
Reese, David
Reese, Wm. G.
Ritchie, James N.
Robinson, Jas. E.
Robinson, Samuel
Robinson, J. J.
Rice, Hezekiah
Rutledge, Jesse
Reid, A. E.
Rice, H. dec'd.
Rice, Amaziah
Roach, Henry
Roach, Forrester
Rice, Sarah
Rampey, Jas. A.
Rainey, John dec'd.
Reid, Eliz.
Reid, Wm.
Rusk, David dec'd.
Reid, Moses?
Reid, Jesse

Roberts, Willis
Reeves, R. W.
Riley, Hezekiah
Richardson, David
Rodgers, Larkin
Rodgers, J_ T.?
Rodgers, John
Rodgers, Jos. T.
Rodgers, W. W.
Riley, Abraham
Richardson, Mat's Jr.
Richardson, Noah
Richardson, Matthias
Richardson, Sion
Rix, Washington
Rea, Elihu
Rankin, Geo.
Ritchie, Wm.
Rodgers, Simeon
Rosamond, John
Robinson, Jane
Robinson, Dr. Wm.
Russell, Thos. H.
Robinson, David
Robinson, Willis
Reese, Carlos
Ritchie, Eliz.
Ross, Rev. A. W.
Richardson, Mrs. M. L.
Richardson, Maria
Richardson, Wade A.
Russell, David
Rice, Ibzan
Robinson, Jane
Rainwater, D. T.
Reid, Andrew
Ragsdale, Francis
Rodgers, Hester
Ritchie, Reuben
Rimmer, Lucinda
Rice, F.
Rice & Earle
Reid, J. B.
Reid, Dr. J. H.
Rice, Thos. A.
Rodgers, Wm.
Rornson?, Wm.
Ruff, David
Reeves, John dec'd.
Reeves, J. A.
Richardson, A. W.
Rice, Jane
Steele, James?
Shirley, Stephen
Smith, Wiley C.
Smith, Samuel
Smith, Nancy
Smith, Wm.
Stone,. Wm. H.
Stone, Geo.
Stanton, Catharine
Stanton, Matthias
Smith, Davis
Smith, Jeremiah
Smith, Joel
Shirley, Obediah
Stone, Hampton
Sailors, Leonard
Sailors, Abram
Sailors, Isaac
Strickland, Mat'w.?
Seawright, Wm. T.
Shirley, Benj.
Sadler, Wm. B.
Spearman, John
Saunders, A.
Saunders, Eli
Simpson, Wm.
Simpson, Arch'd.
Speer, Jas. G.
Simpson, Wm.
Stewart, John
Sullivan, Kelly

Scott, David
Simpson, Thos.
Stewart, Geo.
Stewart, Mary
Stewart, Adam
Stephenson, John
Stewart, James
Steele, Robt. A.
Smith, Whitaker
Smith, Aaron Sr.
Stanton, C. B.
Smith, Nimrod
Smith, Wm. J.
Shirley, Eliz.
Smith, Robinson
Sadler, David
Stephenson, Thos.
Sherrard, Jane
Sadler, John F.
Stephenson, John
Stephenson, Geo. Jr.
Stephenson, John
Smith, Martin H.
Shaw, Wm. S.
Skelton, Thomas
Skelton, Thos. A.
Skelton, A. A.
Swilling, Samuel
Swilling, James
Simmons, Jas.
Simmons, David
Stanley, Ezekiel
Simmons, Thos. H.
Skelton, J. W. B.
Smith, Jesse R .
Snipes, Matthew
Smith, Ed'd.
Stephenson, And'w.
Stephenson, Geo.
Stephenson, John
Smith, Robert
Stott, Williamson
Stott, Drayton
Smith, Wm.
Shirley, Aaron
Spearman, David
Spearman, D. D.
Smith, Basil
Smith, J. C.
Smith, Simeon
Slaton, John
Spearman, Benj.
Smith, Wyatt
Simmons, Chas.
Shumate, Jas. J.
Simpson, Hon.? R. F.
Stephenson, Mary
Sherrard, Wm.
Smith, Jesse R. & Co.
Smith, Philip P.
Smith, Geo. S.
Slaten, Loven
Stanton, Geo. dec'd.
Sitton, John P.
Sitton, Wm.
Sitton, Wm. D.
Smith, Jos. D.
Smith, Griffin
Spearman, F. A.
Stone, James
Smith, Jas. W.
Smith, A. M.
Satterfield, Jer'h.?
Siddell, John
Smith, J. H.
Smith, J. M.
Smith, W. A.
Smith, Sarah
Smith, John A.
Smith, Ephraim
Smith, Jas. D.
Smith, John
Sheriff, Washington

Spruel, Simeon
Shirley, Richard
Shirley, James Jr.
Shirley, Jas. Sr.
Seaborn, Geo.
Sloan, Thomas M.
Sloan, Mrs. Susan
Sloan, B. F.
Sharpe, Elam Jr.
Sharpe, Major E.
Starke, Mrs. E. G.
Sharpe & Warley
Swords, John
Shanklin, J. V.
Smith, T. G.
Siddell, A. L. Y.
Shaw, Peyton
Smith, Aaron
Shearor?, Andrew
   ", Gillam
Skelton, Thos. G.
Smith, Wm.
Smith, Eliz.
Smith, Samuel
Saunders, Wm.
Smith, A. W.
Smith, R. D.
Scott, M. B.
Simpson, D. M.
Smith, Zeph'h
Spee_, Wm. G.
Smith & Brown
Scott, Talliaferro
Sitton, John
Symmes, Dr. F. W.
Scott, Jos. D.
Smith, Ebenezer
Sailor, John
Sloan, John T.
Smith, Mrs. S. N.
Smith, Mary E. N.
Smith, Alice E. D.
Smith, John L. W.?
Smith, Wm. C. Jr.?
Smith, Benj. S.
Solomon, John
Steele, Wm.
Turner, John B.
Tripp, Anne
Telford, Geo. B.
Telford, J. H.
Telford, Wm.
Telford, James
Telford, Isabella dec'd.
Todd, John L.
Trussell, Henley
Trussell, Posey
Tribble, R. O.
Taylor, Elijah
Tate, John A.
Thompson, Jas.
Thompson, Elizabeth
Thompson, Matthew (Dr.)
Taylor, L. H. (S.? H.)
Tucker, Dejarnet
Todd, Andrew
Todd, Olive
Tate, David
Tate, Van
Taylor, James
Tilly, John
Thompson, Dr. A. E.
Tippens, Eliz.
Terry, Henry
Trussel, Wm.
Towers, John R.
Timms, Isaac
Tripp, Nicholas
Thompson, Jas.
Tripp, John H.
Trainer?, Laz's.
Tilly, Mary
Tate, Tillman

Taylor, Richard
Tompkins, John
Tucker, James
Tippen, Geo.
Towns, Wm. W.
Tucker, Wm.
Todd, James
Thompson, John
Tippens, Dennis
Taylor, Wm. G.
Taylor, Jos. D^r
Todd, Mary
Taylor, Jos.
Taylor, J. B. E.
Teague, Elijah
Todd, Wm. P.
Taylor, David S.
Vandiver, Wm.
Vandiver, Thomas
Vandiver, Ed.
Vandiver, Enoch
Voyles, Amos
Vandiver, Aaron
Vandiver, Peter
Warnock, John
Willingham, John
Wardlaw, H.
Wardlaw, J. M.
Wilson, James
Wilson, Bartly
Wilson, Jasper
Wilson, Hugh
Williams, James
Webster, Jane
Wright, Norris
Williamson, M.
Williamson, Wm.
Wilson, Geo. W.
Wright, Turner
Webb, Andrw
Watt, Mary
Watt, Jas. L.
Willbanks, Elijah
Watt, Jas. G.
Watt, Jas. W.
Watt, Thomas
Wiley, James
Watt, James
Watt, Mary
Wiles, Jas. H.
Wiles, Spencer
Watt, John
Whitman, Jacob
Watson, Martha L.
Wilkes, Thomas
Watson, Daniel
Williford, C. R.
Williford, Sarah
Wentons?, Jas. C.
Whitfield, Lewis
Webb, Elisha
Webb, James
Wardlaw, James
Wright, Cath'e
Webb, Clayton
White, Jonathan
Webb, Sam'l. M.
White, Barthol'w
Wilson, Jackson
Webb, Wm.
Williams, M. B.
Welborn, Thomas
Wilbanks, Jas.
Wilson, Jas.
Welborn, Wm.
Welborn, Wm. E.
Welborn, W. E.
Welborn, A. G.?
Waddell, Wm.
Wilson, Wm. M.
Wiggington, Elihu
Wiggington, John
Watson, James

Wyatt, Redman G.
Wilson, Wm. D.
Watkins, Felix
Wilson, John
Walker, John L.(S.)
Watkins, John
Watkins, Wm.
Warley, Mrs. L.(S.)
White, Mrs. S.(L.)
Wilson, Rich'd
Whitaker, H. H.
Wilson, Wm. M.
Wyatt, J. F.
Wyatt, Elijah
Watson, J. B.
Watson, Mary
Wright, W. F.
Wellborn, Jas. M.
Wilson, James
White, Thomas
White, Henry
Wakefield, John
Wallace, Wilson
Warnock, John dec'd.
Watkins, Baylis
Wilson, Sarah
Watson, Maria
Welborn, Sarah
Wilson, John
Williford, S. W.
Webb, C. B.
Webb, Elijah
Whitfield, J. T.
Williams, John
Willbanks, Shad'k
Wakefield, Coon'd
Waller, Miss R. H.
Waller, Miss Mary
Webb, Edmond
Whitmore, J. N.
Wilson, Steph. M.
Waddell, A. H.
Young, Francis A.
Young, William
Yeatgan, Saml.
Young, James
Young, Polly

GREENVILLE:
Lewis, J. W. & J. B.
Acker, P. N.
Seaborn, Geo.
Maverick, Saml.
Avery, E. H.
Arnold, L. T.

LAURENS:
Cox, William
Acker, J. S.(L.)

ABBEVILLE:
Gambrell, James
Davis, John L.
Clemment, Wm. H.
Thompson, Jas.
Kelly, Geo.
Mochat, Jacob
Smith, Robt.
Sharrard, Wm.
Wakefield, John
Norris, Jesse W.
Barmore, Mary
Armstrong, J. B.
Scott, Jas. D.
Dickson, Thos.
Ruff, David
Scott, Mrs. M.
Smith, Mrs. L. N.

CHARLESTON:
Maverick, S. & family
UNION:
Maverick, S. & family

NEWBERRY:
Maverick, S. & family

ORANGE:
Maverick, S. & family

WASSAMASAW:
Maverick, S. & family

GOOSE CR^K:
Maverick, S. & family

PICKENS:
Major, Jas.
Breckenridge, Robt.
Adams, John
Black, John
Norris & Houston
G..mm.s, Jas.
Meredith, A.
Earle, J. B.
Elrod, G. G.
Anderson, Wm. __?
Richardson, M.
Hubbard, Wm.
Watson, A. P.
Bishop, J. & D.
Shanklin, J. N.?(V.)
Keys, R. A.
Calhoun, John
McClure, E. J.
Todd, James
Hall, Wilson
Vandiver, Peter
Lewis, Major (Major, Lewis)
Symmes, Dr. F. W.
Fielding, H. B.
Fretwell, John
Knight, W. W.

#

Anderson, Dr. Wm.
Acker, P. N.
Acker, Susanna
Avery, William
Allen, James E.
Acker, Amos
Armstrong, Jno. R.?
Armstrong, James
Armstrong, Archibald
Ashley, John
Ashley, Wilson
Armstrong, James
Adams, James
Armstrong, A. B.
Adams, Asa
Adams, John
Adams, John Senr
Able, James S.
Able, E.?
Alexander, Robt. B.
Anderson, Micajah
Amick, John D.
Abbott, John
Acker, Wm.
Anderson, David
Adams, Henry
Archer, Wm. M.
Alexander, David
Acker, Halbert
Alewine, Jacob
Ashley, Edward
Acker, Joshua L.?
Arnold, Lawson T.
Armstrong, John B.
Broyles, John T.
Bartley, Nancy
Ballentine, Jesse
Bartley, Josiah
Ballentine, G. dec;d.
Brazeale, Kennon
Brazeale, Williamson
Brazeale, Matthew
Brazeale, David R.?
Brazeale, Griffin
Bartley, Sally
Brown, Dr. G. R.
Brasswell, Nancy
Bagwell, John
Bagwell, Jas. dec'd.
Brock, Hayden
Brock, Meredith
Brock, James
Brasswell, Anderson
Branyan, John A.
Brock, Johnston E.
Benson & Trimmier
Buchanan, Samuel
Beatty, Samuel
Beatty, John
Beatty, Thomas
Brown, Johanna
Bonds, Sugar
Beatty, Martha
Bowie, Charles
Beatty, William dec'd
Burdett, Hiram
Beatty, Margarett
Brooks, Garner
Burton, Blackman
Brown, Samuel
Black, John
Brown, Charles
Bozeman, Lewis
Bozeman, D. T.
Brooks, Thomas
Brown, John
Brown, William P.
Brown, Ezarina
Brown, Mathew A.
Brown, Alvira
Burris, Thos. Junr.

Brooks, James
Brown, Abner
Bowen, Samuel
Burgess, James
Boggs, J. L.?
Boggs, T. H.
Brewer, Wm.
Brewer, Milly
Bailey, Isaac dec'd
Bowen, Robert
Blasingame, Robt.
Blasingame, Thos.
Beco, Antween
Bennett, Wm.
Bryant, Terrell
Burris, Reuben
Barrett, Charles
Burris, John M.
Burris, Wm. R.
Betterton, John
Bellotte, Peter E.
Bellotte, John E.?C.?
Bowden, James
Bishop, Jane & D
Benson, C. B.
Benson, C. B. & son
Brown, Randolph
Bellotte, Jacob
Bradbury, Salathiel
Bradbury, James
Burns, Joseph
Bailey, Allen
Burns, Jordan
Bradbury, Jesse
Bradbury, S. Junr.
Bradbury, Wm.
Bruce, Charles
Bruce, E. P.
Brown, Larkins
Brown, L & C
Bowman, A.
Burris, Thomas
Bowler, A. D.
Brownlee, Maria
Browne, Lide? H.
Brown, Robt.
Brady, Wm. C.
Bagwell, James Senr.?
Brown, Linda
Burroughs, Bryan
Brown, Rachel
Benton, Peyton
Browne, J. M.
Baker, Samuel
Beatty, David
Branyan, Jos.? J.
Branyan, Henry
Browne, Newton
Bruce, Thomas
Browne, L.?(S.?)
Burris, James
Brazsale, R. J.?
Belcher, Manning
Briant, Simon
Ball, Minyard
Brock, Andrew
Bailey, Wm.
Bowlan, Wm. H.?
Burris, Joshua
Brothers, James
Baker, S.? A.
Burris, Milford
Breckenridge, Robt.
Breckenridge, James
Bridwell, J.? W.?
Barton, H. M.
Bell, Samuel
Burris, Jacob
Burris, Mrs. C.?(E.?)
Brazeale, Enoch
Benson, Jno. P.

Boyd, Robert
Brazeale, Gambrell
Brown, Daniel
Brown, Robert
Brown, Samuel
Burris, Elisha
Bennett, Charles
Bennett, Thos. dec'd.
Broyles, O. R.
Campbell, James
Cobb, Henry
Campbell, Alfred
Crymes, B. F.?
Cox, Gabriel
Cole, Hampton
Cox, Thomas
Cumming, David
Crymes, R. D.
Cox, Arris
Clinkscales, Wm. F.?
Clement, Isaac
Clement, Jane
Cullins?, John
Clement, Christopher
Cox, Joel
Cox, R. B.
Cox, Mrs. Frances
Cox, Thomas
Cobb, Martin
Clement, Isaac
Cobb, Ephraim
Cobb, Noah
Clinkscales, John
Clarke, Anne
Clinkscales, Mrs. M.
Clinkscales, __? T.?
Cromer, Philip
Cunningham, Arthur?
Carpenter, J. W.
Chalmers, Rev. J. C.
Casey, Sarah
Casey, Delilah
Campbell, Thomas
Cook, Wm.
Clinkscales, Abner
Clinkscales, Lewis C.
Casey, Mary
Campbell, Jesse
Caldwell, John
Caldwell, James
Corr, Mary
Cunningham, Thos.
Cunningham, Catharine
Connels, James
Cater, Dr. A. P.
Chastian, Renny? Henry?
Cason, Esther
Cobb, Franklin
Clandry?, Joel
Clandry, John
Childress, Nicholas
Clandry, Norman
Carter, Caleb
Carpenter, A. T.
Carpenter, Elizabeth
Carpenter, James M.
Chastian, Stephen
Campbell, Wm.
Campbell, George
Cumming, Harman
Campbell, Alexander
Carpenter, A. M.
Craig, Samuel
Cannon, Isaac
Crenshaw, Thomas
Cherry, Thos. R.
Carne, Martha F.?
Clarke, Henry
Cherry, John C.?
Cherry, L. L.(S. S.?)
Coates, John

Cato, Edward
Coffee, Iley?
Coffin, A.
Cox, John
Carlile, Rev'd Wm.
Carter, J. S.?
Clement, Alexander
Crawford, James
Clarke, J. B. (P.?)
Cooley, Hiram
Cooley, Lucinda
Cochrane, James
Cochrane, D. H.
Chamblee, Moses
Cowan, Hiram
Clarke, J. R.? Junr.
Cannon, Eph. dec'd.
Clarke, Jane
Crawford, Henry
Crawford, Sarah
Campbell, Danl.
Carpenter, John
Chamblee, James
Cox, Wm.
Cox, Elizabeth
Cox, R _? R.
Cox, Joseph
Cox, David
Clement, C. W.
Caldwell, Joseph
Cobb, James
Cox, Jesse
Clement, Wm. K.?
Chamblee, Robert
Chamblee, James
Caesar (Free Negro)
Cobb, A. B.
Coates, J. J.
Cowan, Wm.
Chastian, James
Cox, D. L.
Cox, John dec'd.
Cox, Asa
Cox, Wm. H.
Cobb, Josiah W.?
Cullins, Caleb
Cason, Anderson
Conant, A.
Cresswell, Mrs. L.
Clayton, B. F.?
Cooley, John dec'd.
Cherry, Dr. E. D.
Cox, Abner
Cason, J. A.
Caruth, Miss L. L.
Duckworth, Thomas
Duckworth, Welborn
Duckworth, Benjn.
Dawson, Samuel
Davis, Wm.
Davis, Zachariah
Deane, C. P.
Dunlap, Wm. F.
Davis, John L.
Davis, Moses
Davis, Aaron
Davis, Thomas
Drake, James
Drake, James A.
Drake, Robt. dec'd.
Drake, Enoch
Dunlop, Mathew
Davis, F. W.?
Deane, Thomas
Deane, Samuel A.?
Douthit, James
Dunham, David
Davis, Wm. L.
Dunham, Benajah
Douthit, Benjamin
Davis, Richard
Davis, Charles R.
Dorr, G.? W.

Duckworth, Howard
Dacus, John A.
Dowelle, R. dec'd.
Driven, James
Driven, James Junr.
Dalrymple, Lewis
Dollar, Williamson
Drennan, Wm.
Dobbins, James
Duncan, Thomas
Daniels, W. D. C.
Davis, John B.
Davis, M. N. A. J.
Dupre, Miss S.? H. M.
Dupre, Benjn.
Dickson, Thomas
Dart, Mrs. Mary
Dickson, Mat. dec'd.
Duckworth, Jacob
Duncan, David
Dooley, Wm.
Dalrymple, John
Dobbins, A. C.
Duncan, Robt.
Dobbins, John
Dobbins, Martha
Dalrymple, James
Dalrymple, John
Dalrymple, Mary
Duckworth, Wm.
Dart, Mary
Dart, Henrietta
Duckworth, Ann
Duke, J. J.
Deane, Moses
Elrod, Wm.
Elrod, George
Erskine, Thos.
Erskine, John
Ellison, Miles
Ellison, Joel
Eubanks, Elijah
Elrod, Wm.
Elrod, Thos. P.
Earle & Towers
Earle, Jno. B.
Eaton, Joseph
Earle, Dr. James
Ellison, James
Ellison, Joel
Elrod, Elias
Elrod, Adam
Elrod, Saml.
Elrod, Philip
Estes, Larkin
Elrod, George
Elrod, John
Evans, Edwd. C.
Elliott, Lewis
Elliott, Dr. R. E.
Emberson, James
Esker, Wm.
Evans, Dr. A.
Earle, Elias
Erskine, James
Elrod, Alfred
Elliott, Mary
Erskine, Wm. R.
Erskine, Wm.
Erskine, James dec'd.
Earle, James G.
Earle & Griffin
Fant, Alfred
Fant, Mary
Fant, Elizabeth
Featherston, J. W.
Fisher, S. C.
Fant, Wm. N.
Finley, Elias
Ford?, Wm.
Ford, Stephen
Floyd, A. J.
Forbes, Alanson

Fleming, Richard
Felton, Amariah
Fitzgerald, Thos.
Fant, Jas. R.
Fielding, H. B.
Fretwell, Jos. Y.
Fant, V.? D.
Fant, Abner
Felton, Richard
Felton, Mary
Fant, Abner
Fuller, A.
Golden, John
Garrett, Thomas
Guyon, Guyton
Gambrell, Lettice
Gambrell, D. H.
Gaines, H. M.
Gillespie, Wm.
Gambrell, Mat. T.(L.?)
Griffin, Elijah
Gantt, Wm.
Gantt, Hugh
Gambrell, James
Gambrell, E. B.
Gambrell, Sarah
Green, John
Green, David Junr.
Green, David Senr.
Green, Wm. L.
Gudry, Huldah
Gambrell, Wm.
Gantt, John
Gantt, John G.
Grubbs, George
Green, Wm.
Gable, Levy
Gable, Henry
Gassaway, Benjn.
Gable, Henry
Giles, Dr. Robt.
Gentry, Moody
Gentry, Elizabeth
Gray, A. D.
Gentry, Zachariah
Gregg, Hugh
Glenn, Wm.
Gentry, Reuben
Gentry, Arthur
Gambrell, James R.
Glenn, F. M.
Gambrell, James
Gambrell, Ezekiel
Gambrell, Reid
Givens, Harrison
Guthrie, Nelson
Guthrie, David dec'd.
Guthrie, Benjamin
Guthrie, Stephen
Garrett, John
Garrett, Richardson
Garrett, Jesse
Gilmer, Robt.
Gentry, Daniel
Gentry, _? V.?
Gaillard, W. H. D.
Gaillard, Mrs. R. W.
Grant, Wm.
Gambrell, David
Gantt, Jno.? W.
Cordon, A. J.
Gunnin, James
Gaillard, C. L.
Geer, Solomon
Green, James L.
Green, Thomas
Grubbs, John
Guyton, John W.
Graham, H.? S.?
George, Jesse
Glenn, J. W.
Gambrell, James M.
Galloway, Massey

Geen?, David (Geer?)
Gray, Hezekiah
Gray, Jesse
Gray, John
Gray, E. dec'd.
Gambrell, Matt. dec'd.
Gentry, A. R.? (B.?)
Gray, Robt. D.
Garrison, Henry
Gilmer, James
Gordon, Agnes
Gordon, David
Gray?, James P.
Gilmer, Nancy
Gambrell, H. J.?
Gambrell, L.
Gordon, James
Gantt, James A.
Griffin, James C.
Gaillard, C. D.
Gambrell, Harrison?
Gambrell, James
Gambrell, John
Gambrell, Wm.
Gambrell, Barbara
Goode, P. P.
Gaillard, Josias D.
Gaillard, Miss M. D.
Gaillard, A. D.
Grubbs, Williamson
Gibson, Wm. B.
Gibson & Fant
Graham, J. B.
Hunter, Wm.
Hammond, S. J.
Hammond, W. L.
Hunter, Mrs. Sarah
Holland, John
Holmes, Wm.
Harper, Thomas
Harper, John
Harper, Martha
Horton, Grief
Haskins, John
Holland, Wm.
Harkins, Sarah
Harper, John
Hog, Thompson
Hinton, John
Hanks, Luke
Hunt, William
Hanks, James A.(Tilman is
    written above)
Hall, John
Hopkins, John
Hunt, Samuel
Hopkins, Zachariah
Hall, Mary
Hall, David
Hall, Thomas
Hanna, Hiram
Howard, John
Harkness, John N.
Harkness, Jane
Hamilton, Robt.
Howie, ...
Hayes, John
Howard, D. C.
Hatton, Wm.
Hughens, Wm.
Harris, Nathan
Hill, Thomas O.?
Hall, Lent
Hamilton, Luke
Havine?, Mark
Hall, Martin
Hall, A. J.
Humphreys, Rev'd D.
Hardy, James
Hardy, John
Haley, Reuben
Hardy, R. B.?
Houston, Wm.

Herring, Francis
Herring, James M.
Haney, Charles
Hembree, Wm.
Hembree, James
Hembree, James Junr.
Harper, Asa
Hamilton, D. K.
Hunt, J. J.
Hix, John
Harris, Mrs. M. M.
Harrison, Wm.
Herring, James
Hall, Joseph
Hembree, A. D.
Harris, Nathaniel dec'd.
Hobson, C. G.
Hunter, James
Harbin?, J. B.
Hopkins, Martin
Hamilton, Leonard
Hastie, J & Co.
Hastie, John
Hillhouse, Recd. J.
Holland, Robt.
Holland, Wm.
Herring, Levy
Harris, Sarah
Harris, Thos. N.
Hughes, John
Hix, D. J.
Hix, Wm.
Hagood, L. M.
Harrison, James
Hackett, Albert
Harper, Wm. C.
Hall, John
Hall, Ezekiel
Hall, Wm.
Hall, Samuel
Hix, Daniel
Holland, A. M.?(W.?)
Hodge, R. H. W.
Herring, John
Harring, Ewel?
Harper, Barbara
Hamilton, C. E.
Henderson, Martha
Haney, Stephen
Haney, J. C.
Hall, D. R.
Haslett, M. W.
Hammond, B. F.
Holland, A. B.
Hughens, Robt.
Harris, D. E.
Hall, A. M.
Hall, Aaron
Hall, Joab
Hawkins, Wm. P.
Hall, Wilson
Hall, John
Howard, George
Hall, Wm. S.
Hall, Lemuel
Harris, Joseph P.
Haney, Luke
Haney, Wm.
Hanks, Thos.
Harkins, Hugh
Haney, John
Harrison?, James W.
Herring, Jesse
Hunter, Mary
Harrison & Wynne
Hamilton, John
Hunter, John
Hammond, F.? C.
Jolley, Joseph
Irby, Charles
Johnston, Peter
Ingraham, Delilah
Johnston, Benjn.

Irwin, Mrs. E.
Jones, James
Jones, Thomas
Jones, Wilson
Ingraham, Wm.
Jones, J. W.
Jones, Happy
Ingraham, J. H.
Isaacs, A.
Isbell, Samuel
Isbell, Robert
Jolly, Henry
Johnston, A. B.
Johnston, Milly
Jones, Samuel
Jones, John
Junkin, Margt. dec'd.
Jones, Wm.
Johnston, Allen
Johnston, Joel E.?
Jolly, Wm.
Johnston, Willis
Jeffow?, Mrs. R.
Jolly, James
Jenkins, Dr. Wm. L.
Kay, Wm. M.
Kay, Charles
King, James
King, Peter
King, Robert
King, G. W.
King, Josiah
Kay, Jesse
Kelly, Elisha
Kelly, Allen
Kelly, Elizabeth
Kelly, Barzilla
Kelly, John
Kay, William
Kay, Joel
Kay, Catharine
Kay, Mason
Kay, Wm. P.
Kay, Wm.
Kay, James W.
Knox, John
Kay, Gabriel
Keaton, Wm.
Keown, G. W.
Keown, Wm.
Keys, John
Kennedy, Revd. J. L.
Kelly, Daniel
Keaton, Archibald
Keaton, B. F.
Keys, R. A.
Keaton?, Henry
Knauff, Wm. J.
King, Wm.
King, R. A.
Kay, G. W.
King, Wm. P.
K___?, James D.
King, John G.
Kerr, Wm.
Keys, J. C.
Kay, Strother
Kay, F. M.
King, John
Kay, John
Kay, Henry
Kenton, Wilborn (Keaton?)
Kay, Alexander
Kelly, Alfred
Levels, John
Lewis, J. W. & J. B.
Lewis, J. B.
Loveless, Sophronia
Lewis, James W.
Lewis & Simpson
Lewis & Cox
Lewis, Ep___?
Lucius, Daniel

Lucius, James
Lee, Philip
Lindsay, James
Lattimer, Harrison
Long, Wm. W.
Liverett, Stephen Jr.
Liverett, Wm.
Liverett, Stephen
Latham, Wm.
Long, Harrison
Lathem, Cornelius
Langa, Wm.
Laboon, Joseph
Laboon, Edy
Long, Ezekiel
Longstreet, G.? & Co.
Ledbetter, D. T.
Ledbetter, James
Ledbetter, Joel
Long, Wm.
Lorton, Jno. L.
Lorton, Mrs. F.?
Lewis, Mrs. L. dec'd.
Lewis, Jesse
Liddell, A. _?
Lowry, Jackson
Lewis, Elizabeth
Lewis, Elisha
Leverett, John
Leverett, Thomas
Ledbetter, L. A.
Ledbetter, Mary
Leverett, W.
Lewis, Jesse P. dec'd.
Lewis, Miss H. E.?
Lanier, B.
Martin, Jacob
McCarty, Thomas
Major, Wm.
Massey, Hiram?
Major, James A.
Major, James
Mayfield, Abraham
Mayfield, Eph. dec'd.
Moore, Grant A.
Mauldin, B. F.
McAdams, John
Mattison, Wm.
Mattison, L. J.
Mattison, Elizabeth
Massey, Laban
Maddox, Henry?
McCollum, Danl
Mattison, Archibald
Mattison, O.? N.
Mattison, G. P.
McFee, Washington
May, Daniel
McAllister, John
McPhail, John
McKee, Wm. A.
Martin, Phoebe
McBride, James L.
McCullough, Saml
McCullough, L. T.
McGee, Willis
McCurdy, Sarah
McKee, Archibald
McKee, Wm.
Morgan, John
Major, Daniel
Major, Wm. M.
McClabone?, D & T
McFall, A. N.
McCann, T. H.
Murty?, Margaret
Milford, John
Morgan, Thos.
Mochat, Jacob
McCurdy, Sarah
McMahan, Saml.
Moore, Kno. R.
McGill, S. _? M.

McGill, Mary
McCarley, Robt. B.
McCarley, Joseph
McGee, G. L.
McConnell, Wm.
McAllister, Nathan
McGee, Elias
McFall, Phoebe
McGee, Nancy
McLees, Andrew
McLees, James J.
Moore, John
McGee, John
Milton, Michael
McMurry, Wm. C.
Martin, Chesley
Mulliken, James
McKenny, Martin
Martin, Wm.
Mulliken, Benjn.
McElroy, John
Mitchell, Larkin
Moore, David
McMurry, Joberry
McMurry, Wm.
McMurry, Jane
McElroy, A.
Maxwell, John
Morris, Jesse O.
Miller, Dr. H. C.
McGee, Burrill
Mulliken, Benjn. Junr.
Martin, Fanny
McMahan, Susanna
Martin, Jesse
Merritt, Obadiah
Mulliken, Wm.
Moore, Thos. B.
McHechy?, David
Moore, Elijah
Murphy, Ezekiel
Murphy & Martin
McAllister, John
Murphy, Thos. M.
McMurtry, Wm.
McAllister, James
Moore, Elizabeth
Murphy, John
Martin, Wm.
Martin, Hester
Martin, J. C.
Martin, Chesley
McCarley, H. W.?
McKraken, Susan
Massey, Sion
Mitchell, M. C.
McGregor, J. W.
Masters, G. W.
Major, Elijah
McClure, E. J.
Maxwell, Saml.
McMurtry, James
McMurtry, Rebecca
McCrary, Mary
McCrary, Albert
Maverick, Saml.
Major, Jno. P.
Major, Wesley
Moses, C. B.
Miller, John
Miller, S.F.?M.
Miller, M_
McPhail, Peter
Moss, Samuel
McKay, Martin
Merritt, Jane H.?
Merritt, John
Martin, Matthew
Meredith, A.
McPherson, Eliz'h.
Morris, Saml.
Morris, D. J.
Morris, James

Morris, Jno. C.
Moorehead, Alex'r
Mattison, Wyatt
Moore, Jesse
McGee, A. H.
Martin(Mastin?), H.
McLesky, James
McRay?, James
Mattison, Danl.
Mattison, James
Mills, Benjn.
McCully, Stephen
McGee, Wm.
Merritt, Benj.
Martin, John
Murphy, Mary
Massey, Eliz'th
McKeown, Jno.
Martin, Jno.
Moorehead, Maxey
Moorehead, M. L.
Moorehead, Clara?
Maddox, Thos.
McClinton, W.? G.
McMillion, W. A.
McCee, Jesse C.
Mattison, Jno.
Martin, Saml.
Mitchell, Ephraim
Mitchell, B. L.
McCollum, Saml.
Mattison, Mary
McConnell,
McAllister, Nathan?
McCoy, Ephraim
McConnell, Thos.
McLees, James
McLees, Robt.
McLees, Margt.
McLees, Wm.
Moorehead, Jno.
Mitchell, Caleb
May, Tucker
Milford, Dr. W. T.?
Miller, Jno. C.
McGee, Mitchell
McAllister, Mrs. M.
McFall, Jno.
Millwee, Saml.
Millwee, Wm.
Millwee, E. & M.
Maxwell, R. A.
Nichols, Archibald
Nichols, James
Norris, Robert
Nelson, Wm. R. Junr.
Norris, Ezekiel L.
North, _? C. E.
Newton, Samuel
Newton, Isaac
Newton, J. M.
Newton, Larkin
Newel, George
Newel, Jincey
Nevitt, Wm.
Norris, A. C.
Neil, A. M.?
Newton, Willis
Newton, John
Newel, Thomas A.
Norris, Jesse W.
Norris, Peter R.
Nevitt, Wm. M.
Nelson, Wm. R. Senr.
Norris, John E.(C.?)
Owen, Daniel
Oldham, Wm.
Oldham, Thos.
Owen, Thornton
Obrien, Wm.
Obrien, Jane
Orr, Thomas
Oliver, Martha

389

Owen, Elijah
Orr, James
Orr, Wm. M.
Oliver, Andrew
Owen, Elijah
Owen, John
Orr, John
Orr, Wm.
Orr, Alexander
Owen, Lewis
Osborn, L. A.
Ovenbuy(Overby?), Nicholas
Orr, James L.
Orr, Christopher
Poor, Holland
Poor, Samuel
Pettis, Jane
Poor, J. W.
Poor, Reuben
Poor, Hampton
Poor, Nancy
Poor, John R.
Pierman, Benjamin
Pruett, E. D.
Pruett, Wm.
Pierman, Jonathan
Penel, Thomas
Presseley, David A.
Price, Pennel
Pressley, Ann
Parker, Henry
Parker, Mathew
Prince, Mark
Prince, John
Price, H. P.
Pettigrew, Robt.
Parten, Hubbard (Hubbone)
Pickle, Wm.
Pickle, Chessley
Pegg, John
Pegg, James ?
Pickle, Jacob
Pickens, Rob.t.
Prator, J. P.
Pickens, Wm. Y.?
Pickel, James C.?
Pickle, C. W.
Phillips, Martin
Paget, Elizabeth
Pritchard, Lewis
Poor, John
Pendleton Factory
Pullen, John
Palmer, Wm.
Pullen, Wm.
Pickerd, Jonathan
Pinion, Elizabeth
Philips, Reuben
Philips, John
Poor, George
Poor, William
Parker, Robert?
Posey, Benjamin
Poole, Wm. H.
Poole, Mary
Poole, Elizabeth
Pepper, Elijah
Pickens, Thos. J.
Reid, A. C.
Rodger, Jane dec'd.
Rodger, Larkin
Ragsdale, Daniel
Roberts, Mathias
Reeves, Elizabeth
Ragsdale, John F.?
Reid, Henry
Robinson, John B.
Reese, Wm.
Reese, David
Ritchie, James R.?
Rice, Hezekiah
Rice, Thos.? L.
Robinson, James E.

Robinson, Saml.
Robinson, James
Robinson, John
Rice, Amaziah
Rice, H. dec'd.
Robinson, Jane
Robinson, John A.
Reid, Andrew
Reid, Dr. J. H.
Rampey, James A.
Reid, Wm.
Roach, Henry
Roach, Elias
Roach, Forester
Reid, Elizabeth
Rainey, John dec'd.
Reeves, R. W.
Richardson, David
Robinson, Dr. Wm.
Robinson, Jane
Rodgers, Wm.
Russell, T. H.
Reeves, John A.
Richardson, Mary D.?
Richardson, Wade A.
Robinson, David
Rankin, George
Ritchie, Wm.
Rhea, Elihu
Rice?, G. W.
Rosamond, John
Riley, Abram
Richardson, Matthias?
Richardson, L. T.
Rodgers, W. W.
Rodgers, Jos. T.
Richardson, Noah
Reid, Jesse
Reid, Moses
Ritchie, Elizabeth
Robinson, John A.
Rusk, David
Rodgers, John
Rutledge, Jesse
Rice, Abzan (Ibzan)
Rainwater, D. T.
Riley, Hezekiah
Reid, J. D.?
Rice, F.?
Rice & Towers
Russell, David
Rimmer, Lucinda
Richardson, A. W.
Ranson, Wm.
Rodgers, Elihu
Richardson, Mat
Robinson, J. J. dec'd.
Ritchie, Reuben
Reece, H. D.
Rodgers, Hester?
Ross, Rev'd. A. W.
Steele, James
Smith, Whitaker
Shirley, James Junr.
Shirley, Richard
Shirley, James
Smith, Aaron
Stott, Williamson
Stott, Drayton
Smith, Wiley C.
Shirley, Stephen
Smith, Wm.
Shumate, James L.
Stone, Wm. H.
Stanton, Mathias
Smith, Wm.
Stone, George
Stanton, Catharine
Stanton, Christian
Smith, D.
Smith, A. W.
Smith, Jeremiah
Stone, Hampton

Sailors, Leonard
Sailors, Abraham
Sailors, John
Shirley, Benjamin
Seawright, Margaret
Strickland, Mathew
Saunders, Wm.
Sadler, Wm. B.
Speed, Wm. G.
Sullivan, Kelly
Simpson, Archibald
Spearman, John
Sadler, David
Smith, Wm.
Smith, Samuel
Smith, Nancy
Speer?, James G.
Speer?, John C.
Smith, Aaron Junr.
Simpson, Wm.
Simpson, Thos.
Stewart, John
Sherwood, Jane
Simpson, W. J.
Saunders, A.
Stephenson, Thos.
Sherwood, Wm.
Stephenson, G. J...?
Smith, M. H.
Stewart, James
Stewart, George
Stewart, Mary
Stewart, Adam
Spruel, Simeon
Smith, J. H.
Smith, Sarah
Smith, James D.
Smith, John
Sherriff, Washington
Smith, Ephraim
Smith, John A.
Setton, Wm. D.
Smith, A. M.
Smith, J. C. & J. M.
Smith, J. M.
Smith, Edward
Stanton, G. dec'd.
Sitton, John P.
Siddell, John
Slater, L.
Sitton, Wm.
Stone, James
Stone, Jas. B.
Smith, Thos. G.
Smith, Samuel
Smith & Brown
Simmons, Charles
Sloan, John T.
Symmes, Dr. F. W.
Simpson, Honb'le R. F.?
Slaten, John
Smith, Griffin
Smith, James W.
Spearman, F. A.
Satterfield, Jeremiah
Smith, Basil
Spearman, David
Spearman, D. D.
Shirley, Aaron
Spearman, Benjn.
Smith, John C.
Spence, Robert
Smith, Simeon
Smith, P. P.
Smith, Wyatt
Smith, Wm.
Simmons, David
Simmons, James
Skelton, Thomas
Skelton, T. T.
Simpson, David
Simpson, James
Scott, J. D.

Stephenson, James
Snipes, Mathew
Steele, Robt. A.
Seaborn, George
Sharpe, Elam Junr.
Sharpe, Major E.
Starke, Mrs. E. G.
Sharpe & Warley
Smith, Mrs. L. dec'd.
Smith, Mary Est.
Smith, Alice E. D.
Smith, J. L. N.
Scott, Talliaferro
Scott, M. B.
Smith, Wm. C. Junr.
Smith, Benjn. L.
Smith, Edith A. L.
Swords, John
Shanklin, J. N.(V.?)
Sloan, B. F.?
Sloan, Mrs. Susan
Sloan, Thos. M.
Sitton, John B .
Swilling, Samuel
Stanley, Ezekiel
Simmons, T. H.
Skelton, Thos. A.
Shaw, Wm. S.
Smith, Joel
Smith, Jesse R.
Smith, Jesse R. & Co.
Stephenson, Mary
Stephenson, John
Shirley, O.
Stephenson, George
Skelton, A. B.
Scott, David
Swilling, James
Shaw, P. R.
Smith, Robert
Sadler, J. F.?
Smith, Jane
Stephenson, Andrew
Siddell, A. L. Y.
Sailors, Isaac
Shearer, Andrew
Skelton, John
Seawright, Andrew
Shearer, Gillam
Steele, William
Turner, John B.
Telford, James
Telford, George
Telford, James H.
Telford, William
Treble, R. O.
Trussell, Posey
Trussell, Henley
Towns, W. W.
Todd, John L.
Taylor, Elijah
Thompson, James
Tate, John A.
Thompson, Dr. Mat
Todd, Andrew
Todd, Olive
Tucker, Nancy
Tate, Tillman
Tucker, James
Tucker, Harrison
Tate, David
Tate, Van
Tilley, John R.
Taylor, James
Trainem, L.
Timms, Isaac
Tompkins, John
Tripp, John
Tripp, Nicholas
Thompson, James
Tripp, Anna
Tucker, D.
Thompson, John

Tippen, Wm. dec'd.
Tucker, Wm.
Thompson, Dr. A. C.?
Todd, James
Teague, Elijah
Todd, W. P.
Towers, J. R.
Tippens, George
Taylor, Richard
Tilley, Mary
Thompson, Mrs. E.?(C.?)
Taylor, Wm. J.
Tippens, Dennis
Trussell, Wm.
Taylor, Joseph
Todd, Archibald
Todd, Mary
Taylor, J. B. E.
Terry, Henry
Taylor, D. J. (G.?)
Vandiver, A. P.
Vandiver, Aaron
Vandiver, Wm.
Vandiver, Jeptha
Vandiver, Edward
Vandiver, Enoch
Vandiver, Elizabeth
Voyles?...(blurred)
Vandiver, P. S.(L.?)
Vandiver, Elam
Wilson, James
Willbanks, L.
Wilson, John
Webb, William
Wilson, J. J.
Willingham, John
Wardlaw, James
Wardlaw, H. H.
Wardlaw, J. M.
Wilson, Bartley
Wilson, Hugh
Wilson, Sarah
Webster, Jane
Williams, J. E.
Wilson, George
Williamson, Martin
Williamson, Wm.
Webb, Andrew
Wright, T. T.
Wright, R. N.
Wright, Mrs. F.?(Wm. F.?)
Wakefield, John?
Watt, Joseph L.?
Watt, Mary
Watt, Jas. _?
Watt, Thos._
Willbanks, Elijah
Watt, James G.
Watt, James D.
Wiles, James H.
Wiles, Jesse
Whitman, Jacob
White, Ezekiel
Walker, James
Webb, W. R.
Webb, C. B. dec'd.
Williford, G. S.
Williford, Sarah
Williford, Deane
Watson, Martha L.
Wit_s, Thomas
Watkins, Wm.
Watkins, Joseph
Waddell, Wm.
Watkins, Felix
Wilson, Wm. D.
Wilson, Wm. M.
Wilson, Robt. G.
Watson, James dec'd.
Watkins, Baylis
Welborn, James
Walker, John S.
Wigginton, John

Wilson, John
Wigginton, Elihu
Wilson, W. M.
Welborn, Thomas
Welborn, Halbert
Welborn, Wm. E.
Welborn, A. G.
Wilson, James B.
Willibanks, James
Welborn, N. H.
Welborn, Wm.
White, Bart.
Watson, Daniel
Webb, Samuel
Wilson, Stephen M.
Wilson, R. T.
Warley, Mrs. L.(S.?)
Whitfield, Lewis
Webb, Elisha
Wright, Catharine
Warren, Samuel dec'd.
Wyatt, R. G.
Wilson, Thomas
Wallace, Wilson
Warnock, John
Warnock, John dec'd.
Watson, Mary
Wiley, James
Webb, Elijah
Wilkes, Samuel
Wynne, Samuel
Williford, Sarah W.(Saml.)
Webb, Clayton
Waters, Ibzan
Waters, Rebecca
White, Thos.
White, H. N.
Wilson, James
White, J. W.
Williams, M. B.
Wakefield, C.
Watson, Maria
Watson, J. B.
Williams, John
Wyatt, Elijah
Wyatt, J. F.
Wyatt, Wm. N.
Williams, W. A.
Waddell, Alex.
Webb, Dr. Edmund
Waller, Miss R.? H.
Waller, Miss Mary
Whitfield, J. T.
Whitner, Jos. N.
Williams, Jasper
Walker, Maria T.?
Webb, James
Whitaker, H. H.
Wilson, Elizabeth
Young, F. A.
Young, Wm.
Yeargan, Saml.
Ye_rs?, Polly
Young, James
ABBEVILLE:
Gambrell, James
Cullins, John
Davis, John L.
Fisher, Thos. dec'd.
Morgan, Rebecca
Mochat, Jacob
Sherrard, William
Scott, J. D.
Webb, Saml.
Smith, Mrs. L. N.
Dickson, Thos.
Clement, Wm. R.
Tucker, Wm.
Cunningham, J. J.
Smith, Robt.
Armstrong, J. B.

GREENVILLE: (next page)

391

Lewis, J. W. & J. B.
Jones, James
Seaborn, George
Maverick, S.

LAURENS:
Cox, Wm.
Acker, J. S.(L.?)
Maverick, S.

ST. JAMES SANTEE:
Gaillard & Jenkins

ST. PHILIP & ST. MICHAELS:
Maverick, Saml.

ST. JAMES - GOOSE NECK:
Maverick, Saml.

UNION:
Maverick, Saml.

NEWBERRY:
Maverick, Saml.

ORANGE:
Maverick, Saml.

SUMPTER:
Maverick, Saml.

PICKENS:
Elrod, G. G.
Anderson, Wm.
Major, James
Adams, John
Black, John
Norris, E. S.
Earle, J. B.
Smith, Wm. J.
Hubbard, Wm.
Kennedy, J. L.
Watson, A. P.
Reys, R. A.
McClure, E. J.
Bishop, J. & D.
Shanklin, J. V.
Fielding, H. B.
Gunnin, James
Clement, A.
Zachary, James
Todd, James
Lewis, M. dec'd.
Vandiver, P. L.?
Hall, Wilson
Calhoun, John
Breckenridge, R.

FREE NEGROES IN ANDERSON
DIST.:
Jessup?, Reb & E.
Wilson, M.
Paine, Dru & Ben
Given, John
Givens, L. family
Dennis, Wade & Wife
Wilson, Riley
Padin, A. H. R. & ?
Paden, Joberry & Wife
Bird, Green
Hog, John & Lang
Valentine, R.
Given, J.
Pugh, Polly
Elliott, Emily
Shumate, James

Comptrollers office, September 1848   Wm. T. Laval? for Comptroller.

392

GENERAL TAXES PAID IN ANDERSON DIST. FOR 1848:

Anderson, William
Abbott, John
Amick, John D.
Anderson, Micajah
Avery, William
Allen, James E.
Acker, Holbert
Acker? (blurred), P. N.?
Acker, Mrs. Susan
Acker, Amos
Ashley, Willson?
Ashley, John Senr.? Junr.?
Adams?, James
Adams, Asa
Adams, John
Adams, Jno.? Senr.?
Alexander, Robt.
Able, John
Anderson, David
Alexander, David
Acker, J. G.?
Anderson, M. M.
Alewine, Jacob
Archer, William M.
Acker, William Esq.
Adams, Henry
Armstrong, Archibald
Arnold, Lauren? T.?
Armstrong, James Jr.
Armstrong, Senr.
Armstrong, John R.
Armstrong, Andrew B.
Armstrong, Jno. A.?
Barkley, Josiah M.
Bryant, ___?
Barkley, Miss Nancy
Barkley, Sarah
Bennett, William
Blasengame, Thomas
Bowen, Robt.
Beca, Artwain
Belott, Jacob
Burris, Mrs. Leah
Benson, E. B.
Benson, E. B. & Son
(blurred in crease)
Bishop, Jane & Dorcas(Miss)
Belot, J. E.
Bredwell, J. W.
Burges, James
Brewer, Wm.
Brewer, Mrs. Milly
Brown, Randolph
Belot, Peter E.
Bradbury, Salathiel
Bruce, James R.
Burns, ___(blurred)
Bruce, C. P.
Bradbury, Salathiel Jr.?
Bailey, Allen
Bradbury, Jesse
Bradbury, Wm.
Butler?, Rev.d C. W.?
Bradbury, James
Bruce?, Charles?
Bomar?, Archibald
Betterson, John
B___?, Thomas Sr.?
B___?, Levi
B___? Reuben
B___? Miss Louisa
Buchanan, Saml.
Brooks, J. C.
Baker, L. A.
Brown, John
Brown, Wm. P.
Brown, _nna? Miss?
Brown, Martha Ann
Brown, Elvira
Brown, Charles
Brown, Abner

Brown, Elizabeth
Brazeal, Matthew
Brazeal, Kennon
Brazeal, Williamson
Bolan, Albert
Brazeal, Griffin
Brown, Dr.?
Balentine, Jessa? H.
Bagwell, James
Braswell, Miss Nancy
Bagwell, John
Brock, Haden
Bagwell, Miss Nancy
Burress?, James
Brock, M. H.
Brown, Nathan?
Brown, J. M.?
Branyan, Henry
Belcher, Manning
Benson & Tramel?
Beaty, John W.
Bozeman, Lewis
Bowie, Charles
Bozeman, ___
Beaty, Saml. W.
Beaty, John
Beaty, Thos.
Burdett, Hyram
Beaty, Miss Margaret
Beaty, David
Barton, Labon(Laton?)
Brown,Samuel
Boyd, Robert
Ba___, Elias
Barton, Mrs.? ___
Burress?, Thomas
Brown, Lee? Wm. A.
Brooks, Thomas
Brady, Wm. C.
Ball, Margaret
B___, J. M.
Bo__n, Saml.?
Brock, James
Burns, Jourdan
Bowen?, John
Brown, C. Miss?
Brezeal, Gambrell
Bolt?, Robt
Black, John
Boggs, J. L.?
Blasingame, Robt.
Brient, Francis
Brown, Saml.
Brock, Charles
B___, Milford
B___, Elisha
Brazeal, Cannin Jr.?
Bra_kema_e, Robt.
Banister?, J. G.?
Brown, Larkin
Brazeal, D.K.?
Bryant, Simon
Branyan, Joseph
Burres, W. W.?
Brockart?, James
Brown, Miss Johanna
Breed?, Thos.
Brazeal, Williamson Jr.?
Burres, Jacob
Brown, Miss Elizabeth
Burrass, William
Bennett, C. M.
Baly, William C.
Bennett, Thos. Estate
Bell, Saml.
Bell, James Junr.? (Georgia)
Bruce, John
Brown, R. M.
Boggs, ___
Bailey?, J. J.? Estate
Broyles, Dr. _ _

Broyles, Aaron Estate
Brazeal, Enak
Baker, Saml. N.?
Burress, Elbert
Brown, Danl.
Brown, Robert (Mississippi)
Benson & Cunningham
Burress, Joshua
Brackenna_, J. B.
Branyan, Alexander
B_m_ee, Mrs. Mariah
Branyan, Jno.? A.
Burress?, Bryan
Brown, Miss Rachel
Ballman?, Wm. H.
Benson?, J. P.
Brown, ___ C. Jr.
Bee?, Ann F. Miss?
Banister, Rolley
Brock, Andrew
Bowlin, Thadius?(Bienville)
Bowen, Elizabeth
Bailey, R. G.?
Bennett?, Charles
Chamblee, Moses
Campbell, James
Campbell, Alfred
Cox, Asa
Carter, Caleb
Cobb, Franklin
Clardy?, ___
Clardy, Jno. M.
Clardy, John
Childers, Nicholas
Coly, Wm. M.
Cason, Mrs. Hester
Cherry, L. R.
Cherry, J. C. & C.? H.
Cherry, Dr. E. L.?
Craig, Samuel
Clarke, Henry
Crenshaw?, Henry
C___, Miss L.(S.?) M.
Caruth, Miss Louisa
Clinkscales, Asa Est.
Chastain, Renny
Cato? Edward
Coffee, Iley?
Coffin, Abraham
Campbell, George
Caldwell, John
Cunningham, Thos.
Cunningham, Catharine
Caldwell, James
Caldwell, Joseph
Co_t?, Mrs.(Miss) Mary
Camel?, Thos. _
Camel?, Jesse
Cobb, Hampton
Cobb, Henry Jr.
Cox, Thos.
Clinkscales, Wm. F.?
Clement, Isaac? Junr.
Clement, Miss Sara?
Cummins, David
Clement, Christopher
Cox, Abner
Cox, Aris
Cox, Gabriel
Crymes, R. D.?
Cox, Thomas Senr.
Cullins, Caleb
Cox, R. B.
Cox, Miss Frances
Cox, David
Clement, Isaac Senr.
Cobb, Noah
Cox, John Estate
Cox, Miss Elizabeth
Carpenter, J. W.?
Clark, Miss Ann

393

Clinkscales, Miss Polly
Cromer?, Philip
Casey?, Miss Delila
Casey, Miss Sarah
Chabness?, Revd. J. C.
Cowan, Hyram
Cunningham, Catharine
Casey, Mis Mary
Cook, William
Carpenter, A. L.?
Carpenter, James M.
Carpenter, Mis Eliz'th
Clinkscales, Jno.? Junr.
Carpenter, A. M.
Clinkscales, Abner
Clinkscales, Lewis C.
Carpenter, John
Cox, J. M.
Cummins, Harmon
Clark, Jane?
Cannon, Isaac
Cox, Jesse
Cox, Joseph
Cox & Lewis
Cox, Rachel & Sisters
Campbell, William
Cowan, William
Clark, B. R.?
Carlile, Revd. Wm.
Cooper, Washington
Carter.
Cannon, Ephraim Est.
Cochran, J. P.?
Cochran, D. H.?
Clark?, J. B. Sen.r?
Crawford, Henry
Crawford, Mis Sarah
Chastine?, Stephen
Cox, John
Campbell, Danl./Saml.?
Cramley?, James
Cox, W. H.
Clinkscales, Wm. F. J.?
Coats, James
Coats, John
Clement, Wm. K.?
Chastain, James
Crawford, James
Cooley, Hyram(Bienville?)
Crawford, Mis Frances
Cherry, John
Craylor, L.? F.?
Crayton, B. F. & P. L.?
Creswell, Mis Sarah
Campbell, Alex'd.
Cater, Dr. A. P.
Coble, Henry(Cobb?)
Cobb, Josiah
Conwell, James
Cobb, Martin
Cox, Elizabeth ___ Senr.
Cox, William
Cox, William T__stee (B-
   Ha_per?)
Cowan, & Martin
C___-, John
Cooley, Wm. M.
Clement, C. W.?
Cason, Austin & McCason?
Cason, Jas. J. N.?
Chamblee, Robert
Cesar P of C Estate
Camfield, M.
Davis, Zachariah
Davis, Wm.
Davis, Wm. L.?
Davis, Richard
Dorson?, Saml.
Duckworth, Benjn.
Duckworth, Thos.
Duckworth, Wilbon
Duckworth, Wm.
Duckworth, Howard

Duckworth, Jacob
Dacus, Jno. A.
Douthet, James
Dunham, B.
Dunham, David
Dillworth, Amos
Douthet, Benjamin
Dupree, Mis _ H. M.
Davis, C. R.
D__, W. G.
Dupree, Benjn.
Davis, Jno. B.?
Davis, Mattison
Dart, Mrs. Mary
Dart, Mis Henrietta
Dart, Mis Mary
Duke, J. J.
Dickson, Thos.
Danils, W. D. C.
Dickson, Mathew Est.
Dooley, Wm. (of Ga.)
Dean, S. E.
Dean, Thomas
Dollard, Williamson
Duncan, David
Davis, Jno. L.?
Dunlap, Wm.
Davis, Moses
Drake, James Senr.
Drake, James A.
Drake, Enock
Duncan, Robert
Dunlap, Mathew
Driver, James Junr.
Driver, James Senr.
Duncan, B. F.
Dobbins, James
Dunham, William
Dalrymple, John
Dalrymple, Lewis
Duncan, Martha
Dobbins, Jason C.
Dalrymple, James
Dalrymple, Jno. J.?
Dalrymple, Mis Mary
Davis, F. W.
Dobbins, J. D. M.
Dean, Revd. C. P.
Davis, Thos. W.
Drennan, Wm.
Dean, Moses
Erskine, Thos.
Elrod, Mis Sarah
Elrod, Wm.
Elrod, Jno. M.
Elrod, Saml.
Elrod, Richardson
Estus, Larkin
Elrod, George
Evans, C. C.(E.? C.?)
Elrod, Philip
Ellison, James
Ellison, Joel
Elrod, Adam
Elrod, Elias
Earle, J. W.
Elliott, R. E.
Eaton, Joseph C.
Earle, Jno. B.
Eubanks, Elijah
Ellison, Miles
Ellison, Joel Jr.
Elrod, Wm.
Emerson, James
Emerson (Trustee for Mc-
   Clennon)
Erskine, James
Earle & Towers?
Erskine, John
Erskine, J. P.? M.
Elliott, Mary
Elrod, Thos. L.?
Elrod, Alfred

Eskew, Wm. E.
Erskine, Wm.
Erskine, Wm. R.
Earle, Elias
Evans, Alex'r Dr.
Evans, Thos. A.
Elrod, George C.
Emerson, S. C.
Earle & Griffin
Fant, Alfred
Fant, Mis Mary
Ford, Richard
Floyd, J. _
F____, Alanson
Fant, Jas. R.
Fitzgerald, Mis Martha
Ford, W. H.
Finley, Elias
Finley, Nancy?
Featherston, J. M.?
Felton, Richard
Felton, Mis Mary
Fuller, Alfred
Fant, V. D.
Felton, Amariah
Fretwell, Joseph
Ford, Stephen
Fisher, S. C.
Fant, Alfred
Fant, J. R.
Fant, Abner
Fielding, H. B.
Franks, Miles
Fant, Wm. N.
Garrett, Thos. H.
Garrett, Jesse
Garrett, Richardson
Guthrie, Nelson
Guthrie, Nelson Estate
Guthrie, Stephen B.
Gantt?, John
Guthrie, Benjamin
Golespin?, Edward
Gambrell, Reid
Givens, Harrison
Gambrell, James Sr.
Gambrell, James Jr.
Gambrell, Matthew
Gambrell, Ezekiel
Glenn, F. M.
Gaillard, Mrs? R. W.
Gaillard, W. H. D.?
Gaillard & Sloan
Gaillard, C. L.?
Gentry, Arthur
Grantham, A. J.?
Gantt, J. W.
Gilmer, James Esqr.
Gilmer, Robt. Estate
Gilmer, Robt.
Gunnin, James
Gentry, Moody
Gentry, Mrs Elizabeth
Gains, James M.
Gentry, Zachariah
Golespy, William
Griffin, Elijah
Gambrell, Jno. Senr.
Gambrell, Wm.
Gains, Henry M.
Gambrell, J. M.
Greer, Jno. M.
Gantt, Wm.
Gambrell, James
Gambrell, Sarah Mrs.
Greer, David Jr.
Greer, David Sr.
Greer, Wm. H.
Gray, Mis Huldah
Gambrell, William
Greer, James L.
Grubbs, George
Gantt, Jno. G.

Gantt, Hugh
Gantt, Jno. A. Estate
Gantt & Cox
Gassaway, Benjn.
Gortney, David
Gable, Levi
Gable, Henry
Gable, Henry Senr.
Guyton, J. W. Gent.?
Gray, Ms Elizabeth
Gable, James
Giles, _?
Geer, Wm. E.
Gaillard, J. D.
Gaillard, M. D.
Gray, R. D.
George, Ezekiel
Geer, Solomon
Geer, David
Gambrell, Mathew Est.
Gambrell, Harper
Gambrell, James
Gray, A. D.
Gambrell, David
Guyton, G. & Mother
Geer, Thomas
Gregg, Hugh
Grant, William
Gilbert, Amos
Graham, J. B.
Gilson, W. B.
Gilson & Dart?
Gambrell, David H.
George, Jesse
Gray, Hezekiah
Garrison, H. C.
Grubbs, J. M.
Gray, Jesse
Gorden, Andrew
Glenn, Wm.
Galloway, Mathew
Gentry, Casey
Gentry, David
Gray, John
Gambrell, M. T.
Gambrell, L. G.
Gentry, A. B.
Glenn, J. W.
Gorden, Agnes Mrs.?
Gentry, S. P.?
Green, Wm. W.
Griffin, Mrs.? Sophia
Gray, James L. Est.
Glen?, Solomon Jr.?
Golden, John
Gaillard, A. H.
Griffin, Jno. C.
G__bly, R. W.
Goode, P. P.
Holmes, William
Holland, Jno.
Hunter, Mrs. Sarah
Hunter, Jno. Senr.
Holland, J. B.
Hubbard, Wm.
Hamilton, D. K.
Hendrix, Jno. M.
Hunt, Jeremiah
Harris, N. Estate
Hamilton, Leonora L.
Hastie, J. & Co.
Hastie, J.
Hamilton, Cyrus? E.?
Hobson, E. J.
Hunter, James
Haynie, J. G.?
Harper, Asa
Hembree, Wm.
Hembree, A. D.
Hix, John
Hembree, James Jr.
Hembree, James Sr.
Hillhouse, Joseph Rev.

Holland, William W.
Holland, Robert
Herring, Jessee
Harris, Samuel P.
Herring, Levi
Hughs, B. P.
Harris, Mrs. Sarah G.
Harris, Thomas N.
Harrison, James
Harrison, F. E. & T. B.
 Wynne
Henderson, Mrs. Martha
Haslett, Moses W.
Hermin?, Francis
Hardy, R. B.
Henin?, James M.
Hardy, John
Hardy, James
Hall, Martin
Hall, Lent
Hall, A. J.
Howard, Hiram
Howard, George
Horton, Grief
Harkins, Miss Sarah
Harkins, John
Hog, Thomson
Harper, William C.
Harper, John H.
Hunt, William Sen.
Hanks, Capt. A.
Hanks, Luke
Hanks, Nimrod
Haynie, Luke
Hopkins, John
Hopkins, James M.
Hanks, John
Hammilton, Jane
Hall, Zachariah Esq.
Hall, Mrs. Mary
Hall, David
Hammilton, Luke
Harkness, John
Hanner, Thomas
Herrin, James
Hall, John
Hall, Lemuel
Haynin, Stephen
Hall, James D.
Hall, S. C.
Harkness, John P.
Hall, James A.
Hardy, Miles Estate
Hatten, William
Hall, John Sen.
Hodges, R.H. Co.?
Hill, Thomas
Harris, Nathan
Hughins, William
Herron, Newell
Hammond, S. L.
Herron, John
Hix, Daniel
Haynie, P. C.
Hix, William
Hall, Joseph
Harrison, William
Hall, Aron
Hagood, S. M.
Hollin, William
Hinton, John
Holland, A. M.?
Hammond, B. F.
Hammond, W. L.
Hall, W. S.?
Harbin, J. B.
Harris, Matilda
Haley, Reuben
Harris, Joseph P.
Hawkins, Wm. P.
Hunter, William
Hunter, Mrs. Mary
Hacket, Alfred

Hall, Wilson
Hix, D. J.
Hanks, Thomas
Harkins, Hugh
Humphries, David
Humphries, S. L.
Hall, Joab
Hammond, Herbert
Haynie, John
Haynie, Wm. H.
Hall, Ezekiel
Harrison, J. W.
Hall, A. M.
Harper, Thomas
Harper, John
Harper, Martha Mrs.
Hillhouse, S. P.
Jones, Happy
Jones, John W.
Jenkins, W. L. Dr.
Isaacs, A.
Jones, Wilson
Isbel, Robert
Isbel, Samuel
Jones, Thomas
Johnson, Willis
Johnson, Peter
Ingram, Mrs. Delilah
Johnson, Benjamin
Jolly, J. M.
Irvin, Mrs. E.
Jones, William
Jones, Samuel
Jankins, Mrs. Margart
Jeffers, Mrs. M. L.
Jolly, James
Jones, James
Jones, John H.
Johnson, Allen
Johnson, Joel E.
Jolly, Henry
Jones, H. R.
Johnson, A. B. & Milly
Irby, Charles
Irby, B. H.
Ingrum, William
King, Robert
Knox, John
King, James
King, Peter
King, G. W.
King, John D.
Kelly, Daniel
Kennedy, J. L.
Keasler, Henry
Knauff, W. J.
King, John J.
King, Wm. P.
Kelly, P. J.
Kelly, Elisha
King, John
Kelly, Alfred
Kelly, Elizabeth
Kelly, Allen
Kay, William Sen.
Kay, Mason
Kay, Joel
Kay, Mrs. Catherine
King, Josiah
King, James Senr.?
Kay, Gabriel
Keaton, William
Kay, F. M.
Kay, Alexander
Kay, Wm. P.
Kay, John
Kay, Wm. Est.
Kay, Jessee
Kay, Robert A.
Kay, J. C.
Kay, Strother
King, William
King, Anderson

Kay, S. D.
Keown, William
Keaton, Archibald
Keown, G. W.
Keaton, William
Kay, Jas. W. Est.
Kay, Wm. M.
Keaton, B. F.?
Kay, Charles
Kelly, Mrs. Mary
Kerr, William Est.
Lanear, William
Long, Ezekiel
Laboon, Joseph
Laboon, Edilly
Lorton, J. S.
Lorton, Mrs. Frances
Lewis, Mrs. L. Est.
Lewis, Jessee
Liddle, A. J.
Ledbetter, James
Ledbetter, George
Lewis, Elizabeth Mrs.
Latham, William
Latham, Cornelius
Levell, John
Cooley, Lisandra
Lewis, J. W. & J.B.
Lewis, J. B.
Lewis, J. W.
Lewis & Simpson
Lucious, Daniel
Lucious, Ackayow?
Lucious, James
Leverett, Stephen Jr.
Leverett, Stephen Sr.
Leverett, William
Long, Wm. N.
Long, Harrison
Leverett, John
Lindsey, Jas. L.
Ledbetter, David T.
Ledbetter, Joel
Long, Wm.
Latimore, Harrison
Ledbetter, Miss A.
Long, Wm. W.
Lindsey, Jas. L.(Abbeville)
Lewis, Elisha
Lowry, A. J.
Leverett, Thomas
Lee, Philip
Lewis, Jesse P. Est.
Lewis, Hannah E.
Leverett, Wesley
Major, William
Major, James Sen.
McCoy, E. V.
McCarty, Thomas
Martin, William
Martin, Mrs. Hester
Murphy, Thomas
Murphy, Ezekiel
Murphy, E. & Co.
Murphy, John
McCollister, John
Moore, Wm. S.(L.?)
McMurtry, Wm. (Georgia)
McCollister, James
McCollister, John Senr.?
Martin, J. C.
Moote, Mrs. Elizabeth
Moore, Elijah
Moore, Thomas B.
Merat, Obediat
McNeley, David
Mullikin, Wm.
McCann, T. H.
McCann, T. H. & Co.
McKenney, Mrs. Martha
Martin, Jacob
Mullikin, Benjamin
McMahan, Mrs. ? Susan

Mullikin, James
Martin, Stephen
McMurry, William
McMurry, Mrs. Jane W.
McMurry, J. B.
Miller, John
Miller, S. F. W.
McElroy, A.
Martin, Jessee
McElroy, John
McCrary, Mrs. Mary
McCrary, Albert
Moore, J. A.
Mays, Mrs. Miriam D.
Maxwell, R. A.
McMurtry, James
McMurtry, Mrs. Rebecca
McMurtry, Wm. C.
Melton, Michel
Morris, Samuel
Morris, David J.
Martin, John
Marit, John
Marrit, Benjamin
Marit, J. H.
Maradith, Abraham
Maradith, & Brown
Massey, Silas
McClinton, A. S.
McGee, Samuel
McLees, William
McLees, James
McLees, Mrs. Margaret
McLees, Robert
McPhearson, Elizabeth Est.
McLees, J. J.
McLees, Andrew
Magee, John
McGee, Jesse C.
Moore, John Revd.
McCarley, Robt. B.
McCarley, Joseph
Moore, John R.
McMahan, Samuel
McConnell, William
McGill, Marian & Sarah
McGill, Mrs. Mary
Mayfield, Austin & Abraham
Mayfield, William
Millwee, Dr. Wm. B.
Moore, Grant A.
Maulden, B. F.
Massey, Laban
Morrison, Nace
Mattison, L. J.
Mattison, Mrs. Elizabeth
Mattison, William
McAdams, John
More, Jeremiah
McFee, Washington (Alan__)
McCoy, Jas. M.
Morgan, Miky(a Mat__ trustee)
May, Daniel
Mattison, George
McCollister, John
McPhail, John
McAllister, Nathan
Millford, Mrs. Mary
McAlister, Capt. N.
McGee, G. L.
McBride, Jas. L.
Millford, John
Morgan, John
Morgan, Thomas
McGee, Willis
Mouchit, Jacob
McGee, Elias
McKee, Wm. A.'
McKee, Archibald
McCollough, L. D.
Martin, Jas. O.?

Martin, Mrs. Phebe
McCurdy, Mrs. Sarah
McKee, James
McCraken, Susan E.
McCleskey, James
Masters, G. W.
McGee, Michael
Massey, Abraham
McPhail, John (dec'd?)
McDowel, Polly
McGreger, John W.
Maddock, Thomas
Mills, Berry
Millwee, Samuel
Millwee, E. O. M.
Millwee, Wm. D.?
Morehead, John
Mitchel, Beng. L.
Mitchel, Caleb
Mattison, J. M.
Moss, Samuel
Mattison, James
Mattison, Daniel
Michel, Marion
Mitchel, Ephraim
Murry?, Mrs. Margaret
Major, John P.
Major, John W.
McDavid, James
Mitchel, Larkin
McCay, Martin L.
Major, Enoch
Martin, J. R.
Mager, William
Murphy, Moses Est.
McCulley, Stephen
Morehead, Maxey
Morehead, Sarah
Morehead, Clarissa
Mattison, Charles S.
Miller, John C.
Moore, David
Milford, W. J.? Dr.
Major, Wm. N.
Martin, Chesley
Martin, Abraham
Morehead, Alexander
McCollum, Samuel
McCarley, H. W.
Mctown?, John
Martin, Samuel
Martin, Mathew
Major, Elijah
Major, Daniel
Morris, James
Morris, John Est.
McFall, A. N.
McClure, E. J.
Mor:is, J. C.'
McMillion, W. A.
McCoy, Mary
McFee,Sarah
Massey, Mrs. Elizabeth
Major, James A.
Maxwell, John
Mattison, Wyatt
McGee, Mrs. Nancy
Mills, William
McAllister, Mrs. M. P.
Martin, Col. John
McFall, Col. John
Miller, Mrs. Jane
McPhail, Peter
Maxwell, Samuel E.
Mavorick, Saml. & family
Major(Magee), A. H.
Moses, C. B.
McConnell, Samuel
Magee, Burrell
Nichols, James C.
Newton, Samuel
North, E. E. Mrs.
Newton, Isaac

396

Newton, Larkin
Newton, Isaac M.
Newell, George
Norris, E. G.(L.?)
Norris, E. L.(for Corni__)
Norris, E. L.(for Houston)
Nelson, W. R.
Nelson, William
Nichols, Archibald
Norris, Robert B.
Norris, P. K.?
Norris, J. W.
Newell, Mrs. Jane
Newell, John
Norris, A. O.?
Norris, John E.
Newell, Thos.
Nevitt, William
Nevitt, William Est.
Newton, Willis
Neil, A. M.
Owens, Lewis
Oldham, Thomas
Oldham, William
Orr, Wm. M.
Orr, William
Orr, Alexander
Orr, John
Owen, Daniel
Owen, Elijah
Oliver, Mrs. Martha
Orr, James
Orr, Thomas
Overby, Nicholas
Owen, Elijah Junr.?
Owen, John
Orr, Hon. J. L.
Owen, Thornton
Obrient, William
Obrient, J. Mrs.
Oliver, Andrew
Orsborn, L. A.
Pickell, Jacob
Pickell, William
Pickell, W. C.
Pegg, John
Pegg, James B.
Philips, Martin
Pickens, Robert
Pickell, J. E.
Pendleton Manufacturing Co.
Palmer, William
Pullin, William
Pullin, John
Poor, John
Poor, Samuel
Poor, J. W.
Poor, John B.
Poor, Holland
Poor, George
Poor, Reuben
Pettus, Mrs. Jane
Poor, Hampton
Poor, Nancy
Philips, Reuben
Philips, Wm. L.(S.?)
Penald, Thomas
Pruitt, E. D.
Pruitt, William
Pearmen, Jonathan
Presley, David A.
Price, Pennel
Parker, Mathew
Prince, Mark
Prince, John
Prince, P. R.
Prince, H. P.
Parton, Hubbard
Philips, John
Quails, J. B.
Poole, Elizabeth __?
Padget, J. L. __
Poor, William

Presley, John S.?
Pickell, C. W.
Prater, Joseph
Pearman, Benjamin
Posey, Benjamin
Padget, Mrs. Elizabeth
Philips, Archibald
Pickens, Wm. L.
Pickrell, Jonathan
Parker, Robert
Pinion, Elizabeth
Pettigrew, Robt. __?
Poole, Wm. H.
Poole, Mrs. Mary
Parris?, Henry
Pickens, Thos. J.
Prichard, Lewis
Pendleton Hotel Co.
Pepper, Elijah
Quails, Reuben
Rice, Hezekiah
Rice, T. L.
Ruff, George
Robinson, James
Robinson, James E.
Rochester, Nathaniel
Rogers, John P.
Rogers, Mrs. Elizabeth
Rogers, John
Riley, Abraham
Rogers, Wm. W.
Richardson, N. L.?
Rogers, Larken
Richardson, Mathias
Richison, Sion S.?
Reeks, George W.
Richardson, Mathias Jrn.
Rankin, George
Robinson, David
Rosamond, J. H.
Robinson, Wm. __?
Ross, Rev. A. W.
Robinson, Mrs. Jane
Richison, Mrs. Hester
Reeves, R. W.
Reeves, John A.
Robert, Willis (Georgia)
Rogers, Elihu
Reed, Jessee
Reed, Moses
Rush(Rusk), D. Est.
Reid, William
R_____, Lucinda
Raymie, Malicia
Rampy, Jas. A.
Rawson, William
Ragsdale, Daniel F.
Roberts, Mathias
Robinson, John B.
Reece, William
Reed, Henry
Reece, David R.
Rutledge, Jesse
Robinson, Samuel
Rice, Rev. A.
Roach, Elias
Robinson, John __?
Robinson, Mrs. Jane
Reid, Andrew
Roach, Forester
Rice, Sarah
Reid, Dr. J. H.
Rainwater, D. L.
Reid, Mrs. Elizabeth
Rice, H. Junr.? Est.
Richey, Reuben
Rogers, J. L.
Rice, Ibzan
Ragsdale, Francis A.
Russel, Thos. H.
Rice & Towers
Rice, Fleetwood
Robins, Mary

Russel, David
Richey, Wm.
Reese, C.
Reed, A. E.
Robinson, Willis
Rogers, Mrs. Hester
Richardson, A. W.
Riley, Hezekiah
Rogers, William
Reed, J. P.
Robinson, John
Robinson, Mrs. L. M.
Richey, James N.
Swords, John
Smith, Miss M. E. N.
Smith, Mrs. L. N.(S.?)
Smith, Miss A. E. D.
Smith, J. L. N.
Smith, W. C.
Smith,Simeon
Smith, Bazile
Shirley, Aron?
Spearman, F. A.
Spearman, Benjamin
Spearman, D. D.
Spence, Robert
Smith, J. C.
Smith, J. C. & J. M.
Smith, Philip? P.
Spearman, David
Slaton, John
Siddall, John
Stanton, George
Smith, Griffin
Stone, James
Smith, G. S.
Smith, Joseph
Smith, Thos. G.
Sitton, William
Sitton, Wm. D.
Sitton, John P.
Slaton, Lovene?
Satterfield, Jeremiah
Smith, Andrew
Smith, J. M.
Smith, Mrs. Sarah
Smith, J. H.
Smith, A. M.
Smith, J. D.
Spruill, Simeon
Smith, Ephraim
Sloan, B. F.
Sloan, Mrs. Susan
Symmes, Dr. F. P.?
Sloan, J. T.
Sloan, J. T. & T. J.
Smith, Wm. C. Sr.?
Smith, S. E. A.
Smith, Benjamin S.
Shanklin, J. V.
Steele, James
Smith, Josiah E.
Steele, R. D.?
Sloan, Thos. M.
Sitton, John B.
Shearer, Gillam
Shearer, Malinda
Stanley, Ezekiel
Simmons, Charles
Simmons, C. H.
Simmons, James
Swilling, James
Swilling, Samuel
Skelton, A. B.
Skelton, Thomas Jr.?Sr.?
Simpson, Jas. L.
Shaw, W. S.
Scudday, H. H.
Simpson, David
Steele, William
Smith, M. H.
Stevenson, John A.?
Stewart, George

Stewart, Adam
Stewart, Mrs. Mary
Stevenson, George
Seawright, Andrew
Stone, George
Shirley, Obediah
Stanton, Catherine
Shumate, Jas. J.
Smith, Jeremiah
Smith, Davis
Saylor, Leonard
Saylor, Isaac
Saunders, William
Smith, Samuel
Speed, W. G.
Sadler, Wm. B. (Georgia)
Speer, J. C.
Speer, J. G.
Simpson, William
Spearman, John
Sadler, John L.?
Scott, David
Simpson, Archibald
Sanders, Abraham
Sanders, Elias
Sullivan, Kelly
Seigler, John
Sherard, William
Sadler, David
Stewart, John
Stevenson, Thomas
Sherard, Mrs. Jane
Stevenson, John
Smith, Whitaker
Simmons, David
Skelton, Thos. S.?
Shirley, James Sen?
Shirley, Richard
Shirley, James Jur.
Skelton, John
Smith, Samuel
Smith, Miss Nancy
Smith, William
Smith, Wyatt
Stone, Hampton
Saylors, Abraham
Strickland, Matthew
Stevenson, James
Stone, William
Smith, Aron __?
Shirley, Benj. S.?
Shearer, Andrew
Smith, Joel
Stevenson, Andrew
Sullivan, John
Shaw, Paten R.
Smith, J. R.
Skelton, Thos. A.?
Smith, J. R. & Co.
Simmons, Thomas N.
Snipes, Mathew
Scott, D. M.
Smith, William
Smith, Aron
Smith, Jane
Seaborn, George
Stewart, James
Steele, Henry
Smith, Robert
Stevenson, George
Syddall, A. Y. L.?(S.)
Shirley, Stephen
Sloan, John B.
Shambly, James
Simpson, Hon. R. F.
Scott, L. L.(T.? L.)
Sloan, David Dr.?
Scott, M. B.
Smith & Brown
Saylor, John
Shirley, Benjamin
Sharp, Elam Jr.
Sharp, Elam Maj.

Stark, Mrs. E. G.
Smith, John
Scott, James S.
Seawright, margaret
Smith, A. P.?
Smith, A. W.? for Elizabeth Reese?
Strickland, Mrs. Milly
Smith, William Est.
Simpson, Thomas
Thompson, James
Tripp, Nicholas
Tripp, John N.
Tripp, Mrs. Ann
Tompkins, John
Trainum, Lazarus
Teage, Elijah
Taylor, James
Thomson, A. E.
Tate, David
Todd, Andrew Esq.
Todd, Mrs. Olive
Turner, J. B.
Telford, James
Telford, James H.
Telford, William
Telford, G. B.
Trussel, Posey
Trible, R. O.
Trussel, Henley
Todd, W. P.
Towns, W. W.
Todd, J. L.
Tucker, William
Thomson, M. Dr.
Tate, J. A.
Tucker, Harrison
Taylor, Elijah
Tucker, D.
Thomson, John
Tippen, Dennis
Terry, Henry for R. Webb
Tucker, Nancy
Taylor, Joseph
Timms, Isaac
Taylor, D. S.?
Towers, John R.
Todd, James
Tucker, James
Tate, Tilman
Tilley, Mary
Tilley, John K.?
Thomson, James Maj.
Thomson, Elizabeth Est.
Tippen, George
Todd, Archibald
Todd, Mrs. Mary
Taylor, Wm. J.
Tucker, J. P.
Taylor, Thomas (Abbeville)
Vandiver, William
Vandiver, A. P.
Vandiver, Elam
Voyles, Amos
Vandiver, J. N.
Vandiver, Elizabeth
Vandiver, Aron
Vandiver, Edward
Vandiver, Enoch
Vandiver, P. S.
Welborn, William
Wilson, Bartley
Webster, James Mrs.
Williams, Jas. C.
Wardlaw, James
Wilson, James
Webb, William
Wigington, John
Welborn, Thomas
Welborn, Wm. E.
Wilson, Thomas
Wilson, James B.
Welborn, N. H.

Wilbanks, James
Welborn, A. G.
Wilson, Williams D.
Wilson, John
Wilson, W. M.
Waddle, William
Wigington, Elihu
Wilson, Wm. M. Senr.
Wilson, R. D.
Welborn, Jas. M.
Wadkins, William
Wadkins, Joseph Est.
Wadkins, Felix
Wilson, Stephen M.
Watkins, Baylis
Watson, Mariah Mrs.
Watson, Andrew P.
Warren, Samuel Est.
Whitfield, Lewis
Wright, Catherine Mrs.
Webb, Elisha
Wilkes, L. C.(S.? C.)
Walker, James A.
Wardlaw, J. M.
Wardlaw, H. H.
Williams, Jasper
Williams, Samuel __?
Wilson, Hugh
Wilson, Mrs. Sarah
Williamson, William
Williamson, Mastin
Wyatt, Col. Jas. F.?
Wyatt, Elijah
Wyatt, Wm. N.
Webb, Andrew
Wakefield, Conrad
Wakefield, John
Watt, J. S.
Watt, Mrs. Mary
Watt, Joseph M.(W.?)
Watt, Thomas
Watt, Jas. G.
Watt, Jas. D.
Willbanks, Elijah
Whitman, Jacob
Wyley, James
Watson, Damiel R.
Waters, Ibzan
Webb, C. B. Est.
Webb, Mrs. Eliza A.
Webb, Samuel
Willingham, John
Walker, A. W.
Williford, S. W.
Wright, Wm. F.
White, Bartholomew
Wiles, Jas. H.
Wilborne, Mrs. Sarah
Wilford, Mrs. Sarah
Wyatt, R. G.
Wallace, Wilson
Webb, James
Willbanks, Shadrack
Winton, Jas. C.
White, Sarah
White, Thomas
White, Henry
Wilson, James
Wilson, J. J.
Webb, Clayton
Wilson, John N.
Watson, Mrs. Martha
Williams, John
Wilson, Mrs. Elizabeth
Watson, John B.
Watson, Mrs. Mary
Walker, J. F.?
Webb, Elijah
Whitiker, H. H.
Warnock, John
Warnock, John Est.
Waller, Miss Mary M.
Waller, Mrs. Mariah

Wilks, J. M. Esq.
Webb, Edmund
White, Mrs. Julia
Wilson, George
Warley & Sharp
Warley, Mrs. Sophia
Williams, M. B.
Williford, C. K.
Whitfield, J. L.? Esq.
Williams, Mrs. M. K.
Waddle, Alexander
Whitner, J. N. Esq.
Williams, W. A.
Wilson, John
Wright, R. N.
Young, James
Yeargan, Samuel
Young, F. A.
Young, William
Yoes, Mary
Zachary, James

Davis, Aron
White, Sarah

PROPERTY IN OTHER DISTRICTS

ABBEVILLE:
Mavrick, Samuel
Dickson, Thomas
Davis, John L.
Tucker, William
Smith, Mrs. L. N.
Mouchet, Jacob
Keown, Robt.
Kelly; G. W.
Sherard, William
Waters, Ibzan
Webb, Samuel
Wilson, J. F.
Clement, W. K.
Smith, Robert
Armstrong, John B.
Cunningham, J. J.
Scott, Jas. D.
Hall, Fenton Est.

PICKENS:
Major, James
Anderson, William
Richison, Mathias
Hubbard, William
Kennedy, Rev. J. L.
Bishop, Miss Jane & Dorcas
Shanklin, J. V.
Watson, Andrew P.
Earle, John B.
Calhoun, John
Gunnin, James
Norris & Houston
Turner, George W.
Adams, John Junr.?
Keys, Robt. A.
Black(Beach), John
Burt, F.
Taylor, D. S.
Todd, James
Brackenridge, Robt.
McClure, E. J.
Hall, Wilson
Humphries, David
Vandiver, P. S.
Elrod, George
Maxwell, John

GREENVILLE:
Lewis, J. W. & J. B.
Seaborn, George
Jones, James
Arnold, Lawson T.
Mavrick, Samuel

LAURENS:
Cox, William

LAURENS cont'd:
Mavrick, Samuel

CHARLESTON:
Mavrick, Samuel and family

WASSAMASAW:
Mavrick, Saml. and family

GOOSE CREEK:
Mavrick, Saml. and family

Mavrick, Saml. and family
  also in: LEXINGTON, SPAR-
  TANBURG, NEWBERRY, UNION,
  FAIRFIELD & SUMTER

PENDLETON VILLAGE:
Cherry, Dr. E. D.
Maxwell, J. E.
Bridwell, J. W.
Cherry, T. R.
Cherry, J. C. & C. H.
Carne, Miss L.? (S.) M.
Dupree, Benjamin
Dupree, Mrs. & J. H. M.
Dart, Mrs. Mary
Dart, Miss Henrietta
Dart, Miss Mary
Duke, J. J.
Daniels, W. D. C.
Fitzgerald, Miss(Mrs.?)
Fuller, Alfred
Gaillard, Mrs. R. W.
Gaillard, W. H. D.
Gaillard & Sloan
Harris, N. Est.
Hastie, J. & Co.
Hastie, J.
Hunter, Jas.
Hunter, Mary
Jenkins, Dr.
Isaacs, A.
Knauff, W. J.
Lorton, J. S.
Lorton, Mrs.
Mays, Mrs. M. D.
Maxwell, R. A.
Miller, Mrs. Jane
Mavrick, Samuel
Symmes, Dr. F. W.
Sloan, J. T.(S.?)
Sloan, J. T. & T. J.
Smith, Miss M. E. N.
Smith, Miss A. E. D.
Smith, Benj. S.
Shanklin, J. V.
Sloan, Thos. M.
Sitton, John B.
Warley, Mrs. Sophia
Warley & Sharp
Sharp, Maj. E.
Sharp, E. Jr.
Starke, Mrs. E. G.
Bee, Mrs.
Benson, E. B.
Benson, E. B. & Son
Benson, John B.
Caruth, Mrs.
Bowlin, S. (T.?) Greenville
Mackey?, Edward free negro
Pendleton Hotel Co.

#

GENERAL TAX RETURN IN THE DISTRICT OF ANDERSON COLLECTED FOR THE YEAR 1853-COLLECTED BY
James Mullekin, Tax Coll.

Armstrong, J. B.
Able, John
Alexander, Robert
Adams, Henry
Adams, James C.
Adams, Asa Est.
Avary, Alexander
Anderson, Thos. F.
Acker, Joshua S.
Acker, P. Ga?
Anderson, Dr. William dec'd.
Allen, Willis
Abbott, John dec'd.
Alewine, Jacob
Ashley, Wilson
Ashley, John
Adams, James
Alexander, Mrs. Eliz'th
Armstrong, Andrew
Armstrong, James Sr.
Armstrong, James Jr.
Acker, Capt. W. H.
Acker, Holbert Esq.
Allen, James E.
Acker, Amos
Ashley, John
Acker, Reid & Smith
Acker, P. N.
Acker, Mrs. Susan
Anderson, Thos. H.
Armstrong, Archable
Anderson, David
Arnold, Jna.
Amech?, John D.
Adger, Rev. J. B.
Alexander, Elijah
Arnold, H. B.
Abbott, Miss Eliz'th
Acker, William M.
Avery, Asa
Arnold, L. T.
Armstrong, J. B.
Burns, Jordan
Burns, Joseph
Bradbury, Jesse
Bradbury, Salathiel Jr.
Bradbury, Salathiel Sr.
Bruce, Samuel G.
Burriss, Levi
Burriss, Mrs. Eliz'th
Boil, Martin
Buckhannon, Samuel
Baker, D. L.
Baker, L. A.
Brooks, James C.
Brooks, Thomas
Bozeman, Dan T.
Bozeman, Lewis Esq.
Bozeman, D. Les
Brown, Abner
Beatie, John
Beatie, Thomas
Beatie, John W.
Brown, Mrs. Charity
Buckhannon, Lemuel
Burton, Mrs. Jane
Burriss, Joshua
Brown, H.
Beatie, William A.
Beatie, Mrs. Margaret
Brown, Dr. Jasper
Brown, Jeremiah M.
Beatie, David
Branyan, Joseph T.
Brown, Dr. George R.
Brown, & Broyles
Broyles, A. R.
Brazeale, Mrs. Nancy
Brazeale, David K.
Brazeale, Cannon

Bowen, Thomas
Brazeale, Mathew
Brazeale, Williamson
Brazeale, E. W.
Branyan, T. A.
Brazeale, F. W.
Boon, Dr. John G.
Briant, Simon L.?
Blake, Mrs. Esther
Bartley, Josiah
Barkley, Mrs. Sarah
Briant, Terrell
Blasengame, Thomas
Blasengame, David
Blasengame, Robt. E.
Brown, Roger
Brown, William
Bayley, Isaac S.
Boggs, J. L.
Burriss, Ruben
Burriss, Mrs. Louisa
Burriss, Mrs. Jane
Burriss, Mrs. Sarah
Burriss, Joseph N.
Borstell, Maj. F. C. V.
Brown, Samuel
Brown, J. L.
Barrester(Banester?),James
Brown, Mrs. Eliza'th
Banester, Rolly
Braswell, Mrs. Mary(Nany?)
Brock, Hallom?
Brock, M. H.
Brock, And'w. J.
Bagwell, Mrs. Nancy
Bagwell, James
Brock, And'w
Balentine, J. H.
Brazeale, Griffin
Blake, Caleb A.
Bennett, William
Bennett, Thomas dec'd.
Barnett, D. T.
Bragg, James
Brooks, Garner
Brazeale, Henon Jr.(Kennon)
Brazeale, Enoch Est.
Brownlee, William A.
Burton, P. T.?
Banester, Roley Junr.
Bennett, Charles M.
Barratt, Charles C.
Bowen, Robert
Burriss, J. M.
Brown, E. G.
Brown, C. H.
Bruce, Samuel G.
Bolin, A. D.
Burriss, Elisha
Bonds, J. R.
Burgess, James W.
Boggs, Joseph A.
Bellott, Peter E.
Burriss, Rev. Briant
Boyd, Robert
Bell, Mrs. Eliza'th
Bruce, Thomas
Burdit, Hiram
Busby, James
Bruce, John
Baker, L. H.
Burriss, Milford
Brown?, Mrs. Cinderella
Brackenridge, Robt.
Brackenridge, James
Bagwell, Mrs. Mariah
Brock?, Johnson E.
Bruce, Charles
Boen, Sameul
Brown, John Sen.r Est.

Ballott, Jacob(Belott?)
Baley, Allen
Burton?, William
Boen, William J.
Burriss, William R.
Burgess, James
Benson & Eaton & Co.
Bishop, Miss Jane & Dorcas
Barton, Rev. H. M.?
Bolt, Asa
Barnett, Isaac
Brazelle, F. W.
Brothers, James
Benson, E. B.
Benson, Charles
Baley, William
Brown, C. B.
Brown, Robert (Georgia)
Blake, L. B.
Brown, James
Brown, E. M.(W.?)
Brownlee, Mrs. F. A.
Benson, J. P.
Benson, & Keys
Brown, William P.
Brown, Miss Jane C.
Broyles, Dr. O. R.
Brown, Daniel
Brown, George W.
Burdine, Rev. John
Bee, Col. E. B. Est.
Burt?, Frank Esq.
Bellotte, J. E.
Bellotte, L. D.(T.? D.)
Bellotte, M. A.
Bellotte, J. E. & T. D.
Bozengame, Harrison
Blake, John
Ball, Minyard
Brown, Saml. (Fork?)
Brown Vandiver & Co.
Belcher, Maning
Burriss, Rev. Jacob
Burriss, William
Brown, Maj. Larken
Brock?, Armstrong & Co.
Burns, Mrs. Leah
Branyan, Dr. A. (Abeville)
Bolt, John
Boman, Archable
Berry, L. D.
Blake, E. of Charleston
Blake, J. H. Est.
Corr, Laban
Coats, John
Coats, Dr. J. J.
Cunningham, Thomas
Cunningham, Mrs. Catherine
Corr, Mrs. Mary
Cosper, Mrs. Melissa
Carpenter, J. W.
Carpenter, J. W. & J. M.
Campbell, Jesse
Cazay, Mrs. Dela Ann
Cazay, Mrs. Sarah
Campbell, Thomas
Cunningham, Miss Catherine
Campbell, William J.
Clinkscales, Maj. Abner
Carter, V. T.?
Clinkscales, Lewis C.
Cazay, Mrs. Mary
Clark, Mrs. Ann
Cromer, Phillip
Clinkscales, John
Cobb, Ephraim
Cummings, Robert
Cobb, George
Cummings, David
Cummings, William

Cox, Mrs. Elizabeth
Chamley, Moses
Cox, Asa
Cox, James R.
Cooley, Lewis
Cooley, Spencer
Cobb, Franklin
Clarday, Joab M.
Coats, Anthony(of color)
Coley, Thos. W.
Coley, William M.
Clardy, John
Clardy, Elliott
Childers, Nicholas
Clardy, Norman
Coh___, Daniel
Campbell, George J.
Clinkscales, Mrs. Polley
Cooley, E. F.
Clemmons, Isaac
Crayton & Wright
Cought?, Mrs. Margtt.
Clemmons, William K.
Clemmons, Mrs. Jane
Cobb, Mastine
Cobb, Holbert H.
Cox, Thomas
Cox, Mrs. Francis
Coker, William
Cox, Abner
Cox, Rachel & Rebecca
Cox, R. B. dec'd.
Cox, Avis (Aris?)
Cox, James
Clemmons, C. W.
Cox, William D.
Clemmons, Christopher
Clinkscales, W. F. Esq.
Coker, Beney (Berry?)
Cox, Thomas
Cox, David
Cobb, Hampton
Cox, J. M.
Cox, M. G.
Campbell, Alfred
Cooley, Mrs. Lucinda
Cooley, W. M.
Carter, Caleb
Cobb, Mrs. Elender
Cobb, Josiah W.
Crymmes, Benj. F.
Campbell, George
Campbell, David
Campbell, William dec'd.
Clark, John B.
Carpenter, John
Chamly, James D.
Cox, D. L.
Chalmers, Rev. Jas. C.
Cato, Edward
Carpenter, Mrs. Eliz'th
Carpenter, Mrs. Caroline
Crawford, David
Creamer, Aaron
Chambley, Robert
Crawford, James
Campbell, William
Cook, Thomas D.
Cannon, Isaac
Carlisle, Rev. William
Cowen, William dec'd.
Cooley, Hiram C.
Cox, Joseph Esq.
Crawford, Samuel
Crawford, Henry
Coffin, Abraham
Chambly, James
Cowen, Elijah
Crague, Samuel
Crague, David B.
Cox, David B.
Campbell, A. C.
Campbell, H. E.

Clark, Henry
Campbell, Collin
Crinshaw, Thomas
Cheney?, S. S.(Cherry,?)
Carpenter, F. G.
Cobb, Ephraim
Carter, S. S. Esq.
Cox, George W.
Cox, William
Cox, Mrs. Elizabeth
Campbell, Daniel
Carpenter, James M.
Campbell, Austin
Creswell, Mrs. Sarah
Campbell, Alexander
Campbell, Ephraim dec'd.
Cater, Dr. A. P.
Cheney, R. G.
Crenshaw, W. H.
Cason, Mrs. Esther
Cason, John A.
Cason, James H.
Cason, William A.
Cason, Jas. A. M.
Crymmes, Mrs. Nancy
Calahan, William M.
Crayton, B. F.
Crayton, Thos. S.
Crayton, B. F. & T. S.?
Clark, J. B. Junr.
Capers, Bishop William
Dollar, Williamson
Dean, Thomas
Denniss, Wade H. (of color)
Dunlap, Mathew
Doyle?, R. B.
Davis, William
Davis, Zacheriah
Davis, William L.
Davis, Charles R.
Davis, Richard
Durham, Col. B. dec'd.
Dollard, Amos
Douthitt, Samuel
Douthitt, Mrs. Susannah
Durham, Miles
Durham, William
Dorr, George W.
Dayty?, John
Dalrymple, John
Dalrymple, James
Dobbins, James
Drake, James
Drake, Enoch H.
Drake, James A.
Davis, John L.
Davis, Thomas W.
Davis, Moses
Duckworth, William
Duckworth, Wilborn
Driver, James
Dean, B. D.
Dickson, Mrs.(Miss?) Sarah
Davis, Maddison
Davis, John B.
Dunkin, David
Dawkins?, William
Dean, Samuel A.
Dickson, Miss May & Alenor
Darracott, Herbert, Esq.
Dakes?, John A.
Davenport, Frances
Douthett, Benj'n H.
Dalrymple, Lewis
Dickson, Thomas
Duckworth, Benjamin
Dobbins, John B. M.
Dean, Charles P.
Dobbins, James C.
Dalrymple, Mrs. May(Mary?)
Dobbins, A. C.
Duke, J. J.
Douthett, Benjn. H.

Dean, Moses
Duckworth, Jacob J.
Daviss, Aaron
Dean, Moses J.
Earle, J. R.
Earle, Elias J.
Earle, Mrs. E. H.
Earle, J. W.
Esque, William T.
Ellrod, Samuel
Elrod, George G.
Ellrod, R. O.
Ellrod, E. B.
Ellrod, Rev. Philip
Ellrod, Benjamin L.
Ellison, James
Ellrod, Elias
Ellrod, Adam Esq.
Ellrod, Richard T.?
Ellison, Joel
Ellrod, David L.
Ellison, Emeziah
Erskine, Capt.T. M.
Erskine, W. W.
Ellrod, Alfred
Esque, William E.
Emerson, James Esq.
Eaten, H. L.
Ellison, Miles
Ellison, William
Ellrod, Thos. H.
Ellrod, George
Ellison, Joel Senr.
Esque, Elijah
Ellrod, William
Earle, Dr. S. G.
Ellrod, Thos. T.
Erskine, James
Elliott, Mrs. Mary
Erskine, Thomas
Elgin, J. M.
Emerson, J.(S.?) J.
Erskine, John
Erskine, William
Eaton, Joseph C.
Elliott, Lewis
Earle, J. B.
Eldred, William
Earle, Elias
Evins, Dr. A.
Elliott, Dr. R. E. Est.
Earle, Dr. J. W.
Ervin, Mrs. Ellmore
England, Bleckley & Co.
England, John E.
Evins, Dr. Thos.
Evins, Griffin & Co.
Evins, & Griffin
Ford, William
Fant, James R.
Felton, Mrs. Mary
Finley, John
Fa_t?, Alfred (Farel?)
Floyd, And'w. J.
Fretwell, J. Y.
Featherston, J. W.?
Freeman, M. T.?
Fleming, Richard
Floyd, Z. B.
Fisher, S. C.
Finley, Elias
Finely, John
Fisher, A. M.
Felton, Emeziah
Fisher, Samuel S.
Farmers Hall(for Clerk?)
Fielding, J. W.
Fielding, Henry B.
Fant, V. D.
Ford, Stephen
Foant?, Abner (Fouet?)
Fant, O. H. P.
Felton, Miss Eliza

Gant, William M.
Glenn, William A.
Garrison, Henry
Glenn, Joseph B.
Gillmore, Robert
Gannon, James Esq.
Gentry, Zachariah
Glenn, William
Gregg, Hugh
Gentry, Moody
Gordine, David
Galaway, M. A.
Gillmore, G. W.
Gray, James A.
Gasaway, Jas. S.?
Gable, Levi
Gable, Henry
Gasaway, William H.
Gasaway, Mrs. Margaret
Gambrille, Jas. M.
Griffin, Elijah
Gambrille, P. M.
Garrett, Jesse
Guthrie, Nelson
Guthrie, David dec'd
Guthrie, S. B.
Garrett, Thomas H.
Guthrie, Benjamin
Garrett, John
Garrett, Richardson
Gambrell, James
Gambrell, Ezekial
Gambrell, Mathew
Givens, Harrison
Griffin, John C.
Gambrelle, James Junr.
Gambrelle, Reed
Gore, Joshua
Gore, Ralph
Glenn, F. M.
Gentry, S. N.(V.?)
Guyton, Genl. John W.
Gantt, Asa
Garrett, Samuel
Grice, W. E[
Grice, Thomas
Grubs, R. W.
Gailard, F. W.
Geer, J. M.
Geer, David Senr.
Gambrelle, James
Gambrelle, Mrs. Sarah
Gantt, Hugh
Grey, Mrs. Hulda dec'd.
Gambrelle, William
Gear, David Jrn
Gear, William S.
Gantt, Dr. John
Gantt & Cox
Gantt, William dec'd.
Gear, Jas. L.
Gambrelle, John
Galasby, William
Gambrelle, James
Gambrelle, Harper
Gentry, Daniel
Gentry, A. B.
Gambrelle, D. H.
Greg, Robert D.
Gambrelle, Mrs. Liddia
Gambrelle, Sanford V.
Green, William W.
Geer, David A.
Gentry, John
Grubbs, J. M.
Gambrelle, H. J.
Gambrelle, Mrs. Susan
Geer, S[M.
Gambrelle, Ira G.
Grey, Hezekiah dec'd.
Gains, Nathaniel
Grey, Alex. D.
Garrison, D. V.

Gillmore, Maj. James
Graham, And'w
Griffin, Mrs. Sephronia?
Grey, Jesse
Garland & Sloan
Gailard, W. H. & Co.
Gailard, W. H. Dr.
Gailard, Mrs. R. W.
Gailard, Rev. Charles L.
Gailard, Josiah? D.
Gailard, Mary D.
Gailard, Lewis C.
Golden, Rev. John
Glenn, Mrs. Mary
Gambrelle, J. J.
Geer, David Senr.
Giles, R.
Guyton, Mrs. Margaret
Grubbs, George
Glenn, J. W.
Gambrelle, M. T.
Gray, W. A. & Co.
Holland, Jas. H.
Holland, Robert
Hu__y?, Levi
Hu__y?, Jessee
Harriss, Joseph H.
Harriss, Thomas N.
Hughs, B. P.
Holland, Benjn.
Holland, William
Harrison, F. E.
Hagood, S. M.
Humphries, Rev. David
Henderson, Mrs. Martha
Heringdon, Zapheriah
Harriss, John M.
Haynes, Charles
Howard, Hiram
Hining?, John
Hining?, _ell E.
Howard, D. C.
Howard, George
Hatten, William
Harriss, Nathan
Hutchson, Robert
Hardy, Richard B.
Hardy, James
Hall, Johnson
H-11, Thos. O.
Haley, Ruben
Hall, Lent
Hall, John
Harkins, John
Hall, Lemuel
Hamilton, Mrs. Jane
Hamilton, Luke
Harkness, John N.
Harkness, John
Harper, Mrs. Nancy
Harkness, Hugh
Hall, A. M.
Hunter, Mrs. Sarah
Harrison, Mrs. Happy
Henderson, James Esq.
Hamilton, Cyrus E.
Hamilton, Col. D. K.
Holcomb, David M.
Haynie, Luke
Haynie, William H.
Harper, William C.
Hammond, S. J. Sent.
Hammond, S. J. Junr.
Haynie, John
Hawkins, W. P.
Hunt, William
Hunt, John
Hogg, Thompson
Hall, James A.
Hopkins, James M.
Harper, William N.
Horton, Grief
Holland, William E.

Harper, John
Hicks, Daniel
Harrison, William
Hall, Aaron
Hall, Zachariah Esq.
Hall, Chesley
Hastie, J. & Co.
Holland, Aaron B.
Hewings, William
Hall, Samuel G.(C.?)
Hall, William A. Jnr.
Hanks, Stephen
Harton, B. F.
Harvey?, William D.
Holland, Joshua
Hembree, John H.
Hall, William S.
Hendrix, John
Hanna?, Thomas
Hall, H. A.
Harper, J. J.
Hutchinson, William
Harper, Jepthah
Hembree, James K.
Hering?, Frances
Harriss, B. B.
Harriss, And'w
Harriss, Joseph P.
Haynie?, Robt. B.
Hall, David
Hayney, J. C.
Hopkins, J. H.
Hall, Wilson
Hardy, John
Hembree, William
Hall, Martin
Holland, D. W. F.
Hammond, Col. Herbert
Hammond, William L.
Holland, John
Hall, M. H.
Hopkins, B. F.
Hicks?, D. J.
Hunter?, John Jr.
Harper, Asa
Harper, Newton
Harper, William
Harriss, Mrs. Margaret
Hall, John C.
Hicks?, John
Hicks?, Baylis
Hunter, James
Hunter, Mrs. Mary
Harbin, Capt. J. B.
Hillhouse, Rev. Joseph
Hobson, E. G.
Hillhouse, Maj. S.? P.
Hillhouse, P.
Hubbard, William
Hall, James T.?
Holmes, William
Harper, John H.
Hembree, A. D.
Hall, Joab
Hubbard, B. H.
Hanks, Thomas
Hall, Ezekiel
Hall, John
Harper, Mrs. Barbary
Hammond, B. F.
Hembree, Aaron S.?
Holland, & Sherard
Holland, A. W.
Hackett, Albert
Haskinson, Robert
Harriss, F. A.
Humphries, Mrs. Susan C.
Harriss, Mrs. P. P.
Harper, Thos.
Horton, J. C. Esq.
Harrison, Genl. J. W.
Isbell, Samuel
Jefferson, Robert

402

Jones, J. C.
Jones, James
Jones, William L.
Johnson, James
Irby, Charles Esq.
Jolly, J. M.
Johnson, Capt. Willis
Jordan, Benson
Johnson, Peter
Johnson, Allen
Jones, Samuel B.
Jolly, Levi
Jolly, Albert
Johnson, P. S.(L.?)
Irby, Benjamin T
Jolley, Henry
Jones, Wilson
Jenkins?, Dr. W. L.
Jones, William
Jenkins, Mrs. Malinda
Ingraham, William
Jones, John H.
Jenkins, Margaret dec'd.
Isaac, Aboham?(Abraham?)
Johnson, Jonathan
Jolley, Joseph
Jolley, James
Jones, Adam dec'd.
King, William P.
King, Rev. Robert
King, James
Kay, Strother
King, George W.
King, Peter Sr.
King, Josiah
Knox, John
Kates, Robert T.
Kelly, Capt. Allen
Kelley, Mrs. Sarah
Kenedy, Samuel
Kay, Charles
Keown, G. W.
Keown, William M.
Kay, John
Keaton, Archable
Keaton, B. F.
Keaton, Reuben
Kay, R. G.
King, James
Kay, Mrs. Susannah
Kay, A. W.
Kay, Joel
Kay, William P.
Kay, William P. Senr
Kay, John B.
Kay, James E.
Kay, Mason
Kelly, Mrs. Eliz'th
Kelley, Jasper
King, Col. John D.
Kelley, Joseph
Keaton, William
Keasley, Henry
Hanks, Nimrod
Hanks, Luke
Kelley, Mansell
Kay, Jessee
Kelley, Elisha
Kelley, B. J.
Keaton, William
Keys, Robert A.
Kelley, Mrs. Mary
Kay, F. M.
King, Robert A.
King, William
King, Josiah
Kanauff, W. J.
Kenedy, Rev. J. L.
Keys, J. C.
King, George
Kay, Wm. M.
Ledbetter, George
Lewis, Mrs. Elizabeth

Latham, Mrs. Jane
Lee, Dr. Thomas
Long, William
Long, Harrison
Latham, William
Leverett, William
Latham, John
Lewis & Cox
Lewis, J. B.
Levill, John
Ladd, (Ludd?), Hachah
Lewis, Jessee
Laborn(Laboon?), Joseph
Long, John
Laboon, Ednah
Long, Ezekial
Long, Henry
Lindsey, James S.
Lusk, John
Lee, Phillip
Lallice, Michael
Laviett, Harper & William
Leveritt, Westley
Langston, S. H.
Lowrey, Mrs. Rozanah
Lutia, James
Lorton, John S.
Lorton, J. S. & Co.
Langston, C. C.'
Leverett, Thomas
Laurence, R. G.
Langston, S. H.
Liddle, Mrs. Mary & May(?)
Leverett, Stephen
Lathe?, J. S.
Lewis, J. P. dec'd.-Est.
Long, Capt. James
Long, Ezekiel Junr.
Land, G. W.
Merrett, William M.
Massey, Major
Massey, Silas
McCarty, H. W.
McConnell, David (2)
McClinton, A. S.
McLure, James J.
McLure, And'w
McLure, William
McLure, James
McLure, Mrs. Margarett
McLure, Robert
McGee, Elias
McCurley, Robert B.
McMahan, Samuel
McConnell, William
McGill, Mrs. Mary Ann
McGill, Andrew
McConnell, James H.
McBride, And'w J.
McGee, Willis
McGee, Jessee
Morgan, John
Morgan, Thomas
McMahan, B. S.(L.?)
McCallough, D. S.
McKee, William A.
McKee, Mrs. Eliza'th
McKee, David L.
McLinn, Jas. - Ga.
Martin, Stephen
Milford, Mrs. Mary
McKee, James
Mochatt, Jacob
McCollin, Mrs. Mary
Maddox, Tilman
Maddox, Brazelle & Co,
Mason, Mrs. Peggy
Moore, G. A.
McDowell, G. W.
McDavid, James
McCalister, John
McCalister, James
Martin, Jacob C.

Murphy, John (Georgia)
Murphy, Ezekial Esq.
Murphy, Robert R.
Martin, William
Martin, Mrs. Hester
Martin, B. C.
Martin, Thos. C.
Martin, Chesley
Martin Sandford
Moore, Thomas B.
Merritt, Obadiah
Manley, David
Moore, Elijah
Mullikins, William
Murphy, Thomas M.
Murphy, Chesley
McCann, Thos. H.
McKenny, Mrs. Martha
Martin, Jacob
Martin, Jessee
McMurtry?, William Esq.
McMurrey?, Js. B.
Martin, Stephen
McKenny, Frank P.
McColester, William
Mitchell, Benjn. S.(L.?)
McCartey, Elijah
Mitchell, James H.
Mitchell, Caleb
Maddox, Thomas
Masters, Jessee
Morris, Jessey C.
McMillon, W. A.
Morehead, Alex'r Esq.
McGuh__?, Hugh
M____?, E.
McGregor, Mrs. Marian
McGregor, John W.?
McClis hey?, Jas. Esq.
Major, William N.
Major, Elijah
Major, John C.
Major, Enock dec'd.
MaAdams, John
Massey, Silas
Moore, Jeremiah
Maddison, John M.
Massey, John C.
Maddison, B. F.
Maddison, Mrs. Eliz'th
Maddison, Elias
Massey, J. F. M.
Maddison, O. N.
Mattison, William J.
Mattison, Jackson
McGee, Rev. William
Maulden, Rev. B. F.
Mattison, Daniel
Moore, W. S.(L.?)
Moore, Mrs. Eliz'th
Moore, William J.
McCalister, And'w
McCollister, Mrs. Amy?
Melton, Michael Esq.
McPhail, John Junr.
McPhail, John Senr
McCoy, Helsy C.
McCollister, John
Martin, L.(?) W.
Mattison, Mrs. Eliz'th
Mills, William
McClure, E. J.
Majors, Jas. A.
McCrary, E. A. M.
Maxwell, S. E.(L.? E.)
McGee, Elias
Martin, James
McGee, A. H.
McCord, And'w A.
McAllister, Nathan
Majors, William
McGee, Michael Esq.
McGee, J. P.

Martin, John
McElroy, A. L.
Morris, Samuel
McCown, John
McGee, Burrell dec'd.
McGee, G. W.
McGee, William S.
McGee, L. H.
Millwee, Wm. A.
McPhail, Peter
Mitchell, M. E.
McCay, Martin S.
Majors, E. J.
Mitchell, G. W. L.
Mattison, D. & J. F.
Mattison, J. F.
Martin, Col. John
McAdams, R. B.
Masters, George W.
Martin, J. R.
Maddox, William
McCrary, Mrs. Mary
McCrary, Albert
McMurtrey, James
Miller, John
Martin, Warren
Miller, Mrs. Jane F.
Miller, Miss Charlotte
Miller, J. F. W.
Ma_s, Medy
McElroy, S. R.
Morriss, James
Morris, David J.
Martin, Chesley
McKinney, Perry?(Penny?)
Mullikin, James
Moore, W. S.
McBride, Rev. T. L.
Maverick, Saml. dec'd.
Milford, Dr. W. J.
McFall, Mrs. Phebe
McFall, Col. John
Major, A. J.
Mays, Larkin
Mays, Henry
Martin, Mathew
Moore, Joseph
Majors, Mrs. Mary
Majors, John W.
Miles, Miss Harriet
Murphy, Mrs. Susan
Millwee, Samuel Esq.
Millwee, Miss Eliz'th &
  Mattie?
McCullough, Stephen
Mattison, Mrs. Mary K.
Mattison, C. S.
McCarthie, Thomas
Maxwell, Dr. R. D.
Maxwell, John
Maxwell, R. A.
Mays, Mrs. D. M.
Maxwell, R. A.
Martin, Abraham
Milliken, Benj'n
McCollister, Mrs. Mary
McChlon, T & D.
McAllister, Capt. B. A.
Moorehead, Maxie
Moorehead, Mrs. Sarah
Moorehead, Miss Clarrissa
McFall, A. N. Esq.
McAllister, Mrs. Margaret
Millwee, Dr. W. B.
Martin, William
Newell, George
Norriss, E. S. Esq.
Neal, Julian
Norriss, Robert B.
Nicholas, Archable
Nichols, James C.
Nichols, Miss Martha
Neal, A. M.

Norriss, John E.
Norriss, Col. Jessee W.
Nevvit, William M.
Norriss, Dr. John T.
Newton, Isaac M.
Newton, Samuel
Newton, Isaac Senr.
North, Mrs. E. E.
Norriss, P. K.
Norriss, A. ? Esq.
Newton, Wills
Norriss, T. T.
Newell, Mrs. Jincey
Newell, John
Newell, Thos.
Newell, Ruben
Newton, Larkin
Owens, Elijah
Owens, Miss Judah
Oldham, Thos. Jr.
Oldham, Thos. Sr.
Oldham, William
Orr, Alexander
Owens, Lewis
Orr, William
Orr, John B.
Orr, William M.
Orr, James (Georgia)
Oliver, And'w
Owens, John
Orr, Thomas
Obriant, William
Obriant, Mrs. Rejoice
Osborn, L. A.
Overbay, Nicholas
Oliver, Mrs. Martha
Osborn & Harrison
Osborn, Wm. N.
Orr, Hon. Jas. L.
Palmer, Maddison
Palmer, William
Pullin, Bird
Pullin, William
Pettigrew, Robt. H.
Prince, John
Presley, John S.
Parker, Mathew Est.
Prince, Mark
Payn, Lewis (of color)
Presley, David A.
Price, Benjamin
Poor, Holland
Pegg, James B.
Pegg, John
Pickle, William C.
Pepper, P. L.
Pepper, Mrs. Sarah
Pepper, E. S.
Pepper, Elijah dec'd.
Perkins, Robert
Perkins, Col. William S.
Pickle, Jacob
Pickle, William
Prator, Joseph
Pickens, Robert M.
Pickens, James M.
Price, P. R.
Pennell, Thomas
Pearman, Benjamin
Parker, Robert
Pruet, William
Pruet, E. D.
Philips, Lorenzo Dr.
Phillips, William S.
Petrie, Mrs. Jane(Petho?)
Poor, Hampton
Poor, Mrs. Nancy?
Poor, Samuel
Poor, George
Poor, John B.
Poor, John
Pickle, C. W.
Poor, John W.

Painter, Thos. L.
Philips, Martin
Pruet, William Jr
Pruet, H. P.
Purdie, W. N.
Prince, A. C.
Pew, Abraham
Pickens, A. C.
Paggott, Mrs. Eliz'th
Pickerall, Jonathan Esq.
Parker, W. F.
Pendleton Manf'r Co.
Pendleton Hotel
Philips, William
Prichard, Lewis
Philips, Archable
Poor, Ruben
Prewit, Taliafour
Pool, Mrs. Eliz'th
Pickens, Thos. J.
Potter, Rev. W. T.
Pool, Wm. H.
Pool, Mrs. Mary dec'd.
Paggett, Col. J. L.
Pickle, Jos. E.
Reed, Jessee
Reed, Moses
Rush, David Est.
Rimmer, Mrs. Lucinda
Reed, Mrs. Eliz'th
Reed, And'w Est.
Reed, Dr. J. H.
Reed & Simpson
Rice, Col. A.
Rampie, Peter
Ransom, Robert H.
Roggers, W. W.
Richie, William dec'd
Roggers, John
Roggers, Robert
Richardson, Sion
Richardson, Mathias
Reeks?, John G.
Riley, Abraham
Robertson, Dr. William
Robertson, David
Ranker?, George (Rankin?)
Robertson, Mrs. Jane
Rice, Hezekiah
Reed, A. E.
Richie, Jas. W.
Robertson, John R.?
Robertson, John
Rice, Thos. L.
Robertson, James E.
Robertson, Mrs. L. M.
Robertson, James
Reese, Mrs. Eliza'th
Reed, Henry
Reeves, Noah R.
Reese, William
Reeves, Mrs. Eliz'th
Razor, Ezekiel
Roberts, Mathias
Rochester, Nathaniel
Ragsdale, D. F.
Richardson, Noah T.?
Richie, James
Ragsdale, F. A.
Rice, Jas. T.?
Roggers, Mrs. Eliza'th
Roggers, John P.
Rice, A. E.
Rampey, William
Roggers, David
Rampey, William
Russle, Maj. T.? H.
Russle, David
Richardson, A. W.
Roland, William
Robbins, Miss Poley
Ross, Rev. A. W.
Rolletor, John

Reeves, R. W.
Razor, Rev. Thos.
Roggers, Joseph T.?
Roggers, O. B.
Roggers, Larkin
Roggers, William
Roggers, Mrs. Hester
Richie, R. C.
Rainwater, D. S.?(L.?)
Reeves, J. A.
Riley, Mrs. Ruthy
Rosemon, John H.
Reed, J. P. Esq.
Riley, Benjamin
Robertson, Maj. Willis
Roof, George
Reeves, Josiah
Ramply, Jos. A.
Rice, Fleetwood
Richie, Ruben
Simmons, Rev. David
Simmons, Charles
Simmons, James
Simmons, Charles H.
Sanders, William
Simmons, Thos. H.
Skelton, A. B.
Stephenson, Mrs. Polley
Simpson, William
Simpson, James
Skelton, Thos. T.
Shaw, Col. William S.
Skelton, Mrs. Eliz'th
Stewart, George Sr.
Stewart, Adam
Stewart, George Jr.
Scott, David
Sullivan, Jelly Esq.
Seaglar, John
Sadler, William B.
Sanders, Elias
Sanders, A. N.
Sanders, Abraham
Spear, E. H.
Sherard, J. W.
Stewart, John
Stephenson, Thos.
Sadler, David
Stephenson, Elbert
Sadler, John F[
Spearman, Mrs. Margaret
Stephenson, And'w
Simpson, W. J.
Stephenson, George
Stewart, James
Stephenson, Thos.
Sherrard, Mrs. Jane
Simpson, William
Stephenson, Alexander
Smith, W. M.
Spearman, David D.
Spearman, Benj'n
Smith, Simon
Smith, J. C.
Smith, J. C. & J. M.
Scott, William H.
Stannton, Mrs. Mary
Saterfield, Jeremiah
Smith, John A.
Smith, C. M.
Smith, H. Gee
Smith, A. A.
Smith, George S.
Smith, And'w
Slather, Loven
Sitten, John P.
Sitten, William
Smith, Griffin
Stean?, And'w
Siddle, John
Spearman, F. A.
Spearman, David dec'd.
Smith, Ephraim

Stephenson, And'w
Smith, Mrs. Mariah
Smith, J. M.
Smith, William (Abbeville)
Shearley, Stephen
Shearley, John W.
Saylors, Lenard
Strickland, Mathew?
Sherley, Mrs. Eliz'th
Symms, Thos. (Abbeville)
Sherley, John
Smith, A. W.
Smith, John G.
Stannton, C. B.
Smith, James D.
Smith, James D. & J. C.
Stott, Draton M.
Stone, George
Smith, James
Spence, Robert Sr.
Spence, Robert Jr.
Stephenson, John
Simpson, A. Est.
Steward, J. L.
Skelton, W. B.
Sherriff, John
Smith, Samuel
Stewart, John
Sherrar, Gillam
Sherley, Aaron
Saylers, John
Sherrard, William
Scott, Joseph D.
Snipes, Matthew
Sherley, Benjamin T.
Smith, Aaron Senr.
Sherley, Obadiah
Smith, Mrs. Jane
Smith, Robert
Sherely, James
Stone, W. H.
Smith, A. M.(W.?)
Smith, Robert
Steel, Capt. Robert
Smith, Mrs. Polly
Smith, A. J.
Stephenson, A. F.
Smith, William
Smith, Samuel
Steen r?, L. D.
Sullivan, John
Smith, M. H.
Spear, William H.
Smith, J. R.
Smith, J. R. & Co.
Simpson, Maj. R. F.
Symms, Arthur
Smith, Joel
Smith, Wyatt
Smith, J. G.
Spennel, Simeon
Smith, Daniel
Symms, Dr. F. W.
Smith, Josiah E.
Shanklin, Josh. V. Esq.
Sloan, B. F.
Sloan, Mrs. Susan
Setton, J. B.
Smith, Capt. Aaron
Smith, N. T.
Sords, John S.
Setton, Wm. D. Esq.
Smith, Mrs. Emeline
Stephenson, James
Sharpe, Elam
Starke, Mrs. E. G.
Sharpe, Mrs. Eliz'th
Sharpe, M. L. (Ad nnt?)
Sta_, James
Simpson, William
Simpson, Robert G.
Smith, M. E. N.
Smith, J. L. N.

Smith, W. C.
Smith, S. E. D.
Smith, B. S.
Smith, E. H.
Smith, L. N. Est.
Scott, M. B.
Sherear, And'w
Sloan, J. B.
Sloan, Mrs. Nancy
Simpson, David M.
Stephens, Green
Stephens, Mrs. Sarah
Sharpe, Dr. M. L.
Seaban, Maj. George
Sloan, T. J.
Smith, Samuel
Speed, Wm. G.
Speed, Jas. M.
Speed, Samuel D.
Tubb, Richard (Treble?)
Tilly, L. M.
Todd, And'w Esq.
Todd, Mrs. Ollive
Todd, Robert
Tate, Tilman
Tate, Grief
Tucker, Dejarnet Sr.
Tucker, Dejarnet Jr.
Taylor, Taliafaree
Thompson, Mathew
Thompson, Maj. James
Tadford, James
Tadford, William
Tadford, James H.
Tadford, George B. Esq.
Timms, Isaac
Timms, Elijah
Tripp, Nicholas
Tompkins, John
Tran an, Lazarus
Trible, L. W. Capt.
Tucker, Elias
Towns, William W.
Trussle, Posey
Turner?, G. W.
Trapp, Mrs. Ann
Taylor, Elijah
Tucker, William
Todd, William P.
Tucker, Capt. T. P.
Todd, R. W.
Tucker, Harrison
Taylor, Mrs. Nancy
Thompson, Dr. A. E.
Todd, James
Taylor, Richard
Timno?, Mrs. Eliz'th
Taylor, Col. David S.
Thompson, James
Tucker, Mrs. Nancy
Todd, Mrs. Mary
To___, Henry
Thompson, Mrs. Mary
Taylor, Isham W.
Towers, A. B. & J.
Todd, Archabal
Tucker, James
Teague, Elijah
Towers, A. B
Towers, Joel
Taylor, James M.
Voyles, Amos
Vandiver, Aaron
Vandiver, James
Vandiver, Elam
Vaun, Joel
Vandiver, A. W.
Vandiver, Edward
Vandiver, Enoch
Van Wyck
Vandiver, P. S. Esq.
Vandiver, H. R.
Vandiver, William

Whitfield, Lewis
Wright, Mrs. Catherine
White, Thomas
Williams, William
Walliford, Saml. W.
Walliford, C. K.?
Walliford, Mrs. Sarah
Watson, D. K.
Winter, Jas. C.
Walker, James A.
Watts, John W.
Watts, Joseph S.?(L.)
Watts, Jas. D.
Wonslor?, Dabney
Watt, Samuel
Wakefield, John
Walker, David
Whiteman, Jacob
Wyatt, & Co.
Willingham, John
Wyatt, Elijah
Wyatt, D.? F.
Wyatt, William N.
Wardlaw, H. H.
Wilbanks, Shadrick
Watson, John A.
Wilson, James
Wilborn, Mrs. Sarah
Wilson, James B.
Wilson, Thomas
Wilborn, Col. A. G.
Westmoreland, S. L.
Waddle, William
Woodson, William
Wilson, William M. Senr.
Wilson, Rev. Jackson J.
Walker, John S.
Watson, Mrs. Moriah
Watkins, Willis C.
Watson, And'rw P.
Wilson, William M. (Santi?)
Webb, Elisha
White, Bartholomew
Webb, Samuel M.
Whitaker, Capt. H. H.
Wilson, William N.
Wilson, James
Williams, J. C.
Wilson, G. W.
Williamson, Mrs. Rosa
Williamson, Mastin
Wright, R. N. Esq.
Wright, Wilson & Co.
Webb, And'w
Williams, Humphrey
Wilson, M. (W.?) R.
Wilson, Dr. John
Webster, Mrs. Jane
Welborn, Col. W. E.
Welborn, Aaron
Williams, Austin Esq.
Williams, S. R.
Welborn, Thomas
Williams, Jasper
Wilborn, William
Wilson, Mrs. Eliz'h
Wilson, Capt. Hugh
Wilson, Jasper & Hugh
Wilson, Mrs. Sarah
Walker, A. W.?
Wideman, Thos. A.
Wiles?, James H.
Wiles?, Jessey
Whorton, William L.
Wilson, W. D.
Willbanks, Elijah
Willbanks, Henry
White, Henry N.
Waits, J. C.
Waters, Ibsam
Waters, John
Wallis, Robert R.
Wiley, James

Watkins, David
Williams, John N.
Webb, James
Wakefield, Conrad
Watkins, William
Watkins, Mrs. Jane
Watkins, Joseph dec'd.
Wilson, Jeptha T.?
Watkins, Felix
Watkins, Miss Jane
Williams, John
Webb, Dr. Edmund
Wilbe?, Samuel Esq.
Wells, Thomas
Watson, D. M.
Wilson, William H.
Warren, Samuel Est.
Warley, Mrs. Sophia
Waters, Jessey dec'd.
Welborn, James M.
Webb, Mrs. Eliz'h
Wilson, Rev. James
Watkins, Balis
Wilson, John
Webb, Mrs. Eliz'h D.
Wardlaw, James
Warnock, John
Whitner, Harrison & Co.
Walker, Miss M. M.
Walker, Miss Caroline
Webb, Charles G.
Washington, J. J.?(of color)
Wigganton, Elihu
Wigganton, John
Wyatt, R. G.
Watkins, Maj. Thos.
Wardlaw, John
Wardlaw, Jesse
Williams, M. B.
Whitfield, I.? T.? Esq.
Wearn? & Robertson (Weam?)
Wright, J. C.
Whitaker, D. L.?
Williford, C. K. (2)
Waltie?, Mrs. Sarah
Webb & Horton
Webb, Elijah Esq.
Welborn, Dr. William
Welborn & Hall Dr's.?
Weam, Richard
Watson, Mrs. Mary
Watson, J. B.
Wilson, John
Williams, J. C.
Whitner, Hon. J. N.
Young, William
Yeargan, Rufus
Young, Frances A.?
Young, James Sr.
Quarles, J. B.

PENDLETON VILLAGE - subject
to road tax:
Maxwell, S. E.
Hall, J. C.
Symms, Dr. F. W.
Campbell, H. E.
Shanklin, Joseph V.
Pendleton Hotel
Kanauff, W. J.
Jenkins, Dr. W. L.
Taylor, David S.
Earle, J. B.
Cherry, S. S.
Sharp, Eli___ (Elinor?/Elam)
Stark, Mrs. E. G.
Sharpe, Mrs. Eliz'h
Sharpe, M. L.
Lorton, J. S.
Lorton, J. S. & Co.
Campbell, Collin
Farmers Hall
Gailard & Sloan

Gailard, W. H. & Co.
Gailard, W. H. D.
Gailard, Mrs. R. W.
Miller, Miss Jane F.
Miller, Miss Charlotte
McBride, Rev. J. L.
Benson, E. B.
Maverick, Saml. dec'd.
Sloan, Mrs. Nancy
Cherry, R. G.
Stephens, Mrs. Mary
Maxwell, John
Bellott, M. A.
Bellott, J. E. & L. D.
Duke, J. J.
Isaac, Abraham
Potter, Rev. W. J.

25 Free Negroes

GENERAL TAXES, ANDERSON DISTRICT FOR 1854:

Anderson, Thos. H.
Adams, Henry
Adams, James C.
Alexander, Robert B.
Aylwine, Jacob
Adams, John E.
Anderson, F. F.
Acker, Jas. S. Esq.
Acker, Peter G.
Anderson, R. H.
Anderson, Mrs. Mary D.?
   & R. H.
Anderson, Mrs. Mary D.
Anderson, Mrs. Mary D.
Anderson, Mrs. Mary D.
Anderson, Mrs. Ann
Allen, Willis
Acker, William M.
Armstrong, John
Armstrong, James
Ashley, William
Ashley, John
Armstrong, John B.
Armstrong, Holbert
Acker, Amos
Allen, James E.
Ashley, John
Acker, Reed & Smith
Acker, Holbert Est.
Acker, Capt. Wm. H.
Able, John
Ashley, Joshua
Armstrong, Archable
Anderson, David
Arnold, H. B.
Amick, John D.
Adjer, Rev. J. B.
Alexander, Maj. Elijah
Avery, Asa
Anderson, R. H. & M. D.
Armstrong, A. B.
Arnold, L. T.
Abbott, Miss Eliz'th
Alexander, Mrs. Elizabeth
Anderson, D. F.
Acker, Mrs.? Susannah
Bradberry, Jesser
Bayley, Allen
Bradberry, Salathiel Senr.
Bradberry, Salathiel Junr.
Bowman, Archable
Bowen, William J.
Brooks, Thos.
Baker, D. L.
Baker, Samuel H.
Bozeman, Dan T.?
Bozeman, D. L.
Bozeman, Lewis Esq.
Brown, Abner
Beatie, John
Beatie, Thomas
Beatie, J. W.
Beatie, William A.
Beatie, Mrs. Magarett
Burdet, Hiram
Brown, H. H.
Burton, Mrs. Jane N.?
Brown, Mrs. Charity
Buckhanon, Lemuel
Burriss, Joshua
Burton, Peyton
Bonds, Isham
Black, John
Beatie, David
Brown, J. M.
Brown, Jasper
Brown & Broyles
Bowen, Robert
Branyan, Jasper
Brazeale, Williamson
Branyan, John A.

Brazeale, Matthew
Brazeale, Kennan
Brazeale, D. K.
Brown, Dr. William C.
Brazeale, Mrs. Nancy
Brazeale, S. H.
Brazeale, E. W.
Brown, Dr. George R.
Barkley, Josiah
Barkley, Mrs. Sarah
Briant, Simon S.
Blasengame, Harrison
Blasengame, David
Blasengame, Thomas
Blasengame, Robt. E.
Bowen, Robert
Barley, Isaac S.
Brown, William
Brown, E. M.
Burress, Reuben
Burress, Mrs. Jane dec'd.
Burress, Mrs. Sarah
Burress, J. M.
Burress, Milford
Bowen, Samuel
Burress, L.
Bolt, Asa
Bruce, Dr. H. H.
Benson, John P.
Brazeale, Kennan Junr.?
Brazeale, Mrs. Nancy
Brown, Miss Elvira
Brown, Miss Martha
Benson Sullivan & Co.
Brown, Samuel
Brown, Miss Elizabeth
Brock, M. H.
Banester, James
Branyan, Alexander
Burton?, William
Bagwell, James
Brock, Haydon
Bagwell, Mrs. Nancy
Brock, Anderson
Blake, Caleb A.
Bennett, William
Bennett, Thos. died?
Bruce, P. S. F.
Barnett, D. J. Esq.
Baker, William L.
Brown, Mrs. Lucinda
Bruce, Charles
Brackenridge, James
Brackenridge, Robert
Bolt, Tallaifaroe
Black, J. B.
Brazeale, F. M.
Burns, Jordan
Burns, Joseph
Bowie, Martin A.
Brown, George W.
Brock, And'w. J.
Burress, Elisha
Brazelle, Griffin
Buckhanon, Samuel
Branyan, Ruben
Bolin, A. D.
Brown, Samuel
Brown Vandiver & Co.
Bruce, Thos.
Barton, H. M.
Bonds, Sugar J.
Brownlee, Wm. A.
Ballintine, J. H.
Burriss, Mrs. Elizabeth
Bruce, Saml. G.
Broyles, Dr. O. R.
Burgess, James
Burgis, James W.
Benson & Eaton
Benson, E. B.

Bee, Mrs. Ann
Burt, Gov. Frank
Bishop, Miss Jane & Dorcas
Bellott, Jacob
Bellott, Michael A.
Bellott, Thomas D.
Bellott, J. Est.
Bellott, J. E. & Co.
Barnes, Rev. C. V.?
Boone, Dr. John G.
Bellott, Peter E.
Brown, E. G.
Bolt, Willian
Brown, Danual
Birum?, Joseph
Bagwell, Mrs. Moriah
Beacham, D. S.
Blake, Mrs. Esther
Burriss, J. B.
Barrett, Charles
Burriss, Wm. R.
Burriss, Rev. Briant
Busan?(Beeson?), Charles
Brown, Maj. Larkin
Burriss, J. M.
Bruce, John
Borstell, Maj. F. C. V.?
Burriss, William
Boggs, J. L.
Brown, Roger
Barnett, Isaac
Boggs, William
Brothers, James
Brown, Cornelius
Brown, Capt. C. B.
Berrey?, Spartin dec'd.
Burns, Mrs. Leah
Boggs, And'w J.
Ball, Minyard
Barr, Leroy
Burdine, Rev. John
Belcher, Manning
Brown, Robert
Brown, W. P.
Brown, Miss Jane Z.
Burress, Rev. Jacob
Brock, J. E.
Baley, W. C.
Clark, Henry
Cunningham, Thomas Esq.
Cunningham, Mrs. Catherine
Corr, Mrs. Mary
Casey, Mrs. Dela Ann
Casey, Mrs. Marey
Campbell, W. S.
Cunningham, Miss? Catherine
Casey, Mrs. Sarah
Clinkscales, Lewis
Chalm__, Rev. J. C.
Campbell, Thomas
Clinkscales, Maj. Abner
Campbell, Mrs. Sarah
Cook, Dr. A. G.
Cromer, Philip
Clinkscales, John
Chamberlain, C.
Cox, Abner
Cox, Thomas
Chambley, Moses
Cox, M. G.
Campbell, Alfred
Cooley, Dr. Lewis
Cealy, William
Clordy, John Senr.
Clardy, Elliott
Clardy, Joab M.
Celey, Thos. W.
Childers, Nichols
Coats, Anthony (of color)
Cottrell, W. W.
Cox, Thomas

Creamer, Aaron
Carpenter, John
Clinkscales, Mrs. Mary
Clinkscales, Newton
Cooley, E. P.
Clemmons, C. W.
Clemmons, Isaac
Crayton & Wright
Cobb, George
Callaham, William
Ceught?, Mrs. Margarett
Clinkscales, Wm. F. Esq.
Cobb, Martin
Cobb, Holbert A.
Cox, Ariss
Coker, Berrey
Cox, William D.
Cobb, Ephrim
Cox, Mrs.? Francis
Cummins, David
Cummings, Robert
Cummings, William
Callahan, Wm. M.
Cox, James
Clemmons, Christopher
Cox, Mrs. Elizabeth
Cobb, Hampton
Coker, William
Cox, Mrs. Cynthia
Cox, Capt. Thos. J.
Cooley, Mrs. Lunda?
Cobb, Mrs. Ellenor
Carter, Caleb
Cooley, Wm. M.
Carter, Spencer
Carter, Reuben
Cobb, Mrs. Eliz'th
Crymes, Mrs. Nancy
Crymes, Benj'm F.
Cobb, Josiah W.
Campbell, William
Cox, Maj. G. W.
Carpenter, J. W.
Carpenter, Mrs. Eliz'th
Carpenter, Mrs. Caroline
Cox, Capt. D. L.
Coats, John
Coats, Dr. J. J.
Craft, John M.
Cummings, Thos. J.
Carter, N. J.
Cox, J. M.
Crawford, David
Clark, John B.
Campbell, George
Campbell, David
Cresswell, Mrs. Sarah
Clark, J. B. Junr.
Cromer, Lewis
Cromer, Jacob
Cobb, Frank
Cox, John
Cromer, Elijah
Cox, Asa
Cannon, Isaac
Cox, David
Campbell, Jas. B.
Corr, Laban
Clark, Mrs. Nancy
Cox, William
Cox, Miss Eliz'th
Cox, Mrs. Eliz'th
Clardy, Norman
Chambley, Robert
Campbell, Collin? dec'd.
Cambbale, A. C.
Cranshaw, Thomas
Craigue, Samuel
Craigue, D. J. B.
Carpenter, Jas. L.
Clarke, Henry
Cornish?(Carruth?),Rev.A.H.
Chesley?, L. S.

Campbell, H. E. Est.
Cater, Dr. A. P.
Cummins, Harrison
Cox, Joseph Esq.
Cox, Mrs. Rachele
Cox, Rachael & Rebecca
Cox, Gabrille
Cox, Capt. Jesse
Carpenter, J. M.
Carpenter, J. W. & J. M.
Cason, Mrs. Esther
Cason, Jas. H.
Cason, Austin
Cason, Jas. A.(Jos.?)
Clemmons, William K.?
Clemmons, Stephen
Chambley, James
Crawford, Samuel
Crawford, Henry
Crawford, James
Chastine, Henry Y.
Cox, J. R.
Crayton, B. F. & T. S.
Crayton, Thos. S.
Crayton, B. F.
Cochrane, D. H.?
Carpenter, F. J.
Cherry, George H.
Chastine, John B.
Cason, Jas. A. M.
Carlisle, Rev. William
Campbell, G. J.
Cooley, Hiram
Colwell, F. J. (Union)
Campbell, Alexander
Dennis, W. H. (of color)
Dunlap, Mathew
Davis, W. L.
Davis, William
Davis, Zachariah
Duncan, David
Dailey, John
Douthett, Samuel
Douthett, Mrs. Susan
Davis, Charles R.
Durham, David
Davis, Richard
Dunham, B. Est.
Dillworth, Amos
Durham, William
Dean, B. D.
Driver, James
Drake, Enock
Davis, John L.
Davis, Aaron
Davis, Thos. W.
Dickson, Mrs. Mary
Duckworth, Benj'n
Dollar, Williamson
Davenport, Francis
Dean, Charles P.
Davis, William
Dobbins, A. C.
Dawphine?, William
Dobbins, James
Duckworth, William
Durham, William Junr.
Davis, Moses
Dobbins, James
Drake, James A.
Drake, James Senr.
Douthett, Benj. H.
Dalrymple, Lewis
Dickens, Mrs. Rachel
Davis, John B.
Davis, Maddison
Dickson, Thomas
Deirecott, Herbert Esq.
Dickson, Miss Sarah
Dobbins, John D. M.
Duckworth, Wilborn Esq.
Dalrymple, John
Dalrymple, James

Dorr, George W.
Dean, Charles P.
Dean, W. E.
Dean, M. J.
Doyle, R. B.
Dean, Samuel A.
Dean, Thomas dec'd.
Dean, J. T.
Driver, M. A. J.
Dean, Moses
Duke, Jas. J.
Dannells, Mrs. Francis
Dakus?, John A/
Duckworth, Jacob
Everley?, Alexander
E_oim?, Mrs. Elenor
Esque, Wm. S.?
Elgin, Jas. M.
Erskine, Thomas
Erskine, John
Ellrod, Samuel
Ellrod, R. O.
Ellrod, E. B.
Ellrod, Rev. Philop
Ellrod, Elias
Ellrod, Benjamin
Ellrod, Adam Esq.
Ellrod, David D.
Ellrod, Richard
Ellison, James
Erskine, Capt. William
Eaton, H. L.
Ellison, Miles
Ellison, William
Ellison, Joel
Ellrod, George
Ellrod, Thos. H.
Estes, Larkin
Ellrod, William
Emerson, S.? J.
Emerson, Mrs. Eliz'th
Esque, E.
Erskine, James
Erskine, Capt. J. M.
Erskine, W. W.
Ellrod, Alfred
Esque, William
Earle, Dr. S. G.(J.? G.?)
Eaton, Joseph C.
Earle, J. B.
Edgar, Ezekiel
Earle, Elias
Elliott, Mrs. Mary
Ellrod, William dec'd.
Ellrod, George G.____?
Evins, Griffin & Co.
Evans & Griffin
Evans, Dr. Alex'r
Earle, Dr. James
Ellison, Amaziah
Emerson, James Esq.
England, Bleckley & Co.
England, Jas. E.
Evans, Dr. Thos. A.
Earle, Elias J.
Fant, James R.
Finley, Elias
Finley, Mrs. Nancy
Fisher, Ameziah
Finley, John J.
Finley, Robert
Fisher, S. C. Esq.
Fant, Alfred
Floyd, And'w J.
Fant, O.? H. P.
Fretwell, Capt. J. Y.
Featherston, J. W.
Flemming, Richard
Floyd, Z. B.
Freeman, Martin
Fisher, Saml. S.
Farmers Hall
Ford, Stephen

408

Felton, Ameziah
Felton, Miss Eliza
Felton, Mrs. Mary
Ford, William
Fielding, H. B.
Fant, V. D. Esq. dec'd.
Graham, And'w J.
Gillmore, Robert
Gillmore, A. R. N.
Glenn, William
Gentry, Zacheriah
Glenn, Capt. Will'm A.
Garrison, Henry
Gregg, Hugh
Cordin, David
Grey, Alexander D. Esq.
Gillmore, Washington
Gray, James A.
Gabriell, Henry
Gable, Levi
Gable, Mrs. Margarett
Gaseway, William H.
Gaseway, Mrs. Margarett
Garrett, Richardson
Gutherel, Benjamin
Gutherel, Nelson
Gutherel, Mrs. Mary
Garrett, John
Gambrelle, James Senr.
Garrett, Jesse
Cuthree, S. B.
Gore, Joshua
Gore, Ralph
Giovins, Harrison
Gambrelle, Reed
Gambrelle, James Senr.
Gambrelle, Ezekiel
Gambrelle, Mathew
Gibbs, Dr. Robert
Gentrey, Daniel
Guyton, Genl. John W.
Geer, David
Green, Wm. W.
Geer, Thomas
Grubles, R. W.
Gantt, Hugh
Galard, Franklin
Gambrille, Mrs. Sarah
Gaines, Nathaniel
Geer, David Junr.
Geer, Caleb W.
Gambrelle, Jas. S.
Gantt, Dr. John G.
Ganntt, & Cox
Gantt, Dr. John & Eliz'h
Gray, Mrs. Cynthia
Gambrelle, Jas. M.
Gambrelle, Harper
Garrett, Thos. H.
Garrett, Asa
Gambrille, H. J.
Gambrille, James
Gray, Robert D.
Grissoph, Rebeccah (of color)
Gillmore, Maj. James
Geer, John M.
Geer, David Senr.
Garrison, David V.
Grubles, J. M.
Graves, J. F.
Griffin, Elijah
Gambrelle, J. J.
Gambrelle, P. M.
Gilkerson, William
Gantt, James
Gambrelle, D. H.
Gambrelle, Ira G.
Geer, S. M.
Gentrey, A. B.
Gentrey, John
Gentrey, S. V.
Gambrelle, Mrs. Leticia

Gambrelle, S. V.
Gunnin, James dec'd.
Gambrelle, M. T.
Gaseway, James S.
Garrett, S. L.
Gentrey, Moody
Green, David A.
Gallawey, M. A.
Gailard, W. H. D. & Co.
Gailard, Mrs. R. W.
Gailard, W. H. D.
Gailard, Dr. P. C.
Gray, Jessee
Gailard, Rev. Charles L.
Gailard, J. D.
Gailard, Miss M. D.
Goldin, Rev. John
Gage, E. J.
Guyton, Quit
Griffin, John C.
Gordin, Miss Agness
Glenn, Mrs. Mary
George, Ezekiel
George, John & McFall
Griffin, Mrs. Sophia
Glenn, Franklin M.
Gray, Damarcus
Geer, David A.
Gambrelle, Miss Susannah
Gavin? Cox & Martin
Garland, Lewis
Glenn, J. W.
Gambrelle, James
Gambrelle, John
Harriss, Joseph
Harriss, Thomas N.
Harriss, And'w
Herring, Jessee
Hughes, John
Hicks, Balis
Holland, William
Holland, Robert
Holebrooks, Jessee
Holland, Benjamin
Holland, James
Harrison, Frank E.
Harrison, James
Hagood, Simpson M.
Hayney, Charles
Hardy, R. B.
Hardy, James
Hardy, John
Horress, John M.
Harrison, Nathan
Herring, E. E.
Howard, Hiram
Howard, George
Hall, Lent
Howard, D. C.
Hatten, William
Hall, Johnson
Hewings, William
Hewings, William D.
Hill, Thomas
Huchison, Robert
Howard, Mark W.
Haley, Reuben
Harress, Ezekiel
Hamilton, Mrs. Jane
Hall, Samuel C.
Hall, David
Herring, John
Hall, James D.
Hall, Martin
Hall, Chesley
Harkness, John N.
Harkness, John dec'd.
Horton, J. C. Esq.
Harkins(harknis) John
Harkins(Harnis), Hugh
Holmes, William
Harper, Mrs. Nancey
Hunter, Mrs. Sarah

Holland, Aaron B.
Henderson, James Esq.
Hendrix, John
Hubbard, William
Hamilton, ? D. K.
Holcomb, D. N.
Hembree, Jas. H.
Hembree, John H.
Humphress, Samuel
Hembree, A. D.
Haney, Luke
Haney, James P.
Hawkins, W. P.
Hogg, Thompson
Hopkins, Jas. M.
Hunt, William
Hopkins, H. H.
Hunt, John
Harper, William N.
Holland, John
Hainey, Robert B.
Hembree, A. F.
Hall, William S.
Hall, Lemuel
Harper, Mrs. Barbary
Harress, Esqr. Joseph T.?
Hall, Zackeriah
Hall, Wilson
Hall, John
Hobson, E. G.
Hastie, John
Hastie, & Co.
Hunter, James
Hunter, Mrs. Mary
Hillhouse, Rev. Joseph
Hillhouse, S. P. Esq.
Hainey, W.? A.
Harress, T. A. (Union)
Harress, Mrs. Matilda
Harrison, William
Harper, Asa
Hunter, John
Hale(Hall), John C.
Hackett, Albert
Hushison, Robert
Hall, Ezekiel
Hall, John G.
Herndon, Zephania
Harrison, J. S.?
Hubbard, R. H.
Hall, M. H.
Hammond, W. L.
Holland, Dr. D. T.
Horton, Grief
Holcomb, ineh---?
Holland, William Esq.
Hutchison, William
Hicks, Danuel
Hicks, Danuel J.
Harress, B. B.
Hembrey, William
Hanks, Thos.
Harper, John H.?
Haney, ·J. C.
Hammond, Col. Herbert
Haney, John
Hammond, S. J. Senr.
Hammond, S. J. Junr.
Harper, William C.
Hall, Aaron
Hall, A. J.
Hannah, J. S.?(T.?)
Hall, J. A.
Harkness, J. J.
Harper, Jephtah
Hamilton, Luke
Harbin, Maj. J. B.
Herring, Francis
Hicks, John
Hamilton, Cyrus
Hamilton, Mrs. Elizabeth
Harper, John
Harper, William

Hanks, Nimrod
Hanks, Luke Senr.
Harper, Newton
Helderman, Mathew
Harlow, B. F.
Humphries, Rev. David
Harper, Thomas
Holland, A. M.
Holland, & Sherard
Horton, C. E.
Hammond, B. F.
Hammond, Herbert & Co.
Harrison, Genl. J. W.
Jenkins, Mrs. Milly
Isbell, Rev. Sámuel
Jones, John
Jones, Mrs. Happy
Johnson, James
Johnson, Dr. W. B.
Johnson, P. S.
Johnson, Peter
Johnson, Allen
Jolley, A. M.
Jones, Adam dec'd.
Jones, Rev. Saml. B.
Jones, James
Jolley, Henry
Johnson, Jonathan J.
Jones, W. L.
Isaac, Abraham
Jones, Wilson
Irby, Charles Esq.
Jones, William
Jones, Jas. C.
Jenkins, Dr. W. L.
Jolley, Joseph
Ingraham, William
Jolley, Levi
Jolley, Albert
Irby, Benjamin S.?
Johnson, J. H.
Jordon, Benson
Jolley, James
Jones, John H.
King, John J.
King, William P.
Keaton, Joseph J.
King, Robert
King, Peter
King, James
Knox, John
Kay, George W.
Kay, Strother
Kelley, Jasper
Kelley, Mrs. Sarah
King, Josiah
Kates, Robert S.(T.?)
Kelly, Joseph
Kay, John
Keys, J. C.
Keys, & Benson
Keaton, Archable dec'd.
Keaton, B. F.
Keaton, Welborn
Kay, Mrs. Susannah
Kay, Rich'd G.
Kay, Mrs. Mary
King, James A.
Keaton, Ruben
Kay, William S.?
Kay, John B.
Kay, Mason
Kay, And'w W.
King, Col. John D.
Kay, Charles
Keown, George W.
Kelly, Manuel
Keys, Robert A.
Kay, Jessee
Kay, Thos. M. Senr.
Keaton, Henry
Kay, John
Kay, Robert A.

Kay,Mrs.Martha
Kay, Mrs. Nancy
Kelley, B. J.
Kay, Joel
Kelley, Mrs. Elizabeth
Kelley, Capt. Allen
King, Josiah
Keown, William M.
Kay, William M.
Kennedy, Rev. J. L.
Knauff, W. J.
Kelley, Mrs. Mary
Kay, C. W.
Kay, Silas
King, Peter
Kay, E. H.
Leadbetter, George M.
Latham, Miss Jane
Lee, Dr. Thos.
Long, Harrison
Latham, William
Leverett, William
Latham, John B.
Long, William
Long, John
Long, George
Lowe, Bennett
Long, Henry
Lewis, & Cox
Lewis, J. B.
Labon, Joseph
Laboon, Mrs. Edith
Long, Ezekiel Senr.
Long, Ezekiel, Junr.(2)
Lindsey, James
Leist?, John
Leverett, Westley
Leverett, Harpper Wiliiams
   & Co.
Lipscomb, Thos. C.
Lythgroves, George B.
Lucieus, James
Lewis, Mrs. Rosannah
Leverett, Thos.
Lucieus, Exoda
Lwurence, R. G.
Levvill, John
Lancaster, C. C.
Lorton, John S.
Lorton, J. S. & Co.
Lewis, Jessee P. dec'd.
Lewis, Jessee
Liddle, Miss M. C.
Liggan, Danuel
Lee, Phillop
Leverett, Stephen
Langston, S. H.
Lattie?, J. T.?
Langston, Allison
Long, Capt. James
Long, John
Lewis, Miss Elizabeth
Land, G. W.
Martin, Miss Fanney?
McKenny, P. F.
McMurray, J. B.
McMurray, William Esq.
McKenney, O. P.(2)
Martin, Jacob
Morress, Jesse C.
McColister, And'w
McColister, Miss Amey
McPhail, Peter
Mitchell, Benj'n S.
Moore, Capt. Jas. B.
McGregor, John W.
Millwee, Patsey & Elizabeth
Mills, William
McGee, George W.
McConnell, S. F.
Masters, Rev. Washington
Maddox, Thomas
Major, Col. William

May, J. W.
Maddox, Tilman
Martin, James
McAdams, John
Major, Elijah
Mattison, Wyatt
Massey, Silas
Mattison, B. H.
Mattison, Albert
Mattison, Mrs. Elizabeth
Mattison, Sanford J.
Massey, John C.
Mattison, William
McFall, Mrs. Phoebe
Merrett, George W.
Merrett, William M.
Martin, Mathew
McLure, William
McLure, James
McLure, Mrs. Margarett
McLure, Robert
Massey, Silas
McLure, Andrew
McLure, James J.
McLinton, Alexander S.
McConnell, James
McCarley, Robert B[
McGill, Miss Mary & Sarah
McGill, Mrs. May
McConnell, David
McConnell, William
McMahan, Samuel
McCerley, Elijah
McGee, Willis
McGee, Capt. Jessee
McBride, Jas. L.
McKee, James
Milford, Mrs. Mary
McCullough, L. D.(S.? D.)
Morgan, John
Morgan, Thomas
McGee, Elias
McKee, William A.
McKee, Mrs. Elizabeth
McKee, David
Mochatt, Jacob
McLinn, Jas. G.
Moore, Larkin
McAlister, Nathan
McMahan, Benajah
McPhael, John
McAdams, R. B.
Milford, Dr. W. J.
Major, Mrs. Peggy
Major, H. B.
Major, Joab W.
McDowell, G. W.
McGee, W. S.
Major, William
Moore, G. A.
McDavid, James
Majors, E. A.
McLure?, Rev. John
McLure?, Rev. John
McAllister, Capt. Nathan
McAllister, James
McAllister, John
Murphy, Ezekiel Esq.
Murphy, Robert
Mauldin, R. N.
Martin, Jacob C.
Martin, William
Martin, Chesley
Martin, Sanford V.
Martin, Thomas C.
Merrett, Obediah
McNeely, David
Moore, Elijah
Moore, Thomas B.
Murphy, Thomas
Mullikin, William
McConn, Thos. H.
McKenney, Mrs. Martha

McLillin, J. & D.
Massey, James N.
Mattison, Daniel
Mattison, J. F.
Mattison, D. & J. F.
Mauldin, Rev. B. F.
Mallinax, John B.
Moore, W. S.
Murphy, John (Georgia)
Mattison, O. N.
Moore, Jefferson
Moore, Mrs. Elizabeth
McGee, Rev. William
McCown, John
McCardy, J. W.
Mays, Mada?
Major, J. B.
Majors, John W.
Majors, John P. dec'd.
McFee, Mrs. Sarah
Mattison, Charles S.
Mattison, Mrs. Mary K.
Mitchell, John
Mattison, John M.
McKee, Martin S. Esq.
McCarley, H. W.
Moore, Rev. Albert A.
McMillon, W. A.
McLuar, E. J.
Morehead, Maxey
Morehead, Mrs. Sarah
Morehead, Miss Clarissa
McElroy, A. J.
Moore, Jeremiah
McGee, L. H.
Major, A. J.
Morress, James
McFall, A. N. Esq.
McGee, Mrs. Eliza
McGee, H. L. P.
Mitchell, G. W. L.
McGee, J. P.
McCullin, Samuel
Major, Jas. A!
McCoy, Riley C.
Mattison, Mrs. Eliza
Mitchell, James H.
Murrey, E. F.
Morriss, R. M.
Mitchell, M. E.
Martin, John
Morriss, D. J.
Milton, Michael Esq.
Martin, W. J.
Miller, John F. W.
Miller, Miss Charlotte
Miller, John
Maxwell, D. L. E.
McMaurtrey, James
McElroy, Saml. B.
Morgan, Balis C.
Mahaffy, Hugh
McColister, Mrs. Margaret
Martin, Chesley
Martin, Abraham
Moore, Joseph
Mitchell, Caleb
Martin, William
Maddox, William
Mullikin, James
McCollister, William
Miller, Miss Jane F.
Major, M.
Martin, Jessee
Morehead, Alexander
Martin, Stephen
Milwee, Dr. W. B.
Murphy, Dr. Charles
Morriss, Samuel
Mays, Larkin
McPhail, John
Millwee, Saml. dec'd.
McCown, J. T.

McGee, Burrell dec'd.
McGee, Mrs. Sarah
Masters, Jessee M.
McCukin, Hugh
McColloster, John
McGee, Michael Esq.
McCheskey, James Esq.
Major, J. C.
Maddox, Mrs. Matilda
Martin, William
McFall, Col. John
McCullah, Stephen
McCrarey, Mrs. Mary
McCrarey, Albert
Martin, Col. John
McBride, Rev. J. L.
Martin, Jessee
Maverick, Saml. dec'd.
Maxwell, John
Maxwell, R. A.
Mays, Mrs. D. M.
Mays, Samuel (miner)
Martin, Mrs. Hester dec'd.
Martin, B. C.
Mullikin, Benjamin
McCorthon, Thomas
Martin, Col. John
Martin, Mrs. Phoebe
Miles, Miss H. G.
Merida, Abraham
McGee, Elias
Norriss, P. K.
Norriss, Robert B.
Newton, Willis
Neal, A. M.
Norriss, John E. Esq.
Norris, E. S. Esq.
Norriss, Col. J. W.
Norris, Dr. John T.
Norris, J. T.
Norris, J. W.
Neal, Julian
Newell, Thompson
Newell, Mrs. Jinny
Newell, R. D.
Newell, John
Norriss, A. O. Esq.
Newton, Samuel
Nalley, Abraham
Nichols, Archable
Nichols, James C.
Nichols, Mrs. Martha
Nevitt, Capt. William
Nelson, George
North, Mrs. E. E.
Newton, Larkin
Newton, Isaac Senr.
Newton, Isaac Junr.
Obriant, William
Obriant, Mrs.? Rejoice
Owen, Elijah
Owen, Miss Judah
Owen, Lewis
Orr, William Senr.
Orr, William M.
Orr, James
Olliver, Andrew
Orr, Alexander
Orr, Caswell
Orr, John B.
Orr, Thomas
Oliver, Mrs. Martha
Oldham, Thomas
Oldham, William
Orr, Hon. Jas. L.
Osborn, L. A.
Overbey, Nicholas
Owen, John
Osborn & Harrison
Osborn, Wm. M.
Palmer, William
Pullin, William
Palmer, Maddison

Pickerell, Jonathan Esq.
Prince, J. W.
Prince, Mark
Presley, Dr. John S.
Pettigrew, Robert H.
P_dice, Wm. N.
Presley, David
Price, Benjamin
Poor, John
Poor, John W.
Poor, Samuel
Pettuce, Mrs. Jane
Poor, Holland
Pegg, James B.
Pegg, John
Pepper, E. S.
Phillips, Martin
Pickle, William
Pickens, Robert
Pickens, Robert M.
Pickle, Jacob
Prater, Joseph
Price, P. R.
Parker, Robert
Pruit, William Senr.
Pruit, Elias
Pennall, Thomas
Pruet, William Junr.
Poor, Hampton
Poor, Mrs. Nancy
Poor, John B.
Poor, George
Pepper, Elijah dec'd.
Pepper, Mrs. Sarah
Pepper, P. L.
Pickle, C. W. & Co.
Pickle & Murphy
Pickle, J. E. & Co.
Pickle, J. E.
Phillips, L. D.
Phillips, W. S.
Paggett, Mrs. Elizabeth
Prince, Edward
Pew, Polley (of color)
Pearman, Benjamin
Price, H. P.
Pool, Wm. H.
Pickens, Col. J. M.
Pendleton Factory
Pickens, Dr. T. J.
Pendleton Hotel Co.
Pickens, Mrs. A. C.
Prichard, Lewis
Pickle, W. C.
Pool, Mrs. Eliz'th
Parker, W. F.
Pinckney, Mrs. Eliza
Posey, B. B.
Parker, Mrs. Martha
Parks, Thomas
Pew, Abraham (of color)
Pickens, Col. Thos. J.
Robertson, John dec'd.
Richie, James W.
Reese, Mrs. Elizabeth
Reese, Mrs. Sarah
Razor, Ezekiel
Roggers, H. B.
Roggers, O. B.
Rochester, Nathaniel
Roggers, John P.
Roggers, Mrs. Elizabeth
Painter, Thos. L.
Poore, Reuben
Phillips, Archable
Pickens, Col. Wm. S.
Pruet, Joshua
Roggers, Mrs. Hester
Robertson, James
Riley, Mrs. Ruthy
Robertson, Miss Jane
Ross, Rev. A. W.
Rail Road (Blue Ridge & Co.

411

Reed, Jessee
Reed, Moses
Reed, Mrs. Elizabeth
Rice, Mrs. Sarah
Reed, Dr. J. H.
Reed, And'w Esq.
Ransom, William
Rampie, Peter
Robertson, Mrs. Jane
Ransom, R. H.
Rice, Jas. T.?
Rampie, Mrs. Mary
Reeves, Mrs. Elizabeth
Roberts, Mathias
Reece?, Rev. R. H.
Riley, Abraham
Roggers, W. W.
Roggers, John
Roggers, Joseph T.(S.?)
Ray, Elihu
Roseman, John
Roggers, Robert
Ricks, John G.
Ricks, Mrs. Sarah
Robertson, Dr. William
Rankins, Maj. George
Richie, J. N.
Robertson, David
Roggers, Larkin
Rimmer?, Mrs Lucinda
Rice, Hesekiah
Robertson, John B.
Rolley, Banister
Robertson, Mrs. Cena
Richardson, Noah S.?
Richardson, John
Richardson, Sion T.
Richardson, Mathias Senr.
Roof, George
Ragsdale, D. F.
Razor, Ezekiel
Rayney, William
Rice, A. E.
Russell, Maj. T. H.
Reed, Alfred E.
Robbins, Jessee
Ragsdale, F. A.
Russell, David Esq.
Rice, Rev. Ameziah
Rice, Thos. L. dec'd.
Richardson, A. W.
Robertson, Maj. Willis
Rolleton, John
Rechie, Robert C.
Reaves, R. W.
Reaves, John A.
Roland, William
Rechie, Jabes
Rampley, William
Robertson, Jas. E.
Rainwater, D. T.
Riche, Ruben
Richie, Mrs. Mary
Rechee, John F.? P.
Roggers, William
Rice, Fleetwood
Reed, J. P. Esq.
Sitton, J. B. Esq.
Shearer, Gillane
Simpson, Robt. G.
Slanerley, Obdiah
Smith, Mrs. Moriah
Scott, Mitchell B.
Sharpe, Elam
Smith & Cheatham
Smith & Sullivan
Stephenson, And'w
Smith, Wyatt
Sprewell, Mrs. Nancy
Sprewell, Simeon
Shanklin, J. V. Esq.
Sloan, Capt. J. B. & Co.
Seaborn, Maj. George

Stone, Callaway
Swords, John S.
Stephens, Mrs. Mary
Sherley, Aaron
Sloan, Mrs. T. ? N.
Simpson, D. M.
Sloan, J. B.
Stone, George
Sloan, J. B. Esq.
Smith, M. E. N.
Smith, W. C.
Smith, S. E. D.
Smith, D. S.
Smith, E. H.
Smith, Mrs. S. N. dec'd.
Shain, Col. John T.?
Shearer, And'w
Smith, Robert S.
Sherley, John
Strickland, Mathew
Sherley, John
Symms, Arthur
Saylors, Leonard
Sherley, B. S.?(T.?)
Smith, And'w (Abermarle?)
    (Abeville?)
Smith, Joel
Smith, John G.
Staunton, C. B.
Siny__?, J. R.
Stone, W. H.
Smith, H. G.
Smith, A, A.
Spence, Robert Junr.
Smith, Jas. D.
Smith, J. D. & J. C.
Spence, Robert Senr.
Steel, Capt. Robert A.
Simpson, William
Simmons, C. H.
Simmons, James
Smith, Jas. R.
Smith & Clark
Smith, Wm. M.
Simmons, Charles
Simmons, Rev. David
Shelton, Thos. T.
Shelton, Mrs. Elizabeth
Simpson, William S.
Stewart, George
Stewart, Adam
Stephenson, George
Stephenson, Amaziah
Seiglor, John
Sullivan, Kelly Esq.
Sadler, Wm. B.
Speed, Capt. Wm. G.
Speed, Saml. D.
Speed, James M.
Stephenson, E. J.
Saunders, A. N.
Saunders, Elias
Saunders, Abraham
Spear, E. H.
Simpson, W. J.
Simpson, Thomas
Simpson, Archable Esq.
Sherard, Mrs. Jane
Spearman, Mrs. Margarett
Sadler, David
Stewart, John
Stewart, John W.
Stephenson, Thos.
Spear, Wm. H.
Sherrard, William
Scott, David
Smith, A. W.
Stephenson, And'w
Stephenson, A.
Stone, Wm. H.
Smith, Jessee J.
Spearman, David D.
Spearman, Benjamin

Smith, John C.
Smith, And'w
Sherreff, John
Spearman, F. A.
Spearman, David dec'd.
Smith, Andw. M.
Saterfield, Jeremiah
Staunton, Mrs. Mary
String, And'w
Smith, Griffin
Sitton, William
Sitton, John P.
Smith, George S.
Smith, Caleb
Sitton, Wm. D. Esq.
Siddle, John
Smith, Simeon
Smith, Ephraim
Shaw, Col. William
Smith, J. C. & J. M.
Smith, J. M.
Smith, Mrs. P. E.
Saunders, William
Scott, Wm. H.
Snipes, Mathew
Skelton, J. W. B.
Smith, Aaron
Skelton, A. B.
Stephenson, James
Simpson, J. L.
Stephenson, John J.
Smith, Danuel
Smith, Smith
Stewart, James
Stewart, John
Sherley, Jas. M.
Sadler, J. F.
Smith, William
Stewart, Jas. L.
Sherley, Stephen
Sherley, James
Simpson, Robert
Smith, Samuel
Smith, Mrs. Mary
Smith, And'w J.
Shearer, S. G.
Smith, M. H.
Sloan, Thos. J.
Stott, Drayton M.
Smith, J. G.
Simpson, Maj. R. F.
Sloan, B. F.
Sloan, Mrs. Susan Est.
Sharpe, Mrs. Elizabeth
Sharpe, Dr. M. L.
Starke, Mrs. Elizabeth Est.
Steel, James E.
Smith, Capt. Aaron
Symms, Dr. F. W.
Simpson, William
Smith, Robert
Smith, Nimrod dec'd.
Sherrard, J. W.
Towns, Wm. W.
Treble, L. W.
Thomas, Mrs. Sarah
Taylor, David S.
Tucker, James
Toad, Archable
Toad, R. W.
Timms, Elijah
Teague, Elijah
Terry, Henry
Tilly, Lewis M.
Taylor, Isham W.
Thompson, Mrs. Mary
Taylor, Mrs. Nancy
Towers, A. B. & J.
Towers, A. B.
Towers, Joel
Todd, Jas. A.
Thompson, Dr. Mathew
Tucker, Harrison

Treble, Richard
Treadawey, Washington
Toad, And'w Esq.
Toad, Mrs. Olive
Taylor, Taliafaroe
Tucker, Degarnet
Toad, Robert
Taylor, Elijah
Thompson, Maj. James
Telford, James
Telford, J. H.
Taylor, Jas. M.
Telford, William
Telford, George B. Esq.
Traynham, W. P.
Tompkins, John
Tripp, Nicholas
Traynum, Lazerus dec'd.
Toad, Mrs. Mary
Thompson, Dr. A. E.
Taylor, William J.
Trussell, Posey
Turner, George W.
Tripp, Mrs. Ann
Thompson, James
Tate, Tillman
Tate, Grief
Tucker, J. P.
Toler, Mrs. Nancy
Taylor, James
Todd, Wm. P.
Tucker, William
Todd, James
Tate, Milford
Vandiver, William
Vandiver, Edward
Vandiver, Enoch
Vandiver, Elam
Voyles, Amos
Vandiver, Aaron
Vandiver, A. W.
Van Dick, Wm.
Vaughn, Joel
Vandiver, Peter Esq. dec'd.
Vandiver, H. R.
Vandiver, Peter Esq. dec'd.
Whitfield, Lewis
Wright, Mrs. Catharine
Williams, William
Winter, J. C.
Walker, Jas. A.
Wharton, Wm. L.
Watt, Joseph S.
Watt, John W.
Wharton, Samuel S.
Wiley, James
Winslow, Dabney
Wiley, S. H.
Watt, James D.
Willingham, John
Wardlaw, H. H. Esq.
Wardlaw, James dec'd.
Williams, Humphrey
Wilson, James
Wilborn, Mrs. Sarah
Wilson, James B.
Wilborn, Col. A. G.
Woodson, William
Waddle, William
Wilson, W.? D.
Wynn, Franklin
Wyatt, Redman G.
Woodson, Allen
Wiggenton, Elihu
Wiggenton, John
Wadsworth, Robt. (of color)
Watson, And'w P.
Wilson, William M. Senr.
Wilson, William M. Junr.
Walker, John S.
Watkins, Willis
Wilson, Rev. J. J.
Webb, Samuel M.

Wright, J. C.
Wakefield, John
Wakefield, Conrad
Wilson, John
Walhel?, Mrs. Sarah
Williford, Mrs. Sarah
Williford, C. K.(H.?)
Williford, S. W.
Wilson, George W.
williamson, Mrs. Rosa
Williamson, Master?
Wilson, Riley
Wilson, William
Wilson, James
Wright, R. N. Esq.
Webb, Andr'w
Williams, J. C.
Wilson, Dr. John
Webster, Mrs. Jane
Wright, Wilson & Co.
Wyatt, Col. Jas. F.
Wyatt, Elijah
Welborn, Aaron
Williams, Austin
Wilson, Mrs. Elizabeth
Welborn, Thomas
Wilson, Capt. Hugh
Watkins, Capt. David
Welborn, Col. W. E.
Welborn, William
Welborn, A. F.
Waters, Mrs. Mary
Waters, Mrs. Rebeccah
Willbank, Shadrach
White, Henry N.
White, Thomas dec'd.
Webb, Mrs. Eliza D.
Watson, D. K.
Williams, Ira G.
Westmoreland, S. L.
Webb, James
Wells, Thomas
Whitaker, Capt. H. H.
Wiles, Jessee
Willbanks, Elijah
Willbanks, Henry
White, David
Wideman, Thos. A.
Wilson, William H.
Watkens, Balis
Washington, J. J.(of color)
Wilson, Mrs. Martha
Watkins, William
Watkins, Mrs. Jane
Watkins, Joseph dec'd.
Waller, Miss C. M.
Waller, Miss M. M.
Wearn, Richard
Warnock, John
Williams, Capt. Micajah
Welborn, Westley
Warley, Mrs. Sophia
Wilson, John
Watson, Mrs. Moriah
Wardlaw, John
Wardlaw, Jessee
Williams, W. A. Esq.
Welborn & Hall, Drs.
Welborn & Murphy, Drs.
Whetley, Mrs. Elizabeth
Walker, A. W.
Whitaker, Lounso
Watson, John A.
Wallace, Robert
Wearn & Robertson
Watson, John
Webb, D. H.
Willhete, Dr. P. A.
Watson, David M.
Watson, John B. & Co.
Watson, John B.
Watson, Mrs. Mary
Webb, Elijah Esq.

Webb, Elijah Esq.
Wilson, Rev. James
Wright, Mrs.
Williams, Joseph
Welborn, James M.
Watkens, Maj. Thos. C.
Williams, Jasper
Watkens, Felix
Wilson, Mrs. Sarah
Wilks, Genl. S. M. Esq.
Williams, J. L.
Webb, Elisha
Webb & Horton
Webb, C. G.
Whitner, Hon. J. N.
Wilson, Jepthah F.
Whitefield, J. T. Esq.
Webb, Dr. Edward
Young, James
Young, Frances A.
Young, William
Quals, John B.
Quals, Ruben

Maxwell, Dr. Robert
Hodge, Mrs. Mary
Blake, E. (of Charleston)
Blake, J. H. Est.
Williams, John

27 Free Negroes

GENERAL TAXES COLLECTED IN THE DISTRICT OF ANDERSON FOR THE YEAR 1856 by W. S. SHAW, Tax Collector.

Abel, John
Alexander, R. B.
Adams, Henry
Adams, John
Alewine, Jacob
Adams, J. C.
Aiken, James
Amick, John Dr.
Avay, Asa
Ashley, Rev. Wilson
Ashley, John
Adams, Capt. James
Armstrong, J. B.
Armstrong, James Jr.
Armstrong, Archibald
Armstrong, James Sr.
Acker, Capt. Joshua
Acker, Mrs. Susannah
Acker, McDade & Cox
Anderson, T. F.
Allen, James E.?
Acker, Amos
Acker, Holbert Capt.
Ashley, John
Allen, Capt. Wm. N.?
Acker, Smith & Acker
Alexander, Wm. O.?
Acker, P. G.
Allen, J. E. dec'd. by
   Rev. C. L. Gailard? An-
   derson (very small and
   difficult to read)
Anderson, D. F.
Anderson, Mrs. Mary
Anderson, Miss O. L.
Anderson, Taply
Allen, Willis
Anderson, Miss A. H.?
Anderson, Miss A. V.?
Anderson, W. H.
Anderson, R. H.
Anderson, M. D. & R. H.
Ashmore, Col. J. D.
Austin, Alexander
Ashley, J. T.?
Anderson, T. H.
Arnold, L. T.?
Alexander, Col. E.
Adger, Dr. Geo. B.
Acker, W. M.
Acker, Capt. W. H.
Armstrong, J. R.
Brown, Miss Martha
Brown, Miss Elvira
Buchanan, Saml. Sr.?
Burress, W. R.
Bowen, W. J.
Burress, Miss E.
Baker, D. L.
Brooks, Thomas
Brown, Peter R.
Beatie, Thomas
Beaty, J. W.
Brown, Cornelius
Burton, P. T.?
Brown, J. R.
Burton, J. T.?
Burdock, George
Buchanan, Capt. L.
Burress, Joshua
Beaty, David
Brown, Dr. Jeffers
Brown, J. M.
Branian, Joseph J.
Bozeman, Lewis
Burress, Mrs.Sarah
Burton, Thomas
Bowie, M. A.
Bradberry, Salathiel
Bradberry, Jesse

Burney, Jordan
Burney, Joseph
Bruce, Dr. H. H.
Bruce, Charles
Brown, Maj. Larkin
Bellotte, J.(T.?) E.
Bellotte, S.? Dr.?
Bellotte, M. A.
Bellotte, J. E. & M. A.
Bellotte, Peter E.
Bishop, Miss J. & D.
Boon, Dr. J. G. dec'd.
Black, Mrs. Nancy
Black?, J. B.
Bolt, Asa
Bolt, William
Brown, C. H.
Brown, Capt. C. B.
Barnettee, Isaac
Bowen, Thomas M.
Bowen, E. B.
Banisler, Rolley (Banister)
Banisler, J.
Braniean, R. H.
Bell, William
Bird, Martin
Brock, M. H.
Brogweller, Mrs. Nancy
Brogweller, Mrs. Nancie
Brock, Anderson
Branian, Jno. A.?
Balentine, J__? H.?
Brownson, Norman
Brazeale, Griffin
Blake, C. A.
Blake, Mrs. Esther
Bennett, William
Breazeale, Mathers?
Breazeale, Kennon Jr.?
Brazeale, S. M.
Brazeale, E. W.
Brown, Dr. G. R.
Breazeale, D. R.
Brown, Dr. W. C.
Brazeale, Mrs. Nancy
Berkley, Josiah
Brazeale, Wilimson
Brazeale, Kennon Sr.
Black, John
Brown, Samuel
Boggs, William
Brown, E. M.
Burrow, Andw? M.
Bowland, A. D.
Barkely, Mrs. Sarah
Blasengame, Thomas
Blasengame, David
Blasengame, Robert
Blasengame, Mrs. Mary
Bowen, Robert
Barr, Mrs. Matilda
Barr, Leroy
Briant, Mrs. Margery
Barr, G. D.
Boggs, J. F.
Boggs, Joseph A.
Brown, Capt. William
Burgess, J. Wm.
Brock, Hayden
Burgess, James Sr.
Bagwell, Mrs. Maria
Bozeman, D. T.
Bozeman, D. L.
Bowen, Samuel
Barton, Rev. H. M.
Burdein, Rev. J. M.?(Jno.?)
Briant, Simion
Burress, Jno. M.
Brown, Mrs. Cindrilla?
Brackenridge, Robt.

Blassingame, Franklin
Bynum, Jos. L.
Brackenridge, James
Bagwell, James
Broyles, Maj. J. T.?
Bailey, Allen
Branian, Reuben
Brown, Samuel
Brown, Vandiver & Co.
Belcher, Mannin
Belcher, Mrs. Susan
Burns, Robert M.
Brownlee, Wm. A.
Bruce, John
Burdette, Hiram
Burress, Levi
Burress, Reuben
Burress, Elisha dec'd.
Bruce, Thomas
Brock, J. L. & J. C.
Brock, Jno. C.
Barnette, D. J.·
Bruce, C. C. M.
Branian, Dr. Alexander
Brown, E. G.
Barrett, Charles
Benson, E. B.
Burress, Rev. J__?
Baker, Samuel
Bruce, S. G.
Brothers, J. W.
Brown, Hillery
Benson, Mrs. Catherine
Burress, William
Ball?, Miniard
Burress, Milford
Babb, Rev. R. F.
Brock, James E.
Baily, W. C.
Boyd, R. N.
Brown, W. D.
Brown, Miss J. C.
Burress, Rev. Bryan
Broyles, Dr. O.? R.
Brown, Daniel
Cunningham, Thos. dec'd.
Cunningham, John
Cosper, Mrs. Malissa
Cook, Dr. A. G.
Carpenter, J. W.
Chalmers, Rev. J. C.
Casey, Miss D. A.
Casey, Mrs. Sarah
Campbell, Wm.
Campbell, Wm.(Mrs.?)
Casey, Mrs. Mary dec'd.
Cromer, Philip
Clark, Mrs. Ann
Clinkscales, Mrs. Mary
Cunningham, Miss C.? dec'd.
Campbell, George jr.
Campbell, D. M.
Campbell, George Sr.
Cox, John
Cromer, Elijah
Clark, H.
Corr, Laban
Cromer, Lewis
Coates, Dr. J. J.
Campbell, A. C.
Crenshaw, Thomas
Crenshaw, Wm. H.
Cannon, J. C.
Carpenter, James M.
Craig?, Samuel
Craig?, J. B.
Chastan, Jno. B.
Creamer, Aaron
Chastain, S. F.
Crawford, James Sr.

414

Cowan, Mrs. Elizabeth
Cummins, Robt.
Cobb, Mastine
Cobb, H. A.
Cummins, David
Coker, Berry
Calahan, Wm. M.
Cox, A. R.
Clement, J. J. & C. W.
Clinkscales, W. F.
Cox, James
Cummins, Wm.
Cox, Mrs. Elizabeth
Cox, Mrs. Frances
Cox, Abner
Coker, William
Cox, Mrs. Cynthia
Cox, Wm. D.
Cox, Capt. T. J.
Cheslie, Dr. R. S.
Cobb, Hampton
Cooly, Mrs. Lucinda
Clement, Isaac
Carte, Caleb
Clement, W. K.
Crimes, Mrs. Nancy
Crimes, B. F.
Carlisle, Rev. J. M.
Cobb, J. W.
Cox, Mrs. Elizabeth
Cox, Thomas
Chamblee, Moses
Cobb, Ephraim
Cannon, Ephraim (___?)
Creswell, Mrs. Sarah
Chamblee, Robt. Jr.?
Cox, Col. T. W.
Cox, Mrs. Margaret
Cumming, T. ?J.
Cullins, Caleb
Cox, Asa
Cason, Thomas A.
Cason, Mrs. Esther
Cason, J. H.
Clardy, Joab M.
Cooper, Washington
Cely, Thomas W.
Cely, Wm. M.
Clary, John dec'd.
Clardy, N. S.?
Childers, Nicholas
Cooley, Mrs. Susan
Cason, W. A.
Carte, J. S. (c__?)
Carte, Reuben
Crawford, David
Cochran, Daniel
Clinkscales, John
Cromer, Jacob
Clement, C. W.
Campbell, Thomas G.
Calahan, Wm.
Coates, John
Carpenter, John
Cox, J. M.
Craft, John M.
Cason, J. A. M.
Clardy, Alexander
Clinkscales, L. N.
Caldwell, Joseph
Chamblee, T. B.
Carwile, J. S.
Clinkscales, Reuben
Carpenter, J. M.
Carpenter, Mrs. E.
Carpenter, Miss S. E.
Carroll, James
Chamblin, Capt. W. D.
Cooley, E. T.?
Cox, M. G.
Cowan, J. A.
Clark, Henry
Clinkscales, Col. A.

Cater?, Mrs. Jane
Cooly, W. M.
Campbell, Austin
Cooly, J. J.
Carpenter, F. G.
Crawford, Henry
Cox, David
Chamblee, James
Conner, G. W.
Cooley, Hiram?
Cunningham, Miss C.?
Campbell, Alexander
Cox, Capt. D. L.
Cottrell?, W. M.
Crayton, B. F.
Caldwell, Miss Fannie
Campbell, Alfred
Cater, Dr. A. P.
Chastain, Henry
Carlisle, Rev. W.
Cox, Joseph Esq.
Cox, Joseph & Abner
Cox, Gabriel
Dollar, Williamson
Dunlap, Matthew
Doyel, R. B.
Dawkins, W.
Dickard, Wm.
Dobbins, James
Douthiet, R. H.
Dickson, Thomas
Dickson, Mrs. Sarah
Derricoat, Herbert
Drake, E. H.
Drake, Mrs. Nancy
Dunlap, John M.
Davis, Charles
Davis, Aaron
Davis, John L.
Davis, Moses
Davis, T.? W.
Davis, Zacheriah
Dean, Capt. B. D.
Davis, Wm. L.
Davis, Wm. dec'd.
Dalrymple, Lewis
Duckworth, Welborn
Duckworth, J. J.
Duckworth & Rogers
Durham, David
Douthit, Samuel
Douthit, Mrs. Susannah
Dunham, B. (est.?)
Davis, C. R.
Davis, Richard
Davis, M. A.
Dilworth, Amos
Dilworth, Benjamin
Deavenport, G. W.
Dennis, Wade H.
Dorr, G. W.
Davis, Jno. B.
Davis, M. N. A. J.
Dobbins, James E.?
Dickson, Miss Mary
Dobbins, A. C.
Duckworth, W.
Dalrymple, John
Dalrymple, James
Dean, Rev. C. P.
Dean, W. E.
Driver, M. A. J.?
Duckworth, Benj.
Sean, Saml. Esq.
Duckworth, W. J.
Dacus, Mrs. A. E.
Dean, S. A.
Dobbins, J. D. M.
Dickson, W. C.
Deavenport, Frances
Drake, James A.
Davis, William
Driver, James

Dean, Moses
Dean, Major J.
Davis, Edward
Dean, J. T.?
Dean, Mrs. Elizabeth
Earle, Maj. S. G.
Earle, E. J.
Estes, E. H.
Eurvy, R. H.
Elrod, Wm. Sr.?
Edgar, E. N.
Evette, J. F. J. (est.?)
Eaton, J. C.
Elliot, Mrs. Mary
Eaton, H. L.
Edwards, J. W.
Ellison, Mills
Elrod, E. B.
Ellison, J. E.
Estes, Larkin
Elrod, Cap. T.? H.
Elrod, R. O.
Elrod, Mrs. Elizabeth
Erskine, John
Eskew, W. T.?
Earle, B. J.
Erskine, Thomas
Elgan, J. M.
Elrod, W. B.
Elrod, Samuel
Elrod, John
Elrod, Elias
Elrod, David
Elrod, Rev. Philip
Elrod, Adam (Esq.?)
Elrod, R. T.?
Earle, Dr. J. W.?
Ellison, James
Ellison, James W.
Ellison, Hugh
Ellison, Matthew
Elrod, G. G.
Erskine, W. W.
Eskew, W. E.
Emerson, James (Esq.)
Elrod, Mrs. Dorcas
Earle, Dr. J. W.
Erskine, Capt. W.
Elrod, Do_k?
Elrod, G._G.
Earle, Elias
Emerson, Saml. J.?
Ellison, Amaziah
Evins & Griffin
Evins, Griffin & Co.
Evins, Dr. Alexander
Erskine, James
Findley, Jno. J.
Findley, Rebecha?
Fisher, Amaziah
Felton, Mrs. Mary
Fant, James R.
Fielding, Y.? B.
Featherston, J. W.
Freeman, M. F.
Fisher, Saml. S.?
Fant, Alfred
Fretwell, Capt. J. Y.
Felton, A.
Farmer, Jno. R.
Flemming, Richard
Fielding?, Jno. B.
Ford, Stephen
Ford, W. H.
Floyd, J. A.
Fant, O. H. P.
Findley, Mrs. Nancy
Fant, Abner
Felton, Mrs. Eliza
Fant, Abner (est.?)
Gilmer, Robert
Glenn, Capt. W. A.?
Gilmer, A. R.? N.

Gunnin, Jane Miss
Gunnin, Miss Sarah
Gregg, Hugh
Glover, Dr. B. W.
Giles, Dr. Robert
Gable, Levi
Gassaway, W. H.
Gassaway, Mrs. Margaret
Gentry, Zachariah
Grey?, Alexander
Gentry, Moody
Glenn, William Jr.?
Graham, A. J.
Gray, N. A.
Gambrell, Ora? (Asa)?
Griffin, Mrs. Sophia
Gambrell, Mrs. Sarah
Gambrell, James
Gambrell, James J.(S.?)
Greer, David
Greer, C. W.
Gilkerson, W. D.
Garrison, D. V.
Grubbs, R. W.
Greer, J. M.
Greer, B. C.
Gant, Hugh
Gambrell, Rev. J. M.
Gray, Miss Cynthia
Glines?, Mrs. Frances
Gambrell, Mrs. L. dec'd.
Gambrell, John
Gower, Cox & Gower
Griffin, Elijah
Graves, Joseph
Gambrell, P. M.
Gassaway, James
Garrett, C. W.
Geer, Thomas
Geer, So'lo? M.
Garrett, S.? H.
Garrett, Jesse
Guthrey, Nelson
Guthrey, Mrs. Mary
Garrett, Richardson
Guthrey, Benjamin
Guthrey, S.? B.
Garrett, Thomas
Garrett, W. C.
Gambrell, Matthew
Gore? Joshua
Gore?, Ralph
Gambrell, Ezekiel
Gambrell, James
Gambrell, Reid
Gambrell, James Jr.?
Glenn, F. M.
Golden, Rev. John
Guyton, Gen.? J. W.
Gentry, A. B.
Gentry, John
Gantt, Mrs. Jane
Gantt, Dr. J. G.
Gaines, Rev. Nathaniel
Green, W. W.
Glenn, B. F.
Gambrell, J. J.
Gambrell, H.? J.
Gray, Jesse
Garrett, Asa
Gambrell, M. T.?
Gaillard, J. D.
Gaillard, Miss M. D.
Gray, James A.
Gray, W. D.
Gambrell, Mrs. Susan
Garrett, Rev. S. L.
Guyton, Guyton
Geer, David
Glaspey, William
Gambrell, James Junr
Gambrell, Harper
Gaillard, Dr. C. L.

Gambrell, D. H.
Grubbs, John M. (Esq.)
Guyton, A. W.
Gilmore(Gilmer?), Major James
Crisop, E.
Gordon, Mrs. Agness
Griffin, John C.
Glenn, Mrs. Mary
Gambrelle, S.? V.?
Glenn, Capt. J. W.
Galloway, M. A.
Gordon, David
Haslet, Miss Sarah
Harris, Nathan
Haynie, Charles
Hall, J. G.
Hutchinson, J. A.
Hall, Johnston
Hill, Thomas O.?
Hill, Dr. Frank
Haley, Reuben
Hatten, William
Hall, M. H.
Hall, Zachariah (Esq.)
Hall, Samuel
Harris?, John
Hall, J. D.
Harkness, John N.
Hamilton, Mrs. Jane
Hamilton, Luke
Hall, Ezekiel
Hall, Lemuel
Hall, David
Hall, A. J.
Howard, Hiram
Howard, D. C.
Howard, George
Hall, Lent
Harrison, P. El_le?
Harrison, F. E.
Hughes, B. P.
Holland, Robt.
Holland, James N.?
Holland, Wm. Wm.?
Holland, Dr. N. H.
Holler, David
Holbrooks, Jesse
Holland, Benjamin
Herrin, Jesse
Harris, Andrew
Harris, B. B.
Harris, Joseph H.
Harris, Thomas M.
Haynie, Wm. H.
Harper, Asa
Harper, Newton
Haynie, William
Harper, Mrs. Mary
Hilhouse, Mrs. Harriet
Hicks, John
Hilhouse, Col. S.? P.
Hembree, J. H.
Hembree, A. D.
Haynie, Capt. Jno.
Haynie, Capt. J. C.
Herrin, E. E.
Haynie, R. B.
Hanks, Luke Jr.
Haynie, Luke
Haynie, James P.
Hawkins, Wm. P.
Hall?, James A.
Hawks, John
Hunt, John
Harper?, Wm. M.
Hogg?, Thompson
Harper, John H.
Harper, Wm. C.
Holland, Wm. Esq.
Hyde, Rev. E. F.
Hoke?, F. A. Esq.
Harkins, Hugh

Harper, Mrs. Nancy
Harkins, John
Hammond, Wm. N.
Holmes, William
Hammond, Col. H.
Hunter, Mrs. Sarah
Henderson, James
Hamilton, Col. D. R.
Holland, A. B.
Hendricks, Jno. M.
Hunt, William
Hall, Aaron
Herrin, William Jr.?
Haygood, J. M.
Hayne, W. A.
Hembree, A. F.
Hunter, John
Hicks, Bayles
Hicks, W. J.?
Holland, A. M.
Hammond, S. J. Est.
Hammond, S. J.
Harrison, W.
Hall, C. H.
Harkness, J. J.
Harkness, W. B.
Hamilton, C. E.
Hannah, J. T.
Hobson, E. G.
Hembree, M. B.
Harper, John
Harper, William & Co.
Hall, M. H.
Hardy, R. B.
Hardy, James
Hopkins, J. H.
Hembree, James
Hammond, J. W.
Harris, Wm. K.?
Hopkins, James M.
Horton, Jno. C. Esq.
Harris, Jos. P.
Harbin, Mrs. L.
Hanks, Thomas
Herrin, Frances dec'd.
Herrin, James M.
Hall, John B.
Harris, Ezekiel
Hammond, W. L.
Hammond, B. F.
Hall, W. S.
Humphrey, Rev. David
Hill, Joseph
Hicks, Josiah
Hicks, D. J.
Hicks, Pinckney
Hopkins, Dr. Jno.
Humphrey, S. C.
Hoke, D. & Jno. E.
Harrison, Gen. J. W.
Harlow, B. F.
Harrison, J. T.?
Hutchinson, B. F.
Harper, Thomas
Hacket, Albert
Husterson?, Robt.
Holland, Capt. Jno.
Hanks, Stephen
Hanks, Nimrod
Hall, William
Holcom, Hinton
Harris, Jno. M.
Hall, Wilson
Jones, James
Jones, William
Isbel, Rev. Saml.?
Johnston, Peter
Jenkins, Milly
Jolly, Henry
Jolly, James A.
Jolly, Joseph
Irwin, Mrs. Eleanor
Ingram, Mrs. Delila

416

Jones, Jesse S.?
Jones, Mrs. Happy
Jones, Willson
Johnston, James
Ingraham, W. dec'd.
Jones, Stephen
Johnston, Allen
Johnston, J. A.
Johnston, N. G.
Jones, W. L.
Jolly, Joseph M. dec'd.
Jolly, James
Jones, Rev. J. C.
Irby, Charles Esq.
Irby, Benjamin
Jordon, Harrison
Johnston, Mrs. H.
Jenkins, Dr. W. L.
Johnston, Capt. P. J.?
Jordon, Benson
Jolly, Levi
Jones, Jno. H.
King, Jno. J.
King, Wm. P.
Knauff, Wm. J.
Kelly, Mansel
Keaton, B. F.
Keaton, Welborn
Keaton, Reuben
Kay, R. G.
Kay, Mrs. Mary
King, J. A.
Kay, James E.
Kay, Wm. P.
Kay, Joel
Kay, Mrs. Susan
Kay, John B.
Kay, Mason
Kennedy, Saml.
Kelly, Mrs. Elizabeth
Kelly, Mrs. Mary
King, Rev. Robt.
King, Peter Jr.
King, James
King, Josiah
Kelly, J. B.
Kitsinger, R. S.
Kelly, Mrs. Sarah
Knox, John
Kates, Frances M. & N.
Keys, R. A.
kay, Strother
Kay, John
Kelly, Joseph
King, Col. Jno. D.
King & Richardson
Kay, A. W.?
Kennedy, Rev. J. L.
Kelly, Mrs. Sarah
Kay, Charles
Kay, F. M.
King, Robt. A.
King, Mrs. Nancy
King, Miss Martha
Keesler, Henry
Kelly, Capt. A. dec'd.
Kay, Jesse
Kay, Charles Jr.
Keys, James C.
Jay, C. W.
Kay, E. H.
Kay, W. M.
Keown, W. E.
Kelly, Jasper
King, Peter Junr.
Keown, G. W.
Lewis, Mrs. Elizabeth
Lathem, Mrs. Jane
Lathem, J. B.'
Lathem, W.
Ledbetter, G. M.
Ledbetter, D. A.
Lorton, J. S.?

Lewis, Mrs. J. P.
Liddle, Miss M. C.
Long, William
Long, Henry
Long, John
Long, George
Lee, Philip
Lusk, John
Ligen, Daniel
Lucius, Mrs. Axecy
Leavell, Rev. John
Lewis & Cox
Lewis, J. B.
Laboon, Joseph A.
Laboon, Mrs. Edith
Long, John
Long, Ezekiel
Long, Capt. James
Long, Ezekiel Jr.?
Lee, Dr. Thomas
Lewis, Jessee
Langston, Allison
Lou?, B. F.
Latta, James S.?
Lewis, E. B.
Lawrence, R. G.
Lee, W. C. Esq.
Long, Harrison
Leverett, Thomas
Lythgoe, Gen. George
McClinton, A. S.?
McCarly, R. B.
Massey, Silas Jr.?
McLeese, James
McLeese, Rev. Robt.
McLeese, Mrs. Rebecca
McConnell, David
McConnell, Wm. Jr.?
McGill, Miss M.? A.
McGill, Mrs. Mary
McAlister, O. B.
McAlister, Wm. A.?
Morgan, John
Martin, Mrs. Phoebe
McBride, J. S.
McCullough, D. _?
McKee, Wm. A.
McKee, Mrs. E.
McAlister, G. W.
McConnell, J. H.
McGee, Willis
McGee, Jessee
McMahan, B. S.?
Morgan, Thomas
McPhail, John Jr.?
McAlister, J. A.
Milford, Mrs. Mary
McMahan, Saml. Jr.
Macklin, Mrs. Harriet
McLeese, Andrew
McLeese, J. T.?
Martin, Matthew
Marat, W. M.
Maret, M. H.
Mahaffy, P. S.
Maxwell, Dr. S.? E.
McCrary, Mrs. Mary
McCrary, Albert
Miller, John
Martin, Jesse
Martin, W. J.
McKay, M. S.
Miller, S. F. W.
Morris, Samuel
Morris, R. M.
Major, Capt. J. W.
Mays, Medy
Morris, David J.
McCarly, Capt. H. W.?
McClesky, James Esq.
Major, Elijah
Major, Col. W. N.
Mitchel, G. W. L.

Martin, Samuel
Moore, Jeremiah
Martin, James
Mitchel, Willie
Mattison, John M.
May, G. W.
Mosely, Wesly
Massey, J. F. (Marion)
McAdams, John
Mattison, B. H.
Mattison, William
Mattison, Wyatt
Mattison, Mrs. Elizabeth
Mattison, Albert
Mattison, S. J.
Mattison, J. J.
Mattison, J. F.
Mattison, D. & J. F.
Mattison, Daniel
Mattison, J. R.
Milwee, Dr. Wm. B.
Martin, T. C.
McNeely, R. O.
Major, Mrs. Margaret
Major, H. B.
McDowell, G. Wm.
McGee, G. W.
Moore, G. A.
Moore, W.
Maddox, Tilman
McDavid, James
Major, William
Martin, T. W.
Major, E. J.
McMurtry, James
Morris, J. C.
Maddox, Thomas
McGee, J. P.
Mitchell, Caleb
Moore, Capt. J. B.
McFee, Mrs. Sally
Myers, W. J.
Martin, Sanford
Martin, Wm. Jr.?
McAlister, James
McAlister, Anna
McAlister, John
Murphy, Ezekiel Esq.?)
Martin, Jacob
Martin, W. C.
Martin, Sanford Junr.
Moore, Mrs. Elizabeth
Martin, J. C.
Martin, Chesly Junr.?
Murphy, John
Merrett, Obadiah
Murphy, Thomas M.
Moore, Thomas B.
Moore, John M.
McNeely, David
Moore, Elijah
Mulliken, Capt. Wm.
Maulden, _ucker
Martin, J. W.
Mulliken, James Esq.
Martin, Abram
Martin, Thomas H.
Martin, Miss Fanny
M _ten?, Michael
McAlister, W.
Martin, Stephen
McKinney, R. F.
McKinney, P. F.
McMurry, J. B.
McMurry, William
McKinney, O. P.
Morehead, Alex. Esq.
Morehead, John
Moore, Wm. J.
McPhail, Capt. Peter
McElroy, A. L.
McElroy, S. R.
Milwee, Mrs. S.? C.

417

Milwee, Saml. Est.
McKinney, Mrs. Martha
Meredith, Abraham
McCleland, Saml.
Morse, Rev. A. A.
Major, James A.
Maxwell, R. D.
Maverick, Samuel Est.
Maret, G. W.
McGee, Rev. Wm.
McMillian, W. A.
Mauldin, Rev. B. F.
Martin, John
Mouchet, Jacob
Martin, Robert
McClure?, E. J.
Mattison, Maj. C. S.
Mattison, Mrs. Mary K.
Manly, Mrs. M.
McCoy, Kelson?
Milford, Dr. Wm. J.
McFale, Mrs. Phebe
McAdams, Robinson
Martin, B. C.
McConnele, S. F.
Major, James C.
Major, J. W.
McAlister, Capt. N.
McCooley, Elijah
McGee, Capt. Elias
Masters, James H.
McCully, Stephen
Mosely, J. L.
McGee, W. S.?
McGee, L. H.?
McPhail, Elder John
Mitchel, B. S.
Martin, Chesley
McCown, John
McCown, James
McGukin, Hugh
Moore, W. S.
McGregor, J. W.
Moorhead, Maxey
Moorhead, M. L.
Mitchel, W. N.
Mitchel, Jno. F.
McGee, Michael
Miles?, Miss H.?
Major, Daniel
McCarty, Thomas
McCann, Col. S. H.
Maddox, W.
Mills, William
Martin, W. N.
Moore, Joseph
Maxwell, R. A.
Mays, W. D. M.
Mays, S.(J.?) E.
Martin, Col. Jno.
Mattison, Olley
McGee, W. H.
Milwee, W. A.
Milwee, Misses M. & E.?
McClellan, J.? & T.?
McAlister, A. B.
Milwee, Mrs. Sophia
McFall, Col. Jno.
Morgan, Bayles
Masters, P. A.
Mitchel, M. A.
Martin, Capt. J. R.
McGee, Mrs. Nancy
McGee, Elias
Morris, James
McFall, A. N.
Massey, Jno. C.
McBath, Dr. J. J.
Mulinax, Jno. B.
Mullikin, Mrs. Jane
Massey, Major
Neal, A. M.
Newell, Mrs. Jane

Newell, R. D.
Newton, Issaac
Newton, Samuel
Newton, Maj. L.
Newton, Willis
Nichols, A. D. dec'd.
Nichols, J. C.
Nichols, Mrs. Nancy
Noris, A. O. Esq.
Noris, Col. J. W.
Nevett, Capt. Wm.
Newton, J. W.
Norris, Capt. R. B.
Norris, J. T.?
Neal, Julian
Norris, Jno. E.
Norris, Mrs. Elvira
Norris, Col. J. W. Jr.
Norris, P. H. (K.?)
North, Mrs. Eliza
Norris, E. S. Esq.
Norris, Dr. W. C.
Newell, Jno. J.
Newell, Dr. N. J.
Obriant, William
Obriant, Mrs. Joicey
Owen, John
Oveby, Nicholas
Oldham, Thomas
Oldham, W.
Osheal, Seabron
Owen, Elijah
Owen, Miss Judah
Orr, Jno. B.
Orr, W. M.
Orr, Alexander
Orr, Thomas C.
Orr, William Jr.
Owen, Lewis
Orr, Thomas Jr.
Osborn, Hon. James L.
Oliver, Mrs. Martha
Osborn, L. A.
Partain, J. H.
Prince, J. Wm.
Presley, Rev. Jno. S.?
Presley, D. A.
Price, Pennel
Price, H.
Price, P. R.
Pickeral, Jonathan Esq.
Palmer, Wm. Sr.?
Palmer, Mattison
Pinckney, Roger
Pickens, Mrs. Mary
Prichard, Lewis
Pennell, Thomas
Philips, L. D.
Pettis, Mrs. Jane
Poor, Samuel
Poor, George
Poor, John B.
Poor, John
Poor, George
Poor, J. W.
Poor, Hampton
Poor, Mrs. Nancy
Pew, Polly
Poor, Holland
Pruitt, E. D.
Pickle, Wm. C.
Pickens, Col. Wm. S.
Pegg, James B.
Pegg, John
Pickle, William Jr.
Pickle, Jacob
Prater, Joseph
Pickens, Robt.
Pickens, R. A.
Pullen, W.
Prince, Mark
Philips, Archibald
Philips, W.?

Parker, Robert
Philips, Martin
Pearman, Benjamin
Pruitt, Mrs. Frances
Pruitt, Joshua
Parker, Mrs. M.
Pickle, C. W.
Pepper, Mrs. Sarah
Poor, Mrs. Nixa
Padget, J. A.
Petigrew, Robt.
Pinckney, Mrs. Eliza
Pendleton Factory Co.
Pickens, Hon. T. J.
Poor, Reuben dec'd.
Pool, W. H.
Pool, Mrs. Elizabeth
Powell, F. M.
Pepper, E. S.
Posey, Benjamin
Pruit?, William
Pruit?, Toliver
Pain, Lewis
Pickle, J. E.
Parks, Thomas
Rainey, W. H.
Reid, Miss Elizabeth
Reid, Andrew Esq.
Reid, Dr. J. H.
Reid, Mrs. Sarah
Rice, James F.
Rampy, S. J.
Rice, H.
Rice, T.(S.?) L. dec'd.
Rice, Rev. A.
Robinson, Mrs. Jane
Ranson, William Jr.
Reid, Moses
Reid, Jesse
Ross, Rev. A. W.
Robinson, Willis
Robinson, Mrs. Jane
Rolletter, John
Richie, Jabes
Richie, J. S. P.
Rowland, William
Reeves, R. W.
Reeves, J. A.
Richardson, J. T.
Rawson, R. H.
Robinson, Capt. J. E.
Robinson, Col. James
Robinson, Mrs. L. M.
Robertson, John B.
Reece, Mrs. Elizabeth
Ritchie, James W.
Ragsdale, F. A.
Reece, Mrs. Sarah
Razor, Ezekiel (Roger?)
Rochester, Nathaniel
Reid, George M.
Reily, B.
Rogers, David
Reeves, Mrs. Elizabeth
Roberts, Matthias
Rainwater?, D. C.
Rice, A. E.
Reimer, Mrs. Lucinda
Richardson, A. W.
Rogers, J. D.
Rogers, Larkin
Rogers, Joseph S.
Rogers, John
Rogers, W. W.
Rogers, O. B.
Richardson, N. T.?
Richardson, Jno. & Noah
Richardson, Sion T.?
Richardson, Matthias
Rily, Abraham
Rosamond, John
Recks, Mrs. Sarah
Reeks, John G.

Rankins, Thomas F.
Robinson, David
Robinson, Dr. William
Rankins, Mrs. Mary
Rankins, Miss E. B.
Rankins, Miss M. P.
Rankins, Miss M. J.
Rankins, Miss Mary A.
Rankins, Col. G. W.
Ritchie, J. N.
Reid, Capt. J. P.
Russel, Maj. T. H.
Razor?, E.
Reid, Thomas L.
Ragsdale, D. F.
Reid, A. E.
Reid, A. E. & T.? L.
Robinson, John dec'd.
Rogers, J. P.
Rogers, Mrs. Elizabeth
Rogers, H. P.
Rogers, Robert
Rampley, Rev. W.
Ritchie, R. C.
Robins, Jessee
Rogers, Mrs. Hester
Rice, F.
Roof, George
Ritchie, Wilson
Ritchie, Mrs. Mary
Randell, Col. Carver
Rogers, William
Ritchie, Reubin
Skelton, Thos. S.(T.?)
Skelton, Mrs. Elizabeth
Stewart, George
Stewart, Adam
Strickland, Ansel
Stevenson, George
Sullivan, Kelly Esq.
Seiglet?, John
Speed, Dr. Wm. J.
Speed, James M.
Speer, E. H.
Saddler, David
Saddler, Jno. F.
Stevenson, E. J.
Steuart, John
Steuart, J. W.
Simpson, W.
Sanders, A. N.
Sanders, Miss Sarah
Sanders, Elias
Simpson, Archibald
Simpson, Robert
Simpson, Thomas
Stevenson, Andrew
Simpson, W. J.
Stevenson, Thomas
Simpson, James
Sherrard, J. W.
Sherrard, Mrs. Jane
Sherrard, William
Symmes, Arthur
Scott, David
Stewart, James
Stewart, John
Sanders, Capt. W.
Simpson, W. L.
Simpson, James L.
Simmonds, Rev. David
Simmonds, Charles
Simmonds, James Jr.?
Simmonds, C. H.
Shanklin, J. V.
Swords, John
Symmes, Dr. F. W.
Simpson, W.
Scott, Mrs. Narcissa
Simpson, J. L.
Steele, James
Smith, Daniel
Spruile, Simeon

Spruil, Mrs. Nancy
Smith, Capt. Aaron
Smith, N. T.?
Smith, Mrs. M. E.
Scott, M. B.
Sherrard, Gillam
Smith, Samuel
Shirley, J. W.
Shirley, B. T.?
Shirley, John
Seawright, Mrs. Margaret
Strickland, Matthew
Saylors, Jno. N.
Shirley, Obadiah
Shirley & Lewis?
Shirley, Capt. Jno.
Shaw?, J. H.
Strickland, M. S.
Smith, Joel
Smith, John G.
Smith, R. S.
Snipes, J. R.
Sitton, John
Stone, Hampton
Stone & Armstrong
Smith, J. C.
Smith, A. C. & J. D.
Smith, James dec'd.
Smith & Sullivan
Stevenson, A.
Smith, A. W.
Smith, J. J.
Stringer, A. J.
Smith, W.
Smith, Samuel
Smith, James M.
Smith, John G.
Smith, Aaron
Smith, Mrs. Maria
Smith, W. N.
Spearman, David D.
Spearman, B. J.
Spearman, F. A.
Spearman, David
Stone, George
Spence, Robt.
Spence, Robt. Jr.
Sin_t_?, Simion
Smith, G. S.
Scott, W. H.
Smith, Caleb M.
Smith, H. G.
Smith, A. A.
Smith, Andrew
Sitton, William
Sitton, W. D. Esq.
Satterfield, Jerimias
Sitton, J. P.
Spain, Andrew
Stanton, Miss M. W.
Siddell, John
Sherman, Mrs. Mary
Smith, Griffin
Smith, P. E.
Spiller, Rusel
Smith, Joshua
Smith, Pannell
Smith, Ebenezer
Stevenson, Andrew
Stevenson, Jno. J.
Smith, Mrs. Mary
Smith, A. J.
Shirley, Stephen
Stone, W. H.
Shirly, Aaron
Stanton, C. B.
Slaton, G. P.
Simpson, Sanford
Smith, A. M.
Steele, R. A.
Smith, William
Stevenson, James
Shirley, James

Stringer, L. D.
Sloan, McGee & Co.
Simpson, R. G.
Skelton, J. W. B.
Smith, W. C.
Smith, Mrs. S. E[A.
Smith, B. S.
Smith, Miss E. H.
Smith, Mrs. S. E. N. Est.
Smith & Cheatham
Stott, D. M.
Steuart, James
Smith, Robt. S.
Shirley, Marion
Stevenson, Robert
Shearer, Andrew
Steifer, Dr. G. F.
Seaborn, Maj. George
Smith, Mrs. Sarah
Sloan, Mrs. Susan Est.
Sloan, B. F.
Sitton, Jno. B.
Stone, W. C.
Simpson, Hon. R. F.
Smith, J. E.
Spearman, Mrs. Margaret
Smith, Wyatt
Smith, J. B.
Smith, Jesse R.
Shubick?, Ed T.?
Smith, S. D.
Smith, J. G.
Smith, M. H.
Snipes, Matthew
Skelton, A. B.
Simpson, D. M.
Saylor, John
Shaw, W. S.
Taylor, James
Taylor, Toliver
Tucker, Dejarnet
Tucker, Harrison
Tucker, Capt. J. P.
Tucker, William
Tucker, Mrs. Nancy
Thompson, Col. James
Tucker, James
Trimiers, T. G.
Tate, William
Todd, Andrew Esq.
Todd, Mrs. Olive
Trible, Richard
Taylor, Col. D. S.
Ta_no, William
Terry, Henry
Tate, Grief
Tribble, Capt. L. W.
Taylor, W. J.
Telford, W.
Turner, G. W.
Todd, R. W.
Thompson, James
Thompson, Beverly
Tripp, Mrs. Ann
Trustle, Posey dec'd.
Todd, Capt. W. P.
Tranynham, W. P.
Telford, James
Telford, R. C.
Todd, Dr. James A.
Telford, J. H.
Telford, G. B.
Tripp, Nicholas
Tompkins, John
Trany_m, M. F.? H.
Tower, Capt. Joel
Tims, Isaac
Taylor, Elizabeth
Todd, James
Taylor, Mrs. Nancy
Taylor, Dr. J. W.
Thomson, Dr. A. E.
Tilly, L. M.

Towns, W. W.
Teague, Elijah
Thomson, Mrs. Sarah
Tims, Elijah
Todd, Mrs. Mary
Tate, W. M.
Todd, Robt.
Vandiver, E. & E.
Vandiver, William
Vandiver, Capt. E.
Voyles, Amos
vandiver, Aaron
Vanwyck, S. M.
Vanwyck, Wm.
Vandiver, F.? A.
Vandiver, A. W.
Williford, C. K.
Williford, Mrs. Sarah
West, Robert
Winter, James C.
Welbanks, Elijah
Welbanks, Henry
Watts, Saml. S.
Watts, J. W.
Watts, Joseph S.
Willie, James
Watts, J. D.
Wharton, W. L.
Wakefield, John
Wattis, R. R. dec'd (Watts)
Whitman, Jacob
Walker, James A.
West, S.(T.?) W.
Wright, Mrs. Catherine
Wooten, James
White, Yancy
Whitefield, Lewis
Wright, William
Watkins, Felix
Watkins, William
Watkins, Mrs. Jane
Watkins, Joseph dec'd.
Watkins, Col. T.? C.
Wilson, J. N.
Wilborn, Lemuel
Watter, Mrs. Elvira
Wilborn, Mrs. Caroline
Wideman, T.?(F.?) A.
Wright, T. T.?
Wright, James C.
Wilmson, Mrs. R.
Wilmson, Mastin
Webb, Andrew
Webster, Mrs. Jane
Williams, Humphrey
Wilson, George
Wilson, James
Wilson, M. R.
Wilson, Capt. Hugh
Wilson, Dr. John
Wilson, James Sr.?
Wilborn, Thomas
Wilborn, Aaron
Wilborn, Col. W. E.
Williams, Austin
Williams, Miss H. A.
Williams, John
Wilson, Mrs. Elijah
Williams, Jasper
Willingham, John
Wardlaw, H. H.
Wardlaw, H. C.
Webb, Elijah Esq.
Webb, James
Webb, Samuel
Wallins?, W. C.
Williams, Capt. M.? B.
Welborn, Mrs. Sarah
Wilson, James B.
Wilborn, Col. A. G.
Waddle, William
Woodson, William
Wadsworth, Robt.

Wardlaw, Jesse
Wardlaw, David
Watson, Andrew P.
Wardlaw, J. M.
Wilborn, J. M.
Wilson, Rev. J. J.
Watkins, Baylos
Watkins, Jeptha
Wilson, Hugh Jr.
Wigington, John
Wilson, W. M.
Wilson, W. M. Jr.
Watkins, W. H.
White, Batholemew
White, H. N.
Wilborn, E. C.
Whitaker, L. D.
Wynnes, Franklin
Wilson, William
Wyatt, Col. James F.
Wyatt, Elijah
Walters, Mrs. Mary
Waters, Rebecca
Wyatt, R. G.
Watson, W. A.
Webb, Mrs. E. D.
Wilson, Rev. James
Wells, Thomas
Walker, J. S.
Wilborn, A. F.
Williams, Jno. L.
Williamson, James
Watson, J. M.
Wilborn, Wesley
Woodson, Tucker
Williams, James C.
Wilson, Robt.
Whitaker, H. H.
Warnock, John
Webb, Elisha
Wanslow, Dabner
Williams, W.
Walker, Rev. A. W.
Williams, John Est.
Wilson, Jeptha
Webb, Mrs. Elizabeth
Webb, C. G.
Webb, Dr. Edward
Watson, D. K.
Wallis, Mrs. Sarah
Wilson, W. D.
Williams, Ora C.
Whitner, Hon. J. N.
Watson, Jno. B.
Watson, Mrs. Mary
Willifred, S. W.
Wright, R. N. Esq.
Watson, David M.
Wakefield, Conrad
Westmorland, S. (J.?) L.
Webb, D. H.
Wilborn, William
Williams, James E.(C.?)
Wilson, John
Wiley, J. H.
Watson, John A.
Wootson, Allen
Watkins, David
Young, William

IN THE CITY OF PENDLETON:
Knauff, Wm. J.
Maxwell, Dr. S. E.
Bellotte, J. E. & Co.
Barnes, C. V.
Cobb, E. M.
Campbell, A. C.
Campbell, Collins dec'd.
Hall, J. C.
Hodge, Mrs. Mary
Franklin, (Shanklin) J.V.
Symmes, Dr. F. W. dec'd.
Starks, Mrs. E. dec'd.

Sharpe, Mrs. E.
Sharpe, Elam
Sharpe, Dr.? M. L.
Hunter, James
Hunter, Miss Mary
Hastie, Dr. John
Gaillard, W. H. D.
Gailaird, W. H. D. & Co.
Gailard, Mrs. R. W.
Stephens, Mrs. M. O.
Lorton, John S. & Co.
Miller, Miss Charlot
Miller, Miss Jane
Wilson, Mrs. Martha
Calhoun, Mrs. F.
Blue Ridge R. R. Co.
Calhoun, Mrs. Martha
Campbell, T.? E.
Smith, J. D. & Co.
Lorton, John S.
Cherry, G. R.
Cherry, S. S.
Taylor, Col. D. S.
Washington, J. J.
Vanwyck, W.
Maverick, Saml. Est.
Alexanda, Col. Elijah
McBride, Rev. Dr.
Benson, E. B.
Jenkins, Dr. W. L.
Gilreath, Miss Mary
Sloan, B. F.
Sloan, J. B. E. & Co.
Sitton, Jno. B.
Pendleton Hotel Co.
Maxwell, Dr. Jno. H.
Pickens, Dr. T. J.
Sloan, Mrs. Nancy
Earle, Maj. S. G.
Earle, Mrs.? E. J.
Tucker, Dejarnet
Reid, Dr. J. H.
Earle, C. E.
Simmonds, Rev. David
Haynie?, W. H.
Todd, Archibald
Webb, Elijah
Earle, B. J.
Moore, Maj. Jno. V.
Norris, Dr. Jno. T.
Pegg, James B.
Reid, Capt. J. P.
Sloan, Jo Berry
Sloan & McGowen
Sloan, Col. W.
Milwee, John
Russel, David
Russel, Maj. T. H.
Crawford, Capt. Saml.
Morse, Rev. A. A.
Carpenter, John
Roberts, Benj'a
Vanwyck, Wm.
Holland, A. M.
Holland & Sherrard
Bradley, Mrs. Frances
Peyton, Amazaih
Peyton, Richmond
Bogley, Maj. J. T.
Anderson, David
Murray, E. F[
Wilhite, Dr. P. A.
White, David
McCully, Stephen
George, Ezekiel
Clinkscales, Col. A.
McFall & Hammond
George, John
Whitaker, H. H.
Osborn, L. A.
Riley, Mrs. Ruth
Taylor(Saylor?) & Simpson
Earle, Mrs. Elizabeth

420

Earle, C. E.
Johnston, Elder W. B.
Sloan, Col. Jno. S.?
Fant, G. W.
Gilmer, Maj. James
Webb, Dr. Edward
Arnold, H. B.
Arnold, L. S.? & Co.
Arnold, L. S.?
Bosselle?, Col. F. C. V.
Rice, F.
Walker, J. S.
Wilkes., Gen. S. M.
Orr, Hon. J. L.
Wright, W. T.?
Sampson, Josepheus B.
Hubbard, R. H.
Whitefield, Joseph T.?
Sullivan & Sloan
Sullivan, Capt. N. K.
Earle, Elias
Crayton, Thomas S.?
Crayton, B. F.
Crayton, B. F. & T.? S.
Whitridge, Hon. Jos. N.
Harrison, Gen. J. W.
Cater, Dr. A. P.
Watson, Jno. B. & Co.
Watson, Jno. B.
Smith, Jesse R.
Smith & Clark
Sharpe, W. S.
Clark, J. B.
Osborn, W. M.
Osborn & Harrison
Parker, W. F.
Parker, Langston & Webb
Peyton, Joberry
Byrum, Peter L.
Harlow, B. F.
White & Wynn
Williamson, Elisha
Wilhite, Dr. P. A. & Co.
Horton, C. E. & Co.
England, Bleckley & Co.
England, J. E.
Miller, J. D. (Muller?)
Williams, Mrs. Martha
Langston, Capt. C. C.
Burress, Elder Jas.?
Benson, Mrs. C.
Benson's, Jno. P. Est.
Hering, A.
Sloan, Jno. B.
Evins, Dr. Alex
Gordon, Mrs. Agnes
Leper?, M.
Murray, Elder J. Scott
Towers, A. B.
Towers & Sloan
Garrison, Henry
Golden, Elder Jno.
Dr. Evins & Brown
Evins, Dr. T.? A.
Horsey, Jno. R.
Langston, S. H.
Wearne & Robinson
Wearne, Richard
Williamson & Brown
Lythgoe, Gen. George B.
Whitaker, Hugh G.
Wilson, Jno.
Broyles, Dr. O. R.
Brown, S.? & E. W.
Horton, Grief
Brown, W. J.
Brown, Daniel
Waller, Miss M. M.

Filed the 25th day Dec. 1857

Able, Jno.
Alexander, R. B.
Ashley, J. R.
Adams, J. C.
(next two names blurred)
Ashley, Eld. Wilson
Adams, Capt. James
Ashley, Jno.
Ashley, Joshua
Ashley, Jno. T.?
Alewine, Jac.
Alewine, W.? M.
Armstrong, N. H.
Armstrong, James
Armstrong, Miss M. & E. E.
Armstrong, Wm.
Armstrong, J. B. Estate
(these last three above
may not be Armstrong...
writing very blurred.)
Acker, Capt. J. S.
Allen, Mrs. Mary
Ashley, Jno.
Acker, J. J. & E. H.
Acker, J. J.
Acker, Amos
Anderson, T. F.
Allen, Willis
Allen, Capt. W. H.
Abanatha?, A. L.
Acker, P. G.
Anderson, D. F.
Anderson, R. Q.?
Archar?, W. M.
Avery, Eld. Asa
Anderson, T. H.
Alexander, Mrs. Anna
Arnold, L. T.
Anderson, Capt. W.
Anderson, Rich'd. H.
Anderson & Co.?
Anderson, Mrs. Mary
Anderson, Miss? A. V.?
Anderson, W. H.
Anderson, Miss? A. H.
Alexander, Wm. O.
Armstrong, Jno. R.
Armstrong, James Est.
Armstrong, C. C.
Adger, Eld. J. B.
Adger, Robt.
Adger, J. E.
Archer, R. C.
Ashmore, Col. J.? D.
Armstrong, Arch'd Est.?
Archer, Capt. J. S.?
Archer, Halbert
Acker, W. H. Est.?
Armstrong, J. B. Est.
Beaty, Thomas
Beaty, Mrs. (Miss?) Sarah
Brown, Mrs. Charity
Briant, Jno. L.
Buchanan, Capt. Leml.?
Bozeman, D. T.
Boyel, R. N.
Beaty, David
Beaty, J. S.?
Beaty, R. R.
Burton, P. T.?
Burress, Joshua
Burton, Mrs. J. S.?
Brown, Dr. Jasper
Brown, J. M.
Banister, James
Burress, Mrs. Sarah
Bulman?, W. H.
_____, A. A.
_____rett, Charles
_____rett, S.

_____rett, Jno. J.
Bradberry, Salatheil Jr.?
Barton, Eld. H. M.
Bradberry, Sla'a. Sr.
Bradberry, Anderson
Bruce, J. J.
Brown, Saml.
Brown, Vandiver & Co.
Brown, Jordan
Brown, Maj. Larkin
Brown, Saml.
Bishop, Miss J. & D.
Bellotee, T. D.
Blackman, Z. D.
Brixon?, Charles
Bragwell, Mrs. Nancy
Bell, Wm.
Branian, R. H.
Bagwell, James
Bagwell, Pleasant
Brock, A. F.
Brock, Hayden
Brock, J. H.
Brock, H. N.
Burts, Mitchell
Burres, B. F.
Branian, T. B.
Barmore, W. C.
Barmore, Miss M. M. (W.?)
Brock, Anderson B.
Barkley, Josiah
Barkley, E. H.
Barkley, George R.
Balentine, Jes.(Jos.?) H.
Blake, Miss? Esther
Blake, Caleb
Bennett, Wm.
Bennett, Mrs. Rhoda
Broyles, Maj. J. T.?
Barnett, Maj. D. J.
Berry, Dr. M. G.
Breazeale, Mrs. Nancy
Breazeale, Miss. M. P.
Breazeale, E. Wm.
Breazeale, Matthew Esq.?
Breazeale, W. Est.
Boreland, A. D.? heirs of
Wilson (Bowland?)
Branian, J. A.
Breazeale, D. K.
Breazeale, Mrs. Lucy
Breazeale, Griffin
Balentine, G. N.
Brown, Dr. W. C.
Brown & Cobb
Breazeale, S. H.
Brock, J. E.
Beaty, J. W.
Brown, C. H.
Brown, C. B.
Breazeale, Kenion
Bowland, A. D.
Byrane?, Jos. L.
Branian, J. J.
Briant, Simon
Beaty, C. S.
Bowen, W. J.
Brock, James
Brock & Gantt
Burress, Reuben
Burress, Capt. Wm.
Burress, Levi Jun.?
Burress, Pinckney
Brown, P. R.
Brookes, Asbury
Brown, Miss Elvira
Brown, Miss Martha
Bu_n?, Mrs. Matilda
Burkhead, Eld. DeWitt
Briant, Terrell

Briant, B. R.
Braint, Wm.
Briggs, Russell
Blassengame, Mrs. Sarah
Blassengame, D. W.
Bowen, Robt.
Barr, Jno.
Blassengame, R. E.
Briant, Mrs. Maxsey?
(Massey?)
Barr, G. D.
Burdoine, Eld. Jno.
Boggs, J. L.
Boggs, Jno. A.
Boggs, J. C.
Barr, Le__?
Berry, M. C. & S. M.
Burgess, J. W.
Burgess, Jan'_ B.
Burgess, Milford
Bruce, Mrs. S.
Brown, J. J.
Bruce, Jno.
Bolt, Asa
Bolt, Wm.
Brown, Saml.
Bagwell, Mrs. Maria
Breazeal, B. B.
Brown?, S. F.
Brown?, S. F. & Co.
Burres?, G. W.
Bowen, Elijah
Bailey, Wm. B.
Brown, Mrs. S. R.
Bruce, S. G.
Belcher, Manning
Barrett?, Isaac
Bowers, S.
Bailey, Wm.
Burress, Wm.
Baker, Mrs. Marg't?
Burress, Levi Jr.?
Burress, Wm. R.
Bruce, Thomas
Brown, Mrs. P.
Brown, Miss J. C. Est.
Bellotte, Peter E.
Bellotte, M. A. Est.
Bellotte, J. E. & M. A.
Bellotte, J. E.
Ba__, Mrs. L.
Bailey, R. S.
Braddy, Lorton?
Broyles, Dr. O. R.
Burdett, G. F.
Burdett, Hyram
Brownlee, W. A.
Brackenridge, Robert
Boroughs?, Eld. Bryan?
Buchanan, Wm. M.
Beatie, J. S.
Beatie, R. R.
Burress, Eld. Joe?
Burress, J. M.
Breazeale, F. M.
Black, Jno.
Baker, W. L.
Bird, Martin
Brown, Elias
Brown, Dan'l
Browning, John (Jehn?)
Catlet, Jno.
Cook, Dr. A. G.
Campbell, T. G.
Casey, Miss Malinda
Casey, Miss Delila?
Casey, Miss Sarah
Clinkscales, Col. Abner
Craft?, J. M.
Cunningham, R. L.

422

Clinkscales, L. N.
Clinkscales, Mrs. Mary
Clinkscales, T. L.
Clinkscales, Fleetwood
Cromer, Philip
Campbell, W. J.
Campbell, Mrs. Sarah
Cox, Jno.
Cromer, Ja's?
Capeheart, Mrs. Sarah
Cox, Capt. F.? L.
Clark, H.
Cunninghall?, T. J. Est.
Cox, Mrs. Jane E.
Cates, Dr. J. J.
Clark, Henry
Craig, Saml.
Craig, D. J. B.
Chastain, J. B.
Chastain, James
Clinkscales, Jno.?
Crawford, Henry
Cox, Miss M. A.
Cox, Miss S. J.
Cooper, Mrs. Malissa
Calahan, J. R.
Cowan, Mrs. Eliz'th
Cullen, Caleb
Clement, Mrs. Pricilla
Cobb, Ephraim
Callaham, Wm.
Cobb, H. A.
Cummins, Robt.
Cummins, Wm.
Cox, Thos.
Cox, Mrs. Frances
Cox, Aris
Cox, Jno.
Clement, J. J.
Cummins, David
Campbell, Elihu
Clatworthy, T. J.
Copeland, J. J.?
Cobb, Robinson
Cooker, Berry
Cooker, Joseph
Cox, W. Wm.
Cox, James
Cox, Mrs. Elizabeth(2)
Cox, W. D.
Cooley, Mrs. Lucinda
Cox, Jno. M.
Cox, James M.
Cox, M. G.
Cox, Capt. S. J.
Cox, David
Chapman, C. T.?
Cooley, Hiram
Cooley, Dr. H. C.
Clement, Capt. W. K.?
Crymes, Mrs. Nancy
Cotes, Mrs. Milly
Cox, J. A. J.
Campbell, A. B.
Crymes, B. F.
Carte, Caleb (Catte?)
Carte, Wm. F.   "
Cooley, M.(W.?) M.
Cobb, Martin
Cobb, El_hanah
Cox, Abner
Cox, Miss R. E.
Chamblee, Moses
Chamblee, Elisha
Cobb, Dr. M. C.   ch.?
Cox, Col. G. Wm.
Cox, W. H.
Cox, Thos. Est.
Campbell, Alfred
Campbell, Austin
Cox, Asa
Crawford, David
Crawford, James

Cooley, E. T.?
Caldwell, Jos.
Cunningham, Col. J. J.
Cunningham, Mrs. Eliz'th
Campbell, A. D. & J. L.
Carte, Ruben
Clardy, Joab M.
Cason, J. A.
Cason, J. H.
Cason, Mrs. Esther
Cason, J. A. M.
Coates, Anthony
Clardy, N. S.
Childress, J. B.
Cooper, G. W.?
Ciely, Thos.
Ciely, W. M.
Carpenter, Eld. F. G.
Coleman, Robt.
Carlisle, Eld. W.
Carlisle, L. A.
Chamblee, J. B.
Chamblee, J. M.
Chamblee, D. S.
Chamblee, Jno. Est.
Coates, Jno.
Chamblee, Z. B.
Clark, Mrs. Jane
Cox, Mrs. Margt.
Cox, Miss M. E.
Chamblee, James Z.
Cromer, Lewis
Carpenter, Jno.
Cromer, Elijah
Cox, Mrs. Martha
Cox. J. J.
Carpenter, Mrs. S. C.
Clinkscales, Rueben
Cook, J. T.
Cook, Wm. Est.
Cannon, Ephraim Est.
Cox, Joseph Esq.
Cox, Joseph & Abner
Crymmes, Edward
Crayton, B. F.
Cottrell, W. W.
Cater, Dr. A. P.
Carlisle, J. S.
Cason, W. A.
Chesner?, Dr. R. S.
Cow___, G. W.
Cowan, Capt. J. A.
Campbell, W. W.
Cochran, Robt.
Creswell, Mrs. Sarah
Cooley, J. J.
Campbell, George Jr.?
Campbell, Alex.
Campbell, G. J.?
Cobb, J. A.
Dickward, W.
Dunlap, Matthew
Davis, Edward
Deal, S. D.
Darby?, George
Dixon, Maj. Wm.
Dobbins, James Est.
Douthit, B. H.
Dickson, James
Dickson, Thomas
Darricott, Herbert
Drake, E. H.
Deal, F. A.
Davis, Charles
Davis, Eld. W.
Davis, W. K.
Dunlap, Jno.
Davis, J. H.
Donald, D. L.
Davis, Jno. L.
Davis, J. L. & D. W.
Davis, Moses
Davis, M. A.

Duckworth, J. J.
Davis, W. L.
Davis, Mrs. H. O. & Miss
    Jane
Dawkins, Wm.
Dailey, Jno.
Dalrymple, Lewis
Dean, Moses
Douthit, J. G.
Dean, Capt. B. D.
Dean, R. B.
Dobbins, A. C.
Dobbins, J. T.
Duckworth, A. A.
Duckworth, Benj'n
Duckworth, Wilborn
Durham, Miles
Douthit, Mrs. Susannah
Douthit, Mrs. Emily
Davis, Rich'd
Wilworth, A. A.
Dilworth, Benj'n
Dickson, T. J.
Dougan, Maj. Robt.
Dickson, W. C.
Duckworth, B. Wm.
Duckworth, W. R.
Dacus, Mrs. Anna
Davis, Charles
Davinport, Francis
Dean, Saml. A.
Dean, Mrs. Eliz'th
Dalrymple, Jno.
Dobbins, J. D. M.
Driver, M. A. J.
Driver, James
Dean, Col. T.? J.
Drake, James A.
Drake, J. L. minors
Dean, Eld. C. P.
Duncan, Capt. B. F.
Davis, Benj.
Duckworth, W. J.
Durham, W. C.
Duncan, David
Davenport, H. B.
Davenport, W. M.
Every, R. A.
Elrod, J. W.
Erskins, James
Eaton, Jos. C.
Eaten, J. C. & Co.
Eaten, H. L.
Ellison, Miles
Ellison, Greenleaf
Elrod, Mrs. E.
Elrod, R. O.
Elrod, E. B.
Elrod, A. F.
Elrod, Capt. T. H.
Ellison, Capt. Joel
Ellison, A.
Ellison, Wm.
Erskine, Thos.
Erskine, J. J.
Elliott, Emily
Eskew, W. E.
Earle, Maj. E. J.
Earle, Mrs. E. M.
Earle, C.? E. Est.
Earle, Dr. J. W.
Elrod, Saml.
Elrod, Wm. D.
Elrod, G. C.
Estes, Larkin
Estes, J. J.
Elrod, G. W.
Elrod, Elias
Ellis, Mrs. Sarah
Elrod, E. W.
Elrod, Mrs. S. O.
Elrod, R. T.
Elrod, J.? S.

Ellison, James
Ellison, J. W.
Ellison, Hugh
Ellison, Matthew
Earle, Dr. J. Wm.
Elrod, J. Y.
Elrod, Capt. W. A.
Elgin, J. S.?
Erskine, Mrs. M. M.
Emerson, James Esq.
Emerson, S.? J.
Earle, J. B.
Earle, Elias
Earle, E. P.
Earle, Miss F. L.
Erskine, W. W.
Evins, & Griffin
Evins, Dr. J. A.
Elrod, D. D.
Eskew, W. T.
Fisher, S. S.
Fisher, Amaziah
Fant, James R.
Fisher, Miss C. C.
Featherston, L. P.
Flemming, Rich'd
Fant, Alfred
Fretwell, Capt. J. Y.
Freeman, M. F.
Findley, Robt.
Findley, Jno.
Fisher, T.? M.
Floyd, James
Ford, Stephen
Ford, W. H.
Fielding, H. B.
Fielding, J. W.
Fielding, J. B.
Fielding, W. H.
Fant, O. H. P.
Felton, A.
Findly, Mrs. Nancy
Gray, James A.
Giles, Dr. Robt.
Gable, Levi
Gassaway, Mrs. Mary
Gentry, Moody
Gray, A. D. Esq.
Garrison, Mrs. L. G.
Gibert, Peter
Gilmer, Maj. James
Graham, A. J.
Grubbs, Jno. M. Esq.
Grubbs, Maj. W. M.
Gilbreath, Miss Mary
Gray, Jesse
Griffin, Mrs. Sophia
Green, M. P.
Glenn, Col. W. A.
Geer, L. N.
Green, W. W. Est.
Garrison, D. O.?
Gantt, Hugh
Gambrell, James
Gambrell, Enock
Green, N. A.
Grubbs, R. W.
Gaines, Eld. Nathaniel
Gambrell, Jno. Jr.?
Gambrell, Harper
Gambrell, James
Gambrell, Ez Re?
Gibbs, W.
Greer, Danl.
Glasby?, W.
Gan(r?)ett, Rich'd
Good, S. D.
Gambrell, M. T.?
Griffin, Elijah
Griffin, J. F.
Gassaway, James S.
Geer, S. M.
Geer, David

Galliard, Elder C. L.
Gambrell, J. J.?
Gentry, Jno.
Gantt & Trayham
Gantt, Dr. J. G.
Glenn, Wm. Jr.
Glenn, J. F.
Glenn, G. T.?
Guthrie, Nelson
Ganett, W. C.
Guthrie, Benj'n
Garrett, Mrs. C.
Garrett, Jno.
Gambrell, James Sr.?
Gambrell, Reid
Gambrell, Matthew
Gambrell, J. M.
Ganett, Mrs. Mary
Ganett, Jesse
Gambrell, James Jr.
Glenn, F. M.
Glenn, B. F.
Garrett & Ball
Garrett, W. B.
Guyton, Genl.? J. Wm.
Guyton, Mrs. Margt.
Glenn, Miss M. E.
Geer, Mrs. Elizabeth
Goodlet, S. D.
Gilkerson, J. G.
Greer, Jno. M.
Gambrell, S. O.?
Gray, Mrs. Damaris
Guyton, A. W.
Geer, Thos.
Gilmer, Robt.
Gordon?, Mrs. Jane M.
Glenn, Mrs. M. A.
Gentry, Wm. Jno. (Mrs.?)
Gunnin, Miss Sarah
Gambrell, D. H.
Gambrell, H. J.
Gambrell, Wm.
Gambrell, P. M.
Garrett, Eld. S. L.
Gray, Miss Nancy
Gaines, T. W.
Griffin, Jno. C.
Griffin, J. C. & Co.
Guyton, Guyton
Gray, Jas. M? & Wornin?
Gregg, Hugh
Gilmer, A. R. N.
Glenn, Mrs. Mary Est.
Glenn, Col. A. H.
Glenn, Miss M. E.
Glenn, Miss M. C.
Harris, Nathan'l
Hewins, Wm. Jr.
Hatten, Wm. Est.
Hill, Thos. O.
Hill, Dr. D. F.
Havard, Mark Wm.
Hall, Fenton
Hutchinson, B. F.
Hutchinson, Capt. J. A.
Hall, A. M.
Hutchinson, R. B.
Hall, Johnston
Hall, Ezekiel
Hall, B. D.
Hall, Jno. G.
Hall, A. J.
Hamilton, Mrs. Jane
Hall, Zachariah
Hall, H. M.
Harkness, J. J.
Hamilton, Luke
Hall, Jno.
Hall, Josiah
Harkness, J V.?(J. N.?)
Hale,(Hall?), A. M.
Howard, D. C.

Howard, Hiram
Hall, Lent
Hall, Martin
Howard, George
Holland, W. Wm.?
Hix?, W. J.
Hix, Baylis
Hellies?, David
Hutchins, Thomas
Harriss?, T. N.
Holland, Benj'n
Hayne, Col. W. A.
Hix, W.
Honnicut, Miss E.
Hackett, Albert
Harper, N. M.
Harper, Wm.
Harper, Asa
Huskinson, Mrs. Matilda
Hillhouse, Col. S. P.
Hale, Wm.
Hillhouse, Mrs. Harriet
Hembree, Mrs. Nancy
Hall, D. L.
Hall, Absolem J.
Hall, Mrs. Hannah
Hall, Miss Lucinda
Hawkins, Wm. P.
Haynie, L. B.
Hanks, Thos.
Haynie, Capt. Jno. Est.
Hanks, Christopher
Hanks, Stephen
Haynie, Luke
Haynie, James P.
Hanks, Jno.
Hogg, Thomson
Hopkins, Jno. H.
Hopkins, Jno. Jr.
Hunt, Jno.
Harriss, Ezkiel
Haynie, W. H.
Harper, W. C.
Harper, Jno. H.
Harper, M. J. & D. H.
Harper, W. N.
Hawthorn & Agnew
Hawthorn, D. W.
Horton, Grief
Hunter?, Dr. M. M.
Hamilton, A. M.
Horton, C. E.
Harkness, Hugh
Holmes, Wm.
Holland, Capt. J. H.
Harkness, Jno.
Harkness, Mrs. M. Est.
Harriss?, Mrs. Malinda
Hall, W. S.
Hembree, A. F.
Holland, Robt.
Harrison, Wm.
Holland, Robt.
Holland, E. M.
Hall, Miss? Mary
Hannah, Thos.
Hammond, S. J.
Hammond, Mrs. A. W.
Herring, Jno.
Hall, Lem'l
Hall, Saml C.
Hammond, Col. H.
Hardy, James
Hardy, R. B.
Haynie, Charles
Herring, Mrs. Mary
Herndon, Zeph___?
Holland, A. M.
Hunter, Mrs. Sarah
Holland, A. B.
Hamilton, Col. D. K.
Hallums?, Jno.
Hendrix, Jno. M.

424

Hunt, Wm.
Harper, Jepthah
Harper, Jno.
Harper, Thos.
Hopkins, Dr. Jno.
Hall, Wilson
Horton, J. C. Esq.
Hix, D. J.
Hembree, M. B.
Hall, J. A. Esq.
Hamilton, C. E.
Hall, J. M.
Hall, W. C.
Hall, Aaron
Hall, J. J. H.
Hall, A. O. N.
Hunter, Jno. Jr.?
Harris, Andrew
Harper, Mrs. Ann
Humphries, S. C.
Holden, W. W.(Holder?)
Haynie, Col. J. C.
Herring, Mrs. Mary
Herring, Jesse Sr.?(Jr.?)
Harrison, Hon. J. W.
Holcomb, Kitchen
Holland, J. H.
Humphreys, Eld. David
Hanks, Nimrod
Holland, Dr. W. T.?
Herrin, E. E.
Hutchins, Saml.
Hogg, Langdon
Hallums, A. C.
Hicks, Jno.
Hudgins, Jno.
Harris, Jas. P.
Howard, Jno.
Hammond, B. F.
Hopkins, Jas. M.(Jos.?)
Hay, Eld. Baxter
Hanks, Capt. Luke
Harrison, F.? E.
Hanks, J. T.?
Hewins, P. L.
Jackson, A. C.
Jones, Wm.
Jackson, Nesbet & Co.
Jones, James Est.
Jones, Wilson
Ingram, Jessee
Johnston, Peter
Johnston, J. W.
Jordon, Benson
Isbell, Eld. Saml.
Jolly, James
Jones, Jno. H.
Jolly, Henry
Jolly, Joseph
Jolly, J. Levi
Ingram, Mrs. Delila
Johnston, Wm.
Johnston, Hasting
Jones, Wm.
Jolly, Mrs. Happy
Johnston, Mrs. Sarah
Jameson, Joshua
Jolly, Mrs. A. C.
Jolly, J. L.
Jolly, Albert
Johnston, P. S.? Est.
Jenkins, Mrs. Milly
Jenkins, H. W. L.
Irwin, Mrs. E.
Irby, B. T.?
Irby, Charley
Isbell, Mrs. Sarah
Jordan, Harrison
Kenon, James A.
Kay, F. M.
Keaton, Reuben
Keaton, Jos. Jno.
King, W.? P.

Keasler, Henry
Keaton, B. F.
Kay, R. G.
Kay, Miss M. E.
Kay, Mrs. Mary Est.
Kates, Wm.
King, James
Kay, C. M.
King, Eld. Robt.
Kay, W. P.
Kay, Joel
Kay, Mason
Kay, Charles
Kennedy, Eld. J. L.
Kelly, Mrs. Eliz'th
Knox, Jno.
King, Peter
King, Josiah
Kelly, Mrs. Sarah
King, James
Kates, Miss N. A.
King, R. M.
Kay, Jesse
Keaton, Wilborn
Keown, W. M.
King, Mrs. Nancy
Keys, J. C.
Kay, Strother Est.
Kay, M. P.(W.? P.)
Kay, W. M.
Kay, Tho.
King, Col. J. D.
Kelly, D. C.
King, J. B.
Kay, A. W.
Kelly, Mrs. Mary
King, Jno. Jac?
King, Robt. A.
King, Miss Martha
King, Mrs. Nancy
Kay, Mrs. Susan
Kelly, Mrs. Sarah
Latham, Wm.
Long, Harrison
Long, A. F.
Latham, Jno. B.
Latham, Jno.
Long, G. W.
Lowe, B. F.
Leverett, Elder Stephen
Leverett, Thos. Est.
Long, W.
Long, Jno.
Lee, Dr. Thos.
Lee, W. C. Esq.
Lewis, J. P. Est.
Lewis, Jesse
Lusk, Jno.
Lucius, Mrs. A_y
Lipford, J. J.
Ligon, Saml.(Danl.?)
Lewis, J. B.
Lewis & Cox
Lewis & Brown
Lewis & _tim__?
Lee, E. D.
Level, Elder Jno. (Jos.?)
Long, Wm.
Long, Jo-
Long, Henry
Linsley, Mrs. M. C.
Lewis, J. J.
Long, Col. James
Leonheardt?, Lawrence
Leonheardt?, Rich'd
Long, Ez'kel Sr.
Long, Ez'kel Junr.
Laboon, Mrs. Edith
Laboon, Joseph (Labon)
Long, Maj. Jno.?
Langston, Allison
Lewis, E. B.
Lewis, Mrs. Roda

Ledbetter, Col. D. A.
Lorton, J. S.
Latta, J. T.?
Leverett, Wm.
Lipscomb, T. C.
Latta, J. T.
Leverett, Wesley (minor)
Leverett, Thos. Est.(heirs)
Leverett, Wm.
Long, J. O.
Little, J. R.
Lewis, Mrs. Eliz'th
McClinton, A. P.
McClinton, R. A.
McClinton, J. H.
McClister, O. B.
McClister, G. Wm.
McCollum, Miss Ann
Manning, Mrs. Fresea
McMahan, A. H.
McMahan, Mrs. M. C.
Morgan, Jno.
McCullough, S. D.
Martin, Mrs. Phebe
McCullough, Mrs. E. R.
Milford, Mrs. Mary Est.
McKee, James
McKee, W. A.
McKee, Mrs. E.
Mouchet, Jac.
McBride, J. L.
May, Tuck? W.
McLee, G. L.
McGill, Mrs. Mary
McGill, Mrs. M. & Lalla?
McCornwell?, David
McCornwell?, Wm. Sr.?
Morris, James Sr.?
Morris, Jesse C.
Massey, Silas
McLeese, Andrew
Manning, G. D.
Maret, G. W.
Maret, W. M.
Mahaffey, P. S.
Maxwell, Mrs. Lucy
Maxwell, Capt. Jno.
Maxwell, R. A.
Miller, Jno.
Martin, Jesse
Martin, W. J.
McMurtry, W. H.
McMurtry, J. F.
McPhail, Capt. Peter
Morris, Saml.
Major, Capt. J. W.
Mays?, Medy
Morris, David
McCarly, Capt. H. M.
Martin, Capt. W. C.
Martin, Jno.
Major, D. K.
Major, Capt. Jos.? A.
Mitchell, J. T.?
Mitchell, Willie
Mattison, George Est.
Moore, Jeremiah
Mattison, Mrs. Mary
Madox, Tilman
Mattison, Wm.
Mattison, Wyatt
Mattison, A. E.
Mulliken, W. H.
McAdams, Jno.
Massey, Jno. C.
Mattison, J. J.
Mattison, Jno. R.
Manly, Mrs. S.
Mattison, S. J.
Mattison, Mrs. E.
Mattison, Danl.
Mattison, J. F.
Mattison, D. & J. F.

McNeely, W. & Son
McAlister, Jno.?
McAlister, W. J.
McLane?, James
M t_, Dr. W. B.
Maulding, Eld. B. F.
Maulding, B. F. & Son
Martin, James
Martin, Eld. W. P.
Moseley, Wm. C.
Martin, J. C.
Martin, C. M. Est.
McGee, G. Wm.
McGee, L. H.
McGee, Wm. S.
Moore, G. A.
McDavid, James
McMarty?, James
McMarty?, E. B.
Major, E. _?
McGregor, J. W.
McMillian, W. A.
Madox, Shad.?
McGee, J. P.
McGee, Eld. Wm.
Major, J. P. Est.
Minton?, Thds.
Morse, Elder A. A.
Moorehead, Mary
Mosely, J. L.
McCarly, Elijah(McCarty?)
McCarty?, Capt. R. B.
McGuire?, J. J.
McGee, Elias
McLeese, James
Montgomery, J. A.
Moorehead, Alex. Esq.
Moorehead, Jno.
Moorehead, Robt.
Moore, W. S.?
Mullikin, R. J.
Moore, & Elrod
Mitchell, Aaron
Mitchell, Dr. Caleb
Martin, Chesley
Martin, W. _?
Martin, W. S.
Martin, Sanford V.(O.?)
Martin, B. C.
Martin, T. C.
Murphy, Ezk'le Esq.
Murphy, Thos. M.
McAlister, Anna
McAlister, James
Moore, W. J.
Moore, Elijah
Maulding, R. M.
Moore, Flwd. B.
McNeely, David
Mullikin, W.
Moore, Alex
Moore, Mrs. E.
McCann, Col. T. H.
McKinny, Mrs. Martha
Martin, Stephen
McAlister, Wm.
Mullikin, James Esq.
McKinney, P. F.
Martin, Jac.
Mitchell, Jno. F.
Martin, Thdd. H.
Melton?, Michael Y.?
Martin, Wm.
Martin, James Esq.
Martin, S. M.
McConnell, J. H.
Masters, P. A.
McElroy, S. R.
McElroy, S. J.
Mattison, J. M.
McAlister, J. A.
McFee, Mrs. Sarah
Manly, G. W.

McGukin, Hugh
Milwee, Mrs. S. C.
Milwee, Miss F.
Mitchell, G. W.
Major, Mrs. Margaret
Major, J. W.
Mitchell, W. N.
Major, W.
Martin, Abram
Martin, T. W.
Martin, Capt. T. W.
McClure, E. W.
McClure, E. J.
McDowell, G. W.
McPhail, Jno. Jr.
Mitchell, M. E.
McLin?, Mrs. H. N.
Meredith, Abram
McCartha, Thoms.?
McCartha, Thos.
McConnell, S. F.
Morgan, Baylis
Major, J.? S.
Major, Col. W. N.
Major, Mrs. Nancy
McCully, Stephen
McMahan, Saml. Est.
McFall, Col. Jno.
Moore, Joseph
McCay, W. (M.?) S. Esq.
Mills, Wm.
Martin, Matthews
Martin?, James
McAlister, Capt. N.
McClland, Miss M. & N.
Major, H. B. B.
McCann?, Jno.
McCann?, Jas. T.
McCann, W. T.
Matin, W. A.
Maxwell, S. E.
Miller, S. F. W.
McCreary, E. M.
McCreary, A.
McElroy, A. L. Est.
Moore, Mrs. Nancy
Moore, Capt. Jas. B.
Maverack, Saml. Est.
McGee, Capt. Elias
Mullikin, Mrs. James
Murry?, Eld. J. Est.
McFall, Mrs. Phebe
Milford, Dr. W. J.
McPhail, Jno. Jur.
McFall, Mrs. Rachael
McFall, Miss R. L. (minor)
McFall, W. A.
Martin, Benj'n
McLeese, Eld. R. B.
McLeese, Mrs. Rebecca
McCully, Mrs. E.
Mattison, Mrs. M. K.
McDavid, G. W.
Mattison, Col. C. S.?
Major, Danl.?
McGee, W. D.
McGee, E. J.
Martin, Col. Jno.
Mattison, Olly Est.
McAlister, A. B.
Martin, Robt.
Milwee, W. A.
Milwee, Miss M. & E.
Moorhead, W.
McAlister, Capt. N.
McDavid, Mrs. S.
Martin, J. H.
Morris, R. M.
McGee, Jesse
Major J. V. Moore
Moore, J. M.
Martin, Capt. J. R.
McGee, Capt. Willis

McCoy?, H. C.
Neal, Julian
Nichols, Miss Anna
Newton, J. B.
Newell, R. D.
Newell, Dr. N. J.
Newell, Miss J. A.
Newell, Jno.
Newton, J. N.
Newton, J. S.
Neighbors, J. T.?
Nichols, J. C.
Nichols, W. A.
Norris, Capt. Robt. B.
Norris, J. T.?
Nevett, Capt. Wm.
Nettles?, Joseph
Newton, Saml.
Newton, Willis
Norris, Col. J. W. Sr.
Neal, A. M.
Norris, Mrs. Elvira
Norris, Dr. W. C.
Norris, E. S. Esq.?
Norris, Capt. P. K.
Norris, Mrs. E.
Newton, Maj. Larkin
Norris, J. E.
Norris, A. O. Esq.?
Newell, S. S.
Norris, Col. J. W. Junr.
O'Briant, Wm. O.
Osborn, S.? R.
Owen, Jno.
Overby, Nicholas
Og_, John
Owens, Mrs. Eliz'th
Owens, Miss Pinah
Owens, Elijah
Owens, Miss Judeah?
Oliver, Mrs. Martha
Oliver, Miss M. L.
Oldham, Thos.
Oldham, Wm.
Orr, Capt. Wm. M.
Orr, Wm. H.
Orr, J. B.
Orr, T.? C.
Orr, Alex
Orr, Wm. Sr.
Oneal, James
Owens, Lewis
Orr, Thos.
Oliver, Mrs. Mary
Orr, Capt. James
Orr, J. W. B.?
Orr & Sm_es
Orr, Hon. J. L.
Presley, Dr. J. S.?
Prince, Jno. Wm.?
Prince, Edward
Prince, Mark
Price, H. P.
Pruitt, E. D.
Pruitt, Mrs. Frances
Parker, Robt.
Price, P. R.
Price, Mrs. Jane
Palmer, J. W.
Palmer, Mattison
Pickerel, Jonathen
Palmer, W.
Palmer, S. (T.?) B.
Palmer, Jno.
Pullen, W.
Pendleton Fact. Company
Philip, W.
Poe, Mrs. E. C.?
Pickens, Dr. G.? J.
Pickens, Hon. T. J.
Pickens, J. Miles
Pickens, Col. M. M.
Prichard, Mrs. Harriet

Pennall, Thomas
Pruiett, Wm.
Philip, L. D.
Poor, Saml.
Poor, Mrs. Nancy
Poor, Hamilton
Poor, J. B.
Philip, Reuben
Poor, George
Pickle, J. E.
Pickle, C. W.
Poor, Mrs. Nira?
Poor, J. W.
Pepper, Elijah Est.
Peu, Dolly
Pepper, W. G. & E. H.
Poor, Holland
Pepper, E. K.
Poor, Jno.
Parks, Col. Thos.
Powel, F. M.
Pickens, Col. W. S.
Pickens, J. W.
Pickle, W. Chesley
Pegg, Jno.
Pegg, James B.
Philips, Martin
Philips, Jno.
Pace, Silas
Prater, Joseph
Pickle, W.
Pickens, Capt. R. M.
Prater, F. N.
Prichard, A. C.
Pool, Mrs. Eliz'th
Pearman, Benj'n
Pickens, Robt.
Pool, W. H.
Pagett, J. A.
Pinckney, Mrs. E.
Peyton, Hezkiel
Prater, H.
Petigrew, Mrs. R. H.
Powers, D. T. A.
Philips, Arch'd
Poor, Hugh
Parrott, Nathaniel
Reid, Andrew Esq.
Reid, Dr. _? H.
Reid & Davis
Reid, A. _?
Rice, Eld̄. A.
Ranson, R. H. Est.
Rice, Fleetwood
Rice, A. E.
Rice, Joel T.?
Rice, Miss E. M.
Rice, Enoch B.
Rice, J. L.
Rice, H. F.
Rice, James T.?
Rampy, Mrs. Mary
Ranson, Mrs. Catherine
Reeves, M. E.
Reed, Jesse
Reed, Moses
Rampy, Eld. W. M.
Robinson, Miss Jane
Rowland, Mrs. Frances
Reid, Thos. F.
Robinson, J. B.
Richie, J. W.
Robinson, Mrs. L. M.
Robinson, Col. James
Ragsdale, D. F.
Robinson, S. E.
Rowland, W. W.
Ragsdale, F. A. & J. F.
Ragsdale, F. A.
Ragsdale, J. F.
Ramsey, A. W.
Ramsey, Arch'd
Roberts, Matthias

Rogers, Jos. T.?
Rogers, ? P.
Rogers, W. W.
Rogers, Jno. C.
Rogers, Jno.
Rogers, H. D.
Richardson, N. T.?
Richardson, J. F.
Reid, Leml.
Rogers, Jac? D.
Rogers, David
Rogers, J. B.
Reeves, Mrs. Eliz'th
Reeves, N. R.
Reece, David (heirs minors)
Rochester, Nathan'l
Rainwater, Capt. D. L.?
Reeves, Wilson
Reid, Hon. J. P.
Reeves, J. A.
Robinson, Mrs. Jane Est.
Russell, Col. T.? H.
Reimer, Mrs. Lucinda
Reid, Miss Elizabeth
Rogers, Mrs. Chesley
Rogers, Larkin
Rogers, W. N.
Rogers, O. B.
Richardson, S. T.
Richardson, Matthias
Richardson, S. T. & M.
Ray, Saml.
Richardson, Matthias
Reeks, Mrs. Sarah
Reeks, Jno. G.
Riley, Abram
Rosamond, J. W.
Rosamond, J. H. Est.
Robinson, Mrs. C.
Robinson, T.? S.
Richie, J. N.
Rankin, T. F.
Rankin, Mrs. Mary
Rankin, Miss E. B.
Rankin, Miss M. P.
Rankin, Miss M. J.
Rankin, Miss M. A.
Rankin, Col. G. W.
Richie, Mrs. Mary
Richie, Miss E. A.
Richie, Miss S. J.
Richie, Jabez
Roberts, W. H.
Richardson, G. W.
Reese, Mrs. Sarah
Rogers, Mrs. Eliz'th
Rogers, Jac. F. Est.
Rogers, Mrs. Hester
Rogers, Chesley
Robinson, Richard
Riley, Wm.
Richardson, Mrs. David
Robinson, James M.
Roof, George
Randall, Carver
Ross, Eld. A. W. Est.
Rogers, B. W.
Rogers, W.
Rogers, Miss E. & R. H.
Rice, Mrs. Sarah
Rogers, H. B.
Richie, Reuben
Richie, Jno.
Robins, W. J.
Sanders, A. N.
Sanders, Elias
Sanders, Miss Sarah
Sherard, Mrs. Jane
Simpson, James
Simpson, Wm.
Stewart, Jno.
Spearman, J. W.
Stevenson, E. J.

Sherard, J. W.
Sherard, Capt. S. W.
Sherard, W. S.
Sherard, Wm.
Simpson, J. M.
Simpson, Mrs. Mary
Simpson, Miss S. H.
Sadler, David
Serard, T. A.
Seigler, Jno.
Speerman, J. E.
Simpson, Robt.
Simpson, Mrs. E. J.
Speerman, W. M.
Symms, Jno. & James
Stewart, James
Stewart, Jno.
Stevenson, George
Simpson, W. S.
Sanders, Capt. Wm.
Simpson, James L.
Stewart, J. L.
Simons, David
Smmons, James
Simons, J. T.?
Simons, Chas.
Simons, C. H.
Simpson, Miss E. A.
Shanklin, J. V.
Symms, Dr. G. H.
Sloan, B. F.
Shirley, A. Y.?(T.?)
Simpson, Hon. R. F.
Sloan, B. P.
Simpson, Wm.
Steele, James
Sitton, J. B.
Swords, Mrs. Massey?
Steele, R. A.
Smith, Mrs. Maria
Smith, Wm. N.
Smith, Danl.
Scott, Mrs. Mary
Scott, Mrs. Narcissa
Smith, Capt. Aaron
Smith, Nimrod T.
Smith, Mrs. W.? E.
Se_er, Gillam
Smith, Saml.
Stevenson, J. J.
Shirley, J. W.
Seawright, Mrs. M.
Strickland, Mathew
Shaw, A. J.
Shirley, Obediah
Smith, Joel
Shaw, Hembree
Shirley, Capt. J. J.
Smith, Jno. G.
Southerland, W. F.
Southerland, J. N.
Southerland, Miss N. J.
Stanton?, C. B.
Stanton?, Mathias
Storm, J. D.
Smith, J. D.
Smith, J. C. & J. D.
Stone, Hampton
Stow?, J. P.
Stone & Armstrong
Smith & Sullivan
Strickland, S.
Spencer, Robt. Jr.
Smith & Cheatham
Sullivan, Dr. J. C.
Stansel, F. G.
Smith, J. T.?
Stringer, Cox & McGee
Stringer, A. J.?
Smith, W.
Smith, A. W.
Smith, A. J.
Smith, Mrs. Mary

Smith, Robt. S.
Shirley, Stephens
Spearman, Mrs. Margt.
Simpson, Dr. J. B.
Shelton, J. W. B.
Sherard, D. J.
Stone, Wm.
Smith, Jesse R.
Scott, M. B.
Simpson, James H.
Saber?, A. H.
Saber?, H. F.
Snipes, Elisha
Snipes, Matthew
Smith, Jno. G.
Skelton, A. B.
Stewart, George Jr.
Stewart, Adam
Smith, M. H.
Sullivan, Jelly Esq.
Simpson, D. M.
Stevenson, Robt.
Shirley?, James
Shirley?, Richd.
Steone, G. W.
Speerman, B. J.
Speerman, Jno. W.
Sitton, Jno.
Spearman, David D.
Smith, Jno. C.
Spearman, F. A.
Spearman, David Est.
Stone, George (Stow?)
Slaten, J. C.
Seawright, W. W.
Sherriff, Jno.
Satterfield, Jeremiah
Stra_, Andrew
Siddall, Jno.
Shearman, Mrs. Mary
Smith, Ephraim
Smith, H. G.
Sitten, J. P.
Stornton?, Mrs. M.
Sitton, Wm. D. Esq.
Sitton, Wm.
Smith, George S.
Smith, Griffin
Smith, Andrew
Stone?, Elijah (minor)
Smith, C. M.
Smith, A. A.
Smith, J. F.
Smith, Joshua
Smith, Simeon
Sear?, Wm.
Stewart, Miss L. J.
Smith, P. J.
Simeon Spruil
Smith, W.
Stucky, J. T.
Stevenson, James
Stevenson, Andrew
Smith, J. M.
Smith, Miss T. L.
Shirley, Aaron
Spence, Robt. Jr.
Simpson, W. J.
Smith, Saml.
Smith, Wyatt
Stott?, D. M.
Sullivan, Capt. N. K.
Simpson, Robert
Shirley, J. M.
S__n er?, Wm. P.
Skelton, Thos. T.
Shearer, Andrew
Shearer, J. Wm.
Simpson, J. L.
Smith, B. S.
Smith, Miss E. H.
Smith, Miss S. E. A.
Smith, Miss M. E. N.

Sloan, Caol. J. T.
Seaborn, Maj. George
Sloan, Mrs. S. E.
Spiller, J. R.
Sloan, Ben. Frank
Sadler, James H.
Sadler, David F.
Sadler, Jno. E.
Stevens, Jno. E.
Strickland, Maj. M. S.
Smith, Mrs. Margt.
Smith, Saml. D.
Smith, W. C.
Stringer, L. D.
Saylor, J__?(Jno.?)
Stevenson, Thos.
Shirley, Jno.
Smyres? & Orr?
Shaw, W. S.
Tucker, Dejearnett Sr.?
Tucker, Harrison
Todd, Robert
Tucker, Dejearnett
Taylor, Toliver
Tucker, Wm.
Tucker, Reuben
Tucker, Capt. J. P.
Thomson, Col. James
Taylor, Elijah
Tribble, Richard
Taylor, Col, D. S.
Taylor, Mrs. Nancy
Thomas, B.
Thomas, Mrs. Sallie
Tunno(Turner?), Mrs. E. M.
Terry, Henry
Tribble, Capt. L. W.
Taylor, W. J.
Telford, W.
Tranynham, W. P.
Telford, G. B.
Telford, minors of Jas.
  Telford
Telford, heirs of J. Wil-
  son Est.
Towers, W. W.
Townes, W. W. & Co.
Telford, J. H.
Teague, Elijah
Todd, James
Tate, Tilman
Trimmer, Elijah
Thomson, James
Thomson, B. L.
Thomson, W.
Thomason, J. D.
Tribb(Tripp?), Mrs. Ann
Tribb(Tripp?), Nicholas
Tompkins, Wm.
Tranynham, J. P.
Timms?, Isaac
Timms?, Jesse
Tranynham, Miss M. A.
Todd, Mrs. Mary
Todd, Capt. W. P.
Tate, Grief
Tilly, L. M.
Todd, Andrew Esq.
Todd, Mrs. Olive
ThomLee?, Mrs. E. M.
Taylor, Dr. J. W.
Taylor, Elijah
Tucker, James
Thomson, Dr. A. E.
Taylor, W.?
Telford, R. C.?
Vandiver, Mrs. Susan
Vandiver, Capt. H. R.
Vandiver, Capt. E.
Vandiver, A. W.
Vandiver, H. A.
Vandiver, Aaron
Vandiver, W.

Vanwyck, Wm.
Vandiver, E. & E.
Vandiver, Jno.?
Wiley, James Est.
Watt, Jas. S.
Watt, Jno. Wm.
Watt, S. S. Est.
Watt, Jos. D.
Wharton, W. L.
Wiles, James H.
Waters, Mrs. Mary
Whitman, David
Whitman, E. P.
Whitman, Jac.
Wallace, Georg.?
Welch, C. W.
Wakefield, Capt. Jno.
West, J. N.
West, T.? W.
Waters, Miss Elvira
Warley, Mrs. Sophia
Watkins, Felix
Watkins, B. J.
Watson, Mrs. Maria
Walkins, Col. T.? C.
Williams, Jasper
Welborn, Saml.
Watson, Dr. M.
Williams, Capt. R. L.
Webb, D. H.
Webb, Saml.
Webb, Jno. Jas. & Hannah
Wright, Capt. T. T.
Wright, R. N.
Wilson, G. _?
Wilson, J.?~W.
Wilson, W. N.
Webster, Mrs. Jane
Woods, J. H.
Wilson, W.(M.?) R.
Williams, J. C.
Williams, Humphrey
Watson, Jno. A.
Wilson, Capt. Hugh
Wilson, Dr. John
Wilson, Mrs. Mary
Wilson, Reuben
Williams, Austin
Walker, J. M.
Welborn, Thos.
Welborn, Col. W. E.
Walker, M. T.
Wilson, J. B.
Welborn, Aaron
Welborn, T. M.
Wilson, Mrs. E.
Welborn, J. Y.
Welborn, A. F.
Wilemon?, Martin
Wilemon?, Mrs. Rosa
Wilemon?, Miss Frances
Wilemon?, Wm.
Wilemon?, James
Willingham, A. P.
Willingham, & Major
Willingham, Jno.?
Watson, E. W.
Williams, Ira C.
Williams, T. O. minor
Wardlaw, H. H.
Wardlaw, H. C.
Wardlaw, A. C.
Wardlaw, James Est.
Wright, Wm.
Wright, Mrs. Martha
Webb, James
Wilson, Jepththah F.
Webb, Dr. Edmund
Watkins, W.
Watkins, Miss R. E. & J. C
Watson, W. B.
Winter, J. C.
Williford, C. K.

Wakefield, Mrs. E. E.
White, Mrs. Susan
White, Bartholemew
White, Matthew G.
Wootson, Wm.
Wynne, F.
Wootson, Allen
Waddle, Wm.
Wilson, Mrs. Abby
Walker, J. S.
Wardlaw, J. M.
Wardlaw, J. C.
Wardlaw, D. L.
Williams, S. & G. S.
Wardlaw, Elijah
Wilson, Wm. M.
Williams, Mrs. Eliz'th
Watson, A. P.
Wyatt, Col. J. F.
Wyatt, Mrs. N. A.
Wyatt, R. F.
Wyatt, W. F.
Watkins, W. C.
Wilson, Elder James
Wilson, Eld. J. J.
Wilson, W. H.
Webb, C. G.
Webb, Mrs. Eliz.
Webb, E. Wm.
Williams, Capt. M. B.
Watkins, Bailes
Watkins, Jepththah
Watkins & Harper
Watkins, E. H.
Wilborn, Capt. J. M.
Williford, S. W.
Williford, Mrs. Sarah Est.
Whitaker, H. A.
Whitaker, S. A.
Williams, Mrs. Anna
Watkins, W. H.
Whitefield, P. M.
Whitaker, Eld. D. L.
Warnock, J.
Watson, D. H.
Watson, J. M.
Wat?, J. T. Est.
Wilcox, Mrs. E.
Whitner, Hon. J. N.
Williams, L. & S.? A.
Webb, Elisha
White, T. M.
Webb, Elijah
Wilson, Jno. Esq.
Wilson, Richard
Wamlow?, Mrs. Leander
Walker, Eld. A. W.
Wamlow?, E. minor
Wamlow?, J. W.
Wamlow?, Mary
Wamlow?, Miss Leanora
Wright, J. C.
White, Henry
Wells, Thos.
Wilson, Hugh
Watkins, Capt. David
Welborn, W.
Welborn, R. H.
Welborn, W. W.
Westmoreland, S. L.
Williams, A.
Williams, Allen Est.
Wallace, Mrs. Sarah
Watt, S. A.
Watson, Mrs. Mary
Watson, W. G.
Watson, J. B.
Wigington, Jno. Jr.
Wigington, Elihu
Wigington, E. G.
Williford, Mis. S. E. &
   M. E.

Saml. A. Beam?(Brown?)
W. B. Newell
L. D. Giles & Mrs. R. Wa-
   ters
Robt. Chamblee

Young, Wm.
Yeus?, Polly Est.
Young, James
Yeargan, Jer?

CITY OF PENDLETON:
W. J. Ligon
Cobb, E. M.
J. D. Smith
Smith & Henry?
Mrs. Frances Davis?
R. A. Maxwell
Mrs. Lucy Maxwell
Mrs. D. M. Mays
Dr. Jno. H. Maxwell
T. L. McBride
Mrs. E. C. Shubrick
Maj. Elijah Alexander
J. W. Clark
Dr. W. B. Ceh_ney(Cheney?)
Mrs. F. Calhoun
A. C. Campbell
J. P. Lewis Est.
Miss Eleanor Lewis
Capt. J. L. Shanklin
J. V. Shanklin
Mrs. E. C. Poe
Dr. G. H. Symmes
B. F. Sloan
Miss Mary Hunter
Mrs. N. E. Sloan
Dr. P. H. E. Sloan
Col. D. S. Taylor
Mrs. Nancy Taylor
Mrs. R. A. Boet?
Jos. D. Taylor
Mrs. A. Bacot?
W. W. Hamilton
Jones & Seaborn
Jno. B. Sitton
James Hunter
Dr. T. J. Pickens
Jno. Hastie
J. J. Lewis
Dr. M. L. Sharpe
Mrs. E. Sharpe
J. E. Adger
J. L. Simpson
Col. Jno. T. Sloan
T. B. Benson & Co.
Miss Lucretia Whitaker
Mrs. Sarah Stevens
W. H. D. Gaillard
W. H. D. Gaillard & Co.
Mrs. M. O. Stevens
S. E. Maxwell
Masonic Lodge
W. J. Knauff
Mrs. Susan Knauff
Jno. S. Lorton
Miss. E. F. Lorton
J. L. Lorton & Co.
Miss J. F. Miller
Miss Charlotte Kay
Mrs. Martha Wilson
Mrs. Mary Hodge
Major George Seaborn
C. S. Stevens
Green Stevens
Col. J. B. E. Sloan & Co.
Col. J. B. E. Sloan
B. Frank Sloan
Pen'd Hotel Co.
Miss Sallie Crook?
J. C. Cheney
G. R. Cheney
S. S. Cherry

Miss Mary Symms
Mrs. E. Stark Est.
Carver? Randall
C. V. Barnes
J. E. Bellotte Esq.
J. E. & W. M. Bellotte
Col. W. R. Jones
Jos.? F. Hunter
E. G. Evans
Saml. Maverick Est.
Wm. Vanwyck
Dr. W. L. Jenkins
W. C. Smith
T. B. Benson & Co.
C. J. Bowie?
Miss L. Sloan
Miss R. C. Sloan
A. Simpson Est.
Col. A. Clinkscales
Maj. James Gilmer
James R. Fant
Miss L. O. Daricott
M. H. Brock
Herbert Daricott
Maj. J. L.? Brogly?
Rich'd Partin
D. A. Woodson
Col. F. C. V. Borstell
Joseph L. Byram
James C. Keys
W. M. Archer
Blockley & Crayton
S. Blockley
Mrs. M. W. Williams
J. D. Miller
Eld. Jno. Golden
Mrs. C. Benson
E. B. Sloan
Sloan, Sullivan & Co.
J. P. Sullivan
Mrs. Sarah Creswell
B. L. Roberts
Ezekiel George
Hon. J. P. Reid
J. B. Clark
Mrs. M. J. McFall
Dr. Edmond Webb
Col. T. H. Russell
Jesse R. Smith
Smith & Clark
David Anderson Est.
Gen. Saml. M. Wilkes Est.
Mrs. L. C. Wilkes
H. Riley Est.
J. M. Partlow
G. W. Fant
James B. Pegg
Mrs. M. A. Morris
Mrs. M. P. McAlister
H. H. Whitaker
Capt. N. R. Sullivan
Whitner, B. F.
Stephen McCully
Eld. T. G. Herbert
Jno. D. M. Dobbins
McFall & Hammond
Col. Jno. V. Moore
J. A. Pagett
Dr. Brown & Nardin?
J. C. Whitfield
Maj. J. T. Whitfield Est.
Maj. E. J. Earle
Capt. C. E. Earle Est.
Zach Payton
Capt. J. B. Moore
Moore & Major
England, Blackly & Co.
E. F. Marry?
Wm. Vanwyck
A. Todd Est.
Capt. C. C. Langston
R. H. Hubbard
Evins & Hubbard

W. C. McFall
Dr. T. A. Evins
Hon. J. W. _____ (Harris?)
Hon. J. N. Whitner
Miss F. J. Caldwell
B. F. & J. H. Whitner
Maj. E. W. Bucker?
Dr. Alex. Cowen?
Mrs. R. H. Webb
Mrs. E. N. ThomLee
England & Beverly
W. C. Bewley
England, Jno. E.
O. H. P. Fant
Mrs. E. H. Earle
Capt. Saml. Crawford
Wil_____ & Green
B. F. Crayton
B. F. & T. S. Crayton
Elisha Webb
Elias Earle
Jos Berry Sloan
Mrs. Eliz'th Earle
Eld. J. Scott Murry
Mrs. Nancy Edwards
Dr. O. R. Broyles
Dr. A. P. Cater
S. H. Owen
S. M. White
R. C. Archer?
Col. Jno. T. Sloan
Eld. Jac. Burress
L. A. Osborn
Level & White
Mrs. Sarah Creswell
J. B. Sloan
Sloan & Towers
A. B. Towers
Danl. Brown
Miss M. Waller
Elijah Brown
Miss C. M. Waller
Capt. A. B. Tower
A. B. Tower
R. E. Sloan
O. P. McKinny
Mrs. F.? (T.?) Braddy
Hon. R. Monroe
J. B. Edwards?
Saml. Brown Jr.
S. J. S__man
W. M. Osborn
Jno. B. Watson
Miss? M. J. Watson
Mrs. M. C. Price
D. M. Watson
Sharpe & Watson
Hon. J. L. Orr
Miss Susan Thomson
Jno. Cochran
Mrs. Eliz'th Robinson
Mrs. J. E. Mauldin

18 Free Negroes
Mrs. M. W. Williams
J. C. Cheney
G. R. Cheney
S. Blockley

END OF BOOK OF TAX RETURNS

Pendleton/Anderson Dist., So. Carolina
Prepared by
Colleen Elliott, Randy Linville, Kay Melear & Dorothy Peters
Fort Worth, Texas

Waller, Mariah T. 246,247
  Mary 185
  R. H. 247
  William 184,246,247
Walters, Flemming 104
  Ibzan 104
  Macklin 104
  Rebecca 104
  Williford 104
  W. E. 181
Walton, Jesse 191
Ward, Elizabeth 67
  Jane 83
  John 3
  Mary 22
Wardin, John 20
Wardlaw..12
  Andrew C. 171
  Betsey 113,119
  Betsey Francis 113
  Carral B. 171
  E. A. 119
  Fannie E. 171
  H. C. 120,171
  H. H. 104,171,228,259
  Hugh 4
  Hugh A. 119
  Hugh H. 113,243
  J. 274
  James 19,22,34,119,123, 228,260
  James L. 171
  J. M. 244
  Jesse 256
  John 20
  John M. 113,119
  Lizzie 183
  Margaret 34
  Nancy 20
  Peggy 119
  William 9,199
Wardlow, John 243
Ware, A. N. 225
  Jas. H. 130
  Wm. 228
Warley, J. M. 222
  Jacob 229
Warnck, John 48
Warnock, Alfred 94
  Andrew 6,8,20
  Andrew Jr. 50
  Eleanor 259
  Ellenor 55,95
  Frances 95,234
  James 6,8,94,222,232
  Jane 95,234
  John 7,55,95,115,222, 234,259,276
  Margaret 234
  Joseph 15
  LeRoy 94
  Margaret 95
  Mary 94
  Matilda 94
  Robert 6
  Scipio 259
Warren, Samuel 94,218,222, 223,229,233,247
Wasson, Permelia E. 146
Waters, Armstead 239,261
  Armsted J. 187
  Drury 267
  Elizabeth 110
  Emily C. 187
  Hiram 226
  Ibzan 262
  Jesse 276,282
  Jesse G. 268
  Mary 27
  Philmon 195
  Wiliford 231,268
Waties, Wm. 176
  Zenobia 176

Watkins, B. J. 139,281
  Baylis 260
  David 20,40,248,272
  D. O. 139
  Elizabeth 272
  Felix 252
  Fielding 272
  Fuldix 241
  Jane 272
  Jane C. 272
  Japtha 281
  Jno. 251
  John 40
  Joseph 35,40,241,272
  Rebecca 272
  T. A. 272
  Thos. C. 134,139,251
  William 272
Watson, A. J. 246
  Andrew P. 105,159,265, 266
  A. P. 281
  B. 236
  Belton 183
  Benj. 232
  Corrie 163
  Cynthia 105
  D. K. 187,260
  D. R. 280
  Daniel 97,247,257
  Daniel K. 243
  David 10,53,97,163,179, 222,225,243
  David M. 97,125,162
  David W. 133
  Edward 267
  Elijah 229
  Eliza 105,183
  Esther 260
  J. B. 254
  J. J. 97,243,247,254
  J. G. 254,280
  J. P. 258
  Jackson 97
  James 8,10,105,265,266
  James M. 105
  Jno. 126
  Jno. Sr. 109
  John 28,39,135,261
  John B. 139,163,164, 180,183,243
  John D. 97
  John G. 243
  Jonathan 30,53
  Jonathan J. 243
  L. W. 135
  M. C. 236
  M. L. 254
  Malissa 97
  Martha 270
  Martha E. 183,184
  Mary 97,105,243,254
  Melinda C. 96
  Nancy 53
  Oliver Y. 175
  Polly 105
  Reede 163
  Robert A. 105
  Samuel 105,265
  Sarah Ann 105
  Stephen 53,237,241
  Thomas 25,96,222,223, 235
  Mrs. Willard 260
  William 38,259
  William B. 183,184
  William G. 97,170
  W. H. 135
Watt, J. D. 273
  James D. 136,282
  James G. 266
  James W. 136
  John 223,230,232,238

Watt, Joseph W. 266
  Martha G. 136
  Samuel S. 136
  Thomas 266
  Thomas A. 122
Watters, Early 271
  Fleming 264
  Ibzan 264,266,282
  J. 264
  Julia Ann 141
  Sophia Jane 141
  Wm. E. 172
Watts, Henry 6
  Thomas 6
Waynie, Stephen 15
Wayland, Th. 223
Wayne...223
Weacan, Judey 37
Weatherford, John 216
Weaver, John L. 216
Webb, A. 277
  Andrew 257
  Ann W. 135,162
  Benjamin 162
  Benjamin F. 135
  Betsy 93
  C. 260,264,282,283
  C. B. 222,253,261,267
  Caroline 86,113
  Charles 40,54,71
  Charles B. 239,266
  Charles L. 135
  Charles S. 162
  Chas. W. 185
  Charlotte 162
  Charlotte A. C. T. 135
  Clayton 71,131,232, 256,266,267,283
  Cornelia 123
  Dudley 132
  Dudley H. 123,131,161
  E. 232,237,264,265,272
  Edmund 131,149
  Edward 71
  Elijah 86,88,93,101,104, 107,110,121,130,131,132, 136,138,142,144,148,150, 151,153,161,164,165,167, 184,226,229,232,234,237, 243,247,253,257,258,262, 265,266,268,278,283
  Elijah R. 131
  Elisha 71,123,131,149, 267,271
  Eliza 131,267
  Eliza D. 123
  Elizabeth 24,94,113
  Frances 71
  Francis 131
  Hammond 162
  Hiram 245
  J. 265
  James 115,173,265
  James Warren 131
  Martha Ann 149
  Mary Ann 71,222,236
  Mary Elizabeth 174
  Micajah 71,118,131
  Nancy 71,131
  N. R. 60
  R. C. 185
  R. E. 130
  S. M. 247
  S. N. 280
  Sam'l. M. 244
  Samuel 274
  Samuel J. H. 135
  Samuel M. 283
  Samuel Warren 131
  Simeon 24
  Thomas 71
  Thomas J. 149
  W. 242

The following index of <u>Freed Persons</u>, <u>Bound Persons</u>, <u>Slaves</u>, etc. are listed under
the name of the family in which they were found unless the surname was different.

CPSIA information can be obtained at www.ICGtesting.com
Printed in the USA
LVOW070915010713

340902LV00002B/5/P